The American Journey

Authors

Joyce Appleby, Ph.D.
Alan Brinkley, Ph.D.
James M. McPherson, Ph.D.

NATIONAL
GEOGRAPHIC
SOCIETY

Glencoe
McGraw-Hill

New York, New York   Columbus, Ohio   Woodland Hills, California   Peoria, Illinois

Authors

Joyce Appleby, Ph.D. is Professor of History at UCLA. Dr. Appleby's published works include *Capitalism and a New Social Order: The Jeffersonian Vision of the 1790s* and *Ideology and Economic Thought in Seventeenth-Century England*, which won the Berkshire Prize. She served as president of the Organization of American Historians and chaired the Council of the Institute of Early American History and Culture at Williamsburg. Dr. Appleby is past president of the American Historical Association.

Alan Brinkley, Ph.D. is Professor of American History at Columbia University. His published works include *Voices of Protest: Huey Long, Father Coughlin, and the Great Depression*, which won the 1983 American Book Award, *The End of Reform: New Deal Liberalism in Recession and War*, and *The Unfinished Nation: A Concise History of the American People*. He received the Levenson Memorial Teaching Prize at Harvard University. Dr. Brinkley is a member of the national advisory board for the PBS series "The American Experience."

James M. McPherson, Ph.D. is George Henry Davis Professor of American History at Princeton University. Dr. McPherson is the author of 11 books about the Civil War era. These include *Battle Cry of Freedom: The Civil War Era*, for which he won the Pulitzer Prize in 1989, and *For Cause and Comrades: Why Men Fought in the Civil War*, for which he won the 1998 Lincoln Prize. He is a member of many professional historical associations, including the Association for the Preservation of Civil War Sites and the Civil War Trust.

The **National Geographic Society,** founded in 1888 for the increase and diffusion of geographic knowledge, is the world's largest nonprofit scientific and educational organization. Since its earliest days, the Society has used sophisticated communication technologies and rich historical and archival resources to convey knowledge to a worldwide membership. The Education Products Division supports the Society's mission by developing innovative educational programs—ranging from traditional print materials to multimedia programs including CD-ROMs, videodiscs, and software. "National Geographic Journeys," featured in each unit of this textbook, were designed and developed by the National Geographic Society's Education Products Division.

Glencoe/McGraw-Hill

A Division of The **McGraw·Hill** Companies

Design and Production: DECODE, Inc.

Send all inquiries to:
Glencoe/McGraw-Hill
8787 Orion Place
Columbus, Ohio 43240

ISBN 0-07-825875-8 (Student Edition) ISBN 0-07-825878-2 (Teacher's Wraparound Edition)
Printed in the United States of America.

4 5 6 027/055 05 04 03 02

Academic Consultants

Richard G. Boehm, Ph.D.
Professor of Geography
Southwest Texas State University
San Marcos, Texas

Assad N. Busool, Ph.D.
Professor and Chairman of the
 Department of Arabic Studies
American Islamic College
Chicago, Illinois

Margo J. Byerly, Ph.D.
Assistant Professor of Social
 Studies Methods
Ball State University
Muncie, Indiana

Frank de Varona
Region Superintendent
Dade County Public Schools
Miami, Florida

William E. Nelson, Jr., Ph.D.
Research Professor of Black Studies
 and Professor of Political Science
The Ohio State University
Columbus, Ohio

Bernard Reich, Ph.D.
Professor of Political Science and
 International Affairs
George Washington University
Washington, D.C.

Donald A. Ritchie, Ph.D.
Associate Historian of the United
 States Senate Historical Office
Washington, D.C.

Medal with Andrew Jackson's portrait

Teacher Reviewers

John R. Doyle
Director, Division of Social
 Sciences
Dade County Public Schools
Miami, Florida

David J. Engstrom
American History Teacher
Discovery Junior High School
Fargo, North Dakota

Harry J. Hancock
Social Studies Teacher
Theodore Roosevelt
 Middle School
Kenner, Louisiana

**Elysa E. Toler Robinson,
 Ed.D.**
Program Supervisor
Detroit Public Schools
Detroit, Michigan

Kay R. Selah
Social Studies Teacher
Landmark Middle School
Jacksonville, Florida

Deborah N. Smith
Social Studies Teacher
New Albany Middle School
New Albany, Ohio

Larry John Smith
United States History Teacher
Mt. Savage School
Mt. Savage, Maryland

Cheryl Summers
Clinical Supervisor
Albuquerque Public Schools
Albuquerque, New Mexico

Renée Marie Trufant
Social Studies and
 Communications Skills
 Teacher
Brevard Middle School
Brevard, North Carolina

Shaun Kelley Wallace
Social Studies Teacher
Alexander Middle School
Huntersville, North Carolina

Sonya Lou Weaver
Social Studies Teacher
Greencastle–Antrim
 Middle School
Greencastle, Pennsylvania

Carol Davenport Wood
Social Studies Teacher
Lusher Extension
New Orleans, Louisiana

Table of Contents

Chest brought from the Netherlands, colonial period

Table of Contents

The Victory Ball at Fredericksburg, 1781
by Jean L.G. Ferris

Table of Contents

Fan brought to America from China

World War II Service Star flag

Table of Contents

Appendix

Table of Contents

Civil War songsheet

Table of Contents

Huron box, 17th century

SKILL BUILDER

America's FLAGS

Campaign banner and torch, mid-1800s

Table of Contents

Table of Contents

Maps

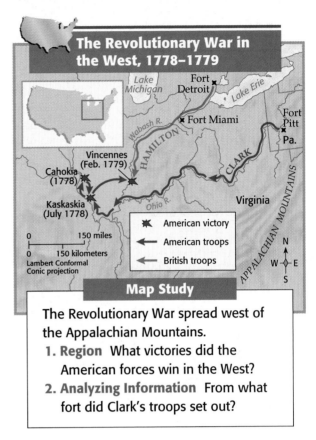

The Revolutionary War in the West, 1778–1779

American victory
American troops
British troops

Map Study

The Revolutionary War spread west of the Appalachian Mountains.
1. **Region** What victories did the American forces win in the West?
2. **Analyzing Information** From what fort did Clark's troops set out?

Table of Contents

The Korean War, 1950–53

UN forces
Chinese Communist and N. Korean forces
N. Korean forces
Truce line, July 1953
Capital city

130°E

PEOPLE'S REPUBLIC OF CHINA

SOVIET UNION

3. Farthest advance of UN forces Nov. 1950

Yalu R.

NORTH KOREA

N
W E
S

Sea of Japan

Pyongyang

38°N

Panmunjom

38th Parallel (Int'l. boundary line)

Seoul
Inchon

2. UN landing Sept. 1950

4. Farthest advance of North Koreans and Chinese Jan. 1951

SOUTH KOREA

Pusan

1. Farthest advance of North Koreans Sept. 1950

Yellow Sea

34°N

0   100 miles
0   100 kilometers
Bonne projection

Korea Strait

JAPAN

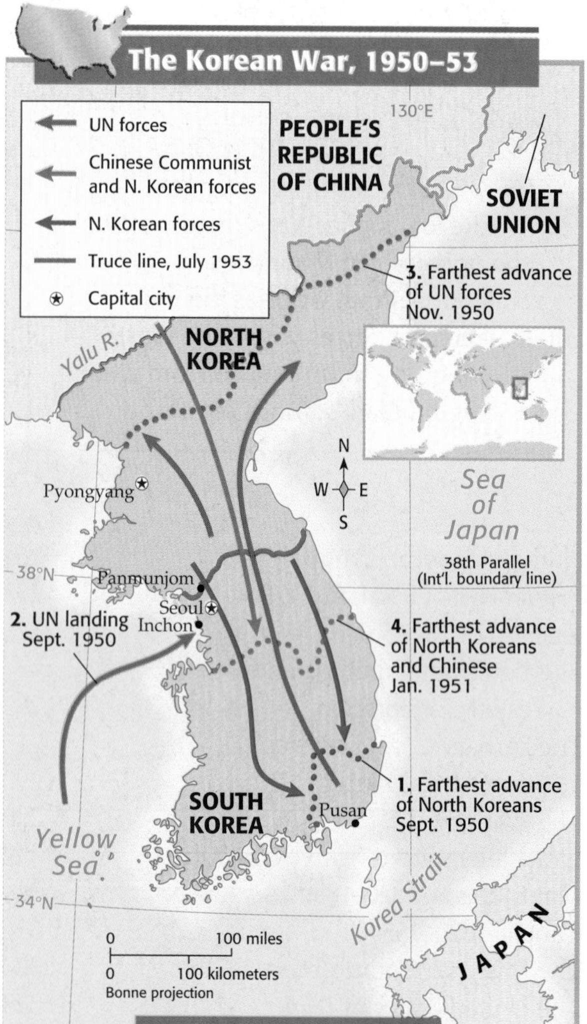

Map Study

The Korean War raged along the Korean Peninsula.
1. **Location** What city is located along the 38th parallel?
2. **Analyzing Information** Whose forces landed at Inchon in September 1950?

Charts, Graphs, and Tables

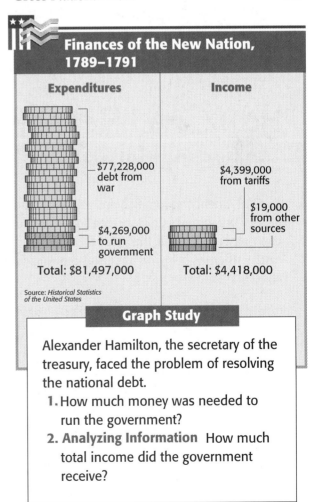

Finances of the New Nation, 1789–1791

Expenditures

$77,228,000 debt from war

$4,269,000 to run government

Total: $81,497,000

Income

$4,399,000 from tariffs

$19,000 from other sources

Total: $4,418,000

Source: *Historical Statistics of the United States*

Graph Study

Alexander Hamilton, the secretary of the treasury, faced the problem of resolving the national debt.

1. How much money was needed to run the government?
2. **Analyzing Information** How much total income did the government receive?

What Is American History?

American history is people, events, places, documents, art, inventions, literature. In other words—American history is everything about the adventures of all Americans—past and present.

Golden spike commemorating completion of transcontinental railroad

New Deal badge

Why Study American History?

Only by learning about the past can you truly understand the present. Only by learning about your nation's past can you understand what it means to be an American today.

Detail from quilt, mid-1800s

How Can I Remember Everything?

The American Journey helps you learn about your nation's past by organizing its history around 10 themes. A *theme* is a concept, or main idea, that happens again and again throughout history. Themes help you understand events in the past and how they affect you today.

Using the Themes in *The American Journey*

To help you learn about your nation's history, the authors have identified major themes for every section of *The American Journey.* You will find these listed under **Chapter Themes** at the beginning of every chapter. You can check your understanding of these themes in every **Section Assess-** **ment.** Finally, in the Reviewing Themes section of every **Chapter Assessment** you are asked questions that help you put it all together to better understand how ideas are connected across time—and to see why history is important to you today. Read more about these themes on the next page.

What Do the Themes in The American Journey Mean?

1. **Culture and Traditions** Being aware of cultural differences helps us understand ourselves and others.

2. **Continuity and Change** Recognizing our historic roots helps us understand why things are the way they are today.

3. **Geography and History** Understanding geography helps us understand how humans interact with their environment.

4. **Individual Action** Recognizing the contributions of men and women in history helps us see patterns of power, influence, and progress.

5. **Groups and Institutions** Identifying how political and social groups and institutions work helps us work together.

6. **Government and Democracy** Understanding the workings of government helps us become good citizens.

7. **Economic Factors** Understanding production, distribution, and consumption helps us see how economic factors influence our lives.

8. **Science and Technology** Understanding the roles of science and technology helps us see their impact on our society today and the roles they will play in the future.

Twig figure found in Grand Canyon

9. **Global Connections** Being aware of global interdependence helps us make decisions and deal with the difficult issues we will encounter.

10. **Civic Rights and Responsibilities** Recognizing America's democratic principles will help us claim and fulfill our own civic duties.

Continental coin

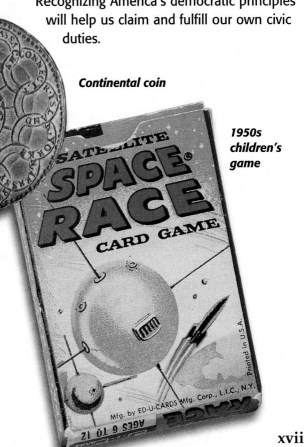

1950s children's game

REFERENCE ATLAS

NATIONAL
GEOGRAPHIC
SOCIETY

ATLAS KEY

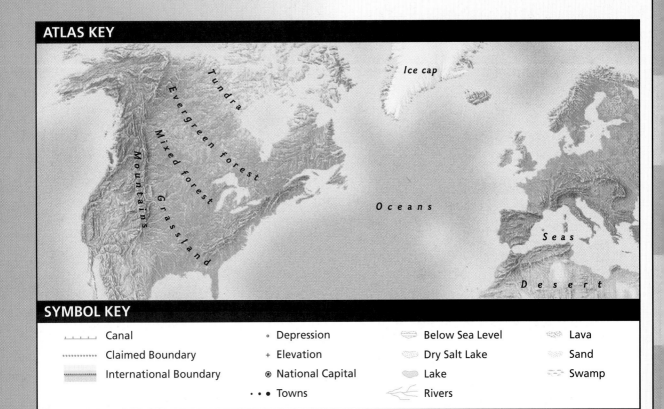

SYMBOL KEY

⊥⊥⊥	Canal	∘	Depression	⬮	Below Sea Level	〰	Lava
··········	Claimed Boundary	+	Elevation	〰	Dry Salt Lake	〰	Sand
▦▦▦	International Boundary	⊛	National Capital	〰	Lake	⇢	Swamp
		• • ●	Towns	≪	Rivers		

A New Nation, 1787

BRITISH NORTH AMERICA

Claimed by U.S. and Great Britain

Claimed by U.S. and Great Britain

Part of Mass.

Claimed by N.H. and N.Y.

NORTHWEST TERRITORY Ceded by Va. to U.S. 1784

Ceded by Mass. to U.S. 1785

Awarded to Pa. from Conn. 1782

Ceded by Mass. to N.Y. 1786

NEW HAMPSHIRE

MASSACHUSETTS

RHODE ISLAND

CONNECTICUT

New York (1787-1790)

Mississippi

Missouri

Ceded by Conn. to U.S. 1786 & 1800

PA.

NEW JERSEY

MD.

DELAWARE

SPANISH

NORTH

AMERICA

SPANISH LOUISIANA

Arkansas

Wabash

Ohio

UNITED

VIRGINIA

STATES

Ceded by New York to U.S. 1782

Claimed by Virginia

NORTH CAROLINA

ALTA CALIFORNIA

Colorado

Claimed by North Carolina

SOUTH CAROLINA

Gila

Ceded by S.C. to Ga. 1787

Claimed by Georgia

GEORGIA

BAJA CALIFORNIA

Rio Grande

WESTERN INTERIOR PROVINCES

Claimed by Ga., Spain and U.S.

SPANISH FLORIDA

EASTERN INTERIOR PROVINCES

	Original 13 states
	Land still claimed by states 1787
	U.S. territory
	British territory
	Spanish territory
– – –	Disputed boundary

Expanding West of the Mississippi, 1803

BRITISH NORTH AMERICA

Claimed by U.S. and Great Britain

OREGON COUNTRY
Claimed by Great Britain, Russia, Spain, and United States

Claimed by U.S. and Great Britain

VERMONT 1791

Mississippi

Missouri

INDIANA

TERRITORY

Philadelphia (1790-1800)

NEW SPAIN
(SPANISH MEXICO)

LOUISIANA PURCHASE
Purchased by U.S. 1803

Wabash

OHIO 1803

Ohio

Washington (new capital 1800)

Arkansas

KENTUCKY 1792

TENNESSEE 1796

Red

Ceded by Georgia to U.S. 1802

Rio Grande

Claimed by U.S. and Spain

MISSISSIPPI TERR.

SPANISH FLORIDA

Claimed by U.S. and Spain

UNITED STATES

TERRITORIAL GROWTH

	States previously in the Union
	States newly admitted

NATIONAL GEOGRAPHIC SOCIETY

Coming of Age, 1821

BRITISH NORTH AMERICA

Columbia

U.S.–British treaty line of 1818

RED RIVER BASIN
To U.S.
1818

Claimed by U.S.
and Great Britain

MAINE
1820

OREGON COUNTRY
U.S.–British agreement
to joint occupation in 1818

Snake

Adams-Onis Treaty line of 1819

*MICHIGAN
TERRITORY*

UNORGANIZED

TERRITORY

Mississippi

Missouri

INDIANA
1816

ILLINOIS
1818

Ohio

Wabash

⊛Washington

**ALTA
CALIFORNIA**

Colorado

Arkansas

MISSOURI
1821

M E X I C O

Gila

Red

ARKANSAS TERRITORY

Rio Grande

MISSISSIPPI
1817

ALABAMA
1819

**BAJA
CALIFORNIA**

TEXAS

LOUISIANA
1812

FLORIDA
To U.S.
1819

Coast to Coast, 1850 and beyond

BRITISH NORTH AMERICA

Treaty line of 1846

Treaty line of 1842

Treaty line of 1842

WASHINGTON
1889

MONTANA
1889

NORTH DAKOTA
1889

MINNESOTA
1858

OREGON TERRITORY
Added to U.S. in 1846

Snake

IDAHO
1890

*MINNESOTA
TERRITORY*

MICHIGAN
1837

OREGON
1859

WISCONSIN
1848

WYOMING
1890

SOUTH DAKOTA
1889

NEVADA
1864

UNORGANIZED

IOWA
1846

UTAH TERRITORY

TERRITORY

NEBRASKA
1867

Missouri

Wabash

Ohio

W. VA.
1863

⊛Washington

CALIFORNIA
1850

UTAH
1896

COLORADO
1876

KANSAS
1861

Arkansas

Colorado

ARIZONA
1912

Gila

**NEW MEXICO
TERRITORY**

OKLAHOMA
1907

ARKANSAS
1836

Red

**GADSDEN
PURCHASE**
To U.S. 1853

NEW MEXICO
1912

Mississippi

RUSSIA

Rio Grande

TEXAS
1845

FLORIDA
1845

ALASKA
1959

*Purchased by U.S.
1867*

M E X I C O

······ States admitted
after 1850

HAWAII
1959

*Annexed by U.S.
1898*

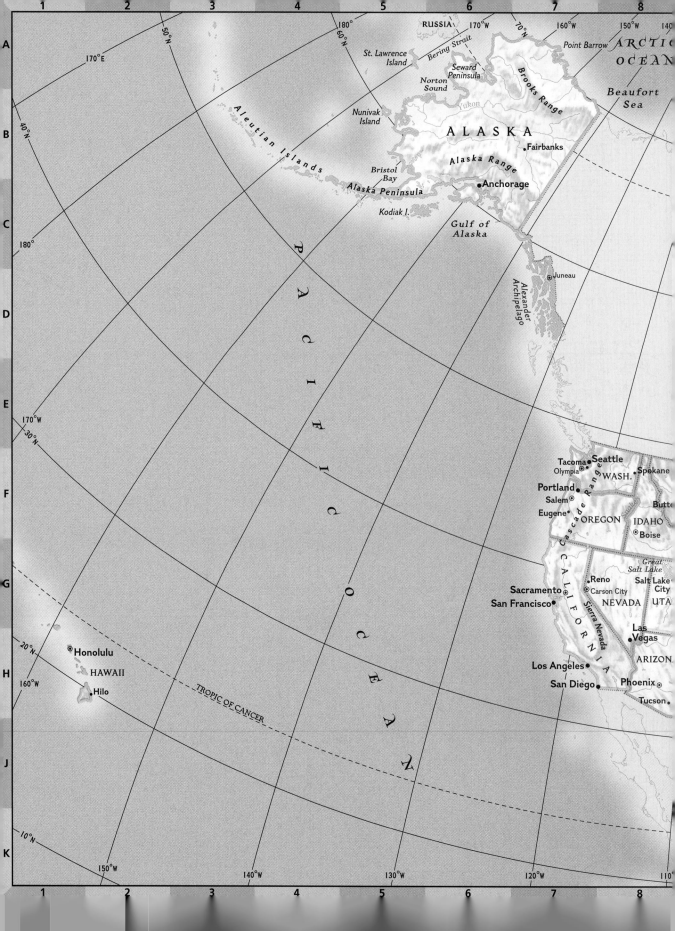

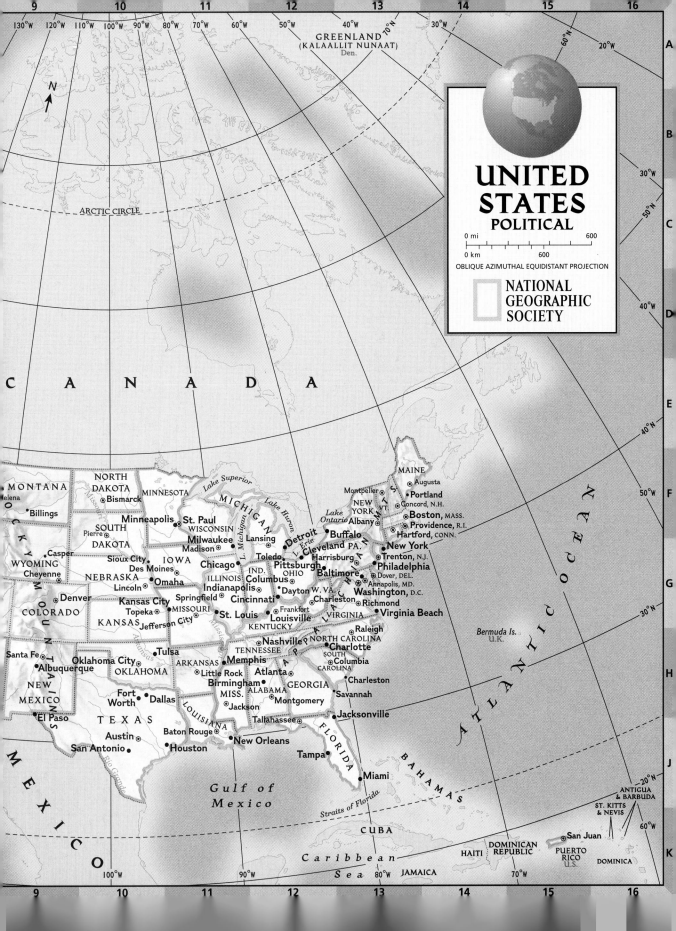

UNITED STATES POLITICAL

0 mi _____ 600

0 km _____ 600

OBLIQUE AZIMUTHAL EQUIDISTANT PROJECTION

NATIONAL GEOGRAPHIC SOCIETY

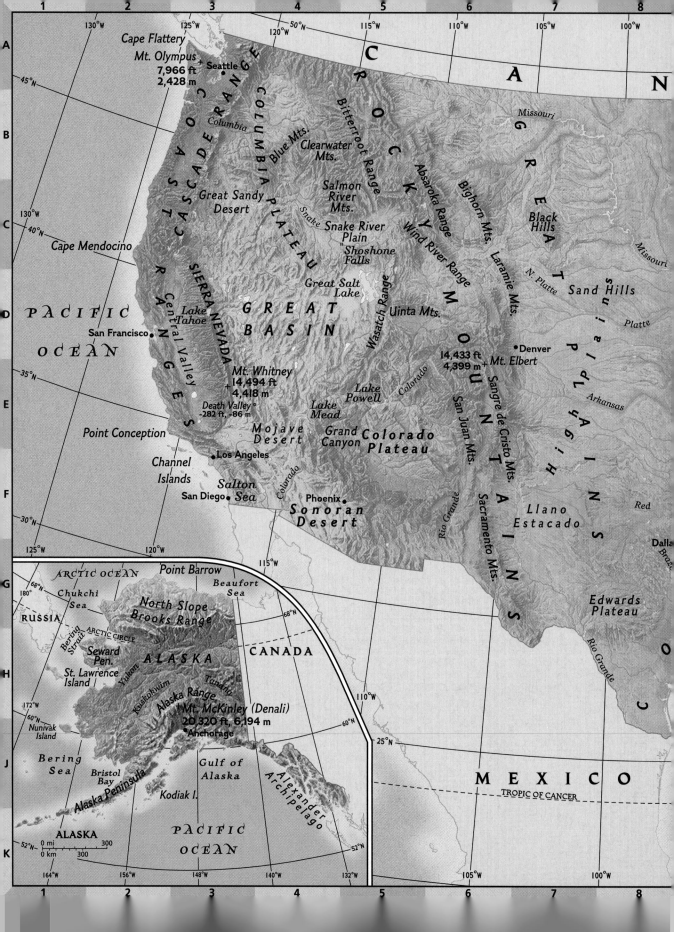

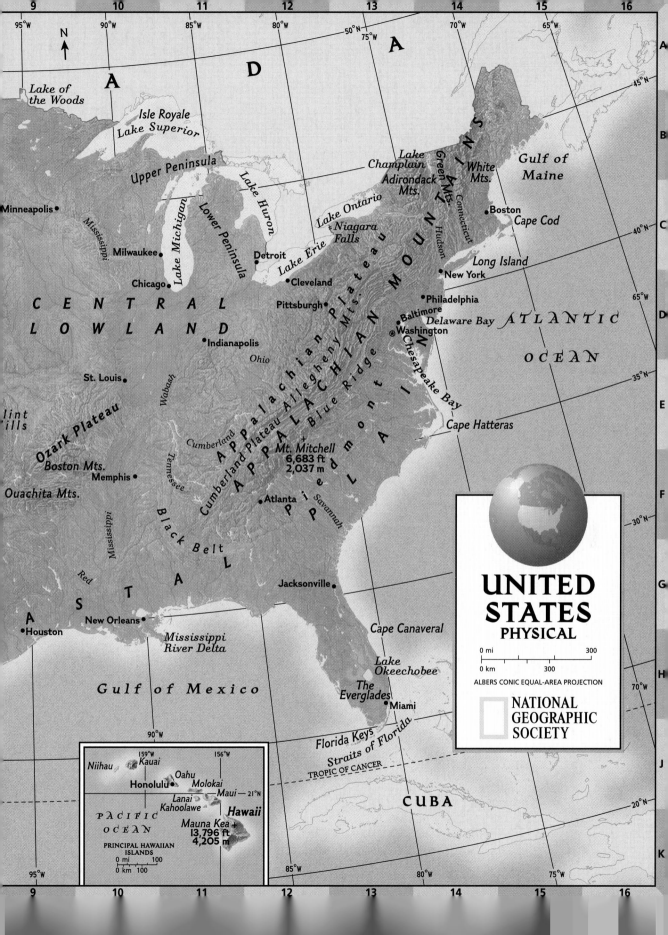

UNITED STATES
PHYSICAL

0 mi   300
0 km   300

ALBERS CONIC EQUAL-AREA PROJECTION

NATIONAL
GEOGRAPHIC
SOCIETY

PRINCIPAL HAWAIIAN ISLANDS

0 mi   100
0 km   100

MIDDLE AMERICA
PHYSICAL/POLITICAL

0 mi   400
0 km   400

AZIMUTHAL EQUIDISTANT PROJECTION

NATIONAL
GEOGRAPHIC
SOCIETY

UNITED STATES

N

Tijuana
Mexicali
Sonoran Desert
Ciudad Juarez
30°N
Baja California
Gulf of California
Chihuahua
Rio Grande
Nuevo Laredo
MEXICO
Sierra Madre Occidental
Sierra Madre Oriental
Monterrey
Matamoros
Gulf of Mexico
La Paz
False Cape
Mazatlan
20°N
Ciudad Madero
Tampico
San Luis Potosi
Leon
Guadalajara
Bay of Campeche
Merida
Cozumel Island
Yucatan Peninsula
Revillagigedo Islands
Mex.
Mexico City
Popocatepetl
17,802 ft
5,426 m
Orizaba
18,855 ft
5,747 m
Veracruz
Sierra Madre del Sur
Isthmus of Tehuantepec
Belmopan
Belize City
BELIZE
Gulf of Hondu
Acapulco
Gulf of Tehuantepec
Sierra Madre
GUATEMALA
Guatemala City
Tegucigalpa
HO
EL SALVADOR
San Salvador
Lee
CENTRA
10°N
AMERIC
PACIFIC
OCEAN
Cocos Isla
C.R.
0°
110°W
100°W
90°W

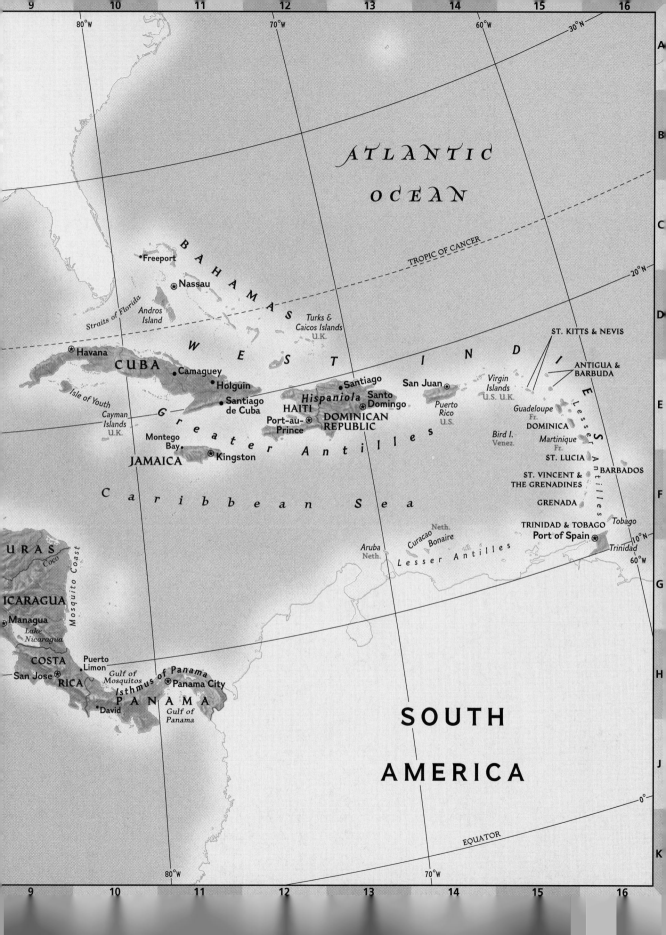

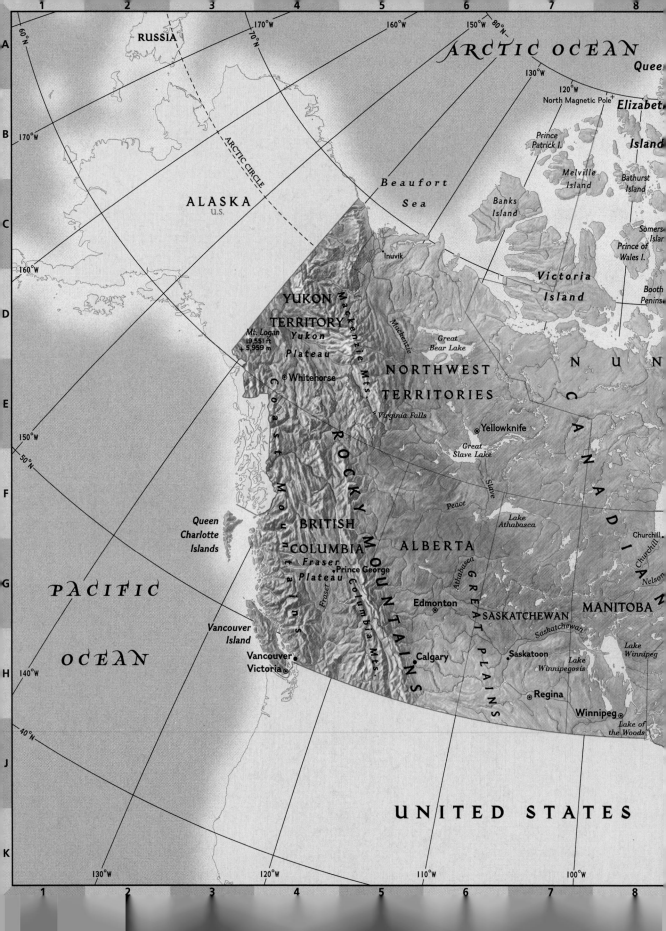

CANADA
PHYSICAL/POLITICAL

0 mi ———————— 400
0 km ———————— 400

AZIMUTHAL EQUIDISTANT PROJECTION

NATIONAL GEOGRAPHIC SOCIETY

Ellesmere Island

evon Island

ICELAND

GREENLAND
(KALAALLIT NUNAAT)
Den.

Baffin Bay

Davis Strait

Melville Peninsula

Foxe Basin

Baffin Island

N U N A V U T

Southampton Island

Iqaluit

Hudson Strait

Labrador Sea

Ungava Bay

Hudson Bay

Belcher Islands

NEWFOUNDLAND

Cartwright

Schefferville
Smallwood Reservoir
Happy Valley-Goose Bay
"Churchill Falls"

LABRADOR

Island of Newfoundland

James Bay

QUEBEC

St. John's
Avalon Peninsula

Manicouagan Reservoir
Sept-Iles

Anticosti I.

St-Pierre & Miquelon
Fr.

SHIELD

Gaspe Pen.

Gulf of St. Lawrence

PRINCE EDWARD ISLAND

Cape Breton I.

ATLANTIC

ONTARIO

Lake Nipigon

Chicoutimi

Charlottetown
NOVA SCOTIA

NEW BRUNSWICK

Thunder Bay
Lake Superior

Rouyn-Noranda

Quebec City
Fredericton
Saint John
Halifax

OCEAN

Sudbury

Montreal
St. Lawrence
Bay of Fundy

Ottawa

Lake Huron

Toronto
L. Ontario
Niagara Falls
London
L. Erie

Lake Michigan

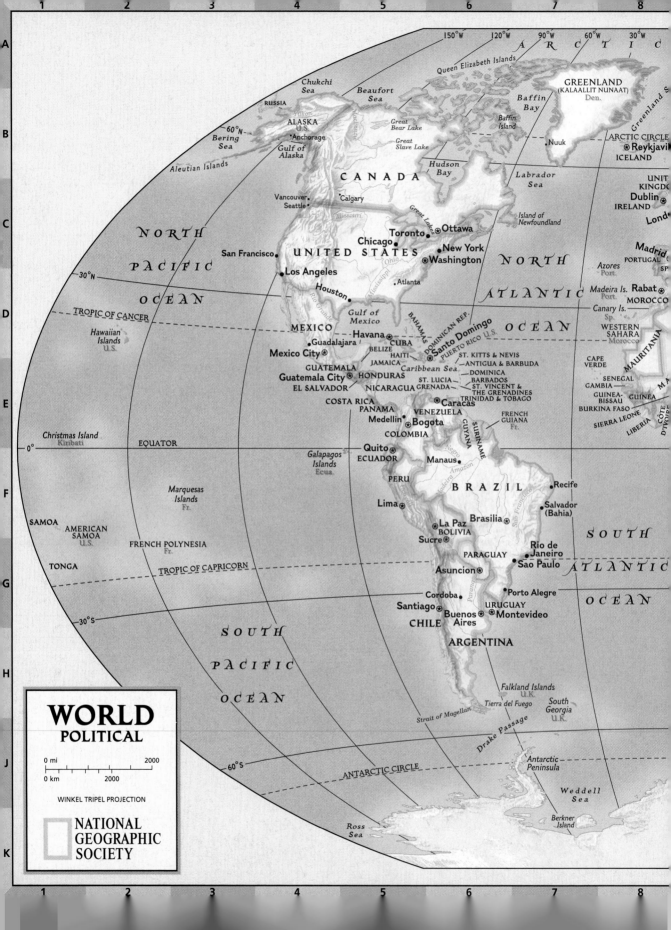

WORLD
POLITICAL

0 mi　　　　　　2000
0 km　　　　　　2000

WINKEL TRIPEL PROJECTION

NATIONAL GEOGRAPHIC SOCIETY

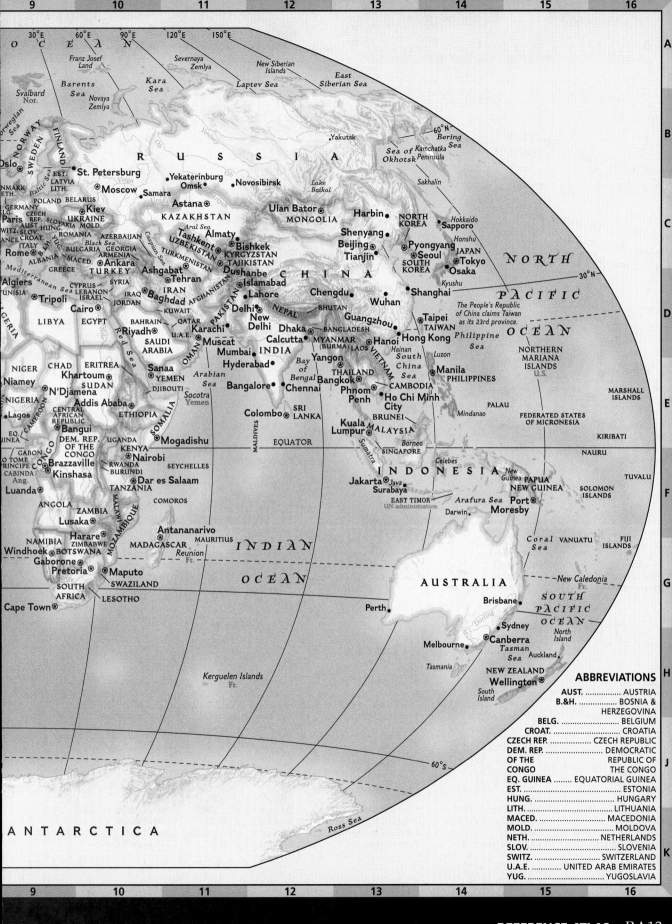

United States Facts

States at a Glance

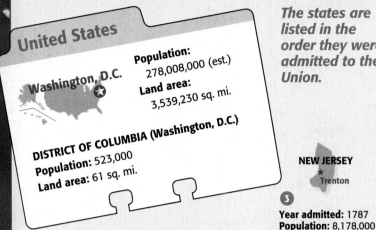

United States

Washington, D.C.

Population: 278,008,000 (est.)

Land area: 3,539,230 sq. mi.

DISTRICT OF COLUMBIA (Washington, D.C.)
Population: 523,000
Land area: 61 sq. mi.

The states are listed in the order they were admitted to the Union.

DELAWARE — Dover
❶
Year admitted: 1787
Population: 768,000
Land area: 1,954 sq. mi.
Representatives: 1

PENNSYLVANIA — Harrisburg
❷
Year admitted: 1787
Population: 12,202,000
Land area: 44,819 sq. mi.
Representatives: 21

NEW JERSEY — Trenton
❸
Year admitted: 1787
Population: 8,178,000
Land area: 7,418 sq. mi.
Representatives: 13

GEORGIA — Atlanta
❹
Year admitted: 1788
Population: 7,875,000
Land area: 57,918 sq. mi.
Representatives: 11

CONNECTICUT — Hartford
❺
Year admitted: 1788
Population: 3,284,000
Land area: 4,845 sq. mi.
Representatives: 6

MASSACHUSETTS — Boston
❻
Year admitted: 1788
Population: 6,199,000
Land area: 7,838 sq. mi.
Representatives: 10

MARYLAND — Annapolis
❼
Year admitted: 1788
Population: 5,275,000
Land area: 9,774 sq. mi.
Representatives: 8

SOUTH CAROLINA — Columbia
❽
Year admitted: 1788
Population: 3,858,000
Land area: 30,111 sq. mi.
Representatives: 6

NEW HAMPSHIRE — Concord
❾
Year admitted: 1788
Population: 1,224,000
Land area: 8,969 sq. mi.
Representatives: 2

VIRGINIA — Richmond
❿
Year admitted: 1788
Population: 6,997,000
Land area: 39,597 sq. mi.
Representatives: 11

NEW YORK — Albany
⓫
Year admitted: 1788
Population: 18,146,000
Land area: 47,223 sq. mi.
Representatives: 31

NORTH CAROLINA — Raleigh
⓬
Year admitted: 1789
Population: 7,777,000
Land area: 48,718 sq. mi.
Representatives: 12

RHODE ISLAND — Providence
⓭
Year admitted: 1790
Population: 998,000
Land area: 1,212 sq. mi.
Representatives: 2

VERMONT — Montpelier
⓮
Year admitted: 1791
Population: 617,000
Land area: 9,249 sq. mi.
Representatives: 1

KENTUCKY — Frankfort
⓯
Year admitted: 1792
Population: 3,995,000
Land area: 39,732 sq. mi.
Representatives: 6

TENNESSEE — Nashville
⓰
Year admitted: 1796
Population: 5,657,000
Land area: 41,219 sq. mi.
Representatives: 9

OHIO — Columbus
⓱
Year admitted: 1803
Population: 11,319,000
Land area: 40,952 sq. mi.
Representatives: 19

LOUISIANA — Baton Rouge
⓲
Year admitted: 1812
Population: 4,425,000
Land area: 43,566 sq. mi.
Representatives: 7

INDIANA — Indianapolis
⓳
Year admitted: 1816
Population: 6,045,000
Land area: 35,870 sq. mi.
Representatives: 10

MISSISSIPPI — Jackson
⓴
Year admitted: 1817
Population: 2,816,000
Land area: 46,913 sq. mi.
Representatives: 5

ILLINOIS — Springfield
㉑
Year admitted: 1818
Population: 12,051,000
Land area: 55,593 sq. mi.
Representatives: 20

ALABAMA — Montgomery
㉒
Year admitted: 1819
Population: 4,451,000
Land area: 50,750 sq. mi.
Representatives: 7

MAINE — Augusta
㉓
Year admitted: 1820
Population: 1,259,000
Land area: 30,864 sq. mi.
Representatives: 2

MISSOURI — Jefferson City
㉔
Year admitted: 1821
Population: 5,540,000
Land area: 68,898 sq. mi.
Representatives: 9

ARKANSAS — Little Rock
㉕
Year admitted: 1836
Population: 2,631,000
Land area: 52,075 sq. mi.
Representatives: 4

MICHIGAN ★ Lansing
Tallahassee ★ **FLORIDA**
TEXAS ★ Austin
IOWA ★ Des Moines
WISCONSIN Madison ★

(26)
Year admitted: 1837
Population: 9,679,000
Land area: 56,809 sq. mi.
Representatives: 16

(27)
Year admitted: 1845
Population: 15,233,000
Land area: 53,997 sq. mi.
Representatives: 23

(28)
Year admitted: 1845
Population: 20,119,000
Land area: 261,194 sq. mi.
Representatives: 30

(29)
Year admitted: 1846
Population: 2,900,000
Land area: 55,874 sq. mi.
Representatives: 5

(30)
Year admitted: 1848
Population: 5,326,000
Land area: 54,313 sq. mi.
Representatives: 9

★ Sacramento **CALIFORNIA**
MINNESOTA Saint Paul ★
Salem ★ **OREGON**
Topeka ★ **KANSAS**
Charleston ★ **WEST VIRGINIA**

(31)
Year admitted: 1850
Population: 32,521,000
Land area: 155,973 sq. mi.
Representatives: 52

(32)
Year admitted: 1858
Population: 4,830,000
Land area: 79,616 sq. mi.
Representatives: 8

(33)
Year admitted: 1859
Population: 3,397,000
Land area: 96,002 sq. mi.
Representatives: 5

(34)
Year admitted: 1861
Population: 2,668,000
Land area: 81,823 sq. mi.
Representatives: 4

(35)
Year admitted: 1863
Population: 1,841,000
Land area: 24,086 sq. mi.
Representatives: 3

NEVADA ★ Carson City
NEBRASKA Lincoln ★
Denver ★ **COLORADO**
NORTH DAKOTA ★ Bismarck
SOUTH DAKOTA ★ Pierre

(36)
Year admitted: 1864
Population: 1,871,000
Land area: 109,805 sq. mi.
Representatives: 2

(37)
Year admitted: 1867
Population: 1,705,000
Land area: 76,877 sq. mi.
Representatives: 3

(38)
Year admitted: 1876
Population: 4,168,000
Land area: 103,729 sq. mi.
Representatives: 6

(39)
Year admitted: 1889
Population: 662,000
Land area: 68,994 sq. mi.
Representatives: 1

(40)
Year admitted: 1889
Population: 777,000
Land area: 75,897 sq. mi.
Representatives: 1

MONTANA ★ Helena
★ Olympia **WASHINGTON**
IDAHO ★ Boise
WYOMING Cheyenne ★
★ Salt Lake City **UTAH**

(41)
Year admitted: 1889
Population: 950,000
Land area: 145,556 sq. mi.
Representatives: 1

(42)
Year admitted: 1889
Population: 5,858,000
Land area: 66,581 sq. mi.
Representatives: 9

(43)
Year admitted: 1890
Population: 1,347,000
Land area: 82,750 sq. mi.
Representatives: 2

(44)
Year admitted: 1890
Population: 525,000
Land area: 97,104 sq. mi.
Representatives: 1

(45)
Year admitted: 1896
Population: 2,207,000
Land area: 82,168 sq. mi.
Representatives: 3

Oklahoma City ★ **OKLAHOMA**
Santa Fe ★ **NEW MEXICO**
ARIZONA ★ Phoenix

(46)
Year admitted: 1907
Population: 3,373,000
Land area: 68,678 sq. mi.
Representatives: 6

(47)
Year admitted: 1912
Population: 1,860,000
Land area: 121,364 sq. mi.
Representatives: 3

(48)
Year admitted: 1912
Population: 4,798,000
Land area: 113,642 sq. mi.
Representatives: 6

U.S. Territories

PUERTO RICO
Population: 3,908,000
Land area: 3,459 sq. mi.
Capital: San Juan

U.S. VIRGIN ISLANDS
Population: 99,000
Land area: 132 sq. mi.
Capital: Charlotte Amalie

GUAM
Population: 171,000
Land area: 209 sq. mi.
Capital: Agana

AMERICAN SAMOA
Population: 69,000
Land area: 77 sq. mi.
Capital: Pago Pago

ALASKA ★ Juneau
Honolulu ★ **HAWAII**

(49)
Year admitted: 1959
Population: 653,000
Land area: 591,004 sq. mi.
Representatives: 1

(50)
Year admitted: 1959
Population: 1,257,000
Land area: 6,432 sq. mi.
Representatives: 2

• Population figures are based on U.S. Bureau of the Census projections for 2000. House of Representatives figures are from the *1997 Information Please Almanac*.
• States are not drawn to scale.

Geography HANDBOOK

The story of the United States begins with **geography**—the study of the earth in all of its variety. Geography describes the earth's land, water, and plant and animal life. It is the study of places and the complex relationships between people and their environments.

The United States is a land of startling physical differences. It is also a nation of diverse groups of people. A study of geography can help explain how the United States acquired its diversity.

The United States—with a total land area of 3,539,230 square miles (9,166,606 sq. km)—is the world's fourth-largest country in size. Only Russia, Canada, and China are larger.

Most of the United States—48 of the 50 states—spans the entire middle part of North America. This group of states touches three major bodies of water—the Atlantic Ocean, the Gulf of Mexico, and the Pacific Ocean. Two states—Alaska and Hawaii—lie apart from the 48 states. Alaska, the largest state, is located in the northwestern part of North America. Hawaii lies in the Pacific Ocean about 2,400 miles (3,862 km) southwest of California.

Within the borders of the United States stretch a rich variety of landscapes—dense forests, hot deserts, rolling grasslands, and snow-capped mountains. Because of its large

Mountains frame the eastern and western coasts of the United States; plains span the center. Here, a lighthouse stands on the Maine coast.

Continental United States: Physical Profile

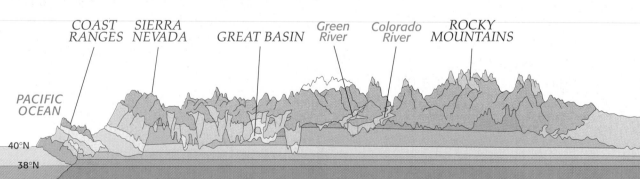

Geographic Facts About the United States

Largest state	Alaska	591,004 square miles (1,530,700 sq. km)
Smallest state	Rhode Island	1,212 square miles (3,139 sq. km)
Most populated state	California	32,521,000
Least populated state	Wyoming	525,000
Longest river	Mississippi	2,348 miles (3,778 km)
Highest waterfall	Yosemite Falls (California)	2,425 feet (739 m)
Points farthest apart	Log Point, Elliot Key, Florida and Kure Island, Hawaii	5,859 miles (9,429 km)
Largest lake	Lake Superior*	31,820 square miles (82,414 sq. km)
Deepest lake	Crater Lake (Oregon)	1,932 feet (589 m)
Highest mountain	Mount McKinley (Alaska)	20,320 feet (6,194 m)
Lowest point	Death Valley (California)	282 feet (86 m) below sea level
Rainiest location	Mt. Waialeale (Hawaii)	460 inches (1,168 cm) rainfall per year
Highest recorded temperature	Death Valley (California)	134° Fahrenheit, on July 10, 1913
Lowest recorded temperature	Prospect Creek (Alaska)	-80° Fahrenheit, on January 23, 1971

*Part of Lake Superior is located in Canada

Population source: *U.S. Bureau of the Census.*

Chart Study

This chart lists geographic facts about the United States.

1. In what state is the highest mountain?

2. What states have both the highest and lowest of something? Name those highs and lows.

size and diverse environments, the United States throughout its history has offered many opportunities. Many historians believe that thousands of years ago, the first Americans migrated across a land bridge from Asia to the countries we now call the United States and Canada. Over the centuries people from Europe, Africa, Asia, and other parts of the Americas followed. Today more than 266 million people make their homes in the United States. They live in crowded metropolitan areas, in towns and villages, and in rural communities.

Coast to Coast This diagram shows the proportionate elevation across the continental United States between 38°N and 40°N latitude.

GREAT PLAINS

CENTRAL LOWLANDS

Mississippi River   Illinois River   Wabash River   Ohio River

APPALACHIAN MOUNTAINS

ATLANTIC COASTAL PLAIN

ATLANTIC OCEAN

40°N

38°N

Five Geography Themes

Geography has shaped the development of the United States. To show the link between history and geography, geographers—the people who study geography—have organized the subject into five broad themes. These themes are location, place, human/environment interaction, movement, and region.

Location

"Where is it?" Every place has an absolute location and a relative location. **Absolute location** is one exact spot on the earth. To pinpoint places exactly, geographers use numbered lines called latitude and longitude lines.

Relative location tells where a place is, compared with one or more other places. Knowing a place's relative location may give us an understanding of how it was settled and how it developed culturally.

Place

"What is it like?" **Place** describes all the features and characteristics that give an area its own special quality. These can be physical characteristics such as landforms, climate, and plant or animal life. They can also be cultural characteristics—language, religion, music, and architecture.

The Rocky Mountain region shares rugged peaks and swift streams.

New York City

Human/Environment Interaction

"How does the relationship between people and their natural surroundings influence the way people live?" This is one of the questions that the theme of **human/environment interaction** answers. This theme also shows how people use the environment and how their actions affect the environment.

Movement

"How do people in one area relate to people in other areas?" Geographers answer this question within the theme of **movement.** People, ideas, goods, and information move from place to place.

The theme of movement shows the connections among different parts of the world. Transportation routes, communication systems, and trade connections linked people and places in the past. They have also helped create a global community today in which the United States plays an important role.

Region

"What common characteristics does a certain area share?" The answer to this question involves the theme of **region.** A region can be an area that has the same climate or physical features. Cultural features such as language, religion, or government can also form a region.

The Land

Like a patchwork quilt, the United States consists of regional stretches of different landscapes. Look at the map below to find the eight physical regions of the United States.

Coastal Plains

A broad lowland runs along the Atlantic Ocean and the Gulf of Mexico. Geographers divide this lowland into two parts: the **Atlantic Coastal Plain** and the **Gulf Coastal Plain.** These plains begin at sea level along the coasts and rise gradually inland to a height of about 1,000 feet (305 m).

The Atlantic Plain borders the Atlantic coast from Massachusetts to Florida. Many of the region's deepwater ports provided excellent harbors for the first settlers' ships. Today a densely populated area of cities and towns stretches along the Atlantic coast from Boston to Washington, D.C. This area of continuous urbanization is called a **megalopolis.**

Much wider than the Atlantic Plain, the Gulf Plain hugs the Gulf of Mexico from Florida to Texas. The Mississippi River—the longest river in the country—drains much of the Gulf Plain.

Physical Regions of the United States

Legend:
- Hawaii
- Intermountain
- Rocky Mountains
- Interior Plains
- Pacific Coast
- Canadian Shield
- Appalachian Highlands
- Coastal Plains

Map Study

The physical features of the United States vary greatly from the Pacific Coast to the Atlantic Coast.

1. **Region** According to the map, in what physical region is Kansas?
2. **Analyzing Information** What physical feature separates the Coastal Plains from the Interior Plains?

Appalachian Highlands

Curving west along the Atlantic Plain are the **Appalachian** (A•puh•LAY•chuhn) **Highlands.** They stretch about 1,500 miles (2,414 km) from Canada to Alabama and contain the forest-covered Appalachian Mountains. The Appalachians, which average about 6,000 feet (1,829 m) in height, are the oldest mountain range in North America. To the east of the Appalachians, the land descends abruptly to the Piedmont, a well-drained rolling land that meets the Coastal Plains.

Interior Plains and Lakes

The central part of the United States is made up of the Interior Plains. The eastern half of these plains, the **Central Lowlands,** consists of thick forests, broad river valleys, rolling flatlands, and grassy hills. The largest group of freshwater lakes in the world—the Great Lakes—lies in the northern part of the Central Lowlands.

The **Canadian Shield**—a vast expanse of huge rocks, low hills, and lakes—extends from central Canada into Minnesota, Michigan, and Wisconsin. Farther west lie the **Great Plains**—a broad, high area blanketed with fields of grain and grassy pasturelands.

Mountains and Basins

The western part of the Great Plains meets the awesome **Rocky Mountains.** The Rockies are the largest mountain range in North America, stretching all the way from Alaska to Mexico. With some peaks rising more than 14,000 feet (4,267 m), the Rocky Mountains are higher and more rugged than the Appalachians.

A ridge of the Rockies, the **Continental Divide,** separates the rivers and streams that flow west to the Pacific Ocean from those flowing east toward the Mississippi River and Gulf of Mexico. Several important rivers—including the Colorado, Missouri, Arkansas, and Rio Grande—begin in the Rocky Mountains.

West of the Rockies stretches the **Intermountain region,** an area of sparsely populated basins, plateaus, and deserts. The Colorado Plateau—in the southern part of the region—has some of the nation's most unusual landforms, including the Grand Canyon and various flat-topped rock formations.

Pacific Areas

The Pacific Ocean forms the western border of the continental United States. Near the coast lie two major mountain ranges: the **Sierra Nevada** and the **Coast Ranges.** Some of the peaks in these chains tower more than 12,000 feet (3,658 m). West of the Pacific mountain ranges are coastal lowlands and fertile valleys.

Alaska is also part of the Pacific region. Islands, bays, and **glaciers,** or large frozen rivers of slowly moving ice, line Alaska's southern coastline. Central and southern mountain ranges are broken up by lowlands and plateaus. Mount McKinley, North America's highest mountain at 20,320 feet (6,194 m), towers over this area.

The huge saguaro cactus grows only in the desert region of the southwestern United States.

Climate

The United States can be divided into 10 climate regions. **Climate** is the usual pattern of weather events that occurs in an area over a long time period. The United States's climates are determined by distance from the Equator, location near large bodies of water, and changing elevations. The climate map below shows the country's various climates.

Midlatitude Climates

Most of the United States lies in the middle latitudes—midway between the Equator and the North Pole. Climates in the midlatitudes are often moderate. Find the areas on the map that have a **humid continental** climate. Winters in these areas are cold and moist; summers are long and hot. In Chicago, January temperatures hover around 12°F (–11°C), whereas July temperatures may exceed 84°F (29°C).

The southeastern United States has a **humid subtropical** climate. Winters here are mild and cool, while summers are hot and humid. January temperatures in New Orleans rarely dip below 40°F (4°C). The city's July temperatures often soar above 90°F (32°C).

The area along the Pacific coast from northern California to southeastern Alaska has a

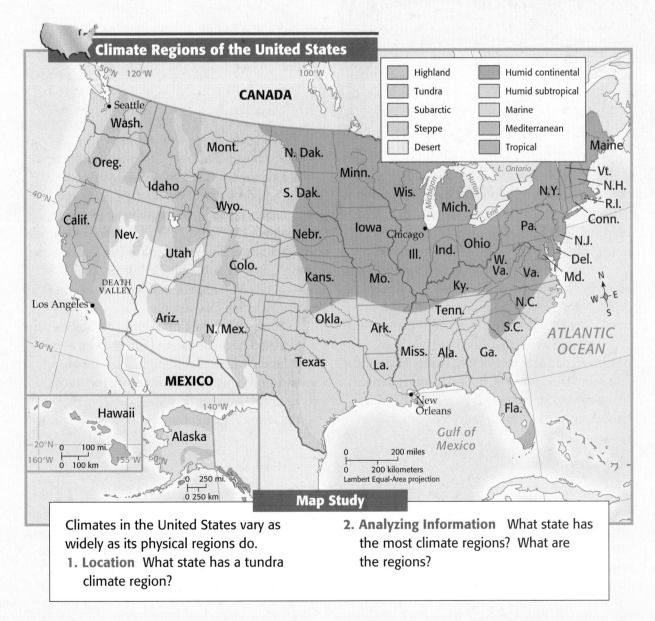

Climate Regions of the United States

Legend:
- Highland
- Tundra
- Subarctic
- Steppe
- Desert
- Humid continental
- Humid subtropical
- Marine
- Mediterranean
- Tropical

Map Study

Climates in the United States vary as widely as its physical regions do.

1. **Location** What state has a tundra climate region?

2. **Analyzing Information** What state has the most climate regions? What are the regions?

Death Valley (below) has a dry desert climate. Denali National Park (right) in Alaska experiences a subarctic climate.

marine climate. Temperatures here are mild year-round. Pacific winds bring plenty of rainfall to the marine climate region. The northwestern part of Washington State, on the Olympic Peninsula, is one of the wettest areas of the nation. More than 140 inches (356 cm) of rain falls there yearly.

Southern California, however, has a **Mediterranean** climate of dry, warm summers and rainy, mild winters. In Los Angeles, January temperatures stay at about 56°F (13°C). In July, temperatures are a moderate 75°F (24°C).

Dry Climates

A dry **desert** climate covers the plateaus and basins between the Pacific mountain ranges and the Rockies. Hot, dry air gets trapped here when the Pacific ranges block moist ocean winds. This region is dotted with deserts. In California's Death Valley—the hottest place in the United

States—summer temperatures often sizzle at 125°F (52°C)!

The western part of the Great Plains, however, has a dry **steppe,** or grasslands, climate. Winters here tend to be very cold, and summers hot and dry.

High Latitude Climates

Some areas of the United States have high latitude, or polar, climates. Alaska has tundra and subarctic climates. The **tundra**—a vast rolling, treeless plain south of the Arctic Circle—has bitterly cold winters in which average temperatures are below –15°F (–26°C). Summer temperatures in the tundra seldom rise above freezing. Farther south, Alaska's **subarctic** climate region has severely cold winters, but temperatures rise above freezing during the summer.

Although mountainous areas in the West are not located near the North Pole, they have a **highland** climate of cold or cool temperatures year-round. The high elevations of the Rockies, for example, cannot hold the heat from the sun, so the temperature drops.

Tropical Climates

Southern Florida and the Hawaiian Islands have **tropical** climates. Humidity and rainfall are high during much of the year. Summers are hot, and winters are warm. In Miami, Florida, January temperatures average more than 67°F (19°C); July temperatures more than 83°F (28°C).

Geography's Impact on United States History

![globe icon] Geographic factors—landforms, waterways, natural resources—have shaped the outcome of America's history. Here are some examples of geography's influences in history that are highlighted in *The American Journey*.

Unit 1 Different Worlds Meet

Native Americans developed various cultures thousands of years ago. Native Americans along the Pacific coast prospered because of the mild climate and the abundance of fish and plants. In the Southwest, Native Americans invented methods of irrigation to farm the dry land. The Great Plains Native Americans depended on herds of buffalo for food, clothing, shelter, and tools. Native Americans living in woodlands hunted a variety of animals and built farming villages.

Unit 2 Colonial Settlement

Europeans settled North America during the 1500s, 1600s, and 1700s. They came seeking land, riches, and the right to live freely. Groups from Spain, France, Great Britain, and other

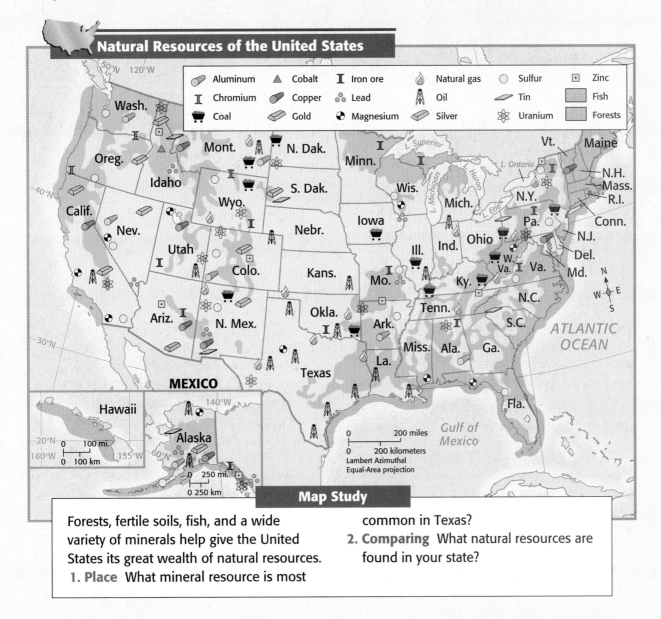

Natural Resources of the United States

Aluminum	Cobalt	Iron ore	Natural gas	Sulfur	Zinc
Chromium	Copper	Lead	Oil	Tin	Fish
Coal	Gold	Magnesium	Silver	Uranium	Forests

Map Study

Forests, fertile soils, fish, and a wide variety of minerals help give the United States its great wealth of natural resources.

1. **Place** What mineral resource is most common in Texas?

2. **Comparing** What natural resources are found in your state?

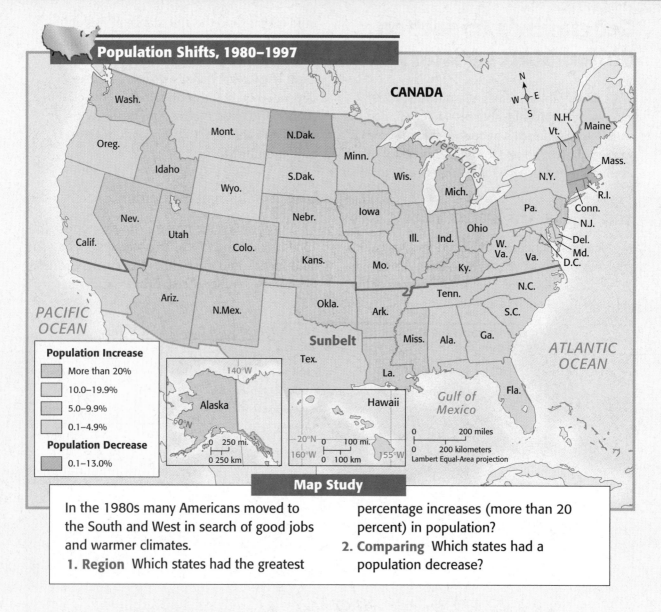

Population Shifts, 1980–1997

Population Increase
- More than 20%
- 10.0–19.9%
- 5.0–9.9%
- 0.1–4.9%

Population Decrease
- 0.1–13.0%

200 miles
200 kilometers
Lambert Equal-Area projection

Map Study

In the 1980s many Americans moved to the South and West in search of good jobs and warmer climates.

1. **Region** Which states had the greatest percentage increases (more than 20 percent) in population?

2. **Comparing** Which states had a population decrease?

countries set up colonies along rivers and other waterways. The British colonies along the Atlantic coast were hemmed in by the Appalachian Mountains—the first physical barrier to the West.

Unit 3 Creating a Nation

During the 1700s British colonists began to think of themselves as Americans. They fought to end the Crown's rule in the American colonies. The American soldiers were outnumbered and poorly equipped. Their knowledge of the environment, however, enabled them to use guerrilla tactics to defeat the stronger British troops.

Unit 4 The New Republic

During the early 1800s, New England launched the nation's Industrial Revolution. Factories began using steam-powered machines to make goods. Industry spread as large supplies of coal in Pennsylvania and Ohio made steam power cheap and manufacturing very profitable. Rivers and canals transported goods.

Unit 5 The Growing Nation

Through wars, treaties, and purchases, the United States gained control of the lands west of the Mississippi River. By the mid-1800s, the discovery of gold and silver drew thousands of settlers to Western territories. Railroads enabled people to overcome geographic barriers.

Unit 6 Civil War and Reconstruction

In the mid-1800s, the demand for cotton by the textile industry in the North made cotton production highly profitable in the agriculturally rich South. Enslaved Africans provided labor for large-scale farming. In 1861 regional differences and a dispute over slavery sparked the Civil War between the North and the South.

Unit 7 Reshaping the Nation

After the Civil War, transcontinental railroads transported goods from the East to the West and carried food products and beef cattle from the West to the East. Factories used electricity to make goods. The workers who advanced this industrial boom were immigrants and people who moved from farms to the cities.

Unit 8 Reform, Expansion, and War

As industry grew in the United States, foreign trade became more important. During and after World War I and World War II, the vast resources of the United States aided allies around the world. Along with weapons and manufactured goods, American culture also spread overseas and changed the way of life in many places.

Unit 9 Turbulent Decades

Environmental disasters during the first part of the 1900s affected the national economy. During the 1930s winds blew away so much of the soil in the Great Plains that the area became known as the Dust Bowl.

Unit 10 Turning Points

After World War II, high-technology industries helped the United States maintain its leadership role in world manufacturing. As

Across the Continent *by Currier and Ives, 1868*

computers and robots entered factories, many American workers learned new skills or started new careers.

Unit 11 Modern America

Always a mobile people, Americans during the 1900s continued to move from place to place. As the map on page 8 shows, industrial growth and a pleasant climate drew people to the South and Southwest in the 1980s and 1990s.

In recent years, the economies of the United States and other countries have become more **interdependent,** or reliant on each other. The movement of ideas and products has transformed the world into a global village.

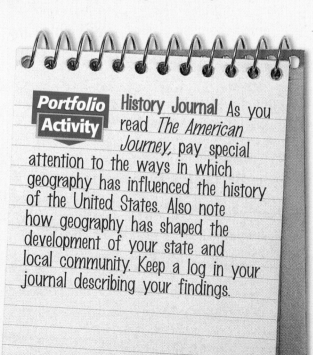

Portfolio Activity History Journal As you read *The American Journey,* pay special attention to the ways in which geography has influenced the history of the United States. Also note how geography has shaped the development of your state and local community. Keep a log in your journal describing your findings.

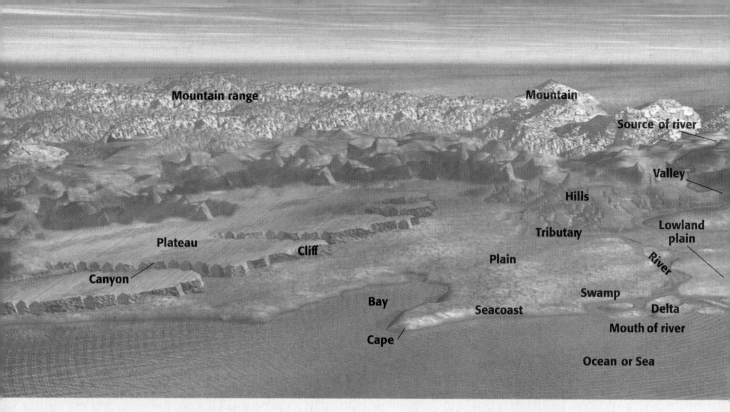

Mountain range   Mountain

Source of river

Valley

Hills

Lowland plain

Tributary

Plateau   Cliff

Plain

River

Canyon

Swamp

Bay   Seacoast

Delta

Cape

Mouth of river

Ocean or Sea

Geographic Dictionary

As you read about America's geography and history, you will encounter most of the terms listed below. Many of the terms are pictured in the diagram above.

absolute location exact location of a place on the earth described by global coordinates

basin area of land drained by a given river and its branches; area of land surrounded by lands of higher elevations

bay part of a large body of water that extends into a shoreline, generally smaller than a gulf

canyon deep and narrow valley with steep walls

cape point of land that extends into a river, lake, or ocean

channel wide strait or waterway between two land-masses that lie close to each other; deep part of a river or other waterway

cliff steep, high wall of rock, earth, or ice

continent one of the seven large landmasses on the earth

cultural feature characteristic that humans have created in a place, such as language, religion, housing, and settlement pattern

delta flat, low-lying land built up from soil carried downstream by a river and deposited at its mouth

divide stretch of high land that separates river systems

downstream direction in which a river or stream flows from its source to its mouth

elevation height of land above sea level

Equator imaginary line that runs around the earth halfway between the North and South Poles; used as the starting point to measure degrees of north and south latitude

glacier large, thick body of slowly moving ice

gulf part of a large body of water that extends into a shoreline, generally larger and more deeply indented than a bay

harbor a sheltered place along a shoreline where ships can anchor safely

highland elevated land area such as a hill, mountain, or plateau

hill elevated land with sloping sides and rounded summit; generally smaller than a mountain

island land area, smaller than a continent, completely surrounded by water

isthmus narrow stretch of land connecting two larger land areas

lake a sizable inland body of water

latitude distance north or south of the Equator, measured in degrees

longitude distance east or west of the Prime Meridian, measured in degrees

lowland land, usually level, at a low elevation

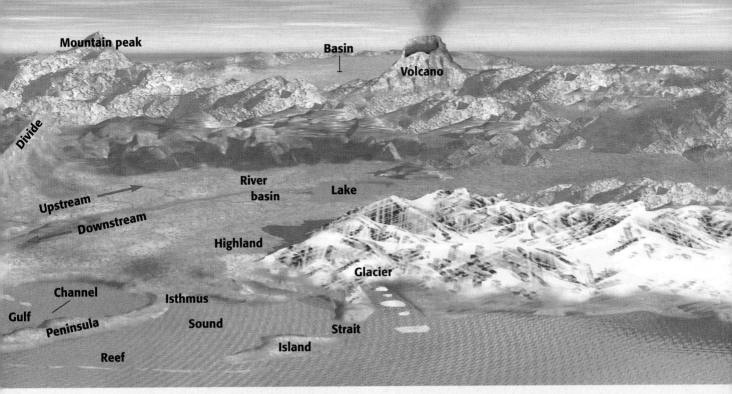

Mountain peak

Basin

Volcano

Divide

River basin

Lake

Upstream

Downstream

Highland

Glacier

Channel

Isthmus

Gulf

Peninsula

Sound

Strait

Island

Reef

map drawing of the earth shown on a flat surface

meridian one of many lines on the global grid running from the North Pole to the South Pole; used to measure degrees of longitude

mesa broad, flat-topped landform with steep sides; smaller than a plateau

mountain land with steep sides that rises sharply (1,000 feet or more) from surrounding land; generally larger and more rugged than a hill

mountain peak pointed top of a mountain

mountain range a series of connected mountains

mouth (of a river) place where a stream or river flows into a larger body of water

ocean one of the four major bodies of salt water that surround the continents

ocean current stream of either cold or warm water that moves in a definite direction through an ocean

parallel one of many lines on the global grid that circle the earth north or south of the Equator; used to measure degrees of latitude

peninsula body of land jutting into a lake or ocean, surrounded on three sides by water

physical feature characteristic of a place occurring naturally, such as a landform, body of water, climate pattern, or resource

plain area of level land, usually a low elevation and often covered with grasses

plateau area of flat or rolling land at a high elevation, about 300–3,000 feet high

Prime Meridian line of the global grid running from the North Pole to the South Pole at Greenwich, England; starting point for measuring degrees of east and west longitude

relief changes in elevation over a given area of land

river large natural stream of water that runs through the land

sea large body of water completely or partly surrounded by land

seacoast land lying next to a sea or ocean

sea level position on land level with surface of nearby ocean or sea

sound body of water between a coastline and one or more islands off the coast

source (of a river) place where a river or stream begins, often in highlands

strait narrow stretch of water joining two larger bodies of water

tributary small river or stream that flows into a large river or stream; a branch of the river

upstream direction opposite the flow of a river; toward the source of a river or stream

valley area of low land between hills or mountains

volcano mountain created as liquid rock or ash erupt from inside the earth

Unit 1

Different Worlds Meet

Beginnings to 1625

"The people of this island [have] such a generosity that they would give away their own hearts."

—CHRISTOPHER COLUMBUS, 1493

interNET CONNECTION

To learn more about this period in history, visit the Glencoe Social Studies Web Site at **www.glencoe.com** for information, activities, and links to other sites.

MAPPING *America*

Portfolio Activity Draw a freehand map of North America, Central America, and South America. As you read Unit 1, draw arrows on your map that show how the first Americans traveled throughout the Americas and where they ultimately settled. Also include the European explorers' routes on your map.

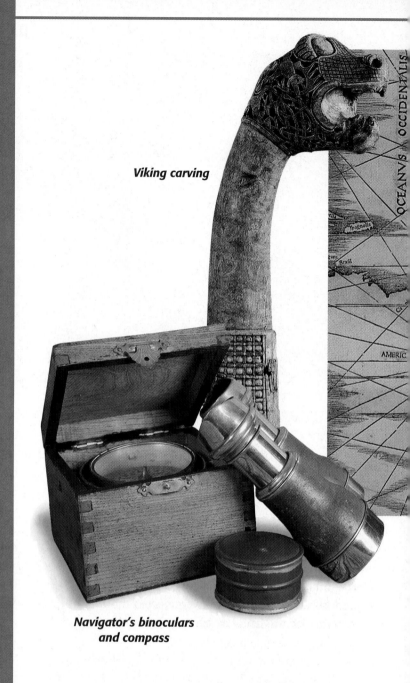

Viking carving

Navigator's binoculars and compass

The Americas

c. 28,000 B.C.
Asian hunters enter North America

7000 B.C.
Farming develops in Mexico

Pre-History

c. 10,000 B.C.
Last Ice Age ends

The World

12

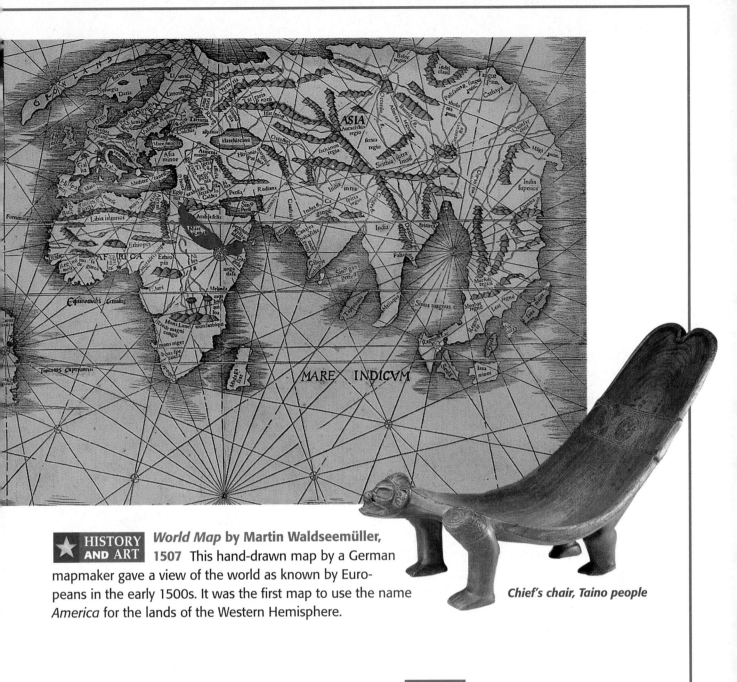

★ **HISTORY AND ART**

World Map by Martin Waldseemüller, **1507** This hand-drawn map by a German mapmaker gave a view of the world as known by Europeans in the early 1500s. It was the first map to use the name *America* for the lands of the Western Hemisphere.

Chief's chair, Taino people

A.D. 1085
Anasazi build pueblos in North America

A.D. 1300
Aztec build Tenochtitlán in Mexico

A.D. 1400s
Inca Empire reaches its height in South America

A.D. 1609
Henry Hudson sails up the Hudson River

A.D. 1492
Columbus lands in the Americas

1050 **1250** **1450** **1650**

A.D. 1295
Italian traveler Marco Polo returns from China

A.D. 1312
Ruler Mansa Musa begins West African kingdom of Mali

A.D. 1517
Luther starts Protestant Reformation

America's LITERATURE

Morning Girl
by Michael Dorris

Michael Dorris, a Modoc Native American, was an educator, a social activist, and an award-winning author. Morning Girl, *his first book for young adults, portrays the lives of the Taino people of the Bahamas.*

▌ READ TO DISCOVER

Morning Girl is the fictional story of a young Native American woman who meets Columbus and his crew as they arrive in the Bahamas in 1492. While reading this passage, think about the ways that Morning Girl's life might change as a result of Columbus's visit.

▌ READER'S DICTIONARY

canoe: a light, narrow boat
surf: waves
Morning Girl: a young Taino woman
drifting: floating smoothly, without effort

Dawn made a glare on the ocean, so I splashed through the shallow surf and dived without looking. I felt the hair lift from around my head, felt a school of tiny fish glide against my leg as I swam underwater. Then, far in the distance, I heard an unfamiliar and frightening sound. It was like the panting of some giant animal, a steady, slow rhythm, dangerous and hungry. And it was coming closer.

I forgot I was still beneath the surface until I needed air. But when I broke into the sunlight, the water sparkling all around me, the noise turned out to be nothing! Only a canoe! The breathing was the dip of many paddles! It was only *people* coming to visit, and since I could see they hadn't painted themselves to appear fierce, they must be friendly or lost.

I swam closer to get a better look and had to stop myself from laughing. The strangers had wrapped every part of their bodies with colorful leaves and cotton. Some had decorated their faces with fur and wore shiny rocks on their heads. Compared to us, they were very round. Their canoe was short and square, and, in spite of all their dipping and pulling, it moved so slowly. What a backward, distant island they must have come from. But really, to laugh at guests, no matter how odd, would be impolite, especially since I was the first to meet them. If I was foolish, they would think they had arrived at a foolish place. . . .

I kicked toward the canoe and called out the simplest thing.

"Hello!"

One of the people heard me, and he was so startled that he stood up, made his eyes small, as fearful as I had been a moment earlier. . . .

Christopher Columbus and the Taino

The man stared at me as though he'd never seen a girl before, then shouted something to his relatives. They all stopped paddling and looked in my direction.

"Hello," I tried again. "Welcome to home. My name is Morning Girl. My mother is She Wins the Race. My father is Speaks to Birds. My brother is Star Boy. We will feed you and introduce you to everyone."

All the fat people in the canoe began pointing at me and talking at once. In their excitement they almost turned themselves over, and I allowed my body to sink beneath the waves for a moment in order to hide my smile. . . .

When I came up they were still watching, the way babies do: wide eyed and with their mouths uncovered. They had much to learn about how to behave.

"Bring your canoe to the beach," I shouted, saying each word slowly so that they might understand and calm themselves. "I will go to the village and bring back Mother and Father. . . ."

. . . The strangers were drifting in the surf, arguing among themselves, not even paying attention to me any longer. They seemed very worried, very confused, very unsure what to do next. It was clear that they hadn't traveled much before.

From *Morning Girl* by Michael Dorris. Text © 1992 by Michael Dorris. Reprinted with permission from Hyperion Books for Children.

RESPONDING TO LITERATURE

1. How does Morning Girl treat the unexpected visitors?
2. Why does Morning Girl think the visitors have poor manners?

Activity

Writing a Play Imagine that explorers from another planet landed in your backyard. How would you respond? Write the dialogue you think would occur between you and the aliens. Then ask a classmate to read the dialogue with you in the form of a play.

Prehistory to 1492

The First Americans

★ Why It's Important

Many groups of Native Americans live in the Americas today. Their history is the story of many different peoples, all of whom helped shape the American society we live in today. They are part of the modern world, yet many of them also preserve the ways of life, customs, and traditions developed by their ancestors centuries ago.

★ Chapter Themes

- *Section 1,* Geography and History
- *Section 2,* Culture and Traditions
- *Section 3,* Groups and Institutions

PRIMARY SOURCES
Library

See pages 936–937 for primary source readings to accompany Chapter 1

★ HISTORY AND ART **Maya Wall Painting** The Maya were one of many Native American peoples living in the Americas before the arrival of Europeans. This wall painting, located at a ceremonial center, shows musicians celebrating a royal birth.

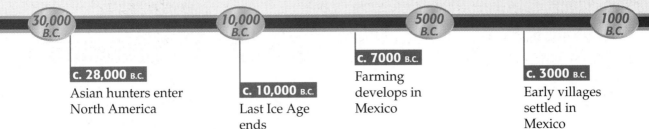

| 30,000 B.C. | 10,000 B.C. | 5000 B.C. | 1000 B.C. |

c. 28,000 B.C.
Asian hunters enter
North America

c. 10,000 B.C.
Last Ice Age
ends

c. 7000 B.C.
Farming
develops in
Mexico

c. 3000 B.C.
Early villages
settled in
Mexico

Section 1

Early Peoples

READ TO DISCOVER . . .
- how the first people arrived in the Americas.
- which discovery changed the lives of the early Native Americans.

TERMS TO LEARN
archaeology   migration
artifact   maize
Ice Age   carbon dating
nomad   culture

⟨The⟩ Storyteller

No one knows for sure why the first people to settle in North America crossed the land bridge that once connected Asia and North America. With spears poised, small bands of hunters may have pursued a mammoth, a large game animal that is now extinct, or other large animals. Later settlers may have come by boat, hunting seals and whales. Over time, these "native Americans" would inhabit both North and South America.

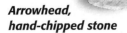

*Arrowhead,
hand-chipped stone*

When Europeans arrived in the Americas in the late 1400s, they found Native Americans living there. The Europeans wondered where these peoples had come from and how they happened to settle in the Americas. Some believed the Native Americans had come from Atlantis, a mythical island that was supposed to have sunk beneath the waves of the Atlantic Ocean.

Modern scientists are still trying to determine when and how the first people appeared in North and South America. The story of the first Americans is still being pieced together by experts in archaeology, the study of ancient peoples. Archaeologists learn about the past from artifacts, things left behind by early people, such as stone tools, weapons, baskets, and carvings. Their most recent discoveries show that the Native Americans *did* come from a land that later sank into the sea. It was not the mythical Atlantis, however, but a stretch of land called **Beringia** that once joined Asia and the Americas.

🌐 Geography

The Journey From Asia

⭐ During its long history, the earth has passed through several Ice Ages, periods of extremely cold temperatures when part of the planet's surface was covered with massive ice sheets. Much of the water from the oceans was frozen into these ice sheets, or glaciers. For that reason the sea levels were much lower during that period than they are today. The lower sea levels exposed large areas of the seabed that would once again be covered with water when the Ice Age ended and the glaciers melted.

Crossing the Land Bridge

The most recent Ice Age began 100,000 years ago and ended about 12,000 years ago. During this period the lower sea level exposed a broad strip of land between Asia and North America. This land bridge ran from **Siberia** in northeastern Asia to present-day **Alaska,** the westernmost part of the Americas. The land bridge, Beringia, now lies under the **Bering Strait.**

Scientists are fairly certain that the first Americans were people from Asia who crossed over Beringia during the last Ice Age. These early peoples probably reached the Americas about 30,000 years ago.

In Search of Hunting Grounds

The early Americans were nomads, people who moved from place to place. They gathered wild grains and fruits but depended on hunting for much of their food. While traveling in search of game or following herds of animals, they crossed Beringia into what are now Alaska and Canada.

The crossing of the land bridge was a migration, a movement of a large number of people into a new homeland. It did not happen in a single journey. As the centuries passed, many groups of people traveled from Asia, either on foot across the land bridge or in boats along its coast. From the north, the migrants gradually moved into new territory. They spread out across the Americas, going as far east as the Atlantic Ocean and as far south as the tip of South America.

---

*F*ootnotes to History

The Land Bridge Beringia takes its name from Vitus Bering, a Danish explorer hired by the Russians to explore the Arctic waters of the Bering Strait in the early 1700s.

Causes and Effects

CAUSES

★ The earth enters a long Ice Age.
★ Water from the oceans freezes into glaciers.
★ Sea levels drop, exposing the Beringia land bridge.

Migration to the Americas

EFFECTS

★ Nomadic hunters from Asia cross into North America.
★ People spread into Central America and South America.
★ The early Americans create many new cultures.

Chart Study

The settlement of the Americas can be traced to a geographic element—the earth's climate.
Analyzing Information When did people from Asia first come to the Americas?

Hunting for Food

 Native American legends tell of giant beasts that roamed the earth in ancient times. When the first Americans arrived from Asia, they did indeed find huge mammals. There was the saber-toothed tiger—a large, flesh-eating cat—the woolly mammoth, and the mastodon. The mammoth and mastodon resembled modern elephants in size and shape but had shaggy fur and tusks up to 13 feet (4 m) long.

The early Americans were skilled at hunting these beasts. The hunters shaped pieces of stone and bone to make tools for chopping and scraping. They chipped rocks into extremely sharp points and fastened them on poles to make spears. Bands of hunters armed with these spears stalked herds of giant bison, mastodons, or mammoths and then charged at the animals, hurling their weapons.

A single mammoth provided tons of meat, enough to feed a group of people for months. The hunters and their families used every part of the animal. They made the skin into clothing, carved the bones into weapons and tools, and may have used the long ribs to build shelters.

About 12,000 years ago the earth's temperatures began to rise. The Ice Age was drawing to an end. As the great glaciers melted, the oceans rose, and Beringia was submerged again. The Americas were cut off from Asia. At the same time, the hunters of America faced a new challenge. The mammoths and other large animals began to die out, either from overhunting or because of changes in the environment. The early Americans had to find other sources of food.

Settling Down

⭐ As the large game animals disappeared, the early Americans found new sources of food. They hunted smaller game, such as deer, birds, and rodents. Those who lived along rivers or near the seacoast learned to catch fish with nets and traps—as Native Americans still do today. They continued to gather wild berries and grains.

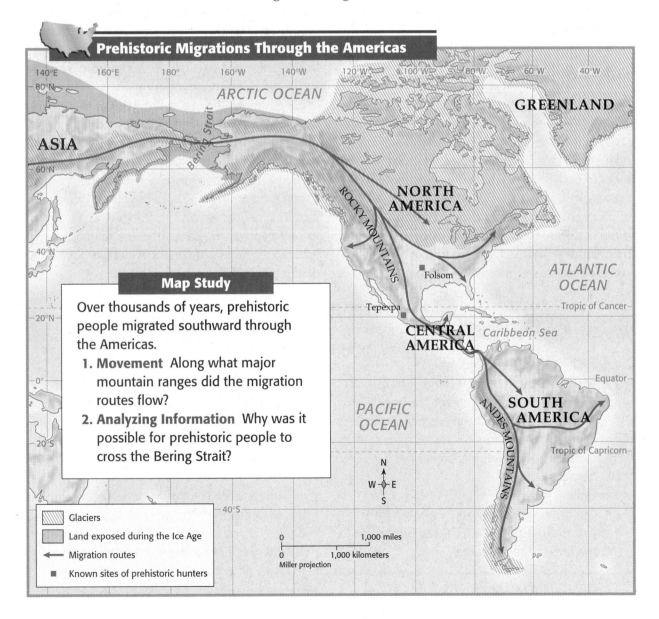

Prehistoric Migrations Through the Americas

Map Study

Over thousands of years, prehistoric people migrated southward through the Americas.

1. **Movement** Along what major mountain ranges did the migration routes flow?
2. **Analyzing Information** Why was it possible for prehistoric people to cross the Bering Strait?

Glaciers

Land exposed during the Ice Age

Migration routes

Known sites of prehistoric hunters

0   1,000 miles

0   1,000 kilometers
Miller projection

★ ★

Planting Seeds

About 9,000 years ago, people living in pres-ent-day **Mexico** made a discovery that would shape the lives of Native Americans for thou-sands of years. They learned to plant and raise an early form of corn called maize. Their harvests of maize provided a steady, reliable source of food. No longer did they have to move from place to place in order to survive.

Early Americans in Mexico also experiment-ed with other kinds of seeds. They planted pump-kins, edible gourds, beans, chili peppers, avocados, and squashes. The people who had once depended on wandering animals for their food were producing more than enough food to feed themselves. The population grew along with the ever-increasing food supply.

Early Communities

With rising numbers of people and a depend-able supply of food, early Americans in Mexico gave up their nomadic way of life and started to form stable communities. Scientists have found traces of early villages that date from about 5,000 years ago.

Scientists use a method called carbon dating to find out how old an artifact is. By measuring the amount of radioactive carbon that remains in something that was once alive—such as a bone or a piece of wood—they can tell how long ago it lived.

Sometime after the early settlements in Mexi-co, people began farming in what is now the southwestern United States. Not all the early peo-ples in the Americas farmed, however. Some re-mained nomadic hunters, and others relied on fishing or trading instead of agriculture.

The Growth of Cultures

Farming allowed people to spend time on ac-tivities other than finding food. Knowing that they would harvest an abundant supply of grains and vegetables, the people of ancient Mexico began to improve their lives in other ways. They built permanent shelters of clay, brick, stone, or wood. They made pottery and cloth and decorat-ed these goods with dyes made from roots and herbs. They also began to develop more complex forms of government and religion.

Agriculture changed the lives of these early people and led to the birth of a new culture, a way of life of a particular group of people. Rather than move from place to place in search of food, the people who farmed were able to settle down. They formed communities and developed common customs, beliefs, artistic styles, and ways of pro-tecting themselves. Over time, the many different groups of people living in the Americas developed distinctive cultures.

★ ★ ★ ★ ★ Section 1 Assessment ★ ★ ★ ★ ★ ★

Checking for Understanding
1. *Identify* Siberia, Alaska, Bering Strait.
2. *Define* archaeology, artifact, Ice Age, nomad, migration, maize, carbon dating, culture.
3. *Explain* how farming changed the lives of nomads.

Reviewing Themes
4. **Geography and History** How did an Ice Age make it possible for Asian hunters to migrate to the Americas?

Critical Thinking
5. **Determining Cause and Effect** How do you think the first Americans discovered that they could grow their own plants?

Activity

Making a Map Create an enlarged version of the map on page 19. Label all landmasses and bodies of water. Add illustrations to the map to tell the story of how the first Americans migrated to North America.

1200 B.C.		B.C./A.D.		A.D. 1200		A.D. 1400

C. 1200 B.C.
Rise of Olmec
in Mexico

C. A.D. 700
Maya civilization
at its height in
Central America

A.D. 1325
Aztec establish
Tenochtitlán
in Mexico

A.D. 1400s
Inca Empire
at its height in
South America

Section 2

Cities and Empires

READ TO DISCOVER . . .
▦ why powerful empires rose up in the Americas.
▦ how the people of each empire adapted to their environment and used their resources.

TERMS TO LEARN
civilization   hieroglyphics
theocracy   terrace

Rumors of a lost city led American historian Hiram Bingham to the mountains of Peru in 1911. Bingham followed a steep mountain trail, pulling himself along by grabbing vines. After many hours of climbing, he reached a clearing. Suddenly he saw acres of huge, crumbling walls and pillars of white stone covered with vines and moss. "It fairly took my breath away," wrote Bingham. He knew that these temples and monuments were the remains of a very advanced people.

A Mayan deity

Long before the arrival of Europeans in the early 1500s, several great civilizations, or highly developed societies, arose in present-day Mexico and in Central and South America. These civilizations built enormous cities in dense jungles and on difficult-to-reach mountaintops. They also developed complex systems of writing, counting, and tracking time.

Among the largest and most advanced of these early civilizations were the **Olmec,** the **Maya,** the **Aztec,** and the **Inca.** Each civilization spread out over hundreds of miles, included millions of people, and thrived for centuries.

The Olmec flourished between 1200 B.C. and 400 B.C. along the Gulf Coast of what are now Mexico, Guatemala, and Honduras. Olmec farmers produced enough food to sustain cities containing thousands of people. Olmec workers sculpted large stone monuments and built stone pavements and drainage systems. Their civilization strongly influenced their neighbors.

The Maya

★ The Maya built their civilization in the dense, steamy rain forests of present-day **Mexico, Guatemala, Honduras,** and **Belize.** Around 1000 B.C. they began clearing the land. They planted maize, beans, sweet potatoes, and other vegetables. They also pulled enormous stones from the earth to build monuments and pyramids that still stand today. Much of this labor was performed by enslaved people, usually prisoners of war.

★ Picturing HISTORY In Tikal and other cities, the Maya built huge pyramids where people could gather for ceremonies honoring the deities. A model of a Mayan city is shown (top left). **How were the Maya governed?**

Mayan Cities

By A.D. 300 the Maya had built many large cities. Each city was dominated by at least one stone pyramid. Some pyramids reached about 200 feet (60 m)—the height of a 20-story building. Steps ran up the pyramid sides to a temple on top. The largest Mayan city, **Tikal,** in present-day Guatemala, was surrounded by six pyramids. The pyramid in **Chichén Itzá** (chih•CHEHN iht•SAH), located on Mexico's Yucatán Peninsula, covered an acre of ground.

The temples on top of the pyramids were religious and governmental centers. Wearing gold jewelry and elaborate headdresses, the priests in the temples performed rituals dedicated to the Mayan gods. On special days, the whole city attended religious festivals. Crowds gathered in the plazas to watch masked dancers, drummers, and flute players perform for the gods.

The Maya believed the gods controlled everything that happened on earth. Because only priests knew the gods' wishes, the priests held great power in Mayan society and made most of the important decisions. The civilization of the Maya was a theocracy, a society ruled by religious leaders.

Mayan Astronomy

The Mayan priests believed that the gods were visible in the stars, sun, and moon. They thought that studying the night sky would help them understand the gods and predict the future. Their intense interest in the workings of the heavens led to an understanding of astronomy. Their desire to measure time advanced their knowledge of mathematics. The priests created a 365-day calendar by which to schedule plantings, harvests, and religious ceremonies.

Mayan priests recorded the movements of the stars, sun, and moon by carving pictures on stones. These images developed into hieroglyphics, pictures or symbols that are used to represent words, sounds, or concepts. The Maya developed a complex vocabulary of hieroglyphics.

Transport and Trade

The Maya did not have wheeled vehicles or horses, so everything they transported overland was carried on human backs. Mayan traders traveled on a network of roads that had been carved out of the jungle. Farmers brought maize and vegetables to outdoor markets in the cities. They exchanged their crops for cotton cloth, pottery, deer meat, and salt.

The Maya also engaged in long-distance trade. At the height of the civilization—from A.D. 300 to A.D. 900—thousands of Mayan canoes traveled up and down Mexico's east coast. The canoes carried jade statues, turquoise jewelry, parrot feathers, cacao beans for making chocolate, and other luxury goods to traders throughout a large area. 💲

Decline of a Civilization

Around A.D. 800 the Maya civilization began to decline. By A.D. 900 the great cities were almost ghost towns. The jungle crept back across the plazas, roads, and fields. No one knows what caused the decline. Perhaps slaves and farmers revolted against their masters. Perhaps the soil became too exhausted by erosion and fire to produce enough food. The Maya civilization collapsed, but descendants of the Maya still live in parts of Mexico and Central America.

The Aztec

★ Centuries after the fall of the Maya, a group of hunters called the Aztec wandered through central Mexico, searching for a perma-

nent home. In 1325 they came upon an island in Lake Texcoco, today part of Mexico City. There the Aztec saw a sign: an eagle sitting on a cactus, a snake in its beak. That meant this island was to be their home.

Tenochtitlán

On this island "amidst the water, in the reeds, in the sugar-canes" emerged **Tenochtitlán** (tay•NAWCH•teet•LAHN), one of the greatest cities in the Americas. Its construction was a miracle of engineering and human labor. Directed

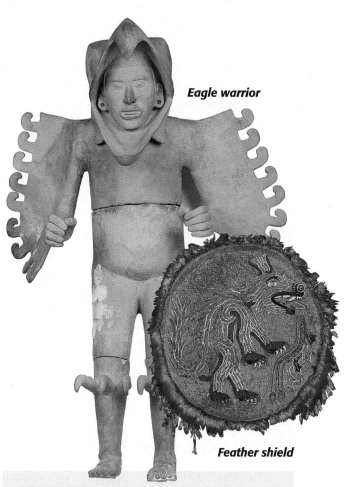

Eagle warrior

Feather shield

★ **Picturing HISTORY** The Aztec were a warrior people, and much of their art reflected military themes. Birds and animals known for their strength and beauty—especially the eagle, jaguar, and coyote—were honored in the Aztec's art and folklore. **How did the Aztec treat the people they conquered?**

by priests and nobles, workers toiled day and night, sometimes until they died of exhaustion. They pulled soil from the bottom of the lake to make causeways, or bridges of earth, linking the island and the shore. They filled parts of the lake with earth so they could grow crops.

In time the Aztec capital expanded to the mainland around the lake. At its height Tenochtitlán was the largest city in the Americas, perhaps the largest in the world. By A.D. 1500 nearly 200,000 people lived there. Tenochtitlán also served as a center of trade, attracting thousands of merchants to its outdoor marketplaces.

War and Religion

The Aztec civilization grew into a military empire. In the 1400s the Aztec army marched through central and southern Mexico, conquering nearly all rival communities. Aztec warriors took everything they could carry from their victims, including maize, cotton cloth, copper, and weapons. Conquered people were forced to work as slaves in Aztec cities and villages.

Like the Maya, the Aztec organized their society around their religion. Aztec priests studied the stars, moon, and sun and created a complex calendar. At the center of the Aztec religion was the powerful sun god. To make sure that the sun god would rise each morning, the priests offered the blood of humans. Thousands of prisoners of war were sacrificed in ceremonies to the sun god.

Eyewitness to HISTORY

A Great City Remembered

The first Europeans to see the Aztec capital were awed by its splendor. In 1519, 550 Spanish soldiers entered Tenochtitlán, led by Hernán Cortés. He wrote:

❝ There are forty towers at least, all of stout construction and very lofty. . . . The workmanship both in wood and stone could not be bettered anywhere. ❞

Bernal Díaz del Castillo, one of the soldiers, marveled at the "great stone towers and temples and buildings that rose straight up out of the water." Tenochtitlán, he explained, was a city of water, and many of the streets were waterways for canoes.

Díaz also admired the gardens, "the diversity of trees and the scents given off by each . . . and the paths choked with roses and other flowers." Some of the Spaniards thought that Tenochtitlán was more magnificent than Rome and other European capitals of the time. 🔍

The Inca

⭐ Another great American civilization developed in the western highlands of South America. The empire of the Inca was the largest of the early American civilizations.

Empire Builders

The Inca founded their capital city of **Cuzco** (KOOS•koh) around A.D. 1200. In 1438 an emperor named Pachacuti (PAH•chah•KOO•tee) Inca Yupanqui came to the throne and began a campaign of conquest against the neighboring peoples. He and his son, Topa Inca, built an empire that stretched from north to south for more than 3,000 miles (4,800 km), from present-day Colombia to northern Argentina and Chile.

The Incan army was a formidable force. All men between 25 and 50 years old could be drafted to serve in the army for up to five years. Their weapons included clubs, short spears, and spiked copper balls on ropes. Using slings of woven cloth, they could throw stones as far as 30 yards (27 m).

Communication and the Empire

At its height, the Inca Empire had a population of more than 6 million, including many conquered peoples. To control this far-flung empire, the Inca built at least 10,000 miles (16,000 km) of stone-paved roads that ran over mountains, across deserts, and through jungles. Rope bridges, made from grass, crossed canyons and rivers.

Runners carrying messages to and from the emperor linked remote outposts of the empire to the capital at Cuzco. The Inca language, Quechua (KEH•chuh•wuh), became the official language for all the different peoples in the empire. Although the Inca did not possess paper or writing, they developed a system of record keeping with string called *quipus* (KEE•poos). Using various lengths and colors of string, knotted in special patterns, the *quipus* carried information about resources such as grain supplies.

Inca ceremonial cup

Agricultural Achievements

Although mountainous land is not well suited for farming, the Inca devised ways to produce a steady supply of food. They cut terraces, or broad platforms, into steep slopes so they could plant crops. They built stone walls on the terraces to hold the soil and plants in place. Incan farmers grew maize, squash, tomatoes, peanuts, chili peppers, melons, cotton, and potatoes.

Religious Beliefs

All land and property within the Inca's domain belonged to the emperor, who was believed to be a descendant of the sun god. Because the Inca thought that the sun god enjoyed displays of gold, they crafted magnificent gold jewelry and temple ornaments. The Inca also built special

Machu Picchu

cities devoted to religious ceremonies. One of these religious centers was **Machu Picchu** (MAH•choo PEE•choo), the mountaintop site discovered by Hiram Bingham in 1911.

The wealth and high achievements of the Inca were remarkable. Inca civilization, however, could not stand up against the Spanish invaders.

Section 2 Assessment
★ ● ★ ● ★ ● ★ ● ★   ★ ★ ★ ★ ★

Checking for Understanding
1. **Identify** Olmec, Maya, Aztec, Inca.
2. **Define** civilization, theocracy, hieroglyphics, terrace.
3. **List** reasons the Maya, Aztec, and Inca were considered advanced civilizations.

Reviewing Themes
4. **Culture and Traditions** What was the connection between religion and astronomy in the Maya civilization?

Critical Thinking
5. **Making Inferences** How does trade help to enrich a civilization? Provide examples in your answer.

Making a Chart Create a chart that lists some of the accomplishments of the Maya, Aztec, and Inca in the areas of communication, science, and math.

Understanding the Parts of a Map

Maps can direct you down the street, or around the world. There are as many different kinds of maps as there are uses for them. Being able to read a map begins with learning about its parts.

Learning the Skill

Maps usually include a key, a compass rose, and a scale bar. The map key explains the meaning of special colors, symbols, and lines used on the map. On a road map, for example, the key tells what map lines stand for paved roads, dirt roads, and interstate highways.

After reading the map key, look for the compass rose. It is the direction marker that shows the cardinal directions of north, south, east, and west. North and south are the directions of the North and South Poles. If you stand facing north, east is the direction to your right—toward the rising sun. West is the direction on your left.

A measuring line, often called a scale bar, helps you estimate distance on a map. The map's scale tells you what distance on the earth is represented by the measurement on the scale bar. For example, 1 inch (2.54 cm) on the map may represent 100 miles (160.9 km) on the earth. Knowing the scale allows you to visualize how large an area is and to measure distances.

Practicing the Skill

The map on this page shows where the ancient Maya, Aztec, and Inca built their empires in North America and South America. Look at the parts of this map, then answer the questions that follow.

1. What information is given in the key?
2. What color shows the Inca Empire?
3. What direction would you travel to go from Tenochtitlán to Chichén Itzá?

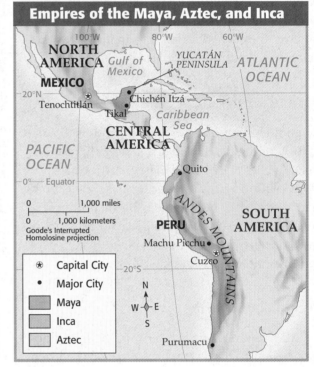

Empires of the Maya, Aztec, and Inca

4. About how many miles long was the Inca Empire?
5. What was the capital of the Aztec Empire?

Applying the Skill

Drawing a Map Picture a mental image of your house or room. Draw a map showing the location of various areas. Include a map key explaining any symbols or colors you use. Also include a scale bar explaining the size of your map compared to the real area. Finally, add a compass rose and title to your map.

Glencoe's **Skillbuilder Interactive Workbook, Level 1** provides instruction and practice in key social studies skills.

C. 1000 B.C.
First ceremonial mounds built

C. A.D. 1085
Anasazi build pueblos in North America

C. A.D. 1100
City of Cahokia is built in Illinois

A.D. 1200
Hohokam civilization of Southwest begins to decline

Section 3

North American Peoples

READ TO DISCOVER . . .
■ why Native Americans built cliff dwellings in canyons in the American Southwest.
■ how different Native American groups adapted to their environments.

TERMS TO LEARN
pueblo   adobe
drought   federation

The Storyteller

In the summer of 1991, a helicopter passenger made an amazing discovery in Arizona's Coconino National Forest. As the helicopter hovered among the sandstone cliffs, the sun shone into a cave 200 feet (60 m) below the rim of one cliff. Standing in the opening of the cave were three large pottery jars.

Up to that moment, no one even knew the cave existed. It had never been spotted from the ground, and it could not be seen from the cliff top. The three jars had been sitting, untouched and unseen, for more than 700 years.

Hohokam jar

The jars and other objects found in the cave were left there by the Sinagua, Native Americans who lived in present-day Arizona hundreds of years ago. The Sinagua are just one of many Native American peoples who are now being studied by archaeologists and historians.

Early Native Americans

Many Native American cultures rose, flourished, and disappeared in North America long before Europeans arrived in the 1500s. Among the most advanced of these early cultures were the Hohokam and Anasazi of the Southwest and the Mound Builders of the Ohio River valley.

The Hohokam

The dry, hot desert of present-day Arizona was home to the **Hohokam** people. They may have come from Mexico about 300 B.C. The Hohokam culture flourished from about A.D. 300 to A.D. 1200 in an area bordered by the Gila and Salt River valleys.

The Hohokam were experts at squeezing every drop of available water from the sun-baked soil. Their way of life depended on the irrigation channels they dug to carry river water into their fields. In addition to hundreds of miles of irrigation channels, the Hohokam left behind pottery, carved stone, and shells etched with acid. The shells came from trade with coastal peoples.

★ Picturing HISTORY Pueblo Bonito had more than 800 rooms and 32 kivas, or underground ceremonial chambers. Today, the ruins of Pueblo Bonito are part of Chaco Culture National Historical Park in northwestern New Mexico. **What other kind of dwellings were built by the Anasazi?**

Kivas at Pueblo Bonito

Anasazi jar

The Anasazi

The **Anasazi** lived around the same time as the Hohokam, roughly A.D. 200 to A.D. 1300, in the area known as the Four Corners (the meeting place of the present-day states of Utah, Colorado, Arizona, and New Mexico). There they built great stone dwellings that the Spanish explorers later called **pueblos** (PWEH•blohs), or villages. **Pueblo Bonito,** one of the most spectacular of the Anasazi pueblos, can still be seen in New Mexico. The huge semicircular structure of stone and sun-dried earth resembles an apartment building. It is four stories high and has hundreds of rooms. Archaeologists have found traces of a complex road system linking Pueblo Bonito with other villages. This suggests that Pueblo Bonito was an important trade or religious center for the Anasazi.

The Anasazi also built dwellings in the walls of steep cliffs. Cliff dwellings were easy to defend and offered protection from winter weather. **Mesa Verde** in Colorado, one of the largest and most elaborate cliff dwellings, held several thousand inhabitants.

In about 1300 the Anasazi began leaving the pueblos and cliff dwellings to settle in smaller communities. Their large villages may have been abandoned because of droughts, long periods of little rainfall, during which their crops dried up.

The Mound Builders

The early cultures of Mexico and Central America appear to have influenced people living in lands to the north. In central North America, prehistoric Native Americans built thousands of mounds of earth that look very much like the stone pyramids of the Maya and the Aztec. Some of the mounds contain burial chambers. Some were topped with temples, as in the Mayan and Aztec cultures.

The mounds are dotted across the landscape from present-day Pennsylvania to the Mississippi River valley. They have been found as far north as the Great Lakes and as far south as Florida. Archaeologists think that the first mounds were built about 1000 B.C. They were not the work of a single group but of many different peoples, referred to as the **Mound Builders**.

Among the earliest Mound Builders were the **Adena**, hunters and gatherers who flourished in the Ohio Valley by 800 B.C. They were followed by the **Hopewell** people, who lived between 200 B.C.

and A.D. 500. Farmers and traders, the Hopewell built huge burial mounds in the shape of birds, bears, and snakes. One of them, the **Great Serpent Mound**, looks like a giant snake winding across the ground. Archaeologists have found freshwater pearls, shells, cloth, and copper in the mounds. The objects indicate a widespread pattern of trade.

Cahokia

The largest settlement of the Mound Builders was **Cahokia** (kuh•HOH•kee•uh) in present-day Illinois. This city, built between A.D. 900 and A.D. 1200 by a people called the Mississippians, may have had 30,000 or more residents. The largest mound in Cahokia, the Monks Mound, rises nearly 100 feet (30 m). When it was built, it was probably the highest structure north of Mexico.

Although nearly 2,000 miles (3,200 km) away from the great cities of Mexico, Cahokia resembled them. The city was dominated by the great pyramid-shaped mound. A temple crowned the summit—perhaps a place where priests studied the movements of the sun and stars or where the priest-ruler of Cahokia lived. A legend of the Natchez people, descendants of the Mississippians, hints of a direct link to Mexico:

❝ Before we came into this land we lived yonder under the sun [the speaker pointed southwest toward Mexico]. . . . Our nation extended itself along the great water [the Gulf of Mexico] where this large river [the Mississippi] loses itself. ❞

Other Native North Americans

★ Although the civilizations of the Hohokam, the Anasazi, and the Mound Builders eventually faded away, other Native American cultures arose to take their place. Around the time that Europeans began arriving, North America was home to dozens of diverse societies.

Peoples of the North

The people who settled in the northernmost part of North America, in the lands around the Arctic Ocean, are called the **Inuit**. Some scientists think that the Inuit were the last migrants to cross the land bridge into North America.

★ **Picturing HISTORY** Workshops, dwellings, mounds, and pyramids developed around the central plaza of Cahokia. Farms stretched along the Mississippi River valley. **In what way did Cahokia resemble Native American cities in Mexico?**

The Inuit possessed many skills that helped them survive in the cold Arctic climate. They may have brought some of these skills from northern Siberia, probably their original home. In the winter the Inuit built igloos, low-lying structures of snow blocks, which protected them from severe weather. Their clothing of furs and sealskins was both warm and waterproof. The Inuit were hunters and fishers. In the coastal waters, they pursued whales, seals, and walruses in small, skin-covered boats. On land they hunted caribou, large deer-like animals of the far north.

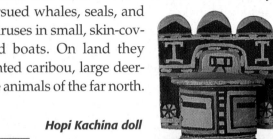

Hopi Kachina doll

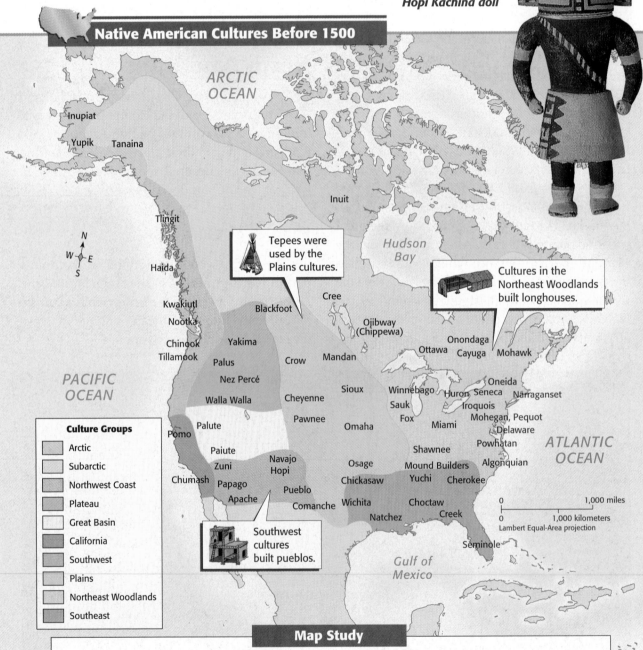

Native American Cultures Before 1500

ARCTIC OCEAN

Inupiat
Yupik
Tanaina

Inuit

Tlingit

Hudson Bay

Haida

Tepees were used by the Plains cultures.

Cultures in the Northeast Woodlands built longhouses.

Cree

Kwakiutl
Nootka
Chinook
Tillamook

Blackfoot

Ojibway (Chippewa)

Onondaga
Ottawa Cayuga Mohawk

Yakima
Palus
Nez Percé
Walla Walla

Crow Mandan

Oneida
Winnebago Huron, Seneca Narraganset
Sauk Iroquois
Fox Miami Mohegan, Pequot
Delaware

Sioux

PACIFIC OCEAN

Palute
Pomo
Paiute
Zuni
Chumash Papago
Apache

Navajo
Hopi

Pueblo

Comanche

Cheyenne
Pawnee

Omaha

Osage
Chickasaw

Shawnee
Mound Builders
Yuchi

Powhatan
Algonquian
Cherokee

ATLANTIC OCEAN

Wichita
Natchez

Choctaw
Creek

Southwest cultures built pueblos.

Seminole

Gulf of Mexico

Culture Groups
- Arctic
- Subarctic
- Northwest Coast
- Plateau
- Great Basin
- California
- Southwest
- Plains
- Northeast Woodlands
- Southeast

0 ___ 1,000 miles
0 ___ 1,000 kilometers
Lambert Equal-Area projection

Map Study

Early Native Americans spread throughout the continent and adapted their way of life to the terrain and climate where they settled.

1. **Region** To which culture group did the Apache and Hopi belong?
2. **Analyzing Information** What type of dwelling did the Iroquois build?

The Inuit made clothing from caribou skins and burned seal oil in lamps.

Peoples of the West

★ The mild climate and dependable food sources of the West Coast created a favorable environment for many different groups.

The peoples of the northwestern coast, such as the **Tlingit** (TLIHNG•kuht), **Haida,** and **Chinook,** developed a way of life that used the resources of the forest and the sea. They built wooden houses and made canoes, cloth, and baskets from tree bark. Using spears and traps, they fished for salmon along the coast and in rivers such as the Columbia. This large fish was the main food of the northwestern people. They preserved the salmon by smoking it over fires.

Salmon was also important for the people of the plateau region, the area between the Cascade Mountains and the Rocky Mountains. The **Nez Perce** (NEHZ PUHRS) and **Yakima** people fished the rivers, hunted deer in forests, and gathered roots and berries. The root of the camas plant, a relative of the lily, was an important part of their diet. The plateau peoples lived in earthen houses.

Present-day California was home to a great variety of cultures. Along the northern coast, Native Americans fished for their food. In the more barren environment of the southern deserts, nomadic groups wandered from place to place collecting roots and seeds. In the central valley, the **Pomo** gathered acorns and pounded them into flour. As in many Indian cultures, the women of the Pomo did most of the gathering and flour making.

In the Great Basin between the Sierra Nevada and the Rocky Mountains, Native Americans found ways to live in the dry climate. The soil was too hard and rocky for farming, so peoples such as the **Ute** (YOOT) and **Shoshone** (shuh• SHOHN) traveled in search of food. They ate small game, pine nuts, juniper berries, roots, and some insects. Instead of making permanent settlements, the Great Basin people created temporary shelters of branches and reeds.

Peoples of the Southwest

Descendants of the Anasazi formed the **Hopi,** the **Acoma,** and the **Zuni.** They built their homes from a type of sun-dried mud brick called adobe. They raised maize, beans, and squash.

In the 1500s two new groups settled in the region—the **Apache** and the **Navajo.** Unlike the other peoples of the Southwest, the Apache and Navajo were hunters. They chased buffalo and other game. Eventually the Navajo settled into stationary communities and built square houses called hogans. Although they grew maize to add to their diet of buffalo meat, they depended primarily on hunting for food.

Peoples of the Plains

The peoples of the Great Plains were nomadic; villages were temporary, lasting only for a growing season or two. When the people moved from place to place, they dragged their homes—cone-shaped skin tents called tepees—behind them. The men hunted antelope, deer, and buffalo. The women tended plots of maize, squash, and beans.

When the Spanish brought horses to Mexico in the 1500s, some got loose. In time horses made their way north, roaming from Texas to the Great Plains. Native Americans captured and tamed the wild horses, and the Apache, the **Dakota**, and other Plains peoples became skilled riders. They learned to use the horses in warfare, attacking their enemies with long spears, and to hunt on horseback.

☆ ☆

Citizenship

Peoples of the East

The Native Americans who lived in the woodlands of eastern North America formed complex political systems to govern their nations. The **Iroquois** (IHR•uh•KWAWIH) and **Cherokee** had formal law codes. They also formed federations, governments that linked different groups.

The Iroquois lived near Canada in what is now northern New York State. There were five Iroquois groups or nations: the **Onondaga,** the **Seneca,** the **Mohawk,** the **Oneida,** and the **Cayuga.** These groups warred with each other until the late 1500s, when they joined in an organization called the Iroquois League.

Iroquois women occupied positions of power and importance in their communities. They owned the land and were responsible for the planting and harvesting of crops. Women also had a strong voice in the community's government. According to the constitution of the Iroquois League, women chose the 50 men who served on the league council.

The Iroquois constitution was written down after the Europeans came to North America. It describes the Iroquois peoples' desire for peace:

❝I am Dekanawidah and with the Five Nations' Confederate Lords I plant the Tree of Great Peace. . . . Roots have spread out from the Tree of the Great Peace, one to the north, one to the east, one to the south and one to the west. The name of these roots is The Great White Roots and their nature is Peace and Strength. **❞**

Peoples of the Southeast

The Southeast was also a woodlands area, but with a warmer climate than the eastern woodlands. The Creek, Chickasaw, and Cherokee were among the region's Native American peoples. Many Creek lived in loosely knit farming communities in present-day Georgia and Alabama. There they grew corn, tobacco, squash, and other crops. The Chickasaw, most of whom lived farther west in what is now Mississippi, farmed the river bottomlands. The Cherokee farmed in the mountains of Georgia and the Carolinas.

Wherever they lived in North America, the first Americans developed ways of life that were well suited to their environments. In the 1500s, however, the Native Americans met people whose cultures, beliefs, and ways of life were different from anything they had known or ever seen. These newcomers were the Europeans, and their arrival would change the Native Americans' world forever.

★ ★ ★ ★ ★ Section 3 Assessment ★ ★ ★ ★ ★

Checking for Understanding

1. *Identify* Hohokam, Anasazi, Mound Builders, Hopewell, Inuit, Iroquois.
2. *Define* pueblo, drought, adobe, federation.
3. *Identify* clues that led archaeologists to believe that the Mound Builders were influenced by other cultures.

Reviewing Themes

4. **Groups and Institutions** What organization did the Iroquois form to promote peace among their people?

Critical Thinking

5. **Making Generalizations** Why was the environment of the West Coast favorable for settlement by so many groups of Native Americans?

Designing a Home Draw a model of a home that a Native American could have built. Use natural materials that exist in the area where you live and label the materials on your diagram. Consider the climate of your area in your design.

Multimedia Activities

ABCNEWS iNTERACTiVE™ Historic America Electronic Field Trips

Field Trip to Cahokia Mounds

Setting up the Video

Work with a group of your classmates to view "Cahokia Mounds" on the videodisc *Historic America: Electronic Field Trips*. The community of Cahokia, built about 1,000 years ago, left huge mounds dotting the surrounding landscape. This mound-building civilization, located in present-day Illinois, may have had 30,000 or more residents. The program shows students working with guides to protect the mounds.

Hands-On Activity

Just as the Cahokia mounds revealed details of the Cahokia people, modern monuments and buildings express who we, as Americans, are today. Create a collage of photographs showing American architecture and monuments. Write captions that explain what the buildings reveal about modern American society.

Side 1, Chapter 3

View the video by scanning the bar code or by entering the chapter number on your keypad and pressing Search.

Surfing the "Net"

Modern Explorers

Many European explorers used primitive navigational instruments to help guide them in finding new places. Today, people explore new and exciting places by using the Internet. To become a modern explorer, follow the instructions below.

Getting There

Pick a country you would like to know more about. Follow these steps to gather information about this place.

1. Use a search engine. Type in the name of the country that you want to learn more about.
2. After the country's name, enter words like the following to find more specific information about this place:

- *geography*
- *maps*
- *population*
- *travel*
- *culture*
- *sports*

3. The search engine will provide you with a number of links to follow. Links are "pointers" to different sites on the Internet and commonly appear as blue underlined words.

What to Do When You Are There

Once you are at the country you have chosen, click on the links to navigate through the pages of information. Gather your findings by creating a fact sheet using a word processor. Using the findings, create an illustrated map of the region you explored. Attach your facts to the map.

Chapter 1

Assessment and Activities

★ Reviewing Key Terms

On a sheet of paper, define the following terms:

archaeology
artifact
Ice Age
nomad
carbon dating

culture
civilization
hieroglyphics
pueblo
federation

★ Reviewing Key Facts

1. Why did Asians cross the land bridge to the Americas?
2. What was the first crop raised by Native Americans in Mexico?
3. What were two advantages of living in cliff dwellings?
4. How did horses change the lives of Native Americans who lived on the Great Plains?

★ Critical Thinking

Analyzing Information

Over time Native Americans formed unique cultures.

1. In what ways did farming contribute to the growth of large empires in Central and South America?
2. How did living in Siberia help the Inuit adapt to life in the Arctic region?

★ Time Line Activity

Create a time line on which you place the following events in chronological order.

- Europeans arrive in the Americas
- Asian hunters cross Beringia
- Inca establish their capital at Cuzco
- Maya civilization begins to decline
- Mound Builders begin building mounds
- Native Americans in Mexico learn to grow maize

★ Reviewing Themes

1. **Geography and History** In what ways did the environment of Native Americans who lived in the Northwest differ from the environment of those who lived in the Southwest?
2. **Culture and Traditions** How do we know that religion was an important part of Native American life?
3. **Groups and Institutions** How did the Inca and Aztec use war to increase their power?

★ Geography Activity

Study the map below and answer the questions that follow.

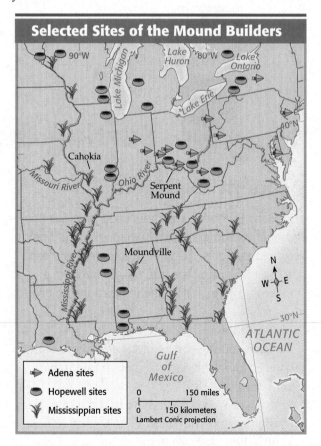

Selected Sites of the Mound Builders

1. **Location** Along what two major rivers did many of the Mound Builders settle?

2. Place Near which river did the Adena build most of their settlements?

3. Movement Of the Adena, Hopewell, and Mississippian cultures, which settled the farthest east?

★ Skill Practice Activity

Understanding the Parts of a Map

Use the key, compass rose, and scale bar on the map of early Ohio villages to answer the questions that follow.

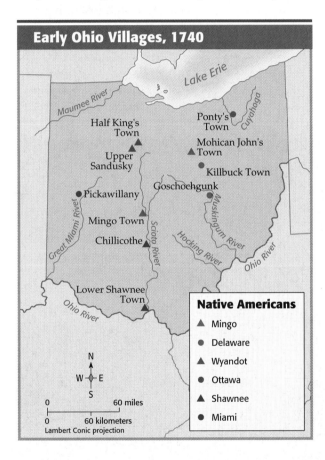

Early Ohio Villages, 1740

1. What does the map key highlight?
2. About how far from Lake Erie was Mohican John's Town?
3. Which Native Americans settled Goschochgunk?
4. Which town was farther west--Pickawillany or Upper Sandusky?
5. What village is located along the Ohio River?

★ Technology Activity

Using the Internet Search the Internet for a Web site created by a modern Native American organization or group. Based on information you find at the Web site, explain the group's purpose or goals. How do you think this group's activities will help to preserve the culture of Native Americans?

★ Cooperative Activity

History and Art Create a Native American artifact museum for your classroom. With a partner, find an existing photo or illustration (or make your own drawing or model) of a Native American artifact created before 1500. Label your artifact with the name of the Native American group that created it, the approximate date it was made, a description of how it was used, and the materials from which it was made. Mount your artifact on cardboard and display it with other artifacts in a classroom "museum."

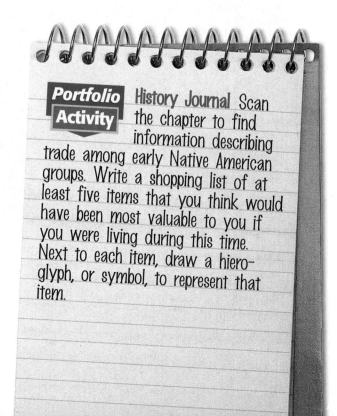

Portfolio Activity History Journal Scan the chapter to find information describing trade among early Native American groups. Write a shopping list of at least five items that you think would have been most valuable to you if you were living during this time. Next to each item, draw a hieroglyph, or symbol, to represent that item.

1400–1625

Exploring the Americas

★ Why It's Important

The Americas today consist of peoples from cultures from around the globe. Although the English have been the dominant influence on United States history, they are only part of the story. The Native Americans, Spanish, Africans, and other peoples who are discussed in this chapter have all played key roles in shaping the culture we now call American.

★ Chapter Themes

- *Section 1*, Culture and Traditions
- *Section 2*, Geography and History
- *Section 3*, Groups and Institutions
- *Section 4*, Global Connections

PRIMARY SOURCES
Library

See pages 938–939 for primary source readings to accompany Chapter 2

★ HISTORY AND ART   *Landing of Columbus* by John Vanderlyn   The European explorations of North America were common subjects for American artists. This painting of Columbus's arrival in the Americas was done by American artist John Vanderlyn in the early 1840s.

1271
Marco Polo travels to China from Italy

1324
Mansa Musa makes a pilgrimage to Makkah

1400s
Renaissance spreads throughout Europe

1500s
Songhai Empire rises in Africa

Section 1

A Changing World

READ TO DISCOVER . . .

■ how the Renaissance and economic and political developments led Europeans to invest in overseas exploration.

■ how technology helped make long sea voyages possible.

■ how great civilizations flourished in Africa.

TERMS TO LEARN

classical
Renaissance
technology
astrolabe

caravel
pilgrimage
mosque

The Storyteller

In 1271 Marco Polo set off from the city of Venice on a great trek across Asia to China. Only 17 years old at the time, Polo journeyed with his father and uncle, both Venetian merchants. Traveling on camels for more than 3 years, the merchants crossed almost 7,000 miles (11,263 km) of mountains and deserts. Finally they reached the palace of Kublai Khan (KOO•bluh KAHN), the Mongol emperor of China. There Marco Polo spent 17 years working for the Khan and learning much about China's advanced culture.

Marco Polo

When **Marco Polo** returned to Venice from China in 1295, he wrote an account of the marvels of Asia. He described exotic lands and peoples, great riches, and splendid cities. Polo called the Chinese city of Hangzhou the greatest city in the world, exclaiming that it had "so many pleasures . . . that one fancies himself to be in Paradise." He wrote of things like paper money and coal that filled Europeans with wonder.

Translated into many languages, Polo's *Travels* was eagerly read throughout western Europe. Almost 200 years later, when Columbus set sail from Spain, he hoped to find the golden roofs of Cipangu (Japan) that Marco Polo had described but never seen.

Expanding Horizons

For centuries after the fall of the Roman Empire, the people of western Europe lived in a fairly self-contained world. This world, dominated by the Catholic Church, was divided into many small kingdoms and city-states.

A Growing Interest

Most Europeans knew little about India, China, or the rest of Asia and had no idea that the Western Hemisphere existed. However, as the story of Marco Polo spread and exotic goods from the East appeared in marketplaces in Europe, more people became interested in these distant lands.

Picturing HISTORY During the 1200s, Europeans created illuminated manuscripts decorated with beautiful lettering and miniature paintings. As shown in this miniature painting, Marco Polo sets sail from Venice for his journey to China in 1271. **What does the painting reveal about life in Venice during the 1200s?**

The Growth of Ideas

In the 1300s a powerful new spirit emerged in the Italian city-states and spread throughout Europe. The development of banking and the expansion of trade with Asia enriched Italian merchants. Wealthy citizens were able to pursue an interest in the region's past, to learn more about the glorious civilizations of ancient Rome and Greece.

Because they wanted to improve their knowledge of people and the world, Italians studied the classical—ancient Greek and Roman—works with new interest. Scholars translated Greek manuscripts on philosophy, poetry, and science. Many thinkers of this period began to take an experimental approach to science, testing new and old theories and evaluating the results.

Influenced by the classical texts, many authors wrote of the individual and the universe in a secular, or nonreligious, way. Artists studied the sculpture and architecture of the classical world. They particularly admired the harmony and balance in Greek art with its realistic way of portraying people.

$ Economics

The Growth of Trade

Merchants could make a fortune selling goods from the Orient. Wealthy Europeans clamored for cinnamon, pepper, cloves, and other spices. They also wanted perfumes, silks, and precious stones from India and Persia. Italian merchants obliged.

Buying the goods from Arab traders in the Middle East, the merchants sent them overland by caravan to the **Mediterranean Sea** and then by ship to Italian ports. The cities of Venice, Genoa, and Pisa prospered as centers of the growing East-West trade. **$**

The Renaissance

This period of intellectual and artistic creativity became known as the Renaissance (REH •nuh•SAHNTS). A French word meaning "rebirth," it refers to the recovery of classical Greek and Roman learning. Over the next two centuries, the Renaissance spread north, south, and west, reaching Spain and northern Europe in the 1400s.

The spirit of the Renaissance dramatically changed the way Europeans thought about themselves and the world. It encouraged them to pursue new ideas and set new goals, paving the way for an age of exploration and discovery.

*F*ootnotes to History

Preserving Meat In the days before refrigeration, salt was used to preserve meats. Europeans wanted pepper and other spices to cover the extremely salty taste or, even worse, the taste of spoiled meat.

Powerful Nations Emerge

During the 1400s the population of western Europe began to increase. Merchants and bankers in the growing cities wanted to expand their business through foreign trade. If they could buy spices and silks from the East directly, without going through the Arab and Italian cities, they could reap huge profits. They looked for alternatives to the overland route through the Middle East.

The development of large nation-states in western Europe helped expand trade and interest in overseas exploration. For many years Europe had been a patchwork of small states. Political power was divided among local lords, and few people traveled outside their region.

By the 1400s, however, a new type of centralized state was emerging in western Europe. Strong monarchs came to power in Spain, Portugal, England, and France. They began to establish national laws, courts, taxes, and armies to replace those of local lords. These ambitious kings and queens sought ways to increase trade and make their countries stronger and wealthier.

Technology's Impact

Advances in technology—the use of scientific knowledge for practical purposes— prepared the way for European voyages of exploration. In the 1450s the invention of movable type and the printing press revolutionized bookmaking. Now more people could have access to books and to new information. After its publication in print form in 1477, Marco Polo's *Travels* gained much wider circulation in Europe.

Geography

Better Maps

Most early maps were wildly inaccurate, drawn from scattered impressions of travelers and traders. Using the reports of explorers and information from Arab geographers, mapmakers made more accurate land and sea maps. These maps showed the direction of ocean currents. They also showed lines of latitude, which indicated distance north and south of the Equator.

Better instruments were developed for navigating the seas. Sailors could determine their latitude while at sea with an astrolabe, an instrument that measured the position of stars. Europeans also improved the magnetic compass, a Chinese invention the Arabs had passed on to Europe in the 1200s. The compass allowed sailors to determine their location when they were far from land.

Linking PAST & PRESENT

Astrolabe to Satellite

"Land ho!" The tools that early explorers used to sail the uncharted seas were much different from the instruments used today. One early navigation tool was the astrolabe. A sailor held the astrolabe vertically, located a star through its sights, and measured the star's elevation above the horizon. A ship's approximate location could be identified this way.

Today navigation satellites do the work of an astrolabe—and more! The NAVSTAR Global Positioning System (GPS) satellites were launched by the United States in 1993. From space the GPS can track the location of a vehicle on the earth to within a few meters of its actual position. What other inventions aided early explorers?

Past
Astrolabe

Present
Satellite

★ ★

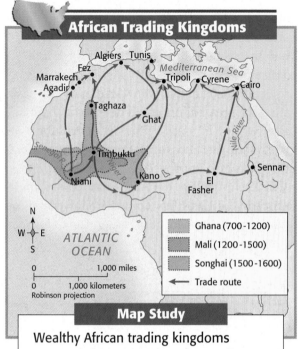

African Trading Kingdoms

Ghana (700–1200)
Mali (1200–1500)
Songhai (1500–1600)
← Trade route

Map Study

Wealthy African trading kingdoms existed long before Europeans sailed west to find riches.

1. **Movement** In which direction would a trading party from Timbuktu travel to reach Ghat?

2. **Comparing** What African kingdom covered the smallest area?

Better Ships

Advances in ship design allowed shipbuilders to construct sailing vessels capable of long ocean voyages. The stern rudder and the triangular sail enabled ships to sail into the wind. Both of these new features came from the Arabs. In the late 1400s, the Portuguese developed the three-masted caravel. The caravel sailed faster than earlier ships and carried more cargo and food supplies. It also could float in shallow water, allowing sailors to explore inlets and beach their ships to make repairs. A Venetian sailor called the caravels "the best ships that sailed the seas."

By the mid-1400s the Italian ports faced increased competition for foreign trade. Powerful countries like Portugal and Spain began searching for sea routes to Asia, launching a new era of exploration. These new voyages took sailors down the west coast of Africa, which Europeans had never visited before.

African Kingdoms

★ Powerful kingdoms flourished in Africa south of the Sahara between 300 and 1600. The region was richly endowed with natural resources. Thus, Africans mined gold, copper, and iron ore. Trade with Islamic societies in North Africa brought wealth and Islamic ideas and customs to the West African kingdoms.

City-states on the east coast of Africa also benefited from trade. There Arab traders from the Middle East brought cotton, silk, and porcelain from India and China to exchange for ivory and metals from the African interior.

The Portuguese started sailing south along the African coastline in the mid-1400s and set up trading posts. From these, they traded for gold and for slaves.

Ghana—A Trading Empire

Between 300 and 1100, a vast trading empire called **Ghana** emerged in West Africa. Well located between the salt mines of the Sahara and the gold mines to the south, Ghana prospered from the taxes its kings imposed on trade.

Caravans with gold, ivory, and slaves from Ghana crossed the Sahara to Morocco. Muslim traders from North Africa loaded caravans with salt, cloth, and brass and headed back to Ghana. As a result of their trading contacts, many West Africans became Muslims.

In 1076 people from North Africa called Almoravids attacked Ghana's trade centers and seized the capital. The Almoravids controlled Ghana for about 10 years. After that Ghana's power declined, and several separate states emerged in the region.

Mali—A Powerful Kingdom

Mali, one of the new states, grew into a powerful kingdom. The people of Mali, under the Almoravids, revived the profitable trade routes with North Africa. By the late 1200s, Mali's expanded territory included the former kingdom of Ghana. The country was mainly agricultural, but well-endowed gold mines enriched the kingdom.

Mali's greatest king, **Mansa Musa,** ruled from 1307 to 1332. He was described at the time as "the most powerful, the richest, the most fortunate, the most feared by his enemies, and the most able to do good to those around him."

In 1324 Musa, a Muslim, made a grand pilgrimage to **Makkah** (also spelled Mecca). A pilgrimage is a journey to a holy place. Arab writers reported that Musa traveled with 12,000 slaves and a huge military escort. Ahead of him marched 500 royal servants who carried staffs of gold to distribute along the way.

Musa returned to Mali with an Arab architect who built great mosques, Muslim houses of worship, in the capital of **Timbuktu.** Under Mansa Musa, Timbuktu became an important center of Islamic art and learning.

The Songhai Empire

Some years later the Songhai (SAWNG•hy) people, who lived along the **Niger River,** rose up against Mali rule. They built a navy to control the Niger and in 1469 captured Timbuktu. In the late 1400s, **Askia Muhammad** brought the Songhai empire to the height of its power. Askia strengthened his country and made it the largest in the history of West Africa. He built many schools and encouraged trade with Europe and Asia.

Mansa Musa

Gold pendant, West Africa

In the late 1500s, the North African kingdom of Morocco sent an army across the Sahara to attack Songhai gold-trading centers. Armed with guns and cannons, the Moroccans easily defeated the Songhai.

Section 1 Assessment

Checking for Understanding

1. **Identify** Marco Polo, Ghana, Mali, Mansa Musa, Makkah, Timbuktu, Askia Muhammad.
2. **Define** classical, Renaissance, technology, astrolabe, caravel, pilgrimage, mosque.
3. **Describe** three technological advances that furthered European exploration.

Reviewing Themes

4. **Culture and Traditions** How did the Islamic religion spread to the early kingdoms of Africa?

Critical Thinking

5. **Drawing Conclusions** Why do you think the Renaissance began in Italy and not in another part of Europe? Provide reasons to support your answer.

Activity

Comparing Paintings Look in a reference book for a painting by an artist of the Renaissance and a painting by an artist of the Middle Ages. Write a paragraph describing the similarities and differences you see in the two paintings.

Motives for Exploration

During the Middle Ages, European merchants journeyed thousands of miles and faced scorching deserts, blinding blizzards, and terrorizing bandits. Why did they do this? They wanted to make a profit.

Europeans of the 1400s wanted to buy fine porcelain, jewels, silk, and spices from East Asia. These items were very expensive, however. Because the Turkish Muslims controlled all the trade routes to Asia, they could also control the prices of goods that traveled along those routes. As Europeans demanded more and more Asian goods, the Muslim merchants raised their prices.

To get these goods for less, the Europeans wanted to find a way to go around the Muslim traders altogether. Their solution was to find their own route to East Asia by sea.

What makes some items more expensive than others? Maybe the product comes from far away and the cost of transporting it is high. Perhaps the item is scarce. For example, gold is expensive because the world supply is limited. Some things are simply much more desirable than others. If many people want to buy the item, the price will probably be high.

Activity

Creating an Advertisement Think of a costly item you have seen in a store. Imagine that you are a merchant who sells the item. Create a newspaper advertisement convincing people to buy the item.

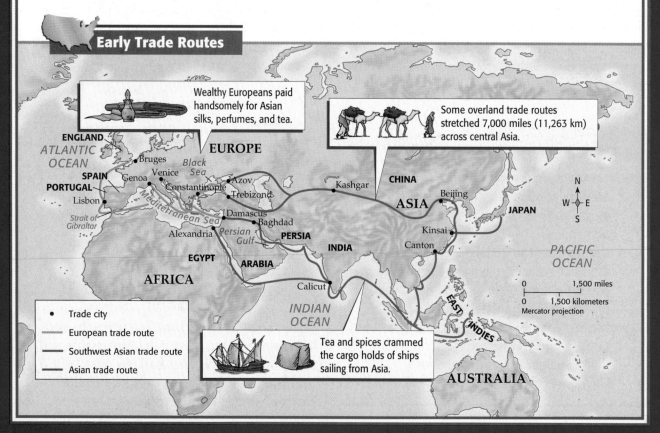

Early Trade Routes

Wealthy Europeans paid handsomely for Asian silks, perfumes, and tea.

Some overland trade routes stretched 7,000 miles (11,263 km) across central Asia.

Tea and spices crammed the cargo holds of ships sailing from Asia.

ENGLAND
ATLANTIC OCEAN
SPAIN
PORTUGAL
Lisbon
Strait of Gibraltar
Bruges
Genoa
Venice
EUROPE
Black Sea
Constantinople
Azov
Trebizond
Damascus
Alexandria
Persian Gulf
Baghdad
PERSIA
EGYPT
ARABIA
AFRICA
Calicut
INDIAN OCEAN
Kashgar
INDIA
CHINA
ASIA
Beijing
Kinsai
Canton
JAPAN
EAST INDIES
AUSTRALIA
PACIFIC OCEAN

N
W   E
S

0   1,500 miles
0   1,500 kilometers
Mercator projection

• Trade city
— European trade route
— Southwest Asian trade route
— Asian trade route

1000
Leif Eriksson lands in present-day Newfoundland

1488
Bartholomeu Dias sets sail

1492
Columbus lands in the Americas

1498
Vasco da Gama reaches India

1519
Magellan begins circumnavigation of the world

Early Exploration

READ TO DISCOVER . . .

- how Portugal led the way in overseas exploration.
- what was Columbus's plan for sailing to Asia.
- why the Europeans explored the Pacific Ocean.

TERMS TO LEARN

line of demarcation   circumnavigate
strait

The Storyteller

More than 150 years after Marco Polo's death, a young Italian sea captain—Christopher Columbus—sat down to read Polo's *Travels* with interest. Columbus read what Polo had to say about the islands of Cipangu, or present-day Japan. According to Polo, Cipangu lay some 1,500 miles (2,414 km) off the eastern shore of Asia. Because the earth is round, Columbus reasoned, a person sailing west from Europe should quickly reach Cipangu. It could be much closer than anyone thought.

Unfortunately, Marco Polo—and therefore Columbus—was wrong.

Compass

The maps that the first European explorers used did not include America. They showed three continents—Europe, Asia, and Africa—merged together in a gigantic landmass. This landmass was bound by oceans. Some explorers assumed that the Western (Atlantic) and Eastern (Pacific) Oceans ran together to form the Ocean Sea. At the time, no one realized that another huge landmass was missing from the maps or that the oceans were as large as they are.

🌐 Geography

Seeking New Trade Routes

⭐ Portugal took the lead in exploring the boundaries of the known world. Because Portugal lacked a Mediterranean port, it could not be part of the profitable trade between Asia and Europe. The country's ambitious rulers wanted to find a new route to China and India.

The Portuguese also hoped to find a more direct way to get West African gold. The gold traveled by caravan across the desert to North Africa, then by ship across the Mediterranean. Portuguese traders needed a better route.

Early Portuguese Voyages

Prince Henry of Portugal laid the groundwork for a new era of exploration. He was fascinated by what lay beyond the known boundaries

Causes and Effects

CAUSES

★ European desire for new trade routes and gold
★ New spirit of adventure
★ Power and wealth of new European nations
★ Competition among European nations
★ Missionaries' desire to convert others to Christianity

European Voyages of Exploration

EFFECTS

★ New knowledge of Africa, Asia, and the Americas
★ Clash of European and Native American cultures
★ Enslavement of Africans
★ New plants and animals in Europe and the Americas
★ Rivalry of European nations in the Americas

Chart Study

The mid-1400s in Europe were a time of adventure, great learning, and curiosity about the world.

Analyzing Information Which explorer sailing for Portugal was the first to land in the Americas?

---

of the world. In about 1420 he set up a center for exploration on the southwestern tip of Portugal, "where endeth land and where beginneth sea." Known as **Henry the Navigator,** the prince brought astronomers, geographers, and mathematicians to share their knowledge with Portuguese sailors and shipbuilders.

The prince encouraged mariners to explore the west coast of Africa. Up to that time, no ship had gone past Cape Bojador into the "green sea of darkness," an area known for its dangerous currents, fog, and strong coastal winds. The Portuguese maneuvered around this treacherous point by sending their ships farther west into the Atlantic. There they reached the **Azores** and the **Canary Islands.** From the islands the ships could pick up favorable winds and currents that carried them down the African coast.

Bartholomeu Dias

As the Portuguese moved south along the coast of West Africa, they traded for gold and ivory and established trading posts. Because of its abundance of gold, the area came to be known as the **Gold Coast.** In 1441 the Portuguese began buying slaves there as well.

King John II of Portugal launched new efforts to realize the Portuguese dream of a trading empire in Asia. If the Portuguese could find a sea route around Africa, they could trade directly with India and China. In the 1480s the king urged Portuguese sea captains to explore farther and farther south along the African coast.

In 1488 the king sent **Bartholomeu Dias** to explore the southernmost part of Africa. As Dias approached the area, he ran into a terrible storm that carried him off course and around the southern tip of Africa. Dias wrote that he had been around the "Cape of Storms." On learning of Dias's discovery, King John II renamed this southern tip of land the Cape of Good Hope—the passage around Africa might lead to a new route to India.

Vasco da Gama

The first Portuguese expedition to India came years later. In July 1497, after much preparation, **Vasco da Gama** set out from Portugal with four ships. Da Gama sailed down the coast of West Africa, rounded the Cape of Good Hope, and visited cities along the coast of East Africa. He engaged an Arab pilot who knew the Indian Ocean well. With the pilot's help, da Gama sailed on to India. He reached the port of Calicut in 1498, completing the long-awaited eastern sea route to Asia.

Columbus Crosses the Atlantic

⭐ **Christopher Columbus** had a different plan for reaching Asia. He thought he could get there by sailing west. Born in Genoa, Italy, in 1451, Columbus became a sailor for Portugal. He had traveled as far north as the Arctic Circle and as far south as the Gold Coast.

In the 1400s most educated people believed the world was round. A more difficult matter was determining its size. Columbus was among those who based their estimates of the earth's size on the work of Ptolemy, an ancient Greek astronomer. Columbus believed Asia was about 2,400 miles (3,800 km) from Europe—a voyage of about two months by ship. Ptolemy, however, had underestimated the size of the world.

The Viking Voyages

Several centuries before Columbus, northern Europeans called **Vikings** had sailed west and

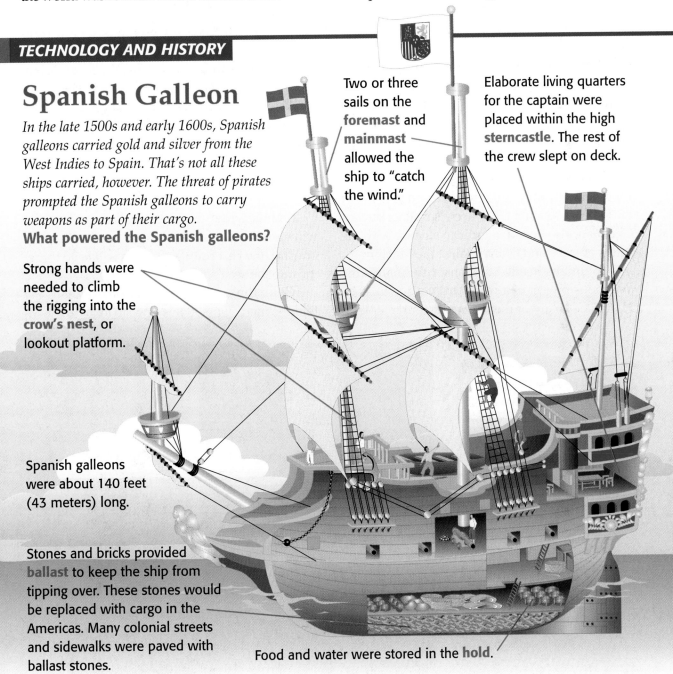

TECHNOLOGY AND HISTORY

Spanish Galleon

In the late 1500s and early 1600s, Spanish galleons carried gold and silver from the West Indies to Spain. That's not all these ships carried, however. The threat of pirates prompted the Spanish galleons to carry weapons as part of their cargo.
What powered the Spanish galleons?

Two or three sails on the **foremast** and **mainmast** allowed the ship to "catch the wind."

Elaborate living quarters for the captain were placed within the high **sterncastle**. The rest of the crew slept on deck.

Strong hands were needed to climb the rigging into the **crow's nest**, or lookout platform.

Spanish galleons were about 140 feet (43 meters) long.

Stones and bricks provided **ballast** to keep the ship from tipping over. These stones would be replaced with cargo in the Americas. Many colonial streets and sidewalks were paved with ballast stones.

Food and water were stored in the **hold**.

reached North America. In the 800s and 900s, Viking ships visited Iceland and Greenland and established settlements. Then in about 1000, a Viking sailor named Leif Eriksson got lost on his way to Greenland and landed in present-day **Newfoundland.** He established a small settlement there, but it did not last.

Although accounts of the Vikings existed in Scandinavian legends, they were unknown in the rest of Europe. Europeans did not "discover" the Americas until Columbus made his great voyage.

Spain Backs Columbus

For most of the 1400s, Spanish monarchs devoted their energy to driving the Muslims out of their country. With the fall of the last Muslim kingdom in southern Spain in 1492, **King Ferdinand** and **Queen Isabella** of Spain could focus on other goals. The Spanish had been watching the seafaring and trading successes of neighboring Portugal with envy. They, too, wanted to share in the riches of Asian trade. Queen Isabella, a devout Christian, also hoped to form an alliance with the rulers of India and China against the Muslims.

Columbus needed a sponsor to finance his ambitious project of a westward voyage to Asia. He visited many of the European courts looking

for support. After many years of frustration, he finally found a sponsor in Spain.

Queen Isabella agreed to finance the expedition. She promised Columbus a share of any riches gained from lands he discovered on his way to Asia. At the time, of course, nobody knew that a great landmass blocked his route to Asia.

Eyewitness to HISTORY

Columbus's First Voyage

On August 3, 1492, Columbus set out from Palos, Spain. He had two small ships, the *Niña* and the *Pinta,* and a larger one, the *Santa María,* carrying a total of about 90 sailors. The small fleet stopped at the Canary Islands for repairs and supplies, then sailed westward into the unknown.

The ships had good winds, but after a month at sea the sailors began to worry. Provisions were running low, and they had not sighted any land. Columbus wrote that he was "having trouble with the crew. . . . I am told that if I persist in going onward, the best course of action will be to throw me into the sea."

Columbus, however, was determined. He told the men, "I made this voyage to go to the In-

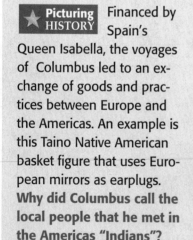

★ Picturing HISTORY Financed by Spain's Queen Isabella, the voyages of Columbus led to an exchange of goods and practices between Europe and the Americas. An example is this Taino Native American basket figure that uses European mirrors as earplugs. **Why did Columbus call the local people that he met in the Americas "Indians"?**

dies, and [I] shall continue until I find them, with God's help." To convince the crew that they had not traveled too far from home, Columbus altered the distances in his ship's log.

"Tierra! Tierra!"

Weeks later, signs of land began to appear—flocks of birds in the air and weeds floating near the ships. On October 12, 1492, at 2:00 in the morning, a lookout shouted, *"Tierra! Tierra!"*— Land! Land! He had spotted a small island, part of the group now called the Bahamas. Columbus went ashore, claimed the island for Spain, and named it San Salvador. He described the island's inhabitants as *"all of good stature, a very handsome people."* Although he did not know it, Columbus had reached the Americas.

Columbus explored the area for several months, convinced he had reached the East Indies, the islands off the coast of Asia. Today the **Caribbean Islands** are often referred to as the **West Indies.** Columbus called the local people Indians. He noted that they regarded the Europeans with wonder and often touched them to find out *"if they were flesh and bones like themselves."*

Columbus returned to Spain in triumph in March 1493. Queen Isabella and King Ferdinand received him with great honor and agreed to finance his future voyages. Columbus had earned the title of Admiral of the Ocean Sea.

Columbus's Later Voyages

Columbus made three more voyages from Spain in 1493, 1498, and 1502. He explored the Caribbean islands of Hispaniola (present-day Haiti and the Dominican Republic), Cuba, and Jamaica, and he sailed along the coasts of Central America and northern South America. He claimed the new lands for Spain and established settlements.

Columbus originally thought the lands he had found were in Asia. Later explorations made it clear that Columbus had not reached Asia at all. He had found a part of the globe unknown to Europeans, Asians, and Africans. In the following years, the Spanish explored most of the

Spain, 1492 Christopher Columbus proudly carried the Spanish banner of Castile and Leon to the shores of the Bahamas. The flag's castle represented Queen Isabella. The lion symbolized her husband, King Ferdinand.

Caribbean region. In time their voyages led to the establishment of the Spanish Empire in the Americas.

The Treaty of Tordesillas

Columbus's voyages fueled the rivalry between Spain and Portugal. The Portuguese king rejected Spanish claims to what Columbus called the Indies. Each country contested the right of the other to explore the new lands.

To keep the peace, Pope Alexander VI worked out an agreement between Spain and Portugal. In 1493 the pope established a **line of demarcation,** an imaginary line running down the middle of the Atlantic from the North Pole to the South Pole. Spain was to have control of all lands to the west of the line, while Portugal was to have control of all lands east of the line. Portugal, however, protested that the division favored Spain. As a result, in 1494 Spain and Portugal signed the **Treaty of Tordesillas** (TAWR•duh•SEE•yuhs), an agreement to move the line of demarcation farther west.

Nobody realized how much land still lay to the west of the line. As it turned out, the Treaty of Tordesillas gave Spain the right to most of North and South America. In 1500 the Portuguese explorer **Pedro Cabral** was blown off course during a storm and landed on the coast of what is now **Brazil.** Because the land lay east of the line of demarcation, Portugal claimed and eventually colonized Brazil.

Geography

The Vast Pacific

Vasco Núñez de Balboa (bal•BOH•uh), governor of a Spanish town in present-day Panama, had heard stories of the "great waters" beyond the mountains. In 1513 he formed an exploring party and tramped through the steaming jungles. After many days of difficult travel, the Spaniard climbed a hill and saw a vast body of water. When he reached the water's edge, Balboa waded in and claimed the **Pacific Ocean** and adjoining lands for the king and queen of Spain.

A Southern Route to Asia

The Spanish wanted to find a sea route through or around South America that would lead

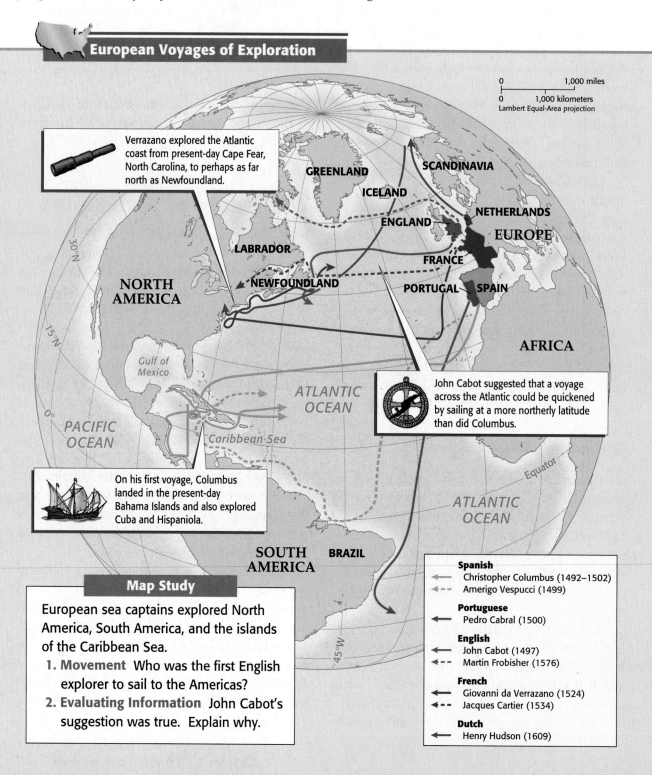

European Voyages of Exploration

Verrazano explored the Atlantic coast from present-day Cape Fear, North Carolina, to perhaps as far north as Newfoundland.

John Cabot suggested that a voyage across the Atlantic could be quickened by sailing at a more northerly latitude than did Columbus.

On his first voyage, Columbus landed in the present-day Bahama Islands and also explored Cuba and Hispaniola.

0   1,000 miles
0   1,000 kilometers
Lambert Equal-Area projection

Spanish
Christopher Columbus (1492–1502)
Amerigo Vespucci (1499)

Portuguese
Pedro Cabral (1500)

English
John Cabot (1497)
Martin Frobisher (1576)

French
Giovanni da Verrazano (1524)
Jacques Cartier (1534)

Dutch
Henry Hudson (1609)

Map Study

European sea captains explored North America, South America, and the islands of the Caribbean Sea.

1. **Movement** Who was the first English explorer to sail to the Americas?
2. **Evaluating Information** John Cabot's suggestion was true. Explain why.

them to Asia. In 1519 they commissioned **Ferdinand Magellan,** a Portuguese mariner, to lead an expedition of five ships. Sailing from Spain, Magellan headed west across the Atlantic and south along the eastern coast of South America.

Searching for a passage that would lead to the Pacific Ocean, the sailors grew restless and rebelled against the long and dangerous journey. Magellan managed to regain command, but one of his ships returned to Spain.

In late November 1520, Magellan finally found and sailed through the narrow, twisting sea passage to the Pacific. This strait still bears his name. Looking over the calm waters at the end of the strait, Magellan exclaimed: "We are about to stand [go] into an ocean where no ship has ever sailed before." He named the ocean the Pacific, which means "peaceful."

Sailing Around the World

Magellan expected to reach Asia in just a few weeks after rounding South America, but the voyage across the Pacific lasted four months. The crew ran out of food and ate sawdust, rats, and the leather of the rigging to stay alive. Magellan was killed in the Philippines in a local war, but some of his crew returned to Spain. Their trip had

Ferdinand Magellan

taken almost 3 years. Only 1 of the 5 original ships and 18 of the 250 crew members completed the difficult journey. These men were the first to circumnavigate, or sail around, the world.

★ ★ ★ ★ ★ Section 2 Assessment ★ ★ ★ ★ ★ ★

Checking for Understanding
1. *Identify* Henry the Navigator, Vasco da Gama, Christopher Columbus, Vikings, King Ferdinand, Queen Isabella, Ferdinand Magellan.
2. *Define* line of demarcation, strait, circumnavigate.
3. *Describe* the accomplishments of Vasco de Balboa and Ferdinand Magellan.

Reviewing Themes
4. **Geography and History** Where did Columbus land on his first voyage?

Critical Thinking
5. **Making Inferences** For many years history books claimed that "Columbus discovered America." Why do you think Native Americans might disagree with the use of the word *discovered* in this statement? What might be a better word choice?

Activity

Drawing a Map Draw a map of the world as you think Columbus might have seen it in 1492. Remember his error in calculating distance.

1519
Hernán Cortés lands in Mexico

1532
Francisco Pizarro captures Atahualpa

1541
De Soto crosses the Mississippi River

1565
Spain establishes fort at St. Augustine, Florida

Section 3

Spain in America

READ TO DISCOVER . . .

- how the great Aztec and Inca Empires came to an end.
- how Spain governed its empire in the Americas.
- why the Columbian Exchange was significant.

TERMS TO LEARN

conquistador
tribute
viceroy
pueblo
mission
presidio
encomienda
plantation
Columbian Exchange

The Storyteller

Would you like to visit a place described in the following way? "A river . . . [stretched] two leagues wide, in which there were fishes as big as horses. . . . The lord of the country took his afternoon nap under a great tree on which were hung a great number of little gold bells. . . . The jugs and bowls were [made] of gold."

"[It was] a land rich in gold, silver, and other wealth . . . great cities . . . and civilized people wearing woolen clothes."

Conquistador's armor

Stories of kingdoms wealthy beyond belief greeted the early Spanish explorers in the Americas. The reports led them far and wide in search of fabulous riches.

Spanish Conquistadors

Known as conquistadors (kahn•KEES •tuh•dawrs), these explorers received grants from the Spanish rulers. They had the right to explore and establish settlements in the Americas. In exchange they agreed to give the Spanish crown one-fifth of any gold or treasure discovered. This arrangement allowed Spanish rulers to launch expeditions with little risk. If a conquistador failed, he lost his own fortune. If he succeeded, both he and Spain gained wealth and glory.

As one conquistador explained, "We came here to serve God and the king, and also to get rich." The story of how the conquistadors destroyed the most powerful empires of the Americas and went on to build a new Spanish empire is one of the most astonishing in history.

Cortés Conquers the Aztec

When **Hernán Cortés** landed on the east coast of what we now know as Mexico in 1519, he was looking for gold and glory. He came with about 500 soldiers, some horses, and a few cannons. Cortés soon learned about the great Aztec Empire and its capital of Tenochtitlán.

In building their empire, the Aztec had conquered many cities in Mexico. These cities were forced to give crops, clothing, gold, and precious stones to the Aztec as **tribute.** Cortés used the resentment of the people of these cities to his advantage. With the help of **Doña Marina,** a Mayan woman who acted as his translator, he formed alliances with nearby cities against the Aztec.

Cortés marched into Tenochtitlán in November with his small army and his Native American allies. The Aztec emperor **Montezuma** (MAHN •tuh•ZOO•muh)—also spelled Moctezuma—welcomed Cortés and his soldiers and provided them with food and a fine palace. However, Cortés took advantage of the Aztec's hospitality and made Montezuma his prisoner.

In the spring the Spaniards heard rumors of rebellion. To crush any spark of resistance, they killed Montezuma and many Aztec nobles. The Aztec had had enough. They rose up and drove the Spaniards from Tenochtitlán. Cortés, however, was determined to retake the city. He waited until more Spanish troops arrived, then attacked and destroyed the Aztec capital in 1521. An Aztec lament describes the awful scene:

❝Without roofs are the houses,
And red are their walls with blood. . . .
Weep, my friends,
Know that with these disasters
We have lost our Mexican nation.❞

The Aztec Empire disintegrated, and Spain seized control of the region.

Pizarro Conquers Peru

In 1530 the conquistador **Francisco Pizarro** sailed down the Pacific coast of South America with about 180 Spanish soldiers. Pizarro had heard tales of the incredibly wealthy Inca Empire in present-day Peru. In 1532 Pizarro captured the Inca ruler, **Atahualpa** (ah•tah•WAHL•pah), and trapped much of the Incan army in a square surrounded by walls. An Incan historian describes what happened:

American Memories

An Aztec Home

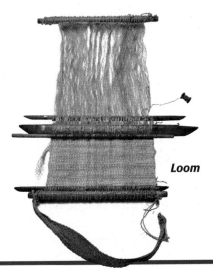

What Was It Like? Aztec homes were simple and built for usefulness rather than beauty. **How do you think the Aztec used each of the household items shown here?**

Grinding stone

Bowl

Loom

> All the Indians were inside like llamas. There were a great many of them and they could not get out, nor did they have any weapons. . . . The Spaniards killed them all—with horses, with swords, with guns. . . . From more than 10,000 men there did not escape 200.

A few months later, the Spanish falsely accused Atahualpa of crimes and executed him. The Inca were used to obeying commands from their rulers. Without leadership they were not able to fight effectively. By 1535 Pizarro had gained control of most of the vast Inca Empire.

Why Spain Succeeded

The conquistadors' victories in Mexico and Peru were quick and lasting. How could Cortés and Pizarro, with only a few hundred Spanish soldiers, conquer such mighty empires?

First, the Spanish arrived with strange weapons—guns and cannons—and fearsome animals. They rode horses and had huge, ferocious dogs. To the Native Americans, the Spanish seemed almost like gods. Second, many Native Americans hated their Aztec overlords and assisted the conquistadors in overthrowing them.

Finally, disease played an extremely large role in the Spanish conquest. Native Americans had no immunity to the diseases the Europeans had, unknowingly, brought with them. Epidemics of smallpox and other diseases wiped out entire communities in the Americas and did much to weaken the Aztec's and Inca's resistance. In Mexico, a Spanish friar recalled, "More than half the population died. They died in heaps, like bedbugs."

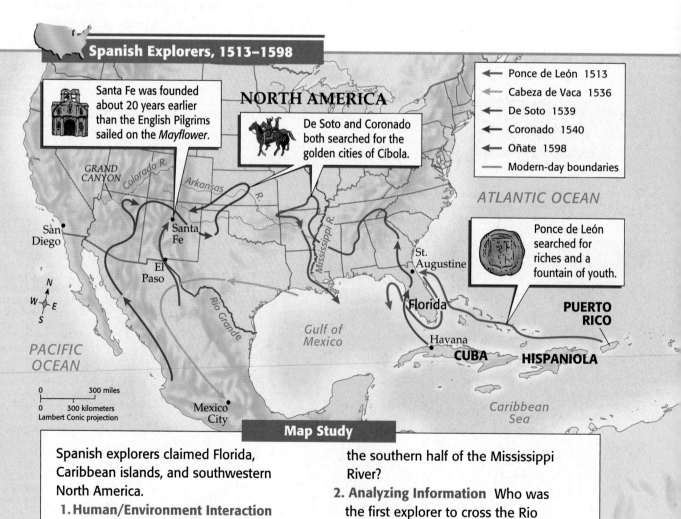

Spanish Explorers, 1513–1598

NORTH AMERICA

Santa Fe was founded about 20 years earlier than the English Pilgrims sailed on the *Mayflower*.

De Soto and Coronado both searched for the golden cities of Cíbola.

→ Ponce de León 1513
→ Cabeza de Vaca 1536
→ De Soto 1539
→ Coronado 1540
→ Oñate 1598
— Modern-day boundaries

ATLANTIC OCEAN

Ponce de León searched for riches and a fountain of youth.

GRAND CANYON • Colorado R. • Arkansas R. • San Diego • Santa Fe • El Paso • Rio Grande • Mississippi R. • St. Augustine • Florida • PUERTO RICO • Gulf of Mexico • Havana • CUBA • HISPANIOLA • PACIFIC OCEAN • Caribbean Sea • Mexico City

0   300 miles
0   300 kilometers
Lambert Conic projection

Map Study

Spanish explorers claimed Florida, Caribbean islands, and southwestern North America.

1. **Human/Environment Interaction** Which Spaniard explored areas along the southern half of the Mississippi River?
2. **Analyzing Information** Who was the first explorer to cross the Rio Grande?

★ ★

Spain in North America

⭐ Mexico and Peru were rich in silver and gold. Hoping to find similar wealth to the north, conquistadors explored the southeastern and southwestern parts of North America.

Ponce de León in Florida

Juan Ponce de León made the first Spanish landing on the mainland of North America. He arrived on the east coast of present-day Florida in 1513. Besides gold, Ponce de León hoped to find the legendary fountain of youth, "a spring of running water of such marvelous virtue" that drinking it "makes old men young again." Ponce de León never found the fountain, but his exploration led to the first Spanish settlement in what is now the United States. In 1565 the Spanish established a fort at **St. Augustine,** Florida, to keep out a group of French settlers in the region.

The Seven Cities of Gold

Many other conquistadors searched for quick riches. None ever achieved this goal, and several lost their lives trying. **Álvar Núñez Cabeza de Vaca** (kuh•BAY•suh duh VAH•kuh) was part of a Spanish expedition to Florida in 1528.

The expedition, led by the conquistador **Pánfilo de Narváez,** failed. Stranded, de Narváez and his followers built several boats and sailed along the coast toward Mexico. However, in November 1528, all but two of the boats were lost in a storm. The two boats that survived went aground on an island near present-day Texas. Within a few months, all but a handful of the shipwrecked explorers died from disease and exposure.

Cabeza de Vaca and his companions survived by adopting Native American ways. Cabeza de Vaca and an enslaved African named **Estevanico** became medicine men. Cabeza de Vaca later wrote that their method of healing was "to bless the sick, breathing on them" and to recite Latin prayers. The Spaniards were praying that the patients would recover and be grateful.

In 1533 the Spaniards set off on foot on a great 1,000-mile journey across the Southwest. Arriving

★★★ **Linking**
PAST & PRESENT

The First Thanksgiving

On April 30, 1598, long before the Pilgrims came to North America, Spanish colonists held a thanksgiving feast near present-day El Paso, Texas. Juan de Oñate had led 400 men and their families across the desert from Mexico. After they reached the Rio Grande, Oñate told them to feast and give thanks for the abundance of the new land.

in Mexico in 1536, Cabeza de Vaca related tales he had heard of seven cities with walls of emerald and streets of gold.

De Soto's Expedition

The stories inspired **Hernando de Soto,** who led an expedition to explore Florida and lands to the west. For three years De Soto and his troops wandered around the southeastern area of the present-day United States, following stories of gold. As the Spaniards traveled, they preyed on the native peoples. Their usual method was to enter a village, take the chief hostage, and demand food and supplies.

De Soto crossed the **Mississippi River** in 1541, describing it as "swift, and very deep." After traveling as far west as present-day Oklahoma, De Soto died of fever. His men buried him in the waters of the Mississippi to keep his death a secret from the Indians.

Coronado and Oñate

Francisco Vásquez de Coronado also wanted to find the fabled seven cities of gold. His expedition included Friar Marcos, who claimed to have seen one of the cities on an earlier trip. After traveling through northern Mexico and present-day Arizona and New Mexico, the expedition reached the Zuni town of Cibola in early summer 1540. They realized at once that the friar's accounts had been false. There was no gold.

Juana Inés de la Cruz

Juan de Oñate (day ohn•YAH•tay) was sent from Mexico to gain control over lands to the north and to convert the natives. In 1598 Oñate founded the province of New Mexico and introduced cattle and horses to the Pueblo people.

Spain, however, remained much more interested in its colonial empire to the south. The West Indies, Mexico, and South America provided the silver and gold that made Spain wealthy.

 **Citizenship**

Spanish Rule

★ The Spanish governed their colonies the way they governed their own country—from the top down. They divided their new lands into five provinces. The wealthiest were New Spain (Mexico) and Peru. The Spanish king established a Council of the Indies that met in Spain and made laws for the colonies. He also appointed a **viceroy** as his representative in each province.

Spanish law called for three kinds of settlements in the Americas—pueblos, missions, and presidios. **Pueblos,** or towns, were established as centers of trade. **Missions** were religious communities that usually included a small town, surrounding farmland, and a church. A **presidio,** or fort, was usually built near a mission.

Social Classes

A complex class system developed in Spain's empire in the Americas. The upper class consisted of people who had been born in Spain, called *peninsulares.* The *peninsulares* owned the land, served in the Catholic Church, and ran the local government. Below them were the creoles, people born in the Americas to Spanish parents. Lower in the class structure were the mestizos (meh•STEE•zohs), people with Spanish and Indian parents. Still lower were the Native Americans, most of whom lived in great poverty. At the very bottom were enslaved Africans.

Men dominated the society, and a woman's place was in the home. One Mexican woman of the 1600s, however, was different. Juana Inés de la Cruz gained renown as a woman of letters. She wrote plays, poetry, and an essay discussing women's place in society.

Native Americans

In the 1500s the Spanish government granted each conquistador who settled in the Americas an *encomienda,* the right to demand taxes or labor from Native Americans living on the land. This system turned the Native Americans into slaves. Grueling labor in the fields and in the gold and silver mines took its toll. Many Native Americans also died from malnutrition and disease.

A Spanish priest named **Bartolomé de las Casas** condemned the cruel treatment of the Native Americans. He reported abuses to the authorities in Spain and pleaded for laws to protect the Native Americans. Las Casas claimed that millions had died because the Spanish "made gold their ultimate aim, seeking to load themselves with riches in the shortest possible time."

Because of Las Casas's reports, in 1542 the Spanish government passed the New Laws, which forbade making slaves of Native Americans. Although not always enforced, the laws did correct the worst abuses.

The Plantation System

Some Spanish settlers made large profits by exporting crops and raw materials back to Spain. In the West Indies, the main exports were tobacco and sugarcane. To raise these crops, the Spanish developed the plantation system. A plantation was a large estate run by the owner or a manager and farmed by workers living on it. The Spanish used Native Americans to work their plantations.

In his effort to help the Native Americans, Las Casas suggested replacing them with enslaved Africans—a suggestion he bitterly regretted later. He thought the Africans could endure the labor better than the Native Americans.

The Slave Trade

The Spanish quickly took up Las Casas's idea and began importing enslaved Africans. By the mid-1500s the Spanish were bringing thousands from West Africa to the Americas. The Portuguese did the same in Brazil.

The Africans who survived the brutal ocean voyage were sold to plantation owners. By the late 1500s, plantation slave labor was an essential part of the economy of the Spanish and Portuguese colonies.

The Columbian Exchange

The voyages of Columbus and other explorers brought together two parts of the globe that previously had had no contact: the continents of Europe, Asia, and Africa in one hemisphere and the Americas in the other. The contact led to an exchange of plants, animals, and diseases that altered life on both sides of the Atlantic. Scholars refer to this as the Columbian Exchange.

New Ways of Life

Europeans brought horses, cattle, pigs, and chickens. These new animals changed the diet and lifestyle of many Indian cultures. In turn the Americas provided many new foods—such as corn, tomatoes, beans, squash, potatoes, and chocolate—that made the European diet more nutritious and varied.

Recall that Europeans brought many diseases to the Americas that Native Americans had no immunity to. As a result many died of smallpox, influenza, measles, and other diseases. When Columbus landed on Hispaniola in 1492, more than 3 million Native Americans lived there. Fifty years later only about 500 remained.

Section 3 Assessment

Checking for Understanding
1. **Identify** Cortés, Montezuma, Pizarro, Atahualpa, Ponce de León, Las Casas.
2. **Define** conquistador, tribute, pueblo, mission, presidio, Columbian Exchange.
3. **Explain** how the Spanish, with so few soldiers, were able to conquer empires.

Reviewing Themes
4. **Groups and Institutions** What groups made up the class system in Spanish America?

Critical Thinking
5. **Identifying Assumptions** "We came to serve God and the king, and also to get rich." In what way do you think conquistadors planned to serve "God and the king"?

Activity

Creating a Menu Using cookbooks as your references, create an all-American dinner menu that includes foods introduced to the Europeans by Native Americans.

3 The Pima accepted Catholicism and welcomed the Spanish missionaries but they did not forget their own rituals. On special occasions today—such as the coming-of-age of a young person—the Pima still wear traditional dress.

Father Kino's Journey

Colorado River

Gila River

N

UNITED STATES

MEXICO

Cerro del Pinacate

Batki village

Sonora

4 This crucifix adorns a container used during Roman Catholic Communion services. It is one of the symbols of the Roman Catholic faith that Father Kino and other missionaries introduced into the Southwest.

Gulf of California

Caborca

5 During his 25 years in the Pimería Alta—the area now known as southern Arizona and northern Mexico—Father Kino baptized thousands of Native Americans. On one journey he traveled among the Pima and Papago.

6 Missionary, mathematician, astronomer, and mapmaker, Kino was also an avid explorer. On his 800-mile trip in 1698, he learned from the Indians that the Gila River met the Colorado River, which flows into the Gulf of California. Father Kino climbed Cerro del Pinacate and—looking west from the mountaintop—saw the river flowing into the gulf. In 1705 he published the first map of this area based on actual exploration.

Arizona

2 Father Kino established 29 missions, including San Xavier del Bac near Tucson, founded in 1700. Today the mission still serves as a church and school for the Papago Indians.

•Tucson

Santa Cruz River

1 In 1687 Father Francisco Eusebio Kino, a Catholic missionary who came to the Americas with the Spanish, established headquarters at Nuestra Señora de los Dolores Mission in northern Mexico. From there, he set out on more than 50 journeys across Sonora and present-day Arizona. On September 22, 1698, he headed northwest to explore the region and to baptize more than 400 Pima and Papago.

Dolores

A Missionary's Journey

66 In this vast and very fertile vineyard of the Indian tribes which they call the Pimas ... I have been able, through the celestial favors of the heavenly saints, to wash about three hundred Indians in the holy water of baptism.... God willing, hundreds, and later, thousands will be gathered into the bosom of our sweet, most holy Mother Church.... In this charge where I am working, a mission [has] been established, and many very suitable rooms of a house [have] been built. We are now occupied in the erection of a new church, with the help of some soldiers, and its walls have ... happily arisen to a height of several feet. 99

—From a letter written by Father Kino, June 30, 1687.

1450	1500	1550	1600

1497
John Cabot lands
in Newfoundland

1517
Martin Luther
starts the Protestant
Reformation

1535
Jacques Cartier sails
up the St. Lawrence
River to Montreal

1609
Henry Hudson
sails the
Hudson River

Section 4

Exploring North America

READ TO DISCOVER . . .

- how the Protestant Reformation affected North America.
- how French, Dutch, and English explorers searched for the Northwest Passage.
- why the activities of early traders encouraged exploration.

TERMS TO LEARN

mercantilism   coureur de bois
Northwest Passage

The Storyteller

In 1517 **Martin Luther,** a German priest, nailed a list of complaints about the Catholic Church on the door of a local church. Luther declared that the Bible was the only true guide for Christians. He rejected many Church practices—even the authority of the pope—because they were not mentioned in the Bible. Luther also believed that faith rather than good deeds was the way to salvation.

Church officials tried to get Luther to take back his statements. "I cannot go against my conscience," he replied. "Here I stand. I cannot do otherwise. God help me."

Martin Luther

Martin Luther's actions led to incredible changes in Europe. Before he voiced his beliefs, the countries of Europe had their differences, but they were bound together by a common church. For centuries, Catholicism had been the main religion of western Europe. In the 1500s, however, Luther's opposition to the policies of the Roman Catholic Church emerged.

A Divided Church

Within a few years, Luther had many followers. They broke away from Catholicism to found their own Christian churches. Martin Luther's protests were the start of a great religious and historical movement known as the **Protestant Reformation.**

Protestantism Spreads in Europe

From Germany Luther's ideas spread rapidly. **John Calvin,** a French religious thinker, also broke away from the Catholic Church. Like Luther, Calvin rejected the idea that good works would ensure a person's salvation. He believed that God had already chosen those who would be saved.

In England King Henry VIII also left the Catholic Church. A dispute with Pope Clement VII over his marriage led to the break. The pope had refused Henry's request to declare his first marriage invalid. In 1534 the English Parliament denied the authority of the pope and recognized the king as head of the Church of England.

During the rule of Henry's daughter, Queen Elizabeth I, further reforms firmly established England as a Protestant nation.

Religious Rivalries in the Americas

Throughout western Europe, people and nations divided into Catholics and Protestants. When these Europeans crossed the Atlantic, they took along their religious differences.

Spanish and French Catholics worked to spread their faith to the Native Americans. The Spanish settled in the southwestern and southeastern regions of North America, and the French in the northeast. Dutch and English Protestants established colonies in lands along the Atlantic coast between the French and the Spanish settlements. Some of the English settlements were founded by Protestants seeking to practice their beliefs in peace.

$ Economics

Economic Rivalry

★ Religion was only one of the factors that pushed European nations across the Atlantic Ocean. The promise of great wealth was equally strong, especially as other Europeans watched Spain draw riches from its colonies.

According to the economic theory of mercantilism, a nation's power was based on its wealth. Rulers tried to increase their nation's total wealth by amassing gold and silver and by developing trade. Mercantilism provided great opportunities for individual merchants to make money. It also increased rivalry between nations.

Several countries in Europe competed for overseas territory that could produce wealth.

They wanted to acquire colonies in the Americas that could provide valuable resources, such as gold and silver, or raw materials. The colonies also served as a place to sell European products. **$**

A Northwest Passage

★ The Treaty of Tordesillas had divided the Americas between Spain and Portugal. It did not allow for claims by other nations—but England, France, and the Netherlands ignored the treaty. During the 1500s and early 1600s, these countries sent explorers to chart the coast of North America. The voyage to Asia—either around the southern tip of Africa or South America—was long and difficult. For this reason, the three countries hoped to discover a Northwest Passage to Asia—a more direct water route through the Americas.

English and French Explorations

In 1497 England sent **John Cabot,** an Italian, to look for a northern route to Asia. Cabot probably landed on the coast of present-day Newfoundland. England used Cabot's voyage as the basis for its claims to North America.

In 1524 France hired an Italian, **Giovanni da Verrazano,** to look for the northern sea route. Verrazano explored the coast of North America from present-day Nova Scotia to the Carolinas.

★ **Picturing HISTORY** In 1676 Kateri Tekakwitha, a 20-year-old Mohawk woman, accepted Christianity from French Catholic missionaries. **What region of North America was settled by the French?**

Eleven years later Frenchman **Jacques Cartier** (KAR•tyay) sailed up the St. Lawrence River hoping it would lead to the Pacific. He got as far as the Huron Indian village of Hochelaga. From the mountain next to the village, wrote Cartier, "one sees a very great distance." He named the peak Mont-Royal, meaning "royal mountain." This is the site of the city now called **Montreal.** Cartier had heard many stories about gold, but he found neither gold nor a sea route to Asia.

Hudson's Discoveries

The Dutch, too, wanted to find a passage through the Americas. They hired **Henry Hudson,** an English sailor, to explore. In 1609 he discovered the river that now bears his name. In his ship, the *Half Moon,* Hudson sailed north on the Hudson River as far as the site of present-day Albany. Deciding that he had not found a passage to India, he turned back. The following year Hudson tried again, this time sent by England.

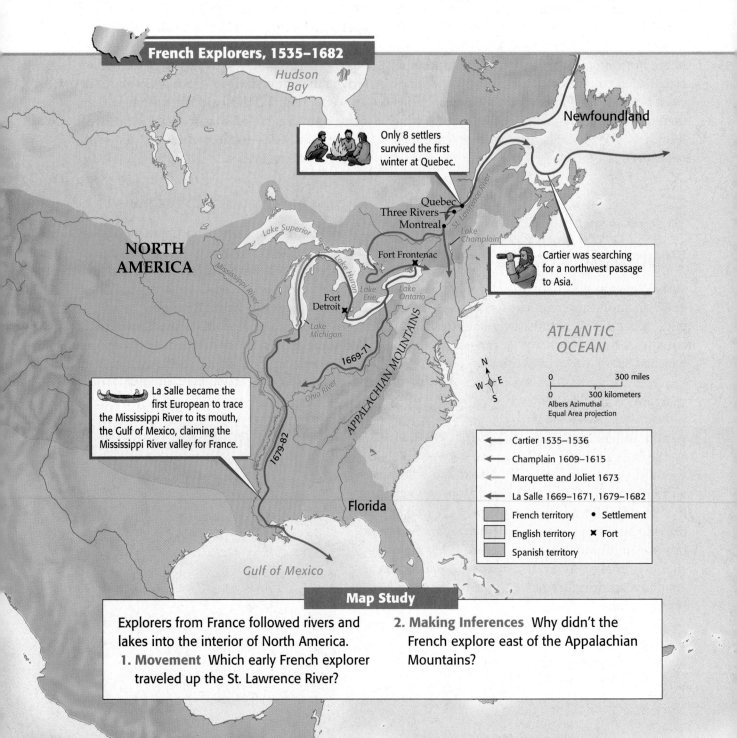

French Explorers, 1535–1682

Hudson Bay

Newfoundland

Only 8 settlers survived the first winter at Quebec.

Quebec
Three Rivers
Montreal

St. Lawrence River

Lake Champlain

NORTH AMERICA

Lake Superior

Mississippi River

Lake Huron

Fort Frontenac

Cartier was searching for a northwest passage to Asia.

Fort Detroit

Lake Michigan

Lake Erie

Lake Ontario

1669-71

APPALACHIAN MOUNTAINS

Ohio River

ATLANTIC OCEAN

La Salle became the first European to trace the Mississippi River to its mouth, the Gulf of Mexico, claiming the Mississippi River valley for France.

1679-82

N W E S

0   300 miles
0   300 kilometers
Albers Azimuthal
Equal Area projection

Florida

→ Cartier 1535–1536
→ Champlain 1609–1615
→ Marquette and Joliet 1673
→ La Salle 1669–1671, 1679–1682
☐ French territory   • Settlement
☐ English territory   ✖ Fort
☐ Spanish territory

Gulf of Mexico

Map Study

Explorers from France followed rivers and lakes into the interior of North America.

1. Movement Which early French explorer traveled up the St. Lawrence River?

2. Making Inferences Why didn't the French explore east of the Appalachian Mountains?

Major European Explorers, 1487-1682

Explorer	Dates of Voyage	Accomplishments
For Portugal		
Bartolomeu Dias	1487–1488	Sailed around the southern tip of Africa
Vasco da Gama	1497–1499	Sailed around Africa to India
Pedro Alvares Cabral	1500	Sailed to Brazil
For Spain		
Christopher Columbus	1492–1504	Explored the islands of the Caribbean Sea
Juan Ponce de León	1508–1509, 1513	Explored Puerto Rico Explored Florida
Ferdinand Magellan	1519–1522	First to sail around the world
Cabeza de Vaca	1530	Explored Spanish northern Mexico and Brazil
Francisco Coronado	1540–1542	Explored southwestern North America
Hernando de Soto	1516–1520, 1539–1543	Explored Central America Led expedition to the Mississippi River
Juan Cabrillo	1542–1543	Explored the west coast of North America
For England		
John Cabot	1497–1501	Rediscovered Newfoundland (east coast of North America)
Henry Hudson	1610–1611	Explored Hudson Strait and Hudson Bay
For the Netherlands		
Henry Hudson	1609	Explored the Hudson River
For France		
Giovanni da Verrazano	1524	Explored the east coast of North America, including New York Harbor
Jacques Cartier	1534–1542	Explored the St. Lawrence River
Samuel de Champlain	1603–1615	Explored the St. Lawrence River Founded Quebec
Jacques Marquette/ Louis Joliet	1673	Explored the Mississippi River
Robert de La Salle	1666–1682	Explored the Great Lakes Founded Louisiana after reaching the mouth of the Mississippi River

Chart Study

Most European explorers reached the Western Hemisphere.

1. Which two countries explored the east coast of North America?

2. **Analyzing Information** Whose expedition was the first to sail around the world?

America's FLAGS

Flag of New France Settlers in New France flew this French flag, which was based on the French Royal Banner, until 1763. White was the French royal color of the time.

Sailing almost due west from northern England, Henry Hudson and his crew discovered a huge bay, now called **Hudson Bay.** Hudson thought he had reached the Pacific Ocean. After months of searching for an outlet from the bay, however, the crew rebelled. Hudson, his son John, and a few sailors were set adrift in a small boat—and never seen again.

Early Traders

France had shown little interest in building an empire in the Americas. Its rulers were preoccupied by political and religious conflicts at home. The French viewed North America as an opportunity for profits from fishing and fur trading rather than a place to settle.

Furs were popular in Europe, and traders could make large profits from beaver pelts acquired in North America. A group of French traders obtained the rights to the fur trade with Native Americans. In 1608 the group sent **Samuel de Champlain** to establish a settlement in **Quebec** in what is now **Canada.** Champlain made several trips to the region and discovered Lake Champlain. He described the beautiful scenery and abundant wildlife and the Native Americans he met there.

From Quebec the French moved into other parts of Canada, where they built trading posts to collect furs gathered by Native Americans and French trappers. The trappers were called **coureurs de bois** (ku•RUHR duh BWAH), meaning "runners of the woods."

In the early 1600s, the Dutch began to set up trading posts along the Hudson River—first at Fort Orange (later Albany) and then at New Amsterdam (site of present-day New York City). For the Netherlands, England, and France, the 1500s were years of early exploration. In the early 1600s, France and the Netherlands established trading posts in the Americas. More serious efforts to discover and develop the possibilities of North America were to come in the years that followed.

★ ★ ★ ★ ★ **Section 4 Assessment** ★ ★ ★ ★ ★ ★

Checking for Understanding

1. *Identify* Martin Luther, Jacques Cartier, Henry Hudson, Samuel de Champlain.
2. *Define* mercantilism, Northwest Passage, coureur de bois.
3. *Summarize* the complaints of Protestants who were opposed to the practices of the Roman Catholic Church.

Reviewing Themes

4. **Global Connections** Why did some European nations hope to find raw materials for industry in the Americas?

Critical Thinking

5. **Making Comparisons** How did the goals of the French in the Americas differ from the goals of other European countries?

Activity

Giving Directions Write a letter to one of the explorers who searched for a Northwest Passage. Provide the explorer with specific directions on how to find a water passage through northern Canada to the Pacific Ocean.

Social Studies
SKILL BUILDER

Reading a Time Line

Knowing the relationship of time to events is important in studying history. A time line is a visual way to show chronological order within a time period. Most time lines are divided into sections representing equal time intervals. For example, a time line showing 1,000 years might be divided into ten 100-year sections. Each event on a time line appears beside the date when the event took place.

Dates at the beginning and the end of a time line mark a time span, or the number of years the time line covers. Events listed on the time line all take place within its time span.

Learning the Skill

To read a time line, follow these steps:
• Find the dates on the opposite ends of the time line to know the time span. Also note the intervals between dates on the time line.
• Study the order of events.
• Analyze relationships among events or look for trends.

Practicing the Skill

Analyze the time line of Magellan's voyage. Use it to answer the questions below.
1. What time span is represented?
2. How many years do each of the sections represent?
3. Did Magellan's voyage to the Spice Islands occur before or after his voyage to the Philippines?
4. How long did Magellan's voyage around the world take?

◆ Applying the Skill ▶

Making a Time Line List 10 key events that have occurred in your life and the dates on which these events occurred. Write the events in chronological order on a time line.

GO TO Glencoe's **Skillbuilder Interactive Workbook, Level 1** provides instruction and practice in key social studies skills.

---

c. 1480
Magellan is born in Sabrosa, Portugal

c. 1490
Spends early years as a page at Portuguese court

1506
Travels to Spice Islands on exploratory expeditions

1510
Promoted to captain

1517
Offers services to king of Spain

1480 — **1490** — **1500** — **1510** — **1520**

Sept. 20, 1519
Sails from Spain with five ships

April 7, 1521
Lands in the Philippines

April 27, 1521
Magellan is killed during inter-island dispute

Sept. 6, 1522
One ship reaches Spain with valuable cargo

Assessment and Activities

★ Reviewing Key Terms

On graph paper, create a word search puzzle using the following terms. Crisscross the terms vertically and horizontally, then fill in the remaining squares with extra letters. Use the terms' definitions as clues to find the words in the puzzle. Share your puzzle with a classmate.

Renaissance
astrolabe
caravel
mosque
strait
conquistador
viceroy
pueblo
Columbian Exchange
mercantilism
Northwest Passage

★ Reviewing Key Facts

1. Why were Europeans interested in Asia?
2. What three large African kingdoms south of the Sahara flourished between 300 and 1600?
3. Which country supported Columbus on his quest to find a water route to Asia?
4. List the major accomplishments of Vasco da Gama, Ponce de León, and John Cabot.
5. What was the main reason the Spanish wanted to conquer the Aztec and Inca?

★ Critical Thinking

Making Comparisons

European nations had different reasons for exploring overseas.
1. How did Portuguese efforts to reach Asia differ from Columbus's efforts?
2. Why was England more interested in North America than Spain was?

★ Time Line Activity

Create a time line on which you place the following events in chronological order.
- Columbus makes his first voyage to the Americas
- Pizarro conquers the Inca
- The Renaissance begins
- Dias sails around the tip of Africa
- Cartier explores Canada

★ Skill Practice Activity

Reading a Time Line

Study the time line below, then answer the following questions.
1. What is the time span covered on this time line?
2. How far apart are the intervals on this time line?
3. Which three events occured in 1492?

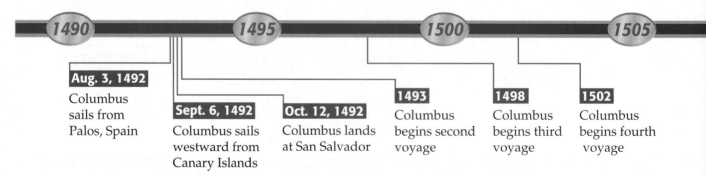

| 1490 | 1495 | 1500 | 1505 |

Aug. 3, 1492
Columbus sails from Palos, Spain

Sept. 6, 1492
Columbus sails westward from Canary Islands

Oct. 12, 1492
Columbus lands at San Salvador

1493
Columbus begins second voyage

1498
Columbus begins third voyage

1502
Columbus begins fourth voyage

★ Geography Activity

Study the map below and answer the questions that follow.

Missions in New Spain by the 1700s

Mission
Presidio
City

1. **Place** In what present-day states were the Spanish missions located?
2. **Location** Near what city was the northern-most Spanish mission located?
3. **Location** In which direction would a traveler leaving Mexico City journey to reach San Diego?

★ Reviewing Themes

1. **Culture and Traditions** Give one example of how trade encouraged an exchange of culture.
2. **Geography and History** Why are the Caribbean Islands often referred to as the West Indies?
3. **Groups and Institutions** How did the development of the Spanish *encomienda* system lead to the enslavement of Africans in America?
4. **Global Connections** What factors motivated voyages of exploration?

★ Technology Activity

Using a Word Processor Search the library for information on boats and sailing. Using a word processor, prepare a report about a navigational instrument that is in use today. Describe how it would have been helpful to an explorer such as Magellan.

★ Cooperative Activity

History and Language Arts Working in a group, research Spanish influence on American culture. Decide how American words, styles of architecture, and foods were influenced by Spain's presence. Other areas of influence might include clothing styles, traditions, and holidays. Present your findings in an illustrated brochure. Use photos, maps, or sketches to add information to your brochure. Include information about locations in the United States where Spanish influence is particularly strong.

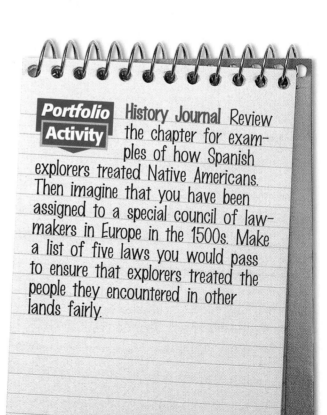

Portfolio Activity History Journal Review the chapter for examples of how Spanish explorers treated Native Americans. Then imagine that you have been assigned to a special council of lawmakers in Europe in the 1500s. Make a list of five laws you would pass to ensure that explorers treated the people they encountered in other lands fairly.

Colonial Settlement

1587–1770

"Rejoyce together, mourne together, labour and suffer together...."

—JOHN WINTHROP, 1630

inter*NET*
CONNECTION

To learn more about colonial settlement, visit the Glencoe Social Studies Web Site at **www.glencoe.com** for information, activities, and links to other sites.

MAPPING
America

Portfolio Activity Draw a freehand outline map of the United States. As you read Unit 2, use map pencils to shade in the various colonial settlements as they are introduced. Plot the important cities on your map, too. Then label the important physical features—mountains, rivers, other bodies of water—on your map.

English colonial chair

Feather pen from the House of Burgesses

Algonquin beaver bowl

United States

1607
English establish first permanent settlement at Jamestown

1620
Pilgrims land at Plymouth Rock

1550

1600

1588
England defeats Spanish Armada

World

★ HISTORY AND ART *Signing the Compact on Board the Mayflower* by Tompkins H. Matteson Pilgrims on board the *Mayflower* signed a compact, or agreement, to set up a civil government and obey its laws.

Pewter pitcher, Plymouth Plantation

1630
Puritans begin settling Massachusetts Bay

1700s
Thousands of Africans are brought to America and enslaved

1718
French establish port of New Orleans

1763
British tighten enforcement of Navigation Acts

1650　**1700**　**1750**　**1800**

1649
King Charles I is beheaded in London

1660
King Charles II is restored to the English throne

1670
Alafin Ajagbo founds Oyo Empire in Nigeria

1701
England and Spain go to war

The Kidnapped Prince

by Olaudah Equiano

Olaudah Equiano (c. 1745–1797) was an 11-year-old boy when he and his sister were kidnapped and brought to the West Indies, where they were enslaved. His life story includes memories of his childhood in Africa. He wrote his story after receiving the name Gustavus Vassa from one of his masters and buying his freedom. Published during the time of the movement to end slavery, Equiano's work became a best-seller.

■ READ TO DISCOVER

In this selection, Olaudah and his sister have been kidnapped and are forced to endure the terrifying trip across the Atlantic Ocean aboard a slave ship. As you read, think about what life must have been like for Africans who were sold into slavery.

■ READER'S DICTIONARY
vessel: ship
Bridgetown: capital of Barbados
parcel: group
lots: groups
toil: work

One day the whites on board gave a great shout, and made many signs of joy to us. We did not know why, but as the vessel drew nearer we plainly saw the island of Barbados and its harbor, and other ships of different kinds and sizes. Soon we anchored among them off Bridgetown.

Many merchants and planters came on board, though it was in the evening. They put us in separate groups, and examined us, and made us jump. They pointed to the land, signifying we were to go there. We thought these ugly men meant they were going to beat us soon. Then we were all put down under the deck again.

There was much dread and trembling among us, and nothing but bitter cries to be heard all night. At last the crew, who heard us, got some old slaves from the land to calm us. They told us no one was going to beat us. We were going to work. Soon we would go on land, and see many of our countrypeople. This report relieved us, and we could sleep. And, sure enough, not long after we landed, Africans of all languages came to talk to us.

Right away we were taken to a merchant's yard, where we were all penned up together like so many sheep. When I looked out at the town, everything was new to me. The houses were built with bricks, in stories, and were completely different from any I had seen in Africa. I was still more astonished at seeing people on horseback. I thought it was more magic, but one of the slaves with me said that the horses were the same kind they had in his country.

Between 1600 and 1850, millions of enslaved Africans were brought to the Americas on ships.

We were not many days in the merchant's custody before we were sold—like this:

Someone beat a drum. Then all the buyers rushed at once into the yard where we were penned to choose the parcel of us that they liked best. They rushed from one group of us to another, with tremendous noise and eager faces, terrifying us all.

Three men who were sold were brothers. They were sold in different lots. I still remember how they cried when they were parted. Probably they never saw each other again.

I didn't know it, but this happened all the time in slave sales. Parents lost their children; brothers lost their sisters. Husbands lost their wives.

We had already lost our homes, our countries, and almost everyone we loved. The people who did the selling and buying could have done it without separating us from our very last relatives and friends. They already could live in riches from our misery and toil. What possible advantage did they gain from this refinement of cruelty?

From *The Kidnapped Prince* by Olaudah Equiano. Adapted by Ann Cameron. Copyright © 1995 by Ann Cameron. Reprinted by permission of Alfred A. Knopf, Inc.

■ RESPONDING TO LITERATURE

1. Where in the Americas was Olaudah Equiano sold into slavery?
2. How were the Africans treated after they landed?

Activity

Writing a Diary Reread the excerpt. Imagine what it must have been like to be separated from family members in the way that Olaudah describes. Write two journal entries as an enslaved person. The first entry should reflect your fears on the day you are sold. The second entry should describe what your life is like one year later.

1587–1770

Colonial America

★ Why It's Important

The early North American colonies were a meeting place of cultures. The Europeans who settled these colonies included Protestants, Catholics, and Jews. Native Americans, the original inhabitants, played an important role in the life of the colonists. Africans were also part of colonial America from the earliest days. The goals and ways of life of these different groups sometimes clashed, ending in conflict. However, America was becoming a place where people of different backgrounds and beliefs could learn to live together peacefully.

★ Chapter Themes

- *Section 1*, Economic Factors
- *Section 2*, Civic Rights and Responsibilities
- *Section 3*, Individual Action
- *Section 4*, Culture and Traditions
- *Section 5*, Culture and Traditions

PRIMARY SOURCES **Library**

See pages 940–941 for primary source readings to accompany Chapter 3

★ **HISTORY AND ART** *View of Boston* by John Smibert John Smibert was a prominent artist in Boston, Massachusetts, during the early 1700s. He painted scenes of Boston as well as portraits of the city's wealthy merchant families.

| 1580 | 1590 | 1600 | 1610 | 1620 |

1583
Sir Humphrey Gilbert
claims Newfoundland
for Queen Elizabeth

1590
Settlers of Roanoke
Island vanish

1607
Colonists
settle at
Jamestown

1619
House of
Burgesses
meets in
Jamestown

Section 1

Early English Settlements

READ TO DISCOVER . . .

▪ why England's first two attempts to start a
colony failed.

▪ what crop saved the Jamestown colony.

▪ how the colonists received political rights.

TERMS TO LEARN

charter   burgesses
joint-stock company

The Storyteller

In the summer of 1588, Spanish warships
sailed toward the coast of England. King Philip
of Spain had sent the armada, or war fleet, of
132 ships to invade England. With 30,000
troops and 2,400 guns, the Spanish Armada
was the mightiest naval force the world had
ever seen. Yet the smaller, swifter English ships
quickly gained the upper hand. The Spanish
Armada fled north to Scotland,
where violent storms de-
stroyed and scattered the
fleet. Only about one-
half of the Spanish
ships straggled home.

English soldier's helmet,
Jamestown

England and Spain had been heading
toward war for years. Trading rivalry and
religious differences divided the two countries. Philip II, Spain's Catholic king, wanted to
put a Catholic ruler on the throne of England and
bring the country back to the Catholic Church. He
did not consider Queen Elizabeth, a Protestant,
the rightful ruler of England.

Attacks on Spanish ships and ports by such
English adventurers as **Sir Francis Drake** infuriat-
ed Philip. He thought that Queen Elizabeth should
punish Drake for his raids. Instead, she honored
Drake with a knighthood. Philip sent the Spanish
Armada to conquer England—but it failed.

The English victory had far-reaching consequences. Although war between England and
Spain continued until 1604, the defeat of the armada marked the end of Spanish control of the seas.
Now the way was clear for England and other European nations to start colonies in North America.

The Lost Colony of Roanoke

The English had made several attempts to
establish a base on the other side of the Atlantic before their victory over Spain. In 1583 **Sir
Humphrey Gilbert** claimed Newfoundland for
Queen Elizabeth. Then he sailed south along the
coast looking for a place to establish a colony. Before finding a suitable site, he died at sea.

The following year Queen Elizabeth gave **Sir
Walter Raleigh** the right to claim any land in

★ ★ ★ ★ ★ ★ ★ ★ ★ ★ ★ ★ ★ ★ ★ ★ ★

★ Picturing HISTORY This map of the late 1500s shows an English ship entering a bay near Roanoke Island. Shipwrecks nearby symbolize the dangers of the North Carolina coast at that time. **Why did English colonists settle at Roanoke Island?**

North America not already owned by a Christian monarch. Raleigh sent an expedition to look for a good place to settle. His scouts returned with an enthusiastic report of **Roanoke Island,** off the coast of present-day North Carolina. The land was good for farming, they said, and the local people were "most gentle, loving and faithful."

Roanoke Settlements

In 1585 Raleigh sent about 100 men to settle on Roanoke Island. After a difficult winter on the island, the unhappy colonists returned to England.

Two years later Raleigh tried again, sending 91 men, 17 women, and 9 children to Roanoke. **John White,** a mapmaker and artist, led the group. The new settlers began building a permanent colony. They needed many supplies, however, and White sailed to England for the supplies

---

*F*ootnotes to History

It's a Girl! Shortly after arriving on Roanoke Island, John White's daughter gave birth to a baby girl. The baby, named Virginia Dare, was the first English child born in North America.

and to recruit more settlers. Although he had hoped to be back within a few months, the war with Spain delayed his return for three years.

When White finally returned to Roanoke, he found it deserted. The only clue to the fate of the settlers was the word *Croatoan* carved on a gatepost. White thought the colonists must have gone to Croatoan Island, about 100 miles to the south. Bad weather kept White from investigating. The Roanoke colonists were never seen again.

Jamestown Settlement

★ Roanoke was Sir Walter Raleigh's last attempt to establish a colony. For a time his failure discouraged others from planning English colonies in North America. However, the idea emerged again in 1606. Several groups of merchants sought charters, the right to organize settlements in an area, from King James I.

The Virginia Company

One group of merchants, the Virginia Company of London, received a charter to "make habitation . . . into that part of America, commonly called Virginia." The Virginia Company was a joint-stock company. Investors bought stock, or part ownership, in the company in return for a share of its future profits.

The company acted quickly. In December 1606, it sent 144 settlers in 3 ships—the *Godspeed,* the *Discovery,* and the *Susan Constant*—to build a new colony in North America. The settlers were to look for gold and attempt to establish trade in fish and furs. Forty of them died during the voyage.

In April 1607, the ships entered **Chesapeake Bay** and then sailed up a river flowing into the bay. The colonists named the river the James and their new settlement **Jamestown** to honor their king.

The settlers built Jamestown on a peninsula so they could defend it from attack. The site had major drawbacks, however. The swampy land teemed with mosquitoes that carried malaria, a disease found in warm, humid climates. Jamestown also lacked good farmland and was surrounded by Native American settlements.

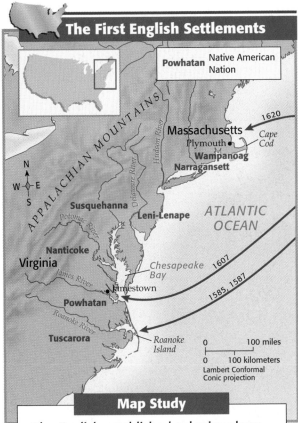

The First English Settlements

Powhatan — Native American Nation

APPALACHIAN MOUNTAINS

1620
Massachusetts
Plymouth • Cape Cod
Wampanoag
Narragansett

Hudson River
Delaware River

Susquehanna
Leni-Lenape
ATLANTIC OCEAN

Potomac River

Nanticoke
Virginia
Chesapeake Bay 1607
James River
Jamestown
Powhatan
1585, 1587

Roanoke River
Tuscarora
Roanoke Island

0   100 miles
0   100 kilometers
Lambert Conformal Conic projection

N W E S

Map Study

The English established colonies along the Atlantic coast in the late 1500s and early 1600s.

1. **Location** Which colony was located farthest north?
2. **Analyzing Information** Which Native American nations lived nearest the Roanoke colonists?

The colonists faced mounting difficulties over the next several months. Many of them were unaccustomed to hard labor. Because the London investors expected a quick profit from their colony, the settlers searched for gold and silver when they should have been growing food. In addition, disease and hunger devastated the colonists. By January 1608, when ships arrived with additional men and supplies, only 38 of the Jamestown colonists remained alive.

Captain John Smith

Governing Jamestown was perhaps the biggest obstacle the colonists faced. The colony survived its second year under the leadership of 27-year-old **Captain John Smith,** a soldier and explorer who arrived in 1608. Smith forced the settlers to work and managed to get corn from the Powhatan people. "It pleased God," he wrote, "to move the Indians to bring us corn . . . when we rather expected they would destroy us."

The Virginia Company replaced Smith with a governor, Lord De La Warr, and a period of strict rule began. The colonists barely survived the winter of 1609–1610, called the "starving time." One settler reported, "Having fed upon horses and other beasts as long as they lasted, we were glad to make shift with [such] vermin as dogs, cats, rats, and mice." Trouble also broke out with the Native Americans, and the 300 desperately hungry colonists had to barricade themselves inside their walls. When new settlers arrived in May, they found only 60 survivors.

💲 Economics

Tobacco Saves the Colony

Although the Virginia colonists found no gold or silver, they did discover another way to make money for the investors. They began to grow tobacco.

Tobacco had become popular in Europe, though some people found smoking unhealthy and disgusting. King James I, for example, called it a "vile and stinking" custom.

One colonist, **John Rolfe,** learned to grow a type of tobacco that was less bitter. The first crop was sold in England in 1614. Soon planters all along the James River were raising tobacco, and the colony of Virginia began to prosper and grow. Relations with the Powhatan also improved after Rolfe married **Pocahontas,** the daughter of Chief Powhatan. 💲

Ætatis suæ 21. A. 1616

Pocahontas

★ **Picturing HISTORY** After landing at Jamestown, the English settlers built homes and a meetinghouse, which was used for religious services. **What difficulties did the Jamestown colonists face during their first months of settlement?**

🔔 **Citizenship**

Representative Government

★ In the early years of the Jamestown colony, nearly all of the settlers were men. They worked for the Virginia Company and lived under strict military rules. The governors imposed rigid discipline and organized the settlers into work gangs.

As the colony grew, the settlers complained about taking orders from the Virginia Company in London. In 1619 the company agreed to let the colonists have some say in their government. It sent a new governor, Sir George Yeardley, to the colony with orders to end military rule.

Yeardley allowed the men of the colony to elect representatives called burgesses to an assembly. The assembly had the right to make local laws for the colony. On July 30, 1619, the **House of Burgesses** met for the first time in a church in Jamestown. 🔔

New Arrivals in Jamestown

★ In 1619 the Virginia Company sent 100 women to Jamestown. As a company report noted: "The plantation can never flourish till families be planted, and the respect of wives and children fix the people on the soil." Colonists who wanted to marry one of the women had to pay a fee of 120 pounds of tobacco. Men still outnumbered women in the colony, but marriage and children began to be part of life in Virginia.

The First Africans in America

A Dutch ship brought another group of newcomers to Jamestown in 1619—20 Africans who were sold to Virginia planters to labor in the tobacco fields. These first Africans may have come as servants—engaged to work for a set period of time—rather than as slaves.

Until about 1640 some African laborers in Jamestown were free and even owned property. William Tucker, the first African American born in the American colonies, was a free man. In the years to follow, however, many more shiploads of Africans would arrive in North America, and those unwilling passengers would be sold as slaves. Slavery was first recognized in Virginia law in 1661.

In the early 1620s, the Virginia Company faced financial troubles. The company had poured all its money into Jamestown, with little return. The colony also suffered a disastrous attack by the Native Americans. In 1624 King James canceled the company's charter and took control of the colony, making it England's first royal colony in America.

Linking PAST & PRESENT

Peddlers to Malls

During the colonial era, families relied on peddlers, or traveling merchants, for many of their goods. Peddlers journeyed throughout the countryside with such items as clocks, shoes, pans, cloth, and even books. Wherever crowds assembled, a peddler selling wares was usually present. Today, crowds of shoppers still assemble—at malls. Malls often are the focus of community life. They attract shoppers, walkers, and moviegoers. **How are peddlers and malls similar?**

Past

Colonial peddler

Present

Mall of America, Bloomington, Minnesota

Section 1 Assessment

Checking for Understanding

1. **Identify** Sir Francis Drake, Sir Walter Raleigh, Roanoke Island, John White, Jamestown, Captain John Smith, John Rolfe, Pocahontas, House of Burgesses.
2. **Define** charter, joint-stock company, burgesses.
3. **List** two reasons Jamestown was a poor location for a colony.

Reviewing Themes

4. **Economic Factors** What economic activity helped save the Virginia colony?

Critical Thinking

5. **Making Inferences** Why do you think the king of England was willing to let a group of merchants try to establish a colony in North America?

Activity

Making a Poster Create a poster that might have attracted early colonists to the area where you live. Focus on the location as well as natural features in your area such as good farmland, forests, waterways, and mineral resources.

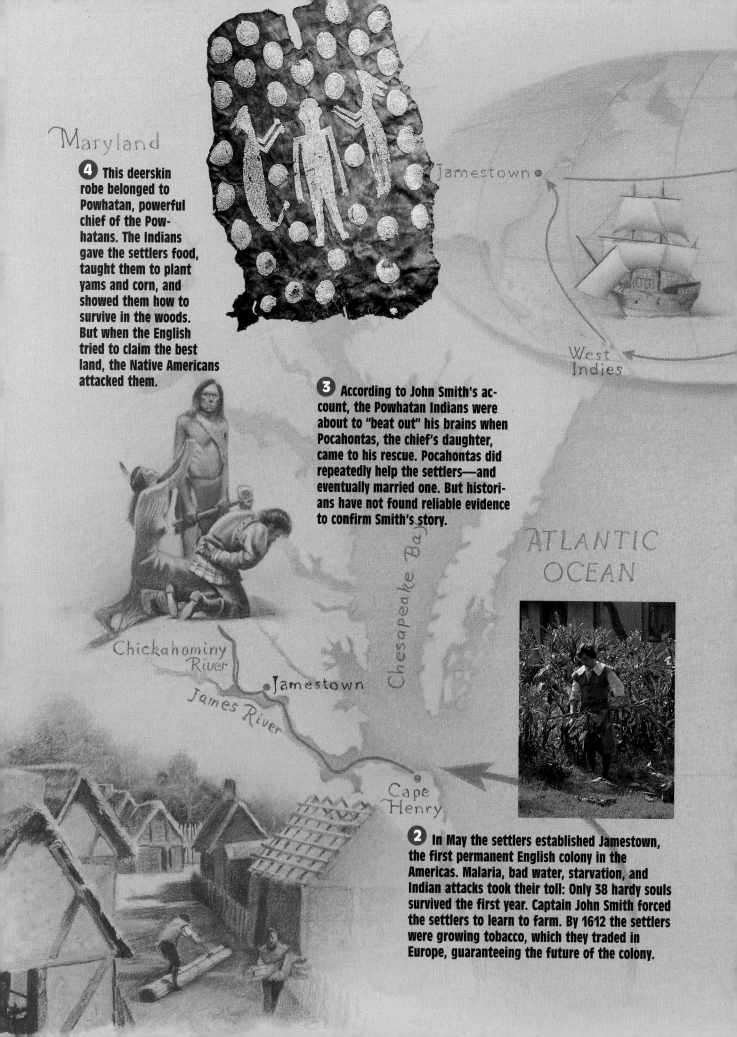

Maryland

4 This deerskin robe belonged to Powhatan, powerful chief of the Powhatans. The Indians gave the settlers food, taught them to plant yams and corn, and showed them how to survive in the woods. But when the English tried to claim the best land, the Native Americans attacked them.

Jamestown

West Indies

3 According to John Smith's account, the Powhatan Indians were about to "beat out" his brains when Pocahontas, the chief's daughter, came to his rescue. Pocahontas did repeatedly help the settlers—and eventually married one. But historians have not found reliable evidence to confirm Smith's story.

ATLANTIC OCEAN

Chickahominy River

Jamestown

James River

Chesapeake Bay

Cape Henry

2 In May the settlers established Jamestown, the first permanent English colony in the Americas. Malaria, bad water, starvation, and Indian attacks took their toll: Only 38 hardy souls survived the first year. Captain John Smith forced the settlers to learn to farm. By 1612 the settlers were growing tobacco, which they traded in Europe, guaranteeing the future of the colony.

NATIONAL GEOGRAPHIC
Journeys

Journey *to* Jamestown

1 Captain John Smith (above) and more than 100 other men left England and set out for the Americas in December 1606. Three ships under the command of Captain Christopher Newport sailed to the Canary Islands and West Indies, before Cape Henry was sighted at the mouth of the Chesapeake Bay in April 1607. Smith also led later explorations beyond Jamestown and around the Chesapeake Bay.

66 From May to September those that escaped [sickness] lived upon sturgeon and sea crabs. Fifty in this time we buried.... Nothing [is] so difficult as to establish a commonwealth so far remote from men and means.... The new [governing council] President ... being little beloved, of weak judgment in dangers and less industry in peace, committed the managing of all things ... to Captain Smith, who by his own example ... set some to mow, others to bind thatch, some to build houses, others to thatch them ... so that in short time he provided most of them lodgings. 99

—From Captain John Smith's History of Virginia. *This excerpt was written by Thomas Studley, a member of the expedition, in the summer and fall of 1607.*

1620
Pilgrims land
at Plymouth

1630
Puritans settle the
Massachusetts
Bay Colony

1636
Thomas Hooker
founds Hartford

1638
Anne Hutchinson
founds Portsmouth

Section 2

New England Colonies

READ TO DISCOVER . . .
■ why the Pilgrims and the Puritans came to America.
■ how the Connecticut, Rhode Island, and New Hampshire colonies began.

TERMS TO LEARN
dissent
persecute
Puritan
Separatist

Pilgrim
Mayflower Compact
toleration

Storyteller

The young man looked around at the other passengers aboard the *Mayflower.* These people had muskets but knew little about shooting. They planned to fish but knew nothing about fishing. They had hoped to settle in Virginia but instead landed in New England without enough supplies to last the winter. The only thing these people had plenty of was courage. They would need it.

*Shoes,
Plymouth Colony*

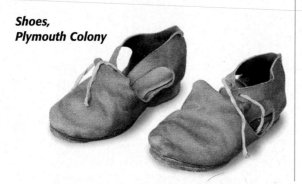

In 1614 Captain John Smith explored and mapped the coast of New England. His map showed a harbor called Patuxet, which was later renamed **Plymouth.** It was here that the next wave of English settlers to America would land. Unlike the Jamestown colonists, many of these settlers did not cross the ocean for riches. They came in search of religious freedom.

Demands for Religious Freedom

★ In the early 1600s, the Protestant Anglican Church was the official church of England, and the English monarch was head of the church. Many people, however, dissented—they disagreed with the beliefs or practices of the Anglicans. English Catholics, for example, still considered the pope the head of the church, and they were often persecuted, or treated harshly, for that reason.

At the same time, some Protestants wanted to change—or reform—the Anglican Church, while others wanted to break away from it altogether. The Protestants who wanted to reform the Anglican Church were called Puritans. Those who wanted to leave and found their own churches were known as Separatists.

The Separatists were persecuted in England, and some fled to the Netherlands. Though they found religious freedom there, the Separatists still had problems. They had difficulty finding work because the local craft guilds did not accept them. The Separatists also worried that their children would lose their English heritage in the Netherlands.

The Pilgrims' Journey

Some Separatists in the Netherlands made an arrangement with the Virginia Company. The Separatists could settle in Virginia and practice their religion freely. In return they would give the company a share of whatever profits they made.

The Separatists considered themselves Pilgrims because their journey had a religious purpose. Only 35 of the 102 passengers who boarded the *Mayflower* in September 1620 were Pilgrims. The others were called "strangers." They were common people—servants, craftspeople, and poor farmers—who hoped to find a better life in America. Because Pilgrim beliefs shaped life in the Plymouth colony, however, all the early settlers are usually called Pilgrims.

The Mayflower Compact

The *Mayflower*'s passengers planned to settle in the Virginia colony. The first land they sighted was **Cape Cod,** well north of their target. Because it was November and winter was fast approaching, the colonists decided to drop anchor in Cape Cod Bay. They went ashore on a cold, bleak day in December at a place called Plymouth. **William Bradford,** their leader and historian, reported that "all things stared upon them with a weather-beaten face."

Plymouth was outside the territory of the Virginia Company and its laws. To provide order in their new colony, the Pilgrims drew up a formal document called the Mayflower Compact. The compact pledged their loyalty to England and declared their intention of forming "a civil body politic, for our better ordering and preservation." The signers also promised to obey the laws passed "for the general good of the colony."

Help from the Native Americans

Their first winter in America, almost half the Pilgrims died of malnutrition, disease, and cold. In the spring a few Native Americans approached

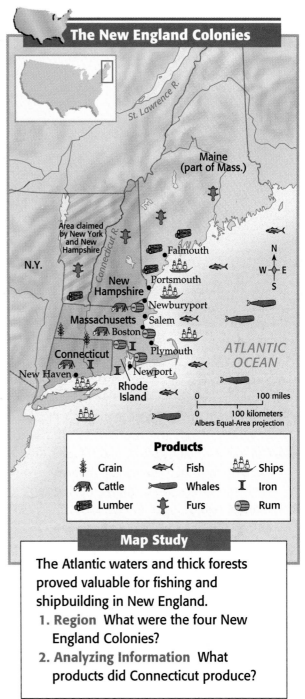

The New England Colonies

Products
- Grain
- Cattle
- Lumber
- Fish
- Whales
- Furs
- Ships
- Iron
- Rum

Map Study

The Atlantic waters and thick forests proved valuable for fishing and shipbuilding in New England.
1. **Region** What were the four New England Colonies?
2. **Analyzing Information** What products did Connecticut produce?

the settlement. Two of them, **Squanto** and **Samoset,** befriended the colonists. Squanto was a Wampanoag who had been kidnapped by an English ship captain and had learned English.

Squanto and Samoset showed the Pilgrims how to grow corn, beans, and pumpkin and where to hunt and fish. Without this help the Pilgrims might not have survived. Squanto and Samoset also helped the Pilgrims make a treaty with the Wampanoag people who lived in the area.

First Thanksgiving by Jennie A. Brownscombe This traditional depiction of the first Thanksgiving shows Pilgrims sharing their bountiful harvest with Native Americans. **What Native American group helped the Pilgrims survive at Plymouth?**

In the autumn of 1621, the Pilgrims invited the Native Americans to celebrate the peace between them. After the losses of the first winter, the Pilgrims also felt relieved to be raising food.

> ❝Our harvest being gotten in, our Governor sent four men on fowling [hunting for fowl], so that we might after a special manner rejoice together after we had gathered in the fruit of our labors. ❞

During the feast the Pilgrims thanked God for the harvest and for their survival.

Massachusetts Bay

★ In 1625 the English throne passed to Charles I. Charles objected to the Puritans' calls for reform in the Anglican Church, and persecution of Puritans increased dramatically. Some Puritans looked for a way to leave England.

In 1628 a group of Puritans formed the **New England Company** and received a royal charter to establish the Massachusetts Bay Colony, north of Plymouth. This was the Puritans' chance to create a new society in America—a society based on the Bible and their own beliefs.

The company chose a well-educated Puritan named **John Winthrop** to be the colony's governor.

In 1630 Winthrop led 1,000 men, women, and children in 11 ships to **Massachusetts Bay.** Most of them settled in a place they called **Boston.** Winthrop explained that the new colony they were building in the wilderness "shall be as a city upon a hill. The eyes of all the people are upon us." Their settlement would provide a model for other Christian communities to follow.

Citizenship

Growth and Government

During the 1630s religious persecution and economic hard times in England drove more than 15,000 Puritans to journey to Massachusetts. This movement of people became known as the **Great Migration.**

An elected group ran the colony through the General Court of the Massachusetts Bay Company. When the settlers insisted on having a larger role in the government, the company created a colonial legislature. Every adult male who owned property and was a church member could vote for the governor and for representatives to the General Court.

The Puritans had come to America to put their religious beliefs into practice. Yet they were unwilling to allow other religious groups the freedom to practice their beliefs. The Puritans had little toleration—they criticized or persecuted people who held other religious views. This lack of toleration led to the creation of new colonies.

Connecticut

The fertile Connecticut River valley, south of Massachusetts, was much better for farming than was the stony soil around Boston. In the 1630s colonists began to settle in this area.

A minister named Thomas Hooker became dissatisfied with Massachusetts. He did not like the way that Winthrop and the other Puritan leaders ran the colony. Also, he had heard good reports of the Connecticut farmland. In 1636 Hooker led his congregation through the wilderness to Connecticut, where he founded the town of **Hartford.** Three years later Hartford and two other towns, Windsor and Wethersfield, agreed to form a colony. They adopted a plan of government called the **Fundamental Orders of Connecticut.** The first written constitution in America, it described the organization of government in detail.

Rhode Island

Good land drew colonists to Connecticut, but Rhode Island was settled by colonists who were forced out of Massachusetts. The first of these was **Roger Williams,** a minister. Williams felt that people should be free to follow any religious practices. In his view the church and the government should be completely separate. Williams also believed it was wrong for settlers to take land away from the Native Americans.

The ideas of Roger Williams deeply disturbed the Massachusetts leaders, and in 1635 they decided he should be banished, or forced to leave the colony. Williams left Massachusetts before the authorities could send him back to England and took refuge with the Wampanoag people. From them he bought land on Narragansett Bay, the site where he later founded the town of Providence.

Roger Williams received a charter in 1644 for a colony east of Connecticut called **Rhode Island.** With its policy of religious toleration, Rhode Island became a safe place for dissenters. It was the first place in America where people of all faiths—including Jews—could worship freely.

Others followed Williams's example, forming colonies where they could worship as they pleased. In 1638 **John Wheelwright** led a group of dissidents from Massachusetts to the north. They founded the town of Exeter in **New Hampshire.** The same year, a group of Puritans settled Hampton. The colony of New Hampshire became fully independent of Massachusetts in 1679.

📖 Biography

Anne Hutchinson Speaks Out

Anne Hutchinson came to Massachusetts with her husband in 1634 and soon held religious meetings in her Boston home. To the horror of the Massachusetts officials, Hutchinson questioned the religious authority of the colony's ministers. She also believed women should have more power.

Puritans were shocked to hear a woman state her ideas so boldly. As Hutchinson gained followers, she was seen as a danger to the colony's stability. In 1637 the Massachusetts leaders put her on trial for heresy—criticizing church officials.

When Hutchinson defended herself, she showed a remarkable knowledge of religion. Her accusers, however, found her guilty of heresy and ordered her to leave the colony as "a woman

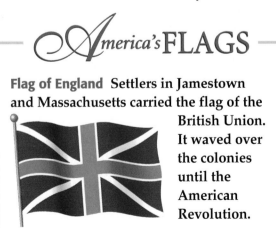

America's FLAGS

Flag of England Settlers in Jamestown and Massachusetts carried the flag of the British Union. It waved over the colonies until the American Revolution.

not fit for our society." With her family and some followers, Hutchinson left Massachusetts and moved to Rhode Island.

Native Americans

Native Americans helped the settlers adapt to the land. They also traded with the settlers—exchanging furs for goods such as iron pots, blankets, and guns. In Virginia the colonists had frequent dealings with Powhatan's confederacy. In New England the settlers met the Wampanoags, Narragansetts, and other groups.

Conflicts arose, however. Usually settlers moved onto Native American lands without permission or payment. English settlers and Native Americans competed fiercely for control of the land throughout the colonial period.

Decline in Population

For the Native Americans of New England, contact with Europeans was deadly. In 1600 about 100,000 Native Americans lived in New England. By 1675 only 10,000 survived. Most died from disease, not war. Chicken pox, smallpox, measles, and other European illnesses proved fatal to the Native Americans, who had no immunity against them.

Wars with Settlers

In 1637 war broke out in Connecticut between settlers and the Pequot people. The English colonists resented the Pequot trading network, which included Dutch settlers from New Amsterdam. The most savage attack of the **Pequot War** was committed by English soldiers. They surrounded a Pequot village and set fire to it. As the village went up in flames, the English killed those trying to escape.

King Philip

In 1675 the settlers of Massachusetts went to war with the Wampanoag people. **Metacomet,** the chief, was known to the settlers as **King Philip.** To keep the English from advancing into their land, the Wampanoag raided frontier outposts. They killed several thousand settlers in three years.

The settlers found an ally in the Mohawk, rivals of the Wampanoag. The Mohawk attacked Wampanoag villages, finally ambushing and killing Metacomet. **King Philip's War,** as the conflict was called, ended in defeat for the Wampanoag. The colonists were now able to enlarge their settlements in Massachusetts.

★ ★ ★ ★ ★ Section 2 Assessment ★ ★ ★ ★ ★

Checking for Understanding
1. *Identify* Great Migration, Roger Williams, Anne Hutchinson, King Philip's War.
2. *Define* dissent, persecute, Puritan, Separatist, Pilgrim, Mayflower Compact, toleration.
3. *Describe* how Native Americans helped the Plymouth colonists to survive.

Reviewing Themes
4. **Civic Rights and Responsibilities** What freedom did Rhode Island offer that other colonies did not?

Critical Thinking
5. **Making Comparisons** What did the Mayflower Compact and the Fundamental Orders of Connecticut have in common?

Activity

Building a Model Work with a small group to select one event from this section, such as the voyage of the *Mayflower*. Use a small box to create a scene illustrating that event. Use small objects and paint to represent buildings, trees, and other details.

Reading a Bar Graph

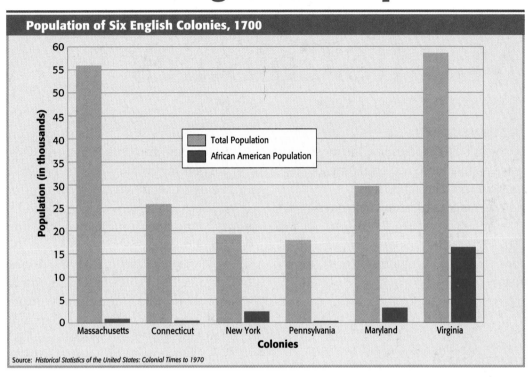

Population of Six English Colonies, 1700

Population (in thousands) vs. Colonies

Legend: Total Population, African American Population

Colonies: Massachusetts, Connecticut, New York, Pennsylvania, Maryland, Virginia

Source: *Historical Statistics of the United States: Colonial Times to 1970*

A bar graph presents numerical information in a visual way. Bars of various lengths stand for different quantities. Bars may be drawn vertically—up and down—or horizontally—left to right. Labels along the axes, or the left side and bottom of the graph, explain what the bars represent.

Learning the Skill

To read a bar graph:
• Read the title to learn the subject of the graph.
• Look at the horizontal and vertical axes to find out what information the graph presents.
• Compare the lengths of the bars on the graph.

Practicing the Skill

Study the bar graph on this page and answer the following questions.
1. What do the numbers along the vertical axis represent?
2. Which colony had the highest total population in 1700? The lowest?

Applying the Skill

Reading a Bar Graph Create a bar graph to represent the number of students in each American history class in your school.

Glencoe's **Skillbuilder Interactive Workbook, Level 1** provides instruction and practice in key social studies skills.

1600		1650		1700

1626
Manhattan Island purchased from the Manhates people

1664
New York has about 8,000 inhabitants

1681
William Penn founds Pennsylvania

1702
New Jersey becomes a royal colony

Section 3

Middle Colonies

READ TO DISCOVER...

- why the Middle Colonies had the most diverse populations in colonial America.
- how New York City got its start.
- who was America's first town planner.

TERMS TO LEARN

patroon   pacifist
proprietary colony

The Storyteller

In 1649, 17-year-old Philip Henry stood near the back of the crowd gathered around a public platform near Whitehall Palace in London. There he watched Charles I, the king of England, prepare to die. The king made a short speech, prayed silently, and then knelt with his head on the block.

With just one blow, the executioner severed the king's head from his body. At that moment, the crowd uttered "such a groan as I never heard before, and desire I may never hear again," Henry wrote in his diary.

Royalty plate

In England the Puritans were engaged in a struggle for power against King Charles I. Soon the country was embroiled in civil war. Led by Puritan Oliver Cromwell, the Parliamentary forces defeated the king. In 1649 the king was beheaded after a parliamentary court convicted him of treason.

A new government was established with Cromwell as Protector. During the years of upheaval and uncertainty, many Puritans left Old England for New England. During the English Civil War, English men and women loyal to the king went to royal colonies like Virginia.

After Cromwell died in 1658, parliament brought back the monarchy—but placed new limits on the ruler's powers. Charles II, son of the beheaded Charles I, became king in 1660. His reign is called the *Restoration* because the monarchy had been restored.

New York

In 1660 England had two clusters of colonies in what is now the United States—Massachusetts, New Hampshire, Connecticut, and Rhode Island in the north and Maryland and Virginia in the south. Between the two groups of English colonies were lands that the Dutch controlled.

In 1624 a group of Dutch merchants had formed the Dutch West India Company to trade in the Americas. Their posts along the Hudson River grew into the colony of New Netherland. The main settlement of the colony was **New Amsterdam,** located on **Manhattan Island.** In 1626 the company bought Manhattan from the Manhates people for a small amount of beads and other goods. Blessed with a good natural port, the city of New Amsterdam soon became a center of shipping to and from the Americas.

The Patroons

To increase the number of permanent settlers in its colony, the Dutch West India Company sent over families from the Netherlands, Germany, Sweden, and Finland. The company gave a large estate to anyone who brought at least 50 settlers to work the land. The wealthy landowners who acquired these riverfront estates were called patroons. The patroons ruled like kings. They could charge whatever rents they wanted to the farmers and other laborers on their estates.

England Takes Over

New Netherland boasted an excellent harbor and thriving river trade. The English wanted to acquire the valuable Dutch colony that lay between England's New England and Southern Colonies. In 1664 the English sent a fleet to attack New Amsterdam.

At the time **Peter Stuyvesant** ruled the colony as governor. His strict rule and heavy taxes turned many of the people in New Netherland against him. When the English ships sailed into New Amsterdam's harbor, the governor was unprepared for a battle and surrendered the colony.

King Charles II gave the colony to his brother, the **Duke of York,** who renamed it **New York.** New York was a proprietary colony, a colony in which the owner, or proprietor, owned all the land and controlled the government. It differed from the New England Colonies, which were run by private corporations under a royal charter.

Most of New York's settlers lived in the Hudson River valley. The Duke of York promised the

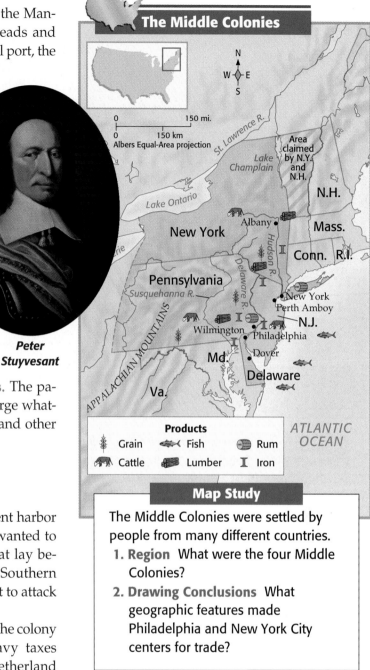

Peter Stuyvesant

The Middle Colonies

Products
🌾 Grain 🐟 Fish 🛢 Rum
🐂 Cattle 🪵 Lumber ⚙ Iron

Map Study

The Middle Colonies were settled by people from many different countries.
1. **Region** What were the four Middle Colonies?
2. **Drawing Conclusions** What geographic features made Philadelphia and New York City centers for trade?

diverse colonists freedom of religion and allowed them to keep their property. As a result, most of the Dutch colonists decided to remain in New York.

The Growth of New York

In 1664 New York had about 8,000 inhabitants. Most were Dutch, but Germans, Swedes, Native Americans, and Puritans from New England lived there as well. The population also included at least 300 enslaved Africans. New

★ **HISTORY AND ART** *Penn's Treaty with the Indians* by Benjamin West In 1682 William Penn made his first treaty with the Delaware people. **Why did Penn see Pennsylvania as a "holy experiment"?**

Amsterdam, now called New York City, was one of the fastest-growing locations in the colony.

By 1683 the colony's population had swelled to about 12,000 people. A governor and council appointed by the Duke of York directed the colony's affairs. The colonists demanded a representative government like the governments of the other English colonies. The duke resisted the idea, but the New Yorkers would not give up. Finally the duke let them form an elected legislature.

New Jersey

★ The Duke of York gave the southern part of his colony, between the Hudson and Delaware Rivers, to **Lord John Berkeley** and **Sir George Carteret.** The proprietors named their colony New Jersey after the island of Jersey in the English Channel, on which Carteret was born.

Berkeley and Carteret hoped to make money from New Jersey by charging their settlers rent. To attract settlers, they offered large tracts of land and generous terms. They also promised freedom of religion, trial by jury, and a representative assembly. The assembly would make local laws and set tax rates. Every man in the colony would have a vote. The assembly held its first meeting in 1688.

Like New York, New Jersey was a place of ethnic and religious diversity. Because New Jersey had no natural harbors, however, it did not develop a major port or city like New York.

The proprietors of New Jersey did not make the profits they had expected from rents. Berkeley sold his share, West Jersey, in 1674. Carteret's share, East Jersey, was auctioned off in 1680.

By 1702 New Jersey had passed back into the hands of the king, becoming a royal colony. But the colonists continued to make local laws.

★ ★

Pennsylvania

⭐ In 1680 **William Penn,** a wealthy English gentleman, presented a plan to King Charles. Penn's father had once lent the king a great deal of money. Penn had inherited the king's promise to repay the loan. Instead of money, however, Penn asked for land in America. Pleased to get rid of his debt so easily, the king gave Penn a tract of land stretching inland from the Delaware River. The new colony, named Pennsylvania, was as large as England.

Penn and the Quakers

William Penn belonged to a Protestant group of dissenters called the Society of Friends, or **Quakers.** The Quakers believed that people had an "inner light" that could guide them to salvation. Each person could experience religious truth directly, which meant that church services and officials were unnecessary. Everybody was equal in God's sight. Though firm in their beliefs, the Quakers were tolerant of the views of others.

Many people found the Quakers' ideas a threat to established traditions. Quakers would not bow or take off their hats to lords and ladies because of their belief that everyone was equal. In addition they were pacifists, people who refuse to use force or to fight in wars. Quakers were fined, jailed, and even executed for their beliefs.

The "Holy Experiment"

William Penn saw Pennsylvania as a "holy experiment," a chance to put the Quaker ideals of toleration and equality into practice. In 1682 he sailed to America to supervise the building of **Philadelphia,** the "city of brotherly love."

Penn had designed the city himself, making him America's first town planner. Penn also wrote Pennsylvania's first constitution.

Penn believed that the land belonged to the Native Americans and that settlers should pay for it. Native Americans held Penn in such high regard that some settled in Pennsylvania.

To encourage European settlers to come to Pennsylvania, Penn advertised the colony throughout Europe with pamphlets in several languages. By 1683 more than 3,000 English, Welsh, Irish, Dutch, and German settlers had arrived. In 1701 in the Charter of Liberties, Penn granted the colonists the right to elect representatives to the legislative assembly.

The southernmost part of Pennsylvania was called the Three Lower Counties. Settled by Swedes in 1638, the area had been taken over by the Dutch and the English before becoming part of Pennsylvania. The Charter of Privileges allowed the lower counties to form their own legislature, which they did in 1703. Thereafter Delaware functioned as a separate colony supervised by Pennsylvania's governor.

★ ★ ★ ★ ★ Section 3 Assessment ★ ★ ★ ★ ★

Checking for Understanding
1. *Identify* Peter Stuyvesant, William Penn, Quakers.
2. *Define* patroon, proprietary colony, pacifist.
3. *Explain* why the English wanted the Dutch settlement of New Netherland.

Reviewing Themes
4. **Individual Action** How did William Penn earn the respect of Native Americans?

Critical Thinking
5. **Making Comparisons** How was the Quaker religion different from that of the Puritans?

Designing a Flag Design a flag for one of the Middle Colonies. Choose one colony, then decide what symbols and colors would be appropriate to represent it.

1632
King Charles I grants Maryland to Lord Baltimore

1676
Bacon's Rebellion occurs

1729
Carolina is divided into two colonies; Baltimore, Maryland, is founded

1733
Georgia is founded

Section 4

Southern Colonies

READ TO DISCOVER . . .

- why the Act of Toleration was passed.
- how North Carolina and South Carolina were different.
- how Georgia was established as a safe place for debtors and the poor.

TERMS TO LEARN

indentured servant   debtor
constitution

The Storyteller

How did it feel to be enslaved on the plantations of the South? In the 1930s, interviewers put this question to African Americans once under slavery. Many of them were approaching 100 years old, and some still carried deep scars on their backs from whippings. To be a slave meant to have no human rights. Elderly Roberta Mason remembered, "Once they whipped my father 'cause he looked at a slave they killed, and cried."

Slave drum, Virginia

Building colonies in North America involved a great deal of work. The settlers had to clear the land, construct homes and churches, plant crops, and tend the fields. As the colonies expanded, the demand for capable workers grew.

Not all people came to work in the colonies of their own free will. Africans were seized and brought over as slaves. English criminals and Scottish and Irish prisoners of war were also shipped to the colonies. They could earn their release by working for a period of time—often seven years. Other colonists complained that their settlements were dumping grounds for "His Majesty's seven-year passengers."

Other men, women, and children came to the colonies as indentured servants. In return for the payment of their passage to America, they agreed to work without pay for a certain period of time.

Catholics in Maryland

Maryland was the dream of **Sir George Calvert, Lord Baltimore,** a Catholic. Calvert wanted to establish a safe place for his fellow Catholics, who were being persecuted in England. He also hoped that a colony would bring him a fortune.

Calvert's dream came true in 1632, when King Charles I gave him a proprietary colony north of Virginia. Calvert died before actually receiving the grant. His son Cecilius Calvert took charge of the colony. It was named Maryland after the English queen, Henrietta Maria.

Establishing the Colony

The younger Calvert—the new Lord Baltimore—never lived in Maryland but sent two of his brothers to run the colony. They reached America in 1634 with two ships and more than 200 settlers. Entering the Chesapeake Bay, they sailed up the **Potomac River** through fertile countryside. A priest in the party described the Potomac as "the sweetest and greatest river I have ever seen." The colonists chose a site for their settlement, which they called St. Mary's.

Knowing that tobacco had saved the Virginia colony, the Maryland colonists turned first to tobacco farming. To keep the colony from becoming too dependent on one crop, however, a Maryland law declared that "every person planting tobacco shall plant and tend two acres of corn." In addition to corn, most Maryland tobacco farmers produced wheat, fruit, vegetables, and livestock to feed their families and their workers. **Baltimore,** founded in 1729, was Maryland's port. Before long Baltimore became the colony's largest settlement.

Aristocrats and Farmers

Lord Baltimore gave large estates to his relatives and other English aristocrats. By doing so he created a wealthy and powerful class of landowners in Maryland.

The colony needed people to work in the plantation fields. To bring settlers to the colony, Lord Baltimore promised land—100 acres to each male settler, another 100 for his wife, 100 for each servant, and 50 for each of his children. As the number of plantations increased and additional workers were needed, the colony imported indentured servants and enslaved Africans to supply the needed labor.

Settling Disputes

For years the Calvert family and the Penn family argued over the boundary between Maryland and Pennsylvania. In the 1760s they hired two British astronomers, Charles Mason and Jeremiah Dixon, to map the line dividing the colonies. It took the two scientists five years to lay out the

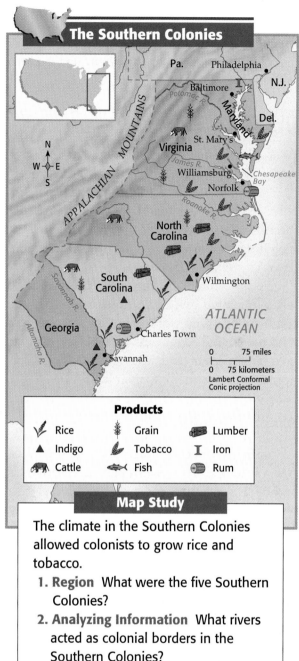

The Southern Colonies

Map Study

The climate in the Southern Colonies allowed colonists to grow rice and tobacco.

1. **Region** What were the five Southern Colonies?
2. **Analyzing Information** What rivers acted as colonial borders in the Southern Colonies?

boundary stones. Each stone had the crest of the Penn family on one side and the crest of the Calverts on the other.

Another conflict was harder to resolve. The Calverts had welcomed Protestants as well as Catholics in Maryland. Protestant settlers outnumbered Catholics from the start.

To protect the Catholics from any attempt to make Maryland a Protestant colony, Baltimore passed a law called the **Act of Toleration** in 1649. The act granted Protestants and Catholics the right to worship freely. It failed to end the tension between Protestants and Catholics, however. In 1692 the colony's Protestant majority repealed the act.

Virginia Expands

While other colonies were being founded, Virginia continued to grow. Wealthy tobacco planters held the best land near the coast, so new settlers pushed inland. Sir William Berkeley, the colony's governor, sent explorers over the Blue Ridge Mountains to open up the backcountry of Virginia to settlement.

As the settlers moved west, they came to lands inhabited by Native Americans. To avoid conflicts, Berkeley worked out an arrangement with the Native Americans in 1644. In exchange for a large piece of land, he agreed to keep settlers from pushing farther into their lands.

Bacon's Rebellion

Nathaniel Bacon, a wealthy young planter, was a leader in the western part of Virginia. He and other westerners opposed the colonial government because it was dominated by easterners. The westerners resented Berkeley's pledge to stay out of Native American territory. Some of them settled in the forbidden lands and then blamed the government in Jamestown for not protecting them from Native American raids.

In 1676 Bacon led the angry westerners in attacks on Native American villages. Governor Berkeley declared Bacon "the greatest rebel that ever was in Virginia." Bacon's army marched to Jamestown, set fire to the capital, and drove Berkeley into exile. Only

Nathaniel Bacon

Bacon's sudden illness and death kept him from taking charge of Virginia. British troops helped Berkeley restore order and end the rebellion.

Bacon's Rebellion had shown that the settlers were not willing to be restricted to the coast. In 1677 the colonial government signed a treaty with the Native Americans that opened up more land to settlement.

Settling the Carolinas

In two charters issued in 1663 and 1665, King Charles II created a large proprietary colony south of Virginia. The colony was called Carolina, which means "Charles's land" in Latin. The king gave the colony to a group of eight prominent members of his court.

The Carolina proprietors carved out large estates for themselves and hoped to make money by selling and renting land to settlers. One of the proprietors convinced his partners to provide money to bring colonists over from England. Settlers began arriving in Carolina in 1670. By 1680 they had founded a city, which they called Charles Town after the king. The name later became **Charleston.**

John Locke, an English political philosopher, wrote a constitution for the Carolina colony. This constitution, or plan of government, covered such subjects as land distribution and social ranking. Carolina, however, did not develop according to plan. The people of northern and southern Carolina soon went their separate ways, creating two colonies.

$ Economics

Northern and Southern Carolina

The northern part of Carolina was settled mostly by farmers from Virginia's backcountry. They grew tobacco and sold forest products such as timber and tar. Because the northern Carolina coast offered no good harbor, the farmers relied on Virginia's ports and merchants to conduct their trade.

Founding the Thirteen Colonies

Colony	Date of Charter	Reasons Founded	Founders or Leaders
New England Colonies			

Massachusetts
  Plymouth
  Mass. Bay Colony
	1620
	1630
		Religious freedom
		Religious freedom
			John Carver, William Bradford, John Winthrop

New Hampshire	1622	Profit from trade and fishing	Ferdinando Gorges, John Mason
Rhode Island	1636	Religious freedom	Roger Williams
Connecticut	1636	Profit from fur trade, farming; religious and political freedom	Thomas Hooker
Middle Colonies			
New York	1624	Expand trade	Dutch settlers
Delaware	1638	Expand trade	Swedish settlers
New Jersey	1664	Profit from selling land	John Berkeley, George Carteret
Pennsylvania	1681	Profit from selling land; religious freedom	William Penn
Southern Colonies			
Virginia	1607	Expand trade	John Smith
Maryland	1632	Profit from selling land; religious freedom	Cecil Calvert
North Carolina	1663	Profit from trade and selling land	Group of eight aristocrats
South Carolina	1663	Profit from trade and selling land	Group of eight aristocrats
Georgia	1732	Religious freedom; protection against Spanish Florida; safe home for debtors	James Oglethorpe

Chart Study

The thirteen colonies were founded over a span of 125 years.

1. What were the two most common reasons for founding these colonies?

2. **Sequencing** What colony was first to be settled? Which was last?

The southern part of the Carolinas was more prosperous, thanks to fertile farmland and a good harbor at Charles Town (later Charleston). Settlements spread, and the trade in corn, lumber, and cattle flourished. In the 1680s planters discovered that rice grew well in the wet coastal lowlands. Rice soon became the colony's leading crop.

In the 1740s a young Englishwoman named Eliza Lucas developed another important Carolina crop—indigo. Indigo, a blue flowering plant, was used to dye textiles. After experimenting with seeds from the West Indies, Lucas succeeded in growing and processing indigo, the "blue gold" of Carolina.

Slave Labor in the Carolinas

Most of the settlers in southern Carolina came from another English colony—the island of Barbados in the West Indies. In Barbados the colonists used enslaved Africans to grow sugar. The colonists brought these workers with them.

A Rice Plantation

Rice basket

Mortar and pestle

Rice hook

What Was It Like? A rice plantation included the owner's large house surrounded by the small dwellings of enslaved Africans. **Of the items shown here, which were used to harvest the rice crop?**

Many enslaved Africans who arrived in the Carolinas worked in the rice fields. Some of them knew a great deal about rice cultivation because they had come from the rice-growing areas of West Africa. Growing rice required much labor, so the demand for slaves increased. By 1700 more than half the people who arrived in Charles Town were enslaved Africans.

Tensions Lead to Division

Tension continued to grow between wealthy planters of southern Carolina and colonists with small farms in the north. In 1719 the settlers seized control of the colony from its proprietors. In 1729 Carolina was formally divided into two colonies—North and South Carolina.

Georgia

Georgia, the last of the British colonies in America to be established, was founded in 1733. A group led by General **James Oglethorpe**

received a charter to create a colony where English debtors and poor people could make a fresh start. In Great Britain, debtors—those unable to repay their debts—were generally thrown into prison.

The British government had another reason for creating Georgia. This colony could protect the other British colonies from Spanish attack. Great Britain and Spain had been at war in the early 1700s, and new conflicts over territory in North America were always breaking out. Located between Spanish Florida and South Carolina, Georgia could serve as a military barrier.

Oglethorpe's Town

Oglethorpe led the first group of "sober, industrial, and moral persons" to Georgia in 1733. They built a town called **Savannah,** as well as forts to defend themselves from the Spanish.

Oglethorpe wanted the people of Georgia to be hardworking, independent, and Protestant. He

During the 1700s, Charles Town was the major port in South Carolina. **Why was South Carolina a prosperous colony?**

kept the size of farms small and banned slavery, Catholics, and rum.

Although Georgia had been planned as a debtors' colony, it actually received few debtors. Hundreds of poor people came from Great Britain. Religious refugees from Germany and Switzerland and a small group of Jews also settled there. Georgia soon had a higher percentage of non-British settlers than any other British colony.

The Colony Changes

Many settlers complained about the limits on the size of landholdings and the law banning slave labor. They also objected to the many rules

Oglethorpe made regulating their lives. The colonists referred to Oglethorpe as "our perpetual dictator."

Oglethorpe grew frustrated by the colonists' demands and the colony's slow growth. He agreed to let people have larger landholdings and lifted the bans against slavery and rum. In 1751 he gave up altogether and turned the colony back over to the king.

By that time British settlers had been in what is now the eastern United States for almost a century and a half. They had lined the Atlantic coast with colonies. The British were not the only Europeans who were colonizing North America, however. Elsewhere on the continent, the Spanish and the French had built settlements of their own.

★ ★ ★ ★ ★ Section 4 Assessment ★ ★ ★ ★ ★

Checking for Understanding

1. **Identify** Sir George Calvert, Lord Baltimore, Act of Toleration, Nathaniel Bacon, Bacon's Rebellion, James Oglethorpe.
2. **Define** indentured servant, constitution, debtor.
3. **Describe** what the Act of Toleration was supposed to prevent.

Reviewing Themes

4. **Culture and Traditions** How did the need for workers contribute to cultural diversity in Maryland?

Critical Thinking

5. **Analyzing Information** Do you think uprisings such as Bacon's Rebellion were a sign of things to come? Explain your answer.

Activity

Making a Bulletin Board Display Work with a group to create a bulletin board display titled "The Southern Colonies." Include slogans and pictures to show the colonies' origins, climate, land, and products.

1608
The French
settle Quebec

1610
Santa Fe
founded by
the Spanish

1663
New France
becomes a
royal colony

1718
French found city
of New Orleans

1769
Junípero Serra
establishes
mission at
San Diego

Section 5

Other European Settlements

READ TO DISCOVER . . .

▪ how France's colony in North America was different from the English colonies.
▪ why Spain built forts in Texas.
▪ who founded the first Catholic mission in California.

TERMS TO LEARN

tenant farmer   mission

The Storyteller

Spring had arrived. The French fur trapper and his Native American partner guided their canoe through the huge chunks of ice bobbing in the St. Lawrence River. The canoes behind them carried other fur trappers. All were headed downriver to Montreal after trapping beaver in the snowy wilderness.

The fur trapper looked over his shoulder at the mound of skins in the canoe. The last time he counted, more than 600 beaver skins filled his cargo.

French fur trapper

When French fur trappers reached Montreal every spring, merchants rushed to the river. They set up booths where they traded muskets, blankets, kettles, and other items for the beaver skins the trappers had caught during the winter. The governor greeted the trappers with a speech, and priests offered sermons. Then came several days of trading and celebrations.

New France

⭐ The French had founded **Quebec** in 1608. At first they had little interest in large-scale settlement in North America. They were mainly concerned with fishing and furs. French trappers and missionaries went far into the interior of North America. French fur companies built forts and trading posts to protect their profitable trade.

In 1663 **New France** became a royal colony. King Louis XIV limited the privileges of the fur companies. He appointed a royal governor, Jean Talon, who strongly supported new explorations.

Down the Mississippi River

In the 1670s two Frenchmen—a fur trader, **Louis Joliet,** and a priest, **Jacques Marquette**—explored the Mississippi River by canoe. Joliet and Marquette hoped to find gold, silver, or other precious metals. They were also looking for a water passage to the Pacific Ocean. The two explorers reached as far south as the junction of the Arkansas and Mississippi Rivers. When they realized that the Mississippi flowed south into the

Picturing HISTORY This painting shows French traders receiving furs from Native Americans at a point along the Mississippi River. **Why did the French generally have good relations with the Native Americans?**

Gulf of Mexico rather than west into the Pacific, they turned around and headed back upriver.

A few years later, **Robert Cavelier Sieur de La Salle** followed the Mississippi River all the way to the Gulf of Mexico. La Salle claimed the region around the river for France. He called this territory Louisiana in honor of King Louis XIV. In 1718 the French governor founded the port of **New Orleans** at the mouth of the Mississippi River. Later French explorers, traders, and missionaries traveled west to the Rocky Mountains and southwest to the Rio Grande.

Growth of New France

Settlement in French America advanced very slowly. Settlement in New France consisted of a system of seigneuries (SEHN•yuh•reez), or estates, along the St. Lawrence River. The estates were much like the patroonships of New Netherland. The seigneurs (SEHN•yehrz), or lords, received land in exchange for bringing settlers to the colony. Known as tenant farmers, the settlers paid their lord an annual rent and worked for him for a fixed number of days each year.

The French had better relations with the Native Americans than did any other Europeans. French trappers and missionaries traveled deep into Indian lands. They lived among the Native American peoples, learned their languages, and respected their ways.

Although the missionaries had come to convert Native Americans to Catholicism, they did not try to change the Indians' customs. Most important, the French colony grew so slowly that Native Americans were not pushed off their lands.

New Spain

In the early 1600s, England, France, and the Netherlands began their colonization of North America. The Spanish, however, still controlled most of Mexico, the Caribbean, and Central and South America. They also expanded into the western and southern part of what would one day be the United States.

The Southwest and the Pacific Coast

Spain was determined to keep the other European powers from threatening its empire in America. To protect their claims, the Spanish sent soldiers, missionaries, and settlers into the north.

Spanish missionaries, soldiers, and settlers founded **Santa Fe** in present-day New Mexico in

1610. Another group of missionaries and settlers went to present-day Arizona in the late 1600s. When France began exploring and laying claim to lands around the Mississippi River, the Spanish moved into what is now Texas. Spain wanted to control the area between the French territory and their own colony in Mexico. In the early 1700s, Spain established San Antonio and seven other military posts in Texas.

Missions in California

Spanish priests built a string of missions along the Pacific coast. Missions are religious settlements established to convert people to a particular faith. The missions enabled the Spanish to lay claim to California.

The Spanish did more than convert Native Americans to Christianity. Spanish missionaries and soldiers also brought the Indians to the missions—often by force—to serve as laborers in fields and workshops.

Biography

Father Junípero Serra

In 1769 **Junípero Serra,** a Franciscan monk, founded a mission at **San Diego.** Over the next 15 years, Father Serra set up 8 more missions

Junípero Serra

in California along a route called *El Camino Real* (The King's Highway)—missions that would grow into such cities as Los Angeles and Monterey.

The distance from one mission to the next was usually a day's walk, and Serra traveled on foot to visit each one and advise the missionaries. Serra also championed the rights of the Indians. He worked to prevent Spanish army commanders in the region from mistreating the Native Americans.

European Conflicts in North America

The rivalries between European nations carried over into the Americas. Britain and Spain fought several wars in the early 1700s. When the two countries were at war in Europe, fighting often broke out between British colonists in Georgia and Spanish colonists in Florida.

France and Great Britain were the great rivals of the colonial period. Both nations were expanding their settlements in North America. In the late 1700s and early 1800s, wars in Europe between the British and the French would shape events across the Atlantic even more decisively.

★ ★ ★ ★ ★ Section 5 Assessment ★ ★ ★ ★ ★

Checking for Understanding
1. **Identify** Louis Joliet, Jacques Marquette, La Salle, Father Junípero Serra.
2. **Define** tenant farmer, mission.
3. **Explain** why settlement in French America was slower than in the English colonies.

Reviewing Themes
4. **Culture and Traditions** Why was France's relationship with the Native Americans better than that of other Europeans?

Critical Thinking
5. **Predicting Consequences** What might have happened to Spain's land claims if it had not built military posts in Texas?

Activity

Making a Map Sketch a map of North America and label the areas claimed by the British, French, and Spanish. Then, using a red pencil or marker, indicate border areas that might be potential hot spots between rival nations.

Multimedia Activities

ABC NEWS INTERACTIVE™ Historic America Electronic Field Trips

Field Trip to St. Augustine

Setting up the Video

With your classmates, view "St. Augustine" on the videodisc *Historic America: Electronic Field Trips*. St. Augustine is the oldest European settlement in the United States. It was founded as a military outpost in 1565 by the Spanish to protect their ships, which were carrying treasures from Mexico and South America to Spain. This program explains the history of St. Augustine and the influences left behind by the Spanish.

Side 1,
Chapter 4

View the video by scanning the bar code or by entering the chapter number on your keypad and pressing Search.

Hands-On Activity

Think of Spanish influences that appear in modern American culture. Organize into five groups, with each group brainstorming several examples of Spanish influences in the areas of: food, language, music, traditions, sports. Hold a "Spanish Legacy Day," with each group bringing samples, artifacts, or videotapes of their topic.

Surfing the "Net"

Tools of the Trade

During the Colonial Era, many remarkable inventions appeared. Benjamin Franklin, one famous inventor of the period, published *Poor Richard's Almanack,* a publication filled with advice on a variety of topics. Many colonists turned to this resource for information. Imagine the Internet was around during Franklin's time. Place yourself in the shoes of a typical colonist and search the Internet for information that is pertinent to your occupation. To assist you on your search, follow the instructions below.

Getting There

Pick a trade that a colonist might have practiced, then research related topics of that trade. For example, if you are a farmer, you might be interested in knowing about the weather and its effect on crop planting.

1. Use a search engine. Type in words that relate to the trade you choose.
2. The search engine will provide you with a number of links to follow. Links are "pointers" to different sites on the Internet and commonly appear as blue underlined words.

What to Do When You Are There

Click on the links to navigate through the pages of information. Print your findings. Using a word processor, create an almanac page that would inform others about your trade and the information you discovered on the Internet.

Assessment and Activities

★ Reviewing Key Terms

On a sheet of paper, define the following terms:
charter
joint-stock company
burgesses
dissent
persecute
Puritan
Separatist
Pilgrim
patroon
proprietary colony
pacifist
indentured servant
constitution
debtor
mission

★ Reviewing Key Facts

1. Why did the Virginia Company create the House of Burgesses?
2. How did the Puritans' and the Pilgrims' view of the Anglican Church differ?
3. Name two things that colonial leaders offered to attract settlers.
4. What were Sir George Calvert's two main reasons for establishing Maryland?
5. Why did Spain send missionaries to the Pacific coast and the Southwest?

★ Critical Thinking

Identifying Central Issues

For colonies to prosper, they needed a large number of settlers.
1. Why did the success of a colony depend on attracting settlers?
2. In what ways did William Penn try to attract settlers?

★ Skill Practice Activity

Reading a Bar Graph

Study the bar graph, then answer these questions:
1. What do the numbers on the vertical axis represent?
2. What was the approximate value of exports to England in 1700?
3. In which years were there more exports than imports?

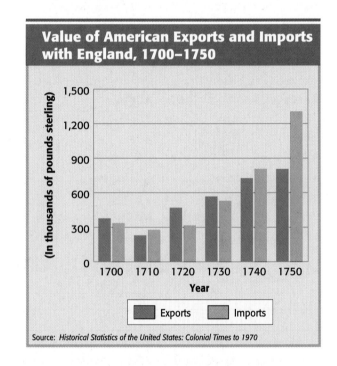

Value of American Exports and Imports with England, 1700–1750

(In thousands of pounds sterling)

Year

Exports ▪ Imports

Source: *Historical Statistics of the United States: Colonial Times to 1970*

★ Time Line Activity

Create a time line on which you place the following events in chronological order.
- *Mayflower* lands at Plymouth
- French found port of New Orleans
- England takes over New Netherland
- Anne Hutchinson founds Portsmouth
- William Penn founds Pennsylvania
- The Spanish settle Santa Fe
- King Philip's War is waged
- Jamestown is established
- Quebec is established

★ Technology Activity

Using a Word Processor Search the library for information about the Canadian cities of Quebec and Montreal. Find historical sites that show the French influence in these cities. Then, on your word processor, create a travel brochure with a brief description of each site.

★ Geography Activity

Study the map below and answer the questions that follow.

1. **Location** Which colonies had the largest areas of settlement before 1660?
2. **Place** During what time period was Boston settled?

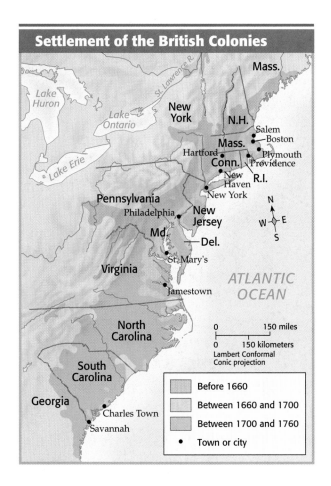

Settlement of the British Colonies

★ Reviewing Themes

1. **Economic Factors** How did the economic activities of the French differ from those of the English in North America?
2. **Civic Rights and Responsibilities** What role did religious freedom play in the founding of Rhode Island and Pennsylvania?
3. **Individual Action** Why did cooperation turn to conflict between the New England settlers and the Native Americans?
4. **Culture and Traditions** Between what two groups in the Carolinas did tension arise?
5. **Culture and Traditions** How did the treatment of Native Americans by Spanish missionaries differ from their treatment by French missionaries?

★ Cooperative Activity

History and Math Working in a group, research the populations of the English colonies in 1700. Create a bar graph to compare the populations of each. Use the graph to determine whether the total population of the New England, Middle, or Southern Colonies was largest.

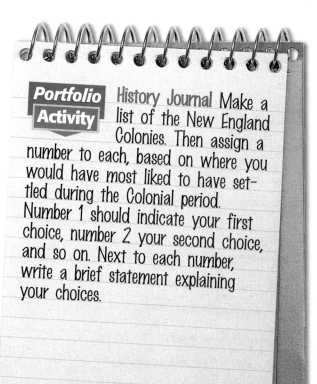

Portfolio Activity History Journal Make a list of the New England Colonies. Then assign a number to each, based on where you would have most liked to have settled during the Colonial period. Number 1 should indicate your first choice, number 2 your second choice, and so on. Next to each number, write a brief statement explaining your choices.

Hands-On HISTORY Lab Activity

Making Soap

Early settlers in North America usually made soap once a year from animal fats collected at butchering time. This soap was used for everything— washing dishes, clothes, and people, too! Try making a bar of soap to understand this aspect of colonial life.

The Way It Was

The average American colonist did not have very much need for a large supply of soap. Most colonists washed their clothing only once a month and bathed even less frequently. They thought that baths were bad for their health. Homemade soap—a harsh mixture of wood ashes, water, and animal fat—was often a strong-smelling, soft, jellylike mass. Soap makers made soap in a large pot over an outdoor fire to keep the fumes away from the house. The fat was heated and stirred for hours until it turned into a smooth, thick liquid. The top layer of fat was skimmed off and poured into wooden tubs. Then lye, made from wood ashes and water, was stirred into the melted fat. It took several hours of stirring to combine the fat and lye to make soap. The soap was then poured into small wooden boxes, allowed to cool, and stored.

Soap Boiler.

 **1 Materials**

- small plastic container
- petroleum jelly
- 1 cup of soap scraps
- cheese grater
- measuring cup
- double boiler, with water in the bottom
- water
- plastic stirring spoon
- small twig

 Believe It Or Not!

The basic recipe for homemade soap included 5 to 6 bushels of wood ashes and about 20 to 25 pounds of animal fat. These ingredients would produce one barrel of soap.

2 **What To Do**

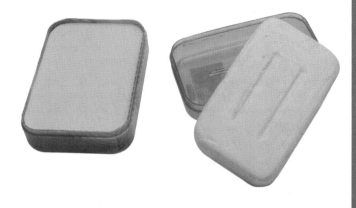

1 Grease the inside of the plastic container with petroleum jelly. Set aside.

2 Grate 1 cup of scraps of soap with the cheese grater until the scraps are about the size of pencil erasers. Put the grated soap into the top of the double boiler.

3 Add 1/2 cup of water.

4 Turn the stove on medium heat. Place the double boiler on the stove and carefully stir the soap and water until the mixture turns into a smooth liquid. Continue stirring and be patient. It may take up to 30 minutes for the soap to melt. SAFETY NOTE: HANDLE HOT MATERIALS CAREFULLY.

5 When the soap is the consistency of honey, stand a small twig in the mixture. If the twig stands up without support, the soap is ready to pour into the plastic container.

6 Allow the soap to cool overnight. After the soap hardens, turn the mold over and slip out the bar of soap.

3 **Lab Report**

1. What were the main ingredients of the colonists' homemade soap?
2. How was the soap you made different from the soap settlers made?
3. Did you use your soap? How would you compare the soap you made with your usual kind of soap?
4. **Drawing Conclusions** What effect do you think modern soap-making methods have had on the way that we live?

Go a Step Further

Find out more about soap making and soap products of the past. Research the ways that Native Americans, Europeans, Asians, and Africans made soap using the materials found in their environments.

1607–1770

The Colonies Grow

★ Why It's Important

The settlers who came to the English colonies were English, Scottish, Irish, Ibo, Mandingo, Yoruba, Portuguese, German, Dutch, French, Swedish, and Finnish. They eventually learned English and adapted to the English traditions of the colonies. At the same time, these peoples made their own contributions. Words from a number of languages, foods from many lands, a variety of religious beliefs and holidays—all became part of the emerging culture of colonial America.

★ Chapter Themes

■ *Section 1,* Economic Factors
■ *Section 2,* Continuity and Change
■ *Section 3,* Groups and Institutions
■ *Section 4,* Individual Action

PRIMARY SOURCES
Library *See pages 942–943 for primary source readings to accompany Chapter 4*

★ **HISTORY AND ART** *The South Side of St. John's Street* by Joseph B. Smith This colonial-era painting depicts a quiet, middle-class neighborhood in New York City during the late 1760s.

1700s
Thousands of enslaved Africans are brought to America

1725
Pennsylvania Quakers speak out against slavery

1750
New England is the center of colonial shipping

1750s
South Carolina and Georgia have the fastest-growing colonial economies

Section 1

Life in the Colonies

READ TO DISCOVER . . .

- what the triangular trade was and how it affected American society.
- how the Tidewater planters and backcountry farmers differed.
- why the use of enslaved workers increased in the colonies.

TERMS TO LEARN

subsistence farming
triangular trade
cash crop
diversity

Tidewater
backcountry
overseer

Storyteller

In 1760 Englishman Andrew Burnaby traveled throughout the North American colonies, observing American life. He could not imagine that these colonies would ever join in union for they were as different from one another as "fire and water," and each colony was jealous of the other. "In short, such is the difference of character, of manners, of religion, of interest, of the different colonies, that I think . . . were they left to themselves, there would soon be a civil war, from one end of the continent to the other."

Colonial spinning wheel

During the 1700s the population of the English colonies grew dramatically. The number of Europeans living in the colonies rose from about 250,000 in 1700 to 2.5 million in 1775—a tenfold increase. The population of African Americans increased at an even faster rate—from 28,000 to more than 500,000.

Colonial Growth

⭐ Immigration was a major factor in this growth. Between 1607 and 1790, almost a million people—600,000 Europeans and 300,000 Africans—came to live in the colonies.

Another reason for the increase was that colonial women tended to marry early and have large families. It was not unusual for a woman to have seven or more children. In addition America, especially New England, turned out to be an unusually healthy place to live. Many babies survived the diseases of childhood to become adults, and many adults lived to an old age.

The New England Colonies

⭐ Most people in New England lived in well-organized towns. In the center of the town stood the meetinghouse, a building used for both church services and town meetings. The meetinghouse faced a piece of land called the green, where cows grazed and the citizen army trained. Farmers lived in the town and worked in fields on its outskirts.

Farming was the main economic activity in all the colonies, but New England farms were smaller than those farther south. Long winters and thin, rocky soil made large-scale farming difficult. Farmers in New England practiced subsistence farming, which means that they generally produced just enough to meet the needs of their families, with little left over to sell or exchange. Most Northern farmers relied on their children for labor, and everyone in the family worked—spinning yarn, preserving fruit, milking cows, fencing in fields, and sowing and harvesting grain.

$ Economics

Commerce in New England

New England also had many small businesses. Some people used the waterpower from the streams on their land to run mills for grinding grain or sawing lumber. Women who made cloth, garments, candles, or soap for their families sometimes produced enough of these products to sell or trade. Large towns attracted skilled craftspeople who set themselves up as blacksmiths, shoemakers, furniture makers, gunsmiths, metalsmiths, and printers.

Shipbuilding was an important local industry. The lumber for building ships came from the forests of New England and was transported down rivers to the shipyards in coastal towns.

Fishing was another major economic activity. New Englanders fished for cod, halibut, crabs, oysters, and lobsters. Some ventured far out to sea to hunt whales for oil and whalebone.

Colonial Trade

As the hub of the shipping trade in America, New England linked the Northern and Southern Colonies and tied America to other parts of the world. New England ships sailed south along the Atlantic coast, trading with the colonies and with islands in the **West Indies.** They crossed the Atlantic carrying fish, furs, and fruit to exchange for manufactured goods in England and Europe.

Triangular Trade

These colonial merchant ships followed many different trading routes. Some ships went directly

★ **HISTORY AND ART** *Needlework* **by Hannah Otis** This scene includes John Hancock (on horseback), who later became the first signer of the Declaration of Independence. **Why was New England important for colonial trade?**

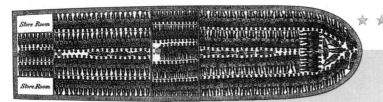

Slaves packed in ship

from the colonies to England and other European ports and back. Others followed routes that came to be called the triangular trade because the routes formed a triangle. On one leg of such a route, ships took fish, grain, meat, and lumber to the West Indies. There the ship's captain traded for sugar, molasses—a syrup made from sugarcane—and fruit, which he then took back to New England. Colonists used the molasses to make rum.

The rum, along with manufactured goods, was then shipped to **West Africa.** There these goods were traded for Africans who had been captured and enslaved by slave traders. On another leg of the route, the ships carried the enslaved Africans back to the West Indies, where planters were in need of workers. With the profits made from selling slaves to the planters, the captain bought more molasses and sugar to ship back and sell in the colonies. A later route brought enslaved Africans directly to the American colonies. 💲

★ **Picturing HISTORY** A deck plan (top left) reveals tightly packed ranks of slaves on a ship bound from Africa to the Americas. Once docked, the ship's human cargo was replaced with rum or molasses. **What does the term *Middle Passage* refer to?**

The Middle Passage

The most inhumane aspect of the triangular trade, shipping enslaved Africans to the West Indies, was known as the **Middle Passage.** Olaudah Equiano, a young African forced onto a ship to America, later described the horror of the voyage across the Atlantic:

❝ I was soon put down under the decks, and there I received such . . . [an odor] in my nostrils as I had never experienced in my life. . . . The closeness of the place, and the heat of the climate, added to the number in the ship, which was so crowded that each had scarcely room to turn himself, almost suffocated us. . . . The shrieks of the women, and the groans of the dying, rendered [made] the whole a scene of horror. ❞

With its trade, shipbuilding, and fishing, New England flourished. Although good farmland

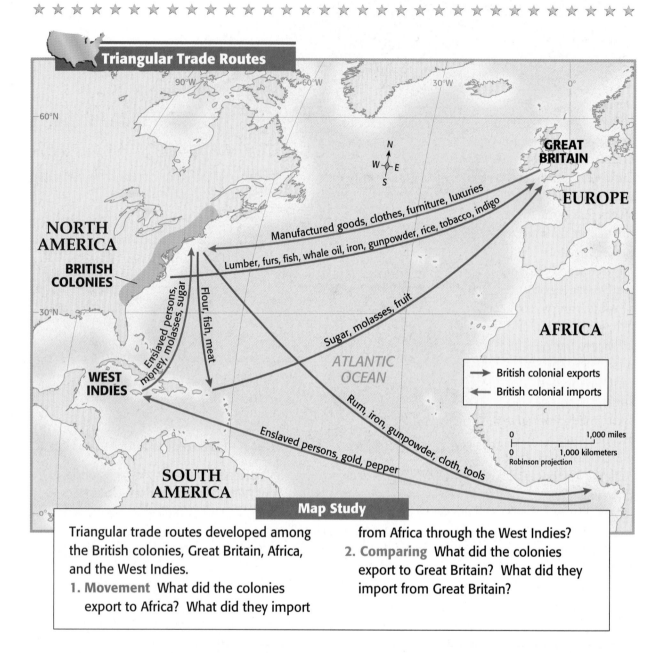

NORTH AMERICA

BRITISH COLONIES

WEST INDIES

SOUTH AMERICA

GREAT BRITAIN

EUROPE

AFRICA

ATLANTIC OCEAN

Manufactured goods, clothes, furniture, luxuries

Lumber, furs, fish, whale oil, iron, gunpowder, rice, tobacco, indigo

Enslaved persons, money, molasses, sugar

Flour, fish, meat

Sugar, molasses, fruit

Rum, iron, gunpowder, cloth, tools

Enslaved persons, gold, pepper

→ British colonial exports
← British colonial imports

0   1,000 miles
0   1,000 kilometers
Robinson projection

Map Study

Triangular trade routes developed among the British colonies, Great Britain, Africa, and the West Indies.

1. **Movement** What did the colonies export to Africa? What did they import from Africa through the West Indies?

2. **Comparing** What did the colonies export to Great Britain? What did they import from Great Britain?

was lacking in much of the region, New England's population expanded and towns and cities developed.

The Middle Colonies

The Middle Colonies enjoyed fertile soil and a slightly milder climate than that found in New England. Farmers in this region cultivated larger tracts of land and produced bigger harvests than did New Englanders. In New York and Pennsylvania, farmers grew large quantities of wheat and other cash crops, crops that could be sold easily in markets in the colonies and overseas.

Farmers sent cargoes of wheat and livestock to New York City and Philadelphia for shipment, and these cities became busy ports. By the 1770s New York, with 25,000 people, and Philadelphia, with 28,000 people, were the largest cities in the American colonies.

Industries of the Middle Colonies

The Middle Colonies—especially New Jersey and Pennsylvania—also had industries. Some were home-based crafts such as carpentry and flour making. Others included commercial ventures such as lumbering, mining, and small-scale manufacturing.

One iron mill in northern New Jersey employed several hundred workers, many of them from Germany. Other smaller ironworks operated in New Jersey and Pennsylvania.

German Immigrants

Most of the 100,000 Germans who came to America during the colonial era settled in Pennsylvania. Using agricultural methods developed in Europe, these immigrants became successful farmers.

The Germans belonged to a number of Protestant sects. Together with the Dutch, Swedish, and other non-English immigrants, they gave the Middle Colonies a cultural diversity, or variety, not found in New England. With the diversity came tolerance.

The Southern Colonies

⭐ With their rich soil and warm climate, the Southern Colonies were well suited to certain kinds of farming. Southern farmers could cultivate large areas of land and produce harvests of cash crops. Because of their profitable lifestyle based on agriculture, the Southern Colonies had little need to develop commerce or industry. For the most part, London merchants rather than local merchants managed Southern trade.

$ Economics

Tobacco and Rice

Tobacco was the principal cash crop of Maryland and Virginia. Most tobacco was sold in Europe, where the demand for it was strong. Growing tobacco and preparing it for sale required a good deal of labor. At first planters used indentured servants to work in the fields. When indentured servants became scarce and expensive, Southern planters used enslaved Africans instead.

Slaveholders with large properties became rich on tobacco. Sometimes, however, a surplus of tobacco on the market caused prices to fall—and so did the growers' profits. After 1745 some tobacco planters switched to growing corn and wheat.

The main cash crop in South Carolina and Georgia was rice. In low-lying coastal areas, planters built dams to create rice fields called paddies. These fields were flooded when the rice was young and drained when the rice was ready to harvest. Work in the rice paddies involved standing knee-deep in the mud all day with no protection from the blazing sun or the biting insects.

Because rice harvesting required so much strenuous work, rice growers relied on slave labor. Rice proved to be even more profitable than tobacco. As it became popular in southern Europe, the price of rice rose steadily. By the 1750s South Carolina and Georgia had the fastest-growing economies in the colonies. 💲

Tidewater and Backcountry

Most of the large Southern plantations were located in the Tidewater, a region of flat, low-lying plains along the seacoast. Plantations, or large farms, were often situated on rivers so crops could be shipped to market by boat.

Each plantation was a self-contained community with fields stretching out around a cluster of buildings. The planter's wife supervised the main

Sugarcane and a rum barrel

★ **HISTORY AND ART** *The Old Plantation* by an unknown artist This watercolor from the 1700s shows a traditional African celebration on a Southern plantation. **What skills were developed by enslaved Africans on plantations and in towns?**

house and the household servants. A plantation also included slave cabins, barns and stables, and such outbuildings as carpenter and blacksmith shops and storerooms. Even kitchens, which frequently caught fire, were in separate buildings. A large plantation might also have its own chapel and school.

West of the Tidewater lay a region of hills and forests climbing up toward the **Appalachian Mountains.** This region, known as the backcountry, was settled in part by hardy newcomers to the colonies. The backcountry settlers grew corn and tobacco on small farms. They usually worked alone or with their families, although some had one or two enslaved Africans to help.

In the Southern Colonies, the independent small farmers of the backcountry outnumbered the large plantation owners. The plantation owners, however, had greater wealth and more influence. They controlled the economic and political life of the region.

Slavery

★ Most enslaved Africans in North America lived on plantations. Some of the Africans did housework, but most worked in the fields and often suffered great cruelty. The large plantation owners hired overseers, or bosses, to keep the slaves working hard.

All the Southern Colonies had **slave codes,** strict rules governing the behavior and punishment of enslaved Africans. Slaves could not leave the plantation without written permission from the master. Enslaved people could not be taught to read or write. They were whipped for minor offenses and hanged or burned to death for serious crimes. Those who ran away were often caught and punished severely.

All white colonists were encouraged to enforce these laws against enslaved Africans. As a result, a person's race determined his or her place in society.

African Traditions

Although the Africans brought to America or born in America had strong family ties, their families were often torn apart. Slaveholders could split up families by selling a spouse, a parent, or a child to another slaveholder. Slaves who worked on plantations found a source of strength in their connection to their African roots. They developed a culture that drew on the languages, customs, and religions of their West African homelands, even as they learned the English ways of the slaveholders.

Some enslaved Africans learned trades such as carpentry, blacksmithing, or weaving. Skilled workers could sometimes set up shops, sharing their profits with the slaveholders. Those lucky enough to be able to buy their freedom joined the small population of free African Americans.

Criticism of Slavery

Slavery was part of colonial life and one of the main reasons for the economic success of the Southern Colonies. That success, however, was built on a profound injustice: the idea that one human being could own another. Some European colonists did not believe in slavery. Many Puritans refused to hold enslaved people. In Pennsylvania, Quakers and Mennonites—a German religious

★ **Picturing HISTORY** Colonists brought traditions from their homelands and developed new ways of life in America. **Where did most German immigrants settle?**

group—condemned slavery. Eventually the debate over slavery would erupt in a bloody civil war, pitting Northerners against Southerners.

Section 1 Assessment

★ ★ ★ ★ ★ ★ ★ ★ ★ ★ ★

Checking for Understanding
1. *Identify* West Indies, West Africa, Middle Passage, Appalachian Mountains.
2. *Define* subsistence farming, triangular trade, cash crop, diversity, Tidewater, backcountry, overseer.
3. *Compare* farming in New England with farming in the Southern Colonies.

Reviewing Themes
4. **Economic Factors** How did New England's natural resources help its commerce?

Critical Thinking
5. **Making Inferences** How do you think plantation owners in the Southern Colonies justified their use of enslaved Africans?

Activity

Writing a Letter Imagine you are from New England and are visiting your cousins on a farm in the Carolinas. Write a letter to a friend at home describing your visit to their farm.

1636
Harvard College
is established

1693
William and Mary
College is founded

1732
Benjamin Franklin
publishes *Poor
Richard's Almanack*

1735
Great Awakening
sweeps through
the colonies

Section 2

Government, Religion, and Culture

READ TO DISCOVER . . .
▪ what the Navigation Acts were and why
they made the colonists angry.
▪ who had the right to vote in colonial
legislatures.

TERMS TO LEARN
mercantilism   charter colony
export   proprietary colony
import   apprentice
smuggling   literacy

Storyteller

"Fish and Visitors stink after three days."
"Beware of little Expenses: a small Leak
   will sink a great Ship."
"No gains without pains."
   Benjamin Franklin wrote these and other
witty sayings for his annual book, *Poor
Richard's
Almanack*. The
last saying—"No
gains without
pains"—was par-
ticularly true in
the American
colonies in the
late 1600s.

***From* Poor Richard's Almanack**

Trouble was brewing in England—and in
the colonies—during the mid-1600s. England's monarchy had been restored under
Charles II, but many people were not satisfied
with his rule. James II, Charles's successor, attempted to seize from Parliament powers that it
had won during the English Civil War. He also
tried to tighten royal control over the colonies.

In 1688 Parliament took action. It ousted
James and placed his daughter Mary and her
Dutch husband, William of Orange, on the
throne. This change, which showed the power of
the elected representatives over the monarch,
came to be known as the **Glorious Revolution.**

William and Mary signed an **English Bill of
Rights** in 1689 guaranteeing certain basic rights to
all citizens. This document became part of the
heritage of English law that the American
colonists shared. It later inspired the people who
created America's own Bill of Rights.

English Colonial Rule

★ England viewed its North American
colonies as an economic resource. The
colonies provided England with raw materials.
English manufacturers used these materials to
produce finished goods, which they sold to the
colonists. This process followed an economic theory called mercantilism, which held that a nation's power depended on expanding its trade

and increasing its gold reserves. To make money from its trade, England had to export, or sell abroad, more goods than it imported, or bought from foreign markets.

To make certain that only England benefited from trade with the colonies, Parliament passed a series of laws in the 1650s called the **Navigation Acts.** These laws directed the flow of goods between England and the colonies. Colonial merchants who had goods to send to England could not use foreign ships—even if those ships offered lower shipping rates. The Navigation Acts also prohibited the colonists from sending certain products, such as sugar or tobacco, outside England's empire.

Some colonists ignored these laws and began smuggling, trading illegally with other nations, in Europe or in the West Indies. Restrictions on trade would later cause more conflict between the colonies and England.

Citizenship

Colonial Government

As the colonies grew, they relied more and more on their own governments to make local laws. By the 1760s there were three types of colonies in America--charter colonies, proprietary colonies, and royal colonies.

Charter Colonies

Connecticut and Rhode Island, the charter colonies, were established by groups of settlers who had been given a charter, or a grant of rights and privileges. These colonists elected their own governors and the members of both houses of the legislature. Although Great Britain had the right to approve the governor's appointment, the colonial governor could not veto the acts of the legislature.

American Memories

A Colonial Home

Ladder-back chair

Iron kettle

Hooded cradle

What Was It Like? The kitchen was the heart of the early American home. What items do you see here that are forerunners of items you might find in a modern kitchen?

Proprietary Colonies

The proprietary colonies—Delaware, Maryland, and Pennsylvania—were ruled by proprietors, individuals or groups to whom Britain had granted land. Proprietors were generally free to rule as they wished. They appointed the governor and members of the upper house of the legislature, while the people elected the lower house.

Royal Colonies

By the 1760s Georgia, Massachusetts, New Hampshire, New Jersey, New York, North Carolina, and Virginia were royal colonies. Britain directly ruled all royal colonies. In each, Parliament appointed a governor and council, known as the upper house. The colonists elected an assembly, called the lower house. The governor and members of the council usually did what the British leaders told them to do. Often, however, this led to conflict with the colonists in the assembly, especially when officials tried to enforce tax laws and trade restrictions.

Voting Rights

Colonial legislatures gave some people a voice in government. Only white men who owned property had the right to vote. Neither women, nor indentured servants, nor landless and poor people, nor enslaved Africans could vote.

TECHNOLOGY AND HISTORY

Colonial Printing Press

Life in the colonies often revolved around local printers who produced pamphlets, small flyers, books, and newspapers. The first printing press in the American colonies was established by Stephen Daye in 1639. **Which of the processes shown here do you think was most time-consuming?**

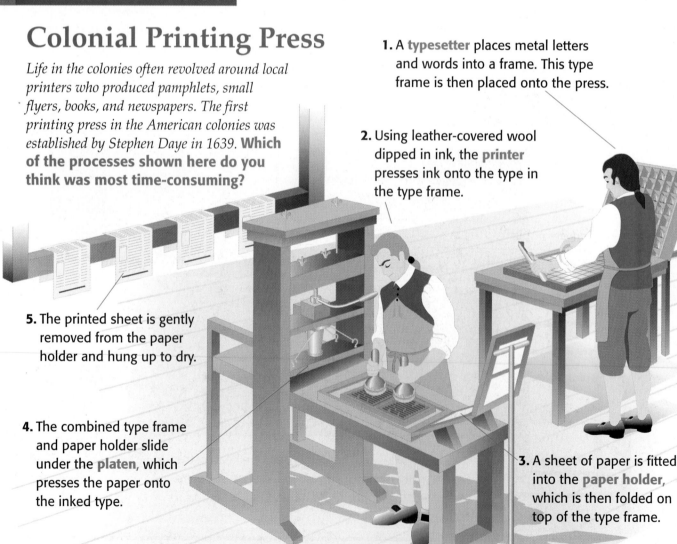

1. A **typesetter** places metal letters and words into a frame. This type frame is then placed onto the press.

2. Using leather-covered wool dipped in ink, the **printer** presses ink onto the type in the type frame.

3. A sheet of paper is fitted into the **paper holder**, which is then folded on top of the type frame.

4. The combined type frame and paper holder slide under the **platen**, which presses the paper onto the inked type.

5. The printed sheet is gently removed from the paper holder and hung up to dry.

Religion in the Colonies

⭐ The Puritans of New England came to America to establish their own kind of Christian religion. Because worship was so central to their lives, they built their towns around the church. The Puritans believed that each congregation should be self-governing. All church members could participate in church decisions such as choosing a minister. Everyone was required to attend church services, and people who played or laughed on Sunday could be punished. Later the Puritans were called Congregationalists.

The Great Awakening

In the 1730s and 1740s, a religious revival called the **Great Awakening** swept through the colonies. In New England and the Middle Colonies, ministers called for "a new birth," a return to the strong faith of earlier days. One of the outstanding preachers of the Great Awakening was **Jonathan Edwards** of Massachusetts. People found his sermons powerful and convincing.

The English preacher **George Whitefield,** who arrived in the colonies in 1739, helped spread the religious revival. During a two-year tour, Whitefield electrified worshipers in churches and open fields from New England to Georgia. The Great Awakening led to the formation of many new churches, especially in the Southern backcountry.

Jonathan Edwards

An Emerging Culture

⭐ Throughout the colonies, people adapted their traditions to the new conditions of life in America. Religion, education, and the arts all contributed to a new American culture.

Family Roles

A colonial farm was both home and workplace. Women cooked, made butter and cheese, and preserved food. They spun yarn, made clothes, and tended chickens and cows. Men worked in the fields and built barns, houses, and fences. Mothers and fathers cared for their children and taught them to do farming tasks. In the backcountry, women worked in the fields next to their husbands. Women also shared fieldwork in the German areas of Pennsylvania.

Men were the formal heads of the households. They managed the farms and represented the family in community affairs. In church matters, however, women also participated in making decisions. Families often arranged for their adolescent boys to work as indentured servants for farmers or to serve as apprentices, or learning assistants, to craft workers who taught them a trade. Married women were considered subject to their husbands' authority and had few rights.

Women in cities and towns sometimes held jobs outside the home. Young unmarried women without income might work for wealthy families as maids, cooks, and nurses. Widows might work as teachers, nurses, and seamstresses. They also opened shops and inns. Widows and women who had never married could run businesses and own property, although they could not vote.

Education

Most colonists placed a high value on education. Children were often taught to read and write at home by their parents, but the daily chores of colonial life left adults little time for giving lessons. In 1647 the Massachusetts Puritans

---

*F*ootnotes to History

Indentured Servants were termed *indentured* because their contract was indented, or folded, along an irregular line and torn in two. Master and servant each kept half.

passed a public education law. Each community had to have a teacher whose wages would be paid through taxes. Although some communities did not comply, most established schools.

During this period New England had a very high level of literacy, the ability to read and write. Perhaps 70 percent of the men and about half of the women could read. *The New England Primer,* first published in 1683, combined lessons in good conduct with reading and writing.

Many colonial schools were "dame schools," run by widows or unmarried women who taught classes in their homes. In the Middle Colonies, some schools were run by Quakers and other religious groups. In the towns and cities, craftspeople set up night schools for their apprentices.

The colonies' early colleges were founded to train ministers. The first was Harvard College, established in 1636 by the Puritans in Cambridge, Massachusetts. Anglicans founded William and Mary College in Virginia in 1693.

The Enlightenment

By the middle of the 1700s, many educated colonists were influenced by **the Enlightenment.** This movement, which began in Europe, spread the idea that knowledge, reason, and science could improve society. Because some religious leaders feared independent thinking, they opposed the reforms proposed under the influence of the Enlightenment. Nevertheless, in colonial cities Enlightenment ideas spread rapidly through newspapers, lectures, and organizations.

Biography

Benjamin Franklin's Contributions

The American who best exemplified the Enlightenment way of thinking was **Benjamin Franklin.** Franklin learned the printer's trade as a young man. By the time he was 23, he owned his own newspaper in Philadelphia. Soon afterward he began publishing *Poor Richard's Almanack,* a calendar filled with advice and wise sayings, such as "Early to bed, early to rise, makes a man healthy, wealthy, and wise."

Franklin was deeply interested in science. His major scientific contribution came from his discoveries about electricity. He invented the lightning rod, bifocal eyeglasses, and the efficient Franklin stove for heating. Energetic and open-minded, Franklin served in the Pennsylvania Assembly for many years. He founded a hospital, a fire department, America's first lending library, and an academy of higher learning that later became the University of Pennsylvania.

Franklin's greatest services to his fellow Americans would come during the 1770s. As a statesman and patriot, Franklin would help guide the colonies toward independence.

★ ★ ★ ★ ★ Section 2 Assessment ★ ★ ★ ★ ★ ★

Checking for Understanding

1. *Identify* Jonathan Edwards, George Whitefield, Benjamin Franklin.
2. *Define* export, charter colony, proprietary colony, apprentice, literacy.
3. *Identify* the only people permitted to vote in the colonies.

Reviewing Themes

4. **Continuity and Change** Why did the Navigation Acts anger the colonists?

Critical Thinking

5. **Making Comparisons** How did the family roles of colonial women and men differ?

Activity

Making an Organizational Chart Draw a chart that shows the structure of a royal colony, a proprietary colony, and a charter colony.

Living in the English Colonies

Settlers in America brought customs and crafts from home, but they also had to learn new skills. They had to make or grow almost everything they used. How would you get along as a settler in the wilderness? As you complete these activities, imagine how each might have been a part of a colonist's everyday life.

Science

Growing an Herb Garden Herbs and other plants were necessary to colonists as flavorings, preservatives, and medicines. Plant several kinds of herbs in flowerpots and monitor their growth. Many, such as basil and parsley, will sprout from seeds in a few days. Investigate each herb's uses and sample each taste and smell. Then present samples to the class.

School-to-Work

Organizing a Settlement You and other settlers decide to leave Massachusetts Bay Colony and form a new town some miles inland. Make a "business plan" for the settlement: the number of workers and artisans needed (farmers, carpenters, and so on); a list of tools, food, and supplies to take along; and things to look for in a site. Sketch a map of the town plan.

Art

Using Natural Dyes Experiment with plant-based dyes like those used in the 1700s. A yellow-orange dye was made from onion skins or turmeric. Blueberries developed a pink to purple dye. Walnut shells made brown, and apple bark a soft yellow.

Wash wool yarn or pieces of cotton cloth. Simmer the plant material or crushed berries in a gallon of water for a half hour. Strain the liquid; cool it, then put in the clean, wet fibers. Simmer the liquid again, stirring gently. Remove the fibers, rinse, and hang to dry. Make a display of the dyes and dyed fibers.

Music

Learning a Colonial Dance Country dances from England took on an American flavor in the colonies. To learn the Virginia reel, choose a traditional dance tune, such as "Turkey in the Straw." Form a double line with partners facing each other. The lead couple alternately swing each other and the other dancers, moving to the other end of the line. There they form an arch with their arms for other couples to pass through. The next couple repeats the pattern.

Gourd fiddle played by enslaved Africans

1713
French and Abenaki massacre settlers at Deerfield, Massachusetts

1753
George Washington sent to Ohio country to protest French actions

1754
Washington returns to Ohio and builds Fort Necessity; Benjamin Franklin proposes Albany Plan of Union

Section 3

France and Britain Clash in America

READ TO DISCOVER . . .
▓ how wars in Europe spread to the American colonies.
▓ what role the Native Americans played in the conflict between Britain and France.
▓ what the Albany Plan of Union was.

TERMS TO LEARN
Iroquois Confederacy   militia

The Storyteller

In 1689 England and France began competing to be the richest and most powerful nation in Europe. This contest for power went on for generations with only short intervals of peace. The long rivalry for the control of North America was a drama played against a backdrop of a vast wilderness. In 1758 Nathaniel Ames wrote, "The parts of North America which may be claimed by Great Britain or France are of as much worth as either kingdom. That fertile country to the west of the Appalachian Mountains [is the] 'Garden of the World'!"

Powderhorn, French and Indian War

As the population of the British colonies grew, some land companies wanted to explore opportunities in the **Ohio River valley.** However, the French, who traded throughout the Ohio country, regarded it as their own territory. They had no intention of letting British colonists share in their profitable fur trade with the Native Americans.

In the 1740s British fur traders from Pennsylvania went into the Ohio country. They built a fort deep in the territory of the Miami people at a place called Pickawillany. Acting quickly, the French attacked Pickawillany and drove the British traders back to Pennsylvania. The governor of New France then built a string of forts along the rivers of the upper Ohio Valley, closer to the British colonies than ever before. Two mighty powers—Great Britain and France—were headed for a showdown in North America.

⊕ Geography
British-French Rivalry

★ Britain and France had been competing for wealth for centuries. By 1700 they were the major powers in North America. Their long rivalry aroused hostile feelings between British and French colonists in North America.

Britain had gained control of Nova Scotia, Newfoundland, and the Hudson Bay region in a treaty in 1713. In the 1740s France attacked Nova Scotia. In response a force of New Englanders went north and captured the important French fortress at **Louisbourg** on Cape Breton Island, north of Nova Scotia. Later Britain returned Louisbourg to France, much to the disgust of the New England colonists.

In North America the French and British fought over resources and land. They clashed over the fur trade and over rights to the rich fishing grounds of the North Atlantic. The French defended the Ohio Valley. The British feared that their colonies would be encircled by French settlements along the lower Mississippi Valley and in Canada.

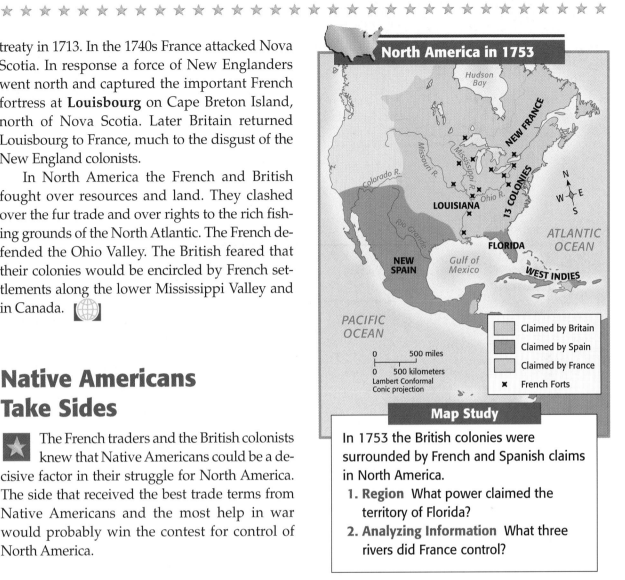

North America in 1753

Claimed by Britain
Claimed by Spain
Claimed by France
✕ French Forts

Map Study

In 1753 the British colonies were surrounded by French and Spanish claims in North America.
1. **Region** What power claimed the territory of Florida?
2. **Analyzing Information** What three rivers did France control?

Native Americans Take Sides

The French traders and the British colonists knew that Native Americans could be a decisive factor in their struggle for North America. The side that received the best trade terms from Native Americans and the most help in war would probably win the contest for control of North America.

The French and the Native Americans

The French had many Native American allies. Unlike the British, the French were interested mainly in trading for furs—not in taking over Native American land. The French were also more tolerant than the British of Native American ways. French trappers and fur traders often married Native American women and followed their customs. French missionaries converted many Native Americans to Catholicism but let them maintain their own cultures.

During the wars between Great Britain and France, Native Americans often helped the French by raiding British settlements. In 1713, for example, the Abenaki people joined the French in an attack on the British frontier outpost at Deerfield, Massachusetts.

The Iroquois Confederacy

The most powerful group of Native Americans in the East was the Iroquois Confederacy, based in New York. When the confederacy was first crafted in about 1570, it included five nations—the Mohawk, Seneca, Cayuga, Onondaga, and Oneida. Other groups later joined or were conquered by the Iroquois.

The Iroquois managed to remain independent by trading with both the British and the French. By skillfully playing the British and French against each other, the Iroquois dominated the area around the Great Lakes.

By the mid-1700s, however, the Iroquois came under increased pressure as the British moved into the Ohio Valley. Eventually the leaders of the

George Washington's telescope

George Washington's compass

George Washington as a Colonel of Virginia Militia by John Gadsby Chapman **Washington may have worn this uniform while fighting the French in the Ohio Valley in the mid-1750s. How was Washington regarded by the colonists after the war?**

Confederacy gave certain trading rights to the British and became their reluctant allies. By taking this step, the Iroquois upset the balance of power between the French and British that they had worked so hard to establish.

American Colonists Take Action

A group of Virginians had plans for settling the Ohio Valley. In the fall of 1753 Governor Robert Dinwiddie of Virginia sent a 21-year-old planter and surveyor named **George Washington** into the Ohio country. Washington's mission was to tell the French that they were trespassing on territory claimed by Great Britain and demand that they leave.

Washington delivered the message, but it did no good. "The French told me," Washington said later, "that it was their absolute design to take possession of the Ohio, and by God they would do it."

Washington's First Command

In the spring of 1754, Dinwiddie made Washington a lieutenant colonel and sent him back to the Ohio country with a militia—a group of civilians trained to fight in emergencies—of 150 men. The militia had instructions to build a fort where the Allegheny and Monongahela Rivers meet to form the Ohio River—the site of present-day

---

*F*ootnotes to History

A Close Call In a skirmish with the French on the way to Fort Duquesne, Washington was nearly killed by his own soldiers. Many years later, Washington said of this incident, "[My life] was in as much jeopardy as it has ever been before or since."

Pittsburgh. When Washington and his troops arrived, they found the French already building Fort Duquesne on that spot.

Washington established a small post called **Fort Necessity** nearby. Although greatly outnumbered, the forces of the inexperienced Washington attacked a French scouting party. The French surrounded Washington's soldiers and forced them to surrender, but the colonists were later released and returned to Virginia. Washington's account of his experience in the Ohio country was published, and his fame spread throughout the colonies and Europe. In spite of his defeat, the colonists regarded Washington as a hero who struck the first blow against the French.

Editorial cartoon promoting colonial unity, c. 1754

The Albany Plan of Union

While Washington struggled with the French, representatives from New England, New York, Pennsylvania, and Maryland met to discuss the threat of war. In June 1754, the representatives assembled in Albany, New York. They wanted to find a way for the colonies to work together to defend themselves from the French. They also hoped to persuade the Iroquois to take their side against the French.

The representatives adopted a plan suggested by Benjamin Franklin. Known as the **Albany Plan of Union,** Franklin's plan called for "one general government" for all the American colonies. A single elected legislature would govern all the colonies and would have the power to collect taxes, raise troops, and regulate trade.

Not a single colonial assembly approved the plan. None of the colonies was willing to give up any of its power. "Everyone cries, a union is necessary," wrote the disappointed Franklin, "but when they come to the manner and form of the union, their weak noodles [brains] are perfectly distracted."

The Albany meeting failed to unite the colonists to fight the French. Washington's defeat at Fort Necessity marked the beginning of a series of clashes and full-scale war. The colonists called it the French and Indian War because they were fighting two enemies—the French and their Native American allies.

Section 3 Assessment

Checking for Understanding
1. *Identify* George Washington, Fort Necessity, Albany Plan of Union.
2. *Define* Iroquois Confederacy, militia.
3. *List* two reasons the French felt threatened by British interest in the Ohio River valley.

Reviewing Themes
4. **Groups and Institutions** Why did colonists consider George Washington a hero, even after he was defeated?

Critical Thinking
5. **Analyzing Primary Sources** Based on Benjamin Franklin's quote above, what was his reaction to the colonies' refusal to accept the Albany Plan of Union?

Preparing an Interview Make a list of three to five questions that a reporter might have wanted to ask Iroquois leaders after they reluctantly sided with the British.

1754
French and Indian War begins

1758
British forces capture Fort Duquesne

1759
British general Wolfe captures Quebec

1763
Proclamation of 1763 forbids colonists to settle west of Appalachians

Section 4

The French and Indian War

READ TO DISCOVER . . .
- how British fortunes improved after William Pitt took over direction of the war.
- how Chief Pontiac united his people to fight for their land.

TERM TO LEARN
speculator

The Storyteller

"These lakes, these woods, and mountains were left us by our ancestors. They are our inheritances, and we will part with them to no one. . . . [Y]ou ought to know that He, the Great Spirit and Master of Life, has provided food for us in these spacious lakes and on the woody mountains. . . ."

These words, spoken by Chief Pontiac, served as a warning to the British colonists who wanted to take Native American lands.

Iroquois mask

In 1754 the governor of Massachusetts fed the fears of that colony's assembly when he announced that the French were on the way to "making themselves masters of this Continent." The British colonists knew that the French were building well-armed forts throughout the Great Lakes region and the Ohio River valley. Their network of alliances with Native Americans allowed the French to control vast interior lands, stretching from the St. Lawrence River all the way south to New Orleans. The French and their Native American allies seemed to be winning control of the American frontier. The final showdown was at hand.

The British Government Takes Action

⭐ During the early stages of the French and Indian War, the British colonists fought the French and the Native Americans with little help from Britain. In 1754, however, the government in London decided to intervene in the conflict. It was alarmed by the new forts the French were building and by George Washington's defeat at Fort Necessity. In the fall of 1754, Great Britain appointed **General Edward Braddock** commander in chief of the British forces in America and sent him to drive the French out of the Ohio Valley.

Braddock Marches to Duquesne

In June 1755, Braddock set out from Virginia with 1,400 red-coated British soldiers and a smaller number of blue-coated colonial militia. George Washington served as one of his guides. It took Braddock's army 32 days to trek through the dense forest to **Fort Duquesne.** Washington reported that Braddock "halted to level every mole-hill and to erect bridges over every brook, by which means we were four days in getting twelve miles."

Washington tried to tell Braddock that his army's formal style of marching was not well suited to fighting in frontier country. Lined up in columns and rows, the troops made easy targets for French and Native American sharpshooters. Braddock ignored the advice.

On July 9 the combined force of Native American warriors and French troops ambushed the British. The Indians fired from behind trees, aiming at the bright uniforms. The British, confused and frightened, could not even see their attackers.

One of the survivors of Braddock's army, Captain Orne, later described the "great confusion" that overcame Braddock's troops when they were attacked. Braddock called for an orderly retreat, "but the panic was so great he could not succeed." Braddock was killed, and the battle ended in a bitter defeat for the British, who lost nearly 1,000 soldiers. Washington led the survivors back to Virginia.

Britain Declares War on France

When news of Braddock's defeat reached London, Britain declared war on France, beginning the

Picturing HISTORY Native American warriors and French troops, protected by rocks and trees, fire into General Braddock's army crammed together on a forest trail. **What weakness of the British army contributed to Braddock's defeat?**

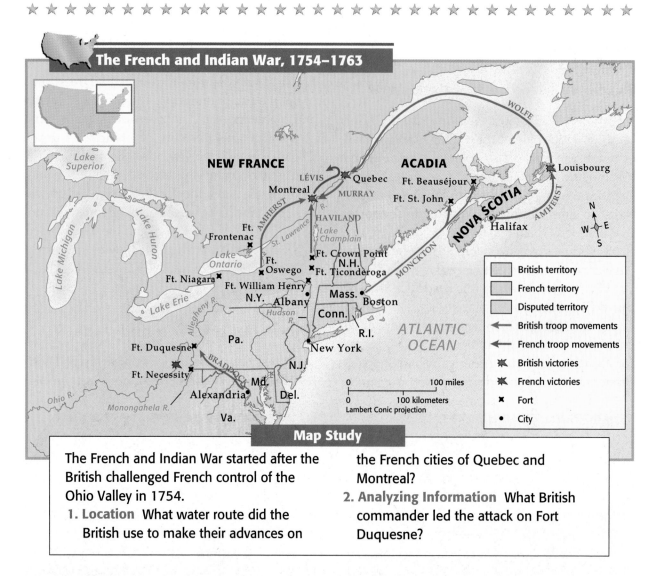

The French and Indian War, 1754–1763

Lake Superior

NEW FRANCE

LÉVIS — Quebec
Montreal
MURRAY

ACADIA

Louisbourg

Ft. Beauséjour
Ft. St. John

WOLFE

AMHERST

NOVA SCOTIA

Halifax

AMHERST

Ft. Frontenac

HAVILAND

Lake Champlain

Ft. Crown Point
N.H.
Ft. Ticonderoga

MONCKTON

Lake Michigan

Lake Huron

Ft. Niagara

Lake Ontario

Ft. Oswego

Ft. William Henry
N.Y.

Albany

Mass.

Boston

Lake Erie

Allegheny R.

Conn.

R.I.

ATLANTIC OCEAN

Hudson R.

Pa.

New York

British territory

French territory

Disputed territory

British troop movements

French troop movements

British victories

French victories

Fort

City

Ft. Duquesne

BRADDOCK

Ft. Necessity

Ohio R.

Monongahela R.

Alexandria

Md.

Del.

N.J.

0   100 miles
0   100 kilometers
Lambert Conic projection

Va.

Map Study

The French and Indian War started after the British challenged French control of the Ohio Valley in 1754.

1. **Location** What water route did the British use to make their advances on the French cities of Quebec and Montreal?

2. **Analyzing Information** What British commander led the attack on Fort Duquesne?

Seven Years' War. During the war, French, British, and Spanish forces clashed in Cuba, the West Indies, India, and the Philippines as well as in North America and Europe.

The first years of the war were disastrous for the British and their American colonies. Native Americans used the roads that Braddock's troops cut and the bridges they built to raid frontier farms from Virginia to Pennsylvania. They killed settlers, burned farmhouses and crops, and drove many families back toward the coast. French forces from Canada captured British forts at Lake Ontario and at Lake George.

Pitt Takes Charge

Great Britain's fortunes improved after **William Pitt** came to power as secretary of state and then prime minister. An outstanding military planner, Pitt knew how to pick skilled commanders. He oversaw the war effort from London.

To avoid having to deal with constant arguments from the colonies about the cost of the war, Pitt decided that Great Britain would pay for supplies needed in the war—no matter the cost. In doing so Pitt ran up an enormous debt. After the French and Indian War, the British raised the colonists' taxes to help pay this debt. Pitt had only delayed the moment when the colonists had to pay their share of the bill.

Pitt wanted more than just a clear path to the Western territories. He also intended to conquer French Canada. He sent British troops to North America under the command of such energetic officers as **Jeffrey Amherst** and **James Wolfe.**

In 1758 Amherst and Wolfe led a British assault that recaptured the fortress at Louisbourg. That same year a group of New Englanders, led by

British officers, captured Fort Frontenac at Lake Ontario. Still another British force marched across Pennsylvania and captured Fort Duquesne.

The Fall of New France

⭐ The year 1759 brought so many British victories that people said the church bells of London wore thin with joyous ringing. The British captured Guadeloupe in the West Indies, the city of Havana in Cuba, defeated the French in India, and destroyed a French fleet that had been sent to reinforce Canada. The greatest victory of the year, though, took place in the heart of New France.

The Battle of Quebec

Perched high atop a cliff overlooking the St. Lawrence River, **Quebec,** the capital of New France, was thought to be impossible to attack. In September 1759, British general James Wolfe found a way.

One of Wolfe's scouts spotted a poorly guarded path up the back of the cliff. Wolfe's soldiers overwhelmed the guards posted on the path and then scrambled up the path during the night. The British troops assembled outside the fortress of Quebec on a field called the **Plains of Abraham.** There they surprised and defeated the French army. James Wolfe died in the battle. The French commander, the Marquis de Montcalm, was mortally wounded and died the next day.

The Treaty of Paris

The fall of Quebec and General Amherst's capture of Montreal the following year brought the fighting in North America between France and Britain to an end. In the **Treaty of Paris** of 1763, France was permitted to keep its sugar-producing islands in the West Indies, but it was forced to give up Canada and its lands east of the Mississippi River to Great Britain. From Spain, France's ally, Great Britain gained Florida. In return, Spain received French lands west of the Mississippi River—the Louisiana Territory—as well as the port of New Orleans.

The Treaty of Paris marked the end of France as a power in North America. The continent was now divided between Great Britain and Spain with the Mississippi River marking the boundary. While the French and British were working out a plan for the future of North America, many Native Americans still lived on the lands covered by the European agreement.

Trouble on the Frontier

⭐ The British victory over the French dealt a blow to the Native Americans of the Ohio River valley. They had lost their French allies and trading partners. Although they continued to trade with the British, the Indians regarded them as enemies. The British raised the prices of their goods and, unlike the French, refused to pay rent for their forts. Worst of all, British settlers began moving into the Monongahela and Susquehanna River valleys in western Pennsylvania.

Pontiac's War

Pontiac, chief of an Ottawa village near Detroit, recognized that the British settlers threatened the Native American way of life. Just as Benjamin Franklin had tried to bring the colonies together with the Albany Plan, Pontiac wanted to join Indian groups to fight the British.

In the spring of 1763, Pontiac put together an alliance of Native American peoples. He laid

Acadians

The French colonists in Nova Scotia were called Acadians. In 1755 the British forced thousands of Acadians to leave Nova Scotia. Some of them made their way to Louisiana. They were the ancestors of today's French-speaking Louisiana Cajuns. The name *Cajun* is derived from the word *Acadian.*

Chief Pontiac

siege to the British fort at **Detroit** while other war parties captured most of the other British outposts in the Great Lakes region. That summer Native Americans killed settlers along the Pennsylvania and Virginia frontiers in a series of raids called **Pontiac's War.**

The Native Americans, however, failed to capture the important strongholds of Niagara, Fort Pitt, and Detroit. The war ended in late October, when Pontiac learned that the French had

signed the Treaty of Paris. He broke off the siege of Detroit. Pennsylvania settlers took their revenge by attacking peaceful Indian villages.

Geography

The Proclamation of 1763

To prevent more fighting, the British government called a halt to the settlers' westward expansion. In the **Proclamation of 1763,** King George III of Great Britain declared that the Appalachian Mountains were the temporary western boundary for all the colonies. Governors were forbidden to grant land west of the Appalachians to settlers without the king's permission.

The proclamation angered many people, especially those who owned shares in land companies, such as the Ohio Company of Virginia. These wealthy speculators, or investors, from the East had already bought property west of the mountains. They were furious with Britain for ignoring their land claims.

Although the end of the French and Indian War brought peace for the first time in many years, the Proclamation of 1763 created friction between Britain and the colonies. More conflicts would soon arise between the government in Britain and the colonists in North America.

Section 4 Assessment

Checking for Understanding

1. **Identify** General Edward Braddock, Fort Duquesne, Seven Years' War, William Pitt, Quebec, Treaty of Paris, Pontiac's War, Proclamation of 1763.
2. **Define** speculator.
3. **Name** the three nations involved in the Seven Years' War and the areas in which the fighting took place.

Reviewing Themes

4. **Individual Action** How did Pontiac plan to protect the people in his village and

other Native Americans from British settlers?

Critical Thinking

5. **Identifying Alternatives** What do you think General Braddock could have done to increase his soldiers' chances of defeating the French?

Activity

Making a Map Sketch a map showing the land claims of Great Britain, France, and Spain in North America after the Treaty of Paris.

Understanding Cause and Effect

Causes and Effects

CAUSES

★ Colonists need to grow cash crops, such as tobacco and rice.
★ European demand for tobacco and rice increases.
★ Growing tobacco and rice requires large labor force.

Slave Trade Emerges

EFFECTS

★ Africans are robbed of basic human rights.
★ African American population grows.
★ Slavery creates feelings of injustice and plants seeds of regional conflict.

You know that if you watch television instead of completing your homework, you will receive poor grades. This is an example of a cause-and-effect relationship. The cause—watching television instead of doing homework—leads to an effect—poor grades.

When you look for why or how an event or a chain of events took place, you are developing the skill of understanding causes and effects.

Learning the Skill

A *cause* is any person, event, or condition that makes something happen. What happens as a result is known as an *effect*. These guidelines will help you identify cause and effect:

• Look for "clue words" that alert you to cause and effect, such as *because, led to, brought about, produced,* and *therefore.*
• Look for logical relationships between events, such as "She did this, and then that happened."

In a chain of historical events, one effect often becomes the cause of other effects. The chart above shows such a chain of events.

Practicing the Skill

Study the cause-and-effect chart on this page. Then answer the questions below.

1. What were some causes of the development of slavery in the colonies?
2. What were some of the short-term effects of enslaving Africans?
3. What was the long-term effect of the development of slavery?

Applying the Skill

Understanding Cause and Effect Read an account of a recent event or chain of events in your community as reported in a local newspaper. Determine at least one cause and one effect of that event. Show the cause-and-effect relationship in a chart.

Glencoe's **Skillbuilder Interactive Workbook, Level 1** provides instruction and practice in key social studies skills.

Assessment and Activities

★ Reviewing Key Terms

On a sheet of paper, define the following terms:

subsistence farming
triangular trade
cash crop
diversity
Tidewater
backcountry
overseer
mercantilism
export
import

smuggling
charter colony
proprietary colony
apprentice
literacy
Iroquois Confederacy
militia
speculator

★ Reviewing Key Facts

1. Why did the population of the English colonies grow rapidly during the 1700s?
2. What differences existed between the Tidewater planters and the backcountry farmers of the Southern Colonies?
3. What was England's reason for passing the Navigation Acts?
4. What was the Enlightenment?
5. What North American land claims were the French forced to give up in the Treaty of Paris?
6. Why did the Proclamation of 1763 cause friction between Great Britain and the colonies?

★ Critical Thinking

Identifying Alternatives

The Albany Plan of Union was an effort to unite the colonies in their war against France.

1. Do you think the plan could have been changed to make it more acceptable to the colonies? Explain.
2. What incentives could have been used to interest the colonies in the Albany Plan?

★ Time Line Activity

Create a time line on which you place the following events in chronological order.

- Puritans found Harvard College
- French and Indian War ends
- England passes Navigation Acts
- French and Indian War begins
- Great Awakening begins

★ Reviewing Themes

1. **Economic Factors** How did the economies of the Northern Colonies and Southern Colonies differ?
2. **Continuity and Change** In what ways did Benjamin Franklin exemplify the Enlightenment way of thinking?
3. **Groups and Institutions** How did the French relationship with Native Americans help the French in their conflicts with the British?
4. **Individual Action** What was George Washington's role in the French and Indian War?

★ Skill Practice Activity

Understanding Cause and Effect

Each sentence below illustrates a cause-and-effect relationship. On a separate sheet of paper, identify the cause(s) and the effect(s) in each sentence.

1. During the 1700s the population of the English colonies grew dramatically as a result of high immigration and a high birthrate.
2. To make certain that only England benefited from trade with the colonies, Parliament passed the Navigation Acts.
3. Because worship was so central to the Puritans, they built their towns around the church.

★ Geography Activity

People in the American colonies came from many different national and cultural backgrounds. Study the map below, which shows the national origins of colonists. Then answer the questions that follow.

1. **Place** What area is shown on the map?
2. **Movement** What group settled mostly along the Appalachian Mountains?
3. **Region** In what colony did most of the Dutch settle?
4. **Region** Which ethnic group was the most common throughout the colonies in 1760?

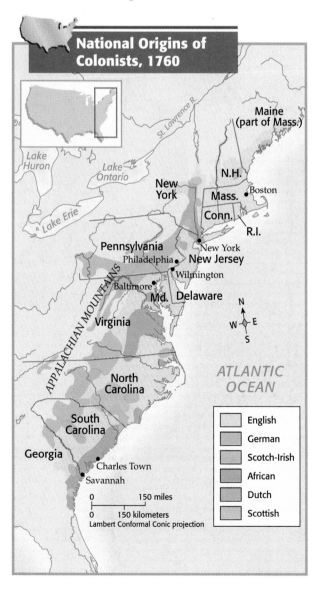

National Origins of Colonists, 1760

Maine (part of Mass.)
Lake Huron
Lake Ontario
N.H.
New York
Mass.
Boston
Conn.
R.I.
Lake Erie
Pennsylvania
New York
Philadelphia
New Jersey
Wilmington
Baltimore
Md.
Delaware
Virginia
APPALACHIAN MOUNTAINS
North Carolina
ATLANTIC OCEAN
South Carolina
Georgia
Charles Town
Savannah

St. Lawrence R.

N W E S

0   150 miles
0   150 kilometers
Lambert Conformal Conic projection

English
German
Scotch-Irish
African
Dutch
Scottish

★ Cooperative Activity

History and Geography Working with a partner, create a map showing a trade route that colonial merchants might use. To get started, examine maps and information from your text and from encyclopedias and historical atlases. Label the approximate points of departure and arrival. Include the physical features that the colonial merchants had to face, including rivers, mountains, lakes, and so on.

★ Technology Activity

Using an Electronic Card Catalog
Search the electronic card catalog of your local or school library for books about Benjamin Franklin. Skim the books to find a little-known fact about Franklin that you think is interesting or unusual. With your class, create a "Believe It or Not" booklet that contains the results of each student's fact-finding mission.

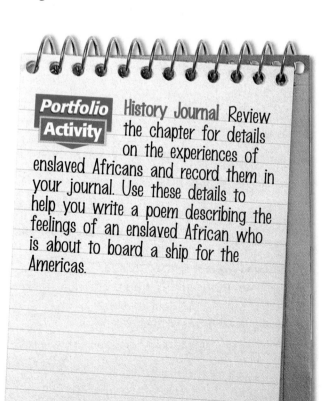

Portfolio Activity History Journal Review the chapter for details on the experiences of enslaved Africans and record them in your journal. Use these details to help you write a poem describing the feelings of an enslaved African who is about to board a ship for the Americas.

Unit 3

Creating a Nation

1763–1791

"Give me liberty, or give me death!"

—PATRICK HENRY, 1775

interNET CONNECTION

To learn more about the period of the American Revolution, visit the Glencoe Social Studies Web Site at www.glencoe.com for information, activities, and links to other sites.

MAPPING America

Portfolio Activity Draw a freehand outline map of the United States. As you read about events during the Revolutionary War, label their locations on your map. Include battles, confrontations, and important meetings. Illustrate at least three of your labels with sketches.

128

American flag, Revolutionary War

Liberty Bell

United States

1765
Stamp Act protests erupt

1770
Boston Massacre

1773
Boston Tea Party

1760

1770

1763
Treaty of Paris ends Seven Years' War in Europe

1772
Captain Cook explores the South Pacific

World

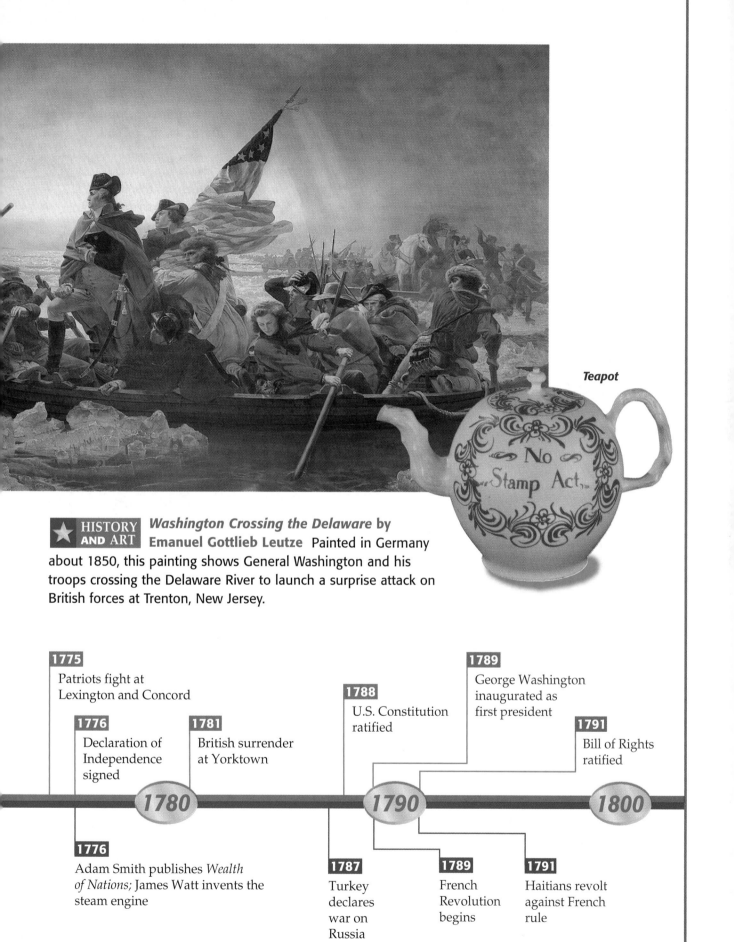

Teapot

No Stamp Act,

⭐ HISTORY AND ART **Washington Crossing the Delaware by Emanuel Gottlieb Leutze** Painted in Germany about 1850, this painting shows General Washington and his troops crossing the Delaware River to launch a surprise attack on British forces at Trenton, New Jersey.

1775
Patriots fight at Lexington and Concord

1776
Declaration of Independence signed

1781
British surrender at Yorktown

1788
U.S. Constitution ratified

1789
George Washington inaugurated as first president

1791
Bill of Rights ratified

1780

1790

1800

1776
Adam Smith publishes *Wealth of Nations;* James Watt invents the steam engine

1787
Turkey declares war on Russia

1789
French Revolution begins

1791
Haitians revolt against French rule

America's LITERATURE

Johnny Tremain

by Esther Forbes

Esther Forbes (1891–1967) wrote a number of books, among them the prize-winning biography Paul Revere and the World He Lived In. *As she researched Paul Revere's life, Forbes learned that many young apprentices played a role in the American Revolution.* Johnny Tremain, *a fictional work, tells the story of such an apprentice. Its setting is Massachusetts, where Forbes was born.*

■ READ TO DISCOVER

In this passage from *Johnny Tremain*, 14-year-old Johnny and his friend Rab have covered themselves with soot and disguised themselves as Mohawks. They race toward Griffin's Wharf in Boston Harbor, where three English ships carrying tea are docked and are unable to leave or unload their cargo.

■ READER'S DICTIONARY

boatswain: officer on a ship
warped: roped
jargon: strange language
hold: place where cargo is stored on a ship
hoists: lifting mechanisms
winch: machine for hauling

They were running so fast it seemed more like a dream of flying than reality.

The day had started with rain and then there had been clouds, but as they reached Griffin's Wharf the moon, full and white, broke free of the clouds. The three ships, the silent hundreds gathering upon the wharf, all were dipped in the pure white light. The crowds were becoming thousands, and there was not one there but guessed what was to be done, and all approved.

Rab was grunting out of the side of his mouth to a thick-set, active-looking man, whom Johnny would have known anywhere, by his walk and the confident lift of his head, was Mr. Revere. "Me Know You."

"Me Know You," Johnny repeated this countersign and took his place behind Mr. Revere. The other boys . . . began arriving. . . . Many who were now quietly joining one of those three groups were acting on the spur of the moment, seeing what was up. They had blacked their faces, seized axes, and come along. They were behaving as quietly and were as obedient to their leaders as those who had been so carefully picked for this work of destruction.

There was a boatswain's whistle, and in silence one group boarded the *Dartmouth*. The *Eleanor* and the *Beaver* had to be warped in to the wharf. Johnny was close to Mr. Revere's heels. He heard him calling for the captain, promising him, in the jargon everyone talked that night, that not one thing should be damaged on the ship except only the tea, but the captain and all his crew had best stay in the cabin until the work was over.

The Boston Tea Party

Captain Hall shrugged and did as he was told, leaving his cabin boy to hand over the keys to the hold. The boy was grinning with pleasure. The "tea party" was not unexpected.

"I'll show you," the boy volunteered, "how to work them hoists. I'll fetch lanterns, Mister."

The winches rattled and the heavy chests began to appear—one hundred and fifty of them. As some men worked in the hold, others broke open the chests and flung the tea into the harbor. But one thing made them unexpected difficulty. The tea inside the chests was wrapped in heavy canvas. . . .

Johnny and a parcel of boys brushed the deck until it was clean as a parlor floor. Then Mr. Revere called the captain to come up and inspect. The tea was utterly gone, but Captain Hall agreed that beyond that there had not been the slightest damage.

It was close upon dawn when the work on all three ships was done. And yet the great, silent audience on the wharf, men, women, and children, had not gone home. As the three groups came off the ships, they formed in fours along the wharf, their axes on their shoulders. Then a hurrah went up and a fife began to play. This was almost the first sound Johnny had heard since the tea party started—except only the crash of axes into sea chests, the squeak of hoists, and a few grunted orders.

Excerpt from *Johnny Tremain* by Esther Forbes. Copyright © 1943 by Esther Forbes Hoskins, © renewed 1971 by Linwood M. Erskine, Jr., Executor of the Estate of Esther Forbes Hoskins. Reprinted by permission of Houghton Mifflin Co. All rights reserved.

■ RESPONDING TO LITERATURE

1. Why was the "tea party" expected?
2. Why do you think Mr. Revere asked the captain to inspect the deck of the ship?

Activity

Making a Poster Imagine you lived in Boston during this time. Your town's government will not let the tea ships unload their cargo. Create a poster that either supports this position or opposes it.

1763–1776

Road to Independence

⭐ Why It's Important

Many of the issues that caused the colonists to declare independence remain important today. Americans still protest unfair taxation and attempts to limit the rights of citizens. The ideals and language of revolutionary America still play a major role in shaping the society we live in today.

⭐ Chapter Themes

- *Section 1*, Civic Rights and Responsibilities
- *Section 2*, Groups and Institutions
- *Section 3*, Groups and Institutions
- *Section 4*, Government and Democracy

PRIMARY SOURCES Library

See pages 944–945 for primary source readings to accompany Chapter 5

⭐ **HISTORY AND ART** *Pulling Down the Statue of George III* by William Walcutt
Patriots celebrating independence pulled down the statue of King George III in New York on July 9, 1776. The statue was later melted down into bullets to be used against the king's troops.

1763	**1764**	**1765**	**1767**
Proclamation of 1763 forbids settlement west of the Appalachians	Parliament passes Sugar Act	Parliament enacts Stamp Act	Townshend Acts tax colonial imports

Section 1

Taxation without Representation

READ TO DISCOVER . . .

■ why the British faced problems in North America after the French and Indian War.

■ why the American colonists objected to the new British laws.

TERMS TO LEARN

revenue	boycott
writs of assistance	nonimportation
resolution	repeal
effigy	

The Storyteller

Huron and Ottawa warriors silently peered from the woods. They watched about 100 British soldiers camped on Lake Erie's shore. The soldiers—sent by the British Crown—had just stopped to rest on their way to Fort Detroit. They were worried about rumors of Native Americans planning war.

Suddenly the warriors rushed from the forest. The British managed to escape in two boats. War raged on the frontier—and the British were in the thick of it!

St. Edward's crown, worn by George III

After winning the French and Indian War, Great Britain acquired a vast territory in North America. This land was not uninhabited. It was home to nearly 500,000 Native Americans. Conflicts over the use of this territory led to a series of Native American raids on British forts and villages along the western frontier. In attempting to resolve its difficulties with Native Americans, Britain created new problems with its American colonies.

Relations with Britain

★ The British took two measures to end the troubles with the Native Americans. First they planned to station 10,000 soldiers in the colonies and on the frontier. Then, in the Proclamation of 1763, they prohibited colonists from moving west of the Appalachian Mountains into Native American territory.

Growing Distrust

In 1763 most colonists were satisfied with the government in London. Few wanted or expected any major changes in their relationship with the king or with Parliament. However, these measures by the British alarmed the colonists. Many feared that the large number of British troops in North America might be used to interfere with their liberties. They saw the Proclamation of 1763

Chapter 5 Road to Independence 133

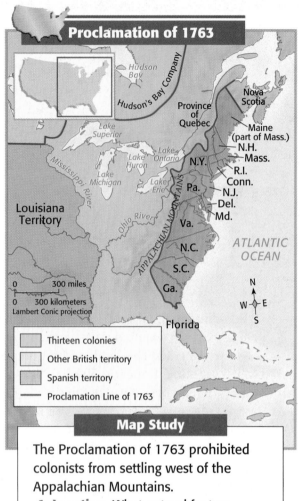

Proclamation of 1763

Map Study

The Proclamation of 1763 prohibited colonists from settling west of the Appalachian Mountains.

1. **Location** What natural feature marked the western boundary of British territory?

2. **Analyzing Information** Who controlled Louisiana Territory in 1763?

as a limit on their freedom. These two measures contributed to the feeling of distrust that was growing between Great Britain and its colonies.

Britain Needs Money

The financial problems of Great Britain complicated the situation. The British had amassed a huge public debt fighting the French and Indian War. Desperate for new revenue, or incoming money, the king and Parliament began to view their American colonies as a source of funds. They began plans to tax them. This decision set off a chain of events that enraged the American colonists and surprised British authorities.

Britain's Trade Laws

In 1764 **George Grenville,** the British finance minister, decided the American colonists should contribute more toward British expenses in North America. His first step was to take action against smuggling in the colonies. For the British smuggling to avoid import taxes meant lost revenue. Britain intended to monitor colonial trading more closely.

Enforcing Trade Laws

To catch colonists involved in smuggling, Grenville allowed customs officers to obtain general writs of assistance. These legal documents enabled the officers to search homes and warehouses for goods that might be smuggled. Many colonists considered Grenville's action as an outrageous abuse of power. They were horrified that government officials could come into their homes without warning.

The Sugar Act

Grenville next turned his attention to tax revenue. In 1764 Parliament passed the **Sugar Act** to stop the smuggling between the colonies and the French West Indies. The act lowered the tax on molasses imported by the colonists. The British hoped the lower tax would encourage colonists to pay the duty on foreign molasses. The British could then collect the tax on molasses and increase their revenues.

The Sugar Act also established special courts to hear smuggling cases. In these courts British-appointed judges, rather than juries, would decide whether accused smugglers were to be jailed. As British citizens, the colonists had enjoyed the right to a jury trial. But now, in the eyes of the colonists, the Sugar Act would take away this basic right.

These measures alarmed the colonists. Never before had their taxes been used to raise money for the British treasury. Leaders of New York's legislature declared, "There can be no liberty, no happiness, no security" with this interference in colonial life.

James Otis, a young lawyer in **Boston**, argued that colonists should not be taxed by Parliament because they could not vote for members of Parliament. Otis coined a memorable slogan for colonial protesters: "Taxation without representation is tyranny."

The Stamp Act

⭐ In 1765 Parliament passed another, even more disturbing, law in an effort to raise money for Britain. This law, the **Stamp Act,** placed a tax on almost all printed material in the colonies—everything from newspapers and pamphlets to wills and playing cards. All printed material had to have a stamp, which was applied by British colonial officials. Because the tax pertained to so many items, it affected everyone in the colonial cities. The Stamp Act was a terrible nuisance, but it also convinced many colonists of the need for united action.

Opposition to the Stamp Act focused on two points. Parliament had interfered in colonial affairs by taxing the colonies directly. In addition, it taxed the colonists without their consent. In passing the Stamp Act without consulting the colonial legislatures, Parliament ignored the colonial tradition of self-government. 💲

Protesting the Stamp Act

⭐ A young member of the **Virginia** House of Burgesses, **Patrick Henry,** persuaded the burgesses to take action against the Stamp Act. When opponents accused him of treason, Henry replied, "If this be treason, make the most of it!" The Virginia assembly passed a resolution—a formal expression of opinion—declaring it had "the only and sole exclusive right and power to lay taxes" on its citizens.

Protest mounted in Boston as well. **Samuel Adams** helped start an organization called the **Sons of Liberty.** Members took to the streets to protest the Stamp Act. People in other cities also organized Sons of Liberty groups. Throughout the summer of 1765, protesters burned effigies—rag figures—representing unpopular tax collectors. They

Revenue stamp

also ransacked and destroyed houses belonging to royal officials and marched through the streets shouting that only Americans had the right to tax Americans.

In the colonial cities, people refused to use the stamps. They urged merchants to boycott—refuse to buy—British and European goods in protest. Thousands of merchants, artisans, and farmers signed nonimportation agreements. In these agreements, they pledged not to import or use goods imported from Great Britain. As the boycott spread, British merchants lost so much business that they begged Parliament to repeal, or cancel, the Stamp Act.

In **New York** Major Thomas James, the officer in charge of the stamps, vowed to enforce the Stamp Act no matter what the consequences. The

---

𝓕ootnotes to History

Friendly Persuasion? The Sons of Liberty had an effective way of getting what they wanted from British officials. They merely sent a note asking: "What think you of . . . ten gallons of liquid tar [poured] on your [head]—with the feathers of a dozen wild geese laid over that to enliven your appearance? Your friends . . . THE COMMITTEE OF TARRING AND FEATHERING."

⭐ **HISTORY AND ART** *Patrick Henry Before the Virginia House of Burgesses* **by Peter F. Rothermel** Patrick Henry gave a fiery speech before the Virginia House of Burgesses in 1765. **Why did Henry deliver the speech?**

consequences turned out to be a rampaging mob that raided his home. An observer reported:

❝The multitude burst open the doors, proceeded to destroy every individual article the house contained: the beds they cut open, and threw the feathers abroad; broke all the glasses, china, tables, chairs, desks, trunks, chests; made a large fire, [and] threw in everything that would burn. ❞

In October delegates from nine colonies met in New York at the **Stamp Act Congress.** They drafted a petition to the king and Parliament declaring that the colonies could not be taxed except by their own assemblies.

Britain Repeals the Stamp Act

In February 1766, Parliament gave in to the colonists' demands and repealed the Stamp Act. Yet the colonists' trust in the king and Parliament was never fully restored.

While the colonists celebrated their victory over the Stamp Act, Parliament passed another act with far-reaching consequences. The **Declaratory Act** of 1766 stated that Parliament had the right to tax and make decisions for the British colonies "in all cases whatsoever." The colonists might have won one battle, but the war over making decisions for the colonies had just begun.

New Taxes

⭐ Soon after the Stamp Act crisis, a new British finance minister, **Charles Townshend,** made another attempt to raise money in the colonies. He thought he knew how to do this without creating another crisis.

The Townshend Acts

Under Townshend's leadership Parliament passed a set of laws in 1767 that came to be known as the **Townshend Acts.** In these acts the British leaders tried to avoid some of the problems the Stamp Act caused. They understood that the colonists would not tolerate internal taxes—those levied or paid inside the colonies. As a result the new taxes applied only to imported goods, with the tax being paid at the port of entry. The goods taxed, however, included basic items—such as

Linking PAST & PRESENT

Boycotts

The boycott has served as a form of protest throughout our country's history. One successful boycott in the twentieth century was the 1955–56 bus boycott in Montgomery, Alabama. African Americans—40,000 a day—refused to ride the city-owned buses until the bus company stopped segregated seating.

glass, tea, paper, and lead—that the colonists had to import because they did not produce them.

New courts were set up to try cases under the Townshend Acts. Some of the tax revenue was to go to pay for these courts. The British authorities planned also to use this revenue to pay the British governors in the colonies. In the past, the governors had been paid by the colonial local assemblies, supported by various taxes paid by the colonists. Under the new plan, the British, not the local assemblies, would pay the governors. The colonists would lose this means of controlling the British officials.

By this time the colonists were outraged by *any* taxes Parliament imposed. They believed that only their own representatives had the right to levy taxes on them. The colonists responded by reviving the boycott that had worked so well against the Stamp Act. The boycott proved to be even more widespread this time.

Colonial Women Organize Protests

Women took an active role in the protest against the Townshend Acts. In towns throughout the colonies, women organized groups to support the boycott of British goods, sometimes calling themselves the **Daughters of Liberty.**

★ **Picturing HISTORY** To protest the Stamp Act, angry colonists burned stamps in the streets. **What group formed in Boston to lead opposition to the act?**

They urged Americans to wear homemade fabrics and produce other goods that were previously available only from Britain. In this way, they believed, the American colonies could become economically independent.

Section 1 Assessment

★ ★ ★ ★ ★   ★ ★ ★ ★ ★

Checking for Understanding
1. *Identify* George Grenville, Sugar Act, Boston, Stamp Act, Virginia, Patrick Henry, Samuel Adams, Sons of Liberty, New York, Townshend Acts, Daughters of Liberty.
2. *Define* revenue, writs of assistance, resolution, effigy, boycott, nonimportation, repeal.
3. *State* two reasons that relations between the British and the colonists began to deteriorate.

Reviewing Themes
4. **Civic Rights and Responsibilities** Why did the colonists think the writs of assistance infringed on their rights?

Critical Thinking
5. **Identifying Cause and Effect** Why did the British think the colonists would tolerate the Townshend Acts when they did not tolerate the Stamp Act?

Activity

Making a Poster Design a poster that encourages colonists to boycott British goods.

Section 2

Building Colonial Unity

READ TO DISCOVER . . .
- why Boston colonists and British soldiers clashed in the Boston Massacre.
- how the British government tried to maintain its control over the colonies.

TERMS TO LEARN
propaganda
committee of correspondence

Storyteller

In the summer of 1768, British customs officials in Boston seized the *Liberty*, a ship belonging to John Hancock, a prominent merchant and protest leader. The ship had docked in Boston Harbor to unload a shipment of wine and take on new supplies. The customs officials, however, charged that Hancock was using the ship for smuggling. As news of the ship's seizure spread through Boston, angry townspeople filled the streets. They shouted against Parliament and the taxes it had imposed on them.

The *Liberty* affair became one of the events that united the colonists against British policies.

DONT TREAD ON ME

American protest banner

In the summer of 1768, nervous customs officers sent word back to Britain that the colonies were on the brink of rebellion. Parliament responded by ordering two regiments of troops to Boston. On October 1, 1768, a fleet of British ships sailed into **Boston Harbor** and docked. Seven hundred soldiers in red uniforms filed out of the ships with "muskets charged, bayonets fixed, colours flying, drums beating and fifes playing." As angry Bostonians jeered, the "redcoats" marched right into the center of the city and set up camp.

Trouble in Boston

Many colonists, especially those living in Boston, felt that the British had pushed them too far. First the British had passed a series of laws that violated colonial rights. Now they sent an army to occupy colonial cities.

Tension Grows

To make matters worse, the soldiers who were stationed in Boston acted rudely and sometimes even violently toward the colonists. Mostly poor men from Ireland, Scotland, and rural England, the redcoats earned little pay. Some of them stole goods from local shops or scuffled with boys who taunted them in the streets. The soldiers competed off-hours for jobs that Bostonians wanted. Fights broke out between redcoats and Bostonians. The townspeople's hatred for the soldiers grew every day.

The Boston Massacre

Throughout the next year, the tense atmosphere between the redcoats and the Boston colonists grew. On March 5, 1770, the tension finally reached a peak.

That day a fight broke out between townspeople and soldiers. This spurred the crowd on. While some British officers tried to calm the crowd, a man shouted, "We did not send for you. We will not have you here. We'll get rid of you, we'll drive you away!"

The angry townspeople moved on through the streets, picking up sticks, stones, shovels, and clubs—any weapon they could find. They pushed forward toward the customshouse on King Street.

As the crowd approached, the sentry on duty panicked and called for help. Seven soldiers stationed nearby rushed into the street to confront the raging crowd. The crowd responded by throwing stones, snowballs, oyster shells, and pieces of wood at the soldiers. "Fire, you bloodybacks, you lobsters," the crowd screamed. "You dare not fire."

After one of the soldiers was knocked down, the nervous and confused redcoats did fire. Seven shots rang out, killing five colonists. One Bostonian cried out: "Are the inhabitants to be knocked down in the streets? Are they to be murdered in this manner?" Among the dead was **Crispus Attucks,** an African American dockworker who some said was the leader of the crowd. The colonists called the tragic encounter the **Boston Massacre.**

The Word Spreads

Colonial leaders used the killings as propaganda—information designed to influence opinion—against the British. Samuel Adams put up posters describing the "Boston Massacre" as a slaughter of innocent Americans by bloodthirsty redcoats. An engraving by **Paul Revere** showed a British officer giving the order to open fire on an orderly crowd. Nearly every colonist in Boston

Restrictions on Colonial Trade, 1650–1750	
Acts	**Restrictions**
Navigation Acts 1650, 1651, 1660–1661, 1696	Only English-owned and -crewed ships could carry on colonial trade. Tobacco, cotton, indigo, and other colonial products could be sent only to England. Colonial trade laws had to agree with the Navigation Acts.
Woolen Act 1699	Prohibited the colonial exports of wool or wool products.
Hat Act 1732	Prohibited the exporting of hats from one colony to another.
Molasses Act 1733	Levied a large duty on foreign sugar, molasses, and rum.
Iron Act 1750	Prohibited building of new colonial iron plants. Prohibited colonial import duties on iron bought from Britain.

Chart Study

British trade acts affected many American products.

1. Which trade act dealt with food products?
2. **Drawing Conclusions** Which trade act was passed to protect the British sheep-farming industry?

saw copies of the engraving. The powerful image inflamed anti-British feeling.

The Boston Massacre led many colonists to call for stronger boycotts on British goods. Aware of the growing opposition to its policies, Parliament repealed all the Townshend Acts taxes except the one on tea. Many colonists believed they had won another victory. They ended their boycotts, except on the taxed tea, and started to trade with British merchants again.

Some colonial leaders, however, continued to call for resistance to British rule. In 1772 Samuel Adams revived the Boston committee of correspondence, an organization used in earlier protests. The committee circulated writings about colonists' grievances against Britain. Soon other

This tea chest and bottled tea were among the items heaved into Boston Harbor at the Boston Tea Party.

TEA THROWN INTO BOSTON HARBOR DEC 16 1773.

committees of correspondence sprang up throughout the colonies, bringing together protesters opposed to British measures.

A Crisis over Tea

★ In the early 1770s, some Americans considered British colonial policy a "conspiracy against liberty." The British government's actions in 1773 seemed to confirm that view.

The British East India Company had acquired much more tea than it could sell in Britain. If it could not sell the extra tea, it faced ruin. For both economic and political reasons, the British government wanted to keep the company in business.

To save the East India Company, Parliament passed the **Tea Act** of 1773. This measure gave the company the right to ship tea to the colonies without paying most of the taxes usually placed on tea. It also allowed the company to bypass colonial

merchants and sell its tea directly to shopkeepers at a low price. This meant that East India Company tea was cheaper than any other tea in the colonies. The Tea Act gave the company a very favorable advantage over colonial merchants.

Colonial Demands

Colonial merchants immediately called for a new boycott on British goods. Samuel Adams and others denounced the British monopoly. The Tea Act, they exclaimed, was just another attempt to crush the colonists' liberty.

At mass meetings in Boston and Philadelphia, colonists vowed to stop the East India Company's ships from unloading. The Daughters of Liberty issued a pamphlet declaring that rather than part with freedom, "we'll part with our tea." Women in Wilmington, North Carolina, marched solemnly through town and burned their tea.

Although some British politicians warned of another crisis with the colonies, Parliament ignored the warnings. The East India Company loaded its ships with the tea and set sail for America. In all colonial ports except Boston, colonists forced the ships' captains to turn around and go back to Great Britain.

The Boston Tea Party

Three tea ships docked in Boston Harbor in December 1773. The royal governor, whose house had been destroyed by Stamp Act protesters, refused to let the ships turn back. When he ordered the tea unloaded, Adams and the Boston Sons of Liberty acted swiftly. On December 16 a group of men disguised as Mohawks and armed with hatchets marched to the wharves. At midnight they boarded the ships and threw 342 chests of tea overboard, an event that became known as the **Boston Tea Party.**

Word of this dramatic act of defiance spread throughout the colonies. Men and women poured into the streets to celebrate the Boston Sons of Liberty for boldly championing the colonial cause. Yet no one spoke of challenging British rule, and colonial leaders continued to press their claims as members of the British empire.

---

*F*ootnotes to History

Tough Defense John Adams, who would become America's second president, served as a defense attorney for the British soldiers accused in the Boston Massacre.

★ ★

The Intolerable Acts

★ When news of the Boston Tea Party reached London, the reaction was quite different. King **George III** realized that Britain was losing control of the colonies. "We must master them or leave them to themselves." Not prepared to give up, the king and Parliament vowed to punish Boston.

Lord North, the British prime minister, decided to make an example of Massachusetts. In the spring of 1774, Parliament passed the **Coercive Acts,** very harsh laws intended to make Massachusetts pay for its resistance.

Punishing Boston

The Coercive Acts closed Boston Harbor until the Massachusetts colonists paid for the ruined tea. This action prevented the arrival of food and other supplies that normally came by ship. Even worse the laws took away many of the rights of the Massachusetts colonists. For example, the laws prohibited most town meetings, an important form of self-government in New England.

As a final insult, the Coercive Acts forced Bostonians to shelter soldiers in their own homes. The British Parliament wished to isolate Boston with these acts. Instead the other colonies sent food and clothing to demonstrate their support

★ **HISTORY AND ART** *King George III* by Johann Zoffany An energetic leader, George III strongly opposed any compromise with the American colonists. **How did George III and Parliament respond to news of the Boston Tea Party?**

for Boston. The feelings of the colonists were made clear by *their* name for the new laws—the Intolerable Acts.

★ ★ ★ ★ ★ Section 2 Assessment ★ ★ ★ ★ ★

Checking for Understanding

1. **Identify** Boston Harbor, Crispus Attucks, Boston Massacre, Paul Revere, Boston Tea Party, George III, Coercive Acts.

2. **Define** propaganda, committee of correspondence.

3. **Explain** how colonial leaders used the Boston Massacre to their advantage.

Reviewing Themes

4. **Groups and Institutions** Why were the committees of correspondence powerful?

Critical Thinking

5. **Drawing Conclusions** Why do you think some saw the Boston Tea Party as a turning point in the relationship between the British and the colonists?

Activity

Drawing a Cartoon Draw a cartoon strip showing the story of the Boston Tea Party. Use at least four cartoon frames to tell the story from your point of view.

1774
First Continental
Congress meets

April 19, 1775
Battles of Lexington
and Concord are
fought

May 10, 1775
Ethan Allen
captures Fort
Ticonderoga

June 17, 1775
Battle of Bunker
Hill is fought

Section 3

A Call to Arms

READ TO DISCOVER . . .
- what happened at the Continental Congress in Philadelphia.
- how the colonists met British soldiers in the first resort to arms.

TERMS TO LEARN
militia   Loyalist
minutemen   Patriot

The Storyteller

At first few colonists wanted a complete break with Britain. One of the most popular songs of the time, "The Bold Americans," called for *both* liberty and continued loyalty to the British king:

We'll honor George, our sovereign, while he
*   sits on the throne.*
If he grants us liberty, no other king we'll own.
If he will grant us liberty, so plainly shall you
*   see,*
We are the boys
*   that fear no*
noise! Success to
*   liberty.*

As tensions mounted, however, a peaceful compromise no longer was possible.

Revolutionary War drum and fife

With the passage of the Intolerable Acts, the colonial leaders realized that they must be more vigorous in protesting the abuses from their British rulers. The outpouring of sympathy for Bostonians demonstrated that the people wanted them to continue resisting new taxes. Bostonians vowed to boycott all British goods, but something new was needed—a gathering of the colonial leaders. From Massachusetts to Virginia, word spread through the committees of correspondence: the colonies must unite in protest or lose their liberties.

Citizenship

The Continental Congress

★ In September 1774, 56 men arrived in Philadelphia. Sent as delegates from all the colonies except Georgia, these men had come to establish a political body to represent the American interests. They called the new organization the **Continental Congress.**

Delegates to the Congress

Major political leaders from all the colonies attended the Congress. Massachusetts sent fiery Samuel Adams and his younger cousin **John Adams,** a successful lawyer. New York sent **John Jay,** another lawyer. From Virginia came **Richard Henry Lee** and **Patrick Henry,** two of the most outspoken defenders of colonial rights, as well as **George Washington.**

Patrick Henry summed up the meaning of the gathering. "The distinctions between Virginians, Pennsylvanians, New Yorkers, and New Englanders are no more," he said. "I am not a Virginian, but an American."

Decisions of the Congress

Although the delegates were hardly united in their views, they managed to work together in behalf of their common interests. First they drafted a statement of grievances calling for the repeal of 13 acts of Parliament passed since 1763. They declared that these laws violated the colonists' rights. Their rights were based on the "laws of nature, the principles of the English constitution, and the several charters" of the colonies. The delegates also voted to boycott all British goods and trade. No British products could be brought into or consumed in the colonies, and no colonial goods could be shipped to Britain.

Perhaps the most important decision the Congress made concerned armed opposition to Britain. After much debate the delegates passed a resolution to form militias, groups of citizen soldiers. If fighting broke out, the colonies would be ready with their own armed forces. People in the colonies and in Britain wondered whether this meant war. The answer came soon after the Continental Congress adjourned in October.

Causes and Effects

CAUSES

★ Colonists' tradition of self-government
★ Americans' desire for a separate identity from Britain
★ Proclamation of 1763
★ British policies toward North America after 1763

Colonies Declare Independence

EFFECTS

★ A long war with Great Britain
★ Self-government for the United States
★ World recognition of United States independence

Chart Study

The conflict between Britain and America worsened after passage of the Intolerable Acts of 1774.
Analyzing Information What did the British learn after the Battle of Bunker Hill?

The First Battles

★ Colonists expected that if fighting against the British broke out, it would begin in New England. Militia companies in Massachusetts held frequent training sessions, made bullets, and stockpiled rifles and muskets. Some companies, known as minutemen, boasted they would be ready to fight on a minute's notice. In the winter of 1774–1775, a British officer stationed in Boston noted in his diary: "The people are evidently making every preparation for resistance. They are taking every means to provide themselves with arms."

*F*ootnotes to History

Midnight Ride In 1861 poet Henry Wadsworth Longfellow described Paul Revere's ride: *"Listen, my children, and you shall hear/ Of the midnight ride of Paul Revere."* For Longfellow, the ride marked a momentous event in the nation's history. *"The fate of a nation was riding that night;/ And the spark struck out by that steed in his flight,/ Kindled the land into flame with its heat."*

Britain Sends Troops

The British, also, prepared for conflict. George III announced to Parliament that the New England colonies were "in a state of rebellion" and said that "blows must decide" who would control America. By April 1775, British general Sir Thomas Gage had 3,000 soldiers under his command in and around Boston, with many more on the way. Gage had instructions to take away the weapons of the Massachusetts militia and arrest the leaders of the colony's resistance movement.

Gage learned that the militia was storing arms and ammunition at **Concord,** a town 20 miles northwest of Boston. He ordered 700 troops under Major John Pitcairn to move out of Boston "to Concord, where you will seize and destroy all the artillery and ammunition you can find."

Alerting the Colonists

On the night of April 18, 1775, Dr. Joseph Warren walked the streets of Boston, looking for any unusual activity by the British army. He saw a regiment form ranks in Boston Common and then begin to march out of the city.

Warren rushed to alert **Paul Revere** and **William Dawes,** leading members of the Sons of Liberty. Revere and Dawes rode to **Lexington,** a town east of Concord, to warn **Samuel Adams** and **John Hancock** that the British were coming.

Revere galloped off across the moonlit countryside, shouting, "The regulars are out!" to the people and houses he passed along the way. When he reached Lexington, he raced to tell Adams and Hancock his news. Adams could barely control his excitement. "What a glorious morning this is!" Adams was ready to fight for American independence.

Fighting at Lexington and Concord

At dawn the redcoats under Major Pitcairn approached Lexington. When they reached the center of the town, they came across a group of

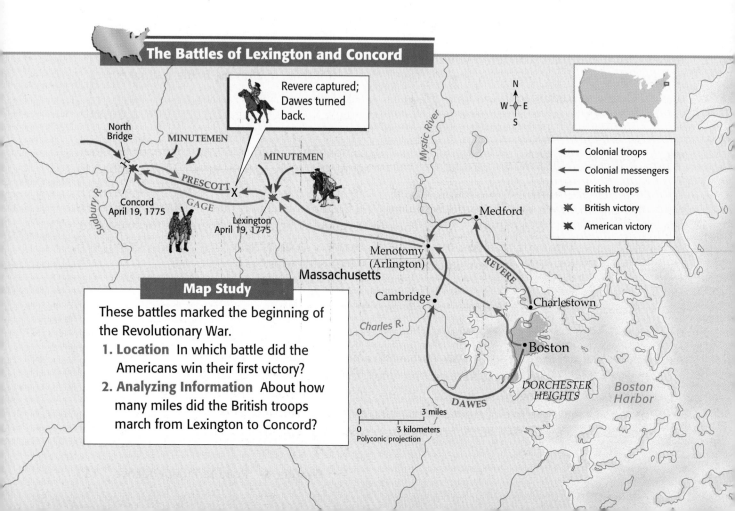

The Battles of Lexington and Concord

Revere captured; Dawes turned back.

Colonial troops
Colonial messengers
British troops
British victory
American victory

Map Study

These battles marked the beginning of the Revolutionary War.

1. **Location** In which battle did the Americans win their first victory?
2. **Analyzing Information** About how many miles did the British troops march from Lexington to Concord?

about 70 minutemen who had been alerted by Revere and Dawes. Led by Captain John Parker, the minutemen had positioned themselves on the town common with muskets in hand.

A minuteman reported, "There suddenly appeared a number of the King's troops, about a thousand . . . the foremost of which cried, 'Throw down your arms, ye villains, ye rebels.'" A shot was fired, and then both sides let loose with a barrage. When the fighting was over, eight minutemen lay dead.

The British troops continued their march to Concord. When they arrived there, they discovered that most of the militia's gunpowder had already been removed. They destroyed the remaining supplies, turned around, and headed back to Boston. Now the minutemen were waiting for them.

Messengers on horseback had spread word of the British movements. All along the road from Concord to Boston, farmers, blacksmiths, saddle makers, and clerks hid behind trees, rocks, and stone fences. As the British marched down the road, the militia fired. A British officer wrote, "These fellows were generally good marksmen, and many of them used long guns made for duck shooting." By the time the redcoats reached Boston, more than 200 were wounded and 73 were dead.

Looking back, the poet Ralph Waldo Emerson wrote in "The Concord Hymn" that the Americans at Lexington and Concord had fired the "shot heard 'round the world." The battle for America's independence from Great Britain had begun. 🔍

More Military Action

★ A few weeks later, on May 10, more fighting broke out. Leading a small group of New Englanders known as the **Green Mountain Boys, Ethan Allen** captured the British **Fort Ticonderoga** on Lake Champlain. The British were caught by surprise. When Allen called for them to surrender "in the name of . . . the Continental Congress," the British commander obeyed.

Building Forces

Following the battles of Lexington and Concord, the committees of correspondence sent out calls for volunteers to join the militias. Soon the colonial militia assembled around Boston was 20,000 strong. For several weeks, the American and British armies waited nervously for the other to make the next move.

 HISTORY AND ART *Battle of Bunker Hill* by **Alonzo Chappel** The Battle of Bunker Hill showed that the untrained American militia could match the professional British army. **Where is Bunker Hill located?**

The Battle of Bunker Hill

On June 16, 1775, about 1,200 militiamen under the command of Colonel William Prescott set up fortifications at Bunker Hill and nearby Breed's Hill, across the harbor from Boston.

The British decided to drive the Americans from their strategic locations overlooking the city. The next day redcoats crossed the harbor and assembled at the bottom of Breed's Hill. Bayonets drawn, they charged up the hill. With his forces low on ammunition, Colonel Prescott reportedly shouted the order, "Don't fire until you see the whites of their eyes." The Americans opened fire, forcing the British to retreat. The redcoats charged two more times, receiving furious fire. In the end the Americans ran out of gunpowder and had to withdraw.

The British won the **Battle of Bunker Hill** but suffered heavy losses—more than 1,000 dead and wounded. As one British officer wrote in his diary, "A dear bought victory, another such would have ruined us." The British had learned that defeating the Americans on the battlefield would not be quick or easy.

Choosing Sides

As American colonists heard about these battles, they faced a major decision. Should they join the rebels or remain loyal to Britain? Those who chose to stay with Britain, the Loyalists, did not consider unfair taxes and regulations sufficient cause for rebellion. The Patriots, on the other hand, were determined to fight the British to the end—until American independence was won.

★ ★ ★ ★ ★ Section 3 Assessment ★ ★ ★ ★ ★

Checking for Understanding
1. *Identify* Continental Congress, John Adams, John Jay, Richard Henry Lee, George Washington, Concord, Paul Revere, Lexington, Ethan Allen, Fort Ticonderoga, Battle of Bunker Hill.
2. *Define* militia, minutemen, Loyalist, Patriot.
3. *Explain* why the British sent troops to Concord.

Reviewing Themes
4. **Groups and Institutions** Which action by the Continental Congress made it obvious that the colonies were preparing for war?

Critical Thinking
5. **Analyzing Ideas** What reasons might Loyalists have had to support Great Britain?

Activity

Writing a Poem Write a poem about one of the events described in this section.

Multimedia Activities

ABCNEWS INTERACTIVE™ Historic America Electronic Field Trips

Field Trip to Lexington and Concord

Setting up the Video

Work with a group of your classmates to view "Lexington and Concord" on the videodisc *Historic America: Electronic Field Trips*. The Battles of Lexington and Concord were the first armed conflicts of the American Revolution. Although the idea of independence from Great Britain was growing popular, some colonists remained unsure. This program reenacts the events during the Battles of Lexington and Concord.

Side 1,
Chapter 6

View the video by scanning the bar code or by entering the chapter number on your keypad and pressing Search.

Hands-On Activity

Organize into groups. Imagine you are colonists faced with making the decision of whether to fight for independence. As a group, decide whether you are pro-independence or wish to remain loyal to the British Crown. Then write and videotape a propaganda commercial designed to influence public opinion in your favor.

Surfing the "Net"

Modern Inventors

Although he is known primarily for writing the Declaration of Independence, Thomas Jefferson was accomplished in many other ways. He was recognized for inventing the moldboard of least resistance (otherwise known as the plow), the cipher wheel, and the spherical sundial. Americans continue to design new innovations to make their lives easier. Information about many of these innovations can be found on the Internet.

Getting There

Pick a subject that you would like to know more about and research recent innovations that are related to that subject. Follow these steps to gather your information.

1. Use a search engine. Type in the subject that you are searching for.
2. Enter words like the following to find specific information about the newest technology: *inventions, innovations, patents, licenses*.
3. The search engine will provide you with a number of links to follow. Links are "pointers" to different sites on the Internet.

What to Do When You Are There

Click on the links to navigate through the pages of information. Gather your findings. Using the findings, create a consumer report highlighting five inventions. Evaluate each invention for its innovation and usability.

May 10, 1775
Second Continental
Congress meets

July 1775
The Congress sends
Olive Branch Petition
to George III

March 1776
George Washington
takes Boston from
the British

July 4, 1776
Declaration of
Independence
is approved

Section 4

Moving Toward Independence

READ TO DISCOVER...
■ what happened at the Second Continental Congress.
■ why the colonists drafted the Declaration of Independence.

TERMS TO LEARN
petition   preamble

The Storyteller

In June 1776, delegates to the Second Continental Congress came to a momentous decision. They agreed to have a committee draw up a document declaring America's independence from Great Britain. Many years later John Adams recalled a conversation with Thomas Jefferson about the writing of the document.

Jefferson: You should do it.
Adams: Oh! no.
Jefferson: Why will you not? You ought to do it. . . .
Adams: You can write ten times better than I can.
Jefferson: Well, if you are decided, I will do as well as I can.

Lap desk invented by Jefferson

Declaring independence was still a long way off when the **Second Continental Congress** assembled for the first time in **Philadelphia.** The Congress held its first meeting on May 10, 1775, just three weeks after the battles at Lexington and Concord. All 13 colonies sent delegates to the Congress.

📖 Biography

Colonial Leaders Emerge

The delegates to the Second Continental Congress included some of the greatest political leaders in America. Among those attending were John and Samuel Adams, Patrick Henry, Richard Henry Lee, and George Washington—all delegates to the First Continental Congress held in 1774. Several distinguished new delegates came as well.

Benjamin Franklin, one of the most accomplished and respected individuals in the colonies, had been an influential member of the Pennsylvania legislature. In 1765, during the Stamp Act crisis, he had acted as a colonial spokesman in London.

John Hancock of Massachusetts, 38 years old, was one of the wealthiest colonists. He funded many of the Patriot groups, including the Sons of Liberty. The delegates chose Hancock as president of the Second Continental Congress.

America's FLAGS

Continental Colors, 1775–77 The Continental Colors, or Grand Union flag, was the first to represent all the colonies. Its 13 stripes stood for the thirteen colonies. The crosses represented the British flag

and symbolized the colonists' loyalty to Great Britain at that time.

Thomas Jefferson, only 32 years old when the Second Continental Congress met, had already acquired a reputation as a brilliant thinker and writer. As a member of the Virginia House of Burgesses, Jefferson had become associated with the movement for independence.

The Congress Becomes a Government

The Second Continental Congress began to govern the colonies. It authorized the printing of money and set up a post office with Franklin in charge. It established committees to communicate with Native Americans and with other countries. Most important, the Congress created the **Continental Army** to fight against Britain in a more organized way than the colonial militias could.

The new army needed a commander. On John Adams's recommendation, the Congress unanimously chose George Washington. Washington had more military experience than any other American, and the delegates admired and trusted him. Washington offered to serve without pay.

The Olive Branch Petition

After Washington left to take charge of the colonial forces in Boston, the delegates offered Britain one last chance to avoid all-out war. In July the Congress sent a petition, or formal request, to George III. Called the **Olive Branch Petition,** it assured the king of the colonists' desire for peace. It asked the king to protect the colonists' rights, which Parliament seemed determined to destroy.

George III refused to receive the Olive Branch Petition. Instead he prepared for war, hiring more than 30,000 German troops to send to America.

The Colonies Take the Offensive

Washington reached Boston in July 1775, a few weeks after the Battle of Bunker Hill. He found the members of the militia growing in number every day, but lacking discipline, organization, and leadership. He began the hard work of shaping these armed civilians into an army.

By March 1776, Washington judged the Continental Army ready to fight. He positioned the army in a semicircle around Boston and gave the order for its cannons to bombard the British forces. The redcoats, under Sir William Howe, hurriedly withdrew from the city and boarded their ships. On March 17 Washington led his jubilant troops into Boston. The British troops sailed to Halifax, Nova Scotia.

Meanwhile the Congress learned that British troops stationed in present-day Canada were planning to invade New York. The Americans decided to strike first. Marching north from Fort Ticonderoga, a Patriot force captured Montreal in November. An American attack on Quebec led by **Benedict Arnold** failed, however. The American

---

★★★ Linking PAST & PRESENT

Symbol of a Traitor

In 1780 Patriot general Benedict Arnold was in debt and beginning to doubt that the Americans could win the war. Papers found on a British spy indicated that Arnold plotted to surrender West Point to the British. In America today, the name *Benedict Arnold* has come to mean "traitor."

forces stayed outside the city of Quebec through the long winter and returned to Fort Ticonderoga in 1776.

Moving Toward Independence

★ Throughout the colonies in late 1775 and early 1776, some Americans still hoped to avoid a total break with Britain. Support for the position of complete independence was growing, however.

In January 1776, **Thomas Paine** published a pamphlet that captured the attention of the American colonists. Called *Common Sense*, it sold 120,000 copies within three months of publication. In bold language, Paine called for complete independence from Britain. He argued that it was

★ HISTORY AND ART *Drafting the Declaration of Independence* by **J. L. G. Ferris** Thomas Jefferson prepared the draft of the Declaration of Independence, while Benjamin Franklin and John Adams made suggestions. **What other leaders were involved in the Second Continental Congress?**

simply "common sense" to stop following the "royal brute," King George III. Paine told the colonists their cause was not just a squabble over taxes but a struggle for freedom—"in great measure the cause of all mankind." *Common Sense* inspired thousands of Americans.

Eyewitness to HISTORY

The Colonies Declare Independence

★ At the Second Continental Congress in Philadelphia, the meeting hall was filled with spirited debate. One central issue occupied the delegates: Should the colonies declare themselves an independent nation, or should they stay under British rule?

In April 1776, North Carolina instructed its delegates to support independence. On June 7 Virginia's Richard Henry Lee proposed a bold resolution:

❝ That these United Colonies are, and of right ought to be, free and independent States . . . and that all political connection between them and the State of Great Britain is, and ought to be, totally dissolved. ❞

The Congress debated the resolution. Some delegates still thought the colonies were not ready to form a separate nation. Others argued that war already had begun and a large portion of the American population wanted to separate from Great Britain. Still others feared Great Britain's power to hold down the rebellion.

Drafting a Declaration

While the delegates debated the issue, the Congress chose a committee to draft a **Declaration of Independence.** The committee included Jefferson, Franklin, John Adams, Roger Sherman of Connecticut, and Robert Livingston of New York. Jefferson was selected to write the document.

Jefferson spent about two weeks writing the document. He later recalled the goal was

Picturing HISTORY Abigail Adams was an advocate for women's rights. **What request did Abigail Adams make in a letter to her husband, John Adams?**

66 . . . to place before mankind the common sense of the subject, in terms so plain and firm as to command their assent. . . . Neither aiming at originality of principle or sentiment, nor yet copied from any particular and previous writing, it was intended to be an expression of the American mind. 99

While the Congress considered a declaration of independence, John Adams received a letter from his wife, **Abigail Adams.** She told Adams the delegates should

66 . . . remember all men would be tyrants if they could. If particular care and attention is not paid to the ladies, we are determined to foment a rebellion, and will not hold ourselves bound by any laws in which we have no voice or representation. 99

John Adams did not circulate Abigail's letter at the Congress.

Congress Votes for Independence

On July 2, 1776, the Congress finally voted on Lee's resolution for independence. Twelve colonies voted for it. New York did not vote but later announced its support. Next the delegates took up Jefferson's draft of the Declaration of Independence. After making some changes, they approved the document on July 4, 1776.

John Hancock, the president of the Congress, was the first to sign the Declaration of Independence. Hancock remarked that he wrote his name large enough for King George to read it without his glasses. Hancock's bold signature stands out on the original document. Eventually 55 delegates signed the paper announcing the birth of the United States.

Copies of the Declaration went out to the newly declared states. Washington had it read to his troops on July 9. In New York American soldiers tore down a statue of George III in celebration. In Worcester, Massachusetts, the reading of the Declaration of Independence was followed by "repeated huzzas [cheers], firing of musketry and cannon, bonfires, and other demonstrations of joy."

*F*ootnotes to History

Divided Loyalties Many colonial families were divided over the issue of loyalty to the Crown. Benjamin Franklin, one of the strongest voices for independence, experienced this division firsthand. Franklin's son William, who was governor of New Jersey, remained loyal to Britain, causing a lifelong rift between father and son.

The Declaration of Independence

★ The Declaration has four major sections. The preamble, or introduction, states that people who wish to form a new country should explain their reasons for doing so. The next two sections list the rights the colonists believed they should have and their complaints against Britain. The final section proclaims the existence of the new nation.

Demanding Basic Rights

The Declaration of Independence states what Jefferson and many Americans thought were universal principles. It begins with a description of basic human rights.

Continental infantryman

 We hold these truths to be self-evident, that all men are created equal, that they are endowed by their Creator with certain unalienable Rights, that among these are Life, Liberty, and the pursuit of Happiness. "

Government exists to protect these rights. If it does not, the Declaration states that "it is the Right of the People to alter or to abolish it and to institute new Government."

Listing British Abuses

The Declaration goes on to list the many grievances Americans held against the king and Parliament. The crimes of George III included "cutting off our trade with all parts of the world" and "imposing taxes on us without our consent." Americans, the Declaration says, had "Petitioned for Redress" of these grievances. These petitions, however, were rejected by Britain.

Declaring Independence

The Declaration ends by announcing America's new status. Now pledging "to each other our Lives, our Fortunes, and our sacred Honor," the Americans declared themselves a new nation. The struggle for American independence—the American Revolution—had begun.

★ ★ ★ ★ ★ **Section 4 Assessment** ★ ★ ★ ★ ★

Checking for Understanding

1. *Identify* Second Continental Congress, Philadelphia, Benjamin Franklin, Thomas Jefferson, Thomas Paine, *Common Sense*, Declaration of Independence, Abigail Adams.
2. *Define* petition, preamble.
3. *Describe* George III's response to the Olive Branch Petition.

Reviewing Themes

4. **Government and Democracy** Why was the Second Continental Congress more like a government than the First?

Critical Thinking

5. **Analyzing Primary Sources** Based on the letter that appears on page 151, what do you think Abigail Adams was asking her husband to include in the Declaration of Independence?

 Activity

Writing an Advertisement Prepare a help-wanted ad to locate a qualified person to write the Declaration of Independence. Describe the responsibilities of the job as well as the experience and character traits needed.

Distinguishing Fact From Opinion

Suppose a friend says, "Our school's basketball team is awesome. That's a fact." Actually, it's not a fact; it is an opinion. Can you tell the difference?

Learning the Skill

A **fact** answers a specific question such as: What happened? Who did it? When and where did it happen? Why did it happen? Statements of fact can be checked for accuracy and proven. If your friend had said, "We have the highest-ranking team in the state," that could be a fact. We can look up the rankings of state teams and determine whether the statement is a fact.

An **opinion,** on the other hand, expresses beliefs, feelings, and judgments. Although it may reflect someone's thoughts, we cannot prove or disprove it.

An opinion often begins with phrases such as *I believe, I think, probably, it seems to me,* or *in my opinion.* It often contains words such as *might, could, should,* and *ought* and superlatives such as *best, worst,* and *greatest.* Judgment words that express approval or disapproval—such as *good, bad, poor,* and *satisfactory*—also usually indicate an opinion.

To distinguish between facts and opinions, ask yourself these questions:

- Does this statement give specific information about an event?
- Can I check the accuracy of this statement?
- Does this statement express someone's feelings, beliefs, or judgment?
- Does it include phrases such as *I believe,* superlatives, or judgment words?

Practicing the Skill

Read each numbered statement below. Tell whether each is a fact or an opinion, and explain how you arrived at your answer.

1. *The Second Continental Congress held its first meeting on May 10, 1775.*

2. *The delegates to the Second Continental Congress included the greatest men in America.*

3. *The Continental Army fought against the British.*

4. *George Washington should have been paid for his services as commander.*

5. *King George III was a foolish king.*

Applying the Skill

Distinguishing Fact from Opinion Analyze 10 advertisements. List at least 3 facts and 3 opinions presented in the ads.

 Glencoe's **Skillbuilder Interactive Workbook, Level 1** provides instruction and practice in key social studies skills.

2 Jefferson traveled for seven days. Colonial inns along the way offered food and a chance to exchange news. And what news there was! General George Washington had chased British troops from Boston in March, and Thomas Paine had called King George III "the Royal Brute of Great Britain" in a pamphlet titled *Common Sense*.

3 Jefferson arrived in Philadelphia on May 14. On June 7, delegate Richard Henry Lee introduced a resolution to declare independence from Great Britain–a crime of treason punishable by death. On June 11, the Congress elected 5 men–including 33-year-old Jefferson–to write a formal declaration of independence.

Pa.   Philadelphia   N.J.

York

Md.

Potomac River   Baltimore

Alexandria

Fredericksburg

Charlottesville

Va.

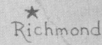

★ Richmond

1 On May 7, 1776, Virginia delegate Thomas Jefferson embarked from his home, Monticello, near Charlottesville, Virginia. He headed toward Philadelphia to join other delegates at the Second Continental Congress. Since May 1775 the delegates had debated the issue of self-rule as a colony versus total independence from Britain. That issue would soon be resolved.

N.Y.

New York

Conn.

4 Jefferson asked John Adams to write the document, but Adams refused, saying, "Reason 1st—You are a Virginian, and a Virginian ought to appear at the head of this business. Reason 2d. I am obnoxious, suspected, and unpopular. You are very much otherwise. Reason 3d. You can write ten times better than I can."

5 On July 2, 1776, the delegates formally voted to accept the first draft of the document. John Adams later wrote to his wife: "The Second Day of July 1776 . . . ought to be solemnized with Pomp and Parade, with Shews, Games, Sports, Guns, Bells, Bonfires, and Illuminations from one End of this Continent to the other from this Time forward forever more." The final draft of the Declaration was adopted on July 4, 1776.

N

ATLANTIC
OCEAN

Journey to Independence

" You inquire why so young a man as Mr. Jefferson was placed at the head of the Committee for preparing a Declaration of Independence? I answer: . . . to place Virginia at the head of every thing. . . . Mr. Jefferson came into Congress, in June 1775, and brought with him a reputation for literature, science, and a happy talent of composition. Writings of his were handed about, remarkable for the peculiar felicity [happiness] of expression. Though a silent member in Congress, he was so prompt, frank, explicit, and decisive upon committees and in conversation . . . that he soon seized upon my heart and upon this occasion I gave him my vote. . . . "

—From a letter written by John Adams to Timothy Pickering, August 22, 1822

The Declaration of Independence

Delegates at the Second Continental Congress faced an enormous task. The war against Great Britain had begun, but to many colonists the purpose for fighting was unclear. As sentiment increased for a complete break with Britain, Congress decided to act. A committee was appointed to prepare a document that declared the thirteen colonies free and independent from Britain. More important, the committee needed to explain why separation was the only fitting solution to long-standing disputes with Parliament and the British Crown. Thomas Jefferson was assigned to write a working draft of this document, which was then revised. It was officially adopted on July 4, 1776. More than any other action of Congress, the Declaration of Independence served to make the American colonists one people.

☆ ☆

The printed text of the document shows the spelling and punctuation of the parchment original. To aid in comprehension, selected words and their definitions appear in the side margin, along with other explanatory notes.

impel *force*

endowed *provided*

People create governments to ensure that their natural rights are protected.

If a government does not serve its purpose, the people have a right to abolish it. Then the people have the right and duty to create a new government that will safeguard their security.

Despotism *unlimited power*

In Congress, July 4, 1776. The unanimous Declaration of the thirteen united States of America,

Preamble

When in the Course of human events, it becomes necessary for one people to dissolve the political bands which have connected them with another, and to assume among the powers of the earth, the separate and equal station to which the Laws of Nature and Nature's God entitle them, a decent respect to the opinions of mankind requires that they should declare the causes which impel them to the separation.—

Declaration of Natural Rights

We hold these truths to be self-evident, that all men are created equal, that they are endowed by their Creator with certain unalienable Rights, that among these are Life, Liberty, and the pursuit of Happiness.—

That to secure these rights, Governments are instituted among Men, deriving their just powers from the consent of the governed,—

That whenever any Form of Government becomes destructive of these ends, it is the Right of the People to alter or to abolish it, and to institute new Government, laying its foundation on such principles and organizing its powers in such form, as to them shall seem most likely to effect their Safety and Happiness. Prudence, indeed, will dictate that Governments long established should not be changed for light and transient causes; and accordingly all experience hath shewn, that mankind are more disposed to suffer, while evils are sufferable, than to right themselves by abolishing the forms to which they are accustomed. But when a long train of abuses and usurpations, pursuing invariably the same Object evinces a design to reduce them under absolute Despotism, it is their right, it is their duty, to throw off such Government, and to provide new Guards for their future security.—

List of Grievances

Such has been the patient sufferance of these Colonies; and such is now the necessity which constrains them to alter their former Systems of Government. The history of the present King of Great Britain is a history of repeated injuries and usurpations, all having in direct object the establishment of an absolute Tyranny over these States. To prove this, let Facts be submitted to a candid world.—

He has refused his Assent to Laws, the most wholesome and necessary for the public good.—

He has forbidden his Governors to pass Laws of immediate and pressing importance, unless suspended in their operation till his Assent should be obtained; and when so suspended, he has utterly neglected to attend to them.—

He has refused to pass other Laws for the accommodation of large districts of people, unless those people would relinquish the right of Representation in the Legislature, a right inestimable to them and formidable to tyrants only.—

He has called together legislative bodies at places unusual, uncomfortable, and distant from the depository of their public Records, for the sole purpose of fatiguing them into compliance with his measures.—

He has dissolved Representative Houses repeatedly, for opposing with manly firmness his invasions on the rights of the people.—

He has refused for a long time, after such dissolutions, to cause others to be elected; whereby the Legislative powers, incapable of Annihilation, have returned to the People at large for their exercise; the State remaining in the meantime exposed to all the dangers of invasion from without, and convulsions within.—

He has endeavoured to prevent the population of these States; for that

usurpations
unjust uses of power

Each paragraph lists alleged injustices of George III.

relinquish *give up*
inestimable *priceless*

Annihilation *destruction*

convulsions
violent disturbances

The Second Continental Congress **by Edward Savage**

Eagle and crossed flags

Naturalization of Foreigners *process by which foreign-born persons become citizens*

purpose obstructing the Laws for Naturalization of Foreigners; refusing to pass others to encourage their migrations hither, and raising the conditions of new Appropriations of Lands.—

He has obstructed the Administration of Justice, by refusing his Assent to Laws for establishing Judiciary powers.—

tenure *term*

He has made Judges dependent on his Will alone, for the tenure of their offices, and the amount and payment of their salaries.—

Refers to the British troops sent to the colonies after the French and Indian War.

He has erected a multitude of New Offices, and sent hither swarms of Officers to harass our people, and eat out their substance.—

He has kept among us, in times of peace, Standing Armies without the Consent of our legislatures.—

He has affected to render the Military independent of and superior to the Civil power.—

Refers to the 1766 Declaratory Act.

He has combined with others to subject us to a jurisdiction foreign to our constitution, and unacknowledged by our laws; giving his Assent to their Acts of pretended Legislation:—

quartering *lodging*

For quartering large bodies of troops among us:—

For protecting them, by a mock Trial, from punishment for any Murders which they should commit on the Inhabitants of these States:—

For cutting off our Trade with all parts of the world:—

For imposing Taxes on us without our Consent:—

For depriving us in many cases, of the benefits of Trial by Jury:—

For transporting us beyond Seas to be tried for pretended offences:—

Refers to the 1774 Quebec Act.
render *make*

For abolishing the free System of English Laws in a neighbouring Province, establishing therein an Arbitrary government, and enlarging its Boundaries so as to render it at once an example and fit instrument for introducing the same absolute rule into these Colonies:—

For taking away our Charters, abolishing our most valuable Laws, and altering fundamentally the Forms of our Governments:—

For suspending our own Legislatures, and declaring themselves invested with power to legislate for us in all cases whatsoever.—

abdicated *given up*

He has abdicated Government here, by declaring us out of his Protection and waging War against us.—

He has plundered our seas, ravaged our Coasts, burnt our towns, and destroyed the Lives of our people.—

He is at this time transporting large Armies of foreign Mercenaries to compleat the works of death, desolation and tyranny, already begun with circumstances of Cruelty & perfidy scarcely paralleled in the most barbarous ages, and totally unworthy the Head of a civilized nation.—

perfidy *violation of trust*

He has constrained our fellow Citizens taken Captive on the high Seas to bear Arms against their Country, to become the executioners of their friends and Brethren, or to fall themselves by their Hands.—

insurrections *rebellions*

He has excited domestic insurrections amongst us, and has endeavoured to bring on the inhabitants of our frontiers, the merciless Indian Savages, whose known rule of warfare, is an undistinguished destruction of all ages, sexes and conditions.

Petitioned for Redress *asked formally for a correction of wrongs*

In every stage of these Oppressions We have Petitioned for Redress in the most humble terms: Our repeated Petitions have been answered only by repeated injury. A Prince, whose character is thus marked by every act which may define a Tyrant, is unfit to be the ruler of a free people.

Nor have We been wanting in attentions to our British brethren. We have warned them from time to time of attempts by their legislature to extend an unwarrantable jurisdiction over us. We have reminded them of the circumstances of our emigration and settlement here. We have appealed to their native justice and magnanimity, and we have conjured them by the ties of our common kindred to disavow these usurpations, which would inevitably interrupt our connections and correspondence. They too have been deaf to the voice of justice and of consanguinity. We must, therefore, acquiesce in the necessity, which denounces our Separation, and hold them, as we hold the rest of mankind, Enemies in War, in Peace Friends.—

unwarrantable jurisdiction *unjustified authority*

consanguinity *originating from the same ancestor*

Resolution of Independence by the United States

We, therefore, the Representatives of the united States of America, in General Congress, Assembled, appealing to the Supreme Judge of the world for the rectitude of our intentions, do, in the Name, and by Authority of the good People of these Colonies, solemnly publish and declare, That these United Colonies are, and of Right ought to be Free and Independent States; that they are Absolved from all Allegiance to the British Crown, and that all political connection between them and the State of Great Britain, is and ought to be totally dissolved; and that as Free and Independent States, they have full Power to levy War, conclude Peace, contract Alliances, establish Commerce, and to do all other Acts and Things which Independent States may of right do.—

And for the support of this Declaration, with a firm reliance on the protection of divine Providence, we mutually pledge to each other our Lives, our Fortunes and our sacred Honour.

rectitude *rightness*

The signers, as representatives of the American people, declared the colonies independent from Great Britain. Most members signed the document on August 2, 1776.

John Hancock
  President from
  Massachusetts

Georgia
Button Gwinnett
Lyman Hall
George Walton

North Carolina
William Hooper
Joseph Hewes
John Penn

South Carolina
Edward Rutledge
Thomas Heyward, Jr.
Thomas Lynch, Jr.
Arthur Middleton

Maryland
Samuel Chase
William Paca
Thomas Stone
Charles Carroll
  of Carrollton

Virginia
George Wythe
Richard Henry Lee
Thomas Jefferson
Benjamin Harrison
Thomas Nelson Jr.
Francis Lightfoot Lee
Carter Braxton

Pennsylvania
Robert Morris
Benjamin Rush
Benjamin Franklin
John Morton
George Clymer
James Smith
George Taylor
James Wilson
George Ross

Delaware
Caesar Rodney
George Read
Thomas McKean

New York
William Floyd
Philip Livingston
Francis Lewis
Lewis Morris

New Jersey
Richard Stockton
John Witherspoon
Francis Hopkinson
John Hart
Abraham Clark

New Hampshire
Josiah Bartlett
William Whipple
Matthew Thornton

Massachusetts
Samuel Adams
John Adams
Robert Treat Paine
Elbridge Gerry

Rhode Island
Stephen Hopkins
William Ellery

Connecticut
Samuel Huntington
William Williams
Oliver Wolcott
Roger Sherman

Assessment and Activities

★ Reviewing Key Terms

On a sheet of paper, define the following terms:

revenue	militia
writs of assistance	minutemen
resolution	Loyalist
effigy	Patriot
boycott	petition
nonimportation	preamble
repeal	
propaganda	
committee of correspondence	

★ Reviewing Key Facts

1. What did the British do to keep colonists from expanding westward?
2. How did the British government use the colonies to raise revenue?
3. What incident caused the British Parliament to pass the Coercive Acts?
4. What was the purpose of the first Continental Congress?
5. If government does not protect the basic rights of the people it governs, what did the Declaration of Independence say that people had the right to do?

★ Critical Thinking

Drawing Conclusions

Colonists created many documents to rouse anti-British feelings and to support the move for independence.

1. Why did the Boston Massacre present a good opportunity for the colonists to use propaganda against the British?
2. Why do you think Thomas Paine chose the title *Common Sense* for his pamphlet? How did the pamphlet encourage the colonists' move toward freedom from Great Britain?

★ Time Line Activity

Create a time line on which you place the following events in chronological order.

- Declaration of Independence written
- Battle of Bunker Hill begins
- Britain passes Stamp Act
- First Continental Congress meets
- The Boston Massacre occurs
- Colonists throw tea into Boston Harbor

★ Reviewing Themes

1. **Civic Rights and Responsibilities** Why did colonists think that the Stamp Act ignored the colonial tradition of self-government?
2. **Groups and Institutions** Give two examples of how colonies gained strength against the British by working in groups.
3. **Groups and Institutions** What did Patrick Henry mean when he said, "I am not a Virginian, but an American"?
4. **Government and Democracy** According to the Declaration of Independence, what are the three basic freedoms to which every person is entitled?

★ Skill Practice Activity

Distinguishing Fact from Opinion

Read the following statements. Tell whether each is a fact or an opinion.

1. Great Britain should not have tried to stop the colonists from settling west of the Appalachians.
2. The Stamp Act placed a tax on almost all printed material in the colonies.
3. The Daughters of Liberty urged Americans to wear homemade fabrics.
4. Thomas Jefferson was a better writer than John Adams was.

★ Geography Activity

Study the map below and answer the questions that follow.

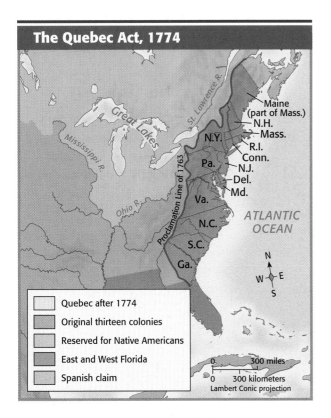

The Quebec Act, 1774

- Quebec after 1774
- Original thirteen colonies
- Reserved for Native Americans
- East and West Florida
- Spanish claim

0   300 miles
0   300 kilometers
Lambert Conic projection

1. **Place** What bodies of water were part of Quebec after the Quebec Act?
2. **Location** What country claimed the land west of Quebec?
3. **Movement** What inland waterways marked the southern and western boundaries of Quebec's new territory?
4. **Region** For whom was land reserved just west of the Appalachian Mountains?

★ Cooperative Activity

History and Citizenship Work with a group of classmates to create your own "Declaration of Independence." Use the original Declaration of Independence on pages 156-159 as a guide to create your document. Outline the basic freedoms that you expect to have as a citizen and describe why these freedoms are important to you. Then write at least three responsibilities and/or sacrifices that citizens should be willing to make to enjoy the freedoms you listed. After your group has completed its Declaration of Independence, have the groups come together as a class. Share all the groups' documents and decide which group best represented the needs of the whole class.

★ Technology Activity

Using the Internet On the Internet, locate the computer address for the National Archives or the Library of Congress in Washington, D.C. Search each site for documents concerning the drafting of the Declaration of Independence and/or photos of pamphlets produced by the colonies in the 1700s. Print a copy of what you find or sketch a likeness to share with the class.

Portfolio Activity History Journal Review the chapter for details about the Boston Massacre, the Battle of Bunker Hill, and the writing of the Declaration of Independence. Record the details in your journal. Use your information to create three headlines for articles that might have run in a colonial newspaper when these events occurred.

1776–1783

The American Revolution

★ Why It's Important

Although the United States declared its independence in 1776, no country recognized it as an independent nation at that time. It took a war and the efforts of American diplomats to win this recognition from Britain, France, Spain, and other European countries. In fighting for the principles set forth in the Declaration, the American Patriots laid the foundation for the United States of America we know today.

★ Chapter Themes

■ *Section 1,* Groups and Institutions
■ *Section 2,* Groups and Institutions
■ *Section 3,* Geography and History
■ *Section 4,* Groups and Institutions

PRIMARY SOURCES
Library   *See pages 946–947 for primary source readings to accompany Chapter 6*

★ HISTORY AND ART   ***Washington's Triumphant Entrance*** **by an unknown artist**
George Washington, commander of the Continental Army, entered New York in triumph after the departure of British troops from the city in November 1783.

April 1776
Battle of
Lexington

December 1776
Patriots capture
Hessians at
Trenton

October 1777
Burgoyne
surrenders
at Saratoga

1778
African
American
regiment forms
in Rhode Island

Section 1

The Early Years

READ TO DISCOVER . . .

- why some Americans supported the British.
- how the British planned to win the war.
- how the Battle of Saratoga marked a turning point of the war.

TERMS TO LEARN

Patriot   mercenary
neutral   recruit
Loyalist   deserter

The Storyteller

The mighty British troops sailed to America, confident that they would quickly and easily crush the rebellious colonists. A British officer wrote to his friend, describing a military skirmish:

September 3, 1776

We landed on Long-Island. . . . [I]t was a fine sight to see with what [eagerness] they dispatched the Rebels with their bayonets after we had surrounded them so that they could not resist. . . . The island is all ours, and we shall soon take New-York, for the Rebels dare not look us in the face. I expect the affair will be over [after] this campaign. . . .

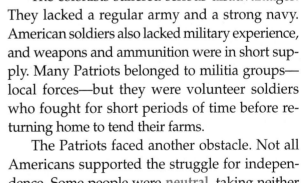

British cannon

Both the British and the Americans expected the war for independence to be short. The British planned to crush the rebellious colonists by force. Most of the Patriots—Americans who supported independence—believed the British would give up after losing one or two major battles. Few Patriots believed John Adams when he predicted in April 1776: "We shall have a long, obstinate, and bloody war to go through."

The Opposing Sides

At first glance the British had an overwhelming advantage in the war. They had the strongest navy in the world; an experienced, well-trained army; and the wealth of a worldwide empire. Britain also had a much larger population than the United States—9 million people in Britain compared to only 2.5 million in the United States.

The colonists suffered serious disadvantages. They lacked a regular army and a strong navy. American soldiers also lacked military experience, and weapons and ammunition were in short supply. Many Patriots belonged to militia groups—local forces—but they were volunteer soldiers who fought for short periods of time before returning home to tend their farms.

The Patriots faced another obstacle. Not all Americans supported the struggle for independence. Some people were neutral, taking neither side in the conflict. The Quakers, for example, would not participate in the war because they opposed all armed conflict. Still other Americans remained loyal to Britain.

Chapter 6   The American Revolution   **163**

Some Americans used force against British sympathizers. **In what regions was Loyalist strength the greatest?**

The Loyalists

Those who remained loyal to Britain and opposed the war for independence were called Loyalists or Tories. Perhaps one American in five was a Loyalist. Some people changed sides during the war, depending on which army was closer. Loyalist strength varied from region to region. In general it was strongest in the Carolinas and Georgia and weakest in New England.

Loyalists supported Britain for different reasons. Some remained loyal because they were members of the Anglican Church, headed by the British king. Some depended on the British for their jobs. Many feared the disorder that would come from challenging the established government. Others simply could not understand what all the commotion was about. No other country, one Loyalist complained, "faced a rebellion arising from such trivial causes."

The issue of independence disrupted normal relations. Friends and families were divided over loyalty to Britain. For example, William Franklin, son of Patriot Benjamin Franklin, was a Loyalist. He had served as the royal governor of New Jersey. As one Connecticut Loyalist observed:

66 Neighbor was against neighbor, father against son and son against father. He that would not thrust his own blade through his brother's heart was called an infamous villain. 99

African Americans in the War

Some African Americans also sided with the Loyalists. At the start of the war, the British appealed to enslaved Africans to join them. Lord Dunmore, the royal governor of Virginia, announced that slaves who fought on the British side would be freed, and many men answered his call. Eventually some of them ended up free in Canada, and others settled the British colony of Sierra Leone in Africa.

Patriot Advantages

The Americans possessed some advantages. They were fighting on their own ground and fought with great determination to protect it. The British, on the other hand, had to wage war in a faraway land and were forced to transport soldiers and supplies 3,000 miles across the Atlantic Ocean.

The nature of the British army in America also helped the Patriots. The British relied on mercenaries—hired soldiers—to fight. The Americans called the mercenaries **Hessians,** after the region in Germany where most of them lived. To gain support for the war effort, Patriots compared their own troops, who were fighting for the freedom of their own land, to the Hessians, who fought for money. The Patriots had a much greater stake in winning the war than the hired soldiers did. This determination to succeed gave the Americans an edge over the Hessians in battle.

Probably the Americans' greatest advantage was their leader, George Washington. Few individuals could match him for courage, honesty, and determination. The war might have taken a different turn without Washington steering its course.

Raising an Army

⭐ The Americans placed great value on liberty and personal freedom. After throwing off the rule of the British Parliament, they hesitated to transfer power to their own Continental Congress. In some ways the American Revolution was really 13 separate wars, with each state pursuing its own interests. As a result Congress experienced difficulty enlisting soldiers and raising money to fight the war.

Although the militia played an essential role in the Patriots' forces, the Americans also needed a regular army—well-trained soldiers who could fight anywhere in the colonies. The Congress established the Continental Army but depended on the states to recruit, or enlist, soldiers.

At first soldiers signed up for one year of army service. General Washington appealed for longer terms. "If we ever hope for success," he said, "we must have men enlisted for the whole term of the war." Eventually the Continental Congress offered enlistments for three years or for the length of the war. Most soldiers, however, still signed up for only a year.

Women also fought with the Patriot forces. Margaret Corbin of Pennsylvania accompanied her husband when he joined the Continental Army. After he died in battle, she took his place. Deborah Sampson of Massachusetts disguised herself as a man so she could fight. When she was wounded, she treated the wounds herself so no one would discover that she was a woman.

Fighting in New York

⭐ Most of the early battles involved few troops. At Bunker Hill, for example, about 2,000 British soldiers fought 1,200 Americans. The British had not yet won a decisive victory over the Patriots, however, and they realized they would need more troops to end the war quickly.

During the summer of 1776, Britain sent 32,000 troops across the Atlantic to New York. The British commander, **General William Howe,** hoped the sheer size of his army would convince the Patriots to give up. He was soon disappointed.

Defeat on Long Island

Although Washington and the Patriots had fewer than 20,000 troops, they were determined to fight. In late August the two sides clashed in the **Battle of Long Island.** Outnumbered and

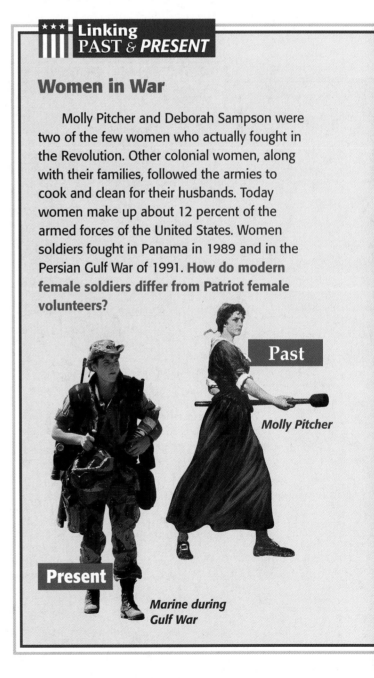

★★★ Linking PAST & PRESENT

Women in War

Molly Pitcher and Deborah Sampson were two of the few women who actually fought in the Revolution. Other colonial women, along with their families, followed the armies to cook and clean for their husbands. Today women make up about 12 percent of the armed forces of the United States. Women soldiers fought in Panama in 1989 and in the Persian Gulf War of 1991. **How do modern female soldiers differ from Patriot female volunteers?**

Past

Molly Pitcher

Present

Marine during Gulf War

outmaneuvered, the Continental Army suffered a serious defeat at the hands of the British forces.

One Patriot, **Nathan Hale,** proved himself a hero at Long Island. A teacher from Connecticut, Hale volunteered to spy on British troops and disguised himself as a Dutch schoolteacher. The British discovered his true identity, however, and hanged him. Hale's immortal last words were, "I only regret that I have but one life to lose for my country."

Although the Americans showed no lack of bravery, they ran short of supplies for the army. In the autumn of 1776, a British officer wrote that many of the Patriot soldiers killed on Long Island had not been wearing shoes, socks, or jackets. "They are also in great want of blankets," he said, predicting that "the Rebel Army must suffer greatly as soon as the severe weather sets in."

After their defeat on Long Island, Washington retreated to Manhattan, pursued by the British. By late November, the Continental Army had retreated across New Jersey into Pennsylvania.

A Low Point

In the winter of 1776 to 1777, the Patriots' cause was near collapse. The size of the Continental Army had dwindled. Some soldiers

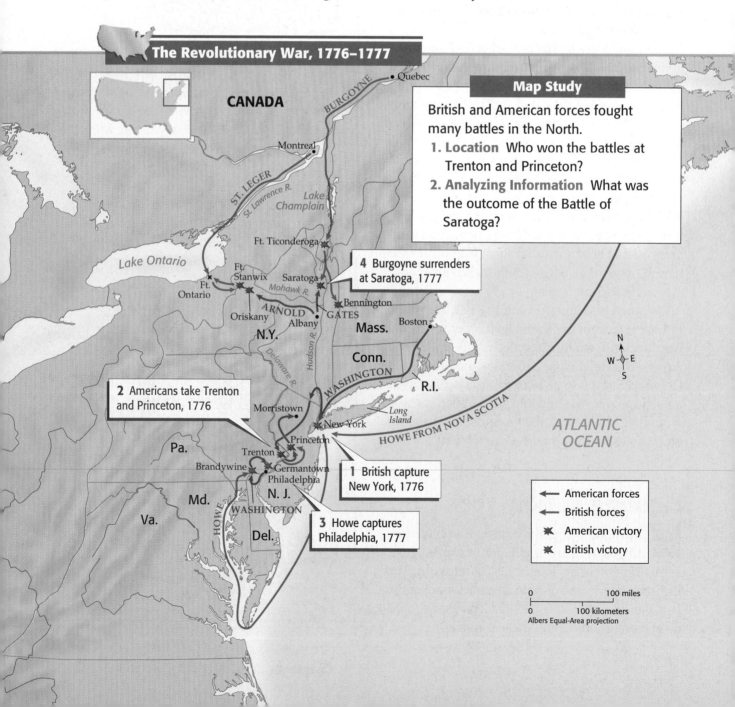

The Revolutionary War, 1776–1777

Map Study

British and American forces fought many battles in the North.
1. **Location** Who won the battles at Trenton and Princeton?
2. **Analyzing Information** What was the outcome of the Battle of Saratoga?

4 Burgoyne surrenders at Saratoga, 1777

2 Americans take Trenton and Princeton, 1776

1 British capture New York, 1776

3 Howe captures Philadelphia, 1777

CANADA

Quebec

Montreal

BURGOYNE

ST. LEGER

St. Lawrence R.

Lake Champlain

Ft. Ticonderoga

Lake Ontario

Ft. Stanwix

Ft. Ontario

Saratoga

Mohawk R.

ARNOLD

GATES

Oriskany

Albany

Bennington

Boston

Mass.

Conn.

R.I.

N.Y.

Hudson R.

Delaware R.

WASHINGTON

Long Island

New York

HOWE FROM NOVA SCOTIA

ATLANTIC OCEAN

Morristown

Princeton

Pa.

Trenton

Brandywine

Germantown

Philadelphia

N. J.

WASHINGTON

Md.

HOWE

Va.

Del.

← American forces
← British forces
✳ American victory
✳ British victory

0   100 miles
0   100 kilometers
Albers Equal-Area projection

completed their terms of service and went home. Others were **deserters,** soldiers who ran away.

Washington wrote his brother that if new soldiers were not recruited soon, "I think the game is pretty near up." Still, Washington could not believe that the fight for liberty would truly fail.

Biography

Thomas Paine and *The Crisis*

In early 1776 **Thomas Paine** wrote a pamphlet, *Common Sense,* that moved many American colonists toward independence. After taking part in the retreat across New York and New Jersey, Paine published another pamphlet to help boost Americans' lagging spirits. In *The Crisis* he reminded Americans that "the harder the conflict, the more glorious the triumph."

> ❝ These are the times that try men's souls. The summer soldier and the sunshine patriot will in this crisis shrink from the service of their country; but he that stands it now deserves the love and thanks of man and woman. ❞

Washington had Paine's encouraging words read to his troops to inspire them to continue the fight. Throughout the colonies people passed copies of *The Crisis* from hand to hand and discussed Paine's stirring ideas.

Patriot Gains

⭐ Washington pleaded with the Continental Congress for more troops. He asked the Congress to enlist free African Americans. Early in the war, the Southern states had persuaded the Congress to bar African American soldiers from the Continental Army. Many white people in the Southern states felt uncomfortable about giving guns to African Americans and allowing them to serve as soldiers. In Southern states with large enslaved populations, whites feared revolts.

Picturing HISTORY About 5,000 African Americans fought for the Americans. **Why did many African Americans support the Americans' cause?**

African Americans Join the Fight

As the need for soldiers grew, some states ignored the ban and enlisted African Americans. Rhode Island raised an all–African American regiment in 1778. By war's end, every state except South Carolina enlisted African Americans to fight.

Historians estimate that as many as 5,000 African Americans joined the Patriots. Among them were **Lemuel Hayes** and **Peter Salem,** who fought at Concord. African Americans fought for the same reasons as other Americans. They believed in the Patriot cause or they needed the money. Some soldiers were enslaved Africans who had run away from slaveholders. Others fought to earn their freedom.

American Victories in New Jersey

The British army settled in New York for the winter of 1776 to 1777, leaving some troops in New Jersey at **Trenton** and **Princeton.** Armies

Hut Camp of the 17th Regiment by John W. Dunsmore A British military camp guards New York City against American attack. **What happened to the Continental Army during the New York campaign of 1776?**

usually called a halt to their wars during the winter, and the British did not expect to fight.

Stationed across the Delaware River from the British camp in New Jersey, Washington saw a chance to catch the British off guard. On Christmas night 1776, Washington took 2,400 troops across the icy river and surprised the enemy at Trenton the next day.

The Americans captured 900 Hessians at Trenton. Washington called the victory "glorious." The British sent reinforcements under Lord Charles Cornwallis, but Washington led his troops away from Cornwallis's men. Washington then marched the army to Princeton, where they drove away the British. One discouraged British soldier wrote in his diary, "A few days ago [the Americans] had given up the cause for lost. Their late successes have turned the scale and now they are all liberty mad again."

A British Plan for Victory

★ The British worked out a battle plan for 1777. They would take **Albany,** New York, and gain control of the Hudson River. This would separate New England from the Middle States.

The plan involved a three-pronged attack. **General John Burgoyne** would lead 8,000 troops south from Canada. A second force, under Lieutenant Colonel Barry St. Leger (leh•ZHAY), would move east from Lake Ontario. A third group, under General Howe, would move north from New York City. The three British forces would meet at Albany and destroy the Patriot troops.

The British Capture Philadelphia

Howe planned to take Philadelphia, the American capital, before marching to Albany. After winning battles in September 1777 at Brandywine and Paoli near Philadelphia, Howe's troops captured the city itself without much of a fight. The Continental Congress fled to the Pennsylvania countryside. In early October Washington attacked the main British camp at nearby Germantown, but he was forced to withdraw. Postponing the move north to Albany, Howe decided to spend the winter in Philadelphia.

Patriots Slow the British

Meanwhile the British plans for moving toward Albany were not going well. In August American soldiers halted St. Leger's advance at Fort Stanwix, New York. Led by **Benedict Arnold**, the Americans forced the British to retreat.

General Burgoyne's army was not making much progress toward Albany either. In July Burgoyne captured Fort Ticonderoga, but his army had trouble advancing after that. Burgoyne, a dashing general who enjoyed good food and drink and fine clothes, traveled with 30 wagons of luxury goods. Loaded down with this heavy baggage, Burgoyne's army moved slowly through the dense forests. To make matters worse, the Americans blocked the British at every opportunity by felling trees across their path.

In need of food and supplies, Burgoyne sent 700 British and Hessian soldiers to capture the military stores at Bennington, Vermont. The British troops' brightly colored uniforms made the soldiers easy targets in the woods. A local militia group, the **Green Mountain Boys,** attacked and defeated them. Having lost part of his army and desperately short of supplies, Burgoyne retreated in October to the town of **Saratoga** in New York.

The Battle of Saratoga

At Saratoga Burgoyne faced serious trouble. He expected British forces from the west and south to join him, but they had not arrived. The Americans had stopped St. Leger's army at Fort Stanwix, and Howe's forces were still in Philadelphia. In addition American troops under the command of **General Horatio Gates** blocked his path to the south. Burgoyne found himself surrounded

America's FLAGS

First Stars and Stripes, 1777–1795 On June 14, 1777, the Continental Congress designed the first Stars and Stripes. The Congress determined that "the Flag of the United States be 13 stripes, alternate red and white; that the Union be 13 stars, white in a blue field representing a new constellation." For Americans past and present,

the color red symbolizes courage; white, purity of ideals; and blue, strength and unity of the states.

by an army about three times as large as his own. Burgoyne made a last desperate attack on October 7, but the Americans held firm. The British were trapped. They had no food, and wounded soldiers lay all around.

On October 17, 1777, General Burgoyne surrendered. As a Patriot band played "Yankee Doodle," 5,700 British soldiers handed their weapons to the Americans. At dinner with Gates, Burgoyne offered a toast to George Washington. The British plan to cut off New England had failed.

Section 1 Assessment

Checking for Understanding
1. *Identify* Hessians, Nathan Hale, Thomas Paine, Benedict Arnold, Saratoga.
2. *Define* Patriot, neutral, Loyalist, mercenary, recruit, deserter.
3. *Compare* the strengths of the British and American military forces.

Reviewing Themes
4. **Groups and Institutions** What problems did the Continental Congress face in raising an army to fight during the American Revolution?

Critical Thinking
5. **Making Critical Judgments** Provide reasons to explain why African Americans wanted to enlist in the Continental Army.

Activity

Making a Recruitment Poster Design a poster that encourages colonists to join the war effort on the side of the Americans.

Reading a Military Map

In your study of American history, you often use maps. A military map shows the area where battles occur, where victories are won, routes soldiers take, and who controls various sites.

Learning the Skill

Military maps use colors, symbols, and arrows to show major battles, troop movements, and defensive positions during a particular battle or over a period of time.

When reading a military map, follow these steps:

• Read the map title. This will indicate the location and time period covered on the map.

• Read the map key. This tells what the symbols on the map represent. For example, battle sites may be symbolized by crossed swords, a burst shell, or a star.

• Study the map itself. This will reveal the actual events or sequence of events that took place. Notice the geography of the area and try to determine how it could affect military strategy.

Practicing the Skill

Analyze the information on the map on this page, then answer the following questions.

1. What is the title of this map?
2. What troops surrounded Boston Harbor? How do you know this?
3. Which commander led the British troops to Breed's Hill?
4. What action did the American forces take after fighting on Bunker Hill?
5. In which direction did the British forces move when they left Boston? What parts of the map help you find this information?

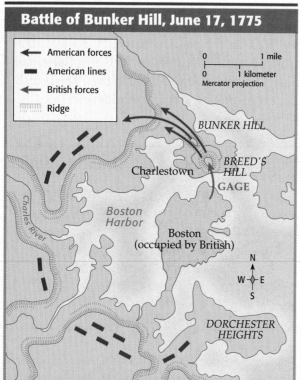

Battle of Bunker Hill, June 17, 1775

American forces
American lines
British forces
Ridge

0   1 mile
0   1 kilometer
Mercator projection

BUNKER HILL
BREED'S HILL
GAGE
Charlestown
Charles River
Boston Harbor
Boston (occupied by British)
DORCHESTER HEIGHTS

N
W—E
S

Applying the Skill

Reading a Military Map Find a map of a specific battle of the American Revolution in an encyclopedia or other reference book. Create a three-dimensional model of the battle and use moveable pieces to represent troops. Then demonstrate troop movements over the course of the battle.

GO TO

Glencoe's **Skillbuilder** Interactive **Workbook, Level 1** provides instruction and practice in key social studies skills.

1777	1778	1779

October 1777
Americans win
Battle of Saratoga

Winter 1777-1778
Patriot troops suffer
at Valley Forge

February 1778
France and U.S.
form an alliance

1779
Spain declares
war on Britain

Section 2

The War Continues

READ TO DISCOVER . . .
- how the Patriots received help from other nations.
- how Washington's troops survived the winter at Valley Forge.
- what challenges Americans faced at home as a result of the war.

TERMS TO LEARN
desert   inflation

The Storyteller

The Continental Congress sent Jonathan Austin of Boston to France to deliver the news of the American victory at Saratoga. Benjamin Franklin was already in France trying to get that country to help the Americans against the British. As soon as Austin arrived, Franklin nervously inquired, "Is Philadelphia taken?" Austin answered, "It is, sir. But, sir, I have greater news than that. General Burgoyne and his whole army are prisoners of war."

The news prompted France to agree to an alliance with America.

French medal showing Benjamin Franklin

The American victory at Saratoga in October 1777 marked a turning point in the war. The European nations, especially France, realized that the United States might actually win its war against Great Britain. Now was the time for the Americans to seek support from Great Britain's rivals.

Gaining Allies

By late 1777 Benjamin Franklin had been in Paris for a year, trying to get the French to support the Americans' fight for independence. With his skill and charm, Franklin gained many friends for the United States. The French gave the Americans money secretly, but they would not commit to an alliance.

France

News of the American victory at Saratoga caused a shift in France's policy. Realizing that the Americans had a chance of defeating Britain, the French announced support for the United States openly. In February 1778, the French and the Americans worked out a trade agreement and an alliance. France declared war on Britain and sent money, equipment, and troops to aid the American Patriots.

Spain and the Netherlands

Other European nations also helped the American cause, mostly because they hated the

British. Although Spain did not recognize American independence until after the Revolution, Spain declared war on Britain in 1779. The Spanish governor of Louisiana, **Bernardo de Gálvez** (GAHL•vez), sent money, rifles, and other supplies to American armies in Virginia and the Ohio Valley. Spanish troops under Gálvez captured five British forts in the Mississippi Valley. The Netherlands also went to war with Britain, and Dutch bankers lent money to the Americans.

A Difficult Winter

★ Word of the French-American alliance did not reach the United States until the spring of 1778. Meanwhile British general Howe and his forces spent the winter in comfort in Philadelphia. Washington set up camp at **Valley Forge,** 20 miles to the west of the British. Washington and his troops endured a winter of terrible suffering, lacking decent food, clothing, and shelter. Washington's greatest challenge at Valley Forge was keeping the Continental Army together.

Eyewitness to HISTORY

Winter at Valley Forge

Joseph Martin, a 17-year-old private from Connecticut, spent the winter at Valley Forge. "We had a hard duty to perform," he wrote years later, "and little or no strength to perform it with." Most of the men lacked blankets, shoes, and shirts. Martin made a rough pair of moccasins for himself out of a scrap of cowhide. Although the moccasins hurt his feet, they were better than going barefoot, "as hundreds of my companions had to do, till they might be tracked by their blood upon the rough, frozen snow."

Not surprisingly, many men **deserted,** or left without permission, the Continental Army while it was camped at Valley Forge. Some officers resigned. The army seemed to be falling apart.

Yet somehow, with enormous determination and effort, the Continental Army survived the winter, and conditions gradually improved. The troops built huts and gathered supplies from the countryside, often by force. Volunteers—including

★ **HISTORY AND ART** *The March to Valley Forge* by William B.J. Trego While waiting for French aid, American soldiers spent a brutal winter at Valley Forge, Pennsylvania. **What were the soldiers' living conditions at Valley Forge?**

Washington's wife, Martha—made clothes for the troops and cared for the sick. Washington declared that no army had ever suffered "such uncommon hardships" with such "patience and fortitude." New soldiers joined the ranks in the spring. "The army grows stronger every day," one officer wrote. "There is a spirit of discipline among the troops that is better than numbers."

In April 1778 Washington told his troops of the Patriots' alliance with France. Everyone's spirits rose at the thought of help from overseas. The Continental Army celebrated with a religious service and a parade. 🔍

Help From Overseas

Among the hardy soldiers who spent the winter at Valley Forge was a French nobleman, the **Marquis de Lafayette** (LAH•fee•EHT). Filled with enthusiasm for the ideas expressed in the Declaration of Independence, Lafayette had bought a ship and set sail for America. He rushed to join the battle for freedom despite a prohibition by King Louis XIV of France.

To his wife and children in France, Lafayette wrote, "The future of America is closely bound up with the future of all mankind." Upon his arrival in Philadelphia, Lafayette offered his services and those of his followers to General Washington. Lafayette became a trusted aide to Washington.

Other Europeans also volunteered to work for the Patriot cause. Two Poles—Thaddeus Kościuszko (kawsh•CHUSH•KOH), an engineer, and **Casimir Pulaski,** a cavalry officer—contributed to the American efforts. Pulaski died in 1780, fighting for the Continental Army in the South.

Friedrich von Steuben (STOO•buhn), a former army officer from Germany, also came to help Washington. Steuben drilled the Patriot troops at Valley Forge, teaching them military

Causes and Effects

CAUSES

★ Long-standing hostility between Britain and France
★ Conflict between Britain and France during French and Indian War
★ Victory at Saratoga boosts French confidence in Patriots

French-American Alliance in 1778

EFFECTS

★ France lends money to the Continental Congress
★ France sends soldiers and ships to help Patriot forces
★ Patriots win the American Revolution

Chart Study

In 1777 Benjamin Franklin negotiated with French leaders for money and support for the American cause. **Drawing Conclusions** Why was it important for France to recognize the independence of the American colonies?

discipline. He turned the ragged Continental Army into a more effective fighting force.

Juan de Miralles (mee•RAH•yays) arrived in Philadelphia in 1778 as a representative of Spain. At his urging, Spain, Cuba, and Mexico sent financial aid to the colonies. Miralles befriended many Patriot leaders and lent them money for their cause.

*F*ootnotes to History

Worthless Paper? The paper dollar bills that the Congress issued were called *Continentals.* People used the expression "not worth a Continental" to describe something of little value.

Linking PAST & PRESENT

Old Allies

France was the first nation to sign a treaty of alliance with the revolutionary United States. France and the United States were allies in the twentieth century, too. They fought on the same side in World War I and World War II. They remain allies today in the North Atlantic Treaty Organization (NATO), an organization formed to defend its members from aggression.

$ Economics

Money Problems

Getting money to finance the war was a major concern. The Continental Congress had no power to raise money through taxes. Although the Congress received some contributions from the states and from foreign countries, much more money was needed.

To pay for the war, the Congress and the states printed hundreds of millions of dollars worth of paper money. These bills quickly lost their value, however, because the amount of bills in circulation grew faster than the supply of gold and silver backing them. This led to inflation, which means that it took more and more money to buy the same amount of goods. The Congress stopped issuing the paper money because no one would use it. However, the Americans had no other way to finance fighting their war for independence. $

Life on the Home Front

★ The war had a major impact on the lives of all Americans, even those who stayed at home. With thousands of men away in military service, women took over the duties that had once been the responsibility of their husbands or

fathers. **Abigail Adams** was just one of many women who managed the family farm while her husband was away.

Other women ran their husband's or their own businesses. According to popular legend, **Betsy Ross**, a seamstress in Philadelphia, made the first American flag for George Washington. Although the story cannot be verified, it is known that a Philadelphia woman named Elizabeth Ross sewed flags for a living.

Changing Attitudes

The ideals of liberty and freedom that inspired the American Revolution caused some women to question their place in society. In an essay on education, **Judith Sargeant Murray** of Massachusetts argued that women's minds are as good as men's. Girls, therefore, should get as good an education as boys. At a time when most girls received little schooling, this was a radical idea.

Abigail Adams also championed women's interests. She wrote to her husband, John Adams, who was a member of the Second Continental Congress:

★ **Picturing HISTORY** Paper notes issued by the Congress and the states rapidly declined in value. By the time these South Carolina bills were printed, their real value was only 10 percent of their face value. **Why did American notes quickly decline in value?**

❝ I cannot say that I think you are very generous to the ladies, for, whilst you are proclaiming peace and good will to men, emancipating all nations, you insist upon retaining an absolute power over wives. **❞**

Treatment of Loyalists

Every state had some Loyalists. Thousands of them fought with the British against the Patriots. To prove their loyalty to Britain, some Loyalists spied and informed on the Patriots.

Many Loyalists, however, fled the American colonies during the Revolutionary War. They packed their belongings and sold whatever they could. Some left hurriedly for England. Others took off for Spanish-owned Florida. Still others journeyed to the frontier beyond the Appalachian Mountains.

Loyalists who remained in the United States faced difficult times. Their neighbors often shunned them. Some became victims of mob violence. Loyalists who actively helped the British could be arrested and tried as traitors. Patriots executed a few Loyalists, but such extreme measures were unusual.

⬗ Citizenship

Hopes for Equality

The Revolutionary War ideals of freedom and liberty inspired some white Americans to question the morality of the institution of slavery. As early as the Stamp Act crisis, the Boston town meeting had voted to condemn slavery. In 1778 Governor William Livingston of New Jersey asked the legislature to free all enslaved people in the state. Slavery, Livingston said, was "utterly inconsistent with the principles of Christianity and humanity."

African Americans made similar arguments. In New Hampshire enslaved Africans asked the legislature for their freedom "so that the name of *slave* may not be heard in a land gloriously contending for the sweets of freedom."

From the beginning of the war—at Lexington, Concord, and Bunker Hill—African American soldiers fought for the American cause. To some fighting for freedom, both African American and white, the Revolution seemed to bring nearer the day when slavery would be abolished. Vermont, New Hampshire, Massachusetts, and Pennsylvania attempted to end slavery in their states. The issue of slavery would remain unsettled for many years, however.

★ ★ ★ ★ ★ **Section 2 Assessment** ★ ★ ★ ★ ★

Checking for Understanding

1. **Identify** Bernardo de Gálvez, Valley Forge, Marquis de Lafayette, Friedrich von Steuben, Abigail Adams, Betsy Ross, Judith Sargeant Murray.
2. **Define** desert, inflation.
3. **Explain** why the French did not publicly support the Americans until after the Battle of Saratoga.

Reviewing Themes

4. **Groups and Institutions** How were the Loyalists treated by the Patriots during the war?

Critical Thinking

5. **Determining Cause and Effect** The Americans claimed they were fighting for the ideals of liberty and freedom. How did these ideals make women and enslaved Americans question their position in society?

Activity

Making a Survival Package Imagine you had friends among the troops at Valley Forge during the winter of 1777–1778. Make a list of five items you would send to them to help them get through the winter.

June 1778
George Rogers
Clark captures
Vincennes

September 1779
The *Serapis*
surrenders to
John Paul Jones

May 1780
British troops
take Charleston

January 1781
Patriots defeat
British at
Cowpens

Section 3

The War Moves West and South

READ TO DISCOVER . . .
- how the war involved Native Americans.
- how the Americans and British waged a war at sea.
- how a new kind of fighting helped the Patriots win battles in the South.

TERMS TO LEARN
blockade   guerrilla warfare
privateer

The Storyteller

On June 28, 1778, one of the hottest days of the summer, General Washington pursued the British and attacked at Monmouth, New Jersey. The battle raged as the heat robbed the Patriots of their energy. Dodging shots, Mary Hays ran back and forth from a nearby spring to her husband's station with water to quench the soldiers' thirst. When her husband collapsed from heatstroke, Mary helped the crew fire the cannon. The British escaped, but the Patriots had fought well—especially with the help of Mary, who earned the nickname Molly Pitcher.

Pack for carrying ammunition

Important battles of the Revolutionary War took place along the western frontier. Much of this fighting involved Native Americans. Although some Indians helped the Patriots, more of them sided with the British. For the Native Americans, the British seemed to present less of a threat than the Americans did. American settlers continued to push westward, threatening the Native Americans' way of life.

Settlement Raids

West of the Appalachian Mountains, the British and their Indian allies were raiding American settlements. Mohawk chief **Joseph Brant** led a number of brutal attacks in southwestern New York and northern Pennsylvania.

Henry Hamilton commanded the main British base in the west, Detroit. Some called Hamilton the "hair buyer" because of rumors that he paid Native Americans for the scalps of settlers.

Geography
Victory at Vincennes

George Rogers Clark, a lieutenant colonel in the Virginia militia, set out to end the British attacks on western settlers. In June 1778, Clark and 175 soldiers sailed down the Ohio River to the mouth of the Tennessee River. After marching 120 miles, the Patriots seized the British post at Kaskaskia (ka•SKAS•kee•uh) in present-day Illinois. Then they captured the town of **Vincennes** (vihn•SEHNZ), in present-day Indiana, from the British.

During Clark's absence in December, British troops under Henry Hamilton's command recaptured Vincennes. Clark vowed to get it back. In February, after marching for days through countrysides flooded with icy waters, Clark and his troops surprised the British, forcing Hamilton to surrender. George Rogers Clark's victory at Vincennes strengthened the American position in the West.

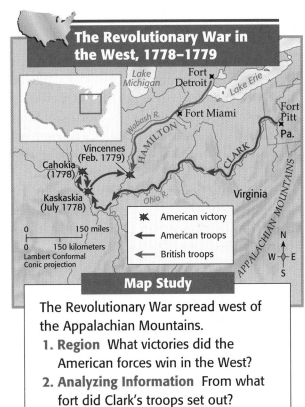

The Revolutionary War in the West, 1778–1779

American victory ✳
American troops ←
British troops ←

Map Study

The Revolutionary War spread west of the Appalachian Mountains.
1. **Region** What victories did the American forces win in the West?
2. **Analyzing Information** From what fort did Clark's troops set out?

Glory at Sea

As fighting continued on the western frontier, other battles raged at sea. Great Britain used its powerful navy to patrol American waterways, keeping the ships of the Patriots and their allies from entering or leaving American harbors. This British blockade prevented supplies and reinforcements from reaching the Continental Army.

Privateers

To break the British naval blockade, the Second Continental Congress ordered the construction of 13 American warships. Few of these, however, sailed to sea. The Americans destroyed 4 of their own ships to keep them out of British hands. Others were quickly captured by the British. Several states maintained their own small fleets, but the American navy was too weak to operate effectively.

American privateers captured more British vessels at sea than did the American navy. The privateers were privately owned merchant ships equipped with weapons. The Congress authorized more than 1,000 ships to sail as privateers and attack enemy shipping. Finding crews for these ships was not difficult. Sailors from the whaling and fishing ports of New England signed on eagerly for the profitable privateering trade.

Biography

John Paul Jones

One of the most daring American naval officers, **John Paul Jones,** raided British ports beginning in 1777. He sailed in an old French ship that Benjamin Franklin had obtained for him. Jones gave the ship a French name, *Bonhomme Richard*, in honor of Franklin's *Poor Richard's Almanack.*

Sailing near the coast of Great Britain in September 1779, the *Bonhomme Richard* met a large fleet of British merchant ships escorted by the warship *Serapis.* The *Bonhomme Richard* moved close to the *Serapis* before attacking. The two ships fought for more than three hours. At one point Jones's ship was so badly damaged that the British captain asked whether Jones wished to surrender. Jones is said to have answered, "I have not yet begun to fight."

In the end the *Serapis* surrendered, but the *Bonhomme Richard* sank not long after the battle. Still, his victory made John Paul Jones a naval hero to the American Patriots.

Struggles in the South

In the early years of the war, the Americans had won some battles in the South. In 1776 they had crushed Loyalists at the Battle of Moore's Creek, near Wilmington, North Carolina, and had saved **Charleston,** South Carolina, from the British. Although a small battle, its impact was great.

By 1778 the British realized that bringing the American colonies back into the empire would not be easy. As a result they changed their strategy and planned a hard-hitting offensive to finish the war.

The British concentrated their efforts in the South, where there were many Loyalists. They hoped to use British sea power and the support of the Loyalists to win decisive victories in the Southern states. Initially the strategy worked.

British Victories

In late 1778 General Henry Clinton sent 3,500 British troops from New York to take Savannah, on the coast of Georgia. The British occupied the city and overran most of the state.

Clinton himself headed south with a large army in early 1780 to attack the port of Charleston, South Carolina. Charleston surrendered in May, and the British took thousands of prisoners. It marked the worst American defeat of the war. A member of Britain's Parliament gloated, "We look on America as at our feet."

Clinton returned to New York, leaving **General Charles Cornwallis** in command of British forces in the South. The Continental Congress sent forces under General Horatio Gates to face Cornwallis. The two armies met at **Camden,** South Carolina, in August 1780. Although the British won,

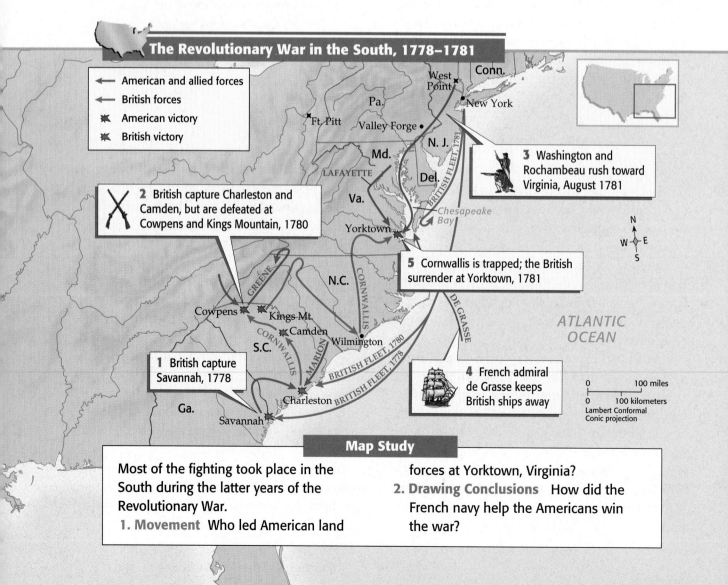

The Revolutionary War in the South, 1778–1781

- ← American and allied forces
- ← British forces
- ✳ American victory
- ✳ British victory

1 British capture Savannah, 1778

2 British capture Charleston and Camden, but are defeated at Cowpens and Kings Mountain, 1780

3 Washington and Rochambeau rush toward Virginia, August 1781

4 French admiral de Grasse keeps British ships away

5 Cornwallis is trapped; the British surrender at Yorktown, 1781

West Point · Conn. · New York · Pa. · Ft. Pitt · Valley Forge · N.J. · Md. · LAFAYETTE · Del. · Va. · BRITISH FLEET, 1781 · Chesapeake Bay · Yorktown · GREENE · N.C. · CORNWALLIS · DE GRASSE · Cowpens · Kings Mt. · Camden · Wilmington · CORNWALLIS · MARION · S.C. · BRITISH FLEET, 1780 · BRITISH FLEET, 1778 · Charleston · Ga. · Savannah · ATLANTIC OCEAN

0   100 miles
0   100 kilometers
Lambert Conformal Conic projection

Map Study

Most of the fighting took place in the South during the latter years of the Revolutionary War.

1. **Movement** Who led American land forces at Yorktown, Virginia?
2. **Drawing Conclusions** How did the French navy help the Americans win the war?

Hat

Clothing

Medal of George Washington

Musket

What Was It Like? Both sides fought furiously, as shown in William T. Ranney's *Tarleton's Cavalrymen in a Skirmish After the Battle of Cowpens.* **Describe the Patriots' clothing and weapons.**

Cornwallis soon found that he could not control the area he had conquered. He and his troops faced a new kind of warfare.

Guerrilla Warfare

The British received less help than they had expected from Loyalists in Southern states. Instead, as British troops moved through the countryside, small forces of Patriots attacked them. These bands of soldiers appeared suddenly, struck their blows, and then disappeared. This hit-and-run technique of guerrilla warfare caught the British off guard.

One successful guerrilla leader, **Francis Marion,** operated out of the swamps of eastern South Carolina. Known as the Swamp Fox, Marion was quick and smart. One British colonel grumbled that "the devil himself" could not catch Marion.

Patriot Victories

The British tried to invade central North Carolina in September 1780. At **Kings Mountain** a British officer and more than 1,000 Loyalists defended an outpost against the attack of Patriot sharpshooters. The Patriots forced the British to retreat. The victory brought new support for

Footnotes to History

The Cure May Be Worse For every Patriot soldier killed by the British, about nine died from disease or poor medical practices. In some cases, doctors drained about three-fourths of a soldier's blood. Then the soldier might be given calomel—a medicine sometimes used as an insecticide—which was sure to kill the already weakened patient.

★ HISTORY AND ART **The "Swamp Fox" and His Men** by William Ranney, c. 1850 Francis Marion, known as the "Swamp Fox," led his troops in quick, surprise strikes. **What is this type of warfare called?**

independence from Americans in the Southern states. They wanted to see an end to the war that was destroying their homes and farms.

In October 1780, **Nathanael Greene** replaced Gates as commander of the Continental forces in the South. Greene split his army in two. In January 1781, one section of the army, led by General Daniel Morgan, defeated the British at **Cowpens,** South Carolina. Another section joined Marion's guerrilla raids. In March Greene reunited his forces to meet Cornwallis's army at **Guilford Courthouse,** in present-day Greensboro, North Carolina. Greene's army was forced to retreat, but the British sustained great losses. General Cornwallis abandoned the Carolina campaign.

British Retreat

Cornwallis retreated north to Virginia in April 1781. His troops carried out raids throughout the state, nearly capturing Governor Thomas Jefferson and the Virginia legislature in June. Jefferson fled on horseback, just ahead of the advancing British troops.

General Washington sent Lafayette and von Steuben south to fight Cornwallis. Meanwhile Cornwallis set up camp at Yorktown, which was located on the Virginia coast, and awaited further orders from Clinton in New York. The battle for control of the South was entering its final phase.

★ ★ ★ ★ ★ **Section 3 Assessment** ★ ★ ★ ★ ★

Checking for Understanding
1. *Identify* George Rogers Clark, John Paul Jones, Charleston, General Charles Cornwallis, Francis Marion, Kings Mountain, Nathanael Greene, Cowpens.
2. *Define* blockade, privateer, guerrilla warfare.
3. *Explain* why most Native Americans sided with the British in the conflict.

Reviewing Themes
4. **Geography and History** How did the location of the colonies aid the British navy?

Critical Thinking
5. **Drawing Conclusions** Why was guerrilla warfare effective against the British?

Creating a Symbol Design a symbol or emblem that captures the spirit of the Patriot soldiers.

The American Revolution

The American Revolution was a time of danger and drama for American colonists. Experience some of the excitement of this period by completing these activities in which you or your group will personally play a role in the Revolutionary Era.

Language Arts

Interviewing the Patriots As a newspaper reporter, you have been assigned to interview delegates to the Second Continental Congress. Choose one or two delegates who interest you. Write a dialogue in which you interview each delegate and record the answers. With a classmate taking the delegate's role, record your interviews to present in class.

Art

Creating a Poster Choose one of the following events of the Revolutionary War period and make a poster that will win people's support for it: the Boston Tea Party, the boycott of British goods, opposition to the Stamp Act, or the recruitment of troops to serve in the Continental Army.

Design the poster with your own artwork or a collage of cut-out letters and images. Arrange a classroom display of all the posters.

Drama

Writing a Play Write a one-act play in which a small group of ordinary men, women, and children in a small town react to the news of the Declaration of Independence. Remember that reactions varied from colony to colony and that not all colonists wanted independence from Great Britain. Practice with a group of classmates and present the play in class.

School-to-Work

Making a Banner Use fabric and your imagination to make a banner or flag honoring an event in the new United States—such as the Declaration of Independence or Paul Revere's ride. Sketch your design. Then use graph paper to draw the patterns you will use for cutting letters, numbers, and symbols from scraps of colorful cloth. Glue or sew the designs on your banner. Attach it to a pole or cord for display in class.

Paul Revere galloped to Lexington with the urgent news that the British redcoats were coming.

July 1780
French troops arrive in colonies

August 1781
Washington advances toward British at Yorktown

October 1781
Cornwallis surrenders at Yorktown

September 1783
Treaty of Paris is signed

Section 4

The War Is Won

READ TO DISCOVER . . .

- how George Washington changed his military strategy.
- why the Americans won the Revolutionary War despite many disadvantages.

TERMS TO LEARN

ratify   ambush

The Storyteller

A popular children's tune in eighteenth-century Britain went like this:

"If ponies rode men and if grass ate the cows,
And cats should be chased into holes by the mouse . . .
If summer were spring and the other way 'round,
Then all the world would be upside down."

This song would hold special meaning for the British troops in America as the Revolution reached its peak.

General Jean Baptiste de Rochambeau, French commander

In July 1780, French troopships appeared in the waters off **Newport,** Rhode Island. The ships carried more than 5,000 soldiers under the command of **General Jean Baptiste de Rochambeau** (ROH•SHAM•BOH). Cheering crowds greeted the French soldiers who were well armed and clad in colorful uniforms and plumed caps. The promised French aid had arrived at last. Unfortunately the British fleet arrived soon afterward and trapped the French ships in Newport.

Victory at Yorktown

In the autumn of 1780, Washington camped north of New York City waiting for a second fleet of French ships. From this position he could keep a close eye on the British army based in New York that General Clinton commanded. Washington planned to attack Clinton's army as soon as this second French fleet arrived from the West Indies. He had to wait a year to put his plan into action, however, because the fleet did not set sail for America until the summer of 1781.

Change in Plans

Washington had followed reports of the fighting in the South during 1780 and 1781. He knew that the British army commanded by Cornwallis was camped in **Yorktown,** Virginia. Washington also knew that Patriot forces under the Marquis de Lafayette were keeping Cornwallis and his troops bottled up on the Yorktown peninsula.

In August 1781, Washington learned that **Admiral François de Grasse,** the French naval commander, was heading toward Chesapeake Bay instead of New York. Washington quickly changed his plans. He would advance on the British at Yorktown rather than at New York City.

Gathering of Forces

Washington took steps to ensure that the new American strategy stayed secret. He wanted Clinton to think the Patriots still planned to attack New York. This, he hoped, would keep Clinton from sending aid to Cornwallis.

General Rochambeau had marched his troops from Newport to join General Washington in July. Washington and Rochambeau then rushed south with their armies. The secrecy was so strict that most of the soldiers did not know where they were going. One soldier wrote, "We do not know the object of our march, and are in perfect ignorance whether we are going against New York, or . . . Virginia."

Washington also ordered Patriot soldiers from the western territories, under the command of **Anthony Wayne,** to march toward Virginia. Three groups—Wayne's troops, Washington's and Rochambeau's main American-French army, and the French fleet under Admiral de Grasse— would meet at Yorktown.

The Siege of Yorktown

Washington wondered whether his complicated plan had fooled Clinton, and whether the French fleet would reach Yorktown in time. On September 5, to his great relief, Washington received news that Admiral de Grasse's ships were nearing Yorktown.

The plan worked perfectly, and the British were thoroughly confused. By the end of September, 17,000 American and French troops had trapped Cornwallis's 8,000 British and Hessian troops at Yorktown. Meanwhile, Admiral de Grasse's fleet kept Cornwallis from escaping by sea. General Clinton and the rest of the British army waited in New York, unable to help the besieged Cornwallis.

★ **Picturing HISTORY** The Marquis de Lafayette (left) relied on James Armistead (right), an enslaved African American, to gather military information about the British. Armistead was later freed and took the name James Armistead Lafayette. **How did the French help the Patriots win the war?**

Cornwallis's Defeat

On October 11 the Americans and French began a tremendous bombardment. A Hessian soldier described the dreadful scene in his diary:

❝One saw men lying nearly everywhere who were mortally wounded and whose heads, arms, and legs had been shot off. . . . Likewise on watch and on post in the lines, on trench and work details, they were wounded by the fearfully heavy fire. ❞

British supplies began running low, and many soldiers were sick. Cornwallis realized the hopelessness of his situation. On October 19 he surrendered. The Patriots had won the **Battle of Yorktown.**

Chapter 6 The American Revolution **183**

 **HISTORY AND ART**

Surrender of Lord Cornwallis at Yorktown by **John Trumbull** Trapped by American and French forces, General Charles Cornwallis surrendered at Yorktown. The victory would guarantee America's independence. **What were the two major terms of the Treaty of Paris?**

Handing over their weapons, the British marched between rows of French and American troops—the French in fancy white uniforms on one side and the raggedly clothed Continental Army on the other. A French band played "Yankee Doodle," and a British band responded with a children's tune called "The World Turned Upside Down." Indeed it had.

The Treaty of Paris

★ The fighting did not really end with Yorktown. The British still held Savannah, Charleston, and New York, and a few more clashes took place on land and sea. The Patriot victory at Yorktown, however, convinced the British that the war was too costly to pursue. In March 1782, King George III appointed new ministers who were prepared to give Americans their independence.

---

*F*ootnotes to History

Two Substitutes Surrender At Yorktown, Washington waited to accept Cornwallis's sword in the gesture of surrender. Cornwallis was not there, instead naming General Charles O'Hara to act in his place. Washington, therefore, selected General Benjamin Lincoln to represent the Americans. Lincoln accepted O'Hara's sword.

The two sides sent delegates to Paris to work out a treaty. **Benjamin Franklin, John Adams,** and **John Jay** represented the United States. The talks began in April 1782, and the British accepted a preliminary agreement written by the Americans six months later. The American Congress ratified, or approved, the preliminary treaty in April 1783. The final **Treaty of Paris** was signed on September 3, 1783. By that time Britain had also made peace with France, Spain, and the Netherlands.

Terms of the Treaty

The Treaty of Paris was a triumph for the Americans. Great Britain recognized the United States as an independent nation. The territory that the new nation claimed extended from the Atlantic Ocean west to the Mississippi River and from Canada in the north to Spanish Florida in the south. The British promised to withdraw all their troops from this expanded American territory. They also agreed to give Americans the right to fish in the waters off the coast of Canada.

The United States, in turn, agreed that British merchants could collect debts owed by Americans. The treaty also stated that the Congress would "earnestly recommend" to the states that property taken from Loyalists be returned to them. Most of this property was never returned, however.

Washington's Farewell

★ British troops left New York City in late November 1783. The war had truly ended, and George Washington could at last give up his command. On December 4 Washington said farewell to his officers at Fraunces' Tavern in Manhattan. "With a heart full of love and gratitude, I now take my leave of you."

Two weeks later Washington formally resigned from the army at a meeting of the Second Continental Congress in Annapolis, Maryland. A witness described the scene: "The spectators all wept, and there was hardly a member of Congress who did not drop tears." Washington said,

❝Having now finished the work assigned me I retire . . . and take my leave of all the employments of public life. ❞

He returned to his home, Mount Vernon, in time for Christmas. There he planned to live quietly with his family.

Why the Americans Won

★ How had the Americans managed to win the Revolutionary War? How had they defeated Britain, the strongest military power in the world?

Fighting on Home Ground

The Americans had several advantages in the war. They fought on their own land, while the British had to bring troops and supplies from thousands of miles away. The siege of Yorktown showed how the British depended on support from the sea. When their ships were blocked, the troops faced American forces without support.

The British succeeded in occupying cities—they held New York for almost the entire war—but had difficulty controlling the countryside. They had not been successful at Saratoga or in the Carolinas. The Patriots, however, knew the local terrain and where to lay an ambush—surprise attack—or what route to take through a forest.

Help from other nations contributed to the American victory. The success at Yorktown would not have been possible without French soldiers and ships. Loans from France helped the Americans win the war. The Spanish also aided the Patriots by attacking the British in the Mississippi Valley and along the Gulf of Mexico.

Washington and the Patriots

George Washington's leadership skills played a critical role in the American victory. Perhaps most important, the American Revolution was a people's movement. Its outcome depended not on any one battle or event but on the determination and spirit of all the Patriots.

★ ★ ★ ★ ★ Section 4 Assessment ★ ★ ★ ★ ★

Checking for Understanding
1. **Identify** General Jean Baptiste de Rochambeau, Yorktown, Admiral François de Grasse, Treaty of Paris of 1783.
2. **Define** ratify, ambush.
3. **Describe** how the French navy helped Washington at Yorktown.

Reviewing Themes
4. **Groups and Institutions** What did the British agree to do in the Treaty of Paris?

Critical Thinking
5. **Analyzing Information** What qualities do you think Washington must have had to generate such loyalty in his soldiers?

▶ **Activity** ◀

Selecting an Appropriate Gift Draw a picture of a gift that you think the Continental Congress might have sent to the French government in appreciation for its help in ending the war.

Assessment and Activities

★ Reviewing Key Terms

On a sheet of paper, define the following terms:

Patriot
neutral
Loyalist
mercenary
recruit
deserter
inflation
blockade
privateer
guerrilla warfare
ratify

★ Reviewing Key Facts

1. Why did the British think its military forces were superior to those of the Americans?
2. What European nations supported the Americans in the war?
3. Why did many Native Americans give their support to the British?
4. What fighting method did the Americans use to keep the British from taking the Southern Colonies?
5. Which battle convinced the British that they could not defeat the Americans?

★ Critical Thinking

Analyzing Primary Sources

When George Washington marched from New York to Yorktown with his soldiers, he pointed to the cheering crowds and said, "We may be beaten by the English . . . but here is an army they will never conquer."

1. To what "army" was George Washington referring?
2. Why did he think they could never be conquered?

★ Time Line Activity

Create a time line on which you place the following events in chronological order.

- France openly supports the Patriots
- The British capture Charleston
- American Revolution begins
- Americans win at Yorktown
- John Paul Jones attacks British warship
- American Revolution ends
- British are defeated at Saratoga
- Patriots suffer at Valley Forge
- British capture Philadelphia

★ Reviewing Themes

1. **Groups and Institutions** What advantage did the Patriots have over the British mercenaries?
2. **Groups and Institutions** How did women help in the war effort?
3. **Geography and History** Why do you think the British found it easier to capture American cities than to take over the American countryside?
4. **Groups and Institutions** Why were the Americans able to defeat the British in the war?

★ Skill Practice Activity

Reading a Military Map

Study the military map on page 178, then answer the questions that follow.

1. What color symbolizes British troop movement?
2. What symbol represents battles?
3. When did the British capture the city of Savannah?
4. Who was victorious at the Battle of Cowpens?

★ Geography Activity

The Treaty of Paris in 1783 established the boundaries of the new United States. The newly independent nation shared land claims on the North American continent with several nations. Study the map below and answer the questions that follow.

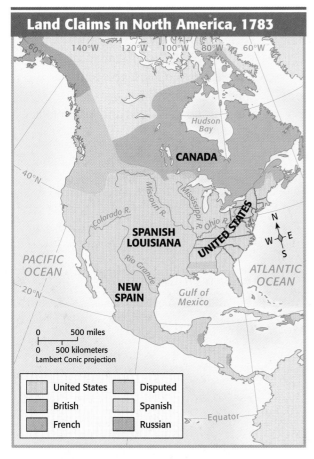

Land Claims in North America, 1783

CANADA

Hudson Bay

SPANISH LOUISIANA

UNITED STATES

PACIFIC OCEAN

NEW SPAIN

Gulf of Mexico

ATLANTIC OCEAN

Colorado R.

Missouri R.

Mississippi R.

Ohio R.

Rio Grande

Equator

0   500 miles
0   500 kilometers
Lambert Conic projection

- United States
- British
- French
- Disputed
- Spanish
- Russian

1. **Location** What natural landmark formed the new western boundary of the United States?
2. **Region** Which country claimed the most land in North America in 1783? The least land?
3. **Location** Which country claimed the land north of the United States?
4. **Location** Which country's land claims lay farthest north?
5. **Region** What nations claimed territory along the Pacific Ocean?

★ Cooperative Activity

History and Language Arts Conduct library research to learn more about the lives of American soldiers during the Revolutionary War. Select either an American soldier or an American regiment. Then organize your group into two smaller groups. One group will write a biography of an American soldier or a description of an American regiment. The other group will make a poster-sized, illustrated map displaying the names and geographic locations where your soldier or regiment fought.

★ Technology Activity

Using a Word Processor Search resources in your library for quotes made by at least five of the people mentioned in the chapter. Then retype and enlarge the quotes on a word processor. Post your quotes on a bulletin board display entitled "What Did They Say?" Add your own drawings of the people quoted.

Portfolio Activity History Journal Scan the chapter for details about people who came to the United States from other countries to help in the war effort. Record the names in your journal. Then create a chart that shows the peoples' names, their home countries, and what they did to aid the Americans.

1777–1790

A More Perfect Union

★ Why It's Important

When the American colonies broke their political ties with Great Britain, they were faced with the task of forming independent governments at both the state and national levels. In 1788 the Constitution became the official plan of American government. Created to meet the growing needs of a changing nation, the Constitution has been the fundamental law of the United States for more than 200 years. Of all the written national constitutions in the world, the United States Constitution is the oldest that is still operating. It has served as a model for many other countries in the world.

★ Chapter Themes

- *Section 1,* Government and Democracy
- *Section 2,* Groups and Institutions
- *Section 3,* Civic Rights and Responsibilities
- *Section 4,* Groups and Institutions

PRIMARY SOURCES Library *See pages 948–949 for primary source readings to accompany Chapter 7*

★ **HISTORY AND ART** *Signing the Constitution of the United States* by Thomas P. Rossiter The delegates sign the final draft of the Constitution in Philadelphia's Independence Hall. Despite mixed feelings, most of those present were hopeful about the future.

1775	1780	1785	1790

1777
Articles of
Confederation
are written

1781
All states approve
Confederation
government

1783
Treaty of Paris
officially ends
American Revolution

1787
Northwest
Ordinance
is passed

Section 1

The Articles of Confederation

READ TO DISCOVER . . .

- how the weaknesses of the Articles of Confederation created instability in the new United States.
- how the Confederation Congress dealt with the western lands.

TERMS TO LEARN

constitution
bicameral
republic

petition
ordinance
depreciate

 The Storyteller

The Revolutionary War had officially ended, but British troops continued to occupy American lands. George Rogers Clark had personally led many attacks against British-backed Native Americans. He boasted in his journal that he and his troops had left five Shawnee villages in Ohio, as well as a British trading post, "in ashes."

Powder horn and sash

Although the Americans won their independence from Britain, they had trouble winning Britain's respect. Ignoring the terms of the Treaty of Paris, the British kept troops at frontier posts within the United States. The British knew the new American government was weak and ineffective. In the years following the Revolution, Britain did not even bother to send a representative to the United States.

Thirteen Independent States

While Americans were fighting for their independence on the battlefield, they were also creating new governments. After rejecting British rule, they needed to establish their own political institutions at both the state and national levels.

State Constitutions

In May 1776 the Continental Congress asked the states to organize their governments, and each moved quickly to adopt a state constitution, or plan of government. By the end of 1776, eight states had drafted constitutions. New York and Georgia followed suit in 1777, and Massachusetts in 1780. Connecticut and Rhode Island retained their colonial charters as state constitutions.

Their experience with British rule made Americans cautious about placing too much power in the hands of a single ruler. For that reason the states adopted constitutions that limited the power of the governor. Pennsylvania even replaced the office of governor with an elected council of 12 members.

The states took further precautions against concentration of power. They divided government functions between the governor (or Pennsylvania's council) and the legislature. Most states established two-house, or bicameral, legislatures to divide the power even further.

The writers of the constitutions not only wanted to stop the abuses of power in the states, but they also wanted to keep power in the hands of the people. State legislators were popularly elected, and elections were frequent.

In most states, only white males over the age of 21 could vote. To qualify as a voter, these citizens also had to own a certain amount of property or pay a certain amount of taxes. Some states allowed free African American males to vote.

Popular Politics

The state constitutions restricted the powers of the governors, which made the legislatures the most powerful branch of government. Western parts of the states got more seats in legislatures, with many more farmers and common men elected than in the Colonial Era. The state legislatures struggled to make taxes more fair, but there were many squabbles between those who represented poor debtors and the wealthier state legislators. Going from dependent colonies to self-governing states brought many new challenges.

Forming a Republic

For Americans, establishing separate state governments was a much easier task than creating a single national government. They agreed that their nation should be a republic, a government in which citizens rule through elected representatives. They could not agree, however, on the organization and powers of their new republic.

At first most Americans favored a weak central government. They assumed the states would be very much like small, independent countries—similar to the way that the colonies had been set up. The states would act independently on most issues, working together through a central government only to wage war and handle relations with other nations.

Planning a New Government

In 1776 the Second Continental Congress appointed a committee to draw up a plan for a new national government. The delegates in the Congress realized they needed a central government to coordinate the war effort against Britain. After much debate the Congress adopted the committee's plan, the **Articles of Confederation,** in November 1777.

The Articles, America's first constitution, provided for a new central government to which the states gave little of their power. For the states the Confederation was "a firm league of friendship" in which each state retained "its sovereignty, freedom and independence."

Under the Articles of Confederation, the national government—consisting of the Confederation

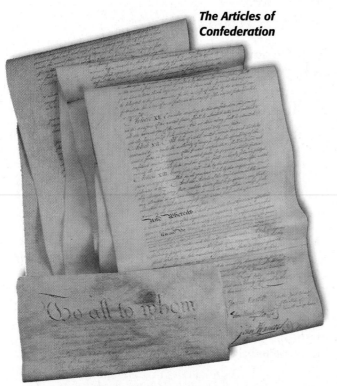

The Articles of Confederation

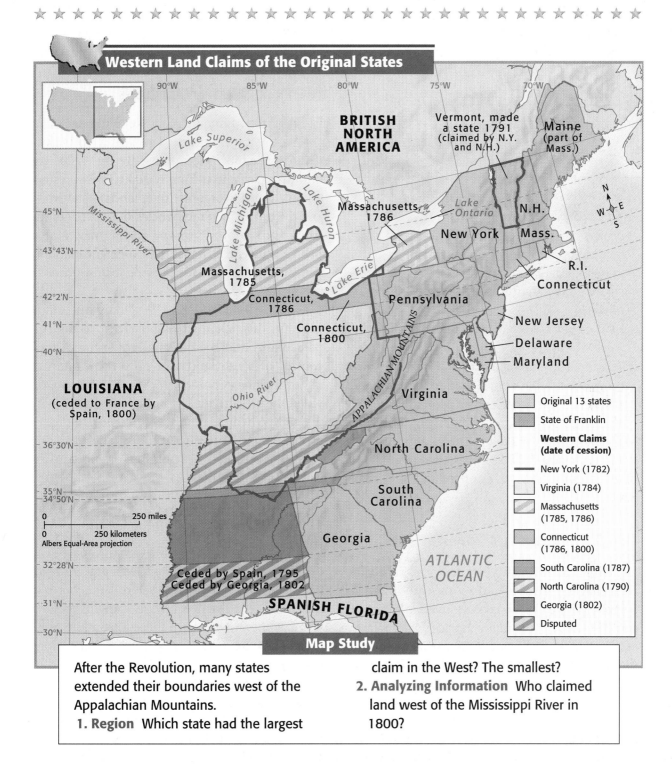

Western Land Claims of the Original States

British North America

Vermont, made a state 1791 (claimed by N.Y. and N.H.)

Maine (part of Mass.)

Massachusetts, 1786

N.H.

New York

Mass.

R.I.

Massachusetts, 1785

Connecticut

Connecticut, 1786

Pennsylvania

Connecticut, 1800

New Jersey

Delaware

Maryland

LOUISIANA (ceded to France by Spain, 1800)

Virginia

North Carolina

South Carolina

Georgia

ATLANTIC OCEAN

Ceded by Spain, 1795
Ceded by Georgia, 1802

SPANISH FLORIDA

0   250 miles
0   250 kilometers
Albers Equal-Area projection

Legend:

- Original 13 states
- State of Franklin
- **Western Claims (date of cession)**
- New York (1782)
- Virginia (1784)
- Massachusetts (1785, 1786)
- Connecticut (1786, 1800)
- South Carolina (1787)
- North Carolina (1790)
- Georgia (1802)
- Disputed

Map Study

After the Revolution, many states extended their boundaries west of the Appalachian Mountains.

1. **Region** Which state had the largest claim in the West? The smallest?
2. **Analyzing Information** Who claimed land west of the Mississippi River in 1800?

Congress—had the authority to conduct foreign affairs, maintain armed forces, borrow money, and issue currency. Yet it could not regulate trade, force soldiers to join the army, or impose taxes. If the Confederation Congress needed to raise money or troops, it had to ask the state legislatures—but the states were not required to contribute. In addition the new national government lacked a chief executive to enforce its laws.

Approving the Articles

All 13 states had to approve the Articles of Confederation before they could go into effect. Under the new plan, each state had one vote in the Confederation Congress. However, the large states thought they should have more votes because of their size and population. The states also argued about rights to western lands. Maryland

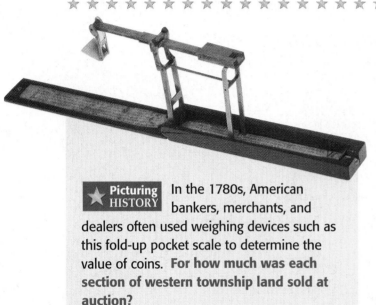

★ Picturing HISTORY In the 1780s, American bankers, merchants, and dealers often used weighing devices such as this fold-up pocket scale to determine the value of coins. **For how much was each section of western township land sold at auction?**

refused to approve the Articles until New York, Virginia, and other states abandoned claims to lands west of the Appalachian Mountains. Finally the states settled their differences, and with Maryland's ratification, all 13 had approved the Articles. On March 1, 1781, the Confederation formally became the government of the United States.

The Confederation Government

Within the next few years, however, it became clear that the Articles had serious problems. To begin with, the Congress had limited authority. It could not pass a law unless 9 states voted in favor of it. Any attempt to change the Articles required the consent of all 13 states. These strict voting requirements made it difficult for the Congress to pass laws when there was any opposition.

Despite its weaknesses, the Confederation did accomplish some important things. Its major accomplishment was winning the war, but it also provided for new states in the West.

🌐 Geography

New Land Policies

★ At the beginning of the Revolutionary War, only a few thousand settlers lived west of the Appalachian Mountains. By the 1780s the number was approaching 100,000. These western settlers hoped to organize their lands as states and join the nation, but the Articles of Confederation contained no provision for adding new states. The Congress realized it had to extend national authority over the frontier and bring order to this territory.

During the 1780s and 1790s, individual states gave up their claims to lands west of the Appalachians, and the national government took control of these lands. In 1784 the Congress, under a plan proposed by Thomas Jefferson, divided the western territory into 10 self-governing districts. When the number of people in a district reached the population of the smallest existing state, that district could petition, or apply to, the Congress for statehood.

The Ordinance of 1785

In 1785 the Confederation Congress passed an ordinance, or law, that established a procedure for surveying and selling the western lands north of the Ohio River. The new law divided this massive territory into townships 6 miles long and 6 miles wide. These townships were to be further divided into 36 sections of 640 acres each that would be sold at auction for at least a dollar an acre.

Land speculators viewed the law as an opportunity to cheaply accumulate large tracts of land. Concerned about lawless people moving into western lands, Richard Henry Lee, the president of the Congress, urged that "the rights of

---

*F**ootnotes to History***

The State of Franklin In 1784 three counties from the western territory of North Carolina formed their own state—Franklin. Named for Benjamin Franklin, the new "state" never met the requirements for admission to the Union. Franklin eventually became part of Tennessee.

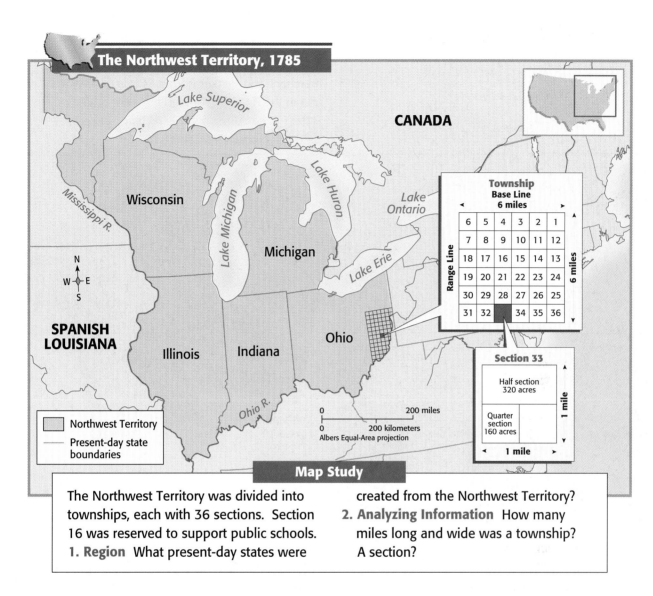

The Northwest Territory, 1785

CANADA

Lake Superior

Lake Huron

Lake Michigan

Lake Erie

Lake Ontario

Mississippi R.

Wisconsin

Michigan

SPANISH
LOUISIANA

Illinois

Indiana

Ohio

Ohio R.

Township
Base Line
6 miles

Range Line

6 miles

6	5	4	3	2	1
7	8	9	10	11	12
18	17	16	15	14	13
19	20	21	22	23	24
30	29	28	27	26	25
31	32	33	34	35	36

Section 33

Half section
320 acres

Quarter
section
160 acres

1 mile

1 mile

N
W—E
S

0   200 miles
0   200 kilometers
Albers Equal-Area projection

Northwest Territory

Present-day state boundaries

Map Study

The Northwest Territory was divided into townships, each with 36 sections. Section 16 was reserved to support public schools.
1. **Region** What present-day states were created from the Northwest Territory?
2. **Analyzing Information** How many miles long and wide was a township? A section?

property be clearly defined" by the government. The Congress drafted another ordinance to protect the interests of hard-working settlers.

The Northwest Ordinance

The Northwest Ordinance, passed in 1787, created a single **Northwest Territory** out of the lands north of the Ohio River and east of the Mississippi River. The lands were to be divided into three to five smaller territories. When the population of a territory reached 60,000, the people could apply for statehood. Each new state would come into the Union on "an equal footing" with the original 13 states.

The Northwest Ordinance included a bill of rights for the settlers, guaranteeing freedom of religion and trial by jury. It also stated, "There shall be neither slavery nor involuntary servitude in said territory." This clause marked the national government's first attempt to stop the spread of slavery.

The Confederation's western ordinances had enormous significance for American expansion and development. These policies opened the way for settlement of the Northwest Territory in a stable and orderly manner.

Trouble on Two Fronts

Despite its accomplishments in dealing with western lands, the Confederation government had so little power that it could not

★ **HISTORY AND ART** *Robert Morris* by Charles Willson Peale Pennsylvania merchant and banker Robert Morris (left) was one of the richest people in the new United States. **What reform did Morris propose to help the country's finances?**

Continental currency

deal with the nation's pressing financial problems. It also failed to resolve problems over land holdings and trade with Britain and Spain.

💲 **Economics**

Financial Problems

By 1781 the money printed during the Revolutionary War had depreciated, or fallen in value, so much that it was almost completely worthless. Unable to collect taxes, both the Continental Congress and the states had printed their own paper money. No gold or silver backed up these bills. For this reason the value of the bills plummeted, while the prices of food and other goods soared. Between 1779 and 1781, the number of Continental dollars required to buy one Spanish silver dollar rose from 40 to 146. In Boston and some other areas, the resulting high prices led to food riots.

Fighting the war left the Confederation Congress with a large debt. The Congress had borrowed money from American citizens and foreign governments during the war. It still owed the Revolutionary soldiers their pay for military service. Lacking the power to tax, the Confederation could not pay its debts. It requested funds from the states, but the states contributed only about one-sixth of the money needed.

Robert Morris's Import Tax

Faced with a total collapse of the country's finances, the Confederation created a department of finance under Philadelphia merchant **Robert Morris.** He proposed collecting a 5 percent tax on imported goods to help pay the national debt.

The plan required that the Articles of Confederation be changed to give the Congress the power to tax. Although 12 states approved the plan, the opposition of Rhode Island killed the measure. A second effort five years later also failed to win approval by all the states. The financial crisis worsened. 💲

Problems with Britain

As the weaknesses of the new American government became clear, the United States developed problems with other countries. In the Treaty of Paris of 1783, Britain had promised to withdraw from the lands east of the Mississippi River. Yet British troops continued to occupy several strategic forts in the Great Lakes region.

British trade policy was another problem. American merchants complained that the British were keeping Americans out of the West Indies and other profitable British markets.

In 1784 the Confederation Congress sent **John Adams** to London to discuss these problems. The British, however, were not willing to talk. They pointed to the failure of the United States to honor *its* promises made in the Treaty of Paris. The British claimed that Americans had agreed to pay Loyalists for the property taken from them during the Revolutionary War. The Congress had, in fact, recommended that the states pay the Loyalists, but the states refused.

Problems with Spain

If American relations with Great Britain were poor, affairs with Spain were worse. Spain, which held Florida as well as lands west of the Mississippi River, was anxious to halt American expansion into the territory it claimed. As a result, Spain closed the lower Mississippi River to American shipping in 1784.

American settlers west of the Appalachian Mountains protested vigorously because this new policy deprived westerners of their major avenue of trade. As **John Jay**, the American secretary of foreign affairs, had noted a few years earlier: "The Americans, almost to a man, believed that God Almighty had made that river a highway for the people of the upper country to go to sea by."

In 1786 American diplomats reached an agreement with Spain to limit American shipping on the Mississippi. In exchange Spain promised to accept the border between Georgia and Spanish Florida proposed by the Americans. The people living in the Southern states, however, rejected the agreement because it would have forced them to give up their right to use the Mississippi River.

The weakness of the Confederation and its inability to deal with problems worried many national leaders. George Washington described the government as "little more than the shadow without the substance." Many Americans began to agree that the country needed a stronger national government.

★ ★ ★ ★ ★ Section 1 Assessment ★ ★ ★ ★ ★

Checking for Understanding

1. *Identify* Articles of Confederation, Northwest Territory, Robert Morris, John Adams, John Jay.
2. *Define* constitution, bicameral, republic, petition, ordinance, depreciate.
3. *List* two weaknesses of the government under the Articles of Confederation.

Reviewing Themes

4. **Government and Democracy** Why did most states limit the power of their governors and divide their legislatures into two bodies?

Critical Thinking

5. **Predicting Consequences** What effects do you think the Northwest Ordinance had on Native Americans?

► Activity ◄

Making a Poster Imagine you are a United States citizen in the 1780s. Create a poster that defends the Articles. Be sure to include reasons the Confederation Congress is needed.

1783
Massachusetts court
rules slavery illegal

January 1787
Daniel Shays
leads rebellion

May 1787
Delegates meet to revise
Articles of Confederation

September 1787
Delegates sign draft
of Constitution

Section 2

Convention and Compromise

READ TO DISCOVER . . .

- how the Constitutional Convention broke the deadlock over the form of the new government.
- how the delegates resolved the issue of representation.

TERMS TO LEARN

depression
manumission
proportional
compromise

By 1786 many Americans observed that the Confederation government was not working. George Washington himself agreed that the United States was really "thirteen Sovereignties [independent nations] pulling against each other."

In the summer of 1787, Washington joined delegates from Virginia and 11 other states in Philadelphia. Rhode Island decided not to participate. The delegates came "for the sole and express purpose of revising the Articles of Confederation."

George Washington

The young nation faced difficult problems. An economic slowdown led to hardships and unrest among the people. Slavery became an issue as some states took action to limit or abolish it. Many Americans believed that the Confederation government was too weak to deal with the tough challenges facing the United States.

Economic Depression

★ After the Revolutionary War ended, the United States went through a depression, a period when economic activity slows and unemployment increases. Southern plantations had been damaged during the war, and rice exports dropped sharply. Trade also fell off as the British closed the profitable West Indian market to American merchants. What little money there was went to pay foreign debts, and a serious currency shortage resulted.

Difficult Times for Farmers

American farmers suffered because they could not sell their goods. They had problems paying the taxes that the states levied to meet Revolutionary War debts. As a result state officials seized farmers' lands to pay their debts and threw many farmers into jail. Grumblings of protest soon grew into revolt.

★ ★

Eyewitness to HISTORY

Shays's Rebellion

Resentment grew especially strong in Massachusetts. Farmers viewed the new government as just another form of tyranny. They wanted the government to issue paper money and make new policies to relieve debtors. In a letter to state officials, some farmers proclaimed: "Surely your honours are not strangers to the distresses [problems] of the people but . . . know that many of our good inhabitants are now confined in [jail] for debt and taxes." In 1786 angry farmers took the law into their own hands. Led by **Daniel Shays,** a former Continental Army captain, they forced courts in western Massachusetts to close so judges could not confiscate farmers' lands.

In January 1787 Shays led more than 1,000 farmers toward the federal arsenal in **Springfield,** Massachusetts, for arms and ammunition. The state militia ordered the advancing farmers to halt, then fired over their heads. The farmers did not stop, and the militia fired again, killing four rebels. Shays and his followers scattered, and the uprising was over.

Shays's Rebellion frightened many Americans. They worried whether the government could control unrest and prevent violence. On hearing of the rebellion, George Washington wondered whether "mankind, when left to themselves, are unfit for their own government." Thomas Jefferson, minister to France at the time, had a different view. "A little rebellion, now and then," he wrote, "is a good thing."

The Issue of Slavery

The Revolutionary War had brought into focus the contradiction between the American battle for liberty and the practice of slavery. Between 1776 and 1786, 11 states—all except South Carolina and Georgia—outlawed or heavily taxed the importing of slaves.

Although slavery was not a major source of labor in the North, it existed and was legal in all the Northern states. However, many individuals and groups worked to end the institution of slavery. In 1775 Quakers in Pennsylvania organized the first American antislavery society. Five years later Pennsylvania passed a law that provided for the gradual freeing of enslaved people.

In 1783 the Massachusetts high court ruled slavery illegal because the state constitution declared that "all men are born free and equal." Between 1784 and 1804, New Hampshire, Connecticut, Rhode Island, New York, and New Jersey also abolished slavery. To help the free African Americans make their way in society, two ministers formed the Free African Society in Philadelphia in 1787.

The states south of Pennsylvania, however, clung to the institution of slavery. The plantation system of the South had been built on the backs of slaves, and many Southerners feared that their economy could not survive without slavery. Nonetheless an increasing number of

★ **Picturing HISTORY** Only through donations was Massachusetts able to raise a militia to defeat Shays. **Why did Shays's Rebellion frighten many Americans?**

Philadelphia preachers Absalom Jones (left) and Richard Allen (right) founded the Free African Society and later set up the first African American churches. **Why was the Free African Society formed?**

slaveholders began freeing their slaves after the war. Virginia passed a law that encouraged manumission, the freeing of individual enslaved persons, and the state's free African American population grew rapidly.

The abolition of slavery in the North divided the states on the critical issue of whether people should be allowed to hold slaves. This division came at the time when many American leaders had decided that the Articles of Confederation needed strengthening. In the summer of 1787, when state representatives assembled to plan a new government, they compromised on this issue. It would take years of debate, bloodshed, and ultimately a war to settle the slavery question.

A Call for Change

★ The American Revolution had led to a union of 13 states; it had not yet created a nation. Some leaders were satisfied with a system of independent state governments that resembled the old colonial governments. Others saw a strong national government as the solution to America's problems. They demanded a reform of the Articles of Confederation.

Significant Voices

Two Americans active in the movement for change were **James Madison,** a Virginia planter, and **Alexander Hamilton,** a New York lawyer. In September 1786, Hamilton proposed calling a convention in **Philadelphia** to discuss trade issues. He also suggested that this convention consider what possible changes were needed to make "the Constitution of the Federal Government adequate to the exigencies [needs] of the Union."

At first George Washington was not enthusiastic about the movement to revise the Articles of Confederation. When he heard the news of Shays's Rebellion, however, Washington changed his mind. He observed, "There are combustibles in every State which a spark might set fire to." After Washington agreed to travel to Philadelphia, the meeting took on greater significance.

The Constitutional Convention

⭐ The Philadelphia meeting began in May 1787 and continued through one of the hottest summers in years. The 55 delegates included planters, merchants, lawyers, college presidents, physicians, generals, and governors. Three of the delegates were under 30 years of age, and one, America's elder statesman Benjamin Franklin, was over 80. Many were well educated. In a time when only one white man in 1,000 went to college, 26 of the delegates had college degrees. Native Americans, African Americans, and women were not considered part of the political process, so none attended.

Virginia's distinguished delegation included **Edmund Randolph**, former governor of Virginia; George Mason, author of the state's bill of rights; Madison, who kept a detailed journal of the convention; and Washington, the nation's hero. Pennsylvania sent the highly regarded Benjamin Franklin, as well as Gouverneur Morris, Robert Morris, and James Wilson. Alexander Hamilton was one of the representatives sent from New York.

The delegates unanimously chose Washington as presiding officer of the convention. Then they decided to close their doors to the public and to keep the proceedings secret. This would allow the delegates to speak freely and change their minds. Each state delegation had only a single vote, and a simple majority vote would be sufficient to make decisions.

📖 Biography

James Madison and the Constitution

James Madison, only 36 at the time, was the best prepared of the delegates. In the months before the convention, he had made a detailed study of government, reading hundreds of books on history, politics, and economics. He also had corresponded with Thomas Jefferson, who was serving as the United States minister to France.

Madison looked for ways to build a strong but fair system of government for the new republic. He knew that republics were considered weaker than monarchies because kings or queens could use their authority to act quickly and decisively. Who would provide the same leadership in a republic? At the same time, Madison was concerned about protecting the people from the misuse of power. As he searched for solutions to these questions, Madison worked out a new plan that included a system of balances among different functions of government. The delegates adopted many of Madison's ideas in what would become the Virginia Plan. 📖

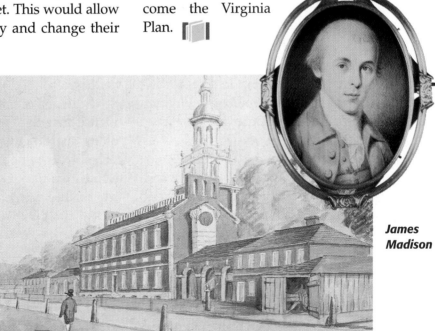

⭐ **Picturing HISTORY** The Pennsylvania State House, later known as Independence Hall, was the site of the signing of the Declaration of Independence and of the Constitutional Convention. **What were some characteristics of the Convention delegates?**

James Madison

Picturing HISTORY Delegate Alexander Hamilton emphasized the need for a stronger central government. **Why did some delegates worry that the Constitution lacked a bill of rights?**

The Virginia Plan

Edmund Randolph proposed that the delegates create a strong national government instead of revising the Articles of Confederation. He introduced the **Virginia Plan,** which was largely the work of Madison. The plan called for a two-house legislature, a chief executive chosen by the legislature, and a court system. The members of the lower house of the legislature would be elected by the people. The members of the upper house would be chosen by the lower house. In both houses the number of representatives would be proportional, or corresponding in size, to the population of each state. This would give Virginia many more delegates than Delaware, the state with the smallest population.

Delegates from Delaware, New Jersey, and other small states immediately objected to the plan. They preferred the Confederation Congress in which all states were represented equally.

The New Jersey Plan

Delegates unhappy with the Virginia Plan rallied around **William Paterson** of New Jersey. On June 15 he presented an alternative plan that modified—but did not completely discard—the Articles of Confederation. His proposal, the **New Jersey Plan**, kept the Confederation's one-house Congress with equal representation. However, Paterson proposed to give the Congress expanded powers to tax and regulate trade.

Compromise Wins Out

★ The convention delegates had to decide whether they were simply revising the Articles or writing a constitution for a new national government. On June 19 the states voted to work toward a national government based on the Virginia Plan. However, they still had to resolve the thorny issue of representation that divided the large and small states.

Discussion and Disagreement

As the convention delegates struggled to deal with difficult questions, tempers and temperatures grew hotter. How were the members of Congress to be elected? How would state representation be determined in the upper and lower houses? Were enslaved Africans to be counted as part of the population on which representation was based?

By the end of June, the disagreements grew so intense that the convention was in danger of falling apart. Benjamin Franklin suggested that each session be opened with a prayer asking for divine guidance. Otherwise, Franklin believed, "We shall be divided by our little partial local interests" and fail to reach agreement.

Footnotes to History

Let's Have Quiet! Philadelphia took great efforts to give the delegates a quiet atmosphere during the convention. The city went so far as to cover the paved road around the hall with dirt to reduce noise.

Citizenship

The Great Compromise

Under Franklin's leadership, the convention appointed a "grand committee" to try to resolve their disagreements. **Roger Sherman** of Connecticut suggested what came to be known as the **Great Compromise.** A compromise is an agreement between two or more sides in which each side gives up some of what it wants.

Sherman proposed a two-house legislature. In the lower house—the House of Representatives—the number of seats for each state would vary according to the state's population. In the upper house—the Senate—each state would have two members.

The Three-Fifths Compromise

A second part of the Great Compromise dealt with counting slaves. Southern states wanted to include enslaved Africans in their population counts to gain delegates in the House of Representatives. Northern states objected to this idea because enslaved people were legally considered property. Some delegates from Northern states argued that slaves, as property, should be counted for the purpose of taxation but not representation. However, neither side considered giving enslaved African Americans the right to vote.

The committee's solution, known as the **Three-Fifths Compromise,** was to count each enslaved person as three-fifths of a free person for both taxation and representation. In other words, every five slaves would equal three "people." On July 16 the convention delegates voted to approve the Great Compromise, breaking the deadlock between large and small states.

---

*F*ootnotes to History

A Man of Many Signatures Roger Sherman was the only man to sign all three major documents of the Revolutionary period. He signed the Declaration of Independence, the Articles of Confederation, and the United States Constitution.

★ **Picturing HISTORY** Connecticut's Roger Sherman proposed what became known as the Great Compromise. **How did the Great Compromise deal with slavery?**

Slave Trade

The convention needed to resolve another difficult issue that divided the Northern and Southern states. Having banned the slave trade within their borders, Northern states wanted to prohibit it throughout the nation. Southern states considered slavery and the slave trade essential to their economies. To keep the Southern states in the nation, Northerners agreed to a compromise. The Congress would not interfere with the slave trade for 20 years. After that, the Congress could limit the slave trade if it chose to.

Bill of Rights

One important issue that the convention did not deal with was that of individual rights. The new state constitutions included sections listing rights of individuals—such as freedom of religion and trial by jury—that government could not take away. Some delegates worried that without the protection of a bill of rights the new national government might abuse its power. However, most of the delegates believed that the Constitution, with its carefully defined listing of government powers, provided adequate protection of individual rights.

Chapter 7 A More Perfect Union **201**

★ **Picturing HISTORY** Delegates to the Constitutional Convention met in this room at Independence Hall. **How many states had to ratify the Constitution before it went into effect?**

Approving the Constitution

★ The committees finished their work on the Constitution in late summer, and on September 17, 1787, the delegates assembled in the Philadelphia State House to sign the document. Franklin made a final plea for approval: "I consent to this Constitution because I expect no better, and because I am not sure, that it is not the best." Three delegates refused to sign—Elbridge Gerry of Massachusetts and Edmund Randolph and George Mason of Virginia. Gerry and Mason would not sign a constitution without a bill of rights.

The convention then sent the approved draft of the Constitution to the states for consideration. The Articles of Confederation had required unanimous approval of the states for the government to act. Getting a unanimous vote had proved slow and frustrating. Therefore, the delegates agreed to change the approval process for the Constitution. When 9 of the 13 states had approved, the new government of the United States would come into existence.

★ ★ ★ ★ ★ **Section 2 Assessment** ★ ★ ★ ★ ★

Checking for Understanding

1. **Identify** Daniel Shays, Springfield, James Madison, Alexander Hamilton, Philadelphia, Edmund Randolph, Virginia Plan, William Paterson, Roger Sherman, Great Compromise, Three-Fifths Compromise.

2. **Define** depression, manumission, proportional, compromise.

3. **Explain** what caused Shays's Rebellion to erupt.

Reviewing Themes

4. **Groups and Institutions** How did the Great Compromise satisfy the small and large states on the question of representation?

Critical Thinking

5. **Media Literacy** You are asked to write a 30-second news broadcast to announce the agreement made in the Great Compromise. What would you include in the broadcast?

Drawing a Political Cartoon Create a political cartoon that illustrates either the Northern states' view or the Southern states' view on how enslaved African Americans should be counted for representation.

Making Comparisons

Suppose you want to buy a portable compact disc (CD) player, and you must choose among three models. You would probably compare characteristics of the three models, such as price, sound quality, and size to figure out which model is best for you. In the study of American history, you often compare people or events from one time period with those from a different time period.

Learning the Skill

When making comparisons, you examine two or more groups, situations, events, or documents. Then you identify any similarities and differences. For example, the chart on this page compares two documents in regard to the powers they gave the federal government. The Articles of Confederation were passed and implemented before the United States Constitution, which took their place.

When making comparisons, you first decide what items will be compared and determine which characteristics you will use to compare them. Then you identify similarities and differences in these characteristics.

Practicing the Skill

Analyze the information on the chart on this page. Then answer the questions.

1. What items are being compared?
2. In what ways are the two documents different?
3. In what ways are the two documents similar?
4. Which document allowed the government to organize state militias?

The Articles of Confederation and the United States Constitution

Powers of Federal Government	Articles of Confederation	United States Constitution
Declare war; make peace	✔	✔
Coin money	✔	✔
Manage foreign affairs	✔	✔
Establish a postal system	✔	✔
Impose taxes		✔
Regulate trade		✔
Organize a court system		✔
Call state militia for service		✔
Protect copyrights		✔
Take other necessary actions to run the federal government		✔

Applying the Skill

Making Comparisons On the editorial page of your local newspaper, find two letters to the editor that express different viewpoints on the same issue. Read the letters and identify the similarities and differences between the two points of view.

Glencoe's **Skillbuilder Interactive Workbook, Level 1** provides instruction and practice in key social studies skills.

1689
English Bill of
Rights established

1690
Locke writes
*Two Treatises on
Civil Government*

1748
Montesquieu writes
The Spirit of Laws

1787
Constitutional
Convention
meets in
Philadelphia

Section 3

A New Plan of Government

READ TO DISCOVER . . .
- how European ideas influenced the Constitution.
- how the Constitution limits the power of government.

TERMS TO LEARN
Enlightenment
federalism
article
legislative branch

executive branch
Electoral College
judicial branch
checks and balances

S toryteller

As the delegates hammered out the Constitution, Benjamin Franklin looked toward the president's chair, at the back of which a rising sun happened to be painted. "I have," said he, "often and often in the course of the Session . . . looked at that [sun] behind the President without being able to tell whether it was rising or setting; but now, at length I have the happiness to know it is a rising and not a setting Sun."

*Rising Sun chair,
Constitutional Convention*

After four long and difficult months, the delegates in **Philadelphia** had produced a new constitution. The document provided the framework for a strong central government for the United States.

Although a uniquely American document, the Constitution had roots in many civilizations. The delegates had studied and discussed the history of political development at length—starting with ancient Greece—so that their new government could avoid the mistakes of the past.

Roots of the Constitution

Many ideas embedded in the Constitution came from the study of European political institutions and political writers. British ideas and institutions particularly influenced the delegates.

The Framers who shaped the document were familiar with the parliamentary system of Britain, and many had participated in the colonial assemblies or the state assemblies that followed. They valued the individual rights guaranteed by the British judicial system. Although the Americans had broken away from Britain, they wanted to continue many British traditions.

British System of Government

Beginning in the 1200s, the English had found ways to limit the power of the monarch. England's lawmaking body, Parliament, emerged as a force that the king had to depend on to pay for wars and to finance the royal government. Like Parliament, the colonial assemblies controlled their colony's funds. For that reason the assemblies had some control over colonial governors.

The English Bill of Rights of 1689 provided another important model for Americans. Many Americans felt that the Constitution also needed a bill of rights.

The Enlightenment

Framers of the Constitution got many ideas on the nature of people and government from European writers of the Enlightenment. The Enlightenment was a movement of the 1700s that spread the idea that knowledge, reason, and science could improve society. James Madison and other architects of the Constitution were familiar with the work of **John Locke** and **Baron de Montesquieu** (MAHN•tuhs•KYOO), two important thinkers who influenced the debate of the Enlightenment period.

Locke, an English philosopher, believed that all people have a natural right to life, liberty, and property. In his *Two Treatises on Civil Government* (1690), he wrote that government is based on an agreement, or contract, between the people and the ruler. The Framers viewed the Constitution as a contract between the American people and their government. The contract protected the people's natural rights by limiting the government's power.

In *The Spirit of Laws* (1748), the French writer Montesquieu declared that the powers of government should be separated and balanced against each other. This separation would keep any one person or group from gaining too much power. The powers of government should also be clearly defined and limited to prevent misuse. Following the ideas of Montesquieu, the Framers of the Constitution carefully described and divided the powers of government.

John Locke, English political thinker, late 1600s

The Federal System

★ The Constitution created a federal system of government that divided powers between the national, or federal, government and the states. Under the Articles of Confederation, the states were much stronger than the national Congress. Under the Constitution the states gave up some of their powers to the federal government while keeping others.

Shared Powers

Federalism, or sharing power between the federal and state governments, is one of the distinctive features of the United States government. Under the Constitution, the federal government gained broad powers to tax, regulate trade, control the currency, raise an army, and declare war. It could also pass laws that were "necessary and proper" for carrying out its responsibilities.

However, the Constitution left important powers in the hands of the states. The states had the power to pass and enforce laws and regulate trade within their borders. They could also establish local governments, schools, and other institutions affecting the welfare of their citizens. Both federal and state governments also had the power to tax and build roads.

The Constitution Becomes Supreme Law of the Land

The Constitution and the laws that Congress passed were to be "the supreme law of the land." No state could make laws or take actions that went against the Constitution. Any dispute between the federal government and the states was to be settled by the federal courts on the basis of the Constitution. Under the new federal system, the Constitution became the final authority.

The Organization of Government

★ Influenced by Montesquieu's idea of a division of powers, the Framers divided the federal government into three branches—legislative, executive, and judicial. The first three articles, or parts, of the Constitution describe the powers and responsibilities of each branch.

The Legislative Branch

Article I of the Constitution established Congress, the legislative, or lawmaking, branch of the government. Congress was composed of the House of Representatives and the Senate. As a result of the Great Compromise between large and small states, each state's representation in the House would be proportional to its population. Representation in the Senate would be equal—two senators for each state.

The powers of Congress would include collecting taxes, coining money, and regulating trade. Congress also could declare war and "raise and support armies." Finally it could make all laws needed to fulfill the functions given to it by the Constitution.

The Executive Branch

Memories of King George III's rule made some delegates reluctant to establish a powerful executive, or ruler. Others believed that the Confederation had failed, in part, because it lacked an executive. They argued that a strong executive would serve as a check on Congress.

Article II of the Constitution established the executive branch, headed by the president, to carry out the nation's laws and policies. The president was to serve as commander in chief of the armed forces and to conduct relations with foreign countries.

The president and a vice president were to be elected indirectly by a special group called the Electoral College, made up of presidential electors. State legislatures would select electors to cast their votes for the president and vice president. Each state was to have as many electors as it had senators and representatives in Congress. The president and vice president chosen by the electors would serve a four-year term.

The Judicial Branch

Article III of the Constitution dealt with the judicial branch, or court system, of the United States. The nation's judicial power was to reside in

Linking PAST & PRESENT

The Election of Senators

The Seventeenth Amendment, adopted in 1913, changed the way senators are elected. Today members of the Senate, like those of the House, are elected directly by the people instead of by state legislatures.

American Memories
America in 1787

Woman's shoes

Boy's home-spun woolen suit

Hepplewhite chair

What Was It Like? Some American families bought imported goods from Europe. For others, however, everyday items were homemade. **What do these photos reveal about life in America in 1787?**

"one supreme Court" and any other lower federal courts that Congress might establish. The Supreme Court and the federal courts were to hear cases involving the Constitution, laws passed by Congress, and disputes between states.

System of Checks and Balances

The most distinctive feature of the United States government is the separation of powers. The Constitution divides government power among the legislative, executive, and judicial branches. To keep any one branch from gaining too much power, the Framers built in a system of checks and balances. The three branches have roles that check, or limit, the others so that no single branch can dominate the government.

Both the House and the Senate must pass a bill for it to become law. The president can check Congress by vetoing, or rejecting, the bill. However, Congress can then check the president by overriding, or voting down, the veto. To override a veto, two-thirds of the members of both houses of Congress must vote for the bill.

The system of checks and balances also applies to the Supreme Court. The president appoints Supreme Court justices, and the Senate must approve the appointments.

---

*F*ootnotes to History

Long-Term Planning When the delegates at the Constitutional Convention established the executive branch, they debated about the number of years a presidential term should be. One suggestion promoted a 15-year term!

Chapter 7 A More Perfect Union **207**

★ **Picturing HISTORY** The Supreme Court has the final say in deciding what the Constitution means. **What types of cases does the Supreme Court hear?**

Sometimes this system of checks and balances prevents the federal government from acting quickly and decisively. Yet for the most part, the system has been successful in maintaining a balance of power among the branches of the federal government and limiting abuses of power.

National Citizens

The Constitution created citizens of the United States. It set up a government in which the people would choose their officials—directly or indirectly. Officials would answer to the people rather than to the states. The new government pledged to protect the personal freedoms of its citizens.

With these revolutionary changes, Americans had shown the world that it was possible for a people to change its form of government through discussion and choice—rather than through chaos, force, or war. The rest of the world regarded the new nation with interest to see whether its experiment in self-government would really work.

★ ★ ★ ★ ★ ★ **Section 3 Assessment** ★ ★ ★ ★ ★ ★

Checking for Understanding

1. **Identify** Philadelphia, John Locke, Baron de Montesquieu.
2. **Define** Enlightenment, federalism, article, legislative branch, executive branch, Electoral College, judicial branch, checks and balances.
3. **Compare** the powers of the national government under the Articles of Confederation and under the Constitution.

Reviewing Themes

4. **Civic Rights and Responsibilities** Why did the Framers of the Constitution believe that a division of powers and a system of checks and balances were necessary in a government?

Critical Thinking

5. **Identifying Central Issues** Why was a powerful national government needed to unite the states?

Activity

Compiling Newspaper Reports Clip three newspaper articles that discuss the three different branches of our national government. Read the articles and discuss them with a classmate.

September 1787
Delegates sign draft
of Constitution

December 1787
Delaware is first state
to ratify Constitution

June 1788
Constitution is ratified
by nine states and goes
into effect

Section 4

Ratifying the Constitution

READ TO DISCOVER . . .
- how the Federalists and Antifederalists differed in their views on government.
- how the arguments for and against a bill of rights affected the vote for ratification.

TERMS TO LEARN
ratify   amendment
Federalist

Storyteller
The

Some voices rang out loud and clear in favor of the Constitution. Merchants shouted for better trade agreements with Britain. Frontier settlers cheered, hoping for more protection from attacks by Native Americans. Others, however, fiercely opposed the Constitution. Why revolt, people asked, simply to fall under a new kind of tyranny? Patrick Henry, one of the most popular leaders in Virginia, was deeply suspicious of centralized power. He warned Americans to "be extremely cautious, watchful, jealous of your liberty; for instead of securing your rights, you may lose them forever."

Desk used by Patrick Henry

Gaining approval of the Constitution with its radical new plan of government was not going to be easy. Supporters and opponents prepared to defend their positions.

Citizenship

The Constitutional Debate

⭐ The Confederation Congress sent the Constitution to the states. Before the Constitution could go into effect, nine states needed to ratify, or approve, it. State legislatures set up special ratifying conventions to consider the document. By late 1787 these conventions started to meet. **Rhode Island** stood apart. Its leaders opposed the Constitution from the beginning and therefore did not call a convention to approve it.

At the same time, a great debate took place throughout the nation. In newspapers, public meetings, and in ordinary conversations, Americans discussed the arguments for and against the new Constitution.

Federalists

Supporters of the new Constitution were called Federalists. Better organized than their opponents, Federalists enjoyed the support of two of the most famous and respected men in America—George Washington and Benjamin Franklin. Three of the nation's most gifted political thinkers—James Madison, Alexander Hamilton, and **John Jay**—also backed the Federalists.

Picturing HISTORY Antifederalist Mercy Otis Warren feared that the Constitution would make the central government too powerful. **What was the biggest criticism of the Constitution by Antifederalists?**

Madison, Hamilton, and Jay teamed up to write a series of essays explaining and defending the Constitution. These essays appeared in newspapers around the country and were widely read by colonists. They were later published as a book called *The Federalist.* Jefferson described the series of essays as "the best commentary on the principles of government which was ever written."

Antifederalists

The Federalists called those who opposed ratification Antifederalists. Although not as well organized as the Federalists, the Antifederalists had some dedicated supporters. Their main argument was that the new Constitution would take away the liberties Americans had fought to win from Great Britain. The Constitution would create a strong central government, ignore the will of the states and the people, and favor the wealthy few over the common people. Antifederalists preferred local government close to the people. Central government, they feared, would be government by a small, educated group of individuals. They agreed with Thomas Paine, who had said, "That government is best which governs least."

Protecting Rights

Perhaps the strongest criticism of the Constitution was that it lacked a bill of rights to protect individual freedoms. Antifederalists believed that no government can be trusted to protect the freedom of its citizens. Several state conventions took a stand and announced that they would not ratify the Constitution without the addition of a bill of rights.

Mercy Otis Warren, a Massachusetts opponent of the Constitution, expressed the problem faced by many Antifederalists. She admitted the need for a strong government but feared it.

❝ We have struggled for liberty and made costly sacrifices . . . and there are still many among us who [value liberty] too much to relinquish . . . the rights of man for the dignity of government. **❞**

In many ways the debate between Federalists and Antifederalists came down to their different fears. Federalists feared disorder without a strong central government and that more uprisings like Shays's Rebellion would occur. They looked to the Constitution to create a national government capable of maintaining order.

The Antifederalists feared government more than disorder. They worried about the concentration of power that would result from a strong national government.

Adopting the Constitution

Despite Antifederalist opposition the ratification of the Constitution proceeded fairly rapidly. On December 7, 1787, Delaware became the first state to approve the Constitution. On June 21, 1788, the ninth state—New Hampshire—ratified. In theory that meant that the new government could go into effect. Without the support of the two largest states—New York and Virginia—however, the future of the new government was not promising. Neither state had ratified yet, and both had strong Antifederalist groups.

In Virginia, **Patrick Henry** gave fiery speeches against the proposed Constitution. It did not, he charged, sufficiently check the power of the federal government. Nevertheless, Washington, Madison, Randolph, and the other Virginia Federalists carried the day. Virginia ratified the Constitution at the end of June 1788, after being assured that the Constitution would include a bill of rights amendment. An amendment is something added to a document.

That left three states—New York, North Carolina, and Rhode Island—to ratify. In July 1788, New York finally ratified by a narrow margin. One reason for its approval was New York City's threat to leave the state and join the Union on its own. North Carolina approved in November 1789 and Rhode Island in May 1790.

Americans Celebrate

After ratification came the celebrations. Boston, New York, and Philadelphia held big pa-

★ **Picturing HISTORY** Ratification of the Constitution set off a wave of celebration. This flag was carried by artisans in a New York City parade in July 1788. **Who were the most well-known Federalists supporting ratification of the Constitution?**

rades accompanied by cannon salutes and pealing church bells. Smaller celebrations took place in hundreds of American towns.

The task of creating the Constitution had ended with its ratification by the state conventions. The Bill of Rights would be added in 1791, after the new government took office. Now it was time for the nation to elect leaders and begin the work of government.

Section 4 Assessment

Checking for Understanding
1. *Identify* Rhode Island, John Jay, *The Federalist*, Patrick Henry.
2. *Define* ratify, Federalist, amendment.
3. *List* three reasons the Antifederalists opposed the Constitution.

Reviewing Themes
4. **Groups and Institutions** Why were the Federalists effective at getting their message across to the public?

Critical Thinking
5. **Predicting Consequences** Although the government could have gone into effect earlier, why was it important for *all* the states to ratify it?

Activity

Creating a Poster Collect photographs from newspapers or magazines that show the freedoms guaranteed in the Bill of Rights. Put your photos on a poster entitled "The Face of Liberty."

Assessment and Activities

⭐ Reviewing Key Terms

On a sheet of paper, define the following terms:

constitution	Enlightenment
bicameral	federalism
republic	legislative branch
ordinance	executive branch
depreciate	judicial branch
depression	checks and balances
proportional	ratify
compromise	amendment

⭐ Reviewing Key Facts

1. What was one achievement under the Articles of Confederation?
2. What caused the depression after the Revolutionary War?
3. How were John Locke's ideas incorporated into the Constitution?
4. What are two powers shared by federal and state governments?
5. Why did some states want a bill of rights added to the Constitution?

⭐ Reviewing Themes

1. **Government and Democracy** Did the state governments or the national government hold most of the power under the Articles of Confederation? Explain.
2. **Groups and Institutions** Were the people who attended the Constitutional Convention representative of the American public? Explain.
3. **Civic Rights and Responsibilities** Why was a system of checks and balances built into the Constitution?
4. **Groups and Institutions** What compromise was needed for Virginia to ratify the Constitution?

⭐ Critical Thinking

Determining Cause and Effect

The state of the economy had a great effect on people's desire to replace the Articles of Confederation.

1. Why did merchants and manufacturers want a stronger national government?
2. Why was it important for a national government to have the power to tax?

⭐ Skill Practice Activity

Making Comparisons

The two statements below reflect the opinions of an Antifederalist and a Federalist toward the Constitution. Read the opinions, then answer the questions that follow.

❝These lawyers, and men of learning, and moneyed men . . . make us poor illiterate people swallow down the pill, expect to get into Congress themselves; they expect to be the managers of this Constitution, and get all the power and all the money into their own hands, and then they will swallow up all us little folks. . . . This is what I am afraid of. ❞

—Amos Singletary, farmer

❝I am a plain man, and get my living by the plough. . . . I did not go to any lawyer, to ask his opinion; I formed my own opinion, and was pleased with this Constitution. . . . I don't think the worse of the Constitution because lawyers, and men of learning, and moneyed men, are fond of it. ❞

—Jonathan Smith, farmer

1. Who is the Antifederalist? How do you know?
2. How are the two opinions similar? How are they different?

⭐ Geography Activity

By 1790 Philadelphia was one of the information capitals of the United States. The map below shows the number of days it took for newspapers in Philadelphia to publish events that occurred elsewhere. Study the map and answer the questions that follow.

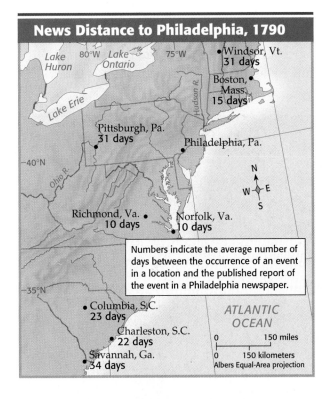

News Distance to Philadelphia, 1790

Lake Huron
Lake Ontario
Lake Erie
80°W 75°W
Windsor, Vt. 31 days
Boston, Mass. 15 days
Pittsburgh, Pa. 31 days
Philadelphia, Pa.
Hudson R.
Ohio R.
40°N
Richmond, Va. 10 days
Norfolk, Va. 10 days
Numbers indicate the average number of days between the occurrence of an event in a location and the published report of the event in a Philadelphia newspaper.
35°N
Columbia, S.C. 23 days
Charleston, S.C. 22 days
Savannah, Ga. 34 days
ATLANTIC OCEAN
N W E S
0 150 miles
0 150 kilometers
Albers Equal-Area projection

1. **Movement** How long, on average, did it take information from Pittsburgh to reach Philadelphia? From Savannah? From Windsor?
2. **Region** What effect do you think this information time lag had on different regions of the country?

⭐ Cooperative Activity

History and Global Issues Working in a small group, select a nation that has emerged in the last 25 years. Write a report that describes this nation's quest for independence.

⭐ Time Line Activity

Create a time line on which you place the following events in chronological order.
- Ninth state ratifies Constitution
- Articles of Confederation adopted
- Constitutional Convention begins
- Daniel Shays leads rebellion
- Congress passes first law regarding settlement of western lands
- Bill of Rights added to Constitution

⭐ Technology Activity

Using E-Mail Search the Internet for the names of your state's representatives in the United States Senate and House of Representatives. Find the E-mail address of one representative. Then write and send an electronic letter to the representative suggesting action on a national issue you feel strongly about.

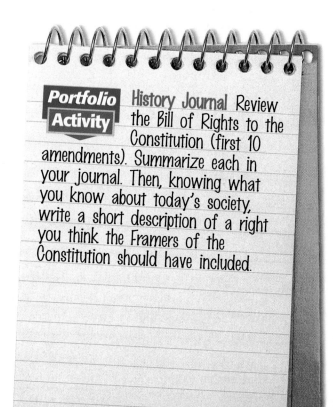

Portfolio Activity History Journal Review the Bill of Rights to the Constitution (first 10 amendments). Summarize each in your journal. Then, knowing what you know about today's society, write a short description of a right you think the Framers of the Constitution should have included.

Civics in Action
A Citizenship Handbook

READ TO DISCOVER . . .
- what goals shape the Constitution.
- the functions of the legislative, executive, and judicial branches.
- what the responsibilities of American citizens are.

TERMS TO LEARN

preamble	implied powers
domestic tranquility	judicial review
popular sovereignty	appropriate
enumerated powers	impeach
reserved powers	constituent
concurrent powers	warrant
amendment	due process of law

 Picturing HISTORY The Constitution—on display in the National Archives—is the nation's most important document. Written in 1787, it set up a system of government that has weathered crisis and change for more than 200 years.

The Constitution

In the summer of 1787, delegates from 12 states assembled in Philadelphia. They had come to address some of the weaknesses in the Articles of Confederation. Instead of changing the Articles, however, the delegates proposed an entirely new system of national government—in the Constitution of the United States. For more than 200 years, the Constitution has provided the framework for the United States government and has helped preserve American citizens' basic rights.

Silver inkwell used in the signing of the Constitution

★ ★

Goals of the Constitution

The Preamble, or introduction, to the Constitution reflects the basic principle of American government—the right of the people to govern themselves. It also lists six goals for the United States government:

> **" . . . to form a more perfect Union, establish Justice, insure domestic Tranquility, provide for the common defence [defense], promote the general Welfare, and secure the Blessings of Liberty to ourselves and our Posterity. "**

These goals guided the Constitution's Framers as they created a new government. They remain as important today as they were when the Constitution was written.

To Form a More Perfect Union

Under the Articles of Confederation, the states functioned almost like independent nations. For the most part, they did not work together on important matters such as defense and finances. This lack of unity could have been dangerous for the nation during times of crisis. To form "a more perfect Union" the Framers be-

lieved the states needed to agree to operate as a single country and cooperate on major issues, for the benefit of all.

To Establish Justice

For the Framers, treating each citizen equally was a fundamental principle on which to build the new nation. The Constitution provides a national system of courts to protect the people's rights and to hear cases involving violations of federal law and disputes between the states.

To Insure Domestic Tranquility

Shays's Rebellion in 1787 shocked Americans. The United States had become a self-governing nation, yet a group of people had resorted to violence to express their anger over government policies. The Constitution provides a strong central government "to insure domestic Tranquility"—that is, to keep peace among the people.

To Provide for the Common Defense

The Articles of Confederation did not provide an army or navy to defend the nation's borders. Its only defense system was the poorly trained militia of individual states. The Constitution gives the federal government the power to maintain armed forces to protect the country and its citizens from attack.

To Promote the General Welfare

The Declaration of Independence states that the purpose of government is to promote "Life, Liberty, and the pursuit of Happiness" for the people of the nation. The Constitution includes measures that promote the general welfare—or well-being—of the people by maintaining order, protecting individual liberties, and by using its laws and resources to ensure, as much as possible, that citizens will be free from poverty, hunger, and disease.

To Secure the Blessings of Liberty

The American colonists fought the Revolutionary War to gain their liberty from Great Britain. The Framers believed that preserving liberty should also be a major goal of the Constitution. The Constitution guarantees that no American's basic rights will be taken away now or for posterity. (Posterity means generations not yet born.)

Underlying Principles

The Constitution's Framers struggled to create a balance between a strong government and the liberties of the people. To achieve this, they adopted four ideas, or principles: popular sovereignty, limited government, federalism, and separation of powers.

Popular Sovereignty

The Declaration of Independence states that governments derive their powers from "the consent of the governed." The opening words of the Constitution, "We the people," reinforce this idea

of popular sovereignty—or "authority of the people." In the Constitution the people of America not only consent to be governed, but they also specify the powers and rules by which they shall be governed.

The Constitution allows the people to hold the final authority, or ruling power, in government. The people grant the government limited powers to act on their behalf, however. They choose representatives who understand and agree with their views to make laws and government policies.

The Constitution

Powers of the National Government	Powers shared by National and State Governments	Powers reserved for State Governments
• Regulate interstate and foreign trade • Raise/support armed forces • Declare war/make peace • Coin and print money • Grant patents/copyrights • Establish federal courts • Govern territories and admit new states • Set weights/measures • Establish a postal system • Regulate immigration	• Collect taxes • Borrow money • Make and enforce laws • Establish and maintain courts • Charter banks • Provide for public welfare	• Regulate trade within the state • Write business/corporation laws • Establish and maintain public schools • Set up local governments • Pass marriage/divorce laws • Conduct elections • Ratify constitutional amendments

Chart Study

The Constitution divides power between state and national levels.

1. Are public universities supported by the national or state government?

2. **Synthesizing Information** What powers shared by national and state governments deal with money?

Limited Government

The Framers saw both benefits and risks in creating a powerful national government. Although they agreed that the nation needed a stronger central authority, they feared misuse of power. They wanted to prevent the government from using its power to give one group special advantages or deprive another group of its rights. By creating a limited government, they restricted the government's authority to specific powers granted by the people.

Article I of the Constitution states the powers that the government has and the powers that it does not have. Other limits on government appear in the Bill of Rights, which guarantees certain rights and liberties to the people.

Limited government can be described as the "rule of law." No people or groups are above the law. Government officials must obey the law.

Federalism

In establishing a strong central government, the Framers did not deprive states of all authority. The states would give up some powers to the national government while retaining others. This principle of shared power is **federalism.**

Types of Powers

The Constitution defines three types of government powers. Certain powers belong only to the federal government. These enumerated powers include the power to coin money, regulate interstate and foreign trade, maintain the armed forces, and create federal courts (Article I, Section 8).

The second kind of powers are those retained by the states, known as reserved powers. They include such rights as the power to establish schools, pass marriage and divorce laws, and regulate trade within a state. Although reserved powers are not listed specifically in the Constitution, the Tenth Amendment says that all powers not specifically granted to the federal government "are reserved to the States."

The third set of powers defined by the Constitution are concurrent powers—powers shared by the state and federal governments. Among these powers are the right to raise taxes, borrow money, provide for public welfare, and administer criminal justice.

When conflicts arise between state law and federal law, the Constitution declares that the Constitution is "the supreme Law of the Land." Such conflicts must be settled in a federal court.

Separation of Powers

To prevent any single group or institution in government from gaining too much authority, the Framers divided the federal government into three branches: **legislative, executive,** and **judicial.** Each branch has its own functions and powers. The legislative branch, Congress, makes the laws. The executive branch, headed by the president, carries out the laws. The judicial branch, consisting of the Supreme Court and other federal courts, interprets and applies the laws.

As an additional safeguard, the Framers established a system of **checks and balances** in which each branch of government can check, or limit, the power of the other branches. This system helps maintain a balance in the power of the three branches. For example, Congress can pass a law. Then the president can reject the law by vetoing it. However, Congress can override, or reverse, the president's veto if two-thirds of the members of both houses vote again to approve the law.

Over the years, the Supreme Court has acquired the power to determine the meaning of the Constitution and to declare that a law or a

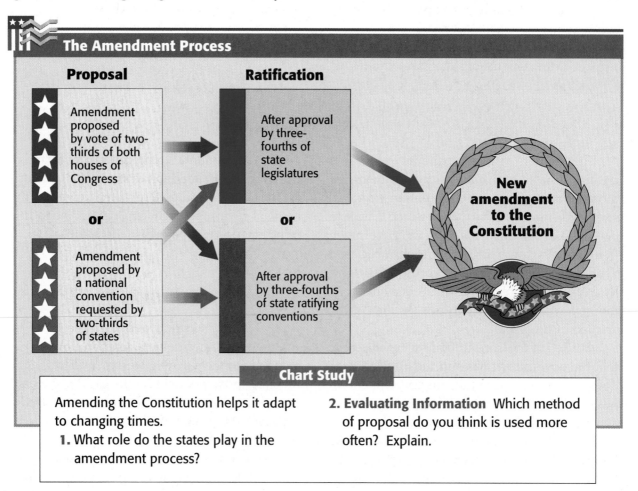

The Amendment Process

Proposal

Amendment proposed by vote of two-thirds of both houses of Congress

or

Amendment proposed by a national convention requested by two-thirds of states

Ratification

After approval by three-fourths of state legislatures

or

After approval by three-fourths of state ratifying conventions

New amendment to the Constitution

Chart Study

Amending the Constitution helps it adapt to changing times.

1. What role do the states play in the amendment process?

2. **Evaluating Information** Which method of proposal do you think is used more often? Explain.

government policy goes against the Constitution. In doing so, the Court provides a check on the powers of Congress and the president. Judicial decisions—those made by the courts—can be overruled by amending the Constitution. The president and the Senate provide a check on the judicial branch through their power to appoint and approve federal judges.

A Living Constitution

Two years after the Constitutional Convention, Benjamin Franklin wrote to a friend: "Our Constitution is in actual operation; everything appears to promise that it will last; but in this world nothing is certain but death and taxes."

Despite Franklin's uncertainty about the Constitution's future, it is still very much alive today. The Constitution has survived because the Framers wrote a document that the nation could alter and adapt to meet changing needs. They accomplished this by making the wording of the Constitution general rather than specific. The result is a flexible document that can be interpreted in different ways in keeping with conditions and thinking of a particular time. The Constitution's flexibility allows the government to deal with matters the Framers never anticipated—such as regulating nuclear power plants or developing a space program. In addition the Constitution contains a provision for amending—changing or adding to—the document.

Amending the Constitution

The Framers made the amendment process difficult to discourage minor or frequent changes being made in the Constitution. Although more than 9,000 amendments—changes to the Constitution—have been proposed since 1788, only 27 have actually become part of the Constitution.

An amendment to the Constitution may be proposed in two ways: by the vote of two-thirds of both houses of Congress or by two-thirds of the state legislatures asking for a special convention on the amendment. The second method has never been used.

The 27th Amendment

The most recent amendment to the Constitution was the Twenty-seventh Amendment. It was proposed on September 25, 1789, but not ratified until May 7, 1992. This amendment prevents Congress from passing immediate salary increases for itself. It delays congressional pay raises until after the next election. Congress passed the amendment in 1789 and sent it to the states for ratification. Because no time limit was set for its ratification, the proposal did not become part of the Constitution until Michigan became the 38th state to ratify it, 202 years later.

Ratification of an amendment requires approval by three-fourths of the states. The Constitution can be ratified by the approval of state legislatures or by special state conventions.

Only the Twenty-first Amendment—which repealed the Eighteenth Amendment, banning the sale of alcoholic beverages—was ratified by state conventions. Voters in each state chose the delegates to the special conventions. Congress chose this method to give the people a direct voice in the decision.

The Bill of Rights and Other Amendments

The Bill of Rights became part of the Constitution in 1791. These first 10 amendments protect basic liberties and rights that you may take for granted—including freedom of speech, freedom of the press, freedom of assembly, freedom of religion, and the right to a trial by jury.

The 17 amendments that follow the Bill of Rights expand the rights of Americans and adjust certain provisions of the Constitution. Included among them are amendments that abolish slavery, define citizenship, guarantee the right to vote to all citizens, authorize an income tax, and set a two-term limit on the presidency.

Medal of Washington

Interpreting the Constitution

The Constitution includes two provisions that give Congress the power to act as needed to meet changing conditions. The first of these provisions is what is known as the "elastic clause" (Article I, Section 8). It directs Congress to "make all Laws which shall be necessary and proper" for executing all the powers of government. Congress has interpreted this clause to mean that it has certain implied powers, powers not specifically defined in the Constitution. Over the years, Congress has drawn on its implied power to pass laws to deal with the needs of a changing society. When Congress created the United States Air Force in 1947, for example, it used the power implied in its authority to maintain an army and navy and to declare war.

The second provision used to expand congressional authority, the "commerce clause" (Article I, Section 8), gives Congress the power to "regulate Commerce with foreign Nations, and among the several States." Congress has used this clause to expand its powers into a number of areas, such as regulation of the airline industry, radio and television, and nuclear energy.

Power of the Presidency

The Constitution describes the role and the powers of the president in general terms. This has allowed the executive branch to extend its powers. In 1803, for example, President Thomas Jefferson approved a treaty with France that enabled the United States to buy an enormous tract of land. The treaty made the people living in the Louisiana Territory citizens of the United States. Although the Constitution gives the president the power to make treaties, it contains no provision granting the president the power to grant citizenship through a treaty.

The Courts

The role of the judicial branch has also grown as powers implied in the Constitution have been put into practice. In 1803 Chief Justice John Marshall expanded the powers of the Supreme Court by striking down an act of Congress in the case of *Marbury* v. *Madison.* In the Court's decision, Marshall wrote: "It is emphatically the province and duty of the judicial department to say what the law is." In that decision the Court defined its right to determine whether a law violates the Constitution. Although not mentioned in the Constitution, judicial review has become a major power of the judicial branch.

The process of amending the Constitution and applying its principles in new areas helps keep our government functioning well. In 1974 Barbara Jordan, an African American member of Congress and a constitutional scholar, spoke in ringing tones of her faith in the Constitution:

> **❝** I felt somehow for many years that George Washington and Alexander Hamilton just left me out by mistake. But through the process of amendment, interpretation, and court decision I have finally been included in 'We, the people.' **❞**

Activity

Analyzing Information The Bill of Rights guarantees certain basic rights to all Americans. Select one of the 10 amendments that make up the Bill of Rights (see pages 242–243) and research its history. Present your findings in a one-page essay.

The Federal Government

The government of the United States has three branches: the legislative branch, the executive branch, and the judicial branch. Each branch has specific powers that it uses to create, enforce, and interpret the nation's laws.

The presidential seal

The Legislative Branch

Congress, the legislative branch of the government, makes the nation's laws. It also has the power to "lay and collect taxes" and to declare war. Congress has two houses, the House of Representatives and the Senate.

The House and Senate

Today the House of Representatives has 435 voting members and 5 nonvoting delegates from the District of Columbia, Puerto Rico, Guam, American Samoa, and the Virgin Islands. The number of representatives from each state is determined by the state's population. Representatives, who must be at least 25 years old, serve 2-year terms.

The Senate consists of 100 senators, 2 from each state. Senators, who must be at least 30 years old, serve 6-year terms. The senators' terms are staggered, which means that one-third of the Senate seats come up for election every 2 years.

The Role of Congress

Congress has two primary functions: to make the nation's laws and to control government spending. The government cannot spend any money unless Congress appropriates, or sets aside, funds. All tax and spending bills must originate in the House of Representatives and gain approval in both the House and the Senate before going to the president for signature.

Congress also serves as a watchdog over the executive branch, monitoring its actions and investigating possible abuses of power. The House of Representatives can impeach, or bring formal charges against, any federal official it suspects of wrongdoing or misconduct. If an official is impeached, the Senate acts as a court and tries the accused official. Officials who are found guilty may be removed from office.

The Senate also holds certain special powers. Only the Senate can ratify treaties made by the president and confirm presidential appointments of federal officials such as department heads, ambassadors, and federal judges.

All members of Congress have the responsibility of representing their constituents, the people of their home states and districts. As a constituent you can expect your senators and representative to promote and protect your state's interests as well as those of the nation.

Congress at Work

Thousands of **bills**—proposed laws—are introduced in Congress every year. Because individual members of Congress could not

EXECUTIVE BRANCH

President Carries Out the Law

Checks on the Judicial Branch:
• Appoints federal judges
• Can grant pardons to federal offenders

Checks on the Legislative Branch:
• Can propose laws
• Can veto laws
• Can call special sessions of Congress
• Makes appointments to federal posts
• Negotiates foreign treaties

Checks on the Executive Branch:
• Can override presidential veto
• Confirms executive appointments
• Ratifies treaties
• Can declare war
• Appropriates money
• Can impeach and remove president

Checks on the Executive Branch:
• Can declare executive actions unconstitutional

JUDICIAL BRANCH

Supreme Court Interprets the Law

Checks on the Judicial Branch:
• Creates lower federal courts
• Can impeach and remove judges
• Can propose amendments to overrule judicial decisions
• Approves appointments of federal judges

LEGISLATIVE BRANCH

Bill

Congress Makes the Law

Checks on the Legislative Branch:
• Can declare acts of Congress unconstitutional

Chart Study

"You must first enable the government to control the governed," wrote Madison, "and in the next place, oblige it to control itself." The control Madison meant is found in the system of checks and balances in the Constitution.

1. How does the executive branch check the judicial branch?
2. **Making Generalizations** Do you think this system of checks and balances works? Explain.

possibly study all these bills carefully, both houses use committees of selected members to evaluate proposed legislation.

Standing committees are permanent committees in both the House and the Senate that specialize in a particular topic, such as agriculture, commerce, or veterans' affairs. These committees usually are broken down into **subcommittees** that focus on a particular aspect of a problem or issue.

The House and the Senate sometimes form temporary **select committees** to deal with issues requiring special attention. These committees meet only until they complete their task.

Occasionally the House and the Senate form **joint committees** with members from both houses. These committees meet to consider specific issues, such as the system of federal taxation. One type of joint committee, a **conference committee,** has a special function. If the House and the Senate pass different versions of the same bill, a conference committee tries to work out a compromise bill acceptable to both houses.

When it receives a bill, a committee can kill it by rejecting it outright, "pigeonhole" it by setting it aside without reviewing it, or prepare it for consideration by the full House or Senate. While preparing bills committees hold public hearings at which citizens can present arguments and documents supporting or opposing the bills.

Once a bill is approved by a committee in either house of Congress, it is sent to the full Senate or House for debate. After debate the bill may be passed, rejected, or returned to committee for further changes.

When both houses pass a bill, the bill goes to the president. If the president approves the bill and signs it, it becomes law. If the president vetoes the bill, it does not become law. Congress, however, may **override**—cancel—the presidential veto by a vote of two-thirds of the members in each house.

The Executive Branch

The executive branch of government includes the president, the vice president, and various executive offices, departments, and agencies. The executive branch carries out the laws that Congress passes.

Chief Executive

The president plays a number of different roles in government, each of which has specific powers and responsibilities. These roles include the nation's chief executive, chief diplomat, commander in chief, chief of state, and legislative leader.

As chief executive the president is responsible for carrying out the nation's laws. Many executive departments and agencies assist the president in this job.

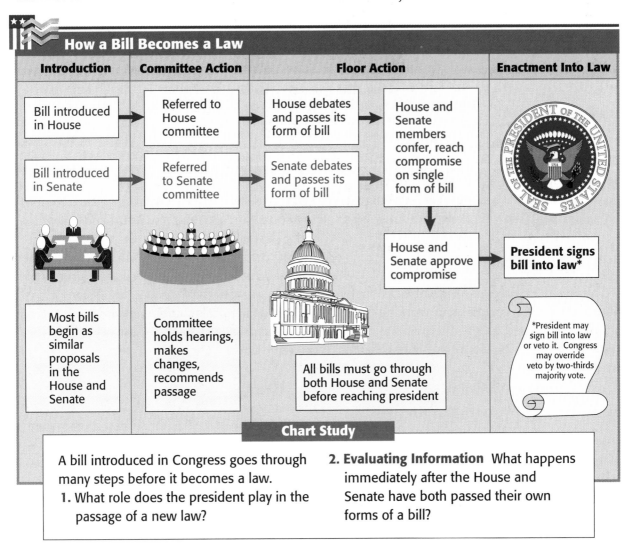

How a Bill Becomes a Law

Introduction	Committee Action	Floor Action	Enactment Into Law

Bill introduced in House → Referred to House committee → House debates and passes its form of bill → House and Senate members confer, reach compromise on single form of bill

Bill introduced in Senate → Referred to Senate committee → Senate debates and passes its form of bill

House and Senate approve compromise

President signs bill into law*

Most bills begin as similar proposals in the House and Senate

Committee holds hearings, makes changes, recommends passage

All bills must go through both House and Senate before reaching president

*President may sign bill into law or veto it. Congress may override veto by two-thirds majority vote.

Chart Study

A bill introduced in Congress goes through many steps before it becomes a law.

1. What role does the president play in the passage of a new law?

2. **Evaluating Information** What happens immediately after the House and Senate have both passed their own forms of a bill?

Chief Diplomat

As chief diplomat, the president directs foreign policy, appoints ambassadors, and negotiates treaties with other nations. Treaties must be approved by a two-thirds vote of the Senate before they go into effect.

Commander in Chief

As commander in chief of the armed forces, the president can use the military to intervene or offer assistance in crises at home and around the world. The president cannot declare war; only Congress holds this power. The president can send troops to other parts of the world for up to 60 days but must notify Congress when doing so. The troops may remain longer only if Congress gives approval or declares war.

President Clinton and Secretary of State Madeleine Albright with Palestinian leader Yassir Arafat

Chief of State

As chief of state, the president serves a symbolic role as the representative of all Americans. The president fulfills this role when receiving foreign ambassadors or heads of state, visiting foreign nations, or bestowing honors on Americans.

Legislative Leader

The president serves as a legislative leader by proposing laws to Congress and working to see that they are passed. In the annual State of the Union address, the president presents goals for legislation.

The Executive Branch at Work

Many executive offices, departments, and independent agencies help the president carry out and enforce the nation's laws. The Executive Office of the President (EOP) is made up of individuals and agencies that directly assist the president. Presidents rely heavily on the EOP for advice and for gathering information needed for decision making.

The executive branch also includes 14 executive departments, each responsible for a different area of government. For example, the Department of State plans and carries out foreign policy, and the Department of the Interior manages and protects the nation's public lands and natural resources. The heads, or secretaries, of these departments are members of the president's **cabinet,** a group that helps the president make decisions and set government policy.

The independent agencies manage federal programs in many fields. These include aeronautics and space, banking, communications, farm credit, and trade. Government corporations are government agencies that are run like privately owned businesses. One government corporation whose services you may use often is the United States Postal Service.

The Judicial Branch

Article III of the Constitution called for the creation of a Supreme Court and "such inferior [lower] courts as Congress may from time to time ordain and establish." In 1789 Congress passed a **Judiciary Act,** which added a series of district courts to the federal court system. Congress added appeals courts, sometimes called circuit courts, in 1891 to ease the workload of the Supreme Court.

Lower Federal Courts

At the lowest level of the federal court system are the United States **district courts.** These courts consider criminal and civil cases that come under federal, rather than state, authority. The criminal cases include such offenses as kidnapping and federal tax evasion. Civil cases cover claims against the federal government and cases

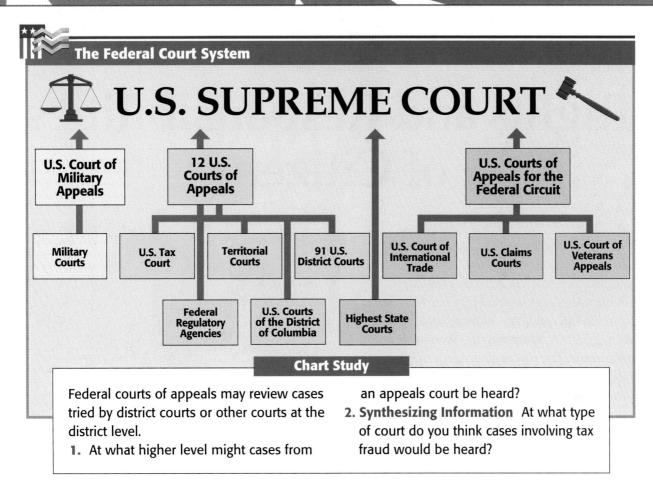

U.S. SUPREME COURT

- U.S. Court of Military Appeals
  - Military Courts
- 12 U.S. Courts of Appeals
  - U.S. Tax Court
    - Federal Regulatory Agencies
  - Territorial Courts
    - U.S. Courts of the District of Columbia
  - 91 U.S. District Courts
    - Highest State Courts
- U.S. Courts of Appeals for the Federal Circuit
  - U.S. Court of International Trade
  - U.S. Claims Courts
  - U.S. Court of Veterans Appeals

Chart Study

Federal courts of appeals may review cases tried by district courts or other courts at the district level.

1. At what higher level might cases from an appeals court be heard?
2. **Synthesizing Information** At what type of court do you think cases involving tax fraud would be heard?

involving constitutional rights, such as free speech. There are 91 district courts in the nation, with at least 1 in every state.

The next level of federal courts, the **appeals courts,** considers district court decisions in which the losing side has asked for a review of the verdict. If an appeals court disagrees with the lower court's decision, it can either overturn the verdict or order a retrial. There are 14 appeals courts in the United States.

The Supreme Court

The **Supreme Court,** the highest court in the federal court system, consists of a chief justice and eight associate justices. Most of the Supreme Court's cases come from appeals of lower-court decisions. Only cases involving foreign ambassadors or disputes between states can begin in the Supreme Court. The Supreme Court hears only about 150 cases each year.

The Supreme Court has the power of judicial review; that is, it can review laws and decide whether they are constitutional—in agreement with the Constitution. Over the years, the Supreme Court has interpreted the Constitution in different ways, sometimes reaching decisions that overturned earlier ones. Supreme Court decisions cannot be appealed, but Congress can modify a law to make it constitutional or propose an amendment to the Constitution.

Activity

Reading a Flowchart Flowcharts are meant to show the steps in a certain process. The flowchart on page 223 shows the movement of a bill through Congress. Use that chart to answer the following questions.

1. In what two places can a bill be introduced?
2. What is used to show the direction in which the bill is moving?
3. Where does a bill go after receiving approval by the House and the Senate?

Rights and Responsibilities of Citizens

Citizens of the United States have both rights and responsibilities. The rights come from the Constitution and its amendments, including the Bill of Rights; from laws enacted by Congress; and from the interpretation of those laws by the courts. State constitutions also confer rights on citizens. The responsibilities derive from each American's role as a member of society.

Citizens taking part in a town meeting

★ ★

The Rights of American Citizens

❝We hold these truths to be self-evident, that all men are created equal, that they are endowed by their Creator with certain unalienable Rights, that among these are Life, Liberty, and the pursuit of Happiness. ❞

These words from the Declaration of Independence have inspired Americans. They have encouraged Americans to pursue the ideals expressed in the Declaration and to create a Constitution and Bill of Rights that protect these rights.

Types of Rights

The rights of Americans fall into three broad categories: the right to be protected from unfair actions of the government, to have equal treatment under the law, and to have basic freedoms.

Parts of the Constitution and the Bill of Rights protect all Americans from abuse, or unfair treatment, by the government or the law. Among these rights are the right to a lawyer when accused of a crime and the right to trial by jury when charged with a crime. In addition the Fourth Amendment to the Constitution offers protection from unreasonable searches and seizures. This provision requires police to have a warrant before searching a person's home for criminal evidence. To obtain the search warrant, the police must have a very strong reason to suspect the person of committing a crime.

Due Process

The Fifth Amendment states that no person shall "be deprived of life, liberty, or property, without due process of law." Due process of law means that the government must follow procedures established by law and guaranteed by the Constitution, treating all people according to these principles.

Equal Protection

All Americans, regardless of race, religion, or political beliefs, have the right to be treated the same under the law. The Fourteenth Amendment requires every state to grant its citizens "equal protection of the laws."

Basic Freedoms

The basic freedoms involve the fundamental liberties outlined in the First Amendment—freedom of speech, freedom of religion, freedom of the press, freedom of assembly, and the right to petition. In addition the Ninth Amendment states that the rights of Americans are not limited to those mentioned in the Constitution. This has allowed basic freedoms to expand over the years through the passage of other amendments and laws. The Twenty-sixth Amendment, for example, extends the right to vote to American citizens 18 to 20 years of age.

Limits on Rights

The rights of Americans are limited, based on the principle of respecting everyone's rights equally.

Consider this situation. Many cities and towns require groups to obtain a permit to march on city streets. You might feel that this restricts your right to freedom of speech and assembly. However, the permit also protects the community by allowing the police to make provisions so that the march will not disturb the lives of other people. A law banning all marches would be unreasonable and in conflict with the First Amendment rights of free speech and assembly. Similarly, a law preventing only certain groups from marching would be unfair because it would not apply equally to everyone.

In this and other cases, the government applies the principle of limiting an individual's rights to protect the rights of others and the community's health and safety. Most Americans are willing to accept some limitations on their rights to gain these protections as long as the restrictions are reasonable and apply equally to all.

Citizens' Responsibilities

Participation in a democratic society involves certain duties and responsibilities. **Duties** are actions required by law. **Responsibilities** are voluntary actions. No law requires you to fulfill responsibilities in the community. Fulfilling both your duties and your responsibilities, however, helps ensure good government and the protection of your rights.

Duties

One of the fundamental duties of all Americans is to obey the law. Laws serve three important functions. They help maintain order; they protect the health, safety, and property of all citizens; and they make it possible for people to live together peacefully. If you disobey laws, for example, you endanger others and interfere with the smooth functioning of society. If you believe a law needs to be changed, you can work through your representatives to improve it.

Americans also have a duty to pay taxes. The government uses tax money to defend the nation, provide health insurance for people over 65, and build roads and bridges. Americans benefit from services provided by the government.

Upon Becoming 18 Years Old

Another duty of citizens is to defend the nation. All males aged 18 and older must register with the government in case the nation needs to call on them for military service. The nation no longer has a **draft,** or required military service, but a war could make the draft necessary again.

The Constitution guarantees all Americans the right to a trial by a jury of their peers. For this reason you should be prepared to serve on a jury when you become eligible at the age of 18. Having a large group of jurors on hand is necessary to guarantee the right to a fair trial. You also have a duty to serve as a witness at a trial if called to do so.

Most states require you to attend school until a certain age. School is where you gain the knowledge and skills needed to be a good citizen. In school you learn to think more clearly, to express

Citizens' demonstration

your opinions more accurately, and to analyze the statements and ideas of others. These skills will help you make informed choices when voting.

Responsibilities

The responsibilities of citizens are not as clear-cut as their duties. Responsibilities are as important as duties, however, because they help maintain the quality of government and society.

One important responsibility is to become well informed. You need to know what is happening in your community, your state, your country, and the world. Knowing what your government representatives are doing and expressing your feelings about their actions can help keep the government responsive to the wishes of the people. You can gain information about public issues and government activities by reading books, newspapers, and magazines and by listening to the news on radio or television. Discussing issues and events with others is another important way of gaining information and understanding.

You also need to be informed about your rights and to exercise them when necessary. Knowing your rights helps preserve them.

Vote, Vote, Vote!

Perhaps your most important responsibility as an American citizen will be to vote when you reach the age of 18. Voting allows you to participate in government and guide its direction. When you vote for people to represent you in govern-

ment, you will be exercising your right of self-government. If you disapprove of the job your representatives are doing, it will be your responsibility to help elect other people in the next election. You can also let your representatives know how you feel about issues through letters, telephone calls, and petitions and by taking part in public meetings or political rallies.

While not everyone holds public office, everyone can participate in government in other ways. Working on a political campaign, volunteering to help in a hospital or a library, and participating in a local park cleanup are all ways to take responsibility and make a contribution to good government and a well-run community.

To enjoy your rights to the fullest, you must be prepared to respect the rights of others. Respecting the rights of others also means respecting the rights of people with whom you disagree. Respecting and accepting others regardless of race, religion, beliefs, or other differences is essential in a democracy. All Americans are entitled to the same respect and treatment.

Activity

Making a Poster One responsibility of being an American citizen is to become involved in the democratic system. Make a poster showing how students can get involved in their community's democracy. Display your poster in a prominent place in the school.

Handbook Assessment

⭐ Reviewing Key Terms

On a sheet of paper, define the following terms:

preamble	implied powers
domestic tranquility	judicial review
popular sovereignty	appropriate
enumerated powers	impeach
reserved powers	constituent
concurrent powers	warrant
amendment	due process of law

⭐ Reviewing Key Facts

Section 1

1. *List* the six goals of government stated in the Preamble.
2. *Name* the three types of powers found in the Constitution.
3. *Explain* why the amendment process is so difficult.

Section 2

4. *Name* the three branches of government.
5. *Explain* how a bill becomes a law.
6. *Identify* the roles of the president of the United States.

Section 3

7. *List* the basic freedoms outlined in the First Amendment.
8. *State* three of the duties and three of the responsibilities of an American citizen.

⭐ Understanding Themes

1. **Government and Democracy** Why did the Framers of the Constitution provide for the separation of powers?
2. **Government and Democracy** What is the power of judicial review?
3. **Civic Rights and Responsibilities** How does due process of law protect individual rights?

⭐ Critical Thinking

1. **Analyzing Information** Review the six goals of the United States government in the Preamble. List them in order of importance as you think they should be carried out. Why did you select your first listed goal as most important? What goal would you eliminate if you had to? Why?
2. **Predicting Consequences** What might have happened to the U.S. republic if the Framers had not provided for a system of checks and balances?
3. **Evaluating Information** Some people have argued that there should be a limit on the number of terms a senator or representative can serve. What are some of the advantages of the present system, which does not limit these terms? What are some of the disadvantages?

⭐ Cooperative Activity

History and Citizenship Working with a partner, draw scenes from your community that show the freedoms guaranteed in the Bill of Rights. Put your drawings on a poster titled "The Face of Liberty."

⭐ Technology Activity

Using a Word Processor Part of your responsibility as an American citizen is to be informed about what the government is doing and to voice your opinion about its actions. On your word processor, compose a letter to the editor of your local newspaper. In your letter, express your opinion about an issue in your community.

The Constitution of the United States

The Constitution of the United States is truly a remarkable document. It was one of the first written constitutions in modern history. The Framers wanted to devise a plan for a strong central government that would unify the country, as well as preserve the ideals of the Declaration of Independence. The document they wrote created a representative legislature, the office of president, a system of courts, and a process for adding amendments. For over 200 years, the flexibility and strength of the Constitution has guided the nation's political leaders. The document has become a symbol of pride and a force for national unity.

The entire text of the Constitution and its amendments follows. For easier study, those passages that have been set aside or changed by the adoption of amendments are printed in blue. Also included are explanatory notes that will help clarify the meaning of each article and section.

The Capitol, Washington, D.C.

Preamble

We, the people of the United States, in Order to form a more perfect Union, establish Justice, insure domestic Tranquility, provide for the common defence, promote the general Welfare, and secure the Blessings of Liberty to ourselves and our Posterity, do ordain and establish this Constitution for the United States of America.

Article I

Section 1

All legislative Powers herein granted shall be vested in a Congress of the United States, which shall consist of a Senate and House of Representatives.

Section 2

1. The House of Representatives shall be composed of Members chosen every second Year by the People of the several States, and the Electors in each State shall have the Qualifications requisite for Electors of the most numerous Branch of the State Legislature.

2. No Person shall be a Representative who shall not have attained to the Age of twenty-five Years, and been seven Years a Citizen of the United States, and who shall not, when elected, be an Inhabitant of that State in which he shall be chosen.

3. Representatives and direct Taxes shall be apportioned among the several states which may be included within this Union, according to the respective Numbers, which shall be determined by adding to the whole Number of free Persons, including those bound to Service for a Term of Years, and excluding Indians not taxed, three-fifths of all other Persons. The actual Enumeration shall be made within three Years after the first Meeting of the Congress of the United States, and within every subsequent Term of ten Years, in such Manner as they shall by Law direct. The Number of Representatives shall not exceed one for every thirty Thousand, but each state shall have at Least one Representative; and until such enumeration shall be made, the State of New Hampshire shall be entitled to chuse three; Massachusetts eight, Rhode Island and Providence Plantations one, Connecticut five, New York six, New Jersey four, Pennsylvania eight, Delaware one, Maryland six, Virginia ten; North Carolina five, South Carolina five, and Georgia three.

4. When vacancies happen in the Representation from any State, the Executive Authority thereof shall issue Writs of Election to fill such Vacancies.

5. The House of Representatives shall chuse their Speaker and other Officers; and shall have the sole Power of Impeachment.

The Preamble introduces the Constitution and sets forth the general purposes for which the government was established. The Preamble also declares that the power of the government comes from the people.

The printed text of the document shows the spelling and punctuation of the parchment original.

Article I. The Legislative Branch

Section 1. Congress

The power to make laws is given to a Congress made up of two chambers to represent different interests: the Senate to represent the states; the House to be more responsive to the people's will.

Section 2. House of Representatives

1. Election and Term of Office

"Electors" means voters. Every two years the voters choose new Congress members to serve in the House of Representatives. The Constitution states that each state may specify who can vote. But the 15th, 19th, 24th, and 26th Amendments have established guidelines that all states must follow regarding the right to vote.

2. Qualifications

Representatives must be 25 years old, citizens of the United States for 7 years, and residents of the state they represent.

3. Division of Representatives Among the States

The number of representatives from each state is based on the size of the state's population. Each state is divided into congressional districts, with each district required to be equal in population. Each state is entitled to at least one representative. The number of representatives in the House was set at 435 in 1929. Since then, there has been a reapportionment of seats based on population shifts rather than on addition of seats.

Only three-fifths of a state's slave population was to be counted in determining the number of representatives elected by the state. Native Americans were not counted at all.

The "enumeration" referred to is the census, the population count taken every 10 years since 1790.

4. Vacancies

Vacancies in the House are filled through special elections called by the state's governor.

5. Officers

The Speaker is the leader of the majority party in the House and is responsible for choosing the heads of various House committees. "Impeachment" means indictment, or bringing charges against an official.

Section 3. The Senate
1. Number of Members, Terms of Office, and Voting Procedure
Originally, senators were chosen by the state legislators of their own states. The 17th Amendment changed this, so that senators are now elected directly by the people. There are 100 senators, 2 from each state.

2. Staggered Elections; Vacancies
One-third of the Senate is elected every two years. The terms of the first Senate's membership was staggered: one group served two years, one four, and one six. All senators now serve a six-year term.

The 17th Amendment changed the method of filling vacancies in the Senate.

3. Qualifications
Qualifications for the Senate are more restrictive than those for the House. Senators must be at least 30 years old and they must have been citizens of the United States for at least 9 years. The Framers of the Constitution made the Senate a more elite body in order to produce a further check on the powers of the House of Representatives.

4. President of the Senate
The vice president's only duty listed in the Constitution is to preside over the Senate. The only real power the vice president has is to cast the deciding vote when there is a tie. However, modern presidents have given their vice presidents new responsibilities.

5. Other Officers
The Senate selects its other officers, including a presiding officer (president pro tempore) who serves when the vice president is absent or has become president of the United States.

6. Trial of Impeachments
When trying a case of impeachment brought by the House, the Senate convenes as a court. The chief justice of the United States acts as the presiding judge, and the Senate acts as the jury. A two-thirds vote of the members present is necessary to convict officials under impeachment charges.

7. Penalty for Conviction
If the Senate convicts an official, it may only remove the official from office and prevent that person from holding another federal position. However, the convicted official may still be tried for the same offense in a regular court of law.

Section 4. Elections and Meetings
1. Holding Elections
In 1842 Congress required members of the House to be elected from districts in states having more than one representative rather than at large. In 1845 it set the first Tuesday after the first Monday in November as the day for selecting presidential electors.

2. Meetings
The 20th Amendment, ratified in 1933, has changed the date of the opening of the regular session of Congress to January 3.

Section 3
1. The Senate of the United States shall be composed of two Senators from each State, chosen by the Legislature thereof, for six Years; and each Senator shall have one Vote.

2. Immediately after they shall be assembled in Consequence of the first Election, they shall be divided as equally as may be into three Classes. The Seats of the Senators of the first Class shall be vacated at the Expiration of the second Year, of the second Class at the Expiration of the fourth Year, and of the third Class at the Expiration of the sixth Year, so that one-third may be chosen every second Year; and if Vacancies happen by Resignations, or otherwise, during the Recess of the Legislature of any State, the Executive thereof may make temporary Appointments until the next Meeting of the Legislature, which shall then fill such Vacancies.

3. No person shall be a Senator who shall not have attained the Age of thirty Years, and been nine Years a Citizen of the United States, and who shall not, when elected, be an Inhabitant of that State in which he shall be chosen.

4. The Vice President of the United States shall be President of the Senate, but shall have no vote, unless they be equally divided.

5. The Senate shall chuse their Officers, and also a President pro tempore, in the absence of the Vice-President or when he shall exercise the Office of the President of the United States.

6. The Senate shall have the sole Power to try all impeachments. When sitting for that purpose they shall be on Oath or Affirmation. When the President of the United States is tried, the Chief Justice shall preside: And no person shall be convicted without the Concurrence of two-thirds of the Members present.

7. Judgment in Cases of Impeachment shall not extend further than to removal from Office, and disqualification to hold and enjoy any Office of Honor, Trust or Profit under the United States: but the Party convicted shall nevertheless be liable and subject to Indictment, Trial, Judgment and Punishment, according to Law.

Section 4

1. The Times, Places, and Manner of holding Elections for Senators and Representatives, shall be prescribed in each state by the Legislature thereof; but the Congress may at any time by Law make or alter such Regulations, except as to the Places of Chusing Senators.

2. The Congress shall assemble at least once in every Year, and such Meeting shall be on the first Monday in December, unless they shall by Law appoint a different Day.

Section 5

1. Each House shall be the Judge of the Elections, Returns and Qualifications of its own Members, and a Majority of each shall constitute a Quorum to do Business; but a smaller Number may adjourn from day to day, and may be authorized to compel the Attendance of absent Members, in such Manner, and under such Penalties as each House may provide.

2. Each House may determine the Rules of its Proceedings, punish its Members for disorderly Behaviour, and, with the Concurrence of two-thirds, expel a Member.

3. Each House shall keep a Journal of its Proceedings, and from time to time publish the same, excepting such Parts as may in their Judgment require Secrecy; and the Yeas and Nays of the Members of either House on any question shall, at the desire of one-fifth of those Present, be entered on the Journal.

4. Neither House during the Session of Congress, shall, without the Consent of the other, adjourn for more than three days, nor to any other Place than that in which the two Houses shall be sitting.

Section 6

1. The Senators and Representatives shall receive a Compensation for their Services, to be ascertained by Law, and paid out of the Treasury of the United States. They shall in all Cases, except Treason, Felony and Breach of the Peace be privileged from Arrest during their attendance at the Session of their respective Houses, and in going to and returning from the same; and for any Speech or Debate in either House, they shall not be questioned in any other place.

2. No Senator or Representative shall, during the Time for which he was elected, be appointed to any civil Office under the Authority of the United States, which shall have been created, or the Emoluments whereof shall have been encreased, during such time; and no Person holding any Office under the United States, shall be a Member of either House during his continuance in Office.

Section 7

1. All Bills for raising Revenue shall originate in the House of Representatives; but the Senate may propose or concur with Amendments as on other bills.

2. Every Bill which shall have passed the House of Representatives and the Senate, shall, before it become a Law, be presented to the President of the United States; If he approve he shall sign it, but if not he shall return it, with his Objections, to that House in which it shall have originated, who shall enter the Objections at large on their Journal, and proceed to reconsider it. If after such Reconsideration two-thirds of that House shall agree to pass the bill, it shall be sent, together with the objections, to the other House, by which it shall likewise be reconsidered, and if approved by two-thirds of that House, it shall

Section 5. Organization and Rules of Procedure

1. Organization

Until 1969 Congress acted as the sole judge of qualifications of its own members. In that year, the Supreme Court ruled that Congress could not legally exclude victorious candidates who met all the requirements listed in Article I, Section 2.

A "quorum" is the minimum number of members that must be present for the House or Senate to conduct sessions. For a regular House session, a quorum consists of the majority of the House, or 218 of the 435 members.

2. Rules

Each house sets its own rules, can punish its members for disorderly behavior, and can expel a member by a two-thirds vote.

3. Journals

In addition to the journals, a complete official record of everything said on the floor, as well as the roll call votes on all bills or issues, is available in the *Congressional Record*, published daily by the Government Printing Office.

4. Adjournment

Neither house may adjourn for more than three days or move to another location without the approval of the other house.

Section 6. Privileges and Restrictions

1. Pay and Privileges

To strengthen the federal government, the Founders set congressional salaries to be paid by the United States Treasury rather than by members' respective states. Originally, members were paid $6 per day. Salaries for senators and representatives are $133,600.

The "immunity" privilege means members cannot be sued or be prosecuted for anything they say in Congress. They cannot be arrested while Congress is in session, except for treason, major crimes, or breaking the peace.

2. Restrictions

"Emoluments" means salaries. The purpose of this clause is to prevent members of Congress from passing laws that would benefit them personally. It also prevents the president from promising them jobs in other branches of the federal government.

Section 7. Passing Laws

1. Revenue Bills

"Revenue" is income raised by the government. The chief source of government revenue is taxes. All tax laws must originate in the House of Representatives. This ensures that the branch of Congress which is elected by the people every two years has the major role in determining taxes. This clause does not prevent the Senate from amending tax bills.

2. How Bills Become Laws

A bill may become a law only by passing both houses of Congress and by being signed by the president. If the president disapproves, or vetoes, the bill, it is returned to the house where it originated, along with a written statement of the president's objections. If two-thirds of each house approves the bill after the president has vetoed it, it becomes law. In voting to override a president's veto, the votes of all members of Congress must be recorded in the journals or official records. If the president does not sign or veto a bill within 10 days (excluding Sundays), it becomes law. However, if Congress has adjourned during this 10-day period, the bill does not become law. This is known as a "pocket veto."

3. Presidential Approval or Veto

The Framers included this paragraph to prevent Congress from passing joint resolutions instead of bills to avoid the possibility of a presidential veto. A bill is a draft of a proposed law, whereas a resolution is the legislature's formal expression of opinion or intent on a matter.

Section 8. Powers Granted to Congress

1. Revenue

This clause gives Congress the power to raise and spend revenue. Taxes must be levied at the same rate throughout the nation.

2. Borrowing

The federal government borrows money by issuing bonds.

3. Commerce

The exact meaning of "commerce" has caused controversy. The trend has been to expand its meaning and, consequently, the extent of Congress's powers.

4. Naturalization and Bankruptcy

"Naturalization" refers to the procedure by which a citizen of a foreign nation becomes a citizen of the United States.

5. Currency

Control over money is an exclusive federal power; the states are forbidden to issue currency.

6. Counterfeiting

"Counterfeiting" means illegally imitating or forging.

7. Post Office

In 1970 the United States Postal Service replaced the Post Office Department.

8. Copyrights and Patents

Under this provision, Congress has passed copyright and patent laws.

9. Courts

This provision allows Congress to establish a federal court system.

10. Piracy

Congress has the power to protect American ships on the high seas.

11. Declare War

While the Constitution gives Congress the right to declare war, the United States has sent troops into combat without a congressional declaration.

become a Law. But in all such Cases the Votes of both Houses shall be determined by Yeas and Nays, and the Names of the Persons voting for and against the Bill shall be entered on the Journal of each House respectively. If any Bill shall not be returned by the President within ten Days (Sundays excepted) after it shall have been presented to him, the Same shall be a Law, in like Manner as if he had signed it, unless the Congress by their Adjournment prevent its Return, in which Case it shall not be a Law.

3. Every Order, Resolution, or Vote to which the Concurrence of the Senate and House of Representatives may be necessary (except on a question of Adjournment) shall be presented to the President of the United States; and before the Same shall take Effect, shall be approved by him, or, being disapproved by him, shall be repassed by two-thirds of the Senate and House of Representatives, according to the Rules and Limitations prescribed in the case of a Bill.

Section 8

The Congress shall have the Power

1. To lay and collect Taxes, Duties, Imposts and Excises, to pay the Debts and provide for the common Defence and general Welfare of the United States; but all Duties, Imposts and Excises shall be uniform throughout the United States;

2. To borrow money on the credit of the United States;

3. To regulate Commerce with foreign Nations, and among the several States, and with the Indian Tribes;

4. To establish an uniform Rule of Naturalization, and uniform Laws on the subject of Bankruptcies throughout the United States.

5. To coin Money, regulate the Value thereof, and of foreign Coin, and fix the Standard of Weights and Measures;

6. To provide for the Punishment of counterfeiting the Securities and current Coin of the United States;

7. To establish Post Offices and post Roads;

8. To promote the Progress of Science and useful Arts, by securing for limited Times to Authors and Inventors the exclusive Right to their respective Writings and Discoveries;

9. To constitute Tribunals inferior to the Supreme Court;

10. To define and punish Piracies and Felonies committed on the high Seas, and Offenses against the Law of Nations.

11. To declare War, grant Letters of Marque and Reprisal, and make Rules concerning Captures on Land and Water;

12. To raise and support Armies, but no Appropriation of Money to that Use shall be for a longer Term than two Years;

13. To provide and maintain a Navy;

14. To make Rules for the Government and Regulation of the land and naval forces;

15. To provide for calling forth the Militia to execute the Laws of the Union, suppress Insurrections, and repel Invasions;

16. To provide for organizing, arming, and disciplining, the Militia, and for governing such Part of them as may be employed in the Service of the United States, reserving to the States respectively, the Appointment of the Officers, and the Authority of training the Militia according to the discipline prescribed by Congress;

17. To exercise exclusive Legislation in all Cases whatsoever, over such District (not exceeding ten Miles square) as may, by Cession of particular States, and the acceptance of Congress, become the Seat of Government of the United States, and to exercise like Authority over all Places purchased by the Consent of the Legislature of the State in which the Same shall be, for the Erection of Forts, Magazines, Arsenals, dock-Yards, and other needful Buildings;—And

18. To make all Laws which shall be necessary and proper for carrying into Execution the foregoing Powers, and all other Powers vested by this Constitution in the Government of the United States, or in any Department or Officer thereof.

Section 9

1. The Migration or Importation of such Persons as any of the States now existing shall think proper to admit, shall not be prohibited by the Congress prior to the Year one thousand eight hundred and eight, but a tax or duty may be imposed on such importation, not exceeding ten dollars for each Person.

2. The privilege of the Writ of Habeas Corpus shall not be suspended, unless when in Cases of Rebellion or Invasion the public Safety may require it.

3. No Bill of Attainder or ex post facto Law shall be passed.

4. No capitation, or other direct, Tax shall be laid unless in Proportion to the Census or Enumeration herein before directed to be taken.

5. No Tax or Duty shall be laid on Articles exported from any State.

6. No Preference shall be given by any Regulation of Commerce or Revenue to the Ports of one State over those of another: nor shall Vessels bound to, or from, one State, be obliged to enter, clear, or pay Duties in another.

12. Army
This provision reveals the Framers' fears of a standing army.

13. Navy
This clause allows Congress to establish a navy.

14. Rules for Armed Forces
Congress may pass regulations that deal with military discipline.

15. Militia
The "militia" is now called the National Guard. It is organized by the states.

16. National Guard
Even though the National Guard is organized by the states, Congress has the authority to pass rules for governing its behavior.

17. Nation's Capital
This clause grants Congress the right to make laws for Washington, D.C.

18. Elastic Clause
This is the so-called "elastic clause" of the Constitution and one of its most important provisions. The "necessary and proper" laws must be related to one of the 17 enumerated powers.

Section 9. Powers Denied to the Federal Government

1. Slave Trade
This paragraph contains the compromise the Framers reached regarding regulation of the slave trade in exchange for Congress's exclusive control over interstate commerce.

2. Habeas Corpus
Habeas corpus is a Latin term meaning "you may have the body." A writ of habeas corpus issued by a judge requires a law official to bring a prisoner to court and show cause for holding the prisoner. The writ may be suspended only during wartime.

3. Bills of Attainder
A "bill of attainder" is a bill that punishes a person without a jury trial. An "ex post facto" law is one that makes an act a crime after the act has been committed.

4. Direct Taxes
The 16th Amendment allowed Congress to pass an income tax.

5. Tax on Exports
Congress may not tax goods that move from one state to another.

6. Uniformity of Treatment
This prohibition prevents Congress from favoring one state or region over another in the regulation of trade.

7. Appropriation Law

This clause protects against the misuse of funds. All of the president's expenditures must be made with the permission of Congress.

8. Titles of Nobility

This clause prevents the development of a nobility in the United States.

Section 10. Powers Denied to the States

1. Limitations on Power

The states are prohibited from conducting foreign affairs, carrying on a war, or controlling interstate and foreign commerce. States are also not allowed to pass laws that the federal government is prohibited from passing, such as enacting ex post facto laws or bills of attainder. These restrictions on the states were designed, in part, to prevent an overlapping in functions and authority with the federal government that could create conflict and chaos.

2. Export and Import Taxes

This clause prevents states from levying duties on exports and imports. If states were permitted to tax imports and exports, they could use their taxing power in a way that weakens or destroys Congress's power to control interstate and foreign commerce.

3. Duties, Armed Forces, War

This clause prohibits states from maintaining an army or navy and from going to war, except in cases where a state is directly attacked. It also forbids states from collecting fees from foreign vessels or from making treaties with other nations. All of these powers are reserved for the federal government.

Article II. The Executive Branch

Section 1. President and Vice President

1. Term of Office

The president is given power to enforce the laws passed by Congress. Both the president and the vice president serve four-year terms. The 22nd Amendment limits the number of terms the president may serve to two.

2. Election

The Philadelphia Convention had trouble deciding how the president was to be chosen. The system finally agreed upon was indirect election by "electors" chosen for that purpose. The president and vice president are not directly elected. Instead, the president and vice president are elected by presidential electors from each state who form the electoral college. Each state has the number of presidential electors equal to the total number of its senators and representatives. State legislatures determine how the electors are chosen. Originally, the state legislatures chose the electors, but today they are nominated by political parties and elected by the voters. No senator, representative, or any other federal officeholder can serve as an elector.

7. No Money shall be drawn from the Treasury, but in Consequence of Appropriations made by Law; and a regular Statement and Account of the Receipts and Expenditures of all public Money shall be published from time to time.

8. No Title of Nobility shall be granted by the United States:—And no Person holding any Office of Profit or Trust under them, shall, without the Consent of the Congress, accept of any present, Emolument, Office, or Title, of any kind whatever, from any King, Prince, or foreign State.

Section 10

1. No State shall enter into any Treaty, Alliance, or Confederation; grant Letters of Marque and Reprisal; coin Money; emit Bills of Credit; make any Thing but gold and silver Coin a Tender in Payment of Debts; pass any Bill of Attainder; ex post facto Law, or Law impairing the Obligation of Contracts, or grant any Title of Nobility.

2. No State shall, without the Consent of the Congress, lay any Imposts or Duties on Imports or Exports, except what may be absolutely necessary for executing its inspection Laws: and the net Produce of all Duties and Imposts, laid by any State on Imports and Exports, shall be for the Use of the Treasury of the United States; and all such Laws shall be subject to the Revision and Controul of the Congress.

3. No State shall, without the Consent of Congress, lay any duty on Tonnage, keep Troops, or Ships of War in time of Peace, enter into any Agreement or Compact with another State, or with a foreign Power, or engage in War, unless actually invaded, or in such imminent Danger as will not admit of delay.

Article II

Section 1

1. The executive Power shall be vested in a President of the United States of America. He shall hold his Office during the Term of four years, and together with the Vice-President chosen for the same Term, be elected, as follows:

2. Each State shall appoint, in such Manner as the Legislature thereof may direct, a Number of Electors, equal to the whole Number of Senators and Representatives to which the State may be entitled in the Congress: but no Senator or Representative, or Person holding an Office of Trust or Profit under the United States, shall be appointed an Elector.

3. The Electors shall meet in their respective States, and vote by Ballot for two Persons, of whom one at least shall not be an Inhabitant of the same State with themselves. And they shall make a List of all the Persons voted for and of the Number of Votes for each; which List they shall sign and certify, and transmit sealed to the Seat of the Government of the United States, directed to the President of the Senate. The President of the Senate shall, in the Presence of the Senate and House of Representatives, open all the Certificates, and the Votes shall then be counted. The Person having the greatest Number of Votes shall be the President, if such Number be a Majority of the whole Number of Electors appointed; and if there be more than one who have such Majority, and have an equal Number of Votes, then the House of Representatives shall immediately chuse by Ballot one of them for President; and if no Person have a Majority, then from the five highest on the List the said House shall in like Manner chuse the President. But in chusing the President, the Votes shall be taken by States, the Representation from each State having one Vote; a quorum for this Purpose shall consist of a Member or Members from two-thirds of the States, and a Majority of all the States shall be necessary to a Choice. In every Case, after the Choice of the President, the Person having the greatest Number of Votes of the Electors shall be the Vice-President. But if there should remain two or more who have equal votes, the Senate shall chuse from them by Ballot the Vice President.

4. The Congress may determine the Time of chusing the Electors, and the Day on which they shall give their Votes; which Day shall be the same throughout the United States.

5. No person except a natural born Citizen, or a Citizen of the United States, at the time of the Adoption of this Constitution, shall be eligible to the Office of President; neither shall any Person be eligible to that Office who shall not have attained to the Age of thirty-five years, and been fourteen Years a Resident within the United States.

6. In Case of the Removal of the President from Office, or of his Death, Resignation, or Inability to discharge the Powers and Duties of the said Office, the same shall devolve on the Vice-President, and the Congress may by Law provide for the Case of Removal, Death, Resignation or Inability, both of the President and Vice-President, declaring what Officer shall then act as President, and such Officer shall act accordingly, until the disability be removed, or a President shall be elected.

7. The President shall, at stated Times, receive for his Services a Compensation, which shall neither be encreased nor diminished during the Period for which he shall have been elected, and he shall not receive within that Period any other Emolument from the United States, or any of them.

8. Before he enter on the execution of his office, he shall take the following Oath or Affirmation "I do solemnly swear (or affirm) that I will faithfully execute the Office of President of the United States, and will to the best of my Ability, preserve, protect and defend the Constitution of the United States."

3. Former Method of Election

This clause describes the original method of electing the president and vice president. According to this method, each elector voted for two candidates. The candidate with the most votes (as long as it was a majority) became president. The candidate with the second highest number of votes became vice president. In the election of 1800, the two top candidates received the same number of votes, making it necessary for the House of Representatives to decide the election. To prevent such a situation from recurring, the 12th Amendment was added in 1804.

4. Date of Elections

Congress selects the date when the presidential electors are chosen and when they vote for president and vice president. All electors must vote on the same day. The first Tuesday after the first Monday in November has been set as the date for presidential elections. Electors cast their votes on the Monday after the second Wednesday in December.

5. Qualifications

The president must be a citizen of the United States by birth, at least 35 years old, and a resident of the United States for 14 years. See Amendment 22.

6. Vacancies

If the president dies, resigns, is removed from office by impeachment, or is unable to carry out the duties of the office, the vice president becomes president. (Amendment 25 deals with presidential disability.) If both the president and vice president are unable to serve, Congress has the power to declare by law who acts as president. Congress set the line of succession in the Presidential Succession Act of 1947.

7. Salary

Originally, the president's salary was $25,000 per year. The president's current salary of $400,000 plus a $50,000 taxable expense account per year was enacted in 1999. The president also receives numerous fringe benefits including a $100,000 nontaxable allowance for travel and entertainment, and living accommodations in two residences—the White House and Camp David. However, the president cannot receive any other income from the United States government or state governments while in office.

8. Oath of Office

The oath of office is generally administered by the chief justice, but can be administered by any official authorized to administer oaths. All presidents-elect except Washington have been sworn into office by the chief justice. Only Vice Presidents John Tyler, Calvin Coolidge, and Lyndon Johnson in succeeding to the office have been sworn in by someone else.

Section 2. Powers of the President
1. Military, Cabinet, Pardons
Mention of "the principal officer in each of the executive departments" is the only suggestion of the president's cabinet to be found in the Constitution. The cabinet is a purely advisory body, and its power depends on the president. Each cabinet member is appointed by the president and must be confirmed by the Senate. This clause also makes the president, a civilian, the head of the armed services. This established the principle of civilian control of the military.

2. Treaties and Appointments
The president is the chief architect of American foreign policy. He or she is responsible for the conduct of foreign relations, or dealings with other countries. All treaties, however, require approval of two-thirds of the senators present. Most federal positions today are filled under the rules and regulations of the civil service system. Most presidential appointees serve at the pleasure of the president. Removal of an official by the president is not subject to congressional approval. But the power can be restricted by conditions set in creating the office.

3. Vacancies in Offices
The president can temporarily appoint officials to fill vacancies when the Senate is not in session.

Section 3. Duties of the President
Under this provision the president delivers annual State of the Union messages. On occasion, presidents have called Congress into special session to consider particular problems.

The president's duty to receive foreign diplomats also includes the power to ask a foreign country to withdraw its diplomatic officials from this country. This is called "breaking diplomatic relations" and often carries with it the implied threat of more drastic action, even war. The president likewise has the power of deciding whether or not to recognize foreign governments.

Section 4. Impeachment
This section states the reasons for which the president and vice president may be impeached and removed from office. (See annotations of Article I, Section 3, Clauses 6 and 7.)

Article III. The Judicial Branch

Section 1. Federal Courts
The term *judicial* refers to courts. The Constitution set up only the Supreme Court but provided for the establishment of other federal courts. There are presently nine justices on the Supreme Court. Congress has created a system of federal district courts and courts of appeals, which review certain district court cases. Judges of these courts serve during "good behavior," which means that they usually serve for life or until they choose to retire.

Section 2
1. The President shall be Commander in Chief of the Army and Navy of the United States, and of the Militia of the several States, when called into the actual Service of the United States; he may require the Opinion, in writing, of the principal Officer in each of the executive Departments, upon any subject relating to the Duties of their respective Offices, and he shall have Power to Grant Reprieves and Pardons for Offences against the United States, except in Cases of Impeachment.

2. He shall have Power, by and with the Advice and Consent of the Senate, to make Treaties, provided two-thirds of the Senators present concur; and he shall nominate, and by and with the Advice and Consent of the Senate, shall appoint Ambassadors, other public Ministers and Consuls, Judges of the supreme Court, and all other Officers of the United States, whose Appointments are not herein otherwise provided for, and which shall be established by Law. But the Congress may by Law vest the Appointment of such inferior Officers, as they think proper, in the President alone, in the Courts of Law, or in the Heads of Departments.

3. The President shall have Power to fill up all Vacancies that may happen during the Recess of the Senate, by granting Commissions which shall expire at the End of their next Session.

Section 3
He shall from time to time give to Congress Information of the State of the Union, and recommend to their Consideration such Measures as he shall judge necessary and expedient; he may, on extraordinary occasions, convene both Houses, or either of them, and in Case of Disagreement between them, with respect to the Time of Adjournment, he may adjourn them to such Time as he shall think proper; he shall receive Ambassadors and other public Ministers; he shall take Care that the Laws be faithfully executed, and shall Commission all the Officers of the United States.

Section 4
The President, Vice-President and all civil Officers of the United States, shall be removed from Office on Impeachment for, and Conviction of, Treason, Bribery, or other high Crimes and Misdemeanors.

Article III

Section 1
The Judicial Power of the United States, shall be vested in one supreme Court, and in such inferior Courts as the Congress may from time to time ordain and establish. The judges, both of the supreme and inferior Courts, shall hold their Offices during good Behaviour, and shall, at stated Times, receive for their Services, a Compensation, which shall not be diminished during their Continuance in Office.

Section 2

1. The judicial Power shall extend to all Cases, in Law and Equity, arising under this Constitution, the Laws of the United States, and treaties made, or which shall be made, under their Authority; to all Cases affecting ambassadors, other public ministers and consuls; to all cases of admiralty and maritime Jurisdiction; to Controversies to which the United States shall be a party; to Controversies between two or more states; between a State and Citizens of another State; between Citizens of different States; between Citizens of the same State claiming Lands under Grants of different States, and between a State, or the Citizens thereof, and foreign States, Citizens or Subjects.

2. In all Cases affecting Ambassadors, other public Ministers and Consuls, and those in which a State shall be Party, the supreme Court shall have original Jurisdiction. In all the other Cases before mentioned, the supreme Court shall have appellate Jurisdiction, both as to Law and Fact, with such Exceptions, and under such Regulations as the Congress shall make.

3. The trial of all Crimes, except in Cases of Impeachment, shall be by Jury; and such Trial shall be held in the State where the said Crimes shall have been committed; but when not committed within any State, the Trial shall be at such Place or Places as the Congress may by Law have directed.

Section 3

1. Treason against the United States, shall consist only in levying War against them, or in adhering to their Enemies, giving them Aid and Comfort. No Person shall be convicted of Treason unless on the Testimony of two Witnesses to the same overt Act, or on Confession in open Court.

2. The Congress shall have power to declare the Punishment of Treason, but no Attainder of Treason shall work Corruption of Blood, or Forfeiture except during the Life of the Person attainted.

Article IV

Section 1

Full Faith and Credit shall be given in each State to the public Acts, Records, and judicial Proceedings of every other State. And the Congress may by general Laws prescribe the Manner in which such Acts, Records, and Proceedings shall be proved, and the Effect thereof.

Section 2. Jurisdiction

1. General Jurisdiction

Use of the words *in law and equity* reflects the fact that American courts took over two kinds of traditional law from Great Britain. The basic law was the "common law," which was based on over five centuries of judicial decisions. "Equity" was a special branch of British law developed to handle cases where common law did not apply.

Federal courts deal mostly with "statute law," or laws passed by Congress, treaties, and cases involving the Constitution itself. "Admiralty and maritime jurisdiction" covers all sorts of cases involving ships and shipping on the high seas and on rivers, canals, and lakes.

2. The Supreme Court

When a court has "original jurisdiction" over certain kinds of cases, it means that the court has the authority to be the first court to hear a case. A court with "appellate jurisdiction" hears cases that have been appealed from lower courts. Most Supreme Court cases are heard on appeal from lower courts.

3. Jury Trials

Except in cases of impeachment, anyone accused of a crime has the right to a trial by jury. The trial must be held in the state where the crime was committed. Jury trial guarantees were strengthened in the 6th, 7th, 8th, and 9th Amendments.

Section 3. Treason

1. Definition

Knowing that the charge of treason often had been used by monarchs to get rid of people who opposed them, the Framers of the Constitution defined treason carefully, requiring that at least two witnesses be present to testify in court that a treasonable act was committed.

2. Punishment

Congress is given the power to determine the punishment for treason. The children of a person convicted of treason may not be punished nor may the convicted person's property be taken away from the children. Convictions for treason have been relatively rare in the nation's history.

Article IV. Relations Among the States

Section 1. Official Acts

This provision ensures that each state recognizes the laws, court decisions, and records of all other states. For example, a marriage license or corporation charter issued by one state must be accepted in other states.

Section 2. Mutual Duties of States

1. Privileges

The "privileges and immunities," or rights of citizens, guarantee each state's citizens equal treatment in all states.

2. Extradition

"Extradition" means that a person convicted of a crime or a person accused of a crime must be returned to the state where the crime was committed. Thus, a person cannot flee to another state hoping to escape the law.

3. Fugitive-Slave Clause

Formerly this clause meant that slaves could not become free persons by escaping to free states.

Section 3. New States and Territories

1. New States

Congress has the power to admit new states. It also determines the basic guidelines for applying for statehood. One state, Maine, was created within the original boundaries of another state (Massachusetts) with the consent of Congress and the state.

2. Territories

Congress has power over federal land. But neither in this clause nor anywhere else in the Constitution is the federal government explicitly empowered to acquire new territory.

Section 4. Federal Protection for States

This section allows the federal government to send troops into a state to guarantee law and order. The president may send in troops even without the consent of the state government involved.

Article V. The Amending Process

There are now 27 amendments to the Constitution. The Framers of the Constitution deliberately made it difficult to amend or change the Constitution. Two methods of proposing and ratifying amendments are provided for. A two-thirds majority is needed in Congress to propose an amendment, and at least three-fourths of the states (38 states) must accept the amendment before it can become law. No amendment has yet been proposed by a national convention called by the states, though in the 1980s a convention to propose an amendment requiring a balanced budget had been approved by 32 states.

Section 2

1. The Citizens of each State shall be entitled to all Privileges and Immunities of Citizens in the several States.

2. A Person charged in any State with Treason, Felony, or other Crime, who shall flee from Justice, and be found in another State, shall on demand of the executive Authority of the State from which he fled, be delivered up, to be removed to the State having Jurisdiction of the crime.

3. No Person held to Service of Labour in one State, under the Laws thereof, escaping into another, shall, in Consequence of any Law or Regulation therein, be discharged from such Service or Labour, but shall be delivered up on Claim of the Party to whom such Service or Labour may be due.

Section 3

1. New States may be admitted by the Congress into this Union; but no new State shall be formed or erected within the Jurisdiction of any other State; nor any State be formed by the Junction of two or more States, or parts of States, without the Consent of the Legislatures of the States concerned as well as of the Congress.

2. The Congress shall have Power to dispose of and make all needful Rules and Regulations respecting the Territory or other Property belonging to the United States; and nothing in this Constitution shall be so construed as to Prejudice any Claims of the United States, or of any particular State.

Section 4

The United States shall guarantee to every State in this Union a Republican Form of Government, and shall protect each of them against Invasion; and on Application of the Legislature, or of the Executive (when the Legislature cannot be convened) against domestic Violence.

Article V

The Congress, whenever two-thirds of both Houses shall deem it necessary, shall propose Amendments to this Constitution, or, on the Application of the Legislatures of two-thirds of the several States, shall call a Convention for proposing Amendments, which, in either Case, shall be valid to all Intents and Purposes, as part of this Constitution, when ratified by the Legislatures of three-fourths of the several States, or by Conventions in three-fourths thereof, as the one or the other Mode of Ratification may be proposed by the Congress; Provided that no Amendment which may be made prior to the Year One thousand eight hundred and eight shall in any Manner affect the first and fourth clauses in the Ninth Section of the first Article; and that no State, without its Consent, shall be deprived of its equal Suffrage in the Senate.

Article VI

1. All Debts contracted and Engagements entered into, before the Adoption of this Constitution, shall be as valid against the United States under this Constitution as under the Confederation.

2. This Constitution, and the Laws of the United States which shall be made in Pursuance thereof; and all Treaties made, or which shall be made, under the Authority of the United States, shall be the supreme Law of the Land; and the Judges in every State shall be bound thereby, any Thing in the Constitution or Laws of any State to the Contrary notwithstanding.

3. The Senators and Representatives before mentioned, and the Members of the several State Legislatures, and all executive and judicial Officers, both of the United States and of the several States, shall be bound by Oath or Affirmation, to support this Constitution; but no religious Test shall ever be required as a Qualification to any Office or public Trust under the United States.

Article VII

The Ratification of the Conventions of nine States shall be sufficient for the Establishment of this Constitution between the States so ratifying the same.

Done in Convention, by the Unanimous Consent of the States present, the Seventeenth Day of September, in the Year of our Lord one thousand seven hundred and Eighty-seven, and of the Independence of the United States of America the Twelfth. In Witness whereof We have hereunto subscribed our Names.

Article VI. National Supremacy

1. Public Debts and Treaties
This section promised that all debts the colonies had incurred during the Revolution and under the Articles of Confederation would be honored by the new United States government.

2. The Supreme Law
The "supremacy clause" recognized the Constitution and federal laws as supreme when in conflict with those of the states. It was largely based on this clause that Chief Justice John Marshall wrote his historic decision in *McCulloch* v. *Maryland*. The 14th Amendment reinforced the supremacy of federal law over state laws.

3. Oaths of Office
This clause also declares that no religious test shall be required as a qualification for holding public office. This principle is also asserted in the First Amendment, which forbids Congress to set up an established church or to interfere with the religious freedom of Americans.

Article VII. Ratification of the Constitution

Unlike the Articles of Confederation, which required approval of all thirteen states for adoption, the Constitution required approval of only nine of thirteen states. Thirty-nine of the 55 delegates at the Constitutional Convention signed the Constitution. The Constitution went into effect in June 1788.

Signers
George Washington, **President and Deputy from Virginia**

New Hampshire
John Langdon
Nicholas Gilman

Massachusetts
Nathaniel Gorham
Rufus King

Connecticut
William Samuel Johnson
Roger Sherman

New York
Alexander Hamilton

New Jersey
William Livingston
David Brearley
William Paterson
Jonathan Dayton

Pennsylvania
Benjamin Franklin
Thomas Mifflin
Robert Morris
George Clymer
Thomas FitzSimons
Jared Ingersoll
James Wilson
Gouverneur Morris

Delaware
George Read
Gunning Bedford, Jr.
John Dickinson
Richard Bassett
Jacob Broom

Maryland
James McHenry
Daniel of St. Thomas Jenifer
Daniel Carroll

Virginia
John Blair
James Madison, Jr.

North Carolina
William Blount
Richard Dobbs Spaight
Hugh Williamson

South Carolina
John Rutledge
Charles Cotesworth Pinckney
Charles Pinckney
Pierce Butler

Georgia
William Few
Abraham Baldwin

Attest: William Jackson,
Secretary

Amendment 1.
Freedom of Religion, Speech, Press, and Assembly (1791)

The 1st Amendment protects the civil liberties of individuals in the United States. The 1st Amendment freedoms are not absolute, however. They are limited by the rights of other individuals.

Amendment 2.
Right to Bear Arms (1791)

The purpose of this amendment is to guarantee states the right to keep a militia.

Amendment 3.
Quartering Troops (1791)

This amendment is based on the principle that people have a right to privacy in their own homes. It also reflects the colonists' grievances against the British government before the Revolution. Britain had angered Americans by quartering (housing) troops in private homes.

Amendment 4.
Searches and Seizures (1791)

Like the 3rd Amendment, the 4th Amendment reflects the colonists' desire to protect their privacy. Britain had used writs of assistance (general search warrants) to seek out smuggled goods. Americans wanted to make sure that such searches and seizures would be conducted only when a judge felt that there was "reasonable cause" to conduct them. The Supreme Court has ruled that evidence seized illegally without a search warrant may not be used in court.

Amendment 5.
Rights of Accused Persons (1791)

To bring a "presentment" or "indictment" means to formally charge a person with committing a crime. It is the function of a grand jury to see whether there is enough evidence to bring the accused person to trial. A person may not be tried more than once for the same crime (double jeopardy).

Members of the armed services are subject to military law. They may be tried in a court martial. In times of war or a natural disaster, civilians may also be put under martial law.

The 5th Amendment also guarantees that persons may not be forced in any criminal case to be a witness against themselves. That is, accused persons may refuse to answer questions on the ground that the answers might tend to incriminate them.

Amendment I

Congress shall make no law respecting an establishment of religion, or prohibiting the free exercise thereof; or abridging the freedom of speech, or of the press; or the right of the people peaceably to assemble, and to petition the Government for a redress of grievances.

Amendment II

A well-regulated Militia, being necessary to the security of a free State, the right of the people to keep and bear Arms, shall not be infringed.

Amendment III

No soldier shall, in time of peace be quartered in any house, without the consent of the Owner, nor in time of war, but in a manner to be prescribed by law.

Amendment IV

The right of the people to be secure in their persons, houses, papers, and effects, against unreasonable searches and seizures, shall not be violated, and no Warrants shall issue, but upon probable cause, supported by Oath or affirmation, and particularly describing the place to be searched, and the persons or things to be seized.

Amendment V

No person shall be held to answer for a capital, or otherwise infamous crime, unless on a presentment or indictment of a Grand Jury, except in cases arising in the land or naval forces, or in the Militia, when in actual service in time of War or public danger; nor shall any person be subject for the same offence to be twice put in jeopardy of life or limb; nor shall be compelled in any criminal case to be a witness against himself, nor be deprived of life, liberty, or property, without due process of law; nor shall private property be taken for public use, without just compensation.

Amendment VI

In all criminal prosecutions, the accused shall enjoy the right to a speedy and public trial, by an impartial jury of the State and district wherein the crime shall have been committed, which district shall have been previously ascertained by law, and to be informed of the nature and cause of the accusation; to be confronted with the witnesses against him; to have compulsory process for obtaining witnesses in his favor, and to have the Assistance of Counsel for his defence.

Amendment VII

In suits at common law, where the value in controversy shall exceed twenty dollars, the right of trial by jury shall be preserved, and no fact tried by a jury, shall be otherwise reexamined in any Courts of the United States, than according to the rules of common law.

Amendment VIII

Excessive bail shall not be required, nor excessive fines imposed, nor cruel and unusual punishments inflicted.

Amendment IX

The enumeration in the Constitution, of certain rights, shall not be construed to deny or disparage others retained by the people.

Amendment X

The powers not delegated to the United States by the Constitution, nor prohibited by it to the States, are reserved to the States respectively, or to the people.

Amendment XI

The Judicial power of the United States shall not be construed to extend to any suit in law or equity, commenced or prosecuted against one of the United States by Citizens of another State, or by Citizens or Subjects of any Foreign State.

Amendment 6.
Right to Speedy, Fair Trial (1791)

The requirement of a "speedy" trial ensures that an accused person will not be held in jail for a lengthy period as a means of punishing the accused without a trial. A "fair" trial means that the trial must be open to the public and that a jury must hear witnesses and evidence on both sides before deciding the guilt or innocence of a person charged with a crime. This amendment also provides that legal counsel must be provided to a defendant. In 1963, the Supreme Court ruled, in *Gideon* v. *Wainwright*, that if a defendant cannot afford a lawyer, the government must provide one to defend him or her.

Amendment 7.
Civil Suits (1791)

"Common law" means the law established by previous court decisions. In civil cases where one person sues another for more than $20, a jury trial is provided for. But customarily, federal courts do not hear civil cases unless they involve a good deal more money.

Amendment 8.
Bail and Punishment (1791)

"Bail" is money that an accused person provides to the court as a guarantee that he or she will be present for a trial. This amendment ensures that neither bail nor punishment for a crime shall be unreasonably severe.

Amendment 9.
Powers Reserved to the People (1791)

This amendment provides that the people's rights are not limited to those mentioned in the Constitution.

Amendment 10.
Powers Reserved to the States (1791)

This amendment protects the states and the people from an all-powerful federal government. It provides that the states or the people retain all powers except those denied them or those specifically granted to the federal government. This "reserved powers" provision is a check on the "necessary and proper" power of the federal government provided in the "elastic clause" in Article I, Section 8, Clause 18.

Amendment 11.
Suits Against States (1795)

This amendment provides that a lawsuit brought by a citizen of the United States or a foreign nation against a state must be tried in a state court, not in a federal court. This amendment was passed after the Supreme Court ruled that a federal court could try a lawsuit brought by citizens of South Carolina against a citizen of Georgia. This case, *Chisholm* v. *Georgia*, decided in 1793, was protested by many Americans, who insisted states would lose authority if they could be sued in federal courts.

Amendment 12.
Election of President and Vice President (1804)

This amendment changes the procedure for electing the president and vice president as outlined in Article II, Section 1, Clause 3.

To prevent the recurrence of the election of 1800 whereby a candidate running for vice president (Aaron Burr) could tie a candidate running for president (Thomas Jefferson) and thus force the election into the House of Representatives, the 12th Amendment specifies that the electors are to cast separate ballots for each office. The votes for each office are counted and listed separately. The results are signed, sealed, and sent to the president of the Senate. At a joint session of Congress, the votes are counted. The candidate who receives the most votes, providing it is a majority, is elected president. Other changes include: (1) a reduction from the five to three candidates receiving the most votes among whom the House is to choose if no candidate receives a majority of the electoral votes, and (2) provision for the Senate to choose the vice president from the two highest candidates if neither has received a majority of the electoral votes.

The 12th Amendment does place one restriction on electors. It prohibits electors from voting for two candidates (president and vice president) from their home state.

United States coins

Amendment 13.
Abolition of Slavery (1865)

This amendment was the final act in ending slavery in the United States. It also prohibits the binding of a person to perform a personal service due to debt. In addition to imprisonment for crime, the Supreme Court has held that the draft is not a violation of the amendment.

This amendment is the first adopted to be divided into sections. It is also the first to contain specifically a provision granting Congress power to enforce it by appropriate legislation.

Amendment XII

The Electors shall meet in their respective States and vote by ballot for President and Vice-President, one of whom, at least, shall not be an inhabitant of the same State with themselves; they shall name in their ballots the person voted for as President, and in distinct ballots the person voted for as Vice-President, and they shall make distinct lists of all persons voted for as President, and of all persons voted for as Vice-President, and of the number of votes for each, which lists they shall sign and certify, and transmit sealed to the seat of the government of the United States, directed to the President of the Senate;—The President of the Senate shall, in the presence of the Senate and House of Representatives, open all the certificates and the votes shall then be counted;—The person having the greatest number of votes for President, shall be the President, if such number be a majority of the whole number of Electors appointed; and if no person have such majority, then from the persons having the highest numbers not exceeding three on the list of those voted for as President, the House of Representatives shall choose immediately, by ballot, the President. But in choosing the President, the votes shall be taken by states, the representation from each state having one vote; a quorum for this purpose shall consist of a member or members from two-thirds of the states, and a majority of all the states shall be necessary to a choice. And if the House of Representatives shall not choose a President whenever the right of choice shall devolve upon them, before the fourth day of March next following, then the Vice-President shall act as President, as in the case of the death or other constitutional disability of the President.—The person having the greatest number of votes as Vice-President, shall be the Vice-President, if such number be a majority of the whole number of Electors appointed, and if no person have a majority, then from the two highest numbers on the list, the Senate shall choose the Vice-President; a quorum for the purpose shall consist of two-thirds of the whole number of Senators, and a majority of the whole number shall be necessary to a choice. But no person constitutionally ineligible to the office of President shall be eligible to that of Vice-President of the United States.

Amendment XIII

Section 1
Neither slavery nor involuntary servitude, except as a punishment for crime whereof the party shall have been duly convicted, shall exist within the United States, or any place subject to their jurisdiction.

Section 2
Congress shall have power to enforce this article by appropriate legislation.

Amendment XIV

Section 1

All persons born or naturalized in the United States, and subject to the jurisdiction thereof, are citizens of the United States and of the State wherein they reside. No State shall make or enforce any law which shall abridge the privileges or immunities of citizens of the United States; nor shall any State deprive any person of life, liberty, or property, without due process of law, nor deny to any person within its jurisdiction the equal protection of the laws.

Section 2

Representatives shall be apportioned among the several States according to their respective numbers, counting the whole number of persons in each State, excluding Indians not taxed. But when the right to vote at any election for the choice of electors for President and Vice-President of the United States, Representatives in Congress, the Executive and Judicial officers of a State, or the members of the Legislature thereof, is denied to any of the male inhabitants of such State, being twenty-one years of age, and citizens of the United States, or in any way abridged, except for participation in rebellion, or other crime, the basis of representation therein shall be reduced in the proportion which the number of such male citizens shall bear to the whole number of male citizens twenty-one years of age in such State.

Section 3

No person shall be a Senator or Representative in Congress, or elector of President and Vice-President, or hold any office, civil or military, under the United States, or under any State, who, having previously taken an oath, as a member of Congress, or as an officer of the United States, or as a member of any State legislature, or as an executive or judicial officer of any State, to support the Constitution of the United States, shall have engaged in insurrection or rebellion against the same, or given aid or comfort to the enemies thereof. But Congress may by a vote of two-thirds of each House, remove such disability.

Section 4

The validity of the public debt of the United States incurred for payment of pensions and bounties for service, authorized by law, including debts in suppressing insurrections or rebellion, shall not be questioned. But neither the United States nor any State shall assume or pay any debt or obligation incurred in aid of insurrection or rebellion against the United States, or any claim for the loss or emancipation of any slave; but all such debts, obligations and claims shall be held illegal and void.

Amendment 14.
Rights of Citizens (1868)

The clauses of this amendment were intended (1) to penalize Southern states that refused to grant African Americans the vote, (2) to keep former Confederate leaders from serving in government, (3) to forbid payment of the Confederacy's debt by the federal government, and (4) to ensure payment of the war debts owed the federal government.

Section 1. Citizenship Defined By granting citizenship to all persons born in the United States, this amendment granted citizenship to former slaves. The amendment also guaranteed "due process of law." By the 1950s, Supreme Court rulings used the due process clause to protect civil liberties. The last part of Section 1 establishes the doctrine that all citizens are entitled to equal protection of the laws. In 1954 the Supreme Court ruled, in *Brown* v. *Board of Education of Topeka*, that segregation in public schools was unconstitutional because it denied equal protection.

Section 2. Representation in Congress This section reduced the number of members a state had in the House of Representatives if it denied its citizens the right to vote. This section was not implemented, however. Later civil rights laws and the 24th Amendment guaranteed the vote to African Americans.

Section 3. Penalty for Engaging in Insurrection The leaders of the Confederacy were barred from state or federal offices unless Congress agreed to revoke this ban. By the end of Reconstruction all but a few Confederate leaders were allowed to return to public life.

Section 4. Public Debt The public debt incurred by the federal government during the Civil War was valid and could not be questioned by the South. However, the debts of the Confederacy were declared to be illegal. And former slaveholders could not collect compensation for the loss of their slaves.

Section 5. Enforcement Congress was empowered to pass civil rights bills to guarantee the provisions of the amendment.

Amendment 15.
The Right to Vote (1870)
Section 1. Suffrage for African Americans The 15th Amendment replaced Section 2 of the 14th Amendment in guaranteeing African Americans the right to vote; that is, the right of African Americans to vote was not to be left to the states. Yet, despite this prohibition, African Americans were denied the right to vote by many states by such means as poll taxes, literacy tests, and white primaries.

Section 2. Enforcement Congress was given the power to enforce this amendment. During the 1950s and 1960s, it passed successively stronger laws to end racial discrimination in voting rights.

Amendment 16.
Income Tax (1913)
The origins of this amendment went back to 1895, when the Supreme Court declared a federal income tax unconstitutional. To overcome this Supreme Court decision, this amendment authorized an income tax that was levied on a direct basis.

Amendment 17.
Direct Election of Senators (1913)

Section 1. Method of Election The right to elect senators was given directly to the people of each state. It replaced Article I, Section 3, Clause 1, which empowered state legislatures to elect senators. This amendment was designed not only to make the choice of senators more democratic but also to cut down on corruption and to improve state government.

Section 2. Vacancies A state must order an election to fill a Senate vacancy. A state may empower its governor to appoint a person to fill a Senate seat if a vacancy occurs until an election can be held.

Section 3. Time in Effect This amendment was not to affect any Senate election or temporary appointment until it was in effect.

Section 5
The Congress shall have power to enforce, by appropriate legislation, the provisions of this article.

Amendment XV

Section 1
The right of citizens of the United States to vote shall not be denied or abridged by the United States or by any State on account of race, color, or previous condition of servitude.

Section 2
The Congress shall have power to enforce this article by appropriate legislation.

Amendment XVI
The Congress shall have power to lay and collect taxes on incomes, from whatever source derived, without apportionment among several States, and without regard to any census or enumeration.

Amendment XVII

Section 1
The Senate of the United States shall be composed of two Senators from each State, elected by the people thereof, for six years; and each Senator shall have one vote. The electors in each state shall have the qualifications requisite for electors of the most numerous branch of the state legislatures.

Section 2
When vacancies happen in the representation of any State in the Senate, the executive authority of such State shall issue writs of election to fill such vacancies: *Provided*, that the legislature of any State may empower the executive thereof to make temporary appointments until the people fill the vacancies by election as the legislature may direct.

Section 3
This amendment shall not be so construed as to affect the election or term of any Senator chosen before it becomes valid as part of the Constitution.

Amendment XVIII

Section 1

After one year from ratification of this article the manufacture, sale, or transportation of intoxicating liquors within, the importation thereof into, or the exportation thereof from the United States and all territory subject to the jurisdiction thereof for beverage purposes is hereby prohibited.

Section 2

The Congress and the several states shall have concurrent power to enforce this article by appropriate legislation.

Section 3

This article shall be inoperative unless it shall have been ratified as an amendment to the Constitution by the legislatures of the several States, as provided in the Constitution, within seven years from the date of the submission hereof to the states of the Congress.

Amendment XIX

Section 1

The right of citizens of the United States to vote shall not be denied or abridged by the United States or by any state on account of sex.

Section 2

Congress shall have power to enforce this article by appropriate legislation.

Amendment XX

Section 1

The terms of the President and Vice President shall end at noon on the 20th day of January, and the terms of the Senators and Representatives at noon on the 3rd day of January, of the years in which such terms would have ended if this article had not been ratified; and the terms of their successors shall then begin.

Section 2

The Congress shall assemble at least once in every year, and such meeting shall begin at noon on the 3rd day of January, unless they shall by law appoint a different day.

Amendment 18.
Prohibition of Alcoholic Beverages (1919)

This amendment prohibited the production, sale, or transportation of alcoholic beverages in the United States. Prohibition proved to be difficult to enforce, especially in states with large urban populations. This amendment was later repealed by the 21st Amendment.

Amendment 19.
Woman Suffrage (1920)

This amendment, extending the vote to all qualified women in federal and state elections, was a landmark victory for the woman suffrage movement, which had worked to achieve this goal for many years. The women's movement had earlier gained full voting rights for women in four Western states in the late nineteenth century.

Amendment 20.
"Lame-Duck" Amendment (1933)

Section 1. New Dates of Terms This amendment had two major purposes: (1) to shorten the time between the president's and vice president's election and inauguration, and (2) to end "lame-duck" sessions of Congress.

When the Constitution first went into effect, transportation and communication were slow and uncertain. It often took many months after the election in November for the president and vice president to travel to Washington, D.C., and prepare for their inauguration on March 4. This amendment ended this long wait for a new administration by fixing January 20 as Inauguration Day.

Section 2. Meeting Time of Congress "Lame-duck" sessions occurred every two years, after the November congressional election. That is, the Congress that held its session in December of an election year was not the newly elected Congress but the old Congress that had been elected two years earlier. This Congress continued to serve for several more months, usually until March of the next year. Often many of its members had failed to be reelected and were called "lame-ducks." The 20th Amendment abolished this lame-duck session, and provided that the new Congress hold its first session soon after the November election, on January 3.

Section 3. Succession of President and Vice President
This amendment provides that if the president-elect dies before taking office, the vice president-elect becomes president. In the cases described, Congress will decide on a temporary president.

Section 4. Filling Presidential Vacancy
If a presidential candidate dies while an election is being decided in the House, Congress may pass legislation to deal with the situation. Congress has similar power if this occurs when the Senate is deciding a vice-presidential election.

Section 5. Beginning the New Dates
Sections 1 and 2 affected the Congress elected in 1934 and President Roosevelt, elected in 1936.

Section 6. Time Limit on Ratification
The period for ratification by the states was limited to seven years.

Amendment 21.
Repeal of Prohibition Amendment (1933)
This amendment nullified the 18th Amendment. It is the only amendment ever passed to overturn an earlier amendment. It remained unlawful to transport alcoholic beverages into states that forbade their use. It is the only amendment ratified by special state conventions instead of state legislatures.

Section 3
If, at the time fixed for the beginning of the term of the President, the President elect shall have died, the Vice President elect shall become President. If a President shall not have been chosen before the time fixed for the beginning of his term, or if the President elect shall have failed to qualify, then the Vice President elect shall act as President until a President shall have qualified; and the Congress may by law provide for the case wherein neither a President elect nor a Vice President elect shall have qualified, declaring who shall then act as President, or the manner in which one who is to act shall be selected, and such person shall act accordingly until a President or Vice President shall have qualified.

Section 4
The Congress may by law provide for the case of the death of any of the persons from whom the House of Representatives may choose a President whenever the right of choice shall have devolved upon them, and for the case of the death of any of the persons from whom the Senate may choose a Vice President whenever the right of choice shall have devolved upon them.

Section 5
Sections 1 and 2 shall take effect on the 15th day of October following the ratification of this article.

Section 6
This article shall be inoperative unless it shall have been ratified as an amendment to the Constitution by the legislatures of three-fourths of the several States within seven years from the date of its submission.

Amendment XXI

Section 1
The eighteenth article of amendment to the Constitution of the United States is hereby repealed.

Section 2
The transportation or importation into any State, Territory, or possession of the United States for delivery or use therein of intoxicating liquors, in violation of the laws thereof, is hereby prohibited.

Section 3
This article shall be inoperative unless it shall have been ratified as an amendment to the Constitution by conventions in the several States, as provided in the Constitution, within seven years from the date of the submission hereof to the States by the Congress.

Amendment XXII

Section 1

No person shall be elected to the office of the President more than twice, and no person who had held the office of President, or acted as President, for more than two years of a term to which some other person was elected President shall be elected to the office of the President more than once.

But this Article shall not apply to any person holding the office of President when this Article was proposed by the Congress, and shall not prevent any person who may be holding the office of President, or acting as President, during the term within which this Article becomes operative from holding the office of President or acting as President during the remainder of such term.

Section 2

This article shall be inoperative unless it shall have been ratified as an amendment to the Constitution by the legislatures of three-fourths of the several States within seven years from the date of its submission to the States by the Congress.

Amendment XXIII

Section 1

The District constituting the seat of Government of the United States shall appoint in such manner as the Congress may direct:

A number of electors of President and Vice President equal to the whole number of Senators and Representatives in Congress to which the District would be entitled if it were a State, but in no event more than the least populous State; they shall be in addition to those appointed by the States, but they shall be considered, for the purposes of the election of President and Vice President, to be electors appointed by a State; and they shall meet in the District and perform such duties as provided by the twelfth article of amendment.

Section 2

The Congress shall have power to enforce this article by appropriate legislation.

Amendment 22.
Limit on Presidential Terms (1951)

This amendment wrote into the Constitution a custom started by Washington, Jefferson, and Madison, whereby presidents limited themselves to two terms in office. Although both Ulysses S. Grant and Theodore Roosevelt sought third terms, the two-term precedent was not broken until Franklin D. Roosevelt was elected to a third term in 1940 and then a fourth term in 1944. The passage of the 22nd Amendment ensures that no president is to be considered indispensable. It also provides that anyone who succeeds to the presidency and serves for more than two years of the term may not be elected more than one more time.

Presidential campaign button

Amendment 23.
Presidential Electors for the District of Columbia (1961)

This amendment granted people living in the District of Columbia the right to vote in presidential elections. The District casts three electoral votes. The people of Washington, D.C., still are without representation in Congress.

Amendment 24.
Abolition of the Poll Tax (1964)

A "poll tax" was a fee that persons were required to pay in order to vote in a number of Southern states. This amendment ended poll taxes as a requirement to vote in any presidential or congressional election. In 1966 the Supreme Court voided poll taxes in state elections as well.

Amendment 25.
Presidential Disability and Succession (1967)

Section 1. Replacing the President The vice president becomes president if the president dies, resigns, or is removed from office.

Section 2. Replacing the Vice President The president is to appoint a new vice president in case of a vacancy in that office, with the approval of the Congress.

The 25th Amendment is unusually precise and explicit because it was intended to solve a serious constitutional problem. Sixteen times in American history, before passage of this amendment, the office of vice president was vacant, but fortunately in none of these cases did the president die or resign.

This amendment was used in 1973, when Vice President Spiro Agnew resigned from office after being charged with accepting bribes. President Richard Nixon then appointed Gerald R. Ford as vice president in accordance with the provisions of the 25th Amendment. A year later, President Nixon resigned during the Watergate scandal, and Ford became president. President Ford then had to fill the vice presidency, which he had left vacant upon assuming the presidency. He named Nelson A. Rockefeller as vice president. Thus both the presidency and vice presidency were held by men who had not been elected to their offices.

Section 3. Replacing the President With Consent If the president informs Congress, in writing, that he or she cannot carry out the duties of the office of president, the vice president becomes Acting president.

Section 4. Replacing the President Without Consent If the president is unable to carry out the duties of the office but is unable or unwilling to so notify Congress, the cabinet and the vice president are to inform Congress of this fact. The vice president then becomes acting president. The procedure by which the president may regain the office if he or she recovers is also spelled out in this amendment.

Amendment XXIV

Section 1

The right of citizens of the United States to vote in any primary or other election for President or Vice President, for electors for President or Vice President, or for Senator or Representative in Congress, shall not be denied or abridged by the United States or any State by reason of failure to pay any poll tax or other tax.

Section 2

The Congress shall have power to enforce this article by appropriate legislation.

Amendment XXV

Section 1

In case of the removal of the President from office or his death or resignation, the Vice President shall become President.

Section 2

Whenever there is a vacancy in the office of the Vice President, the President shall nominate a Vice President who shall take the office upon confirmation by a majority vote of both houses of Congress.

Section 3

Whenever the President transmits to the President pro tempore of the Senate and the Speaker of the House of Representatives his written declaration that he is unable to discharge the powers and duties of his office, and until he transmits to them a written declaration to the contrary, such powers and duties shall be discharged by the Vice President as Acting President.

Section 4

Whenever the Vice President and a majority of either the principal officers of the executive departments or of such other body as Congress may by law provide, transmit to the President pro tempore of the Senate and the Speaker of the House of Representatives their written declaration that the President is unable to discharge the powers and duties of his office, the Vice President shall immediately assume the power and duties of the office of Acting President.

Thereafter, when the President transmits to the President pro tempore of the Senate and the Speaker of the House of Representatives his written declaration that no inability exists, he shall resume the powers and duties of his office unless the Vice President and a majority of either the principal officers of the executive departments or of such other body as Congress may by law provide, transmit within four days to the President pro tempore of the Senate and the Speaker of the House of Representatives their written declaration that the President is unable to discharge the powers and duties of his office. There-upon Congress shall decide the issue, assembling within forty-eight hours for that purpose if not in session. If the Congress within twenty-one days after receipt of the latter written declaration, or, if Congress is not in session, within twenty-one days after Congress is required to assemble, determines by two-thirds vote of both houses that the President is unable to discharge the powers and duties of his office, the Vice President shall continue to discharge the same as Acting President; otherwise, the President shall resume the power and duties of his office.

Amendment XXVI

Section 1

The right of citizens of the United States, who are eighteen years of age or older, to vote shall not be denied or abridged by the United States or by any State on account of age.

Section 2

The Congress shall have power to enforce this article by appropriate legislation.

Amendment XXVII

No law, varying the compensation for the services of Senators and Representatives, shall take effect, until an election of Representatives shall have intervened.

Amendment 26.
Eighteen-Year-Old Vote (1971)

This amendment made 18-year-olds eligible to vote in all federal, state, and local elections. Until then, the minimum age had been 21 in most states.

Amendment 27.
Restraint on Congressional Salaries (1992)

Any increase in the salaries of members of Congress will take effect in the subsequent session of Congress.

Joint meeting of Congress

Unit 4

The New Republic

1789–1825

"I walk on untrodden ground."

—GEORGE WASHINGTON, 1789

interNET
CONNECTION

To learn more about the new American republic, visit the Glencoe Social Studies Web Site at **www.glencoe.com** for information, activities, and links to other sites.

MAPPING *America*

Portfolio Activity Draw a freehand outline map of the United States. As you read about the expansion of the United States's borders in this unit, note this expansion on your map. Include the boundaries of the Louisiana Purchase, the 10 states admitted to the Union between 1791 and 1821, and the movement of settlers into western lands.

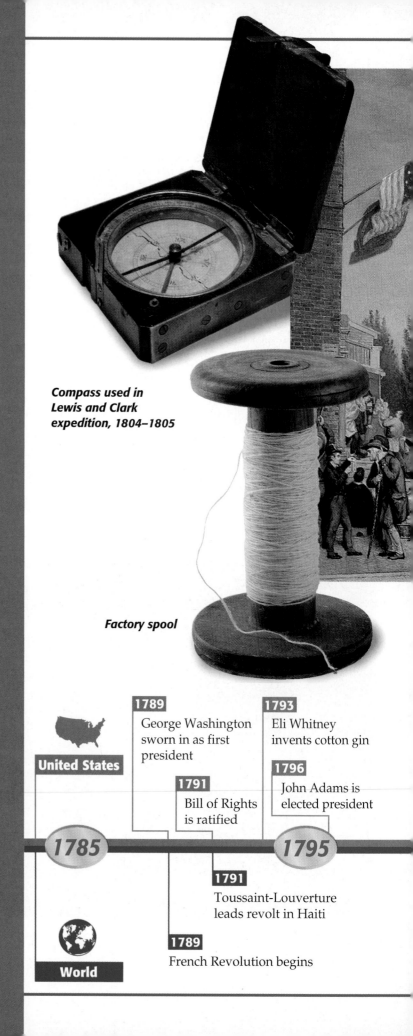

Compass used in Lewis and Clark expedition, 1804–1805

Factory spool

United States

1789
George Washington sworn in as first president

1791
Bill of Rights is ratified

1793
Eli Whitney invents cotton gin

1796
John Adams is elected president

1785

1795

1791
Toussaint-Louverture leads revolt in Haiti

World

1789
French Revolution begins

★ HISTORY AND ART ***Election Day in Philadelphia* by John Krimmel**
An Election Day crowd gathers in front of the Pennsylvania State House (Independence Hall) in Philadelphia. With the ratification of the Constitution, the United States set out to establish a new government.

Pitcher honoring Washington's inauguration, 1789

1801 Thomas Jefferson becomes president

1803 United States buys Louisiana Territory

1811 Native Americans defeated at Battle of Tippecanoe

1814 Treaty of Ghent ends War of 1812

1820 Missouri Compromise is reached

1825 Erie Canal opens

1805

1815

1825

1804 Napoleon Bonaparte becomes emperor of France

1807 Slave trade is abolished in British Empire

1819 Simón Bolívar elected president of Greater Colombia

1820 Liberia is founded in Africa

1821 Mexico declares independence from Spain

America's LITERATURE

Night Flying Woman
by Ignatia Broker

Born on the White Earth Ojibway Reservation in Minnesota, Ignatia Broker (1919–1987) grew up hearing the stories of her people. She decided that one day she would tell others about Ojibway traditions. Through her writing, Broker passed on many Ojibway tales about "the purity of man and nature and keeping them in balance."

■ READ TO DISCOVER

Night Flying Woman tells the story of Oona, Ignatia Broker's great-great-grandmother. Oona was still a child when the Ojibway were forced to leave their land and find a new home. As you read, look for the ways in which Oona overcomes her fears. What gives the Ojibway people faith that they will continue as a people?

■ READER'S DICTIONARY
Gitchi Manito: Great Spirit
Anishinabe: Ojibway name for "people"

On this, the fifth night of their travels, after the people had given thanks and eaten the evening meal, there was a firelight council. The people decided to stay on this small lake for two days while three of the men went deep into the forest to look for the new place.

The next morning, very early, Grandfather, Oldest Uncle, and Father walked into the thick forest. Oona did not see them leave, for she was sleeping soundly. When Mother told her that they were gone, Oona looked at the forest fearfully. It seemed very unfriendly. She thought, "It has swallowed up my grandfather and father." She became fretful.

Mother said, "Daughter, look at the forest again but do not look and see only the dark and shadows. Instead, look at the trees, each one, as many as you can. Then tell me what you think."

Oona looked at the trees. Then she walked to the forest's edge to see them better. There were many, many kinds of trees. Some were tall, so tall that they must surely touch the sky, thought Oona. Instead of leaves they had needles that were long and pointed like porcupine quills. Beneath these tall trees smaller ones reached up, as if in friendship. As Oona looked at the trees, she heard the si-si-gwa-d—the murmuring that the trees do when they brush their branches together. It was a friendly sound, and the sun sent sparkles through the si-si-gwa-d that chased the shadows. Suddenly the forest seemed different to Oona, and she knew that Grandfather, Oldest Uncle, and Father had gone into a friendly place.

"Mother," said Oona, "I have the feeling now that the trees are glad we are

Pine forest, northern Minnesota

here. The forest is happy and I know that we will be happy, too."

"That is good, my daughter, for I also have the feeling that this will be a good and happy place." A-wa-sa-si and Grandmother, who had been listening, nodded their heads in agreement.

A-wa-sa-si said, "The forests have never failed the Ojibway. The trees are the glory of the Gitchi Manito. The trees, for as long as they shall stand, will give shelter and life to the Anishinabe and the Animal Brothers. They are a gift. As long as the Ojibway are beneath, the trees will murmur with contentment. When the Ojibway and the Animal Brothers are gone, the forest will weep and this will be reflected in the sound of the si-si-gwa-d. My grandmother told me this is so, and her grandmother told her. When the forest weeps, the Anishinabe who listen will look back at the years. In each generation of Ojibway there will be a person who will hear the si-si-gwa-d, who will listen and remember and pass it on to the children. Remembering our past and acting accordingly will

ensure that we, the Ojibway, will always people the earth. The trees have patience and so they have stood and have seen many generations of Ojibway. Yet will there be more, and yet will they see more."

From *Night Flying Woman: An Ojibway Narrative* by Ignatia Broker. Copyright © 1983 by the Minnesota Historical Society. Reprinted by permission.

■ RESPONDING TO LITERATURE

1. Why did Oona's father, uncle, and grandfather go into the forest?
2. What sound did Oona hear in the forest? How did the sound affect Oona's feelings about the forest?

Activity

Making an Illustration Create a painting or drawing that shows the forest as Oona saw it. Use symbols to hint at the coming of the Europeans.

1789–1800

A New Nation

★ Why It's Important

The Washington administration faced the huge task of establishing a new government. The Constitution had created the office of the presidency, but it was Washington who established the procedures and customs that succeeding presidents would follow. He tried also to set a precedent for not getting involved in the political affairs of foreign nations. In the 1790s revolution and war raged throughout Europe. Despite the efforts of Washington and of John Adams, who followed him, the United States did become involved in disputes with European powers.

★ Chapter Themes

- *Section 1,* Government and Democracy
- *Section 2,* Civic Rights and Responsibilities
- *Section 3,* Economic Factors
- *Section 4,* Groups and Institutions

PRIMARY SOURCES
Library   *See pages 950–951 for primary source readings to accompany Chapter 8*

★ **HISTORY AND ART**   *The Republican Court* by Daniel Huntington President George Washington and his wife, Martha, entertained guests at formal receptions.

April 6, 1789
George Washington
is elected president

April 30, 1789
Washington takes
the oath of office

September 1789
Judiciary Act sets up
federal court system

December 1791
Bill of Rights added
to the Constitution

Section 1

The First President

READ TO DISCOVER . . .
■ what actions Washington and Congress
took to launch the new government.
■ how Hamilton proposed to strengthen the
nation's credit and economy.

TERMS TO LEARN
inauguration
precedent
cabinet
national debt
bond
speculator
unconstitutional
tariff

Storyteller

Celebrations erupted in the streets of
Philadelphia, New York, Boston, and
Charleston in 1789. News about the Constitution's ratification was greeted with relief and
enthusiasm. All that was needed now was a
leader to guide the new nation.

On April 6 the new Senate counted the
presidential ballots. To no one's surprise, the
votes were unanimous. Senator John Langdon
wrote to General
George Washington:
"Sir, I have the honor
to transmit to Your Ex-
cellency the informa-
tion of your unanimous
election to the office of
President of the United
States of America."

Washington banner

The 57-year-old president-elect made his
way slowly toward **New York City,** the nation's temporary capital, and the job he had
never wanted. After the Constitutional Convention, **George Washington** had looked forward to
the peace and quiet of retirement at his beloved
estate of Mount Vernon. Instead his fellow citizens summoned him to assume the highest office
in the land. On April 30, 1789, Washington took
the oath of office as the first president of the United States. **John Adams** became vice president.
This inauguration ceremony took place at Federal Hall on the island of Manhattan.

Biography

President Washington

Perhaps no office in the new government created more suspicion among the people than the
office of president. Although many Americans
feared that a president would try to become king,
they trusted Washington. They believed that his
leadership had brought them through the Revolutionary War to victory. Most political leaders
agreed with Alexander Hamilton's assessment of
the new president: "He consulted much, pondered much, resolved slowly, resolved surely."

Washington was aware of the "ocean of difficulties" he faced. He knew that the precedents, or
traditions, he established as the nation's first president would shape the future of the United States.
"No slip will pass unnoticed," he remarked. One
precedent he established concerned the way

Picturing HISTORY President Washington relied on the expert advice of his cabinet. Henry Knox is seated at left. Next to him are Thomas Jefferson, Edmund Randolph (back turned), Alexander Hamilton, and Washington himself. **Who was the first secretary of state?**

relations with other nations, the Treasury Department would deal with financial matters, and the War Department would provide for the nation's defense. Congress also created the office of attorney general to handle the government's legal affairs and the office of postmaster general to oversee the postal service.

To head the departments, Washington chose leading political figures of the day—**Thomas Jefferson** as secretary of state, **Alexander Hamilton** as secretary of the treasury, and **Henry Knox** as secretary of war. He appointed **Edmund Randolph** as attorney general. Washington met regularly with the three department heads and the attorney general, who together became known as the cabinet.

The First Congress

★ Congress created the executive departments; however, opinion was divided on how much power the president should have over them. For example, should the president be able to replace an official he had appointed and the Senate had confirmed? Senators were evenly divided in voting on the issue.

Vice President Adams broke the tie by voting to allow the president the authority to dismiss cabinet officers without the Senate's approval. This decision strengthened the president's position. It also helped create a greater separation between the legislative and executive branches of government by establishing the president's authority over the executive branch.

Judiciary Act

The first Congress also had to decide how to set up the nation's court system. The Constitution briefly mentioned a supreme court but had left further details about the courts to Congress.

A dispute arose between those favoring a uniform, national legal system and those favoring state laws. The two groups reached a compromise in the **Judiciary Act of 1789.** With this act, Congress established a federal court system with 13 district courts and 3 circuit courts in the nation.

people should address him. Vice President Adams suggested "His Highness the President of the United States," but Washington decided that "Mr. President" would be appropriate.

Washington and the new Congress also had many decisions to make about the structure of government. For example, the Constitution gave Congress the power to establish departments, but it did not specify whether the department heads would report to the president or to Congress. 📖

Washington's Cabinet

During the summer of 1789, Congress set up three departments in the executive branch of government. The State Department would handle

State laws would remain, but the federal courts would have the power to reverse state decisions.

The Supreme Court would be the final authority on many issues. Washington nominated **John Jay** to lead the Supreme Court as chief justice, and the Senate approved Jay's nomination. With the Judiciary Act, Congress had taken the first steps toward creating a strong and independent judiciary.

The Bill of Rights

Americans had long feared strong central governments. They had fought a revolution to throw off one and did not want to replace it with another. Some people thought the best protection lay in stronger state governments. Others insisted the Constitution needed to include specific statements guaranteeing personal liberties. Some states had supported the Constitution on the condition that a bill of rights be added.

After studying hundreds of proposals for protecting "essential rights," James Madison presented a list of possible constitutional amendments to Congress. Congress passed 12 amendments, and the states ratified 10 of them. In December 1791, these 10 amendments were added to the Constitution and became known as the Bill of Rights.

Among the liberties guaranteed in the Bill of Rights are freedom of speech, press, and religion. The Tenth Amendment protects the rights of states

*John Jay,
first chief justice
of the United States*

and individuals by saying that powers not specifically given to the federal government "are reserved to the States respectively, or to the people."

$ Economics

Financial Problems

⭐ The first president rarely proposed laws, and he almost always approved the bills that were passed by Congress. Washington focused his attention on foreign affairs and military matters and left the government's economic policies to his dynamic secretary of the treasury, Alexander Hamilton.

The new nation faced serious financial problems. The national debt—the amount the nation's government owed—was growing. Hamilton tried to find a way to improve the government's financial reputation and to strengthen the nation at the same time.

Hamilton's Plan

In 1790 Hamilton issued a "Report on the Public Credit." He proposed that the new government pay off the millions of dollars in debts owed by the Confederation government to other countries and to individual American citizens.

The states had fought for the nation's independence, Hamilton argued, so the national government should pay for the cost of their help. Hamilton also believed that federal payment of state debts would give the states a strong interest in the success of the national government.

Opposition to the Plan

Congress agreed to pay money owed to other nations. However, Hamilton's plan to pay off the debt to American citizens unleashed a storm of protest. When the government had borrowed money during the American Revolution, it had issued bonds—paper notes promising to repay

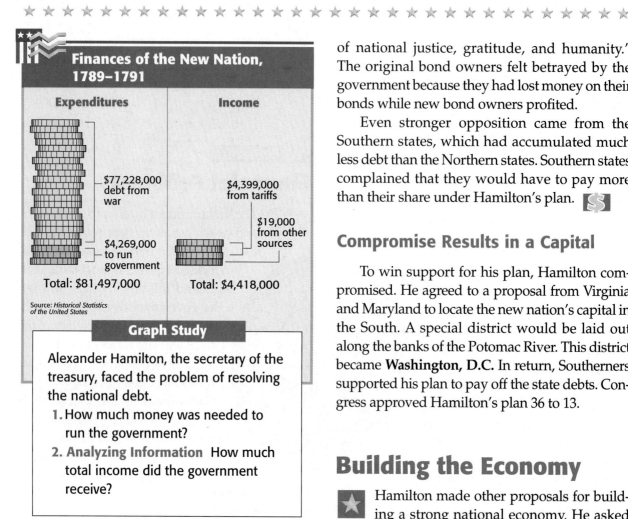

Finances of the New Nation, 1789–1791

Expenditures	Income
$77,228,000 debt from war	$4,399,000 from tariffs
	$19,000 from other sources
$4,269,000 to run government	
Total: $81,497,000	**Total: $4,418,000**

Source: *Historical Statistics of the United States*

Graph Study

Alexander Hamilton, the secretary of the treasury, faced the problem of resolving the national debt.

1. How much money was needed to run the government?
2. **Analyzing Information** How much total income did the government receive?

of national justice, gratitude, and humanity." The original bond owners felt betrayed by the government because they had lost money on their bonds while new bond owners profited.

Even stronger opposition came from the Southern states, which had accumulated much less debt than the Northern states. Southern states complained that they would have to pay more than their share under Hamilton's plan.

Compromise Results in a Capital

To win support for his plan, Hamilton compromised. He agreed to a proposal from Virginia and Maryland to locate the new nation's capital in the South. A special district would be laid out along the banks of the Potomac River. This district became **Washington, D.C.** In return, Southerners supported his plan to pay off the state debts. Congress approved Hamilton's plan 36 to 13.

Building the Economy

Hamilton made other proposals for building a strong national economy. He asked Congress to create a national bank, the Bank of the United States. Both private investors and the national government would own the Bank's stock.

The Fight Over the Bank

Until this time only three banks existed in the nation—in Boston, New York City, and Philadelphia. All three had been established by state governments. Madison and Jefferson opposed the idea of a national bank. They believed it would benefit the wealthy. They also charged that the Bank was unconstitutional—that the Constitution had no provision for creating such

money in a certain length of time. During hard times, many of the original bond owners—shopkeepers, farmers, and soldiers—had sold the bonds for less than their value. They were purchased by speculators, people who risk money in order to make a larger profit. Hamilton proposed that these bonds be paid off at their original value. Opponents believed that Hamilton's plan would make speculators rich at the expense of average Americans.

Opposition to the plan went beyond political leaders. In the view of one Pennsylvania farmer, Hamilton's plan was "established at the expense

---

*F*ootnotes to History

Presidential Design Pierre-Charles L'Enfant of France planned the city of Washington. Helping L'Enfant lay out the boundaries of the new capital was Benjamin Banneker, the son of free African Americans. Recommended by Thomas Jefferson, Banneker was a mathematician and inventor and also published an almanac.

an institution. Hamilton argued that although the Constitution did not specifically say that Congress could create a bank, Congress still had the power to do so.

Washington asked Hamilton and Jefferson to write opinions on the question. In the end the president agreed with Hamilton and signed the bill creating the national bank.

Tariffs and Taxes

At the time, most Americans earned their living by farming. Hamilton thought the development of manufacturing industries would make America stronger. He proposed a tariff—a tax on imports—to encourage people to buy American products. This **protective tariff** would protect American industry from foreign competition.

The South, having little industry to protect, opposed protective tariffs. Hamilton did win support in Congress for some low tariffs to raise money rather than to protect industries. By the 1790s the revenue from tariffs provided 90 percent of the national government's income.

The final portion of Hamilton's economic program concerned the creation of national taxes. The government needed additional funds to operate and to make interest payments on the

America's FLAGS

Betsy Ross Flag, 1790 Legend holds that Philadelphia seamstress Betsy Ross stitched the first Stars and Stripes. Historical record does not support this account, however. The popular "Betsy Ross flag," with 13 stars arranged in a circle, did not appear until the early 1790s.

national debt. At Hamilton's request Congress approved a variety of taxes, including one on whiskey distilled in the United States.

Hamilton's economic program gave the national government new financial powers and protected the investments and interests of well-to-do Americans. However, his proposals split Congress and the nation. The opponents—including Jefferson and Madison—feared a national government with strong economic powers dominated by the wealthy class. They had a very different vision of what America should become.

Section 1 Assessment

Checking for Understanding

1. **Identify** George Washington, John Adams, Alexander Hamilton, Judiciary Act of 1789.
2. **Define** inauguration, precedent, cabinet, national debt, bond, speculator, unconstitutional, tariff.
3. **Name** three things that Hamilton wanted to do to strengthen the economy.

Reviewing Themes

4. **Government and Democracy** How did Congress try to balance power between the state and federal courts?

Critical Thinking

5. **Analyzing Primary Sources** About Washington, Hamilton said: "He consulted much, pondered much, resolved slowly, resolved surely." Did this make Washington a good first president? Explain.

Activity

Mock Interview Imagine that you must choose the first cabinet members. Write a job description for the secretary of state, treasury, or war. Then interview a classmate to see if he or she would be good for the position.

November 1791
Little Turtle defeats St. Clair's forces

April 1793
Washington issues Proclamation of Neutrality

July 1794
Western farmers revolt in Whiskey Rebellion

August 1794
Battle of Fallen Timbers occurs

October 1795
Spain opens Mississippi River to American shipping

Section 2

Early Challenges

READ TO DISCOVER . . .
- how the federal government asserted its power in the West.
- how the United States tried to stay out of European conflicts.

TERMS TO LEARN
neutrality   impressment

The Storyteller

Far removed from the bustle of trade and shipping along the Atlantic coast, farmers on the western frontier moved at a slower pace. In fact, western ways seemed almost primitive to travelers from the East. They seemed to notice only the poor roads and the boring diet of corn and salted pork. Living in scattered, isolated homesteads, frontier farmers were proud of their self-reliance. They wanted no "eastern" tax collectors heading their way.

Tax collector

Hamilton's taxes led to rebellion in western Pennsylvania. The farmers were in an uproar over paying a special tax on the whiskey they made from surplus corn. In the backcountry most farmers lived by bartering—exchanging whiskey and other items they produced for goods they needed. They rarely had cash. How could they pay a tax on whiskey?

The Whiskey Rebellion

The farmers' resistance was mostly peaceful until July 1794, when federal officers stepped up efforts to collect the tax. Then a mob of about 500 people armed with swords, guns, and pitchforks attacked tax collectors and burned down buildings. Some chanted a slogan from the French Revolution—"Liberty, Equality, Fraternity"—and waved a flag symbolizing an independent "country" in western Pennsylvania.

The armed protest, called the **Whiskey Rebellion,** alarmed government leaders. President Washington personally led an army of about 13,000 soldiers to crush the challenge. The rebellion collapsed as soon as the army crossed the **Appalachian Mountains.**

The Whiskey Rebellion set a milestone in determining how far people could go in protesting the laws of the new nation. By his action, Washington served notice on those who opposed government actions. If citizens wished to change the law, they had to do so peacefully, through constitutional means. Government would meet with force any threats to disturb the social order.

Geography

Struggle Over the West

★ The new government faced problems in the West that were not easy to resolve. The Native Americans who lived between the Appalachian Mountains and the Mississippi River denied that the United States had any authority over them. On many occasions Native Americans turned to Britain and Spain to help them in their cause. Both countries welcomed the opportunity to prevent American settlement of the region.

Foreign Powers in the West

Washington worried about European ambitions in the Northwest Territory. His goal was to remove that threat, "in peace if I can, and to be prepared for war if I cannot." He hoped that signing treaties with Native Americans would lessen the influence of the British and Spanish.

American settlers, however, ignored the treaties and continued to move onto lands promised to the Indians. Fighting broke out between the settlers and Native Americans.

Washington sent a large military expedition under General Arthur St. Clair to restore order in the Northwest Territory. In November 1791, St. Clair's forces were badly beaten by Little Turtle, chief of the Miami people. More than 600 American troops died in a battle by the Wabash River.

Many Americans believed that an alliance with France would enable them to defeat the combined forces of the British, Spanish, and Native Americans in the West. The British, who still had forts in the region, wanted to hold on to the profitable fur trade. The possibility of French involvement in the region pushed the British to make a bold bid for control of the West. In 1794 the British governor of Canada urged Indians to destroy American settlements west of the Appalachians. The British also began building a new fort in Ohio.

American Victories in the West

Washington sent John Jay to Britain to try to halt the nation's slide toward war. He also instructed **General Anthony Wayne** to gain control over the Native Americans in the Ohio River valley. Wayne used his knowledge of Native American customs to gain an important advantage. Aware that Indians usually fasted before a battle, he spread rumors that he planned to attack on August 17. Then he delayed his attack. Expecting the battle to begin at any moment, the Native Americans continued to fast. Finally on August 20, 1794, Wayne attacked and defeated Shawnee chief Blue Jacket and his warriors—weakened by hunger—at the **Battle of Fallen Timbers.**

A year later Wayne forced 12 Indian nations in the Great Lakes region to sign the **Treaty of Greenville.** The treaty opened most of Ohio to white settlement.

★ **Picturing HISTORY** Upon signing the Treaty of Greenville, 12 Indian nations received $20,000 worth of goods to share. **What did white settlers receive?**

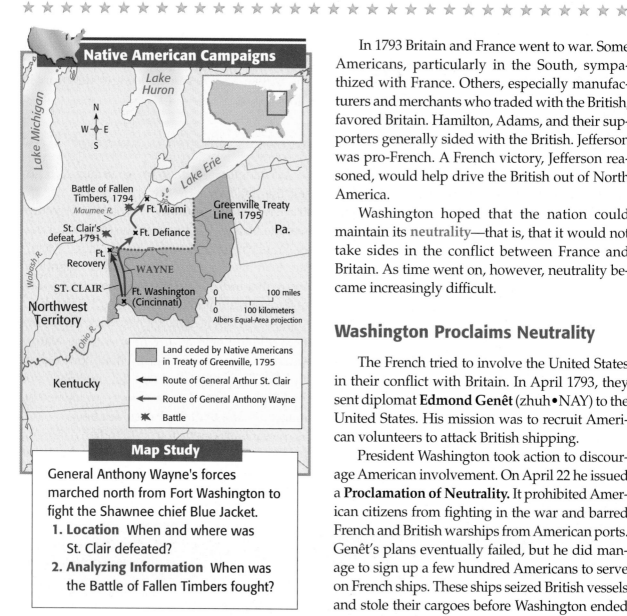

Native American Campaigns

Map Study

General Anthony Wayne's forces marched north from Fort Washington to fight the Shawnee chief Blue Jacket.

1. **Location** When and where was St. Clair defeated?
2. **Analyzing Information** When was the Battle of Fallen Timbers fought?

The French Revolution

In 1789 the French rebelled against their king, Louis XVI, and overthrew the government. At first most Americans cheered the news. The French had helped the Americans in their struggle for independence, and their revolution seemed to embody many of the ideals of the American Revolution.

By 1793, however, the French Revolution had turned bloody. The leaders had executed the king and queen of France and thousands of French citizens. Public opinion in the United States started to divide. The violence of the French Revolution, as well as its attack on religion and disregard of individual liberties, offended many Americans.

In 1793 Britain and France went to war. Some Americans, particularly in the South, sympathized with France. Others, especially manufacturers and merchants who traded with the British, favored Britain. Hamilton, Adams, and their supporters generally sided with the British. Jefferson was pro-French. A French victory, Jefferson reasoned, would help drive the British out of North America.

Washington hoped that the nation could maintain its neutrality—that is, that it would not take sides in the conflict between France and Britain. As time went on, however, neutrality became increasingly difficult.

Washington Proclaims Neutrality

The French tried to involve the United States in their conflict with Britain. In April 1793, they sent diplomat **Edmond Genêt** (zhuh•NAY) to the United States. His mission was to recruit American volunteers to attack British shipping.

President Washington took action to discourage American involvement. On April 22 he issued a **Proclamation of Neutrality.** It prohibited American citizens from fighting in the war and barred French and British warships from American ports. Genêt's plans eventually failed, but he did manage to sign up a few hundred Americans to serve on French ships. These ships seized British vessels and stole their cargoes before Washington ended their adventures by closing American ports.

Outraged by the French attacks at sea, the British began seizing American ships that traded with the French. The British also stopped American merchant ships and forced their crews into the British navy. This practice, known as impressment, infuriated the American government and people. British attacks on American ships and sailors, along with the challenge in the West, pushed the nation closer toward war with Great Britain.

A Controversial Treaty

General Wayne's victory at the Battle of Fallen Timbers persuaded the British in November 1794 to accept many of the American demands presented by the negotiator, John Jay. In **Jay's Treaty** the British agreed to withdraw from American soil, to pay damages for ships they had seized, and to allow some American ships to trade with British colonies in the Caribbean. The treaty also provided for settlement of debts from before 1776.

Despite these gains few Americans approved of Jay's Treaty. Most considered it dishonorable. They protested that the treaty did not deal with the issue of impressment and did not mention British interference with American trade.

Crowds marched in the streets and burned images of John Jay. When Hamilton tried to speak in support of the treaty, people threw stones at him. Although Washington found fault with the treaty, he realized it would end an explosive crisis with Great Britain. He sent the treaty to the Senate, which narrowly approved it after a fierce debate.

Success with Spain

In 1795 the United States signed an agreement with Spain known as **Pinckney's Treaty.** American victories west of the Appalachians had convinced the Spanish to make peace. The Spanish gave the Americans unrestricted access to the Mississippi River and promised to dismantle all forts on American territory.

Washington's Farewell

★ In the spring of 1796, Washington announced he would not seek a third term. By choosing to serve only two terms, Washington set a precedent that later presidents would follow.

Plagued with a variety of ailments, the 64-year-old president looked forward to retirement at Mount Vernon. He also felt troubled over the divisions in American politics and with what he considered a grave danger to the new nation—the growth of political parties.

Washington's "Farewell Address" was published in a Philadelphia newspaper. In it he attacked the evils of political parties and entanglement in foreign affairs. He also urged his fellow citizens to "observe good faith and justice toward all nations" while avoiding "passionate attachment" and "permanent alliances" with any. Washington's parting words had great influence on the nation's foreign policy for more than 100 years. The text is still read aloud in the U.S. Senate each year on Washington's birthday.

*F*ootnotes to History

A Hero Passes Washington died on December 14, 1799. He became ill with what was probably pneumonia.

Section 2 Assessment

Checking for Understanding
1. *Identify* Whiskey Rebellion, Anthony Wayne, Treaty of Greenville.
2. *Define* neutrality, impressment.
3. *Explain* the message that Washington was sending to the American people by using force to stop the Whiskey Rebellion.

Reviewing Themes
4. **Civic Rights and Responsibilities** How did the Treaty of Greenville affect the rights of Native Americans?

Critical Thinking
5. **Predicting Consequences** What did the United States have to gain by remaining neutral?

Activity

Writing a Tribute A tribute is a speech showing respect and gratitude. Write a one-paragraph tribute that you might have delivered if you had been asked to speak at President George Washington's funeral.

1796
Federalists nominate
John Adams for president;
Democratic-Republicans
nominate Jefferson for president

1797
John Adams takes
the office of president

Section 3

The First Political Parties

READ TO DISCOVER . . .
- how political parties got started and what positions they supported.
- how John Adams and Thomas Jefferson became candidates of opposing parties in the election of 1796.

TERMS TO LEARN
partisan   caucus
implied powers

The Storyteller

The Washington presidency was known for its dignity and elegance. The president rode in a coach drawn by horses and accompanied by mounted attendants. He and his wife, Martha, lived in the finest house in Philadelphia, the new nation's capital. They entertained a great deal, holding weekly receptions. Each year a ball was held on Washington's birthday. The president wore a black velvet suit with gold buckles, yellow gloves, powdered hair, an ostrich plume in his hat, and a sword in a white leather sheath. Despite these extravagances, Washington's character and military record were admired by most Americans.

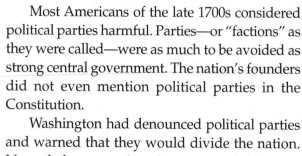

Pennsylvania ballot box

Although hailed by Americans as the nation's greatest leader, George Washington did not escape criticism during his two terms as president. From time to time, harsh attacks on his policies and on his personality appeared in newspapers. One paper even called Washington "the scourge and the misfortune of his country."

Opposing Views

The attacks on Washington had come from supporters of Thomas Jefferson. They were trying to discredit the policies of Washington and Hamilton by attacking the president. By 1796 Americans were beginning to divide into opposing groups and to form political parties.

Distrust of Political Parties

Most Americans of the late 1700s considered political parties harmful. Parties—or "factions" as they were called—were as much to be avoided as strong central government. The nation's founders did not even mention political parties in the Constitution.

Washington had denounced political parties and warned that they would divide the nation. Nevertheless as various issues arose in the new republic, it was only natural that people would disagree about them and that people of similar views would band together.

In Washington's cabinet Hamilton and Jefferson increasingly took opposing sides on issues.

★ Picturing HISTORY Both Federalists and Republicans used newspaper articles, editorials, and cartoons to influence public opinion. **What were the major differences between Federalists and Republicans?**

They disagreed on economic policy and foreign relations, on the power of the federal government, and on interpreting the Constitution. Even Washington had been partisan—favoring one side of an issue. Although he believed he stood above politics, Washington usually supported Hamilton's positions.

Political Parties Emerge

In Congress and the nation at large, similar differences existed. By the mid-1790s, two distinct political parties had taken shape.

The name **Federalist** had first described someone who supported ratification of the Constitution. By the 1790s the word was applied to a group of people who generally supported the policies of Alexander Hamilton. One man who called himself a Federalist declared he was a "friend of order, of government, and of the present administration."

Generally Federalists stood for a vigorous federal government. They admired Britain, because of its stability, and distrusted France, because of the violent changes following the French Revolution. Federalist policies tended to favor banking and shipping interests. Federalists received the strongest support in the Northeast, especially in New England, and from wealthy plantation owners in the South.

Efforts to turn public opinion against Federalist policies began seriously in late 1791 when Philip Freneau began publishing the *National Gazette* in **Philadelphia.** Jefferson, then secretary of state, helped the newspaper get started. Later he and Madison began to organize people who disagreed with Hamilton's policies. They called their party the **Republicans,** or the **Democratic-Republicans.**

The Republicans wanted to leave as much power as possible to the state governments. They feared that a strong federal government would endanger people's liberties. They supported the French and condemned what they regarded as the Washington administration's pro-British policies. Republican policies appealed to small farmers and urban workers, especially in the Middle Atlantic states and the South.

*F*ootnotes to History

Modern Political Parties Today's Democratic Party traces its roots to Jefferson's Democratic-Republicans. The modern Republican Party, however, was not founded until 1854.

✒ Citizenship

Views of the Constitution

One difference between Federalists and Republicans concerned the basis of government power. In Hamilton's view the federal government had **implied powers,** powers that were not specifically mentioned in the Constitution.

Hamilton used the idea of implied powers to justify a national bank. He argued that the Constitution gave Congress the power to issue money and regulate trade, and a national bank would clearly help the government carry out these responsibilities. Therefore, creating a bank was within the constitutional power of Congress.

Jefferson and Madison disagreed. They believed in a strict interpretation of the Constitution. In their view, unless the Constitution specifically mentioned government powers in a particular area, the government had no authority to act.

Differences Between the First Political Parties

Federalists	Democratic-Republicans
Leader: Alexander Hamilton	Leader: Thomas Jefferson
Favored:	**Favored:**
★ Rule by the wealthy class	★ Rule by the people
★ Strong federal government	★ Strong state governments
★ Emphasis on manufactured products	★ Emphasis on agricultural products
★ Loose interpretation of the Constitution	★ Strict interpretation of the Constitution
★ British alliance	★ French alliance
★ National bank	★ State banks
★ Protective tariffs	★ Free trade

Chart Study

Hamilton and Jefferson represented the beliefs of opposition parties.
1. Which leader would have encouraged trade with France? Explain.
2. **Analyzing Information** Which leader would American business owners be more likely to favor?

The People's Role

The differences between the parties, however, went even deeper. Federalists and Republicans had sharply opposing views on the role ordinary people should play in government.

Federalists supported representative government, in which elected officials ruled in the people's name. They did not believe that it was wise to let the public become too involved in politics. "The people are turbulent and changing," Hamilton said. "They seldom judge or determine right."

Public office, Federalists thought, should be held by honest and educated men of property who would protect everyone's rights. Ordinary people were too likely to be swayed by agitators.

In contrast, the Republicans feared a strong central government controlled by a few people. They believed that liberty would be safe only if ordinary people participated in government. As Jefferson explained: "I am not among those who fear the people; they, and not the rich, are our dependence [what we depend on] for continued freedom." ✒

Washington's Dilemma

Washington tried to get his two advisers to work out their differences. Knowing Jefferson was discontented, Washington wrote:

❝ I have a great sincere esteem and regard for you both, and ardently wish that some line could be marked out by which both [of] you could walk. ❞

Nevertheless, by 1793 Jefferson was so unhappy that he resigned as secretary of state. Alexander Hamilton resigned, too. The rival groups and their points of view moved further apart.

The Election of 1796

★ In the presidential election of 1796, candidates sought office for the first time as members of a party rather than as individuals. To

Causes and Effects

CAUSES		EFFECTS
★ Different philosophies of government		★ Federalists and Democratic-Republicans propose different solutions
★ Conflicting interpretations of the Constitution	**Political Parties Emerge**	★ The two parties nominate candidates
★ Different economic and regional interests		★ Political parties become a way of American life
★ Disagreement over foreign affairs		

Chart Study

Thomas Jefferson and Alexander Hamilton emerged as the leaders of the two opposing parties.

Analyzing Information Which political party favored rule by the wealthy and educated class?

prepare for the election, the Federalists and the Republicans held meetings called caucuses. At the caucuses members of Congress and other leaders chose their party's candidates for office.

The Federalists nominated Vice President Adams as their candidate for president and Charles Pinckney for vice president. The Republicans put forth former secretary of state Jefferson for president and Aaron Burr for vice president. Adams and Jefferson, who had been good friends, became rivals. The Federalists expected to carry New England. The Republicans' strength lay in the South, which would give most of its votes to Jefferson.

In the end Adams received 71 electoral votes, winning the election. Jefferson finished second with 68 votes. Under the provisions of the Constitution at that time, the person with the second-highest number of electoral votes became vice president. Jefferson therefore became the new vice president even though he represented a different party from the elected president. The administration that took office on March 4, 1797, had a Federalist president and a Republican vice president.

★ ★ ★ ★ ★ Section 3 Assessment ★ ★ ★ ★ ★

Checking for Understanding
1. **Identify** Federalist, Philadelphia, Democratic-Republican.
2. **Define** partisan, implied powers, caucus.
3. **Compare** the Federalists' and Republicans' views of the Constitution.

Reviewing Themes
4. **Economic Factors** Which party was most popular with middle-class urban workers and farmers? Explain.

Critical Thinking
5. **Synthesizing Information** Do you think the development of political parties was necessary? Why or why not?

Activity

Making a Campaign Poster Choose the candidate that you would have voted for in the election of 1796 and make a campaign poster using words and illustrations to promote your candidate.

March 1797
John Adams becomes president

1798
Congress passes Alien and Sedition acts

May 1798
Congress establishes the Navy Department

1800
France makes peace with the United States

Section 4

President John Adams

READ TO DISCOVER . . .

■ why the United States fought an undeclared war with France.
■ why the Alien and Sedition acts divided the country.

TERMS TO LEARN

alien
sedition
deport

states' rights
nullify

The Storyteller

Before John Adams was inaugurated, he had been widely criticized in the newspapers. At one time he had worked on the idea of titles for high government officials. Perhaps the president should be called "His Mightiness," Adams offered.
This suggestion earned Adams great ridicule, including being rudely dubbed "His Rotundity" —a comment on his stout figure.

Pitcher honoring John Adams, 1797

John Adams became the second president of the United States on March 4, 1797. The new president was a man of great intelligence and ability. Reserved and somewhat rigid, he felt more comfortable with ideas than with people. In the emotionally charged political atmosphere of the day, the nation needed a strong leader.

The XYZ Affair

Early in his administration, Adams faced a crisis with France. The French regarded Jay's Treaty, signed in 1794, as an American attempt to help the British in their war with France. To punish the United States, the French seized American ships that carried cargo to Britain.

Adams wanted to avoid war with France. In the fall of 1797, he sent a delegation to Paris to try to resolve the dispute. French foreign minister **Charles de Talleyrand,** however, refused to meet with the Americans. Instead, Talleyrand sent three agents who demanded a bribe and a loan for France from the Americans. "Not a sixpence," the Americans replied and sent a report of the incident to the United States. Adams was furious. Referring to the three French agents as X, Y, and Z, the president urged Congress to prepare for war. The incident became known as the **XYZ affair.**

Undeclared War With France

Congress responded with a program to strengthen the armed forces. It established the Navy Department in May 1798 and set aside money for building warships. Congress also increased the size of the army. George Washington was appointed commanding general.

Between 1798 and 1800, American and French naval forces fought an undeclared war. The Americans seized more than 90 French armed ships. No fighting took place on land.

For most Americans France had become an enemy. The Republican Party, friendly toward France in the past, hesitated to turn around and condemn France. As a result, in the 1798 elections, Americans voted many Republicans out of office.

Alien and Sedition Acts

The threat of war with France made Americans more suspicious of aliens, immigrants living in the country who were not citizens. Many Europeans who came to the United States in the 1790s endorsed the ideals of the French Revolution. Some became active supporters of the Republican Party. Some Americans questioned whether these aliens would remain loyal in the event of a war with France.

Federalists in Congress responded with strict laws to protect the nation's security. In 1798 they passed a group of measures known as the **Alien and Sedition acts.** Sedition refers to activities aimed at weakening established government. Adams had not asked for these laws, but he went along with the Federalist majority in Congress.

The Alien Act

The Alien Act gave the president the power to deport, or send out of the country, aliens he considered dangerous. Another law, the **Naturalization Act,** made it difficult for white aliens—African Americans could not even apply—to become citizens. Individuals would have to live in

Picturing HISTORY In Congress, Federalist Roger Griswold, wielding a cane, fights with Republican Matthew Lyon, a victim of the Sedition Act of 1798. **What was the aim of the Sedition Act?**

the country for 14 years—instead of 5 years—before applying for citizenship. This law was aimed at preventing foreigners, who were likely to join the Republicans, from becoming citizens.

The Sedition Act

The Sedition Act made it a crime to speak, write, or publish "false, scandalous and malicious" criticisms of the government, Congress, or the president. The Federalists, who controlled Congress, pointedly omitted mention of the vice president in the law because Thomas Jefferson—a Republican—held the office.

Nobody was deported under the Alien Act, which expired in 1802. The government did use the Sedition Act, however, to prosecute a number

*F*ootnotes to History

The Laundry Room When John and Abigail Adams moved into the White House in 1800, the house was largely unfinished. Because there was no place to dry the family laundry, Mrs. Adams strung up a clothesline in the East Room.

of people—mostly Republican newspaper editors. One Republican representative, Matthew Lyon of Vermont, even went to jail for criticizing Adams. In all, 25 people were arrested and 10 convicted of violating the law.

Citizenship
States' Rights

For some Americans, fears of a strong central government abusing its power seemed to be coming true. The Republicans looked to the states to preserve the people's liberties and stand up to what they regarded as Federalist tyranny. Madison and Jefferson wrote two resolutions on the rights of states that were endorsed by the legislatures of **Virginia** and **Kentucky**.

The **Virginia** and **Kentucky Resolutions** of 1798 and 1799 spelled out a theory of states' rights. According to the resolutions, states had the right to judge the constitutionality of federal laws. The Kentucky Resolutions further suggested that states might nullify—that is, legally overturn—federal laws considered unconstitutional.

The Virginia and Kentucky Resolutions posed a direct challenge to the constitutional authority of the national government. The prospect of state militias fighting with federal army troops seemed real at the time to many people. Although no other states adopted similar resolutions, the Resolutions revealed the extent of people's fears about a strong federal government interfering with their rights. The issue of states' rights would arise again and again in the nation's early history, leading in time to a division of the states into opposing camps and to civil war.

Peace With France

As the election of 1800 approached, the Federalists found themselves under attack. They urged Adams to step up the war with France. They hoped to benefit politically from the patriotic feelings that war would unleash.

Adams refused to rush to war, especially for his own political gain. Instead he appointed a new commission to seek peace with France. In 1800 the French agreed to a treaty and stopped attacks on American ships.

Although the agreement with France was in the best interest of the United States, it divided the Federalists and hurt Adams's chance for reelection. Rather than benefiting from a conflict with France, Hamilton and his supporters were now in open opposition to their own president.

With the Federalists split, the Republican prospects for capturing the presidency improved. The way was prepared for Thomas Jefferson in the election of 1800.

Section 4 Assessment

Checking for Understanding
1. *Identify* John Adams, XYZ affair, Alien and Sedition acts, Kentucky Resolution.
2. *Define* alien, sedition, deport, states' rights, nullify.
3. *Explain* why the Federalists passed the Alien and Sedition acts.

Reviewing Themes
4. **Groups and Institutions** What did the Virginia and Kentucky Resolutions uphold?

Critical Thinking
5. **Determining Cause and Effect** How did President Adams's decision to avoid a war with France divide the Federalists and help the Republicans?

Drawing a Political Cartoon Draw a political cartoon that criticizes the Alien and Sedition acts of 1798.

Reading a Flowchart

Sometimes determining a sequence of events can be confusing, particularly when many events are occurring at the same time. Reading a flowchart can help you understand what is going on.

Learning the Skill

Flowcharts show the steps in a process or a sequence of events. A flowchart could be used to show the movement of goods through a factory, of people through a training program, or of a bill through Congress. The following steps explain how to read a flowchart:

- Read the title or caption of the flowchart to find out what you are studying.
- Read all of the labels or sentences on the flowchart.
- Look for numbers indicating a sequence, or arrows showing the direction of movement.
- Evaluate the information in the flowchart.

Practicing the Skill

Read the flowchart on this page. It shows a sequence of events that took place in the Northwest Territory. Analyze the information in the flowchart, then answer the following questions.

1. What is the title of this flowchart?
2. What symbol is used to show the direction in which the events are moving?
3. What actions taken by the British set off the sequence of events that are reflected in the title of the chart?
4. What action did Washington take in response to trouble in the Ohio Valley?
5. What information from the chapter could you add to the flowchart to show a further sequence of events?

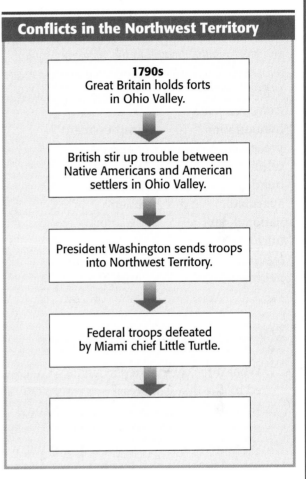

Conflicts in the Northwest Territory

1790s
Great Britain holds forts in Ohio Valley.

⬇

British stir up trouble between Native Americans and American settlers in Ohio Valley.

⬇

President Washington sends troops into Northwest Territory.

⬇

Federal troops defeated by Miami chief Little Turtle.

⬇

Applying the Skill

Making a Flowchart Imagine that a student who is new to your school asks you how to sign up for a sport or social club. Draw a flowchart outlining the steps the student should follow.

Glencoe's **Skillbuilder Interactive Workbook, Level 1** provides instruction and practice in key social studies skills.

Assessment and Activities

★ Reviewing Key Terms

On graph paper, create a word search puzzle using the following terms. Crisscross the terms vertically and horizontally, then fill in the remaining squares with extra letters. Use the terms' definitions as clues to find the words in the puzzle. Share your puzzle with a classmate.

inauguration	impressment
precedent	partisan
cabinet	implied powers
bond	caucus
speculator	alien
national debt	sedition
unconstitutional	deport
tariff	states' rights
neutrality	nullify

★ Reviewing Key Facts

1. What three cabinet departments were created by the first Congress?
2. Why did many people think Hamilton's proposal to sell bonds was unfair?
3. Why did many Americans support the French Revolution at first but later oppose it?
4. What was the main reason for the formation of political parties?
5. What actions by France led to an undeclared war with the United States?

★ Critical Thinking

Identifying Assumptions

The issue of states' rights versus national rights was a problem that would plague the new nation for many years.

1. Why did some Americans fear a strong central government?
2. How did the Alien and Sedition acts increase these fears?

★ Time Line Activity

Create a time line on which you place the following events in chronological order.

- John Adams is elected president
- Twelve Native American nations sign the Treaty of Greenville
- Bill of Rights is added to the Constitution
- Congress passes Alien and Sedition acts
- George Washington becomes the first president of the United States
- Undeclared war between America and France ends

★ Geography Activity

The British held on to their frontier outposts until the Jay Treaty. Study the map below, then answer the questions that follow.

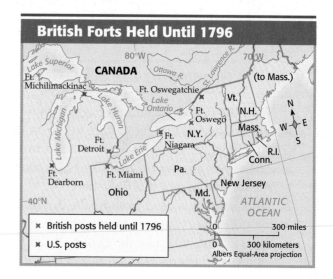

British Forts Held Until 1796

1. **Location** What two British forts were located in New York?
2. **Movement** Along what natural transportation route were British forts located?
3. **Location** About how many miles apart were the easternmost and westernmost U.S. posts?

★ Skill Practice Activity

Reading a Flowchart

Alexander Hamilton promoted the creation of a national bank. Study the flowchart below, then answer the questions that follow.

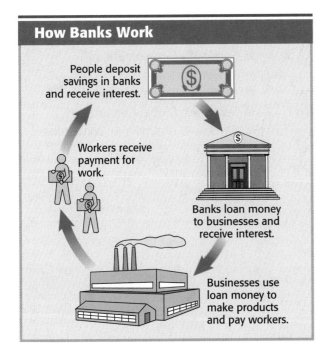

How Banks Work

People deposit savings in banks and receive interest.

Workers receive payment for work.

Banks loan money to businesses and receive interest.

Businesses use loan money to make products and pay workers.

1. What is the title of this flowchart?
2. What is used to show the direction in which the events are moving?
3. What happens after workers receive payment for their work?
4. What two parts on this flowchart show who receives interest on their money?

★ Cooperative Activity

History and Journalism Working in pairs, scan newspapers to find five articles that, as written, would have been considered a violation of the Sedition Act in 1798. Clip each article and highlight the information you think would have violated the Sedition Act.

★ Reviewing Themes

1. **Government and Democracy** How did the Tenth Amendment strengthen the rights of individual states?
2. **Civic Rights and Responsibilities** What advice did President Washington give Americans in his Farewell Address?
3. **Economic Factors** How did Federalists justify Congress's creation of a national bank?
4. **Groups and Institutions** How did the XYZ affair increase bad feelings between France and the United States?

★ Technology Activity

Using a Computerized Card Catalog
Search your local library's computerized card catalog for sources on Mount Vernon, George Washington's home. Find the sources on the library shelves, then use the information you find to write a two-paragraph description that Washington might have written if he had ever wanted to sell his home.

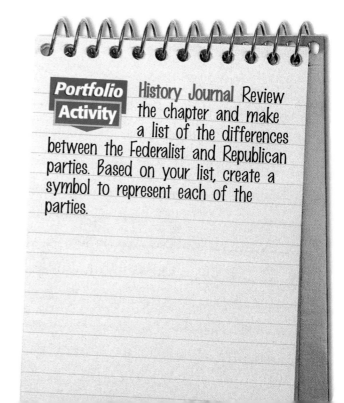

Portfolio Activity History Journal Review the chapter and make a list of the differences between the Federalist and Republican parties. Based on your list, create a symbol to represent each of the parties.

1800–1816

The Jefferson Era

★ Why It's Important

In 1801 the Democratic-Republican Party took control of the nation's government. The Federalists—the party of George Washington, Alexander Hamilton, and John Adams— were now on the sidelines and played the role of critics to the Republican administration. Today politicians operate within the party system that took shape at that time. While the two main parties have changed, each still works to win votes and gain power. If the people vote to change the party in power, the newly elected representatives take office peacefully and the government continues.

★ Chapter Themes

- Section 1, Government and Democracy
- Section 2, Geography and History
- Section 3, Global Connections
- Section 4, Groups and Institutions

PRIMARY SOURCES
Library   *See pages 952–953 for primary source readings to accompany Chapter 9*

★ HISTORY AND ART   *Launching of the Ship* Fame *by George Ropes* During Jefferson's term, the United States experienced rapid expansion. The launching of this ship in 1802 symbolized growth of the nation's naval forces.

1800
Thomas Jefferson and John Adams contend for presidency

1801
Judiciary Act expands court system

March 1801
Jefferson is inaugurated

1803
Marbury v. *Madison* sets precedent for judicial review

Section 1

The Republicans Take Power

READ TO DISCOVER . . .

- how the election deadlock of 1800 was resolved.
- how John Marshall strengthened the Supreme Court of the United States.

TERMS TO LEARN

laissez-faire   judicial review
customs duties

Storyteller

In 1801 Washington, D.C., was slowly rising from a swampy site on the Potomac River. The nation's new capital had only two noteworthy buildings—the president's mansion (later called the White House) and the still-unfinished Capitol. Between them stretched a mile and a half of muddy streets on which pigs and chickens roamed freely.

Very few people liked being in Washington. It was hot and steamy in the summer, and the river and swamps were a breeding ground for mosquitoes. Abigail Adams called the new capital "the very dirtiest Hole."

Surveyor's tools

The Federalist and Republican parties fought a bitter election campaign in 1800. Federalists supported President Adams for a second term and Charles Pinckney of South Carolina for vice president. Republicans nominated **Thomas Jefferson** for president and **Aaron Burr** of New York as his running mate.

The Election of 1800

The election campaign of 1800 differed greatly from campaigns of today. Neither Adams nor Jefferson traveled around the country making speeches about why he should be elected. That would have been considered in bad taste. Instead the candidates and their allies wrote hundreds of letters to leading citizens and friendly newspapers to publicize their views. The letter-writing campaign, however, was not polite.

Federalists charged the Republican Jefferson, who believed in freedom of religion, as being "godless." Republicans warned that the Federalists would bring back the monarchy. Federalists, they claimed, represented the interests of wealthy people with property.

Election Deadlock

When members of the Electoral College voted, Jefferson and Burr each received 73 votes. Because of this tie, the House of Representatives

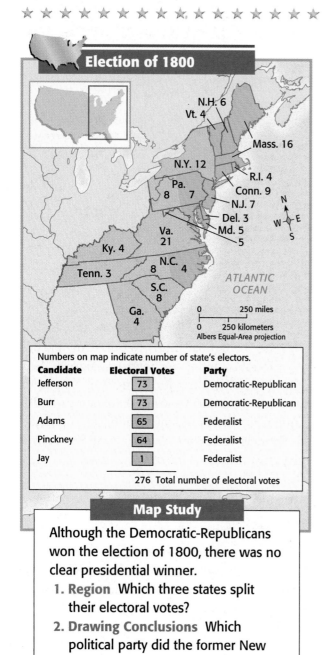

Election of 1800

Numbers on map indicate number of state's electors.

Candidate	Electoral Votes	Party
Jefferson	73	Democratic-Republican
Burr	73	Democratic-Republican
Adams	65	Federalist
Pinckney	64	Federalist
Jay	1	Federalist

276 Total number of electoral votes

Map Study

Although the Democratic-Republicans won the election of 1800, there was no clear presidential winner.

1. **Region** Which three states split their electoral votes?
2. **Drawing Conclusions** Which political party did the former New England Colonies support?

To prevent another showdown between a presidential and a vice-presidential candidate, Congress passed the Twelfth Amendment to the Constitution in 1803. This amendment, ratified in 1804, requires electors to vote for the president and vice president on separate ballots.

Jefferson's Inauguration

On March 4, 1801, the day of the inauguration, Jefferson dressed in everyday clothes. He left his boardinghouse and walked to the Senate to be sworn in as president. President Adams did not attend the ceremony. He had slipped out of the presidential mansion at 4:00 A.M. and left the city so he would not have to watch Thomas Jefferson become president.

In his Inaugural Address, Jefferson tried to bridge the gap between the developing political parties and reach out to Federalists with healing words. "We are all Republicans, we are all Federalists," he said. Then he outlined some of his goals, which included "a wise and frugal government," and "the support of state governments in all their rights." Jefferson had long been a supporter of states' rights. He believed that a large federal government threatened liberty and that strong states could best protect freedom.

Jefferson also believed in a policy called laissez-faire (LEH•SAY FEHR). This French term means "let (people) do (as they choose)." A laissez-faire government plays only a small part in the economic concerns of a country.

had to decide the election. At the time the electors voted for each presidential and vice-presidential candidate individually rather than voting for a party's candidates as a team.

In the House, Federalists saw a chance to prevent the election of Jefferson by supporting Burr. For 35 ballots, the election remained tied. Finally, at Alexander Hamilton's urging, one Federalist decided not to vote for Burr. Although he was no friend of Jefferson's, Hamilton greatly distrusted Burr. Jefferson became president and Burr became vice president.

Jefferson's Policies

Thomas Jefferson was a man of contradictions. He had proclaimed in the Declaration of Independence that "all men are created equal"—but he was a slaveholder. He thought the United States should be a nation of small farmers—but he himself was a wealthy landowner with a huge estate at Monticello, Virginia. A political philosopher, he excelled as a practical politician. In addition he designed buildings and loved to tinker with gadgets and with his own inventions.

Jefferson's Cabinet

When Jefferson entered office, he surrounded himself with men who shared his Republican principles. His secretary of state was his friend and fellow Virginian James Madison. For secretary of the treasury, he chose **Albert Gallatin.** This Pennsylvanian had a grasp of financial matters that equaled Alexander Hamilton's.

The new government soon ended two unpopular Federalist measures. It allowed the Alien and Sedition acts to expire and repealed the Naturalization Act. For Republicans both acts were symbols of a big federal government that threatened individual liberties.

Cutting Costs

Jefferson and Gallatin aimed to reduce the huge national debt of $83 million that the Federalists had left. They scaled down military expenses. They cut the army by one-third and reduced the navy from 25 to 7 ships. By slashing spending Jefferson and Gallatin significantly lowered the national debt within a few years.

Jefferson and Gallatin also persuaded Congress to repeal all federal internal taxes, including the hated whiskey tax. At that point government funds would come only from customs duties—taxes on foreign imported goods—and from the sale of western lands.

The entire federal government in 1801 consisted of only a few hundred people, and some of these were part-time workers. This was exactly how Jefferson thought it should be. In his view the responsibilities of government should be limited to delivering the mail, collecting customs duties, and conducting a census every 10 years.

Jefferson and the Courts

 Jefferson hoped that some Federalists would support his policies. However, bitter feelings between the parties continued during his administration. Much of the ill will resulted from a fight over control of the federal courts.

 **Citizenship**

Judiciary Act of 1801

Before Jefferson took office, the Federalists passed the Judiciary Act of 1801. The act set up regional courts for the United States with 16 judges and many other judicial officials. In his last days as president, John Adams made hundreds of appointments to these positions, and the Federalist-controlled Congress approved them. Adams also asked **John Marshall,** his secretary of state, to serve as chief justice of the United States after

★ HISTORY **AND** ART

***Washington, D.C., 1803* by Nicholas King** Washington, D.C., at the time of Jefferson's presidency, did not resemble the capital city familiar to citizens today. **How did Abigail Adams describe the city?**

Chief Justice Oliver Ellsworth resigned. By these actions Adams shut President-elect Jefferson out of the appointment process and ensured that Federalists would control the courts.

"Midnight Judges"

Adams and Marshall worked around the clock in the final hours of the Federalist government, processing the papers for these judicial appointments. The appointments could not take effect, however, until the papers (commissions) for these last-minute "midnight judges" were delivered. When Jefferson became president on March 4, a few of the commissions had not been delivered. He told Secretary of State Madison not to send them out. One commission was addressed to William Marbury.

Marbury v. *Madison*

To force the delivery of his commission, Marbury took his case directly to the Supreme Court, which he claimed had jurisdiction as a result of the Judiciary Act of 1789. Chief Justice John Marshall, a

Chief Justice John Marshall

Federalist, wrote an opinion turning down Marbury's claim. He noted that the Constitution did not give the Court jurisdiction to decide Marbury's case.

In *Marbury* v. *Madison* Justice Marshall had for the first time exercised the right of the Supreme Court to review and rule on acts of the other branches of government. Known as judicial review, this power has become a basic part of the system of checks and balances of our government today.

The Marshall Court

John Marshall served as chief justice until 1835. He made the Supreme Court an equal partner in government with the executive and legislative branches by declaring the Court's right to review the actions of the other branches.

Under Marshall the Court usually upheld the power of the national government over the rights of states. The Federalists had lost the presidency and Congress, but the Marshall Supreme Court incorporated many Federalist beliefs in the American system of government.

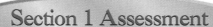

Section 1 Assessment

Checking for Understanding

1. **Identify** Washington, D.C., Thomas Jefferson, Aaron Burr, Albert Gallatin, John Marshall, *Marbury* v. *Madison*.
2. **Define** laissez-faire, customs duties, judicial review.
3. **Explain** how Jefferson cut government spending.

Reviewing Themes

4. **Government and Democracy** How did the judicial branch under Jefferson serve as a check on the executive and legislative branches?

Critical Thinking

5. **Identifying Central Issues** How was the deadlock in the presidential election of 1800 finally resolved?

Activity

Turning Words into Pictures Draw a picture of what you think the city of Washington, D.C., might have looked like on the day of Jefferson's inauguration.

1804   1805   1806   1807

December 1803
United States buys
Louisiana Territory

May 1804
Lewis and Clark
expedition sets off
from St. Louis

September 1806
Lewis and Clark
return to St. Louis

November 1806
Zebulon Pike
sights Pikes Peak

Section 2

The Louisiana Purchase

READ TO DISCOVER . . .

- how the United States expanded in the early 1800s.
- how Lewis and Clark led an expedition to explore the Louisiana Territory.

TERMS TO LEARN

Conestoga wagon   secede

The Storyteller

Why did Americans risk everything they had to travel west? An English visitor, Harriet Martineau, observed: "The pride and delight of Americans is in their quantity of land. . . . The possession of land is the aim of all action . . . and the cure for all social evils. . . . If a man is disappointed in politics or love, he goes and buys land. If he disgraces himself, he betakes himself to a lot in the West. . . ."

Conestoga wagon

American pioneers in search of land and adventure headed over the mountains into Kentucky and Tennessee and the less settled areas of the Northwest Territory. Most of these pioneers were farmers. They made a long and exhausting journey over the Appalachian Mountains. Pioneers had to trudge along crude, muddy roads or cut their way through dense forests.

Settlers loaded their household goods in Conestoga wagons, sturdy vehicles topped with white canvas. For these westward-bound pioneers, their two most valued possessions were a rifle for protection and hunting and an ax to hack their way through the dense forests.

Western Territory

In 1800 the territory of the United States extended only as far west as the Mississippi River. The area to the west of the river—known as the **Louisiana Territory**—belonged to Spain. It was an enormous area of land, anchored to the south by the city of New Orleans and extending west to the Rocky Mountains. Its northern boundaries remained undefined.

Many of the pioneers settled down and established farms along rivers that fed into the upper Mississippi River. They needed the river to ship their crops to markets. The Spanish allowed the Americans to sail on the lower Mississippi and trade in **New Orleans.** For the western farmers, this right was vital. The goods they sent downriver were unloaded in New Orleans and sent by ship to markets on the East Coast.

★ ★

The French Threat

In 1802 the Spanish suddenly changed their policy. They refused to allow American goods to move into or past New Orleans. Representatives in Washington muttered about taking New Orleans by force. That same year, President Jefferson learned that Spain and France had made a secret agreement that transferred the Louisiana Territory to France. This agreement posed a serious threat for the United States. France's leader, **Napoleon Bonaparte,** had plans for empires in Europe and the Americas.

Jefferson was alarmed. He believed French control would jeopardize American trade on the Mississippi River. Jefferson sent James Monroe to France as his special representative. In a letter to **Robert Livingston**, U.S. ambassador to France, Jefferson declared:

❝ There is on this globe one single spot, the possessor of which is our natural . . . enemy. It is New Orleans. ❞

Jefferson authorized American diplomats to offer as much as $10 million for New Orleans and West Florida. Jefferson believed that France had gained Florida as well as Louisiana in its secret agreement with Spain.

Revolt in Santo Domingo

Napoleon was forced to abandon his plans for an American empire. In 1802 Napoleon sent troops to the Caribbean island of Santo Domingo (now Haiti and the Dominican Republic) to crush a major revolt against French rule. The leader of the revolt, **Toussaint-Louverture** (TOO•SAN LOO•vuhr•TYUR), was the grandson of an African chief and a fiercely determined ex-slave. He had helped drive the British and Spanish from the island and end

slavery. The French captured Toussaint-Louverture but could not regain control of the island. Thousands of French troops died in the effort, many from disease.

The Nation Expands

★ The situation in Santo Domingo helped the United States. Stunned by their losses, the French feared that Britain might persuade the United States to join forces against them. Also, the French needed money to finance Napoleon's plans for war against Britain. The French believed they had something for sale that the United States might want to buy.

French foreign minister Charles de Talleyrand informed the American diplomats that the whole Louisiana Territory was for sale. Monroe and Livingston were taken completely by surprise. Accepting the offer went far beyond what they were authorized to do, but the deal was too good to pass up. After a few days of negotiation, the parties agreed on a price of $15 million.

Legality of the Purchase

The Louisiana Purchase pleased Jefferson. The new territory would provide cheap and abundant land for farmers for generations to come. He worried, however, whether the purchase was legal. The Constitution said nothing about acquiring new territory. By what authority could he justify the purchase? Livingston wrote from Paris, urging Jefferson to accept the deal before Napoleon changed his mind. Jefferson decided the government's treaty-making powers allowed the purchase of the new territory. The Senate gave its approval in October 1803. With the signing of the treaty, the size of the United States doubled.

Toussaint-Louverture

Geography

Lewis and Clark

⭐ Jefferson wanted to know more about the mysterious lands west of the Mississippi. Even before the Louisiana Purchase was complete, he persuaded Congress to sponsor an expedition to explore the new territory. Jefferson was particularly interested in the expedition as a scientific venture. Congress was interested in commercial possibilities and in sites for future forts.

To head the expedition, Jefferson chose his private secretary, 28-year-old **Meriwether Lewis.**

Lewis was well qualified to lead this journey of exploration. He had joined the militia during the Whiskey Rebellion and had been in the army since that time. The expedition's coleader was **William Clark,** 32, a friend of Lewis's from military service. Both Lewis and Clark were knowledgeable amateur scientists and had conducted business with Native Americans. Together they assembled a crew that included expert river men, gunsmiths, carpenters, scouts, and a cook. Two men of mixed Native American and French heritage served as interpreters. An African American named York rounded out the group.

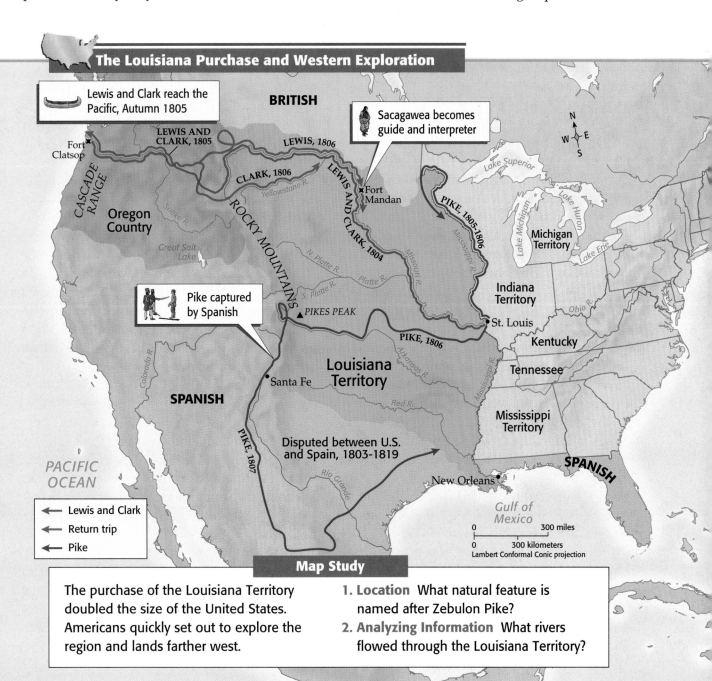

The Louisiana Purchase and Western Exploration

Lewis and Clark reach the Pacific, Autumn 1805

BRITISH

Sacagawea becomes guide and interpreter

Fort Clatsop

LEWIS AND CLARK, 1805

LEWIS, 1806

CLARK, 1806

Yellowstone R.

LEWIS AND CLARK, 1804

Fort Mandan

PIKE, 1805–1806

Lake Superior

Lake Michigan

Lake Huron

Lake Erie

CASCADE RANGE

Oregon Country

Snake R.

Great Salt Lake

ROCKY MOUNTAINS

N. Platte R.

S. Platte R.

Platte R.

Missouri R.

Mississippi R.

Michigan Territory

Indiana Territory

Ohio R.

St. Louis

Pike captured by Spanish

▲ PIKES PEAK

PIKE, 1806

Arkansas R.

Kentucky

Tennessee

Colorado R.

SPANISH

Santa Fe

Louisiana Territory

Red R.

Mississippi R.

Mississippi Territory

PIKE, 1807

Disputed between U.S. and Spain, 1803–1819

Rio Grande

New Orleans

SPANISH

PACIFIC OCEAN

Gulf of Mexico

N W E S

0   300 miles
0   300 kilometers
Lambert Conformal Conic projection

← Lewis and Clark
← Return trip
← Pike

Map Study

The purchase of the Louisiana Territory doubled the size of the United States. Americans quickly set out to explore the region and lands farther west.

1. **Location** What natural feature is named after Zebulon Pike?
2. **Analyzing Information** What rivers flowed through the Louisiana Territory?

The President's Instructions

Jefferson instructed the explorers to find a route across the Rocky Mountains to the Pacific Ocean. They were also to learn as much as they could about the Native Americans who lived in the new territory and to treat them "in the most friendly and conciliatory manner." In addition Lewis and Clark were to collect plant and animal specimens and chart the geography of the region.

The Journals of Lewis and Clark

The expedition left **St. Louis** in the spring of 1804, slowly working its way up the **Missouri River.** Lewis and Clark kept a journal of their voyage, making notes on what they saw and did.

By the time the cold weather of October came, Lewis and Clark had reached a site near present-day **Bismarck, North Dakota.** There they camped for the winter with the Mandan people. The Mandan survived by hunting buffalo and raising corn, squash, and beans. Long known as shrewd traders, the Mandan acted as go-betweens for the fur traders and other Native American peoples.

Before Lewis and Clark began the next leg of their journey, they hired a French trapper as a guide. The trapper was married to a young Shoshone woman named **Sacagawea** (SA•kuh •juh•WEE•uh). At first Lewis and Clark thought that having a woman and her infant son in their party would be a burden. As it turned out, Sacagawea proved invaluable. She served as an interpreter and helped the explorers survive.

When Lewis and Clark reached the **Rocky Mountains** in the summer of 1805, Sacagawea's presence was essential. This was the land she had come from. At first the Shoshone warriors they met reacted to the white men with suspicion. To the explorers' relief, the Shoshone chief turned out to be Sacagawea's older brother, Cameahwait. He helped Lewis and Clark secure horses and supplies and provided directions for the difficult journey over the Rockies.

To the Pacific and Back

After 18 months and nearly 4,000 miles, Lewis and Clark reached the Pacific Ocean at the mouth of the **Columbia River** in November 1805. After spending the winter there, they headed back east along separate routes. Both explorers arrived in St. Louis in September 1806, and Jefferson greeted the news of their return "with unspeakable joy." The expedition collected valuable information on people, plants, animals, and the geography of the West. Perhaps most important, the journey provided inspiration to a nation of people eager to move westward.

Pike's Expedition

★ Even before Lewis and Clark returned, Jefferson sent others to explore the wilderness. Lieutenant **Zebulon Pike** led two expeditions between 1805 and 1807, traveling through the upper Mississippi River valley and into the region that now is **Colorado.** In Colorado he found a snow-capped mountain he called Grand Peak. Today this mountain is known as Pikes Peak. During his expedition Pike was captured by the Spanish but was eventually released.

Federalists Plan to Secede

★ Many Federalists opposed the Louisiana Purchase. They feared that the agricultural states carved out of the new territory would become Republican, reducing the Federalists' power. A group of Federalists in Massachusetts plotted to secede—withdraw—from the Union. They wanted New England to form a separate "Northern Confederacy."

Aaron Burr

The plotters realized that to have any chance of success, the Northern Confederacy would have to include New York. The Massachusetts Federalists needed a powerful friend in that state who would back their plan. They turned to Aaron Burr, who had been cast aside by the Republicans for his refusal to withdraw from the 1800 election. The Federalists gave Burr their support in 1804, when he ran for governor of New York.

The Hamilton-Burr Feud

Alexander Hamilton had never trusted Aaron Burr. Now Hamilton was concerned about rumors that Burr had secretly agreed to lead New York out of the Union. Hamilton accused Burr of plotting treason. When Burr lost the election for governor, he blamed Hamilton and challenged him to a duel. In July 1804, the two men—armed with pistols—met in Weehawken, New Jersey. Hamilton fired first and missed Burr, probably deliberately. Burr, however, aimed to hit. Seriously wounded, Hamilton died the next day. Burr fled to avoid arrest.

★ ★ ★ ★ ★ **Section 2 Assessment** ★ ★ ★ ★ ★ ★

Checking for Understanding
1. **Identify** Louisiana Territory, New Orleans, Toussaint-Louverture, Meriwether Lewis, William Clark, Sacagawea, Zebulon Pike.
2. **Define** Conestoga wagon, secede.
3. **Explain** why France agreed to sell the Louisiana Territory to the United States.

Reviewing Themes
4. **Geography and History** Why was the Mississippi River and New Orleans important to the United States?

Critical Thinking
5. **Determining Cause and Effect** How do you think the Lewis and Clark expedition helped to prepare people who wanted to move west?

Recording Details Accurate descriptions and drawings in their journals made Lewis and Clark's observations valuable. Find an example of plants or animals nearby. Carefully draw and describe what you see.

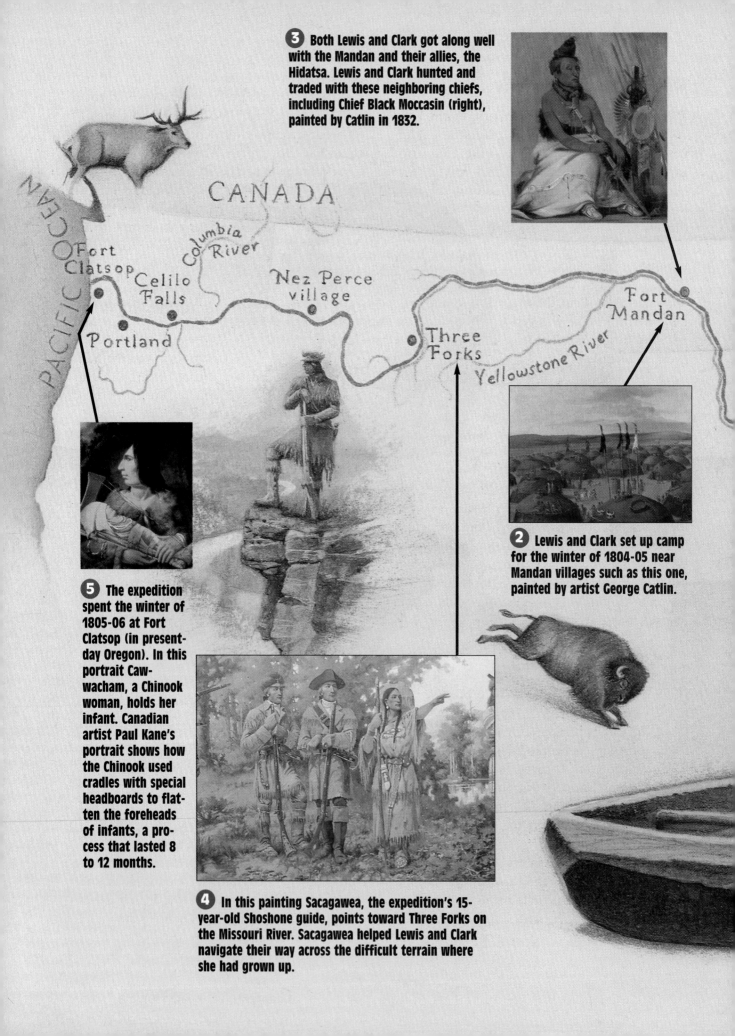

3 Both Lewis and Clark got along well with the Mandan and their allies, the Hidatsa. Lewis and Clark hunted and traded with these neighboring chiefs, including Chief Black Moccasin (right), painted by Catlin in 1832.

CANADA

PACIFIC OCEAN

Fort Clatsop

Columbia River

Celilo Falls

Portland

Nez Perce village

Three Forks

Yellowstone River

Fort Mandan

2 Lewis and Clark set up camp for the winter of 1804-05 near Mandan villages such as this one, painted by artist George Catlin.

5 The expedition spent the winter of 1805-06 at Fort Clatsop (in present-day Oregon). In this portrait Caw-wacham, a Chinook woman, holds her infant. Canadian artist Paul Kane's portrait shows how the Chinook used cradles with special headboards to flatten the foreheads of infants, a process that lasted 8 to 12 months.

4 In this painting Sacagawea, the expedition's 15-year-old Shoshone guide, points toward Three Forks on the Missouri River. Sacagawea helped Lewis and Clark navigate their way across the difficult terrain where she had grown up.

NATIONAL GEOGRAPHIC

Journeys

Lewis & Clark

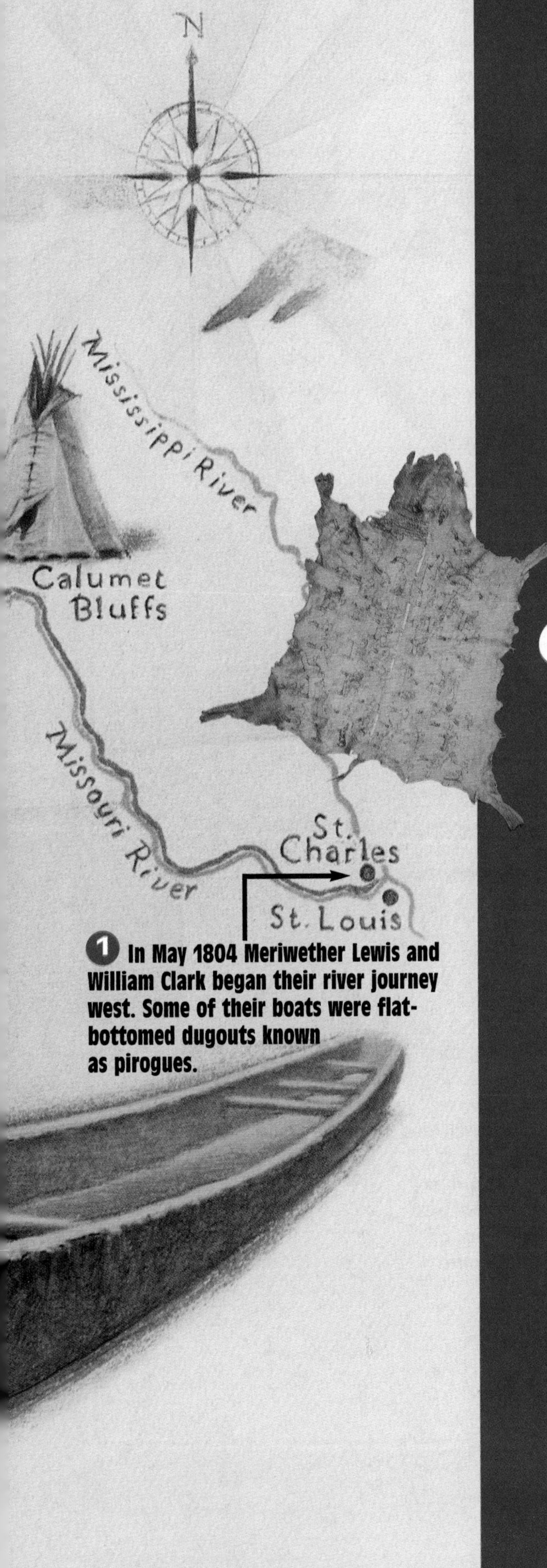

1 In May 1804 Meriwether Lewis and William Clark began their river journey west. Some of their boats were flat-bottomed dugouts known as pirogues.

66 Our vessels consisted of six small canoes and two large pirogues. This little fleet, altho' not quite so respectable as those of Columbus or Capt. Cook, was still viewed by us with much pleasure.... We were about to penetrate a country at least two thousand miles in width, on which the foot of civilized man had never trodden; the good or evil it had in store ... was for experiment yet to determine.... The picture which now presented itself to me was a most pleasing one.... I could but esteem this moment of ... departure as among the most happy of my life. 99

— From an April 1805 entry in the journal of Meriwether Lewis, as he prepares to leave Fort Mandan.

A New Frontier

What lay in the vast Louisiana Territory? How far was it to the Pacific Ocean? The Lewis and Clark expedition had both scientific and political goals. Its scientific mission was to explore the Louisiana territory—its plants, animals, geology, climate and terrain. Its political mission was to establish an American claim to Oregon territory.

The two explorers carefully mapped the entire trip, which covered about 8,000 miles (12,900 km). William Clark constructed 60 maps—some eight feet in length—depicting the expedition's route. The maps included the latitude and longitude of natural features such as rapids and islands. Both Lewis and Clark packed their journals with descriptions and sketches of all they saw.

Many of the local animals and plants were new to Lewis and Clark. They collected and preserved specimens such as a prairie dog, jackrabbit, black-tailed deer, pronghorn, and mountain sheep. Huge grizzly bears were a frequent threat and at least 43 bears were killed by the explorers. In 1816 the American scientist George Ord read Lewis and Clark's journals and gave the grizzly its scientific name: *Ursus arctos horribilis,* or "terrible bear."

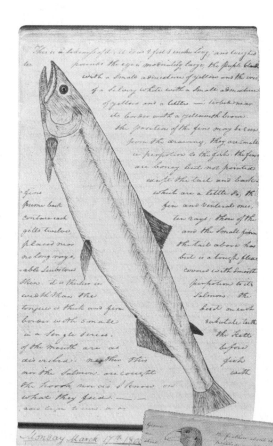

White salmon trout

Heath cock

While exploring the Louisiana Territory with Meriwether Lewis, William Clark recorded his observations in a journal. The pages of Clark's journal also include drawings of the animals found in the area.

Activity

Writing a Journal Entry Imagine you are a member of the Lewis and Clark expedition. Write a day's journal entry that details the route you take and what you see.

1804	1808	1812

1804
Barbary pirates
seize the U.S.
warship *Philadelphia*

1807
The British navy attacks
the American vessel
Chesapeake; Congress
passes the Embargo Act

1811
Harrison defeats
the Prophet at
Tippecanoe

1812
Madison asks
Congress to declare
war on Britain

Section 3

A Time of Conflict

READ TO DISCOVER . . .
- why Jefferson sent American ships to the Mediterranean Sea.
- why the Embargo Act of 1807 proved to be a disaster.
- why Tecumseh built a confederacy among tribes in Indiana, Ohio, and Michigan.
- why the War Hawks wanted to go to war with Britain.

TERMS TO LEARN
tribute
neutral rights
impressment

embargo
War Hawks
nationalism

The Storyteller

The floors of the oceans are littered with the remains of once mighty ships and the unmarked graves of unlucky sailors who sank with them in the 1700s. Seafarer Francis Rogers described the terror of a storm in this journal entry: "The sky seemed all on fire and [all around] were such swift darting rays of lightning, flying in long bright veins, with inexpressible fury as was very frightful."

Shipbuilder's tool bag and tools

In 1785 the American ship *Empress of China* returned to New York from China with a highly prized cargo of tea and silk. The goods sold for a fabulous profit. Soon ships from New York, Philadelphia, and especially New England were sailing regularly to China and India carrying furs and other goods. In the following years, American merchant ships sailed far and wide, making calls in South America, Africa, and lands along the Mediterranean Sea.

Americans in Foreign Seas

War between the French and British in the mid-1790s gave an additional boost to American shipping. Rather than risk capture or destruction by the enemy, many French and British merchant ships remained at home. American shippers profited from the situation and increased their trade. By 1800 the United States was second only to Great Britain in the number of merchant ships trading around the world.

Barbary Pirates

Sailing in foreign seas was not without danger. In the Mediterranean, for example, ships had to be on guard for pirates from Tripoli and the other **Barbary Coast states** of North Africa. For years these Barbary pirates had been terrorizing the Mediterranean. They demanded tribute, or protection money, from European governments to let their ships pass safely. The United States, too, had paid tribute—but not enough.

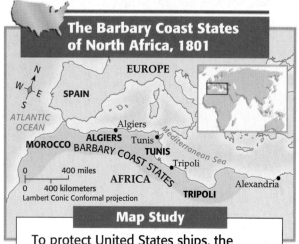

The Barbary Coast States of North Africa, 1801

Map Study

To protect United States ships, the American government paid a yearly bribe to the rulers of the Barbary States.

1. **Location** What bodies of water bordered the Barbary Coast states?
2. **Analyzing Information** About how many miles is it from the port of Algiers to the port of Tunis?

War With Tripoli

In 1801 the ruler of Tripoli asked for more money from the United States. When President Jefferson refused, the ruler chopped down the flagpole of the American consulate—a declaration of war. Jefferson sent ships to the Mediterranean and blockaded, or closed off, Tripoli. The American fleet, however, was not powerful enough to defeat the Barbary pirates, and the conflict continued.

In 1804 the pirates seized the U.S. warship *Philadelphia* and towed it into Tripoli Harbor. They threw the captain and crew into jail. Then **Stephen Decatur,** a 25-year-old United States Navy captain, took action. Slipping into the heavily guarded harbor with a small raiding party, Decatur burned the captured ship to prevent the pirates from using it. A British admiral praised the deed as the "most bold and daring act of the age."

Negotiations finally ended the conflict with Tripoli in June 1805. Tripoli agreed to stop demanding tribute, but the United States had to pay a ransom of $60,000 for the release of the American prisoners.

Freedom of the Seas

Riding the wave of four successful years as president, Jefferson won reelection easily in 1804. Jefferson received 162 electoral votes to only 14 for his Federalist opponent, Charles Pinckney. His second term began with the nation at peace. Across the sea, however, Great Britain and France were already involved in a war that threatened to interfere with American trade.

The thriving foreign trade of the United States depended on being able to sail the seas freely. The nation had resolved the threat from the Barbary pirates. Now it was challenged at sea by the two most powerful nations in Europe.

Neutral Rights Violated

When Britain and France went to war in 1803, America enjoyed a prosperous commerce with both countries. As long as the United States remained neutral, shippers could continue doing business. A nation not involved in a conflict had neutral rights—the right to sail the seas and not take sides.

For two years American shipping continued to prosper. By 1805, however, the warring nations had lost patience with American "neutrality." Britain blockaded the French coast and threatened to search all ships trading with France. France announced that it would search and seize ships caught trading with Britain.

American Sailors Kidnapped

The British needed sailors for their naval war. However, conditions in the British navy were terrible. Sailors were poorly paid, poorly fed, and badly treated. Many of them deserted. Desperately in need of sailors, the British often used force to get them. British naval patrols claimed the right to stop American ships at sea. They seized any sailors on board suspected of being deserters from the British navy and forced them into service.

This practice, known as impressment, was a clear violation of neutral rights. While some of those taken were deserters from the British navy, the British also impressed thousands of native-born and naturalized American citizens.

⭐ ⭐ ⭐ ⭐ ⭐ ⭐ ⭐ ⭐ ⭐ ⭐ ⭐ ⭐ ⭐ ⭐ ⭐ ⭐

Attack on the *Chesapeake*

Quite often the British would lie in wait for American ships outside an American harbor. This happened in June 1807 off the coast of **Virginia.** A British warship intercepted the American vessel *Chesapeake* and demanded to search the ship for British deserters. When the *Chesapeake*'s captain refused, the British opened fire, killing 3, wounding 18, and crippling the American ship.

As news of the attack spread, Americans reacted with an anti-British fury not seen since the Revolutionary War. Secretary of State **James Madison** called the attack an outrage. Many demanded war against Britain. Although President Jefferson did not intend to let Great Britain's actions go unanswered, he sought a course of action other than war.

President Bans Trade

⭐ Britain's practice of impressment and its violation of America's neutral rights had led Jefferson to ban some trade with Britain. The attack on the *Chesapeake,* however, triggered even stronger measures.

A Disastrous Trade Ban

In December 1807, the Republican Congress passed the **Embargo Act.** An embargo prohibits trade with another country. Although Great Britain was the target of this act, the embargo banned imports from and exports to *all* foreign countries. Jefferson wanted to prevent Americans from using other countries as go-betweens in the forbidden trade.

By using the embargo, Jefferson and Madison hoped to hurt Britain but avoid war. They believed the British depended on American agricultural products. As it turned out, the embargo of 1807 was a disaster. The measure wiped out all American commerce with other nations. Worse, it proved ineffective against Britain. The British simply traded with South America for its agricultural goods. Even worse, the embargo divided the American people.

⭐ **Picturing HISTORY** Americans resented the British method of recruiting for their navy by impressment. **How did the United States respond when the British ship *Leopard* attacked the American frigate *Chesapeake*?**

Opposition to the Trade Ban

Federalist New England, the heart of the American shipping industry, complained the loudest about the embargo. With ships stuck in their ports, unemployment began to rise, and protests flooded Washington. The feeling of frustration was summed up in a bitter poem:

Our ships all in motion,
Once whiten'd the ocean;
They sail'd and return'd with a Cargo;
Now doom'd to decay
They are fallen a prey,
To Jefferson, worms, and EMBARGO.

New England was not the only region hurt by the embargo. In the South tobacco meant for Europe rotted on the docks, and cotton went unpicked. In the West the price of wheat declined, and river traffic came to a halt. At first, however, these Republican regions continued to support Jefferson.

The embargo proved difficult to enforce also. Before long American shippers began smuggling

Building Warships

Plane

Hammer

Saw

What Was It Like? During the early 1800s, shipbuilding was a major economic activity and was important for national defense. **What were some of the tools used to build early ships?**

their goods—as they had done in the days of the Revolutionary War. Public opinion started to turn against the president and the Republicans. Having suffered a disastrous setback in the 1804 elections, the Federalists now gained support from the surge of feeling against the embargo.

Jefferson Leaves Office

Following Washington's precedent, Jefferson made it clear in mid-1808 that he would not be a candidate for a third term. With Jefferson's approval the Republicans chose James Madison as their candidate for president. The Federalists nominated Charles Pinckney and hoped that anger over the embargo would gain support for their party. Pinckney carried most of New England, but the Federalist ticket collected little support from the other regions. Madison won with 122 electoral votes to Pinckney's 47 votes.

The embargo clearly had not worked. On March 1, 1809, Congress repealed it. In its place Congress enacted the much weaker **Noninter-**course Act. The new act prohibited trade only with Britain and France and their colonial possessions. It was no more popular or successful than the Embargo Act.

War Fever

★ James Madison did not take office as president under the most favorable conditions. Called "Little Jemmy" by his enemies—he stood only 5 feet 4 inches tall—Madison had to follow in the imposing footsteps of Thomas Jefferson. At home and abroad, the nation was mired in the embargo crisis. Meanwhile Britain continued to claim the right to halt American ships, and cries for war with Britain grew louder and louder.

Closer to War

In 1810 the Nonintercourse Act expired and Congress replaced it with a complicated new law. This law permitted direct trade with either France or Britain, depending on which country first lifted its trade restrictions against America. Napoleon seized the opportunity and promised to end France's restrictions.

Unfortunately for Madison, Napoleon had tricked the American administration. The French continued to seize American ships, selling them and pocketing the proceeds. Americans were deeply divided. To some it seemed as if the nation was on the verge of war—but it was hard to decide if the enemy should be Britain or France. Madison knew that France had tricked him, but he continued to see Britain as the bigger threat.

Frontier Conflicts

While Madison was trying to decide how to resolve the difficulties with European powers, news arrived about problems in the West. **Ohio** had become a state in 1803. Between 1801 and 1810, white settlers continued to press for more land in the Ohio Valley. Native Americans had given up some 100 million acres. Now the settlers were moving onto lands that had been guaranteed to Native Americans by treaty.

Tecumseh and the Prophet

As tensions increased, some Native Americans began renewing their contacts with British agents and fur traders in Canada. Others pursued a new strategy. A powerful Shawnee chief named **Tecumseh** (tuh•KUHM•suh) built a confederacy among Native American nations in Indiana, Ohio, and Michigan. Tecumseh believed that a strong alliance—with the backing of the British in Canada—could put a halt to white movement onto Native American lands.

A commanding speaker, Tecumseh possessed great political skills. In his view the United States government treaties with individual nations were worthless. "The Great Spirit gave this great island to his red children," he said. No one nation had the right to give it away.

Tecumseh had a powerful ally—his brother, known as **the Prophet.** The Prophet urged Native Americans everywhere to return to the customs

of their ancestors. They should, he said, give up practices learned from the white invaders—wearing western dress, using plows and firearms and, especially, drinking alcohol. The Prophet attracted a huge following. He founded a village at a site in northern Indiana, near present-day Lafayette, where the Tippecanoe and Wabash Rivers meet. It was called Prophetstown.

A Meeting With Harrison

The American governor of the Indiana Territory, **General William Henry Harrison,** became alarmed by the growing power of the two Shawnee brothers. He feared they would form an alliance with the British.

In a letter to Tecumseh, Harrison warned that the United States had many more warriors than all the Indian nations could put together. "Do not think that the redcoats can protect you; they are not able to protect themselves." Tecumseh sent word that he would reply in person.

A few weeks later, Tecumseh arrived at the river across from Fort Knox, accompanied by 400 armed warriors in canoes. He spoke to the white people assembled there:

❝ Brothers: Since the peace was made, you have killed some of the Shawnees, Winnebagoes, Delawares, and Miamis, and you have taken our land from us; and I do not see how we can remain at peace if you continue to do so. You try to force the red people to do some injury; it is you who are pushing them on to do mischief. You try to keep the tribes apart, and make distinctions among them. You wish to prevent the Indians from uniting. ❞

The Battle of Tippecanoe

In 1811 while Tecumseh was in the South trying to expand his confederacy, Harrison decided to attack Prophetstown on the Tippecanoe River.

After a two-hour battle, the Prophet's forces fled the area in defeat. The **Battle of Tippecanoe** was proclaimed a glorious victory for the Americans. Harrison acquired the nickname "Tippecanoe" and used it as a patriotic rallying cry when he ran for president in 1840.

The American victory at the Battle of Tippecanoe, however, resulted in something the American people had hoped to prevent. Tecumseh now joined forces with the British troops. White settlers in the region claimed that the British had supplied Tecumseh's confederacy with guns. As a result, the rallying cry of the settlers became "On to Canada!"

War Hawks

★ Back in the nation's capital, President Madison faced demands for a more aggressive policy toward the British. The most insistent voices came from a group of young Republicans elected to Congress in 1810. Known as the War Hawks, they came from the South and the West. The War Hawks pressured the president to declare war with Britain.

While the War Hawks wanted to avenge British actions against Americans, they were also eager to expand the nation's power. Their nationalism appealed to a renewed sense of

TECHNOLOGY AND HISTORY

The Conestoga Wagon

By the mid-1700s, sturdy Conestoga wagons transported settlers and their freight over the Appalachian Mountains. These wagons were first built in the Conestoga Creek region of Lancaster, Pennsylvania. As people pushed even farther westward, the Conestoga was seen rolling across the plains toward Oregon and California. **Why did Conestoga wagons have a high front and back?**

A white canvas cloth stretches over hoops, or **wagon bows**. This cover protects passengers and cargo from heat, rain, and snow.

The boat-shaped wagon's high front and back keep goods from falling out on steep mountain trails.

A **toolbox** attached to the side of the wagon holds spare parts for needed repairs.

Six to eight draft horses or a dozen oxen pull the wagon. The driver rides or walks beside the animals.

The average Conestoga wagon was 21 feet long, 11 feet high, and 4 feet in width and depth. It could carry up to 12,000 pounds of cargo.

Broad **wheels** help keep the heavy wagon from being mired in the mud.

Picturing HISTORY The Battle of Tippecanoe began a series of conflicts between Native Americans and white settlers. **How did Harrison's victory at Tippecanoe affect Tecumseh (right) and his Native American forces?**

American patriotism. The leading War Hawks were **Henry Clay** from Kentucky and **John Calhoun** from South Carolina, both in their 30s.

Preparing for War

With the support of the other War Hawks, Clay was elected Speaker of the House of Representatives in 1811. This was an extraordinary step in view of his youth and lack of experience. The War Hawks urged major spending to strengthen the United States military. Through their efforts Congress quadrupled the army's size. During all these preparations, the Federalists in the Northeast remained strongly opposed to war.

Declaring War

By the spring of 1812, Madison concluded that war with Britain was inevitable. In a message to Congress on June 1, he cited "the spectacle of injuries and indignities which have been heaped on our country" and asked for a declaration of war.

In the meantime the British had decided to end their policy of search and seizure of American ships. Unfortunately, because of the amount of time it took for news to travel across the Atlantic, this change in policy was not known in Washington. Word of the breakthrough arrived too late. Once set in motion, the war machine could not be stopped.

Section 3 Assessment

Checking for Understanding
1. *Identify* James Madison, Embargo Act, Tecumseh, the Prophet, Henry Clay.
2. *Define* tribute, neutral rights, impressment, embargo, War Hawks, nationalism.
3. *Describe* the negotiations that ended the war with Tripoli.

Reviewing Themes
4. **Global Connections** How did conflict in Europe help American shipping prosper?

Critical Thinking
5. **Identifying Cause and Effect** How did battles on the frontier with Native Americans intensify Americans' anti-British feelings?

Activity

Drawing a Political Cartoon Choose a side in the argument about war with Great Britain. Draw a political cartoon supporting your point of view.

1812	1813	1814	1815

June 1812
United States declares war on Britain

September 1813
Perry defeats the British navy on Lake Erie

August 1814
The British burn Washington, D.C.

January 1815
American forces win the Battle of New Orleans

Section 4

The War of 1812

READ TO DISCOVER . . .

- how the American plan to invade Canada failed.
- how the British seized Washington, D.C.
- why Andrew Jackson fought a battle after the war was over.

TERMS TO LEARN

frigate   privateer

Storyteller

While President Madison awarded peace medals to Native Americans who supported the United States against the British, Congressional War Hawks could be heard singing:

Ye Parliaments of England,
Ye lords and commons, too,
Consider well what you're
    about,
And what you're
    goin' to do;
You're now at war
    with Yankees,
And I'm sure you'll rue
    the day
Ye roused the sons of
    liberty,
In North Americay.

Madison peace medal

The War Hawks predicted that the war with Great Britain would last no more than 30 days. Their plan was to invade Canada and keep the fighting on land; the Royal Navy was too powerful to challenge at sea.

In following this course of action, the Americans committed a series of blunders that showed how unprepared they were for war. The regular army now consisted of fewer than 7,000 troops. The states had nearly 700,000 militia, but the units were poorly trained, and many states opposed "Mr. Madison's war." The military commanders, veterans of the American Revolution, were too old for warfare, and the government in Washington provided no leadership. In addition the Americans underestimated the strength of the British and their Native American allies.

The Canadian Campaign

The war started in July 1812, when **General William Hull** led the American army from **Detroit** into Canada. Hull was met by Tecumseh and his warriors. Fearing a massacre by the Native Americans, Hull retreated and surrendered Detroit to a small British force.

The Americans made three more attempts at invasion. One ended in defeat. The second never got off the ground because some of the state militia troops refused to cross the border into Canada. A third attempt by General William Henry Harrison had no more success. Harrison decided that the Americans could make no headway in Canada as long as the British controlled Lake Erie.

Lake Erie

Oliver Hazard Perry, commander of the **Lake Erie** naval forces, had his orders. He was to assemble a fleet and seize the lake from the British. From his headquarters in Put-in-Bay, Ohio, Perry could watch the movements of the enemy ships. The showdown came on September 10, 1813, when the British ships sailed out to face the Americans. In the bloody battle that followed, Perry and his ships destroyed the British naval force. "We have met the enemy, and they are ours," Perry reported.

Thames and Toronto

With Lake Erie in American hands, the British and their Native American allies tried to pull back from the Detroit area. Harrison and his troops cut them off. In the fierce **Battle of the Thames** on October 5, the great leader Tecumseh was killed.

The Americans also attacked the town of York (present-day **Toronto,** Canada), burning the parliament buildings. Canada remained unconquered, but by the end of 1813 the Americans had won some victories on land and at sea.

Naval Battles

★ To lower the national debt, the Republicans had reduced the size of the navy. However, the navy still boasted three of the fastest frigates, or warships, afloat. Americans exulted when the *Constitution*, one of these frigates, destroyed two British vessels—the *Guerrière* in August 1812 and the *Java* four months later. After seeing a shot bounce off the *Constitution*'s hull during battle, a sailor nicknamed the ship "Old Ironsides."

American privateers, armed private ships, also staged spectacular attacks on British shipping and captured numerous vessels. These victories were more important for morale than for their strategic value.

The British hit back with a devastating blockade of the American coast from the Chesapeake Bay to New York Harbor. In a divide-and-conquer strategy, the British left the New England coast open. They were well aware of the war's unpopularity in Federalist New England. Madison fumed about Federalist disloyalty, but the New Englanders did not join the British. Finally in 1814 the British extended the blockade to New England as well.

Setbacks for Native Americans

★ With the death of Tecumseh at the Battle of the Thames in 1813, hopes for an Indian confederation died. In his travels two years before his death, Tecumseh had discussed plans for a confederation with the Creeks in the Mississippi Territory.

In March 1814, a lanky Tennessee planter named **Andrew Jackson** attacked the Creeks. Jackson's forces slaughtered more than 550 men, women, and children. Known as the **Battle of Horseshoe Bend,** the defeat broke the Creeks' resistance and forced them to give up most of their lands to the United States.

★ **HISTORY AND ART** *Perry's Victory on Lake Erie* **by William Birch**
During the War of 1812, Oliver Hazard Perry led 10 small ships on an attack against the British. **What was the result of the Battle of Lake Erie?**

The British Offensive

British military fortunes improved in the spring of 1814. They had been fighting a war with Napoleon and had finally won. Now they were free to concentrate their forces against the United States. The British soon discovered, however, that American forces had been toughened by their earlier defeats.

In August 1814, the British sailed into Chesapeake Bay. Their destination was Washington, D.C. **Dolley Madison** waited at the president's mansion on August 24 for word from her husband. "We have had a battle, or skirmish, near Bladensburg [Maryland], and I am still here within sound of the cannon!" she wrote her sister.

A messenger arrived with news that the British were fast approaching. The First Lady refused to leave. First, she insisted, she must see that the portrait of George Washington was removed from the wall and sent to safety.

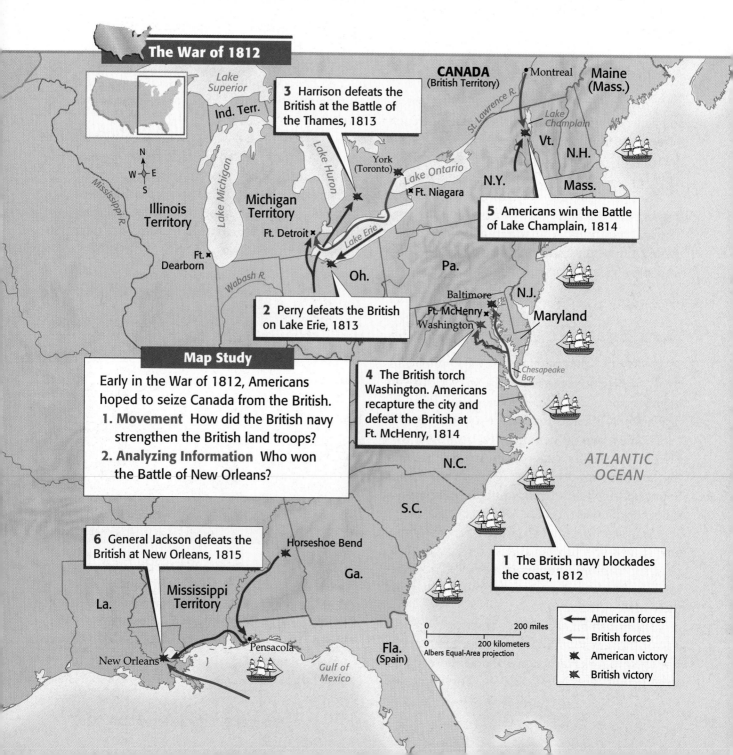

The War of 1812

3 Harrison defeats the British at the Battle of the Thames, 1813

5 Americans win the Battle of Lake Champlain, 1814

2 Perry defeats the British on Lake Erie, 1813

4 The British torch Washington. Americans recapture the city and defeat the British at Ft. McHenry, 1814

6 General Jackson defeats the British at New Orleans, 1815

1 The British navy blockades the coast, 1812

Map Study

Early in the War of 1812, Americans hoped to seize Canada from the British.

1. **Movement** How did the British navy strengthen the British land troops?
2. **Analyzing Information** Who won the Battle of New Orleans?

CANADA (British Territory)

Lake Superior · Ind. Terr. · Lake Michigan · Lake Huron · York (Toronto) · Lake Ontario · Ft. Niagara · Montreal · St. Lawrence R. · Lake Champlain · Maine (Mass.) · Vt. · N.H. · N.Y. · Mass. · Michigan Territory · Ft. Detroit · Lake Erie · Oh. · Pa. · Ft. Dearborn · Wabash R. · Illinois Territory · Mississippi R. · Baltimore · Ft. McHenry · Washington · N.J. · Maryland · Chesapeake Bay · N.C. · S.C. · ATLANTIC OCEAN · Horseshoe Bend · Ga. · Mississippi Territory · La. · New Orleans · Pensacola · Fla. (Spain) · Gulf of Mexico

0 — 200 miles
0 — 200 kilometers
Albers Equal-Area projection

→ American forces
→ British forces
✴ American victory
✴ British victory

Attack on Washington

Meanwhile on the outskirts of Washington, D.C., the British troops quickly overpowered the American militia and then marched into the city. "They proceeded, without a moment's delay, to burn and destroy everything in the most distant degree connected with government," reported a British officer.

The Capitol and the president's mansion were among the buildings burned. Watching from outside the city, President Madison and his cabinet saw the night sky turn orange. Fortunately a violent thunderstorm put out the fires before they could do more damage. August 24, 1814, was a low point for the American side.

Baltimore Holds Firm

Much to everyone's surprise, the British did not try to hold Washington. They left the city and sailed north to Baltimore. Baltimore, however, was ready and waiting—with barricaded roads, a blocked harbor, and some 13,000 militiamen. The British attacked in mid-September. They were kept from entering the town by a determined defense and ferocious bombardment from Fort McHenry in the harbor.

During the night of September 13–14, a young attorney named **Francis Scott Key** watched as the bombs burst over Fort McHenry. Finally "by the dawn's early light," Key was able to see that the American flag still flew over the fort. Deeply moved by patriotic feeling, Key wrote a poem called "The Star-Spangled Banner."

Defeat at Plattsburgh

Meanwhile in the north, **General Sir George Prevost** led more than 10,000 British troops into New York State from Canada. The British had every advantage—trained soldiers, superior firepower, cavalry, and professional leaders. Nevertheless in September 1814, the British suffered a humiliating defeat in the **Battle of Plattsburgh.** Demoralized by this unexpected loss, Prevost abandoned the campaign. The American victory secured the northern border of the United States.

★ **Picturing HISTORY** After sailing up Chesapeake Bay, British troops captured and burned Washington, D.C. **How did Dolley Madison, as First Lady, respond to the British attack?**

After Plattsburgh, British leaders in London came to the conclusion that the war in North America was too costly and unnecessary. They had achieved their goal in Europe with the removal of Napoleon. To continue a minor war in America with little to gain no longer seemed worth the effort.

The War Ends

★ American and British representatives signed a peace agreement in December 1814 in Ghent, Belgium. The **Treaty of Ghent** did not change any existing borders. Nothing was mentioned about the impressment of sailors, but with Napoleon's defeat, neutral rights had become a dead issue.

The Battle of New Orleans

Before word of the treaty had reached the United States, one final—and ferocious—battle occurred at New Orleans. In December 1814, a British army under **General Sir Edward Pakenham** moved toward New Orleans, located between Lake Ponchartrain and the Mississippi River. Awaiting them behind earthen fortifications was an American army led by Andrew Jackson.

America's FLAGS

The First Star-Spangled Banner, 1779–1818
The Stars and Stripes flag gained two more stars and two more stripes in 1795, after Kentucky and Vermont had joined the Union. This flag flew over Fort McHenry during the War of 1812 and inspired Francis Scott Key to write "The Star-Spangled Banner."

Congress realized that the flag would become too large if a stripe were added for every new state. It decided to keep the

stripes at 13—for the thirteen original colonies—and to add a star for each new state.

On January 8, 1815, Pakenham's troops advanced. The redcoats were no match for Jackson's soldiers, who shot from behind bales of cotton. In an hour of gruesome bloodshed, about 700 British soldiers, including Pakenham, were killed. At the **Battle of New Orleans,** Americans achieved a decisive victory in the War of 1812. Andrew Jackson became a hero, and his fame helped him win the presidency in 1828.

Federalist Disgrace

New England Federalists had opposed "Mr. Madison's war" from the start. In December 1814, disgruntled New England Federalists gathered in Connecticut at the **Hartford Convention.** A few favored secession. Most wanted to remain within the Union, however. To protect their interests, they drew up a list of proposed amendments to the Constitution.

After the convention broke up, word came of Jackson's spectacular victory at New Orleans, followed by news of the peace treaty. In this moment of triumph, the Federalist grievances seemed unpatriotic. The party lost respect.

American Triumph

Americans celebrated the end of the War of 1812 with candlelight parades, fireworks, and public prayers. The war brought a new spirit of nationalism throughout the country, even in New England. Americans felt pride in their new and more equal relationship with their former homeland.

Perhaps the biggest winners were the War Hawks, who took up the banner of the Republican party and carried it in new directions. These young Republicans favored trade, western expansion, the energetic development of the economy, and a strong army and navy.

Section 4 Assessment

Checking for Understanding
1. **Identify** Lake Erie, Toronto, Andrew Jackson, Dolley Madison, Treaty of Ghent, Battle of New Orleans.
2. **Define** frigate, privateer.
3. **State** the importance of the Battle of Plattsburgh.

Reviewing Themes
4. **Groups and Institutions** Why did Americans consider the War of 1812 a glorious victory?

Critical Thinking
5. **Determining Relevance** What impact did the Battle of New Orleans have on the outcome of the war?

Writing a Song Imagine that Francis Scott Key had been at the Battle of New Orleans instead of in Baltimore. Rewrite the first verse of "The Star-Spangled Banner" based on what occurred in that battle.

Writing a Journal

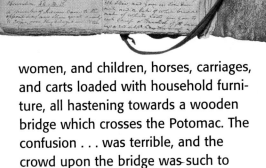

William Clark's journal

As you can see from William Clark's journal, journal writing is personal writing with a casual style. What you write *on* is not as important as what you write *about*—your experiences, interests, and even your feelings.

Learning the Skill

A journal is a written account that records what you have learned or experienced. In the journal you can express your feelings about a subject, summarize key topics, describe difficulties or successes in solving particular problems, and draw maps or other visuals. To help you get started writing in your journal, follow these steps:

- As you read your textbook, jot down notes or questions about a specific topic or event. Then look for details and answers about it as you continue reading.
- Describe your feelings as you read a selection or look at a photograph. Are you angry, happy, frustrated, sad? Explain why.
- Ask yourself if drawing a map or flow-chart would help you understand an event better. If so, draw in your journal.

women, and children, horses, carriages, and carts loaded with household furniture, all hastening towards a wooden bridge which crosses the Potomac. The confusion . . . was terrible, and the crowd upon the bridge was such to endanger its giving way. **99**

1. What is particularly interesting about this description?
2. What are your feelings as you read the excerpt?
3. Draw a map or other visual to help you understand the situation described here.

Practicing the Skill

The following excerpt describes the burning of Washington, D.C., during the War of 1812. Read the excerpt, then use the following questions to help you write entries in your own journal.

66 . . . [T]his was a night of dismay to the inhabitants of Washington. They were taken completely by surprise. . . . The first impulse of course tempted them to fly. . . . [T]he streets were . . . crowded with soldiers and senators, men,

Applying the Skill

Writing a Journal Imagine that you have had the chance to take part in an American adventure—for instance, accompanying Lewis and Clark, or fighting Barbary pirates. Make notes for a journal entry describing what you have done and seen.

Glencoe's **Skillbuilder Interactive Workbook, Level 1** provides instruction and practice in key social studies skills.

Assessment and Activities

★ Reviewing Key Terms

On a sheet of paper, define the following terms:
laissez-faire
judicial review
secede
tribute
impressment
neutral rights
embargo
War Hawks
nationalism
frigate
privateer

★ Reviewing Key Facts

1. What did Congress do to prevent an election deadlock between a presidential and vice-presidential candidate?
2. Why was Jefferson alarmed by the secret agreement that Spain made with France regarding the Louisiana Territory?
3. How did the Embargo Act of 1807 hurt the United States?
4. Who were the War Hawks?
5. Why was the Battle of Lake Erie fought?

★ Critical Thinking

Analyzing Information

The Republicans were in power for the first time with Jefferson's election to the presidency in 1801.

1. Why did Alexander Hamilton help his political foe, Thomas Jefferson, win the presidential election of 1800?
2. Why was *Marbury* v. *Madison* a victory for the Federalists over the Republicans?

★ Time Line Activity

Create a time line on which you place the following events in chronological order.

- Lewis and Clark begin their expedition
- Treaty of Ghent ends War of 1812
- United States purchases Louisiana
- Thomas Jefferson becomes president
- Tecumseh is killed
- James Madison is elected president

★ Geography Activity

Study the map below and answer the following questions.

1. **Region** During which of the three time periods was the largest amount of land taken along the Atlantic coast?
2. **Movement** During what years was land taken from the Iroquois?
3. **Location** Which Native American nations still held on to their land after 1810?

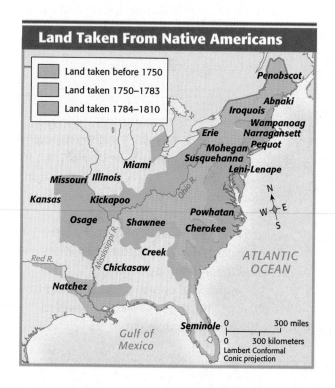

Land Taken From Native Americans

Land taken before 1750
Land taken 1750–1783
Land taken 1784–1810

Penobscot
Abnaki
Iroquois
Wampanoag
Erie   Narragansett
Mohegan Pequot
Susquehanna
Miami   Leni-Lenape
Missouri Illinois
Kansas   Kickapoo
Osage   Shawnee   Powhatan
Cherokee
Creek
Red R.   Chickasaw   ATLANTIC
OCEAN
Natchez

Seminole   0   300 miles
Gulf of   0   300 kilometers
Mexico   Lambert Conformal
Conic projection

★ Reviewing Themes

1. **Government and Democracy** What was the importance of the *Marbury* v. *Madison* decision?
2. **Geography and History** What were the boundaries of the Louisiana Territory?
3. **Global Connections** Why were American merchants eager to trade with countries in Asia?
4. **Groups and Institutions** How did the War Hawks and Federalists differ in their views of war?

★ Skill Practice Activity

Writing a Journal

By the late 1700s, more than 55,000 Americans had crossed the mountains into Kentucky and Tennessee. They endured terrible hardships in their trek to the "Promised Land." One person wrote the following excerpt about the journey. Read the excerpt, then in your journal answer the questions that follow.

> ❝Women and Children in the Month of [December], Travelling a Wilderness through Ice and Snow, passing large rivers and Creeks without Shoe or Stocking, and barely as many raggs as covers their Nakedness. . . . Here is Hundreds Travelling hundreds of Miles, they know not what for Nor Whither, except its to Kentucky . . . the Land of Milk and Honey. ❞

1. What questions do you have about the excerpt?
2. What are your feelings as you read the excerpt?
3. Why do you think settlers would endure such hardships to move to new land? Explain your reasoning.
4. Draw a visual to illustrate the situation described in the excerpt.

★ Cooperative Activity

History and Geography Work in small groups to prepare an international trade map. Your map should show United States imports during the early 1800s from each of the major continents. What major ports were merchants sailing to during this time? What products were they bringing back to the United States? Your map should include the names of important ports, the countries where they were located, symbols to represent the different products, a map key to explain the symbols, and other information such as distances or major shipping routes.

★ Technology Activity

Using a Spreadsheet Search the library for information about the modern city of New Orleans. Make a spreadsheet with the following headings: Spanish Street Names, French Street Names, Spanish Buildings, French Buildings, Spanish Foods, French Foods, and other sites that reflect Spanish and French influences in the area.

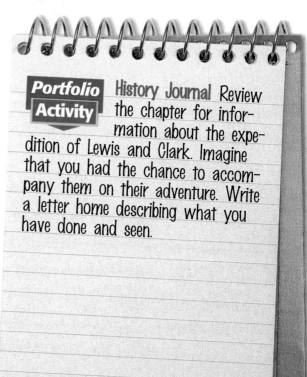

Portfolio Activity History Journal Review the chapter for information about the expedition of Lewis and Clark. Imagine that you had the chance to accompany them on their adventure. Write a letter home describing what you have done and seen.

1790–1825

Growth and Expansion

★ Why It's Important

Between 1790 and 1825, manufacturing took on an important role in the American economy. During the same period, people moved westward across the continent in larger and larger numbers. In 1823 the United States proclaimed its dominant role in the Americas with the Monroe Doctrine. These three developments were major factors in shaping the nation. Today the United States is one of the leading economic and military powers in the world.

★ Chapter Themes

■ *Section 1*, Economic Factors
■ *Section 2*, Science and Technology
■ *Section 3*, Individual Action
■ *Section 4*, Global Connections

PRIMARY SOURCES
Library   *See pages 954–955 for primary source readings to accompany Chapter 10*

★ **HISTORY AND ART**   *Globe Village* **by Francis Alexander** Changes in the countryside came during the Industrial Revolution of the early 1800s. In New England, factories were built along the falls and rapids of rivers.

1793
Eli Whitney invents the cotton gin

1807
Congress passes the Embargo Act

1814
Francis Lowell opens textile plant in Massachusetts

1816
Second National Bank is chartered

Section 1

Economic Growth

READ TO DISCOVER . . .

- how the Industrial Revolution began in the United States and what its effects were.
- how the United States changed as it became more economically independent.

TERMS TO LEARN

Industrial Revolution
capital
technology
cotton gin

patent
factory system
interchangeable parts

The Storyteller

Both men and women in the early 1800s valued hard work. An English journalist described the farmers of Long Island in 1818: "Every man can use an axe, a saw, and a hammer. Scarcely one who cannot do any job at rough carpentering, and mend a plough and wagon. . . . " Another European noted the daily activities of American women in 1823: "They take care of everything pertaining to the domestic economy, for example making candles, boiling soap, preparing starch, canning berries, fruit and cucumbers, baking, and spinning, sewing, and milking the cows."

Paddles used to prepare cotton for spinning

During the colonial era, workers were in short supply. Americans learned to develop tools that made work easier and more efficient. American methods and inventions won the admiration of Europeans. One observer exclaimed:

❝ The axe here [in America] . . . is a combination axe, wedge, and sledgehammer; what an accomplished woodchopper can do with this instrument! There are some among them who can chop and split five and one-half loads of wood a day, including stacking them. ❞

$ Economics

The Growth of Industry

★ People working in their homes or in workshops made cloth and most other goods. Using hand tools, they produced furniture, farm equipment, household items, and clothing.

In the mid-1700s, however, the way goods were made began to change. These changes appeared first in Great Britain. British inventors created machinery to perform some of the work involved in cloth making, such as spinning. The machines ran on waterpower, so British cloth makers built mills along rivers and installed the machines in these mills.

People left their homes and farms to work in the mills and earn wages. This meant a new way

The cotton gin's crank turned a cylinder that drew cotton fibers, but not cotton seeds, through small slots. **How did the cotton gin transform the production of cotton?**

Cotton gin

Eli Whitney

of working as well as a new way of producing goods. The changes this system brought about were so great that this time in history is known as the Industrial Revolution.

The Industrial Revolution in New England

The Industrial Revolution began to take root in the United States around 1800, appearing first in **New England.** The New England states—Massachusetts, Rhode Island, Connecticut, Vermont, and New Hampshire—offered ideal conditions for the development of factories. New England's soil was poor, and farming was difficult. As a result, people were willing to leave their farms to find work elsewhere. Also, New England had many rushing rivers and streams. These provided the waterpower necessary to run the machinery in the new factories.

New England's geographic location also proved to be an advantage. It was close to other resources, including coal and iron from nearby Pennsylvania. Equally important, New England had many ports. Through these ports passed the cotton shipped from Southern states to New England factories as well as the finished cloth bound for markets throughout the nation.

Most important of all, merchants in New England had capital—money for investment. The merchants of Boston and Providence had grown wealthy as American shipping thrived in the 1790s and early 1800s. Their capital was essential for developing needed machinery and building industries. 💲

New Technology

Workers, waterpower, location, and capital all played key roles in New England's Industrial Revolution. Yet without the invention of new machines and new technology—the application of scientific discoveries to practical use—the Industrial Revolution could not have taken place.

In Great Britain inventors devised new machinery and methods that revolutionized the textile industry, totally changing the way cloth was manufactured. Inventions such as the spinning jenny and the water frame—which spun thread—and the power loom—which wove the thread into cloth—made it possible to perform many steps in making cloth by machine, saving time and money.

Because these new machines ran on waterpower, most mills were built near rivers. In 1785, for the first time, a steam engine provided power for a cotton mill.

The United States also had its share of inventors. **Oliver Evans** of Delaware improved the steam engine and developed a mechanical flour mill. His flour mill needed only two workers: one to empty a bag of wheat into it and another to roll away the barrels of flour. In 1793 **Eli Whitney** of Massachusetts invented the cotton gin, a simple machine that quickly and efficiently removed the cotton seeds from the fiber. The cotton gin enabled one worker to clean cotton as fast as 50 people working by hand.

In 1790 Congress passed a patent law to protect the rights of those who developed "useful and important inventions." A patent gives an inventor the sole legal right to the invention and its profits for a certain period of time. One of the first patents went to Jacob Perkins for a machine to make nails.

New England Factories

★ The British tried to keep their new industrial technology a secret. They even passed laws prohibiting their machinery as well as their skilled mechanics from leaving the country. However, a few enterprising workers managed to slip away to the United States.

In Britain **Samuel Slater** had worked in a factory that used machines invented by Richard Arkwright for spinning cotton threads. Slater memorized the design of Arkwright's machines and slipped out of Britain in 1789.

Once in the United States, Slater took over the management of a cotton mill in Pawtucket, Rhode Island. There he duplicated all of Arkwright's machines. Using these machines the mill made cotton thread. Women working in their homes wove the thread into cloth.

The establishment of Slater's mill marked an important step in the Industrial Revolution in America. In 1790 Slater had 10 people working for him. By 1800 his Pawtucket factory employed more than 100 workers, mostly women and young children.

Lowell's Mills

In 1811 **Francis Cabot Lowell,** a wealthy New Englander, traveled to Great Britain, where he visited many textile mills. At night in his hotel room, he made detailed drawings of the factories and machines. After returning home, Lowell borrowed $400,000 to start the Boston Manufacturing Company. Lowell improved on the design of the British power looms and made plans to put his design to use.

In 1814 Francis Lowell's company opened a textile plant in Waltham, Massachusetts. The plan he implemented went several steps beyond Slater's mill. As one of Lowell's partners explained, the factory used "an entirely new arrangement, in order to save labor, in passing from one process to another." For the first time, all the stages of cloth making were performed under one roof. Lowell's mill launched the factory system, a system bringing manufacturing steps together in one place to increase efficiency. The factory system was a significant development in the way goods were made—and an important part of the Industrial Revolution.

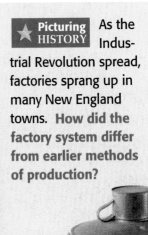

★ **Picturing HISTORY** As the Industrial Revolution spread, factories sprang up in many New England towns. **How did the factory system differ from earlier methods of production?**

Lunch pail

Lowell Girls

Lowell's mills drew about 80 percent of their workers from unmarried women between the ages of 15 and 30—and some were even younger. Known as the "Lowell girls," they left their farms and headed to the factories in towns for the opportunity to earn a wage and the adventure of working on their own.

The company built boardinghouses for the Lowell girls and tried to ensure their safety. These young women were carefully supervised and were expected to attend church regularly and to observe curfews. Most of them worked for a few years in the mill and either sent their pay home to their parents or saved their wages for the day when they would marry. After marrying, many left the mill to care for their families.

The young women who worked in Lowell's mills endured difficult working conditions. They put in long hours—from sunrise to sunset—for low wages. The volume of the factory machinery was earsplitting, and the work was monotonous and required little skill. The women usually performed one task over and over again. Sometimes the only skill necessary was the ability to tie a knot in thread that had broken.

Lucy Larcom started working in the mills when she was 11 years old. She later recalled her life at Waltham:

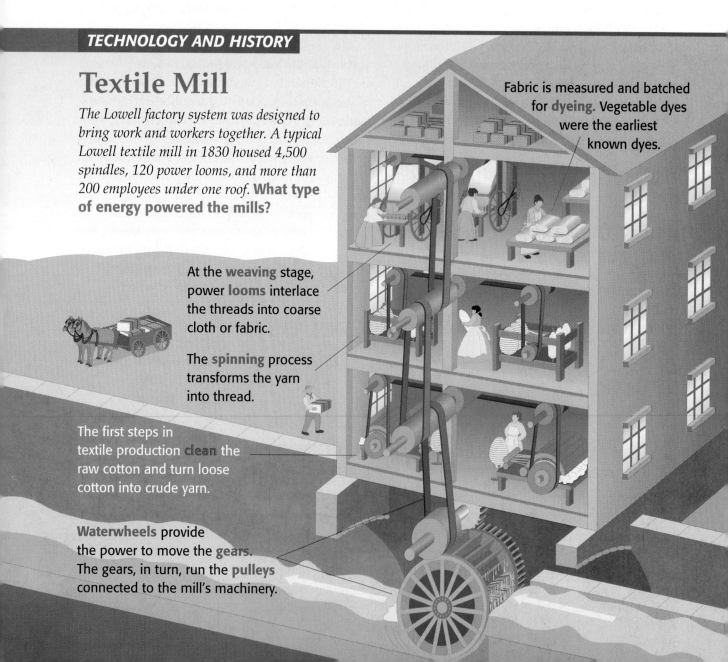

TECHNOLOGY AND HISTORY

Textile Mill

The Lowell factory system was designed to bring work and workers together. A typical Lowell textile mill in 1830 housed 4,500 spindles, 120 power looms, and more than 200 employees under one roof. **What type of energy powered the mills?**

Fabric is measured and batched for dyeing. Vegetable dyes were the earliest known dyes.

At the weaving stage, power looms interlace the threads into coarse cloth or fabric.

The spinning process transforms the yarn into thread.

The first steps in textile production clean the raw cotton and turn loose cotton into crude yarn.

Waterwheels provide the power to move the gears. The gears, in turn, run the pulleys connected to the mill's machinery.

> We did not call ourselves ladies. We did not forget that we were working girls, wearing aprons suitable to our work, and that there was some danger of our becoming drudges. **"**

When the noisy machinery got to her, Lucy would

> . . . lean far out of the window, and try not to hear the unceasing clash of sound inside. **"**

To many visitors, the mills seemed a promising opportunity for the women who worked there. For the women themselves, however, the daily drudgery of the mills was not so wonderful. Many eventually abandoned their work there and sought jobs as teachers or maids. By the 1830s and 1840s, factory workers—often immigrants—labored under even harsher conditions at textile mills and other factories.

Interchangeable Parts

Revolutionary changes occurred in other industries beyond cloth making. In 1798 Eli Whitney received a contract from the United States government to make 10,000 rifles in 28 months. To produce this enormous quantity in such a short time, Whitney devised a manufacturing method that would produce interchangeable parts. The idea was to make large quantities of uniform pieces that could replace any other identical pieces.

Whitney made a mold for each part of the rifle, and the pieces that came out of the molds were supposed to be identical and interchangeable. The pieces were fairly crude, however, and had to be finished by hand.

For Whitney, the new system had its flaws. It took 10 years to complete the government's order. Later, the development of more precise machines that could turn out uniform pieces made interchangeable parts a reality. Interchangeable parts opened the way for producing many different kinds of goods on a mass scale and for reducing the price of the goods.

Agriculture Expands

Although many New Englanders went to work in factories, most Americans still lived and worked on farms. In the 1820s more than 65 percent of Americans were farmers.

In the Northeast, farms tended to be small, and the produce was usually marketed locally. In the South, cotton production increased dramatically. The demand for cotton had grown steadily with the development of the textile industries of New England and Europe. Southern plantation owners used enslaved workers to plant, tend, and pick the cotton. The cotton gin—which made it possible to clean the cotton much faster and more cheaply than by hand—encouraged the planters to raise larger crops. Between 1790 and 1820, cotton production soared from 3,000 to more than 300,000 bales a year.

In the West, agriculture also expanded. Southern farmers seeking new land moved west to plant cotton. Western farmers north of the Ohio River concentrated on raising pork and cash crops such as corn and wheat.

Economic Independence

★ As more cotton and wool factories went into operation, Americans came to rely less on British-made cloth. The Industrial Revolution helped make the United States more independent economically. In the early 1800s, foreign relations also affected the American economy.

Embargo, War, and Tariffs

In 1807 Congress passed the Embargo Act, which cut off all foreign trade for two years. In 1812 the United States went to war with Great Britain. During the war the British blockaded American ports.

The embargo and the blockades sharply reduced America's overseas trade. At the same time, these factors contributed to the nation's quickly growing economic independence. With

Fire bucket

★ **Picturing HISTORY** As industry grew, Philadelphia, shown here in the early 1800s, increased its population from about 91,000 in 1810 to about 161,000 in 1830. **What problems did Northeast cities face as a result of the growth of industry?**

foreign goods difficult to acquire, new American industries emerged to meet local needs. Some New England merchants put the money they made before the embargo into building new factories and machinery to increase production.

As soon as the War of 1812 ended, British goods began to pour into the United States. British manufacturers often sold these goods at very low prices to take business away from American manufacturers. To protect the new American industries from British competition, Congress passed the **Tariff of 1816.** The new law placed a tax on imported goods, making the ironware, paper, and woolen and cotton goods from Britain more expensive than products made in the United States.

The Second National Bank

Most new industries were financed by small investors—merchants, shopkeepers, and farmers. These people invested some of their money in the hope of earning profits if the new businesses succeeded.

Businesses that needed a larger amount of capital had to obtain it from banks. The charter of the First Bank of the United States had expired in 1811. The Bank had faced fierce opposition from Republicans when it was established 20 years earlier, and some people still believed Congress had no authority to create such a bank. However, Republican president Madison came to accept the Federalist view of national economic development and supported a new bank.

In 1816 Congress chartered the **Second Bank of the United States.** The Bank had the power to establish a national currency and to make large loans to businesses. It, too, helped strengthen the economic independence of the nation.

Cities Come of Age

★ The growth of factories and trade spurred the growth of towns and cities, especially in the Northeast. Along with this development, however, came new problems: overcrowding, unsanitary conditions, disease, and the threat of fire.

Urban Growth

The new industrial towns grew quickest. Many developed along rivers and streams because of waterpower. Older cities like New York, Boston, and Baltimore also grew as centers of commerce and trade. In the West, towns like Pittsburgh, Cincinnati, and Louisville profited from their locations on major rivers. As farmers in the West shipped more and more of their products by water, these towns grew rapidly.

City Life

Cities and towns looked quite different from modern urban areas. Buildings were made of wood or brick. Streets and sidewalks were unpaved, and barnyard animals often roamed freely. No sewers carried waste and dirty water away, and as a result, the threat of such diseases as cholera and yellow fever always loomed over city dwellers. In 1793, for example, a yellow fever epidemic in Philadelphia killed thousands of people.

Fire posed another threat to cities. Sparks from a fireplace or chimney could easily ignite a wooden building and spread to others. Few towns or cities had organized fire companies, and fires could be disastrous.

Cities and towns of the period also had advantages, however. Some people left farming

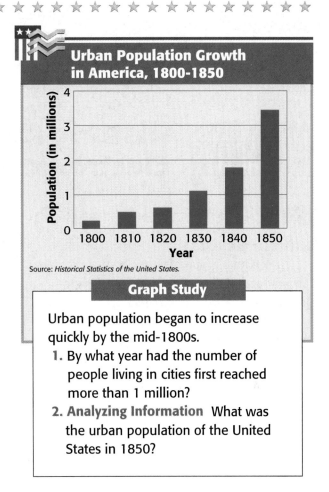

Urban Population Growth in America, 1800-1850

Source: *Historical Statistics of the United States.*

Graph Study

Urban population began to increase quickly by the mid-1800s.
1. By what year had the number of people living in cities first reached more than 1 million?
2. **Analyzing Information** What was the urban population of the United States in 1850?

because cities and towns offered a variety of jobs and steady wages. As cities grew they added libraries, museums, and shops that were unavailable in the countryside. For many, the jobs and attractions of city life outweighed any dangers.

Section 1 Assessment

Checking for Understanding
1. *Identify* Eli Whitney, Samuel Slater.
2. *Define* Industrial Revolution, capital, technology, cotton gin, patent, factory system, interchangeable parts.
3. *List* three reasons New England was ideal for the development of factories.

Reviewing Themes
4. **Economic Factors** How did the cotton gin affect production?

Critical Thinking
5. **Determining Cause and Effect** Was new technology necessary for the Industrial Revolution to take place? Explain your point of view.

Activity

Making a State Map Make an outline map of your state showing the three largest cities and the geographic features you think might have contributed to their growth.

Multimedia Activities

ABCNEWS INTERACTIVE™ Historic America Electronic Field Trips

Field Trip to the Lowell Factories

Setting up the Video

Work with a group of your classmates to view "Lowell Factories" on the videodisc *Historic America: Electronic Field Trips*.

The Lowell textile mill was one of the first mechanized factories in the country. The program reveals a letter written by a young woman named Mary who experienced the hardships of factory work firsthand.

Hands-On Activity

Call your local chamber of commerce for a list of manufacturing companies in your area. Find out how many employees each company employs. Create a circle graph to show the percentage of people from your community that depend on factories for their livelihood.

Side 2,
Chapter 4

View the video by scanning the bar code or by entering the chapter number on your keypad and pressing Search.

Surfing the "Net"

E-Mail Your Government Officials

The legislative branch of the U.S. government consists of the House of Representatives and the Senate. With the Internet, constituents can communicate with their representatives quickly. To find out how you can E-mail your representatives, follow the instructions below.

2. After typing in *Congress,* enter words like the following to focus your search: *E-mail address, state's name, representative's name.*
3. The search engine will provide you with a number of links to follow.

Getting There

Find out who your representatives are in Congress. Think of any issues, concerns, or questions you might like to discuss with one of your elected representatives.

1. Use a search engine. Type in the word *Congress.*

What to Do When You Are There

Click on the links to navigate through the pages to find your representative's E-mail address. Using your E-mail service, compose and send a letter to your representative that expresses your interests or concerns. When you receive your response, share your news with your class.

1806
Congress approves funds for a national road

1807
Robert Fulton's *Clermont* steams to Albany

1820
The U.S. population stands at 10 million

1825
The Erie Canal is completed

Section 2

Westward Bound

READ TO DISCOVER . . .

- how land and water transportation improved in the early 1800s.
- how settlements in the West affected economic and political developments in the nation.

TERMS TO LEARN

census   canal
turnpike   lock

The Storyteller

During the early 1800s, settlers poured into the frontier west of the Appalachians. The typical frontier family moved from place to place as the frontier pushed ever westward. Their home often consisted of a three-sided shack or a log cabin with a dirt floor and no windows or door. A pile of leaves in the loft of the cabin often served as a bed. Loneliness, poverty, and an almost primitive lifestyle were daily companions to many frontier people.

Mug honoring the first census

The first census—the official count of the population—of the United States in 1790 revealed a population of nearly 4 million. Most of the Americans counted lived east of the Appalachian Mountains and within a few hundred miles of the Atlantic coast.

Within a few decades this changed. The number of settlers heading west increased by leaps and bounds. In 1811 a Pennsylvania resident reported seeing 236 wagons filled with people and their possessions on the road to Pittsburgh. A man in Newburgh, New York, counted 60 wagons rolling by in a single day. In 1820, just 30 years after the first census, the population of the United States had more than doubled to about 10 million people, with nearly 2 million living west of the Appalachians.

Geography

Moving West

Traveling west was not easy in the late 1790s and early 1800s. The 370-mile trip from **New York City** to **Buffalo** could take as long as three weeks. A pioneer family heading west with a wagonload of household goods faced hardship and danger along the way.

Roads and Turnpikes

The nation needed good inland roads for travel and for the shipment of goods to and from seaports. Private companies built many roads as

Chapter 10 Growth and Expansion **313**

turnpikes, or toll roads. The fees travelers paid to use those roads helped offset construction costs. Many of the roads had a base of crushed stone. In areas where the land was often muddy, companies built "corduroy roads," consisting of logs laid side by side like the ridges of corduroy cloth.

Many pioneers from New York and Philadelphia began their trip west on the Lancaster Turnpike, built in the 1790s from Philadelphia to Lancaster, Pennsylvania. From there they could continue west on rough dirt roads to Pittsburgh and then switch to a barge and sail down the **Ohio River** toward Ohio and Kentucky.

When Ohio joined the Union in 1803, the new state asked the federal government to build a road to connect it with the East. In 1806 Congress approved funds for a **National Road** to the West and agreed on the route five years later. Because work on the road stopped during the War of 1812, the first section, from Maryland to western Virginia, did not open until 1818. In later years the National Road reached Ohio and continued on to Vandalia, Illinois. Congress viewed the National Road as a military necessity, but it did not undertake other road-building projects.

River Travel

River travel had definite advantages over wagon and horse travel. It was far more comfortable than travel over the bumpy roads, and pioneers could load all their goods on river barges—if they were heading downstream in the direction of the current.

River travel had two problems, however. The first related to the geography of the eastern United States. Most major rivers in the region flowed in a north-south direction, not east to west, where most people and goods were headed. Second, traveling upstream by barge against the current was extremely difficult and slow.

Steamboats

Steam engines were already being used in the 1780s and 1790s to power boats in quiet waters. Inventor James Rumsey equipped a small boat on the Potomac River with a steam engine, and David

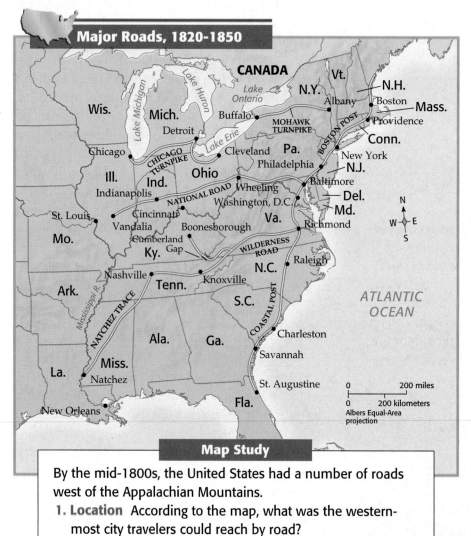

Major Roads, 1820–1850

Map Study

By the mid-1800s, the United States had a number of roads west of the Appalachian Mountains.

1. **Location** According to the map, what was the western-most city travelers could reach by road?

2. **Analyzing Information** Through what states did the National Road run?

Cotton and wool dress

Children's shoes

Man's overcoat

What Was It Like? The lavish clothing and elegant carriages of wealthy Americans in the early 1800s may not seem comfortable by modern standards. **What problems did travelers face during this period?**

Fitch, another inventor, built a steamboat that navigated the Delaware River. Neither of these boats, however, had enough power to withstand the strong currents and shifting winds found in large rivers or open bodies of water.

In 1802 Robert Livingston, a political and business leader, hired **Robert Fulton** to develop a steamboat with a powerful engine. Livingston wanted the steamboat to carry cargo and passengers up the **Hudson River** from New York City to **Albany.**

In 1807 Fulton had his steamboat, the *Clermont*, ready for a trial. Powered by a newly designed engine, the *Clermont* made the 150-mile trip from New York to Albany in the unheard-of time of 32 hours. Using only sails, the trip would have taken four days.

About 140 feet long and 14 feet wide, the *Clermont* offered great comforts to its passengers. They could sit or stroll about on deck, and at night they could relax in the sleeping compartments below deck. The engine was noisy, but its power provided a fairly smooth ride.

Steamboats ushered in a new age in river travel. They dramatically improved the transport of goods and passengers along major inland rivers. Shipping goods became cheaper and faster. Steamboats also contributed to the growth of river cities like Cincinnati and St. Louis.

Canals

Although steamboats represented a great improvement in transportation, their routes depended on the existing river system. Steamboats could not effectively tie the eastern and western parts of the country together.

In New York business and government officials led by **De Witt Clinton** came up with a plan to link New York City with the Great Lakes region. They would build a canal—an artificial waterway—across New York State, connecting Albany on the Hudson River with Buffalo on **Lake Erie.** Clinton declared the canal would "create the greatest inland trade ever witnessed."

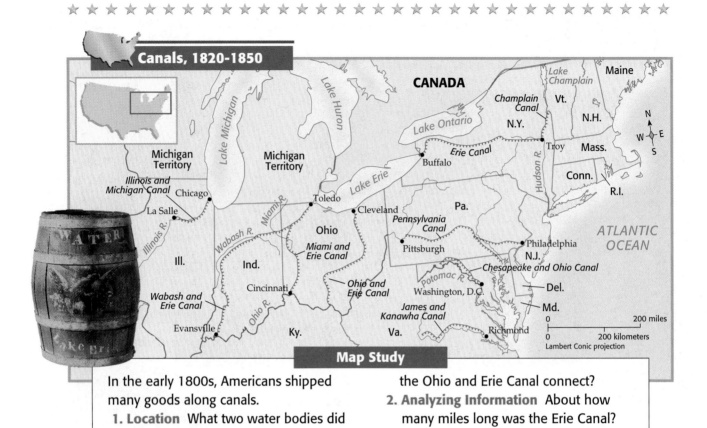

Canals, 1820–1850

CANADA

Lake Champlain
Maine
Champlain Canal
Vt.
N.H.
N.Y.
Lake Ontario
Troy
Mass.
Erie Canal
Buffalo
Conn.
R.I.
Hudson R.
ATLANTIC OCEAN

Michigan Territory
Michigan Territory
Lake Michigan
Lake Huron

Illinois and Michigan Canal
Chicago
La Salle
Illinois R.
Toledo
Lake Erie
Cleveland
Pa.
Pennsylvania Canal
Philadelphia
N.J.
Miami R.
Wabash R.
Ohio
Miami and Erie Canal
Pittsburgh
Chesapeake and Ohio Canal
Del.

Ill.
Ind.
Cincinnati
Ohio and Erie Canal
Potomac R.
Washington, D.C.
Md.

Wabash and Erie Canal
Ohio R.
James and Kanawha Canal
200 miles
200 kilometers

Evansville
Ky.
Va.
Richmond
Lambert Conic projection

Map Study

In the early 1800s, Americans shipped many goods along canals.

1. **Location** What two water bodies did the Ohio and Erie Canal connect?

2. **Analyzing Information** About how many miles long was the Erie Canal?

Building the Erie Canal

Thousands of laborers, many of them Irish immigrants, worked on the construction of the 363-mile **Erie Canal.** Along the canal they built a series of locks—separate compartments where water levels were raised or lowered. Locks provided a way to raise and lower boats where canal levels changed significantly. Many people made fun of the canal, calling it Clinton's Ditch.

In 1825 Clinton boarded a barge in Buffalo and journeyed on the canal to New York City. Officials poured water from Lake Erie into the Atlantic Ocean. The East and Midwest were joined.

In its early years, the canal did not allow steamboats because their powerful engines could damage the earthen embankments along the canal. Instead teams of mules or horses hauled the boats and barges. A 2-horse team pulled a 100-ton barge about 24 miles in one day—astonishingly fast compared to travel by wagon. In the 1840s the canal banks were reinforced to accommodate steam tugboats pulling barges.

The success of the Erie Canal led to an explosion in canal building. By 1840 the United States had more than 3,300 miles of canals, 20 times more than it had in 1817. Canals lowered the cost of shipping goods. They brought prosperity to the towns along their routes. Perhaps most important, they helped unite the growing country.

Western Settlement

Americans moved westward in waves. The first wave began before the 1790s and led to the admission of four new states between 1791 and 1803—Vermont, Kentucky, Tennessee, and Ohio. During the next 13 years, only one new state, Louisiana, entered the Union. The westward movement slowed during the War of 1812. After the war, however, a second wave of westward growth began. Between 1816 and 1821, five new western states were created—Indiana, Illinois, Mississippi, Alabama, and Missouri.

The new states reflected the dramatic population growth of the region west of the Appalachians. Ohio, for example, had only 45,000 Americans in 1800. By 1820 the population had soared to 581,000.

Building Communities

Pioneers usually migrated as families rather than as individuals. They tended to settle in communities along the great rivers, such as the Ohio and the Mississippi, so that they could ship their crops to market. The expansion of canals, which crisscrossed the land in the 1820s and 1830s, allowed people to live farther away from the rivers.

People also tended to settle with others from their home communities. Indiana, for example, was settled mainly by Southerners moving north from Kentucky and Tennessee, while Michigan's pioneers came mostly from New England.

Life in the West

Western families often gathered together for social events. Men took part in sports such as wrestling and pole jumping, a sport similar to present-day pole vaulting. Women met for quilting and sewing parties. Both men and women participated in cornhuskings—gatherings where farm families shared the work of stripping the husks from ears of corn.

Life in the West did not include the conveniences of Eastern town life. The pioneers, however, had not come west to be pampered. They wanted to make a new life for themselves and their families. America's population continued to travel westward in the years ahead.

Linking PAST & PRESENT

"Modern" Medicine

In the mid-1800s, a visit to the doctor's office was viewed with suspicion. Faced with "cures" that were often fatal, people started using patent medicines—those they could buy in stores. One popular remedy, Snake Oil, was a mixture of wintergreen and white gasoline.

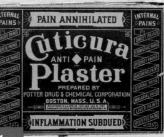

Past

Patent medicine

Today artificial hearts, cameras that move through veins, and other products have greatly improved Americans' health. **Why did settlers turn to patent medicines to cure their ills?**

Present

Genetic engineer

Section 2 Assessment

Checking for Understanding

1. *Identify* National Road, Robert Fulton, *Clermont*, De Witt Clinton, Erie Canal.
2. *Define* census, turnpike, canal, lock.
3. *Describe* the improvements in transportation in the early 1800s.

Reviewing Themes

4. **Science and Technology** How did steam-powered boats improve river travel?

Critical Thinking

5. **Drawing Conclusions** How did better transportation affect westward expansion?

Activity

Making a Chart Create a chart that lists the major means of transportation that helped the United States grow. Include the advantages and disadvantages of each type of transportation.

1816
James Monroe
is elected
president

1819
McCulloch v. *Maryland*
strengthens national
government

1820
Missouri
Compromise
passed

1824
Henry Clay
promotes the
American System

Section 3

Unity and Sectionalism

READ TO DISCOVER . . .

■ why the period of James Monroe's
presidency was called the Era of Good
Feelings.

■ why sectional differences intensified in the
1820s.

■ what roles Daniel Webster, John Calhoun,
and Henry Clay played in 1820s politics.

TERMS TO LEARN

sectionalism   American System
internal improvements

The Storyteller

Following the War of 1812, Americans felt
buoyed by a new sense of pride and faith in
the United States. In his Inaugural Address on
March 4, 1817, President James
Monroe expressed this feeling
of proud nationalism: "If we
look to the history of
other nations, ancient
or modern, we find
no example of a
growth so rapid,
so gigantic, of a
people so prosper-
ous and happy."

James Monroe pocket watch

The absence of major political divisions after
the War of 1812 helped forge a sense of national unity. In the 1816 presidential election, Republican candidate **James Monroe** faced
almost no opposition. The Federalists, weakened
by doubts of their loyalty during the War of 1812,
barely existed as a national party. Monroe won
the election by an overwhelming margin.

The Era of Good Feelings

★ Although the Federalist Party had almost
disappeared, many of its programs gained
support. Republican president James Madison,
Monroe's predecessor, had called for tariffs to
protect new industries, for a national bank, and
for some national development programs.

Political differences seemed to fade away,
causing a Boston newspaper to call these years
the **Era of Good Feelings.** The president himself
symbolized these good feelings.

Eyewitness to HISTORY

Monroe Tours the Nation

Monroe had been involved in national politics since the American Revolution. He wore
breeches and powdered wigs—dress no longer in
fashion. With his sense of dignity, Monroe represented a united America free of political strife.

Early in his presidency, Monroe toured the
nation. No president since George Washington

had done this. He paid his own expenses and tried to travel without an official escort. Everywhere Monroe went, local officials greeted him and celebrated his visit.

Monroe arrived in Boston, the former Federalist stronghold, in the summer of 1817. About 40,000 well-wishers cheered him, and John Adams, the second president, invited Monroe to his home. Abigail Adams commended the new president's "unassuming manner."

Monroe did not think the demonstrations were meant for him personally. He wrote Madison that they revealed a "desire in the body of the people to show their attachment to the union."

Two years later Monroe continued his tour, traveling as far south as Savannah and as far west as Detroit. In 1820 President Monroe won reelection, winning all but one electoral vote. 🔍

Sectionalism Grows

★ The Era of Good Feelings did not last very long. Regional differences came to the surface, ending the period of national harmony.

Most Americans felt a strong allegiance to the region where they lived. They thought of themselves as Westerners or Southerners or Northerners. This sectionalism, or loyalty to their region, became more intense as differences arose over national policies.

The conflict over slavery, for example, always simmered beneath the surface. Most white Southerners believed in the necessity and value of slavery. Northerners increasingly opposed it. To protect slavery, Southerners stressed the importance of states' rights, defending the powers of the states over the power of the federal government.

Footnotes to History

The White House Because the British had burned the president's mansion during the War of 1812, the sooty exterior had been painted white. People began calling the building "the White House," although that name did not become official until 1901.

America's FLAGS

Flag of 1818 By 1818 the number of states had reached 20. In April President Monroe signed a bill that set the basic design of the flag. Each newly admitted state added a star to the field of blue. The addition of a new star took place on the Fourth of July following the state's year of entry.

The Great Star Flag Congress did not state how the stars should be arranged, so flagmakers used various designs. The Great Star Flag placed the stars in the form of a five-pointed star.

The different regions also disagreed on the need for tariffs, a national bank, and internal improvements. Internal improvements were federal, state, and privately funded projects, such as canals and roads, to develop the nation's transportation system. Three powerful voices emerged in Congress in the early 1800s as spokespersons for their regions: John C. Calhoun, Daniel Webster, and Henry Clay.

John C. Calhoun

John C. Calhoun, a planter from South Carolina, was one of the War Hawks who had called for war with Great Britain in 1812. Calhoun remained a nationalist for some time after the war. He favored support for internal improvements and developing industries and backed a national bank. At the time, he believed these programs would benefit the South.

In the 1820s, however, Calhoun's views started to change, and he emerged as one of the

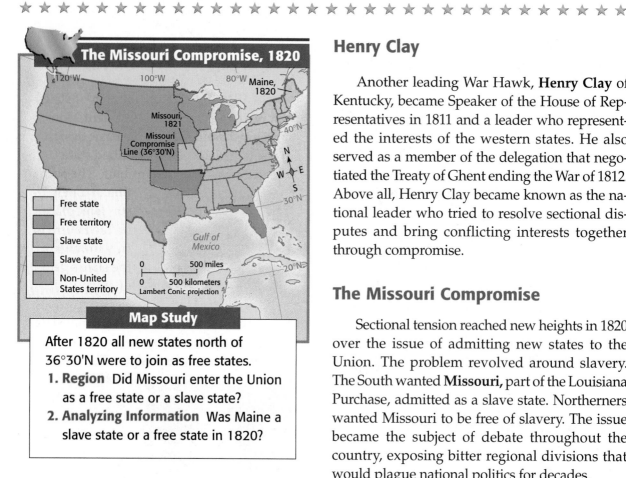

The Missouri Compromise, 1820

Maine, 1820

Missouri, 1821

Missouri Compromise Line (36°30'N)

- Free state
- Free territory
- Slave state
- Slave territory
- Non-United States territory

Gulf of Mexico

0 500 miles
0 500 kilometers
Lambert Conic projection

Map Study

After 1820 all new states north of 36°30'N were to join as free states.

1. **Region** Did Missouri enter the Union as a free state or a slave state?
2. **Analyzing Information** Was Maine a slave state or a free state in 1820?

foremost advocates of states' rights. Calhoun became a strong opponent of nationalist programs such as high tariffs. He believed them to be against the agricultural and slavery interests of Southerners.

Daniel Webster

First elected to Congress in 1812 to represent his native New Hampshire, **Daniel Webster** later served in both the House and Senate representing Massachusetts. Webster began his political career as a supporter of free trade and the shipping interests of New England. In time, however, Webster came to favor the **Tariff of 1816**—which protected American industries from foreign competition—and other policies that he thought would strengthen the nation and help the North.

Webster gained fame as one of the greatest orators of his time. As a United States senator, he spoke eloquently in defense of the nation as a whole against sectional interests. In one memorable speech Webster declared: "Liberty and Union, now and forever, one and inseparable."

Henry Clay

Another leading War Hawk, **Henry Clay** of Kentucky, became Speaker of the House of Representatives in 1811 and a leader who represented the interests of the western states. He also served as a member of the delegation that negotiated the Treaty of Ghent ending the War of 1812. Above all, Henry Clay became known as the national leader who tried to resolve sectional disputes and bring conflicting interests together through compromise.

The Missouri Compromise

Sectional tension reached new heights in 1820 over the issue of admitting new states to the Union. The problem revolved around slavery. The South wanted **Missouri,** part of the Louisiana Purchase, admitted as a slave state. Northerners wanted Missouri to be free of slavery. The issue became the subject of debate throughout the country, exposing bitter regional divisions that would plague national politics for decades.

While Congress considered the Missouri question, Maine—still part of Massachusetts—also applied for statehood. The discussions about Missouri now broadened to include Maine.

Some observers feared for the future of the Union. Eventually Henry Clay helped work out a compromise that preserved the balance between North and South. The **Missouri Compromise,** reached in March 1820, provided for the admission of Missouri as a slave state and Maine as a free state. The agreement banned slavery in the remainder of the Louisiana Territory north of the 36°30' parallel.

The American System

Though he was a spokesperson for the West, Henry Clay believed his policies would benefit *all* sections of the nation. In an 1824 speech, he called his program the American System. The American System included a protective tariff to stimulate the growth of the nation's industries; a program of internal improvements, especially the building of roads and canals, to stimulate trade; and a national bank to promote one currency throughout the nation and to lend money to build developing industries.

Clay believed that the three parts of his plan would work together. The tariff would protect American industries but would also provide the government with money to build roads and canals. Healthy businesses could use their profits to buy more agricultural goods from the South, then ship these goods northward along the nation's efficient new transportation system.

Not everyone, however, saw Clay's program in such positive terms. Former president Jefferson believed the American System favored the wealthy manufacturing classes in New England. Many people in the South agreed with Jefferson. They saw no benefits to the South from the tariff or internal improvements.

Henry Clay

In the end little of Clay's American System went into effect. Congress eventually adopted some internal improvements, though not on the scale Clay had hoped for. Congress had created the Second National Bank in 1816, but it remained an object of controversy.

The Supreme Court

The Supreme Court also became involved in sectional and states' rights issues at this time. The state of Maryland imposed a tax on the Baltimore branch of the Second Bank of the United States—a federal institution. The Bank refused to pay the state tax, and the case, *McCulloch* v. *Maryland*, reached the Court in 1819.

Speaking for the Court, Chief Justice **John Marshall** ruled that Maryland had no right to tax the Bank because it was a federal institution. He argued that the Constitution and the federal government received their authority directly from the people, not by way of the state governments. The Bank was a legal creation of the federal government because the Constitution gave Congress the power to issue and borrow money. The states therefore had no right to interfere with the Bank.

The Supreme Court's ruling strengthened the national government. It also contributed to the debate over sectional issues. People who supported states' rights believed the decision was a threat to individual liberties. Strong nationalists welcomed the decision's support for national power.

Section 3 Assessment

Checking for Understanding

1. *Identify* James Monroe, John C. Calhoun, Daniel Webster, Henry Clay, *McCulloch* v. *Maryland*, John Marshall.
2. *Define* sectionalism, internal improvements, American System.
3. *Summarize* the disagreement between the North and South that resulted in the Missouri Compromise.

Reviewing Themes

4. **Individual Action** What action did Daniel Webster take that shows he placed his concerns for the nation above his sectional interests?

Critical Thinking

5. **Analyzing Information** How did sectionalism destroy the Era of Good Feelings?

Activity

Creating a Flag Design a flag to represent either the North, South, or West during the early 1800s. Use photos, symbols, or mottoes that might have been popular with the people who lived in these regions.

1815	1820	1825

1817
Rush-Bagot Treaty limits ships in Great Lakes

1818
Convention of 1818 fixes U.S.–Canada boundary

1819
Adams-Onís Treaty cedes Florida to the U.S.

1823
Monroe Doctrine prohibits European colonization

Section 4

The Monroe Doctrine

READ TO DISCOVER . . .
- how John Quincy Adams influenced American foreign policy.
- what effect the Monroe Doctrine had on foreign policy.

TERMS TO LEARN
disarmament court-martial
demilitarize

The Storyteller

The War of 1812 heightened Americans' pride in their country. Abigail Adams, wife of John Adams, wrote from England to her sister back in Massachusetts: "Do you know that European birds have not half the melody of ours? Nor is their fruit half so sweet, nor their flowers half so fragrant, nor their manners half so pure, nor their people half so virtuous."

At the same time, many Americans realized that the United States needed peace with Britain to grow and develop. It had to put differences aside and establish a new relationship with the "Old World."

Brass eagle mounted on tortoiseshell box

In the years following the War of 1812, President Monroe and his secretary of state, John Quincy Adams, moved to resolve long-standing disputes with Great Britain and Spain.

Relations With Britain

In 1817, in the **Rush-Bagot Treaty,** the two nations agreed to set limits on the number of naval vessels each could have on the Great Lakes. The treaty provided for the disarmament—the removal of weapons—along an important part of the border between the United States and British **Canada.**

The second agreement with Britain, the **Convention of 1818,** set the official boundary between the United States and Canada at the 49th parallel. The convention created a secure and demilitarized border—one without armed forces. Through Adams's efforts, Americans also gained the right to settle in the **Oregon Country.**

Relations With Spain

Spain owned East Florida and also claimed West Florida. The United States contended that West Florida was part of the Louisiana Purchase. In 1810 and 1812, Americans simply added parts of West Florida to the states of Louisiana and Mississippi. Spain objected but took no action.

In April 1818, General **Andrew Jackson** invaded Spanish East **Florida,** seizing control of two Spanish forts. Jackson had been ordered to

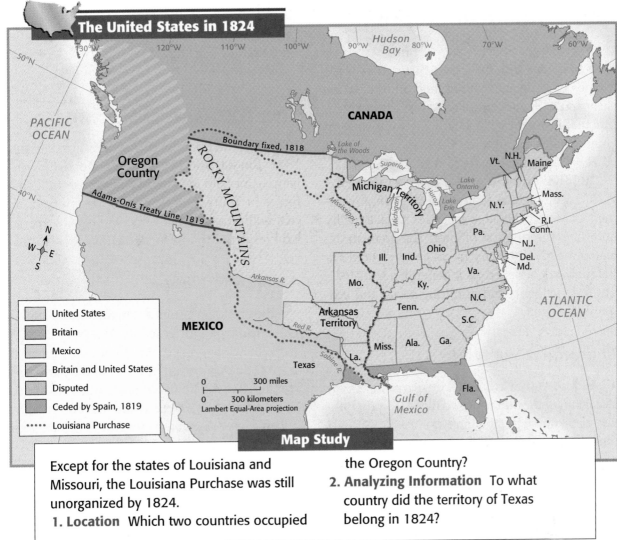

The United States in 1824

PACIFIC OCEAN

Oregon Country

Boundary fixed, 1818

ROCKY MOUNTAINS

Adams-Onís Treaty Line, 1819

CANADA

Hudson Bay

Lake of the Woods

L. Superior

Michigan Territory

Lake Ontario

Lake Erie

Lake Huron

L. Michigan

Mississippi R.

Vt. N.H. Maine

N.Y. Mass.

Pa. R.I. Conn.

Ill. Ind. Ohio N.J.

Mo. Ky. Va. Del. Md.

MEXICO

Arkansas R.

Arkansas Territory

Red R.

Sabine R.

Tenn. N.C.

S.C.

Miss. Ala. Ga.

La.

Texas

Fla.

ATLANTIC OCEAN

Gulf of Mexico

Legend:
- United States
- Britain
- Mexico
- Britain and United States
- Disputed
- Ceded by Spain, 1819
- ····· Louisiana Purchase

0   300 miles
0   300 kilometers
Lambert Equal-Area projection

Map Study

Except for the states of Louisiana and Missouri, the Louisiana Purchase was still unorganized by 1824.

1. Location Which two countries occupied the Oregon Country?

2. Analyzing Information To what country did the territory of Texas belong in 1824?

stop Seminole raids on American territory from Florida. In capturing the Spanish forts, however, Jackson went beyond his instructions.

Luis de Onís, the Spanish minister to the United States, protested forcefully and demanded the punishment of Jackson and his officers. Secretary of War Calhoun said that Jackson should be court-martialed—tried by a military court—for overstepping instructions. Secretary of State John Quincy Adams disagreed.

Geography

Adams-Onís Treaty

Although Secretary of State Adams had not authorized Jackson's raid, he did nothing to stop it. Adams guessed that the Spanish did not want

war and that they might be ready to settle the Florida dispute. He was right. For the Spanish the raid had demonstrated the military strength of the United States.

Already troubled by rebellions in **Mexico** and South America, Spain signed the **Adams-Onís Treaty** in 1819. Spain gave East Florida to the United States and abandoned all claims to West Florida. In return the United States gave up its claims to Spanish Texas and took over responsibility for paying the $5 million that American citizens claimed Spain owed them for damages.

The two countries also agreed on a border between the United States and Spanish possessions in the West. The border extended northwest from the Gulf of Mexico to the 42nd parallel and then west to the Pacific, giving the United States a large piece of territory in the Pacific Northwest. America had become a transcontinental power.

Latin American Republics

While the Spanish were settling territorial disputes with the United States, they faced a series of challenges within their empire. In the early 1800s, Spain controlled a vast colonial empire that included what is now the southwestern United States, Mexico and Central America, and all of South America except Brazil.

In 1810 a priest, Miguel Hidalgo (ee• DAHL• goh), led a rebellion against the Spanish government of Mexico. Hidalgo called for racial equality and the redistribution of land. The Spanish defeated the revolutionary forces and executed Hidalgo. Mexico gained its independence in 1821, but independence did not bring social and economic change.

Bolívar and San Martín

Independence in South America came largely as a result of the efforts of two men—**Simón Bolívar,** also known as "the Liberator," led the movement that won freedom for the present-day countries of Venezuela, Colombia, Panama, Bolivia, and Ecuador. **José de San Martín** successfully achieved independence for Chile and Peru. By 1824 the revolutionaries' military victory was complete, and most of South America had liberated itself from Spain. Portugal's large colony of Brazil gained its independence peacefully in 1822.

Spain's empire in the Americas had shrunk to Cuba, Puerto Rico, and a few other islands in the Caribbean.

The Monroe Doctrine

In 1822 Spain had asked France, Austria, Russia, and Prussia—the Quadruple Alliance—for help in its fight against revolutionary forces in South America. The possibility of increased European involvement in North America led President Monroe to take action.

A Notice to Europe

The president issued a statement, later known as the **Monroe Doctrine,** on December 2, 1823. While the United States would not interfere with any existing European colonies in the Americas, Monroe declared, it would oppose any new ones. North and South America "are henceforth not to be considered as subjects for future colonization by any European powers."

In 1823 the United States did not have the military power to enforce the Monroe Doctrine. The Monroe Doctrine nevertheless became an important element in American foreign policy and has remained so for more than 170 years. It was another example of America flexing its muscles and expressing its nationalistic feelings.

★ ★ ★ ★ ★ Section 4 Assessment ★ ★ ★ ★ ★

Checking for Understanding

1. **Identify** Convention of 1818, Andrew Jackson, Adams-Onís Treaty, Monroe Doctrine.
2. **Define** disarmament, demilitarize, court-martial.
3. **Explain** how Adams helped solve border disputes with Canada.

Reviewing Themes

4. **Global Connections** What warning was issued in the Monroe Doctrine?

Critical Thinking

5. **Synthesizing Information** Explain the following statement: The Monroe Doctrine was a product of United States nationalism.

Writing an Editorial Write a newspaper editorial supporting or rejecting the ideas of the Monroe Doctrine.

Reading a Diagram

Suppose you buy a new bicycle and discover that you must assemble the parts before you can ride it. A *diagram,* or drawing that shows how the parts fit together, would make this job much easier.

Learning the Skill

To read a diagram, follow these steps:
- Read the title or caption to find out what the diagram shows.
- Read all labels carefully to determine their meanings.
- Read the legend and identify symbols and colors used in the diagram.
- Look for numbers indicating a sequence of steps, or arrows showing movement.
- Summarize the information in the diagram in a brief statement.

Practicing the Skill

Analyze the diagram of the *Clermont,* then answer the following questions.
1. How long did the *Clermont's* round-trip between New York City and Albany take?
2. What type of energy was used to power this ship?

Applying the Skill

Making a Diagram Draw a diagram showing either how to make macaroni and cheese or how to tie a pair of shoes. Use clear drawings and labels in your diagram.

GO TO

Glencoe's **Skillbuilder Interactive Workbook, Level 1** provides instruction and practice in key social studies skills.

The *Clermont* Steamboat

On August 17, 1807, the Clermont *steamed up the Hudson River from New York City on its way to Albany, New York. It returned to New York City 62 hours later—a commercial success!*

Water is heated into steam inside the **boiler.** The *Clermont's* boiler was made by Paul Revere.

The steam is released from the boiler as pressurized energy, which was used to power the **pistons** that moved the paddle wheels.

Two side **paddle wheels** pushed the steamboat upriver.

The *Clermont* was about 140 feet (43 m) long and 14 feet (4.3 m) wide.

Assessment and Activities

★ Reviewing Key Terms

On a sheet of paper, create a crossword puzzle using the following terms. Use the terms' definitions as your crossword clues.

Industrial Revolution
factory system
interchangeable parts
sectionalism
internal improvements
American System
disarmament
demilitarize
court-martial

★ Reviewing Key Facts

1. What problems faced cities as a result of their rapid growth during the Industrial Revolution?
2. How did canals boost the economy of the Great Lakes region?
3. Why did people who migrated to the West usually settle near rivers?
4. What had happened to the Federalist Party by the time James Monroe became president?
5. How did Andrew Jackson help to secure Florida from Spain?

★ Critical Thinking

Making Generalizations

Political and regional differences in the North, South, and West brought an end to the Era of Good Feelings.

1. How did the economy of the North and South differ?
2. Why do you think many people who were moving to the West might have favored states' rights?

★ Geography Activity

Study the map below and answer the questions that follow.

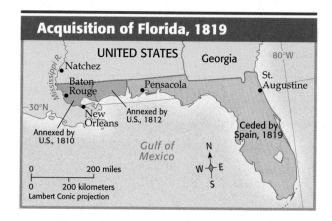

Acquisition of Florida, 1819

1. **Region** When was the largest portion of Florida acquired from Spain?
2. **Movement** In what direction did the United States acquire the various parts of Florida?
3. **Location** What body of water blocked further expansion of Florida to the west?

★ Reviewing Themes

1. **Economic Factors** How did the Industrial Revolution help to make the United States more economically independent in the early 1800s?
2. **Science and Technology** How did the development of roads boost the growth of the United States?
3. **Individual Action** What three men were considered the spokespersons for the North, South, and West regions in the early 1800s?
4. **Global Connections** Why did Secretary of State John Adams do nothing to stop General Andrew Jackson's invasion into Spanish East Florida in 1818?

★ Time Line Activity

Create a time line on which you place the following events in chronological order.

- Spain gives Florida to the United States
- Erie Canal opens
- President Monroe issues Monroe Doctrine
- Samuel Slater starts textile mill using British technology
- Eli Whitney invents cotton gin
- Francis Lowell opens textile plant
- Congress charters the Second Bank of the United States

★ Skill Practice Activity

Reading a Diagram

Study the diagram of the textile mill on page 308. Use the diagram to answer the questions below.

1. What is the first step in the production of textiles?
2. At what stage does the thread become cloth?
3. What process turns the yarn into thread?
4. When would a cotton gin be necessary in this process?

Now choose one of the inventions mentioned in the chapter. Prepare a diagram that traces the development of that invention to a similar device in use today. For example, you might diagram the development of a modern cruise ship showing all the improvements made from start to finish. Use illustrations, short descriptions, and dates to diagram the improvements.

★ Technology Activity

Using the Internet Search the Internet for information about how to apply for a patent for an invention. Create a step-by-step list of directions describing the process.

★ Cooperative Activity

History and Language Arts Organize into a group to produce a song about traveling and living in the West during this time. Part of your group can write the lyrics. Another part can write the melody and decide on the instruments. Be sure to include a chorus, which is repeated between each stanza. Record the song and play it for the class.

The following song was popular after the Erie Canal opened. You may want to follow its style when your group writes its own song.

> I've got a mule, her name is Sal,
> Fifteen miles on the Erie Canal.
> She's a good old worker and a good old pal,
> Fifteen miles on the Erie Canal.
> We've hauled some barges in our day,
> Filled with lumber, coal, and hay,
> And we know every inch of the way
> From Albany to Buffalo.
>
> CHORUS
> Low bridge, everybody down!
> Low bridge, for we're going through a town;
> And you'll always know your neighbor,
> You'll always know your pal,
> If you ever navigated on the Erie Canal.

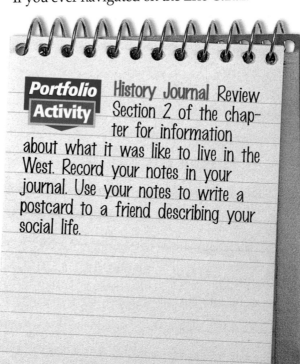

Portfolio Activity History Journal Review Section 2 of the chapter for information about what it was like to live in the West. Record your notes in your journal. Use your notes to write a postcard to a friend describing your social life.

Unit 5

The Growing Nation

1820–1860

"It is an extraordinary era in which we live."

—DANIEL WEBSTER, 1847

inter NET
CONNECTION

To learn more about the growth and expansion of the United States, visit the Glencoe Social Studies Web Site at **www.glencoe.com** for information, activities, and links to other sites.

 MAPPING *America*

Portfolio Activity Draw an outline map of the United States. As you read this unit, draw and label the new territories that were added to the Union. Add symbols to your map showing what economic activities took place in the new areas. Include a key to explain your symbols.

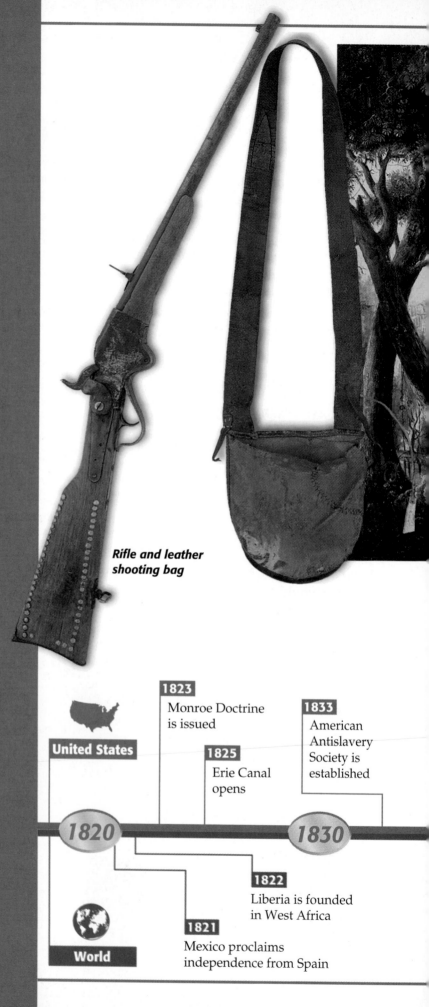

Rifle and leather shooting bag

United States

1823
Monroe Doctrine is issued

1825
Erie Canal opens

1833
American Antislavery Society is established

1820

1830

1822
Liberia is founded in West Africa

1821
Mexico proclaims independence from Spain

World

Slave identification tags

St. Louis in 1846 by Henry Lewis During this era, the United States was a nation of change, a nation on the move—socially, economically, and politically.

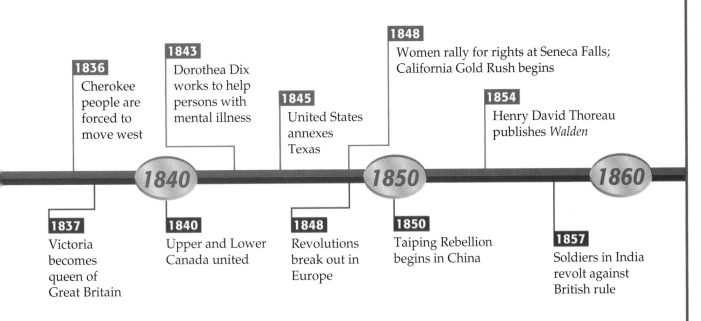

1836 Cherokee people are forced to move west

1843 Dorothea Dix works to help persons with mental illness

1845 United States annexes Texas

1848 Women rally for rights at Seneca Falls; California Gold Rush begins

1854 Henry David Thoreau publishes *Walden*

1840

1850

1860

1837 Victoria becomes queen of Great Britain

1840 Upper and Lower Canada united

1848 Revolutions break out in Europe

1850 Taiping Rebellion begins in China

1857 Soldiers in India revolt against British rule

America's LITERATURE

A Son of the Middle Border

by Hamlin Garland

Hamlin Garland (1860–1940) was born in rural Wisconsin and grew up on farms in Iowa and South Dakota. At the age of 24, he moved to Boston to begin his writing career. Although he gave up the life of a prairie farmer, Garland's work—fiction and nonfiction—reflects his background and his concern for the hard, lonely lives of pioneer men and women.

■ READ TO DISCOVER

A Son of the Middle Border is Garland's autobiography. The following excerpt describes one of the many westward moves that the Garland family made. As you read, pay attention to the emotions that the author expresses when he sees the plains for the first time.

■ READER'S DICTIONARY

middle border: the advancing frontier across the Mississippi River
habitation: residence
blue-joint: type of prairie grass
primeval: ancient or primitive
clarion: brilliantly clear
poker: metal rod for stirring a fire
sod: grass-covered surface of the ground
billow: to rise or roll in waves
russet: reddish-brown
fleck: mark

Late in August my father again loaded our household goods into wagons, and with our small herd of cattle following, set out toward the west, bound once again to overtake the actual line of the middle border.

This journey has an unforgettable epic charm as I look back upon it. Each mile took us farther and farther into the unsettled prairie until in the afternoon of the second day, we came to a meadow so wide that its western rim touched the sky without revealing a sign of man's habitation other than the road in which we travelled.

The plain was covered with grass tall as ripe wheat and when my father stopped his team and came back to us and said, "Well, children, here we are on The Big Prairie," we looked about us with awe, so endless seemed this spread of wild oats and waving blue-joint.

Far away dim clumps of trees showed, but no chimney was in sight, and no living thing moved save our own cattle and the hawks lazily wheeling in the air. My heart filled with awe as well as wonder. The majesty of this primeval world exalted me. I felt for the first time the poetry of the unplowed spaces. It seemed that the "herds of deer and buffalo" of our song might, at any moment, present themselves—but they did not, and my father took no account even of the marsh fowl.

"Forward march!" he shouted, and on we went.

Hour after hour he pushed into the west, the heads of his tired horses hanging ever lower, and on my mother's face the shadow deepened, but her chieftain's voice cheerily urging his team lost

Pioneer families on the prairies built their homes using squares of hard sod—the dense top layer of earth.

nothing of its clarion resolution. He was in his element. He loved this shelterless sweep of prairie. This westward march entranced him, I think he would have gladly kept on until the snowy wall of the Rocky Mountains met his eyes, for he was a natural explorer.

Sunset came at last, but still he drove steadily on through the sparse settlements. Just at nightfall we came to a beautiful little stream, and stopped to let the horses drink. I heard its rippling, reassuring song on the pebbles. Thereafter all is dim and vague to me until my mother called out sharply, "Wake up, children! Here we are!"

Struggling to my feet I looked about me. Nothing could be seen but the dim form of a small house.—On every side the land melted into blackness, silent and without boundary.

Driving into the yard, father hastily unloaded one of the wagons and taking mother and Harriet and Jessie drove away to spend the night with Uncle David who had preceded us, as I now learned, and was living on a farm not far away. My brother and I were left to camp as best we could with the hired man.

Spreading a rude bed on the floor, he told us to "hop in" and in ten minutes we were all fast asleep.

The sound of a clattering poker awakened me next morning and when I opened my sleepy eyes and looked out a new world displayed itself before me.

The cabin faced a level plain with no tree in sight. A mile away to the west stood a low stone house and immediately in front of us opened a half-section of unfenced sod. To the north, as far as I could see, the land billowed like a russet ocean with scarcely a roof to fleck its lonely spread. . . .

Once more and for the sixth time since her marriage, [my mother] Belle Garland adjusted herself to a pioneer environment. . . . No doubt she also congratulated herself on the fact that she had not been carried beyond the Missouri River. . . .

■ RESPONDING TO LITERATURE

1. Give two details that Garland uses to describe "The Big Prairie" at the beginning of the selection.
2. How do Garland's parents feel about moving west?

Activity

Writing a Poem The vast prairie fills Garland with awe because the land is empty and untouched. Write a poem about a vast empty place that you know, or base your poem on a place about which you have read.

Chapter 11

1824–1845

The Jackson Era

★ Why It's Important

The struggle for political rights took shape in the 1820s and 1830s, when many people questioned the limits of American democracy. In the years since the Jackson era, women, African Americans, and other minorities have won the right to vote and to participate in the political process. Today every United States citizen aged 18 or older, regardless of gender, race, or wealth, has the right to vote.

★ Chapter Themes

■ *Section 1,* Continuity and Change
■ *Section 2,* Government and Democracy
■ *Section 3,* Groups and Institutions
■ *Section 4,* Economic Factors

PRIMARY SOURCES
Library

See pages 956–957 for primary source readings to accompany Chapter 11

 HISTORY AND ART

Stump Speaking **by George Caleb Bingham** Bingham's series of election paintings in the 1850s expressed faith in the growth of democracy.

1825
John Quincy Adams wins presidency in House election

1826
Adams attends the first congress of American nations in Panama

1828
Andrew Jackson is elected president

1834
National Republicans change their name to Whigs

Section 1

From Adams to Jackson

READ TO DISCOVER . . .
- why the nation's sixth president was chosen by the House of Representatives.
- why the Republican Party split into two parties.

TERMS TO LEARN
favorite son   mudslinging
majority   landslide
plurality

The Storyteller

The presidential campaign of 1828 was one of the most vicious in American history. Supporters of John Quincy Adams in Philadelphia distributed a pamphlet titled "An Account of Some of the Bloody Deeds of General Jackson." One illustration in the pamphlet showed a ferocious-looking Andrew Jackson plunging his sword through the body of a helpless civilian. Meanwhile Jackson's supporters falsely accused John Quincy Adams of kidnapping a young American girl and selling her to the ruler of Russia.

Jackson sewing box

From 1816 to 1824, the United States had only one political party—the Jeffersonian Republicans. However, within the party differences arose among various groups with their own views and interests.

In 1824 James Monroe was finishing his second term as president. Following the example of earlier presidents, Monroe declined to run for a third term. Four candidates from the Republican Party competed for the presidency.

The Election of 1824

The four candidates' opinions differed on the role of the federal government. They also spoke for different areas of the country. The Republican Party nominated **William H. Crawford,** a former congressman from Georgia. He called for a limited federal government and strong state powers. He also defended slavery. However, Crawford's poor health weakened him as a candidate.

The other three Republicans in the presidential race were favorite son candidates, meaning they received the backing of their home states rather than that of the national party. Two of these candidates—**Andrew Jackson** and **Henry Clay**—came from the West. Clay of Kentucky was Speaker of the House of Representatives. Clay fought for his program of internal improvements, high tariffs, and a stronger national bank.

General Andrew Jackson of Tennessee was not a Washington politician but a hero of the War of 1812. Raised in poverty by his widowed mother,

***President
John Quincy Adams***

Jackson claimed to speak for the Americans who had been left out of politics. His supporters included farmers in the hill country of the South, settlers trying to carve out a life in the West, and struggling laborers in the cities of the East.

John Quincy Adams of Massachusetts, son of former president John Adams, received support from merchants of the Northeast. Adams believed that the federal government should actively help the nation shift from an economy based on farming to one based on manufacturing.

Striking a Bargain

In the election Jackson received the largest number of popular votes. However, no candidate received a majority, or more than half, of the electoral votes. Jackson won 99 electoral votes, which gave him a plurality, or largest single share. Under the terms of the Twelfth Amendment to the Constitution, when no candidate receives a majority of electoral votes, the House of Representatives selects the president.

While the House was preparing to vote on the next president, Henry Clay met with Adams. Clay agreed to use his influence as Speaker of the House to defeat Jackson. In return Clay may have hoped to gain the position of secretary of state.

With Clay's help Adams received enough votes in the House to become president. Adams quickly named Clay as secretary of state, traditionally the stepping-stone to the presidency. Jackson's followers accused the two men of making a **"corrupt bargain"** and stealing the election.

The Adams Presidency

In **Washington, D.C.,** the "corrupt bargain" had cast a shadow over Adams's presidency. Outside the capital Adams's policies

ran against popular opinion. Adams wanted a stronger navy and government funds for scientific expeditions. Adams also wanted the federal government to direct economic growth.

Such ideas horrified those who desired a more limited role for the federal government, and Congress turned down many of Adams's proposals. This was especially true after the congressional elections of 1826, when Adams's enemies controlled both the House and Senate.

The Election of 1828

In 1828 Andrew Jackson tried again for the presidency. He ran against John Quincy Adams in a bitter election campaign.

In 1824 all four presidential candidates had run as Republicans. By the time of the election of 1828, the party had divided into two separate parties: the **Democratic-Republicans,** who supported Jackson, and the **National Republicans,** who supported Adams. Jackson's Democratic-Republicans, or Democrats, favored states' rights and mistrusted strong central government. Many Democrats were individualists from the frontier, immigrants, or laborers in the big cities.

Election of 1824

Candidate	Electoral Vote	Popular Vote	House Vote
Jackson	99	153,544	7
Adams	84	108,740	13
Crawford	41	46,618	4
Clay	37	47,136	—

Chart Study

The presidential election of 1824 was decided in the House of Representatives.

1. How many more popular votes did Jackson have than Adams?
2. **Analyzing Information** Which candidate received the most electoral votes? The least?

The National Republicans wanted a strong central government. They supported federal measures, such as road building and the Bank of the United States, that would shape the nation's economy. Many were merchants or successful farmers.

A Vicious Campaign

During the campaign both parties resorted to mudslinging, attempts to ruin their opponent's reputation with insults. The Democratic-Republicans accused Adams of betraying the interests of the people. They put out a handbill calling the election a contest "between an honest patriotism, on the one side, and an unholy and selfish ambition, on the other."

The National Republicans fought back. They created a vicious campaign song to play up embarrassing incidents in Jackson's life. One involved Jackson's order in the War of 1812 to execute several soldiers who had deserted. Adams himself referred to Jackson as "a barbarian and a savage."

Mudslinging was not the only new element introduced in the 1828 campaign. Election slogans, rallies, buttons, and events such as barbecues were also used to arouse enthusiasm, mostly by Jackson's supporters. All of these new features became a permanent part of American political life.

Jackson campaign poster

Jackson Triumphs

In the election of 1828, Jackson received most of the votes cast by voters of the new frontier states. He also received many votes in the South, where his support for states' rights was popular. **John C. Calhoun** of South Carolina, who had served as Adams's vice president, switched parties to run with Jackson. Calhoun also championed states' rights. Jackson won the election in a landslide, an overwhelming victory, with 56 percent of the popular vote and 178 electoral votes.

★ ★ ★ ★ ★ Section 1 Assessment ★ ★ ★ ★ ★ ★

Checking for Understanding

1. **Identify** Andrew Jackson, Henry Clay, John Quincy Adams, Democratic-Republicans, National Republicans.
2. **Define** favorite son, majority, plurality, mudslinging, landslide.
3. **Compare** and contrast the Democratic-Republicans and the National Republicans.

Reviewing Themes

4. **Continuity and Change** What election

practices used in the 1828 presidential campaign are still in use today?

Critical Thinking

5. **Identifying Central Issues** What was the main reason President Adams was not popular with the Democratic-Republicans?

Drawing a Political Cartoon Draw a political cartoon to illustrate your opinion of the "corrupt bargain."

1828	1830	1832	1834

1828
Congress passes
the Tariff of
Abominations

1830
Webster and
Hayne debate

1832
South Carolina
threatens to
secede

1833
Congress passes
the Force Bill

Section 2

Jacksonian Democracy

READ TO DISCOVER . . .

■ why Andrew Jackson was a popular leader.
■ what changes President Jackson brought to the American political system.
■ why South Carolina threatened to withdraw from the United States in 1832.

TERMS TO LEARN

suffrage   tariff
bureaucracy   nullify
spoils system   secede
caucus   states' rights
nominating convention

The Storyteller

Andrew Jackson was everything most Americans admired—a patriot, a self-made man, and a war hero. On March 4, 1829, thousands of farmers, laborers, and other ordinary Americans crowded into the nation's capital to hear Jackson's Inaugural Address. After Jackson's speech a crowd joined him at a White House reception. They filled the elegant rooms of the mansion, trampling on the carpets with muddy shoes, spilling food on sofas and chairs. They were there to shake the hand of the general who seemed just like them.

Goblet showing Jackson's log cabin

Like many of his supporters, Andrew Jackson had been born in a log cabin. His parents, poor farmers, died before he was 15. As a teenager Jackson fought with the Patriots in the American Revolution. Before he was 30, he was elected to Congress from Tennessee.

Jackson gained fame during the War of 1812. He defeated the Creek Nation in the Battle of Horseshoe Bend and led the Americans to victory at New Orleans. His troops called him "Old Hickory" because he was as tough as a hickory stick.

Small farmers, craft workers, and others who felt left out of the expanding American economy loved Jackson. They felt that his rise from a log cabin to the White House demonstrated the American success story. His popularity with the common man changed politics in Washington, D.C.

A New Era in Politics

★ President Andrew Jackson promised "equal protection and equal benefits" for all Americans—at least for all white American men. During his first term, a spirit of equality spread through American politics.

🔖 Citizenship

New Voters

In the nation's early years, most states had limited suffrage, or the right to vote, to men who owned property or paid taxes. Starting in 1815

Western and Eastern states alike loosened the property requirements for voting. In the 1820s democracy expanded as people who had not been allowed to vote voted for the first time. Between 1824 and 1828, the percentage of white males voting in presidential elections increased from 36.9 to 57.6 percent. For the first time, white male sharecroppers, factory workers, and many others were brought into the political process.

The expansion of suffrage continued, and by 1840 more than 80 percent of white males voted in the presidential election. However, women still could not vote, and African Americans and Native Americans had few rights of any kind.

Another important development in the broadening of democracy involved presidential electors. By 1828, 22 of the 24 states changed their constitutions to allow the people, rather than the state legislatures, to choose presidential electors.

The Spoils System

Democrats carried the spirit of democracy into government. They wanted to open up government jobs to people from all walks of life. They were disturbed that the federal government had become a bureaucracy, a system in which nonelected officials carry out laws. Democrats argued that ordinary citizens could handle any government job.

President Jackson fired many federal workers and replaced them with his supporters. The discharged employees protested vehemently. They charged that Jackson was acting like a tyrant, hiring and firing people at will. Jackson responded that a new set of federal employees would be good for democracy.

One Jackson supporter explained it another way: "To the victors belong the spoils." In other words, because the Jacksonians had won the election, they had the right to the spoils—benefits of victory—such as handing out government jobs to supporters. The practice of replacing government employees with the winning candidate's supporters became known as the spoils system.

Electoral Changes

Jackson's supporters worked to make the political system more democratic as well. They abandoned the unpopular caucus system. In this system major political candidates were chosen by committees made up of members of Congress. The caucuses were replaced by nominating conventions in which delegates from the states selected the party's presidential candidate.

The Democrats held their first national party convention in 1832 in **Baltimore, Maryland.** The convention drew delegates from each state in the Union. The delegates decided to nominate the candidate who could gather two-thirds of the vote, and Jackson won the nomination. This system allowed many people to participate in the selection of political candidates.

 **Picturing HISTORY** Carriages, wagons, and thousands of people followed Jackson to the White House for his inauguration reception. **What change in politics did Jackson's presidency represent?**

★ **Picturing HISTORY** In an 1832 political cartoon, Andrew Jackson (right) plays a card game with his political enemies. **What major issue divided Jackson and his opponents in 1832?**

💲 **Economics**

The Tariff Debate

★ Americans from different parts of the country disagreed strongly on some issues. One such issue was the tariff, a fee paid by merchants who imported goods. While president, Jackson faced a tariff crisis that tested the national government's powers.

In 1828 Congress passed a very high tariff on manufactured goods from Europe. Manufacturers in the United States—mostly in the Northeast—welcomed the tariff. Because tariffs made European goods more expensive, American consumers were more likely to buy American-made goods.

Southerners, however, hated the new tariff. They called it the Tariff of Abominations—something detestable. The South traded cotton to Europe for manufactured goods, and the new tariff would make these items more expensive. 💲

The South Protests

Southern politicians and plantation owners were outraged over the high tariff. Vice President John C. Calhoun argued that a state or group of states had the right to nullify, or cancel, a federal law it considered unconstitutional.

Some Southerners called for the Southern states to secede, or break away, from the United States and form their own government. When Calhoun explored this idea, troubling questions arose. The United States had been a nation for nearly 50 years. What if a state disagreed with the federal government? Did a state have the right to go its own way?

Calhoun said yes. In his view the states had created the federal government, so they should have the last word on decisions affecting them. Calhoun's argument grew out of the broad idea of states' rights—that the states have many rights and powers that are independent of the federal government. Many Northerners disagreed with Calhoun.

🔍 **Eyewitness to HISTORY**

The Webster–Hayne Debate

In January 1830, Senator **Daniel Webster** delivered a stinging attack on states' rights. Webster stood on the floor of the Senate to challenge a speech given by Robert Hayne, a young senator from South Carolina. Hayne had defended the idea that the states had a right to nullify acts of the federal government, and even to secede.

In his response, Webster defended the Constitution and the Union. He argued that nullification could only mean the end of the Union. Webster closed with the ringing statement, "Liberty and union, now and forever, one and inseparable!"

Jackson Takes a Stand

Nobody knew exactly where President Jackson stood on the issue of states' rights. Many Southerners hoped that Jackson might side with them. In April 1830 supporters of states' rights invited the president to speak at a dinner. The guests, including Calhoun, waited anxiously for Jackson to speak. Finally, the president rose to his feet and spoke directly to Calhoun. "Our federal union . . . must be preserved!"

The states' rights supporters were shocked and disappointed, but Calhoun answered the president's challenge. He raised his glass and said, "The Union—next to our liberty, most dear." He meant that the fate of the Union must take second place to a state's liberty to make its own laws.

Calhoun realized that Jackson would not change his views. Wishing to return to Congress to speak for Southern interests, Calhoun won election to the Senate in December 1832. Two weeks later he resigned the vice presidency.

The Nullification Crisis

★ Southern anger over the tariff continued to build. The Union seemed on the verge of splitting apart. In 1832 Congress passed a new, lower tariff, hoping that the protest in the South would die down. It did not.

South Carolina, Calhoun's home state, had led the fight against the so-called Tariff of Abominations. Now South Carolina took the battle one step further. The state legislature passed the **Nullification Act,** declaring that it would not pay the "illegal" tariffs of 1828 and 1832. The South Carolina legislators threatened to secede from the Union if the federal government tried to interfere with their actions.

The Crisis Passes

"The Nullifiers of the South have run mad," Jackson said. "It leads directly to civil war and bloodshed." To ease the crisis, Jackson supported a compromise bill proposed by Henry Clay that would greatly lower the tariff. At the same time, Jackson made sure that the South would accept Clay's compromise. Early in 1833 he persuaded Congress to pass the **Force Bill,** which allowed the president to use the United States military to enforce acts of Congress. The message was clear: If South Carolina did not give in, it would face the army.

South Carolina quickly accepted the compromise tariff and agreed to set aside the Nullification Act. For the time being, the crisis between a state and the federal government was over. Yet South Carolina and the rest of the South would remember the lesson of the nullification crisis—that the federal government would not allow a state to go its own way without a fight.

Section 2 Assessment

Checking for Understanding
1. *Identify* Nullification Act, Force Bill.
2. *Define* suffrage, bureaucracy, spoils system, caucus, nominating convention, tariff, nullify, secede, states' rights.
3. *Explain* why President Jackson was popular with the average citizen.

Reviewing Themes
4. **Government and Democracy** How did the method of choosing electors change during Jackson's administration?

Critical Thinking
5. **Demonstrating Reasoned Judgment** Do you agree or disagree with Calhoun's statement, "The Union—next to our liberty, most dear"? Explain your answer.

Activity

Formulating Questions Prepare a list of five questions that you might have asked President Jackson if you were able to interview him.

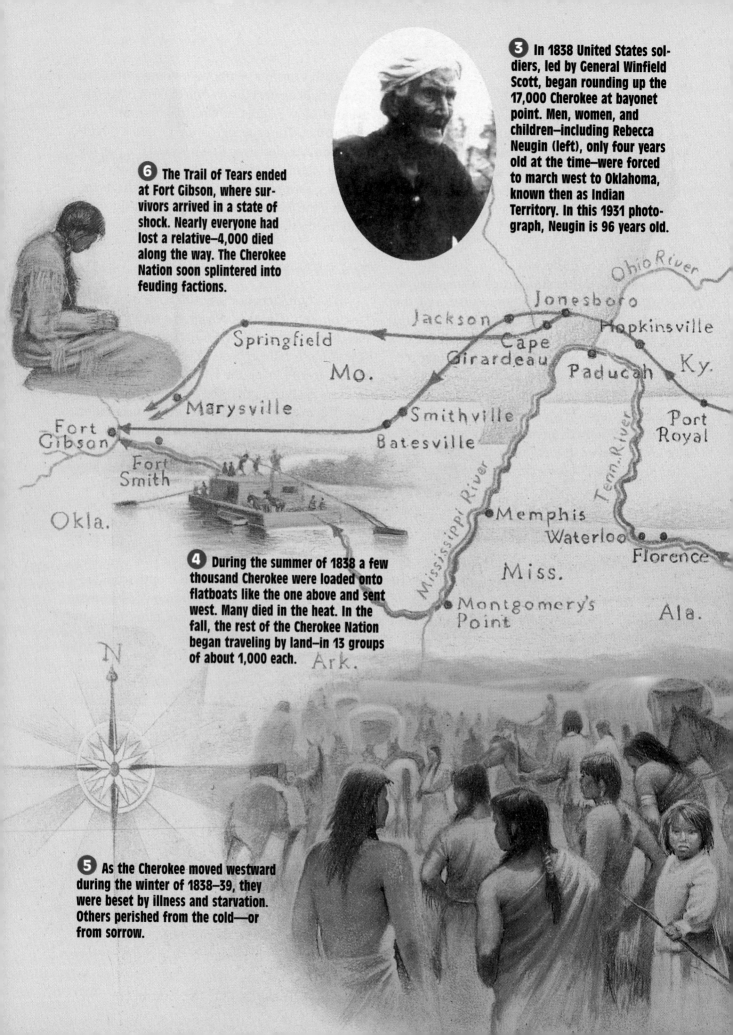

6 The Trail of Tears ended at Fort Gibson, where survivors arrived in a state of shock. Nearly everyone had lost a relative—4,000 died along the way. The Cherokee Nation soon splintered into feuding factions.

3 In 1838 United States soldiers, led by General Winfield Scott, began rounding up the 17,000 Cherokee at bayonet point. Men, women, and children—including Rebecca Neugin (left), only four years old at the time—were forced to march west to Oklahoma, known then as Indian Territory. In this 1931 photograph, Neugin is 96 years old.

Ohio River

Jonesboro

Jackson

Cape Girardeau

Hopkinsville

Ky.

Paducah

Springfield

Mo.

Marysville

Smithville

Batesville

Port Royal

Fort Gibson

Fort Smith

Tenn. River

Okla.

Mississippi River

Memphis

Waterloo

Florence

4 During the summer of 1838 a few thousand Cherokee were loaded onto flatboats like the one above and sent west. Many died in the heat. In the fall, the rest of the Cherokee Nation began traveling by land—in 13 groups of about 1,000 each.

Miss.

Montgomery's Point

Ala.

N

Ark.

5 As the Cherokee moved westward during the winter of 1838–39, they were beset by illness and starvation. Others perished from the cold—or from sorrow.

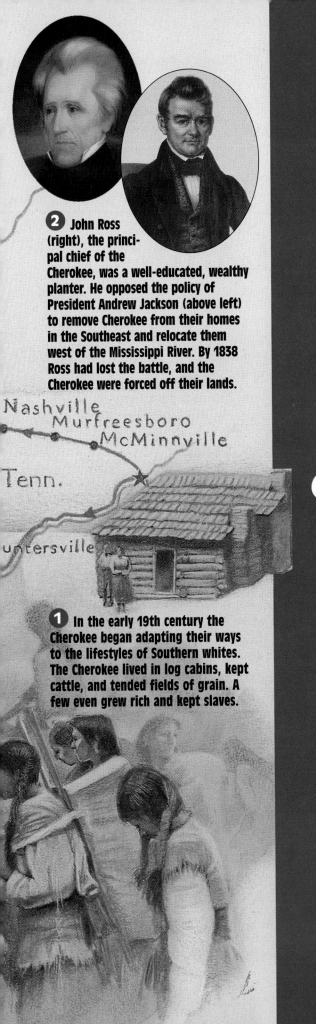

2 John Ross (right), the principal chief of the Cherokee, was a well-educated, wealthy planter. He opposed the policy of President Andrew Jackson (above left) to remove Cherokee from their homes in the Southeast and relocate them west of the Mississippi River. By 1838 Ross had lost the battle, and the Cherokee were forced off their lands.

Nashville
Murfreesboro
McMinnville

Tenn.

untersville

1 In the early 19th century the Cherokee began adapting their ways to the lifestyles of Southern whites. The Cherokee lived in log cabins, kept cattle, and tended fields of grain. A few even grew rich and kept slaves.

NATIONAL GEOGRAPHIC
Journeys

Trail *of* Tears

❝ When [the] soldier came to our house, my father wanted to fight, but my mother told him that the soldiers would kill him if he did, and we surrendered without a fight. They drove us out of our house to join other prisoners in a stockade.... The people got so tired of salt pork on the journey that my father would walk through the woods as we traveled [in the wagon], hunting for turkeys and deer, which he brought into camp to feed us.... There was much sickness among the emigrants and a great many little children died of whooping cough. ❞

— From the recollections of Rebecca Neugin, as told to historian Grant Foreman in the 1930s.

1830
Congress passes the Indian Removal Act

1832
Black Hawk leads Sauk and Fox people to Illinois

1835
Seminole refuse to leave Florida

1838
Cherokee driven from their homelands on the Trail of Tears

Section 3

Conflicts Over Land

READ TO DISCOVER . . .
- how Native American peoples were forced off their lands in the Southeast.
- how President Jackson defied the Supreme Court.

TERMS TO LEARN
relocate   guerrilla

Storyteller

Following the defeat of his forces, Sauk and Fox leader Black Hawk said: "We always had plenty; our children never cried from hunger, neither were our people in want. . . . The rapids of Rock River furnished us with an abundance of excellent fish, and the land being very fertile, never failed to produce good crops of corn, beans, pumpkin, and squash. . . . If a prophet had come to our village in those days and told us that the things were to take place which have since come to pass, none of our people would have believed him."

Medal given to Native Americans

While the United States had expanded westward by the 1830s, large numbers of Native Americans still lived in the eastern part of the country. In Georgia, Alabama, Mississippi, and Florida, the Cherokee, Creek, Choctaw, Chickasaw, and Seminole held valuable lands.

Moving Native Americans

Because the area west of the Mississippi was dry and seemed unsuitable for farming, few white Americans lived there. Many settlers wanted the federal government to relocate Native Americans living in the Southeast, to force them to leave their land and move west of the Mississippi River. President Andrew Jackson, a man of the frontier himself, supported the settlers' demand for Native American land. In his presidential campaign he had promised to back white settlers who wanted Native American lands.

Indian Removal Act

Congress responded by passing the **Indian Removal Act** in 1830. The act allowed the federal government to pay Native Americans to move west. Jackson then sent federal officials to negotiate treaties with Indians of the Southeast. Most accepted payment for their lands and agreed to move. In 1834 Congress created the **Indian Territory,** an area in present-day Oklahoma, for Native Americans from the Southeast.

The Cherokee Nation

The Cherokee Nation, however, refused to give up its land. In treaties of the 1790s, the federal government had recognized the Cherokee people in the state of Georgia as a separate nation with its own laws. Georgia, however, refused to recognize Cherokee laws.

The Cherokee sued the state government and eventually took their case to the Supreme Court.

In *Worcester* v. *Georgia* (1832), Chief Justice John Marshall ruled that Georgia had no right to interfere with the Cherokee. The Native Americans, he said, were protected by the federal government and the Constitution.

President Jackson had supported Georgia's efforts to remove the Cherokee. He vowed to ignore the Supreme Court's ruling. "John Marshall has made his decision," Jackson reportedly said. "Now let him enforce it."

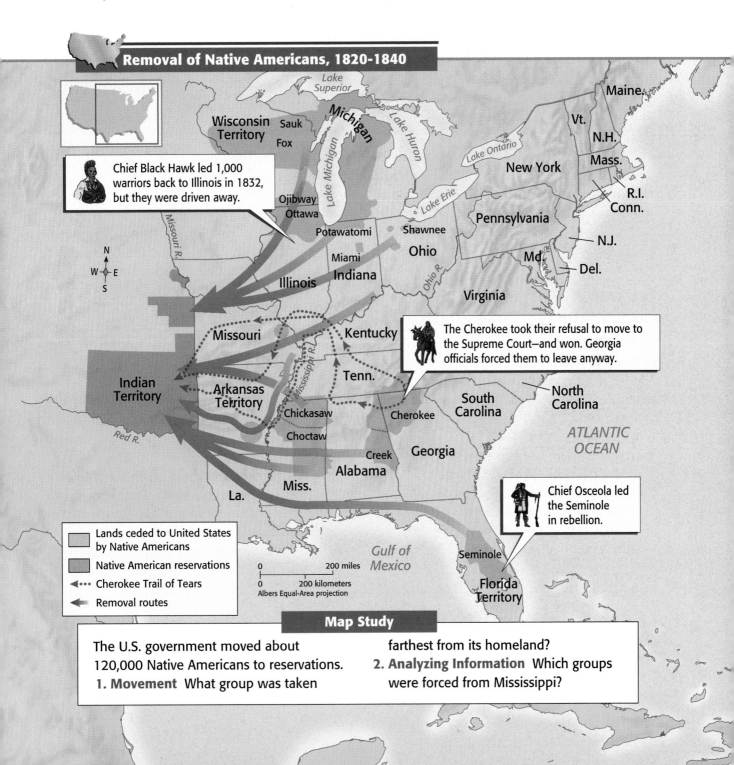

Removal of Native Americans, 1820-1840

Chief Black Hawk led 1,000 warriors back to Illinois in 1832, but they were driven away.

The Cherokee took their refusal to move to the Supreme Court—and won. Georgia officials forced them to leave anyway.

Chief Osceola led the Seminole in rebellion.

Lands ceded to United States by Native Americans

Native American reservations

Cherokee Trail of Tears

Removal routes

0   200 miles
0   200 kilometers
Albers Equal-Area projection

Map Study

The U.S. government moved about 120,000 Native Americans to reservations.
1. **Movement** What group was taken farthest from its homeland?
2. **Analyzing Information** Which groups were forced from Mississippi?

HISTORY AND ART *Trail of Tears* by Robert Lindneux Native Americans who were forced from their land traveled west in the 1830s. **Why did the Cherokee call the forced march the "Trail of Tears"?**

Eyewitness to HISTORY

The Trail of Tears

In 1835 the federal government persuaded a few Cherokee to sign a treaty giving up their people's land. Yet most of the 17,000 Cherokee refused to honor the treaty. They wrote a protest letter to the government and people of the United States.

" We are aware that some persons suppose it will be for our advantage to [re]move beyond the Mississippi. . . . Our people universally think otherwise. . . . We wish to remain on the land of our fathers. "

The Cherokee plea for understanding did not soften the resolve of President Jackson or the white settlers of the area. In 1838 **General Winfield Scott** and an army of 7,000 federal troops came to remove the Cherokee from their homes and lead them west.

Scott threatened to use force if the Cherokee did not leave. He told them he had positioned troops all around the country so that resistance and escape were both hopeless. "Chiefs, head men, and warriors—Will you then, by resistance, compel us to resort to arms?"

The Cherokee knew that fighting would only lead to their destruction. Filled with sadness and anger, their leaders gave in, and the long march to the West began. One man in Kentucky wrote of seeing hundreds of Cherokee marching by:

Footnotes to History

Native American Alphabet In 1821 Sequoya (sih•KWAWIH•uh), a Cherokee, invented an alphabet based on the spoken language of his people. Once they had a written language, many Cherokee learned to read. The Cherokee were the first Native Americans to publish a newspaper.

★ ★

> 66 Even [the] aged . . . nearly ready to drop in the grave, were traveling with heavy burdens attached to their backs, sometimes on frozen ground and sometimes on muddy streets, with no covering for their feet. 99

Brutal weather along the way claimed thousands of Cherokee lives. Their forced journey west became known to the Cherokee people as the Trail Where They Cried. Historians call it the **Trail of Tears.**

this area, which had been given up in a treaty. The Illinois state militia and federal troops responded with force, killing hundreds of Sauk and Fox and chasing the survivors over the border into present-day **Iowa.** The troops pursued the retreating Indians and slaughtered most of them.

Seminole leader Osceola

Native American Resistance

In 1832 the Sauk chieftain, **Black Hawk,** led a force of Sauk and Fox people back to **Illinois,** their homeland. They wanted to recapture

The Seminole Wars

The Seminole people of Florida were the only Native Americans who successfully blocked their removal. Although they were pressured in the early 1830s to sign treaties giving up their land, the Seminole chief, **Osceola,** and some

American Memories

Eastern Native American Life

Clothes

Blanket

Cooking kettle

What Was It Like? Eastern Native American men did most of the hunting and fishing, while the women farmed and gathered berries and nuts. **What do these items reveal about how eastern Native Americans met their other needs?**

HISTORY AND ART

***Black Hawk and Whirling Thunder* by John Wesley Jarvis** This portrait of the 66-year-old Sauk leader Black Hawk (left) with his son was painted in 1833. **Why did Illinois settlers and militia use force against Black Hawk?**

of his people refused to leave Florida. The Seminole decided to go to war against the United States instead.

In 1835 the Seminole joined forces with a group of African Americans who had run away to escape slavery. Together they attacked white settlements along the Florida coast. They used guerrilla tactics, making surprise attacks and then retreating back into the forests and swamps.

By 1842 more than 1,500 of the 10,000 American soldiers who fought in the Seminole wars had died, mostly from disease. The government gave up and allowed the Seminole to remain in Florida. Many Seminole, however, had died in the long war, and many more were captured and forced to move westward. After 1842 only a few scattered groups of Native Americans lived east of the Mississippi.

Section 3 Assessment

Checking for Understanding
1. *Identify* Indian Removal Act, General Winfield Scott, Trail of Tears, Black Hawk, Osceola.
2. *Define* relocate, guerrilla.
3. *Describe* how President Jackson reacted to the Supreme Court decision regarding the Cherokee.

Reviewing Themes
4. **Groups and Institutions** How were the Seminole able to resist relocation?

Critical Thinking
5. **Drawing Conclusions** Do you think it was fair for white Americans to force Native Americans to relocate? Why or why not?

Activity

Writing a Letter Imagine that you were a member of the Cherokee Nation. Write a letter to Andrew Jackson telling him why you should be allowed to stay in your homeland.

Analyzing Primary Sources

How do historians determine what happened in the past? They do some detective work. They comb through bits of evidence from the past to reconstruct events. These bits of historical evidence—both written and illustrated—are called *primary sources*.

Learning the Skill

Primary sources are records of events made by the people who witnessed them. They include letters, diaries, photographs and pictures, news articles, and legal documents.

Primary sources yield several important kinds of information. Often they give detailed accounts of events. However, the account reflects only one perspective. For this reason, you must examine as many perspectives as possible before drawing any conclusions. To analyze primary sources, follow these steps:

- Identify the author of the document.
- Identify when and where the document was written.
- Read the document for its content and try to answer the five "W" questions: <u>W</u>ho is it about? <u>W</u>hat is it about? <u>W</u>hen did it happen? <u>W</u>here did it happen? <u>W</u>hy did it happen?
- Identify the author's opinions.
- Determine what kind of information may be missing from the primary source.

Practicing the Skill

The primary source that follows comes from Speckled Snake, an elder of the Creek Nation, in 1829. He was more than 100 years old at the time he said these words. Read the quote, then answer the questions that follow.

> ❝Brothers! I have listened to many talks from our Great Father. When he first came over the wide waters, he was but a little man. . . . But when the white man had warmed himself before the Indians' fire and filled himself with their hominy, he became very large. With a step he bestrode the mountains and his feet covered the plains and the valleys. His hand grasped the eastern and the western sea, and his head rested on the moon. Then he became our Great Father. He loved his red children, and he said, 'Get a little further, lest I tread on thee. . . .' Brothers, I have listened to a great many talks from our Great Father. But they always began and ended in this—'Get a little further; you are too near me.'❞

1. When was this document written?
2. What events are described?
3. Who was affected by these events?
4. What is the general feeling of the person who stated this opinion?

Applying the Skill

Analyzing Primary Sources Find a primary source from your past—a photo, a report card, an old newspaper clipping, or your first baseball card. Bring this source to class and explain what it shows about that time in your life.

Glencoe's **Skillbuilder Interactive Workbook, Level 1** provides instruction and practice in key social studies skills.

1830   1835   1840   1845

1832
Andrew Jackson
challenges the Bank
of the United States

1836
Martin Van Buren
is elected president

1837
Panic of 1837
strikes the nation

1841
Vice President
John Tyler
becomes
president

Section 4

Jackson and the Bank

READ TO DISCOVER . . .
- why Jackson wanted to destroy the Bank of the United States.
- why the Whigs came to power in 1840.

TERMS TO LEARN
veto

depression

laissez-faire

log cabin campaign

The Storyteller

President Andrew Jackson made many enemies. His most outspoken rivals, the Whigs, were strong in Congress. They accused "King Andrew" of increasing his power and spreading corruption with the spoils system. In response, Jackson declared that the president was responsible for the protection of "the liberties and rights of the people and the integrity of the Constitution against the Senate, or the House of Representatives, or both together."

Bank note issued in the mid-1800s

Jackson had another great battle during his presidency. For years, he had attacked the Bank of the United States as being an organization of wealthy Easterners over which ordinary citizens had no control. The Bank of the United States was a powerful institution. It held the federal government's money and controlled much of the country's money supply. Although the Bank had been chartered by Congress, it was run by private bankers rather than elected officials.

The Bank's president, **Nicholas Biddle,** represented everything Jackson disliked. Jackson prided himself on being a self-made man who started with nothing. Biddle, on the other hand, came from a wealthy family and had a fine education and social standing.

War against the Bank

In 1832 Jackson's opponents gave him the chance to take action against the Bank. Senators **Henry Clay** and **Daniel Webster,** friends of Biddle, planned to use the Bank to defeat Jackson in the 1832 presidential election. They persuaded Biddle to apply early for a new charter—a government permit to operate the Bank—even though the Bank's current charter did not expire until 1836.

Clay and Webster believed the Bank had popular support. They thought that an attempt by Jackson to veto its charter would lead to his defeat and allow Henry Clay to be elected president.

When the bill to renew the Bank's charter came to Jackson for signature, he was sick in bed.

Jackson told his friend **Martin Van Buren,** "The bank, Mr. Van Buren, is trying to kill me. But I will kill it!" Jackson vetoed, or rejected, the bill.

In a message to Congress, Jackson angrily denounced the Bank for favoring the rich and hurting the poor. Jackson argued that

> 66 . . . when laws . . . make the rich richer and the potent more powerful, the humble members of society—the farmers, mechanics, and laborers—who have neither the time nor the means of securing like favors to themselves, have a right to complain of the injustice of their Government. 99

The Election of 1832

Webster and Clay were right about one thing. The Bank of the United States did play a large part in the campaign of 1832. Their strategy for gaining support for Clay as president, however, backfired. Most people supported Jackson's veto of the bank charter bill. Jackson was reelected, receiving 55 percent of the popular vote and collecting 219 electoral votes to Clay's 49. Martin Van Buren was elected vice president.

Once reelected, Jackson decided on a plan to "kill" the Bank ahead of the 1836 schedule. He ordered the withdrawal of all government deposits from the Bank and placed the funds in smaller state banks. By 1836 Nicholas Biddle was forced to close the Bank.

Politics after Jackson

★ When Jackson decided not to run for a third term in 1836, the Democrats selected Martin Van Buren of **New York,** Jackson's friend and vice president, as their candidate. Van Buren faced bitter opposition from the **Whigs,** a new political party that included former National Republicans and other anti-Jackson forces. Jackson's great popularity and his personal support of Van Buren helped Van Buren easily defeat several Whig opponents. Van Buren was inaugurated in 1837.

★ **Picturing HISTORY** Nicholas Biddle was a noted writer, legislator, and diplomat as well as a brilliant financier. **What major institution did Nicholas Biddle head?**

The Panic of 1837

Two months after Van Buren took office, the country entered a severe economic depression, a period in which business and employment fall to a very low level. The depression began with the **Panic of 1837,** a time when land values dropped sharply, investments declined suddenly, banks failed, and people lost confidence in the economic system.

Within a few weeks, thousands of businesses had closed and hundreds of thousands of people lost their jobs. Prices rose so high that poor people could not afford food or rent. In February 1837, people in New York put up signs voicing their anger:

66 Bread, Meat, Rent, and Fuel!
Their prices must come down!
The Voice of the People shall be heard
and will prevail! 99

The Depression Continues

President Van Buren did little to solve the economic problems causing the depression. He believed in the principle of laissez-faire—that government should interfere as little as possible in the nation's economy. As the situation worsened, the administration did take a few steps, such as borrowing money to pay off government debts. These steps had little effect on the economic crisis, however. The depression lasted for about six years. The laborers, farmers, and small businesspeople who had enthusiastically supported Jackson now turned against President Van Buren. 💲

The Whigs Come to Power

★ The Democrats had controlled the presidency for 12 years. However, with the country still in the depths of depression, the Whigs thought they had a chance to win the election in 1840. They nominated **William Henry Harrison,** a hero of the War of 1812, to run against President Van Buren. **John Tyler,** a planter from

Virginia, was Harrison's running mate. Because Harrison had gained national fame defeating Tecumseh's followers in the Battle of Tippecanoe, the Whigs' campaign slogan was "Tippecanoe and Tyler too."

The Election of 1840

To win the election, Harrison had to gain the support of the laborers and farmers who had voted for Jackson. The Whigs adopted a log cabin as their symbol. Political cartoons appeared in newspapers showing Harrison, a wealthy man from an upper-class Virginia family, in front of a log cabin. The Whigs wanted to show that their candidate was a "man of the people."

The Whigs also ridiculed Van Buren as "King Martin," a wealthy snob who had spent the people's money on fancy furniture for the White House. The log cabin campaign seemed to work, and Harrison went on to defeat Van Buren by a wide margin.

Disappointment in Office

William Henry Harrison was inaugurated in 1841 as the first Whig president. The Whigs were still celebrating their victory four weeks later, when Harrison died of pneumonia. John Tyler of Virginia became the first vice president to gain the presidency because the elected president died in office.

★ **Picturing HISTORY** In this political cartoon, President Jackson tries to kill the bank-serpent before it destroys him. **Why did Jackson oppose the Bank of the United States?**

★ ★

★ Picturing HISTORY In the 1840 election campaign, the Whigs marched in street parades, often carrying miniature log cabins on poles. **Why did Harrison's supporters make the log cabin their symbol?**

William Henry Harrison

Miniature log cabin

Although Tyler had been elected vice president as a Whig, he had once been a Democrat. As president, Tyler disagreed with many Whig policies. A strong supporter of states' rights and an independent thinker, Tyler quickly vetoed several bills sponsored by Whigs in Congress, including a bill to recharter the Bank of the United States. His lack of party loyalty outraged Whigs. Most of Tyler's cabinet resigned, and Whig leaders in Congress expelled Tyler from the party.

It seemed that the Whigs could not agree on their party's goals. Increasingly, Whigs voted according to sectional ties—North, South, and West—not party ties. This division may explain why the Whig candidate, Henry Clay, lost the election of 1844 to Democratic candidate **James Polk.** After only four years, the Whigs were out of power again.

★ ★ ★ ★ ★ **Section 4 Assessment** ★ ★ ★ ★ ★

Checking for Understanding

1. **Identify** Nicholas Biddle, Henry Clay, Daniel Webster, Martin Van Buren, Whigs, Panic of 1837, William Henry Harrison, James Polk.
2. **Define** veto, depression, laissez-faire, log cabin campaign.
3. **List** Jackson's reasons for wanting to "kill" the Bank of the United States.

Reviewing Themes

4. **Economic Factors** Why did President Van Buren do little to solve the nation's economic problems caused by the depression?

Critical Thinking

5. **Evaluating Information** What tactics did the Whigs borrow from Jackson's campaign to win the election of 1840?

Activity

Designing a Campaign Button Write a campaign slogan for Van Buren or Harrison in the election of 1840. Then design a campaign button that incorporates your slogan.

Assessment and Activities

★ Reviewing Key Terms

On a sheet of paper, use each of the following terms in a sentence:

favorite son
majority
plurality
mudslinging
landslide
suffrage
spoils system
nominating convention
nullify
secede
states' rights
depression
laissez-faire

★ Reviewing Key Facts

1. How did the supporters of Jackson and Adams differ in their beliefs?
2. Which Americans were prohibited from voting in most states before the 1800s?
3. How did nominating conventions make the selection of political candidates more democratic?
4. What did the government promise Native Americans in exchange for their land?
5. Why was Harrison's log cabin campaign successful?

★ Critical Thinking

Recognizing Bias

President Andrew Jackson promised "equal protection and equal benefits" for all Americans.
1. Who were the "Americans" that he was referring to?
2. Do you think he considered Indians to be Americans? Why or why not?

★ Reviewing Themes

1. **Continuity and Change** How have United States voters' rights been expanded since the 1800s?
2. **Government and Democracy** How did President Jackson justify his use of the spoils system?
3. **Groups and Institutions** What agreement did the Cherokee Nation make with the federal government that Georgia refused to recognize?
4. **Economic Factors** What did Andrew Jackson do after he was elected president in 1832 to "kill" the Bank of the United States?

★ Skill Practice Activity

Analyzing Primary Sources

In an annual message to Congress in 1835, President Andrew Jackson spoke the words below. Read the excerpt, then answer the questions that follow.

❝All preceding experiments for the improvement of the Indians have failed. It seems now to be an established fact that they cannot live in contact with a civilized community and prosper. . . . A country West of Missouri and Arkansas has been assigned to them, into which the white settlements are not to be pushed. **❞**

1. Whose opinion is stated in the excerpt?
2. When and on what occasion were these words spoken?
3. What is the speaker's attitude toward the Indians?
4. According to the speaker, why should the Indians be assigned to a country west of Missouri and Arkansas?

⭐ Geography Activity

Study the map below and answer the questions that follow.

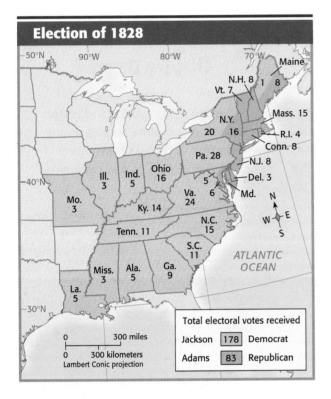

Election of 1828

Total electoral votes received
Jackson 178 Democrat
Adams 83 Republican

0 300 miles
0 300 kilometers
Lambert Conic projection

1. **Region** Which general areas of the United States voted for Andrew Jackson in the election of 1828?
2. **Location** Which candidate won more votes in Adams's home state of Massachusetts?
3. **Place** Which three states divided their total electoral count between the two candidates?

⭐ Cooperative Activity

History and Geography With the members of your group, research and compare the geography of the southeastern United States to that of Oklahoma—the Indian Territory. Use your research to create a how-to booklet that will tell the Cherokee and other Native Americans who were forced from their homes what they will find in this new region.

⭐ Technology Activity

Using a Word Processor Search historical references to find an event that occurred in another part of the world during the time Andrew Jackson was president of the United States. On your word processor, write a headline that might have appeared at the time to describe the event. Then in a paragraph, answer the five "W" questions about the event: Who is it about? What is it about? When did it happen? Where did it happen? Why did it happen?

⭐ Time Line Activity

Create a time line on which you place the following events in chronological order.
- Congress passes the Indian Removal Act
- Harrison is elected president
- Andrew Jackson is elected president
- John Quincy Adams becomes president
- Cherokee walk the Trail of Tears
- South Carolina threatens to secede

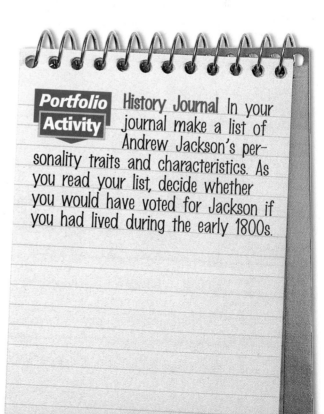

Portfolio Activity History Journal In your journal make a list of Andrew Jackson's personality traits and characteristics. As you read your list, decide whether you would have voted for Jackson if you had lived during the early 1800s.

1818–1853

Manifest Destiny

★ Why It's Important

The tremendous expansion during the first half of the 1800s left a lasting imprint on the United States. It transformed the shape of the nation—and the national character. Thousands of pioneers moved west, adding their struggles and triumphs to the American story. At the same time, the Native Americans and Spanish-speaking peoples of the West became part of the United States. They made their own contributions to the American character.

★ Chapter Themes

■ *Section 1,* Economic Factors
■ *Section 2,* Geography and History
■ *Section 3,* Culture and Traditions
■ *Section 4,* Global Connections
■ *Section 5,* Groups and Institutions

PRIMARY SOURCES
Library *See pages 958–959 for primary source readings to accompany Chapter 12*

★ **HISTORY AND ART** *Advice on the Prairie* by William T. Ranney Ranney was a leading painter of the American frontier during the mid-1800s. Many of his works show pioneers crossing the vast, empty West.

1819
Adams-Onís
Treaty is signed

1836
Marcus Whitman
builds mission
in Oregon

1840s
"Oregon fever"
sweeps through
Mississippi
Valley

1846
U.S. and Britain
set the Oregon
boundary at 49°N

Section 1

The Oregon Country

READ TO DISCOVER . . .
■ why large numbers of settlers headed for
  the Oregon country.
■ how the idea of Manifest Destiny contributed to the growth of the United States.

TERMS TO LEARN
joint occupation   emigrant
mountain man   Manifest Destiny
rendezvous

The Storyteller

On an April morning in 1851, 13-year-old
Martha Gay said good-bye to her friends, her
home, and the familiar world of Springfield,
Missouri. She and her family were beginning
a long, hazardous journey. The townsfolk
watched as the Gays left in four big wagons
pulled by teams of oxen. "Farewell sermons
were preached and prayers offered for our
safety," Martha wrote years later. "All
places of business and the school
were closed . . . and everybody
came to say good-bye to us."
This same scene occurred
many times in the 1840s
and 1850s as thousands
of families set out for
the Oregon country.

Doll owned by a
young pioneer

The **Oregon country** was the huge area that
lay between the Pacific Ocean and the
Rocky Mountains north of **California.** It included all of what is now Oregon, Washington,
and Idaho plus parts of Montana and Wyoming.
The region also contained about half of what became the Canadian province of British Columbia.

Geography

Rivalry in the Northwest

★ In the early 1800s, four nations laid claim to
the vast, rugged land known as the Oregon
country. The United States based its claim on
Robert Gray's discovery of the **Columbia River**
in 1792 and on the Lewis and Clark expedition.
Great Britain based its claim on British explorations of the Columbia River. Spain, which had
also explored the Pacific coast in the late 1700s,
controlled California to the south. Russia had settlements that stretched south from **Alaska** into
Oregon.

Many Americans wanted control of the Oregon country to gain access to the Pacific Ocean.
Secretary of State **John Quincy Adams** played a
key role in promoting this goal. In 1819 he negotiated the **Adams-Onís Treaty** with Spain. In the
treaty the Spanish agreed to set the limits of their
territory at what is now California's northern border and gave up any claim to Oregon. In 1824
Russia also surrendered its claim to the land
south of Alaska. Only Britain remained to challenge American control of Oregon.

In 1818 Adams had worked out an agreement with Britain for joint occupation of the area. This meant that people from both the United States and Great Britain could settle there. When Adams became president in 1825, he proposed that the two nations divide Oregon along the 49° line of latitude. Britain refused, insisting on a larger share of the territory. Unable to resolve their dispute, the two countries agreed to extend the joint occupation. In the following years, thousands of Americans streamed into Oregon, and they pushed the issue toward settlement. 🌐

Mountain Men

⭐ The first Americans to reach the Oregon country were not farmers but fur traders. They had come to trap beaver, whose skins were in great demand in the eastern United States and in Europe. The British established several trading posts in the region, as did American merchant **John Jacob Astor.**

At first the merchants traded for furs that the Native Americans supplied. Gradually American adventurers joined the trade. These people, who spent most of their time in the Rocky Mountains, came to be known as mountain men.

Traders and Trappers

The tough, independent mountain men made their living by trapping beaver. Many had Native American wives and adopted Native American

ways. They lived in buffalo-skin lodges and dressed in fringed buckskin pants, moccasins, and beads.

Some mountain men worked for fur-trading companies; others sold their furs to the highest bidder. Whatever the arrangement, they spent most of the year alone in the wild. Throughout the spring and early summer, they ranged across the mountains, setting traps and then collecting the beaver pelts. In late summer they gathered for a rendezvous (RAHN•dih•VOO), or meeting.

For the mountain men, the annual rendezvous was the high point of the year. They met with the trading companies to exchange their "hairy banknotes"—beaver skins—for traps, guns, coffee, and other goods. They spent what cash they received on food and drink or on ornaments for their wives and children. They met old friends and exchanged news. They relaxed by competing in races and other contests—including swapping stories about who had the most exciting adventures.

From Trappers to Guides

As they roamed far and wide searching for beaver, the mountain men explored the mountains, valleys, and trails of the West. **Jim Beckwourth,** an African American from Virginia, explored Wyoming's Green River. Robert Stuart and Jedediah Smith both found the **South Pass,** a broad break through the Rockies. South Pass later became the main route that settlers took to Oregon.

To survive in the wilderness, a mountain man had to be skillful and resourceful. Trapper Joe Meek told how, when faced with starvation, he once held his hands "in an anthill until they were covered with ants, then greedily licked them off." The mountain men took pride in joking about the dangers they faced.

In time the mountain men killed off most of the beaver and could no longer trap. Some went to settle on farms in Oregon. With their knowledge of the western lands, though, some mountain men found new work. Jim Bridger, Kit Carson, and others acted as guides to lead the parties of settlers now streaming west.

Buckskin jacket

Beaded pouch

 Encampment on Green River by Alfred Jacob Miller Miller's painting shows a rendezvous on the Green River in Wyoming. **What was the purpose of a rendezvous?**

Settling Oregon

Americans began traveling to the Oregon country to settle in the 1830s. Reports of the fertile land persuaded many to make the journey. Economic troubles at home made new opportunities in the West look attractive.

The Whitman Mission

Among the first settlers of the Oregon country were missionaries who wanted to bring Christianity to the Native Americans. Dr. Marcus Whitman and his wife, Narcissa, went to Oregon in 1836 and built a mission among the Cayuse people near the present site of Walla Walla, Washington.

New settlers unknowingly brought measles to the mission. An epidemic killed many of the Indian children. Blaming the Whitmans for the sickness, the Cayuse attacked the mission in November 1847 and killed them and 12 others. Despite this tragedy the flood of settlers continued.

The Oregon Trail

In the early 1840s, "Oregon fever" began to sweep through the towns of the Mississippi Valley. People formed societies to gather information about Oregon and to plan and make the long journey.

The first large-scale migration took place in 1843, when 120 wagons carrying more than 1,000 pioneers left Independence, Missouri, for Oregon. In the years that followed, tens of thousands of Americans made the trip. These pioneers were called emigrants because they left the United States to go to Oregon.

To reach Oregon these pioneers undertook a difficult 2,000-mile journey. Gathering in Independence or other towns in Missouri, they followed the **Oregon Trail** across the Great Plains along the Platte River and through the South Pass of the Rocky Mountains. On the other side, they took the trail north and west along the Snake and Columbia Rivers into the Oregon country.

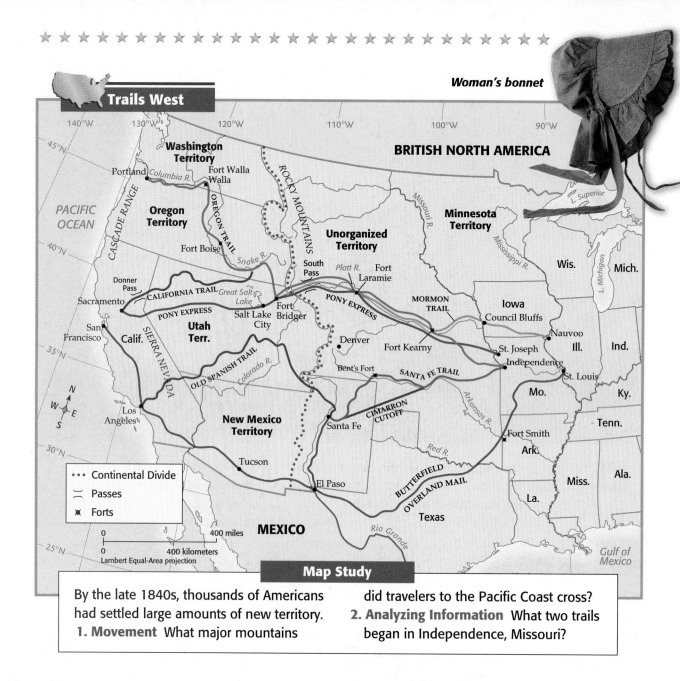

Trails West

Woman's bonnet

BRITISH NORTH AMERICA

Washington Territory

Portland · *Columbia R.* · Fort Walla Walla

ROCKY MOUNTAINS

PACIFIC OCEAN

CASCADE RANGE

Oregon Territory

OREGON TRAIL

Fort Boise

Snake R.

Minnesota Territory

Unorganized Territory

Missouri R.

Mississippi R.

L. Superior

Wis.

L. Michigan

Mich.

South Pass

Platt R. Fort Laramie

Donner Pass

CALIFORNIA TRAIL *Great Salt Lake*

Sacramento

PONY EXPRESS

PONY EXPRESS

MORMON TRAIL

Iowa

Council Bluffs

Salt Lake City

Fort Bridger

San Francisco

Calif.

SIERRA NEVADA

Utah Terr.

Denver

Fort Kearny

St. Joseph

Nauvoo

Ill.

Ind.

Independence

St. Louis

OLD SPANISH TRAIL

Colorado R.

Bent's Fort

SANTA FE TRAIL

Mo.

Ky.

Los Angeles

New Mexico Territory

Santa Fe

CIMARRON CUTOFF

Arkansas R.

Fort Smith

Tenn.

Tucson

Red R.

Ark.

El Paso

BUTTERFIELD OVERLAND MAIL

Miss.

Ala.

La.

MEXICO

Texas

Rio Grande

Gulf of Mexico

··· Continental Divide
≍ Passes
✳ Forts

0   400 miles
0   400 kilometers
Lambert Equal-Area projection

N W E S

Map Study

By the late 1840s, thousands of Americans had settled large amounts of new territory.
1. Movement What major mountains did travelers to the Pacific Coast cross?
2. Analyzing Information What two trails began in Independence, Missouri?

Life on the Trail

The journey lasted five or six months. The pioneers had to start in the spring and complete the trip before winter snows blocked the mountain passes. They usually traveled in large groups, often of related families. They stuffed their canvas-covered wagons, called **prairie schooners,** with supplies and everything they owned. From a distance, these wagons looked like schooners (ships) at sea. Most people walked alongside the wagons. Only pregnant women, sick people, and very old or very young people rode in the wagons.

The trail crossed difficult terrain. The pioneers walked across seemingly endless plains, forded swift rivers, and labored up high mountains. One man described crossing the Platte River in Nebraska:

> ❝A more foaming mad[d]ening river I never saw . . . and the water the color of soapsuds you cannot see the bottom where it is not more than six inches deep. ❞

If families fell behind on the trail or faced a very steep climb, they sometimes decided to lighten their wagons. They would unload a piece of furniture or a family treasure and sadly abandon it at the side of the trail.

Everyone worked hard. Men drove the wagons, tended the animals, and hunted. Women, after walking all day, had more work to do at night. They cared for the children and cooked the meals. They carried on with their chores in all kinds of weather. Making bread in the rain, a woman kneaded her dough, then "watched and nursed the fire and held an umbrella over the fire and her skill[e]t . . . for near two hours."

The pioneers' food supplies often ran low. Fresh water always had to be conserved. The pioneers might not launder their clothes more than two or three times during the entire trip.

At night the travelers arranged their wagons in a square or circle for protection, with the people and horses on the inside. Although the pioneers feared attacks by Native Americans, such attacks rarely occurred. More often Native Americans assisted the pioneers, serving as guides and trading necessary food and supplies. Most of the emigrants who died on the trail perished from disease, overwork, hunger, or accidents.

The Division of Oregon

Most pioneers headed for the fertile **Willamette Valley** south of the Columbia River. Between 1840 and 1845, the number of American settlers in the area increased from 500 to 5,000, while the British population remained at about 700. The question of ownership of Oregon arose again.

Expansion of Freedom

Since colonial times many Americans had believed their nation had a special role to fulfill. For years people thought the nation's mission should be to serve as a model of freedom and democracy.

In the 1800s that vision changed. Many believed that the United States's mission was to spread freedom by occupying the entire continent. In 1819 John Quincy Adams expressed what many Americans were thinking when he called expansion to the Pacific a "law of nature," saying it was as inevitable "as that the Mississippi should flow to the sea."

Manifest Destiny

In the 1840s New York newspaper editor John O'Sullivan put the idea of a national mission in more specific words. O'Sullivan declared it was America's "manifest destiny to overspread and to possess the whole of the continent which Providence has given us." O'Sullivan meant that the United States was clearly destined—set apart for

HISTORY AND ART *The Pioneers* by **William T. Ranney** Emigrants in search of a better life headed west in large numbers during the mid-1800s. **Why were emigrants attracted to Oregon?**

Chest of clothing

James K. Polk

Henry Clay

James K. Polk received the Democratic Party's nomination for president, partly because he supported American claims for sole ownership of Oregon. Democrats campaigned using the slogan "Fifty-four Forty or Fight." The slogan referred to the line of latitude that Democrats believed should be the nation's northern border in Oregon.

Henry Clay of the Whig Party, Polk's principal opponent, did not take a strong position on the Oregon issue. Polk won 50 percent of the popular vote and 170 electoral votes to Clay's 48 percent and 105 electoral votes.

a special purpose—to extend its boundaries all the way to the Pacific. This idea of a national mission gained widespread support by 1844 and played a role in that year's presidential election.

"Fifty-four Forty or Fight"

The settlers in Oregon insisted that the United States should have sole ownership of the area. More and more Americans agreed. As a result Oregon became an issue in the 1844 presidential election.

Reaching a Settlement

Filled with the spirit of Manifest Destiny, President Polk was determined to make Oregon part of the United States. Britain would not accept a border at "Fifty-four Forty," however. To do so would have meant giving up its claim entirely. Instead, in June 1846, the two countries compromised, setting the boundary between the American and British portions of Oregon at latitude 49°. The two nations had finally resolved the Oregon issue.

During the 1830s Americans sought to fulfill their Manifest Destiny by looking much closer to home than Oregon. Much attention at that time also focused on Texas.

★ ★ ★ ★ ★ Section 1 Assessment ★ ★ ★ ★ ★

Checking for Understanding

1. *Identify* John Quincy Adams, Oregon Trail, James K. Polk, Henry Clay.
2. *Define* joint occupation, mountain man, rendezvous, emigrant, Manifest Destiny.
3. *Name* the four countries that laid claim to the Oregon country.

Reviewing Themes

4. **Economic Factors** How did the fur trade in Oregon aid Americans who began settling there?

Critical Thinking

5. **Analyzing Information** How did the notion of Manifest Destiny help Americans justify their desire to extend the United States to the Pacific Ocean?

 Activity

Writing a Letter Imagine you are traveling with your family to the Oregon country in the 1840s. A friend will be making the same trip soon. Write a letter telling your friend what to expect on the journey.

Understanding Latitude and Longitude

Mapmakers use lines of latitude and longitude to pinpoint locations on maps and globes.

Learning the Skill

The imaginary horizontal lines that circle the globe from east to west are called lines of **latitude.** Because the distance between the lines of latitude is always the same, they are also called *parallels.* The imaginary vertical lines that intersect the parallels are lines of **longitude,** also called *meridians.*

Parallels and meridians are numbered in degrees. The Equator, located halfway between the North and South Poles, is at 0°. Moving north or south of the Equator, the number of degrees increases until reaching 90°N or S latitude at the poles.

The Prime Meridian is 0° longitude. Moving east or west of the Prime Meridian, the number of degrees east or west increases up to 180°. The 180° line of longitude is located on the opposite side of the globe from the Prime Meridian and is called the *International Date Line.*

The point at which parallels and meridians intersect is the grid address, or coordinates, of an exact location. The coordinates for Salt Lake City, for example, are 41°N and 112°W.

Practicing the Skill

Analyze the information on the map on this page, then answer the following questions.

1. What are the approximate coordinates of Fort Victoria?
2. At what line of latitude was the Oregon country divided between the United States and Britain?
3. What geographic feature lies at about 42°N and 109°W?

Oregon Country

Alaska (Claimed by Russia)

British North America

Area settled by 1840

54°40'N

50°N
49°N

Vancouver Island

Oregon

Fort Victoria ✖

Boundary (1846) Boundary (1818)

Country

PACIFIC OCEAN

Astoria
Fort Vancouver

Columbia River

Missouri R.

United States

Champoeg

Yellowstone R.

Willamette R.

42°N

Snake R.

South Pass

OREGON TRAIL

40°N

Mexico

Great Salt Lake

Salt Lake City

0   400 miles
0   400 kilometers
Albers Equal-Area projection

N W E S

Applying the Skill

Understanding Latitude and Longitude
Turn to the Atlas map of the United States on pages RA6 and RA7. Find your city or the city closest to it. What are its coordinates? Now list the coordinates of five other cities and ask a classmate to find the cities based on your coordinates.

GO TO

Glencoe's **Skillbuilder Interactive Workbook, Level 1** provides instruction and practice in key social studies skills.

1820		1830			1840

1821
Moses Austin receives
land grant in Texas

1833
Santa Anna
becomes president
of Mexico

March 1836
The Alamo falls
to Mexican troops

September 1836
Sam Houston is
elected president
of Texas

Section 2

Independence for Texas

READ TO DISCOVER . . .

- why problems arose between the Mexican government and the American settlers in Texas.
- how Texas achieved independence from Mexico and later became a state.

TERMS TO LEARN

Tejano   decree
empresario   annex

The Storyteller

Davy Crockett was a backwoodsman from Tennessee. His skill as a hunter and storyteller helped get him elected to three terms in Congress. But when he started his first political campaign, Crockett was doubtful about his chances of winning. "The thought of having to make a speech made my knees feel mighty weak and set my heart to fluttering." Fortunately for Crockett, the other candidates spoke all day and tired out the audience. "When they were all done," Crockett boasted, "I got up and told some laughable story, and quit. . . . I went home, and didn't go back again till after the election was over." In the end, Crockett won the election by a wide margin.

Davy Crockett

Davy Crockett of Tennessee won notice for his frontier skills, his sense of humor, and the shrewd common sense he often displayed in politics. When he lost his seat in Congress in 1835, he did not return to Tennessee. Instead he went southwest to Texas.

Crockett thought he could get a new start there. He also wanted to give the Texans "a helping hand on the high road to freedom"—winning their independence from Mexico. Little did he know his deeds in Texas would bring him greater fame than his adventures on the frontier or his years in Congress.

A Clash of Cultures

⭐ Conflict over Texas began in 1803, when the United States bought the Louisiana Territory from France. Americans claimed that the land in present-day Texas was part of the purchase. Spain protested. In 1819, in the **Adams-Onís Treaty**, the United States agreed to drop any further claim to the region.

Land Grants

At the time, few people lived in Texas. Some settlers came from the United States. Most residents—about 3,000—were Tejanos (teh•HAH•nohs), or Mexicans who claimed Texas as their home. Native Americans from the North also ventured into the area.

Because the Spanish wanted to promote the growth of Texas, they offered vast tracts of land to people who agreed to bring families to settle on the land. The people who arranged for these settlements were called **empresarios.**

Moses Austin heard about the Spanish plan. Austin, who had made a fortune in lead mining in Missouri, applied for and received the first land grant in 1821.

Americans Move In

Before Moses Austin could establish his colony, however, Mexico declared its independence from Spain. Austin died while waiting for the new Mexican government to confirm his land grant. The confirmation went instead to his son, **Stephen F. Austin,** who began to organize the colony.

Stephen F. Austin recruited 300 American families to settle the fertile land along the **Brazos River** and the **Colorado River** of Texas. He picked his settlers carefully, and they came to be called the **Old Three Hundred.** These first families received 960 acres, with additional acres for each child. Austin's success made him a leader among the American settlers in Texas.

From 1823 to 1825, Mexico passed three colonization laws. All these laws offered new settlers large tracts of land at extremely low prices and no taxes for four years. In return the colonists agreed to learn Spanish, convert to Catholicism—the religion of Mexico—and obey Mexican law.

Mexican leaders hoped to attract settlers from all over, including other parts of Mexico. Most Texas settlers, however, came from the United States.

Growing Tension

By 1830 Americans in Texas far outnumbered Mexicans. Further, these American colonists had not adopted Mexican ways. In the meantime the United States had twice offered to buy Texas from Mexico.

The Mexican government viewed the growing American influence in Texas with alarm. In 1830 the Mexican government issued a **decree,** or official order, that stopped all immigration from the United States. At the same time, the decree

encouraged the immigration of Mexican and European families with generous land grants. Trade between Texas and the United States was discouraged by placing a tax on goods imported from the United States.

These new policies angered the Texans. The prosperity of many citizens depended on trade with the United States. Many had friends and relatives who wanted to come to Texas. In addition, those colonists who held slaves were uneasy about the Mexican government's plans to end slavery.

Stephen F. Austin

Attempt at Reconciliation

Some of the American settlers called for independence. Others hoped to stay within Mexico but on better terms. In 1833 **General Antonio López de Santa Anna** became president of Mexico. Stephen F. Austin traveled to Mexico City with the Texans' demands—to remove the ban on American settlers and to make Texas a separate state.

Santa Anna agreed to the first request but refused the second. Austin sent a letter back to Texas, suggesting that plans for independence get under way. The Mexican government intercepted the letter and arrested Austin.

While Austin was in jail, Santa Anna named himself dictator and overthrew Mexico's constitution of 1824. Without a constitution to protect their rights, Texans felt betrayed. Santa Anna reorganized the government, placing greater central control over the regions—including Texas. This loss of local power dismayed many people.

The Struggle for Independence

⭐ During 1835 unrest grew among Texans and occasionally resulted in open conflict. Santa Anna sent an army into Texas late that year

★ **Picturing HISTORY** This painting depicts the last moments of the Battle of the Alamo, before the remaining Texans were finally forced to surrender. **What three noted Western leaders fought for Texas at the Alamo?**

to punish the rebels. Some Mexican troops tried in October to seize a cannon held by Texans at the town of **Gonzales.** During the battle the Texans decorated the front of the cannon with a white flag that bore the words "Come and Take It." After a brief struggle, Texans drove back the Mexican troops. Texans consider this the first fight of the Texan Revolution.

Early Victories

The Texans called on volunteers to join their fight. They offered free land to anyone who would help. Davy Crockett and many others—including a number of African Americans and Tejanos—answered that call.

In December 1835, the Texans scored an important victory. They liberated **San Antonio** from the control of a larger Mexican force. The Mexicans retreated to the other side of the Rio Grande.

Despite these victories, the Texans encountered problems. With the Mexican withdrawal, some Texans left San Antonio, thinking the war was won. Various groups argued over who was in charge and what course of action to follow. In early 1836, when Texas should have been making preparations to face Santa Anna, nothing was being done.

🔍 **Eyewitness to HISTORY**

The Battle of the Alamo

Santa Anna marched north, furious at the loss of San Antonio. When his army reached San Antonio in late February 1836, it found a small Texan force barricaded inside a nearby mission called **the Alamo.**

Although the Texans had cannons, they lacked gunpowder. Worse, they had only about 150 soldiers to face Santa Anna's army of several thousand. The Texans did have brave leaders, though, including Davy Crockett, who had arrived with a band of sharpshooters from Tennessee, and a tough Texan named Jim Bowie. The commander, William B. Travis, was only 25 years old, but he was determined to hold his position.

Travis managed to send messages out through Mexican lines. In a now famous letter of February 24, 1836, Travis wrote:

❝ The enemy has demanded surrender. . . . I have answered that demand with a cannon shot, and our flag still waves proudly from the walls. *I shall never surrender or retreat. . . . Victory or Death!* ❞

For 12 long days, the defenders of the Alamo kept Santa Anna's army at bay with rifle fire. The Mexicans launched two assaults but had to break them off. During the siege, 32 volunteers from Gonzales slipped through the Mexican lines to join the Alamo's defenders.

They were too few, however. Davy Crockett's journal entry for March 3 read:

> ❝We have given over all hopes of receiving assistance. . . . Colonel Travis harangued [commanded] the garrison . . . to fight to the last gasp. . . . This was followed by three cheers. ❞

On March 6, 1836, Mexican cannon fire smashed the Alamo's walls, and the Mexicans launched an all-out attack. The Alamo defenders killed many Mexican soldiers as they crossed open land and tried to mount the Alamo's walls. The Mexicans were too numerous to hold back, however, and they finally entered the fortress, killing William Travis, Davy Crockett, Jim Bowie, and all the other defenders. Only a few women and children and some servants survived to tell of the battle.

In the words of Santa Anna's aide, "The Texans fought more like devils than like men." The defenders of the Alamo had killed hundreds of Mexican soldiers. But more important, they had bought Texans some much needed time.

Texas Declares Its Independence

During the siege of the Alamo, Texan leaders were meeting at Washington-on-the-Brazos, where they were drawing up a new constitution. There, on March 2, 1836—four days before the fall of the Alamo—American settlers and Tejanos firmly declared the independence of the Republic of Texas.

Sam Houston Leads the Fight

The provisional government of the new republic named **Sam Houston** as commander in chief of the Texas forces. Houston had come to Texas in 1833. Raised among the Cherokee people, he became a soldier, fighting with Andrew Jackson against the Creek people. A politician as well, Houston had served in Congress and as governor of Tennessee.

Houston wanted to prevent other forts from being overrun by the Mexicans. He ordered the troops at **Goliad** to abandon their position. As they retreated, however, they came face to face with Mexican troops. After a fierce fight, several hundred Texans surrendered. On Santa Anna's orders, the Texans were executed a few days later. This action outraged Texans, who called it the "Goliad Massacre."

Texas War for Independence, 1835–1836

Map Study

In 1836 General Santa Anna led Mexico's main forces across the Rio Grande into Texas.
1. **Location** At which places did Texans win victories?
2. **Analyzing Information** What battle immediately followed the Alamo?

★ Picturing HISTORY This painting shows San Antonio in the late 1840s, after Texas had become part of the United States. **Why was the admission of Texas to the Union delayed for several years?**

The Battle of San Jacinto

Houston moved his small army eastward about 100 miles, watching the movements of Santa Anna and waiting for a chance to strike. Six weeks after the Alamo, he found the opportunity.

America's FLAGS

Texas Republic, 1839 For its first six years, this Lone Star flag symbolized the independent nation of the Republic of Texas. Texans kept the Lone Star banner as their official state flag after joining the Union in 1845.

After adding some new troops, Houston gathered an army of about 800 at **San Jacinto** (SAN huh•SIN•tuh), near the site of present-day Houston. Santa Anna was camped nearby with an army of more than 1,300. On April 21 the Texans launched a surprise attack on the Mexican camp, shouting, "Remember the Alamo! Remember Goliad!" They killed more than 600 soldiers and captured about 700 more—including Santa Anna. On May 14, 1836, Santa Anna signed a treaty that recognized the independence of Texas.

The Lone Star Republic

★ Texans elected Sam Houston as their president in September 1836. He sent a delegation to Washington, D.C., asking the United States to annex—take control of—Texas. President Andrew Jackson refused, however, because the addition of another slave state would upset the balance of slave and free states in Congress.

General Sam Houston

For the moment Texas would remain an independent country.

Despite rapid population growth, the new republic faced political and financial difficulties. The Mexican government refused to honor Santa Anna's recognition of independence, and fighting continued between Texas and Mexico. In addition Texas had an enormous debt of $7 million and no money to repay it.

The Annexation Debate

Many Texans still hoped to join the United States. Southerners favored the annexation of Texas, but Northerners objected that Texas would add another slave state to the Union. President Martin Van Buren, like Jackson, did not want to inflame the slavery issue or risk war with Mexico. He put off the question of annexing Texas.

John Tyler, who became president in 1841, supported adding Texas to the Union and persuaded Texas to reapply for annexation. However, the Senate was divided over slavery and failed to ratify the annexation treaty.

Texas Becomes a State

The situation changed with the 1844 presidential campaign. The feeling of Manifest Destiny was growing throughout the country.

The South favored annexation of Texas. The North demanded that the United States gain control of the Oregon country from Britain. The Democratic candidate, James K. Polk, supported both actions. The Whig candidate, Henry Clay, initially opposed adding Texas to the Union. When he finally came out for annexation, it lost him votes in the North—and the election.

After Polk's victory, supporters of annexation pressed the issue in Congress. They proposed and passed a resolution to annex Texas. On December 29, 1845, Texas officially became a state of the United States.

Section 2 Assessment

Checking for Understanding

1. **Identify** Davy Crockett, Stephen F. Austin, the Alamo, Sam Houston, John Tyler.
2. **Define** Tejano, empresario, decree, annex.
3. **Name** the three things that American settlers agreed to do in exchange for receiving land in Texas.

Reviewing Themes

4. **Geography and History** Why did Northerners and Southerners disagree on the annexation of Texas?

Critical Thinking

5. **Predicting Consequences** Why did Mexico's plan to colonize Texas backfire?

Activity

Creating an Advertisement Imagine you are Stephen Austin and you are recruiting settlers to colonize Texas. Draw an advertisement that would attract American settlers.

1820
Twenty-one missions exist in California

1821
William Becknell reaches Santa Fe

1840s
Americans settle in California

1845
President Polk offers to buy California and New Mexico

Section 3

New Mexico and California

READ TO DISCOVER . . .

- why Americans began to settle in the Southwest after Mexican independence.
- why California became a source of conflict between the United States and Mexico.

TERMS TO LEARN

rancho   ranchero

The Storyteller

Long lines of covered wagons stretched as far as the eye could see. "All's set!" a driver called out. "All's set!" everyone shouted in reply.

"Then the 'Heps!' of drivers—the cracking of whips—the trampling of feet—the occasional creak of wheels—the rumbling of wagons—form a new scene of [intense] confusion," reported Josiah Gregg. Gregg was one of the traders who traveled west on the Santa Fe Trail in the 1830s to sell cloth, knives, and other goods in New Mexico.

Wagon wheel

I n the early 1800s, **New Mexico** was the name of a vast region sandwiched between the Texas and California territories. It included all of present-day New Mexico, Arizona, and Nevada and parts of Colorado and Utah.

The New Mexico Territory

Native American peoples had lived in the area for thousands of years. Spanish conquistadors began exploring there in the late 1500s and made it part of Spain's colony of Mexico. In 1609 the Spanish founded the settlement of **Santa Fe.** Missionaries followed soon after.

When Mexico won its independence in 1821, it inherited the New Mexico province from Spain. The Mexicans, however, had little control over the distant province. The inhabitants of New Mexico mostly governed themselves.

The Spanish had tried to keep Americans away from Santa Fe, fearing that Americans would want to take over the area. The Mexican government changed this policy, welcoming American traders into New Mexico. It hoped that the trade would boost the economy of the province.

🌐 Geography

The Santa Fe Trail

William Becknell, the first American trader to reach Santa Fe, arrived in 1821 with a pack of mules laden with goods. Becknell sold the

Mexican American Cowhand

Silver-inlaid spurs

Riding whip, religious medal, blanket, and knife

What Was It Like?
Vaqueros in a Horse Corral by James Walker shows a typical day on a ranch in the Southwest. What do the objects shown here reveal about the kind of work vaqueros did?

Vaquero's hat

merchandise he brought for many times what he would have received for it in St. Louis.

Becknell's route came to be known as the **Santa Fe Trail.** The trail left the Missouri River near Independence, Missouri, and crossed the prairies to the Arkansas River. It followed the river west toward the Rocky Mountains before turning south into New Mexico Territory. Because the trail was mostly flat, Becknell used wagons to carry his merchandise on later trips.

Other traders followed Becknell, and the Santa Fe Trail became a busy trade route for hundreds of wagons. Americans brought textiles and firearms, which they exchanged in Santa Fe for silver, furs, and mules. The trail remained in use until the arrival of the railroad in 1880.

As trade with New Mexico increased, Americans began settling in the region. In the United States, the idea of Manifest Destiny captured the popular imagination, and many people saw New Mexico as territory worth acquiring. At the same time, they eyed another prize—the Mexican territory of California, which would provide access to the Pacific.

California's Spanish Culture

⭐ Spanish explorers and missionaries from Mexico had been the first Europeans to settle in California. In the 1760s Captain Gaspar de Portolá and Father Junípero Serra began building a string of missions that eventually extended from San Diego to San Francisco.

The Mission System

The mission system was a key part of Spain's plan to colonize California. The Spanish used the missions to convert Native Americans to Christianity. By 1820, 21 missions dotted California, with about 20,000 Native Americans living in them.

In 1820 American mountain man Jedediah Smith visited the San Gabriel Mission east of present-day Los Angeles. Smith reported that the Indians farmed thousands of acres and worked at weaving and other crafts. He described the missions as "large farming and grazing establishments." Another American in Smith's party called the Indians "slaves in every sense of the word."

★ ★

California after 1821

After Mexico gained its independence from Spain in 1821, **California** became a state in the new Mexican nation. At the time only a few hundred Spanish settlers lived in California, but emigrants began arriving from Mexico. The wealthier settlers lived on ranches devoted to raising cattle and horses.

In 1833 the Mexican government passed a law abolishing the missions. The government gave some of the lands to Native Americans and sold the remainder. Mexican settlers bought these lands and built huge properties called ranchos.

The Mexican settlers persuaded Native Americans to work their lands and tend their cattle in return for food and shelter. The California ranchos were similar to the plantations of the South, and the rancheros—ranch owners—treated Native American workers almost like slaves.

Americans Eye California

Americans had been visiting California for years. Most arrived on trading or whaling ships, although a few hardy travelers like Jedediah Smith came overland from the East. Soon more began to arrive.

At first the Mexican authorities welcomed Americans in California. The newcomers included agents for American shipping companies, fur traders from Oregon, and merchants from New Mexico. In the 1840s families began to arrive in California to settle. They made the long journey from Missouri on the Oregon Trail and then turned south after crossing the Rocky Mountains. Still, by 1845 the American population of California numbered only about 700. Most Americans lived in the Sacramento River valley.

Manifest Destiny and California

Some American travelers wrote glowing reports of California. **John C. Frémont,** an army officer who made several trips through California in the 1840s, wrote of the region's mild climate, scenic beauty, and abundant resources.

Americans began to talk about adding California to the nation. Shippers and manufacturers hoped to build ports on the Pacific coast for trade with China and Japan. Many Americans saw the advantage of extending United States territory to the Pacific. That way the nation would be safely bordered by the sea instead of by a foreign power.

In 1845 Secretary of War William Marcy wrote that "if the people [of California] should desire to unite their destiny with ours, they would be received as brethren [brothers]." Polk twice offered to buy California and New Mexico from Mexico, but Mexico refused. Before long the United States would take over both regions by force.

★ ★ ★ ★ ★   Section 3 Assessment   ★ ★ ★ ★ ★

Checking for Understanding

1. **Identify** William Becknell, Santa Fe Trail, John C. Frémont.
2. **Define** rancho, ranchero.
3. **Explain** why Mexico, at first, welcomed Americans to New Mexico.

Reviewing Themes

4. **Culture and Traditions** Why did the Spanish establish missions in the Southwest?

5. **Identifying Assumptions** State the hidden message in this statement: "If the people [of California] should desire to unite their destiny with ours, they would be received as brethren."

Activity

Creating a Picture Map Create an enlarged version of the map on page 358. Then add illustrations to tell the story of the Santa Fe Trail.

Traveling West

In the early 1800s many Americans believed that they would find their fortune on the frontier, even though the way west was long and dangerous. Imagine yourself as a pioneer as you complete these activities about traveling west.

Art

Picturing the West Painters and photographers were amazed by the spectacular scenery of the West. Research the work of painters such as Albert Bierstadt and Frederic Remington or photographers such as William H. Jackson or Ansel Adams. Then create your own painting or photograph that conveys the majestic scenery of the West.

Science

Keeping a Science Log Settlers traveling west encountered new wildlife, vegetation, and landforms. Some, like Lewis and Clark, wrote careful descriptions, drew sketches, and collected samples—feathers, bones, rocks. Choose one region of the West and investigate it as a traveling scientist would. List plants and animals you would see there. Draw sketches of characteristics such as leaves or pawprints. If possible, collect samples for your log. Write a "naturalist's report" to the class, summarizing what you have observed.

Music

Learning a Western Song Many classic American folk songs come from the Old West. Organize a group of classmates who sing or play guitar, banjo, or another instrument. Then learn the words and music to a traditional song such as "Red River Valley," "Shenandoah," or "Home on the Range." Plan a performance for your class.

School-to-Work

Building a Western Town Set designers for movies and television have made the typical Western town a familiar scene—a dusty main street with general store, saloon, corral, and a few houses. Imagine you are a set designer. Plan and build a model of a Western town to be used for constructing scenery for an upcoming movie. First design the layout of the town, then assemble small buildings out of wood or cardboard. Add shutters and colorful signboards. Paint the streets brown and sprinkle sand on the wet paint. Set up your town on a table in the classroom.

Miner with tools of the trade

1845	1846	1847	1848

1845
The United States annexes Texas

1846
Congress declares war on Mexico

1847
General Winfield Scott reaches Mexico City

1848
Treaty of Guadalupe Hidalgo signed

Section 4

War with Mexico

READ TO DISCOVER . . .

■ how the idea of Manifest Destiny contributed to the outbreak of war.

■ how the United States acquired New Mexico and California.

TERMS TO LEARN

Californios   cede

The Storyteller

John Kenly from Maryland had volunteered to fight in the Mexican War. He and other soldiers led by General Zachary Taylor attacked the Mexican city of Monterrey. Bright cannon fire lit up nearby mountains. As he advanced with the other troops, Kenly saw heavy fighting near the bishop's palace. In his diary, Kenly later wrote: "How my heart beat! For I felt that if they could carry the palace, the town was ours." The Americans pushed forward and entered the palace. The Mexican flag was lowered, and a mighty cheer erupted from American forces remaining on the plain below.

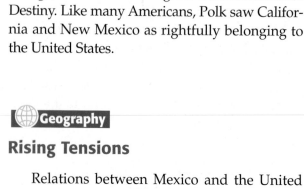

Case showing General Zachary Taylor

After Mexico refused to sell California and New Mexico, President **James K. Polk** plotted to pull the Mexican provinces into the Union through war. He wanted, however, to provoke Mexico into taking military action first. This way Polk could justify the war to Congress and the American people.

The Outbreak of the War

★ Polk was determined to get the California and New Mexico territories from Mexico. Their possession would guarantee that the United States had clear passage to the Pacific Ocean—an important consideration because the British still occupied part of Oregon. Polk's main reason, though, involved fulfilling the nation's Manifest Destiny. Like many Americans, Polk saw California and New Mexico as rightfully belonging to the United States.

🌐 Geography

Rising Tensions

Relations between Mexico and the United States had been strained for some years. When the United States annexed Texas in 1845, the situation worsened. Mexico, which had never recognized the independence of Texas, charged that the annexation was illegal.

Another dispute concerned the Texas-Mexico border. The United States insisted that the **Rio**

Grande formed the border. Mexico claimed that the border lay along the **Nueces** (nu•AY•suhs) **River**, 150 miles farther north. Because of this dispute, Mexico had stopped payments on the more than $2 million it owed to American citizens for losses suffered during outbreaks of fighting in Mexico.

Polk sent an agent, John Slidell, to Mexico to propose a deal. Slidell was authorized to offer $30 million for California and New Mexico in return for Mexico's acceptance of the Rio Grande as the Texas boundary. In addition, the United States would take over payment of Mexico's debts to American citizens.

The Mexican government refused to discuss the offer and announced its intention to reclaim Texas for Mexico. In response Polk ordered General **Zachary Taylor** to march his soldiers across the disputed borderland between the Nueces River and the Rio Grande. Taylor did so and built a fort there on his arrival. A month later, on April 24, Mexican soldiers attacked a small force of Taylor's soldiers. Taylor sent the report the president wanted to hear: "Hostilities may now be considered as commenced."

Polk called an emergency meeting of his cabinet, and the cabinet agreed that the attack was grounds for war with Mexico. On May 11, 1846, the president told Congress that Mexico had "invaded our territory and shed American blood upon the American soil." Congress passed a declaration of war against Mexico.

American Attitudes toward the War

The American people were divided over the Mexican War. Polk's party, the Democrats, generally supported the war. Many Whigs opposed it, calling Polk's actions aggressive and unjust. Northerners accused Democrats of waging the war to spread slavery.

Illinois congressman Abraham Lincoln demanded to know the exact spot where the first attack against American troops had occurred. Lincoln, like many who opposed the war, claimed that the spot was clearly in Mexico and that Polk therefore had no grounds for blaming the war on Mexico.

Frederick Douglass, an African American leader in the antislavery movement, called the war "disgraceful" and "cruel." Douglass shared the belief that if the United States expanded into the West, the Southern states would carry slavery into the new territories.

Newspapers generally supported the war, and volunteers quickly signed up for military service. As time went on, however, antiwar feeling grew, particularly in the North.

American soldier, Mexican War

Polk's War Plan

President Polk had a three-part plan for the war with Mexico. First, American troops would drive Mexican forces out of the disputed border region in Texas and make the border secure. Second, the United States would seize New Mexico and California. Finally, American forces would take **Mexico City,** the capital of Mexico.

Zachary Taylor accomplished the first goal. Crossing the Rio Grande in September 1846, Taylor's army captured the town of **Monterrey.** In February 1847, Taylor defeated the Mexicans again at Buena Vista. The Texas border was secure.

Conquering New Mexico and California

While Taylor made progress in northern Mexico, American forces also advanced farther west. General **Stephen Watts Kearny** led his troops to New Mexico and California.

The Fall of New Mexico

In the summer of 1846, Kearny led about 1,500 cavalry soldiers along the Santa Fe Trail from Missouri to New Mexico. The Mexican

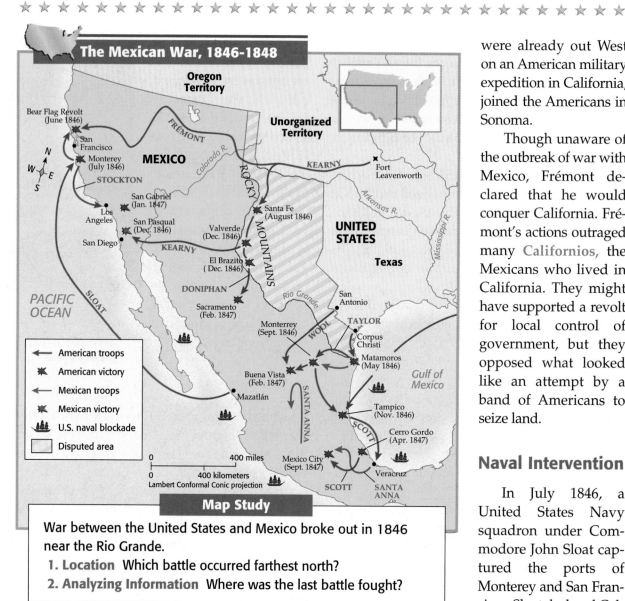

The Mexican War, 1846–1848

Map Study

War between the United States and Mexico broke out in 1846 near the Rio Grande.
1. **Location** Which battle occurred farthest north?
2. **Analyzing Information** Where was the last battle fought?

were already out West on an American military expedition in California, joined the Americans in Sonoma.

Though unaware of the outbreak of war with Mexico, Frémont declared that he would conquer California. Frémont's actions outraged many Californios, the Mexicans who lived in California. They might have supported a revolt for local control of government, but they opposed what looked like an attempt by a band of Americans to seize land.

Naval Intervention

In July 1846, a United States Navy squadron under Commodore John Sloat captured the ports of Monterey and San Francisco. Sloat declared California annexed to the United States, and the American flag replaced the Bear Flag in California.

Commodore Sloat's fleet sailed for **San Diego,** carrying Frémont and Carson. The Americans captured San Diego and moved north to Los Angeles. Carson headed east with the news of California's annexation. On his way he met and joined Kearny's force, marching west from Santa Fe.

After Sloat's ships left, many Californios in San Diego rose up in arms against the Americans who had taken over the city. General Kearny and his troops arrived in the midst of the rebellion. Exhausted from their journey across the desert, they faced a stiff fight but eventually won. By January 1847, California was fully controlled by the United States.

governor fled, allowing the Americans to capture New Mexico's capital, Santa Fe, on August 18, 1846, without firing a shot. Kearny and his army then headed across the deserts of New Mexico and Arizona to California.

California and the Bear Flag Republic

In June 1846, a small group of Americans had seized the town of Sonoma north of San Francisco and proclaimed the independent Republic of California. They called the new country the **Bear Flag Republic** because their flag showed a bear and a star on a white background. **John C. Frémont** and mountain man **Kit Carson,** who

★ ★

The End of the War

★ With their victories in New Mexico and California, the Americans met their original goals in the war. President Polk then launched the third part of his war plan—an attack on Mexico City.

The Capture of Mexico City

Polk gave the task of capturing Mexico City to General **Winfield Scott.** Scott devised a brilliant campaign that brought the Mexican War to a speedy conclusion. In March 1847, Scott's army landed on the coast of the Gulf of Mexico, near the Mexican port of **Veracruz.** Scott captured Veracruz after a 3-week siege and then set out to march the 300 miles to Mexico City.

The Americans had to fight their way toward Mexico City, battling not only the Mexican army but also bands of armed peasants. Scott reached the outskirts of Mexico City with his troops at the end of August 1847.

The Mexican high command was in disorder, but a few divisions of the Mexican army—and a group of boys from the Mexican Military College—fought heroically to defend the capital. Scott's forces overcame the Mexican resistance, however, and by mid-September the Americans had taken Mexico City. The Mexican government surrendered.

California Bear Flag

The United States lost 1,721 men to battle and more than 11,000 to disease in the Mexican War. Mexico's losses were far greater. The war cost the United States nearly $100 million, but here, too, Mexico paid a higher price. The war would cost Mexico half its territory.

The Peace Treaty

Peace talks between the United States and Mexico began in January 1848. The **Treaty of Guadalupe Hidalgo** (GWAH•duhl•OOP hih•DAL•goh) was signed in February 1848.

In the treaty Mexico gave up all claims to Texas and agreed to the Rio Grande as the border between Texas and Mexico. Furthermore, in what was called the **Mexican Cession,** Mexico ceded—gave—its provinces of California and New Mexico to the United States. In return the United States gave Mexico $15 million.

In 1853 the United States paid Mexico an additional $10 million for the **Gadsden Purchase,** a strip of land along the southern edge of the present-day states of Arizona and New Mexico. With the Gadsden Purchase, the United States mainland reached its present size. All that remained was to settle the newly acquired territories.

★ ★ ★ ★ ★ **Section 4 Assessment** ★ ★ ★ ★ ★

Checking for Understanding

1. **Identify** James K. Polk, Zachary Taylor, John C. Frémont, Winfield Scott, Mexican Cession, Gadsden Purchase.
2. **Define** Californios, cede.
3. **Summarize** President Polk's three-part plan in the war with Mexico.

Reviewing Themes

4. **Global Connections** What were the terms of the Treaty of Guadalupe Hidalgo?

Critical Thinking

5. **Drawing Conclusions** Why do you think President Polk wanted to make it seem as if Mexico had started the war?

Writing a Diary Entry Imagine you are a Mexican living on lands acquired in the Mexican Cession. Write a diary entry in which you record your feelings on learning the terms of the Treaty of Guadalupe Hidalgo.

Section 5

New Settlers in California and Utah

READ TO DISCOVER . . .
- how the hope of getting rich quick drew thousands of people to California.
- how the search for religious freedom led to the settlement of Utah.

TERMS TO LEARN
forty-niners
boomtown
vigilante

The Storyteller

James Marshall was building a sawmill on the South Fork of the American River in California. He worked for John Sutter, who owned a vast tract of land about 40 miles from present-day Sacramento. On January 24, 1848, Marshall saw something shining in a ditch. "I reached my hand down and picked it up," he wrote later. "It made my heart thump, for I was certain it was gold." Looking around, he found other shiny pieces. Marshall rushed to show the glittering pieces to Sutter, who determined that they were gold. Sutter tried to keep the discovery a secret, but word soon leaked out. The great California Gold Rush was under way!

Gold miner's cradle

People from all over the world flocked to California in search of quick riches. An official in Monterey reported that "the farmers have thrown aside their plows, the lawyers their briefs, the doctors their pills, the priests their prayer books, and all are now digging gold." By the end of 1848, these farmers, lawyers, doctors, and priests had taken $6 million in gold from the American River.

 **Geography**

California Gold Rush

⭐ Nearly 100,000 people came to California looking for gold in 1848 and 1849. Those who arrived in 1849 were called forty-niners.

Many came by sea. In February 1849 alone, 130 ships left the East Coast for San Francisco. Other forty-niners came overland, traveling on the Oregon Trail or the Santa Fe Trail and then pushing westward through California's **Sierra Nevada** mountain range.

Americans made up more than half of the forty-niners. Others came from Mexico, South America, Europe, and Australia. About 300 men arrived from China, the first large group of Asian immigrants to come to America. Although some eventually returned to China, others remained, establishing California's Chinese American community.

★ ★

Boomtowns

As people rushed to a new area to look for gold, they built new communities, called boomtowns, almost overnight. At one site on the Yuba River where only two houses stood in September 1849, a miner arrived the next year to find a town of 1,000 people "with a large number of hotels, stores, groceries, bakeries, and . . . gambling houses." The miners gave some of the boomtowns colorful names such as Shinbone Peak, Murderers' Gulch, and Whiskey Diggings.

Cities also flourished during the Gold Rush. As ships arrived daily with gold seekers and adventurers, **San Francisco** grew from a tiny village to a city of about 20,000 people.

A Hard Life

Miners found gold along a 150-mile stretch of the western slope of the Sierra Nevada. Any stream or canyon might contain the precious metal. Most of the hopeful forty-niners had no experience in mining. Rushing furiously from place to place, they attacked hillsides with pickaxes and shovels and spent hours bent over streambeds, "washing" or "panning" the water to seek gold dust and nuggets.

The California Gold Rush more than doubled the world's supply of gold. For all their effort, however, very few of the forty-niners achieved lasting wealth. Most of the miners found little or no gold. Many of those who did lost their riches through gambling or wild spending.

Merchants, however, made huge profits. They could charge whatever they liked because the miners had no place else to go to buy food and other essential items. Eggs sold for $10 a dozen. A Jewish immigrant named **Levi Strauss** sold the miners sturdy pants made of denim. His "Levi's" made him rich.

Gold Rush Society

Very few women lived in the mining camps, which were populated by men of all races and walks of life. Lonely and suffering from the hardships of mining, many men spent their free hours

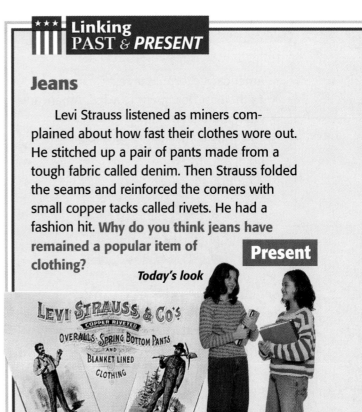

★★★ **Linking**
PAST & PRESENT

Jeans

Levi Strauss listened as miners complained about how fast their clothes wore out. He stitched up a pair of pants made from a tough fabric called denim. Then Strauss folded the seams and reinforced the corners with small copper tacks called rivets. He had a fashion hit. **Why do you think jeans have remained a popular item of clothing?**

Today's look

Present

LEVI STRAUSS & Co's
COPPER RIVETED
OVERALLS. SPRING BOTTOM PANTS
AND
BLANKET LINED
CLOTHING

Past

Early Levi pants ad

drinking, gambling, and fighting. Songs such as "O Susanna" and "Sweet Betsy from Pike" reminded them of the women they missed.

> **❝** Oh, don't you remember sweet Betsy from Pike,
> Who crossed the wide mountains with her lover Ike,
> With two yoke of cattle, a large yellow dog,
> A tall shanghai rooster and a one-spotted hog. **❞**

The camps lacked law and order. One miner wrote, "Robberies and murders were of daily occurrence. Organized bands of thieves existed in the towns and in the mountains." Concerned citizens formed vigilance committees for security. The **vigilantes** (VIH•juh•LAN•tees) took the law into their own hands, acting as police, judge, jury, and sometimes executioner.

Causes and Effects

CAUSES

★ Americans accept Manifest Destiny.
★ As the East becomes crowded, Americans want more land.
★ The West contains furs, lumber, and precious metals.

Westward Movement

EFFECTS

★ Native Americans are forced off lands.
★ The United States wars with Mexico.
★ America extends from sea to sea.

Chart Study

Americans believed the United States had the right to expand to the Pacific Ocean.
Analyzing Information What event drew settlers to California?

Economic and Political Progress

The Gold Rush ended within a few years but had long-lasting effects on California's economy. Agriculture, shipping, and trade expanded to meet the miners' needs for food and other goods.

Many people who had come looking for gold stayed in the area to farm or run a business. California's population soared, increasing from about 20,000 in 1848 to more than 220,000 only 4 years later.

Such rapid growth brought the need for more effective government. Zachary Taylor, the Mexican War hero and now president, urged the people of California to apply for statehood. They did so, choosing representatives to write a constitution in September 1849. Once their constitution was approved, Californians elected a governor and state legislators.

California applied to Congress for statehood in March 1850. Because California's constitution banned slavery, however, the request caused a crisis in Congress. The Southern states objected to making California a state because it would upset the balance of free and slave states. California did not become a state until Congress worked out a compromise six months later.

A Religious Refuge in Utah

★ A visitor to the Utah Territory in the 1850s wrote admiringly: "The whole of this small nation occupy themselves as usefully as the working bees of a hive." This account described the **Mormons,** or members of the Church of Jesus Christ of Latter-day Saints. Mormons had come to Utah to fulfill their vision of the godly life.

★ **Picturing HISTORY** Mormon pioneers traveled across the country and from other parts of the world to settle in the Great Salt Lake area. **Who was the Mormon leader who brought the first Mormon settlers to Utah?**

The First Mormons

Joseph Smith founded the Mormon church in 1830 in New York State. He had visions that led him to launch a new Christian church. He hoped to use these visions to build an ideal society.

Smith formed a community in New York, but unsympathetic neighbors disapproved of the Mormons' religion. They forced the Mormons to move on. From New York the Mormons went to Ohio, then to Missouri, and then Illinois.

In 1844 a mob in Illinois killed Smith, and **Brigham Young** took over as head of the Mormons. Young decided the Mormons should move again, this time near the **Great Salt Lake** in Utah. Although part of Mexico, no Mexicans had settled in the region because of its harsh terrain.

A Haven in the Desert

The Mormon migration to the Great Salt Lake area started in 1846. About 12,000 Mormons made the journey—the largest single migration in American history. In the midst of the desert, they founded a community they called **Deseret.** Later they changed the name to **Salt Lake City.**

With hard work and determination, the Mormons made Deseret flourish. They planned their towns carefully and built irrigation canals to water their farms. They also founded industries so they could be self-sufficient. Mormon merchants sold supplies to the forty-niners who passed through Utah on their way to California.

Picturing HISTORY Mormon settlers brought their possessions overland to Utah in covered wagons. By the end of the 1860s, more than 51,000 Mormons had journeyed to the Salt Lake Valley. **How did the Mormons make their Salt Lake settlements flourish?**

Utah Joins the United States

In 1848 the United States acquired the Salt Lake area as part of the settlement of the Mexican War. Two years later Congress established the Utah Territory, and President Millard Fillmore made Brigham Young its governor.

Utah was not easily incorporated into the United States. The Mormons wanted to be left alone and resisted federal authority. In 1857 and 1858, war almost broke out between the Mormons and the United States Army. Utah did not become a state until 1896.

★ ★ ★ ★ ★ **Section 5 Assessment** ★ ★ ★ ★ ★

Checking for Understanding
1. **Identify** Levi Strauss, Mormons, Joseph Smith, Brigham Young.
2. **Define** forty-niners, boomtown, vigilante.
3. **Describe** how the Gold Rush helped California's economy grow.

Reviewing Themes
4. **Groups and Institutions** What was the goal of Mormons who migrated to Utah?

Critical Thinking
5. **Identifying Alternatives** How might the history of California have been different if the Gold Rush had not occurred?

Drawing a Historical Scene Draw a scene that might have existed in a mining boomtown.

Assessment and Activities

★ Reviewing Key Terms

On a sheet of paper, define the following terms:

joint occupation
mountain man
rendezvous
emigrant
Manifest Destiny
Tejano
empresario
annex
ranchero
cede
forty-niners
vigilante

★ Reviewing Key Facts

1. What agreement did the United States and Canada reach about the Oregon Territory?
2. Why did President Jackson refuse to annex Texas?
3. Why did some Americans think that making California part of the United States would strengthen its security?
4. Summarize the two main causes of the United States's war with Mexico.
5. Why did merchants earn such large profits during the Gold Rush?

★ Time Line Activity

Create a time line on which you place the following events in chronological order.

- California Gold Rush begins
- Gadsden Purchase sets present-day boundaries of mainland United States
- Texas declares independence from Mexico
- Mexico gains independence from Spain
- Mexican War begins
- California becomes a state

★ Critical Thinking

Recognizing Bias

The belief in Manifest Destiny helped the American government and people to justify many of their actions during the 1830s and 1840s.

1. Do you think the United States would have been interested in the Oregon country, New Mexico, and California if the notion of Manifest Destiny had not existed? Explain your answer.
2. What reactions do you think the governments of Canada and Mexico had to the American idea of Manifest Destiny?
3. What do you think your attitude toward Manifest Destiny would have been if you were a farmer in Virginia in the early 1800s?
4. What do you think your attitude toward Manifest Destiny would have been if you were a Native American in the early 1800s?

★ Reviewing Themes

1. **Economic Factors** How did economic troubles in the East affect settlement in the Oregon area?
2. **Geography and History** Before Stephen Austin established a colony in Texas, who inhabited the area?
3. **Culture and Traditions** What work did Native Americans perform at the Spanish missions?
4. **Global Connections** How did the negotiations between the United States and Britain over the Oregon Territory differ from those between the United States and Mexico over the Southwest?
5. **Groups and Institutions** Why did rapid growth create the need for a more effective government in California?

★ Geography Activity

Study the routes of the western trails shown on the map below. Then answer the questions that follow.

The Oregon and California Trails

1. **Region** Which mountains did settlers have to cross to reach Oregon's Pacific coast? To reach California's Pacific coast?
2. **Location** In what city did the Oregon Trail begin? In what city did it end?

★ Cooperative Activity

History and Economics Imagine that a large deposit of gold has been discovered in the area where you live. You and a partner have decided to open a business to serve miners. Create a business plan detailing what type of product, store, or service might be most profitable. Then write a letter to a local bank describing the business, how much money you think you will need to borrow, and a list of what you will use the money for. Explain why you think your enterprise is sure to make money.

★ Skill Practice Activity

Understanding Latitude and Longitude

Turn to the map on page 358. Use it to answer the following questions.

1. What are the latitude and longitude coordinates of Fort Laramie in Unorganized Territory?
2. In general, between what lines of longitude did the Pony Express run?
3. What city lies at about 37°N, 90°W?

★ Technology Activity

Using an Electronic Card Catalog
Search your library's card catalog for books containing information about Salt Lake City and the state of Utah. Use this information to make an alphabetical directory of historic sites that someone who is a Mormon might like to visit. Your list might include museums, sites of Mormon activities, Mormon businesses, or other places of interest.

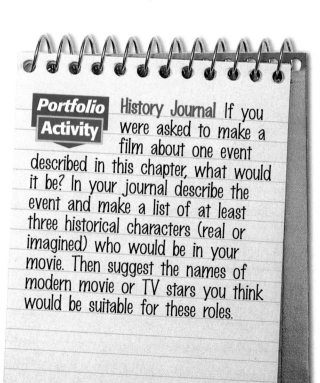

Portfolio Activity History Journal If you were asked to make a film about one event described in this chapter, what would it be? In your journal describe the event and make a list of at least three historical characters (real or imagined) who would be in your movie. Then suggest the names of modern movie or TV stars you think would be suitable for these roles.

Go for the Gold

You're off to the gold fields! It's 1849 and the California Gold Rush is on. Will you find your fortune? Make your own sluice box to see how some California forty-niners searched for gold nearly 150 years ago.

The Way It Was

In the mid-1800s, a call echoed across the United States. "There's gold in California!" Prospectors and adventurers by the thousands headed west hoping to make their fortunes. Teachers, farmers, businesspeople, and merchants armed themselves with picks and shovels. They attacked streambeds and gravel beds, searching for shiny gold dust, flakes, and nuggets. Because much of this valuable mineral washed down from California's mountains, panning for gold in rivers became a common choice for prospecting.

California gold miners

Materials

- 1/2 gallon empty milk or juice carton
- sand, dirt, gravel, with 3 or 4 heavy metal screw nuts (gold nuggets)
- 3 small dowel rods about 6 inches long
- modeling clay
- large baking pan
- water
- scissors

Believe It Or Not!

Stories of gold in California were not new in 1849. In 1842 a rancher in southern California found gold dust on the roots of a wild onion he dug up for lunch. No one paid much attention until James Marshall found gold while building a sawmill on John Sutter's property in 1848.

2 What To Do

1. Use the modeling clay to form a ridge about 1 inch high at one end of the baking pan. Cut off the top end and one side of the milk or juice carton.

2. At the bottom end of the carton, cut a U-shaped opening. Leave about 1/2 inch around 3 sides. Turn the carton so that the cut-away side is up, forming a trough.

3. Insert the 3 dowel rods through two sides of the trough, close to the bottom of the trough. (Use the trough on this page as a model.) Make 2 small holes near the bottom of the trough about 2 inches away from the U-shaped end for the water to drain.

4. Place the trough in the cake pan with the open end on the clay ridge.

5. Place a handful of sand, dirt, gravel, and metal screw nuts at the upper end of your trough. Pour water down your trough and look for "gold nuggets."

6. Repeat the process in step 5 several times. Now you are sluicing for "gold."

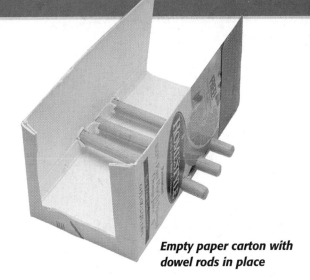

Empty paper carton with dowel rods in place

3 Lab Report

1. Which materials tended to wash all the way down the trough?
2. What happened to the heavier "gold nuggets"?
3. How efficient do you think sluicing was as a mining method?
4. **Drawing Conclusions** How much mining experience and money for equipment do you think the average forty-niner brought to the gold fields?

Go a Step Further

Find out more about the discovery of gold at Sutter's Mill near Sacramento in 1848. Write a series of diary entries that you think John Sutter might have made about the discovery of gold and the arrival of miners.

1820–1860

North and South

★ Why It's Important

Many of the differences between the North and the South have disappeared since the 1800s. Differences still exist, but no longer are there sharp economic and cultural distinctions between the two regions. The South now has many industries, while many cities in the North now have fewer factories than they did in the 1800s. Mass communication and the migration of people from one region to another have also erased regional differences.

★ Chapter Themes

- *Section 1*, Economic Factors
- *Section 2*, Geography and History
- *Section 3*, Science and Technology
- *Section 4*, Culture and Traditions

PRIMARY SOURCES Library *See pages 960–961 for primary source readings to accompany Chapter 13*

 HISTORY AND ART *On the Saint Johns River* by John Bunyan Bristol Most Southerners did not own plantations. Many were poor farmers, living off the crops they raised.

1830   1840   1850   1860

1834
Cyrus McCormick
patents reaper

1844
Samuel Morse
sends first
telegraph message

1847
Elias Howe
introduces the
sewing machine

1860
About 3,000
steamboats
are operating

Section 1

The North's Economy

READ TO DISCOVER . . .

- how advances in technology shaped the economy of the North.
- how new kinds of transportation and communication spurred economic growth.

TERMS TO LEARN

clipper ship   Morse code
telegraph

The Storyteller

In the 1840s, telegraph wires and railroads began to cross the nation. But traveling by rail had its discomforts, as writer Charles Dickens describes: "[T]here is a great deal of jolting, a great deal of noise, a great deal of wall, not much window, a locomotive engine, a shriek, and a bell. . . . In the center of the carriage there is usually a stove . . . which is for the most part red-hot. It is insufferably close; and you see the hot air fluttering between yourself and any other object you may happen to look at, like the ghost of smoke. . . ."

Samuel Morse's telegraph key

In the Northern states, technology changed the way Americans worked, traveled, and communicated. By the mid-1800s, power-driven machinery performed many tasks that were once done by hand, and factories had largely replaced cottage industries.

Technology and Industry

⭐ The industrialization of the North developed in three phases. In the first, manufacturers made products by dividing the tasks involved among the workers. One worker would spin thread all day and another would weave cloth—instead of having one person spinning and then weaving. During the second phase, manufacturers built factories to bring specialized workers together. This allowed products to be made more quickly than before.

In the third phase, factory workers used machinery to perform some of their work. Many of the new machines ran on waterpower or steam power. For example, power-driven looms took over the task of weaving. The worker's job was no longer to weave but to tend the machine, which produced more products in less time.

Mass Production

Mass production of cotton textiles began in New England in the early 1800s. After **Elias Howe** invented the sewing machine in 1846, machine operators could produce clothing on a large scale from textiles made by machine. Other types

A clipper ship, the *Flying Cloud*, set a new record by sailing from New York to California in less than 90 days. **How did clipper ships get their name?**

of industries developed during the same period. By 1860 the Northeast's 74,000 factories produced about two-thirds of the country's manufactured goods.

Improved Transportation

★ Improvements in transportation contributed to the success of many of America's new industries. Between 1800 and 1850, construction crews built thousands of miles of roads and canals. The canals opened new shipping routes by connecting many lakes and rivers. The growth of railroads in the 1840s and 1850s produced another means to speed the flow of goods.

 **Geography**

Steamboats and Steamships

Inventor **Robert Fulton** changed river travel in 1807 with his steamboat. Steamboats carried goods and passengers more cheaply and quickly along inland waterways than flatboats or sail-powered vessels could do.

★ ★ ★ ★ ★ ★ ★ ★ ★ ★ ★ ★ ★ ★ ★ ★ ★ ★

In the 1840s canal builders began to widen and deepen canals to accommodate steamboats. By 1860 about 3,000 steamboats traveled the major rivers and canals of the country as well as the Great Lakes. Steamboats spurred the development of cities such as Cincinnati, Buffalo, and Chicago.

Before long, steam also powered ships across the ocean. One of the first steam-powered ocean-going vessels was an iron ship called the *Great Western*. On its first voyages between the United States and Great Britain in 1838, the *Great Western* carried a supply of sails in case the steam engine broke down in midocean.

Clipper Ships

In the 1840s sailing ships were improved. The clipper ships—with their sleek hulls and tall sails—were the pride of the open seas. They could sail an average of 300 miles per day, as fast as most steamships of the day. The ships got their name because they "clipped" time from long journeys. Before the clippers, the voyage from New York to Great Britain took about 21 to 28 days. A clipper ship could usually make that trip in half the time.

Famous clipper ships included the *Flying Cloud*, the *Sea Witch*, and the *Cutty Sark*. In 1853 the *Champion of the Seas* set a new record, sailing 465 miles in 24 hours. No steamship matched this speed for more than 25 years. 🌐

Locomotives

The development of railroads in the United States began with short stretches of tracks that connected mines with nearby rivers. Early trains were drawn by horses rather than by locomotives. The first steam-powered locomotive, the *Rocket*, began operating in Britain in 1829.

Peter Cooper designed and built the first American steam locomotive in 1830. Called the *Tom Thumb*, it got off to a bad start. In a race against a horse-drawn train in **Baltimore,** the *Tom Thumb*'s engine failed. Engineers soon improved the engine, and within 10 years steam locomotives were pulling trains in the United States.

A Railway Network

In 1840 the United States had some 3,000 miles of railroad track. By 1860 it had almost 31,000 miles, mostly in the North and the **Midwest.** One railway linked New York City and Buffalo. Another connected Philadelphia and Pittsburgh. Still another linked Baltimore with Wheeling, Virginia (now West Virginia).

Railway builders tied these eastern lines to lines being built farther west in Ohio, Indiana, and Illinois. By 1860 a network of railroad track united the Midwest and the East.

Moving Goods and People

Along with canals, the railways transformed trade in the nation's interior. The changes began with the opening of the Erie Canal in 1825 and the first railroads of the 1830s. Before this time agricultural goods were carried down the Mississippi River to New Orleans and then shipped to other countries or to the East Coast of the United States.

The development of the east-west canal and the rail network allowed grain, livestock, and dairy products to move directly from the Midwest to the East. Because goods now traveled

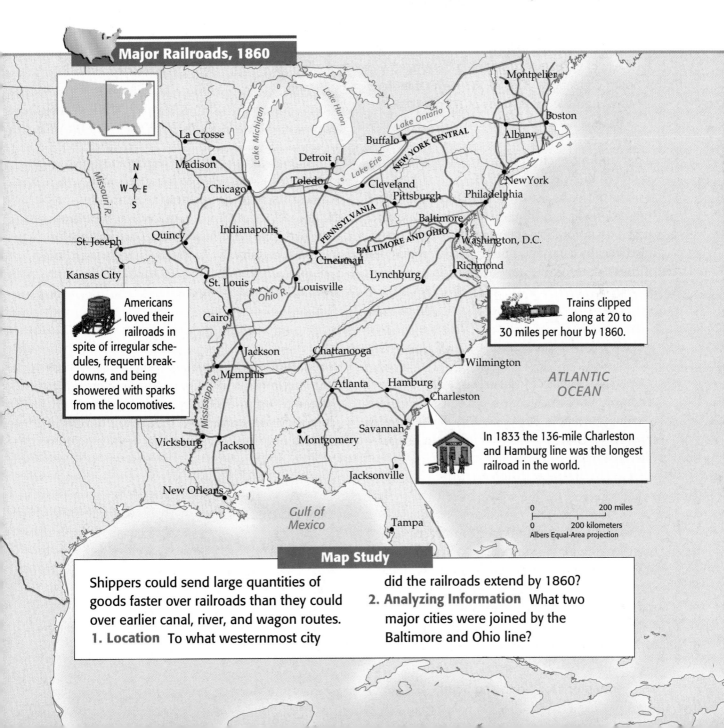

Major Railroads, 1860

Americans loved their railroads in spite of irregular schedules, frequent breakdowns, and being showered with sparks from the locomotives.

Trains clipped along at 20 to 30 miles per hour by 1860.

In 1833 the 136-mile Charleston and Hamburg line was the longest railroad in the world.

ATLANTIC OCEAN

Gulf of Mexico

0   200 miles
0   200 kilometers
Albers Equal-Area projection

Map Study

Shippers could send large quantities of goods faster over railroads than they could over earlier canal, river, and wagon routes.

1. Location To what westernmost city did the railroads extend by 1860?

2. Analyzing Information What two major cities were joined by the Baltimore and Ohio line?

Picturing HISTORY The defeat of the train *Tom Thumb* in 1830 did not mean the end of the steam engine. The first successful use of a steam locomotive in the United States took place in South Carolina in 1831. In 1860 which regions of the United States had the most miles of railroad track?

faster and more cheaply, merchants in the East could sell them at lower prices.

The railroads also played an important role in the settlement and industrialization of the Midwest. Fast, affordable train travel brought people into Ohio, Indiana, and Illinois. As the population of these states grew, new towns and industries developed.

Faster Communication

★ The growth of industry and the new pace of travel created a need for faster methods of communication. The telegraph—an apparatus that used electric signals to transmit messages—filled that need.

Lines of Communication

Samuel Morse, an American inventor, had been seeking to win support for a system of telegraph lines for five years. Finally, in 1843 Congress set aside $30,000 to build an experimental line from Baltimore, Maryland, to Washington, D.C.

On May 24, 1844, Morse got the chance to demonstrate that he could send messages instantly along wires. As a crowd in the U.S. capital watched, Morse tapped in the words, "What hath God wrought!" A few moments later, the telegraph operator in Baltimore sent the same message back in reply. The telegraph worked! Soon telegraph messages were flashing back and forth between Washington and Baltimore.

Morse transmitted his message in Morse code, a series of dots and dashes representing the letters of the alphabet. A skilled Morse code operator could rapidly tap out words in the dot-and-dash alphabet.

Americans adopted the telegraph eagerly. A British visitor marveled at the speed with which Americans formed telegraph companies and erected telegraph lines. Americans, he wrote, were driven to "annihilate [wipe out] distance" in their vast country. By 1860 the United States had constructed more than 50,000 miles of telegraph lines.

Spreading the News

In 1846 Richard Hoe invented the steam cylinder rotary press, a new kind of printing press that printed newspapers quickly and inexpensively. The rotary press prompted the start of dozens of newspapers.

Revolution in Agriculture

★ The railroads gave farmers access to new markets where they could sell their products. Advances in technology allowed farmers to greatly increase the size of the crops they produced.

Farm Technology

Very few farmers ventured into the treeless **Great Plains** west of Missouri, Iowa, and Minnesota in the early 1800s. Even areas of mixed forest and prairie west of Ohio and Kentucky seemed too difficult for farming. Settlers worried that their wooden plows could not break the prairie's matted sod and that the soil was not fertile.

Three revolutionary inventions of the 1830s changed farming methods and encouraged settlers to cultivate larger areas of the West. One was the **steel-tipped plow** that **John Deere** invented in 1837. Far sturdier than the wooden plow, Deere's plow easily cut through the hard-packed sod of the prairies. Equally important were the **mechanical reaper,** which sped up the harvesting of wheat, and the **thresher,** which quickly separated the grain from the stalk.

Biography

McCormick's Reaper

Born on a Virginia farm, **Cyrus McCormick** became interested in machines that would ease the burden of farmwork. After years of tinkering, McCormick designed and constructed the mechanical reaper and made a fortune manufacturing and selling it. After patenting the reaper in 1834, McCormick opened a factory in Chicago in 1847 to mass-produce the machine. By 1860 he had sold 100,000 reapers.

For hundreds of years, farmers had harvested grain with handheld sickles. McCormick's reaper could harvest grain four times faster than the sickle. Because farmers could harvest wheat so quickly, they began planting more of it. Growing wheat became profitable. McCormick's reaper ensured that raising wheat would remain the main economic activity in the Midwestern prairies.

Cash Crops

American farmers had always kept some of their crops for themselves and sold some for cash. New agricultural machines and railroads helped farmers plant more acres in cash crops and sell those crops in distant markets. Midwestern farmers began growing wheat in large quantities and shipping it east by train and canal barge. Farmers in the Northeast and the Middle Atlantic states also increased their production of cash crops, concentrating on the fruits and vegetables that grew well in Eastern soils.

Despite improvements in agriculture, however, the North turned increasingly toward industry. It was difficult making a living farming the rocky soil of New England, but industry flourished in the area. The number of people who worked in factories continued to rise—and so did problems connected with factory labor.

Section 1 Assessment

Checking for Understanding
1. *Identify* Robert Fulton, Samuel Morse, John Deere, Cyrus McCormick.
2. *Define* clipper ship, telegraph, Morse code.
3. *Identify* the three phases of industrialization in the North.

Reviewing Themes
4. **Economic Factors** How did improvements in transportation affect the price of goods?

Critical Thinking
5. **Determining Cause and Effect** How did the steel-tipped plow aid settlers on the Great Plains?

Activity

Making a Graph Research the number of acres of wheat harvested in the United States before and after McCormick introduced his reaper. Then create a chart or graph to illustrate your findings.

1827
Freedom's Journal, first African American newspaper, is published

1834
The General Trades Union of New York is formed

1853
Know-Nothing Party is formed

1860
Population of New York City reaches 1 million

Section 2

The North's People

READ TO DISCOVER . . .
- how working conditions in industries changed.
- why workers began forming trade unions.
- how immigration affected American economic, political, and cultural life.

TERMS TO LEARN
trade union	discrimination
strike	famine
prejudice	nativist

The Storyteller

"At first the hours seemed very long, but I was so interested in learning that I endured it very well; when I went out at night the sound of the mill was in my ears," a Northern mill worker wrote in 1844. The worker compared the noise of the cotton mill to the ceaseless, deafening roar of Niagara Falls. The roar of machinery was only one feature of factory life workers had to adjust to. Industrialization created new challenges for the men, women, and children who worked in the nation's factories.

12-year-old factory worker

Between 1820 and 1860, more and more of America's manufacturing shifted to mills and factories. Machines took over many of the production tasks.

Northern Factories

 In the early 1800s, in the mills established in **Lowell, Massachusetts,** the entire production process was brought together under one roof—setting up the factory system. In addition to textiles and clothing, factories now produced such items as shoes, watches, guns, sewing machines, and agricultural machinery.

Working Conditions

As the factory system developed, working conditions worsened. Factory owners wanted their employees to work longer hours in order to produce more goods. As the workday grew longer—by 1840 factory workers averaged 11.4 hours a day—on-the-job accidents became more common.

Factory work involved some dangerous conditions. For example, the long leather belts that connected the machines to the factory's water-powered driveshaft had no protective shields. Workers often suffered injuries such as lost fingers and broken bones from the rapidly spinning belts. Young children working on machines with powerful moving parts were especially at risk.

Workers often labored under unpleasant conditions. In the summer factories were miserably hot and stifling. The machines gave off heat, and air-conditioning had not yet been invented. In the winter workers suffered because most factories had no heating.

Factory owners showed more concern for profits than for the comfort and safety of their employees. They knew that they could easily replace an unhappy worker with someone else eager for a job. No laws existed to regulate working conditions or to protect workers.

The owners of the Lowell mills had built simple but clean lodging for employees in an effort to attract young women workers to the new industry. By the 1840s, however, factory owners no longer provided this benefit. Workers had to find their own lodging. Because of low wages, most workers ended up living in slums near the factories.

Attempts to Organize

By the 1830s workers began organizing to improve working conditions. Fearing the growth of the factory system, skilled workers had formed trade unions—organizations of workers with the same trade, or skill. Steadily deteriorating conditions led unskilled workers to organize as well.

In the mid-1830s skilled workers in New York City staged a series of strikes, refusing to work to put pressure on employers. Workers struck to get higher wages and to limit their workday to 10 hours. In 1834 groups of skilled workers formed the General Trades Union of New York.

The Right to Strike

In the early 1800s, going on strike was illegal. Striking workers could be punished by the law, or they could be fired from their jobs. In 1842 a Massachusetts court ruled that workers did have the right to strike. It would be many years, however, before workers received other legal rights.

African American Workers

Slavery had largely disappeared from the North by 1820. However, racial prejudice—an unfair opinion not based on facts—and discrimination—unfair treatment of a group—remained in Northern states. For example, in 1821 New York eliminated the requirement that white men had to own property in order to vote—yet few African Americans were allowed to vote. Both Rhode Island and Pennsylvania passed laws prohibiting free African Americans from voting.

Most communities would not allow free African Americans to attend public schools and barred them from public facilities as well. Often African Americans were forced into segregated, or separate, schools and hospitals.

Another damaging effect of prejudice in the North was that African Americans had to take the lowest-paying jobs. William J. Brown, a free African American who lived in Rhode Island in the 1830s, later wrote:

 To drive carriages, carry a market basket after the boss, and brush his boots . . . was as high as a colored man could rise. 〞

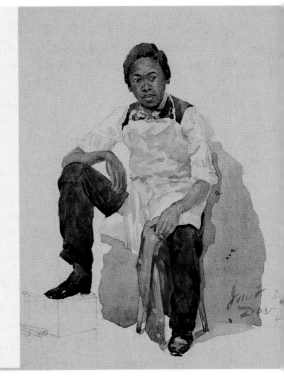

★ HISTORY AND ART

***Young Man in White Apron* by John Mackie Falconer** The artist of this painting was known for his watercolors depicting New York City workers such as this African American clerk. **How did prejudice affect the lives of African Americans in the North?**

A few African Americans in the North became well-to-do businesspeople. Henry Boyd owned a furniture manufacturing company in Cincinnati, Ohio. In 1827 Samuel Cornish and John B. Russwurm founded *Freedom's Journal,* the first African American newspaper, in New York City. In 1845 Macon B. Allen became the first African American licensed to practice law in the United States. The overwhelming majority of African Americans, however, were extremely poor. Although better off than the enslaved people of the South, Northern African Americans still suffered the cruel and lasting effects of discrimination.

Women Workers

Women had played a major role in the developing mill and factory systems. However, employers discriminated against women, paying them less than male workers. When men began to form unions, they excluded women. Male workers wanted women kept out of the workplace so that more jobs would be available for men.

Some female workers attempted to organize in the 1830s and 1840s. In Massachusetts the Lowell Female Labor Reform Organization, founded by a weaver named **Sarah G. Bagley,** petitioned the state legislature for a 10-hour day in 1845. Because most of the petition's signers were women, the legislature did not consider the petition.

Most of the early efforts by women to achieve equality and justice in the workplace failed. They paved the way, however, for later movements to correct the injustices against female workers.

The Rise of Cities

The growth of factories went hand in hand with the growth of Northern cities. People looking for work flocked to the cities, where most of the factories were located. In 1840, 14 percent of the population of the Northern states lived in cities. By 1860 that figure had grown to 26 percent. The population of New York City, the nation's largest city, reached 1 million, and Philadelphia, more than 500,000 in 1860.

City life could be difficult and dangerous. Unable to afford decent housing, new workers usually lived in overcrowded, run-down buildings with no plumbing or heat. Disease spread quickly in such conditions. Fire was also a constant danger in the closely spaced wooden buildings.

Immigration

Immigration—the movement of people into a country—to the United States increased dramatically between 1840 and 1860. American manufacturers welcomed the tide of immigrants, many of whom were willing to work for long hours and for low pay.

Newcomers From Ireland

The largest group of immigrants to the United States at this time traveled across the Atlantic from Ireland. Between 1846 and 1860, more than 1.5 million Irish immigrants arrived in the country, settling mostly in the Northeast.

The Irish migration to the United States was brought on by a terrible potato famine. A famine is an extreme shortage of food. Potatoes were the mainstay of the Irish diet, eaten for breakfast, lunch, and dinner. When a devastating blight, or disease, destroyed Irish potato crops in the 1840s, starvation struck the country. More than 1 million people died.

Although most of the immigrants had been farmers in Ireland, they were too poor to buy land

*F*ootnotes to History

Birth of the Chip In 1853 a diner at an elegant resort in Saratoga Springs, New York, refused an order of potatoes that were "too thick." The chef, Native American George Crum, sliced and fried a batch so thin that they could not be picked up with a fork. The guest loved the crisp potatoes, and the "potato chip" was born!

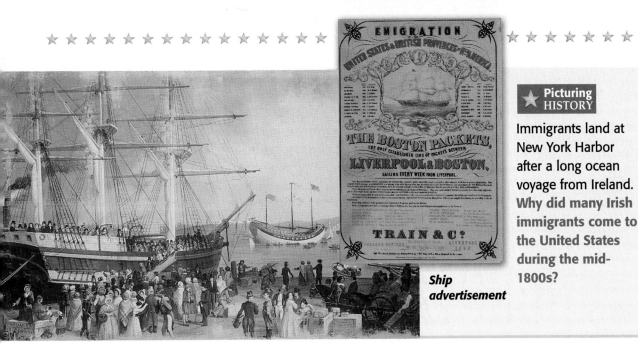

EMIGRATION
UNITED STATES & BRITISH PROVINCES OF AMERICA

THE BOSTON PACKETS,
THE ONLY ESTABLISHED LINE OF PACKETS BETWEEN
LIVERPOOL & BOSTON,
SAILING EVERY WEEK FROM LIVERPOOL.

TRAIN & C.º

Ship advertisement

★ **Picturing HISTORY**

Immigrants land at New York Harbor after a long ocean voyage from Ireland. **Why did many Irish immigrants come to the United States during the mid-1800s?**

in the United States. For this reason many Irish immigrants took low-paying factory jobs in Northern cities. The men who came from Ireland worked in factories or performed manual labor, such as digging ditches and working on the railroads. The women, who accounted for almost half of the immigrants, became servants and factory workers. By 1850 one-third of all workers in Boston were Irish.

German Immigrants

The second-largest group of immigrants in the United States between 1820 and 1860 came from Germany. Some sought work and opportunity. Others had left their homes because of the failure of a democratic revolution in Germany in 1848.

Between 1848 and 1860, more than 1 million German immigrants—mostly men—settled in the United States. Many arrived with enough money to buy farms or open their own businesses. They prospered in many parts of the country, founding their own communities and self-help organizations. Some German immigrants settled in New York and Pennsylvania, but many moved to the Midwest and the western territories.

The Impact of Immigration

The immigrants who came to the United States between 1820 and 1860 changed the character of the country. These people brought their languages, customs, religions, and ways of life with them. Various features soon filtered into American culture.

Before the early 1800s, the majority of immigrants to America had been either Protestants from Great Britain or Africans brought forcibly to America as slaves. At the time, the country had relatively few Catholics, and most of these lived around Baltimore, New Orleans, and St. Augustine. Most of the Irish immigrants and about one-half of the German immigrants were Roman Catholics.

Many Catholic immigrants settled in cities of the Northeast. The church gave the newcomers more than a source of spiritual guidance. It also provided a center for the community life of the immigrants.

The German immigrants brought their language as well as their religion. When they settled, they lived in their own communities, founded German-language publications, and established musical societies.

Immigrants Face Prejudice

In the 1830s and 1840s, anti-immigrant feelings rose. Some Americans feared that immigrants were changing the character of the United States too much.

People opposed to immigration were known as nativists because they felt that immigration threatened the future of "native"—American-

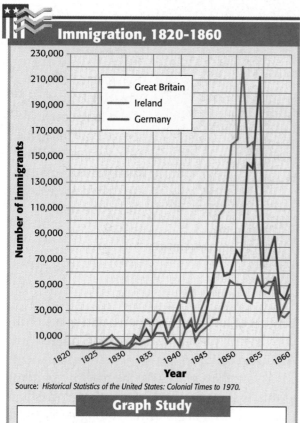

Immigration, 1820–1860

Source: *Historical Statistics of the United States: Colonial Times to 1970.*

Graph Study

Immigration to the United States increased dramatically between 1820 and 1860.

1. Which country provided the most immigrants?
2. **Analyzing Information** What was the highest number of German immigrants before 1855?

born—citizens. Some nativists accused immigrants of taking jobs from "real" Americans and were angry that immigrants would work for lower wages. Others accused the newcomers of bringing crime and disease to American cities. Immigrants who lived in crowded slums served as likely targets of this kind of prejudice.

A New Political Party

The nativists formed secret anti-Catholic societies, and in the 1850s they joined to form a new political party: the American Party. Because members of nativist groups often answered questions about their organization with the statement "I know nothing," their party came to be known as the **Know-Nothing Party.**

The Know-Nothings urged Americans to fight the "alien menace." They called for stricter citizenship laws—extending the immigrants' waiting period for citizenship from 5 to 14 years—and wanted to ban foreign-born citizens from holding office. In 1856 the Know-Nothings supported former president **Millard Fillmore** as their presidential candidate. He lost to the Democratic candidate, **James Buchanan.**

In the mid-1850s the Know-Nothing movement split into a Northern branch and a Southern branch over the question of slavery. At this time the slavery issue was also dividing the Northern and Southern states of the nation.

Section 2 Assessment

Checking for Understanding

1. **Identify** Sarah G. Bagley, Know-Nothing Party.
2. **Define** trade union, strike, prejudice, discrimination, famine, nativist.
3. **List** three reasons workers formed unions in the 1830s.

Reviewing Themes

4. **Geography and History** How did German and Irish immigrants differ in where they settled?

Critical Thinking

5. **Making Inferences** How do you think nativists would have defined a "real" American?

Making a Poster Design a campaign poster for a Know-Nothing Party candidate.

Reading a Circle Graph

Have you ever watched someone dish out pieces of pie? When the pie is cut evenly, everybody gets the same size slice. If one slice is cut a little larger, however, someone else gets a smaller piece. A **circle graph** is like a pie cut in slices. Often, a circle graph is called a *pie chart.*

Learning the Skill

In a circle graph, the complete circle represents a whole group—or 100 percent. The circle is divided into "slices," or wedge-shaped sections representing parts of the whole.

The size of each slice is determined by the percentage it represents.

To read a circle graph, follow these steps:
- Read the title of the graph to find out what the subject is.
- Study the labels or key to determine what the parts or "slices" represent.
- Compare the parts of the graph to draw conclusions about the subject.
- When two or more circle graphs appear together, read their titles and labels. Then compare the graphs for similarities and differences.

Practicing the Skill

Read the graphs on this page, then answer the following questions.
1. What do the four graphs represent?
2. What percentage of workers were in agriculture in 1840? In 1870?
3. During what decade did the percentage of workers in manufacturing increase the most?

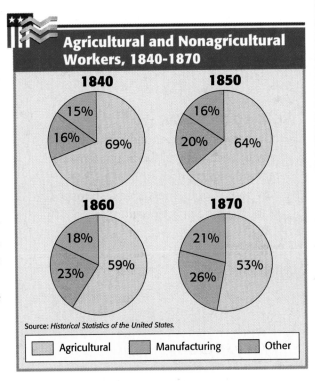

Agricultural and Nonagricultural Workers, 1840–1870

1840
15%
16%
69%

1850
16%
20%
64%

1860
18%
23%
59%

1870
21%
26%
53%

Source: *Historical Statistics of the United States.*

☐ Agricultural   ☐ Manufacturing   ☐ Other

4. In what year did manufacturing workers surpass 20 percent?
5. In what year did agricultural workers make up 59 percent of all workers?
6. What can you conclude from the graphs about the relationship between manufacturing and agricultural workers from 1840 to 1870?

Applying the Skill

Reading a Circle Graph Find a circle graph related to the economy in a newspaper or magazine. Compare its sections. Then draw a conclusion about the economy.

Glencoe's **Skillbuilder Interactive Workbook, Level 1** provides instruction and practice in key social studies skills.

1793
Eli Whitney
invents
cotton gin

1800s
Removal of Native
Americans spurs expansion
of cotton production

1860
The South remains
largely rural and
dependent on cotton

Section 3

Southern Cotton Kingdom

READ TO DISCOVER . . .
- how settlement expanded in the South.
- why the economy of the South remained primarily agricultural.
- why some Southerners tried to boost manufacturing in their region.

TERMS TO LEARN
cotton gin   capital

The Storyteller

Cotton was "king" in the South before 1860. "Look which way you will, you see it; and see it moving," wrote a visitor to Mobile, Alabama. "Keel boats, ships, brigs, schooners, wharves, stores, and press-houses, all appeared to be full." Cotton was also the main topic of conversation: "I believe that in the three days that I was there . . . I must have heard the word *cotton* pronounced more than 3,000 times."

Stem of cotton

In 1790 the South seemed to be an underdeveloped agricultural region with little prospect for future growth. Most Southerners lived along the Atlantic coast in Maryland, Virginia, and North Carolina in what came to be known as the **Upper South.**

By 1850 the South had changed. Its population had spread inland into the **Deep South**—a band of states spreading from Georgia through South Carolina, Alabama, Mississippi, Louisiana, Missouri, Arkansas, and Texas. The economy of the South was thriving. Slavery, which was disappearing from the North, grew stronger than ever in the South. Cotton had transformed the stagnant economy of the South into a prosperous, robust economy.

Rise of the Cotton Kingdom

⭐ Cotton had not always been the South's leading cash crop. In colonial times tobacco was the most profitable crop in Virginia. Georgia and South Carolina produced ever-increasing quantities of rice and indigo.

Both tobacco and rice had drawbacks. Tobacco depended on foreign markets, so its price varied wildly. Tobacco also wore out land quickly because it stripped the soil of important nutrients. Rice could not be grown in the dry climate of inland areas.

Sugarcane, another Southern crop, was raised in southeastern Louisiana. To grow sugarcane, farmers needed to invest large sums of money in irrigation canals and machinery. Sugarcane was therefore considered a "rich man's crop."

The Cotton Gin

The growth of the British textile industry in the late 1700s had created a huge demand for cotton. Unfortunately cotton was difficult to process. After harvest, workers had to painstakingly separate the plant's sticky seeds from the cotton fibers.

Cotton production was revolutionized when **Eli Whitney** invented the cotton gin in 1793. The cotton gin was a machine that removed seeds from cotton fibers, dramatically increasing the amount of cotton that could be processed. A worker could clean 50 pounds of cotton a day with the machine—instead of 1 pound by hand. Furthermore the gin was small enough for one person to carry from place to place.

Whitney's invention had far-reaching consequences for the South. The cotton gin led to the demand for more slaves. Because the cotton gin processed cotton fibers so quickly, farmers wanted to grow more cotton. Many Southern planters relied on slave labor to perform these tasks.

New Lands for Cotton

The removal of Native Americans from the Southeast in the early 1800s opened the way for expanding cotton production across the Deep

---

TECHNOLOGY AND HISTORY

The Cotton Gin

In 1793 Eli Whitney visited Catherine Greene, a Georgia plantation owner. She asked him to build a device that removed the seeds from cotton pods. Whitney called the machine the cotton gin—"gin" being short for engine. **How did the invention of the cotton gin affect slavery?**

2. A hand **crank** turns a **cylinder** with wire teeth. The teeth pull the cotton past a grate.

1. Cotton bolls are dumped into the **hopper**.

3. Slots in the **grate** allow the cotton but not its seeds to pass through.

4. A second cylinder with **brushes** pulls the cotton off the toothed cylinder and sends it out of the gin.

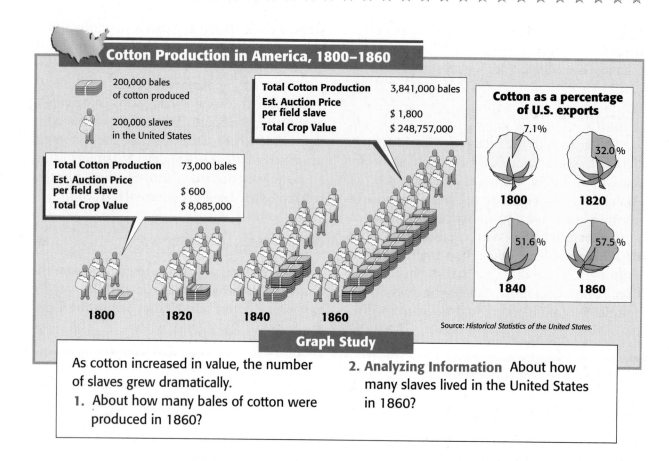

Cotton Production in America, 1800–1860

200,000 bales of cotton produced

200,000 slaves in the United States

Total Cotton Production	73,000 bales
Est. Auction Price per field slave	$ 600
Total Crop Value	$ 8,085,000

Total Cotton Production	3,841,000 bales
Est. Auction Price per field slave	$ 1,800
Total Crop Value	$ 248,757,000

Cotton as a percentage of U.S. exports

7.1% — 1800
32.0% — 1820
51.6% — 1840
57.5% — 1860

1800   1820   1840   1860

Source: *Historical Statistics of the United States.*

Graph Study

As cotton increased in value, the number of slaves grew dramatically.

1. About how many bales of cotton were produced in 1860?

2. **Analyzing Information** About how many slaves lived in the United States in 1860?

South. Settlers swept into the regions of Alabama and Mississippi after 1815.

With wet springs and summers and dry autumns, the Deep South was well suited for cotton production. Farmers without cotton gins or slaves could make a profit growing cotton even on small farms. They could succeed without actually owning a cotton gin because gins could be rented, and enslaved African Americans could be hired from slaveholders.

On large plantations, however, cotton growing went hand in hand with slavery. Using slave labor, the planters could plant and tend vast fields of cotton.

Cotton Rules the Deep South

Intense demand for cotton in Great Britain kept the price of cotton high in the years before 1860. By that year the economies of the Deep South and the Upper South had developed in different ways. Both parts of the South were agricultural, but the Upper South still produced tobacco, hemp, wheat, and vegetables. The Deep South

was committed to cotton and, in some areas, to rice and sugarcane.

The value of enslaved people increased because of their key role in producing cotton and sugar. The Upper South became a center for the sale and transport of enslaved people throughout the region.

$ Economics

Industry's Limited Role in the South

The economy of the South prospered between 1820 and 1860. Unlike the industrial North, however, the South remained overwhelmingly rural, and its economy became increasingly different from the Northern economy. The South accounted for only a small percentage of the nation's manufacturing in the 1850s. In fact, the entire South produced fewer manufactured goods than the state of Massachusetts.

Barriers to Industry

Why was there little industry in the South? One reason was the boom in cotton sales. Because agriculture was so profitable, Southerners remained committed to farming rather than starting new businesses.

Another stumbling block was the lack of cap-ital—money to invest in businesses—in the South. To develop industries required money, but many Southerners had their wealth invested in land and slaves. Planters would have had to sell slaves to raise the money to build factories. Most wealthy Southerners were unwilling to do this. They believed that an economy based on cotton and slavery would continue to prosper, and they saw no reason to risk their resources in new industrial ventures.

In addition the market for manufactured goods in the South was smaller than it was in the North. A large portion of the Southern population consisted of enslaved people with no money to buy merchandise. So the limited local market discouraged industries from developing.

Yet another reason for the lack of industry in the South is that some Southerners simply did not want industry to flourish there. One Texas politi-cian summed up the Southerners' point of view this way:

❝We want no manufactures; we desire no trading, no mechanical or manufac-turing classes. As long as we have our rice, our sugar, our tobacco and our cotton, we can command wealth to purchase all we want. ❞

Southern Factories

While most Southerners felt confident about the future of the cotton economy, some leaders wanted to develop industry in the region. These promoters of industry believed that, by remain-ing rural and committed to cotton production, the South was becoming dependent on the North for manufactured goods. These Southerners also ar-gued that factories would revive the economy of the Upper South, which was less prosperous than the cotton states.

One Southerner who shared this view was **William Gregg**, a merchant from Charleston, South Carolina. After touring New England's

Slave Market in Richmond, Virginia by Eyre Crowe A British ob-server, Crowe showed the dignity of enslaved people. His work, however, fails to show the inhumanity of the slave market. **What role did the Upper South play in promoting slavery?**

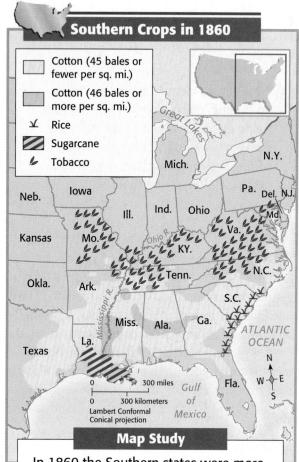

Southern Crops in 1860

Legend:
- Cotton (45 bales or fewer per sq. mi.)
- Cotton (46 bales or more per sq. mi.)
- Rice
- Sugarcane
- Tobacco

Map Study

In 1860 the Southern states were more agricultural than industrial.

1. **Location** In what state was the most sugarcane grown?
2. **Analyzing Information** What crop was grown most extensively throughout the South?

textile mills in 1844, Gregg opened his own textile factory in South Carolina.

In Richmond, Virginia, **Joseph Reid Anderson** took over the Tredegar Iron Works in the 1840s and made it one of the nation's leading producers of iron. Years later during the Civil War, Tredegar provided artillery and other iron products for the Southern forces.

The industries that Gregg and Anderson built stood as the exception rather than the rule in the South. In 1860 the region remained largely rural and dependent on cotton. 💲

Southern Transportation

Natural waterways provided the chief means for transporting goods in the South. Most towns were located on the seacoast or along rivers. There were few canals, and roads were poor.

The railroad boom that the North experienced in the 1840s and 1850s did not take hold in the South until late in the period. Southern rail lines were short and local and did not connect all parts of the region in a network. As a result Southern cities grew more slowly than cities in the North and Midwest, where railways provided the major routes of commerce and settlement.

By 1860 only about one-third of the nation's rail lines lay within the South. The railway shortage would have devastating consequences for the South during the Civil War.

Section 3 Assessment

Checking for Understanding

1. **Identify** Eli Whitney, William Gregg, Joseph Reid Anderson.
2. **Define** cotton gin, capital.
3. **Compare** agriculture in the Upper South and Deep South.

Reviewing Themes

4. **Science and Technology** Why did the invention of the cotton gin increase the demand for enslaved Africans?

Critical Thinking

5. **Predicting Consequences** If slavery had been outlawed, how do you think it would have affected the South's economy?

Activity

Creating an Advertisement Design an advertisement to sell the newly invented cotton gin.

1800	1820	1840	1860

1808
Congress outlaws
the slave trade

1831
Nat Turner leads
rebellion in Virginia

1859
Arkansas
orders free
blacks to leave

1860
Population
of Baltimore
reaches
212,000

Section 4

The South's People

READ TO DISCOVER . . .
- how people lived on Southern plantations.
- what roles different people played on plantations.
- how enslaved African Americans maintained strong family and cultural ties.

TERMS TO LEARN

yeoman	overseer
tenant farmer	spiritual
fixed cost	slave code
credit	

The Storyteller

Planters gathered in the bright Savannah sunshine. They were asked to bid on a strong slave who could plow their fields. Fear and grief clouded the enslaved man's face because he had been forced to leave his wife and children. Later, he wrote this letter: "My Dear wife I [write] . . . with much regret to inform you that I am Sold to a man by the name of Peterson. . . . Give my love to my father and mother and tell them good Bye for me. And if we Shall not meet in this world, I hope to meet in heaven. My Dear wife for you and my Children my pen cannot express the [grief] I feel to be parted from you all."

Plow

Popular novels and films often portray the South before 1860 as a land of stately plantations owned by rich white slaveholders. In reality most white Southerners were either small farmers without slaves or planters with a handful of slaves. Only a few planters could afford the many enslaved Africans and the lavish mansions shown in fictional accounts of the Old South. Most white Southerners fit into one of four categories: yeomen, tenant farmers, the rural poor, or plantation owners.

Small Farmers and the Rural Poor

The farmers who did not have slaves—yeomen—made up the largest group of whites in the South. Most yeomen owned land. Although they lived throughout the region, they were most numerous in the Upper South and in the hilly rural areas of the Deep South, where the land was unsuited to large plantations.

A yeoman's farm usually ranged from 50 to 200 acres. Yeomen grew crops both for their own use and to sell, and they often traded their produce to local merchants and workers for goods and services.

Not all Southern whites owned land. Some rented land or worked as tenant farmers on landlords' estates. Others—the rural poor—lived in crude cabins in wooded areas where they could clear a few trees, plant some corn, and keep a hog or a cow. They also fished and hunted for food.

The poor people of the rural South were stubbornly independent. They refused to take any job that resembled the work of enslaved people. Although looked down on by other whites, the rural poor were proud of being self-sufficient.

Plantations

★ A large plantation might cover several thousand acres. Well-to-do plantation owners usually lived in comfortable but not luxurious farmhouses. They measured their wealth partly by the number of enslaved people they controlled and partly by such possessions as homes, furnishings, and clothing. A small group of plantation owners—about 12 percent—held more than half of the slaves. About half of the planters held fewer than five enslaved workers.

Plantation Owners

The main economic goal for large plantation owners was to earn profits. Such plantations had fixed costs—regular expenses such as housing and feeding workers and maintaining cotton gins and other equipment. Fixed costs remained about the same year after year.

Cotton prices, however, varied from season to season, depending on the market. To receive the best prices, planters sold their cotton to agents in cities such as **New Orleans, Charleston,** Mobile, and Savannah. The cotton exchanges, or trade centers, in Southern cities were of vital importance to those involved in the cotton economy. The agents of the exchanges extended credit—a form of loan—to the planters and held the cotton for several months until the price rose. Then the agents sold the cotton. This system kept the planters always in debt because they did not receive payment for their cotton until the agents sold it.

Plantation Wives

The wife of a plantation owner generally had charge of watching over the enslaved workers who toiled in her home and tending to them when they became ill. Her responsibilities also included supervising the plantation's buildings and the fruit and vegetable gardens. Some wives served as accountants, keeping the plantation's financial records.

Women often led a difficult and lonely life on the plantation. When plantation agriculture spread westward into Alabama and Mississippi, many planters' wives felt they were moving into a hostile, uncivilized region. Planters traveled frequently to look at new land or to deal with agents in New Orleans or **Memphis.** Their wives spent long periods alone at the plantation.

Work on the Plantation

Large plantations needed many different kinds of workers. Some enslaved people worked in the house, cleaning, cooking, doing laundry, sewing, and serving meals. They were called domestic slaves. Other African Americans were trained as blacksmiths, carpenters, shoemakers, or weavers. Still others worked in the pastures, tending the horses, cows, sheep, and pigs.

Most of the enslaved African Americans, however, were field hands. They worked from sunrise to sunset planting, cultivating, and picking cotton and other crops. They were supervised by an overseer—a plantation manager. $

Life Under Slavery

★ Enslaved African Americans endured appalling hardship and misery. They worked hard, earned no money, and had little hope of freedom. One of their worst fears was being resold to another planter and separated from their loved ones. In the face of these brutal conditions, enslaved African Americans maintained their family life as best they could and developed a culture all their own. They resisted slavery through a variety of ingenious methods, and they looked to the day when they would be liberated.

Enslaved Workers

Overseers rang the wake-up bell or horn well before dawn. The enslaved workers reached the fields before the sun came up, and they stayed there until after sundown.

Planters wanted to keep the slaves busy all the time, which meant long and grueling days in the fields. Enslaved women as well as men were required to do heavy fieldwork. Young children carried buckets of water. By the age of 10, they were considered ready for fieldwork. Enslaved people who reached old age—60 or older—performed lighter chores such as weaving or caring for children.

Eyewitness to HISTORY

Life in the Slave Cabins

Enslaved people had few comforts beyond the bare necessities. Josiah Henson, an African American who escaped from slavery, described the quarters where he had lived.

❝We lodged in log huts and on the bare ground. Wooden floors were an unknown luxury. In a single room were huddled, like cattle, ten or a dozen persons, men, women and children. . . . Our beds were collections of straw and

★ **Picturing HISTORY** A family of enslaved workers gathers in front of their cabin on a plantation near Savannah, Georgia. **How did enslaved people cope with the injustices in their lives?**

African American Life in the South

Cotton kerchief

Water gourd

Workingman's shoe

What Was It Like? Although enslaved people had few personal possessions, their lives were marked by a strong shared spirit. **Which of the items shown here reflect the African traditions of enslaved people?**

old rags, thrown down in the corners and boxed in with boards, a single blanket the only covering. . . . The wind whistled and the rain and snow blew in through the cracks, and the damp earth soaked in the moisture till the floor was miry [filthy] as a pigsty. 99

Enslaved people lived on a diet consisting mostly of cornmeal, pork fat, and molasses. Many plantation owners allowed enslaved people to have their own gardens. The slaves grew greens and yams to supplement their diet. They usually had enough to eat, but their diet often was not well balanced or nutritious.

Family Life

Enslaved people faced constant uncertainty and danger. American law in the early 1800s did not protect enslaved families. At any given time a husband or wife could be sold away, or a slaveholder's death could lead to the breakup of an enslaved family. Although marriage between enslaved people was not recognized by law, many couples did marry. Their marriage ceremonies included the phrase "until death or separation do us part"—recognizing the possibility that a marriage might end with the sale of one spouse.

To provide some measure of stability in their lives, enslaved African Americans established a network of relatives and friends, who made up their extended family. If a husband or wife were sold away, an aunt, uncle, or close friend could raise the children left behind. Large, close-knit extended families became a vital feature of African American culture.

African American Culture

Enslaved African Americans endured their hardships by extending their own culture, fellowship, and community. They fused African and American elements into a new and distinctive culture.

The growth of the African American population came mainly from children born in the United States. In 1808 Congress had outlawed the slave trade. Although slavery remained legal in the South, no new slaves could enter the United States. By 1860 almost all the enslaved people in the South had been born there.

These native-born African Americans held on to their African customs. They continued to practice African music and dance. They passed traditional African folk stories and proverbs on to their children. Some wrapped colored cloths around their heads in the African style. Although a large number of enslaved African Americans accepted Christianity, they often followed the religious beliefs and practices of their African ancestors as well.

African American Christianity

For many enslaved African Americans, Christianity became a religion of hope and resistance. They prayed fervently for the day when they would be free from bondage.

The passionate beliefs of the Southern slaves found expression in the spiritual, an African American religious folk song. Spirituals provided a way for the enslaved African Americans to communicate secretly among themselves. Many spirituals combined Christian faith with laments about earthly suffering. The song "Didn't My Lord Deliver Daniel," for example, refers to the biblical story of Daniel who was saved from the lions' den.

❝Didn't my Lord deliver Daniel,
 deliver Daniel, deliver Daniel,
Didn't my Lord deliver Daniel,
An' why not every man? **❞**

Slave Codes

Between 1830 and 1860, life under slavery became even more difficult because the slave codes—the laws in the Southern states that controlled enslaved people—became more severe. In existence since the 1700s, slave codes aimed to prevent the event white Southerners dreaded

most—the slave rebellion. For this reason slave codes prohibited slaves from assembling in large groups and from leaving their master's property without a written pass.

Slave codes also made it a crime to teach enslaved people to read or write. White Southerners feared that a literate slave might lead other African Americans in rebellion. A slave who did not know how to read and write, whites believed, was less likely to rebel.

Resistance to Slavery

Some enslaved African Americans did rebel openly against their masters. One was **Nat Turner,** a popular religious leader among his fellow slaves. Turner had taught himself to read and write. In 1831 Turner led a group of followers on a brief, violent rampage in Southhampton County, Virginia. Before being captured Turner and his followers killed at least 55 whites. Nat Turner was hanged, but his rebellion frightened white Southerners and led them to the passage of more severe slave codes.

Armed rebellions were rare, however. African Americans in the South knew that they would only lose in an armed uprising. For the most part, enslaved people resisted slavery by working slowly or by pretending to be ill. Occasionally resistance took more active forms, such as setting fire to a plantation building or breaking tools. Resistance helped enslaved African Americans endure their lives by striking back at white masters—and perhaps establishing boundaries that white people would respect.

Escaping Slavery

Some enslaved African Americans tried to run away to the North. A few succeeded. **Harriet Tubman** and **Frederick Douglass,** two African American leaders who were born in slavery, gained their freedom when they fled to the North.

Yet for most enslaved people, getting to the North was almost impossible, especially from the Deep South. Most slaves who succeeded in running away escaped from the Upper South. The **Underground Railroad**—a network of "safe

Frederick Douglass

Life in the Cities

⭐ Although the South was primarily agricultural, it was the site of several large cities by the mid-1800s. By 1860 the population of **Baltimore** had reached 212,000 and that of New Orleans 168,000. Other cities on the rise included Charleston, **Richmond,** and Memphis. The population of Southern cities included white city dwellers, some enslaved workers, and a large share—about 250,000—of the South's free African Americans.

Free African Americans

The cities provided free African Americans with opportunities to form their own communities. African American barbers, carpenters, and small traders offered their services throughout their communities. Free African Americans founded their own churches and institutions. In New Orleans they formed an opera company.

Although some free African Americans prospered in the cities, their lives were far from secure. Between 1830 and 1860, Southern states passed laws that limited the rights of free African Americans. Most states would not allow them to migrate from other states. In 1859 Arkansas ordered all free African Americans out of the state. Although spared the horrors of slavery, free African Americans were denied an equal share in economic and political life.

houses" owned by free blacks and whites who opposed slavery—offered assistance to runaways.

Some slaves ran away to find relatives on nearby plantations or to escape punishment. Rarely did they plan to make a run for the North. Most runaways were captured and returned to their masters. Discipline was severe; the most common punishment was whipping.

⭐ ⭐ ⭐ ⭐ ⭐ **Section 4 Assessment** ⭐ ⭐ ⭐ ⭐ ⭐

Checking for Understanding

1. *Identify* Nat Turner, Harriet Tubman, Frederick Douglass, Underground Railroad.
2. *Define* yeoman, tenant farmer, fixed cost, credit, overseer, spiritual, slave code.
3. *List* two differences between yeomen and plantation owners.

Reviewing Themes

4. **Culture and Traditions** Why were extended families vital to African American culture?

Critical Thinking

5. **Making Generalizations** If you were a plantation owner, what would you tell your son or daughter if they asked why you held slaves?

Illustrating Differences Draw scenes that illustrate differences between planters and enslaved people in the 1800s.

Thoreau—The Abolitionist

"If a man does not keep pace with his companions, perhaps it is because he hears a different drummer. Let him step to the music he hears, however measured and far away." These are the words of a man who believed strongly in personal freedom. He believed that if a government, company, or society interferes with a person's life, that person has a right to protest.

This man was Henry David Thoreau (1817–1862). While living in a small cabin on Walden Pond near Concord, Massachusetts, Thoreau devoted himself to the study of nature and to writing about social issues. When he saw something in society that he thought was unjust, he spoke out.

In the mid-1800s, Thoreau became very active in the abolitionist movement. He helped fugitive slaves who were following the Underground Railroad. Horrified by slavery, Thoreau never missed an opportunity to speak out against the government that allowed slavery to continue.

" How does . . . a man behave toward this American government today? I answer that he cannot without disgrace be associated with it. I cannot for an instant recognize that political organization as *my* government which is the *slave's* government also.
. . . [W]hen a sixth of the population of a nation which has

undertaken to be the refuge of liberty are slaves . . . I think that it is not too soon for honest men to rebel and revolutionize.

. . . There are thousands who are *in opinion* opposed to slavery and to the [Mexican] war, who yet in effect do nothing to put an end to them; who, esteeming themselves children of Washington and Franklin, sit down with their hands in their pockets, and say that they know not what to do, and do nothing. . . . "

Thoreau wrote these ideas in an essay called "Civil Disobedience." His powerful message later influenced Martin Luther King, Jr., and Indian leader Mohandas Gandhi.

Activity

Designing a Poster What is there in your community that needs changing? Perhaps homeless people need help or litter needs cleaning up. Design a poster to convince people in your community to take action.

Henry David Thoreau

Walden Pond

Assessment and Activities

★ Reviewing Key Terms

On graph paper, create a word search puzzle using the following terms. Crisscross the terms vertically and horizontally, then fill in the remaining squares with extra letters. Use the terms' definitions as clues to find the words in the puzzle. Share your puzzle with a classmate.

telegraph
Morse code
trade union
prejudice
nativist
cotton gin
yeoman
credit
overseer
slave code

★ Reviewing Key Facts

1. How did the development of the canal and rail network alter the trade route between the Midwest and the East Coast?
2. How did the the telegraph influence long-distance communication?
3. In what ways were women in the work-force discriminated against?
4. Why was there little industry in the South?
5. What was the purpose of the slave codes?

★ Critical Thinking

Comparing and Contrasting

The difference in the economies of the North and South was reflected in the way people lived.
1. Why did the North have more large cities than the South?
2. How did the lives of Northern African Americans differ from those of Southern African Americans?

★ Reviewing Themes

1. **Economic Factors** How did improvements in transportation affect the economy in the North?
2. **Geography and History** Discuss one advantage and one disadvantage of city life in the North.
3. **Science and Technology** Compare the use of railroads in the North and South before 1860.
4. **Culture and Traditions** Describe ways in which enslaved African Americans held on to their African customs.

★ Geography Activity

Study the map below and answer the questions that follow.

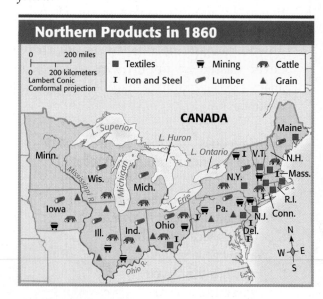

Northern Products in 1860

1. **Place** What products were developed in Ohio?
2. **Location** In general, where were most textile mills located?
3. **Region** How do the products shown here differ from the South's products as shown on the map on page 400?

★ Skill Practice Activity

Reading a Circle Graph

Study the circle graphs below, then answer the questions that follow.

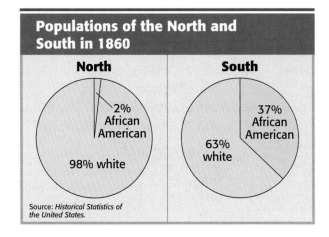

Populations of the North and South in 1860

North — 98% white, 2% African American

South — 63% white, 37% African American

Source: *Historical Statistics of the United States.*

1. What does the information in the two graphs represent?
2. What percentage of the population in the North was white in 1860?
3. In which part of the country did African Americans make up more than one-third of the population?
4. What can you conclude from the graphs about the total population of the North and South?

★ Cooperative Activity

History and Art With members of your group, create a model of what you think a Southern plantation might have looked like. Your model should include a planter's home, slave quarters, farm fields, a cookhouse, barns for the horses, and other details. Research to find illustrations to help you construct your model. Draw a design of your plantation on grid paper. Then gather scrap materials from home to construct your model. You will also need markers, glue, tape, and a large piece of stiff cardboard on which to build your model.

★ Technology Activity

Using a Word Processor Search encyclopedias and other library resources for information about the world's cotton industry today. Find out the countries that grow cotton, quantities grown, and the types of fertilizer used, if any. Gather this information and create a minireport of interesting cotton facts on your word processor. Share your report with the rest of the class.

★ Time Line Activity

Create a time line on which you place the following events in chronological order.

- Nat Turner leads a rebellion
- Elias Howe invents the sewing machine
- Samuel Morse sends the first telegraph message
- First steam-powered locomotive operates
- Cyrus McCormick patents the mechanical reaper
- Know-Nothing Party is formed

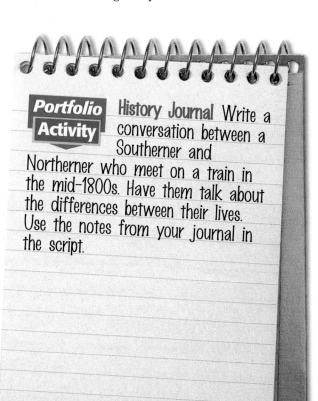

Portfolio Activity History Journal Write a conversation between a Southerner and Northerner who meet on a train in the mid-1800s. Have them talk about the differences between their lives. Use the notes from your journal in the script.

1820–1860

The Age of Reform

⭐ Why It's Important

The idea of reform—the drive to improve society and the lives of individuals—runs like a continuous thread through American history. During the mid-1800s, American reformers attacked such social problems as cruelty toward people with mental illness. They worked to make education available to more young people. Many also crusaded against slavery or for women's rights. These movements paved the way for later social changes.

⭐ Chapter Themes

- *Section 1*, Civic Rights and Responsibilities
- *Section 2*, Individual Action
- *Section 3*, Groups and Institutions

PRIMARY SOURCES
Library

See pages 962–963 for primary source readings to accompany Chapter 14

 HISTORY AND ART   *The Country School* by Winslow Homer   Homer painted scenes of rural American life in the 1800s. This painting shows a classroom in a rural public school.

1825
Robert Owen
establishes New
Harmony, Indiana

1835
Oberlin College
admits African
Americans

1837
Horace Mann
initiates education
reform

1843
Dorothea Dix
reveals abuses
of mentally ill

Section 1

Social Reform

READ TO DISCOVER . . .

- how religious and philosophical ideas inspired various reform movements.
- why educational reformers thought all citizens should go to school.
- how a new American style developed in art and literature.

TERMS TO LEARN

utopia
revival
temperance

normal school
Transcendentalist

Storyteller

Henry David Thoreau sat on the hard, wooden bench in the jail cell, but he did not complain about its stiffness. He felt proud that he had stood up for his beliefs. Thoreau had refused to pay a one-dollar tax to vote, not wanting his money to support the Mexican War. As he looked through the cell bars, he heard a voice. "Why are you here?" asked his friend Ralph Waldo Emerson. Thoreau replied, "Why are you *not* here?" He would later write, "Under a government which imprisons any unjustly, the true place for a just man is also a prison."

Ralph Waldo Emerson

A new reforming spirit arose in America in the early 1800s. The men and women who led the reform movement wanted to extend the nation's ideals of liberty and equality to all Americans. They believed the nation should live up to the noble goals stated in the Declaration of Independence and the Constitution.

The Reforming Spirit

The spirit of reform brought changes to American religion, politics, education, art, and literature. Some reformers sought to improve society by forming utopias, communities based on a vision of a perfect society. In 1825 **Robert Owen** established **New Harmony, Indiana,** a village dedicated to cooperation rather than competition among its members.

The Shakers, the Mormons, and other religious groups also built their own communities. Founded on high hopes and sometimes impractical ideas, few of the utopian communities lasted more than a few years. Only the Mormons established a stable, enduring community.

The Religious Influence

In the early 1800s, a wave of religious fervor—known as the **Second Great Awakening**—stirred the nation. The first Great Awakening had spread through the colonies in the mid-1700s.

The new religious movement began with frontier camp meetings called revivals. People came from miles around to hear eloquent preachers, such as **Charles Finney,** and to pray, sing, weep, and shout. The experience often made men and women eager to reform both their own lives and the world. The Second Great Awakening increased church membership, especially among Methodists and Baptists. It also inspired people to become involved in missionary work and social reform movements.

War Against Alcohol

Religious leaders stood at the forefront of the war against alcohol. Public drunkenness was common in the early 1800s. Alcohol abuse was widespread, especially in the West and among urban workers. **Lyman Beecher,** a Connecticut minister and crusader against the use of alcohol, wanted to protect society against "rum-selling, tippling folk, infidels and ruff-scruff."

Reformers blamed alcohol for poverty, the breakup of families, crime, and even insanity. They called for temperance, drinking little or no alcohol. The movement gathered momentum in 1826 when the American Society for the Promotion of Temperance was formed.

Beecher and other temperance crusaders used lectures, pamphlets, and revival-style rallies to warn people of the dangers of liquor. The **temperance movement** gained a major victory in 1851, when Maine passed a law banning the manufacture and sale of alcoholic beverages. Other states passed similar laws. Many Americans resented these laws, however, and most were later repealed, or canceled.

The temperance movement would reemerge in the early 1900s and lead to a constitutional amendment banning alcohol. You will read about this amendment and its repeal in Chapter 21.

Reforming Education

Reformers also focused on education. They argued that the poor state of education threatened the nation's well-being. Thomas Jefferson had stated that a democracy could not survive without educated citizens.

In the early 1800s, only New England provided free elementary education. In other areas parents had to pay fees or send their children to schools for the poor—a choice some parents refused out of pride. Some communities had no schools at all.

📖 Biography

Horace Mann

The leader of educational reform was **Horace Mann,** a lawyer who became the head of the Massachusetts board of education in 1837. During his term Mann lengthened the school year to six months, made improvements in the school curriculum, doubled teachers' salaries, and developed better ways of training teachers.

Mann shared Jefferson's belief that education was vital to democracy:

★ **Picturing HISTORY** During the 1800s, many Americans on the frontier attended religious camp meetings. At these gatherings, preachers gave rousing messages that stirred the listeners' emotions. **What two religious groups gained members as a result of the camp meetings?**

★ ★

66 If we do not prepare our children to be good citizens, then our republic must go down to destruction, as others have gone before it. 99

Partly due to Mann's efforts, Massachusetts in 1839 founded the nation's first state-supported normal school, a school for training high-school graduates as teachers. Other states soon adopted the reforms that Mann had pioneered. ▮

Education for Some

By the 1850s all states had accepted three basic principles of public education—that schools should be free and supported by taxes, that teachers should be trained, and that children should be required to attend school.

These principles did not immediately go into effect. Opposition to compulsory education slowed the development of public schools in many places. In addition schools were poorly funded, and many teachers lacked training.

Most females received a limited education. Parents often kept their daughters from school because of the belief that a woman's primary role was to become a wife and mother and that this role did not require an education. When girls did go to school, they often studied music or needlework rather than science, mathematics, and history—considered "men's" subjects.

In the West, where settlers lived far apart, many children had no school to attend. And African Americans in all parts of the country had few opportunities to go to school.

Higher Education

Dozens of new colleges and universities were created during the age of reform. Most admitted only men. Religious groups founded many colleges between 1820 and 1850, including Amherst and Holy Cross in Massachusetts and Trinity and Wesleyan in Connecticut.

Slowly, higher education became available to groups who were previously denied the opportunity. Oberlin College of Ohio, founded in 1833, admitted both women and African Americans to

★ Picturing HISTORY In 1862 Mary Jane Patterson, the first African American woman to receive a bachelor's degree, graduated from Oberlin College in Ohio. **Why were educational opportunities limited for women during the mid-1800s?**

the student body. In 1837 a teacher named Mary Lyon in Massachusetts opened Mount Holyoke, the first permanent women's college in America. The first college for African Americans—Ashmun Institute, which later became Lincoln University—opened in Pennsylvania in 1854.

People with Special Needs

Some reformers focused on the problem of teaching people with disabilities. **Thomas Gallaudet** (ga•luh•DEHT), who developed a method of educating people who were hearing impaired, opened the Hartford School for the Deaf in Connecticut in 1817.

At about the same time, Dr. **Samuel Gridley Howe** advanced the cause of those who were visually impaired. He developed books with large raised letters that people with sight impairments could "read" with their fingers. Howe headed the Perkins Institute, a school for the blind, in Boston.

*F*ootnotes to History

Braille Howe's raised-letter system was later replaced by Braille, a method invented by Louis Braille of France, in which raised dots represent letters.

Author Nathaniel Hawthorne explored themes of guilt and innocence, and good and evil. **What American writer of the mid-1800s focused on the supernatural?**

New Attitudes Toward Mental Illness

When schoolteacher **Dorothea Dix** visited a women's jail in Cambridge, Massachusetts, she found that some women confined there had committed no crime. They were mentally ill. These "lunatics," as the jailers called them, were locked up in the back of the jail in cold, dark cells.

Dix spent 18 months visiting the jails, poorhouses, and asylums of Massachusetts. She took notes on what she saw and made a report to the Massachusetts legislature. People were shocked by her vivid description of mentally ill people kept in pens, cellars, and cages, "chained, naked, beaten with rods and lashed into obedience."

Massachusetts lawmakers agreed to spend the money needed to provide better care for the mentally ill. Dix then began a lifelong crusade to improve the care of people with mental illness—one of many reforms dedicated to transforming American society in the mid-1800s.

Cultural Trends

★ The changes in American society influenced art and literature. Earlier generations of American painters and writers looked to Europe for their inspiration and models. Beginning in the 1820s American artists developed their own style and explored American themes.

Painters

American painters started choosing subjects that were specifically American. One group of painters, known as the Hudson River School, painted landscapes of the Hudson River valley in New York.

George Catlin painted hundreds of pictures of Native American life in the West. George Caleb Bingham of Missouri celebrated contemporary river and frontier life. In a series of elegant paintings and sketches, **John James Audubon** portrayed the birds of America.

Transcendentalists

The American spirit of reform influenced Transcendentalists. Transcendentalists stressed the relationship between humans and nature as well as the importance of the individual conscience. Writers such as **Margaret Fuller, Ralph Waldo Emerson,** and **Henry David Thoreau** were leading Transcendentalists. Through her life and writings, Fuller supported rights for women. In his poems and essays, Emerson urged people to listen to the inner voice of conscience and to break the bonds of prejudice. Thoreau put his beliefs into practice through **civil disobedience**—refusing to obey laws he thought were unjust. In 1846 Thoreau went to jail rather than pay a tax to support the Mexican War.

Other Writers

The Transcendentalists were not the only important writers of the period. Two of the most popular authors of the early 1800s were **James Fenimore Cooper** and **Washington Irving.** In novels such as *The Deerslayer* and *The Last of the Mohicans,* James Fenimore Cooper wrote of the clash between the values of the white settlers on the frontier and those of Native Americans. Washington Irving wrote tales, such as "The Legend of Sleepy Hollow" and "Rip Van Winkle," set in the Hudson River valley of New York.

Nathaniel Hawthorne, a descendant of early Massachusetts colonists, wrote of moral struggles in Puritan New England in *The Scarlet Letter.*

Using his experiences at sea, **Herman Melville** wrote *Moby Dick,* an epic tale of a whaling captain's search for revenge. In stories such as "The Tell-Tale Heart," **Edgar Allan Poe** explored the world of the supernatural. Poe perfected the modern detective story and has been called the "father of the modern short story."

American Poets

Many poets created impressive works during this period. **Henry Wadsworth Longfellow** wrote narrative, or story, poems, such as *The Song of Hiawatha,* on American themes. **Walt Whitman** captured the American impulse for self-improvement and equality in *Leaves of Grass* and other poetry. He wrote of a growing, confident people.

Emily Dickinson wrote simple, deeply personal poems. In a poem called "Hope," written in 1861, she compares hope with a bird:

> 66 'Hope' is the thing with feathers—
> That perches in the soul—
> And sings the tune without the words—
> And never stops—at all— 99

Women writers of the period were generally not taken seriously, yet they were the authors of the most popular fiction. **Harriet Beecher Stowe**

 Picturing HISTORY First printed as a series in a newspaper, Harriet Beecher Stowe's *Uncle Tom's Cabin* came out as a book in 1852. **What was the major topic of *Uncle Tom's Cabin?***

wrote the most successful best-seller of the mid-1800s, *Uncle Tom's Cabin.* Stowe's novel explores the injustice of slavery—an issue that took on new urgency during the age of reform.

★ ★ ★ ★ ★ Section 1 Assessment ★ ★ ★ ★ ★ ★

Checking for Understanding

1. **Identify** Horace Mann, Dorothea Dix, Ralph Waldo Emerson, Henry David Thoreau, Emily Dickinson, Harriet Beecher Stowe.
2. **Define** utopia, revival, temperance, normal school, Transcendentalist.
3. **Explain** the link between religion and reform in the early 1800s.

Reviewing Themes

4. **Civic Rights and Responsibilities** How did Thoreau act on his beliefs?

Critical Thinking

5. **Drawing Conclusions** What did Thomas Jefferson mean when he said that the United States could not survive as a democracy without educated and well-informed citizens?

Activity

Conducting an Interview Interview your grandparents or other adults who are more than 50 years old to find out what they remember about their public school days.

| 1815 | 1830 | 1845 | 1860 |

| 1817 | 1822 | 1831 | 1847 |
American Colonization Society is formed | First African Americans settle in Liberia | William Lloyd Garrison founds *The Liberator* | Liberia becomes an independent country

Section 2

The Abolitionists

READ TO DISCOVER . . .

■ how some Americans—African Americans and whites—fought to eliminate slavery.

■ why many Southerners and some Northerners feared the end of slavery.

TERMS TO LEARN

abolitionist   Underground Railroad

Storyteller

William Lloyd Garrison, a dramatic and spirited man, fought strongly for the right of African Americans to be free. On one occasion Garrison was present when Frederick Douglass, an African American who had escaped from slavery, spoke to a white audience about life as a slave. Douglass electrified his listeners with a powerful speech. Suddenly Garrison leaped to his feet. "Is this a man," he demanded of the audience, "or a thing?" Garrison shared Douglass's outrage at the notion that people could be bought and sold like objects.

Antislavery banner

THE ALMIGHTY HAS NO ATTRIBUTE, THAT CAN TAKE SIDES WITH THE SLAVEHOLDER.

The spirit of reform that swept the United States in the early 1800s was not limited to improving education and expanding the arts. It also included the efforts of abolitionists— members of the growing band of reformers who worked to abolish, or end, slavery.

Early Efforts to End Slavery

Even before the American Revolution, some Americans had tried to limit or end slavery. At the Constitutional Convention in 1787, the delegates had reached a compromise on the difficult issue, agreeing to let each state decide whether to allow slavery. By the early 1800s, Northern states had ended slavery, but it continued in the South. The North and the South then engaged in a heated debate over the issue of slavery.

The religious revival and the reform movement of the early and mid-1800s gave new life to the antislavery movement. Many Americans came to believe that slavery was wrong. Yet not all Northerners shared this view. The conflict over slavery continued to build.

Quakers for Freedom

Many of the men and women who led the antislavery movement came from the Quaker faith. One Quaker, **Benjamin Lundy** of New Jersey, founded a newspaper in 1815 to spread the abolitionist message. Lundy wrote, "I heard the wail of the captive. I felt his pang of distress, and the iron entered my soul."

American Colonization Society

The first large-scale antislavery effort was not aimed at abolishing slavery but at resettling African Americans in Africa or the Caribbean. The **American Colonization Society,** formed in 1817 by a group of white Virginians, worked to free enslaved workers gradually by buying them from slaveholders and sending them abroad to start new lives.

The society raised enough money from private donors, Congress, and the Virginia and Maryland legislatures to send several groups of African Americans out of the country. Some went to the west coast of Africa, where the society had acquired land for a colony. In 1822 the first African American settlers arrived in this colony, called **Liberia,** Latin for "place of freedom."

In 1847 Liberia became an independent country. American emigration to Liberia continued until the Civil War. Some 12,000 to 15,000 African Americans settled in the new country between 1822 and 1865.

Problems With Resettlement

The American Colonization Society did not halt the growth of slavery. The number of enslaved people continued to increase at a steady pace, and the society could only resettle a small number of African Americans. Furthermore, most African Americans did not want to go to Africa. Many were from families that had lived in America for several generations. They simply wanted to be free in American society. African Americans feared that the society aimed to strengthen slavery.

The Movement Changes

Reformers realized that the gradual approach to ending slavery had failed. Moreover, the numbers of enslaved persons had sharply increased because the cotton boom in the

William Lloyd Garrison, 1825

Deep South made planters increasingly dependent on slave labor. Beginning in about 1830, the American antislavery movement took on new life. Soon it became the most pressing social issue for reformers.

Biography

William Lloyd Garrison

Abolitionist **William Lloyd Garrison** stimulated the growth of the antislavery movement. In 1829 Garrison left Massachusetts to work for the country's leading antislavery paper in Baltimore. Impatient with the paper's moderate position, Garrison returned to Boston in 1831 to found his own newspaper, *The Liberator.*

Garrison was the first white abolitionist to call for the "immediate and complete emancipation [freeing]" of enslaved people. Promising to be "as harsh as truth, and as uncompromising as justice," he denounced the slow, gradual approach of other reformers. In the first issue of his paper he wrote: "I will not retreat a single inch—AND I WILL BE HEARD."

Picturing HISTORY This song sheet commemorates Frederick Douglass's 1838 escape from slavery. **What role did Frederick Douglass play in the abolitionist movement?**

Garrison *was* heard. He attracted enough followers to start the New England Antislavery Society in 1832 and the American Antislavery Society a year later. The **abolitionist movement** grew rapidly. By 1838 the antislavery societies Garrison started had more than 1,000 chapters, or local branches.

Americans Against Slavery

Among the first women who spoke out publicly against slavery were **Sarah** and **Angelina Grimké.** Born in South Carolina to a wealthy slaveholding family, the sisters moved to Philadelphia in 1832.

In the North the Grimké sisters lectured and wrote against slavery. At the National Anti-Slavery Convention in Philadelphia in 1838, Angelina Grimké exclaimed, "As a Southerner, I feel that it is my duty to stand up . . . against slavery. I have seen it! I have seen it!"

The Grimkés persuaded their mother to give them their share of the family inheritance. Instead of money or land, the sisters asked for several of the enslaved workers, whom they immediately freed.

Angelina Grimké and her husband, abolitionist Theodore Weld, wrote *American Slavery As It Is* in 1839. This collection of firsthand accounts of life under slavery was one of the most influential abolitionist publications of its time.

African American Abolitionists

Although white abolitionists drew public attention to the cause, African Americans themselves played a major role in the abolitionist movement from the start. The abolition of slavery was an especially important goal to the free African Americans of the North, who numbered about 250,000 in 1850.

Most African Americans in the North lived in poverty in cities. Excluded from most jobs and often attacked by white mobs, a great many of these African Americans were nevertheless intensely proud of their freedom and wanted to help those who were still enslaved.

Fighting Slavery

African Americans took active part in organizing and directing the American Antislavery Society, and they subscribed in large numbers to William Lloyd Garrison's *The Liberator.* In 1827 Samuel Cornish and John Russwurm started the country's first African American newspaper, *Freedom's Journal.* Most of the other newspapers that African Americans founded before the Civil War also promoted abolition.

Born a free man in North Carolina, writer **David Walker** of Boston published an impassioned argument against slavery, challenging African Americans to rebel and overthrow slavery by force. "America is more our country than it is the whites'—we have enriched it with our blood and tears," he wrote.

In 1830 free African American leaders held their first convention in Philadelphia. Delegates met "to devise ways and means for the bettering of our condition." They discussed starting an African American college and encouraging free African Americans to emigrate to Canada.

Frederick Douglass

Frederick Douglass, the most widely known African American abolitionist, was born enslaved in Maryland. After teaching himself to read and write, he escaped from slavery in Maryland in 1838 and settled first in Massachusetts and then in New York.

As a runaway, Douglass could have been captured and returned to slavery. Nevertheless he joined the Massachusetts Antislavery Society and traveled widely to address abolitionist meetings. A powerful speaker, Douglass often moved listeners to tears with his message. At an Independence Day gathering he told the audience:

> 66 What, to the American slave, is your Fourth of July? I answer: a day that reveals to him, more than all other days in the year, the gross injustice and cruelty to which he is the constant victim. To him, your celebration is a sham . . . your national greatness, swelling vanity; your sounds of rejoicing are empty and heartless . . . your shouts of liberty and equality, hollow mockery. 99

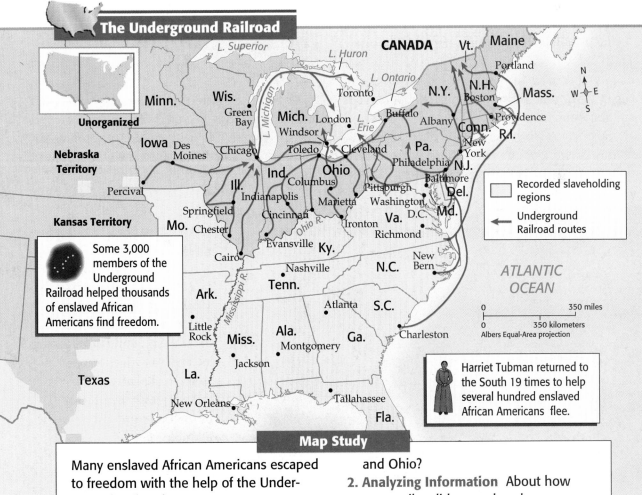

The Underground Railroad

Some 3,000 members of the Underground Railroad helped thousands of enslaved African Americans find freedom.

Recorded slaveholding regions

← Underground Railroad routes

Harriet Tubman returned to the South 19 times to help several hundred enslaved African Americans flee.

Map Study

Many enslaved African Americans escaped to freedom with the help of the Underground Railroad.

1. **Movement** Which river did enslaved persons cross before reaching Indiana and Ohio?

2. **Analyzing Information** About how many miles did an enslaved person travel from Montgomery, Alabama, to Windsor, Canada?

For 16 years, Douglass edited an antislavery newspaper called the *North Star.* Douglass won admiration as a powerful and influential speaker and writer. He traveled abroad, speaking to huge antislavery audiences in London and the West Indies. Douglass returned to the United States believing abolitionists must fight slavery at its source. He insisted that African Americans receive not just their freedom but full equality with whites as well. In 1847 friends helped Douglass purchase his freedom from the slaveholder he had fled in Maryland.

Sojourner Truth

"I was born a slave in Ulster County, New York," Isabella Baumfree began when she told her story to audiences. Called "Belle," she lived in the cellar of her master's house. When New York banned slavery in 1827, her owner insisted she stay a year longer. Instead, she fled.

In 1843 Belle chose a new name. "**Sojourner Truth** is my name," she said, "because from this day I will walk in the light of [God's] truth." She began to work in the movements for abolitionism and for women's rights.

Sojourner Truth had never been taught to read or write, but she spoke with wit and wisdom. In 1852 at a gathering of Ohioans, a rowdy farmer challenged her: The Constitution did not oppose slavery. Was she against the Constitution?

In answer, Sojourner used an example the farmer could understand. She knew that insects called weevils had eaten that year's wheat crop in Ohio. So she described walking near a wheat field and touching the tall, healthy-looking stalks but finding no grain there. "I says, 'God, what's the matter with this wheat?' And he says to me, 'Sojourner, there's a little weevil in it.'"

The farmer started to interrupt, but Sojourner continued to speak: "I hears talk about the Constitution and rights of man. I come up and I takes hold of this Constitution. It looks mighty big. And I feels for my rights. But they not there. Then I says, 'God, what ails this Constitution?' And you know what he says to me? . . . 'Sojourner, there's a little weevil in it.'"

The Underground Railroad

★ Some abolitionists risked prison—even death—by secretly helping enslaved Africans escape. The network of escape routes out of the South came to be called the Underground Railroad.

The Underground Railroad by Charles T. Weber This 1850s painting shows fugitives arriving at a station of the Underground Railroad in Indiana. **Why was Harriet Tubman considered the most famous "conductor" of the Underground Railroad?**

The Underground Railroad had no trains or tracks. Instead, passengers on this "railroad" traveled through the night, often on foot, and went north—guided by the North Star. The runaway slaves followed rivers and mountain chains, or felt for moss growing on the north sides of trees.

Songs such as "Follow the Drinkin' Gourd" encouraged runaways on their way to freedom. A hollowed-out gourd was used to dip water for drinking. Its shape resembled the Big Dipper, which pointed to the North Star.

> 66 When the river ends in between two
>   hills,
> Follow the drinkin' gourd,
> For the Ole Man's waitin' for to carry you
>   to freedom.
> Follow the drinkin' gourd. 99

During the day passengers rested at "stations"—barns, attics, church basements, or other places where fugitives could rest, eat, and hide until the next night's journey. The railroad's "conductors" were whites and African Americans who helped guide the escaping slaves to freedom in the North.

In the early days, many people made the journey north on foot. Later they traveled in wagons, sometimes equipped with secret compartments. One runaway, Henry "Box" Brown, traveled from Richmond, Virginia, to Philadelphia, Pennsylvania, hidden in a crate.

African Americans on the Underground Railroad hoped to settle in a free state in the North or to move on to Canada. Once in the North, however, fugitives still feared capture. Henry Bibb, a runaway who reached Ohio, arrived at "the place where I was directed to call on an Abolitionist, but I made no stop: so great were my fears of being pursued."

Harriet Tubman

Harriet Tubman escaped from slavery to become the most famous conductor on the Underground Railroad. She made many dangerous trips into the South and guided hundreds of enslaved people, including her parents, to freedom.

Slaveholders offered a large reward for Tubman's capture or death. "There was one of two things I had a right to, liberty or death," she said. "If I could not have one, I would have the other; for no man should take me alive." Tubman was never captured and lived to an old age.

Harriet Tubman

The Underground Railroad helped only a tiny fraction of the enslaved population. Most who used it as a route to freedom came from the border states, not the Deep South. Still the Underground Railroad gave hope to those who suffered in slavery. It also provided abolitionists with a way to help some enslaved people to freedom.

Clashes over Abolitionism

★ The antislavery movement led to an intense reaction against abolitionism. Southern slaveholders—and many Southerners who did not have slaves—opposed abolitionism because they believed it threatened the South's way

---

*F*ootnotes to History

Early Freedom Rider During the Civil War, Sojourner Truth tried to desegregate public transportation. Desegregated public transportation would not exist until almost 100 years later, in the 1950s.

of life, which depended on enslaved labor. Many people in the North also opposed the abolitionist movement.

Opposition in the North

Even in the North, abolitionists never numbered more than a small fraction of the population. Many Northerners saw the antislavery movement as a threat to the nation's social order. They feared the abolitionists could bring on a destructive war between the North and the South. They also claimed that, if the enslaved African Americans were freed, they could never blend into American society.

Economic fears further fed the backlash against abolitionism. Northern workers worried that freed slaves would flood the North and take jobs away from whites by agreeing to work for lower pay.

Violence against Abolitionists

Opposition to abolitionism sometimes erupted into violence against the abolitionists themselves. In the 1830s a Philadelphia mob burned the city's antislavery headquarters to the ground and set off a bloody race riot. In Boston a mob attacked abolitionist William Lloyd Garrison and threatened to hang him. Authorities saved his life by locking him in jail.

Elijah Lovejoy was not so lucky. Lovejoy edited an abolitionist newspaper in Illinois. Three times angry whites invaded his offices and wrecked his presses. Each time Lovejoy installed new presses and resumed publication. The fourth time the mob set fire to the building. When Lovejoy came out of the blazing building, he was shot and killed.

The South Reacts

Southerners fought abolitionism by mounting arguments in defense of slavery. They claimed that slavery was essential to economic progress and prosperity in the South. Slave labor, they said, had allowed Southern whites to reach a high level of culture and civilization. Southerners also argued that they treated enslaved people well, and that for African Americans slavery was preferable to factory work in the North.

Other defenses of slavery were based on racism. Many whites believed that African Americans were better off under white care than on their own. "Providence has placed [the slave] in our hands for his own good," declared one Southern governor.

The conflict between proslavery and antislavery groups continued to mount. At the same time, a new women's rights movement was growing, and many leading abolitionists were involved in that movement as well.

Section 2 Assessment

Checking for Understanding

1. *Identify* Liberia, William Lloyd Garrison, Sarah and Angelina Grimké, Frederick Douglass, Sojourner Truth, Harriet Tubman.
2. *Define* abolitionist, Underground Railroad.
3. *Discuss* the American Colonization Society's solution to slavery.

Reviewing Themes

4. **Individual Action** What role did Harriet Tubman play in the antislavery movement?

Critical Thinking

5. **Making Comparisons** Compare the arguments of Northerners and Southerners who opposed abolitionism.

Creating a Political Cartoon Find a political cartoon that depicts abolitionists or expresses an abolitionist sentiment. Use it as a model to create your own cartoon about the antislavery movement.

Multimedia Activities

 **Historic America
Electronic Field Trips**

Field Trip to Frederick Douglass's Home

Setting up the Video

With a group of your classmates, view "Frederick Douglass's Home" on the videodisc *Historic America: Electronic Field Trips*. Frederick Douglass's efforts to abolish slavery make him one of America's greatest civil rights leaders. This program focuses on different aspects of Douglass's life and contributions he made during his lifetime.

Hands-On Activity

Create a map of the United States. Include its borders as they appeared just before the Civil War. Color-code the map to reflect both free and slave states. Draw symbols for the agricultural and economic resources of each state. Include these symbols in your map key.

Side 1,
Chapter 9

View the video by scanning the bar code or by entering the chapter number on your keypad and pressing Search.

Surfing the "Net"

The Underground Railroad

The Underground Railroad was a secret, widespread network of people and places that helped enslaved people reach freedom in the North. Many conductors of the Underground Railroad, such as Harriet Tubman, used Polaris—the fixed star in the northern sky—to guide them to the North. To find out more about the Underground Railroad's famous history, travel the Internet.

Getting There

Follow these steps to gather information about the Underground Railroad.

1. Use a search engine. Type in the phrase *Underground Railroad.*

2. After typing in the phrase, enter words like the following to focus your search: *maps, stations, fugitives, slaves.*
3. The search engine should provide you with a number of links to follow. Links are "pointers" to different sites on the Internet.

What to Do When You Are There

Click on the links to navigate through the pages of information. Locate information about escape routes and stations that fugitive slaves used. Then use a large wall map of North America and trace the various routes that fugitive slaves used to reach freedom in the North. Place pins on the map to represent the location of stations.

1837
Mary Lyon establishes Mount Holyoke Female Seminary

1848
First women's rights convention held in Seneca Falls, New York

1857
Elizabeth Blackwell founds the New York Infirmary for Women and Children

1890
Wyoming grants women the right to vote

Section 3

The Women's Movement

READ TO DISCOVER . . .
- how the antislavery and the women's rights movements were related.
- what progress women made toward equality during the 1800s.

TERMS TO LEARN
feminist   coeducation
suffrage

The Storyteller

Women who fought to end slavery began to recognize their own bondage. On April 19, 1850, about 400 women met at a Quaker meetinghouse in the small town of Salem, Ohio. They came together "to assert their rights as independent human beings." One speaker stated: "I use the term *Woman's Rights,* because it is a technical phrase. I like not the expression. It is not Woman's *Rights* of which I design to speak, but of Woman's *Wrongs.* I shall claim nothing for ourselves because of our sex. . . . [W]e should demand *our* recognition as equal members of the human family. . . ."

Antislavery drawstring purses

In the early 1800s, American women lacked many of the rights that men enjoyed. The British system of law, which the American states had adopted after independence, made men the guardians of women. The law treated women like children who needed to be looked after and cared for. Unmarried women came under the authority of their fathers or nearest male relatives. Married women came under their husbands' authority. Widows and single women could own property and make wills. When they married, however, control of their property and earnings passed to their husbands.

Women and Reform

Women played a major role in all the American reform movements of the 1800s, but they were especially active in the campaign to end slavery. The female abolitionists, however, were often pushed aside or excluded by the men in the movement.

Some men believed that women should not speak in public or publish their writings. When American women attended a world antislavery meeting in London in 1840, they had to sit behind a curtain that separated them from the all-male meeting.

The Birth of the Movement

Gender prejudice turned many female abolitionists into champions of women's rights. "We have good cause to be grateful to the slave,"

★ ★ ★ ★ ★ ★ ★ ★ ★ ★ ★ ★ ★ ★ ★ ★

wrote reformer Abby Kelley. "In striving to strike his irons off, we found most surely, that we were manacled [chained] *ourselves.*"

Women abolitionists became the first American **feminists,** people who work for women's rights. Seeking to improve women's lives and win equal rights, they launched a continuing struggle.

Like many of the women reformers, **Lucretia Mott** was a Quaker. Quaker women, who enjoyed a certain amount of equality in their own communities, were particularly disturbed by the sexism in the antislavery movement. Mott gave lectures in Philadelphia calling for temperance, peace, workers' rights, and abolition. Mott also helped fugitive slaves and organized the Philadelphia Female Anti-Slavery Society.

At the world antislavery convention in London, Mott met **Elizabeth Cady Stanton.** There the two female abolitionists joined forces to work for women's rights.

Feminists Meet Opposition

The abolitionist sisters **Angelina** and **Sarah Grimké** were early supporters of women's rights. Some men in the movement criticized the Grimkés for engaging in "unfeminine" activities, but the sisters continued their work. "Men and women were CREATED EQUAL," they declared, ". . . and whatever is right for man to do, is right for woman to do."

Sojourner Truth also met opposition as she traveled throughout the North speaking about women's rights and slavery. When she addressed a women's meeting in New York City, a hostile crowd forced its way into the hall to jeer at the women. Truth told the mob,

❝ We'll have our rights; see if we don't; and you can't stop us from them; see if you can. You may hiss as much as you like, but it is comin'. ❞

Sojourner Truth

Eyewitness to HISTORY

The Seneca Falls Convention

In July 1848, Elizabeth Cady Stanton, Lucretia Mott, and a few other women organized the first women's rights convention in **Seneca Falls, New York.** About 200 women and 40 men attended.

The convention issued a Declaration of Sentiments and Resolutions modeled on the Declaration of Independence. The women's document declared: "We hold these truths to be self-evident: that all men and women are created equal."

Just as the Declaration of Independence had listed Americans' complaints against King George III, the Seneca Falls declaration listed women's grievances against men. It read,

❝ He [man] has endeavored, in every way he could, to destroy her [woman's] confidence in her own powers, to lessen her self-respect, and to make her willing to lead a dependent and . . . [miserable] life. ❞

*F*ootnotes to History

Women Physicians The first American medical school for women, the Boston Female Medical School, opened in 1848 with an enrollment of 12 students.

★ Picturing HISTORY Lucretia Mott (left) and Susan B. Anthony were leaders in the effort to allow women a greater role in American society. **What changes did the Seneca Falls declaration demand?**

The women's declaration called for an end to all laws that discriminated against women. It demanded that women be allowed to enter the all-male world of trades, professions, and businesses. The most controversial issue at the Seneca Falls Convention concerned suffrage, or the right to vote.

Elizabeth Stanton insisted that the declaration include a demand for **woman suffrage,** but delegates thought the idea of women voting was too radical. Lucretia Mott told her friend, "Lizzie, thee will make us ridiculous." After a heated debate, however, the convention voted to include the demand for woman suffrage in the United States. As Stanton later reasoned:

❝ Having decided to petition for a redress of grievances, the question is *for what shall you first petition*? For the exercise of your right to elective franchise [vote]—nothing short of this. The grant to you of this right will secure all others, and the granting of every other right, whilst this is denied,

is a mockery. For instance: What is the right to property, without the right to protect it? **❞**

The Movement Grows

The Seneca Falls Convention paved the way for the growth of the **women's rights movement.** During the 1800s women held several national conventions. Many reformers—including William Lloyd Garrison—joined the movement.

Susan B. Anthony, the daughter of a Quaker abolitionist in rural New York, worked for women's rights, temperance, and the reform of New York property and divorce laws. She called for equal pay for women, college training for girls, and coeducation—the teaching of boys and girls together. Excluded from a group called the Sons of Temperance, Anthony organized the country's first women's temperance association, the Daughters of Temperance.

Susan B. Anthony met Elizabeth Cady Stanton at a temperance meeting in 1851. They became lifelong friends and partners in the struggle for women's rights. For the rest of the century, Anthony and Stanton led the women's movement. They worked with other women to win the right to vote. Beginning with Wyoming in 1890,

★★★ Linking PAST & PRESENT

Ladies' Legwear Creates Scandal

In the early 1850s, women's rights worker Amelia Jenks Bloomer thought that huge hoops and long skirts kept women from moving about easily and naturally. She began wearing a pair of loose trousers gathered at the ankles. The trousers—invented by Elizabeth Miller but commonly called "bloomers" —caused quite a scandal. Some men shouted taunts, while others hurled sticks. Eighty years later, in the 1930s, wearing pants became commonplace for women.

several states granted women the right to vote. It was not until 1920, however, that woman suffrage became a reality everywhere in the United States.

Progress by American Women

In the 1800s most Americans believed that girls should not have advanced education. Some even questioned whether girls should be taught to read and write. Education, people feared, might make young women dissatisfied with their lives.

Without institutions that would offer them advanced education degrees, women were stopped from expanding their professional horizons. Before the 1830s no university or college in the United States would accept female students. Many men and women alike believed that it was useless and even dangerous for women to learn such subjects as mathematics. The stress of studying such subjects, some felt, might cause delicate women to have nervous breakdowns.

The only schools for women beyond elementary schools at that time offered courses for women on how to be good wives and mothers. Some young women, however, began to make their own opportunities. They broke barriers to female education and helped other women do the same.

Education

After her marriage **Emma Willard** educated herself in subjects considered suitable only for boys, such as science and mathematics. In 1821 Willard established the Troy Female Seminary in upstate New York. Catharine Beecher, the daughter of temperance crusader Lyman Beecher, founded schools to teach women about homemaking in Connecticut and Ohio. **Mary Lyon** established Mount Holyoke Female Seminary (later Mount Holyoke College) in Massachusetts in 1837. She modeled its curriculum on that of nearby Amherst College.

Marriage and Family Laws

During the 1800s women made some gains in the area of marriage and property laws. New York, Pennsylvania, Indiana, Wisconsin, Mississippi, and the new state of California recognized the right of women to own property after their marriage.

Some states passed laws permitting women to share the guardianship of their children jointly with their husbands. Indiana was the first of several states that allowed women to seek divorce if their husbands were chronic abusers of alcohol.

Breaking Barriers

In the 1800s women had few career choices. They could become elementary teachers—although school boards often paid much lower salaries to women than to men. Breaking into fields such as medicine and the ministry was far more difficult. Some strong-minded women, however, succeeded in entering these all-male professions.

Hoping to study medicine, **Elizabeth Blackwell** applied to—and was turned down

★ Picturing HISTORY Mary Lyon was a gifted teacher and a pioneer in the cause of higher education for women. **What institution did Mary Lyon found?**

 Picturing HISTORY Maria Mitchell won world-wide recognition for her achievements in astronomy. **What other notable women made contributions in fields once closed to women?**

New York Infirmary for Women and Children, staffed entirely by women.

One of Blackwell's sisters-in-law, Antoinette Brown, became the first ordained female minister in the United States. Blackwell's other sister-in-law, **Lucy Stone,** an Oberlin College graduate, became an influential lecturer on abolitionism and women's rights. To symbolize her equality with her husband, Stone kept her maiden name after she married and encouraged other women to do the same.

Maria Mitchell, a librarian, taught herself astronomy. Mitchell gained world renown when she discovered a comet in 1847. She became a professor of astronomy at Vassar College and the first woman elected to the American Academy of Arts and Sciences.

Sarah Hale, editor of a popular magazine called *Godey's Lady's Book,* influenced thousands of American women. Hale mixed articles on fashions and other traditional female subjects with a call for women to stand up for their rights.

Despite the accomplishments of notable women, some gains in education, and changes in state laws, women in the 1800s remained limited by social customs and expectations. The early feminists—like the abolitionists, temperance workers, and other activists of the age of reform—had just begun the long struggle to achieve their goals.

by—more than 20 schools. Finally accepted by Geneva College in New York, Blackwell graduated at the head of her class. She went on to become the first woman to receive a medical degree in the United States or Europe. In 1857 she founded the

---

Section 3 Assessment

★ ★ ★ ★ ★   ★ ★ ★ ★ ★

Checking for Understanding
1. *Identify* Lucretia Mott, Elizabeth Cady Stanton, Susan B. Anthony, Mary Lyon, Elizabeth Blackwell, Maria Mitchell.
2. *Define* feminist, suffrage, coeducation.
3. *Summarize* how the fight to end slavery helped to spark the women's movement.

Reviewing Themes
4. **Groups and Institutions** Discuss three specific goals of the women's rights movement.

Critical Thinking
5. **Making Generalizations** What qualities do you think women such as Sojourner Truth, Susan B. Anthony, Elizabeth Cady Stanton, and Elizabeth Blackwell shared?

Activity
Composing a Song Write and record a song designed to win supporters for the women's rights movement. Include lyrics that will draw both men and women supporters.

Using a Computerized Card Catalog

How many times have you had to go to the library to research a report or paper? Skill in using a computerized card catalog will help you find the information you need.

Learning the Skill

Go to the card catalog computer in your school or local library. What do you want to know about? Type in the name of an author or performer; the title of a book, videotape, audiocassette, or CD; or a subject heading. You will access the on-line, or computerized, card catalog that lists all the library's resources for that topic. The computer will list on screen the titles, authors, or whatever you requested.

The "card" that appears on screen will provide other information as well, including the year the work was published, who published it, what media type it is, and the language it is written or recorded in. Use this information to determine if the material meets your needs. Then check to see if the item is available. In addition, find the classification (biography, travel, etc.) and call number under which it is shelved.

Practicing the Skill

This chapter discusses abolitionists. These steps will help you use the computerized card catalog to find additional information on the subject "abolitionists":

1. Type "s/abolitionists."
2. From the list of subjects that appears on the screen, determine which might apply to abolitionists in the United States during the years between 1820 and 1860.
3. Follow the instructions on the computer screen to display all the titles under each

In antislavery newspapers, abolitionists showed the horrors of a slave auction.

subject you selected. For example, the instructions might be to type the line number next to the subject and press RETURN.
4. Determine which of the books, videos, audiocassettes, and CDs now on the screen you want to learn more about.
5. What do the instructions on the screen tell you to do to find more details?
6. What do the instructions on the screen tell you to do if you want to find out how many copies of the title the library owns and if and where a copy is available?

Applying the Skill

Using a Computerized Card Catalog Use the computerized card catalog in your school or local library to identify four resources—books, videotapes, CDs, or audiocassettes—you can use to write two reports, one on Elizabeth Cady Stanton and the other on public education in the 1800s.

Assessment and Activities

★ Reviewing Key Terms

On graph paper, create a word search puzzle using the following terms. Crisscross the terms vertically and horizontally, then fill in the remaining squares with extra letters. Use the terms' definitions as clues to find the words in the puzzle. Share your puzzle with a classmate.

utopia
revival
temperance
normal school
Transcendentalist
civil disobedience
abolitionist
Underground Railroad
feminist
suffrage
women's rights movement
coeducation

★ Reviewing Key Facts

1. What were the founders of utopias hoping to achieve?
2. What problems in society did leading reformers in the temperance movement blame on the manufacture and sale of alcoholic beverages?
3. What were the three basic principles of public education?
4. What was unique about the subject matter that American artists and writers of the mid-1800s used?
5. How did William Lloyd Garrison's demands make him effective in the anti-slavery movement?
6. What purposes did the Underground Railroad serve besides helping runaway slaves?
7. How were women viewed under the American system of law in the early 1800s?

★ Time Line Activity

Create a time line on which you place the following events in chronological order.

- Oberlin College admits women and African Americans
- William Lloyd Garrison founds abolitionist newspaper
- Horace Mann introduces major changes in schools
- Seneca Falls Convention held in New York
- First African American settlers arrive in Liberia
- Dorothea Dix files report revealing abuses of people with mental illness

★ Reviewing Themes

1. **Civic Rights and Responsibilities** How did Dorothea Dix win rights for people with mental illness?
2. **Individual Action** Summarize Frederick Douglass's role in the abolitionist movement.
3. **Groups and Institutions** What was the significance of the Seneca Falls Convention?

★ Skill Practice Activity

Using a Computerized Card Catalog
Use the card catalog computer in your school or local library to find out more about American poets of the early 1800s.

1. Type "s/poetry."
2. From the list of subjects that appears on the screen, determine which might apply to the United States during the years 1820 to 1860.
3. Follow the instructions on the computer screen to display all the titles under each subject you selected.
4. Which of the books on the screen do you want to learn more about?

★ Critical Thinking

Analyzing Information

Emily Dickinson's special talent was to write about great subjects—life, death, nature—using concrete images from everyday experience. Read the poem below, then answer the questions that follow.

> **"'Nature' is what we see"**
>
> "Nature" is what we see—
> The Hill—the Afternoon—
> Squirrel—Eclipse—the Bumble bee—
> Nay—Nature is Heaven—
> Nay—Nature is what we hear—
> The Bobolink—the Sea—
> Thunder—the Cricket—
> Nay—Nature is Harmony—
> Nature is what we know—
> Yet have no art to say—
> So impotent [weak] our Wisdom is
> To her Simplicity.

1. What does the poet say nature is in line 1? In line 4?
2. In your own words explain what the last four lines suggest about nature.
3. Write your own poem describing "What Nature Is."

★ Geography Activity

Use the map on page 419 to answer the following questions.

1. **Movement** About how many enslaved African Americans found freedom through the Underground Railroad?
2. **Location** From what Southern ports did African Americans flee by ship?
3. **Location** What "stations" of the Underground Railroad were situated on the Ohio River?
4. **Movement** How many times did Harriet Tubman risk her life to help slaves escape?

★ Technology Activity

Using the Internet Search the Internet for a modern organization whose goal is to support women's rights. Write a brief description of the organization, including its name, location, and a description of its purpose or activities.

★ Cooperative Activity

History and Language Arts Work in small groups to create a deck of "author cards" for your class. With members of your group, create a card for each of the 11 writers and poets discussed in the chapter. The front of each card should show a sketch of the author and a memorable line from one of that author's works. The back of each card should contain biographical information, a list of some of the author's titles, and other interesting facts about the author's life or writing style. Combine the cards of all the groups. Then work with your group to come up with a set of rules to play a game using your cards.

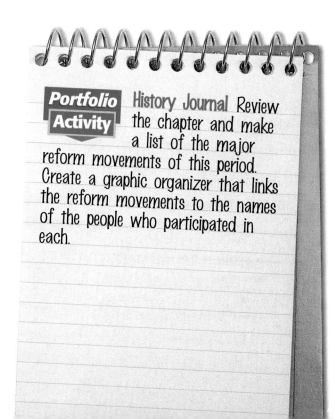

Portfolio Activity History Journal Review the chapter and make a list of the major reform movements of this period. Create a graphic organizer that links the reform movements to the names of the people who participated in each.

Unit 6

Civil War and Reconstruction

1846–1896

"A house divided against itself cannot stand."

—ABRAHAM LINCOLN, 1858

interNET
CONNECTION

To learn more about the Civil War and Reconstruction, visit the Glencoe Social Studies Web Site at **www.glencoe.com** for information, activities, and links to other sites.

MAPPING *America*

Portfolio Activity Draw a freehand outline map of the United States as it existed in 1850. As you read the unit about the Civil War and Reconstruction, note important events such as battles, government actions, or even cultural events. Plot the location of these events on your map and label them.

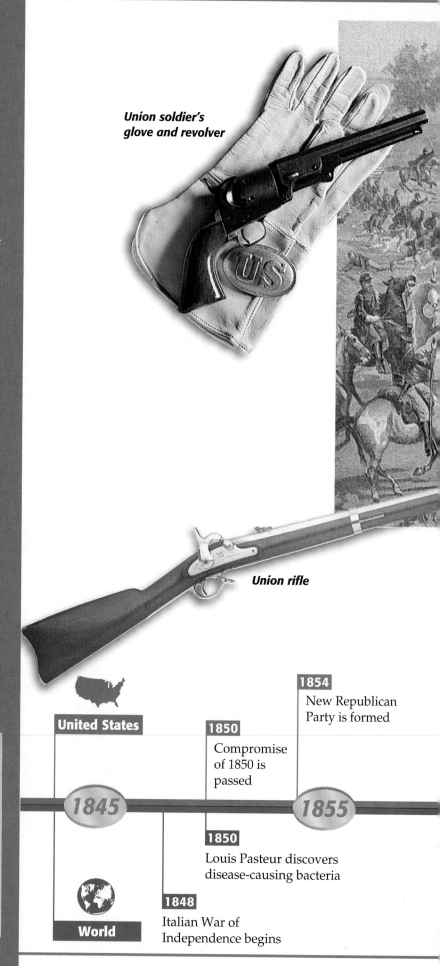

Union soldier's glove and revolver

Union rifle

United States

1850 Compromise of 1850 is passed

1854 New Republican Party is formed

1845

1855

1850 Louis Pasteur discovers disease-causing bacteria

World

1848 Italian War of Independence begins

432

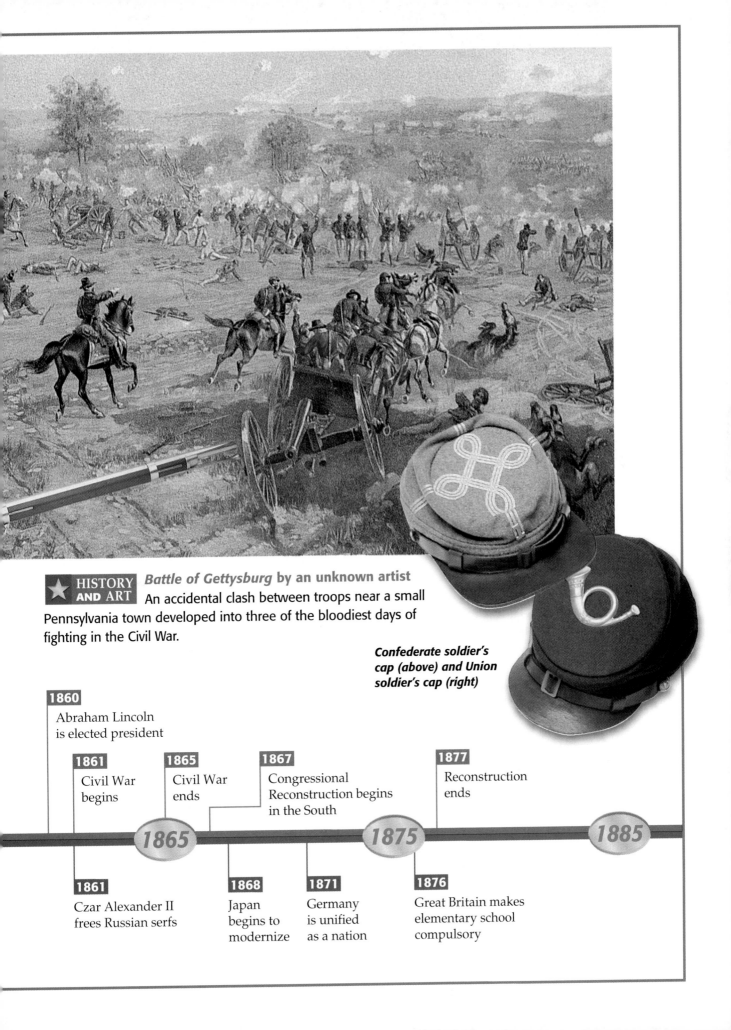

★ HISTORY AND ART **Battle of Gettysburg** by an unknown artist An accidental clash between troops near a small Pennsylvania town developed into three of the bloodiest days of fighting in the Civil War.

Confederate soldier's cap (above) and Union soldier's cap (right)

1860
Abraham Lincoln is elected president

1861
Civil War begins

1865
Civil War ends

1867
Congressional Reconstruction begins in the South

1877
Reconstruction ends

1865

1875

1885

1861
Czar Alexander II frees Russian serfs

1868
Japan begins to modernize

1871
Germany is unified as a nation

1876
Great Britain makes elementary school compulsory

America's LITERATURE

The Red Badge of Courage

by Stephen Crane

Stephen Crane (1871–1900) began his career in journalism while still in his teens. Later, as a reporter, Crane covered several wars in the late 1890s. He had not yet seen a battlefield, however, when he wrote The Red Badge of Courage. *Even so, he described the experience of war so realistically that even combat veterans admired his work. Critics still consider his novel* The Red Badge of Courage *a masterpiece.*

■ READ TO DISCOVER

What is it like to be a soldier facing battle for the first time? Henry Fleming, the young recruit in *The Red Badge of Courage,* offers some answers as he thinks about his role in the war. What battle does Henry fight with himself before he fights in an actual Civil War battle?

■ READER'S DICTIONARY

veterans: experienced soldiers
valor: bravery
Huns: soldiers known for their fierce fighting
despondent: sad
haversack: bag soldiers used to carry personal items
tumult: uproar

Various veterans had told him tales. Some talked of gray, be-whiskered hordes who were advancing with relentless curses, and chewing tobacco with unspeakable valor—tremendous bodies of fierce soldiery who were sweeping along like the Huns. Others spoke of tattered and eternally hungry men who fired despondent powders. "They'll charge through hell's fire an' brimstone t' git a holt on a haversack, an' sech stomachs ain't a-lastin' long," he was told. From the stories, the youth imagined the red, live bones sticking out through slits in the faded uniforms.

Still, he could not put a whole faith in veterans' tales, for recruits were their prey. They talked much of smoke, fire, and blood, but he could not tell how much might be lies. They persistently yelled "Fresh fish!" at him, and were in no wise to be trusted.

However, he perceived now that it did not greatly matter what kind of soldiers he was going to fight, so long as they fought, which fact no one disputed. There was a more serious problem. He lay in his bunk pondering upon it. He tried to mathematically prove to himself that he would not run from a battle.

Previously he had never felt obliged to wrestle too seriously with this question. In his life he had taken certain things for granted, never challenging his belief in ultimate success, and bothering little about means and roads. But here he was confronted with a thing of moment. It had suddenly appeared to him that perhaps in a battle he might run. He was forced to admit that as far as war was concerned he knew nothing of himself.

Military engineers of Company K, 8th New York State Militia

A sufficient time before he would have allowed the problem to kick its heels at the outer portals of his mind, but now he felt compelled to give serious attention to it.

A little panic-fear grew in his mind. As his imagination went forward to a fight, he saw hideous possibilities. He contemplated the lurking menaces of the future, and failed in an effort to see himself standing stoutly in the midst of them. He recalled his visions of broken-bladed glory, but in the shadow of the impending tumult he suspected them to be impossible pictures.

He sprang from the bunk and began to pace nervously to and fro. "Good Lord, what's th' matter with me?" he said aloud.

He felt that in this crisis his laws of life were useless. Whatever he had learned of himself was here of no avail. He was an unknown quantity. He saw that he would again be obliged to experiment as he had in early youth. He must accumulate information of himself, and meanwhile he resolved to remain close

upon his guard lest those qualities of which he knew nothing should everlastingly disgrace him. "Good Lord!" he repeated in dismay.

■ RESPONDING TO LITERATURE

1. How did Henry view the veterans and their war tales?
2. Why did Henry express doubts about his belief in himself?
3. What feelings do you think you might have just before going to battle?

Activity

Drawing Draw a picture showing items you think a young Civil War recruit would carry in a soldier's haversack. Include an item that might give the soldier courage.

1820–1861

Road to Civil War

★ Why It's Important

Slavery was a major cause of the worsening division between the North and the South in the decades preceding the Civil War. The struggle between the North and South turned more hostile, and there was talk of disunion and civil war. Americans today are still struggling with the legacy of slavery.

★ Chapter Themes

- *Section 1,* Government and Democracy
- *Section 2,* Civic Rights and Responsibilities
- *Section 3,* Continuity and Change
- *Section 4,* Geography and History

PRIMARY SOURCES **Library** *See pages 964–965 for primary source readings to accompany Chapter 15*

★ HISTORY AND ART *View of Harpers Ferry* by Ferdinand Richardt Danish artist Ferdinand Richardt captured a peaceful view of Harpers Ferry, Virginia (now West Virginia). The town was the location of the arsenal targeted for attack by abolitionist John Brown in 1859.

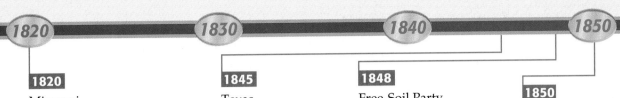

1820	1830	1840	1850

1820
Missouri
Compromise
is passed

1845
Texas
becomes
a state

1848
Free-Soil Party
nominates
Martin Van Buren

1850
Compromise of
1850 diverts war

Section 1

Slavery and the West

READ TO DISCOVER . . .

■ how the debate over slavery was related to the admission of new states.

■ what the Compromise of 1850 accomplished.

TERMS TO LEARN

sectionalism   secede

fugitive   abstain

The Storyteller

"The deed is done. The . . . chains of slavery are forged for [many] yet unborn. Humble yourselves in the dust, ye high-minded citizens of Connecticut. Let your cheeks be red as crimson. On *your* representatives rests the stigma of this foul disgrace." These biting, fiery words were published in a Connecticut newspaper in 1820.

They were in response to members of Congress who had helped pave the way for the admission of Missouri as a slaveholding state.

CAUTION!!
COLORED PEOPLE
OF BOSTON, ONE & ALL,
You are hereby respectfully CAUTIONED and advised, to avoid conversing with the
Watchmen and Police Officers of Boston,
For since the recent ORDER OF THE MAYOR & ALDERMEN, they are empowered to act as
KIDNAPPERS
AND
Slave Catchers,
And they have already been actually employed in KIDNAPPING, CATCHING, AND KEEPING SLAVES. Therefore, if you value your LIBERTY, and the Welfare of the Fugitives among you, Shun them in every possible manner, as so many HOUNDS on the track of the most unfortunate of your race.
Keep a Sharp Look Out for **KIDNAPPERS**, and have
TOP EYE open.
APRIL 24, 1851.

Warning to African Americans

The request by slaveholding **Missouri** to join the Union in 1819 caused an angry debate that worried former president Thomas Jefferson and Secretary of State John Quincy Adams. Jefferson called the dispute "a fire-bell in the night" that "awakened and filled me with terror." Adams accurately predicted that the bitter debate was "a mere preamble—a title-page to a great tragic volume."

The Missouri Compromise

★ Many Missouri settlers had brought enslaved African Americans into the territory with them. By 1819 the Missouri Territory included about 50,000 whites and 10,000 slaves. When Missouri applied to Congress for admission as a state, its constitution allowed slavery.

In 1819, 11 states in the Union permitted slavery and 11 did not. The Senate—with two members from each state—was therefore evenly balanced between slave and free states. The admission of a new state would upset that balance.

In addition, the North and the South, with their different economic systems, were competing for new lands in the western territories. At the same time, a growing number of Northerners wanted to restrict or ban slavery. Southerners, even those who disliked slavery, opposed these antislavery efforts. They resented the interference by outsiders in Southerners' affairs. These differences between the North and the South grew into sectionalism—an exaggerated loyalty to a particular region of the country.

Clay's Proposal

Henry Clay of Kentucky, then Speaker of the House of Representatives, proposed a solution to the Missouri question. Clay suggested that Congress admit Missouri as a slave state and Maine as a free state. Maine, formerly part of Massachusetts, had also applied for admission to the Union. Clay also sought to settle the issue of slavery in the territories for good. His proposal would prohibit slavery from any territory acquired in the Louisiana Purchase that was north of 36°30'N latitude—except Missouri.

This proposal, known as the **Missouri Compromise,** passed in 1820. It preserved the balance between slave and free states in the Senate and brought about a lull in the bitter debate in Congress over slavery.

New Western Lands

For the next 25 years, Congress managed to keep the slavery issue in the background. In the 1840s, however, this heated debate moved back into Congress. Once again the cause of the dispute was the issue of slavery in new territories. The territories involved were **Texas,** which had won its independence from Mexico in 1836, and **New Mexico** and **California,** which were still part of Mexico.

Many Southerners hoped to see Texas, where slavery already existed, join the Union. As a result the annexation of Texas became the main issue in the presidential election of 1844. Democrat **James Polk** of Tennessee won the election and pressed forward on acquiring Texas, and Texas became a state in 1845. At the same time, support for taking over New Mexico and California also grew in the South. The federal government's actions on these lands led to war with Mexico.

Conflicting Views

Just months after the Mexican War began, Representative David Wilmot of Pennsylvania introduced a proposal in Congress. Called the **Wilmot Proviso,** it specified that slavery should be prohibited in any lands that might be acquired from Mexico. Southerners protested furiously. They wanted to keep open the possibility of introducing slavery to California and New Mexico.

Senator **John C. Calhoun** of South Carolina countered with another proposal. It stated that neither Congress nor any territorial government had the authority to ban slavery from a territory or regulate it in any way.

Neither Wilmot's nor Calhoun's proposal passed, but both caused bitter debate. By the time of the 1848 presidential election, the United States had gained the territories of California and New Mexico from Mexico but had taken no action on the issue of slavery in those areas.

Polk campaign banner

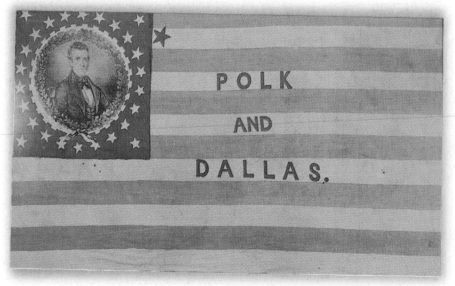

The Free-Soil Party

The debate over slavery led to the formation of a new political party. In 1848 the Whigs chose **Zachary Taylor,** a Southerner and a hero of the Mexican War, as their presidential candidate. The Democrats selected Senator Lewis Cass of Michigan. Neither candidate took a stand on slavery in the territories.

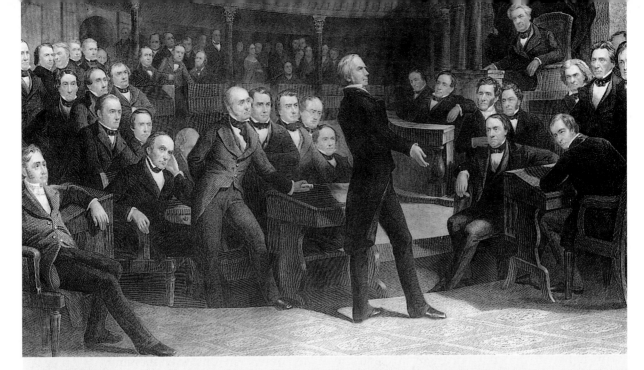

This engraving shows the great Senate debate in 1850 about Clay's compromise bill. **What did Clay's plan propose about slavery?**

This failure to take a position angered voters. Many antislavery Democrats and Whigs left their parties and joined with members of the old Liberty Party to form the **Free-Soil Party.** The new party proclaimed "Free Soil, Free Speech, Free Labor, and Free Men," and endorsed the Wilmot Proviso. The party nominated former president **Martin Van Buren** as its presidential candidate.

Whig candidate Zachary Taylor won the election by successfully appealing to both slave and free states. Taylor defeated Cass 163 to 127 in electoral votes. Van Buren captured only 14 percent of the popular vote in the North, but 13 candidates of the Free-Soil Party won seats in Congress.

California

Once in office President Taylor hoped to avoid congressional debate on the slavery question in California and New Mexico. He urged leaders in the two territories to apply for statehood immediately. Once these lands had become states, he reasoned, their citizens could decide whether to allow slavery. New Mexico did not apply for statehood, but California did in 1849.

Taylor's plan ran into trouble when California's statehood became tangled up with other issues before Congress. Antislavery forces wanted to abolish slavery in the District of Columbia, the nation's capital. Southerners wanted a strong national law requiring states to return fugitive, or runaway, slaves to their masters. Another dispute involved the New Mexico–Texas border.

The greatest obstacle to Taylor's plan, however, was renewed Southern concern over the balance of power in the Senate. In 1849 the nation included 15 slave states and 15 free states. If California entered as a free state—and New Mexico, Oregon, and Utah followed as free states, which seemed likely—the South would be hopelessly outvoted in the Senate. As tension reached a dangerous level, some Southerners began talking about having their states secede from, or leave, the United States.

A New Compromise

★ In January 1850, Henry Clay, now a senator, presented a five-part plan to settle all the issues dividing Congress. First, California would be admitted as a free state. Second, the New Mexico Territory would have no restrictions on slavery. Third, the New Mexico–Texas border dispute would be settled in favor of New Mexico. Fourth, the slave trade, but not slavery itself, would be abolished in the District of Columbia. Finally, Clay pushed for a stronger fugitive slave law.

The Great Debate

Clay's proposal launched an extremely emotional debate in Congress that raged for seven months. Opening that debate were Clay and two other distinguished Senators—John C. Calhoun of South Carolina and **Daniel Webster** of Massachusetts.

Calhoun opposed Clay's plan. Almost 70 and too ill to deliver his own speech, he asked Senator James Mason of Virginia to read it for him. Calhoun believed that the only way to save the Union was to protect slavery. If Congress admitted California as a free state, Calhoun warned, the Southern states had to leave the Union.

Three days later Webster gave an eloquent speech in support of Clay's plan. He claimed to speak "not as a Massachusetts man, nor as a Northern man, but as an American." What was most important was to preserve the Union.

❝I would rather hear of natural blasts and mildews, war, pestilence, and famine, than to hear gentlemen talk of secession. **❞**

The Compromise of 1850

Clay's plan could not pass as a complete package. Too many members of Congress objected to one part of it or another. President Taylor also opposed the plan and threatened to use force against the South if states tried to secede.

Then in July President Taylor suddenly died, the second president to die in office. The new president and Taylor's vice president, **Millard Fillmore,** supported some form of compromise. At the same time, **Stephen A. Douglas,** a young senator from Illinois, took charge of efforts to resolve the crisis. Douglas divided Clay's plan into a series of measures that Congress could vote on separately. In this way members of Congress would not have to support proposals they bitterly opposed.

During months of complicated bargaining, President Fillmore persuaded several Whig representatives to abstain—not to cast votes—on measures they opposed. Congress finally passed a series of five separate bills in August and September of 1850. Taken together these laws, known as the **Compromise of 1850,** contained the five main points of Clay's original plan. Fillmore called the compromise a "final settlement" of the conflict between North and South. The president would soon be proved wrong.

★ ★ ★ ★ ★ ⟨ Section 1 Assessment ⟩ ★ ★ ★ ★ ★

Checking for Understanding

1. **Identify** Henry Clay, Wilmot Proviso, John C. Calhoun, Zachary Taylor, Free-Soil Party, Daniel Webster, Stephen A. Douglas.
2. **Define** sectionalism, fugitive, secede, abstain.
3. **List** the provisions of the Missouri Compromise.

Reviewing Themes

4. **Government and Democracy** Why was the Free-Soil Party created?

Critical Thinking

5. **Media Literacy** Use the computerized card catalog in your library to list three subject headings you could investigate to learn more about the Missouri Compromise.

◆ Activity ◆

Designing a Campaign Poster Create a campaign poster for the Free-Soil Party presidential candidate. Include slogans or symbols to gain popular support.

Recognizing Bias

Cats make better pets than dogs. If you say this—without ever having owned a dog—then you are stating a bias. A bias is a prejudice. It can prevent one from looking at a situation in a reasonable or truthful way.

Learning the Skill

Most people have feelings and ideas that affect their point of view. This viewpoint, or *bias,* influences the way they interpret events. For this reason, an idea that is stated as a fact may really be only an opinion. Recognizing bias will help you judge the accuracy of what you read.

To recognize bias, follow these steps:

- Identify the author of the statement and examine his or her views and possible reasons for writing the material.

- Look for language that reflects an emotion or opinion—words such as *all, never, best, worst, might,* or *should.*

- Examine the writing for imbalances—leaning only to one viewpoint and failing to provide equal coverage of other possible viewpoints.

- Identify statements of fact. Factual statements usually answer the Who? What? Where? and When? questions.

- Determine how the author's bias is reflected in the work.

Practicing the Skill

Read the excerpts on this page. The first excerpt is from a speech by Senator John C. Calhoun of South Carolina. The second is from an 1858 newspaper editorial. Then answer the four questions that follow.

> 66 ... [T]he two great divisions of society are not rich and poor, but white and black; and all the former, the poor as well as the rich, belong to the upper classes, and are respected and treated as such. 99
>
> —Senator Calhoun

> 66 Popular sovereignty for the territories will never work. Under this system, each territory would decide whether or not to legalize slavery. This method was tried in the territory of Kansas and all it produced was bloodshed and violence. 99
>
> —*The Republican Leader,* 1858

1. Is Senator Calhoun expressing a proslavery or antislavery bias?
2. What statements indicate the racism in Calhoun's bias?
3. What political party's view does the editorial represent?
4. What biases or beliefs are expressed in the editorial?

Applying the Skill

Recognizing Bias Look through the letters to the editor in your local newspaper. Write a short report analyzing one of the letters for evidence of bias.

Glencoe's **Skillbuilder Interactive Workbook, Level 1** provides instruction and practice in key social studies skills.

1850
Fugitive Slave
Act is passed

1852
Uncle Tom's Cabin
is published

1854
Kansas-Nebraska
Act is passed

1856
"Bleeding Kansas"
erupts in violence

Section 2

A Nation Dividing

READ TO DISCOVER . . .

■ why the Fugitive Slave Act and the Kansas-Nebraska Act made the division between North and South worse.

■ how popular sovereignty led to violence.

TERMS TO LEARN

popular sovereignty   civil war
border ruffians

The Storyteller

On May 24, 1854, the people of Boston erupted in outrage. Federal officers had seized Anthony Burns, a runaway slave who lived in Boston, to send him back to slavery. Abolitionists tried to rescue Burns from the federal courthouse, and city leaders attempted to buy his freedom. All efforts failed. More than 1,000 militia joined the marines and cavalry in Boston to keep order. Federal troops escorted Burns to a ship that would carry him back to Virginia and slavery. In a gesture of bitter protest, Bostonians draped buildings in black and hung the American flag upside down.

Anthony Burns

The calm that followed passage of the Compromise of 1850 did not last long. Many in the North could not accept the Fugitive Slave Act, a key part of the compromise.

The Fugitive Slave Act

The **Fugitive Slave Act** of 1850 required all citizens to help catch runaways. Anyone who aided a fugitive could be fined—up to $1,000—or imprisoned. People in the South believed the law would force Northerners to recognize the rights of Southerners. Instead enforcement of the law led to mounting anger in the North, convincing more people of the evils of slavery.

Resistance to the Law

After passage of the Fugitive Slave Act, slaveholders stepped up their efforts to catch runaway slaves. They even tried to capture runaways who had lived in freedom in the North for years. Sometimes they seized African Americans who were not runaways and forced them into slavery.

In spite of the penalties, many Northerners refused to cooperate with the law's enforcement. The **Underground Railroad,** a network of free African Americans and whites, helped runaways make their way to freedom. Antislavery groups tried to rescue African Americans who were being pursued or to free those who were captured. In Boston members of one such group followed federal agents shouting, "Slave hunters—there go the slave hunters." People contributed funds to

★ ☆

buy the freedom of African Americans. Northern juries refused to convict those accused of breaking the Fugitive Slave Law.

📖 Biography

Uncle Tom's Cabin

Writer **Harriet Beecher Stowe** called the Fugitive Slave Act a "nightmare abomination." The daughter of a New England minister and wife of a religion professor, Stowe was active in antislavery work for much of her life. She wrote a novel about the evils of slavery. Her book, *Uncle Tom's Cabin,* was published in 1852. Packed with dramatic incidents and vivid characters, the novel shows slavery as a brutal, cruel system. In one scene Simon Legree, a slaveholder, tries to justify why Tom is a slave.

Harriet Beecher Stowe

❝Didn't I pay down $1,200 cash. . . ? An't yer mine, now, body and soul?" he said, giving Tom a violent kick with his heavy boot. "Tell me!" . . . "No! no! no! my soul an't yours . . . [Tom replied]. You haven't bought it—ye can't buy it! ❞

Uncle Tom's Cabin quickly became a sensation, selling more than 300,000 copies within its first year.

Proslavery writers responded with works that defended slavery. They argued that enslaved African Americans in the South lived better than free factory workers in the North. These books had little effect on the growing antislavery sentiment in the North. 📖

The Kansas–Nebraska Act

⭐ Franklin Pierce, a New Hampshire Democrat who supported the Fugitive Slave Law, became president in 1853. Pierce intended to enforce the Fugitive Slave Law, and his actions hardened the opposition.

In 1854 the dispute over slavery erupted in Congress again. The cause was a bill introduced by Stephen A. Douglas, the Illinois senator who had forged the Compromise of 1850.

Hoping to encourage settlement of the West and open the way for a transcontinental railroad, Douglas proposed organizing the region west of Missouri and Iowa as the territories of **Kansas** and **Nebraska.** Douglas was trying to work out a way for the nation to expand that both the North and the South would accept, but his bill reopened the conflict about slavery in the territories. In this new sectional crisis, violence began to infect the political debate.

Repeal of the Missouri Compromise

Because of their location, Kansas and Nebraska seemed likely to become free states. Both lay north of 36°30'N latitude, the line established in the Missouri Compromise as the boundary of slavery. Douglas knew that Southerners would object to having Kansas and Nebraska become free states because it would give the North an advantage in the Senate. As a result Douglas proposed abandoning the Missouri Compromise and letting the settlers in each territory vote on whether to allow slavery. He called this popular sovereignty—allowing the people to decide.

Passage of the Act

Many Northerners protested strongly. Douglas's plan to repeal the Missouri Compromise would allow slavery into areas that had been free for more than 30 years. Opponents of the bill demanded that Congress vote down the bill.

Southerners in Congress, however, provided solid support for the bill. They expected that Kansas would be settled in large part by

The Compromise of 1850

Oregon Territory
Wisc. 1848
Mich. 1837
Minnesota Territory
Utah Territory
Unorganized Territory
Iowa 1846
Calif. 1850
New Mexico Territory
Texas 1845

N W E S

Kansas-Nebraska Act, 1854

Washington Territory
Oregon Territory
Minnesota Territory
Nebraska Territory
Utah Territory
Kansas Territory
New Mexico Territory

N W E S

Free states
Slave states
Territory closed to slaveholding
Territory open to slaveholding
Indian Territory

0   400 miles
0   400 kilometers
Lambert Conformal
Conic projection

Map Study

The Kansas-Nebraska Act provided that the question of slavery should be decided by popular sovereignty.

1. **Region** How did the Kansas-Nebraska Act affect the agreement reached in the Compromise of 1850?

2. **Analyzing Information** What territories were nonslaveholding in 1854?

compromise with the South was no longer possible. Sam Houston, senator from Texas, predicted that the bill "will convulse [upset] the country from Maine to the Rio Grande."

Conflict in Kansas

Right after passage of the Kansas–Nebraska Act, proslavery and antislavery groups rushed supporters into Kansas. In the spring of 1855, when elections took place in Kansas, a proslavery legislature was elected.

Although only about 1,500 voters lived in Kansas at the time, more than 6,000 people cast ballots in the elections. Thousands of proslavery supporters from Missouri had crossed the border just to vote in the election. These Missourians traveled in armed groups and became known as border ruffians.

Soon after the election, the new Kansas legislature passed laws supporting slavery. One law even restricted political office to proslavery candidates. The antislavery people refused to accept these laws. Instead they armed themselves, held their own elections, and adopted a constitution that banned slavery.

By January 1856, rival governments existed in Kansas, one for and one against slavery. Each asked Congress for recognition. To confuse matters further, the president and the Senate favored the proslavery government, while the House backed the forces opposed to slavery.

"Bleeding Kansas"

With proslavery and antislavery forces in Kansas arming themselves, the outbreak of violence became inevitable. In May 1856, 800 slavery supporters attacked the town of Lawrence, the antislavery capital. They sacked the town, burned the hotel and the home of the governor, and destroyed two newspaper offices. Soon after, forces opposed to slavery retaliated.

John Brown, a fervent abolitionist, believed God had chosen him to end slavery. Brown had recently come to Kansas from Ohio with six sons and a son-in-law. When he heard of the attack on

slaveholders from Missouri who would vote to keep slavery legal. With some support from Northern Democrats and the backing of President Pierce, Congress passed the **Kansas–Nebraska Act** in May 1854.

Northern Democrats in the House split evenly on the vote, revealing deep divisions in the party. Many Northerners became convinced that

Lawrence, Brown went into a rage. He vowed to "strike terror in the hearts of the proslavery people." One night Brown led four of his sons and two other men along Pottawatomie Creek, where they seized and killed five supporters of slavery.

More violence followed as armed bands roamed the territory. Newspapers began referring to "Bleeding Kansas" and "the Civil War in Kansas." A civil war is a conflict between citizens of the same country. Not until the fall of 1856 could the United States Army stop the bloodshed in Kansas. By then more than 200 people had been killed.

Violence in Congress

The violence that erupted in Kansas spread to Congress as well. Abolitionist senator **Charles Sumner** of Massachusetts delivered a speech entitled "The Crime Against Kansas." Sumner lashed out against proslavery forces in Kansas. He also criticized proslavery senators, repeatedly attacking Andrew P. Butler of South Carolina.

Two days after the speech, Butler's distant cousin, Representative **Preston Brooks,** walked into the Senate chamber. He hit Sumner again and again over the head and shoulders with a cane. Sumner fell to the floor, unconscious and bleeding. He suffered injuries so severe that he did not

John Brown Calls Down the Storm of the Civil War, *a painting by John Steuart Curry*

return to the Senate for several years. The Brooks-Sumner incident and the fighting in "Bleeding Kansas" revealed the rising level of hostility between North and South.

Section 2 Assessment

★ ★ ★ ★ ★   ★ ★ ★ ★ ★ ★

Checking for Understanding

1. **Identify** Fugitive Slave Act, *Uncle Tom's Cabin*, John Brown, Charles Sumner.
2. **Define** popular sovereignty, border ruffians, civil war.
3. **Describe** how the Northern abolitionists reacted to the Fugitive Slave Act.

Reviewing Themes

4. **Civic Rights and Responsibilities** How did popular sovereignty lead to violence in Kansas?

Critical Thinking

5. **Predicting Consequences** Do you think the violence in Kansas could have been prevented if Congress had not abandoned the Missouri Compromise? Explain your answer.

Activity

Producing a Play With members of your class, choose a scene from *Uncle Tom's Cabin* to portray in a one-act play. Write a short script, assign roles, and present it to the class.

Harriet Tubman's Journey

5 Born into slavery in Maryland, Harriet Tubman escaped to the North where she became the most celebrated leader of the Underground Railroad. Called the Moses of her people, she made more than 19 trips back to the South to conduct hundreds of other slaves north, using underground stations through New York State. This map traces her own journey to freedom in the 1840s from near Cambridge, Maryland, to Philadelphia, then to New York, and on to Canada.

4 The Fugitive Slave Act of 1850 required runaways to be returned to their owners. After the passage of the law, many slaves fled to Canada. "I would not trust Uncle Sam with my people no longer," Tubman said. "I brought them all clear off to Canada." Tubman herself settled in Auburn, New York, in 1857.

Auburn

Philadelphia

CANADA

Mich.

Rochester

Niagara Falls

Port Huron

Detroit

Cambridge Md.

Iowa

Toledo

Ohio

Columbus

Ind.

2 Levi Coffin was known as "President of the Underground Railroad." A Quaker born in the South, he moved to the North in 1826 and became an active abolitionist. For 33 years he received into his house more than 100 enslaved persons a year.

Ill.

W.U

Ky.

Vol. III. No. VII.   JULY, 1837.   Whole No. 31.

This picture of a poor fugitive is from one of the stereotype cuts manufactured in this city for the southern market, and used on handbills offering rewards for runaway slaves.

THE RUNAWAY.

3 This printed handbill pictures a runaway slave. Southern slaveholders posted such handbills in newspapers, offering rewards to anyone who would capture and return runaways.

Tenn.

N.C.

S.C.

Ala.

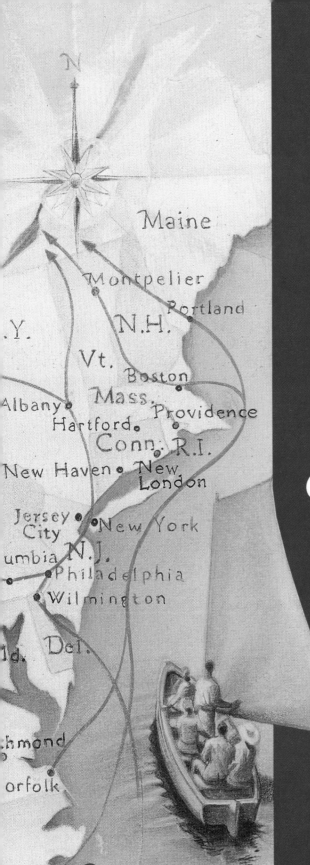

Underground Railroad

66 We knew not what night or what hour of the night we would be roused from slumber by a gentle rap at the door.... Outside in the cold or rain ... would be a two-horse wagon loaded with fugitives.... I would invite them, in a low tone, to come in, and they would follow me into the house without a word.... When they were all safely inside and the door fastened, I would cover the windows, strike a light, and build a good fire.... The fugitives would rest on pallets before the fire the rest of the night. 99

— *From* Reminiscence *by Levi Coffin, published 1876.*

1 Many slaves fled north by water. Some seized small sailing boats; others were taken by ferry operators. Most stowed away on ships bound for Northern ports.

447

1854   1856   1858   1860

1854
Republican Party
is formed

1856
James Buchanan
is elected president

1857
Dred Scott decision
states that all slaves
are property

1859
John Brown raids
Harpers Ferry, Virginia

Section 3

Challenges to Slavery

READ TO DISCOVER . . .

- why the Republican Party was formed.
- how the *Dred Scott* decision, the Lincoln-Douglas debates, and John Brown's raid affected Americans in the North and the South.

TERMS TO LEARN

arsenal   martyr

The Storyteller

Many people considered John Brown to be a radical murderer, while others viewed him as a fighter for the cause of freedom. When he was executed in 1859, the *Anglo-African Magazine* wrote: "On leaving the jail, John Brown had on his face an expression of calmness and serenity characteristic of the patriot who is about to die with a living consciousness that he is laying down his life for the good of his fellow creatures. . . . As he stepped out of the door, a black woman, with a little child in her arms, stood near his way. . . . He stopped for a moment in his course, stooped over, and with the tenderness of one whose love is as broad as the brotherhood of man, kissed the child affectionately."

***Kansas
Free-Soil poster***

Anger over the Kansas–Nebraska Act changed the structure of American politics. The Democratic Party began to divide along sectional lines, with Northern Democrats leaving the party. The death of Whig leaders Henry Clay and Daniel Webster in 1852 had discouraged the party. Differing views over the slavery issue destroyed the party.

In 1854 antislavery Whigs and Democrats joined forces with Free-Soilers to form the **Republican Party.** The new party was determined to "rally as one man for the establishment of liberty and the overthrow of the Slave Power."

The Republican Party

The Republicans began to challenge the proslavery Whigs and Democrats, choosing candidates to run in the state and congressional elections of 1854. Their main message was that the government should ban slavery from new territories.

Gaining Ground in 1854

The Republican Party quietly showed its strength in the North. In the election, the Republicans won control of the House of Representatives and of several state governments. In the South the Republicans had almost no support.

Northern Democrats suffered a beating. Almost three-fourths of the Democratic candidates from free states lost in 1854. The party was increasingly becoming a Southern party.

The Election of 1856

Democrats and Republicans met again in the presidential election of 1856. The Whig Party, disintegrating over the slavery issue, did not offer a candidate of its own.

The Republicans chose **John C. Frémont** of California as their candidate for president. Frémont had gained fame as an explorer in the West and a champion of free California. Party strategists considered Frémont's lack of a political record an asset and hoped that "the romance of his life" would win votes.

The Democrats decided not to nominate President Franklin Pierce because of Pierce's role in the Kansas troubles. Instead the Democrats chose **James Buchanan** of Pennsylvania, who had been minister to Great Britain at the time and was not tainted by Kansas. The Democrats supported popular sovereignty. They attacked the Republicans as a sectional party and accused them of being abolitionists.

A third party, the **American Party** or Know-Nothings, supported former president Millard Fillmore as their candidate in 1856. The party took its name from an organization that opposed immigration. Its members, when questioned about their organization, replied, "I know nothing." The Know-Nothing Party appealed to voters who disliked the growing number of immigrants, but it was divided on the subject of slavery.

Southern votes secured the presidency for Buchanan. Frémont won about one-third of the popular vote even though he received almost no votes in the South. Fillmore carried only the state of Maryland. Soon after this election, the Know-Nothings who opposed slavery joined forces with the Republicans.

★ Picturing HISTORY James Buchanan and John Frémont campaigned for the 1856 presidential election. **Whose support enabled Buchanan to win the election?**

The *Dred Scott* Decision

★ President Buchanan took office on March 4, 1857. Two days later the Supreme Court announced a decision about slavery and the territories that shook the nation.

The *Dred Scott* Case

Dred Scott was an enslaved African American bought by an army doctor in Missouri, a slave state. In the 1830s the doctor moved his household to **Illinois,** a free state, and then to the Wisconsin Territory, where slavery was banned by the Northwest Ordinance of 1787. Later the family returned to Missouri, where the doctor died. In 1846, with the help of antislavery lawyers, Scott sued for his freedom. He claimed he should be free because he had once lived on free soil. Eleven years later, in the midst of growing anger over the slavery issue, the case reached the Supreme Court.

The case attracted enormous attention. While the immediate issue was Dred Scott's status, the Court also had the opportunity to rule on the question of slavery in territories. Many Americans hoped that the Court would resolve the issue for good.

*F*ootnotes to History

A Humble Start Two presidents, Millard Fillmore and Andrew Johnson, were once indentured as apprentices. Andrew Johnson ran away from his master. Fillmore bought his freedom for $30.

★ **Picturing HISTORY** The Supreme Court ruled that Dred Scott had no right to sue for his freedom in the federal courts because he was not a citizen. **What did the Supreme Court rule unconstitutional in the *Dred Scott* case?**

The Court's Decision

The Court's decision electrified the nation. Chief Justice **Roger B. Taney** (TAW•nee) said that Dred Scott was still a slave. As a slave, Scott was not a citizen and had no right to bring a lawsuit. Taney could have stopped there, but he decided to address the broader issues.

Taney wrote that Scott's residence on free soil did not make him free. An enslaved person was property, and the Fifth Amendment prohibits Congress from taking away property without "due process of law."

Finally, Taney wrote that Congress had no power to prohibit slavery in any territory. The Missouri Compromise—which had banned slavery north of 36°30'N latitude—was unconstitutional. For that matter, so was popular sovereignty. Not even the voters in a territory could prohibit slavery because that would amount to taking away a person's property. In effect, the decision meant that the Constitution protected slavery.

Reaction to the Decision

Rather than settling the issue, the Supreme Court's decision divided the country even more. Many Southerners were elated. The Court had reaffirmed what many in the South had always maintained: Nothing could legally prevent the spread of slavery. Northern Democrats were pleased that the Republicans' main issue—restricting the spread of slavery—had been ruled unconstitutional.

Republicans and other antislavery groups were outraged, calling the *Dred Scott* decision "a wicked and false judgment" and "the greatest crime" ever committed in the nation's courts. Several state legislatures passed resolutions declaring that the decision was "not binding in law and conscience." Republicans promised that if they won the presidency in 1860 they would change the Supreme Court—by appointing new justices—and reverse the decision.

African American abolitionist **Frederick Douglass** looked to the future. He hoped that the decision would begin a "chain of events" that would produce a "complete overthrow of the whole slave system."

Lincoln and Douglas

★ In the congressional election of 1858, the Senate race in Illinois was the center of national attention. The contest pitted the current senator, Democrat Stephen A. Douglas, against Republican challenger **Abraham Lincoln.** People considered Douglas a likely candidate for president in 1860. Lincoln was nearly an unknown.

The Candidates

Douglas, a successful lawyer, had joined the Democratic Party and won election to the House in 1842 and to the Senate in 1846. Short, stocky, and powerful, Douglas was called "the Little Giant." He disliked slavery but thought that the controversy over it would interfere with the nation's growth. He believed the issue could be resolved through popular sovereignty.

Born in the poor backcountry of Kentucky, Abraham Lincoln moved to Indiana as a child and later moved to Illinois. Like Douglas, Lincoln was intelligent, ambitious, and a successful lawyer. He had little formal education—but excellent political instincts. Although Lincoln saw slavery as morally wrong, he admitted there was no easy way to eliminate slavery where it already existed. He was certain, though, that slavery should not be allowed to spread.

Eyewitness to HISTORY

The Lincoln–Douglas Debates

Not as well known as Douglas, Lincoln challenged the senator to a series of debates. Douglas reluctantly agreed. The two met seven times in August, September, and October of 1858 at locations all over Illinois. Thousands came to these debates. The main topic, of course, was slavery.

Lincoln had launched his campaign in June with a memorable speech, in which he declared:

> 66 'A house divided against itself cannot stand.' I believe this Government cannot endure permanently half *slave* and half *free.* 99

In the debates, Douglas accused Lincoln of contributing to the breakup of the Union.

> 66 [If the states] cannot endure thus divided, then [he] must strive to make them all free or all slave, which will inevitably bring about a dissolution of the Union. 99

During the debate at Freeport, Lincoln pressed Douglas about his views on popular sovereignty. Could the people of a territory legally exclude slavery before achieving statehood? Douglas replied that the people could exclude slavery by refusing to pass laws protecting slaveholders' rights. Douglas's response, which satisfied antislavery followers but lost him support in the South, became known as the **Freeport Doctrine.**

Douglas claimed that Lincoln wanted African Americans to be fully equal to whites. Lincoln denied this. Still, Lincoln said, "in the right to eat the bread . . . which his own hand earns, [an African American] is *my equal and the equal of [Senator] Douglas, and the equal of every living man.*" The real issue, Lincoln said, is "between the men who think slavery a wrong and those who do not think it wrong. The Republican Party thinks it wrong."

★ **Picturing HISTORY** Thousands attended the Lincoln-Douglas debates. Douglas sits to Lincoln's right in the debate at Charleston, Illinois, in September 1858. **What was the Freeport Doctrine?**

Lincoln Emerges as a Leader

Following the debates Douglas won reelection to the Senate in 1858. However, he lost support in other areas. By saying that voters could keep slavery out of a territory, Douglas further angered the South. In 1860 he lost Southern support in the presidential election. Lincoln, by contrast, lost the Senate race, but his performance in the Illinois debates catapulted him into the national spotlight. He campaigned for Republican candidates in other states and gained support as a candidate for president.

The Raid on Harpers Ferry

Political tensions heightened after the election of 1858. Southerners felt threatened by growing Republican power. In October 1859, an act of violence further fed their fears.

John Brown's Raid

On October 16 the abolitionist John Brown led 18 men, both whites and free African Americans, on a raid on **Harpers Ferry, Virginia.** His target was an arsenal, a storage place for weapons and ammunition. Brown—who had killed 5 proslavery Kansans in 1856—was encouraged and financed by some abolitionists to carry out his plan.

Brown had the idea to seize the federal arsenal and spark an uprising of enslaved people, whom he would arm with the weapons he captured. The plan failed. No slaves rebelled, and United States Marines under the command of Colonel Robert E. Lee captured Brown and several of his followers. During Brown's raid, which lasted only 36 hours, 10 of his men—including 2 of Brown's sons—were killed. One marine, 4 civilians, and 2 slaves also were killed in the fighting.

Brown was tried and found guilty of murder and treason and was sentenced to hang on December 2, 1859. Six of his followers met the same fate over the next few months.

Sectional Response

Brown's trial and execution created an uproar in the North. Some antislavery Northerners, including Republican leaders, denounced Brown for promoting violence. To some Northerners, though, Brown was a great hero. Writer Ralph Waldo Emerson called Brown a martyr—a person who dies for a great cause—who would "make the gallows as glorious as the cross."

John Brown's death became a rallying point for abolitionists. When Southerners learned of Brown's connection to abolitionists, their fears of a great Northern conspiracy against them seemed to be confirmed. The nation was on the brink of disaster.

★ ★ ★ ★ ★   **Section 3 Assessment**   ★ ★ ★ ★ ★

Checking for Understanding

1. **Identify** Republican Party, John C. Frémont, James Buchanan, Dred Scott, Roger B. Taney, Abraham Lincoln.
2. **Define** arsenal, martyr.
3. **Discuss** the stages in the development of the Republican Party.

Reviewing Themes

4. **Continuity and Change** How did the *Dred Scott* decision reverse a previous decision made by Congress?

Critical Thinking

5. **Making Inferences** Why did Lincoln emerge as a leader after the Douglas–Lincoln debates?

Activity

Creating a Political Cartoon Draw a political cartoon that illustrates Lincoln's statement "A house divided against itself cannot stand."

1860
Abraham Lincoln
is elected president;
South Carolina secedes

February 1861
Southern states form
the Confederate States
of America

April 1861
Confederate forces
attack Fort Sumter;
the Civil War begins

Section 4

Secession and War

READ TO DISCOVER . . .
- how the 1860 election led to the breakup of the Union.
- why secession led to the outbreak of the Civil War.

TERMS TO LEARN
secession   states' rights

The Storyteller

In April 1861, Emma Holmes witnessed the Confederates' attack on Fort Sumter. About 4:30 in the afternoon—just 12 hours after the first shot was fired—she observed that bullets and shells were still "pouring into Fort Sumter from Fort Stevens where our 'Palmetto boys' [South Carolina soldiers] have won the highest praise. . . . Though every shot is distinctly heard and shakes our house, I feel calm and composed. . . . The great body of the citizens seem to be so impressed with the justice of our Cause that they place entire confidence on the God of Battles. . . ."

Secessionist ribbon

Would the Union break up? That was the burning question in the months before the presidential election of 1860. Tensions between the North and the South had risen to dangerous levels. In the North antislavery sentiment took on new strength. In the South the Alabama legislature declared that the state would secede if a Republican became president.

The Election of 1860

Despite heightening tensions, efforts to save the Union continued. "One after another," wrote a Mississippian, "the links which have bound the North and South together have been severed . . . [but] the Democratic Party looms gradually up . . . and waves the olive branch over the troubled waters of politics." The party tried to make peace between the two sides but, like the nation, the Democrats were deeply divided.

The Candidates

The Democrats met in Charleston, South Carolina, in April 1860 to choose their presidential candidate. Many Democrats supported Stephen A. Douglas, but Southern delegates insisted that the party promise to protect slavery in the territories. When Douglas and most Northern delegates refused, many Southern delegates walked out. The convention adjourned.

The Democrats met again in Baltimore in June. Northern and Southern factions still could not agree on the slavery issue. When anti-Douglas

The portraits of Lincoln and Douglas on these 1860 campaign ribbons were photographed by Mathew Brady. **What other candidates participated in the 1860 presidential election?**

Southerners walked out again, the party loyalists who remained chose Douglas and endorsed popular sovereignty.

Southern Democrats met in Richmond, Virginia, and Baltimore, Maryland. They nominated **John Breckinridge** of Kentucky, the current vice president, as their candidate. They adopted the position that neither Congress nor territorial legislatures could prevent citizens from taking "their property"—enslaved people—into a territory.

The Republicans, meanwhile, met in Chicago in May to choose their candidate. The leading contenders for the nomination were Senator **William Seward** of New York and **Abraham Lincoln** of Illinois. Although Seward had long been a leader in the Republican Party, the Republicans chose Lincoln because of his more moderate views. The party did, however, declare its opposition to the "legal existence of Slavery in any Territory."

A fourth candidate entered the campaign. **John Bell** of Tennessee was nominated by moderates from both the North and the South who had formed the Constitutional Union Party. This party took no position on slavery.

The campaign stirred political forces in both the South and the North. Many Southerners feared that a Republican victory would encourage abolitionist radicals—inspired by John Brown—to start slave revolts. Douglas campaigned tirelessly, urging moderation.

The Election Outcome

With the Democrats divided, Lincoln won a clear majority of the electoral votes—180 out of 303. He received only 40 percent of the popular vote,

but this was more than any other candidate. Douglas was second with 30 percent of the popular vote.

The vote was along purely sectional lines. Lincoln's name did not even appear on the ballot in most Southern states, but he won every Northern state. Breckinridge swept the South, and Bell took most border states. Douglas won only the state of Missouri and three of New Jersey's seven electoral votes.

In effect, the more populous North had outvoted the South. The victory for Lincoln was a short-lived one, however, for the nation Lincoln was to lead would soon disintegrate.

The South Secedes

★ Lincoln and the Republicans had promised not to disturb slavery where it already existed. Nevertheless, many people in the South mistrusted the party, fearing that the Republican government would not protect Southern rights and liberties. On December 20, 1860, the South's long-standing threat to leave the Union became a reality when South Carolina held a special convention and voted to secede.

Attempt at Compromise

Even after South Carolina's action, many people still wished to preserve the Union. The question was *how*. As other Southern states debated secession—withdrawal from the Union—leaders in Washington, D.C., worked frantically to fashion a last-minute compromise. Senator **John Crittenden** of Kentucky proposed a series of amendments to the Constitution. Central to Crittenden's plan was a provision to protect slavery south of 36°30'N latitude—the line set by the Missouri Compromise—in all territories "now held or hereafter acquired."

Republicans considered this unacceptable. They had just won an election on the principle that slavery would not be extended in any territories. "Now we are told," Lincoln said, "the government shall be broken up, unless we surrender to those we have beaten."

Leaders in the South also rejected the plan. "We spit upon every plan to compromise," exclaimed one Southern leader. "No human power can save the Union," wrote another.

The Confederacy

By the first of February 1861, Texas, Louisiana, Mississippi, Alabama, Florida, and Georgia had joined South Carolina and also seceded. Delegates from these states and South Carolina met in Montgomery, Alabama, on February 4 to form a new nation and government. Calling themselves the **Confederate States of America,** they chose **Jefferson Davis,** a senator from Mississippi, as president.

Southerners justified secession with the theory of states' rights. The states, they argued, had voluntarily chosen to enter the Union. They defined the Constitution as a contract among the independent states. Now because the national government had violated that contract—by refusing to enforce the Fugitive Slave Act and by denying the Southern states equal rights in the territories—the states were justified in leaving the Union.

Reactions to Secession

Many Southerners welcomed secession. In Charleston, South Carolina, people rang church bells, fired cannons, and celebrated in the streets. A newspaper in Atlanta, Georgia, said the South "will never submit" and would defend its liberties no matter what the cost.

Other Southerners, however, were alarmed. A South Carolinian wrote, "My heart has been rent [torn] by . . . the destruction of my country—the dismemberment of that great and glorious Union." Virginian Robert E. Lee expressed concern about the future. "I see only that a fearful calamity is upon us," he wrote.

In the North some abolitionists preferred allowing the Southern states to leave. If the Union could be kept together only by compromising on

Linking PAST & PRESENT

From Hardtack to Unmeltable Chocolate

Feeding troops has always been a problem of warfare. During the Civil War, rations typically consisted of dried salt pork, hardtack (a saltless, hard flour biscuit) or cornmeal, and coffee.

Soldier's hardtack

Past

With age, hardtack could become infested with weevils. Some soldiers thought it better to eat it in the dark. Rations for today's soldier are far different. Meals Ready to Eat (MREs) were distributed to soldiers during the Persian Gulf War. MREs are dehydrated foods in airtight containers. Soldiers add hot water to make them edible. The military even found a way to make unmeltable chocolate! **Why is it important for modern soldiers to have dehydrated foods?**

Present

MREs

slavery, they declared, then let the Union be destroyed. One Republican newspaper wrote of the Southern states, "Let the erring sisters depart in peace."

Most Northerners, however, believed that the Union must be preserved. For Lincoln the issue was "whether in a free government the minority have the right to break up the government whenever they choose."

Presidential Responses

Lincoln had won the election, but he was not yet president. James Buchanan's term ran until March 4, 1861. In December 1860, Buchanan sent a message to Congress saying that the Southern states had no right to secede. Then he added that he had no power to stop them from doing so.

Lincoln disagreed. He believed it was the president's duty to enforce the laws of the United States. That meant preserving the government. He warned that "no state . . . can lawfully get out of the Union."

As Lincoln prepared for his inauguration on March 4, 1861, people in both the North and the South wondered what he would say and do. They wondered, too, what would happen in Virginia,

North Carolina, Kentucky, Tennessee, Missouri, and Arkansas. These slave states had chosen to remain in the Union, but the decision was not final. If the United States used force against the Confederate States of America, the remaining slave states also might secede.

In his Inaugural Address, the new president mixed toughness and words of peace. He said that secession would not be permitted, vowing to hold federal property in the South and to enforce the laws of the United States. At the same time, Lincoln pleaded with the South for reconciliation:

❝We are not enemies, but friends. We must not be enemies. Though passion may have strained, it must not break our bonds of affection.❞

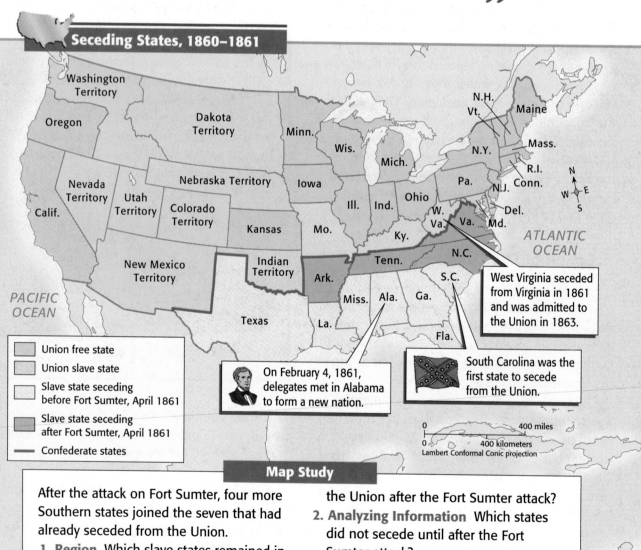

Seceding States, 1860–1861

Washington Territory
Oregon
Dakota Territory
Minn.
Wis.
Mich.
N.H.
Vt.
Maine
N.Y.
Mass.
R.I.
Conn.
Nevada Territory
Utah Territory
Colorado Territory
Nebraska Territory
Iowa
Ill.
Ind.
Ohio
Pa.
N.J.
Del.
Calif.
Kansas
Mo.
W. Va.
Va.
Md.
ATLANTIC OCEAN
New Mexico Territory
Indian Territory
Ark.
Ky.
Tenn.
N.C.
S.C.
PACIFIC OCEAN
Miss.
Ala.
Ga.
Texas
La.
Fla.

West Virginia seceded from Virginia in 1861 and was admitted to the Union in 1863.

On February 4, 1861, delegates met in Alabama to form a new nation.

South Carolina was the first state to secede from the Union.

- ▢ Union free state
- ▢ Union slave state
- ▢ Slave state seceding before Fort Sumter, April 1861
- ▢ Slave state seceding after Fort Sumter, April 1861
- — Confederate states

0 ___ 400 miles
0 ___ 400 kilometers
Lambert Conformal Conic projection

Map Study

After the attack on Fort Sumter, four more Southern states joined the seven that had already seceded from the Union.

1. Region Which slave states remained in the Union after the Fort Sumter attack?

2. Analyzing Information Which states did not secede until after the Fort Sumter attack?

Fort Sumter

★ The South soon tested President Lincoln's vow to hold federal property. Confederate forces had already seized some United States forts within their states. Although Lincoln did not want to start a war by trying to take the forts back, allowing the Confederates to keep them would amount to admitting their right to secede.

On the day of his inauguration, Lincoln received a dispatch from the commander of **Fort Sumter,** a United States fort on an island guarding Charleston Harbor. The message warned that the fort was low on supplies and that the Confederates demanded its surrender.

The War Begins

Lincoln responded by sending a message to Governor **Francis Pickens** of South Carolina. He informed Pickens that he was sending an unarmed expedition with supplies to Fort Sumter. Lincoln promised that Union forces would not "throw in men, arms, or ammunition" unless they were fired upon. The president thus left the decision to start shooting up to the Confederates.

Confederate president Jefferson Davis and his advisers made a fateful choice. They ordered their forces to attack Fort Sumter before the Union supplies could arrive. Confederate guns opened fire on the fort on April 12, 1861. Union captain Abner Doubleday witnessed the attack from inside the fort:

Jefferson Davis

66 Showers of balls . . . and shells . . . poured into the fort in one incessant stream, causing great flakes of masonry to fall in all directions. 99

High seas had prevented Union relief ships from reaching the besieged fort. The Union garrison held out for 33 hours before surrendering on April 14. Thousands of shots were exchanged during the siege, but there was no loss of life on either side.

News of the attack galvanized the North. President Lincoln issued a call for 75,000 troops to fight to save the Union, and volunteers quickly signed up. Meanwhile, Virginia, North Carolina, Tennessee, and Arkansas voted to join the Confederacy. The Civil War had begun.

★ ★ ★ ★ ★ ★ **Section 4 Assessment** ★ ★ ★ ★ ★ ★

Checking for Understanding

1. **Identify** John Breckinridge, William Seward, John Bell, John Crittenden, Jefferson Davis, Fort Sumter.
2. **Define** secession, states' rights.
3. **Explain** how Southern states used the theory of states' rights to justify secession.

Reviewing Themes

4. **Geography and History** What role did sectionalism play in Lincoln's winning the 1860 election?

Critical Thinking

5. **Identifying Assumptions** Do you think either Northerners or Southerners believed that secession would not lead to war? Explain.

▶ **Activity**

Creating a Political Slogan Make up a campaign slogan or song for Abraham Lincoln, Stephen A. Douglas, John C. Breckinridge, or John Bell in the 1860 presidential election.

Chapter 15

Assessment and Activities

⭐ Reviewing Key Terms

On a sheet of paper, define the following terms:
sectionalism
fugitive
secede
popular sovereignty
border ruffians
civil war
arsenal
martyr
secession
states' rights

⭐ Reviewing Key Facts

1. What was the purpose of the Missouri Compromise?
2. List the five parts of the Compromise of 1850.
3. What was Stephen Douglas's solution to the slavery issue in the Kansas and Nebraska territories?
4. What was the *Dred Scott* decision?
5. How did Lincoln plan to prevent secession?

⭐ Critical Thinking

Drawing Conclusions

Even after South Carolina seceded, the nation's leaders worked hard to come up with a last-minute compromise to save the Union.

1. Why did newly elected Republicans refuse to compromise any further on the slavery issue?
2. Why do you think people in the South rejected compromise efforts altogether by saying "We spit upon every plan to compromise"?

⭐ Time Line Activity

Create a time line on which you place the following events in chronological order.
- Civil War begins
- *Dred Scott* decision
- Missouri Compromise passes
- Lincoln is elected president
- *Uncle Tom's Cabin* is published
- Kansas–Nebraska Act is passed

⭐ Skill Practice Activity

Recognizing Bias

The excerpt below was written by Dr. Martin R. Delany, an abolitionist, to the mayor of Pittsburgh about his opinion of the Fugitive Slave Law of 1850. Read the excerpt, then answer the questions.

❝Honorable mayor, whatever ideas of liberty I may have, have been received from reading the lives of your revolutionary fathers. I have therein learned that a man has a right to defend his castle with his life, even unto the taking of life. Sir, my house is my castle. . . . If any man approaches that house in search of a slave—I care not who he may be, whether constable or sheriff, magistrate or even judge of the Supreme Court . . . with the Declaration of Independence waving above his head as his banner . . . —if he crosses the threshold of my door, and I do not lay him a lifeless corpse at my feet. . . . O, no! he cannot enter that house and we both live. **❞**

1. Who is the author?
2. What is his view toward slavery?
3. What language reflects emotion or opinion?
4. What is the author's bias toward the Fugitive Slave Law?

★ Geography Activity

Study the map below, then answer the questions that follow.

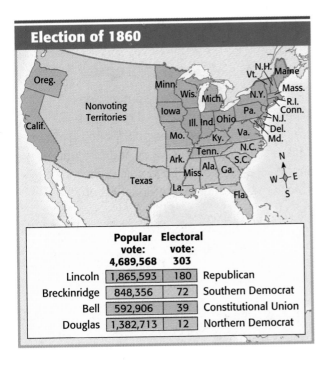

Election of 1860

	Popular vote: 4,689,568	Electoral vote: 303	
Lincoln	1,865,593	180	Republican
Breckinridge	848,356	72	Southern Democrat
Bell	592,906	39	Constitutional Union
Douglas	1,382,713	12	Northern Democrat

1. **Location** Which states supported Douglas?
2. **Region** In what region(s) was the Republican Party strongest?
3. **Region** In what region did Breckinridge find support?

★ Reviewing Themes

1. **Government and Democracy** Why was the balance of free and slave states in the Senate such an important issue?
2. **Civic Rights and Responsibilities** Why did Northerners protest Douglas's plan to repeal the Missouri Compromise?
3. **Continuity and Change** How did pro- and antislavery groups change the structure of political parties in the 1850s?
4. **Geography and History** How did the North's larger population give it an edge over the South in the 1860 election?

★ Technology Activity

Using a Word Processor Search the Internet or your library for a list of political parties in existence today. Using your word processor, make a table that briefly summarizes each party's current goals. Then research to find the date that the party was founded and who its first and prominent party leaders have been. Include this information on your table, too. Then compare your table to the political parties discussed in Chapter 15.

★ Cooperative Activity

History and Citizenship With a partner, think of a controversial issue that is a source of disagreement today. Take opposite sides on the issue, then work together to come up with a list of three compromises that would make the solution to this problem acceptable to both sides. Share the issue and your compromises with the class.

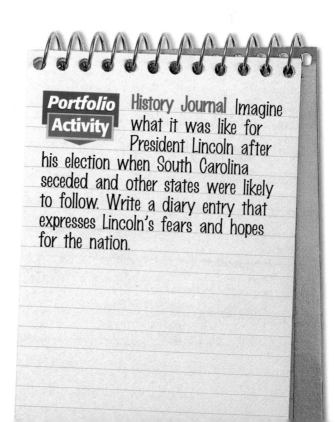

Portfolio Activity History Journal Imagine what it was like for President Lincoln after his election when South Carolina seceded and other states were likely to follow. Write a diary entry that expresses Lincoln's fears and hopes for the nation.

1861–1865

The Civil War

★ Why It's Important

The Civil War—a war in which Americans fought other Americans—transformed the United States. It devastated the economy of the South while contributing to the rapid economic growth of the North and the West. African Americans gained freedom as slavery was abolished, but the war left a legacy of bitterness between North and South that lasted for generations. In addition the war established the power of the federal government over the states.

★ Chapter Themes

- *Section 1*, Government and Democracy
- *Section 2*, Geography and History
- *Section 3*, Groups and Institutions
- *Section 4*, Economic Factors
- *Section 5*, Individual Action

PRIMARY SOURCES
Library

See pages 966–967 for primary source readings to accompany Chapter 16

 HISTORY AND ART   *Fight for the Colors* by Don Troiani Troiani has painted several dramatic Civil War scenes, such as this one of the Battle of Gettysburg.

February 1861
The Confederacy is formed

April 1861
Four more states join the Confederacy

Summer 1861
Rebel soldiers total about 112,000; Yankees number about 187,000

1863
West Virginia is admitted to the Union

Section 1

The Two Sides

READ TO DISCOVER . . .

- why the border states played an important role in the war.
- how the North and the South compared in terms of population, industry, resources, and war aims.

TERMS TO LEARN

border state   Rebel
blockade   Yankee
offensive

The Storyteller

Union sergeant Driscoll led his troops up Malvern Hill on July 1, 1862. The enemy fought fiercely, especially one young Confederate soldier. Driscoll raised his rifle, took aim, and shot the boy. As he passed the spot where the boy had fallen, Driscoll turned the daring soldier over to see what he looked like. The boy opened his eyes and faintly murmured, "Father," then his eyes fluttered shut, never to open again. A Union captain later wrote, "I will forever recollect the frantic grief of Driscoll; it was harrowing to witness. He [had killed] his son, who had gone South before the war."

Union cavalry cap

By February 1861, seven states had left the Union and formed the Confederacy. After the Confederate bombardment of Fort Sumter, President **Abraham Lincoln** issued a call for troops to save the Union. His action caused Virginia, North Carolina, Tennessee, and Arkansas to join the Confederacy. These four states brought needed soldiers, animals, industry, and food to the Confederacy, greatly increasing its chances of winning independence. For its capital, the Confederacy chose **Richmond,** Virginia, a city only about 100 miles from the Union capital of **Washington, D.C.**

⊕ Geography

Choosing Sides

Four states that allowed slavery—Missouri, Kentucky, Maryland, and Delaware—remained in the Union. The people of these border states were divided over whether to support the Union or join the Confederacy. Missouri, Kentucky, and Maryland had such strong support for the South that the three states teetered on the brink of secession.

Losing the border states would seriously damage the North. All had strategic locations. Missouri could control parts of the **Mississippi River** and major routes to the West. Kentucky controlled the Ohio River. Delaware was close to the important Northern city of Philadelphia.

Maryland, perhaps the most important of the border states, was close to Richmond. Vital railroad lines passed through Maryland. Most significantly, Washington, D.C., lay within the state. If Maryland seceded, the North's government would be surrounded.

Maryland's key role became clear in April 1861—just a month after Lincoln's inauguration as president. A mob in Baltimore attacked Northern troops marching through the city. Then, Confederate sympathizers burned railroad bridges and cut the telegraph line to Washington, isolating the capital from the rest of the North. Northern troops soon arrived, but the nation's capital had suffered some anxious days.

Remaining With the Union

Lincoln had to move cautiously to avoid antagonizing people in the border states. If he announced that he aimed to end slavery, for instance, groups supporting the Confederacy might take their states out of the Union. If he ordered Northern troops into Kentucky, Confederate sympathizers there would claim the state had been invaded and swing it to the South.

In some ways Lincoln acted boldly. He suspended some constitutional rights and used his power to arrest people for active support of secession. Lincoln supported rebellion against Missouri's pro-Confederate state government. In the end Lincoln's approach worked. The four border states stayed in the Union—although thousands of their citizens left to join the armies of the South.

A Secession from the South

Most white Southerners favored secession. Still, pockets of Union support existed in eastern Tennessee and western Virginia. People in the Appalachian region generally opposed secession.

In western Virginia a movement to secede from the state and rejoin the Union grew. In 1861, 48 Virginia counties organized themselves as a separate state called **West Virginia.** Congress admitted this state to the Union in 1863.

Comparing North and South

⭐ When the war began, both sides had advantages and disadvantages. How they would use those strengths and weaknesses would determine the war's outcome.

Northern Strengths and Weaknesses

The North enjoyed the advantages of a larger population to support the war effort, more industry, and more abundant resources than the South. It had a better banking system, which helped in raising money for the war. The North also possessed more ships, though most of them were old, and almost all the members of the regular navy remained loyal to the Union. Finally, the North had a larger and more efficient railway network.

⭐ HISTORY AND ART

7th New York Militia at Jersey City on April 19, 1861 by E.L. Henry. The 7th New York Militia was one of the first fully equipped and trained units at war's outbreak. **Why were troops ordered to the nation's capital in early 1861?**

The North also faced disadvantages. Bringing the Southern states back into the Union would be a difficult task. The North would have to invade and hold the South—a large area filled with a hostile population. Furthermore, public opinion in the North was divided over the war, and support for the war remained shaky until very near the end. Recalling the example of the American Revolution, when the smaller, weaker colonies had won independence from wealthy Great Britain, many people believed the South had a good chance of winning.

One Northern advantage was not obvious until later. Both sides greatly underestimated Abraham Lincoln. His dedication, intelligence, skill, and humanity led the North to victory.

Southern Strengths and Weaknesses

One of the main advantages of the South was the strong support its white population gave the war. Southerners also had the advantage of fighting in familiar territory—defending their land, their homes, and their way of life.

The military leadership of the South, at least at first, was superior to the North's. Southern families had a strong tradition of military training and service, and military college graduates provided the South with a large pool of officers. Overseeing the Southern effort was Confederate president **Jefferson Davis,** a West Point graduate and experienced soldier who took a keen interest in the activities of his War Department.

The South faced material disadvantages. It had a smaller population of free men to draw upon in building an army. It also possessed very few factories to manufacture weapons and other supplies, and it produced less than half as much food as the North. With less than half the miles of railroad tracks and vastly fewer trains than the North, the Confederate government had difficulty delivering food, weapons, and other supplies to its troops.

The belief in **states' rights**—a founding principle of the Confederacy—also hampered the South's efforts. The individual states refused to give the Confederate government enough power to fight the war effectively.

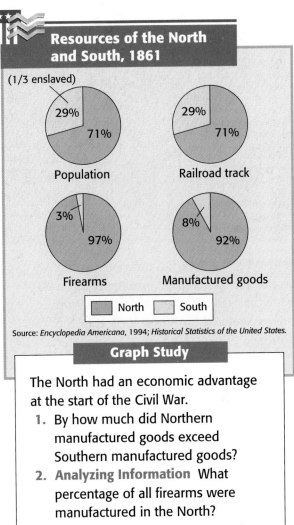

Resources of the North and South, 1861

(1/3 enslaved)

Population: 29% / 71%
Railroad track: 29% / 71%
Firearms: 3% / 97%
Manufactured goods: 8% / 92%

North   South

Source: *Encyclopedia Americana, 1994; Historical Statistics of the United States.*

Graph Study

The North had an economic advantage at the start of the Civil War.
1. By how much did Northern manufactured goods exceed Southern manufactured goods?
2. **Analyzing Information** What percentage of all firearms were manufactured in the North?

War Aims and Strategy

The North and the South entered the Civil War with different war aims. To achieve these aims and win the war, each side devised its own strategy.

Northern Aims and Strategies

The main goal of the North at the outset was to win the war and bring the Southern states back into the Union. Ending slavery was not a major Northern goal at first, but this changed as the war continued.

The Union's plan for winning the war included three main strategies. First, using its superior navy, the North would blockade, or close, Southern ports to prevent supplies from reaching the South—and to prevent the South from earning

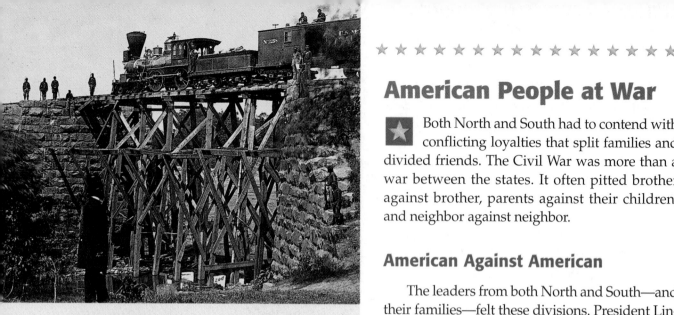

One advantage the North enjoyed over the South was better railroad tracks and trains. **What other advantages did the North have over the South?**

money by exporting cotton. Second, the Union intended to gain control of the Mississippi River to cut Southern supply lines and to split the Confederacy. Third, the North planned to capture Richmond, the Confederate capital.

Southern Aims and Strategies

For the South the primary aim of the war was to win recognition as an independent nation. Independence would allow Southerners to preserve their traditional way of life—a way of life that included slavery.

To achieve this goal, the South devised a defensive strategy. It planned to defend its homeland, holding on to as much territory as possible until the North tired of fighting and agreed to recognize the independence of the Confederacy. The South expected that Britain and France, which imported large quantities of Southern cotton, would pressure the North to end the war so that their cotton supply would be restored.

During the war Southern leaders sometimes changed strategy and took the offensive—went on the attack. They would move their armies northward to threaten Washington and other Northern cities, hoping to persuade the North that it could not win the war.

American People at War

★ Both North and South had to contend with conflicting loyalties that split families and divided friends. The Civil War was more than a war between the states. It often pitted brother against brother, parents against their children, and neighbor against neighbor.

American Against American

The leaders from both North and South—and their families—felt these divisions. President Lincoln's wife, Mary Todd Lincoln, had a brother, three half brothers, and three brothers-in-law who fought in the Confederate army. John Crittenden, a senator from Kentucky, had two sons who became generals in the war—one for the Confederacy and one for the Union. Officers on both sides—including Confederate president Davis, Confederate general Robert E. Lee, and Union generals George McClellan and William Tecumseh Sherman—had attended the United States Military Academy at West Point, never dreaming that they would one day command forces against each other.

Sometimes, family members actually faced each other in combat. In one battle a Union regiment commanded by a man from West Virginia attacked a Confederate regiment from Virginia commanded by his cousin.

Who Were the Soldiers?

Most of the solders were inexperienced, and many were young. The average age of a recruit was about 25 years, but about 40 percent were 21 years or younger. Ted Upson of Indiana was only 16 when he begged his father to let him join the Union army. "This Union your ancestors and mine helped to make must be saved from destruction," he said.

William Stone from Louisiana rushed to join the Confederate army after the attack on Fort Sumter. His sister Kate wrote that he was

❝ . . . wild to be off to Virginia. He so fears that the fighting will be over before he can get there. ❞

Soldiers came from all parts of both sections of the country and all walks of life. Most, though, came from farms. Almost half of the North's troops and more than 60 percent of the South's had owned or worked on farms. The Union army did not permit African Americans to join at first, but they did serve later.

Early terms of enlistment were short. After the shelling of Fort Sumter, Lincoln asked state governors to supply soldiers for 90 days. When the conflict did not end quickly, soldiers' terms became longer. In the first year of the war, leaders in both the North and the South asked volunteers to sign up for 3 years of service.

By the summer of 1861, the Confederate army had about 112,000 soldiers, who were sometimes called **Rebels.** The Union had about 187,000 soldiers, or **Yankees** as they were also known. By the end of the war, about 850,000 men fought for the Confederacy and about 2.1 million men fought for the Union. The Union number included just under 200,000 African Americans. Approximately 10,000 Hispanic soldiers fought in the conflict.

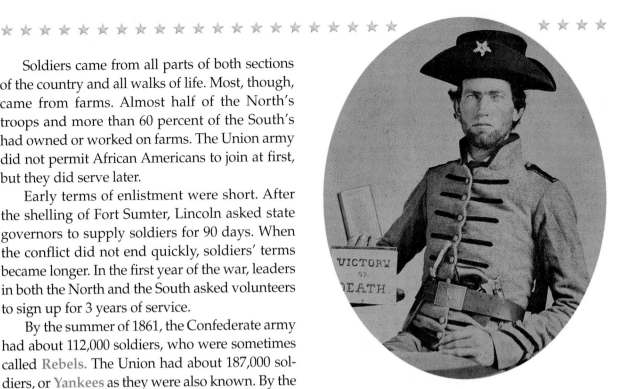

Confederate soldier

False Hopes

When the war began, each side expected a brief conflict and an early victory. Many Southerners believed that Northern soldiers lacked the conviction needed to win the war. A Confederate soldier from Alabama expected the war to be over within a year because "we are going to kill the last Yankee before that time if there is any fight in them still." Northerners were just as confident that they would beat the South quickly—"in thirty days," according to one newspaper.

Some leaders saw the situation more clearly. Northern general William Tecumseh Sherman wrote, "I think it is to be a long war—very long—much longer than any politician thinks." The first spring of the war proved that Sherman's prediction was accurate.

★ ★ ★ ★ ★   Section 1 Assessment   ★ ★ ★ ★ ★

Checking for Understanding
1. **Identify** Abraham Lincoln, states' rights.
2. **Define** border state, blockade, offensive, Rebel, Yankee.
3. **List** the North's three main strategies for winning the war.

Reviewing Themes
4. **Government and Democracy** How did a belief in states' rights hamper the South during the war?

Critical Thinking
5. **Predicting Consequences** What do you think would be the South's greatest advantage in the war? Explain your answer.

Activity

Keeping a Journal Imagine that you are a Southerner or a Northerner in 1861. Write a journal entry that explains your reasons for joining the Confederate or Union army.

1861		1862		1863

July 1861
Confederates win
First Battle of Bull Run

February 1862
Grant captures
Fort Henry and
Fort Donelson

April 1862
Union wins
Battle of Shiloh

September 1862
Battle of Antietam
boosts Union morale

Section 2

Early Years of the War

READ TO DISCOVER...

- what successes and failures the North and the South had in the early years of the Civil War.
- how the North's naval blockade hurt the South.

TERMS TO LEARN

blockade runner
ironclad
casualty

The Storyteller

Sunday, July 21, 1861, was a pleasant, sunny day in Washington, D.C. Hundreds of cheerful residents, food baskets in hand, left the city and crossed the Potomac River to spend the day in Virginia. They planned to picnic while watching the first battle between the Union and the Confederate armies. Expecting to see the Union troops crush the Rebels, they looked forward to a quick victory. The Confederate soldiers also expected a quick victory. They "carried dress suits with them, and any quantity of fine linen. Every soldier, nearly, had a servant with him, and a whole lot of spoons and forks, so as to live comfortably and elegantly in camp...."

1st Virginia Infantry flag

The first major battle of the Civil War was fought in northern Virginia, about 5 miles from a town called Manassas Junction near Bull Run— a small river in the area. Usually called the **First Battle of Bull Run,** it began when about 30,000 inexperienced Union troops commanded by General Irvin McDowell attacked a slightly smaller, equally inexperienced Confederate force led by General **P. G. T. Beauregard.**

Eyewitness to HISTORY

First Battle of Bull Run

The Yankees drove the Confederates back at first. Then the Rebels rallied, inspired by reinforcements under General Thomas Jackson. Jackson, who was seen holding out "like a stone wall," became known thereafter as **"Stonewall" Jackson.** The Confederates unleashed a savage counterattack that forced the Union lines to break.

The Confederates surged forward with a strange, unearthly scream that came to be known as the Rebel yell. Terrified, the Northern soldiers began to drop their guns and packs and run. One observer, Representative Albert Riddle, reported:

❝ A cruel, crazy, mad, hopeless panic possessed them. . . . The heat was awful . . . the men were exhausted—their mouths gaped, their lips cracked and blackened with the powder of the cartridges they had bitten off in the battle, their eyes staring in frenzy. **❞**

General Thomas "Stonewall" Jackson

Picturing HISTORY Union troops fled in panic from Bull Run (Manassas) after a fierce Confederate counterattack led by General Thomas "Stonewall" Jackson. What Confederate action on the battlefield frightened Union forces into fleeing?

The Union army began an orderly retreat that quickly became a mad stampede when the retreating Union troops collided with the civilians, fleeing in panic back to Washington.

The Confederates, though victorious, were too disorganized and weakened to pursue the retreating Yankees. Regardless, the South rejoiced. Edmund Ruffin of Virginia thought it meant "the close of the war."

A Shock for the North

The outcome of the battle shocked the North. Northerners began to understand that the war could be a long, difficult, and costly struggle. Although discouraged by the results, President Abraham Lincoln was also determined. Within days he issued a call for more volunteers for the army. This time he requested 1 million soldiers who would serve for 3 years. Volunteers soon crowded into recruiting offices. Lincoln also appointed a new general, **George B. McClellan,** to head the Union army of the East—called the **Army of the Potomac**—and organize the troops.

War at Sea

Even before Bull Run, Lincoln had ordered a planned naval blockade of Southern ports. An effective blockade would prevent the South from exporting its cotton and importing the supplies necessary to continue the war.

Enforcing the Blockade

When the war began, the North did not have enough ships to blockade the South's entire 3,500-mile coastline. Many Confederate ships, called blockade runners, could sail in and out of Southern ports. In time, the North built more ships and became better able to enforce the blockade.

The blockade caused serious problems for the South. Although the blockade could never close off all Southern trade, it did reduce the trade by two-thirds. Goods such as coffee, shoes, nails, and salt—as well as guns and ammunition—were in short supply throughout the war.

*F*ootnotes to History

Different Names, Same Battle Many Civil War battles have two names. The Union named battles after the nearest body of water. The Confederacy named them after the nearest settlement. Therefore, the battle called the Battle of Bull Run (a river) in the North was known as the Battle of Manassas (a settlement) in the South.

The *Monitor* Versus the *Merrimack*

The South did not intend to let the blockade go unchallenged. Southerners salvaged the *Merrimack*, a Union warship that Northern forces had abandoned when Confederate forces seized the naval shipyard in **Norfolk, Virginia.** The Confederates rebuilt the wooden ship, covered it with thick iron plates, and renamed it the *Virginia.*

On March 8, 1862, this ironclad warship attacked a group of Union ships off the coast of Virginia. The North's wooden warships could not damage the Confederate ship—shells simply bounced off its sides.

Some Northern leaders feared the South would use the ironclad warship to destroy much of the Union navy, steam up the Potomac River, and bombard Washington, D.C. However, the North had already built an ironclad ship of its own, the *Monitor.* Described as looking like a "tin can on a shingle," the *Monitor* rushed south to engage the Confederate ship in battle.

On March 9, the two ironclads exchanged fire, but neither ship could sink the other. The Union succeeded in keeping the *Merrimack* in the harbor, so it never again threatened Northern ships. The battle marked a new age in naval warfare—the first battle between two metal-covered ships.

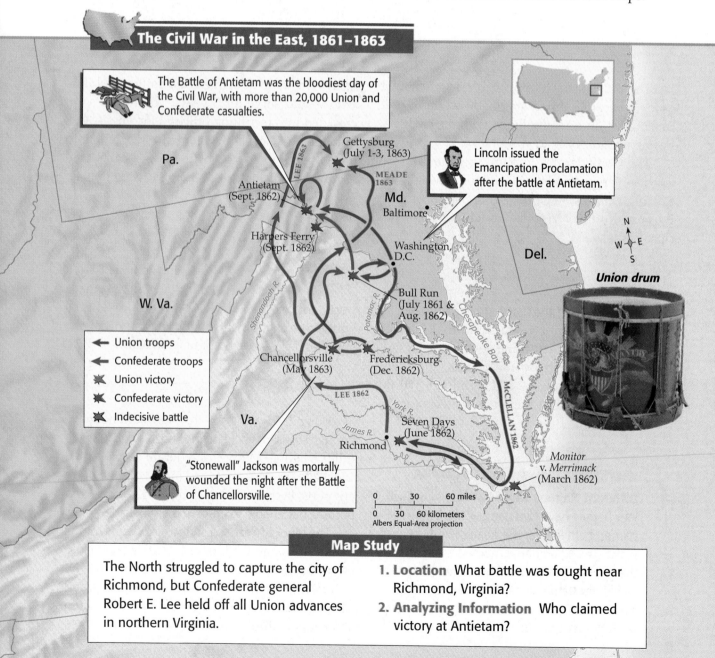

The Civil War in the East, 1861–1863

The Battle of Antietam was the bloodiest day of the Civil War, with more than 20,000 Union and Confederate casualties.

Gettysburg (July 1-3, 1863)

Lincoln issued the Emancipation Proclamation after the battle at Antietam.

Pa.

MEADE 1863

Md.

Antietam (Sept. 1862)

Baltimore

Harpers Ferry (Sept. 1862)

Washington, D.C.

Del.

Union drum

W. Va.

Bull Run (July 1861 & Aug. 1862)

Union troops
Confederate troops
Union victory
Confederate victory
Indecisive battle

Chancellorsville (May 1863)

Fredericksburg (Dec. 1862)

LEE 1862

Va.

Seven Days (June 1862)

Richmond

Monitor v. Merrimack (March 1862)

"Stonewall" Jackson was mortally wounded the night after the Battle of Chancellorsville.

0   30   60 miles
0   30   60 kilometers
Albers Equal-Area projection

Map Study

The North struggled to capture the city of Richmond, but Confederate general Robert E. Lee held off all Union advances in northern Virginia.

1. **Location** What battle was fought near Richmond, Virginia?

2. **Analyzing Information** Who claimed victory at Antietam?

War in the West

⭐ After the First Battle of Bull Run in July 1861, military operations in the East settled into a long stalemate as each side built up its strength. Generals focused on training their raw recruits, trying to turn civilians into disciplined soldiers. For a while the action shifted to the West.

Early Victories for the North

One of the North's primary goals in the West was to gain control of the Mississippi and Tennessee Rivers. This would split the Confederacy and hinder Southern efforts to transport goods.

In February 1862, Union forces under General **Ulysses S. Grant** captured Fort Henry on the **Tennessee River** and Fort Donelson on the **Cumberland River,** both in northern Tennessee. Grant's victories helped secure the lower Tennessee River. They also opened a path for Union troops to march into Tennessee, Mississippi, and Alabama. The victories drove the Confederates out of Kentucky, where the South had been attempting to persuade Kentuckians to secede.

Union drummer boy at Shiloh

Geography

The Battle of Shiloh

General Grant and about 40,000 troops then headed south along the Tennessee River toward Corinth, Mississippi, an important railroad junction. In early April the Union army camped at Pittsburg Landing, 20 miles from Corinth. Nearby was a small church named Shiloh. Additional Union forces started from Nashville to join Grant.

Confederate leaders decided to strike first before the reinforcements arrived. Early in the morning of April 6, Confederate forces led by Albert Sidney Johnston and P. G. T. Beauregard launched a surprise attack on the Union troops. The **Battle of Shiloh** lasted 2 days, with some of the most bitter and bloody fighting of the war. On the first day of battle, the Confederates drove Grant and his troops back to the Tennessee River. On the second day, the Union forces recovered. Aided by the 25,000 troops from Nashville and shelling by gunboats on the river, they defeated the Confederates, who withdrew to Corinth.

The losses in the Battle of Shiloh were enormous. Together the two armies suffered 20,000 casualties—people killed or wounded. Confederate general Johnston also died in the bloodbath. One Confederate soldier lamented that the battle "was too shocking [and] too horrible."

After their narrow victory at Shiloh, Union forces gained control of Corinth on May 30. Memphis, Tennessee, fell to Union armies on June 6. The North seemed well on its way to controlling the Mississippi River. 🌐

New Orleans Falls

A few weeks after Shiloh, the North won another important victory. On April 25, 1862, Union naval forces under **David Farragut** captured **New Orleans,** Louisiana, the largest city in the South. Farragut, who was of Spanish descent, had grown up in the South but remained loyal to the Union.

His capture of New Orleans, near the mouth of the Mississippi River, meant that the Confederacy could no longer use the river to carry its crops to sea. Coupled with Grant's victories to the north, Farragut's capture of New Orleans gave Union forces control of almost all the Mississippi River.

War in the East

⭐ In the East General McClellan was training the Army of the Potomac to be an effective fighting force. An expert at training soldiers, McClellan showed great caution when faced with

Picturing HISTORY While Lincoln searched desperately for a general who could win in the East, the Confederates remained under the able command of General Robert E. Lee. **Which Union general did Lee oppose in the Seven Days battles?**

the prospect of battle, and he worried continually that his troops were not ready. He also hesitated to fight because of reports that overestimated the size of the Rebel forces. Finally, in March 1862, the Army of the Potomac was ready for action. Its goal was to capture Richmond, the Confederate capital.

Union Defeat at Richmond

Instead of advancing directly overland to Richmond as Lincoln wished, McClellan moved his huge army by ship to a peninsula between the York and the James Rivers southeast of the city. From there he began a major offensive known as the **Peninsula Campaign.** The operation took many weeks.

Time passed and opportunities to attack slipped away as General McClellan readied his troops and tried to evaluate the enemy's strength. Lincoln, constantly prodding McClellan to fight, ended one message with an urgent plea: "*You must act.*" Complaining of his difficult situation, McClellan did not attack. His delays allowed the Confederates to prepare their defense of Richmond.

McClellan and his army inched slowly toward Richmond, getting so close that the troops could hear the city's church bells ringing. At the end of June, the Union forces finally met the Confederates in a series of encounters known as the **Seven Days battles.**

In these battles Confederate general **Robert E. Lee** took command of the army opposing McClellan. Before the battles began, Lee's cavalry leader, **James E.B. (J.E.B.) Stuart,** performed a daring tactic. He led his 1,200 troopers in a circle around the Union army, gathering vital information about Union positions and boosting Southern morale. Stuart lost only one man in the action. General Lee then boldly countered Union advances and eventually drove the Yankees back to the James River. The Union troops had failed to capture Richmond.

Gloom in the North

Reports from Richmond disheartened the North. Despite the good news in the West, failure to take the Confederate capital left Northerners with little hope. There was another call for volunteers—300,000 this time—but the response was slow. The Southern strategy of making the North weary of war seemed to be working.

The defeat had not been complete, however. McClellan's army had been pushed back, but it was still larger than Lee's and still only 25 miles from Richmond. When McClellan failed to renew the attack, President Lincoln ordered him to move his army back to northern Virginia and join the troops led by Major General **John Pope.**

The bold Lee sent Stonewall Jackson's forces north to attack Pope's supply base at Manassas. Jackson's troops marched 50 miles in 2 days and were then joined by the rest of Lee's army. On

August 29 Pope attacked the approaching Confederates and started the **Second Battle of Bull Run.** This battle, like the first, ended in a Confederate victory. Richmond was no longer threatened. Indeed the situation of the 2 sides was completely reversed. Lee and the Confederates now stood only 20 miles from Washington, D.C.

The Battle of Antietam

Following these Southern victories, Confederate president **Jefferson Davis** ordered Lee to launch an offensive into Maryland northwest of Washington. He hoped another victory would win aid from Great Britain and France. Davis also issued a proclamation urging the people of Maryland to join the Confederacy, but he received no response.

As Lee's army marched into Maryland in September 1862, McClellan and 80,000 Union troops moved slowly after them. On September 13 the North had an extraordinary piece of good luck. In a field near Frederick, Maryland, 2 Union soldiers found a copy of Lee's orders for his army wrapped around 3 cigars. The small bundle had probably been dropped by a careless Southern officer. Now McClellan knew exactly what Lee planned to do. He also learned that Lee's army was divided into 5 parts, providing McClellan with an opportunity to overwhelm Lee's army one piece at a time.

Once again, however, McClellan was overly cautious. He waited four days before he decided to attack the Confederates. This enabled Lee to gather most of his forces together near Sharpsburg, Maryland, along the Antietam Creek.

The Union and the Confederate armies clashed on September 17 in the **Battle of Antietam.** It was the single bloodiest day of the entire war. A Union officer wrote that "the slain lay in rows precisely as they had stood in their ranks a few minutes before." By the time the fighting ended, close to 6,000 soldiers lay dead or dying, and another 17,000 were seriously wounded. Although both armies suffered heavy losses, neither was destroyed.

The day after the battle, Lee withdrew to Virginia. The Confederate retreat allowed the Union troops to claim victory. However, McClellan, who had been ordered by President Lincoln to "destroy the rebel army," did not pursue the Confederate troops. The president, disgusted with McClellan's failure to follow up his victory, removed McClellan from his command in November. Lincoln placed General **Ambrose Burnside** in command of the Army of the Potomac.

Antietam had a profound impact on the war. The Army of the Potomac finally gained some confidence, having forced Lee and his soldiers back south. More important, the battle marked a major change in Northern war aims. President Lincoln used the battle to take action against slavery.

Section 2 Assessment

Checking for Understanding
1. **Identify** George B. McClellan, *Monitor* and *Merrimack*, Ulysses S. Grant, David Farragut, Robert E. Lee.
2. **Define** blockade runner, ironclad, casualty.
3. **Explain** why the North wanted to blockade Southern ports.

Reviewing Themes
4. **Geography and History** What were the North's main goals in the West?

Critical Thinking
5. **Analyzing Information** Why was Union general McClellan not effective as a military commander?

Activity

Drawing a Cartoon Draw a cartoon that would accompany a front-page story describing the battle between the *Merrimack* and *Monitor*.

1862
African Americans allowed to serve in the Union army

January 1863
Lincoln signs the Emancipation Proclamation

July 1863
Half of the 54th Massachusetts Regiment is wiped out

1865
Thirteenth Amendment is ratified by the Union

Section 3

A Call for Freedom

READ TO DISCOVER . . .
- why Lincoln issued the Emancipation Proclamation.
- what role African Americans played in the Civil War.

TERMS TO LEARN
emancipate   ratify

The Storyteller

The rain poured on the little cabin in South Carolina. Inside, old and young slaves filled the room, sitting around a large, wooden table. One held a watch in his hand, staring at it intently. A young boy held a lit torch so a Yankee officer could see to read the president's Proclamation of Freedom. As the watch ticked closer to midnight, a deep silence fell. The holder of the watch counted: five, four, three, two, . . . Just then a loud strain of a banjo was heard. Free! They were free Americans at last!

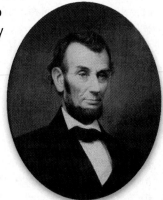

Lincoln portrait by artist Peter Baumgras

From the start of the war through the brutal Battle of Antietam, the Northerners' main goal was to preserve the Union rather than to destroy slavery. Abolitionists did not control the North, or even the Republican Party. Abraham Lincoln and other Republican leaders insisted on many occasions that they would act only to prevent the expansion of slavery.

Although Lincoln considered slavery immoral, he hesitated to move against slavery because of the border states. Lincoln knew that making an issue of slavery would divide the people—both in the border states and in the North—and make the war less popular.

In August 1862, Abraham Lincoln responded to pressure to declare an end to slavery with a public letter stating his views.

❝ If I could save the Union without freeing *any* slave, I would do it; and if I could save it by freeing *all* the slaves, I would do it; and if I could save it by freeing some and leaving others alone, I would also do that. ❞

That was, Lincoln added, his official position. His personal wish was "that all men everywhere could be free."

Emancipation

As the war went on, attitudes toward slavery began to change. More and more Northerners believed that slavery was helping the war effort in the South. The 3.5 million slaves in the Confederacy formed the backbone of the Southern economy. They raised much of the crops used to feed the armies, and they did the heavy work in the trenches at the army camps. In their view anything that weakened slavery struck a blow against the Confederacy.

As early as May 1861, some African Americans in the South escaped slavery by going into territory held by the Union army. In 1861 and 1862, Congress passed laws that freed enslaved people who were used to support the Confederate war effort or held by people active in the rebellion against the Union.

✎ Citizenship

The Emancipation Proclamation

Lincoln was keenly aware of the shifts in public opinion. He also knew that striking a blow against slavery would make Britain and France less likely to aid the South. Moreover, Lincoln became convinced that slavery helped the South continue fighting. Every enslaved person who worked enabled a white Southerner to fight in the Confederate army.

Lincoln had political reasons as well for taking action on slavery. He believed it was important that the president rather than the antislavery Republicans in Congress make the decision on ending slavery. Lincoln told his cabinet, "I must do the best I can, and bear the responsibility."

By the summer of 1862, Lincoln had decided to emancipate, or free, all enslaved African

Americans in the South. He waited, however, for the right moment. He did not want to appear to be acting in desperation when the North seemed to be losing the war.

After the Union forces turned back the Confederate troops at the Battle of Antietam, Lincoln decided to act. Five days after that battle, on September 22, 1862, he announced his plan to issue an order freeing all enslaved people in the Confederacy. On January 1, 1863, Lincoln formally signed the **Emancipation Proclamation,** which said that

❝ . . . all persons held as slaves within any state . . . in rebellion against the United States, shall be then, thenceforward, and forever free. **❞**

Effects of the Proclamation

Because the Emancipation Proclamation applied only to areas that the Confederacy controlled, it did not actually free anyone. Lincoln knew, however, that many enslaved people would hear about the proclamation. He hoped that knowledge of it would encourage them to run away from their slaveholders. Even before the Emancipation Proclamation, some 100,000 African Americans had left slavery for the safety of Union lines.

Despite the limitations of the Emancipation Proclamation, African Americans in the North greeted it joyfully. On the day it was signed, a crowd of African Americans gathered at the White House to cheer the president. Frederick

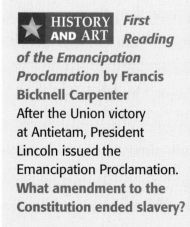

★ HISTORY AND ART *First Reading of the Emancipation Proclamation* by Francis Bicknell Carpenter After the Union victory at Antietam, President Lincoln issued the Emancipation Proclamation. **What amendment to the Constitution ended slavery?**

Frederick Douglass's son, Charles, was a member of the 54th Massachusetts Regiment.

Douglass wrote, "We shout for joy that we live to record this righteous decree."

The proclamation had the desired effect in Europe as well. The Confederacy had been seeking support from its longtime trading partners, Britain and France. However, the British took a strong position against slavery. Once Lincoln proclaimed emancipation, Britain—and France as well—decided to withhold recognition of the Confederacy.

In 1864 Republican leaders in Congress prepared a constitutional amendment to abolish slavery everywhere in the United States. In 1865 Congress passed the **Thirteenth Amendment,** which was ratified, or approved, the same year by states loyal to the Union. It was this amendment that truly freed the slaves in the United States.

African Americans Help

The Emancipation Proclamation and the Thirteenth Amendment changed the status of enslaved African Americans. Meanwhile, in both the South and the North, the war changed the lives of all African Americans.

In the South

When the Civil War began, about 3.5 million enslaved people lived in the Confederacy. Making up almost 40 percent of the region's population and the bulk of its workforce, slaves labored on plantations and in the vital iron, salt, and lead mines. Some also worked as nurses in military hospitals and cooks in the army. By the end of the war, about one-fourth of the enslaved population had fled to areas controlled by Union armies.

The possibility of a slave rebellion terrified white Southerners. For this reason most Southerners refused to consider using African Americans as soldiers—for then they would be given weapons.

Near the end of the war, however, the military situation of the Confederacy became desperate. Robert E. Lee and some other leaders supported using African Americans as soldiers and believed that those who fought should be freed. The Confederate Congress passed a law in 1865 to enlist enslaved people, although the law did not include automatic freedom. The war ended before any regiments could be organized.

Helping the North

The story was different in the North. At the start of the war, African Americans were not permitted to serve as soldiers in the Union army. This was a bitter disappointment to thousands of free African Americans living in the North who volunteered to fight for the Union.

Yet African Americans who wished to help the war effort found ways to do so. Although the army would not accept African American volunteers, the Union navy did. African Americans who had escaped slavery often proved to be especially useful to the North as guides and spies because of their knowledge of the South. Some women helped in this way as well. **Harriet Tubman,** who had helped hundreds escape slavery by way of the Underground Railroad, repeatedly spied behind Confederate lines.

In 1862 Congress passed a law allowing African Americans to serve in the Union army. As a result both free African Americans and those who had escaped slavery began enlisting. In the Emancipation Proclamation, Lincoln supported

Footnotes to History

A Soldier's ID Heavy death tolls in battle led Civil War soldiers to devise the first dog tags for identification if they were killed. Soldiers printed their names and addresses on handkerchiefs or paper, which they pinned to their clothing before going into battle.

the use of African American soldiers, and this helped increase the movement of African Americans into the military.

By the end of the war, African American volunteers made up nearly 10 percent of the Union army and 20 percent of the navy. In all, more than 200,000 African Americans served. About 37,000 lost their lives defending the Union.

By becoming soldiers, African Americans were taking an important step toward securing civil rights. Abolitionist Frederick Douglass, himself an escaped slave, understood the point well:

66 [Just] once let the black man get upon his person the brass letters, *U.S.;* let him get an eagle on his button, and a musket on his shoulder and bullets in his pocket, and there is no power on earth which can deny that he has earned the right to citizenship. **99**

African American Soldiers

African American soldiers were organized into regiments separate from the rest of the Union army. Most commanding officers of these regiments were white. African Americans received lower pay than white soldiers at first, but protests led to equal pay in 1864.

One of the most famous African American regiments was the **54th Massachusetts,** led by white abolitionists. On July 18, 1863, the 54th spearheaded a dramatic attack on a Confederate fortification near Charleston, South Carolina. With Colonel Robert Gould Shaw shouting, "Forward Fifty-Fourth!" the troops charged ahead and battled their way to the top of the fort. The Confederates drove them back with heavy fire. Nearly half of the soldiers in the 54th were wounded, captured, or killed. Their bravery under fire won respect for African American troops.

Lincoln's political opponents criticized the use of African American soldiers. Lincoln replied by quoting General Grant. Grant had written him that African Americans "will make good soldiers and taking them from the enemy weakens him in the same proportion they strengthen us."

Many white Southerners, outraged by the African American soldiers, threatened to execute any that they captured. In a few instances, this threat was carried out. However, slaves were overjoyed when they saw that the Union army included African American soldiers. As one African American regiment entered Wilmington, North Carolina, a soldier wrote, "Men and women, old and young, were running throughout the streets, shouting and praising God. We could then truly see what we have been fighting for."

Section 3 Assessment

Checking for Understanding

1. *Identify* Emancipation Proclamation, Thirteenth Amendment, Harriet Tubman.
2. *Define* emancipate, ratify.
3. *Summarize* President Lincoln's reasons for issuing the Emancipation Proclamation.

Reviewing Themes

4. **Groups and Institutions** Why did abolitionist Frederick Douglass think it was important for African Americans to be allowed to fight in the Civil War?

Critical Thinking

5. **Making Comparisons** How did President Lincoln's political and personal stands on slavery differ during the war?

Activity

Sewing a Banner Imagine that you are an enslaved African American and you learn about the passage of the Thirteenth Amendment. Using material, thread, beads, and/or felt letters, sew a banner that you anticipate carrying in a parade after the Civil War is over.

1861
Union Congress
passes income tax

April 1862
Confederate
Congress passes
draft law

March 1863
The Union passes
draft law

July 1863
Angry mobs
oppose the draft
in New York City

Section 4

Life During the Civil War

READ TO DISCOVER . . .
- what life was like for soldiers in the Civil War.
- what role women played in the war.
- how the war affected the economies of the North and the South.

TERMS TO LEARN

habeas corpus   greenback
draft   inflation
bounty

Storyteller

A soldier's life was not easy—whether in battle or in the mess tent! A Louisiana soldier wrote, "No soldier will forget his first horse-meat breakfast. It was comical to see the facial expression as they viewed the platters of hot steak fried in its own grease or the 'chunk' of boiled mule as it floated in a bucket of 'stew.' However, there seemed to be perfect good humor as they one after the other 'tackled the job.' . . . Occasionally would some stalwart fellow throw back his head and utter a long and loud 'Ye-ha, ye-ha, ye-haw!' in imitation of a . . . mule."

Union soldier and family

In both the North and the South, civilians and soldiers suffered terrible hardships and faced new challenges. In touching letters to their families and friends at home, soldiers described what they saw and how they felt—their boredom, discomfort, sickness, fear, and horror.

The Lives of Soldiers

At the start of the war, men in both the North and the South rushed to volunteer for the armies. Their enthusiasm did not last.

Most of the time, the soldiers lived in camps. Camp life had its pleasant moments of songs, stories, letters from home, and baseball games. Often, however, a soldier's life was dull, a routine of drills, bad food, marches, and rain.

During lulls between battles, Confederate and Union soldiers sometimes forgot that they were enemies. A Southern private described a Fourth of July on the front lines in 1862:

❝ Our boys and Yanks made a bargain not to fire at each other . . . and talked over the fight, and traded tobacco and coffee and newspaper as peacefully and kindly as if they had not been engaged . . . in butchering one another. ❞

The Reality of War

In spite of the fleeting moments of calm, the reality of war was never far away. Both sides suffered terrible losses in the fighting. The new rifles used during the Civil War fired with greater accuracy than the muskets of earlier wars.

Both sides used trench warfare. Soldiers dug trenches in the ground to hold their positions; they often inflicted great damage on attackers. Some generals, however, continued to launch charge after charge toward the trenches, resulting in thousands of casualties.

Medical facilities were overwhelmed by the thousands of casualties in each battle. After the Battle of Shiloh, many wounded soldiers lay in the rain for more than 24 hours waiting for treatment. A Union soldier reported, "Many had died there, and others were in the last agonies as we passed. Their groans and cries were heart-rending."

Faced with such horrors, many men deserted. About one of every 11 Union soldiers and one of every 8 Confederates ran away because of fear, hunger, or sickness.

Rebel soldiers suffered from a lack of food and supplies that worsened during the war. One reason for Lee's invasion of Maryland in 1862 was to allow his hungry army to feed off Maryland crops. A woman who saw the Confederates march to Antietam recalled the "gaunt starvation that looked from their cavernous eyes."

Women and the War

★ Many Northern and Southern women took on new responsibilities during the war. They became teachers, office workers, salesclerks, and government workers. They worked in factories and managed farms. They also suffered the loss of husbands, fathers, sons, and brothers. As Southerner **Mary Chesnut** wrote:

❝ Does anyone wonder [why] so many women die? Grief and constant anxiety kill nearly as many women at home as men are killed on the battle-field. ❞

Aiding the Troops

Women performed many jobs that helped the soldiers and the armies. They rolled bandages, wove blankets, and made ammunition. Many women collected food, clothing, and medicine for distribution to the troops. They also raised money to buy needed supplies.

Some women served as spies. While Harriet Tubman spied for the North, **Rose O'Neal Greenhow** entertained Union leaders in Washington, D.C., picking up information about Union plans that she passed to the South. Greenhow was caught, convicted of treason, and exiled, eventually going to Britain. **Belle Boyd** of Front Royal, Virginia, kept Confederate generals informed of Union army movements in the Shenandoah Valley. A few women even disguised themselves as men and became soldiers. **Loretta Janeta Velázquez** fought for the South at the First Battle of Bull Run and at Shiloh. Later the Havana, Cuba, native became a spy for the Confederacy.

Treating the Sick and Wounded

In the Civil War, for the first time, thousands of women served as nurses. At first many doctors did not want women nurses on the grounds that women were too delicate for such work. Men also

★ **Picturing HISTORY** This 1862 photo shows a Union soldier with his family at the front near Washington, D.C. Most soldiers on both sides, however, faced long separations from their families. **What other hardships did Civil War soldiers face?**

In The Hospital, 1861
by William Sheppard

Soldier-artist William Sheppard portrays a fashionably dressed Southern woman visiting a wounded soldier after the Battle of Bull Run (Manassas). **In what other ways did women help in the war effort?**

disapproved of women doing what was considered male work, and they felt it was improper for women to tend the bodies of unknown men.

Strong-minded women disregarded these objections. In the North **Dorothea Dix** organized large numbers of women to serve as military nurses. Another Northerner, **Clara Barton,** became famous for her work with wounded soldiers. Barton later founded the American Red Cross. In the South **Sally Tompkins** established a hospital for soldiers in Richmond, Virginia.

Nursing was not easy work. Kate Cummings of Alabama, who nursed the wounded in Corinth after the Battle of Shiloh, wrote, "Nothing that I had ever heard or read had given me the faintest idea of the horrors witnessed here." Yet women did a remarkable job in the war.

Opposition to the War

★ The war efforts of the Union and the Confederate governments faced opposition. Politicians objected to wartime policies, and ordinary citizens protested the way the war affected their lives.

Opposition in the North

When the war began, Northern Democrats split into two groups. One group supported most of Lincoln's wartime policies. The other, the "Peace Democrats," opposed the president and favored negotiating with the Confederacy. The Peace Democrats warned that continuing the war would lead to "terrible social change and revolution." They also appealed to racist feelings among Northern whites. Republican newspapers likened the Peace Democrats to poisonous snakes, calling them **Copperheads.** When Union armies fared poorly, support for the Copperheads rose.

Some Republicans suspected Copperheads of actively aiding the Confederates. The president ordered the arrest of anyone who interfered with the war effort—such as discouraging men from enlisting in the army. Several times Lincoln suspended the right of habeas corpus, which guarantees accused individuals the right to a hearing before being jailed. Lincoln defended his actions by asking, "Must I shoot a simple-minded soldier boy who deserts while I must not touch a hair of a wily agitator who induces him to desert?"

Enlistments Decline

As the war dragged on, the numbers of volunteers declined in both the North and the South. Enlisting enough soldiers became a problem, and both sides tried new measures.

In April 1862, the Confederate Congress passed a draft law that required men between ages 18 and 35 to serve in the army for three years. A person could avoid the draft by hiring a substitute. Later, certain groups—including slaveholders with 20 or more slaves—were exempted from the draft. This led ordinary people to complain of "a rich man's war but a poor man's fight." In reality people from all levels of society served in the Confederate and Union armies.

Union states encouraged enlistment by offering bounties—payments of $100 or more—to volunteers. In March 1863, when this system failed, the North turned to a draft. All men over 20 and under 45 had to register, and the army drew the soldiers it needed from this pool of names. A person could avoid the draft by hiring a substitute or by paying the government $300.

Resistance to the Draft

Draft laws aroused opposition in both the North and the South, with protests erupting into riots in several Northern cities. The worst disturbance took place in **New York City** in July 1863. Angry mobs opposed to the draft and to fighting to free African Americans went on a rampage of burning, looting, and killing. After 4 days of terror, more than 100 people, including about 15 African Americans, were dead. Troops from the Army of the Potomac had to be rushed in to end the rioting.

No disturbance as severe took place in the South, but many opposed the draft. The strong opposition led the president of the Confederacy, Jefferson Davis, to proclaim military law and suspend habeas corpus as Lincoln had done early in the war. Davis's action outraged Southerners who feared that they would lose the liberties for which they had gone to war.

TECHNOLOGY AND HISTORY

Civil War Camera

Mathew Brady and his many assistants recorded the camps, lives, and deaths of Union soldiers in more than 10,000 photos. **What is the biggest difference between this camera and a modern one?**

1. The photographer looks at the soldier through a **glass plate** at the **back panel** and the **lens** at the front.

2. A **plate holder** carrying another glass plate coated with light-sensitive chemicals is inserted into the back panel.

4. The plate holder and the exposed wet plate are removed from the back panel, then developed into a negative in the photographer's "traveling" **darkroom.**

3. The photographer opens the **lens.** Light reflects from the soldier and passes through the lens. The lens creates a reversed, upside-down image on the "wet" plate.

The **body** of the camera protects the wet plate from all light except that which enters through the lens when a picture is taken.

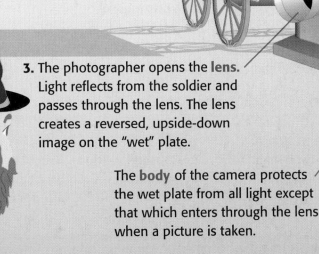

$ Economics

War and the Economy

★ The Civil War strained the Northern and the Southern economies. The North, with its greater resources, was better able to cope with wartime demands.

Both the Union and the Confederacy financed the war by borrowing money, increasing taxes, and printing paper money. The North borrowed more than $2 billion, mainly by selling war bonds that promised high interest. The South borrowed more than $700 million. It issued so many bonds that people stopped buying them.

Both sides imposed new taxes as well. The Union passed an income tax in 1861. When Southern states did not provide sufficient funds, the Confederacy also imposed an income tax.

Because neither borrowing nor taxes raised enough money to pay for the war, both sides simply began printing paper money. Northern money was called greenbacks because of its color. The Confederacy also issued paper money, several times the amount printed in the North.

The North Prospers

During the war prices rose faster than wages in the North. This inflation—general increase in prices—caused great hardship for working people. Overall, however, the Northern economy boomed. Railroad traffic increased, as did the production of coal, iron, and clothing. The need for a steady supply of food for Union troops helped farmers prosper. Industry and agriculture responded to wartime needs by adopting new, more efficient methods of production.

Economic Troubles in the South

The economy of the South suffered far more than that of the North. Because most fighting occurred in the South, Southern farmland was overrun and rail lines were torn up. By the end of the war, large portions of the South lay in ruins, thousands of people were homeless, and many Southern cities were burned.

The North's blockade of Southern ports caused severe shortages of essential goods. A scarcity of food led to riots in Atlanta, Richmond, and other cities. Inflation, too, was much worse in the South. During the course of the war, prices rose 9,000 percent—compared to a rise of 80 percent in the North.

These conditions affected soldiers. Worries about their families caused many men to desert. A Mississippi soldier who overstayed his leave to help his family wrote the governor: "We are poor men and are willing to defend our country but our families [come] first." **$**

★ ★ ★ ★ ★ **Section 4 Assessment** ★ ★ ★ ★ ★

Checking for Understanding
1. **Identify** Dorothea Dix, Clara Barton, Sally Tompkins, Copperheads.
2. **Define** habeas corpus, draft, bounty, greenback, inflation.
3. **Name** three ways that the North raised money for the war.

Reviewing Themes
4. **Economic Factors** How did war affect the economy of the South?

Critical Thinking
5. **Making Inferences** Why do you think President Lincoln believed the Copperheads were a threat to the Union war effort?

Activity

Creating a Travel Brochure Create a travel brochure of a Civil War battlefield site that you would like to visit. Include the name, location, and other activities in the area.

Technology
SKILL BUILDER

Using a CD-ROM

You have probably listened to your favorite music on compact discs. There is another type of compact disc, called a CD-ROM, that holds information. Learning how to use a CD-ROM can help you research information without spending a long time or using many resources.

Learning the Skill

CD-ROM stands for *Compact Disc, Read-Only Memory*. A CD-ROM stores huge amounts of information that a computer equipped with a CD-ROM drive can access in both audio and video form. This makes a CD-ROM a perfect storage place for games, simulations, dictionaries, encyclopedias, and other reference books. Using a CD-ROM disc or software loaded on your computer, you can "view" the information on your computer screen in many forms—words, pictures, video images, and even sounds.

Practicing the Skill

Follow these steps to use a CD-ROM to get information about the Civil War:

1. Check out a CD-ROM encyclopedia at your local library, and insert it into your CD-ROM drive.
2. Find your topic by using the mouse to click on the Search button in the main toolbar, typing in "Civil War," and clicking on the word *Search*. (If there is no Search button, click the Help button to learn what features are available and how to use them.)
3. Use the arrow key to scroll—move up, down, left, or right—through the list of article titles on the screen. If you double-click while pointing to an article title, the article

will appear on the screen. Click the Print button on the toolbar to print the article.
4. To find out what photos are available on the Civil War, click the Picture Index button on the toolbar. When the list of picture titles appears, double-click the title of the picture you want to see. Click the Caption button to read the picture's caption.
5. Each encyclopedia is different. Check the Help menu to see how to access sound clips, videos, animations, outlines, or any other features that may be available to give you information on the Civil War.

Applying the Skill

Using a CD-ROM Using the steps just described and a CD-ROM encyclopedia, find enough information about Abraham Lincoln to tell a classmate where and when he was born, what he looked like, what his role was during the Civil War, and what he said in one of his speeches.

1862   1863   1864   1865

December 1862
Lee wins the Battle
of Fredericksburg

July 1863
Battle of Gettysburg
crushes Lee's troops

March 1864
Grant takes over
Union command

April 1865
Lee surrenders
to Grant

Section 5

The Way to Victory

READ TO DISCOVER . . .
- what great battles turned the tide of the war in 1863.
- what events led the South to surrender in 1865.

TERMS TO LEARN
entrenched   total war

The Storyteller

"My shoes are gone; my clothes are almost gone. I'm weary, I'm sick, I'm hungry. My family have been killed or scattered, and may be now wandering helpless and unprotected in a strange country. And I have suffered all this for my country. I love my country. I would die—yes, I would die willingly because I love my country. But if this war is ever over, I'll . . . [n]ever love another country!" So wrote a Confederate soldier in 1863.

Cannon at Bull Run (Manassas) battlefield

Gone were the parades and masses of volunteers, the fancy uniforms and arrogance of the first years of the war. From 1862 until 1865, the soldiers and civilians faced a grim and grinding conflict marked by death, destruction, and wrenching change. Hopes were raised and dashed. What endured on each side was a fierce dedication to the cause for which it fought.

Southern Victories

The winter of 1862–1863 saw gloom in the North and hope in the South as Robert E. Lee's **Army of Northern Virginia** seemed unbeatable. With bold plans, quick movements, and knowledge of the countryside, Lee managed to surprise and defeat weak Union generals.

Fredericksburg and Chancellorsville

Lee needed little skill to win the **Battle of Fredericksburg.** On December 13, 1862, Union general **Ambrose Burnside** clashed with Lee near the Virginia town. Burnside had the larger army, but the Confederates were entrenched, or set up in a strong position, on a number of hills south of the town. Repeated attacks failed to overcome Lee's troops as thousands of Union soldiers fell on the hillside. A newspaper report concluded, "It can hardly be in human nature for men to show more valor [bravery], or generals to manifest less judgment." Devastated by his failure, Burnside resigned his command and was replaced by General **Joseph Hooker.**

Hooker rebuilt the army and then, in early May 1863, launched a campaign against Lee. Before Hooker could mount a major attack, Lee struck at **Chancellorsville,** Virginia, a few miles west of Fredericksburg.

Boldly dividing his troops for an assault on the Union forces, Lee won another victory—but it proved costly. The battle's heavy casualties included General **Stonewall Jackson.** On May 2 Jackson and his troops attacked Union troops just before dark. One of the Confederate companies fired on Jackson's party by mistake, wounding the general in the left arm. Jackson's arm had to be amputated and he died a week later.

The Tide of War Turns

Despite his own heavy losses, Lee decided to invade the North. Another victory—one on Northern soil—might persuade Britain and France to aid the Confederacy and convince the North to give up.

The Battle of Gettysburg

In June Lee began moving north with an army of 75,000. Confederate spirits were high. A Richmond newspaper wrote, "We can . . . carry our armies far into the enemy's country, exacting peace by blows leveled at his vitals."

Union general Hooker wanted to advance against Richmond, but Lincoln told him, "I think Lee's Army, and not Richmond, is your true objective." When Hooker started to make excuses for not attacking the Confederate forces, Lincoln replaced him with General **George Meade.** Meade's mission was to find and fight Lee's forces and, at the same time, to protect Washington and Baltimore from Confederate attack. Meade began moving his army to meet the enemy.

The two armies met by accident on July 1, 1863, near the small town of Gettysburg, Pennsylvania. The three-day **Battle of Gettysburg** began when Union cavalry surprised Rebel infantry raiding the town for shoes. Outnumbered, the Northerners fought desperately to hold the town before retreating to Cemetery Ridge, a line

America's FLAGS

Confederate Battle Flag, 1861 During Civil War battles, soldiers had difficulty distinguishing between the Confederate and Union flags. As a result, Southern soldiers began to carry this battle flag. It had 13 stars, although there were only 11 states in the Confederacy. The other two stars represented the border states

of Kentucky and Missouri, whose pro-Confederate minority governments had been admitted to the Confederacy.

Seventeenth Flag of the Union, 1863 The Union flag of 1863 held 35 stars. Like all the union flags of the Civil War, it retained stars for the seceded Southern states. Thus it supported Lincoln and the North's claim that the Union could not be broken.

of hills south of Gettysburg. They established strong positions along the ridge and prepared to defend it. The following day the Rebels launched another major assault and almost overran part of the Yankee line, but a counterattack saved the Union position.

Eyewitness to HISTORY

Pickett's Charge

On the third and final day of battle, Lee's boldness proved his undoing. He decided to launch one more attack, determined to "create a panic and virtually destroy the [Union] army."

This last attack, led by General George Pickett, is remembered as **Pickett's Charge.** About 13,000 Confederate soldiers advanced across about one-half mile of open ground toward the Union lines. Faced with this bold attack, the Union soldiers rushed to defend their position.

Confederate soldiers made easy targets for Union fire as they marched across the open fields. Few of the Rebels reached the center of the Union lines, and barely half returned from the charge. The next day a Union officer said:

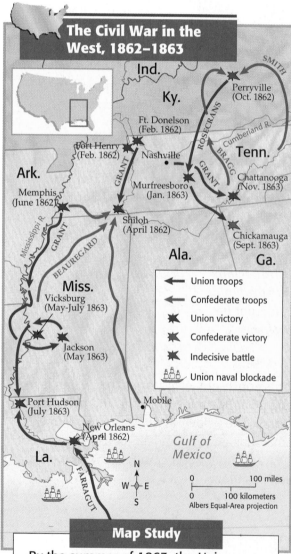

The Civil War in the West, 1862–1863

Ind.

Ky.

Perryville (Oct. 1862)

SMITH

ROSECRANS

Ft. Donelson (Feb. 1862)

Cumberland R.

Fort Henry (Feb. 1862)

Nashville

BRAGG

Tenn.

GRANT

Ark.

Memphis (June 1862)

Murfreesboro (Jan. 1863)

GRANT

Chattanooga (Nov. 1863)

Mississippi R.

GRANT

Shiloh (April 1862)

Chickamauga (Sept. 1863)

BEAUREGARD

Ala.

Ga.

Miss.

Vicksburg (May–July 1863)

Jackson (May 1863)

Union troops

Confederate troops

★ Union victory

★ Confederate victory

★ Indecisive battle

⛵ Union naval blockade

Port Hudson (July 1863)

Mobile

New Orleans (April 1862)

Gulf of Mexico

La.

FARRAGUT

N W E S

0   100 miles
0   100 kilometers
Albers Equal-Area projection

Map Study

By the summer of 1863, the Union controlled the lower Mississippi River.

1. **Location** What battle in Georgia did Union forces lose?
2. **Analyzing Information** Who led the Union troops at Shiloh, Tennessee?

> **❝** I tried to ride over the field but could not, for dead and wounded lay too thick to guide a horse through them. **❞**

Lee knew the battle was lost. "It's all my fault," he told his troops. He waited one day for a counterattack that never came and then painfully retreated to Virginia.

General Meade was proud of the victory, but Lincoln was disappointed. Upset that the Union army had once again allowed Lee and his soldiers to get away, Lincoln exclaimed, "We had them in our grasp. We had only to stretch forth our hands and they were ours."

Victory at Vicksburg

While Confederate and Union troops were fighting at Gettysburg, a great battle was also taking place at **Vicksburg, Mississippi.** Vicksburg stood on a high bluff above the Mississippi River. To gain control of the river, one of the North's major war goals, the Union needed to seize Vicksburg. For several months, Union forces under Ulysses S. Grant had laid siege to the town. Finally, on July 4, 1863, Vicksburg surrendered.

With the surrender of Vicksburg and then Port Hudson—another Confederate fort in Louisiana—the Union now held the entire Mississippi River. Texas, Louisiana, and Arkansas were sealed off from the rest of the Confederacy.

The Union victories at Gettysburg and Vicksburg marked a turning point in the war. They drove Lee's army out of Pennsylvania, secured the Mississippi as a Union highway, and cut the South in two. Nevertheless, the South still had troops and a will to fight. The war would continue for two more terrible years.

Lincoln at Gettysburg

On November 19, 1863, at a ceremony dedicating a cemetery at Gettysburg, Edward Everett, a prominent scholar, gave a two-hour address. Then President Lincoln rose to speak. In a two-minute speech, called the **Gettysburg Address,** Lincoln beautifully expressed what the war had come to mean:

★ **Picturing HISTORY** The Union won an important victory at the Battle of Chattanooga when forces under General Ulysses S. Grant (right) drove the Confederates from the high ground around the city. **To what military position did Lincoln name Grant after Chattanooga?**

66 It is for us the living . . . to be here dedicated to the great task remaining before us . . . that these dead shall not have died in vain—that this nation, under God, shall have a new birth of freedom—and that government of the people, by the people, for the people shall not perish from the earth. 99

The speech helped war-weary Americans look beyond the images of the battlefield and focus on their shared ideals.

Final Phases of the War

★ In November 1863, Grant and General **William Tecumseh Sherman** won an important victory at Chattanooga, Tennessee. Following the Northern triumphs at Vicksburg and Gettysburg, Chattanooga further weakened the Confederates. The following March, President Lincoln turned to Grant for help.

📖 Biography
Grant Takes Command

Ulysses S. Grant was small and unimpressive in appearance. His early army career was not impressive either, and in 1854 he had been forced to resign because of a drinking problem. When the Civil War broke out, he rejoined the army. Grant's victories in the West and his willingness to attack hard and keep fighting impressed President Lincoln. "I can't spare this man," the president said. "He fights." After the victory at Chattanooga, Lincoln named Grant commander of all the Union armies.

Grant devised a plan to attack the Confederacy on all fronts at once. The Army of the Potomac would try to crush Lee's army in Virginia. The western army, under Sherman, would advance to **Atlanta, Georgia,** and crush the Confederate forces in the Deep South. If the plan succeeded, they would destroy the Confederacy.

Virginia Battles

Grant soon put his strategy into effect. In May and June of 1864, his army of 115,000 men smashed into Lee's 65,000 troops in a series of 3 battles near Richmond—the Battles of the Wilderness, Spotsylvania Courthouse, and Cold Harbor. Each time, Confederate lines held, but each time, Grant quickly resumed the attack.

The battles were vicious, costing the North more than 60,000 men. Critics called Grant a butcher, but he said, "I propose to fight it out on this line if it takes all summer." Lincoln supported him, knowing that Lee could not afford the continuing casualties in his army.

After Cold Harbor, Grant swung south of Richmond to attack **Petersburg,** an important railroad center. If it fell, Richmond would be cut off from the rest of the Confederacy. Petersburg, however, had strong defenses. Grant's assault turned into a nine-month siege.

The Election of 1864

To the war-weary North, the events of the first half of 1864 looked like yet another stalled offensive. Grant was stuck outside Richmond and Petersburg, and Sherman was stuck outside Atlanta. Sentiment for a negotiated peace grew.

The Democrats wanted to make peace with the South, even though that might result in Confederate independence. Lincoln was determined to push for restoring the Union and ending slavery. In the summer of 1864, Lincoln's chances for reelection did not look good. "I am going to be beaten and unless some great change takes place, badly beaten," he said.

Great changes did take place. In August David Farragut, now an admiral, led a Union fleet into **Mobile Bay,** braving the Confederate defenses. Union control over the Gulf of Mexico was now complete. Then, in early September, news arrived

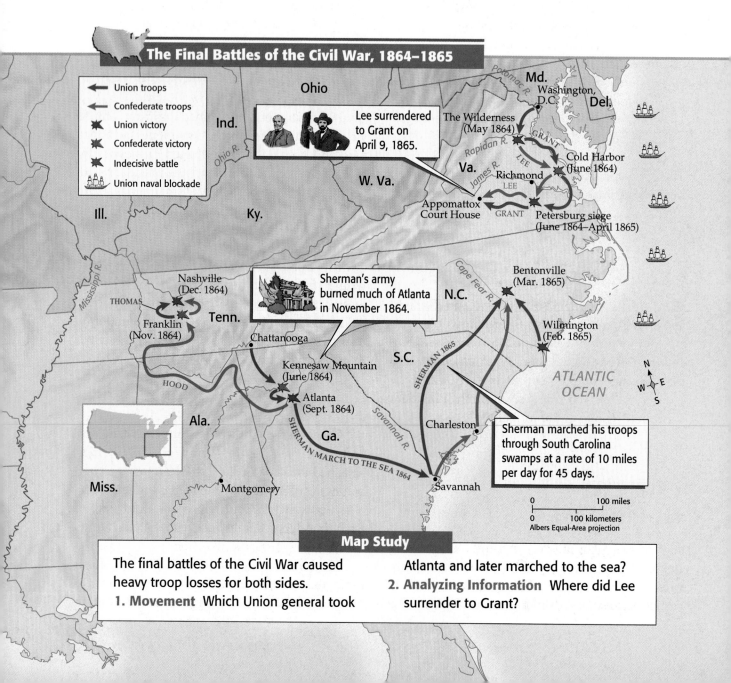

The Final Battles of the Civil War, 1864–1865

← Union troops
← Confederate troops
✸ Union victory
✸ Confederate victory
✸ Indecisive battle
⛵ Union naval blockade

Lee surrendered to Grant on April 9, 1865.

Sherman's army burned much of Atlanta in November 1864.

Sherman marched his troops through South Carolina swamps at a rate of 10 miles per day for 45 days.

Ohio
Md.
Washington, D.C.
Del.
Ind.
The Wilderness (May 1864)
Va.
Richmond
Cold Harbor (June 1864)
W. Va.
Appomattox Court House
Petersburg siege (June 1864–April 1865)
Ill.
Ky.
Nashville (Dec. 1864)
THOMAS
Bentonville (Mar. 1865)
N.C.
Franklin (Nov. 1864)
Tenn.
Chattanooga
Wilmington (Feb. 1865)
HOOD
Kennesaw Mountain (June 1864)
S.C.
ATLANTIC OCEAN
Atlanta (Sept. 1864)
Charleston
Ala.
Ga.
SHERMAN MARCH TO THE SEA 1864
Miss.
Montgomery
Savannah

0   100 miles
0   100 kilometers
Albers Equal-Area projection

Map Study

The final battles of the Civil War caused heavy troop losses for both sides.
1. **Movement** Which Union general took Atlanta and later marched to the sea?
2. **Analyzing Information** Where did Lee surrender to Grant?

that Sherman had captured Atlanta. More news followed in October, when General Sheridan's Union force completed a campaign that drove the Rebels out of the Shenandoah Valley in Virginia. The North's mood changed. With the end of the war in sight, Lincoln easily won reelection, taking 55 percent of the popular vote.

The fall of Atlanta created a deep sense of gloom in the South. "Since Atlanta I have felt as if all were dead within me, forever," Mary Chesnut wrote. "We are going to be wiped off the earth."

Richmond, Virginia, April 1865

Total War

Leaving Atlanta in ruins, Sherman convinced Grant to let him try a bold plan. Sherman's army began a historic "march to the sea" to **Savannah, Georgia.** As the army advanced, it abandoned its supply lines and lived off the land it passed through. Union troops took what food they needed, tore up railroad lines and fields, and killed animals in an effort to destroy anything useful to the South. They cut a path of destruction 50 miles wide. This method of waging war is known as total war. Sherman said:

> **❝** We are not only fighting hostile armies, but a hostile people, and must make old and young, rich and poor, feel the hard hand of war. **❞**

After capturing Savannah in December, Sherman turned north. The army marched through South Carolina, devastating the state. Sherman planned to join Grant's forces in Virginia.

Richmond Falls

Throughout the fall and winter of 1864, Grant continued the siege of Petersburg. Lee and his troops desperately defended the town, but sickness, hunger, casualties, and desertion weakened them. Finally, on April 2, 1865, the Confederate lines broke and Petersburg fell to the Union.

Richmond fell the same day. Rebel troops, government officials, and many residents fled the Confederate capital. They set fire to much of the city to keep it from falling into Union hands.

On April 4 Lincoln visited Richmond. As he walked its streets, African Americans crowded around him. One elderly man approached the president, took off his hat, and bowed. With tears rolling down his cheeks, he said, "May God bless you." Lincoln removed his own hat and bowed in return.

Victory for the North

In his second Inaugural Address on March 4, 1865, Lincoln spoke of the coming peace:

> **❝** With malice toward none, with charity for all . . . let us strive on to finish the work we are in, to bind up the nation's wounds . . . to do all which may achieve and cherish a just and lasting peace among ourselves and with all nations. **❞**

*F*ootnotes to History

No Escaping Wilmer McLean could not escape the Civil War, which started in his front yard and ended in his front parlor! The First Battle of Bull Run was fought on his property, and his home became headquarters for several Confederate generals. McLean tried to escape the devastation of war by moving to Appomattox Court House, Virginia. On April 9, 1865, Grant and Lee discussed the terms of surrender in his parlor.

Surrender of the Confederate Flag at Appomattox by **Richard Norris Brooke** At Appomattox Court House Confederate troops sadly and carefully folded their battle-torn flag and laid it on the ground. **What kind of surrender terms did Grant make to Lee's troops?**

Surrender at Appomattox

Lee moved his army west of Richmond, hoping to link up with the small Confederate force that was trying to stop Sherman's advance. But the Union army blocked his escape route. Realizing that the situation was hopeless, Lee said:

66 There is nothing left for me to do but go and see General Grant, and I would rather die a thousand deaths. 99

On April 9 Lee and his troops surrendered to Grant in a small Virginia village called **Appomattox Court House.** Grant's terms were generous. The Confederate soldiers had to lay down their arms but then were free to go home. Grant allowed them to keep their horses so that they could, as he said, "put in a crop to carry themselves and their families through the next winter." Grant also ordered three days' worth of food to be sent to Lee's hungry troops.

Several days after Lee's surrender, the Confederate forces in North Carolina surrendered to General Sherman. Jefferson Davis, the president of the Confederacy, was captured in Georgia on May 10. The Civil War was over at last.

Results of the War

★ The Civil War was the most devastating conflict in American history. More than 600,000 soldiers died, and the war caused billions of dollars of damage, most of it in the South. The war also created bitter feelings among defeated Southerners that lasted for generations.

The war had other consequences as well. The North's victory saved the Union. The federal government was strengthened and was now clearly more powerful than the states. Finally, the war freed millions of African Americans. How the nation would treat these new citizens remained to be seen.

★ ★ ★ ★ ★ Section 5 Assessment ★ ★ ★ ★ ★

Checking for Understanding
1. *Identify* Gettysburg Address, William Tecumseh Sherman, Appomattox Court House.
2. *Define* entrenched, total war.
3. *Identify* the reasons that Gettysburg and Vicksburg were important battles.

Reviewing Themes
4. **Individual Action** Why did President Lincoln name Ulysses S. Grant commander

of all the Union armies?

Critical Thinking
5. **Drawing Conclusions** How did the Union victory in the war strengthen the federal government?

 Activity

Composing a Poem Write a poem that a Civil War soldier might have written after hearing that the war was over.

Multimedia Activities

Historic America Electronic Field Trips

Field Trip to Gettysburg

Setting up the Video

With a group of your classmates, view "Gettysburg" on the videodisc *Historic America: Electronic Field Trips*.

During the Civil War, one of the most devastating battles was the battle at Gettysburg, Pennsylvania. The battle lasted 3 days, and about 40,000 soldiers died or were wounded. The program gives different perspectives of the battle and its results.

Hands-On Activity

Civil War soldiers and prisoners of war played chess and card games while stationed in military camps. Some soldiers made their own chess sets. Make your own Civil War chess set labeled with the names of presidents, generals, spies, doctors, drummers, and foot soldiers from both the Union and the Confederacy.

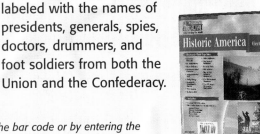

Side 1, Chapter 8

View the video by scanning the bar code or by entering the chapter number on your keypad and pressing Search.

Surfing the "Net"

Abraham Lincoln

Abraham Lincoln was the nation's sixteenth president. During his presidency, he had the task of guiding our country through one of the most difficult experiences in its history—the Civil War. Many historians regard him as one of our greatest presidents. To research more about Lincoln's presidency, look on the Internet.

Getting There

Follow these steps to gather information about Abraham Lincoln's presidency.

1. Use a search engine. Type in the phrase *Abraham Lincoln*.
2. After typing in the subject *Abraham Lincoln*, enter words like the following to focus your

search: *Civil War, Library of Congress, history, presidency*.
3. The search engine will provide you with a number of links to follow. Links are "pointers" to different sites on the Internet and commonly appear as blue underlined words.

What to Do When You Are There

Use the Internet to research Abraham Lincoln and his presidency. Click on the links to navigate through the pages of information. Gather your findings. Then, using a word processor, write a research report on the presidency of Abraham Lincoln. Be sure to cite the various web page sources.

Assessment and Activities

⭐ Reviewing Key Terms

On a sheet of paper, define the following terms:

border state
blockade
offensive
Rebel
Yankee
blockade runner
ironclad
casualty
emancipate
habeas corpus
draft
bounty
greenback

⭐ Reviewing Key Facts

1. What three advantages did the South have in the Civil War?
2. What did most Northerners expect to happen at the First Battle of Bull Run?
3. Why did Lincoln hesitate to make a move against slavery in the early stages of the war?
4. What roles did women play in the war?
5. How did the war help to strengthen the economy of the North?

⭐ Critical Thinking

Analyzing Information

Sherman's "march to the sea" left a wide path of destruction in the South.

1. Do you think waging total war at this stage of the fighting was necessary? Why or why not?
2. How do you think Sherman's actions would affect the South's ability to rebuild its economy after the war?

⭐ Time Line Activity

Create a time line on which you place the following events in chronological order.

- Lincoln elected to second term as president
- Battle between the *Monitor* and *Merrimack*
- Jefferson Davis is captured
- First Battle of Bull Run
- Confederate army surrenders at Appomattox Court House
- Lincoln issues Emancipation Proclamation
- Battle of Gettysburg

⭐ Skill Practice Activity

Using a CD-ROM

Using the steps described on page 481 and a CD-ROM encyclopedia, find enough information about the Battle of Shiloh to tell a classmate where and when it took place, who were the generals involved, what their role was during the battle, and what was the outcome of the battle. Compare what you find to the details shown in this painting. Is the art accurate? Explain.

Battle of Shiloh

⭐ Geography Activity

Study the map below and answer the questions that follow.

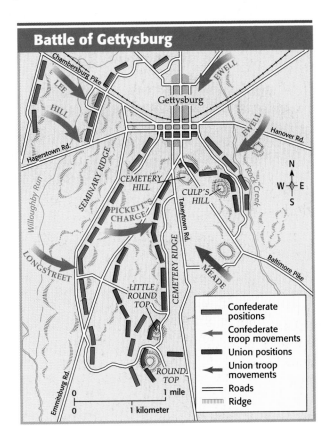

1. **Location** Along what ridge were the Union troops positioned? The Confederate troops?
2. **Movement** Who led the attack on Union troops at Little Round Top?
3. **Movement** What five Confederate commanders are shown on the map?

⭐ Cooperative Activity

History and Geography Work with members of your group to create a three-dimensional relief map of one of the battle sites described in the chapter. Do research to find out the geography of the area and use clay, cardboard, or other materials to construct your map. Then use different colored objects to demonstrate troop movements.

⭐ Technology Activity

Using the Internet Search the Internet for a list of museums that have Civil War artifact and photo collections. Make a map to show the names and locations of the museums.

⭐ Reviewing Themes

1. **Government and Democracy** How did the people of western Virginia respond to Virginia's secession from the Union?
2. **Geography and History** Why was controlling the Mississippi River vital to both the North and the South?
3. **Groups and Institutions** What two government orders changed the status of enslaved African Americans during the war?
4. **Economic Factors** How did inflation affect the lives of people during the war?
5. **Individual Action** Why was General Lee such an effective military leader?

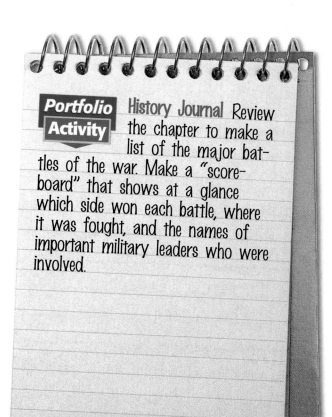

Portfolio Activity History Journal Review the chapter to make a list of the major battles of the war. Make a "scoreboard" that shows at a glance which side won each battle, where it was fought, and the names of important military leaders who were involved.

Hands-On HISTORY Lab Activity

Morse Code

"What hath God wrought!" On May 24, 1844, Samuel Morse tapped this message on his telegraph and sent it across wire from Washington, D.C., to Baltimore, Maryland. A few seconds later the operator in Baltimore tapped back the same message. Americans were astonished. Astonish yourself by building your own simple telegraph.

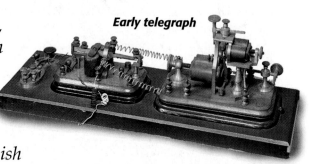

Early telegraph

The Way It Was

Armies in the Civil War made use of the newest communication system—the telegraph. Inventor Samuel Morse sent the first long-distance message in 1844, using a code of short and long (dot-dash) electrical signals invented by Morse and Alfred Vail. Telegraph operators throughout the world began using this Morse code to send messages. By 1846 more than 5,000 miles (8,045 km) of telegraph wire had been strung, and 3,000 more miles (4,827 km) were under construction.

International Morse Code

a	. _	n	_ .
b	_ . . .	o	_ _ _
c	_ . _ .	p	. _ _ .
d	_ . .	q	_ _ . _
e	.	r	. _ .
f	. . _ .	s	. . .
g	_ _ .	t	_
h	. . . .	u	. . _
I	. .	v	. . . _
j	. _ _ _	w	. _ _
k	_ . _	x	_ . . _
l	. _ . .	y	_ . _ _
m	_ _	z	_ _ . .

Materials

- Size D battery
- tape
- 2 feet of insulated wire, cut into 3 pieces
- 1 metal paper clip
- 2 metal thumbtacks
- flashlight-sized lightbulb and holder
- piece of thick cardboard about 1 foot square

Believe It Or Not!

The fastest speed recorded for a hand-key transmission of Morse code is 175 symbols a minute. A member of the United States Army Signal Corps accomplished this feat in 1942.

❷ What To Do

① Push one thumbtack into the cardboard.

② Trap the end of one piece of wire under the thumbtack and tape the other end to one terminal of the battery.

③ Tape another piece of wire to the other battery terminal and connect it to the lightbulb holder.

④ Connect a third piece of wire to the lightbulb holder and to a second tack about 1 inch from the first tack.

⑤ Trap a paper clip under the first thumbtack and bend the end up at an angle. The paper clip will act as a telegraph key. Tap the bent paper clip down on the second thumbtack and observe what happens.

❸ Lab Report

1. What happened when you touched the paper clip to the thumbtack in Step 5?
2. Was it easy or difficult to send a coded message with your paper clip? Explain why.
3. **Drawing Conclusions** How do you think the use of the telegraph might have affected the outcome of the Civil War?

Go a Step Further

Use the Morse code dot-dash symbols listed on page 492 to tap a message to a friend. Then have someone tap you a message. For easier translation, write down the dot-dashes as the light flashes. Decipher the message after you have written down the entire code of dots and dashes.

1865–1896

Reconstruction and Its Aftermath

★ Why It's Important

Reconstruction raised questions about government and the rights of citizens that remained long after it ended. Debate over the rightful power of the federal government and the states continues to this day. Americans continue to wrestle with the problem of providing civil rights and equal opportunity to all American citizens.

★ Chapter Themes

- *Section 1,* Groups and Institutions
- *Section 2,* Civic Rights and Responsibilities
- *Section 3,* Continuity and Change
- *Section 4,* Individual Action
- *Section 5,* Economic Factors

PRIMARY SOURCES
Library

See pages 968–969 for primary source readings to accompany Chapter 17

★ **HISTORY AND ART** *Sunday Morning in Virginia* by **Winslow Homer** Artist Winslow Homer skillfully painted everyday scenes in the lives of rural Southerners during Reconstruction. This African American family shares a reading from the Bible.

1864   1865   1866

July 1864
Congress passes
Wade-Davis Bill

March 1865
Freedmen's
Bureau is
established

April 9, 1865
Lee surrenders

April 14, 1865
President Lincoln
is assassinated

Section 1

Reconstruction Plans

READ TO DISCOVER . . .

▪ how the Reconstruction plans of Lincoln and the Radical Republicans differed.
▪ what were Johnson's Reconstruction plans.

TERMS TO LEARN

Reconstruction
amnesty

radical
freedmen

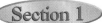

Storyteller

About a month after President Lincoln began his second term of office, the Civil War ended, and the soldiers returned to their homes. One Illinois veteran wrote upon reaching the family farm, "The morning after my arrival, September 29th, I [took off] my uniform of first lieutenant, put on some of my father's old clothes, and proceeded to wage war on the standing corn. The feeling I had while engaged in this work was sort of [odd]. It almost seemed, sometimes, as if I had been away only a day or two, and had just taken up the farm work where I had left off."

Lincoln's second Inaugural Address

The end of the Civil War raised many difficult questions. For example, should the slaveholding Southerners be punished or forgiven? What rights should be granted to the freed African Americans? How could the war-torn nation be brought back together?

Reconstruction Debate

★ The war had left the South with enormous problems. Most of the major fighting had taken place in the South. Towns and cities were in ruin, plantations burned, and roads, bridges, and railroads destroyed.

More than 258,000 Confederate soldiers had died in the war, and illness and wounds weakened thousands more. Many Southern families faced the task of rebuilding their lives with few resources and without the help of adult males.

People in all parts of the nation agreed that the devastated Southern economy and society needed rebuilding. They disagreed bitterly, however, over how to accomplish this. This period of rebuilding is called Reconstruction. This term also refers to the various plans for accomplishing the rebuilding.

Lincoln's Plan

President Lincoln offered the first plan for accepting the Southern states back into the Union. In December 1863, during the Civil War, the president announced what came to be known as the **Ten Percent Plan.** When 10 percent of the voters of a state took an oath of loyalty to the Union, the

Chapter 17   Reconstruction and Its Aftermath   **495**

state could form a new government and adopt a new constitution that had to ban slavery.

Lincoln wanted to encourage Southerners who supported the Union to take charge of the state governments. He believed that punishing the South would serve no useful purpose and would only delay healing the torn nation.

The president offered amnesty—a pardon—to all white Southerners, except Confederate leaders, who were willing to swear loyalty to the Union. Lincoln also supported granting the right to vote to African Americans who were educated or had served in the Union army. He would not force the Southern states to give rights held by white Americans to African Americans.

In 1864 three states that the Union army occupied—**Louisiana, Arkansas,** and **Tennessee**—established governments under Lincoln's plan. These states then became caught in a struggle between the president and Congress when Congress refused to seat the states' representatives.

A Rival Plan

A group of Republicans in Congress considered Lincoln's plan too mild. They argued that Congress, not the president, should control Reconstruction policy. Because these Republicans favored a tougher and more radical, or extreme, approach to Reconstruction, they were called **Radical Republicans.** A leading Radical Republican, **Thaddeus Stevens,** declared that Southern institutions "must be broken up and relaid, or all our blood and treasure have been spent in vain."

Controlled by the Radical Republicans, Congress voted to deny seats to representatives from any state reconstructed under Lincoln's plan. Then Congress began to create its own plan.

The Wade-Davis Bill

In July 1864, Congress passed the **Wade-Davis Bill.** The bill offered a plan much harsher than Lincoln's. First, 50 percent of the white males in a state had to swear loyalty to the Union. Second, a state constitutional convention could be held, but only white males who swore they had never taken up arms against the Union could vote for delegates to this convention. Former Confederates were also denied the right to hold public office. Finally, the convention had to adopt a new state constitution that abolished slavery. Only then could a state be readmitted to the Union.

Lincoln refused to sign the bill into law. He wanted to encourage the formation of new state governments so that order could be restored quickly. Lincoln realized that he would have to compromise with the Radical Republicans.

The Freedmen's Bureau

More progress was made on the other great issue of Reconstruction—helping African Americans freed from slavery. In March 1865, during the

The Return to Fredericksburg After the Battle **by David English Henderson** A Virginia family returns to its home in war-shattered Fredericksburg. **Why do you think the painting shows no men of military age?**

final weeks of the war, Congress and the president established a new government agency to help former enslaved persons, or freedmen. Called the **Freedmen's Bureau,** this agency was actually part of the army.

In the years following the war, the Freedmen's Bureau played an important role in helping African Americans make the transition to freedom. The agency distributed food and clothing and also provided medical services that lowered the death rate among freed men and women.

The Freedmen's Bureau achieved one of its greatest successes in the area of education. The bureau established schools, staffed mostly by teachers from the North. It also gave aid to new institutions of higher learning, such as Atlanta University, Howard University, and Fisk University.

The bureau helped freed people acquire land that had been abandoned by owners or seized by Union armies. It offered African Americans free transportation to the countryside where laborers were needed, and it helped them obtain fair wages. Although its main goal was to aid African Americans, the bureau also helped Southerners who had supported the Union.

Lincoln Assassinated!

A terrible event soon threw the debates over Reconstruction into confusion. On the evening of April 14, 1865, President and Mrs. Lincoln attended the play *Our American Cousin* at Ford's Theater in **Washington, D.C.** It was just five days after the surrender of Lee's army and four years to the day after the fall of Fort Sumter.

As the Lincolns watched the play from a private box in the balcony, **John Wilkes Booth,** an actor and Confederate sympathizer, entered the box without anyone seeing him. Booth shot the president in the back of the head, then leaped to

★ Picturing HISTORY

Actor John Wilkes Booth used this pistol to shoot Lincoln at Ford's Theater. The wanted poster promises a large reward for help in capturing Booth. **How was Booth finally captured?**

the stage and escaped during the chaos that followed the shooting. Aides carried the wounded president to the nearby house of William Petersen, a tailor. Lincoln died there a few hours later, without ever regaining consciousness.

After escaping from Ford's Theater, Booth fled on horseback to Virginia. Union troops tracked him down and on April 26 cornered him in a barn near Port Royal, Virginia. When Booth refused to surrender, he was shot to death.

Booth was part of a small group that plotted to kill high officials of the United States government. On the night of Lincoln's assassination, a fellow conspirator attacked Secretary of State William Seward, wounding him seriously. Another conspirator went to kill Vice President Andrew Johnson but failed to carry out the assignment. A military court convicted eight people of taking part in the plot. Four were hanged and the others imprisoned for life.

News of Lincoln's assassination shocked the nation. African Americans mourned the death of

*F*ootnotes to History

Your Name Is *Mud* During his escape, John Wilkes Booth broke his leg and was treated by Dr. Samuel Mudd. The doctor was later imprisoned for giving aid to the president's assassin. "Your name is mud" came to mean having a damaged reputation.

the man who had helped them win their freedom. Northern whites grieved for the leader who had saved the Union.

A New President

When Lincoln died, Vice President **Andrew Johnson** became president. Formerly a Democratic senator from Tennessee, Johnson had been the only Southern senator to support the Union during the Civil War.

Soon after taking office, President Johnson revealed his plan for Reconstruction. He resented the slaveholders who had dominated the South and wished to punish them. As a result Radicals thought Johnson would create a harsh plan they could accept. Johnson, however, believed in giving the states control over many decisions, and he had no desire to help African Americans.

"Restoration"

Johnson announced his plan, which he preferred to call "Restoration," in the summer of 1865—while Congress was in recess. Under his plan, most Southerners would be granted amnesty once they swore an oath of loyalty to the Union. High-ranking Confederate officials and wealthy landowners, however, could be pardoned only by applying personally to the president. This provision was Johnson's attack on the wealthy leaders who he believed had tricked the average people of the South into seceding.

Johnson also appointed governors to Southern states and required them to hold elections for state constitutional conventions. Only whites who had sworn their loyalty and been pardoned would be allowed to vote. Johnson opposed granting freed African Americans equal rights or letting them vote. He believed that each Southern state should decide what to do about freed people, saying, "White men alone must manage the South."

Before a state could reenter the Union, its constitutional convention had to denounce secession and abolish slavery. States also had to ratify the **Thirteenth Amendment** to the Constitution, which Congress had passed in January 1865. This amendment abolished slavery in all parts of the United States.

By the end of 1865, all the former Confederate states had formed new governments under Johnson's plan and were ready to rejoin the Union. President Johnson declared that "Restoration" was almost complete.

Section 1 Assessment

Checking for Understanding

1. **Identify** Radical Republicans, Wade-Davis Bill, John Wilkes Booth, Andrew Johnson, Thirteenth Amendment.
2. **Define** Reconstruction, amnesty, radical, freedmen.
3. **Compare** Lincoln's Ten Percent Plan to the Radical Republicans' Wade-Davis Bill.

Reviewing Themes

4. **Groups and Institutions** Why do you think both Lincoln and the Radical Republicans excluded former Confederate officials from their Reconstruction plans?

Critical Thinking

5. **Recognizing Bias** Do you think President Johnson's early ties to the South influenced his treatment of African Americans in his Reconstruction plans? Explain your answer.

Creating a Table of Contents What would it have been like for an enslaved African American to be in control of his or her life for the first time? Prepare a table of contents for a booklet to help African Americans make an easier transition to freedom.

1865	1867	1869	1871

1865
First black codes passed

March 1867
Radical Reconstruction begins

1868
Ulysses S. Grant is elected president

February 1870
Fifteenth Amendment extends voting rights

Section 2

Radicals in Control

READ TO DISCOVER . . .
- what some Southerners did to deprive freed people of their rights and how Congress responded.
- what the main features of Radical Reconstruction were.

TERMS TO LEARN
black codes   impeach
override

The **S**toryteller

For three days in May 1866, white mobs in Memphis, Tennessee, burned African American churches, schools, and homes. Forty-eight people, all but two of them African American, were killed in the rioting. Many Northerners saw the rampage as an attempt by whites to terrorize African Americans and keep them from exercising their new freedoms. This incident and similar riots in other Southern cities helped convince Radical Republicans that President Johnson's Reconstruction plans were not strong enough.

Ku Klux Klan flag

During the fall of 1865, the Southern states created new governments that met the rules President Johnson laid down, and Southern voters elected new representatives to Congress. More than two dozen of these representatives had been high-ranking officials in the Confederacy—including the Confederacy's vice president, Alexander H. Stephens. When the newly elected Southern representatives arrived in Washington, D.C., Congress refused to seat them. Many Republicans refused to readmit the Southern states on such easy terms and rejected Johnson's claim that Reconstruction was complete.

African Americans' Rights

To many in the North, it seemed that Johnson's plan for Reconstruction was robbing the Union of its hard-won victory. In addition Northerners realized that the treatment of African Americans in Southern states was not improving.

Black Codes

In 1865 and early 1866, the new Southern state legislatures passed a series of laws called black codes. Key parts of these laws aimed to control freed men and women and to enable plantation owners to exploit African American workers.

Modeled on laws that had regulated free African Americans before the Civil War, the black codes of each Southern state trampled the rights of African Americans. Some laws allowed local officials to arrest and fine unemployed African

His First Vote by Thomas Waterman Wood Wood's oil painting emphasized the importance of the ballot to African American voters. How did African American males gain the right to vote?

Americans and make them work for white employers to pay off their fines. Other laws banned African Americans from owning or renting farms. One law allowed whites to take orphaned African American children as unpaid apprentices. To freed men and women and many Northerners, the black codes reestablished slavery in disguise.

Challenging the Black Codes

In early 1866 Congress extended the life of the Freedmen's Bureau and granted it new powers. The Freedmen's Bureau now had authority to set up special courts to prosecute individuals charged with violating the rights of African Americans. These courts provided African Americans with a form of justice where they could serve on juries.

Congress also passed the **Civil Rights Act of 1866.** This act granted full citizenship to African Americans and gave the federal government the power to intervene in state affairs to protect their rights. The law overturned the black codes. It also contradicted the 1857 *Dred Scott* decision of the Supreme Court, which had ruled that African Americans were not citizens.

President Johnson vetoed both the Freedmen's Bureau bill and the Civil Rights Act, arguing that the federal government was overstepping its proper authority. He also said that the laws were

unconstitutional because they were passed by a Congress that did not include representatives from all the states. By raising the issue of representation, Johnson indirectly threatened to veto any law passed by this Congress.

Republicans in Congress had enough votes to override, or defeat, both vetoes, and the bills became law. As the split between Congress and the president grew, the possibility of their working together faded. The Radical Republicans abandoned the idea of compromise and drafted a new Reconstruction plan—one led by Congress.

The Fourteenth Amendment

Congress wanted to ensure that African Americans would not lose the rights that the Civil Rights Act granted. Fearing the Civil Rights Act might be overturned in court, Congress in June 1866 passed a new amendment to the Constitution.

The **Fourteenth Amendment** granted full citizenship to all individuals born in the United States. Because most African Americans in the United States had been born there, they became full citizens. The amendment also stated that no state could take away a citizen's life, liberty, and property "without due process of law," and that every citizen was entitled to "equal protection of the laws." States that prevented any adult male citizen from voting could lose part of their representation in Congress. The Fourteenth Amendment was interpreted as not including members of the Native American tribes.

The amendment did not include voting rights for African Americans—a right granted only in a

America's FLAGS

The 37-Star Flag By 1866 Nebraskans had ratified their state's constitution. The state was admitted into the Union on March 1, 1867.

few Northern states. The amendment also barred prominent former Confederates from holding national or state office unless pardoned by a vote of two-thirds of Congress.

Congress declared that Southern states had to ratify the amendment to be readmitted to the Union. Of the 11 Southern states, only Tennessee ratified the Fourteenth Amendment. The refusal of the other states to ratify the amendment delayed its adoption until 1868.

Republican Victory

The Fourteenth Amendment became a major issue in the congressional elections of 1866. Johnson urged Northern and Southern state legislatures to reject it. He also campaigned vigorously against Republican candidates. Many Northerners were disturbed by the nastiness of Johnson's

campaign. They also worried about violent clashes between whites and African Americans, such as the riots that erupted in Memphis, Tennessee, and New Orleans, Louisiana.

The Republicans won a decisive victory, increasing their majorities in both houses of Congress. The Republicans also gained control of the governments in every Northern state. The election gave Congress the signal to take Reconstruction into its own hands.

Radical Reconstruction

The Republicans in Congress quickly took charge of Reconstruction. President Johnson could do little to stop them because Congress could easily override his vetoes. Thus began a period known as Radical Reconstruction.

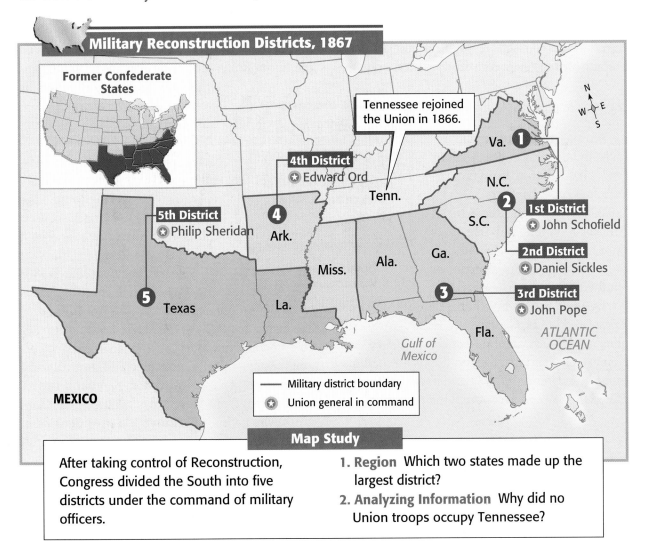

Military Reconstruction Districts, 1867

Former Confederate States

Tennessee rejoined the Union in 1866.

Va. **1**

N.C.

4th District
⭐ Edward Ord

5th District
⭐ Philip Sheridan

Tenn.

1st District
⭐ John Schofield

S.C.

2nd District
⭐ Daniel Sickles

4 Ark.

Ga.

Ala.

Miss.

5 Texas

La.

3

3rd District
⭐ John Pope

Fla.

ATLANTIC OCEAN

Gulf of Mexico

MEXICO

— Military district boundary
⭐ Union general in command

Map Study

After taking control of Reconstruction, Congress divided the South into five districts under the command of military officers.

1. **Region** Which two states made up the largest district?
2. **Analyzing Information** Why did no Union troops occupy Tennessee?

Reconstruction Act of 1867

On March 2, 1867, Congress passed the **First Reconstruction Act.** The act called for the creation of new governments in the 10 Southern states that had not ratified the Fourteenth Amendment. Tennessee, which had ratified the amendment, kept its government, and the state was quickly readmitted to the Union.

The act divided the 10 Southern states into 5 military districts and placed each under the authority of a military commander until new governments were formed. The act also guaranteed African American males the right to vote in state elections, and it prevented former Confederate leaders from holding political office.

To gain readmission to the Union, the states had to ratify the Fourteenth Amendment and submit their new state constitutions to Congress for approval. A **Second Reconstruction Act,** passed a few weeks later, required the military commanders to begin registering voters and to prepare for new state constitutional conventions.

Readmission of States

Many white Southerners refused to take part in the elections for constitutional conventions and state governments. Almost 750,000 newly registered African American voters did use their right to vote. In the elections, Republicans gained control of Southern state governments.

By 1868 seven Southern states—Alabama, Arkansas, Florida, Georgia, Louisiana, North Carolina, and South Carolina—had established new governments and met the conditions for readmission to the Union. Virginia and Texas were readmitted in 1869 and Mississippi the year after.

Challenge to Johnson

Strongly opposed to Radical Reconstruction, President Johnson had the power as commander in chief of the army to direct the actions of the military governors. For this reason Congress passed several laws to limit the president's power.

One of these laws, the **Tenure of Office Act** of March 1867, was a deliberate challenge. It prohibited the president from removing government officials, including members of his own cabinet, without the Senate's approval. The act violated the tradition that presidents controlled their cabinets, and it threatened presidential power.

Impeaching the President

The conflict between Johnson and the Radicals grew more intense. In August 1867—when Congress was not in session—Johnson suspended Secretary of War **Edwin Stanton** without the Senate's approval. When the Senate met again and refused to approve the suspension, Johnson removed Stanton from office—a deliberate violation of the Tenure of Office Act. Johnson angered the Republicans further by appointing some generals the Radicals opposed as commanders of Southern military districts.

Outraged by Johnson's actions, the House of Representatives voted to impeach—formally charge with wrongdoing—the president. The House accused Johnson of misconduct and sent the case to the Senate for trial.

The trial began in March 1868 and lasted three months. Johnson's defenders claimed that the president was exercising his right to challenge laws he considered unconstitutional. The impeachment, they argued, was politically motivated and thus contrary to the spirit of the Constitution. Samuel J. Tilden, a Democrat from New York, claimed that Congress was trying to remove the president from office without accusing him of a crime "or anything more than a mere difference of opinion."

Johnson's accusers argued that Congress should retain the supreme power to make the laws. Senator Charles Sumner of Massachusetts declared that Johnson had turned "the veto

Ticket to Johnson's impeachment trial

power conferred by the Constitution as a remedy for ill-considered legislation . . . into a weapon of offense against Congress."

In May, as the nation waited anxiously, the senators cast their votes. The result was 35 to 19 votes to convict the president—one vote short of the two-thirds majority required by the Constitution for conviction. Several moderate Republicans voted for a verdict of not guilty, because they did not believe a president should be removed from office for political differences. As a result, Johnson stayed in office until the end of his term in March 1869.

Election of 1868

By the presidential election of 1868, most Southern states had rejoined the Union. Many Americans hoped that conflicts over Reconstruction and sectional divisions were behind them.

Abandoning Johnson, the Republicans chose General **Ulysses S. Grant,** the Civil War hero, as their presidential candidate. The Democrats nominated Horatio Seymour, a former governor of New York.

Grant won the election, gaining 214 of 294 electoral votes. He also received most of the 500,000 votes of African Americans in the South. The 1868 election was a vote on Reconstruction, and the voters supported the Republican approach to the issue.

 Picturing HISTORY

A cloth banner from the 1868 election shows presidential candidate Ulysses S. Grant. **How many electoral votes did Grant receive?**

The Fifteenth Amendment

After the election Republicans added their last major piece of Reconstruction legislation. In February 1869, Congress passed the **Fifteenth Amendment**. It prohibited the state and federal governments from denying the right to vote to any male citizen because of "race, color, or previous condition of servitude."

African American men won the right to vote when the Fifteenth Amendment was ratified and became law in February 1870. Republicans thought that the power of the ballot would enable African Americans to protect themselves. That belief, it turned out, was too optimistic.

★ ★ ★ ★ ★ Section 2 Assessment ★ ★ ★ ★ ★

Checking for Understanding
1. *Identify* Fourteenth Amendment, First Reconstruction Act, Edwin Stanton, Ulysses S. Grant, Fifteenth Amendment.
2. *Define* black codes, override, impeach.
3. *Discuss* two ways Southerners violated Lincoln's plan for Reconstruction.

Reviewing Themes
4. **Civic Rights and Responsibilities** How did Congress challenge the black codes set up by Southern states?

Critical Thinking
5. **Distinguishing Fact from Opinion** If you had been a member of the Senate, would you have voted for or against convicting President Andrew Johnson? Explain your decision.

Activity

Creating a Political Cartoon Imagine you are an African American during Reconstruction. Draw a political cartoon critical of the black codes.

1865
Freedmen's Bank
is established

1866
Ku Klux Klan
is formed

1869
African Americans
serve in House of
Representatives

1870
First African American
is elected to the Senate

Section 3

The South During Reconstruction

READ TO DISCOVER . . .

■ what groups participated in Reconstruction
in the South.
■ how Southern life changed during
Reconstruction.

TERMS TO LEARN

scalawag
carpetbagger
corruption

integrate
sharecropping

The Storyteller

"The dust of our fathers mingles with yours in the same graveyards. . . . This is your country, but it is ours too." So spoke an emancipated African American after the Civil War. Most former slaves did not seek revenge or power over whites, only respect and equality. The petition of an African American convention in 1865 stated: "We simply ask that we shall be recognized as *men;* . . . that the same laws which govern *white men* shall govern *black men;* . . . that, in short, we be dealt with as others are—in equity and justice."

Cane honoring freedom for
African Americans

The Republicans who controlled Southern state governments did their best to change and rebuild the South. However, former Confederates resisted, urging white Southerners to take back "their" governments and to restore their "birthright" [heritage].

New Groups Take Charge

⭐ During Reconstruction the Republican Party came to dominate Southern politics. The party consisted mainly of three groups—African Americans, white Southerners who supported Republican policies, and white settlers from the North. These groups dominated the state constitutional conventions and state governments.

African Americans in Government

African Americans played an important role in Reconstruction politics both as voters and as elected officials. In states where African American voters were the majority, they contributed heavily to Republican victories.

African Americans did not control the government of any state, although they briefly held a majority in the lower house of the South Carolina legislature. In other Southern states, they held important positions but never in proportion to their numbers.

Revels and Bruce

At the national level, 16 African Americans served in the House of Representatives and 2 in the Senate between 1869 and 1880. **Hiram Revels,** one of the African American senators, was an ordained minister. During the Civil War, he had recruited African Americans for the Union army, started a school for freed African Americans in St. Louis, Missouri, and served as chaplain of an African American regiment in Mississippi. Revels remained in Mississippi after the war and was elected to the Senate in 1870. He served a year in the Senate, where he declared he received "fair treatment."

Blanche K. Bruce, the other African American senator, also came from Mississippi. A former runaway slave, Bruce had established a school for African Americans in Missouri when the war began. In 1869 he went to Mississippi, entered politics, and became a superintendent of schools. He was elected to the Senate in 1874, serving there for six years.

Scalawags and Carpetbaggers

Some Southern whites supported Republican policy throughout Reconstruction. Many were nonslaveholding farmers or business leaders who had opposed secession in the first place. Former Confederates despised them for siding with the Republicans and called them scalawags, a term meaning "scoundrel" or "worthless rascal."

Many Northern whites who moved South after the war also supported the Republicans and served as Republican leaders during Reconstruction. Critics called these Northerners carpetbaggers because they arrived with all their belongings in cheap suitcases made of carpet fabric. Although some of the carpetbaggers were greedy and took advantage of the situation in the South, most did not. Many carpetbaggers were former Union army soldiers or members of the Freedmen's Bureau who liked the South and wanted to settle there. Others were reformers from the North—including lawyers, doctors, and teachers—who wanted to help reshape Southern society.

★ **Picturing HISTORY** The first African American United States senators were Blanche K. Bruce (left) and Hiram R. Revels (right), shown here with Frederick Douglass. **What political party did most African Americans support during Reconstruction?**

Government Corruption

Many Southerners ridiculed the Reconstruction governments and accused them of corruption—dishonest or illegal actions—and financial mismanagement. While some officials made money illegally, the practice was hardly widespread. Indeed, there was probably less corruption in the South than in the North.

Resistance to Reconstruction

★ Most white Southerners opposed efforts to expand African Americans' rights. Carl Schurz, a Republican from Missouri who toured the South right after the war, reported:

❝ Wherever I go—the street, the shop, the house, the hotel, or the steamboat—I hear the people talk in such a way as to indicate that they are yet unable to conceive of the Negro as possessing any rights at all. ❞

African American Family Life

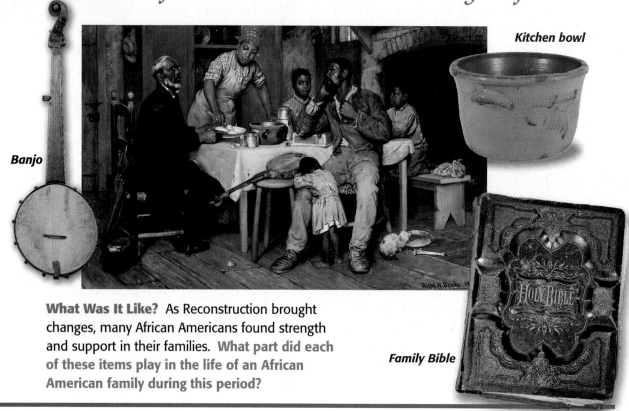

Banjo

Kitchen bowl

Family Bible

What Was It Like? As Reconstruction brought changes, many African Americans found strength and support in their families. **What part did each of these items play in the life of an African American family during this period?**

Plantation owners tried to maintain control over freed people in any way they could. Many told African Americans they could not leave the plantations. Most refused to rent land to freedmen.

Other white Southerners also made life difficult for African Americans. Store owners refused them credit, and employers refused to give them work. As in the days of slavery, some whites also used fear and force to keep freedmen in line.

The Ku Klux Klan

Violence against African Americans and their white supporters became commonplace during Reconstruction. Much of this violence was committed by secret societies organized to prevent freed men and women from exercising their rights and to help whites regain power.

The most terrifying of these societies, the **Ku Klux Klan,** was formed in 1866. Wearing white sheets and hoods, members of the Klan launched "midnight rides" against African Americans, burning their homes, churches, and schools. The

Klan killed as well. In Jackson County, Florida, the Klan murdered more than 150 people over a 3-year period. Klan violence increased before elections, as the group tried to scare African Americans to keep them from voting.

The tactics of the Klan and other violent groups had the support of many Southerners, especially planters and Democrats. These Southerners, who had the most to gain from the reestablishment of white supremacy, saw violence as a defense against Republican rule.

Taking Action against Violence

Southerners opposed to terrorism appealed to the federal government to do something. In 1870 and 1871, Congress passed several laws to try to stop the growing violence of the Klan. These laws had limited success. Most white Southerners refused to testify against those who attacked African Americans and their white supporters. Still, enough arrests were made to restore order for the 1872 presidential election.

Some Improvements

⭐ Despite the violence, Reconstruction brought important changes throughout the South. This was especially true in education.

Education improved for both African Americans and whites. African Americans saw education as an important step to a better life. In many regions they created their own schools, contributing both labor and money to build the schools.

The Freedmen's Bureau and private charities played a major role in spreading education. Northern women and free African Americans came South to teach in these schools. By 1870 about 4,000 schools had been established with 200,000 students. More than half the teachers in these schools were African American.

Public Schools

In the 1870s Reconstruction governments began creating public school systems for both races, which had not existed in the South before the war. Within a few years, more than 50 percent of white children and about 40 percent of African American children in the South were enrolled in public schools. Northern missionary societies also established academies offering advanced educa-

Mother and daughter reading

tion for African Americans. Some academies developed into colleges and universities, such as Morehouse College and Atlanta University.

Generally African American and white students attended different schools. Only three states—Louisiana, South Carolina, and Florida—required that schools be integrated—include whites and African Americans—but the laws were not enforced.

Farming the Land

Along with education, most freed people wanted land. Some African Americans were able to buy land with the assistance of the Freedmen's Bank, established in 1865. Most, however, failed to get their own land.

The most common form of farmwork for freed individuals was sharecropping. In this system a landowner rented a plot of land to a sharecropper, or farmer, along with a crude shack, some seeds and tools, and perhaps a mule. In return sharecroppers shared a percentage of their crop with the landowner.

After paying the landowners, sharecroppers often had little or nothing left to sell. Sometimes there was barely enough to feed their families. For many sharecropping was little better than slavery.

Section 3 Assessment

Checking for Understanding

1. **Identify** Hiram Revels, Blanche K. Bruce, Ku Klux Klan.
2. **Define** scalawag, carpetbagger, corruption, integrate, sharecropping.
3. **Name** the three groups that made up the Southern Republican Party.

Reviewing Themes

4. **Continuity and Change** What two groups spread education in the South?

Critical Thinking

5. **Determining Relevance** Why was voting and holding political office so important to newly freed African Americans?

Activity

Planning a Speech Imagine you have been asked to discuss changes you would like to see in the South's new public schools during the late 1860s. Write an outline of the speech that you would make.

1870		1875	1880

May 1872
The Amnesty Act pardons most former Confederates

1872
President Grant wins reelection

March 1877
Electoral committee names Hayes president

1877
Reconstruction ends

Section 4

Reconstruction Ends

READ TO DISCOVER . . .
- why interest in Reconstruction declined.
- what changes occurred in the South during the last years of Reconstruction.
- how Reconstruction ended.

TERMS TO LEARN
reconciliation   commission

The Storyteller

In 1875 the carpetbag governor of Mississippi faced growing violence between whites and African Americans in his state. He appealed to President Grant for troops to restore order. The president's attorney general responded: "The whole public are tired out with these . . . outbreaks in the South, and the great majority are now ready to condemn any interference on the part of the government. . . . Preserve the peace by the forces in your own state. . . ."
Sharp in tone, the attorney general's letter reflected the government's desire to end Reconstruction.

Struggle for the speaker's chair in a southern statehouse, 1875

By 1876 Southern Democrats were regaining political and economic control in the South. Some freed men and women went back to work for landholders because they had no other way to make a living.

Reconstruction Declines

⭐ During the Grant administration, Northerners began losing interest in Reconstruction. Many believed it was time for the South to solve its own problems.

Business leaders in the North wanted to end Reconstruction because they believed it was holding back Southern economic expansion. Some conservative Republicans saw the federal actions as a violation of states' rights. In addition the continuing violence in the South disturbed Northerners.

Southerners protested what they called "bayonet rule"—the use of federal troops to support Reconstruction governments. President Grant had sent federal troops to the South to stop violence or to enforce the law only when absolutely necessary. Generally, though, he tried to avoid any clashes with the South. The troops remained to protect African Americans and white Republicans.

Republican Revolt

President Grant had difficulties enough within his own party. In the early 1870s, reports of corruption in his administration and in Reconstruction governments spread throughout the nation. Some Republicans split with the party over the issue of corruption. Another group of Republicans broke with the party over Reconstruction, proposing peaceful reconciliation—coming together again—with Southern whites. Calling themselves Liberal Republicans, these two groups nominated **Horace Greeley,** a newspaper editor from New York, to run against Grant in the 1872 presidential election.

The Democrats also supported Greeley for president—despite his long opposition to their party—because he offered a chance to defeat the Republicans. Despite the division in the Republican ranks, however, Grant won a decisive victory in the election.

The Amnesty Act

During the 1872 election campaign, Liberal Republicans called for expanded amnesty for white Southerners. In May 1872, Congress passed the **Amnesty Act,** which pardoned most former Confederates. Nearly all white Southerners could vote and hold office again. The amnesty changed the political balance in the South by restoring full rights to people who supported the Democratic Party.

Democrats Regain Power

In Southern states such as **Virginia** and **North Carolina,** where a majority of voters were white, Democrats soon regained control of state governments. In states where African Americans held a majority or where white and African American populations were nearly equal, the Ku Klux Klan and other violent groups helped the Democrats take power by terrorizing Republican voters.

In an election in Mississippi in 1875, Democrats won by a 30,000 majority, although the Republicans had held a 30,000 majority in the previous election. The Democrats used threats to pressure white Republicans to become Democrats. As one Republican put it:

❝No white man can live in the South in the future and act with any other than the Democratic Party unless he is willing and prepared to live a life of social isolation. ❞

The Democrats also used violence to persuade African Americans not to vote. By 1876 Republicans held only three Southern states—Florida, South Carolina, and Louisiana.

Republican Decline

During these years the Republicans had other problems they could not blame on the Democrats. In 1873 a series of political scandals came to light. Investigations uncovered top government officials making unfair business deals, scheming to withhold public tax money, and accepting bribes. One scandal involved the vice president, and another the secretary of war. These scandals shocked the public and further damaged the Grant administration and the Republicans. At the same time, the nation suffered an economic depression. Blame for the hard times fell on the Republicans.

By the time of the congressional elections in 1874, charges of corruption and economic mismanagement had badly weakened the Republican

★ **Picturing HISTORY** Problems in the Grant administration hurt the Republican Party. **What happened in 1873 to make Republicans focus on the economy?**

Party. Democrats gained seats in the Senate and won control of the House. For the first time since the Civil War, the Democratic Party controlled a part of the federal government. This situation further weakened Congress's commitment to Reconstruction and protecting the rights of newly freed African Americans. Although Congress would pass a Civil Rights Act in 1875, many people evaded the law.

The End of Reconstruction

President Grant considered running for reelection in 1876. Most Republican leaders preferred a new candidate—one who could win back the Liberal Republicans and unite the party.

The Election of 1876

The Republicans nominated **Rutherford B. Hayes,** a former member of Congress and governor of Ohio, for president. A champion of political reform, Hayes had a reputation for honesty, and he held moderate views on Reconstruction. The Democrats nominated New York governor **Samuel Tilden.** Tilden had gained national fame for fighting political corruption in New York City.

After the election, Tilden appeared to be the winner, receiving almost 250,000 more votes than Hayes. However, disputed returns from Florida, Louisiana, and South Carolina—representing 20 electoral votes—kept the outcome in doubt. Tilden had 184 electoral votes, only one short of what he needed to win. Yet if Hayes received all

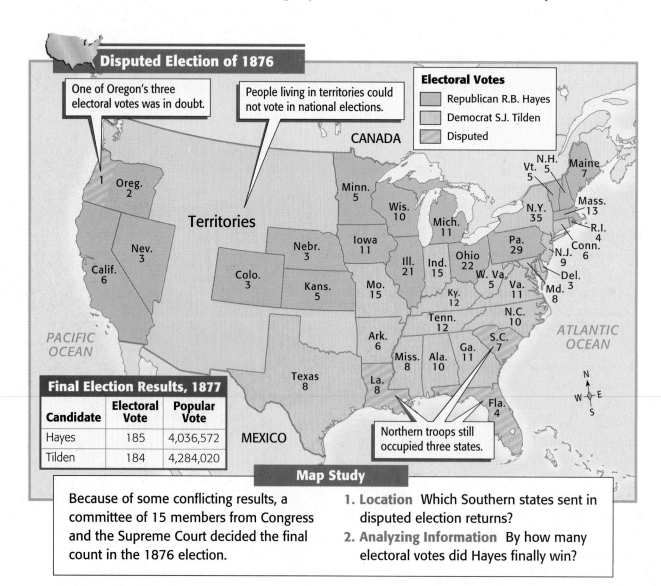

Disputed Election of 1876

One of Oregon's three electoral votes was in doubt.

People living in territories could not vote in national elections.

CANADA

Electoral Votes
- Republican R.B. Hayes
- Democrat S.J. Tilden
- Disputed

Oreg. 2 — 1

Territories

Nev. 3

Calif. 6

Colo. 3

Nebr. 3

Kans. 5

Minn. 5

Iowa 11

Mo. 15

Wis. 10

Mich. 11

Ill. 21

Ind. 15

Ohio 22

Ky. 12

Tenn. 12

Ark. 6

Miss. 8

Ala. 10

Ga. 11

S.C. 7

N.C. 10

Va. 11

W. Va. 5

Pa. 29

N.Y. 35

Md. 8

Del. 3

N.J. 9

Conn. 6

R.I. 4

Mass. 13

Vt. 5

N.H. 5

Maine 7

Texas 8

La. 8

Fla. 4

PACIFIC OCEAN

ATLANTIC OCEAN

MEXICO

Northern troops still occupied three states.

Final Election Results, 1877		
Candidate	**Electoral Vote**	**Popular Vote**
Hayes	185	4,036,572
Tilden	184	4,284,020

Map Study

Because of some conflicting results, a committee of 15 members from Congress and the Supreme Court decided the final count in the 1876 election.

1. **Location** Which Southern states sent in disputed election returns?
2. **Analyzing Information** By how many electoral votes did Hayes finally win?

20 of the disputed votes, he would have the 185 electoral votes required for victory.

Americans worried that the dispute would upset the political stability of the nation. In January Congress created a special commission, or group, of seven Republicans, seven Democrats, and one independent to review the election results. But the independent resigned, and a Republican took his place. After examining the reports of state review boards, the commission voted 8 to 7 to award all 20 disputed votes to Hayes. The vote followed party lines.

Democrats in Congress threatened to fight the verdict. Republican and Southern Democratic leaders met secretly to work out an agreement that would allow the Democrats to accept Hayes as president. On March 2, 1877—almost four months after the election—Congress confirmed the verdict of the commission and declared Hayes the winner. He was inaugurated president two days later.

Compromise of 1877

The deal congressional leaders made to settle the election dispute, the **Compromise of 1877,** included various favors to the South. The new government would give more aid to the region and withdraw all remaining troops from Southern states. The Democrats, in turn, promised to maintain African Americans' rights.

In his Inaugural Address, Hayes declared that what the South needed most was the restoration

Picturing HISTORY

The Republicans nominated Rutherford B. Hayes of Ohio, and the Democrats selected Samuel J. Tilden of New York for president in 1876. **What were the results of the election?**

of "wise, honest, and peaceful local self-government." During a goodwill trip to the South, Hayes announced his intention of letting Southerners handle racial issues. In Atlanta he told an African American audience:

Hayes paper lantern

66 . . . your rights and interests would be safer if this great mass of intelligent white men were left alone by the general government. 99

Hayes's message was clear. The federal government would no longer attempt to reshape Southern society or help Southern African Americans. Reconstruction was over.

Section 4 Assessment

Checking for Understanding
1. *Identify* Horace Greeley, Rutherford B. Hayes, Samuel Tilden, Compromise of 1877.
2. *Define* reconciliation, commission.
3. *Explain* how the Amnesty Act helped the Democratic Party regain its strength.

Reviewing Themes
4. **Individual Action** Why did the Republicans choose Hayes as a presidential candidate?

Critical Thinking
5. **Identifying the Main Idea** Why was Reconstruction largely unsuccessful?

Activity

Illustrating a Quote Create a drawing to illustrate the meaning of the quote by the Republican on page 509.

Struggling for Liberty

After the Civil War the Thirteenth, Fourteenth, and Fifteenth Amendments were ratified. These amendments prohibited slavery, gave citizenship to African Americans, and guaranteed them the right to vote. But most African Americans continued to be extremely poor and to suffer discrimination, including violent prejudice.

In 1883 Frederick Douglass, the great abolitionist, spoke to the National Convention of Colored Men in Louisville, Kentucky. He explained that African Americans needed to continue to fight for their liberty.

This 1892 political cartoon shows how African Americans were denied the right to vote.

❝ With apparent surprise, astonishment and impatience we have been asked: 'What more can the colored people of this country want than they now have, and what more is possible to them?' It is said they were once slaves, they are now free . . . they were once outside of all American institutions, they are now inside of all and are a recognized part of the whole American people. . . .

If the six millions of colored people of this country, armed with the Constitution of the United States . . . have not sufficient spirit and wisdom to organize and combine to defend themselves from outrage, discrimination and oppression, it will be idle for them to expect that the Republican Party or any other political party will . . . care what becomes of them. . . . [W]e are men and must speak for ourselves, or we shall not be spoken for at all.

[African American voters] have marched to the ballot-box in face of gleaming weapons, wounds and death. They have been abandoned by the Government and left to the laws of nature. So far as they are concerned, there is no Government or Constitution of the United States. **❞**

Activity

Analyzing Current Events Bring newspapers to class and search for stories that show groups of people struggling for their rights throughout the United States and the world. After reading the articles aloud in class, post the items on the bulletin board with the heading "Let Freedom Ring."

1889
Poll taxes and literacy tests are initiated

1890s
Southern mills produce nearly 20 percent of nation's iron and steel

1896
Plessy v. *Ferguson* rules segregation constitutional

Section 5

Change in the South

READ TO DISCOVER . . .

- how the economy changed in the "New South."
- what policies the "Redeemers" supported.
- how Southern states denied African Americans their rights.

TERMS TO LEARN

cash crop   grandfather clause
poll tax   segregation
literacy test   lynching

The Storyteller

"I am treated, not as an American citizen, but as a brute. . . . [A]nd for what? Not that I am unable or unwilling to pay my way; not that I am obnoxious in my personal appearance or disrespectful in my conduct; but simply because I happen to be of a darker complexion." These words were spoken by John Lynch, a member of Congress who had once been enslaved. At the end of Reconstruction, many African Americans faced lives of poverty, indignity, and despair.

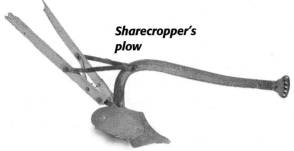

Sharecropper's plow

Many Southern whites hated Republicans because of their role in the Civil War and in Reconstruction. When Reconstruction ended, political power in the South shifted to the Democrats.

A New Ruling Party

⭐ In some regions, the ruling Democrats were the large landowners and other groups that had held power before the Civil War. In most areas, however, a new ruling class took charge. Among their ranks were merchants, bankers, industrialists, and other business leaders who supported economic development and opposed Northern interference. These Democrats called themselves **"Redeemers"** because they had "redeemed," or saved, the South from Republican rule.

The Redeemers adopted conservative policies such as lower taxes, less public spending, and reduced government services. They drastically cut, or even eliminated, many social services started during Reconstruction, including public education. Their one-party rule and conservative policies dominated Southern politics well into the 1900s.

The Southern Economy

⭐ For many years after the Civil War ended, the South continued to lag behind the rest of the nation economically. Despite efforts to industrialize, it remained a poor, rural economy.

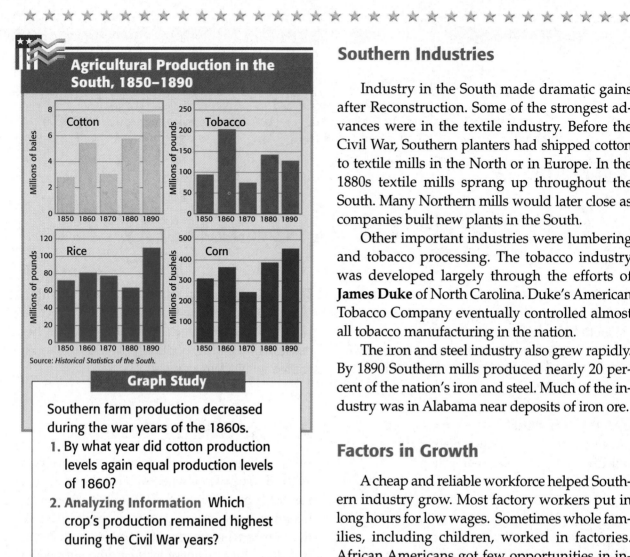

Agricultural Production in the South, 1850–1890

Cotton (Millions of bales): 1850, 1860, 1870, 1880, 1890

Tobacco (Millions of pounds): 1850, 1860, 1870, 1880, 1890

Rice (Millions of pounds): 1850, 1860, 1870, 1880, 1890

Corn (Millions of bushels): 1850, 1860, 1870, 1880, 1890

Source: *Historical Statistics of the South.*

Graph Study

Southern farm production decreased during the war years of the 1860s.

1. By what year did cotton production levels again equal production levels of 1860?
2. **Analyzing Information** Which crop's production remained highest during the Civil War years?

Rise of the "New South"

By the 1880s forward-looking Southerners were convinced that their region must develop a strong industrial economy. They argued that the South had lost the Civil War because its industry and manufacturing did not match the North's. **Henry Grady,** editor of the *Atlanta Constitution,* headed a group that urged Southerners to "out-Yankee the Yankees" and build a "New South." This New South would have industries based on coal, iron, tobacco, cotton, lumber, and the region's other abundant resources. Southerners would create this new economy by embracing a spirit of hard work and regional pride. In 1886 Grady told a Boston audience that industrial development would allow the New South to match the North in a peaceful competition.

Southern Industries

Industry in the South made dramatic gains after Reconstruction. Some of the strongest advances were in the textile industry. Before the Civil War, Southern planters had shipped cotton to textile mills in the North or in Europe. In the 1880s textile mills sprang up throughout the South. Many Northern mills would later close as companies built new plants in the South.

Other important industries were lumbering and tobacco processing. The tobacco industry was developed largely through the efforts of **James Duke** of North Carolina. Duke's American Tobacco Company eventually controlled almost all tobacco manufacturing in the nation.

The iron and steel industry also grew rapidly. By 1890 Southern mills produced nearly 20 percent of the nation's iron and steel. Much of the industry was in Alabama near deposits of iron ore.

Factors in Growth

A cheap and reliable workforce helped Southern industry grow. Most factory workers put in long hours for low wages. Sometimes whole families, including children, worked in factories. African Americans got few opportunities in industry except in the lowest-paying jobs.

A railroad-building boom also aided industrial development. By 1870 the Southern railroad system, which had been destroyed during the war, was largely rebuilt. Track mileage more than doubled between 1880 and 1890.

Still, the South did not develop an industrial economy as strong as the North's. The North was still industrializing more rapidly. The South remained primarily agricultural.

 **Economics**

Rural Economy

Henry Grady and other New South advocates hoped to change Southern agriculture as well as industry. They pictured small, profitable farms raising a variety of crops rather than large plantations devoted to growing cotton.

A different economy emerged, however. Some plantations were broken up, but many large landowners kept control of their property. When estates were divided, much of the land went to sharecropping and tenant farming, neither of which was profitable.

Debt caused problems as well. Poor farmers had to buy on credit to get the food and supplies they needed. The merchants who sold on credit charged high prices for their goods, increasing the farmers' debt. The quickest way for farmers to repay that debt, they thought, was to grow cash crops—crops that could be sold for money. As in the past, the biggest cash crop was cotton. An oversupply of cotton forced prices down, however. The farmers then had to grow even more cotton to try to recover their losses.

Sharecropping and reliance on a single cash crop hampered the development of a more modern agricultural economy. Instead, the rural South sank deeper into poverty and debt.

A Divided Society

As Reconstruction ended, African Americans' dreams for freedom faded. In the last 20 years of the 1800s, racism became firmly entrenched, and individuals took steps to keep African Americans separated from whites and to deny them basic rights.

Voting Restrictions

The Fifteenth Amendment prohibited any state from denying an individual the right to vote because of race. Southern leaders, however, found ways to get around the amendment and prevent African Americans from voting.

Many Southern states required a poll tax, a fee that people had to pay before voting. Because many African Americans could not afford the tax, they could not vote. The tax also prevented many poor whites from voting. Another approach was to make prospective voters take a literacy test, in which they had to read and explain difficult parts of state constitutions or the federal Constitution. Because most African Americans had little education, literacy tests prevented many from voting.

Literacy tests could also keep some whites from voting. For this reason some states passed grandfather clauses. These laws allowed individuals who did not pass the literacy test to vote if their fathers or grandfathers had voted before Reconstruction. Because African Americans could not vote until 1867, they were excluded.

Georgia enacted a poll tax and other limits as early as 1870, but such laws did not become widespread until after 1889. African Americans continued to vote in some states until the end of the 1800s. Because of restrictive voting laws and the constant threat of violence, however, African American voting drastically declined.

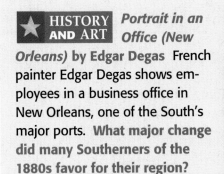

HISTORY AND ART *Portrait in an Office (New Orleans)* by Edgar Degas French painter Edgar Degas shows employees in a business office in New Orleans, one of the South's major ports. **What major change did many Southerners of the 1880s favor for their region?**

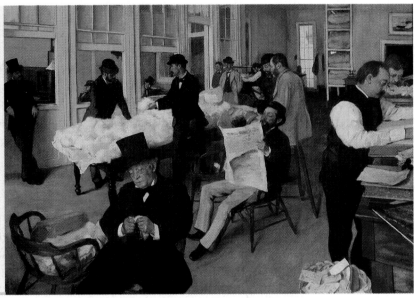

Jim Crow Laws

Another set of laws hurt African Americans. By the 1890s segregation, or the separation of the races, was a prominent feature of life in the South.

The Southern states formed a segregated society by passing so-called **Jim Crow laws.** Taking their name from a character in a song, Jim Crow laws required African Americans and whites to be separated in almost every public place where they might come in contact with each other.

In 1896 the Supreme Court upheld Jim Crow laws and segregation in *Plessy v. Ferguson.* The case involved a Louisiana law requiring separate sections on trains for African Americans. The Court ruled that segregation was legal as long as African Americans had access to public facilities or accommodations equal to those of whites.

The problem, however, was that the facilities were separate but in no way equal. Southern states spent much more money on schools and other facilities for whites than on those for African Americans. This "separate but equal" doctrine provided a legal foundation for segregation in the South that lasted for more than 50 years.

Violence against African Americans

Along with restrictions on voting rights and laws passed to segregate society, white violence against African Americans increased. This violence took many terrible forms, including lynching, in which an angry mob killed a person by hanging. African Americans were lynched because they were suspected of committing crimes—or because they did not behave as whites thought they should.

Reconstruction's Impact

Reconstruction was both a success and a failure. It helped the South recover from the war and begin rebuilding its economy. Yet economic recovery was far from complete. Although Southern agriculture took a new form, the South was still a rural economy, and that economy was still very poor.

Under Reconstruction African Americans gained greater equality and began creating their own institutions. They joined with whites in new governments, fairer and more democratic than the South had ever seen. This improvement for African Americans did not last long, however.

The biggest disappointment of Reconstruction was that it did not make good on the promise of true freedom for freed African Americans. The South soon created a segregated society. In the words of African American writer and civil rights leader **W.E.B. Du Bois,** "The slave went free; stood a brief moment in the sun; then moved back again toward slavery."

Section 5 Assessment

Checking for Understanding
1. *Identify* "Redeemers," *Plessy* v. *Ferguson.*
2. *Define* cash crop, poll tax, literacy test, grandfather clause, segregation, lynching.
3. *State* how some Southern states' efforts to keep African Americans from voting violated the Fifteenth Amendment.

Reviewing Themes
4. **Economic Factors** In what industries did the South make great gains after Reconstruction?

Critical Thinking
5. **Determining Cause and Effect** How did the Redeemers' efforts to cut government services affect freed African Americans?

Activity

Researching Statistics Research to find out how many African Americans hold seats in Congress today. Make a list of their names and states of residence.

Identifying the Main Idea

As you read about American history, you come across historical dates, events, and names. These details are easier to understand and remember when they are connected to one main idea. Understanding the main ideas allows you to grasp the whole picture or story. The details then become more easily understood.

Poor Southern farmers struggled to make a living during Reconstruction.

Learning the Skill

Follow these steps to identify a main idea:
• Before you read the material, find out the setting of the article or document: the time, the place, and who the writer is.
• Read the material and ask, "What is the purpose of this information?"
• Study any photographs or illustrations that accompany the material.
• Ask, "What are the most forceful statements in this material?"
• Identify supporting details.
• Identify the main idea, or central issue.

Practicing the Skill

The passage that follows is from a history of Reconstruction by W.E.B. Du Bois, an African American scholar. In it he describes the attitudes of people in Charleston, South Carolina, just after the Civil War. Read the passage and answer the questions that follow.

❝The economic loss which came through war was great, but not nearly as influential as the psychological change, the change in habit and thought. . . .

The hatred of the Yankee was increased. The defeated Southern leaders were popular heroes. Numbers of Southerners planned to leave the country, and go to South America or Mexico. . . .

The labor situation, the prospect of free Negroes, caused great apprehension. It was accepted as absolutely true by most planters that the Negro could not and would not work without a white master. ❞

1. Du Bois begins by naming two kinds of losses from the war. What are they? Which does he say was greater?
2. What is the main idea of this passage?
3. What details are provided that support the main idea?
4. How does the photograph support or negate Du Bois's main idea?

Applying the Skill

Identifying the Main Idea Bring a news article about a current event to class. Identify the main idea and supporting details in the article.

Glencoe's **Skillbuilder Interactive Workbook, Level 1** provides instruction and practice in key social studies skills.

Assessment and Activities

★ Reviewing Key Terms

On a sheet of paper, define the following terms:

Reconstruction
amnesty
freedmen
black codes
impeach
scalawag
carpetbagger
sharecropping
poll tax
literacy test
grandfather clause
segregation
lynching

★ Reviewing Key Facts

1. What services did the Freedmen's Bureau provide?
2. How was the Fourteenth Amendment supposed to help African Americans?
3. What role did African Americans play in early Reconstruction politics in the South?
4. What tactic did the Ku Klux Klan use to influence elections in the South?
5. What conservative policies did the Redeemers adopt in the South?

★ Critical Thinking

Analyzing Illustrations

The Freedmen's Bureau set up hundreds of schools attended by African American adults and children. Analyze the painting to the right, then answer the questions below.

1. What ages do the students in this school appear to be?
2. How would you characterize the attitude toward learning of the students in this school?

★ Time Line Activity

Create a time line on which you place the following events in chronological order.

- Civil Rights Act passed
- President Johnson's impeachment trial held
- Radical Republicans pass Wade-Davis Bill
- Reconstruction ends
- Fifteenth Amendment passed
- Lincoln assassinated

★ Reviewing Themes

1. **Groups and Institutions** Why did the Freedmen's Bureau consider education to be so important for freed African Americans?
2. **Civic Rights and Responsibilities** How did the black codes deny rights?
3. **Continuity and Change** Explain the following quote as it applies to Reconstruction: "The slave went free; stood a brief moment in the sun; then moved back again toward slavery."
4. **Individual Action** What president brought an end to Reconstruction?
5. **Economic Factors** Why did growing cotton after the Civil War send many Southern farmers into debt?

Freedmen's Bureau school

★ Skill Practice Activity

Identifying the Main Idea

The excerpt below was written by Charlotte Forten, one of many African American teachers who went south to teach freed individuals during the period of Reconstruction. Read the excerpt, which describes her first days of teaching school, then answer the questions that follow.

66 . . . I never before saw children so eager to learn, although I had had several years' experience in New England schools. Coming to school is a constant delight and recreation to them. They come here as other children go to play. The older ones, during the summer, work in the fields from early morning until eleven or twelve o'clock, and then come to school, after their hard toil in the hot sun, as bright and as anxious to learn as ever.

. . . The majority learn with wonderful rapidity. Many of the grown people [want to learn] to read. It is wonderful how a people who have been so long crushed to the earth . . . can have so great a desire for knowledge, and such a capacity for attaining it. . . . **99**

1. What points in this passage are stated most forcefully?
2. What is the main idea of this passage?
3. What details support the main idea of this passage?

★ Cooperative Activity

History and Citizenship Laws about voter registration vary from place to place. Working with a partner, contact your local election board to find out what the requirements for voter registration are in your community. Then design a brochure that encourages citizens to register to vote.

★ Technology Activity

Using a Word Processor Search your library for information about Lincoln and the assassination. Then, using a word processor, write a brief radio announcement about the event that might have been broadcast if radio had been invented by that time.

★ Geography Activity

Turn to the map on page 510 to answer the following questions.

1. **Location** Electoral votes are based on population. What were the six most populous states in 1876?
2. **Region** Which political party gained the most votes in the western states?
3. **Place** How many electoral votes were in dispute?

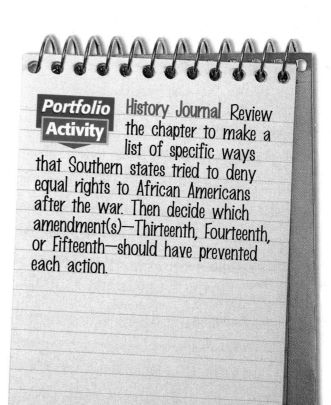

Portfolio Activity History Journal Review the chapter to make a list of specific ways that Southern states tried to deny equal rights to African Americans after the war. Then decide which amendment(s)—Thirteenth, Fourteenth, or Fifteenth—should have prevented each action.

Unit 7

Reshaping the Nation

1858 – 1914

*"America!
America! . . .
From sea to
shining sea!"*
—KATHERINE LEE BATES,
1893

MAPPING *America*

Portfolio Activity Draw a freehand
outline map of the United States. Include state and territorial borders. As
you read this unit about the settlement of the West and the growth of
industries and cities, highlight major
events on your map. Plot the location
of these events on your map and
label them. You may want to include
mining and ranching areas, routes of
the railroads, and the journeys of immigrants.

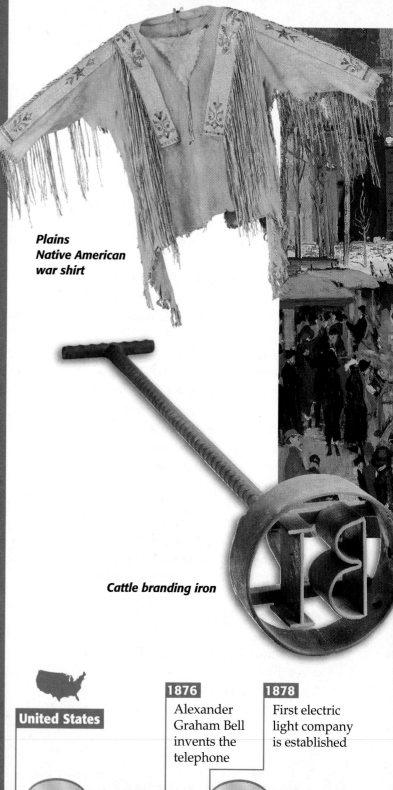

*Plains
Native American
war shirt*

Cattle branding iron

United States

1876
Alexander
Graham Bell
invents the
telephone

1878
First electric
light company
is established

1870

1880

1871
Germany
unifies
under
Bismarck

1881
Czar Alexander II
of Russia is
assassinated

World

New York by George Bellows
As pioneers continued to spread across the continent and immigrants flocked to the cities, Americans adapted to their rapidly changing environment.

Traveler's trunk

1890
Sherman Antitrust Act passed

1896
Henry Ford builds his first automobile

1901
Theodore Roosevelt becomes president

1907
Oklahoma becomes forty-sixth state

1913
Sixteenth and Seventeenth Amendments are ratified

1890

1900

1910

1920

1894
Sino–Japanese War begins

1895
Cubans revolt against Spanish rule

1901
First transatlantic wireless message sent

1911
China becomes a republic

1914
World War I begins

America's Literature

Life on the Mississippi
by Mark Twain

Mark Twain, who was born Samuel Langhorne Clemens in 1835, spent his early life in Hannibal, Missouri. There he became a printer and later a riverboat pilot. So much did he love life on the Mississippi River that he later chose a pen name that would link him with the river forever. "Mark twain!" was a river call meaning "two fathoms," or that the water was deep enough for safe passage.

■ READ TO DISCOVER

Mark Twain's boyhood dreams and memories are the sources of *Life on the Mississippi.* The work begins with a vivid description of the arrival of a riverboat. As you read this excerpt, think about the importance of the riverboat's arrival to the town and to young Twain.

■ READER'S DICTIONARY

packet: boat that carries mail, passengers, and freight at fixed times over a fixed route

Keokuk: town at the southeastern tip of Iowa

drayman: driver of a dray—a low sturdy cart with removable sides

texas deck: the deck adjoining the officers' cabins was called *texas* because the cabins there were the largest on the ship

forecastle: upper deck

stage: plank for loading and unloading cargo and passengers

gauge-cock: measuring instrument

Once a day a cheap, gaudy packet arrived upward from St. Louis, and another downward from Keokuk. Before these events, the day was glorious with expectancy; after them, the day was a dead and empty thing. Not only the boys, but the whole village, felt this. After all these years I can picture that old time to myself now, just as it was then: the white town drowsing in the sunshine of a summer's morning; the streets empty, or pretty nearly so; one or two clerks sitting in front of the Water Street stores, . . . the great Mississippi, the majestic, the magnificent Mississippi, rolling its mile-wide tide along, shining in the sun; the dense forest away on the other side; the "point" above the town, and the "point" below. . . . Presently a film of dark smoke appears above one of those remote "points"; instantly a . . . drayman, famous for his quick eye and prodigious voice, lifts up the cry, "S-t-e-a-m-boat a-comin'!" and the scene changes! The . . . clerks wake up, a furious clatter of drays follows, every house and store pours out a human contribution, and all in a twinkling the dead town is alive and moving. Drays, carts, men, boys, all go hurrying from many quarters to a common center, the wharf. Assembled there, the people fasten their eyes upon the coming boat as upon a wonder they are seeing for the first time. And the boat *is* rather a handsome sight, too. She is long and sharp and trim and pretty; she has two tall, fancy-topped chimneys, with a gilded device of some kind swung between them; a fanciful pilot-house, all glass and "gingerbread," perched on top of the "texas" deck behind them; the paddle-boxes are gorgeous with a picture

George Catlin's painting On the River *shows one of the steamboats that traveled on the Mississippi River during the 1800s.*

or with gilded rays above the boat's name; the boiler-deck, the hurricane-deck, and the texas deck are fenced and ornamented with clean white railings; there is a flag gallantly flying from the jack-staff; the furnace doors are open and the fires glaring bravely; the upper decks are black with passengers; the captain stands by the big bell, calm, imposing, the envy of all; great volumes of the blackest smoke are rolling and tumbling out of the chimneys; . . . the crew are grouped on the forecastle; the broad stage is run far out over the port box, and an envied deck-hand stands picturesquely on the end of it with a coil of rope in his hand; the pent steam is screaming through the gauge-cocks; the captain lifts his hand, a bell rings, the wheels stop; then they turn back, churning the water to foam, and the steamer is at rest. Then such a scramble as there is to get aboard, and to get ashore, and to take in freight and to discharge freight, all at one and the same time; and such a yelling! . . .

Ten minutes later the steamer is under way again, with no flag on the jack-staff and no black smoke issuing from the chimneys. After ten more minutes the town is dead again.

■ RESPONDING TO LITERATURE

1. What adjectives does Twain use to describe the Mississippi River?
2. What major event transpires once a day? Why is the event so important?

Activity

"Painting" Literature Reread Twain's descriptions of the Mississippi River, a steamboat, or the crowd rushing to the wharf. Then draw a picture of one of the scenes. Be sure to add details that reflect Twain's words.

1858–1896

The Western Frontier

★ Why It's Important

Although Native Americans on the Plains tried to resist the advance of American settlers, the newcomers came in overwhelming numbers. With the 1890 census, the government declared that no line could be drawn that clearly marked the end of settlement. For the first time in the nation's history, there was no western frontier. With the settlement of the Great Plains and the closing of this last frontier, the United States fulfilled the dream of Manifest Destiny.

★ Chapter Themes

- Section 1, Geography and History
- Section 2, Economic Factors
- Section 3, Culture and Traditions
- Section 4, Groups and Institutions

PRIMARY SOURCES Library

See pages 970–971 for primary source readings to accompany Chapter 18

HISTORY AND ART   *The Mirage* by Thomas Moran Moran painted the mountains, canyons, and plains of the West during the late 1800s. Many of his scenes show the magnificence and vastness of the region.

1855		1865		1875		1885

1858
Gold is discovered
at Pikes Peak

1869
Transcontinental
railroad links East
and West

1876
Colorado joins
the Union

1883
Nation is
divided into
four time zones

Section 1

The Mining Booms

READ TO DISCOVER . . .
- how the rush to find gold and silver created new communities in the West.
- how the railroad network expanded.
- how the development of railroads affected the nation.

TERMS TO LEARN
lode
ore
vigilante

ghost town
subsidy
transcontinental

The Storyteller

"We'll cross the bold Missouri, and we'll steer
    for the West,
And we'll take the road we think is the
    shortest and the best,
We'll travel over plains where the wind is
    blowing bleak,
And the sandy wastes shall echo with—
    Hurrah for Pikes Peak."
              —"The Gold Seeker's Song"

    Miners sang this
hopeful song in 1859
as they headed for Pikes
Peak, Colorado, where
gold had been
discovered.

Gold nuggets

By the mid-1850s the California Gold Rush had ended. Disappointed miners, still hoping to strike it rich, began prospecting in other parts of the West.

In 1858 a mining expedition found gold on the slopes of **Pikes Peak** in the Colorado Rockies. Newspapers claimed that miners were making $20 a day panning for gold—a large sum at a time when servants made less than a dollar a day. By the spring of 1859, about 50,000 prospectors had flocked to Colorado. Their slogan was "Pikes Peak or Bust." Most went home no richer than when they had arrived.

$ Economics

Mining Is Big Business

Prospectors skimmed gold dust from streams or scratched particles of gold from the surface of the land. Most of the gold, however, was deep in underground lodes, rich streaks of ore sandwiched between layers of rock. Mining this rock, or ore, and then extracting the gold required expensive machinery, many workers, and business organization. Companies made up of several investors had a better chance of getting rich in the goldfields than individual miners did. At most gold rush sites, mining companies soon replaced the lone miner.

Gold and silver mining attracted foreign as well as American investors. The British, for example, invested heavily in the American mining industry.

America's FLAGS

Twentieth Flag of the Union, 1876
Statehood for Colorado in 1876 brought the number of stars in the flag to 38. This was the Twentieth Flag.

The Comstock Lode

In 1858 several prospectors found a rich lode of gold-bearing ore on the banks of the Carson River in Nevada. The discovery was called the **Comstock Lode** after Henry Comstock, who owned a share of the claim.

Thousands of mines opened near the site, but only a few were profitable. Mining companies reaped the largest share of the profits. When Comstock sold his share of the claim, he received $11,000 and two mules—a huge sum at the time. It was, however, just a tiny fraction of the $300 million worth of gold and silver pulled from the Comstock Lode strike.

The Mining Frontier

★ The gold strikes created **boomtowns**— towns that grew up almost overnight around mining sites. The Comstock boomtown was **Virginia City, Nevada.** In 1859 the town was a mining camp. Two years later it had a stock exchange, hotels, banks, an opera company, and five newspapers.

---

*F*ootnotes to History

Gold Rush Words Many of the terms used during the gold rush found their way into our daily language. These include *pay dirt, pan out, to stake a claim,* and *to strike it rich.*

Boomtowns were lively, untamed places filled with people from far-off regions. Gold and silver strikes attracted eager prospectors from Mexico, China, and other countries.

Money came quickly—and was often lost just as quickly through extravagant living and gambling. A fortunate miner could earn as much as $2,000 a year, about four times the annual salary of a teacher at that time. Still food, lodging, clothing, and other goods cost dearly in the boomtowns, draining the miners' earnings.

Violence was part of everyday life in boomtowns, where many people carried large amounts of cash and guns. Cheating and stealing were common. Few boomtowns had police or prisons so citizens sometimes took the law into their own hands. These vigilantes dealt out their own brand of justice without benefit of judge or jury, often hanging the accused person from the nearest tree.

Women in the Boomtowns

Boomtowns were largely men's towns in the early days. Men outnumbered women by two to one in Virginia City, and children made up less than 10 percent of the population.

Eager to share in the riches of the boomtowns, some women opened businesses. Others worked as laundresses, cooks, or dance-hall entertainers. Women added stability to the boomtowns, founding schools and churches and working to make the communities safer and more orderly.

Boom and Bust

Many mining "booms" were followed by "busts." When the mines no longer yielded ore, people left the towns. At its peak in the 1870s, Virginia City had about 30,000 inhabitants. By 1900 its population had dropped below 4,000.

Many boomtowns turned into ghost towns— deserted as prospectors moved on to more promising sites or returned home. Some can still be seen in the West today, relics of the glory days of the mining frontier.

Toward the end of the rush, gold and silver mining gave way in some sites to the mining of other metals. Copper became the key metal found in Montana, New Mexico, and Arizona in the 1870s. In the 1890s people began mining lead and zinc in some former silver-mining towns of Colorado. In its final stage, the mining frontier became part of American industry, providing raw materials for manufacturers.

Many people who went west to seek their fortunes in gold or silver settled there permanently. Frontier areas around the boomtowns eventually became states. Colorado joined the United States in 1876. North Dakota, South Dakota, Washington, and Montana became states in 1889. Wyoming and Idaho were admitted to the Union in 1890.

Railroads Connect East and West

★ The western mines operated far from the industrial centers of the East and Midwest. For this reason transportation played a vital role in the survival of mining communities. Gold and silver had little value unless they could reach factories, ports, and markets. At the same time, the miners and others in the boomtowns needed shipments of food and other supplies.

Wagon trains and stagecoach lines could not move people and goods fast enough to meet these demands. Railroads could—and did. The nation's railroad network expanded rapidly between 1865 and 1890. In that period the miles of track in the United States soared from about 35,000 to more than 190,000.

Government and the Railroads

Railroad construction was made possible by large government subsidies—financial aid and land grants from the government. Railroad executives argued that their companies should receive free public land on which to lay track because a rail network would benefit the entire nation.

The national government—and states, too— agreed. In all, the federal government granted more than 130 million acres of land to the railroad companies. Much of the land was purchased or obtained by treaty from Native Americans.

The government grants included the land for the tracks plus strips of land along the railway, 20 to 80 miles wide. Railroad companies sold those strips of land to raise additional money for construction costs.

States and local communities also helped the railroads. Towns offered cash subsidies to make sure that the railroads came to their communities. For example, Los Angeles gave the Southern Pacific Railroad money and paid for a passenger terminal to ensure that the railroad would come to the town.

Spanning the Continent

The search for a route for a transcontinental rail line—one that would span the continent and connect the Atlantic and Pacific coasts—began in the 1850s. Southerners wanted the route to run through the South, and Northerners through the North. During the Civil War, the Union government chose a northerly route. The government offered land grants to railroad companies willing to build the transcontinental line.

The challenge was enormous—laying track for more than 1,700 miles across hot plains and

★ **Picturing HISTORY** The boomtown of Leadville, Colorado, surrounds a settler's cabin that sits in the middle of the main street. **Why did boomtowns develop almost overnight in the West after 1850?**

★ ★

through rugged mountains. Two companies accepted the challenge. The Union Pacific Company began laying track westward from **Omaha, Nebraska,** while the Central Pacific Company worked eastward from **Sacramento, California.**

The two companies competed fiercely. Each wanted to cover a greater distance in order to receive more of the government subsidies.

The Central Pacific hired about 10,000 Chinese laborers to work on its tracks. The Union Pacific relied on Irish and African American workers. All workers toiled for low wages in harsh conditions.

In the choking heat of summer and the icy winds of winter, they cleared forests, blasted tunnels through mountains, and laid hundreds of miles of track. In the end the Union Pacific workers laid 1,038 miles of track, and the Central Pacific workers laid 742 miles. However, the Central Pacific covered a much harsher terrain.

The Transcontinental Railway

On May 10, 1869, construction was completed. The two sets of track met at **Promontory Point** in Utah Territory. **Leland Stanford,** governor of

TECHNOLOGY AND HISTORY

Steam Locomotive

Since 1825, when the first steam locomotive was built in the United States, trains have crisscrossed the country. As America's transportation needs increased, so did the miles of railroad track linking its people.
Why do you think steam power was the first power source for locomotives?

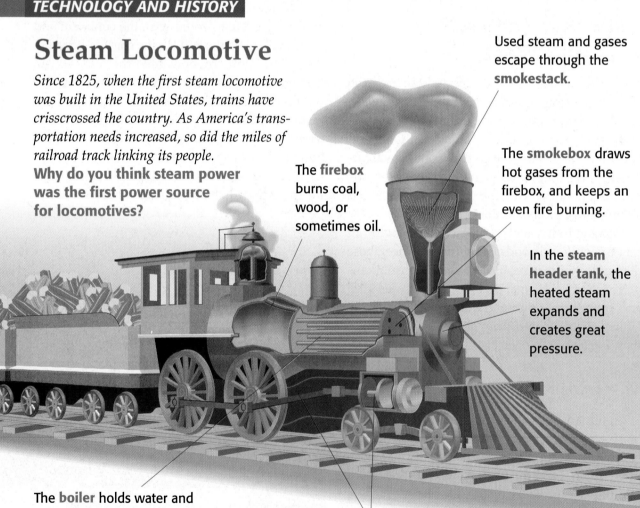

Used steam and gases escape through the **smokestack**.

The **firebox** burns coal, wood, or sometimes oil.

The **smokebox** draws hot gases from the firebox, and keeps an even fire burning.

In the **steam header tank**, the heated steam expands and creates great pressure.

The **boiler** holds water and sits in front of the firebox. The water, heated by gases from the firebox, creates steam.

Hot steam from the steam header tank is piped to the **pistons**. The pistons power the **drive rods** which in turn push the **drive wheels**.

★ ★ ★ ★ ★ ★ ★ ★

California, drove a final golden spike into a tie to join the two railroads. Almost as the event occurred, telegraph lines flashed the news across the country: "The last rail is laid . . . the last spike driven. . . . The Pacific Railroad is completed."

⑤ Economics

Effects of the Railroads

By 1883 two more transcontinental lines and dozens of shorter lines connected cities in the West with the rest of the nation. The economic consequences were enormous. The railroads brought thousands of workers to the West. Trains carried metals and produce east and manufactured goods west. As more tracks were laid, more steel was needed, and the demand boosted the nation's steel industry. Coal producers, railroad car manufacturers, and construction companies also flourished as the railroads spread across the West.

Towns sprang up along the rail lines that carried the settlers' agricultural goods to market. Some of these towns eventually became large cities.

★ **Picturing HISTORY** A Union Pacific work train approaches a bridge being built over the Green River in Wyoming Territory in 1868. **Which railroad companies helped build the first transcontinental railroad?**

The railroads also brought the next wave of new settlers to the West—cattle ranchers and farmers.

Railroads even changed how people measured time. Before railroads, each community kept its own time. Clocks in Boston, for example, were 11 minutes ahead of clocks in New York. The demand for sensible train schedules, however, changed that. In 1883 the railroad companies divided the country into four **time zones.** All communities in each zone would share the same time, and each zone was exactly one hour apart from the zones on either side of it. Congress passed a law making this practice official in 1918. **⑤**

★ ★ ★ ★ ★ **Section 1 Assessment** ★ ★ ★ ★ ★

Checking for Understanding
1. **Identify** Pikes Peak, Promontory Point, Leland Stanford.
2. **Define** lode, ore, vigilante, ghost town, subsidy, transcontinental.
3. **Describe** life in a typical boomtown.

Reviewing Themes
4. **Geography and History** What physical features and climate made building the transcontinental railroad difficult?

Critical Thinking
5. **Determining Cause and Effect** How did the construction of the transcontinental railroad influence settlement of the Great Plains?

Activity

Making a Map Draw a map of what you think a boomtown would look like. Be sure to label all the buildings in the town.

Multimedia Activities

ABCNEWS INTERACTIVE™ Historic America Electronic Field Trips

Field Trip to Sutter's Mill

Setting up the Video

Work with a group of your classmates to view "Sutter's Mill" on the videodisc *Historic America: Electronic Field Trips*. Gold was discovered on John Sutter's land near Sacramento, California, in 1848. Thousands of people rushed westward to try their luck at getting rich. This program explains how the discovery of gold helped California obtain statehood.

Hands-On Activity

Create a poster advertising the discovery of gold in 1848. Think of a colorful name for a boomtown, and advertise how one can become rich quick there! Use a word processor to create letters of different sizes and font styles on your poster.

Side 1, Chapter 11

View the video by scanning the bar code or by entering the chapter number on your keypad and pressing Search.

Surfing the "Net"

How to Become a Citizen

Between 1865 and 1914, the United States experienced a massive influx of immigrants. Today immigrants enter the country on a limited basis. People who legally reside in the United States but are not citizens are called *aliens*. The process by which aliens become citizens is called *naturalization*. Learn more about this process on the Internet.

Getting There

Follow these steps to gather information about the naturalization process.
1. Use a search engine. Type in the word *naturalization*.
2. Enter words like the following to focus your search: *immigration, citizenship skills, alien, INS* (Immigration and Naturalization Service).
3. The search engine will provide you with a number of links to follow. Links are "pointers" to different sites on the Internet.

What to Do When You Are There

Click on the links to navigate through the pages of information. Gather your findings. Using a word processor, create an information pamphlet on how to become a citizen through the naturalization process. Include sample questions asked of immigrants by immigration examiners. These questions determine knowledge about the United States.

1860	1870	1880	1890

1862
Homestead Act
gives free land
to settlers

1866
Missouri Pacific
Railroad reaches
Missouri

1867
Abilene, Kansas,
is founded

1889
Oklahoma
land rush
occurs

Section 2

Ranchers and Farmers

READ TO DISCOVER . . .

■ how the railroads helped create a "Cattle Kingdom" in the Southwest.

■ how women contributed to the settling of the Great Plains.

TERMS TO LEARN

open range   homestead
brand   sodbuster
vaquero   dry farming

The Storyteller

An old Texas cowhand, E. C. Abbott, recalled the early days of riding the trail:

"Here [were] all these cheap long-horned steers overrunning Texas; here was the rest of the country crying for beef—and no railroads to get them out. So we trailed them out, across hundreds of miles of wild country that was thick with Indians. . . . In 1867 the town of Abilene was founded at the end of the Kansas Pacific Railroad and that was when the trail really started."

Cattle ranching book, 1880s

When the Spanish settled Mexico and Texas, they brought a tough breed of cattle with them. Called **longhorns** because of their prominent horns, these cattle gradually spread across Texas. By 1865 the longhorns numbered about 5 million.

Cattle on the Plains

★ At this time much of Texas was open range—not fenced or divided into lots. Huge ranches covered other areas of the state. Ranchers added to their own herds by rounding up wild cattle. The ranchers burned a brand, or symbol, into the animals' hides to show who owned the cattle.

Railroads and Cow Towns

Although Texas ranchers had plenty of cattle, the markets were in the North and the East. In 1866 the Missouri Pacific Railroad reached Missouri, and Texas cattle suddenly increased in value. The cattle could be loaded on trains in Missouri for shipment north and east. Some Texans drove their combined herds—about 260,000 head of cattle—north to **Sedalia, Missouri,** the nearest rail point. Longhorns that had formerly been worth $3 each quickly rose in value to $40.

Cattle drives to **cow towns**—railroad towns for marketing and shipping cattle—turned into a yearly event. Over the next decade, cow towns such as **Abilene** and **Dodge City, Kansas,** and **Cheyenne, Wyoming,** became important stations.

★ HISTORY AND ART **Jerked Down** by Charles Russell Celebrated for his detailed and dramatic scenes of Western life, Charles Russell depicts cowhands on their surefooted horses lassoing cattle. **Where did the traditions of cattle herding begin?**

🌐 Geography
The Long Drive

The sudden increase in the longhorns' value set off what became known as the **Long Drive**—the herding of cattle 1,000 miles or more to meet the railroads. The drives left Texas in the spring, when there was enough grass along the way to feed the cattle. The longhorns had to remain well fed because underweight cattle could not be sold.

Some of the largest Long Drives led from central Texas to Abilene on the **Chisholm Trail.** The **Goodnight-Loving Trail,** named for ranchers Charlie Goodnight and Oliver Loving, swung west through New Mexico Territory and then turned north. During the heyday of the "Cattle Kingdom," from the late 1860s to the mid-1880s, the trails carried more than 5 million cattle north. 🌐

Life on the Trail

★ The cattle drives and the cowhands who worked on them captured the imagination of the nation. Contrary to the popular view, however, cattle driving was hard work. Cowhands rode in the saddle up to 15 hours every day, in driving rain, dust storms, and blazing sun. The life was lonely too. Cowhands saw few outsiders.

Spanish Influence

Many cowhands were veterans of the Confederate army. Some were African Americans who moved west in search of a better life after the Civil War. Others were Hispanics. In fact, the traditions of cattle herding began with Hispanic ranch hands in the Spanish Southwest. These vaqueros developed many of the skills—riding, roping, and branding—that cowhands used on the drives. Much of the language of the rancher today is derived from Spanish words used by vaqueros for centuries. Even the word *ranch* comes from the Spanish word *rancho.*

The cowhand's gear was based on the vaquero's equipment too. Cowhands wore wide-brimmed hats to protect themselves from the sun and leather leggings, called **chaps,** to shield their legs from brush and mishaps with cattle. They used ropes called **lariats** to lasso cattle that strayed from the herd.

Hazards on the Trail

On the trail for many months, the cowhands faced violent storms, "rustlers" who tried to steal cattle, and many other dangers. They had to drive the herds across swift-flowing rivers, where cattle could be lost.

Spurs

One of the greatest dangers on the trail was the **stampede,** when thousands of cattle ran in panic. Any sudden sound—a roar of thunder or the crack of a gunshot—could set off the cattle. The cowhands had to race on horseback with the stampeding cattle and bring them under control.

The "Wild West"

African American, Native American, Hispanic, and Anglo cowhands all met and worked together. Yet discrimination existed in the West just as it did elsewhere. Members of minorities rarely became trail bosses and often received less pay for their work. Some towns discriminated against Hispanics, segregated African Americans, and excluded Chinese cowhands altogether.

After many tiring weeks on the trail, the cowhands delivered their cattle and enjoyed some time off in cow towns. Cowhands drank and gambled and got involved in fistfights and gunplay. Places such as Dodge City and Abilene were rowdy, lawless, and violent. Eventually, though, they grew into settled, businesslike communities.

The Cattle Kingdom Ends

As profits from cattle increased, cattle ranching spread north from Texas. On the northern Plains, ranchers crossbred longhorns with fatter Hereford and Angus cattle to produce hardy, plumper new breeds.

Ranching on the northern Plains began to replace the Long Drive. The sturdy crossbred cattle multiplied on open-range ranches. When cattle prices "boomed" in the early 1880s, ranchers became rich. The boom, however, was soon followed by a bust. Overgrazing depleted the grasslands. In addition, too many cattle glutted the market and prices fell. Then came the bitterly cold winters of 1885 and 1886, which killed large numbers of cattle.

The price collapse of the mid-1880s marked the end of the "Cattle Kingdom." Ranchers built fences and grew hay to feed their cattle during the harsh winters. Another group of settlers would rise on the Plains—the farmers.

Farmers Settle the Plains

The early pioneers who reached the Great Plains did not believe they could farm the dry, treeless area. In the late 1860s, however, farmers began settling there and planting crops. In a surprisingly short time, the Plains changed from "wilderness" to farmland. In 1872 a Nebraska settler wrote,

66 One year ago this was a vast houseless, uninhabited prairie. . . . Today I can see more than thirty dwellings from my door. 99

Several factors brought settlers to the Plains. The railroads made the journey west easier and cheaper. New laws offered free land. Finally, above-average rainfall in the late 1870s made the Plains better suited to farming.

★ Picturing HISTORY European immigrants on a flatcar view land open for settlement on the Great Plains. In moving to the area, settlers were often influenced by advertising. **Which groups used advertising to promote settlement of the Great Plains?**

A group of "Exodusters" wait along a Southern waterway for a steamboat to carry them westward. **Why did the "Exodusters" move west?**

The Homestead Act

In 1862 Congress passed the **Homestead Act,** which gave 160 free acres of land to a settler who paid a filing fee and lived on the land for 5 years. This federal land policy brought farmers to the Plains to homestead—earn ownership of land by settling on it.

Homesteading lured thousands of new settlers to the Great Plains. Some were immigrants who had begun the process of becoming American citizens and were eligible to file for land. Others were women. Although married women could not claim land, single women and widows had the same rights as men—and they took advantage of the Homestead Act to acquire property. In Colorado and Wyoming, 12 percent of all those who filed homestead claims were women.

Promoting the Plains

Homesteaders came to the Plains to own land and be independent. They were also swayed by advertising paid for by railroads, steamship companies, land speculators, and western states and territories.

Railroad companies wanted to sell the strips of land alongside the rail lines to raise cash. Steamship companies went to great lengths to advertise the Plains in Scandinavia. In 1882 alone more than 105,000 Swedes and Norwegians settled in the northern Plains—Minnesota and the Dakotas—where the Scandinavian influence remains strong today.

African American Settlers

Thousands of African Americans also migrated from the Southern states into Kansas in the late 1870s. They called themselves **"Exodusters,"** from the biblical book of Exodus, which describes the Jews' escape from slavery in Egypt.

The end of Reconstruction in 1877 had meant the end of federal protection for African Americans. Fearing for their safety in former slave regions, freed people sought land farther west. By 1881 more than 40,000 African Americans had migrated to Kansas. Some, however, had to return to the South because they lacked the money to start new farms or businesses.

The Farmers' Frontier

★ A pioneer woman on the Great Plains described her surroundings as "a new world, reaching to the far horizon without break of tree or chimney stack; just sky and grass and grass and sky." Farmers wondered how they could survive in such an environment.

 **Geography**

The "Soddie"

To survive on the Plains, settlers needed to find new ways of doing things. To begin with, they had to build houses that did not require lumber on this treeless land. The pioneers carved

---

*F*ootnotes to History

Rain on the Roof Sod roofs often leaked after rains. Even during dry periods, dirt and grass fell like raindrops from the roof.

dugouts in the sides of hills, over which they built houses made of sod. The **sod,** densely packed soil held together by grass roots, was cut into rectangles resembling bricks. It made a useful building material. A Plains family's first home was usually a sod house, called a "soddie." Some sod houses lasted for years, until farmers could afford to buy lumber, which was scarce and expensive.

Other Challenges

The climate of the Plains presented farmers with their greatest challenge. Generally there was little rainfall, but in some years rain came down in torrents, destroying crops and flooding homesteads. The other extreme—drought—also threatened crops and lives. Fire was another enemy. In times of drought, brushfires swept rapidly through a region, destroying crops, livestock, and homes.

Summer might bring plagues of grasshoppers. Several times during the 1870s, swarms of the insects swept over the Plains. Thousands of grasshoppers would land on a field of corn. When they left, not a stalk would remain.

Winters presented even greater dangers. Winds howled across the open Plains, and deep snow could bury animals and trap families in their homes. Farm families had to plan ahead and store food for the winter.

Farm Families

Farming on the Great Plains was a family affair. Men labored hard in the fields. Women often did the same work, but they also cared for the children. A farm wife sewed clothing, made candles, and cooked and preserved food. In the absence of doctors and teachers, she also tended to the children's health and education. When her husband was away—taking the harvest to town or buying supplies—she bore all responsibility for keeping the farm running. She also had to endure the isolation of the Plains.

When children grew old enough, they too worked the farm. Children helped in the fields, tended animals, and did chores around the house. Farmwork often kept children from attending school.

Although separated by great distances, farm families socialized whenever they could. People took great pleasure in getting together for weddings, church services, picnics, and other occasions.

New Farming Methods

The Plains could not be farmed by the usual methods of the 1860s. Most parts of the region had little rainfall and too few streams for irrigation. The Plains farmers, known as sodbusters, needed new methods and tools.

One approach, called dry farming, was to plant seeds deep in the ground where there was some moisture. Wooden plows could not penetrate the tough layer of sod, but farmers could use the lightweight steel plows invented in the late 1870s to do the job.

The sodbusters had other tools to help them conquer the Plains—windmills to pump water

★ **Picturing HISTORY** Evelyn Cameron moved from England to the plains of eastern Montana where she photographed the settlers. This 1904 photo shows Cameron kneading dough. **What kind of life did most women experience on the Great Plains?**

★ Picturing HISTORY Wagons line up just before the start of the largest—and last—Oklahoma land rush in 1893. **What important development did the federal government announce soon after the Oklahoma land rushes?**

from deep in the ground and a new fencing called **barbed wire.** With no wood to build fences, farmers used these wire fences to protect their land.

Dry farming, however, did not produce large crop yields, and the 160-acre grants were too small to make a living. Most farmers needed at least 300 acres as well as advanced machinery to make a Plains farm profitable. Many farmers went into debt. Others lost ownership of their farms and then had to rent the land.

The Oklahoma Land Rush

The last part of the Plains to be settled was the Oklahoma Territory, which Congress had designated as "Indian Territory" in the 1830s. In 1889, after years of pressure from land dealers and settlers' groups, the federal government opened Oklahoma to homesteaders.

On the morning of April 22, 1889—the official opening day—more than 10,000 people lined up on the edge of this land. At the sound of a bugle, the homesteaders charged across the border to stake their claims. The eager **boomers,** as the homesteaders were called, discovered to their dismay that some settlers had already slipped into Oklahoma. These so-called **sooners** had already claimed most of the best land. Within a few years, all of Oklahoma was opened to settlement.

Closing the Frontier

Not long after the Oklahoma land rush, the government announced in the 1890 census that the frontier no longer existed. Settlement had changed the Plains dramatically. No one felt these changes more keenly than the Native Americans who had lived on the Plains for centuries.

★ ★ ★ ★ ★ **Section 2 Assessment** ★ ★ ★ ★ ★

Checking for Understanding
1. **Identify** Long Drive, Chisholm Trail, Goodnight-Loving Trail, Homestead Act, "Exodusters."
2. **Define** open range, brand, vaquero, homestead, sodbuster, dry farming.
3. **Explain** why cow towns developed.

Reviewing Themes
4. **Economic Factors** Discuss two developments that contributed to the collapse of cattle prices during the mid-1880s.

Critical Thinking
5. **Analyzing Information** What opportunities did settlement on the Plains provide for women and African Americans?

Making a Poster Create a poster that the United States government might have used to encourage farmers to move west.

SKILL BUILDER

Reading a Special-Purpose Map

Maps that show information on specialized subjects, or themes, are called special-purpose maps. They differ from general-purpose maps in that they show more than basic physical features or political boundaries. Special-purpose maps can contain physical, economic, climatic, historic, or cultural information—almost anything that can be expressed geographically.

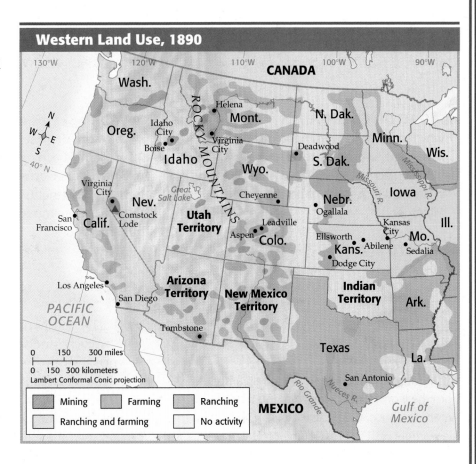

Western Land Use, 1890

130°W   120°W   110°W   CANADA   100°W   90°W

Wash.

Oreg.   Idaho City   Helena   Mont.   N. Dak.   Minn.

40° N   Boise   Virginia City   Deadwood   Wis.

Idaho   Wyo.   S. Dak.   Iowa

Virginia City   Great Salt Lake   Cheyenne   Nebr.   Ill.

San Francisco   Calif.   Comstock Lode   Nev.   Utah Territory   Leadville   Ogallala   Kansas City   Mo.

Aspen   Colo.   Ellsworth   Abilene   Sedalia

Los Angeles   Kans.   Dodge City

San Diego   Arizona Territory   New Mexico Territory   Indian Territory   Ark.

PACIFIC OCEAN   Tombstone

0   150   300 miles
0   150   300 kilometers
Lambert Conformal Conic projection

Texas   La.

Rio Grande   San Antonio   Nueces R.   Gulf of Mexico

| Mining | Farming | Ranching |
| Ranching and farming | No activity |

MEXICO

Learning the Skill

Begin by reading the map title and labels to determine the subject and purpose of the map. Then study the map key. Identify each symbol and color shown in the key and locate these on the map. Use this information to look for similarities and differences in the region shown on the map.

Practicing the Skill

1. What is the subject of the map above?
2. What do the colors represent?
3. What is the most common use of land in Texas?

Applying the Skill

Reading a Special-Purpose Map Look at the map on page 540. Where were Indian reservations placed in relation to productive ranching and farming land in 1890?

Glencoe's **Skillbuilder Interactive Workbook, Level 1** provides instruction and practice in key social studies skills.

1864
Sand Creek
massacre occurs

1876
Sioux victorious
at Little Bighorn

1886
Geronimo
surrenders
to the army

1890
300 Lakota Sioux killed
at Wounded Knee

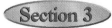
Section 3

Native American Struggles

READ TO DISCOVER . . .

- why the federal government forced Native Americans to move to reservations.
- how conflict between Native Americans and whites led to a series of battles on the Plains.

TERMS TO LEARN

nomadic   reservation

The Storyteller

In May 1876, George Crook led an army from the North Platte River to round up Native American bands. Chief Crazy Horse urged on his warriors with the cry, "Come on Dakotas, it's a good day to die." The two sides fought until midafternoon. Then the Native Americans began to drift away. "They were tired and hungry, so they went home," one warrior later explained. . . . The Native Americans retired to a large camp on the Little Bighorn River. Great leaders were there—Sitting Bull, Gall, Crazy Horse. A vast pony herd grazed nearby; the grass was green; there was dancing at night. . . .

Sioux buffalo shield

Starting in the mid-1850s, miners, railroads, cattle drives, and farmers came to the Plains. Each new group dealt another blow to Native Americans living there. The Sioux chief Red Cloud lamented, "The white children [settlers] have surrounded me and left me nothing but an island."

Following the Buffalo

The southern Plains were home to the Apache and Comanche. The Arapaho and Pawnee lived in the central Plains. The Crow, Cheyenne, and Sioux lived in the northern Plains.

The Sioux led a lifestyle typical of the Plains Indians. The Sioux adopted horses from the Spanish and used them to hunt the huge buffalo herds that roamed the Plains. They lived a nomadic life, settling in one place for only part of the year—although they generally returned to traditional grounds. Most of the time, they followed the buffalo across the vast Plains region north of the Arkansas River. Their culture depended on the horse, the buffalo, and open land.

Village and Family Life

The buffalo provided most of the essentials of Sioux life. The Sioux used buffalo skin to make tepees, clothes, and bags for carrying food. They dried the meat into **jerky** for winter food. They shaped the bones into tools such as hoes, knives, and fishhooks. They used dried manure, called **buffalo chips,** for fuel.

Life of Plains Native Americans

Arapaho adult's and child's moccasins

Sioux bow case with bow and arrows

Sioux beaded robe

What Was It like? Native Americans of the Great Plains settled in one place for only part of the year. **What do the images reveal about how the Plains Native Americans obtained their food?**

The Sioux were also traders, exchanging buffalo and beaver skins for food farmed by more settled Plains Indians. With white people, the Sioux traded for pots, knives, and firearms.

Life for the Sioux, as for other Plains groups, revolved around extended families and community ties. Families joined forces to hunt and plant. Extended families set up large camps near hunting grounds in the summer and established small villages in sheltered areas for the winter months.

Indian women had many responsibilities. They raised the children and taught them their people's traditions. They also prepared food and made clothing and tools. Women rarely joined in the hunt, however.

Threats to the Buffalo

The Plains Indians had millions of buffalo to supply their needs. After the Civil War, though, American hunters hired by the railroads began slaughtering the animals to feed the crews building the railroad. The railroad companies also wanted to prevent huge herds of buffalo from blocking the trains. William Cody, hired by the Kansas Pacific Railroad, boasted that he had killed 4,280 buffalo in less than 18 months. He became known as Buffalo Bill.

Some people traveled west to kill buffalo for the sport of hunting, often shooting from the windows of trains. Starting in 1872 hunters targeted buffalo to sell the hides to the East, where tanneries made them into leather goods.

Between 1872 and 1875, whites killed more than 9 million buffalo for their hides, often leaving the carcasses to rot on the Plains. Government officials encouraged the slaughter. By destroying the buffalo, they thought, they could change the way the Plains Indians lived. The Native Americans wanted to preserve their nomadic life, but the government wanted them to become farmers. A clash seemed inevitable.

Footnotes to History

Where the Buffalo Roamed Between 1830 and 1895, the millions of buffalo on the Great Plains were reduced to just 800.

Government Policy

★ As long as white people regarded the Plains as the "Great American Desert," they left the Native Americans who lived there more or less alone. When whites began settling the Plains, the situation changed. In the late 1860s, the government tried a new Indian policy.

Reservation Policy

In 1867 the federal government appointed the Indian Peace Commission to develop a new policy toward Native Americans. The commission recommended moving the Native Americans to a few large reservations—tracts of land set aside for them. Moving Native Americans to reservations was not a new policy, but the government now increased its efforts in that direction.

One large reservation was in **Oklahoma,** the "Indian Territory" that Congress had created in the 1830s for Native Americans relocated from the Southeast. Another one, meant for the Sioux people, was in the **Dakota Territory.** Managing the reservations would be the job of the federal Bureau of Indian Affairs.

Government agents often used trickery to persuade Native American groups to move to the

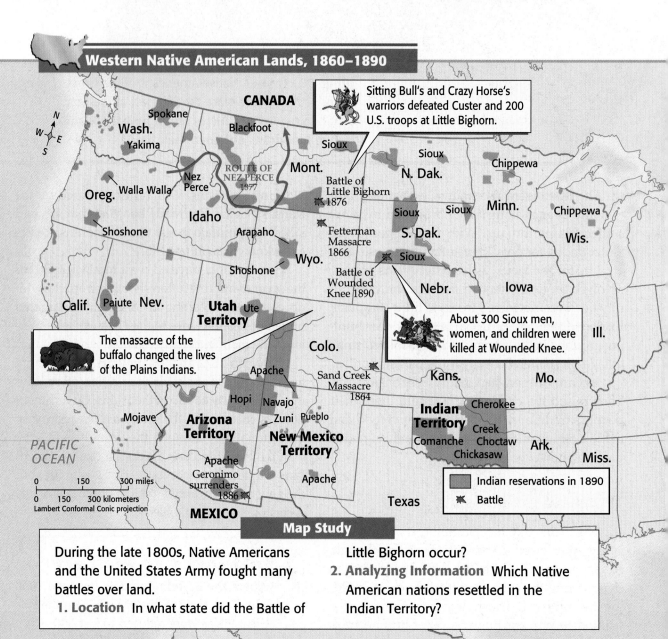

Western Native American Lands, 1860–1890

Sitting Bull's and Crazy Horse's warriors defeated Custer and 200 U.S. troops at Little Bighorn.

The massacre of the buffalo changed the lives of the Plains Indians.

About 300 Sioux men, women, and children were killed at Wounded Knee.

CANADA

Spokane
Wash.
Yakima
Blackfoot
Sioux
Sioux
Chippewa

Oreg.
Walla Walla
Nez Perce
ROUTE OF NEZ PERCE 1877
Mont.
Battle of Little Bighorn 1876
N. Dak.

Idaho
Arapaho
Fetterman Massacre 1866
Sioux
Sioux
Minn.
Chippewa
Wis.

Shoshone
S. Dak.

Wyo.
Shoshone
Battle of Wounded Knee 1890
Sioux
Nebr.
Iowa

Calif.
Paiute
Nev.
Utah Territory
Ute
Colo.
Kans.
Mo.
Ill.

Mojave
Arizona Territory
Hopi
Navajo
Zuni
Pueblo
New Mexico Territory
Sand Creek Massacre 1864
Apache
Indian Territory
Cherokee
Creek
Comanche
Choctaw
Chickasaw
Ark.
Miss.

PACIFIC OCEAN
Apache
Geronimo surrenders 1886
Apache
Texas

MEXICO

0   150   300 miles
0   150   300 kilometers
Lambert Conformal Conic projection

Indian reservations in 1890
✳ Battle

Map Study

During the late 1800s, Native Americans and the United States Army fought many battles over land.

1. Location In what state did the Battle of Little Bighorn occur?

2. Analyzing Information Which Native American nations resettled in the Indian Territory?

reservations. Many reservations were located on poor land—land that white settlers did not want. In addition the government often failed to deliver promised food and supplies, and the goods that were delivered were of poor quality.

A great many Native Americans accepted the reservation policy at first. Many southern Kiowa, Comanche, Cheyenne, and Arapaho agreed to stay on the Oklahoma reservation. Thousands of Sioux agreed to move onto the Dakota reservation in the north.

Pockets of resistance remained, however. Some Native Americans refused to make the move, and some who tried reservation life abandoned it. The stage was set for conflict.

Chief Joseph of the Nez Perce (left) and Sitting Bull

The Indian Wars

Armed clashes between Native Americans and whites had taken place since the 1850s. Congress had appointed the Indian Peace Commission in the hope of ending the fighting, but Native American resistance grew stronger after the reservation policy took effect. The Cheyenne and the Sioux were among the most determined opponents.

Tragedy at Sand Creek

The fighting with the Cheyenne began in the mid-1860s, when a group of Cheyenne refused to move to a reservation. In November 1864, Colonel **J.M. Chivington** swooped down on a Cheyenne camp near **Sand Creek, Colorado,** with a group of volunteer militia. Although the Cheyenne tried to surrender, the militia killed more than 100 men, women, and children.

Enraged by the Chivington massacre, **Chief Black Kettle** led Cheyenne warriors to battle. Fearing another massacre, most Cheyenne moved to a reservation in 1867. Black Kettle, however, continued to fight. In November 1868 Cheyenne resistance came to an end when troops led by Civil War veteran **George Armstrong Custer** defeated Black Kettle along the Washita River in Indian Territory, killing him and most of his followers.

Little Bighorn

The Sioux also began to fight in the 1860s. Although an 1868 treaty was supposed to bring peace, tensions remained and erupted in more fighting a few years later.

This time the conflict arose over the **Black Hills** of the Dakotas. The government had promised that "No white person or persons shall be permitted to settle upon or occupy" or even "to pass through" these hills. However, the hills were rumored to contain gold. In 1874 Custer led an army expedition to check on the rumors and confirmed that there was gold, "from the grass roots down." Prospectors swarmed into the area.

The Sioux protested against the trespassers. Instead of protecting the Sioux's rights, the government tried to buy the hills. **Sitting Bull,** an important leader of the Lakota Sioux, refused. "I do not want to sell any land. Not even this much," he said, holding a pinch of dust.

Sitting Bull gathered Sioux and Cheyenne warriors along the **Little Bighorn River** in present-day Montana. They were joined by **Crazy Horse,** another Sioux chief, and his forces. The United States Army planned a three-pronged attack. One force, the Seventh Cavalry, was led by Custer, who was ordered to scout the Native American encampment.

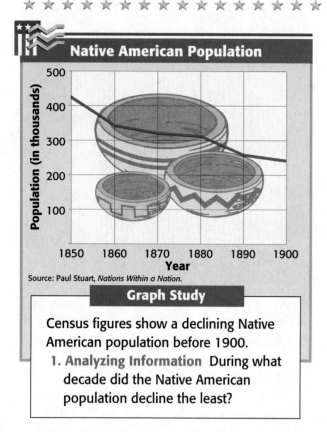

Native American Population

Population (in thousands) vs **Year** (1850–1900)

Source: Paul Stuart, *Nations Within a Nation.*

Graph Study

Census figures show a declining Native American population before 1900.

1. **Analyzing Information** During what decade did the Native American population decline the least?

Custer wanted the glory of leading a major victory. He divided his regiment and attacked the Indians on June 25, 1876. He had seriously underestimated their strength, however. With about 250 soldiers, Custer faced a Sioux and Cheyenne force of thousands. He and all his troops were killed. News of the army's defeat shocked the nation.

The Indians' triumph at Little Bighorn was short-lived. The army, with its greater firepower, soon crushed the uprising, sending most of the Native Americans to reservations. Sitting Bull and his followers fled north to Canada. By 1881, exhausted and starving, the Lakota and Cheyenne agreed to live on a reservation.

The Nez Perce

The **Nez Perce** Indians, who lived in present-day Idaho, Oregon, and Washington, raised horses and hunted buffalo. They also fished and planted crops. By the late 1870s, all but one group of the Nez Perce had yielded their lands and were living on reservations.

In 1877 the army ordered this last group to the reservation. Under their leader, **Chief Joseph,** they began to move. However, a few young warriors, bitterly angry about the relocation, attacked and killed several white settlers. The army came to punish the Nez Perce.

Fearing for the safety of his people, Chief Joseph told them—men, women, and children—to set out for Canada. With the army in close pursuit, the Nez Perce traveled through rugged mountains and lush valleys. They fought, and won, four battles along the way. Then, in northern Montana, just 30 miles short of the Canadian border, they were surrounded by an overwhelming force. Chief Joseph finally surrendered, saying:

> **❝**I am tired of fighting. . . . Hear me, my chiefs. I am tired: my heart is sick and sad. From where the sun now stands, I will fight no more forever.**❞**

The Apache Wars

Trouble also broke out in the Southwest. The Chiracahua Apache had been moved from their homeland to the San Carlos reservation in Arizona in the mid-1870s. Many Apache resented confinement to this reservation. The Apache leader, **Geronimo,** escaped from San Carlos and fled to Mexico with a small band of followers. During the 1880s he led raids against settlers and the army in Arizona.

Thousands of troops pursued Geronimo and his warriors. Several times he went back to the reservation. "Once I moved about like the wind. Now I surrender to you," Geronimo said, but again he left the reservation. In 1886 Geronimo finally gave up—the last Native American to surrender formally to the United States.

A Changing Culture

Many things contributed to changing the traditional Native American way of life—the movement of whites onto Indian lands, the slaughter of the buffalo, United States Army attacks, and the reservation policy. More change came from well-meaning reformers who wanted to abolish reservations and absorb the Indians into American life.

The Dawes Act

American reformers such as **Helen Hunt Jackson** were horrified by the massacres of Native Americans and by the cruelty of the reservation system. Describing the whites' treatment of Native Americans in her 1881 book, *A Century of Dishonor,* Jackson wrote:

❝It makes little difference . . . where one opens the record of the history of the Indians; every page and every year has its dark stain. **❞**

Congress changed government policy in the **Dawes Act** in 1887. The law aimed to eliminate what Americans regarded as the two weaknesses of Native American life: the lack of private property and the nomadic tradition.

The Dawes Act proposed to break up the reservations and to end Indian identification with a tribal group. Each Native American would receive a plot of reservation land. The goal was to encourage the Indians to become farmers. Eventually they would become American citizens. Native American children would be sent to white-run boarding schools. Some of the reservation lands would be sold to support this schooling.

Over the next 50 years, the government divided up the reservations. Speculators acquired most of the valuable land. Indians got dry, gravelly plots that were not suited to farming.

Ghost Dance

The Dawes Act changed forever the Native American way of life and weakened Indian cultural traditions. In their despair the Sioux turned in 1890 to **Wovoka,** a prophet. Wovoka claimed that the Sioux could regain their former greatness if they performed a ritual known as the **Ghost Dance.**

The Ghost Dance was a way for the Sioux to express their culture that was being destroyed. As the ritual spread, reservation officials became alarmed and decided to ban the dance. Believing that Sitting Bull was the leader of the movement, police went to his camp to arrest him. During a scuffle, they shot and killed Sitting Bull.

Wounded Knee

Several hundred Lakota Sioux fled in fear after Sitting Bull's death. They gathered at a creek called **Wounded Knee** in southwestern South Dakota. On December 29, 1890, the army went there to collect the Sioux's weapons. The Indians were starving and freezing in the December winter. No one knows how the fighting started, but when a pistol shot rang out, the army responded with fire. Using machine guns, soldiers killed more than 300 Lakota.

Wounded Knee marked the end of armed conflict between Americans and Indians. The Native Americans had lost their long struggle.

Section 3 Assessment

Checking for Understanding
1. **Identify** Sitting Bull, Crazy Horse, Chief Joseph, Geronimo, Dawes Act, Wovoka.
2. **Define** nomadic, reservation.
3. **Describe** the lifestyle of Native Americans on the Plains.

Reviewing Themes
4. **Culture and Traditions** What two weaknesses of Native American life was the Dawes Act supposed to eliminate?

Critical Thinking
5. **Identifying Central Issues** In what ways did the government reservation policy ignore the needs of Native Americans?

Activity

Making a Graphic Organizer With the buffalo at the center, create a graphic organizer that shows the importance of this animal in the everyday life and culture of the Plains Indians.

1870 | 1880 | 1890 | 1900

1870s
The Grange works to reduce shipping costs

1880s
Farmers' Alliances seek federal support

1892
Alliance members form the Populist Party

1896
William McKinley is elected president

Section 4

Farmers in Protest

READ TO DISCOVER . . .
- why farmers were suffering in the late 1800s.
- how new organizations and political parties tried to solve farmers' problems.

TERMS TO LEARN
National Grange
cooperative

Populist Party
free silver

Storyteller

In the last decades of the 1800s, farmers suffered from falling prices and rising costs. They expressed their frustration in a popular song:

"When the banker says he's broke
And the merchant's up in smoke
They forget that it's the farmer feeds
    them all. . . .
The farmer is the man,
Lives on credit till the fall;
With the interest
    rates so high,
It's a wonder he
    don't die,
For the mortgage
    man's the one
    who gets it all."

Poster celebrating the farmer, 1876

I FEED YOU ALL

After the Civil War, farming expanded in the West and the South, and more land came under cultivation. The supply of crops grew faster than the demand for them, however, and prices fell steadily. In 1866 a bushel of wheat sold for $1.45. By the mid-1880s the price had dropped to 80 cents and by the mid-1890s to 49 cents. At the same time, farmers' expenses—for transporting their goods to market, for seed, and for equipment and other manufactured goods—remained high.

Farmers' Problems

⭐ The farmers' plight gave rise to bitter feelings. Farmers blamed their troubles on three groups in particular. They resented the railroad companies, which charged farmers more to ship crops than they charged manufacturers to ship goods. They were angry at the Eastern manufacturers, who charged high prices for their products. They also disliked bankers.

Farmers needed to borrow money to buy seed, equipment, and other goods. After they sold their crops, they had to pay the high interest rates set by bankers. When crops failed and farmers could not repay the loans, they were in danger of losing their farms.

Farmers with small and middle-sized holdings struggled to survive. Senator William A. Peffer of Kansas summed up the farmers' plight when he noted that the railroad companies "took possession of the land" and the bankers "took possession of the farmer."

The Farmers Organize

⭐ Farmers began to organize in an effort to solve their problems. Within a short time, they had created a mass political movement.

The Grange

The first farmers' organization of this period was a network of local self-help organizations that eventually came to be called the National Grange. The Grange offered farmers education, fellowship, and support. For inexperienced farmers, the Grange provided a library with books on planting and livestock raising. For lonely farm families, it organized social gatherings.

Above all, the Grange tried to encourage economic self-sufficiency. It set up "cash-only" cooperatives, stores where farmers bought products from each other. The cooperatives charged lower prices than regular stores and provided an outlet for farmers' crops. The purpose of the "cash-only" policy was to remove the burden of credit buying that threatened farmers.

In the 1870s the Grange tried to cut farmers' costs by getting state legislatures to limit railroad shipping rates. Many Midwestern states did pass such laws. By 1878, however, the railroads had put so much pressure on state legislatures that these states repealed the rate regulations.

The Grange cooperatives also failed. Farmers were always short of cash and had to borrow money until their next crop was sold. The cash-only cooperative could not work if borrowing was necessary.

By the late 1870s, the Grange had declined. Rural reformers tried to help farmers through the Farmers' Alliances.

The Farmers' Alliances

The **Farmers' Alliances** were networks of organizations that sprang up in the West and the South in the 1880s. The Southern Alliance was founded in Texas when farmers rallied against the railroads and against "money power."

Alliance leaders extended the movement to other states. By 1890 the Southern Alliance had

⭐ **Picturing HISTORY** The Grange worked to promote better agricultural methods and to improve farmers' lives. **What did state legislatures do to help the Grange?**

more than 3 million members, and the Colored Farmers' National Alliance, a separate organization of African American farmers, had 1 million members. An Alliance movement developed in the Plains states as well.

Like the Grange, the Farmers' Alliances sponsored education and cooperative buying and selling. The Alliances also proposed a plan in which the federal government would store farmers' crops in warehouses and lend money to the farmers. When the stored crops were sold, the farmers would pay back the government loans. Such a plan would reduce the power that railroads, banks, and merchants had over farmers and would offer farmers some federal protection.

If the Alliances had remained united, they would have been a powerful political force. Regional differences and personality clashes kept the groups apart, however.

⭐⭐⭐ Linking PAST & PRESENT

The Grange

More than 350,000 farmers in 37 states belong to the Grange today. The organization still pursues its original goals of providing educational and social support to farmers.

Chapter 18 The Western Frontier **545**

Populist Party ribbon

★ Picturing HISTORY For many farmers in isolated areas, Populist meetings like this one in Dickinson County, Kansas, provided fellowship and a chance to promote political ideas. **Why did Populists favor a flexible currency system based on free silver?**

A Party of the People

★ In the 1890 election, the Alliances became active in political campaigns. Candidates they supported won 6 governorships, 3 seats in the United States Senate, and 50 seats in the House of Representatives.

The Populist Party

Pleased with such successes, Alliance leaders worked to turn the movement into a national political party. In February 1892, Alliance members formed the People's Party of the U.S.A., also known as the Populist Party. Its goals were rooted in **populism,** or appeal to the common people.

The new party claimed that the government, not private companies, should own the railroads and telegraph lines. The Populists also wanted to replace the country's gold-based currency system with a flexible currency system that was based on free silver—the unlimited production of silver coins. They believed that putting more silver coins into the economy would give farmers more money to pay their debts.

The Populist Party supported a number of political and labor reforms. They wanted election reforms such as limiting the president and vice president to a single term, electing senators directly, and introducing the use of secret ballots. They also called for shorter hours for workers and the creation of a national income tax.

Populist Gains and Problems

At a convention in **Omaha, Nebraska,** in July 1892, the Populist Party nominated **James B. Weaver** of Iowa to run for president. In the election Weaver received more than 1 million votes—8.5 percent of the total—and 22 electoral votes. **Grover Cleveland,** the Democratic candidate, won the election, but the Populists had done well for a third party.

The Populists made a strong showing in the state and local elections of 1894 and had high hopes for the presidential election of 1896. The party nominated a number of energetic candidates, but it lacked money and organization.

 **Economics**

Free Silver

To make matters worse, antagonism between the North and the South plagued the Populist Party. In addition many white Southerners could not bring themselves to join forces with African American Populists.

Another blow against populism was struck by the Democratic Party in the South. In the 1890s Democrat-controlled Southern state legislatures placed strict limits on the rights of African Americans to vote. Many freedmen—who might have supported the Populists—were unable to vote.

The Populist crusade for free silver and against the "money power" continued, however. Banking and business interests warned that coining unlimited amounts of new currency would lead to inflation and ruin the economy.

Farmers were joined by debtors in supporting free silver, hoping that loans could be repaid more cheaply. Silver-mining companies in the West also supported the cause. If the government coined large quantities of silver, they had a place to sell their metal.

In the mid-1890s Democrats from farm and silver-producing states took up the free silver issue. This created a problem for Populists. Should they ally themselves with these Democrats? Or should they remain a separate party and risk dividing the free-silver vote?

The Election of 1896

President Grover Cleveland, a Democrat, opposed free silver. At their 1896 convention, however, the Democrats chose a candidate for president who supported free silver and other Populist goals. He was 36-year-old **William Jennings Bryan,** known as the Great Commoner because of his appeal to average Americans. Bryan passionately believed in the farmers' causes.

The Populists decided to endorse Bryan as their candidate for president and to nominate their own candidate, Tom Watson of Georgia, for vice president. The Republicans nominated **William McKinley** of Ohio for president. A former representative and governor of Ohio, McKinley was a shrewd politician who opposed free silver.

A fiery speaker, Bryan proved to be an outstanding campaigner. He crossed the nation giving one dynamic speech after another, attacking bankers and other money interests.

Bryan's strenuous campaigning was in vain. By the time of the election, an economic depression that had slowed business in the early 1890s was nearly over. Voters believed that good times were returning, and they put their trust in McKinley, who represented stability. Even the economic situation of the farmers was improving. The Populists' message no longer seemed urgent. McKinley won 271 electoral votes to Bryan's 176. The Populist ticket received only 222,600 popular votes and won no electoral votes.

The Populist Legacy

In one sense, however, the Populists were victorious. Reformers adopted many Populist ideas and succeeded in getting many new laws passed. In the 1900s, the United States abandoned the gold standard, adopted an eight-hour workday, and introduced an income tax. Election reforms brought in the secret ballot and direct election of senators. These were Populist goals.

★ ★ ★ ★ ★ **Section 4 Assessment** ★ ★ ★ ★ ★ ★

Checking for Understanding

1. *Identify* Farmers' Alliances, James B. Weaver, Grover Cleveland, William Jennings Bryan, William McKinley.
2. *Define* National Grange, cooperative, Populist Party, free silver.
3. *Name* the groups on which farmers of the late 1800s blamed their problems.

Reviewing Themes

4. **Groups and Institutions** Why were granges and alliances formed?

Critical Thinking

5. **Making Inferences** Why do you think the Populists considered themselves to be a party of the people?

Activity

Creating a Bumper Sticker Write a campaign slogan for a Populist candidate who is running for office, and make a bumper sticker displaying your slogan.

Assessment and Activities

★ Reviewing Key Terms

On a sheet of paper, define the following terms:

lode	cooperative
ore	Populist Party
vigilante	free silver
subsidy	dry farming
transcontinental	nomadic
open range	reservation

★ Reviewing Key Facts

1. In what ways did the transcontinental railroad help to boost the American economy?
2. What attracted farmers to the Great Plains?
3. What actions by whites destroyed the buffalo population?
4. What was the goal of the Dawes Act?
5. What political reforms did the Populists support?

★ Critical Thinking

Drawing Conclusions

Many Americans in the 1800s viewed the West as free, open land awaiting civilization by white people.

1. Why was this attitude a threat to the Native Americans?
2. How did new technology encourage settlement of the West?

★ Time Line Activity

Create a time line on which you place the following events in chronological order.

- First transcontinental railroad completed
- Comstock Lode discovered in Nevada
- Congress passes Homestead Act
- Custer defeated at Little Bighorn

★ Technology Activity

Using E-mail Use an on-line address book to locate a modern farming organization. Copy the E-mail address of this organization and contact it through E-mail. Explain that you would like to know more about the organization. Ask what services or support the organization provides to farmers today.

★ Geography Activity

Study the map below, then answer the questions.

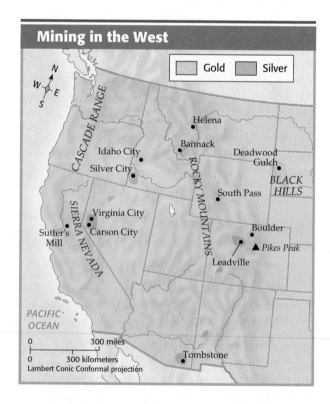

Mining in the West

1. **Region** What is the topic of this map?
2. **Place** What minerals were mined near the Black Hills?
3. **Location** Near what mountain range was Sutter's Mill located?

★ Skill Practice Activity

Reading a Special-Purpose Map

Study the special-purpose map below, then answer the questions that follow it.

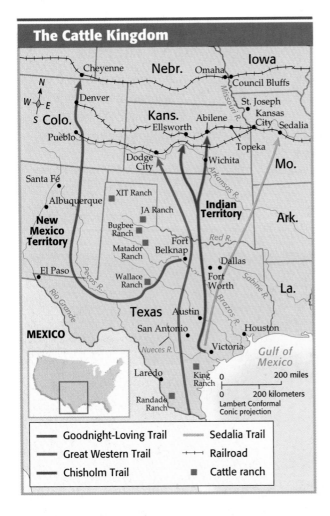

The Cattle Kingdom

Goodnight-Loving Trail
Great Western Trail
Chisholm Trail
Sedalia Trail
Railroad
Cattle ranch

1. What is the subject of the map?
2. What geographic region is shown?
3. What do the different colored lines represent?
4. In what part of Texas were most of the large cattle ranches found?
5. Along which two trails did several major Texas cities develop?
6. Where did a majority of the trails end? Explain why.
7. In which state did the Chisholm Trail end?

★ Reviewing Themes

1. **Geography and History** How did the rush to find gold and silver spark the creation of new communities in the West?
2. **Economic Factors** Why was the "Cattle Kingdom" dependent on the railroads?
3. **Culture and Traditions** What actions by the United States government and white settlers brought an end to the traditional Native American way of life?
4. **Groups and Institutions** What problems led farmers to organize granges and alliances?

★ Cooperative Activity

History and Economics Today many Native Americans still live on reservations. Some reservations have developed their own businesses and industries to help make them more self-sufficient. With a partner research to find information about a reservation in the United States today. Write a report describing one of the major businesses on that reservation.

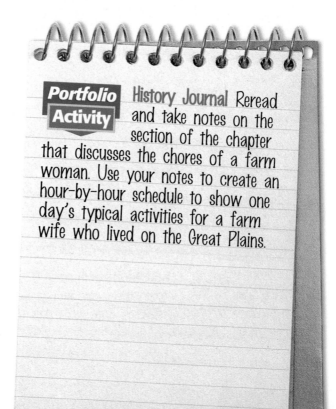

Portfolio Activity

History Journal Reread and take notes on the section of the chapter that discusses the chores of a farm woman. Use your notes to create an hour-by-hour schedule to show one day's typical activities for a farm wife who lived on the Great Plains.

1865–1914

The Growth of Industry

★ Why It's Important

By the early 1900s, many changes had taken place in the nation's economy. Large, powerful corporations had developed, and labor had organized into unions to protect workers' interests. Business owners and employees struggled to establish new ways of working together. The years also brought change to everyday life. Inventions such as the telephone and the automobile revolutionized society in the United States and around the world.

★ Chapter Themes

- *Section 1,* Geography and History
- *Section 2,* Science and Technology
- *Section 3,* Economic Factors
- *Section 4,* Groups and Institutions

PRIMARY SOURCES
Library

See pages 972–973 for primary source readings to accompany Chapter 19

 HISTORY AND ART

***Steel Mills At Night* by Aaron Henry Gorson** Gorson's painting depicts the changes that industrial growth brought to America's landscape during the late 1800s.

1869
First transcontinental
railroad completed

1880s
Standard width
for railroad
tracks adopted

1883
Northern
Pacific
Railroad
opens

1890s
Five railway
lines cross
the country

Section 1

Railroads Lead the Way

READ TO DISCOVER . . .
- how the railroad barons made fortunes.
- how the national railroad system changed the American economy.

TERMS TO LEARN
consolidation   rebate
standard gauge   pool

S̲toryteller

Rugged construction gangs labored on the Union Pacific and other railways during the transportation boom of the late 1800s. A favorite song was:

> Well, every morning at seven o'clock
> There were 20 tarriers [drillers] a-workin' at the rock,
> And the boss comes around and he says "Kape still!"
> And come down heavy on the cast iron drill,
> And drill, ye tarriers, drill!"
> Drill, ye tarriers, drill!
> For it's work all day for sugar in your tay,
> Down behind of the railway and,
> Drill, ye tarriers, drill!
> And blast!
> And fire!

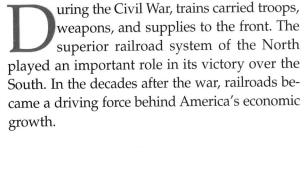

Train song sheet

During the Civil War, trains carried troops, weapons, and supplies to the front. The superior railroad system of the North played an important role in its victory over the South. In the decades after the war, railroads became a driving force behind America's economic growth.

Railroad Expansion

The first transcontinental railroad, completed in 1869, was soon followed by others. By the 1890s five railway lines crossed the country, and hundreds of smaller lines branched off from them. The railroad system grew rapidly. In 1860 the United States had about 30,000 miles of railroad track. By 1900, 163,000 more miles of track had been laid.

Work songs such as "John Henry" and "I've Been Working on the Railroad" were popular among those who labored to build these miles of track. They sang:

> ❝I've been working on the railroad,
> All the live-long day,
> I've been working on the railroad,
> Just to pass the time away. ❞

The expansion of the railroad system was accompanied by consolidation—the practice of combining separate companies—in the industry. Large railroad companies expanded by buying smaller companies or by driving them out of business. Consolidation made the large companies

A train steams through a Rocky Mountain pass on its way to California.

transported produce from farming areas to the cities.

The national railroad system encouraged the expanding economy in many other ways. At first the demand for iron tracks and locomotives helped the iron mining and processing industries grow. Around 1880 railroad companies began using tracks of **steel**—a stronger metal made by adding carbon and other elements to refined iron. The use of steel in railroad tracks stimulated America's steel industry.

The railroads also helped other industries to thrive. The lumber industry, which supplied wood for railway ties, and the coal industry, which provided fuel for locomotives, saw extraordinary growth. In addition railroad companies provided work for thousands of people who laid tracks and built stations and for those who manufactured railway cars and equipment.

more efficient. After consolidating the railroad industry, a few powerful individuals known as **railroad barons** controlled the nation's rail traffic.

Railroad Barons

New Yorker **Cornelius Vanderbilt,** one of the first railroad barons, gained control of the New York Central line and then made a fortune by consolidating several companies. His railroad empire stretched from **New York City** to the Great Lakes. To Vanderbilt, having money was a source of great power.

Another railroad baron, **James J. Hill,** built the Great Northern line between **Minnesota** and **Washington State. Collis P. Huntington, Leland Stanford,** and two other partners founded the Central Pacific, which connected California and Utah.

Improving the Railroads

Increased use made it necessary for railroads to expand and unify their systems. While railroads were being built across the country, different lines used rails of different gauges, or widths. As a result trains of one line could not use another line's tracks. Many early local lines carried goods for short distances and did not even connect with other lines. The gaps in service between the various lines made long-distance railroad travel slow and inefficient.

As the railroad companies consolidated, railroad barons saw the advantages of being part of a national railroad network. By the late 1880s, almost all companies had adopted a standard gauge of 4 feet, 8.5 inches as the width of the railroad track. A standard gauge allowed faster shipment of goods at a reduced cost. It was no longer necessary to load and unload goods from one train to another. One train could make the entire journey.

$ Economics

Railroads Stimulate the Economy

The fast-growing national rail system created new economic links in the country. The railroads carried raw materials such as iron ore, coal, and timber to factories. They also carried manufactured goods from factories to markets and

Railroad Technology

Railway transportation also improved with the introduction of new technology. Four developments were particularly important. Inventor **George Westinghouse** devised air brakes that improved the system for stopping trains, making train travel safer. Janney car couplers, named after inventor **Eli H. Janney,** made it easier for railroad workers to link cars. Refrigerated cars, developed by **Gustavus Swift,** enabled the railroads to ship meat and other perishable goods over long distances. Finally, **George M. Pullman**

developed the Pullman sleeping car—a luxury railway car with seats that converted into beds for overnight journeys. Pullman also introduced improved dining cars, raising train travel to a new level of comfort.

Competing for Customers

As the railroad network expanded, the railroad companies competed fiercely with one another to keep old customers and to win new ones. Large railroads offered secret discounts called rebates to their biggest customers. Smaller

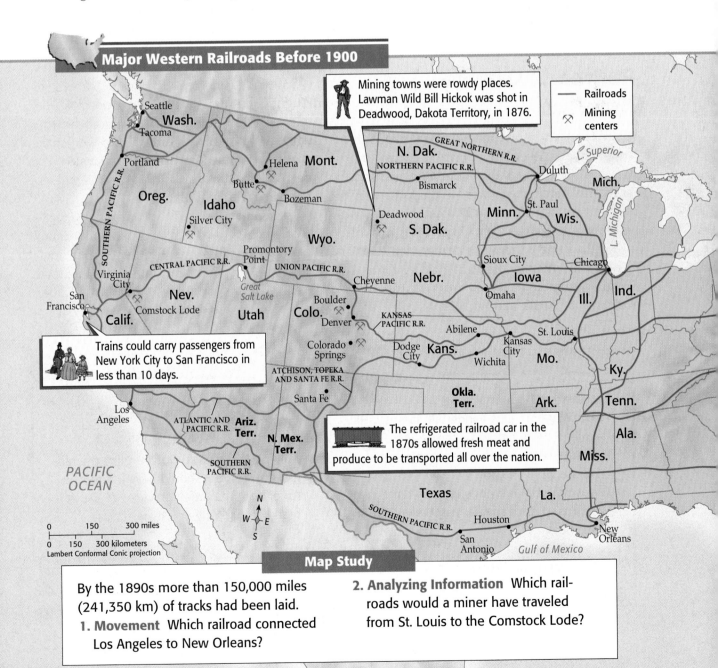

Major Western Railroads Before 1900

Mining towns were rowdy places. Lawman Wild Bill Hickok was shot in Deadwood, Dakota Territory, in 1876.

Railroads

Mining centers

Trains could carry passengers from New York City to San Francisco in less than 10 days.

The refrigerated railroad car in the 1870s allowed fresh meat and produce to be transported all over the nation.

0 150 300 miles
0 150 300 kilometers
Lambert Conformal Conic projection

Map Study

By the 1890s more than 150,000 miles (241,350 km) of tracks had been laid.

1. **Movement** Which railroad connected Los Angeles to New Orleans?

2. **Analyzing Information** Which railroads would a miner have traveled from St. Louis to the Comstock Lode?

railroads that could not match these rebates were often forced out of business. Giving discounts to big customers raised freight rates for farmers and other customers who shipped small amounts of goods.

The railroad barons also made secret agreements among themselves, known as **pools**. They divided the railway business among their companies and set rates for a region. With no other competition in its region, a railroad could charge higher rates and earn greater profits. Although Congress and some states passed laws to regulate the railroads, these laws did little to curb the railroad barons.

Railroads Change America

The growing railroad network paved the way for American industry to expand into the West. The center of the flour milling industry, for example, shifted westward in the 1800s, moving from the East Coast to Ohio, to Minneapolis, and finally to Kansas City. Other industries followed the same pattern. As farmers settled the Great Plains, the manufacturing center for agricultural equipment moved from central New York State to Illinois and Wisconsin.

Linking PAST & PRESENT

Return of the Train

Rising fuel costs and environmental concerns have revived interest in trains. Trains use less energy per passenger than do cars, airplanes, and buses. As a result, trains help conserve energy as more passengers use them.

Railroads also touched the lives of thousands of Americans. Trains redistributed the population. They carried homesteaders into the Great Plains and the West. Trains also made it easy for people to move from rural areas to the cities.

Railroads affected the way Americans thought about time as well. As train travel became more common, people began measuring distances by how many hours the trip would take rather than by the number of miles traveled. The spread of the railroad system led to a national system of time with four time zones.

The railroads opened the entire United States to settlement and economic growth and united the different regions of the country into a single network. At the same time, inventions that revolutionized transportation and communication brought Americans together in new ways.

Section 1 Assessment

Checking for Understanding
1. **Identify** Cornelius Vanderbilt, James J. Hill, Collis P. Huntington, Gustavus Swift.
2. **Define** consolidation, standard gauge, rebate, pool.
3. **Describe** the methods used by railroad barons to drive smaller companies out of business.

Reviewing Themes
4. **Geography and History** How did the railroad pave the way for the expansion of industry in the West?

Critical Thinking
5. **Making Inferences** Do you think the federal government should have intervened to regulate the unfair practices of the railroad barons? Why or why not?

Designing an Advertisement Create an ad with words and pictures to announce the development of the new Pullman sleeping car.

Social Studies
SKILL BUILDER

Reading a Time Zones Map

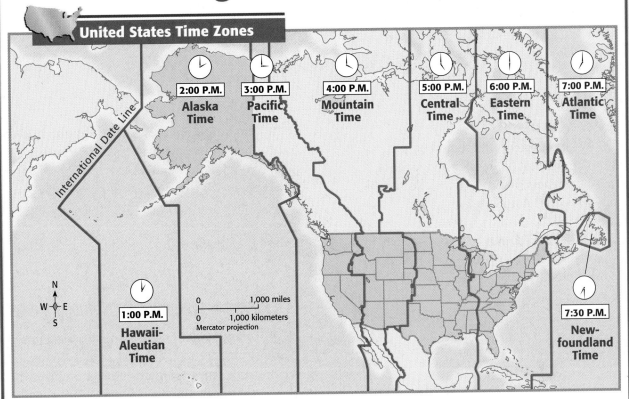

United States Time Zones

2:00 P.M.	3:00 P.M.	4:00 P.M.	5:00 P.M.	6:00 P.M.	7:00 P.M.
Alaska Time	Pacific Time	Mountain Time	Central Time	Eastern Time	Atlantic Time

International Date Line

1:00 P.M.
Hawaii-Aleutian Time

0   1,000 miles
0   1,000 kilometers
Mercator projection

7:30 P.M.
New-foundland Time

Learning the Skill

Earth's surface is divided into 24 time zones. Each zone represents 15° longitude, or the distance the earth rotates in 1 hour. The 0° line of longitude—the Prime Meridian—is the starting point for figuring time around the world. Traveling west from the Prime Meridian, it becomes 1 hour earlier; traveling east, it becomes 1 hour later. To read a time zones map, follow these steps:

- Locate a place where you know what time it is and select another place where you wish to know the time.
- Notice the time zones you cross between these places.
- If the second place lies east of the first, add an hour for each time zone. If it lies west, subtract an hour for each zone.

Practicing the Skill

1. What U.S. time zone lies farthest west?
2. If it is 6:00 P.M. in Washington, D.C., what time is it in San Diego, California?

Applying the Skill

Reading a Time Zones Map It takes two hours to fly from Denver, Colorado, to Chicago, Illinois. If you leave Denver at 2:00 A.M., what time will it be in Chicago when you arrive?

Glencoe's **Skillbuilder Interactive Workbook, Level 1** provides instruction and practice in key social studies skills.

1868
Christopher Sholes invents the typewriter

1876
Alexander Bell develops the telephone

1879
Edison develops first practical lightbulb

1903
The Wright brothers fly at Kitty Hawk

1908
Henry Ford introduces the Model T

Section 2

Inventions

READ TO DISCOVER . . .

- what changes in transportation and communication transformed America.
- how laborsaving inventions affected the lives of all Americans.

TERMS TO LEARN

assembly line
mass production

The Storyteller

In the early 1900s, American songwriters were caught up in the public fascination with new inventions. One of the most popular songs of 1905, "In My Merry Oldsmobile," celebrated the automobile:

"Come away with me Lucile,
In my merry Oldsmobile.
Down the road of life we'll fly,
Automobubbling you and I.
To the church we'll swiftly steal,
Then our wedding bells will peal;
You can go as far as you like, . . .
In my merry Oldsmobile."

Hood ornament

The automobile, the electric light, and the telephone were all invented after 1870. Within a generation they had become part of everyday life for millions of people. These and hundreds of other new inventions, along with new ways of buying and selling goods, transformed the American way of life.

Communication Changes

New inventions helped people communicate more quickly and easily over long distances. Improvements in communication helped unify the different regions of the country and promoted economic growth.

The Telegraph

Samuel F.B. Morse had introduced the telegraph in 1844. By 1860 the United States had thousands of miles of telegraph lines, controlled for the most part by the Western Union Telegraph Company. At telegraph offices, trained operators transmitted people's messages in Morse code. Telegrams offered almost instant communication and had many uses. Shopkeepers relied on telegrams to order goods, and reporters used them to transmit stories to their newspapers. Americans also began sending personal messages by telegram.

The telegraph soon linked the United States and Europe. In the 1860s news from Europe traveled to this country by ship and took several weeks. **Cyrus Field** wanted to speed up the process. After several unsuccessful attempts, Field managed to lay a telegraph cable across the Atlantic Ocean in 1866. The new transatlantic telegraph carried messages in a matter of seconds, bringing the United States and Europe closer together.

Inventions of the Late 1800s

Inventor	Date	Invention
Elisha Otis	1852	elevator brake
Henry Bessemer	1856	Bessemer process
George Pullman	1864	rail sleeping car
Thaddeus Lowe	1865	ice machine
George Westinghouse	1868	air brake
Stephen Dudley Field	1874	electric streetcar
Alexander Graham Bell	1876	telephone
Thomas Alva Edison	1877	phonograph
Anna Baldwin	1878	milking machine
Thomas Alva Edison	1879	incandescent lightbulb
James Ritty	1879	cash register
Lewis Howard Latimer	1882	improved lightbulb filament
Jan E. Matzeliger	1883	shoemaking machine
Sarah E. Goode	1885	folding cabinet bed
Granville T. Woods	1887	automatic air brake
Charles and J. Frank Duryea	1893	gasoline-powered car
John Thurman	1899	vacuum cleaner

Chart Study

Inventions helped the American economy prosper and expand in the late 1800s.

1. Which of the above inventions still affects your life today?
2. **Comparing** How many of the inventions listed above were used outside of the home?

Biography

The Telephone Rings In

Alexander Graham Bell invented a device that revolutionized communications even more than Morse's telegraph. Born and educated in Scotland, Bell moved to the United States, where he studied ways of teaching people who were hearing impaired to speak. At the same time, he experimented with sending voices through electrical wires.

By 1876 Bell developed a device that transmitted speech—the telephone. While Bell was preparing to test the device, he accidentally spilled some battery acid on his clothes. In panic Bell called out to his assistant in another room: "Mr. Watson, come here. I want you!" Watson heard Bell's voice coming through the telephone. The invention was a success.

Eastman camera

Bell's phone transmitter

Bell formed the Bell Telephone Company in 1877. By the 1890s he had sold nearly 500,000 phones. Most early telephone customers were businesses. Before long, though, telephones became common in homes.

The Genius of Invention

The late 1800s saw a burst of inventiveness in the United States. Between 1860 and 1890, the United States government granted more than 400,000 patents for new inventions.

Many of the inventions helped businesses operate more efficiently. Among these were Christopher Sholes's typewriter (1868) and William Burroughs's adding machine (1888).

Other inventions affected everyday life. In 1888 **George Eastman** invented a small camera

Thomas Edison displays his phonograph

that made it easier and less costly to take photographs. **John Thurman** developed a vacuum cleaner in 1899 that simplified housework.

Thomas Alva Edison

Thomas Alva Edison was born in Ohio in 1847. While still in his 20s, Edison decided to go into the "invention business." In 1876, Edison set up a workshop in **Menlo Park, New Jersey.** His goal was to produce "a minor invention every ten days and a big thing every six months or so." Edison usually had 30 or 40 projects under way at one time. His workshop was the country's first industrial research laboratory.

Edison received more than 1,000 patents in his lifetime. Out of his laboratory came the phonograph, the motion picture projector, the telephone transmitter, the storage battery, and the dictating machine. Edison's most important invention was the electric lightbulb.

Edison developed the first practical lightbulb in 1879. He then designed power plants that could produce electric power and distribute it to lightbulbs. For Christmas 1880, Edison used 40 bulbs to light up Menlo Park. Visitors flocked to see the "light of the future." He built the first central electric power plant in 1882 in New York City—illuminating 85 buildings. 📖

Electricity Transforms the Nation

Inventor **George Westinghouse** took Edison's work a step further. In 1885 Westinghouse developed and built transformers that could send electric power more cheaply over longer distances. Soon electricity powered factories, trolleys, streetlights, and lamps all over America.

African American Inventors

A number of African Americans contributed to the era of invention. **Lewis Howard Latimer,** an engineer, developed an improved filament for the lightbulb and joined Thomas Edison's company. **Granville Woods,** an electrical and mechanical engineer from Ohio, patented 35 inventions. Among them were an electric incubator and railroad improvements such as an electromagnetic brake and an automatic circuit breaker. **Elijah McCoy** invented a mechanism for oiling machinery.

Jan E. Matzeliger, another African American inventor, developed a shoemaking machine that performed many steps previously done by hand.

Lewis Howard Latimer and his patent drawing of a lamp fixture

His device, which revolutionized the shoe industry, was adopted in shoe factories in the United States and overseas.

Transportation Changes

In the 1900s two inventions ushered in a new era of transportation. After a period of experimentation, the automobile became a practical method of getting from place to place. Then the airplane forever changed long-distance travel.

Henry Ford's Automobiles

Henry Ford wanted to build an inexpensive car that would last a lifetime. While working as an engineer in **Detroit, Michigan,** in the 1890s, Ford had experimented with an automobile engine powered by gasoline. In 1903 he established an automaking company and began designing cars.

Model T Ford

In 1906 Ford had an idea for a new type of car. He told Charles Sorenson, later Ford's general superintendent, "We're going to get a car now that we can make in great volume and get the prices way down." For the next year, Ford and Sorenson worked on the **Model T,** building the car and testing it on rough roads. In 1908 Ford introduced the Model T to the public. Sorenson described the sturdy black vehicle as

66 . . . a car which anyone could afford to buy, which anyone could drive anywhere, and which almost anyone could keep in repair. 99

These qualities made the Model T immensely popular. During the next 18 years, Ford's company sold 15 million Model T's. Henry Ford also pioneered a new, less expensive way to manufacture cars—the **assembly line.** On the assembly line, each worker performed an assigned task again and again at a certain stage in the production of the automobile. The assembly line revolutionized industry, enabling manufacturers to produce large quantities of goods more quickly. This **mass production** of goods decreased manufacturing costs, so products could be sold more cheaply.

Taking to the Air

Inventors experimented with engine-powered aircraft in the 1800s, but the age of air travel did not begin until 1903 at **Kitty Hawk, North Carolina. Orville** and **Wilbur Wright,** brothers and bicycle mechanics, built a wood-and-canvas plane with a 12-horsepower engine. On the morning of December 17, Orville Wright took off in their plane and flew a distance of 120 feet.

Section 2 Assessment

Checking for Understanding

1. *Identify* Cyrus Field, Alexander Graham Bell, Thomas Alva Edison, Granville Woods, Henry Ford, Orville and Wilbur Wright.
2. *Define* assembly line, mass production.
3. *Name* two inventions that changed the way people communicated in the 1800s.

Reviewing Themes

4. **Science and Technology** How was transportation improved during the early 1900s?

Critical Thinking

5. **Determining Relevance** Which invention do you think brought about the most dramatic change in people's lives? Explain.

Activity

Making a Chart Design a chart of inventors discussed in this section. Your chart should include inventors' names, what each invented and when, and a drawing of each of their inventions.

1859
Oil discovered in Titusville, Pennsylvania

1870
Rockefeller organizes the Standard Oil Company

1890
Sherman Antitrust Act prohibits monopolies

1900
Andrew Carnegie rules the steel industry

Section 3

An Age of Big Business

READ TO DISCOVER . . .

▓ how new discoveries and inventions helped the steel and oil industries grow.

▓ why the development of large corporations brought both benefits and problems.

TERMS TO LEARN

corporation
stock
shareholder
dividend
horizontal integration

trust
monopoly
vertical integration
philanthropy
merger

The Storyteller

John D. Rockefeller, a young oil man, never tired until he got what he wanted. One person commented: "The only time I ever saw John Rockefeller enthusiastic was when a report came in . . . that his buyer had secured a cargo of oil at a figure much below the market price. He bounded from his chair with a shout of joy, danced up and down, hugged me, threw up his hat, acted so like a mad-man that I have never forgotten it. . . . "

John D. Rockefeller

In the hills of western Pennsylvania, a sticky black substance—petroleum—seeped from the ground. For a while promoters sold the oil as medicine. Then in the 1850s researchers found they could burn petroleum to produce heat and smoke-free light. It could also be used to lubricate machinery. Suddenly oil became valuable.

A former railroad conductor named Edwin L. Drake believed that he could find petroleum by digging a well—just as he might dig a well for water. People thought Drake was wrong. Few people knew that pools of oil did indeed exist underground.

In 1859 Drake decided to test his belief. He drilled a well in **Titusville, Pennsylvania,** and struck oil. This led to the creation of a multimillion-dollar petroleum industry.

With the economy growing after the Civil War, many railroads and other businesses looked for ways to expand. To do so they had to raise capital, or money. They needed capital to buy raw materials and equipment, to pay workers, and to cover shipping and advertising costs.

💲 Economics

The Corporation

⭐ One way a company could raise capital was by becoming a corporation—a company that sold shares, or stock, of its business to the public. The people who invested in the corporation by buying stock were its shareholders, or partial owners.

In good times shareholders earned dividends—cash payments from the corporation's profits—on the stock they owned. If the company prospered, its stock rose in value, and the shareholders could sell it for a profit. If the company failed, however, the shareholders lost their investment. Hundreds of thousands of people shared in corporate profits by buying and selling stocks in special markets known as **stock exchanges.**

Growth of Corporations

Railroads were the first businesses to form corporations, or incorporate. Soon manufacturing firms and other businesses were incorporating as well. The growth of corporations helped fuel America's industrial expansion in the years following the Civil War.

Banks played a major role in this period of economic growth. Businesses borrowed money from banks to start or expand their operations. The banks, in turn, made profits on the loans.

The Oil Business

The oil industry grew rapidly in the late 1800s. Edwin Drake's Titusville well produced 15 barrels of petroleum a day. As word of his success spread, prospectors and investors hurried to western Pennsylvania. "Oil rush" towns with names such as Oil City and Petroleum Center sprang up overnight. The oil boom expanded as prospectors struck oil in Ohio and West Virginia.

Biography

John D. Rockefeller

Born in Richford, New York, in 1839, **John D. Rockefeller** made his fortune from oil. When Rockefeller was 26 years old, he and four partners set up an oil refinery—a plant to process oil—in **Cleveland, Ohio.**

Picturing HISTORY Cartoons of the day often portrayed Standard Oil as a "monopoly monster," with its arms reaching out to control government and suppliers.
How did Standard Oil gain a monopoly of the oil industry?

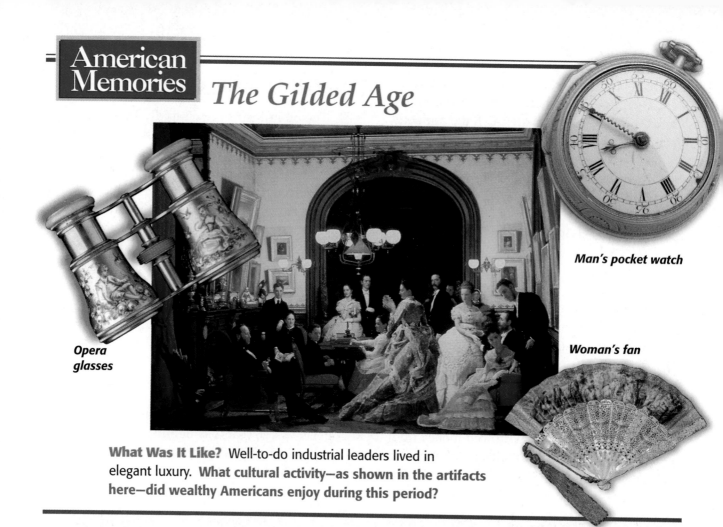

American Memories

The Gilded Age

Man's pocket watch

Opera glasses

Woman's fan

What Was It Like? Well-to-do industrial leaders lived in elegant luxury. What cultural activity—as shown in the artifacts here—did wealthy Americans enjoy during this period?

In 1870 Rockefeller organized the Standard Oil Company of Ohio and set out to dominate the oil industry. He acquired most of the oil refineries in Cleveland and other cities.

One method Rockefeller used to build his empire was horizontal integration—the combining of competing firms into one corporation. The corporation produced and used its own tank cars, pipelines, and even its own wooden barrels—made from forests owned by Standard Oil. Standard Oil grew in wealth and power, becoming the most famous corporate empire of the day.

The Standard Oil Trust

To strengthen Standard Oil's position in the oil industry, Rockefeller lowered his prices to drive his competitors out of business. In addition he pressured customers not to deal with rival oil companies, and he persuaded the railroads to grant him rebates in exchange for his business.

Rockefeller increased his control of the oil industry in 1882 by forming a trust, a group of

companies managed by the same board of directors. First he acquired stock in many different oil companies. Then the shareholders of these companies traded their stock for Standard Oil stock, which paid higher dividends. This gave Standard Oil's board of directors ownership of the other companies' stock and the right to manage those companies. Rockefeller had created a monopoly—total control by a single producer—of the oil industry.

The Steel Business

Steel also became a huge business in the late 1800s. A form of iron treated with carbon, steel is strong and long-lasting—the ideal material for railroad tracks, bridges, and many other products. Before the 1860s, however, steel was not widely used because of the high cost of manufacturing it. The development of new manufacturing techniques helped to overcome this problem.

Steel Industry Growth

Two new methods of making steel—the Bessemer process, developed by Henry Bessemer of England, and the open-hearth process—changed the industry. With the new methods, mills could produce steel at affordable prices and in large quantities.

In the 1870s large steel mills emerged in western Pennsylvania and eastern Ohio, close to sources of iron ore. **Pittsburgh, Pennsylvania,** became the steel capital of the United States. Cleveland, Chicago, Detroit, and Birmingham, Alabama, also became centers of steel production.

Andrew Carnegie

The leading figure in the early years of the American steel industry was **Andrew Carnegie,** son of a Scottish immigrant. Starting as a telegraph operator, Carnegie worked his way up to become manager of the Pennsylvania Railroad. In 1865 he left that job to invest in the growing iron industry.

Carnegie soon realized that steel would have an enormous market. After learning about the Bessemer process, he built a steel plant near Pittsburgh that used the new process. Carnegie named the plant the J. Edgar Thompson Steel Works, after the president of the Pennsylvania Railroad—his biggest customer.

Vertical Integration

By 1890 Andrew Carnegie dominated the steel industry. His company became powerful through vertical integration, acquiring companies that provided the equipment and services he needed. Carnegie bought iron and coal mines, warehouses, ore ships, and railroads to gain control of all parts of the business of making and selling steel. When Carnegie combined all his holdings into the Carnegie Steel Company in 1900, he was producing one-third of the nation's steel.

In 1901 Carnegie sold his steel company to banker **J. Pierpont Morgan** for $450 million. Morgan combined the Carnegie company with other businesses to form the United States Steel Corporation, the world's first billion-dollar corporation.

Philanthropists

Andrew Carnegie, John D. Rockefeller, and other industrial millionaires of the time grew interested in philanthropy—the use of money to benefit the community. The philanthropists founded schools, universities, and other civic institutions across the United States.

Carnegie donated $350 million to various organizations. He built Carnegie Hall in New York City, one of the world's most celebrated concert halls; the Carnegie Foundation for the Advancement of Teaching; and more than 2,000 libraries worldwide. Rockefeller used his fortune to establish the University of Chicago in 1892 and New York's Rockefeller Institute for Medical Research.

Corporations Grow Larger

★ In 1889 New Jersey encouraged the trend toward business monopolies by allowing holding companies to obtain charters, a practice

Andrew Carnegie

that some states prohibited. A holding company buys controlling interests in the stock of other companies instead of purchasing the companies outright. Rockefeller formed Standard Oil of New Jersey so the corporation could expand its holdings. Other states also passed laws that made corporate mergers—the combining of companies—easier.

Corporate Mergers

Mergers concentrated economic power in a few giant corporations and a few powerful individuals, such as Rockefeller and banker J. Pierpont Morgan. By 1900 one-third of all American manufacturing was controlled by just 1 percent of the country's corporations. These giant corporations were the driving force behind the great economic growth of the period, but they also posed problems.

Opposition to Big Business

Defenders of big business claimed that monopolies and trusts benefited society because they reduced competition and brought greater economic stability. According to this view, competition ruined many small businesses and threw great numbers of people out of work. Trusts helped consumers because large corporations could sell goods for lower prices than could smaller companies.

However, a growing number of Americans opposed trusts and monopolies. These people argued that a lack of competition hurt consumers. Without competition, corporations had no reason to keep their prices low or to improve their goods and services.

Government Regulation

State governments responded to the growing opposition to trusts and monopolies. During the 1880s, 15 states passed laws restricting business combinations that limited competition. Corporations, however, avoided these laws by incorporating in states that had no such laws.

Public pressure for a federal law to prohibit trusts and monopolies led Congress to pass the **Sherman Antitrust Act** in 1890. The law sought "to protect trade and commerce against unlawful restraint and monopoly." The act did not clearly define either "trusts" or "monopolies," however.

In its early years, the Sherman Antitrust Act did little to curb the power of big business. By contrast, in the 1890s the government did use the act to stop a strike by railroad workers that threatened to "restrain" the nation's mail delivery.

Section 3 Assessment

Checking for Understanding

1. **Identify** John D. Rockefeller, Andrew Carnegie, J. Pierpont Morgan, Sherman Antitrust Act.
2. **Define** corporation, stock, shareholder, dividend, horizontal integration, trust, monopoly, vertical integration, philanthropy, merger.
3. **List** three reasons railroads and other businesses needed to raise capital after the Civil War.

Reviewing Themes

4. **Economic Factors** Summarize the steps that John D. Rockefeller took to gain total control of the oil industry.

Critical Thinking

5. **Determining Cause and Effect** Why is competition among businesses beneficial to consumers?

Researching Local Philanthropists Research to find a philanthropist who has provided benefits to the community in which you live—in the past or present. Share your findings with the class.

Inventions of the Late 1800s

In the late 1800s, changes in industry and the growth of cities marked the beginning of the modern world. Experience some of these changes as you build, design, and write about developments in that fast-changing world.

Language Arts

Writing an Advertisement Americans in the late 1800s had a dazzling array of new inventions to buy for their homes and businesses. Imagine that you are an advertising manager selling one of these products: sewing machine, telephone, typewriter, telegraph, or phonograph (gramophone or talking machine). Remember that these products are new to your customers. Write and illustrate your advertisement. Display it in class.

Science

Engineering the Panama Canal The Panama Canal, opened in 1914, was an amazing feat of science and technology. Research the engineering design of the canal, and draw a cross-section diagram illustrating how ships are raised and lowered through locks in order to cross the mountains. Then make a map of the canal's path across Panama. Use your diagram and map to explain the canal system to the class.

School-to-Work

Starting a Small Business Some inventions of the late 1800s were the basis for new businesses. Choose a popular invention of this period—the bicycle, sewing machine, or typewriter, for example—and think of a business that uses the new

technology. Make a business plan that includes the number and kind of machines and employees you would need, the kinds of services or products you would offer, and the prices you would charge. Think of a name and symbol for your company and make a small display to introduce it in class.

Speech

Reporting a Sports Event By the 1890s both amateur and professional sports—football, baseball, bicycling, and the new game of basketball—were immensely popular. Although radio had not yet been invented in the 1890s, imagine that you are a radio sportscaster. Choose a sport, research its history, and prepare a short broadcast in which you report from a game or race. Tape it for the class or present it as a "live" broadcast.

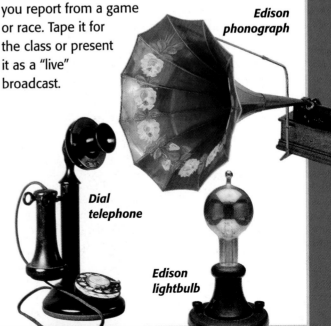

Edison phonograph

Dial telephone

Edison lightbulb

1869
Knights of Labor
organized

1877
Railroad
workers
on strike

1881
National trade
unions form
the AFL

1886
Riots erupt
in Haymarket
Square

Section 4

Industrial Workers

READ TO DISCOVER . . .
- why workers demanded changes in their working conditions and wages.
- how labor unions helped workers gain economic and political power.

TERMS TO LEARN
sweatshop   strikebreaker
trade union   injunction
collective bargaining

The **Storyteller**

On a spring day in 1886, about 12,000 workers in a Chicago manufacturing district were on strike. Nearly all were immigrants, and many wore small red ribbons on their jackets. At 2 o'clock a man climbed up on an empty freight car near the crowd. He moved to the edge of the roof and waved frantically at the crowd below. "Stand firm," he yelled. "Let every man stand shoulder to shoulder and we will win this fight. We must have our rights. Strike while the iron is hot. . . ."

***Haymarket Riot
news report***

Industrial growth in the late 1800s created new jobs and raised the standard of living for many American workers. Yet workers paid a price for economic progress. Factories had once been small workplaces where employers and employees knew one another and often worked side by side. As mass production spread, however, factories became larger and less personal.

Industrial laborers worked for 10 or 12 hours a day, 6 days a week. They could be fired at any time for any reason. Many lost their jobs during business downturns or were replaced by immigrants who were willing to work for lower pay.

Working Conditions

★ Factories and mines were noisy, unhealthy, and unsafe. Accidents were common. Steel workers suffered burns from spills of hot steel. Coal miners died in cave-ins and from the effects of gas and coal dust. Textile workers' lungs were damaged by airborne lint. Garment workers toiled in crowded urban factories called sweatshops, where they ruined their eyesight by sewing for hours in poor light. Filled with flammable materials, the sweatshops were also terrible firetraps.

Women Workers

Although the majority of working women in the late 1800s had jobs as domestic servants, women also joined the industrial workforce, especially the textile industry. By 1900 more than 1 million women worked in industry. However,

★ ★

because no laws regulated workers' salaries, women generally received about half of what men earned for the same work.

Child Labor

Industries also hired children. In 1900 hundreds of thousands of children under 16 years of age worked in factories. Concerned groups brought child labor to the attention of their state legislatures. As a result many states passed child-labor laws. These laws stated that children working in factories had to be at least 12 years old and should not work more than 10 hours a day. Employers widely ignored child-labor laws, however. Also, the laws did not apply to agriculture, which employed about 1 million children.

Labor Unions Form

★ Dissatisfied workers organized into groups—labor unions—to demand better pay and working conditions from their employers. Earlier in the 1800s, skilled workers had formed unions to represent workers in certain crafts or trades, such as carpentry. These trade unions had little influence because each represented only one trade. By the mid-1800s labor leaders looked to expand their unions.

The Knights of Labor

In 1869 garment cutters in Philadelphia founded the Noble and Holy Order of the **Knights of Labor.** Employers fired workers who joined labor organizations, so the Knights met secretly and used special handshakes to identify each other. Under the leadership of **Terence V. Powderly,** the Knights of Labor became a national labor organization in the 1880s. Unlike most unions, the Knights recruited people who had been kept out of trade unions, including women, African Americans, immigrants, and unskilled laborers.

The Knights of Labor grew rapidly, boasting more than 700,000 members by 1886. However, a wave of strikes turned public opinion against the union, and it lost members and power in the 1890s.

The American Federation of Labor

In 1881 a group of national trade unions formed a federation that 5 years later became known as the **American Federation of Labor** (AFL). The AFL represented skilled workers in various crafts. In 1886 the AFL consisted of 12 national unions with a membership of about 150,000.

The AFL was led by **Samuel Gompers,** the tough, practical-minded president of the Cigar Makers' Union. The organization pressed for higher wages, shorter hours, better working conditions, and the right to bargain collectively with employers. In collective bargaining, unions represent workers in bargaining with management.

Although violent strikes turned public feeling against workers and unions in the late 1880s, the AFL survived and grew. By 1904 the AFL claimed more than 1.6 million members.

Women and the Unions

Many unions would not admit women workers, so some women formed their own unions. **Mary Harris Jones,** better known as Mother Jones, spent 50 years fighting for workers' rights.

In 1911 a fire broke out at the **Triangle Shirtwaist Company** factory, a crowded sweatshop

Young coal miners in Kingston, Pennsylvania

in New York City. The workers, mostly young immigrant women, could not escape from the building because the company had locked the doors to prevent employees from leaving early. Nearly 150 workers died in the fire. The disaster led the **International Ladies' Garment Workers Union** (ILGWU) to push for a safer working environment.

The Unions Act

Economic depressions in the 1870s and the 1890s led companies to fire workers and lower wages. Unions responded with large strikes that sometimes sparked violence.

Railroad Strike of 1877

Economic depression hit the nation following the Panic of 1873. To cut costs, companies forced their workers to take pay cuts. In July 1877 angry strikers burned rail yards, ripped up track, and destroyed railroad property.

The companies hired strikebreakers to replace the striking workers. After weeks of riots, federal troops restored order.

Haymarket Riot of 1886

Antilabor feeling grew stronger after a bloody clash between police and strikers in **Chicago's Haymarket Square** on May 4, 1886. Striking

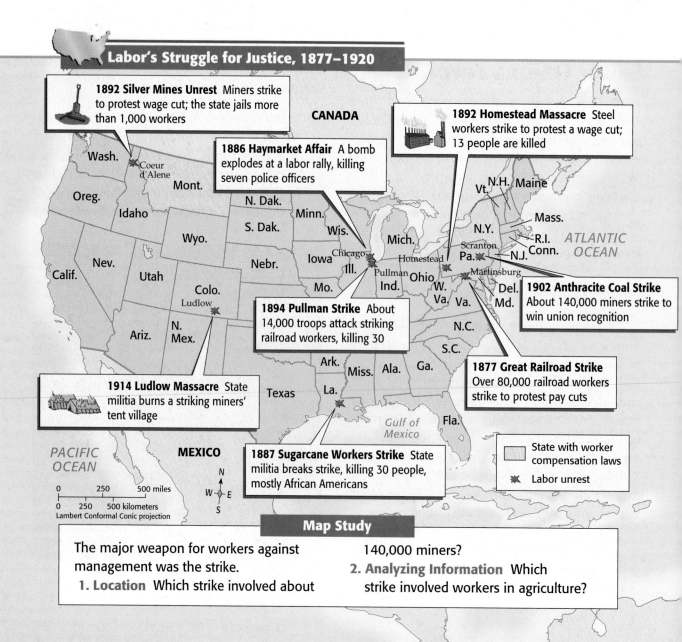

Labor's Struggle for Justice, 1877–1920

1892 Silver Mines Unrest Miners strike to protest wage cut; the state jails more than 1,000 workers

1886 Haymarket Affair A bomb explodes at a labor rally, killing seven police officers

1892 Homestead Massacre Steel workers strike to protest a wage cut; 13 people are killed

1902 Anthracite Coal Strike About 140,000 miners strike to win union recognition

1894 Pullman Strike About 14,000 troops attack striking railroad workers, killing 30

1877 Great Railroad Strike Over 80,000 railroad workers strike to protest pay cuts

1914 Ludlow Massacre State militia burns a striking miners' tent village

1887 Sugarcane Workers Strike State militia breaks strike, killing 30 people, mostly African Americans

CANADA

Wash. — Coeur d'Alene
Oreg.
Mont.
Idaho
N. Dak.
Minn.
Wyo.
S. Dak.
Wis.
Mich.
Vt. N.H. Maine
Nev.
Utah
Nebr.
Iowa Chicago Ill.
Calif.
Colo. Ludlow
Mo.
Ind. Ohio
Pullman
N.Y.
Scranton Pa. N.J. Conn. R.I. Mass.
ATLANTIC OCEAN
Homestead
Martinsburg
W. Va. Va.
Del. Md.
Ariz.
N. Mex.
Ark.
Miss. Ala. Ga.
N.C.
S.C.
Texas La.
Gulf of Mexico
Fla.

PACIFIC OCEAN
MEXICO

0   250   500 miles
0   250   500 kilometers
Lambert Conformal Conic projection

N
W—E
S

State with worker compensation laws

✳ Labor unrest

Map Study

The major weapon for workers against management was the strike.

1. Location Which strike involved about 140,000 miners?

2. Analyzing Information Which strike involved workers in agriculture?

workers from the McCormick Harvester Company gathered to protest the killings of four strikers the previous day. When police ordered the crowd to break up, an unidentified person threw a bomb that killed seven police officers. Following the **Haymarket Riot,** many middle-class Americans associated the labor movement with terrorism and disorder.

Homestead Strike of 1892

In 1892 workers went on strike at Andrew Carnegie's steel plant in **Homestead, Pennsylvania.** Plant managers had cut workers' wages, hoping to weaken the steelworkers' union. When the union called a strike, Homestead managers hired nonunion workers and brought in 300 armed guards to protect them. A fierce battle left at least 13 people dead.

Pennsylvania's governor sent the state's militia to Homestead to restore order. The plant reopened with nonunion workers, protected by the troops. After the failure of the **Homestead Strike,** the steelworkers' union dwindled.

Pullman Strike of 1894

The employees of George Pullman's railway-car plant near Chicago went on strike in May 1894, when the company cut wages. Pullman

National railroad strike of 1877

responded by closing the plant. One month later, workers in the American Railway Union supported the strikers by refusing to handle Pullman cars, paralyzing rail traffic.

Pullman and the railroad owners fought back. They persuaded U.S. Attorney General Richard Olney to obtain an injunction, or court order, to stop the union from "obstructing the railways and holding up the mails." The workers and their leader, **Eugene V. Debs,** refused to end the strike. Debs was sent to jail.

President **Grover Cleveland** sent federal troops to Chicago, and within a month the strike was over. The failure of the **Pullman Strike** dealt another major blow to the labor union movement.

Section 4 Assessment

Checking for Understanding

1. **Identify** Terence V. Powderly, Samuel Gompers, Eugene V. Debs, Pullman Strike.
2. **Define** sweatshop, trade union, collective bargaining, strikebreaker, injunction.
3. **Summarize** the reasons that workers wanted to organize into unions.

Reviewing Themes

4. **Groups and Institutions** What were the goals of the American Federation of Labor?

Critical Thinking

5. **Drawing Conclusions** Why do you think many Americans did not immediately support the labor unions?

Activity

Designing a Board Game Design a board game in which players can experience the ups and downs of factory work in the late 1800s. Include spaces such as "Workday extended to 12 hours. Miss a turn," and "Your union wins a pay hike. Collect $5."

Assessment and Activities

★ Reviewing Key Terms

On a sheet of paper, create a crossword puzzle using the following terms. Use the terms' definitions as your clues.

consolidation
standard gauge
rebate
pool
assembly line
mass production
corporation
stock
shareholder
dividend
horizontal integration
trust
monopoly
vertical integration
philanthropy
merger
sweatshop
trade union
collective bargaining
strikebreaker
injunction

★ Reviewing Key Facts

1. What improvements in railway transportation were brought about by new technology?
2. What were four of Thomas Edison's inventions?
3. What manufacturing methods did Henry Ford use to make his new automobile affordable?
4. What did the government do to control trusts and monopolies in response to pressure from the public?
5. What were the results of the Haymarket Riot of 1886?

★ Critical Thinking

Making Inferences

New transportation and communication technologies transformed the lives of the American people in the late 1800s and early 1900s.

1. How did improved communication "shrink" the country and the world?
2. How did more efficient manufacturing processes affect the average American buyer?

★ Time Line Activity

Create a time line on which you place the following events in chronological order.

- Henry Ford introduces the Model T
- Thomas Edison develops the first practical lightbulb
- Wright brothers make their first machine-powered flight
- Alexander Graham Bell invents the telephone
- Congress passes the Sherman Antitrust Act
- Rally at Haymarket ends in violence

★ Reviewing Themes

1. **Geography and History** How did the growing railroad network help American industry?
2. **Science and Technology** Describe the contributions of African American inventors in the late 1800s.
3. **Economic Factors** How did horizontal integration differ from vertical integration?
4. **Groups and Institutions** Why did workers think that forming organized labor unions would help them get what they wanted from employers?

★ Geography Activity

Study the map below and answer the questions that follow.

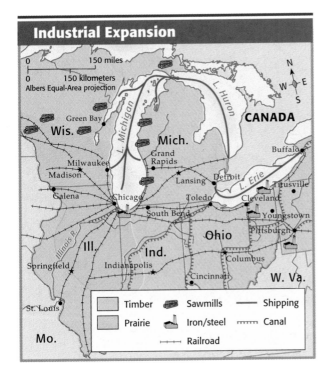

Industrial Expansion

1. **Movement** What forms of transportation moved goods into and out of this region?
2. **Human/Environment Interaction** What industry grew in the timbered regions of Wisconsin and Michigan?
3. **Location** Identify the major iron/steel manufacturing centers shown on the map.

★ Skill Practice

Reading a Time Zones Map

Study the time zones map on page 555. Use the map to answer the following questions.

1. If you traveled from Florida to California, what time zones would you cross?
2. If it is 6:00 A.M. in Maine, what time is it in Hawaii?
3. If it is 3:00 P.M. in Texas, what time is it in Alaska?

★ Cooperative Activity

History and Economics Today's corporations often control many smaller companies. With a partner choose one large corporation and research to find out what other companies are under its control. On poster board make a flowchart to show the relationship and links among some of the companies. Also include the major service or product that each company provides. Display your charts for viewing by the rest of the class.

★ Technology Activity

Using a Spreadsheet Become an imaginary shareholder in a corporation. Search for stock market data in a daily newspaper. Choose one stock to follow for a two-week period. Track the performance of the stock on a spreadsheet by marking its daily increases and decreases. Compare your spreadsheet with classmates' results and decide if you made a good investment.

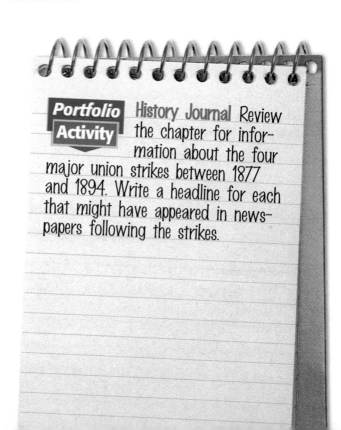

Portfolio Activity History Journal Review the chapter for information about the four major union strikes between 1877 and 1894. Write a headline for each that might have appeared in newspapers following the strikes.

Hands-On HISTORY Lab Activity

Retrieving Oil

United States industrial production in 1900 depended on abundant oil reserves. How did the oil barons retrieve oil from the earth? In this lab activity, imagine you are an oil driller who must pump as much oil as possible from a particular site.

The Way It Was

In 1543 the survivors of the De Soto expedition stopped on the Texas coast to caulk—make watertight—the seams of their leaking boats. On the shores they found a black sticky material—tar—which worked quite well. Native Americans used oil-based tar to waterproof bowls and utensils and probably used oil products for medical purposes. Pioneers used oil to grease the axles on their wagons.

In the 1840s a Canadian scientist discovered kerosene, a fuel that could be made from coal or oil. Kerosene became widely used for lamps and lanterns. People started to use oil to lubricate machinery. As the demand grew, operators eagerly began to drill for oil.

Spindletop Hill near Beaumont, Texas

 **Materials**

- clear plastic bottle with spray pump
- clear plastic tubing
- 100-ml graduated cylinder
- 1–2 cups of small, clean pebbles
- liquid detergent
- 100 ml vegetable oil
- 100 ml hot water
- 50 ml cold water
- eyedropper

Believe It Or Not!

On January 10, 1901, an oil well on Spindletop Hill in Texas began spewing mud. Then, with an explosive roar, the mud turned first to gas and then to oil. The gusher roared out nearly one-half million barrels of oil for six days before being capped.

2 What To Do

❶ The spray bottle will be your well. Place the pebbles inside the spray bottle. Insert the plastic tubing deep into the pebbles and through the opening of the spray bottle. Keep several inches of the tubing protruding out of the sprayer.

❷ Pour 100 ml of oil into your well. Seal your well. Pump as much oil as you can get out of your well into a graduated cylinder. Measure the amount.

❸ Empty the oil back into your well. Rinse your cylinder thoroughly. Pour 50 ml of cold water into your well. Observe what happens in the bottle.

❹ Again, pump out as much oil as you can. Give the oil and water time to separate in the graduated cylinder, then record the amount of oil you recovered. Empty the cylinder into a separate container.

❺ Using 50 ml of hot water, repeat Step 4.

❻ Using 50 ml of hot water and 8 drops of liquid detergent, repeat Step 4.

Step 6

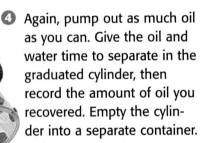

3 Lab Report

1. How many milliliters of oil did you retrieve by pumping alone?
2. What did the oil do when you added the cold water to your well? How much oil did you pump out?
3. How much oil did you pump out using hot water?
4. How much oil did you pump out using hot water and detergent?
5. **Analyzing Information** What method of pumping oil would you recommend to an oil well owner—pumping just oil or pumping using added materials such as hot or cold water? Explain.

Go a Step Further

What do you think the results would be if you used detergent alone in your well? Make a prediction.

1865–1914

Toward an Urban America

Why It's Important

The modern urban nation we live in started to take shape between 1865 and 1914. By 1914 as many Americans lived in cities as in rural areas. The cities faced many of the same problems that American cities face today—poverty, crime, inadequate housing, and conflicts among people of different backgrounds. During these years of urban growth, many aspects of modern life emerged in the cities, including daily newspapers, spectator sports, public parks, and libraries.

Chapter Themes

■ *Section 1,* Culture and Traditions
■ *Section 2,* Science and Technology
■ *Section 3,* Continuity and Change

PRIMARY SOURCES
Library   *See pages 974–975 for primary source readings to accompany Chapter 20*

HISTORY AND ART   *The Bowery at Night* **by W. Louis Sonntag, Jr.** As the United States became a nation of cities, public services expanded to serve the needs of the people.

1882
Chinese Exclusion
Act is passed

1886
Statue of Liberty
is erected

1892
Ellis Island starts
processing
immigrants

1917
Immigration Act of
1917 requires literacy

Section 1

The New Immigrants

READ TO DISCOVER . . .
▇ what opportunities and difficulties
immigrants found in the United States.
▇ how the arrival of new immigrants in the
1880s changed American society.

TERMS TO LEARN
emigrate   sweatshop
ethnic group   assimilate
steerage

The Storyteller

In the 1870s two young brothers left Italy
for America. "We were so long on the water
that we began to think we should never get to
America. . . . We were all landed on an island
and the bosses there said that Francisco and I
must go back because we had not enough
money, but a man named Bartolo came up and
told them that . . . he was our uncle and would
take care of us. . . . We came to Brooklyn to a
wooden house on Adams Street that was full of
Italians from Naples. Bartolo had a room on the
third floor and there were
fifteen men in the room,
all boarding with Bartolo.
. . . It was very hot in the
room, but we were
soon asleep, for we
were very tired."

Immigrant's ticket

Before 1865 most immigrants to the United
States—except for enslaved African Americans—came from northern and western
Europe. The greater part of these "old" immigrants were Protestant, spoke English, and blended readily into American society.

A Flood of Immigrants

★ After the Civil War, growing numbers of
immigrants made the journey to the United States. The tide of newcomers reached a peak
in 1907, when nearly 1.3 million people came to
America.

🌐 Geography

New Immigration

In the mid-1880s the pattern of immigration
started to change. Large groups of "new" immigrants arrived from eastern and southern Europe.
Greeks, Russians, Hungarians, Italians, Turks,
and Poles were among the newcomers. At the
same time, the number of "old" immigrants started to decrease. By 1907 only about 20 percent of
the immigrants came from northern and western
Europe, while 80 percent came from southern and
eastern Europe.

Many of the newcomers from eastern and
southern Europe were Catholics or Jews. Few
spoke English. Because of this, they did not blend
into American society as easily as the "old"

Picturing HISTORY Immigrants arrive in New York from Hamburg, Germany, in 1906.
Where did most immigrants to America come from after 1880?

immigrants had. Many felt like outsiders, and they clustered together in urban neighborhoods made up of people of the same nationality.

After 1900 immigration from Mexico also increased. In addition many people came to the United States from China and Japan. They, too, brought unfamiliar languages and religious beliefs and had difficulty blending into American society.

Leaving Troubles Behind

Why did so many people leave their homelands for the United States in the late 1800s and early 1900s? They were "pushed" away by difficult conditions at home and "pulled" to the United States by new opportunities.

Many people **emigrated,** or left their homelands, because of economic troubles. In Italy and Hungary, overcrowding and poverty made jobs scarce. Farmers in Croatia and Serbia could not own enough land to support their families. Sweden suffered major crop failures. New machines such as looms put many craft workers out of work.

Persecution also drove people from their homelands. In some countries the government passed laws or followed policies against certain **ethnic groups**—minorities that spoke different languages or followed different customs from most people in a country. Members of these ethnic groups often emigrated to escape discrimination or unfair laws. Many Jews fled persecution in Russia in the 1880s and came to the United States.

Seeking Opportunity

Immigrants saw the United States as a land of opportunity and jobs, plentiful and affordable land, and a chance for a better life. Although some immigrants returned to their homelands after a few years, most came to America to stay.

*F*ootnotes to History

The Price Is Right By the mid-1800s, a one-way ticket in steerage cost as little as $12 from Liverpool, England, to New York City. It cost less than $10 from Dublin, Ireland.

The Journey to America

Immigrants often had a difficult journey to America. Many had to first travel to a seaport to board a ship. Often they traveled for hundreds of miles on foot or on horseback and through foreign countries to get to the port cities.

Then came the long ocean voyage to America—12 days across the Atlantic or 60 days across the Pacific. Immigrants usually could afford only the cheapest tickets, and they traveled in steerage, cramped, noisy quarters on the lower decks.

The Statue of Liberty

Most European immigrants landed at New York City. After 1886 the magnificent sight of the **Statue of Liberty** greeted the immigrants as they sailed into **New York Harbor.** The statue, a gift from France, seemed to promise hope for a better life in the new country. On the base of the statue, the stirring words of **Emma Lazarus,** an American poet, welcomed immigrants from Europe:

66 Give me your tired, your poor,
Your huddled masses yearning to
breathe free,
The wretched refuse of your teeming shore.
Send these, the homeless, tempest-
tossed to me,
I lift my lamp beside the golden door! 99

Entering America

Bianca De Carli arrived from Italy in 1913 as a young girl. Many years later she remembered how she felt as her ship reached New York City:

66 We all trembled because of the strangeness and the confusion and the unknownness. Some were weak from no movement and exercise, and some were sick because of the smells and the unfresh air. But somehow this did not matter because we now knew it was almost over. 99

Before the new arrivals could actually pass through the "golden door" to America, they had to register at government reception centers. In the East immigrants were processed at Castle Garden, a former fort on Manhattan Island, and after 1892 at **Ellis Island** in New York Harbor. Most Asian immigrants arrived in America on the West Coast and went through the processing center on **Angel Island** in **San Francisco Bay.**

Entrance Examinations

Examiners at the centers recorded the immigrants' names—sometimes shortening or simplifying a name they found too difficult to write. The examiners asked the immigrants where they came from, their occupation, and whether they had relatives in the United States. The examiners also gave health examinations. Immigrants with contagious illnesses could be refused permission to enter the United States.

The new arrivals often found this process bewildering. Nina Goodenov, who came from Russia in 1911, later wrote:

66 It was a nightmare. After all, none of us spoke English. We had no idea where we were going and no idea what was to be done to us. . . . There were hundreds and hundreds of people and they were treated exactly like sheep. . . . It took a day and a night. . . . You had to sleep on the benches, just sitting up. 99

Arriving at Ellis Island

Picturing HISTORY Jacob Riis photographed many aspects of immigrant life in New York City. The classroom was the major place where the immigrants' children learned American ways. **How did immigrants contribute to American society?**

The Immigrant Experience

★ After passing through the reception centers, most immigrants entered the United States. Where would they go? How would they live? Some had relatives or friends to stay with and to help them find jobs. Others knew no one and would have to strike out on their own.

Finding Work

An immigrant's greatest challenge was finding work. Sometimes organizations in his or her homeland recruited workers for jobs in the United States. The organization supplied American employers with unskilled workers who worked at unloading cargo or digging ditches.

Some of America's fastest-growing industries hired immigrant workers. In the steel mills of Pittsburgh, for example, most of the common laborers in the early 1900s were immigrant men. They might work 12 hours a day, 7 days a week.

Women and Children at Work

Many immigrants, including women and children, worked in sweatshops in the garment industry. These were dark, crowded workshops where workers made clothing. The work was repetitious and hazardous, the pay low, and the hours long.

Pauline Newman, who later became an official in the International Ladies' Garment Workers Union, worked in a New York sweatshop as a child. She recalled:

❝ We started work at seven-thirty in the morning, and during the busy season we worked until nine in the evening. They didn't pay you any overtime and they didn't give you anything for supper money. Sometimes they'd give you a little apple pie if you had to work very late. ❞

Adjusting to America

In their new homes, immigrants tried to preserve some aspects of their own cultures. At the same time, most wanted to assimilate, or become part of the American culture. These two desires sometimes came into conflict.

Tensions arose between parents and children or between men and women. Some immigrants found that their American-born children had little interest in the culture of their European or Asian homeland. Most children wanted to assimilate as quickly as possible.

Language highlighted the differences between generations of families. Many immigrant parents continued to speak their original languages at home. Their children spoke English at school and with friends, but they, too, spoke their original language at home. On the other hand, many immigrants' grandchildren spoke only English.

The role of immigrant women also changed in the United States, where women generally had more freedom than women in European and Asian countries. New lifestyles conflicted with traditional ways and sometimes produced friction. Immigrant women who worked in factories and at other jobs made friends and developed interests that their families did not always understand.

Building Communities

Most of the new immigrants were from rural areas. Because they lacked the money to buy farmland in America, however, they often settled in industrial cities. With little or no education, they usually worked as unskilled laborers.

Relatives who had immigrated earlier helped new arrivals get settled, and people of the same ethnic group naturally tended to form communities. As a result neighborhoods of Jewish, Italian, Polish, Chinese, and other groups quickly developed in New York, Chicago, San Francisco, and other large cities.

The immigrants sought to re-create some of the life they had left behind. The communities they established revolved around a number of traditional institutions. Most important were the houses of worship—the churches and synagogues—where worship was conducted and holidays were celebrated as they had been in their homelands. Priests and rabbis often acted as community leaders.

The immigrants published newspapers in their native languages, opened stores and theaters, and organized social clubs. Ethnic communities and institutions helped the immigrants preserve their cultural heritage.

Native-born Americans React to Immigrants

★ Assimilation was also slowed by the attitudes of many native-born Americans. Although employers were happy to hire immigrant workers at low wages, some American-born workers resented the immigrants. These Americans feared that the immigrants would take away their jobs or drive down everyone's wages by accepting lower pay.

Anti-Immigrant Sentiment

Ethnic, religious, and racial differences contributed to tensions between Americans and the new immigrants. Some Americans argued that the new immigrants—with their foreign languages, unfamiliar religions, and distinctive customs—did not fit into American society.

People found it easy to blame immigrants for increasing crime, unemployment, and other problems in American society. The **nativist** movement, for example, had opposed immigration since the 1830s. Nativism gained strength in the late 1800s. Some Americans formed groups to restrict the rights of immigrants. Some communities passed

★ **Picturing HISTORY** An employment agency in New York City attracts immigrants with its advertisements for jobs. **What kinds of jobs did most immigrants hold?**

laws banning immigrants from holding certain jobs and denying them other rights. Jewish immigrants, for example, were denied admission to certain universities. In addition, immigrants faced physical attack. In 1880, for example, white citizens of Denver, Colorado, attacked Chinese residents and destroyed many of their homes and businesses. Calls for restrictions on immigration mounted.

New Immigration Laws

Lawmakers responded quickly to the tide of anti-immigrant feeling. In 1882 Congress passed the first law to limit immigration—the **Chinese Exclusion Act.** This law prohibited Chinese workers from entering the United States for 10 years. Congress extended the law in 1892 and again in 1902.

In 1908 the federal government and Japan came to a "gentleman's agreement." The Japanese agreed to limit the number of immigrants to the United States, while the Americans pledged fair treatment for Japanese Americans already in the United States.

Other immigration laws affected immigrants from all nations. An 1882 law made each immigrant pay a tax and also barred criminals from entering the country. In 1897 Congress passed a bill requiring immigrants to be able to read and write in some language. Although President Cleveland vetoed the bill as unfair, some years later Congress passed the **Immigration Act of 1917,** which included a similar literacy requirement.

Immigrants' Contributions

Despite some anti-immigrant sentiment, many Americans—including **Grace Abbott** and **Julia Clifford Lathrop,** who helped found the Immigrants' Protective League—spoke out in support of immigration. These Americans recognized that the United States was a nation of immigrants and that the newcomers made lasting contributions to their new society.

The new immigrants supplied the country's growing industries with the workers that were necessary for economic growth. At the same time, the new immigrants and their children—like the old immigrants before them—helped shape American life. They gave the nation its major religious groups—Protestants, Catholics, and Jews. While becoming part of the society around them, they enriched that society with their own customs and cultures, language and literature.

The effects of immigration were most visible in the cities, with their fast-growing ethnic neighborhoods. The flow of immigrants was one of the factors that transformed America's cities in the late 1800s and the early 1900s.

Section 1 Assessment

Checking for Understanding

1. **Identify** Emma Lazarus, Ellis Island, Angel Island, Chinese Exclusion Act, Immigration Act of 1917.
2. **Define** emigrate, ethnic group, steerage, sweatshop, assimilate.
3. **Explain** how the pattern of immigration changed in the 1880s.

Reviewing Themes

4. **Culture and Traditions** What were some of the cultural differences that immigrants had to adjust to in the United States?

Critical Thinking

5. **Identifying Central Issues** Why do you think some Americans blamed the "new" immigrants for many of society's problems?

Activity

Making a Collage Create a collage illustrating the origins of immigrants who came to the United States after 1880. Clip photographs from advertisements and newsmagazines to make your collage.

Reading a Line Graph

Graphs are a way of showing numbers visually, making them easier to read and understand. Graphs are often used to compare changes over time or differences between places, groups of people, or related events.

Learning the Skill

On a line graph, numbers usually appear along the left side of the graph, or the vertical axis. Time is usually shown along the bottom of the graph, or the horizontal axis. A line on the graph shows whether the numbers go up or down over time. Sometimes a graph contains more than one line, recording two or more related quantities.

To read a line graph, follow these steps:
- Read the title of the graph.
- Read the information on the horizontal axis and the vertical axis.
- Study the points where the line intersects the grid on the line graph. This step tells you what amount existed at a given time.
- Study the changes over time that the line on the graph illustrates. Look for increases, decreases, and sudden shifts.
- Draw conclusions from the statistics presented. What trends or patterns appear?

Practicing the Skill

Study the line graph on this page and answer the following questions.
1. What is the subject of this line graph?
2. What information is presented on the horizontal axis? On the vertical axis?
3. In about what year did immigration from northern and western Europe peak?
4. In about what year was immigration from Asia, Africa, and South America the lowest?

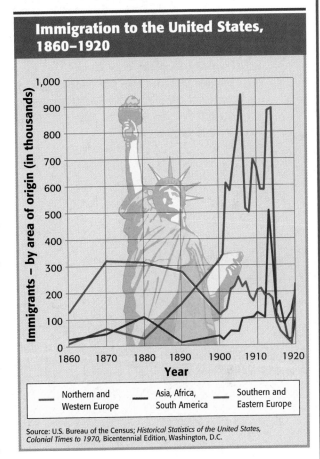

Immigration to the United States, 1860–1920

—— Northern and Western Europe	—— Asia, Africa, South America	—— Southern and Eastern Europe

Source: U.S. Bureau of the Census; *Historical Statistics of the United States, Colonial Times to 1970*, Bicentennial Edition, Washington, D.C.

5. During what two decades did immigration from southern and eastern Europe peak?

4 In 1890 Lee Chew (below) headed for Chicago. Here he stands in front of the Chinese Merchants Association, which later became the Chinatown City Hall. "I had a laundry for three years," he wrote, and "increased my capital to $2,500. After that I was four years in Detroit." In 1897 he returned to China for a year.

1 Chinese bound for the United States crowded the decks of steamships after the discovery of gold in California in 1848. Like many seeking their fortunes, 16-year-old Lee Chew left his farm in China and booked passage on a steamer about 1880. When he and other Chinese immigrants arrived in San Francisco, they confronted a great wave of anti-Asian feeling.

CANADA

Calif.　Nev.　Wyo.

Nebr.　Chicag

San Francisco

Utah　Colo.　Kans.　Ill.

Mo.

CHINA

2 In San Francisco's Chinese quarter, immigrants ran markets, laundries, and other small shops. Chew worked for an American family and saved his earnings for two years. "Chinese laundrymen [like me] were taught by American women," he said. "There are no laundries in China."

MEXICO

PACIFIC OCEAN

3 With his savings Lee Chew and a partner opened a laundry serving railroad crews "in a town about 500 miles" from San Francisco. For three years the partners followed Chinese and Irish immigrants, like those above, who built the early railroads. Then the two moved on to the mines, where rough miners "came into our [laundry] to shoot and steal shirts...."

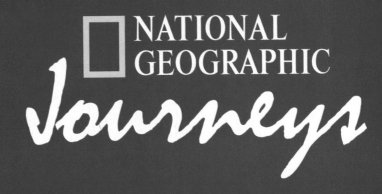

5 In 1898, after opening a laundry in Buffalo, New York, Chew moved on to New York City's Chinatown (above). There Lee made his fortune in an import store where he sold silks, teas, clothes, and Chinese food. But he still had to battle anti-Asian prejudice.

An Immigrant's Journey

> **"** My father gave me $100, and I ... got steerage passage on a steamer.... I did not like [the food] at all.... The thought of what [it] might be made of, by the wicked wizards of the ship, made me ill. Of the great power of these people I saw many signs. The engines that moved the ship were wonderful monsters, strong enough to lift mountains. When I got to San Francisco ... I was half-starved, because I was afraid to eat the provisions of the barbarians.... A man got me work as a house servant ... and my start was the same as that of almost all the Chinese in this country. **"**

—From recollections of Lee Chew, published in Plain Folk: The Life Stories of Undistinguished Americans by David Katzman and William Tuttle, 1982.

1870		1880			1890

1873
Twain's *The Gilded Age* is published

1879
The Salvation Army originates

1883
The Brooklyn Bridge opens

1884
First skyscraper constructed in Chicago

Section 2

Moving to the City

READ TO DISCOVER . . .

- how American cities grew and changed.
- what life was like in the cities.
- what problems cities faced and how people tried to solve them.

TERMS TO LEARN

tenement
slum
suburb

The Gilded Age
settlement house

The Storyteller

A train pulling into Chicago in 1884 carried a young passenger named Hamlin Garland. For Garland, who had grown up on a farm, the big city was a bewildering sight. Garland later became famous for his stories about the Midwest. In one novel he described his feeling of dismay when he first saw Chicago. "The mere thought of a million people stunned my imagination." Garland wondered, "How can so many people find a living in one place?"

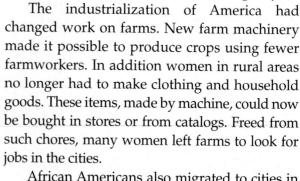

Migrant's suitcase and Bibles

American cities grew rapidly after the Civil War. In 1870, 1 American in 4 lived in cities with 2,500 or more people. By 1910 nearly half of the American population were city dwellers. The United States was changing from a rural to an urban nation.

🌐 Geography

Growth of Cities

⭐ Immigrants played an enormous part in the growth of cities. In major urban centers such as New York, Detroit, and Chicago, immigrants and their children made up 80 percent or more of the population in 1890.

Native-born Americans also contributed to urban growth. Americans moved in huge numbers from farming areas to cities, looking for jobs.

The industrialization of America had changed work on farms. New farm machinery made it possible to produce crops using fewer farmworkers. In addition women in rural areas no longer had to make clothing and household goods. These items, made by machine, could now be bought in stores or from catalogs. Freed from such chores, many women left farms to look for jobs in the cities.

African Americans also migrated to cities in large numbers. The vast majority of the country's African American population lived in the rural South in great poverty. Many African Americans began moving to Southern cities in search of jobs and to escape debt, injustice, or discrimination.

After 1914 a large number of African Americans moved to Northern cities, which offered more jobs in industry and manufacturing than Southern cities did. Many African Americans also hoped to find less discrimination and violence in the North.

★ **Picturing HISTORY** These children lived in a Pittsburgh neighborhood. An advertisement (inset) promotes the sale of a middle-class home in the Chicago suburbs. **How did the dwellings of poor and middle-class Americans differ during the industrial age?**

Transportation and Resources

America's expanding railroad network fed the growth of the cities. Railroads helped people move to the cities and transported the raw materials for industry. Trains carried cattle to Chicago and **Kansas City,** making these cities great meatpacking centers.

Some cities flourished because of nearby resources. **Pittsburgh** developed rapidly as a center for iron and steel manufacturing because both iron ore and coal—to fuel the industry's huge furnaces—were found in the area.

Seaports such as **New York** and **San Francisco** developed as American trade with the rest of the world increased. In addition the immigrant population of these cities provided a large pool of workers who were available for low wages.

City Life

★ Cities were exciting places that offered jobs, stores, and entertainment. But there was also substandard housing and desperate poverty. The gap between the rich and the poor was staggering.

Tenement Living

People poured into the cities faster than housing could be built to accomodate them. In the biggest, most crowded cities, the poorest residents—including most immigrants—lived in tenements. Originally a tenement was simply a building in which several families rented rooms. By the late 1800s, however, a tenement had come to mean an apartment building in the slums—poor, run-down urban neighborhoods.

Tenements had many small, dark rooms. One young immigrant from Poland spoke of living in the dimly lit rooms in the back of a New York City tenement:

Footnotes to History

*F*ootnotes to History

A Cosmopolitan City By 1900, New York City had more Italians than the cities of Florence, Genoa, and Venice, Italy, put together. Almost as many Irish lived there as in Dublin, Ireland. And more Russians lived in New York City than in Kiev, Russia.

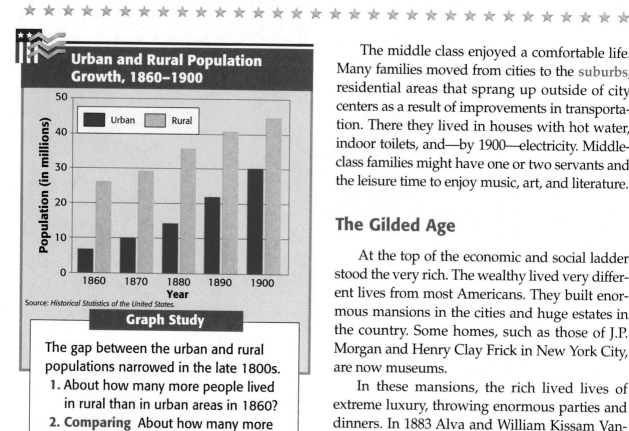

Urban and Rural Population Growth, 1860–1900

Source: *Historical Statistics of the United States.*

Graph Study

The gap between the urban and rural populations narrowed in the late 1800s.

1. About how many more people lived in rural than in urban areas in 1860?
2. **Comparing** About how many more people lived in urban areas in 1900 than in 1860?

> ❝We would so like to live in the front, but we can't pay the rent. . . . Why, they have the sun in there. When the door is opened the light comes right in your face.❞

Three, four, or more people lived in each room. Usually several families had to share a cold-water tap and a toilet. Few tenement houses had hot water or bathtubs. A government inspector wrote of the "filthy and rotten tenements" of the Chicago slums in 1896, where children filled "every nook, eating and sleeping in every windowsill, pouring in and out of every door."

Middle-Class Comfort

The cities also had a growing middle class. The middle class included the families of professional people such as doctors, lawyers, and ministers. An increasing number of managers and salaried office clerks also became part of the middle class.

The middle class enjoyed a comfortable life. Many families moved from cities to the suburbs, residential areas that sprang up outside of city centers as a result of improvements in transportation. There they lived in houses with hot water, indoor toilets, and—by 1900—electricity. Middle-class families might have one or two servants and the leisure time to enjoy music, art, and literature.

The Gilded Age

At the top of the economic and social ladder stood the very rich. The wealthy lived very different lives from most Americans. They built enormous mansions in the cities and huge estates in the country. Some homes, such as those of J.P. Morgan and Henry Clay Frick in New York City, are now museums.

In these mansions, the rich lived lives of extreme luxury, throwing enormous parties and dinners. In 1883 Alva and William Kissam Vanderbilt gave a party for more than 1,000 guests at their New York mansion. The party was estimated to have cost $250,000—equal to about $3 million today.

Mark Twain and Charles Dudley Warner published a novel in 1873 called *The Gilded Age.* The name—which refers to something covered with a thin layer of gold—became associated with America of the late 1800s. The Gilded Age suggested both the extravagant wealth of the time and the terrible poverty that lay underneath.

Cities in Crisis

The rapid growth of the cities produced serious problems. Among these were overcrowding, public health dangers, and crime.

Living Conditions

The terrible overcrowding in tenement districts created sanitation and health problems. Garbage and horse manure accumulated in city streets, and the sewers could not handle the flow of human waste. Filth created a breeding ground for disease.

Diseases spread rapidly through the crowded districts. In a poor Chicago neighborhood in 1900, many babies died—of whooping cough, diphtheria, or measles—before their first birthday. A section of New York was called the "lung block" because so many residents had tuberculosis.

In an effort to control disease, New York City began to screen schoolchildren for contagious diseases and to provide visiting nurses to mothers with young children. The city also established public health clinics for those who could not pay for medical care.

Urban Crime

The poverty in the cities inevitably led to crime. Orphaned and homeless children sometimes resorted to picking pockets and other minor crimes to survive. Gangs roaming the poor neighborhoods committed more serious crimes. **Jacob Riis,** a New York journalist, reported:

66 The gang is an institution in New York. The police deny its existence while nursing the bruises received in nightly battles with it. . . . The gang is the ripe fruit of tenement-house growth. It was born there. 99

Seeking Solutions

The problems of the cities did not go unnoticed. Many dedicated people worked to improve urban life and help the poor.

In 1890 Jacob Riis wrote *How the Other Half Lives.* With words and photographs, Riis's book showed the terrible conditions of the tenements. His book helped establish housing codes to prevent the worst abuses.

Religious groups aided the poor. The **Salvation Army,** started in the United States in 1879, set up soup kitchens to feed the hungry and opened shelters for homeless people. Some religious

The New American City

Child's doll

Seed-beaded handbag

What Was It Like? The growth of American cities during the late 1800s and early 1900s changed the way people lived. **How do each of the items pictured here reflect American life during this period?**

Blue wool dress, c. 1885

HISTORY AND ART

Concert in Central Park by Jerome Myers Central Park in New York City opened in 1859. It soon became a popular place for recreational activities. **Why were public parks designed and built in American cities during the late 1800s?**

orders helped the poor in orphanages, prisons, and hospitals. Organizations such as the **YMCA** (Young Men's Christian Association) and **YWCA** (Young Women's Christian Association) offered recreation centers where city youngsters could meet and play.

Settlement Houses

The poor also received assistance from establishments called settlement houses. The settlement house movement had spread to the United States from Britain. Located in poor neighborhoods, settlement houses provided medical care, playgrounds, nurseries, and libraries as well as classes in English, music, and arts and crafts. Settlement workers—mostly women—also tried to get better police protection, garbage removal, and public parks for poor districts.

One of the most famous settlement houses was Chicago's **Hull House,** founded by **Jane Addams** in 1889. Addams explained:

66 We were ready to perform the humblest neighborhood services.

Jane Adddms

We were asked to wash the new-born babies, and to prepare the dead for burial, to nurse the sick, and to 'mind the children.' 99

The Changing City

⭐ Urban growth led to important, new developments. In the late 1800s, cities saw the introduction of a new type of building, new kinds of public transportation, and public parks.

Building Up—Not Out

Because of the limited space in cities, imaginative architects began building upward rather than outward. In the 1860s architects started to use iron frames to strengthen the walls of buildings. Iron supports—together with the safety elevator that **Elisha Otis** invented in 1852—made taller buildings possible.

In 1884 **William LeBaron Jenney** constructed a 10-story office building in Chicago. Supported by an iron-and-steel frame, it was the world's first **skyscraper.** Architect **Louis Sullivan** gave style to the skyscraper. "It must be every inch a proud and soaring thing, rising in sheer exultation," he said. Sullivan and his colleagues changed the face of America's cities.

Soon people built even higher structures. New York's **Woolworth Building,** completed in 1913, soared an incredible 55 stories—nearly 800 feet (273 m) high. People called the building the Cathedral of Commerce.

Some people looked to reshape the urban landscape. A group known as the "City Beautiful" movement believed city dwellers should be able to enjoy the beauties of nature. **Frederick Law Olmsted,** a leader in this movement, designed New York's Central Park as well as several parks in Boston.

New Forms of Transportation

As cities grew, people needed new means of transportation. Mark Twain complained in 1867 that

❝ New York is too large. You cannot accomplish anything . . . without devoting a whole day to it. . . . The distances are too great. ❞

Streetcars, which horses pulled on tracks, provided public transportation at the time. Horses were slow, however, and left piles of manure. In 1873 San Francisco began construction of cable-car lines. A large underground cable powered by a motor at one end of the rail line moved passengers along. In 1888 Richmond, Virginia, pioneered the use of the trolley car, a motorized train that was powered by electricity supplied through overhead cables. In 1897 Boston opened the nation's first subway, or underground railway.

Building Bridges

Bridge construction provided another improvement in urban transportation. Many American cities were divided or bounded by rivers. Using new construction technology, architects and engineers designed huge steel bridges to link sections of cities. The 520-foot (156-m) **Eads Bridge** across the Mississippi River in St. Louis opened in 1873. Ten years later New York's majestic **Brooklyn Bridge,** 1,600 feet (488 m) long, connected Manhattan and Brooklyn. Both bridges remain in use today.

The new forms of transportation not only helped people travel within the cities, but they also helped the cities grow. Middle-class suburbs developed along train or trolley lines stretching away from city centers. People who moved out of the city centers could easily travel downtown to work or shop.

The increase in immigration and the growth of the cities went hand in hand with other changes in American life. Education, culture, and recreation were changing too.

★ ★ ★ ★ ★ **Section 2 Assessment** ★ ★ ★ ★ ★

Checking for Understanding
1. **Identify** Jacob Riis, Jane Addams, Elisha Otis, Louis Sullivan, Frederick Law Olmsted.
2. **Define** tenement, slum, suburb, The Gilded Age, settlement house.
3. **List** three serious problems facing American cities in the late 1800s.

Reviewing Themes
4. **Science and Technology** What improvements in transportation in the late 1800s

helped cities and suburbs to grow?

Critical Thinking
5. **Analyzing Information** How did the efforts of religious groups help those living in poverty?

Activity

Creating a Postcard Imagine that you were an immigrant living in New York City in the early 1900s. Draw the front of a postcard that shows a scene of the city.

1862
Morrill Act
is passed

1879
Carlisle Indian
Industrial School
is founded

1881
Booker T. Washington
opens the Tuskegee
Institute

1883
Joseph Pulitzer
purchases the
New York *World*

Section 3

A Changing Culture

READ TO DISCOVER . . .
- how education became more widely available to Americans.
- what new trends shaped American literature.
- how Americans spent their hours of leisure time.

TERMS TO LEARN

land-grant college   regionalism
yellow journalism   ragtime
realism   vaudeville

Storyteller

Mary Antin, a young girl who came to the United States from Russia in 1894, never forgot her first day of school. "Father himself conducted us to school. He would not have delegated that mission to the president of the United States." For her father, Mary explained, education was "the essence of American opportunity, the treasure no thief could touch, not even misfortune or poverty. . . . The door stood open for every one of us."

A student's award

Most Americans in 1865 had attended school for an average of only four years. Government and business leaders and reformers believed that for the nation to progress, the people needed more schooling. Toward the end of the 1800s, the "treasure" of education became more widely available to Americans.

Expanding Education

By 1914 nearly every state required children to have at least some schooling. More than 80 percent of all children between the ages of 5 and 17 were enrolled in elementary and secondary schools.

Public Schools

The expansion of public education was particularly notable in high schools. The number of public high schools increased from 100 in 1860 to 6,000 in 1900 to 12,000 in 1914. Despite this huge increase, however, only a small percentage of teenagers attended high schools. Boys often went to work to help their families instead of attending school. The majority of high school students were girls.

The benefits of a public school education were not shared equally by everyone. In the South many African Americans received little or no education. In many parts of the country, African American children had no choice but to attend segregated elementary and secondary schools.

Around 1900 a new philosophy of education emerged in the United States. Supporters of this "progressive education" wanted to shape students' characters and teach them good citizenship as well as facts. They also believed children should learn through the use of "hands-on" activities. These ideas had the greatest effect in elementary schools. **John Dewey,** the leading spokesperson for progressive education, criticized schools for overemphasizing memorization of knowledge. Instead, Dewey argued, schools should relate learning to the interests, problems, and concerns of students.

Higher Education

Colleges and universities also changed and expanded. An 1862 law called the **Morrill Act** gave the states large amounts of federal land that could be sold to raise money for education. The states used these funds to start dozens of schools called land-grant colleges. Wealthy individuals also established and supported colleges and universities. Some schools were named for the donors—for example, Cornell University for Ezra Cornell and Stanford University for Leland Stanford.

Women and Higher Education

In 1865 only a handful of American colleges admitted women. The new land-grant schools admitted women students, as did new women's colleges—Vassar, Smith, Wellesley, and Bryn Mawr—founded in the late 1800s. By 1890 women could attend a wide range of schools, and by 1910 almost 40 percent of all American college students were women.

Minorities and Higher Education

Some new colleges, such as Hampton Institute in Virginia, provided higher education for African Americans and Native Americans. Howard University in Washington, D.C., founded shortly after the Civil War, had a largely African American student body.

One Hampton Institute student, **Booker T. Washington,** became an educator. In 1881 Washington founded the Tuskegee Institute in Alabama to train teachers and to provide practical education for African Americans.

Schools for Native Americans

Reservation schools and boarding schools also opened to train Native Americans for jobs. The Carlisle Indian Industrial School in Pennsylvania was founded in 1879, and similar schools opened in the West. Although these schools provided Native Americans with training for jobs in industry, they also isolated Native Americans from their tribal traditions. Sometimes, boarding schools were located hundreds of miles away from a student's family.

 Picturing HISTORY Scientist George Washington Carver (center) supervises students at Tuskegee Institute. In 1974 Congress established the Tuskegee Institute National Historical Site, which includes the George Washington Carver Museum. The school became Tuskegee University in 1985. **What was the goal of the Tuskegee Institute?**

A Nation of Readers

![star icon] As opportunities for education grew, a growing number of Americans became interested in reading. Public libraries opened across the nation, and new magazines and newspapers were created for the reading public.

Public Libraries

In 1881 **Andrew Carnegie,** the wealthy steel industrialist, made an extraordinary announcement. He pledged to build a public library in any city that would agree to pay its operating costs. In the next 30 years, Carnegie donated more than $30 million to found more than 2,000 libraries throughout the world. With gifts from Carnegie and others and the efforts of state and local governments, every state in the Union established free public libraries.

Spreading the News

Technological advances in printing, paper making, and communications made it possible to publish a daily paper for a large number of readers. The growing cities provided readers for the newspapers.

In 1883 **Joseph Pulitzer** purchased the New York World and created a new kind of newspaper. The paper grabbed the reader's attention with illustrations, cartoons, and sensational stories with huge, scary headlines—such as "ANOTHER MURDERER TO HANG." Under Pulitzer's management, the *World* built up its circulation to more than 1 million readers every day.

Other newspapers soon imitated Pulitzer's style. **William Randolph Hearst's** New York *Morning Journal* became even more successful than the *World,* attracting readers by exaggerating the dramatic or gruesome aspects of stories. This style of sensational writing became known as yellow journalism—a name that came from the paper's popular comic strip, "The Yellow Kid."

Ethnic and minority newspapers thrived as well. By 1900 there were 6 daily Jewish-language newspapers operating in New York City. African Americans started more than 1,000 newspapers between 1865 and 1900.

More magazines took advantage of printing improvements and mass circulation techniques to reach a national market. Between 1865 and 1900, the number of magazines in the United States rose from about 700 to 5,000. Some magazines of that era—the *Atlantic Monthly, Harper's,* and *Ladies' Home Journal*—are still published today.

Changes in Literature

Many writers of the late 1800s and the early 1900s explored new themes and subjects. Their approach to literature was called realism because they sought to describe the real lives of people of the time. Related to realism was regionalism, writing that focused on a particular region of the country.

Mark Twain was a realist and a regionalist. Many of his books, including *Adventures of Huckleberry Finn* and *The Adventures of Tom Sawyer,* are set along the Mississippi River, where Twain grew up. In *Life on the Mississippi,* Twain described the excitement created

★ **Picturing HISTORY** Glossy magazines, such as the *Woman's Home Companion,* combined stories and feature articles with appealing advertisements. **How were magazines able to reach a national market?**

by the arrival of a steamboat in Hannibal, Missouri, his hometown:

> ❝ Assembled there, the people fasten their eyes upon the coming boat as upon a wonder they are seeing for the first time. And the boat *is* rather a handsome sight, too. She is long and sharp and trim and pretty. . . . The captain lifts his hand, a bell rings, the wheels stop; then they turn back, churning the water to foam, and the steamer is at rest. ❞

Stephen Crane wrote about city slums in *Maggie* and about the Civil War in *The Red Badge of Courage.* In books such as *The Call of the Wild* and *The Sea Wolf,* **Jack London** portrayed the lives of miners and hunters in the far Northwest. **Edith Wharton** described the joys and sorrows of the upper-class Easterners in *The House of Mirth* and *The Age of Innocence.*

Paul Laurence Dunbar, the son of former slaves, wrote poetry and novels that used the dialects and folktales of Southern African Americans. Dunbar was one of the first African American writers to gain fame worldwide.

Paperback Books

Paperback books appeared for the first time in the late 1800s, and these inexpensive books helped expand the reading public. Many paperbacks featured lively adventure tales or stories of athletic boys and girls.

Horatio Alger wrote a successful series of young adult books with such titles as *Work and Win* and *Luck and Pluck.* Based on the idea that hard work and honesty brought success, Alger's books sold about 40 million copies.

Art and Music

★ For most of the 1800s, the work of American artists and musicians reflected a European influence. After the Civil War, Americans began to develop a uniquely American style.

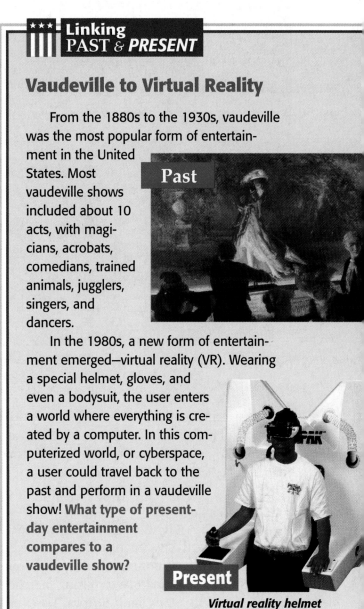

★★★ **Linking**
PAST & PRESENT

Vaudeville to Virtual Reality

From the 1880s to the 1930s, vaudeville was the most popular form of entertainment in the United States. Most vaudeville shows included about 10 acts, with magicians, acrobats, comedians, trained animals, jugglers, singers, and dancers.

Past

In the 1980s, a new form of entertainment emerged—virtual reality (VR). Wearing a special helmet, gloves, and even a bodysuit, the user enters a world where everything is created by a computer. In this computerized world, or cyberspace, a user could travel back to the past and perform in a vaudeville show! **What type of present-day entertainment compares to a vaudeville show?**

Present

Virtual reality helmet

American Artists

Some American painters pursued realist themes. **Thomas Eakins** painted the human anatomy and surgical operations. One of Eakins's students, **Henry Tanner**, depicted warm family scenes of African Americans in the South. **Frederic Remington** portrayed the American West, focusing on subjects such as cowhands and Native Americans. **Winslow Homer** painted Southern farmers, Adirondack campers, and stormy sea scenes. **James Whistler**'s *Arrangement in Grey and Black*, commonly known as *Whistler's Mother*, is one of the best-known American paintings. **Mary**

HISTORY AND ART

Girls with Lobster by Winslow Homer Homer painted scenes of people enjoying the New Jersey and New England seashores. **What themes did American painters pursue in their works?**

Cassatt was influential in the French Impressionist school of painting. Impressionists tried to capture the play of light, color, and patterns as they made immediate impressions on the senses.

Music in America

More distinctively American kinds of music were also becoming popular. Bandleader **John Philip Sousa** composed many rousing marches, including "The Stars and Stripes Forever." African American musicians in **New Orleans** in the late 1800s developed an entirely new kind of music—jazz. **Jazz** combined elements of work songs, gospel music, spirituals, and African rhythms. Related to jazz was ragtime music. For about 20 years, beginning around the turn of the century, ragtime—with its complex rhythms—was the dominant force in popular music. One of the best-known ragtime composers is **Scott**

Joplin. He wrote "Maple Leaf Rag" and many other well-known works.

The symphony orchestras of New York, Boston, and Philadelphia—all founded before 1900—were among the world's finest. Great singers and conductors came from all over the world to perform at New York's Metropolitan Opera House.

Leisure Time

Although sweatshop workers labored long hours for six or even seven days a week, middle-class people and even some factory workers enjoyed increasing amounts of leisure time. Unlike round-the-clock farmwork, professional and industrial jobs gave people hours and even days of free time. Americans developed new forms of recreation for their leisure time.

---

*F*ootnotes to History

The Olympics The first Olympics were held in 776 B.C. to celebrate amateur sports. In 1896, the first modern games were held in Athens, Greece. Women first competed in the Olympics in 1900.

The World of Sports

A version of baseball was played as early as the 1830s. After the Civil War, baseball and other sports—including football, basketball, and boxing—gained popularity. Leagues of sports teams were organized in the late 1800s, and they drew large audiences for the time. Attending these **spectator sports** and rooting for the home team or a local star became a favorite pastime.

Improvements in the bicycle in the late 1800s helped bicycle riding take the country by storm. One romantic song celebrated the bicycle:

❝ It won't be a stylish marriage,
   I can't afford a carriage,
   But you'll look sweet on the seat of a
   bicycle built for two. ❞

Theatrical Entertainment

Large cities had many theaters. Plays performed ranged from serious dramas by Shakespeare to vaudeville shows, variety shows with dancing, singing, comedy, and magic acts. Many people could afford the price of a ticket, and in the early 1900s, vaudeville offered the most popular shows in town. The circus also attracted large crowds. In 1910 the United States had about 80 traveling circuses.

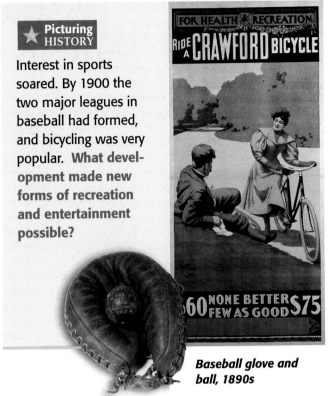

★ **Picturing HISTORY**

Interest in sports soared. By 1900 the two major leagues in baseball had formed, and bicycling was very popular. **What development made new forms of recreation and entertainment possible?**

Baseball glove and ball, 1890s

Early Movies

Thomas Edison invented "moving pictures" in the 1880s. The "movies" soon became enormously popular. Some theaters, called nickelodeons, charged 5 cents to see short films. The nickelodeons were the beginning of today's multimillion-dollar film industry, one of the most influential forms of mass communication in history.

Section 3 Assessment

★ ★ ★ ★ ★   ★ ★ ● ★ ★ ★

Checking for Understanding
1. **Identify** Booker T. Washington, Andrew Carnegie, Joseph Pulitzer, Paul Laurence Dunbar, Mary Cassatt.
2. **Define** land-grant college, yellow journalism, realism, regionalism, ragtime, vaudeville.
3. **Summarize** the new philosophy of education that emerged around 1900.

Reviewing Themes
4. **Continuity and Change** What sparked an increase in the number of newspapers, magazines, and books in the late 1800s?

Critical Thinking
5. **Determining Cause and Effect** Explain the connection between leisure time and development of the arts.

Activity

Making a Motion Picture Create your own moving picture by making a series of drawings on 2-inch by 4-inch slips of paper. Staple the slips of paper together on one side, then flip through them slowly to view your motion picture.

Assessment and Activities

★ Reviewing Key Terms

On a sheet of paper, define the following terms:

ethnic group
assimilate
tenement
suburb
The Gilded Age
settlement house
land-grant college
yellow journalism
realism
ragtime
vaudeville

★ Reviewing Key Facts

1. Why did so many people want to leave their homelands to immigrate to the United States in the late 1800s and early 1900s?
2. How did overcrowding in the cities affect public health?
3. Describe some of the ways in which reformers tried to help the urban poor.
4. What was the purpose of the Morrill Act?
5. What new forms of music emerged during the late 1800s and early 1900s?

★ Critical Thinking

Synthesizing Information

The flood of immigrants who came to the United States during the late 1800s and early 1900s were searching for new opportunities.

1. Do you think the United States government should have allowed so many immigrants into the country at that time? Why or why not?
2. What advice would you have given to a person who wanted to come to America at that time?

★ Time Line Activity

Create a time line on which you place the following events in chronological order.

- Jane Addams founds Hull House
- Ellis Island opens as immigrant center
- Salvation Army established
- World's first skyscraper completed
- First subway built
- Joseph Pulitzer purchases New York *World*

★ Skill Practice Activity

Reading a Line Graph

Study the line graph below, then answer the questions that follow.

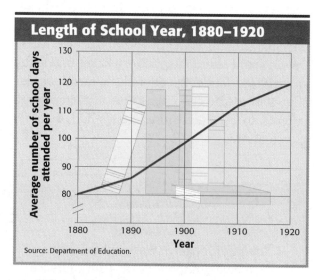

Length of School Year, 1880–1920

Average number of school days attended per year

Year

Source: Department of Education.

1. What is the subject of this line graph?
2. What information is presented on the horizontal axis? On the vertical axis?
3. How many years does this graph cover?
4. What are the time intervals on the horizontal axis?
5. About how many days were students in school in 1880?
6. What was the average number of school days in 1920?
7. What trend is shown in this line graph?

⭐ Technology Activity

Using a Word Processor Research the life of one of the writers, artists, or musicians discussed in Section 3. Using your word processor, prepare a one-page biography of that person to share with the class.

⭐ Geography Activity

Study this map and answer the questions below.

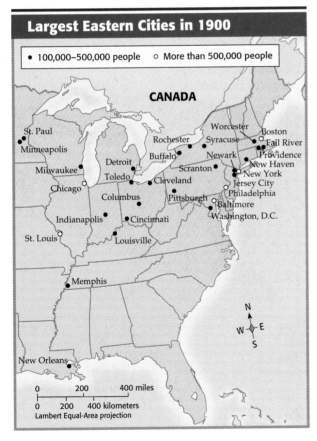

Largest Eastern Cities in 1900

● 100,000–500,000 people   ○ More than 500,000 people

1. **Location** Which cities had more than 500,000 people in 1900?
2. **Place** About how many people lived in Washington, D.C., in 1900?
3. **Location** What is similar about the location of the cities with more than 500,000 people?

⭐ Reviewing Themes

1. **Culture and Traditions** How did immigrants try to preserve their cultural heritage?
2. **Science and Technology** Why did so many people move from farms to cities in the late 1800s and early 1900s?
3. **Continuity and Change** What new styles of writing did American authors adopt during this period?

⭐ Cooperative Activity

History and Citizenship Immigrants who want to become United States citizens today must pass a written test to qualify. Many of the questions on the test deal with United States history and customs. Work with members of your group to design a 15-question test that you think prospective citizens should be required to pass. After completing your test, exchange it with another group. Have each member of the group take the test. Score each test and report the results to the class.

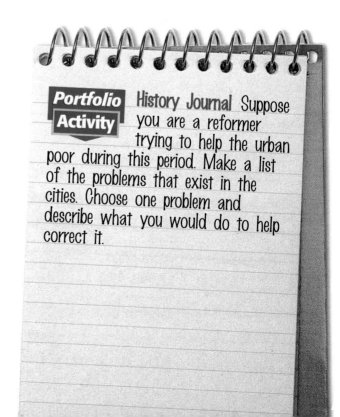

Portfolio Activity History Journal Suppose you are a reformer trying to help the urban poor during this period. Make a list of the problems that exist in the cities. Choose one problem and describe what you would do to help correct it.

Unit 8

Reform, Expansion, and War

1865–1920

"Speak softly and carry a big stick; you will go far."

—THEODORE ROOSEVELT, 1901

*inter*NET CONNECTION

To learn more about this period in history, visit the Glencoe Social Studies Web Site at **www.glencoe.com** for information, activities, and links to other sites.

MAPPING *America*

Portfolio Activity Trace a map of the world onto a piece of paper. As you read this unit about expansion and war, draw and shade in the boundaries of the countries discussed. Add the names of the countries mentioned, then label the events that occurred there.

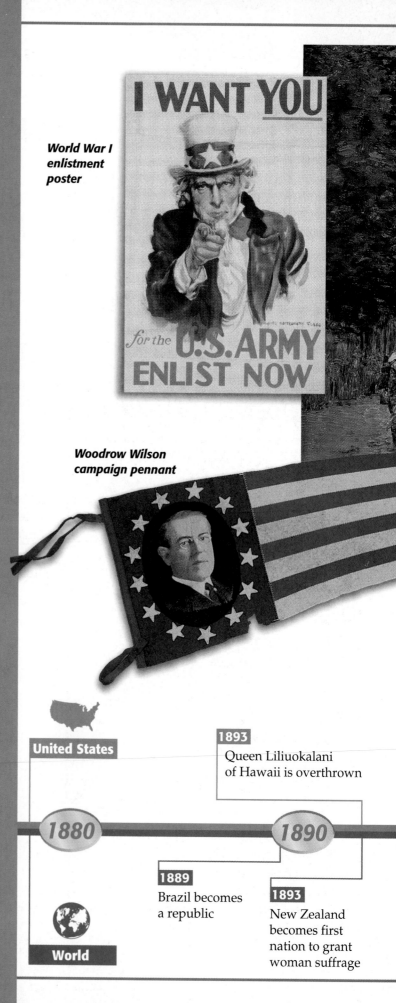

World War I enlistment poster

I WANT YOU *for the* **U.S. ARMY ENLIST NOW**

Woodrow Wilson campaign pennant

United States

1880

1890

1893
Queen Liliuokalani of Hawaii is overthrown

1889
Brazil becomes a republic

1893
New Zealand becomes first nation to grant woman suffrage

World

Theodore Roosevelt tin tray

⭐ HISTORY AND ART *Regimental Band and U.S. Infantry Marching, Paris* by J. F. Boucher Americans provided soldiers, weapons, and the moral support that the Allies needed to win World War I.

1901
Theodore Roosevelt becomes president

1909
National Association for the Advancement of Colored People (NAACP) is formed

1917
U.S. declares war on Germany

1920
Prohibition begins nationwide; ratification of woman suffrage

1900

1910

1920

1898
Spanish-American War begins

1900
Boxer Rebellion occurs in China

1908
Belgium establishes control over the Congo

1914
World War I begins

1917
Russian Revolution begins

1919
Treaty of Versailles signed

Patriotic Songs

George M. Cohan

As the United States entered World War I, rousing songs helped bolster the spirits of soldiers and civilians alike. Composer George M. Cohan wrote "Over There"—the most popular patriotic song of the war—in 1917. He was later awarded the Congressional Medal of Honor for writing it and for writing "You're a Grand Old Flag," *another enthusiastic war song. Edward Bushnell, who wrote* "Uncle Sam!" *in 1917, also touched the hearts and spirits of war-torn America with his patriotic lyrics.*

■ READ TO DISCOVER

As you read the lyrics for the following songs, think about their purpose. How might they have helped the country's war effort? What words used by the composers are especially patriotic?

■ READER'S DICTIONARY

pine: suffer
Hun: a negative word for a German
tyrant: an absolute ruler
Kaiser: German emperor

Over There
by George M. Cohan

Johnnie get your gun, get your gun,
　get your gun,
Take it on the run, on the run, on the run;
Hear them calling you and me;
Ev'ry son of liberty.
Hurry right away, no delay, go today,
Make your daddy glad, to have had such
　a lad,
Tell your sweetheart not to pine,
To be proud her boy's in line.

CHORUS
Over there, over there,
Send the word, send the word over there
That the Yanks are coming, the Yanks
　are coming,
The drums rum-tumming ev'rywhere
So prepare, say a pray'r,
Send the word, send the word to beware,
We'll be over, we're coming over,
And we won't come back till it's over
　over there.

Johnnie get your gun, get your gun,
　get your gun,
Johnnie show the Hun, you're a son
　of a gun,
Hoist the flag and let her fly,
Like true heroes do or die.
Pack your little kit, show your grit,
　do your bit,
Soldiers to the ranks from the towns and
　the tanks,
Make your mother proud of you,
And to liberty be true.

American soldiers eating at mess call, 1918

Uncle Sam
by Edward Bushnell

So you've drawn your sword again, Uncle Sam!
You're lined up with fighting men, Uncle Sam!
For when freedom is at stake,
You will fight for honor's sake,
And you'll fight till tyrants quake, Uncle Sam!

We know war is not your game, Uncle Sam!
'Twas at peace you made your fame, Uncle
   Sam!
And 'tis always with regret
That you make a war-like threat;
But they've never whipped you yet, Uncle Sam!

We will sail on all the seas, Uncle Sam!
Without saying "if" or "please," Uncle Sam!
We'll not wear the Kaiser's tag,
And we'll fly no checkered rag,
For Old Glory is our flag, Uncle Sam!

Let the Eagle flap his wings, Uncle Sam!
These are sorry days for kings, Uncle Sam!
And the Kaiser and his crew
Will be missing when they're through
With the old Red, White and Blue, Uncle Sam!

■ RESPONDING TO LITERATURE

1. According to Cohan, who waiting at home will be proud of the soldiers?
2. What does Bushnell's song say about the willingness of the United States to go to war?

Activity

Writing a Patriotic Song What are some issues facing the United States today that need public support? Choose an issue you believe in and write the lyrics for a song that will encourage people to support that issue. Your song can be brief, but should be enthusiastic, patriotic, and easy for people to learn and remember. You can choose a familiar tune or write a new tune for your song. Then present your composition to the class.

1877–1920

Progressive Reforms

★ Why It's Important

The reform spirit gained strength during the late 1800s and flourished during the early 1900s. Some reformers believed that rapid social and economic change had resulted in a disordered and corrupt society. These reformers, called *progressives,* believed that the efforts of individuals and government could make society better and more fair. As progressive leaders reached positions of power in government, they passed laws affecting government employees, business practices, and public health. These progressive laws form the basis for modern ideas of the role of government.

★ Chapter Themes

■ *Section 1,* Government and Democracy
■ *Section 2,* Groups and Institutions
■ *Section 3,* Economic Factors
■ *Section 4,* Civic Rights and Responsibilities

PRIMARY SOURCES
Library   *See pages 976–977 for primary source readings to accompany Chapter 21*

HISTORY AND ART   *Hester Street* **by George Luks** Hester Street in New York City was part of a Jewish immigrant community in the early 1900s.

1887
Interstate Commerce
Commission is set up

1890
Congress passes
Sherman Antitrust Act

1906
Upton Sinclair
writes *The Jungle*

1912
Congress
passes the
Seventeenth
Amendment

Section 1

Progressive Movement

READ TO DISCOVER . . .

- how journalists helped shape the progressives' reform movement.
- how cities, states, and Congress answered the call for reform of the government.

TERMS TO LEARN

political machine
patronage
civil service
trust
muckraker

primary
initiative
referendum
recall

The Storyteller

Newspaper reporter Jacob Riis shocked Americans in 1890 with his book *How the Other Half Lives.* With words and powerful photographs, Riis vividly portrayed immigrant life in New York City's crowded tenements. Said Riis: "We used to go in the small hours of the morning into the worst tenements to count noses and see if the law against over-crowding was violated and the sights I saw there gripped my heart until I felt that I must tell of them, or burst."

Book on urban life by Jacob Riis

Many Americans called for reform in the late 1800s. The reformers had many different goals. Progressive reformers focused on urban problems, government, and business. They claimed that government and big business were taking advantage of the American people rather than serving them.

Fighting Corruption

Political machines—powerful organizations linked to political parties—controlled local government in many cities. In each ward, or political district, within a city, a machine representative controlled jobs and services. This representative was the **political boss.** The bosses gained votes for their parties by doing favors for people such as offering turkey dinners and summer boat rides, providing jobs for immigrants, and helping needy families. A political boss was often a citizen's closest link with local government. Although they did help people, many bosses were dishonest.

Corrupt politicians found numerous ways to make money. They accepted bribes from tenement landlords in return for overlooking violations of city housing codes. They received campaign contributions from contractors hoping to do business with the city. They also accepted kickbacks. A **kickback** was an arrangement in which contractors padded the amount of their bill for city work and paid, or "kicked back," a percentage of that amount to the bosses.

Some politicians used their knowledge of city business for personal profit. A person who knew where the city planned to build a road could buy land there before the route became public knowledge. Later the land could be sold for a huge profit.

Boss Tweed

One of the most corrupt city bosses, William M. Tweed, known as **Boss Tweed,** headed New York City's Democratic political machine in the 1860s and 1870s. Tweed and a network of city officials—the Tweed ring—controlled the police, the courts, and some newspapers. They collected millions of dollars in illegal payments from companies doing business with the city. Political cartoonist Thomas Nast exposed the Tweed ring's operations in his cartoons for *Harper's Weekly.* Tweed went to prison in 1872.

Citizenship

New Ways to Govern Cities

To break the power of political bosses, reformers founded organizations such as the National Municipal League, formed in Philadelphia. These groups worked to make city governments more honest and efficient

Cities troubled by poor management or corruption tried new forms of government. After the tidal wave of a hurricane devastated **Galveston, Texas,** in 1900, the task of rebuilding the city overwhelmed the mayor and city council. Galveston's citizens persuaded the Texas state legislature to approve a new charter that placed the city government in the hands of five commissioners. The new commission efficiently rebuilt the city. By 1917 commissions governed nearly 400 cities. Many other cities, mostly small ones, hired professional city managers.

One successful civic reformer was **Tom Johnson,** mayor of **Cleveland, Ohio,** from 1901 to 1909. He battled corporations and party bosses to lower streetcar fares, improve food inspections, and build parks. Because of Johnson's reforms, Cleveland became known as the best-governed city in the United States.

Fighting the Spoils System

The spoils system—rewarding political supporters with jobs and favors—had been common practice since the time of Andrew Jackson. Whenever a new president came to power, job seekers flooded the nation's capital.

The spoils system—also called patronage— existed at all levels of government and led to numerous abuses. Many who received government jobs were not qualified. Some were dishonest.

"WHO STOLE THE PEOPLE'S MONEY?" — DO TELL . N.Y.TIMES 'TWAS HIM.

★ **Picturing HISTORY** Cartoonist Thomas Nast criticized William "Boss" Tweed (left foreground) and his corrupt Democratic political machine. **What city did Tweed's political machine control?**

Tammany savings bank

Presidents **Rutherford B. Hayes** (1877–1881) and **James Garfield** (1881) wanted to change the spoils system. Hayes tried to do this by reforming the civil service—the body of nonelected government workers—but neither the Democratic nor the Republican Party supported his efforts.

Garfield also hoped to reform the civil service. He believed that people should be appointed to government jobs not as a reward for political support but because of their qualifications. Garfield took office in 1881 but was assassinated by an unsuccessful office seeker before he could launch his reforms.

When Vice President **Chester A. Arthur** succeeded Garfield, he tried to end the spoils system. In 1883 Congress passed the **Pendleton Act,** which established the **Civil Service Commission** to set up competitive examinations for federal jobs. Applicants had to demonstrate their abilities in this examination. By 1900 the commission controlled the hiring of more than half of all federal employees.

★ **Picturing HISTORY** This political cartoon blames the government for allowing the trusts to benefit from high tariffs at the expense of the American people. **How did high tariffs affect American shoppers?**

Economics

Controlling Business

★ During the late 1800s, many Americans came to believe that trusts, or combinations of companies, were becoming too large. They believed these trusts had too much control over the economy and the government. This public concern led to new laws regulating big business.

A National Antitrust Law

In 1890 Congress passed the **Sherman Antitrust Act,** the first federal law to control trusts and monopolies. Supporters of the law hoped it would keep trusts from limiting competition. During the 1890s, however, the government rarely used the Sherman Act to curb business. Instead, it applied the act against labor unions, claiming that union strikes interfered with trade. Not until the early 1900s did the government win cases against trusts with the Sherman Act.

Reining in the Railroads

The railroads functioned as an **oligopoly**—a market structure in which a few large companies control the prices of the industry. Reformers called for regulations on railroad rates, but the Supreme Court ruled that only Congress could enact legislation to regulate commerce that crossed state lines.

So in 1887 Congress passed the **Interstate Commerce Act,** which required railroads to charge "reasonable and just" rates and to publish those rates. The act also created the **Interstate Commerce Commission** (ICC) to supervise the railroad industry and, later, the trucking industry.

Lowering Tariffs

The reform movement also wanted to lower tariffs. Many people believed that high tariffs led to higher prices for goods. In 1890 the Republicans raised tariffs sharply to protect American businesses from international competition. Voters showed their opposition to high tariffs by sending many Democrats to Congress. When **Grover Cleveland** became president in 1893, he also supported lower tariffs. 💲

Picturing HISTORY Writing for *McClure's*, Ida Tarbell revealed the unfair practices of the oil trust. In *The Jungle*, Upton Sinclair described horrible conditions in Chicago's meatpacking plants. **What muckraker exposed corrupt practices in government?**

The New Reformers

In the early 1900s, new ideas for correcting injustice and solving social problems emerged among American reformers. Socialism and progressivism were two such ideas.

The Socialists and Progressives

Socialists believed a nation's resources and major industries should be owned and operated by the government on behalf of all the people—not by individuals and private companies for their own profit. **Eugene V. Debs** helped found the American Socialist Party in 1898. Under Debs's leadership the party won some support in the early 1900s. Debs ran for president five times but never received more than 6 percent of the popular vote.

During the same period, progressives brought new energy to the reform movement. Progressivism was not a single organization, goal, or outlook. It represented several overlapping beliefs and ideas. Like the socialists, many progressives were alarmed by the concentration of wealth and power in the hands of a few. Progressives rejected the socialist idea of government ownership of industries. Instead, they supported government efforts to regulate industry.

They also sought to reform government, to make it more efficient and better able to resist the influence of powerful business interests. Progressives also believed that society had an obligation to protect and help all its members. Many progressive reforms aimed to help those who lacked wealth and influence.

Muckrakers Expose Problems

Journalists aided the reformers by exposing injustices, corruption, and political favors. Investigative reporters wrote shocking newspaper and magazine stories that brought problems to the attention of the public—and gained readers. These journalists were called muckrakers because they "raked" (brought to light) the "muck" (dirt and corruption) underlying society.

One of the most effective muckrakers, **Lincoln Steffens,** reported for *McClure's Magazine*. Steffens exposed corrupt machine politics in New York, **Chicago,** and other cities. His articles, collected in a book called *The Shame of the Cities* (1904), strengthened the demand for urban reform.

Focus on Industry

Ida Tarbell, also writing for *McClure's*, laid bare the unfair practices of the oil trust. Her articles led to public pressure for more government control over big business. In her 1904 book, *The History of the Standard Oil Company*, she warned of the giant corporation's power.

In his novel *The Jungle* (1906), **Upton Sinclair** described the horrors of the meatpacking industry in Chicago. Although Sinclair's aim was to arouse sympathy for the workers, his vivid descriptions shocked Americans. The uproar caused by Sinclair's book helped persuade Congress to pass the **Meat Inspection Act** in 1906. That same year Congress also passed the **Pure Food and Drug Act,** requiring accurate labeling of food and medicine and banning the sale of harmful food.

★ ★

✒️ Citizenship

Expanding Democracy

⭐ In the early 1900s, progressives backed a number of reforms designed to increase the people's direct control of the government. These reforms changed the nature of American democracy.

The Wisconsin Idea

Robert La Follette led Wisconsin's reform-minded Republicans. "Fighting Bob," as he was called, won the support of farmers and workers with his fiery attacks on big business and the railroads. He served as Wisconsin's governor from 1900 until 1906 and then served four terms in Washington, D.C., as one of Wisconsin's senators.

While governor, La Follette brought about significant reforms—raising taxes for corporations and improving the civil service. "Fighting Bob's" greatest achievement, however, was reforming the state electoral system. Candidates for general elections in Wisconsin had been chosen at state conventions run by party bosses. La Follette introduced a direct primary election, allowing the state's voters to choose their party's candidates. Reformers in other states copied this "Wisconsin idea."

The Oregon System

Oregon also made changes in the political process to give voters more power and to limit the influence of political parties. The reforms included a direct primary election and the initiative, the referendum, and the recall.

The initiative allowed citizens to place a measure or issue on the ballot in a state election. The referendum gave voters the opportunity to accept or reject measures that the state legislature enacted. The recall enabled voters to remove unsatisfactory elected officials from their jobs. These reforms were called the **Oregon System.** Other western states soon adopted the reforms.

The Seventeenth Amendment

Progressives also changed the way United States senators are elected. The Constitution had given state legislatures the responsibility for choosing senators, but party bosses and business interests often controlled the selection process. Progressives wanted to give the people an opportunity to vote for their senators directly. Support for this idea grew. In 1912 Congress passed the **Seventeenth Amendment** to the Constitution to provide for the direct election of senators. Ratified in 1913, the amendment gave the people a voice in selecting their representatives. ✒️

⭐ ⭐ ⭐ ⭐ ⭐ **Section 1 Assessment** ⭐ ⭐ ⭐ ⭐ ⭐

Checking for Understanding

1. **Identify** Boss Tweed, James Garfield, Pendleton Act, Grover Cleveland, Ida Tarbell, Upton Sinclair, Robert La Follette.
2. **Define** political machine, patronage, civil service, trust, muckraker, primary, initiative, referendum, recall.
3. **Explain** how the Civil Service Commission helped to eliminate the spoils system.

Reviewing Themes

4. **Government and Democracy** What five reforms gave the American people more direct control of the government?

Critical Thinking

5. **Making Comparisons** Compare socialist and progressive views on industry.

Activity

Making a Campaign Poster Come up with a slogan for a progressive candidate for a local, state, or federal office. Use the slogan to create a campaign poster.

Multimedia Activities

Historic America Electronic Field Trips

Field Trip to Seneca Falls

Setting up the Video

Work with a group of your classmates to view "Seneca Falls" on the videodisc *Historic America: Electronic Field Trips*. In 1848 hundreds of women attended the Seneca Falls Convention, which met to improve women's rights. Many women felt that equality started with the right to vote. This program discusses the importance of voting today and what women's lives were like before the Nineteenth Amendment was ratified.

Side 2, Chapter 6

Hands-On Activity

Go to your public library and research current salaries earned by women in various occupations. Compare these numbers with men's salaries in the same occupations. Create a line graph showing the comparison and share your results with the class.

View the video by scanning the bar code or by entering the chapter number on your keypad and pressing Search.

Surfing the "Net"

Women and the Progressive Movement

The first women's rights convention took place in Seneca Falls, New York, in 1848. The result of this meeting was a written document—modeled after the Declaration of Independence—claiming that "all men and women are created equal." To find out more information about women, their struggle for equality, and the Progressive movement, search the Internet.

Getting There

Follow these steps to gather information about the Progressive movement.

1. Use a search engine. Type in the phrase *Progressive movement.*
2. After typing that phrase, enter words like the following to focus your search: *suffrage, women's rights, history.*
3. The search engine will provide you with a number of links to follow.

What to Do When You Are There

Click on the links to navigate through the pages of information and gather your findings. Then, using large poster paper, create a time line that highlights significant events that took place for the cause of women's rights from 1848 to 1920. Include illustrations and written captions for all important events. You should also include a map of the United States that pinpoints where these events took place.

1890   1900   1910   1920

1890
National American
Woman Suffrage
Association emerges

1896
National Association
of Colored Women
is formed

1919
The Eighteenth
Amendment
is ratified

1920
The Nineteenth
Amendment
is ratified

Section 2

Women and Progressives

READ TO DISCOVER . . .

- how the role of women in American society changed during the Progressive Era.
- how women fought for the right to vote.
- why the manufacture and sale of alcohol became illegal.

TERMS TO LEARN

suffragist   prohibition

The Storyteller

Nurse Lillian Wald followed a young girl up a rickety staircase in a filthy tenement house on New York City's Lower East Side. The girl had begged Wald to help her mother who had just given birth to a baby. A doctor had refused to treat the girl's mother because she could not pay his fee. The sight of the desperate mother and her baby was a turning point in Wald's life. Wald dedicated herself to helping poor people and educating them about health care. Eventually Wald became a national reform leader who liked to say, "The whole world is my neighborhood."

Lillian D. Wald

The situation of middle-class women changed during the late 1800s. Their responsibilities at home lessened as families became smaller, more children spent the day at school, and men worked away from home. These women also had more free time as technology made housework easier.

Women's Roles Change

Many more middle-class women were gaining higher education. About 40 percent of all college students in 1910 were women. Women were also starting professional careers—mostly in teaching but also in nursing, medicine, and other fields. Between 1890 and 1910, the number of women working outside the home increased from 4 million to nearly 7.5 million.

These changes created the "new woman"—a popular term for educated, up-to-date women who pursued interests outside their homes. Many such women became role models.

As you read in Chapter 20, **Jane Addams** established Hull House, a settlement house, in **Chicago.** Working there gave Addams an outlet for her energy and intelligence, as well as a sense of satisfaction in helping poor people.

Settlement workers such as Addams gained notice as writers, public speakers, fund-raisers, and reformers. Many young women followed the example of these talented public figures. Others found inspiration in the life of **Mother Cabrini,** an Italian nun who came to the United States to work with the poor.

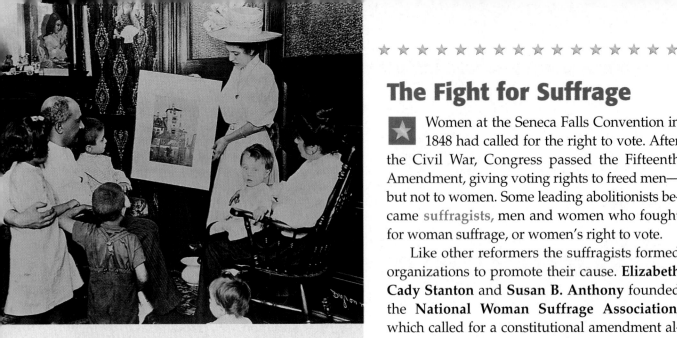

A worker from a New York charity organization discusses health care with an Italian family. **In what two fields did women of the early 1900s increasingly find work?**

Women's Clubs

Women found another outlet for their talent and energy in women's clubs, which rapidly increased in number. At first the clubs focused on such cultural activities as music and painting. Many clubs gradually became more concerned with social problems. Middle-class clubwomen tried to help working-class women and children.

Women's clubs offered many opportunities for self-improvement. A club in Buffalo, New York, ran a library and held classes in typing and bookkeeping. The clubs also gave their members a chance to continue their education and to develop new skills.

When some clubs refused to admit African Americans, African American women established their own network of clubs. Clubs such as the Phyllis Wheatley Club of New Orleans organized classes, recreation activities, and social services. In 1896 women from these clubs formed the **National Association of Colored Women.** Its first president, **Mary Church Terrell,** was an active leader for women's rights. The association established homes for orphans, founded hospitals, and worked for woman suffrage, fulfilling their motto, "Lifting As We Climb."

The Fight for Suffrage

★ Women at the Seneca Falls Convention in 1848 had called for the right to vote. After the Civil War, Congress passed the Fifteenth Amendment, giving voting rights to freed men—but not to women. Some leading abolitionists became suffragists, men and women who fought for woman suffrage, or women's right to vote.

Like other reformers the suffragists formed organizations to promote their cause. **Elizabeth Cady Stanton** and **Susan B. Anthony** founded the **National Woman Suffrage Association,** which called for a constitutional amendment allowing women to vote in national elections. A second organization, the American Woman Suffrage Association, focused on winning woman suffrage in state elections.

In 1890 the two groups merged to form the National American Woman Suffrage Association. Led by **Anna Howard Shaw,** a minister and doctor, and **Carrie Chapman Catt,** an educator and newspaper editor, this organization grew to more than 2 million members by 1917. In a speech to the association in 1902, Catt declared:

❝The whole aim of the [women's] movement has been to destroy the idea that obedience is necessary to women; to train women to such self-respect that they would not grant obedience and to train men to such comprehension of equity [fairness] they would not exact [demand] it. ❞

Opposition to Woman Suffrage

Groups formed to protest the idea of giving women the vote. These organizations—supported by some women as well as by men—claimed that woman suffrage would upset society's "natural" balance and lead to divorce and neglected children.

The suffrage movement gained strength, however, when respected public figures such as Jane Addams spoke out in support of the vote for women. Alice Duer Miller brought humor to the struggle for the right to vote:

❝ Said Mr. Jones in 1910:
'Women, subject yourselves to men.'
Nineteen-Eleven heard him quote:
'They rule the world without the vote.'

....

By Nineteen-Thirteen, looking glum,
He said that it was bound to come.

....

By Nineteen-Fifteen, he'll insist
He's always been a suffragist. ❞

First Suffrage Victories

The suffragists won their early victories in the West. First as a territory in 1869 and then as a state in 1890, **Wyoming** led the nation in giving women the vote. Between 1910 and 1913, six other states adopted woman suffrage. By 1919 women could vote in at least some elections in 39 of the 48 states.

📖 **Biography**

Continuing the Fight

In the meantime suffragists continued their struggle to win the vote everywhere. **Alice Paul,** a Quaker who founded the National Woman's Party in 1916, was a forceful leader of the suffragist movement. She sought greater economic and legal equality as well as suffrage for women.

During a visit to Great Britain, Paul saw suffragists use protest marches and hunger strikes to call attention to their cause. When she returned to the United States, she, too, used these methods in the fight for suffrage.

In 1917 Alice Paul met with President **Woodrow Wilson** but failed to win his support for woman suffrage. Paul responded by leading women protestors in front of the White House. Day after day they marched carrying banners demanding votes for women. When Paul and other

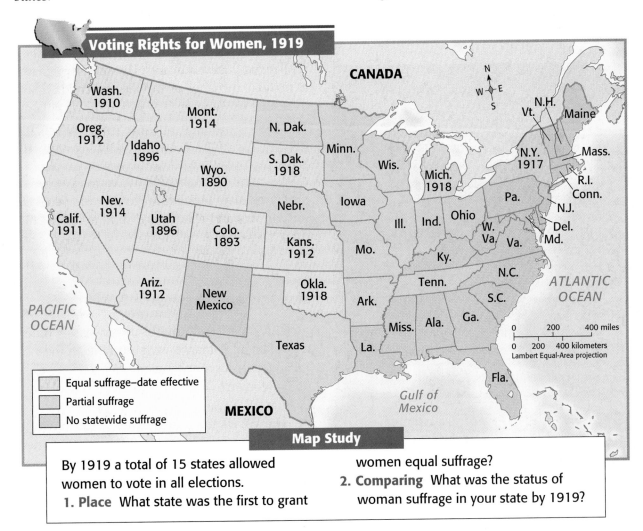

Voting Rights for Women, 1919

Wash. 1910
Oreg. 1912
Idaho 1896
Mont. 1914
N. Dak.
Minn.
S. Dak. 1918
Wis.
Mich. 1918
N.Y. 1917
Vt.
N.H.
Maine
Mass.
R.I.
Conn.
Nev. 1914
Calif. 1911
Utah 1896
Wyo. 1890
Nebr.
Iowa
Ill.
Ind.
Ohio
Pa.
N.J.
Del.
Md.
W. Va.
Va.
Colo. 1893
Kans. 1912
Mo.
Ky.
Ariz. 1912
New Mexico
Okla. 1918
Ark.
Tenn.
N.C.
S.C.
Ga.
Miss.
Ala.
Texas
La.
Fla.
CANADA
PACIFIC OCEAN
ATLANTIC OCEAN
Gulf of Mexico
MEXICO

0   200   400 miles
0   200   400 kilometers
Lambert Equal-Area projection

☐ Equal suffrage–date effective
☐ Partial suffrage
☐ No statewide suffrage

Map Study

By 1919 a total of 15 states allowed women to vote in all elections.
1. Place What state was the first to grant women equal suffrage?
2. Comparing What was the status of woman suffrage in your state by 1919?

protestors were arrested for blocking the sidewalk, they started a much-publicized hunger strike. Alva Belmont, one of the protestors, proudly declared that all the women had done was to stand there "quietly, peacefully, lawfully, and gloriously."

Women Vote Nationally

By 1917 the national tide was turning in favor of woman suffrage. Two states with large populations—New York and Illinois—gave women the vote that year. Meanwhile Congress began debating the issue, and President Wilson agreed to support an amendment to the Constitution.

In 1919 Congress voted in favor of the **Nineteenth Amendment,** which allowed woman suffrage. The amendment was ratified in 1920, in time for women to vote in that year's presidential election. For the first time, American women were able to participate in the election of their national leaders.

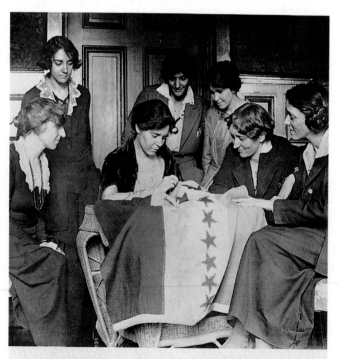

★ **Picturing HISTORY** Alice Paul sews a star on the flag of the National Woman's Party in celebration of the ratification of the Nineteenth Amendment in 1920. **What did this amendment achieve?**

Women and Social Reform

★ During the Progressive Era, women involved themselves in many reform movements besides woman suffrage. In 1912, for example, pressure from women's clubs helped persuade Congress to create the Children's Bureau in the Labor Department. The bureau's task was to develop federal policies that would protect children.

Working for a Better Life

While they struggled to gain rights for themselves, middle-class women of the Progressive Era also worked to improve the lives of working-class people, immigrants, and society as a whole. They supported and staffed libraries, schools, and settlement houses and raised money for hospitals and parks.

Some women promoted other causes. They challenged business interests by sponsoring laws to regulate the labor of women and children and to require government inspection of workplaces. Women also played an important role in the movement to reform and regulate the food and medicine industries.

In many states across the country, women pressured state legislatures to provide pensions for widows and abandoned mothers with children. These pensions later became part of the Social Security system.

Women and the Labor Movement

Reform efforts brought upper-class women reformers into alliance with working women. In 1903 women's groups joined with working-class union women to form the **Women's Trade Union League** (WTUL).

The WTUL encouraged working women to form women's labor unions. It also supported laws to protect the rights of women factory workers. WTUL members raised money to help striking workers and to pay bail for women who were arrested for participating in strikes.

The Temperance Crusade

A crusade against the use of alcohol had begun in New England and the Midwest in the early 1800s. The movement continued throughout the late 1800s. Protestant churches strongly supported the antialcohol movement.

Two driving forces in the crusade were the **Woman's Christian Temperance Union** (WCTU), established in 1873, and the **Anti-Saloon League,** founded 20 years later. They called for temperance, urging individuals to stop drinking, and prohibition, the passing of laws to prohibit the making or selling of alcohol.

Leaders of the Crusade

In 1879 **Frances Willard** became head of the WCTU. Willard led a campaign to educate the public about the links between alcohol abuse and violence, poverty, and unemployment. She turned the WCTU into a powerful organization with chapters in every state. By 1911 it was the largest women's organization the United States had yet known, with 245,000 members.

The WCTU's main goal was prohibition. However, the WCTU also supported other causes,

Temperance poster

including prison reform, woman suffrage, improved working conditions, and world peace. Through WCTU chapters, thousands of women combined their traditional role as guardians of the family and home with social activism.

Carry Nation was an especially colorful crusader for temperance. Nation began lecturing first in Kansas, then in other states, about the evils of "demon rum" and singing hymns outside saloons. Her most dramatic protests occurred when she pushed her way into saloons and broke bottles and kegs with an ax.

The Prohibition Amendment

The antialcohol movement grew steadily during the early 1900s. By 1916, 19 states had adopted prohibition laws.

Progressive reformers who wanted to ban alcohol for social reasons were joined by Americans who opposed alcohol for religious or moral reasons. In 1917 they persuaded Congress to pass a constitutional amendment making it illegal to make, transport, or sell alcohol in the United States. The **Eighteenth Amendment,** known as the Prohibition Law, was ratified in 1919.

Section 2 Assessment

Checking for Understanding

1. **Identify** Jane Addams, Mary Church Terrell, Susan B. Anthony, Carrie Chapman Catt, Alice Paul, Woodrow Wilson, Nineteenth Amendment, Frances Willard, Carry Nation, Eighteenth Amendment.
2. **Define** suffragist, prohibition.
3. **Summarize** the reasons middle-class women had more free time in the 1800s.

Reviewing Themes

4. **Groups and Institutions** How did women's clubs help to change the role of women?

Critical Thinking

5. **Drawing Conclusions** Why do you think the right to vote was important to women?

Activity

Current Events Find a newspaper article that deals with the role of women in today's society. Rewrite the article to reflect how this information might have been presented in the late 1800s and early 1900s.

1 Jeannette Rankin launched her political journey when she joined the suffragists. As a student she became actively involved in the campaign for voting rights for women. Later she traveled to several states to help women win the vote and eventually sought a national platform. As a representative from Montana from 1917 to 1919, Jeannette Rankin was the first woman to serve in Congress.

Missoula

Mont.

N. Dak.

S. Dak.

Idaho

Wyo.

5 Rankin's journey was a journey for all women. At long last they headed to the polls to cast their ballots in the presidential election of 1920. Years of struggle by thousands of suffragists had finally paid off: The 19th Amendment to the Constitution guaranteeing woman suffrage was ratified on August 19, 1920.

Wis.

Nev.

Nebr.

Iowa

Ill.

Mo.

3 These women from St. Louis, Missouri, joined a demonstration in 1916 to demand representation. In 1916 the tide turned—the public was beginning to agree with the suffragists. When Rankin joined the suffragists, women composed more than one-fifth of the nation's workforce but could vote in only four states.

② In 1912 suffragists took to the streets of New York City to demand their rights. Rankin traveled to New York and 15 other states to help promote voting rights for women.

A Suffragist's Journey

④ Jeannette Rankin addresses fellow representatives in her first speech before Congress in May 1917. Rankin served two terms in Congress—from 1917 to 1919 and again from 1941 to 1943. In her first term she worked on a committee that drafted a woman suffrage amendment to the Constitution.

❝ [My aunt] who had been active nationally in the movement came home to Montana to head a ... drive for woman suffrage in 1911.... The details differed from Butte to Broadus, but in essence the ladies moved in on a town tacking up notices of a public meeting.... They generally chose the street corner ... across from the most popular saloon in town. At the advertised hour, a speaker would mount a real soapbox. There would be a gaggle of children, a sprinkling of housewives ... and gradually the men ... would move out of the saloon to see what the commotion was all about. ❞

—From a reminiscence written by Mackey Brown, a niece of Jeannette Rankin, in Montana Business Quarterly, Autumn 1971.

1900   1910   1920

1901
President
McKinley
is assassinated

1905
Roosevelt proposes
the U.S. Forest Service

1913
Federal Reserve
Act creates 12
regional banks

1914
Congress establishes
the Federal Trade
Commission

Section 3

Progressive Presidents

READ TO DISCOVER . . .
■ how President Theodore Roosevelt took on big business and became a "trustbuster."
■ why the progressives formed their own political party.

TERMS TO LEARN
trustbuster   laissez-faire
arbitration   conservation
square deal

Storyteller

"We were still under a heavy fire and I got together a mixed lot of men and pushed on from the trenches and ranch houses which we had just taken, driving the Spaniards through a line of palm-trees, and over the crest of a chain of hills. . . ." With these words, a young lieutenant colonel named Theodore Roosevelt described his military adventures in Cuba during the Spanish-American War. Known for his vigor, enthusiasm, and a colorful personality, Roosevelt became president in 1901 upon the assassination of President William McKinley.

Theodore Roosevelt board game

The wave of progressive reform that began to sweep across the United States in the late 1800s eventually reached the level of presidential politics. When a young, energetic, reform-minded president named **Theodore Roosevelt** moved into the White House in 1901, he brought progressivism with him.

📖 Biography

Theodore Roosevelt

⭐ Theodore Roosevelt came from a prosperous **New York** family. Once a sickly child, Roosevelt set out to improve his health with exercise and personal discipline. As an adult he was proud of his strength and stamina.

After studying law, young Theodore Roosevelt entered politics. He served in the New York State assembly, headed New York City's police commission, and became assistant secretary of the navy. In 1898 Roosevelt organized the **Rough Riders,** a volunteer cavalry regiment that fought in the Spanish-American War. He gained fame for leading his regiment in a charge at the Battle of San Juan Hill. A few months later, Roosevelt the war hero was elected governor of New York.

Roosevelt's efforts to clean up corruption in New York State politics did not make him popular with local Republican bosses. So to remove him as governor, they promoted Roosevelt's nomination for vice president in 1900, to run with President **William McKinley.**

Ohio senator Mark Hanna, chairman of McKinley's reelection campaign did not approve. Hanna considered Roosevelt too impulsive for national offices. When Hanna heard of the Roosevelt nomination he shouted, "Don't any of you realize that there's only one life between that madman and the presidency?"

McKinley and Roosevelt won the election in November 1900. Less than a year later, President McKinley was assassinated. Suddenly, 42-year-old Theodore Roosevelt became president—the youngest president in the nation's history. 📖

Tackling Big Business

President McKinley had favored big business, but President Roosevelt was known to support business regulation and other progressive reforms. In a speech to Congress, Roosevelt declared, "There is a widespread conviction in the minds of the American people that the great corporations known as trusts are . . . hurtful to the general welfare."

In 1902 Roosevelt ordered the Justice Department to take legal action against certain trusts that had violated the Sherman Antitrust Act. His first target was the **Northern Securities Company,** a railroad monopoly formed by financiers J.P. Morgan and James J. Hill to control transportation in the Northwest. Northern Securities fought the government's accusations of illegal activity all the way to the Supreme Court. Finally, in 1904 the Justice Department won its case. The Supreme Court decided that Northern Securities had illegally limited trade and ordered the trust to be taken apart.

---

*F*ootnotes to History

Teddy Bears Once when President Theodore Roosevelt was hunting, he supposedly refused to shoot a bear cub. A *Washington Post* cartoonist drew a cartoon of Roosevelt turning away from the helpless cub. Seeing the cartoon, Morris Michtom began to make toy bear cubs in 1903, naming them "Teddy Bears."

The "Trustbuster"

The Northern Securities case was a victory for the Progressive movement and earned Roosevelt the nickname trustbuster. During his presidency, Roosevelt directed the Justice Department to act against a number of trusts, including the beef trust, the tobacco trust, and Standard Oil—a petroleum trust.

Roosevelt wanted to prove that the federal government had authority over big business. Unlike some reformers who dreamed of returning to the days before big business, however, Roosevelt knew that large corporations had become a permanent part of America's economy. "We do not wish to destroy corporations," he said, "but we do wish to make them [serve] the public good."

Labor Crisis

In 1902 Roosevelt faced a major labor crisis. More than 100,000 Pennsylvania coal miners, members of the **United Mine Workers,** went on strike. They demanded better pay, an 8-hour workday, and recognition of the union's right to represent its members in discussions with mine owners.

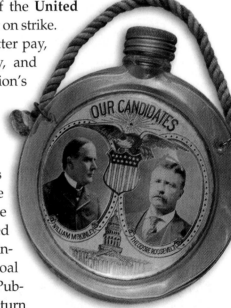

The mine owners refused to negotiate with the workers. The **coal strike** dragged on for months. As winter approached, coal supplies dwindled. Public opinion began to turn against the owners. As public pressure mounted, Roosevelt invited

McKinley/Roosevelt glass canteen, 1900

representatives of the owners and miners to a meeting at the White House. Roosevelt was outraged when the owners refused to negotiate. He threatened to send federal troops to work in the mines and produce the coal. The owners finally agreed to arbitration—settling the dispute by agreeing to accept the decision of an impartial outsider. Mine workers won a pay increase and a reduction in hours, but they did not gain recognition for the union.

Roosevelt's action marked a departure from normal patterns of labor relations at the time. Earlier presidents had used troops against strikers, but Roosevelt had used the power of the federal government to force the company owners to negotiate. In other labor actions, however, Roosevelt supported employers in disputes with workers.

Roosevelt's Square Deal

Roosevelt ran for the presidency in 1904, promising the people a square deal—fair and equal treatment for all. He was elected with more than 57 percent of the popular vote.

Roosevelt's "square deal" called for a considerable amount of government regulation of business. This contrasted with an attitude toward business that dated back to the presidency of Thomas Jefferson, which was summed up in the phrase laissez-faire (LEH•say FEHR). This French term means, generally, "let people do as they choose."

Roosevelt introduced a new era of government regulation. He supported the **Meat Inspection** and **Pure Food and Drug acts** that gave the Department of Agriculture and the Food and Drug Administration the power to visit businesses and inspect their products. Roosevelt also supported new laws giving the Interstate Commerce Commission more power to regulate the railroads.

Conserving the Wilderness

Roosevelt held a lifelong enthusiasm for the great outdoors and the wilderness. He believed in the need for conservation, the protection and preservation of natural resources.

As president, Roosevelt took steps to conserve the country's forests, mineral deposits, and water resources. In 1905 he proposed the **U.S. Forest Service.** He pressured Congress to set aside millions of acres of national forests and created the nation's first wildlife sanctuaries. Roosevelt also formed the National Conservation Commission, which produced the first survey of the country's natural resources.

Roosevelt has been called America's first environmental president. While he made conservation an important public issue, Roosevelt also recognized the need for economic growth and development. He tried to strike a balance between business interests and conservation.

William Howard Taft

No president before had ever served more than two terms. Roosevelt decided not to run for reelection in 1908. Wanting to continue his progressive programs, he persuaded the Republican Party to nominate his secretary of war, **William Howard Taft,** for president. In the election of 1908, Taft easily defeated Democrat William Jennings Bryan. Taft failed to win the public affection that Roosevelt had enjoyed, however. A quiet, cautious man, Taft seemed timid in comparison with the lively, outspoken Roosevelt.

★ **Picturing HISTORY** President Theodore Roosevelt (fourth from left) visits California's Yosemite National Park in 1903. **What steps did Roosevelt take to conserve the country's natural resources?**

Roosevelt campaign button, 1904

Continuing Progressive Reform

Although he had none of Roosevelt's flair, Taft carried out—and went beyond—many of Roosevelt's policies. Taft used the Sherman Antitrust Act to file lawsuits against dozens of large corporations. The Taft administration won more antitrust cases in four years than Roosevelt had won in seven. Taft also favored the introduction of safety standards for mines and railroads.

Taft supported the **Sixteenth Amendment,** which gave Congress the power to tax people's incomes to generate revenue for the federal government. Progressives hoped the income tax would enable the government to lower tariffs. In their view high tariffs led to higher prices for goods, which caused hardship for the poor. Progressives believed that taxes based on income were fairer. The Sixteenth Amendment, added to the Constitution in 1913, did not specify how income would be taxed. Congress passed additional laws so that higher incomes were taxed at a higher rate than lower incomes.

Taft Loses Support

Despite his progressive reforms, President Taft disappointed progressives in two important areas—tariffs and conservation. He failed to fight for a lower tariff, and he modified some conservation policies so that they favored business.

In 1910 Roosevelt returned from a long trip to Africa to find that progressives were disappointed with Taft. Roosevelt claimed that Taft had "completely twisted around" his own policies. In the congressional elections of 1910, Roosevelt campaigned for progressive Republicans. In a speech in Kansas, Roosevelt set forth his own progressive principles, declaring that social justice was possible only with a strong federal government to act as "steward [manager] of the public welfare."

The Bull Moose Party

Everywhere he went, Roosevelt was greeted by cheering crowds. This encouraged him to return to politics, and in 1912 he challenged Taft for the Republican presidential nomination.

★ Picturing HISTORY Theodore Roosevelt was a vigorous campaigner. **Who were the candidates in the 1912 election?**

The showdown between Roosevelt and Taft came at the Republican national convention in Chicago in June. Although Roosevelt won every primary and had many supporters, Taft had the backing of Republican Party leaders and influential business interests who controlled the party machinery. In disputes over seating rival delegations, Taft received the votes of all but 19 of the 254 contested delegates.

A fiery Roosevelt led his supporters out of the convention hall. He and his followers formed a new party, the **Progressive Party.** In August the Progressives held their own convention in Chicago and nominated Roosevelt for president.

When a reporter asked Roosevelt about his health, the candidate thumped himself on the chest and declared, "I feel as strong as a bull moose!" From then on, the Progressive Party was known as the **Bull Moose Party.**

The Election of 1912

The split in the Republican Party hurt both Taft and Roosevelt. While Republicans and Progressives battled each other at the polls, Democrat **Woodrow Wilson** gathered enough support to defeat them in the election. Wilson had acquired a reputation as a progressive reformer while serv-

America's FLAGS

Twenty-fifth Flag, 1912 **Statehood for Arizona and New Mexico increased the number of stars to 48 in 1912. This flag served from 1912 to 1959, more years than any other flag.**

ing as president of Princeton University and governor of New Jersey.

Wilson gained only 42 percent of the popular vote, with Roosevelt receiving 27 percent and Taft 23 percent. However, Wilson won the presidency by the largest electoral majority up to that time, sweeping 435 of the 531 electoral votes.

Wilson's Reforms

★ During his campaign Woodrow Wilson had criticized big government as well as big business. Wilson called his program the "New Freedom."

In 1913 Wilson achieved a long-awaited progressive goal—tariff reform. He persuaded the Democrat-controlled Congress to adopt a lower tariff on imported goods such as sugar, wool, steel, and farm equipment. Wilson believed that the pressure of foreign competition would lead American manufacturers to improve their products and lower their prices. The government income lost by lowering tariffs would be replaced by the new income tax.

That same year Congress also passed the **Federal Reserve Act** to regulate banking. By creating 12 regional banks supervised by a central board in **Washington, D.C.,** the act gave the government more control over banking activities. Banks that operated nationally were required to join the Federal Reserve System and abide by its regulations.

Regulating Business

Wilson also worked toward strengthening government control over business. In 1914 Congress established the **Federal Trade Commission** (FTC) to investigate corporations for unfair trade practices. Wilson also supported the **Clayton Antitrust Act** of 1914, which joined the Sherman Antitrust Act as one of the government's chief weapons against trusts.

By the end of Wilson's first term, progressives had won many victories. The Progressive movement lost some of its momentum as Americans turned their attention to world affairs—especially the war that had broken out in Europe in 1914.

★ ★ ★ ★ ★ **Section 3 Assessment** ★ ★ ★ ★ ★

Checking for Understanding
1. *Identify* Theodore Roosevelt, William McKinley, William Howard Taft, Sixteenth Amendment, Woodrow Wilson.
2. *Define* trustbuster, arbitration, square deal, laissez-faire, conservation.
3. *Describe* two progressive ideas that Roosevelt supported.

Reviewing Themes
4. **Economic Factors** Why did progressives support an income tax?

Critical Thinking
5. **Media Literacy** If you were creating a 30-second television commercial to recruit volunteers for Roosevelt's Rough Riders, what would you say and show?

 Activity

Drawing a Political Cartoon Draw a political cartoon that supports Theodore Roosevelt's actions as a "trustbuster."

Interpreting a Political Cartoon

You've probably heard the saying, "A picture is worth a thousand words." For more than 200 years, political cartoonists have drawn pictures to present their opinions about a person or event. Learning to interpret political cartoons can help you understand issues of both the past and present.

Learning the Skill

Political cartoons state opinions about particular subjects. To illustrate those opinions, cartoonists provide clues using several different techniques. They often exaggerate a person's physical features or appearance in a special effect called *caricature*. A caricature can be positive or negative, depending on the artist's point of view.

Cartoonists also use symbols to represent something else. The bald eagle is often shown in political cartoons as a symbol of the United States. Sometimes cartoonists help readers interpret their message by adding labels or captions.

To interpret a political cartoon, follow these steps:

- Read the caption and any other words printed in the cartoon.
- Analyze each element in the cartoon.
- Identify the clues: What is happening in the cartoon? Who or what is represented by each part of the drawing? What or whom do the figures represent? To what do the symbols refer?
- Study all these elements to decide the point the cartoonist is making.

Practicing the Skill

The cartoon on this page shows Theodore Roosevelt looking in a window at President Taft. Analyze the cartoon, then answer the following questions.

1. What is going on in this picture?
2. What caricatures are included in this cartoon?
3. What symbols are depicted? What do these symbols represent?
4. What point is the cartoonist making?

Applying the Skill

Interpreting a Political Cartoon Bring to class a copy of a political cartoon from a recent newspaper or magazine. Explain the cartoonist's point of view and the tools used to make the point.

Glencoe's **Skillbuilder Interactive Workbook, Level 1** provides instruction and practice in key social studies skills.

1887
American Protective
Association targets
Catholics

1907
Gentlemen's
Agreement
restricts Japanese
immigration

1909
W.E.B.
Du Bois
helps form
the NAACP

1915
Ku Klux Klan
reappears

Section 4

Excluded From Reform

READ TO DISCOVER . . .

- why progressive reforms did little to help African Americans and other minorities.
- how minorities worked to combat prejudice and move toward greater equality.

TERMS TO LEARN

discrimination   barrio

The Storyteller

Prejudice against Asians and African Americans ran deep in the early 1900s. Many Asian immigrants were detained upon arrival in the United States. Held at an immigration station in San Francisco Bay, a Chinese immigrant carved the following poem on the wall of the barracks:

I used to admire the land of the Flowery
    Flag as a country of abundance.
I immediately raised money and started
    my journey.
For over a month, I have experienced
    enough wind and waves. . . .
I look up and see Oakland so
    close by. . . .
Discontent fills
    my belly and
    it is difficult
    for me to
    sleep. . . .

*Chinese shopkeeper
in California*

In 1908 violence erupted in **Springfield, Illinois,** when a white woman claimed to have been attacked by an African American man. Authorities jailed the man. The woman then admitted that her accusation was untrue. By that time, white townspeople had formed an angry mob.

Armed with axes and guns, the mob stormed through African American neighborhoods, destroying businesses and driving people from their homes. Rioters lynched two African American men and injured dozens more. Yet no one was ever punished for these violent crimes.

The Springfield riot shocked the nation and highlighted the deep racial divisions in American life. The riot took place in the hometown of Abraham Lincoln, the president who signed the Emancipation Proclamation. African Americans were no longer enslaved—but they were still pursued by prejudice and racial hatred.

Prejudice and Discrimination in America

During the 1800s the overwhelming majority of Americans were white, Protestant, and had been born in the United States. Many Americans believed that the United States should remain a white, Protestant nation. Nonwhite, non-Protestant, and non-native residents often faced discrimination—unequal treatment because of their race, religion, ethnic background, or place of birth. The government rarely interfered with this discrimination.

Chinese Immigrant Life

Padded robe

Hat made of black silk

What Was It Like? By the late 1800s, busy shops and restaurants dotted the streets of San Francisco's Chinatown. **What parts of Chinese culture shown here are included in your life today?**

Pair of children's shoes

Anti-Catholicism

Some Americans faced discrimination because of their religion. America's largely Protestant population feared that Catholic immigrants threatened the "American" way of life. Anti-Catholic Iowans formed the American Protective Association (APA) in 1887. By the mid-1890s, the APA claimed a membership of 2 million across the nation. Among other activities, the APA spread rumors that Catholics were preparing to take over the country.

Anti-Semitism

Many Jewish immigrants came to the United States to escape prejudice in their homelands. Some of them found the same anti-Semitic attitudes in America. Landlords, employers, and schools discriminated against Jews. Eastern European Jews faced prejudice both as Jews and as eastern Europeans, whom many Americans regarded as more "foreign" than western Europeans.

Anti-Asian Policies

Discrimination was also based on race. In California and other western states, Asians struggled against prejudice and resentment. White Americans claimed that Chinese immigrants, who worked for lower wages, took away jobs. Congress passed the Chinese Exclusion Act in 1882 to prevent Chinese immigrants from entering the United States.

America's westward expansion created opportunities for thousands of Japanese immigrants who came to the United States to work as railroad or farm laborers. Like the Chinese before them, Japanese immigrants encountered prejudice. California would not allow them to become citizens. In 1906 in **San Francisco,** the school board tried to make Japanese children attend a separate school for Asians until President Roosevelt stepped in to prevent such segregation.

Roosevelt yielded to a rising tide of anti-Japanese feeling, however, and authorized the **Gentlemen's Agreement** with Japan in 1907. This accord restricted Japanese immigration to the United States, but it did not bring an end to anti-Japanese feeling. In 1913 California made it illegal for Japanese immigrants to buy land. Other Western states passed similar laws.

Discrimination Against African Americans

African Americans faced discrimination in both the North and the South. Although officially free, African Americans were systematically denied basic rights and restricted to second-class citizenship.

Four-fifths of the nation's African Americans lived in the South. Most worked as rural sharecroppers or in low-paying jobs in the cities. They were separated from white society in their own neighborhoods, schools, parks, restaurants, theaters, and even cemeteries. In 1896 the Supreme Court legalized segregation in the case of *Plessy* v. *Ferguson,* which recognized "separate but equal" facilities.

The **Ku Klux Klan,** which had terrorized African Americans during Reconstruction, was reborn in Georgia in 1915. The new Klan wanted to restore white Protestant America. The Klan lashed out against minorities—Catholics, Jews, and immigrants, as well as African Americans. Calling for "100 percent Americanism," the Klan

kept growing and claimed more than 2 million members by 1924, many of them in Northern cities and towns.

Racial Violence

People who lost their jobs during the economic depressions of 1893 and 1907 sometimes unleashed their anger against African Americans and other minorities. More than 2,600 African Americans were lynched between 1886 and 1916, mostly in the South. Lynchings were also used to terrorize Chinese immigrants in the West.

Progressivism and Prejudice

In the late 1800s and the early 1900s, many Americans held biased views. They believed that white, male, native-born Americans had the right to make decisions for all of society.

Most of the progressive reformers came from the middle and upper classes. They saw themselves as moral leaders working to improve the lives of people less fortunate than themselves. The reforms they supported often discriminated against one group as they tried to help another group, however.

Trade unions often prohibited African Americans, women, and immigrants from joining. Skilled laborers, these unions argued, could

★ **Picturing HISTORY**

A Ku Klux Klan pamphlet (right) promotes the Klan's hate campaign against immigrants. Meanwhile, opponents of lynching called for an end to racial murders. **What two groups experienced the terror of lynching?**

Booker T. Washington (seated, second from left) founded the National Negro Business League. Why did Washington stress economic power among African Americans?

obtain better working conditions for themselves if they did not demand improved conditions for all workers.

Sometimes reforms instituted by the progressives were efforts to control a particular group. The temperance movement, for example, was partly an attempt to control the behavior of Irish Catholic immigrants. Civil service reforms required job applicants to be educated—this reduced the political influence that immigrants had begun to have in some cities. In spite of their contradictions, progressive reforms did succeed in improving conditions for many Americans.

Struggle for Equal Opportunity

⭐ Often excluded from progressive organizations because of prejudice, minorities battled for justice and opportunity on their own. African Americans, Hispanics, and Native Americans took steps to improve their lives.

African American Response

African Americans rose to the challenge of achieving equality. **Booker T. Washington,** who had been born enslaved and taught himself to read, founded the Tuskegee Institute in 1881. The institute taught African Americans farming and industrial skills.

Washington believed that if African Americans had more economic power, they would be in a better position to demand social equality and civil rights. Washington founded the **National Negro Business League** to promote business development among African Americans. In Washington's autobiography, *Up from Slavery*, he counseled African Americans to work slowly, patiently, and peacefully toward equality.

Equality Through Separation

Some African Americans thought that they would be better off in separate societies, either in the United States or in Africa. They founded organizations to establish African American towns and promoted a back-to-Africa movement. These movements were not popular, however, and their goals gained few supporters.

African American Women Take Action

African American women worked together through groups such as the National Association of Colored Women to fight the practice of lynching and other forms of racial violence. **Ida B. Wells,** the editor of an African American newspaper in Memphis, Tennessee, was forced to leave town after publishing the names of people involved in a lynching. The incident started Wells on a national crusade against the terrible practice of lynching.

Ida B. Wells

W.E.B. Du Bois

In her 1894 book, *A Red Record,* Wells showed that lynching was used primarily against African Americans who had become prosperous or who competed with white businesses. "Can you remain silent and inactive when such things are done in your own community and country?" she asked. As she traveled the country lecturing, Wells inspired the growth of the African American women's club movement.

📖 **Biography**

Equality for African Americans

W.E.B. Du Bois was one of the most important African American leaders of the time. Born in Great Barrington, Massachusetts, Du Bois proved to be a gifted debater and writer. At 15, he wrote a regular column for the *New York Globe.* Du Bois graduated from Fisk University at Nashville with honors and received a Ph.D. from Harvard University.

Du Bois urged African Americans to fight for civil rights. Under no circumstances, he said, should they accept segregation. He disagreed with Booker T. Washington's approach to improving the lives of African Americans. In *The Souls of Black Folk* (1903), Du Bois wrote:

❝ So far as Mr. Washington preaches Thrift, Patience, and Industrial Training . . . we must hold up his hands and strive with him. . . . But so far as Mr. Washington apologizes for injustice, North or South, does not rightly value the privilege and duty of voting, belittles the [devastating] effect of caste distinctions, and opposes the higher training and ambition of our brighter minds . . . we must unceasingly and firmly oppose [Washington's ideas]. ❞

In 1905 Du Bois helped organize a meeting of African American teachers, writers, and business leaders in the Canadian town of **Niagara, Ontario.** The meeting launched the **Niagara Movement,** which called for immediate economic and political equality for African Americans.

Four years later Du Bois and members of the Niagara Movement combined with other African Americans and some whites to form the **National Association for the Advancement of Colored People** (NAACP). For much of the century, this interracial group has remained at the forefront of efforts to gain legal and economic equality for African Americans. 📖

Other Successes

During the early 1900s African Americans achieved success in a variety of professions. Chemist **George Washington Carver,** director of agricultural research at Tuskegee Institute, helped improve the economy of the South through his discoveries of plant products. **Maggie Lena** founded the St. Luke Penny Savings Bank in Richmond, Virginia. She was the first American woman to serve as a bank president.

Native Americans Seek Justice

The federal government's efforts to assimilate Native Americans into white society threatened to break down traditional native cultures. In 1910–1911 Native American leaders from around the country formed the **Society of American Indians** to seek justice for Native Americans, to improve their living conditions, and to educate white Americans about different Native American cultures.

One of the society's founding members was **Dr. Carlos Montezuma,** an Apache who had been raised by whites. After graduating from medical school, Montezuma worked for the United States Indian Service.

Convinced that federal policies were hurting Native Americans, Montezuma turned to activism, exposing government abuse of Indian rights. Montezuma believed that Native Americans should leave the reservations and make their own way in white society.

Mexican Americans Work Together

Immigrants from Mexico had long come to the United States as laborers, especially in the West and Southwest. Between 1900 and 1914, the Mexican American population grew dramatically as people crossed the border to escape revolution and economic troubles in Mexico.

★ **Picturing HISTORY** Mexican Americans found work in the mines of the American Southwest during the 1890s. **How did Mexican Americans deal with the challenges they faced?**

Like the Japanese and other immigrant groups, Mexican Americans encountered discrimination and violence. Relying on themselves to solve their problems, they formed *mutualistas*—self-defense associations—to raise money for insurance and legal help. In labor camps and Mexican neighborhoods called **barrios,** they organized self-help groups to deal with overcrowding, poor sanitation, and inadequate public services.

Widespread prejudice excluded Mexican Americans and other minorities from many reform groups. Yet these groups produced dynamic leaders and created organizations to improve their circumstances and fight for justice.

Assessment and Activities

★ Reviewing Key Terms

On a sheet of paper, use each of the following terms in a sentence.

political machine
patronage
civil service
trust
muckraker
primary
initiative
referendum
recall
suffragist
arbitration
laissez-faire
conservation
discrimination
barrio

★ Reviewing Key Facts

1. How did corrupt political bosses get voters for their parties?
2. Why were journalists important to the reform movement?
3. What was the Eighteenth Amendment?
4. Why did progressives form their own political party?
5. What did Dr. Carlos Montezuma think about Native American reservations?

★ Critical Thinking

Determining Cause and Effect

Corruption in politics and business eventually led to stronger government regulation.

1. What conditions brought about the passage of the Meat Inspection Act?
2. Why was the railroad industry subject to so many government regulations?

★ Time Line Activity

Create a time line on which you place the following events in chronological order.

- Woodrow Wilson is elected president
- American Socialist Party is formed
- Women earn the right to vote
- Congress passes the Pendleton Act
- Theodore Roosevelt becomes president
- Congress passes the Meat Inspection and Pure Food and Drug acts

★ Reviewing Themes

1. **Government and Democracy** How did the Seventeenth Amendment give people a greater voice in government?
2. **Groups and Institutions** What did upper-class women and working women accomplish when they joined forces in the labor movement?
3. **Economic Factors** What was the purpose of the Federal Reserve Act?
4. **Civic Rights and Responsibilities** Why was the NAACP formed?

★ Geography Activity

The Federal Reserve System divided the nation into 12 districts. Each district served as a single "bank for bankers." Study the map on page 629 and answer the questions below.

1. **Location** Where is the Federal Reserve Bank in District 1?
2. **Location** Where is the Federal Reserve Bank in District 11?
3. **Place** How many states make up the largest Federal District?
4. **Region** In which Federal District do you live? In what city is the Federal Reserve Bank closest to you?

Regions of the Federal Reserve System

Numbered Federal Reserve Districts

■ Federal Reserve Bank

• Federal Reserve Branch Bank

⭐ Skill Practice Activity

Interpreting a Political Cartoon

Study the cartoon on page 605, then answer the following questions.

1. What figures are shown in the cartoon?
2. Is symbolism or caricature used in this cartoon? Explain.
3. What does the cartoon suggest about big business?
4. What title would you give this cartoon?

⭐ Technology Activity

Using E-Mail Research the names of five modern organizations that have some of the same goals as the progressive reformers of the late 1800s and early 1900s. Choose one organization that interests you and make contact through E-mail to get more information about the group.

Cooperative Activity

History and Geography Work with members of a group to research another country that is currently dealing with problems generated by discrimination and prejudice. Present an oral report to the class that describes specific incidents that have occurred in the country and the groups of people who are involved. Explain what is at the root of the prejudices that exist and compare it to prejudice and discrimination that exists in the United States. Use maps and other visual aids to make your presentation interesting and informative.

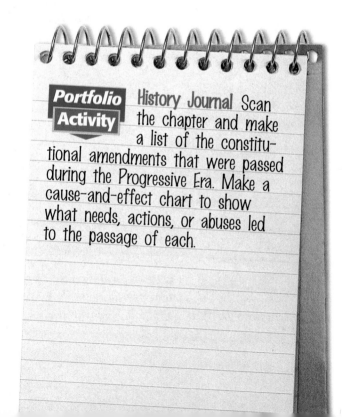

Portfolio Activity History Journal Scan the chapter and make a list of the constitutional amendments that were passed during the Progressive Era. Make a cause-and-effect chart to show what needs, actions, or abuses led to the passage of each.

1865–1917

Overseas Expansion

★ Why It's Important

Some of the territories that the United States acquired in the late 1800s and early 1900s have now gained their independence, and Hawaii and Alaska have joined the United States. Today United States overseas possessions include the Commonwealth of Puerto Rico and the U.S. Virgin Islands in the Caribbean, and Guam and American Samoa in the Pacific. Each of them sends a nonvoting delegate to the United States House of Representatives.

★ Chapter Themes

- *Section 1*, Economic Factors
- *Section 2*, Geography and History
- *Section 3*, Continuity and Change
- *Section 4*, Global Connections

PRIMARY SOURCES Library

See pages 978–979 for primary source readings to accompany Chapter 22

★ HISTORY AND ART **Battle of Santiago de Cuba** by James G. Tyler In 1898 Tyler painted a dramatic moment in the final sea battle of the Spanish-American War. The painting focuses on the newest weapon of war, the battleship.

1850		1870	1890

1853
Matthew Perry steams into Tokyo Bay

1854
Japan signs Treaty of Kanagawa

1867
William Seward signs treaty to buy Alaska

1889
Pan-American Union established

Section 1

Expanding Horizons

READ TO DISCOVER . . .

- what factors contributed to the growth of American imperialism.
- how the United States expanded its economic and political influence in the late 1800s.

TERMS TO LEARN

isolationism   imperialism
expansionism

The Storyteller

In the late 1800s and early 1900s, Americans looked beyond their borders and yearned for an empire. Merchants desired overseas markets, and adventurers wanted another frontier to conquer. Senator Albert Beveridge voiced the feelings of many when he proclaimed in 1900: "The Philippines are ours forever. . . . And just beyond the Philippines are China's illimitable markets. We will not retreat from either. . . . The Pacific is our ocean."

Patriotic song sheet, 1898

When President George Washington published his Farewell Address in 1796, he advised Americans to increase trade with other countries but to have "as little political connection as possible." Above all else, he warned Americans to "steer clear of permanent alliances with any portion of the foreign world."

These principles guided American foreign policy for about 100 years. However, various people interpreted Washington's words in different ways. Some believed he meant that the United States should follow a policy of isolationism, or noninvolvement, in world affairs. Others pointed out that Washington supported commercial ties and was not proposing complete isolation from the world.

American Foreign Policy

★ Americans have always had mixed feelings about their nation's role in world affairs. While striving to maintain their independence, merchants, farmers, and business leaders in the early United States relied on trade with other countries to obtain needed goods and to sell their own products.

American Expansionism

For many years Americans were absorbed in the dream of expanding their territory from ocean to ocean. Seeking land and better opportunities, many Americans moved to territories in the West

Chapter 22 Overseas Expansion **631**

Foreign Trade

In the mid-1800s, American merchants carried on a profitable trade with China and hoped to expand trade in other areas of the world. Many wanted to open trading relations with **Japan,** which had long been isolated from the West.

In 1853 President Millard Fillmore sent Commodore **Matthew Perry** on a mission to Japan. After steaming into Tokyo Bay with four warships, Perry asked the Japanese to open up their ports to U.S. ships. He told them he would return in several months for their answer.

The American show of force alarmed the Japanese. When Perry returned in 1854, the Japanese signed the **Treaty of Kanagawa** and opened two ports to American ships. Perry's successful mission began a period of trade between Japan and the United States. It also marked the start of greater American involvement in Asia.

HISTORY AND ART *Perry's First Landing in Japan at Kurihama* by **Gessan Ogata** A Japanese artist depicts Commodore Matthew Perry's 1853 arrival in Japan. **Why was Perry sent on a mission to Japan?**

and the South. This expansionism was a driving force in American history. While the nation was being torn apart during the Civil War, expansion came to a halt. After the war the United States began rebuilding and expanding again.

Americans settled the vast Great Plains, built railroads, and created large cities booming with people and busy factories. In 1890, as the nation spanned the North American continent from the Atlantic Ocean to the Pacific Ocean, the government issued a report announcing the end of the "frontier." Although areas of empty land remained, settlements could now be found from coast to coast.

To many Americans the frontier meant growth and opportunity. The idea that the frontier was no more was alarming. Americans began to look beyond the nation's borders to frontiers overseas where they could expand trade and compete for political influence.

An Age of Imperialism

★ The United States was not the only Western nation expanding its trade and influence in Asia and other parts of the world. The late 1800s and the early 1900s were called an age of imperialism, a time when powerful European nations created large empires by exercising economic and political control over weaker regions.

The search for materials and markets drove imperialism. The industrial nations of Europe needed raw materials from Asia and Africa. The

Trade with Japan

The amount of goods exchanged between Japan and the United States has grown tremendously since the 1850s. By the mid-1990s, trade between the two nations totaled about $175 billion a year. After Canada, Japan is America's most important trading partner.

Europeans also sought new markets for the goods they manufactured. In their drive for raw materials and new markets, European powers competed with one another for power and influence in Asia and Africa.

Toward an Empire

★ American interest in political as well as economic expansion developed after the Civil War. Some Americans wanted the nation to build an empire. By annexing new lands, they argued, the United States would join the ranks of the world's great powers and take its rightful place at the center of power.

Secretary of State **William H. Seward,** appointed by Abraham Lincoln, supported this view. Seward pictured an American empire that dominated the Caribbean, Central America, and the Pacific. Holding this empire together would be a canal across Central America linking the Atlantic and Pacific Oceans, a thriving transcontinental railroad system, and rapid communication by means of the telegraph.

The Purchase of Alaska

Seward took a major step toward making his vision a reality with the purchase of **Alaska.** In 1867 Seward signed a treaty with Russia to buy the Russian colony for $7.2 million—an extraordinary bargain for a territory that was twice the size of Texas.

At the time many people ridiculed Seward's purchase. They regarded Alaska as a barren, icebound land. Newspapers mocked the purchase as "Seward's Ice Box" and a "polar bear garden." After gold was discovered in Alaska in the 1890s, however, Seward's "folly" began to seem more like a wise purchase. In 1912 Alaska became a territory of the United States.

A Sense of Mission

Some Americans had another reason for imperialist expansion. They had a sense of mission—a belief that they could "lift up" people they considered "uncivilized" by sharing Christianity and Western civilization with the rest of the world. **Josiah Strong,** a Congregational minister, proposed an "imperialism of righteousness," with Americans bringing their religion and their culture to the peoples of Africa, Asia, and the United States's closest neighbor, Latin America.

American Interest in Latin America

Since colonial times, the United States had carried on a flourishing trade with Latin America, including the Caribbean region. Fear of European influence in the region was a factor that led to the Monroe Doctrine in 1823, when President James

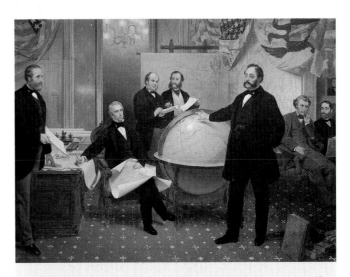

★ **Picturing HISTORY** Secretary of State William Seward (second from left) oversees the signing of the Alaska Purchase Treaty on March 30, 1867. **What country sold Alaska to the United States?**

*F*ootnotes to History

Seward's Revenge At about 2 cents an acre, the purchase of Alaska has paid for itself many times over with the gold, copper, and oil resources discovered there. The "polar bear garden" became a literal "gold mine."

Monroe warned European nations not to attempt to establish new colonies in North or South America.

United States merchants used the Monroe Doctrine to their advantage. In 1884 **James G. Blaine,** then the Republican nominee for president, declared:

❝ While the great powers of Europe are steadily enlarging their colonial domination in Asia and Africa, it is the [particular] province of this country to improve and expand its trade with the nations of America. ❞

Meanwhile, the United States signed treaties with a number of Latin American countries, allowing American businesses to influence those nations' economies.

As secretary of state in 1889, Blaine invited Latin American countries to attend a Pan-American Conference held in Washington, D.C. Blaine hoped to develop economic and political ties among the nations of the region. Although many Latin American countries worried about American domination, they decided to attend the meeting. The conference did establish the **Pan-American Union** to share information among member nations.

Building Sea Power

As the United States looked to expand its horizons, Captain **Alfred Thayer Mahan,** president of the Naval War College, called for improving and enlarging the navy. Mahan argued that sea power would protect shipping and provide access to world markets. "Sea power is essential to the greatness of every splendid people," Mahan declared. To maintain a powerful navy, the United States would need overseas colonies where ships could be refueled.

Transforming and expanding the navy began in 1883, when Congress authorized construction of the first steel-hulled warships. In the following years, the navy gradually shifted from sails to steam power and from wood to steel hulls. By the early 1900s, the United States had the naval power it needed to back up an expanded role in foreign affairs.

Senator Albert Beveridge of Indiana summed up the feeling of many American expansionists:

❝ We will establish trading posts throughout the world as distributing points for American products. We will cover the ocean with our merchant marine. We will build a navy to the measure of our greatness. . . . ❞

Section 1 Assessment

Checking for Understanding

1. **Identify** Matthew Perry, William H. Seward, James G. Blaine, Pan-American Union, Alfred Thayer Mahan.
2. **Define** isolationism, expansionism, imperialism.
3. **Discuss** the main points of the Monroe Doctrine.

Reviewing Themes

4. **Economic Factors** What two economic needs drove American imperialism?

Critical Thinking

5. **Identifying Assumptions** Some Americans who favored imperialist expansion believed it was their mission to "civilize" the "uncivilized" people of the world. What do you think these people meant by the term *uncivilized?*

◆ Activity ▶

Making a Resource Map Research the natural resources of Alaska. Draw a map of the state and use symbols to represent each resource and show its location in the state.

1890	1900	1910

1893
American planters overthrow Queen Liliuokalani

1899
U.S., Britain, and Germany divide Samoa

1900
Hawaii becomes a U.S. territory

1907
The Great White Fleet begins its voyage

Section 2

Imperialism in the Pacific

READ TO DISCOVER . . .

- how the United States gained control of Hawaii and Samoa.
- how competition for influence in China and the Pacific region led to new policies.

TERMS TO LEARN

annexation
spheres of influence

Open Door policy

The Storyteller

As more Americans arrived in Honolulu, many Hawaiians feared that time was running out for their people. Kaona, a local judge in Honolulu, had visions that the end of the world was near. When volcanoes erupted and earth tremors plagued the island, his visions seemed to be coming true. Kaona and his followers prepared for the end. They dressed in flowing white robes and prayed loudly. Kaona had indeed been correct. The world that he and native Hawaiians had known would soon end.

Hawaiian stamp

Secretary of State **William H. Seward** believed the United States could build its empire through peaceful means, with American trade leading the way. The Pacific region played a key part in Seward's plan for expansion. In 1867—the same year he bought Alaska—Seward acquired the two small Pacific islands of **Midway.** He thought that these islands, more than 3,000 miles (4,800 km) west of California, would serve as an important stopping place for American ships en route to China.

American merchants and the United States Navy would need more than two small islands, however, to establish a secure foothold in the vast stretches of the Pacific. Seward believed the United States should also acquire **Hawaii.**

🌐 Geography

Hawaii

⭐ The lush Hawaiian Islands, a chain of 8 large and 100 or so smaller islands, lay about 2,000 miles (3,200 km) west of California. The Hawaiian people dwelled in independent communities, each with its own chieftain, and lived by farming and fishing. American trading ships and whalers often stopped at the islands to take on supplies and fresh water.

In the 1790s Americans began trading with the Hawaiians for local resources such as sandalwood, which the Americans traded in China. About that same time, King Kamehameha I unified the islands. Villages with good ports such as

Honolulu and **Lahaina** (luh•HY•nuh) began to grow in importance, and trade increased. However, American and European ships also brought infectious diseases to the islands. These diseases devastated the island population just as they had once devastated the Native Americans.

Missionaries and Sugar Growers

In 1820 Christian missionaries from the United States began arriving in Hawaii. They established schools, created a written Hawaiian alphabet, and translated the Bible into Hawaiian. Increasing numbers of American merchants in the whaling trade came to settle there, too.

An American firm introduced sugarcane in Hawaii in the 1830s, and the missionaries and traders began buying land and establishing sugar plantations. The sugar industry grew quickly, and plantation owners brought in thousands of immigrants from Japan, China, and other Pacific lands to work in the fields. Gradually the Americans took control of most of the land and businesses. They also exerted strong influence in Hawaiian politics, serving as advisers to the Hawaiian ruling family. Although the United States recognized Hawaiian independence in 1842, the islands came increasingly under American influence.

In 1875 the United States agreed to allow Hawaiian sugar to enter the country without tariffs. As sugar exports to the United States soared, American planters in Hawaii reaped enormous profits. In 1887, in return for renewal of the trade agreement, the United States pressured King Kalakaua (kah•LAH•KAH•u•ah) to allow it to establish a naval base at **Pearl Harbor,** the best seaport in the islands.

In the early 1890s, under pressure from American sugar producers, Congress revised the tariff laws and eliminated the exemption for Hawaiian sugar. As a result, Hawaiian sugar planters had to drop their prices drastically in order to sell any sugar. Sugar exports to the United States dropped sharply. Facing financial ruin, the planters plotted a way to avoid the new tariff. They decided to make Hawaii a territory of the United States.

American Planters' Revolt

The Hawaiians, meanwhile, had begun to resist the growing influence of Americans. In 1891 Queen **Liliuokalani** (lih•LEE•uh•woh•kuh•LAH•nee) came to the throne. The new ruler wanted Hawaiians to regain economic control of their islands, and she took away powers that the American sugar planters had held. In response, the white planters overthrew Liliuokalani and set up their own **provisional,** or temporary,

Queen Liliuokalani

Japanese workers tended the boiler furnaces of Hawaii's American-run sugar industry. **What happened to Hawaii in 1900?**

government in 1893. The queen left under protest: "Now, to avoid any collision of armed forces and perhaps the loss of life, I . . . yield my authority."

Annexation

The success of the planters' revolt stemmed in part from the support of the chief American diplomat in Hawaii, **John Stevens,** who arranged for marines from the warship *Boston* to assist in the uprising. Stevens immediately recognized the new government, which sent a delegation to Washington to seek a treaty of annexation that would add Hawaii to the United States. President Benjamin Harrison signed the treaty during the final days of his administration and forwarded it to the Senate for approval.

However, the Senate did not act quickly enough. It failed to ratify the treaty before Harrison left office. The new president, **Grover Cleveland,** opposed annexation and withdrew the treaty from the Senate after discovering that Hawaiians did not support the revolt. Cleveland called American interference in the Hawaiian revolution "disgraceful."

Although most of the Hawaiians and the Asian immigrants in Hawaii opposed annexation, their opposition made no difference. A small, powerful group of American sugar growers, traders, and missionaries—and their Hawaiian allies, along with influential people in the United States—had the final word. Congress approved the annexation of Hawaii in 1898, after William McKinley became president. In 1900 Hawaii became a territory of the United States.

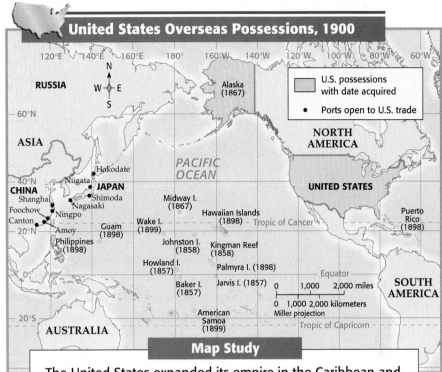

United States Overseas Possessions, 1900

Map Study

The United States expanded its empire in the Caribbean and the Pacific from the 1850s to 1900.
1. **Location** Locate Puerto Rico, Guam, and the Philippines. Which of these is the farthest from the continental United States?
2. **Analyzing Information** When were the Hawaiian Islands acquired?

The Islands of Samoa

About 3,000 miles (4,800 km) south of Hawaii lay the **Samoa Islands,** directly on the trade route linking Australia and the United States. As early as the 1830s, missionaries from the United States landed in Samoa and began converting the people to Christianity.

In 1878 Samoa agreed to give Americans special trading rights and permission to build a naval station at the port of **Pago Pago.** Great Britain and Germany also wanted a stake in the Samoa Islands, and they secured trading rights, too. During the 1880s, tensions mounted as the three rivals competed for power in Samoa.

In 1899 the United States, Great Britain, and Germany met in Berlin and—without consulting the Samoans—decided to divide up the islands. The United States and Germany split Samoa between them, while Great Britain agreed to

View of Peking After the Boxer Rebellion by Yoshikazu Ichikawa
American soldiers march through the Chinese capital after the Boxer Rebellion. **What policy did the United States want for China?**

withdraw from the area in return for rights on other Pacific islands. The Americans annexed their portion of Samoa the same year.

China and the Open Door

 For Americans the island territories in the Pacific, while important in themselves, represented stepping-stones to a larger prize—**China.** Torn apart by warring factions and lacking industry, China was too weak to resist the efforts of foreign powers that wanted to exploit its vast resources and markets.

Rivalries in China

By the late 1890s, Japan and the leading European powers had carved out spheres of influence in China—sections of the country where each of the foreign nations enjoyed special rights and powers. Japan held the island of Formosa and parts of the Chinese mainland. Germany controlled the Shandong area in east-central China. Great Britain and France held a number of Chinese provinces, and Russia moved into **Manchuria** and other areas in northern China.

In the United States, some government and business leaders worried about being squeezed out of the profitable China trade. Although the United States could not force the other foreign powers out of China, Secretary of State **John Hay** wanted to protect and expand American trading interests in the country. Hay proposed an Open Door policy under which each foreign nation in China could trade freely in the other nations' spheres of influence.

The Boxer Rebellion

The other major powers were reluctant to accept a policy that would benefit the United States most of all. The situation soon changed, however. By late 1899 a secret Chinese martial art society, known as the **Boxers,** led a violent uprising against the "foreign devils" in China. About 200 foreigners died in the **Boxer Rebellion;** for nearly 2 months, hundreds more were trapped in the besieged capital city of **Beijing.** Finally, in August 1900, foreign troops broke the siege and defeated the Boxers.

Out of the Boxer Rebellion came a second Open Door proposal, which stressed the importance of maintaining China's independence and respecting its borders. Alarmed by the rebellion, the other foreign powers accepted Hay's policy. They also forced China to sign new commercial treaties as compensation for the rebellion's damage.

Japan

★ Eager to expand its power in Asia, Japan began to ignore the Open Door policy. Japan's actions led to war with Russia and conflict with the United States.

Russo-Japanese War

In the early 1900s, Japan and Russia clashed over their interest in Manchuria, a Chinese province rich in natural resources. On February 8, 1904, Japan launched an attack on the Russian fleet at **Port Arthur** in southern Manchuria, starting the **Russo-Japanese War.** The Japanese scored a series of victories, destroying the Russian fleet. By the spring of 1905, both Japan's and Russia's resources were nearly exhausted, and both countries were eager to make peace. President **Theodore Roosevelt** offered to meet with their leaders in **Portsmouth, New Hampshire,** to help settle the conflict. In September 1905, Japan and Russia signed the **Treaty of Portsmouth,** which recognized Japan's control of Korea in return for a pledge by Japan to halt its expansion.

Roosevelt hoped the treaty would preserve a balance of power in Asia, but it failed to do so. Japan emerged from the war as the strongest naval power in the Pacific, and it challenged the United States for influence in the region. Relations between the two nations deteriorated steadily.

Strained Relations

During the Russo-Japanese War, Japanese immigration to the United States—especially to California—increased. Many Americans resented the Japanese newcomers, claiming that they took jobs from Americans. Anti-Asian feeling mounted.

As you read in Chapter 21, in 1906 the San Francisco Board of Education ordered that all Asian students attend separate schools. The Japanese government protested. An 1894 treaty had guaranteed that Japanese living in the United States would be treated well. The Japanese felt that the treaty had been broken.

President Roosevelt forced the San Francisco school board to change its policies. In return, he persuaded Japan to consent to a **gentlemen's agreement,** promising to restrict emigration. The Japanese resented the Gentlemen's Agreement and relations between the two nations worsened. Some Americans called for war.

The "Great White Fleet"

Although President Roosevelt had no plan for war, in 1907 he sent 16 gleaming white battleships on a cruise around the world to display the nation's naval power. The **"Great White Fleet"** greatly impressed the Japanese. By the time the fleet returned to America in 1909, the United States and Japan had resolved many of their differences.

Section 2 Assessment

★ ★ ★ ★ ★ ★ ★ ★ ★ ★

Checking for Understanding
1. **Identify** Liliuokalani, John Hay, Gentlemen's Agreement, Great White Fleet.
2. **Define** annexation, spheres of influence, Open Door policy.
3. **Name** three Pacific islands that the United States acquired in the late 1800s and early 1900s.

Reviewing Themes
4. **Geography and History** Why were American political leaders so interested in the Pacific islands in the late 1800s?

Critical Thinking
5. **Making Inferences** Why do you think Roosevelt considered the cruise of the Great White Fleet to be "the most important service [he] rendered for peace"?

Activity

Making a Diagram Research the process of turning sugarcane into refined sugar. Draw a diagram showing the steps involved.

1894	1896	1898	1900

1895
José Martí leads revolt in Cuba

1897
William McKinley becomes president

1898
The *Maine* explodes; the Spanish-American War takes place

1900
Foraker Act sets up new government in Puerto Rico

Section 3

Spanish-American War

READ TO DISCOVER . . .

- why the Spanish-American War began.
- what territory the United States gained in the war.
- how the United States's role in the world expanded after the Spanish-American War.

TERMS TO LEARN

yellow journalism   protectorate
armistice

The Storyteller

Spanish authorities arrested José, a young Cuban teenager, for supporting Cuban independence. They sentenced him to hard labor in Havana's stone quarry. At the stone quarry, an angry guard struck José with a heavy iron chain, causing him to walk with a limp for the rest of his life. But young José wrote a play in which the main character stated: "I will be the one to free my anguished country." José Martí would, indeed, be the one to lead his people to independence from Spain.

Cuban patriot José Martí

The people of **Cuba** had lived under Spanish rule for centuries. Several times in the late 1800s, the Cubans rebelled. But each time, the Spanish overpowered them and smashed their dreams of independence. **José Martí,** one of the heroes of the Cuban independence movement, fled to the United States to gather money, arms, and troops. In 1895, as economic conditions in Cuba worsened, Martí returned to Cuba to lead his people in a new revolt.

The Cuban Rebellion

⭐ Martí's revolution led to terrible losses in human life and property. The rebels burned sugarcane fields and destroyed buildings in hopes of forcing the Spaniards to leave. In retaliation Spanish troops herded more than 300,000 Cubans into fortified towns and camps to separate them from the rebels and to break their morale. Thousands of Cubans died of starvation and disease.

War Fever

The Cuban people's struggle against Spain attracted much sympathy in the United States. Businesspeople worried about the destruction of trade and their loss of investments in Cuba. Government leaders were concerned about a rebellion so close to the United States. Finally, many Americans were horrified by the atrocities against Cuban citizens and called for the government to do something about it.

President Grover Cleveland opposed any American involvement in Cuba. In March 1897, **William McKinley** became president. He, too, hoped the conflict could be settled peacefully.

The American press reported the unfolding tragedy in Cuba in graphic detail, and its coverage intensified the debate over America's role in the crisis. Newspapers, including **Joseph Pulitzer's** *World* and **William Randolph Hearst's** *Journal,* tried to outdo each other with shocking reports on the revolution. Hearst supposedly told an artist who was illustrating a story on Cuba, "You furnish the pictures, and I'll furnish the war." This type of sensational, biased, and often false reporting—known as yellow journalism— played a major role in fanning the flames of pro-war sentiment in the United States.

"Remember the *Maine*"

The pressure on President McKinley to take action seemed to grow by the hour. After rioting broke out in the Cuban capital of Havana in January 1898, McKinley sent the battleship *Maine* to protect the lives and property of American citizens.

The ship remained quietly at anchor in Havana Harbor for 3 weeks. Then, on the night of February 15, 1898, an enormous explosion shattered the *Maine,* killing about 260 officers and crew members. American newspapers immediately blamed the Spanish, and the slogan "Remember the *Maine*" became a rallying cry for

revenge. Spain denied responsibility for the explosion. Much later, evidence indicated that the explosion may have been accidental, but at the time, Americans clamored for war with Spain.

After the *Maine* incident, President McKinley sent the Spanish a strong note demanding a truce and an end to brutality against the Cubans. The Spanish agreed to some American demands, but not enough to satisfy McKinley or Congress. On April 19 Congress recognized Cuban independence. It also demanded the withdrawal of Spanish forces and authorized the president to use the army and navy to enforce American aims. On April 25, 1898, Congress declared war on Spain.

War in the Philippines

Although events in Cuba triggered the Spanish-American War, the war's first military actions happened thousands of miles away in the Spanish colony of the **Philippines.** These islands served as a base for part of the Spanish fleet. In late February 1898, Assistant Secretary of the Navy **Theodore Roosevelt** had wired Commodore **George Dewey** and his squadron of navy vessels to prepare for action in the Philippines "in the event of declaration of war." In the early morning hours of May 1, Dewey launched a surprise attack on the Spanish fleet in Manila Bay, destroying most of the ships.

American troops arrived in July. With the help of Filipino rebels led by **Emilio Aguinaldo** (AH•gee•NAHL•doh), the Americans captured

 Picturing HISTORY Yellow journalism helped build American public support for war with Spain. **What two publishers presented shocking reports of the Cuban revolt?**

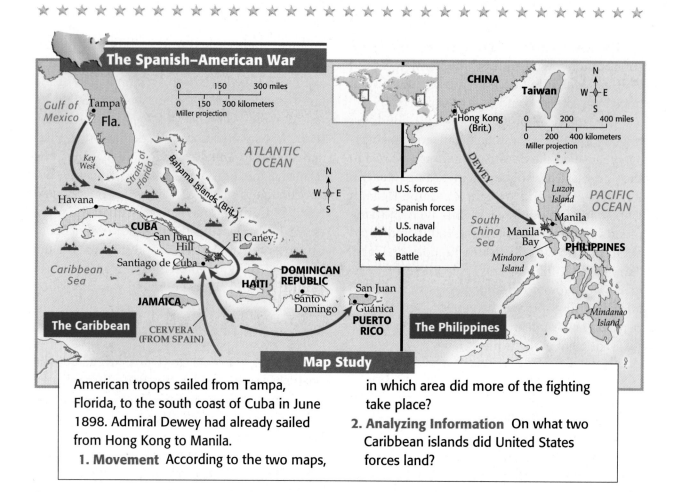

The Spanish–American War

0   150   300 miles
0 150 300 kilometers
Miller projection

Gulf of Mexico
Tampa
Fla.

Key West

Straits of Florida

Havana

CUBA

San Juan Hill

Santiago de Cuba

Caribbean Sea

JAMAICA

Bahama Islands (Brit.)

ATLANTIC OCEAN

El Caney

DOMINICAN REPUBLIC

HAITI

Santo Domingo

San Juan

Guánica

PUERTO RICO

The Caribbean   CERVERA (FROM SPAIN)

Legend:
← U.S. forces
← Spanish forces
⚓ U.S. naval blockade
✳ Battle

CHINA
Taiwan
Hong Kong (Brit.)

0   200   400 miles
0 200 400 kilometers
Miller projection

DEWEY

South China Sea

Luzon Island

Manila
Manila Bay

PACIFIC OCEAN

Mindoro Island

PHILIPPINES

Mindanao Island

The Philippines

Map Study

American troops sailed from Tampa, Florida, to the south coast of Cuba in June 1898. Admiral Dewey had already sailed from Hong Kong to Manila.

1. **Movement** According to the two maps, in which area did more of the fighting take place?

2. **Analyzing Information** On what two Caribbean islands did United States forces land?

---

the city of Manila. As in Cuba, the Filipino rebels had struggled for years to win independence from Spain. Using American-supplied arms, they seized the main island of **Luzon,** declared independence, and created a democratic republic. The rebels expected the United States to support their independence. However, the United States debated what to do with the islands.

Fighting in Cuba

Meanwhile in the Caribbean, a Spanish fleet entered the harbor of **Santiago** on the southeastern shore of Cuba on May 19. Several days later, an American naval force blockaded the coast, trapping the Spanish in the harbor.

An American land force of about 17,000—nearly a quarter of them African American—landed near the city of Santiago. The inexperienced, ill-equipped Americans disembarked while forces under Cuban general Calixto García drove off the Spanish soldiers. When the Cuban and American forces advanced, wrote Sergeant Major Frank W.

Pullen, Jr., they faced "a perfect hailstorm of bullets, which, thanks to the poor marksmanship of the Spaniards, 'went high.'" Heavy fighting followed, however.

The Rough Riders

Theodore Roosevelt resigned his position as assistant secretary of the navy to join the fighting in Cuba. He led the First Regiment of U.S. Cavalry Volunteers, an assorted group of former cowhands and college students, popularly known as the **Rough Riders.** On July 1 the Rough Riders, with African American soldiers of the Ninth and Tenth Cavalries, joined the **Battle of San Juan Hill.** "I waved my hat and we went up the hill with a rush," Roosevelt wrote later.

The Americans captured San Juan Hill after intense fighting. Two days later the Spanish fleet attempted to break out of Santiago. In a battle that lasted about four hours, the Spanish fleet was completely destroyed. This defeat ended Spanish resistance in Cuba.

The United States then turned its attention to the Spanish colony of **Puerto Rico,** east of Cuba. American troops landed on Puerto Rico in late July and quickly took control of the island. Then on August 12 the Spanish signed an armistice—a peace agreement—ending the war.

"A Splendid Little War"

Secretary of State **John Hay** called the **Spanish-American War** "a splendid little war." The war lasted fewer than 4 months, and only 460 Americans were killed in battle or died from wounds received in the fighting.

Yet the war had other aspects that were not at all "splendid." More than 5,000 Americans died of diseases such as yellow fever, malaria, and other diseases contracted in the tropical climate. The 10,000 African Americans who served faced the additional burden of discrimination. Serving in segregated units, African Americans battled alongside the Cuban rebel army, in which black and white troops fought as equals.

In the Caribbean

The United States and Spain signed the Treaty of Paris on December 10, 1898, marking the official end of the war. The treaty dissolved most of the Spanish empire. Cuba became an American protectorate, a country that is technically independent but actually under the control of another country. Puerto Rico and the Pacific island of **Guam** became territories of the United States. Spain also surrendered the Philippines to the United States in exchange for $20 million. The American empire had become a reality, and with the empire came new responsibilities.

Cuban Protectorate

Americans debated what to do about Cuba. Many congressional leaders believed that the Cubans were not ready for complete self-government. American business leaders feared that leaving Cuba might weaken the political stability of Cuba and jeopardize American interests there.

While Congress considered the matter, American troops remained in Cuba. Finally in 1901 the United States agreed to grant Cubans full independence, but only if their new constitution included clauses giving the United States certain rights. Known as the **Platt Amendment,** these clauses prohibited Cuba from making treaties with other nations and gave America control of a naval base at **Guantanamo Bay.** The Platt Amendment also gave the United States the right to intervene in Cuban affairs if the country's independence was threatened.

Major Charles Young

★ HISTORY AND ART **Charge of the Rough Riders at San Juan Hill** by **Frederic Remington** Rough Riders, led by Theodore Roosevelt (on horseback), fight the Battle of San Juan Hill. Major Charles Young, the highest-ranking African American officer, commanded four units of African American troops in Cuba. **What was the outcome of the Cuban campaign?**

New Government for Puerto Rico

After the war, Puerto Rico remained under direct military rule. Then in 1900 the United States set up a new Puerto Rican government under the **Foraker Act.** The American government controlled the new administration. In 1917 the Jones Act made Puerto Rico a territory of the United States and granted American citizenship to all Puerto Ricans. However, many Puerto Ricans still wanted independence.

Acquiring the Philippines

The United States gained possession of the Philippines in the treaty that ended the Spanish-American War. But acquisition of the Philippines aroused fierce debate.

American Anti-Imperialism

During the 1890s some people—**anti-imperialists**—opposed the American enthusiasm for foreign expansion and the Spanish-American War. After the war the anti-imperialists fought approval of the treaty. Some argued that American rule of the Philippines contradicted the principles on which the United States was founded. Others

opposed the large standing army that would be necessary to control the Philippines. Still others feared competition from Filipino laborers.

Many Americans—including Carl Schurz, Andrew Carnegie, and Mark Twain—joined the anti-imperialist campaign. The imperialists, led by Senators Henry Cabot Lodge and Albert Beveridge, eventually won out, however. The Senate ratified the Treaty of Paris on February 6, 1899.

Resistance to Takeover

In February 1899, Emilio Aguinaldo's forces began a long, bloody revolt against American rule. This conflict became a mammoth undertaking for the United States. More than 4,000 Americans died. Filipinos suffered far greater casualties—at least 50,000 died.

Except for sporadic fighting, the rebellion ended in March 1901 with the capture of Aguinaldo. He declared his allegiance to the United States and urged his followers to stop fighting.

In the summer of 1901, the United States transferred authority in the Philippines from the military to a civilian government headed by **William Howard Taft.** Taft set out to prepare the islands for eventual self-rule. However, the Philippines did not achieve full independence until 1946.

★ ★ ★ ★ ★ Section 3 Assessment ★ ★ ★ ★ ★ ★

Checking for Understanding

1. **Identify** José Martí, Emilio Aguinaldo, Rough Riders, Platt Amendment.
2. **Define** yellow journalism, armistice, protectorate.
3. **Summarize** how yellow journalism influenced Americans' views of going to war with Spain.

Reviewing Themes

4. **Continuity and Change** How did the United States govern Puerto Rico and the Philippines?

Critical Thinking

5. **Making Critical Judgments** Do you think the United States should have taken permanent control of Cuba and made it part of its empire? Why or why not?

Creating a News Report Write a 45-second television news report to convince viewers that they should pressure the United States president to get involved in a war with Spain over Cuba. Use "yellow journalism" to help sway your listeners. Present your report to the class.

Developing Multimedia Presentations

You want to present a research report to the rest of your class, and you want to really hold their attention. How do you do it? Your presentation can be exciting if you use various media.

computer graphic tools and draw programs, animation programs that make still images move, and authoring systems that tie everything together. Your computer manual will tell you which tools your computer can support.

Learning the Skill

At its most basic, a multimedia presentation involves using several types of media. To discuss life in the Philippines, for example, you might show photographs of the country. You could also play a recording of the country's language and music, or present a video showing the Filipino people at work and at play.

You can also develop a multimedia presentation on a computer. Multimedia as it relates to computer technology is the combination of text, video, audio, and animation in an interactive computer program.

In order to create multimedia productions or presentations on a computer, you need to have certain tools. These may include traditional

Practicing the Skill

This chapter focuses on the overseas expansion of the United States in the late 1800s and early 1900s. Ask yourself questions like the following to develop a multimedia presentation on the people, politics, and industries of that era:

- Which forms of media do I want to include? Video? Sound? Animation? Photographs? Graphics? Other?
- Which of these media forms does my computer support?
- What kind of software programs or systems do I need? A paint program? A draw program? An animation program? A program to create interactive, or two-way, communication? An authoring system that will allow me to change images, sound, and motion?
- Is there a "do-it-all" program I can use to develop the kind of presentation I want?

Applying the Skill

Developing Multimedia Presentations
Keeping in mind the four guidelines given above, write a plan describing a multimedia presentation you would like to develop. Indicate what tools you will need and what steps you must take to make the presentation a reality.

1900   1910   1920

1904   **1911**   **1914**   **1916**
Roosevelt   Revolution   Panama   Francisco "Pancho"
Corollary   occurs   Canal   Villa launches
is issued   in Mexico   opens   uprising in Mexico

Section 4

Latin American Policies

READ TO DISCOVER . . .
- what shaped the policies the United States followed in Latin America.
- where and how the United States intervened in Latin America.

TERMS TO LEARN
isthmus   dollar diplomacy
anarchy

The Storyteller

On August 15, 1914, something described as the "greatest liberty that Man has taken with Nature" occurred. On that day, the first ship, the *Ancon,* traveled through the newly built Panama Canal. The world barely noticed, however. Most eyes were watching Europe, where World War I was gearing up. As the ship passed the words on the great seal of the Panama Canal Zone—THE LAND DIVIDED, THE WORLD UNITED— the world was setting out to tear itself to pieces.

Canal brochure

Americans and Europeans had long dreamed of building a canal across Central America to connect the Atlantic and Pacific Oceans and to eliminate the long and hazardous sea voyage around South America. Now that the United States controlled territory in both oceans, a canal that would allow faster and easier access to American interests overseas became increasingly important.

In 1879 a French company had acquired a 25-year lease from the government of Colombia to construct a canal across its province of **Panama.** Panama was an isthmus—a narrow strip of land connecting two larger bodies of land—about 50 miles (80 km) wide. Wedged between the Caribbean Sea and the Pacific Ocean, Panama seemed like the perfect site for the canal.

The United States in Panama

French efforts to build a canal ended in financial disaster, and in 1901 the United States bought the lease from the French for $40 million. In 1903 Secretary of State John Hay negotiated a treaty with Colombia that granted the United States a 99-year lease on a strip of land across Panama in return for a payment of $10 million and an annual rent of $250,000.

In Colombia, widespread opposition to the low price offered by the Americans led the Colombian senate to reject the treaty. In a fit of anger, President Roosevelt referred to the Colombians who rejected the treaty as "inefficient bandits." He believed the canal was essential to America's national defense.

Revolution in Panama

Roosevelt began looking for other ways to get land for the canal, and he wrote that he would "be delighted if Panama were an independent state." The Panamanians had staged revolts against Colombia in the past, but never with success. This time, however, the Panamanians had reason to believe that the Americans would support them in a revolt against Colombia.

On November 2, 1903, the American warship *Nashville* steamed into the port of Colón on the Caribbean coast of Panama. Encouraged by this show of support, the Panamanians revolted the next day and declared their independence. When Colombia sent forces to stop the revolt, the United States intervened and turned them back.

The Panama Canal

On November 6, the United States recognized Panama's independence. Less than two weeks later, Hay signed a treaty with the new nation of Panama. It gave the United States a 10-mile (16-km) strip of land across the country for the same amount offered earlier to Colombia. The United States now had land to build a canal.

Roosevelt's actions in Panama horrified many Latin Americans and angered some members of Congress and other Americans. The president, however, took great pride in his accomplishment. "I took the canal zone and let Congress debate," he said later, "and while the debate goes on, the canal does also."

Building the Canal

The United States could now start work on the canal—not an easy undertaking. Disease ran rampant among the workers. An English writer described Panama as "a damp, tropical jungle, intensely hot, swarming with mosquitoes." These mosquitoes carried two deadly diseases—yellow fever and malaria.

Colonel **William Gorgas,** an army physician who had helped eliminate yellow fever in Cuba, went to Panama to fight the diseases. Gorgas instructed workers to drain swamps, spray insecticides, spread oil on stagnant pools of water, and cut grassy marshes in order to kill mosquito eggs and destroy mosquito breeding places. By 1906 these measures had eliminated yellow fever and greatly reduced the number of malaria

Workers building the Panama Canal

HISTORY AND ART

Work Trains, Miraflores by Alson Skinner Clark The building of the Panama Canal was a tribute to the skill of American engineers. What challenges did American engineers face in building the canal?

The United States used the Monroe Doctrine to warn Great Britain and other European powers not to intervene in Latin America. **What was the purpose of the Roosevelt Corollary?**

cases. Without controlling disease, the United States could not have built the canal.

The Panama Canal was regarded as one of the great engineering feats of the time. About 40,000 workers, including many African Americans from the West Indies, struggled to carve a path through the dense jungle and over mountains. They dug out enormous amounts of earth and rock and used them to build a dam. They created a huge lake and constructed giant locks to raise and lower ships from sea level over the mountains and then back to sea level again on the other side of the isthmus.

The Grand Opening

The Panama Canal opened on August 15, 1914, and a cargo ship, the *Ancon*, made the first trip through the canal. A great success from the start, the canal reduced shipping costs by cutting more than 7,000 miles off the voyage from New York to San Francisco. The canal also helped increase and extend American naval power by allowing the United States fleet to move freely between the Atlantic and Pacific Oceans.

In the long run, the canal guaranteed a strong American presence in Latin America, where the United States now had a valuable property it intended to protect. Yet many Latin Americans remained bitter over how the Canal Zone was acquired. This resentment helped sour relations between the United States and Latin America for years.

Policing the Western Hemisphere

★ When Theodore Roosevelt became president in 1901, one of his major goals was to consolidate America's territorial gains in the Pacific and the Caribbean. In Roosevelt's view, the United States had both a duty and a right to intervene in these and other regions that fell under its influence.

The president often quoted an African proverb, "Speak softly and carry a big stick." He believed the United States should respond to foreign crises not by threats but by military action. Roosevelt became known for his "big stick" approach to foreign affairs. America must exercise "an international police power," he maintained, to preserve order and prevent the world from falling into anarchy—disorder and lawlessness.

Roosevelt Corollary

Roosevelt worried that instability in the Caribbean region would lead European powers to intervene. Two incidents confirmed his fears. In 1902, when **Venezuela** failed to meet payments on its loans, European nations imposed a blockade. The following year a revolution in the **Dominican Republic** toppled the government, causing concern that European powers would step in to protect their financial interests there.

The president responded to these incidents in 1904 by asserting America's right to act as a "policeman" in Latin America, intervening "however reluctantly . . . in cases of wrongdoing." This policy, known as the **Roosevelt Corollary,** was a significant addition to the Monroe Doctrine. Up to that time, the United States had used the Monroe Doctrine only to prevent European intervention in Latin America. Under the Roosevelt Corollary, the United States now claimed the right to intervene in the domestic affairs of Latin American nations whenever those nations seemed unstable.

The United States first applied the Roosevelt Corollary in 1905, when it took control of the Dominican Republic's finances. This arrangement continued for more than 30 years. The United States used the policy again in 1906, when troops were sent to Cuba to stop a revolution there.

Dollar Diplomacy

Theodore Roosevelt thought of American power primarily in military terms. His successor in the White House, **William Howard Taft,** took a more commercial view of American interests. Taft hoped to modify American foreign policy by "substituting dollars for bullets."

President Taft was willing to intervene in other nations whenever American prosperity and business interests were threatened. He believed that American investments would bring stability to troubled areas of the world, as well as profit and power to the United States, without the need for force. Taft's policy of linking American business interests to diplomatic interests abroad was known as dollar diplomacy.

Encouraged by dollar diplomacy, American investments in Latin America grew dramatically in the early 1900s. American investments helped build roads, railroads, and harbors, which stimulated trade and brought benefits to both Latin American countries and the United States.

Dollar diplomacy also resulted in greater United States involvement overseas. Large American companies gained great power in Latin America and controlled the politics of some nations in the region. Furthermore, when American business interests were endangered, military intervention often followed. In 1912, when a revolution in Nicaragua threatened American business interests, the United States quickly sent marines to restore peace. Such interference led to increased anti-American feelings throughout Latin America.

Relations with Mexico

★ In the early 1900s, **Mexico** was a poor country run by a tiny group of rich landholders. Investors in the United States poured more than $2 billion into Mexican oil wells and other businesses. Then, in 1911, Mexico entered a turbulent period in its history—one that threatened American investments, revealed the weaknesses of dollar diplomacy, and led to military intervention by the United States.

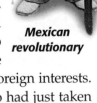

Mexican revolutionary

War in Mexico

In 1911 a popular Mexican reformer named **Francisco Madero** (muh•DEHR•oh) led a revolution to overthrow Mexico's brutal dictator **Porfirio Díaz** (DEE•AHS). Although foreign business and some Mexican politicians and landowners had prospered under the rule of Díaz, the lives of most Mexicans had grown worse.

Two years after taking power, Madero was overthrown and killed by General **Victoriano Huerta** (WEHR•tuh), who—like Díaz—favored the wealthy and foreign interests. President **Woodrow Wilson,** who had just taken office, refused to recognize Huerta's "government of butchers."

Wilson's "Moral Diplomacy"

A sincere believer in the ideals of democracy, Wilson thought the United States had a duty "to teach the South American republics to elect good men." Like Roosevelt and Taft, Wilson recognized the importance of military power and economic interests. Yet Wilson also attempted to follow a foreign policy based on moral principles.

Wilson's "moral diplomacy" faced a serious challenge in Mexico. After Huerta took power, a civil war broke out in Mexico. Wilson hoped that the Huerta government, without American support, would fall. When that did not happen, Wilson authorized arms sales to Huerta's rival, **Venustiano Carranza** (kuh•RAN•ZUH).

In April 1914, after Huerta's troops arrested some American sailors, Wilson ordered United States troops to seize the port of **Veracruz.** This show of force strengthened Carranza's position and forced Huerta to flee in August. Carranza took power, and American troops withdrew.

*F*ootnotes to History

Hollywood Revolution In 1914 Mexican revolutionary Francisco "Pancho" Villa made a deal with a Hollywood film company to film his battles in exchange for a $25,000 advance and 50 percent of the profits. He agreed to carry out his major raids during daylight so that the film crew could gather good footage.

Francisco "Pancho" Villa

Huerta's resignation did not end civil war in Mexico. Rebel leader **Francisco "Pancho" Villa** launched an uprising against Carranza. In January 1916, Villa seized and shot 16 Americans because of United States support for the Carranza government. Villa hoped his action would damage relations between the United States and the Carranza government, but the United States did not take steps against Mexico. Then Villa and his rebels crossed the border into **New Mexico** and burned the town of Columbus, killing 19 Americans there.

Villa's actions outraged the American public. The president sent General **John J. Pershing** with a large force of troops across the border into Mexico to capture Pancho Villa. For almost a year, Pershing's troops pursued Villa across Mexico, but the Mexican people protected Villa.

In 1917, when America's attention turned to the war raging in Europe, President Wilson withdrew the troops from Mexico. Mexico and the United States had come close to war, and American actions had caused great resentment in Mexico. America's experience in Mexico, like its policies in the Caribbean, showed that the nation would willingly use its power when it believed its interests or honor was threatened.

Section 4 Assessment

★ ★ ★ ★ ★ ★ ★ ★ ★ ★

Checking for Understanding

1. *Identify* William Gorgas, Roosevelt Corollary, William Howard Taft, Francisco "Pancho" Villa, John J. Pershing.
2. *Define* isthmus, anarchy, dollar diplomacy.
3. *Describe* how the United States used Panama's desire for independence to its advantage.

Reviewing Themes

4. **Global Connections** Compare the different diplomacy styles of Presidents Roosevelt, Taft, and Wilson.

Critical Thinking

5. **Making Generalizations** Do you think our government follows Roosevelt's, Taft's, or Wilson's diplomatic ideas in setting foreign policy today? Explain.

Making a Protest Poster Create a poster that a person from Mexico might have used to protest American involvement in Mexico in the early 1900s.

The Panama Canal Locks

How The Panama Canal Works

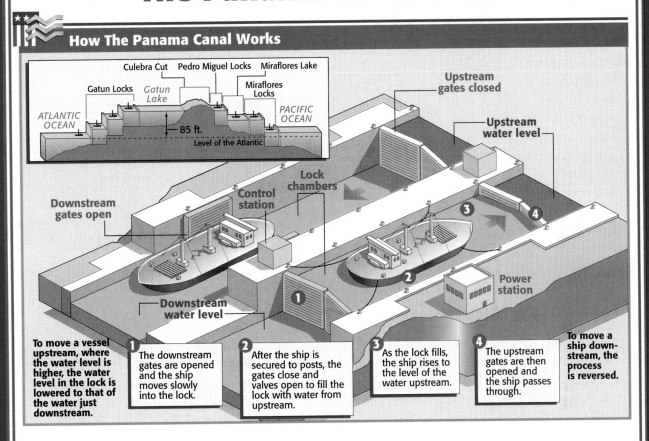

Culebra Cut   Pedro Miguel Locks   Miraflores Lake

Gatun Locks   *Gatun Lake*   Miraflores Locks

ATLANTIC OCEAN

PACIFIC OCEAN

85 ft.

Level of the Atlantic

Upstream gates closed

Upstream water level

Downstream gates open

Control station

Lock chambers

Power station

Downstream water level

To move a vessel upstream, where the water level is higher, the water level in the lock is lowered to that of the water just downstream.

① The downstream gates are opened and the ship moves slowly into the lock.

② After the ship is secured to posts, the gates close and valves open to fill the lock with water from upstream.

③ As the lock fills, the ship rises to the level of the water upstream.

④ The upstream gates are then opened and the ship passes through.

To move a ship downstream, the process is reversed.

Still considered one of the greatest engineering feats in the world, the Panama Canal cuts more than 50 miles through the Isthmus of Panama. An average of 34 oceangoing vessels travel through the Panama Canal each day—about 12,500 ships every year. How do the canal locks work?

The three sets of locks in the Panama Canal are rectangular chambers, the largest concrete structures on the earth. They enable ships to move from one water level to another by changing the amount of water in the locks. Because water flows in and out of the locks by gravity, no pumps are needed. The locks are capable of raising and lowering vessels about 85 feet—the height of a 7-story building.

The locks are operated by 700-ton watertight doors or gates situated at both ends. The gates are 7 feet thick, 65 feet long, and from 47 to 82 feet high. They weigh up to 730 tons.

A ship maneuvers through the canal in about 8 hours. Before the canal was built, a ship had to travel 60 days around South America.

Activity

Canal Technology Using modeling clay, plastic containers, and toy ships, build a model canal. Present your model to the class and explain how the water levels change as you open the gates.

Assessment and Activities

★ Reviewing Key Terms

On a sheet of paper, define the following terms:
isolationism
expansionism
imperialism
annexation
spheres of influence
Open Door policy
yellow journalism
armistice
protectorate
isthmus
anarchy
dollar diplomacy

★ Reviewing Key Facts

1. Why did the United States turn from internal expansion to foreign expansion in the late 1800s and early 1900s?
2. Summarize how the United States gradually gained control of Hawaii.
3. How did the United States gain access to trade in China?
4. What were the terms of the Treaty of Paris?
5. What was the purpose of the Roosevelt Corollary?

★ Critical Thinking

Drawing Conclusions

Presidents Roosevelt, Taft, and Wilson had different opinions on how the United States should handle foreign policy.
1. Which type of diplomacy—"big stick," "dollar," or "moral"—do you think was most effective during this period? Why?
2. Which type of diplomacy do you think would be the least popular with foreign nations? Why?

★ Time Line Activity

Create a time line on which you place the following events in chronological order.
- Japan opens ports to American ships
- Spanish-American War begins
- President Wilson orders troops into Mexico to capture Pancho Villa
- Seward buys Alaska from Russia
- Hawaii becomes United States territory
- Panama Canal is completed

★ Reviewing Themes

1. **Economic Factors** What economic reasons did the United States have for expanding its foreign interests?
2. **Geography and History** What was the main cause of the Russo-Japanese War?
3. **Continuity and Change** What reasons did the anti-imperialists give for opposing American expansion and the Spanish-American War?
4. **Global Connections** Name two actions taken by the United States in Latin America that would damage future relations in this area.

★ Skill Practice Activity

Developing Multimedia Presentations

Study the list of topics below. Choose one of the topics and explain how you would use at least three types of media in a presentation to best teach the topic to your class.
1. Matthew Perry's mission to Japan
2. The development of the American navy
3. How the United States changed Hawaii forever
4. The Battle of San Juan Hill
5. Building the Panama Canal

⭐ Geography Activity

The building of the Panama Canal was regarded as a great engineering feat. Study the map of the canal below, then answer the questions that follow.

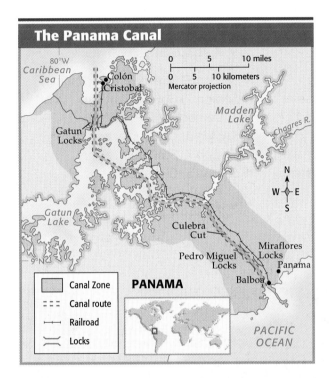

The Panama Canal

1. **Location** What cities are located near the path of the canal?
2. **Movement** In which direction would a ship en route to Cristobal from Balboa travel?
3. **Human/Environment Interaction** What does the location of Panama tell you about the climatic conditions the canal workers faced?

Now compare the map above with the diagram of the Panama Canal locks on page 651. Use this comparison to answer these questions.

4. **Location** Which of the locks are located at the highest elevation, or height above sea level?
5. **Place** Which natural waterway, of those shown on the diagram, is located at the highest elevation? Which is at the lowest elevation?

⭐ Cooperative Activity

History and Economics Work with a partner to create a map showing all of the areas acquired by the United States during the late 1800s and early 1900s. Research to find out about the natural resources that existed in each area and the importance of the area's location in world trade. Then, based on these two factors, rank each of the areas on your map as to their economic value to the United States. The area ranked number "1" should be the most valuable. Compare your maps and rankings with other members of the class and create a chart of the overall ratings.

⭐ Technology Activity

Using the Internet Search the Internet for a news report about the United States that was written in another nation. Decide if the article expresses a positive, negative, or neutral view of the United States. Print the article and underline passages that support your opinion. Think about why this nation might have formed this opinion.

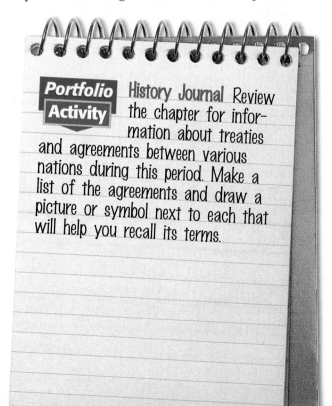

Portfolio Activity **History Journal** Review the chapter for information about treaties and agreements between various nations during this period. Make a list of the agreements and draw a picture or symbol next to each that will help you recall its terms.

1914–1919

World War I

★ Why It's Important

World War I changed the world. The people of the time called the conflict the Great War, and they believed that never again would there be another like it. Although the United States tried to remain neutral, it was drawn into the conflict. The war had a profound effect on the nation, touching on all aspects of life. When the fighting was over, the United States emerged as one of the greatest powers in the world.

★ Chapter Themes

- *Section 1*, Science and Technology
- *Section 2*, Government and Democracy
- *Section 3*, Geography and History
- *Section 4*, Economic Factors
- *Section 5*, Global Connections

PRIMARY SOURCES Library *See pages 980–981 for primary source readings to accompany Chapter 23*

ON THE JOB FOR VICTORY
UNITED STATES SHIPPING BOARD   EMERGENCY FLEET CORPORATION

 **HISTORY AND ART** *On the Job for Victory* During World War I, artists created colorful posters to encourage public support for the war effort.

1914	1915	1916

June 1914
Franz Ferdinand
is assassinated

July 1914
Austria-Hungary
declares war on
Serbia

August 1914
Germany declares
war on Russia and
France

1916
France and
Germany fight the
Battle of Verdun

Section 1

War in Europe

READ TO DISCOVER . . .

- what factors led to World War I.
- how the early fighting progressed in Europe.
- what new weapons were used in the war.

TERMS TO LEARN

nationalism alliance system
militarism entente

The Storyteller

On June 28, 1914, Gavrilo Princip went to great lengths to secure Bosnia's freedom from Austria. His friend described Princip's actions: "As the [Archduke's] car came abreast he [Princip] stepped forward from the curb, drew his automatic pistol from his coat and fired two shots. The first struck the wife of the Archduke, the Archduchess Sofia, in the abdomen. . . . She died instantly. The second bullet struck the Archduke close to the heart.

He uttered only one word, 'Sofia'—a call to his stricken wife. Then his head fell back and he collapsed. He died almost instantly. . . .

The next day they put chains on Princip's feet, which he wore till his death."

Archduke Franz Ferdinand

The people of **Sarajevo** crowded the streets of their city on the morning of June 28, 1914. They wanted to see **Archduke Franz Ferdinand,** the heir to the throne of the **Austro-Hungarian Empire,** as he drove by with his wife in an open car. The royal couple had come on a state visit to **Bosnia,** an Austrian province.

Suddenly shots rang out. The archduke and his wife were hit and died soon after. The assassination destroyed the delicate balance of European stability. Within weeks Europe was at war.

Troubles in Europe

The tensions that led to World War I had roots that went back many years. The conflicts grew as European nations pursued dreams of empire, built up their armies, and formed alliances.

Nationalism

Nationalism, a feeling of intense loyalty to one's country or group, caused much of the tension in Europe. In the late 1800s and the early 1900s, nationalism served as both a unifying and a disruptive force. On the one hand, nationalism encouraged new nations, such as **Italy** and **Germany**, to unify and to establish their power in the world. Italy had become a kingdom in the 1860s, and the German states had united in the 1870s. Their actions challenged the position of older nations such as **Great Britain** and **France.**

On the other hand, nationalism inspired certain groups of people to break away from existing nations. Some of these **ethnic groups**—people who share a common language and traditions—demanded independent nations of their own.

Imperial Expansion

Tension in Europe also grew out of the desire of nations to expand their empires. **Imperialism** led to competition for colonies in Africa, Asia, and other parts of the world. These colonies not only brought new markets and raw materials; they also added to a nation's prestige.

Great Britain and France already possessed large overseas empires, but they wanted to expand them even more. Germany, Italy, and **Russia** wanted to increase their colonial holdings as well. Because few areas were left to colonize, however, expansion by one European nation often brought it into conflict with another imperial power.

Military Buildup

As European nations competed for colonies, they strengthened their armies and navies to protect their interests. If one nation increased its military strength, its rivals felt threatened and built up their own military in response. In this atmosphere of militarism, Germany, France, and Russia developed huge armies in the early 1900s.

Great Britain, an island nation, had the world's largest and strongest navy. When Germany began to challenge British naval supremacy in the early 1900s, a bitter rivalry developed between the two nations. The rivalry led to an arms race that threatened European stability.

Linking PAST & PRESENT

Nationalism

Nationalism remains a strong force in the world today. Nationalist movements were a factor that led to the collapse of the Soviet Union in 1991. Soon after, Yugoslavia split because its ethnic groups—Slovenes, Croatians, and Bosnians—desired independence.

Forming Alliances

Along with militarism came a strengthening of the alliance system, or the defense agreements among nations. By 1914 two major alliances had been established. Germany, Austria-Hungary, and Italy banded together in the **Triple Alliance,** while Great Britain, France, and Russia joined in the **Triple Entente.** An entente is an understanding between nations.

The members of each alliance pledged to go to each other's aid in times of crisis. Some also agreed to protect smaller countries allied to them. The alliances aimed to keep peace by creating a **balance of power**—a system that prevents any one country from dominating the others. Yet the alliance system actually posed a great danger. An attack on one nation was all that was needed to trigger a war involving many countries.

Europe was like a powder keg. One American diplomat noted that it would take "only a spark to set the whole thing off." That spark was ignited in the **Balkans.**

Crisis in the Balkans

The Balkan Peninsula in southeastern Europe was a hotbed of nationalist and ethnic rivalries in the early 1900s. The nations of Greece, Albania, Romania, and Bulgaria argued over territory, while Slavic nationalists hoped to unite all the Slavic peoples in the region. Especially bitter was the dispute between Austria-Hungary, whose Slavic people desired independence, and the neighboring nation of Serbia, which supported the Slavs and opposed the empire.

An Assassination Leads to War

On June 28, 1914, Archduke Franz Ferdinand, heir to the throne of Austria-Hungary, was assassinated while on a goodwill visit to **Sarajevo,** the capital of the Balkan kingdom of Bosnia. The assassin, **Gavrilo Princip,** was a member of a Serbian nationalist group, the Black Hand. Princip and other terrorists had plotted the murder to advance the cause of the unification of Slavic peoples.

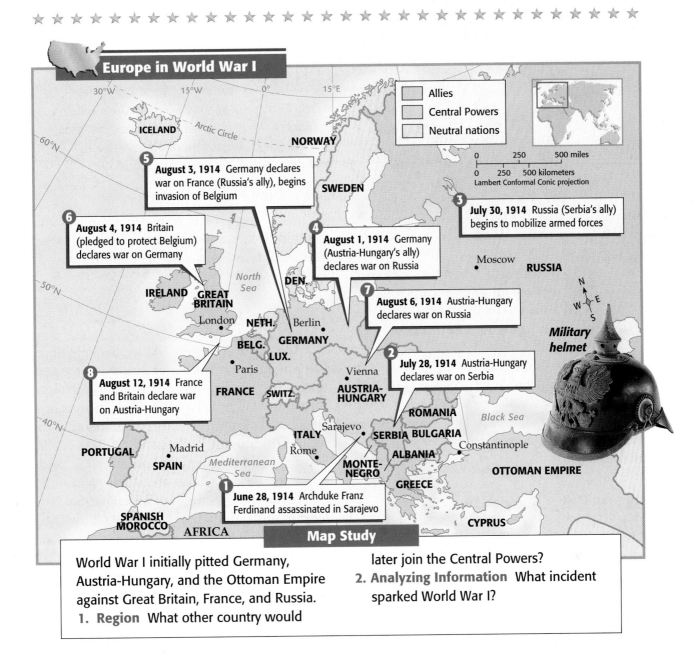

Europe in World War I

Allies
Central Powers
Neutral nations

5 August 3, 1914 Germany declares war on France (Russia's ally), begins invasion of Belgium

6 August 4, 1914 Britain (pledged to protect Belgium) declares war on Germany

3 July 30, 1914 Russia (Serbia's ally) begins to mobilize armed forces

4 August 1, 1914 Germany (Austria-Hungary's ally) declares war on Russia

7 August 6, 1914 Austria-Hungary declares war on Russia

8 August 12, 1914 France and Britain declare war on Austria-Hungary

2 July 28, 1914 Austria-Hungary declares war on Serbia

1 June 28, 1914 Archduke Franz Ferdinand assassinated in Sarajevo

Military helmet

Map Study

World War I initially pitted Germany, Austria-Hungary, and the Ottoman Empire against Great Britain, France, and Russia.

1. **Region** What other country would later join the Central Powers?
2. **Analyzing Information** What incident sparked World War I?

The rulers of Austria-Hungary blamed the Serbian government for the assassination and moved to crush the Serbian nationalist movement. After making sure its ally, Germany, supported its decision, Austria-Hungary delivered a letter to Serbia listing harsh demands. When Serbia refused the conditions, Austria-Hungary declared war on Serbia on July 28, 1914.

Europe's system of alliances caused the war to spread. Russia, which had agreed to protect Serbia, prepared for war. This brought Germany to the side of its ally, Austria-Hungary. Germany declared war on Russia on August 1, 1914. Knowing France was an ally of Russia, Germany declared war on France on August 3.

A day later, Germany invaded **Belgium** as part of a plan to sweep across eastern and northern France. In doing so, Germany violated a treaty signed in 1839 guaranteeing Belgium's neutrality. The invasion of Belgium prompted Great Britain to honor its pledge to protect Belgium, and Britain declared war on Germany.

A World War Begins

The "Great War" had begun. On one side were the **Allied Powers,** or the Allies—Great Britain, France, and Russia. On the other were the **Central Powers**—Germany, Austria-

★ Picturing
HISTORY Airplanes were first used in combat during World War I. Meanwhile German U-boats challenged Great Britain's control of the seas by firing torpedoes that sank surface ships. **What other new and deadly weapons were introduced in World War I?**

Hungary, and the Ottoman (Turkish) Empire, which joined the war in October 1914 because it had fought Russia in the past and feared new aggression. **Japan,** a rival of Germany in Asia, joined the Allies in late August 1914. Italy refused to honor its alliance with Germany and Austria-Hungary. Instead, it joined the Allies in 1915 after being promised territory in Austria after the war.

Battle of the Marne

In launching an offensive through Belgium, Germany hoped to defeat France quickly and destroy the French armies. This would allow Germany to move troops east against Russia.

The plan almost succeeded. The Belgians, however, held out heroically for nearly three weeks against the powerful German army. This delay gave the French and British time to mobilize their forces.

After defeating the Belgians, the Germans marched into France and advanced to within 15 miles of **Paris.** The British and French finally managed to stop the German advance at the **Marne River** just a few miles east of the city. The **Battle of the Marne,** fought between September 5 and

12, 1914, saved Paris from the Germans and boosted French morale. It also made it clear that neither side was capable of winning the war quickly or easily.

Trench Warfare

After the Battle of the Marne, the fighting in western Europe reached a stalemate. For the next three years, the opposing armies faced each other across an elaborate network of deep trenches. Trenches along the front lines provided some protection from flying bullets and artillery shells. Support trenches behind the lines served as headquarters, first-aid stations, and storage areas.

Life in the trenches was miserable. Soldiers lived in dirt and mud for months at a time, their lives filled with terrible fear and endless boredom. Between the enemy lines lay a "no-man's-land" of barbed wire and land mines. Endless days of shelling the enemy might sometimes be interrupted by an attempt to "break out" of the trenches and advance into enemy territory.

Verdun and the Somme

In 1916 both sides attempted to break the deadlock of trench warfare by launching major offensives. The German offensive, the **Battle of Verdun** in northeastern France, began in February and continued on and off until December. At first the Germans made small gains, but these

---

*F*ootnotes to History

Holiday Truce On Christmas Day 1914, fighting stopped, and British and German soldiers met in no-man's-land to chat, play soccer, and pose for photographs. Officers quickly ended these goodwill meetings, and the soldiers returned to war.

were lost after the French counterattacked. Verdun was one of the longest and bloodiest battles of the war. When it was over, more than 750,000 French and German soldiers had lost their lives.

While the Battle of Verdun raged, the British and French launched their own offensive in northern France in July—the **Battle of the Somme**. Again the number of casualties was extremely high. The Allies gained only about 7 miles (11.2 km) in the offensive.

Deadly Technology

New and more deadly weapons accounted for the terrible slaughter during these battles. Improved cannons and other artillery fired larger shells greater distances than ever before. Better rifles enabled soldiers to hit targets with greater accuracy. A new, improved machine gun fired a burst of bullets in just a few seconds.

Poison gas, another new and devastating weapon, was first used by the Germans over Allied lines in April 1915. The gas could kill or seriously injure anyone who breathed it. "They fought with terror, running blindly in the gas cloud, and dropping . . . in agony," wrote a British officer of troops overcome by poison gas. The Allies began to use poison gas also, and gas masks became necessary equipment in the trenches.

The armored tank, invented by the British, proved effective for crossing battle lines to fire on the enemy at close range. Tanks also could crush barbed wire, providing an easier route for advancing troops. After the Germans saw the effectiveness of tanks, they produced them too.

The most dramatic new weapon—the airplane—added a new dimension to fighting in World War I. Both sides used airplanes for watching troop movements and bombing enemy targets. Daring pilots waged duels in the skies called "dogfights." The most famous pilots included Germany's "Red Baron," **Baron von Richthofen,** and America's **Eddie Rickenbacker,** who served in the French air force. The Germans used **zeppelins,** or airships, to bomb Allied cities.

On the Seas

With their land armies deadlocked in western Europe, both sides looked to the sea to gain an advantage in the war. Great Britain blockaded all ports under German control, eventually causing serious shortages. Many Germans suffered from malnutrition and illness because of lack of food and other supplies.

Germany had an effective naval weapon of its own: the submarine. Known as **U-boats**—from the German word for submarine, *Unterseeboot*—submarines prevented supplies, including food, from reaching Great Britain. U-boat attacks on ships at sea eventually affected the United States and changed the course of the war.

★ ★ ★ ★ ★ Section 1 Assessment ★ ★ ★ ★ ★

Checking for Understanding
1. *Identify* Archduke Franz Ferdinand, Allied Powers, Central Powers.
2. *Define* nationalism, militarism, alliance system, entente.
3. *Discuss* how militarism led Europe into World War I.

Reviewing Themes
4. **Science and Technology** Why were casualties so high in World War I?

Critical Thinking
5. **Identifying Central Issues** How did forming alliances increase the likelihood of war in Europe?

▶ **Activity** ◀

Building a Model Research the inventions that were developed in World War I. Using clay, papier-mâché, or other materials, build a model of the invention you researched.

August 1914

Europe goes
to war

May 1915

Germany torpedoes
the *Lusitania*

March 1917

Zimmermann
telegram
angers U.S.

April 1917

U.S. declares
war on Germany

Section 2

America's Road to War

READ TO DISCOVER . . .

- how Americans responded to the war in Europe.
- what led to American involvement in the war.
- how America raised an army to fight.

TERMS TO LEARN

propaganda   autocracy

The Storyteller

President Wilson struggled to remain neutral, even after Americans had been killed at the outbreak of World War I. Others felt differently. An American businessman cabled the president after the *Laconia* was sunk by Germans: "My beloved mother and sister . . . have been foully murdered on the high seas. . . . I call upon my government to preserve its citizens' self-respect and save others of my countrymen from such deep grief as I now feel. I am of military age, able to fight. If my country can use me against these brutal assassins, I am at its call. If it . . . [remains] passive under outrage, I shall seek a man's chance under another flag." Remaining neutral grew more and more difficult.

Magazine cover, 1914

When Europe went to war in August 1914, most Americans believed that the war did not concern them. Many shared the view expressed in an editorial in the *New York Sun*:

❝ There is nothing reasonable in such a war, and it would be folly for the country to sacrifice itself to the frenzy of dynastic policies and the clash of ancient hatreds which is urging the Old World to destruction. ❞

President Wilson agreed. He declared that the United States would be neutral in the war and called on Americans to be "neutral in fact as well as in name, impartial in thought as well as in action."

American Neutrality

Despite Wilson's plea to remain neutral, Americans soon began to take sides. More than one-third of the nation's 92 million people were either foreign-born or the children of immigrants. Many of these people naturally sympathized with their countries of origin. Some of the 8 million Americans of German or Austrian descent and the 4.5 million Irish Americans—who hated the British because they ruled Ireland—favored the Central Powers.

Even more Americans, however, including President Wilson, felt sympathetic to the Allies. Ties of language, customs, and traditions linked the United States to Great Britain, and many

⭐ **Picturing HISTORY** The *Lusitania* left New York for England on May 1, 1915. Germany had placed a warning notice in American newspapers, but few people took it seriously. **How did the United States respond to German U-boat attacks?**

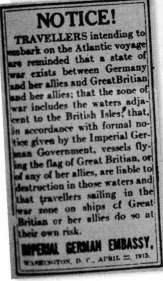

NOTICE!

TRAVELLERS intending to embark on the Atlantic voyage are reminded that a state of war exists between Germany and her allies and Great Britian and her allies; that the zone of war includes the waters adjacent to the British Isles; that, in accordance with formal notice given by the Imperial German Government, vessels flying the flag of Great Britian, or of any of her allies, are liable to destruction in those waters and that travellers sailing in the war zone on ships of Great Britian or her allies do so at their own risk.

IMPERIAL GERMAN EMBASSY,
WASHINGTON, D. C., APRIL 22, 1915.

Americans were of British descent. President Wilson told the British ambassador: "Everything I love most in the world is at stake." A German victory "would be fatal to our form of government and American ideals."

Using Propaganda

To gain the support of Americans, both sides in the war used propaganda—information designed to influence opinion. Allied propaganda emphasized the German invasion of neutral Belgium and included horror stories of German atrocities. It called the Germans "Huns" and pictured them as savage barbarians.

The propaganda from the Central Powers was equally horrible, but because of British sympathies, the Allied propaganda was more effective in influencing Americans.

America's Early Involvement

Trade between the United States and the Allies helped build support for the Allied cause. As a neutral nation, America sought to trade with both sides, but Britain's blockade of Germany made this difficult.

The British navy stopped and searched American ships headed for German ports, often seizing the ships' goods. The United States protested that its ships should be able to pass without interference. The British responded with the defense that they were fighting for their survival. "If the American shipper grumbles," wrote a London paper, "our reply is that this war is not being conducted for his pleasure or profit." The United States government could do nothing about the blockade. Barred from trading with Germany, it continued trading with Britain.

Indeed, American trade with the Allies soared—from about $825 million in 1914 to about $3.2 billion in 1916. In addition Great Britain and France borrowed billions of dollars from American banks to help pay for their war efforts. All this business caused an economic boom in the United States. It also upset the Germans, who watched the United States—supposedly a neutral nation—become the arsenal of the Allies.

Submarine Warfare

To stop American economic assistance to Britain, Germany announced in February 1915 that it would use its U-boats to sink any vessels that entered or left British ports.

The United States protested the policy. President Wilson warned that America would hold

Germany responsible for any American lives lost in submarine attacks. Determined to cut off supplies to Great Britain, the Germans ignored this threat.

On May 7, 1915, a German U-boat torpedoed the British passenger liner **Lusitania** off the coast of Ireland. W.T. Turner, the ship's captain, reported:

> 66 I saw the torpedo speeding towards us. Immediately I tried to change our course, but was unable to maneuver out of its way. There was a terrible impact as the torpedo struck the starboard side of the vessel. . . . It was cold-blooded murder. 99

The *Lusitania* sank in about 15 minutes. More than 1,000 people died, including 128 United States citizens. Americans were outraged, and President Wilson denounced the attack. Later it was learned that the ship carried war materials.

Several months later a German U-boat torpedoed the unarmed French passenger ship *Sussex*, injuring several Americans. The United States denounced the attack as a violation of international law, and Wilson threatened to end diplomatic relations with Germany. Fearing that the Americans might enter the war, Germany offered to compensate Americans injured on the *Sussex* and promised to warn neutral ships and passenger vessels before attacking. The Sussex Pledge, as it was called, seemed to resolve the issue.

TECHNOLOGY AND HISTORY

Submarine

During World War I, German U-boats, or submarines, became the terror of the seas. **What part of the craft guided the submarine up and down?**

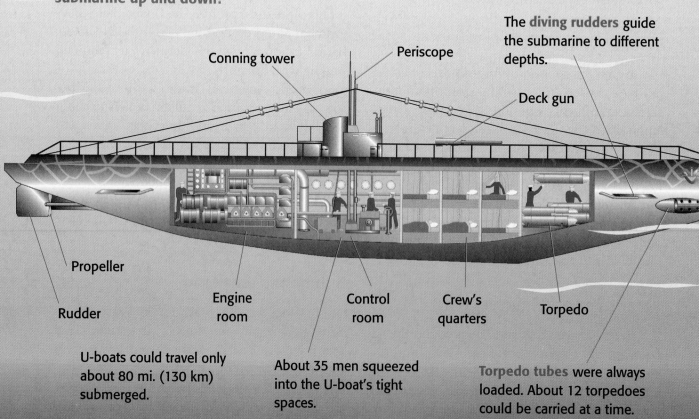

Conning tower

Periscope

The **diving rudders** guide the submarine to different depths.

Deck gun

Propeller

Rudder

Engine room

Control room

Crew's quarters

Torpedo

U-boats could travel only about 80 mi. (130 km) submerged.

About 35 men squeezed into the U-boat's tight spaces.

Torpedo tubes were always loaded. About 12 torpedoes could be carried at a time.

The End of Neutrality

⭐ The crisis over submarine warfare prompted the United States to take steps to strengthen its military forces. In the summer of 1916, Congress passed legislation that doubled the size of the army and provided funds to build new warships. President Wilson still hoped, however, to stay out of the war.

Antiwar sentiment remained very strong. Some Americans criticized the nation's military buildup, seeing it as a major step toward involvement in the war. A popular song in 1915 expressed this opposition:

> ❝I didn't raise my boy to be a soldier,
> I brought him up to be my pride and joy.
> Who dares place a musket on his shoulder,
> To shoot some other mother's
> darling boy? ❞

The 1916 Election

Antiwar sentiment was strong at the 1916 Democratic national convention, where all references to the president's efforts to keep the country out of war brought wild applause. After Wilson was nominated for a second term, the phrase "He Kept Us Out of War" became the Democrats' slogan. Wilson narrowly defeated the Republican presidential candidate, Charles Evans Hughes. The question of neutrality divided the Republicans, and Hughes avoided discussing the issue.

On the Brink of War

In January 1917, Germany reversed its policy on submarine warfare. It announced that it would sink on sight all merchant vessels, armed or unarmed, sailing to Allied ports. While realizing that their policy might bring the Americans into the war, the Germans believed they could defeat the Allies before the United States became heavily involved. An angry President Wilson broke off diplomatic relations with Germany.

A few weeks later, a secret telegram—intercepted by the British government—set off a new wave of anti-German feeling. In late February the

Linking PAST & PRESENT

The Draft

The United States used a military draft in both world wars, the Korean War, the cold war, and the Vietnam War. In 1973 Congress ended the draft, but since 1981 men have still been required to register for military service at age 18.

German foreign minister, Arthur Zimmermann, sent a telegram to **Mexico** with an offer to the Mexican government:

> ❝MAKE WAR TOGETHER, MAKE PEACE TOGETHER, GENEROUS FINANCIAL SUPPORT, AND AN UNDERSTANDING ON OUR PART THAT MEXICO IS TO RECONQUER THE LOST TERRITORY IN TEXAS, NEW MEXICO, AND ARIZONA. ❞

Newspapers published the secret **Zimmermann telegram** on March 1, and Americans reacted angrily to the German action.

Revolution in Russia

In the weeks following publication of the Zimmermann telegram, dramatic events pushed the United States to the brink of war. First, a revolution took place in **Russia.** Following a period of rioting and strikes, the Russian people overthrew the monarchy. In its place they established a provisional democratic government.

Many Americans believed that the new Russian government, which vowed to defeat Germany, would help the Allies. With Russia's change to a democratic form of government, Wilson could now claim that the Allies were fighting a war of democracy against autocracy—rule by one person with unlimited power.

Other critical events took place at sea. On March 18, German U-boats sank three American merchant ships without warning and with heavy loss of life. President Wilson concluded that the United States could no longer remain neutral.

America Enters the War

On the cold, rainy evening of April 2, 1917, President Wilson stood before a special session of Congress to ask for a declaration of war against Germany.

Jeannette Rankin

> ❝The world must be made safe for democracy. . . . It is a fearful thing to lead this great peaceful people into war, into the most terrible and disastrous of all wars. . . . But the right is more precious than peace, and we shall fight for the things which we have always carried nearest our hearts—for democracy. ❞

Congress passed a declaration of war, and Wilson signed it on April 6. Fifty-six members of the House and Senate voted against war, including Representative Jeannette Rankin of Montana—the first woman to serve in Congress.

Raising an Army

★ The United States had to raise an army quickly. On May 18, Congress passed the **Selective Service Act,** establishing a military draft. Unlike the draft during the Civil War that led to riots, this draft had the support of most of the American public.

Men aged 21 to 30 (later the draft age was extended from 18 to 45) registered by the millions. By the end of the war, some 24 million men had registered. Of those, about 3 million were called to serve; another 2 million joined the armed forces voluntarily.

In addition thousands of women enlisted in the armed forces—the first time they were allowed to do so. All the women did noncombat work, serving as radio operators, clerks, and nurses.

Many African Americans also wanted to serve their country. More than 300,000 joined the army and navy—the marines would not accept them. African Americans faced discrimination and racism in the armed forces just as they did in civilian life. Most held low-level jobs on military bases in the United States. Among the 140,000 African American soldiers sent to Europe, 40,000 saw actual combat. Many served with distinction. An African American regiment received medals for bravery from the French government. One of its members, Henry Johnson, was the first American to receive the French Croix de Guerre [Cross of War] for bravery.

★ ★ ★ ★ ★ Section 2 Assessment ★ ★ ★ ★ ★

Checking for Understanding

1. *Identify* Lusitania, Zimmermann telegram, Selective Service Act.
2. *Define* propaganda, autocracy.
3. *Explain* how the war in Europe brought about an economic boom in the United States.

Reviewing Themes

4. **Government and Democracy** What steps did President Wilson have to take to make an official declaration of war?

Critical Thinking

5. **Drawing Conclusions** Why was it difficult for many Americans to remain neutral during the war?

Making a List Imagine you enlisted in the World War I army. List the four things you would miss most about civilian life.

| **June 1917** | **March 1918** | **June 1918** | **November 1918** |
| American troops land in France | Russia withdraws from the war | American Expeditionary Force begins to fight | Armistice ends World War I |

Section 3

Americans Join the Allies

READ TO DISCOVER . . .
- what was happening in Europe when the United States entered the war.
- what role American troops played in the fighting.

TERMS TO LEARN

convoy   armistice
front

The Storyteller

Drafted into the United States Army in 1917, Alvin York was reluctant to serve. "I was worried clean through," he said. "I didn't want to go and kill." York had grown up in the mountains of Tennessee, where he learned to shoot while hunting wild turkeys. Applying his sharpshooting skills in World War I, York killed 17 German soldiers with 17 shots. He also took 132 Germans prisoner and captured 35 enemy machine guns. For his actions and bravery in combat, Sergeant York received the Congressional Medal of Honor.

Congressional Medal of Honor

In 1917 the Allies desperately needed the help of American soldiers. Years of trench warfare had exhausted the Allied armies, and some French troops refused to continue fighting after a failed offensive in 1917. The British had started to run out of war supplies and food; their people were starving. Furthermore, German submarines were taking a deadly toll on Allied shipping—sinking one of every four ships that left British ports.

Supplying the Allies

⭐ The American entry into the war made an immediate difference. To ensure that needed supplies reached Great Britain, the United States Navy took two steps. First, it helped the British find and destroy German submarines. Then **convoys**—teams—of navy destroyers escorted groups of merchant ships across the Atlantic. The convoy system worked well. In one year it reduced Allied shipping losses from 900,000 to 300,000 tons a month. With the convoy system, not one American soldier bound for Europe was lost to submarine attack.

Russian Withdrawal

The Allies needed more troops because of a second revolution in Russia. In November 1917, the **Bolsheviks,** a group of communists, overthrew the democratic Russian government established in March 1917.

Led by **Vladimir Lenin,** the Bolsheviks wanted to end Russia's participation in the war so they

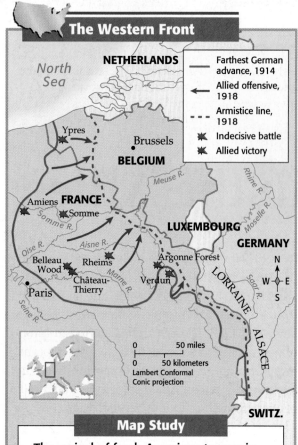

The Western Front

North Sea

NETHERLANDS

Legend:
— Farthest German advance, 1914
← Allied offensive, 1918
- - - Armistice line, 1918
✹ Indecisive battle
✸ Allied victory

Ypres

Brussels

BELGIUM

Meuse R.

Amiens **FRANCE**

Somme

Somme R.

Oise R.

Aisne R.

LUXEMBOURG

Rhine R.

Moselle R.

GERMANY

Belleau Wood

Rheims

Argonne Forest

Château-Thierry

Verdun

Marne R.

Paris

Seine R.

Saar R.

LORRAINE

ALSACE

0   50 miles
0   50 kilometers
Lambert Conformal
Conic projection

N W E S

SWITZ.

Map Study

The arrival of fresh American troops in Europe in 1917 helped turn the Allies toward victory.

1. **Location** About how close to Paris was the battle of Château-Thierry?
2. **Analyzing Information** What country was the site of most Western Front battles?

hammered at Allied lines, pushing them back to within 50 miles (80 km) of Paris. After years of stalemate along the Western Front—the area along the French-German border—it suddenly looked as if Germany might win the war.

American Troops in the War

★ Although the first American soldiers had reached France in June 1917, many months passed before they were ready for battle. When they finally began to fight, the Americans helped turn the war around.

Eyewitness to HISTORY

The American Expeditionary Force

General **John J. Pershing** led the American troops in Europe, the **American Expeditionary Force** (AEF). American correspondent Floyd Gibbons described the tremendous welcome the French gave Pershing and his troops in Paris:

❝ The sooty girders of the Gare du Nord [railroad station] shook with cheers when the special train pulled in. . . . A minute later, there was a terrific roar from beyond the walls of the station. The crowds outside had heard the cheering within. . . . Paris took Pershing by storm. ❞

The AEF reached full strength in Europe in the spring of 1918. The French and British wanted to use the American soldiers to build up their own troops, but General Pershing refused. He preferred to keep the AEF a separate force.

could focus their energies and resources on setting up a new Communist state. Lenin took Russia out of the war in December. In March 1918, he signed the **Treaty of Brest-Litovsk** with Germany, surrendering Poland, the Ukraine, and other territory to the Germans. Russia's withdrawal from the war allowed the Germans to move hundreds of thousands of troops from the Eastern Front—line of battle—to the Western Front in France.

New German Offensive

Reinforced by the transfer of troops, the Germans now launched a powerful offensive against the Allies. Between March and June 1918, they

Americans Go into Action

The American Expeditionary Force saw its first serious fighting in early June 1918. It helped turn back a German offensive at **Château-Thierry** on the **Marne River** east of Paris. The American

Trench checkers

Shaving kit

Soldier's gas mask and pack

What Was It Like? Soldiers lived in the trenches for weeks, fighting boredom and terror. How do you think they passed the time between attacks?

troops then advanced to nearby **Belleau Wood.** For 24 hours a day for the next 3 weeks, American forces fought their way through the forest against a solid wall of German machine-gun fire. In July the Americans and the French fought back German attacks on Allied forces along the Marne and the Somme Rivers.

By the middle of July, the Allies had stopped the German offensive. The battles, General Pershing wrote, had "turned the tide of war." The Allies now began an offensive of their own. In mid-September 550,000 "doughboys"—the nickname given to American soldiers—fighting alone, defeated the Germans at Saint Mihiel, east of **Verdun.** Later in the month, more than 1 million American troops joined the Allies in the **Battle of the Argonne Forest,** west of Verdun.

The Battle of the Argonne Forest raged for nearly seven weeks, with soldiers struggling over the rugged, heavily forested ground. Rain, mud, barbed wire, and withering fire from German machine guns hindered the Allies' advance, and many lives were lost.

American lieutenant Elden Betts wondered if he would survive the battle and wrote home—in case "I get mine tomorrow." He said he hoped his family would be proud of him, ending with "Now good-bye, and thank you Pop, Edie and Margie." Four days later Betts was killed.

The Battle of the Argonne Forest ended in early November, when the Allies finally pushed back the Germans and broke through the enemy lines. The Germans now were faced with an invasion of their own country.

Footnotes to History

Repaying a Debt The AEF marched through Paris to the grave of the Marquis de Lafayette, the Frenchman who had helped the Patriots win the American Revolution. An American officer, Colonel Charles Stanton, heard a great cheer from the Paris crowd when he stated, "Lafayette, we are here!" Indeed, it was time to repay the debt.

Allies Day, May 1917 by Childe Hassam The artist captured the flags of Allied nations during a New York City celebration in 1917. **When did the armistice go into effect?**

The End of the War

With their troops in retreat, German military leaders realized they had little chance of winning the war. The Allied forces were now fortified by the Americans. In addition, the Germans suffered from severe shortages of food and other essential supplies.

Request for an Armistice

On October 4, 1918, the German government appealed to President Wilson for an armistice—an agreement to end the fighting. Wilson consented under certain conditions. Germany must accept his plan for peace and promise not to renew hostilities. All German troops must leave Belgium and France. Finally, Wilson would deal only with civilian leaders, not with the military.

While German leaders considered Wilson's demands, political unrest erupted in Germany. On November 9, the German **kaiser,** or emperor, **Wilhelm II,** was forced to give up his throne. Germany became a republic, and its new leaders quickly agreed to Wilson's terms for the armistice.

Peace Begins

The armistice began on November 11, 1918. Germany agreed to withdraw all land forces west of the **Rhine River,** withdraw its fleet to the Baltic Sea, and surrender huge amounts of equipment.

With the signing of the armistice, the Great War ended. President Wilson announced:

❝Everything for which America fought has been accomplished. It will now be our duty to assist by example, by sober, friendly counsel, and by material aid in the establishment of just democracy throughout the world. ❞

★ ★ ★ ★ ★ Section 3 Assessment ★ ★ ★ ★ ★

Checking for Understanding
1. *Identify* Bolsheviks, Vladimir Lenin, Treaty of Brest-Litovsk, Wilhelm II.
2. *Define* convoy, front, armistice.
3. *List* three reasons the Allies needed the help of the American forces by 1917.

Reviewing Themes
4. **Geography and History** What terms did Germany agree to in the armistice?

Critical Thinking
5. **Predicting Consequences** Do you think the Allies would have won the war if the United States had not intervened? Why or why not?

Activity

Preparing a Radio Broadcast Write the text for a French radio broadcast announcing the arrival of American soldiers in Paris in 1917.

INTERDISCIPLINARY
Activities

The Great War

Although other major wars have been fought since 1918, World War I is still known as "the Great War" because of the overwhelming destruction and change it brought. Experience what people did and thought during that period as you complete these activities.

Art

Designing a Propaganda Poster Dramatic posters did a great deal to win people's support for wartime efforts. Study posters of the era and notice their style. Then design your own poster about one of these themes: Buy Liberty Bonds; Join the Army (or Navy); Conserve Resources (steel, textiles, fuel); Promote Patriotism; Take a Factory Job; Observe Meatless (or Wheatless) Days; Plant a Victory Garden.

Science

Studying War Technology Partly because of new technology, World War I caused a horrifying number of casualties. Research one of the following technologies and prepare a report on its development, wartime use, and effects: poison gas, tanks, airplanes, dirigibles, machine guns, or submarines. Photocopy pictures from books and encyclopedias to illustrate your report, and present it in class.

Mathematics

Charting War Casualties Millions of soldiers—mostly Europeans—were killed in World War I. Use an encyclopedia or almanac to supply statistics for a double bar graph in which you compare the number of troops mobilized by a given country with the number of dead and wounded. Include these nations: Austria-Hungary, Belgium, the British Empire, France, Germany, Italy, Russia, Turkey, and the United States. Which countries had, proportionately, the greatest losses? Display your graph in the classroom.

Language Arts

Writing a Poem World War I produced a number of soldier-poets. Read some poems by Rupert Brooke or Stephen Spender. Then imagine that you were fighting in World War I as a soldier, or nurse, or ambulance driver. Write a poem giving your feelings and impressions. You may want to put your poem in the form of a letter home. Share your poetry with the class.

World War I helmet

World War I infantry boots

July 1917
Race riots
occur in
East St. Louis

April 1918
National War
Labor Board
is set up

June 1918
Congress passes
Sabotage and
Sedition acts

Section 4

The War at Home

READ TO DISCOVER . . .
- what steps the United States took to organize and prepare for World War I.
- how the war affected the American people.
- how Americans treated opponents of the war.

TERMS TO LEARN
mobilization   pacifist
dissent   espionage
socialist   sabotage

The Storyteller

"Over there, over there,
Send the word, send the word over there
That the Yanks are coming, the Yanks are
   coming,
The drums rum-tumming ev'rywhere
So prepare, say a pray'r,
Send the word, send the word to beware,
We'll be over, we're coming over,
And we won't come back till it's over over
   there."
   George M. Cohan
wrote this rousing song to
help create enthusiasm for
America's participation in
World War I. "Over There"
was performed at rallies to
raise money for the war.

"Over There" sheet music

After declaring war on Germany in 1917, Americans immediately focused their energies on getting ready to fight a war. Mobilization—the gathering of resources and the preparation for war—affected almost every part of American life.

Mobilizing the Nation

To ensure production of vital war materials and to resolve labor disputes, the government created the **National War Labor Board** in April 1918. Made up of representatives of business, labor, and the public, the board pressured businesses to grant some of the workers' pressing demands. As a result workers won an 8-hour working day, extra pay for overtime, equal pay for women, and the right to form unions. In return workers agreed not to go on strike.

Workers during the War

The American participation in the war led the nation's industry to expand to meet the need for supplies and weapons. At the same time, however, the workforce grew smaller, creating a labor shortage. Millions of men left their jobs in industry to serve in the armed forces, and few European immigrants—who might have taken these jobs—came to the United States during the war.

The labor shortage provided new job opportunities for women and minorities. Many women joined the workforce for the first time. Women were hired for jobs previously held by men.

The prospect of finding good jobs also brought hundreds of thousands of African Americans to Northern cities from the rural South. In addition thousands of Mexicans migrated to the United States in search of jobs.

Paying for the War

World War I cost the United States an enormous amount of money—about $32 billion. Two-thirds of this money was raised by selling the American people war bonds, or **Liberty Bonds.** To persuade people to buy the bonds, the government created colorful posters advertising the bonds and organized public events featuring actors and popular celebrities. George M. Cohan wrote his song "Over There" for a Liberty Bond rally. Children bought more than $1 billion worth of "thrift stamps," which they could paste into books and exchange for a war bond.

The federal government also raised money for the war by increasing taxes and requiring a greater number of Americans to pay income taxes. It taxed wealthy Americans at rates as high as 70 percent of their income. The government also imposed steep taxes on business profits.

$ Economics

Producing Supplies

The United States had to produce food not only for its own needs but also for the Allies. President Wilson appointed **Herbert Hoover,** who had helped organize food for war refugees in Europe, to head a new **Food Administration.** This agency launched a campaign to encourage American farmers to produce more and to persuade the public to eat less. The agency urged people to observe "Wheatless Mondays," "Meatless Tuesdays," and "Porkless Thursdays," and to add to their own store of food by planting "victory gardens." With slogans such as "Serve Just Enough" and "Use All Leftovers," it reminded Americans to conserve food.

The Food Administration also imposed price controls on various agricultural products to encourage voluntary **rationing**—limitation of use.

As a result of such efforts, Americans consumed less food, expanded food production, and increased food exports.

Another government agency, the **War Industries Board,** headed by Bernard Baruch, supervised and coordinated the nation's industrial production. The board's responsibilities included distributing raw materials to industries, converting factories to the production of war-related goods, and setting prices for key products. **$**

Mobilizing Support

The federal government also needed to mobilize public support for the war because antiwar sentiment remained strong even after the United States entered the war. President Wilson appointed journalist **George Creel** to head the **Committee on Public Information.** Its mission was to persuade Americans that the war represented a battle for democracy and freedom.

The Committee on Public Information distributed millions of pro-war pamphlets, posters, articles, and books. It provided newspapers with government accounts of the war and

These women workers replaced males on the Great Northern Railway

advertisements. It arranged for short patriotic talks, called Four-Minute Speeches, to be presented before plays and movies. The committee hired speakers, writers, artists, and actors to build support for the war. It was the greatest propaganda campaign in the history of the nation.

Americans and the War

World War I provided a boost for the American economy. Yet the war had harmful effects on American society as well. In the interest of national unity, the government stifled voices of dissent, or opposition. Racial and other tensions remained, and many Americans became intolerant of those who were "different."

Causes and Effects

CAUSES

* ★ Nationalistic pride
* ★ Competition for colonies
* ★ Military buildup
* ★ Tangled web of alliances
* ★ Assassination of Franz Ferdinand

World War I

EFFECTS

* ★ Destruction in Europe
* ★ Boom in the American economy
* ★ Suppression of dissent in U.S.
* ★ Allied victory
* ★ Defeated empires lose their colonies

Chart Study

After World War I, the United States was established as a world leader and an economic giant.
Analyzing Information How did World War I affect the economy of the United States?

African American Migration

From 1914 to 1920, between 300,000 and 500,000 African Americans left their homes in the rural South to seek jobs and settle in Northern cities. Known as the **Great Migration,** this tremendous population movement continued the northward migration begun in the late 1800s.

African Americans headed north for several reasons. Many wanted to escape the harsh economic and political conditions they faced in the South. They saw advertisements in their local papers for jobs in the North, and they listened eagerly to the stories of African Americans who had already moved there. Some Northern factory owners even sent recruiting agents to promote jobs and to encourage African Americans to come to work for them.

Many African American workers who traveled north—"Bound for the Promised Land" as they wrote on the sides of railroad cars—did find jobs. Their new lives were not easy. Often they lived in tiny, crowded apartments in segregated neighborhoods, and they found that racial prejudice continued to haunt their lives in the North. When expanding African American neighborhoods pushed up against white neighborhoods, racial hostility sometimes erupted in violence.

Terrible race riots took place in several Northern cities during the war years. One of the worst occurred in **East St. Louis, Illinois.** In July 1917, a white mob attacked an African American neighborhood, burning houses and firing on residents as they tried to escape. During the riot, as many as 40 African Americans died and thousands lost their homes.

Controlling Public Opinion

When the war began, a majority of Americans thought the United States should stay out of it. Even after America entered the war, opposition to it remained strong. Some German Americans and Irish Americans sympathized with the Central Powers. Many socialists—people who believe industries should be publicly owned—opposed the war because they thought it would only help rich business owners and hurt working people. Also

★ ★ ★ ★ ★ ★ ★ ★ ★ ★ ★ ★ ★ ★ ★ ★

against the war were pacifists—people opposed to the use of violence.

Some of the strongest antiwar sentiment came from women's groups. The **Women's Peace Party,** founded in 1915, worked to keep the nation out of the war. Some women—including social worker Jane Addams and women's rights leader Alice Paul—continued to voice their opposition after America entered the war.

During the course of the war, the Committee on Public Information began trying to silence dissent and portrayed people who were against the war as unpatriotic. The **Espionage Act** that Congress passed in 1917 gave the government a new weapon to combat dissent to the war. The law provided stiff penalties for espionage, or spying, as well as for aiding the enemy or interfering with army recruiting. Congress passed even harsher measures in 1918—the **Sabotage Act** and the **Sedition Act.** These laws made it a crime to say, print, or write almost anything perceived as negative about the government. Such acts would be considered sabotage—secret action to damage the war effort.

The government used the laws to stifle all political opposition. Thousands of people—especially immigrants, socialists, pacifists, and labor activists—were convicted under the laws.

Suspicion of disloyalty led to spying on neighbors, opening mail, and even outbreaks of violence by vigilante groups. People became suspicious of German Americans and persecuted

★ **Picturing HISTORY** African American soldiers served in segregated regiments, commanded for the most part by white officers. **What major change affected African Americans at home during the war years?**

them. A few communities prohibited such activities as performing German music and teaching the German language in schools. As a result some German Americans concealed their ancestry. They even gave patriotic names—such as "liberty cabbage" and "liberty sausage"—to German-sounding words such as *sauerkraut* and *frankfurter.*

Some people spoke out against these laws and the intolerance they produced. Most Americans, however, believed that, in wartime, no measure can be "too drastic" toward traitors and disloyal Americans.

★ ★ ★ ★ ★ Section 4 Assessment ★ ★ ★ ★ ★

Checking for Understanding

1. **Identify** Herbert Hoover, Great Migration.
2. **Define** mobilization, dissent, socialist, pacifist, espionage, sabotage.
3. **Describe** the role of the Committee on Public Information.

Reviewing Themes

4. **Economic Factors** Where did the United States government get most of the money to finance the war?

Critical Thinking

5. **Analyzing Information** Do you think it was necessary for the government to take such extreme measures against people who opposed the war? Explain.

Activity

Writing an Advertisement Design an advertisement that a Northern industry might have placed in a Southern newspaper to attract job applicants.

1919	1920	1921

1919
Paris Peace Conference begins;
Treaty of Versailles is signed

1920
Senate rejects
the League of
Nations

1921
U.S. signs separate
peace treaty with
Central Powers

Section 5

Searching for Peace

READ TO DISCOVER . . .
▓ what principles Woodrow Wilson proposed
as the basis for world peace.
▓ what terms were included in the peace
treaty.
▓ why some Americans opposed the Treaty of
Versailles.

TERMS TO LEARN
Fourteen Points   reparations
League of Nations

Storyteller

The most brutal war of history had ended.
As jubilant crowds celebrated in front of London's Buckingham Palace, British general
Henry Wilson spotted an elderly woman sobbing. Wilson asked, "Is there anything that I
can do for you?" The distressed woman
replied, "Thank you. No. I am crying, but I am
happy, for now I know that all my three sons
who have been killed in the war have not died
in vain." It was up to the
Allied leaders and President Woodrow Wilson
to make sure that the
woman's words were
true—that so many soldiers and civilians had
not died in vain.

*Peace song
honoring Wilson*

In January 1919, world leaders met in **Paris,
France,** to try to resolve the complicated issues
arising from World War I. President **Woodrow
Wilson** led the American delegation to the Paris
Peace Conference. When Wilson arrived in the
city, enormous crowds cheered him. Well-wishers
threw flowers in his path and unfurled banners
that read "Long Live Wilson!" With great hope,
Europeans looked to Wilson to help build a better
postwar world. Yet enormous problems lay ahead.

After the War

★ In the aftermath of the war, Europe lay in
ruins. Much of its landscape was devastated, its farms and towns destroyed. The human
losses were terrible. Great Britain, France, Russia,
Germany, and Austria-Hungary each lost between 1 and 2 million people in the fighting. Millions more were wounded. More than 50,000
Americans were killed in battle, while another
60,000 soldiers died from disease. Estimates for
the whole war placed the number of soldiers and
civilians killed worldwide at 10 million and those
wounded at 20 million.

Europe also faced social and political turmoil.
Millions of people found themselves homeless
and hungry. Civil war raged in Russia. Poles,
Czechs, and other peoples struggled to form independent nations out of the collapsed empires of
Turkey, Russia, and Austria-Hungary. The overseas colonies of some European nations also
sought independence. These problems complicated the search for peace and stability.

War-torn Europe

World War I Casualties*		
Country	Killed	Wounded
Allied Powers		
Russia	1,700,000	4,950,000
France	1,358,000	4,266,000
British Empire	908,400	2,090,000
Italy	650,000	947,000
Romania	335,700	120,000
United States	116,500	234,400
Central Powers		
Germany	1,773,000	4,216,000
Austria-Hungary	1,200,000	3,620,000
Turkey	325,000	400,000
Bulgaria	87,500	152,400

*Figures are approximate. Not all countries are listed.

Chart Study

World War I devastated many countries.
1. Which two countries suffered most of the casualties?
2. **Analyzing Information** Which side—the Allied or Central Powers—had more people killed?

A Vision of Peace

Woodrow Wilson had a vision of a just and lasting peace. A reformer and scholar, Wilson had served as the president of Princeton University and as governor of New Jersey before being elected U.S. president in 1912.

Wilson's Fourteen Points

Wilson outlined his peace plan in a proposal known as the Fourteen Points. Several of the points concerned the adjustment of boundaries in Europe and the creation of new nations. These points reflected Wilson's belief in the right of peoples to **"national self-determination"**—the right to decide how to be governed.

Wilson also proposed a number of principles for conducting international relations. These included calls for free trade, freedom of the seas, an end to secret treaties or agreements, reductions and limits on arms, and the peaceful settlement of disputes over colonies.

League of Nations

Wilson's final point, the one he considered most important, concerned the creation of a "general association of nations." This League of Nations would meet regularly to resolve international disputes. The League's member nations would help preserve peace and prevent future wars by pledging to respect and protect each other's territory and political independence.

Wilson's Fourteen Points reflected his strong—and perhaps unrealistic—faith in the ability of governments to resolve their problems fairly. At first many Europeans welcomed Wilson's ideas. Then problems arose when the plan interfered with the competing interests of the individual nations—in determining how to divide up territory. Also, some of Wilson's points were vague. They did not propose concrete solutions to difficult questions—such as how to achieve self-determination in regions where many different ethnic groups lived closely together.

The Peace Conference

The victorious Allies dominated the talks at the Paris Peace Conference. The Allies did not invite either Germany or Russia—now ruled by the Bolsheviks—to participate. The major figures in the negotiations were the Big Four—President Wilson, Prime Minister **David Lloyd George** of Great Britain, Premier **Georges Clemenceau** of France, and Prime Minister **Vittorio Orlando** of Italy.

The Allies Disagree

Wilson faced a difficult task. Although Europeans cheered him, their leaders showed little enthusiasm for the Fourteen Points. The European leaders were more concerned with the narrow interests of their own countries than with Wilson's call for a "peace without victory."

While Wilson opposed punishing the defeated nations, the European Allies sought revenge. Clemenceau wanted to make sure that Germany, which had invaded France twice in his lifetime, could never invade his country again. He believed that Germany should be broken up into smaller countries. Both he and Lloyd George demanded that Germany make large reparations, or payments, for the damage Germans caused in the war.

At the same time, the Allies had to decide how to deal with the new Bolshevik government of Russia. Fearing the spread of communism, France, Britain, and the United States supported anti-Bolshevik forces fighting for control of Russia. All three countries sent troops to Russia.

Lenin, the Bolshevik leader, had issued a statement of goals for the end of the war. Wilson's Fourteen Points came partly as a response to the Russian proposal. Although Wilson struggled to uphold the principles of his Fourteen Points at the Paris meeting, he was forced again and again to compromise or give in to the demands of the other Allies.

The Treaty of Versailles

On June 28, 1919, after months of difficult negotiations, the Allies and Germany signed a treaty at the Palace of Versailles outside Paris. The harsh terms of the **Treaty of Versailles** shocked the Germans. In defeat, however, they had no choice but to sign.

Under the terms of the treaty, Germany had to accept full responsibility for the war and to pay billions of dollars in reparations to the Allies. Germany also had to disarm completely and give up all its overseas colonies and some territory in Europe.

The treaty carved up the Austro-Hungarian and Russian Empires to create or restore the nations of **Austria, Hungary, Czechoslovakia,**

Europe After World War I

ICELAND
Arctic Circle
30°W   15°W   0°   15°E   30°E
60°N
0   250   500 miles
0   250   500 kilometers
Lambert Conformal Conic projection
SWEDEN   FINLAND
NORWAY
North Sea
ESTONIA
LATVIA   Moscow
DENMARK   LITHUANIA   RUSSIA
IRELAND   GREAT BRITAIN   GER.
London   NETH.   Berlin
BELG.   GERMANY   POLAND
ATLANTIC OCEAN   Paris   LUX.
Versailles   CZECHOSLOVAKIA
FRANCE   SWITZ.   AUSTRIA   Vienna
HUNGARY
ROMANIA
Black Sea
YUGOSLAVIA
ITALY   Sarajevo   BULGARIA
40°N   Madrid
PORTUGAL   SPAIN   Rome   ALBANIA   Constantinople
GREECE   TURKEY
Mediterranean Sea
SPANISH MOROCCO   AFRICA
New nations
Baltic Sea
50°N

Map Study

The outcome of World War I brought great changes to Europe and the Middle East as new nations and colonies were created.

1. **Region** What new nations bordered on Germany?
2. **Analyzing Information** Which new nations lacked access to a major sea or ocean?

Henry Cabot Lodge

Woodrow Wilson on tour

Yugoslavia, Poland, Finland, Estonia, Lithuania, and **Latvia.** The emergence of these nations fulfilled part of Wilson's vision of "national self-determination." Many of the borders of the new countries were disputed, however, and this led to future conflicts.

Though deeply disappointed by the rejection of much of his Fourteen Points, Wilson did succeed in having the League of Nations included in the peace treaty. He believed that the League would be able to correct any mistakes in the rest of the treaty.

Opposition at Home

⭐ Wilson presented the Treaty of Versailles to the United States Senate for ratification on July 10, 1919. "Dare we reject it and break the heart of the world?" he asked. In spite of his eloquent plea, a difficult struggle lay ahead.

Many Americans had doubts about the treaty. Some, German Americans in particular, thought the treaty dealt too harshly with Germany. A great many Americans worried about participation in the League of Nations, which marked a permanent American commitment to international affairs. Critics charged that membership in the League would prevent the nation from setting its own foreign policy.

Debate over the Treaty

In 1919 the Republicans controlled the Senate, which had to ratify the treaty. Some Republican senators saw the ratification issue as a chance to embarrass President Wilson, a Democrat, and to weaken the Democratic Party before the upcoming elections of 1920. The fact that Wilson had not included any Republicans in the negotiating team he took to Paris cost him some Republican support. Other senators had sincere concerns about the treaty, particularly the League of Nations. A few senators opposed signing any treaty.

The most powerful opponent of the treaty was **Henry Cabot Lodge** of Massachusetts, head of the Senate Foreign Relations Committee. Lodge, a longtime foe of President Wilson, claimed that membership in the League would mean that

❝American troops and American ships may be ordered to any part of the world by nations other than the United States, and that is a proposition to which I for one can never assent.❞

Lodge delayed a vote on the treaty so that opponents could present their cases. He then proposed a number of reservations that would limit America's obligations under the treaty. One reservation, for example, stated that the League would have no say about situations arising from the

Monroe Doctrine. Wilson refused to accept these changes and described Senate opponents of the League as "contemptible, narrow, selfish, poor little minds that never get anywhere."

In September, Wilson went on a national speaking tour to rally support for the treaty and the League of Nations. Traveling 8,000 miles in 22 days, Wilson pleaded for his vision and warned that the League could not be effective without American participation. If the United States did not join, he believed a terrible war would come again.

On September 25, Wilson collapsed after giving a speech. The rest of his tour was canceled. Back in Washington Wilson suffered a stroke that left him partially paralyzed. During the president's illness, his wife, Edith Wilson, tried to shield him from the pressures of responsibility and took a leading role in deciding which issues were important enough to raise with him.

The Treaty Is Rejected

In the months following Wilson's stroke, opposition to the treaty grew. Yet Wilson remained unwilling to compromise. In March 1920, when the Senate voted on the treaty with Lodge's changes, Wilson ordered loyal Democrats to vote against it. He told his wife:

66 Better a thousand times to go down fighting than to dip your colours to dishonourable compromise. 99

Opposed by most Republicans and deserted by former supporters, the Treaty of Versailles—along with the League of Nations—was rejected in the Senate. Wilson hoped the 1920 election would be a "great and solemn referendum" on the League. He even considered running for a third term. In the end, however, Wilson did not run. In 1921 the United States signed a separate peace treaty with each of the Central Powers, and it never joined the League of Nations.

A Society in Turmoil

While the nation argued over the treaty, other issues were causing turmoil in American society. Relations between African Americans and whites turned increasingly violent, with lynchings in the South and race riots in the North. Economic problems led to labor disputes, which contributed to another source of turmoil—a fear of radicals.

President Wilson, concerned with the peace treaty and then seriously ill, never gave much attention to these problems. However, the troubles at home made Americans less sympathetic to the treaty and the League of Nations.

Section 5 Assessment

Checking for Understanding

1. **Identify** Woodrow Wilson, David Lloyd George, Georges Clemenceau, Vittorio Orlando, Treaty of Versailles, Henry Cabot Lodge.
2. **Define** Fourteen Points, League of Nations, reparations.
3. **Summarize** the provisions of the Treaty of Versailles.

Reviewing Themes

4. **Global Connections** How did President Wilson think that the League of Nations would help maintain world peace?

Critical Thinking

5. **Determining Relevance** Some Americans thought the Treaty of Versailles was too hard on Germany. What terms would you have proposed for Germany?

Activity

Comparing Maps Compare a map of Europe after World War I to a map of Europe today. Make a list of the significant border changes that have occurred since that time.

Study and Writing
SKILL BUILDER

Outlining

To sketch a scene, you first draw the rough shape, or outline, of the picture. Then you fill in this rough shape with details. Outlining written material is a similar process. You begin with the rough shape of the material and gradually fill in the details.

Learning the Skill

There are two kinds of outlines—formal and informal. An informal outline is similar to taking notes. You write only words and phrases needed to remember main ideas.

A formal outline has a standard format. In a formal outline, label main heads with Roman numbers, subheads with capital letters, and details with Arabic numerals and lowercase letters. Each level should have at least two entries and should be indented from the level above. All entries use the same grammatical form. If one entry is a complete sentence, all other entries at that level must also be complete sentences.

When outlining written material, first read the material to identify the main ideas. In textbooks, section heads provide clues to main topics. Then identify the subheads. Place supporting details under the appropriate head.

Outline of Chapter 23, Section 3

I. European Allies need help.
  A. Allied armies are exhausted.
    1. Trench warfare depletes supplies.
    2. Morale is low.
  B. Civilians are in trouble.
    1. People are starving.
    2. Supply ships are sunk by Germans.
II. Americans enter the war.
  A. United States Navy patrols seas.
    1. German U-boats are destroyed.
    2. Convoys protect Allied ships.
      a. Losses are reduced by two-thirds.
      b. No American soldiers are killed.
  B. American Expeditionary Force (AEF) lands in Europe.
    1. Germans lose at Château-Thierry.
    2. Germans are defeated at Belleau Wood.
III. Allies take the offensive.
  A. Battle of Argonne Forest is fought.
  B. President Wilson lists conditions for armistice.

Practicing the Skill

Study the partial outline of Section 3 on this page. Then answer the following questions.

1. Is this a formal or an informal outline?
2. What are the three main topics?
3. If you wanted to add two facts about the AEF, where would you put them in the outline? Would you use numbers or letters to label the facts?

Applying the Skill

Outlining Following the guidelines above, prepare an outline for Section 2 of Chapter 23.

GO TO

Glencoe's **Skillbuilder Interactive Workbook, Level 1** provides instruction and practice in key social studies skills.

Assessment and Activities

★ Reviewing Key Terms

On a sheet of paper, define the following terms:
nationalism
militarism
entente
propaganda
convoy
front
armistice
mobilization
dissent
socialist
pacifist
espionage
sabotage
Fourteen Points
League of Nations
reparations

★ Reviewing Key Facts

1. Why did European nations form alliances?
2. Why did the Zimmermann telegram push the United States toward war?
3. How did Russia's withdrawal affect World War I?
4. In what ways did the war help improve conditions for American workers?
5. What was Henry Cabot Lodge's greatest concern about the League of Nations?

★ Critical Thinking

Making Inferences

Many Americans wanted the United States to remain neutral during the war.
1. Why do you think many Americans feared war?
2. How did economic interests affect the United States's inability to remain neutral?

★ Skill Practice Activity

Outlining

On a separate sheet of paper, add supporting details to the outline of Section 1 below.

Steps Leading to World War I
I. Nationalism
   A. As a unifying force
   B. As a disruptive force
II. Imperial Expansion
III. Military Buildups
IV. Forming Alliances
   A. Triple Alliance members
   B. Triple Entente members

★ Reviewing Themes

1. **Science and Technology** What advantages did airplanes provide in the war?
2. **Government and Democracy** How did President Wilson use Russia's democratic revolution to gain support for the war?
3. **Geography and History** How did the Treaty of Brest-Litovsk affect the war?
4. **Economic Factors** What caused the labor shortage in the United States during the war?
5. **Global Connections** What four nations dominated the Paris Peace Conference?

★ Technology Activity

Using the Internet Search the Internet to find out more details about the "Great War"—World War I. Use the information you find to create a chart titled 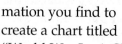 "World War I—A Closer Look." Focus on causes of the war, methods of warfare, and the outcome of the war for various countries. Include numbers of casualties and costs of rebuilding.

★ Geography Activity

Study the map below, then answer the questions that follow.

The Eastern Front

1. **Location** Which Central Powers victories took place in East Prussia?
2. **Place** When was Warsaw, Poland, defeated by the Central Powers?
3. **Movement** Which line gave the Central Powers more territory—the armistice line of 1917 or the treaty line of Brest-Litovsk, 1918?

★ Time Line Activity

Create a time line on which you place the following events in chronological order.

- U.S. declares war against Germany
- Archduke Ferdinand is assassinated
- Battle of Verdun begins
- *Lusitania* torpedoed
- Treaty of Versailles signed

★ Cooperative Activity

History and Music With members of your group, research the life of George M. Cohan. Get copies of the lyrics to his songs, as well as recordings of the music if possible. Then find excerpts such as the following from soldiers who fought in World War I:

❝ As far as the eye could see was a mass of black mud with shell holes filled with water. . . . [H]ere and there a horse's carcase [carcass] sticking out of the water; here and there a corpse. The only sign of life was a rat or two swimming about to find food and a patch of ground. At night a yellow mist hung over the mud; the stench was almost unbearable. When gas shells came over the mist turned to brown. It smelt like violets. The smell of violets was the sign of danger. ❞

—Private H. Jeary, British forces

Use Cohan's music as well as words and pictures from actual soldiers to create a multimedia presentation of "The Great War."

Portfolio Activity **History Journal** Review the chapter for names of committees and organizations created by the United States government to handle war-related concerns. Make a list that describes the responsibilities of each committee or organization.

Hands-On HISTORY Lab Activity

Taffy Pull

Making candy was often a social event in the 1800s and early 1900s. Young people would gather and, as a group, make candy to be enjoyed for the evening. Try to recreate a taffy pull.

Early taffy pull

The Way It Was

Because candy was a luxury that was rarely available in the stores, taffy pulls were a popular gathering for young people. Guests would pull the golden, warm taffy into ropes and then cut the candy and eat it. Candy making, especially taffy pulls, became a family or social event because it required constant attention and many hands to stir and pull the taffy.

 **Materials**

- 2 cups sugar
- 1 cup light corn syrup
- 1 cup water
- 1 1/2 teaspoons salt
- 2 tablespoons butter or margarine, softened
- 2 teaspoons vanilla
- food coloring (optional)
- extra butter
- large flat pan or cookie sheet
- 2-quart saucepan
- candy thermometer
- kitchen scissors
- waxed paper
- stove

Believe **It Or Not!**

The average American eats 18 pounds of candy annually. More than 2,000 different kinds of candy are manufactured in the United States, and more than half of these candies are made with chocolate!

2 What To Do

① Butter the cookie sheet. In the saucepan combine the sugar, corn syrup, water, and salt. Heat the mixture to boiling over medium heat. Carefully stir until the sugar is dissolved.

② Place the candy thermometer in the pan and heat the mixture until the temperature reaches 262°F. SAFETY NOTE: HANDLE HOT MATERIALS CAREFULLY. Remove the pan from the heat. Stir in the butter, vanilla, and food coloring (if desired).

③ Pour the mixture onto the cookie sheet and let it cool 10 to 15 minutes until the taffy is cool enough to handle.

④ Wash your hands very well and coat your hands with butter. Divide the mixture in half with your hands.

⑤ With a partner pull and twist each half until the candy holds its shape. Pull the taffy into long ropes about 3/4 inch in diameter.

⑥ Butter the blades of kitchen scissors and cut the rope into 1 inch pieces. Wrap each piece of candy in waxed paper.

Hardened taffy pieces

3 Lab Report

1. Why do you think it was necessary to pull the taffy instead of just letting it cool on the cookie sheet?
2. Was making taffy easier or more difficult than you thought it would be? Explain your answer.
3. **Drawing Conclusions** How long did it take to make the taffy? How often do you think making candy would occur today if it took this long to make?

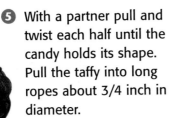

Go a Step Further

Find out more about the making of candy. Research the techniques that the Swiss, Germans, and Dutch used to make their famous chocolates. Draw a diagram showing the various steps involved in turning cacao beans into chocolate candy bars.

Turbulent Decades

1919–1945

"The only thing we have to fear is fear itself."

—FRANKLIN DELANO ROOSEVELT, 1933

interNET CONNECTION

To learn more about the Great Depression and World War II, visit the Glencoe Social Studies Web Site at www.glencoe.com for information, activities, and links to other sites.

MAPPING America

Portfolio Activity Draw a freehand outline map of the United States. Sketch the state borders, including Hawaii. As you read this unit about turbulent decades in American history, note major events. Include sites of labor and racial disputes, the extent of the drought that caused the "Dust Bowl," and the bombing of Pearl Harbor. Plot the location of these events on your map and label them.

General George A. Patton's helmet

WPA poster, mid-1930s

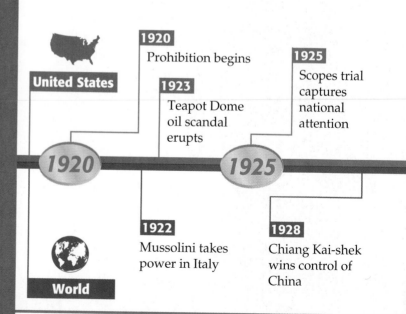

United States

1920
Prohibition begins

1923
Teapot Dome oil scandal erupts

1925
Scopes trial captures national attention

1920

1925

1922
Mussolini takes power in Italy

1928
Chiang Kai-shek wins control of China

World

Life *magazine cover, 1926*

★ HISTORY AND ART *Betio's Red Beach Three* **by Tom Lovell**
American marines plunge into the sea for the assault on Japanese-held islands in 1943.

1929
Stock market crashes, triggering Great Depression

1933
President Franklin D. Roosevelt launches New Deal

1937
Dust Bowl develops in Great Plains

1941
Japanese attack Pearl Harbor; U.S. enters World War II

1944
Allies storm Normandy beaches

1930

1935

1940

1945

1930
Uruguay wins soccer's first World Cup

1933
Hitler becomes chancellor of Germany

1935
Pope Pius XI condemns Nazi atrocities

1939
World War II begins in Europe

1945
Atomic bombs level Hiroshima and Nagasaki

The Invisible Thread

by Yoshiko Uchida

Yoshiko Uchida (1921–1992) grew up in California in the 1930s. As a Japanese American, she sometimes felt very different from the people around her. She wanted to be a "typical" American and often resented the Japanese ways of her family. Eventually Uchida learned to value the "invisible thread" that linked her to her heritage.

■ READ TO DISCOVER

Yoshiko Uchida's family, like many Japanese Americans, were patriotic citizens during World War II. Many Japanese Americans, however, were treated as enemies because of their heritage. During the war, the American government relocated to camps those Japanese people living in the West. How did Yoshiko and her sister, Kay, spend their time in the internment camp?

■ READER'S DICTIONARY

Tanforan: horse racing park used as a camp for Japanese Americans
mess hall: military-style dining area
canteen: a general store at a military camp
contraband: forbidden items
diversion: entertainment

Gradually we became accustomed to life in Tanforan, especially to standing in long lines for everything. We lined up to get into the mess hall or to use a laundry tub or to buy something at the canteen (finding only shoelaces when we got in) or to get into the occasional movies that were shown.

We got used to rushing back to our stall after dinner for the 6:00 P.M. head count (we were still in bed for the morning count), and to the sudden unexpected campwide searches for contraband by the FBI when we were confined to our stalls for several hours.

For diversion we could also go to talent shows, recorded concerts, discussion groups, Saturday night dances, softball games, art classes, and hobby shows exhibiting beautiful handicraft made by resourceful residents from scrap material.

Soon visitors from the outside were allowed to come in as far as the grandstand, and many of our friends came laden with cakes, fruit, candy, cookies, and news from the outside.

Representatives from the university, the YMCA and YWCA, and various church groups also came to give us their support and help. They were working on arrangements to get students out of camp and back into schools as soon as possible.

One day our neighbor Mrs. Harpainter came to see us, bringing all sorts of snacks along with flowers from her garden for Mama. Her boys, however, were not allowed inside because they were under sixteen.

When Kay and I heard they were waiting outside the gate, we hurried to the fence to talk to them.

Japanese Americans unload supplies at an internment camp during World War II.

"Teddy! Bobby!"

We ran to greet them, squeezing our fingers through the chain links to touch their hands.

But an armed guard quickly shouted, "Hey, you two! Get away from the fence!"

Kay and I stepped back immediately. We didn't want to tangle with anyone holding a gun. Bobby and Teddy watched us in total horror, and told us later that they thought we were going to be shot right before their eyes.

When my mother's good friend, Eleanor Knight, came to see us, we asked her to see how Laddie was getting along. Each day we wondered about him, but the boy who had promised to write hadn't even sent us a post-card. And then we learned why he had not written.

"I'm so sorry," Eleanor wrote, "but your dear Laddie died just a few weeks after you left Berkeley."

I was sure he had died of a broken heart, thinking we had abandoned him. I ran outside to find a place to cry, but there were people wherever I turned. I didn't want to see anybody, but there was no place to hide. There was no place to be alone—not in the latrine or the showers or anywhere in the entire camp.

Reprinted with the permission of Simon & Schuster Books for Young Readers, an imprint of Simon & Schuster Children's Publishing Division from *The Invisible Thread* by Yoshiko Uchida. Copyright © 1991 by Yoshiko Uchida.

■ RESPONDING TO LITERATURE

1. Why were Teddy and Bobby not allowed inside the camp?
2. Why did representatives from churches and other groups visit the camp?
3. How do you think you would feel in Uchida's place in the internment camp?

Activity

Designing a Memorial Draw plans for a community memorial suitable for remembering Japanese Americans treated unfairly during World War II.

1919–1929

The Jazz Age

★ Why It's Important

People called the 1920s the Jazz Age—in part because of the popular new music, but also because of the restless, carefree spirit of the time. The economy boomed and many Americans prospered. Not all Americans benefited from the economic progress, however. The 1920s saw a growth in racial unrest and intolerance toward foreigners. During these years, the traditional values of an older, predominately rural society clashed with the new values of a modern, urban nation.

★ Chapter Themes

- *Section 1,* Groups and Institutions
- *Section 2,* Global Connections
- *Section 3,* Economic Factors
- *Section 4,* Science and Technology
- *Section 5,* Culture and Traditions

PRIMARY SOURCES Library *See pages 982–983 for primary source readings to accompany Chapter 24*

 HISTORY AND ART *Music in the Plaza* **by John Sloan** A crowd of evening strollers enjoy band music in the main square of Santa Fe, New Mexico, during the 1920s.

1914
Marcus Garvey founds Universal Negro Improvement Association

1917
Bolsheviks seize control of Russia

1920
Thousands arrested during Palmer raids

1921
Sacco and Vanzetti declared guilty

Section 1

Time of Turmoil

READ TO DISCOVER . . .

■ what factors contributed to a fear of foreigners in the 1920s.

■ how labor and racial unrest in the 1920s affected the nation.

TERMS TO LEARN

capitalism   deport
anarchist

The Storyteller

On a hot summer day in 1920, about 50,000 African Americans marched through the streets of Harlem in New York City. Thousands more lined the sidewalks, cheering the marchers. Their leader, Marcus Garvey, stirred new hope in African Americans, saying: "We are descendants of a people determined to suffer no longer." A participant at the march later recalled, "It was the greatest demonstration of [African American unity] in American history. . . ." Most of the 1920s were anything but unified, however.

Marcus Garvey

After World War I ended, President Woodrow Wilson went to Paris to try to carry through his vision of world peace. In 1919 Wilson and the world leaders attending the peace conference signed the **Treaty of Versailles.** Despite Wilson's efforts, however, the Senate refused to ratify the treaty. A great many Americans hardly seemed to notice. Tired of war and world responsibilities, Americans were eager to return to normal life. They grew more and more suspicious of foreigners and of foreign ideas, as well as of those who held views very different from their own.

Fear of Radicalism

During World War I, the United States government had taken away some of the liberties of American citizens. Many people who opposed the war were arrested. After the war an atmosphere of distrust remained.

At about the same time, the Russian Revolution deeply disturbed some Americans. As you have read in Chapter 23, the Bolsheviks took control of Russia in November 1917 and began establishing a Communist state. They encouraged workers around the world to overthrow capitalism—an economic system based on private property and free enterprise—anywhere it existed. Many Americans feared that "bolshevism" threatened American government and institutions.

Fanning those fears were the actions of anarchists—people who believe there should be no

government. A series of anarchist bombings in 1919 frightened Americans. A number of public officials—mayors, judges, and the United States attorney general—received packages containing bombs. One bomb blew off the hands of the maid of a United States senator. Many of the anarchists were foreign-born, which contributed to the fear of foreigners that was sweeping the country.

The Red Scare

This wave of fear led to the **Red Scare,** a period when the government went after "Reds"—as Communists were known—and others with radical views. In late 1919 and early 1920, Attorney General **A. Mitchell Palmer** and his deputy J. Edgar Hoover ordered the arrest of people suspected of being Communists and anarchists. Palmer and Hoover also staged raids on the headquarters of various "suspicious" groups. In the raids, the government arrested more than 4,000 people, ransacked homes and offices, and seized records. They did not find the large stockpiles of weapons and dynamite they claimed they were seeking.

Palmer said the raids were justified. "The blaze of revolution was sweeping over every American institution of law and order," he declared, "burning up the foundations of society." The government deported—expelled from the United States—about 500 of the aliens it had arrested but quickly released many others for lack of evidence. In time people realized that the danger of revolution was greatly exaggerated. The Red Scare passed—but the fear underlying it remained.

Sacco and Vanzetti

Antiforeign and antiradical feelings surfaced in a criminal case in Massachusetts in 1920. Two men robbed a shoe factory in South Braintree, Massachusetts, shooting and killing a guard and paymaster. Soon afterward the police arrested Italian immigrants **Nicola Sacco** and **Bartolomeo Vanzetti** for the crime. Tried and convicted in July 1921, the two were sentenced to death.

The Sacco and Vanzetti case created a furor. Both men were anarchists, and Sacco owned a pistol similar to the murder weapon. Neither had a criminal record, however, and the evidence against them was weak. Future Supreme Court justice Felix Frankfurter wrote a defense of the two men. William Howard Taft, chief justice of the United States, attacked Frankfurter for "vicious propaganda."

Caught up in antiforeign fever, many Americans demanded that the death sentence be carried out. In 1927 a special commission appointed by the governor of Massachusetts upheld the verdict. Sacco and Vanzetti—still proclaiming their innocence—were executed. While historians continue to debate the verdict, the case suggested the depth of antiforeign and antiradical feelings in the United States in the 1920s.

Labor Unrest

★ Antiforeign and antiradical sentiment also affected American workers and the labor movement. During the war years, labor and management had put aside their differences. A sense of patriotism, high wages, and wartime laws kept conflict to a minimum. When the war ended, conflict flared anew. American workers demanded increases in wages to keep up with rapidly rising prices, launching more than 2,500 strikes in 1919. The wave of strikes fueled American fears of Bolsheviks and radicals, whom many considered to be the cause of the labor unrest.

Workers on Strike

A long and bitter strike—the largest in American history to that point—occurred in the steel industry. Demanding higher wages and an 8-hour workday, about 350,000 steelworkers went on strike in September 1919. Using propaganda techniques learned during the war, the steel companies started a campaign against the strikers. In newspaper ads they accused the strikers of being "Red agitators." The Communist label cost the strikers public support and helped force them to end the strike—but not before violence had occurred on both sides. Eighteen strikers had died in a riot in Gary, Indiana.

In September 1919, police officers in **Boston** went on strike, demanding the right to form a union. This strike by public employees angered many Americans, and they applauded the strong stand Massachusetts governor **Calvin Coolidge** took against the strikers. Coolidge said, "There is no right to strike against the public safety by anybody, anywhere, any time." When the strike collapsed, officials fired the entire Boston police force. Most Americans approved.

Antiunion Feelings Grow

Workers found themselves deeper in debt because of rising prices and unchanged wages. Still labor unions failed to win wide support among working families. Many Americans connected unions with radicalism and bolshevism. A growing feeling against unions, together with strong pressure from employers and the government not to join unions, led to a sharp drop in union membership in the 1920s.

A. Philip Randolph

During this period of union decline, a dynamic African American, **A. Philip Randolph,** started the Brotherhood of Sleeping Car Porters. Made up mostly of African Americans, this union of railroad workers struggled during its

A. Philip Randolph

early years but began to grow in the 1930s, when government policy encouraged unions. In the 1950s and the 1960s, Randolph would emerge as a leader of the civil rights movement.

Racial Unrest

★ During World War I, more than 500,000 African Americans had left the South for new jobs in the North. Many Northern whites resented African American competition for jobs.

★ **Picturing HISTORY** Strikes, such as the 1919 Chicago steel strike, lessened public support for labor unions. Labor leader A. Philip Randolph, however, was able to found the Brotherhood of Sleeping Car Porters. **How did unions fare during the 1920s?**

Violent Reactions

In 1919 rising racial tensions erupted in outbreaks of violence across the country. In the South more than 70 African Americans were lynched. In Chicago a violent riot broke out after a group of whites stoned an African American youth who was swimming in Lake Michigan. The youth drowned, and the incident set off rioting in the city's African American neighborhoods. For two weeks African American and white gangs roamed city streets, attacking each other and burning buildings. The riot left 15 whites and 23 African Americans dead and more than 500 people injured.

Biography

Marcus Garvey

Many African Americans turned to **Marcus Garvey** for answers. Marcus Garvey was born to a poor family in Jamaica, the youngest of 11 children. He worked a variety of jobs growing up, including as a printer's apprentice and on plantations. Educated as a journalist and filled with ambition, Garvey arrived in New York City at the age of 28. A powerful leader with a magnetic personality, Garvey opposed integration. Instead he supported a "back-to-Africa" movement, urging African Americans to establish their own country in Africa. Garvey founded the **Universal Negro Improvement Association** (UNIA) in 1914 to promote racial unity and pride.

During the 1920s Garvey gained an enormous following and great influence, especially among the urban poor. Garvey told audiences that "to be a Negro is no disgrace, but an honor." With branches in many states, the UNIA organized rallies and parades to build pride and confidence among African Americans. It helped African Americans start businesses. One African American newspaper summed up Garvey's achievements: "He taught [African Americans] to admire and praise black things and black people."

Hoping for Peace

For Americans the years following World War I were unsettling. Increasing racial tensions, the wave of strikes, and worries about the growing influence of radicals and foreigners in the United States disturbed many Americans. Most longed for an end to the turmoil.

★ ★ ★ ★ ★ **Section 1 Assessment** ★ ★ ★ ★ ★

Checking for Understanding
1. **Identify** Red Scare, A. Mitchell Palmer, Nicola Sacco, Bartolomeo Vanzetti, Calvin Coolidge, A. Philip Randolph, Marcus Garvey, Universal Negro Improvement Association.
2. **Define** capitalism, anarchist, deport.
3. **Explain** how the fear of radicals and foreigners affected the outcome of the Sacco and Vanzetti trial.

Reviewing Themes
4. **Groups and Institutions** Why was there a sharp drop in union membership during the 1920s?

Critical Thinking
5. **Media Literacy** Imagine you were making a video about the life of Marcus Garvey. If he could speak to American youth today, what statement might he make?

Activity

Describing an Era Make a list of five to seven adjectives that you think describe the mood of the country during the 1920s. Draw or paint these adjectives on poster board in a way that conveys the words' meanings.

1920 — 1925 — 1930

1920
Warren G. Harding
is elected president

1922
Senate investigates
Teapot Dome lease

1923
Calvin Coolidge
becomes president

1928
Kellogg-Briand Pact
aims to outlaw war

Section 2

Desire for Normalcy

READ TO DISCOVER . . .
- what problems President Harding and his administration faced.
- what policies Presidents Harding and Coolidge followed toward business and foreign affairs.

TERMS TO LEARN

lease   isolationism

Storyteller

Warren G. Harding attracted attention with his friendly personality, fine voice, and handsome appearance. These glowing assets could easily make Harding president, thought political strategist Harry Daugherty. As Harding's campaign manager, Daugherty took credit for prodding Harding into the 1920 presidential race: "I found him sunning himself, like a turtle on a log, and I pushed him into the water."

Harding/ Coolidge decal, 1920

In the summer of 1920, the Republicans gathered in Chicago to nominate a candidate for president. Although confident of victory in the upcoming election, they had no outstanding leaders to head the party ticket. As one Republican noted, "There ain't any first raters this year." So party bosses chose "the best of the second raters" as their presidential candidate—Senator **Warren G. Harding** of Ohio. Harding had earned a reputation as a loyal Republican, and Ohio political boss Harry Daugherty pushed through his nomination.

The Harding Presidency

Sensing Americans' longing for calm and stability after decades of progressive reform and world war, Harding declared in his campaign that "America's present need is not heroics, but healing." He promised a return to "normalcy." What Harding meant by *normalcy* was not really clear, but the word sounded reassuring to those Americans who wanted an end to foreign involvement and domestic turmoil.

As Harding's running mate, the Republicans nominated Massachusetts governor **Calvin Coolidge,** celebrated for his firm stand in the Boston police strike. The Harding-Coolidge ticket won a landslide victory in November 1920—the first presidential election in which women could vote. The Republicans defeated the Democratic candidate, Governor **James Cox** of Ohio, and his young running mate, **Franklin Delano Roosevelt** of New York. The Republicans also made large gains in Congress.

Harding admitted having doubts about his qualifications for the presidency. He reportedly told a friend, "I knew that this job would be too much for me." He tried to compensate by appointing several talented people to the cabinet—**Charles Evans Hughes,** a former Supreme Court justice, as secretary of state; **Andrew Mellon,** a prominent Pittsburgh banker and financier, to head the Treasury Department; and **Herbert Hoover,** a talented organizer, as secretary of commerce.

The "Ohio Gang"

President Harding also gave jobs in government to many of his friends and political supporters—the so-called **Ohio Gang.** He appointed **Harry Daugherty** attorney general. He named Senator **Albert Fall** of New Mexico, a close friend, secretary of the interior. **Charles Forbes,** another friend, became head of the Veterans Bureau. Other friends of Harding filled offices throughout the administration.

Many of these appointees were unqualified; some turned out to be corrupt. By 1922 Washington buzzed with rumors of scandals within the Harding administration. Forbes, convicted of stealing funds from the Veterans Bureau, fled to avoid imprisonment. Daugherty was accused of receiving bribes but refused to resign.

1924 recording of a Coolidge speech

Teapot Dome Scandal

The biggest scandal of the Harding administration involved Albert Fall. In 1922 Fall secretly leased, or rented, government oil reserves in Elk Hills, California, and Teapot Dome, Wyoming, to the owners of two oil companies. In exchange Fall received more than $400,000. After the scandal became public, Fall was convicted of bribery and sent to prison—the first cabinet officer ever to go to jail. **Teapot Dome** became a symbol of the corruption in the Harding administration and of government corruption and scandal in general.

Harding himself was not directly involved in any scandals, but as the rumors spread, he grew increasingly distressed. "I have no trouble with my enemies," he said. "But my friends . . . they're the ones that keep me walking the floor nights!"

In the summer of 1923, before the full story of the scandals came out, Harding escaped the stresses of Washington, D.C., by taking a trip west. During the trip he became ill, suffered a heart attack, and died.

Calvin Coolidge

Vice President Calvin Coolidge was visiting his father in Vermont when he was awakened in the early morning hours of August 3, 1923, with the news of President Harding's death. Coolidge's father, a justice of the peace, administered the presidential oath of office. Then the new president—in characteristic Coolidge fashion—calmly turned off the lights and went back to bed.

📖 **Biography**

Honesty Returns to the White House

⭐ Calvin Coolidge was in many ways the complete opposite of Harding. While Harding loved to talk and meet people, Coolidge said very little and earned the name "Silent Cal." In addition, Coolidge had a reputation for honesty. After becoming president, he allowed the investigations into the Harding scandals to proceed without interference. He fired Daugherty and replaced the remaining members of the Ohio Gang with honest officials.

Although Coolidge and Harding differed in style, they held similar political views. Coolidge believed that the best government was the least government and that government should not interfere in the life of the nation. He once said approvingly, "If the federal government should go out of existence, the common run of the people would not detect the difference for a considerable length of time." 📖

A Friend to Business

Under President Coolidge the government took an active role in supporting business. As the president explained, "The chief business of the American people is business. . . . The man who builds a factory builds a temple."

Coolidge and the Republican-dominated Congress aimed to create a favorable climate for business to promote the nation's economic prosperity. The government lowered income tax rates on the wealthiest Americans and on corporate profits and cut government spending. It also raised tariffs protecting American business while overturning laws regulating child labor and wages for women.

Coolidge Is Reelected

Coolidge seemed to be exactly what the country wanted. At the Republican national convention in 1924, the president was nominated without opposition for a term of his own. The Democrats, deeply divided, took more than 100 ballots to nominate a little-known lawyer, John W. Davis of West Virginia, as their presidential candidate. Wisconsin senator Robert La Follette led a

★ **Picturing HISTORY** The Coolidge administration had close ties with business. **How did Coolidge and Congress create a favorable climate for business?**

third party, the Progressives, in the race. Coolidge swept the 1924 presidential election with 54 percent of the popular vote. For the first time in America's history, women won governors' races—**Nellie Taylor Ross** in Wyoming and **Miriam Ferguson** in Texas.

Foreign Policy

★ Harding and Coolidge both favored a limited role for the nation in world affairs. They desired world peace but did not want the nation to join the League of Nations or become involved in international disagreements. Harding had promised the American people that he would not lead them into the League "by the side door, back door, or cellar door." Many Americans supported this policy of isolationism.

---

*F*ootnotes to History

Silent Cal Calvin Coolidge did not believe in wasting money or words. Once a young lady sitting next to him at a White House dinner said, "Mr. President, I have made a bet I can get more than three words out of you during the meal." Without even looking at her he said, "You lose."

United States Marines in Nicaragua display a skull-and-crossbones flag captured from Nicaraguan revolutionaries. **Why did the United States intervene in Latin America during the early 1900s?**

Promoting Peace

The Harding administration made serious efforts to promote peace. After the war the United States, Great Britain, and Japan began a naval arms race. In 1921 Secretary of State Hughes invited Japan and Britain to Washington, D.C., to discuss the problem. In February 1922 the three nations, along with France and Italy, signed the **Five-Power Treaty** to limit the size of the nations' navies. The treaty marked the first time in modern history that world powers agreed to disarm.

The United States continued working for peace. In August 1928, it joined 14 other nations in signing the **Kellogg-Briand Pact,** which called for outlawing war. Within a few years, 48 other nations had signed the pact, but it lacked any means of enforcing peace.

A More Friendly Neighbor

In the early 1900s, the United States had intervened in Latin American countries several times to support American business interests. When Harding took office, American troops were stationed in Haiti, the **Dominican Republic,** and **Nicaragua,** and relations with Mexico were tense.

After the Dominican Republic and Nicaragua held elections in the mid-1920s, the United States withdrew its troops from those countries.

At about the same time, American investors asked President Coolidge to send troops into Mexico after its government threatened to take over foreign-owned oil and mining companies. Coolidge chose to negotiate instead, and the United States reached a settlement with Mexico.

★ ★ ★ ★ ★ **Section 2 Assessment** ★ ★ ★ ★ ★

Checking for Understanding

1. **Identify** Warren G. Harding, Ohio Gang, Teapot Dome, Kellogg-Briand Pact.
2. **Define** lease, isolationism.
3. **Discuss** the factors that led to Harding's election to the presidency in 1920.

Reviewing Themes

4. **Global Connections** What actions did the United States take to promote world peace in the 1920s?

Critical Thinking

5. **Making Comparisons** What role did Harding and Coolidge think the government should play in people's lives?

 Activity

Drawing a Political Cartoon Draw a political cartoon that illustrates an example of the corruption that took place during Warren G. Harding's administration.

Critical Thinking
SKILL BUILDER

Making Generalizations

If you say, "We have a great football team," you are making a generalization, or general statement, about your team. If you go on to say that your team has not lost a game this season and is the top-ranked team, you are providing evidence to support your generalization. When studying history, it is often necessary to put together pieces of information—supporting statements—to arrive at a full picture.

Learning the Skill

In some cases, authors provide only supporting statements and you will need to make the generalizations on your own.

To make generalizations, follow these steps:
- Identify the subject matter.
- Gather facts and examples related to it.
- Identify similarities or patterns among these facts.
- Use these similarities or patterns to form some general ideas about the subject.

Practicing the Skill

Read the passage and the generalizations about the automobile on this page. Then answer the questions that follow.

By 1927, 4 out of 5 cars had closed tops, compared with only 1 in 10 in 1919. Now protected from the weather, many families hopped into their cars for short day trips. With "auto-mobility," many city workers moved to houses in the new suburbs. Car owners now traveled easily to once distant places, bringing far-flung Americans together for the first time.

Traffic jam, 1920s

Generalizations about the Automobile
a. Automobiles were too expensive to buy.
b. The automobile changed American culture in many ways.
c. Many businesses grew from the need to service the newly mobile nation.
d. Suburbs grew as a result of the automobile.

1. Which of the generalizations above are supported by the details in this passage?
2. Write one or two statements that support each of these generalizations.
3. Which of the generalizations are not supported by the passage? Explain.

Applying the Skill

Making Generalizations Make a general statement about your class that describes it. Then write three or four supporting details for that generalization.

Glencoe's **Skillbuilder Interactive Workbook, Level 1** provides instruction and practice in key social studies skills.

1920		1925		1930

1920s
Stock market booms

1922
GNP reaches $70 billion

1924
Model T sells for less than $300

1929
Electricity runs 70 percent of factories

Section 3

A Booming Economy

READ TO DISCOVER . . .
- how the prosperity of the 1920s affected the nation and the American people.
- what impact the automobile had on American life.

TERMS TO LEARN

recession
gross national product

productivity
installment buying

The Storyteller

During the "golden age of the automobile" in the 1920s, the car became a vital part of many Americans' lives. A mother of nine children said that her family "would rather do without clothes than give up the car." In the past, they had wanted to visit her sister-in-law, but by the time the children were "shoed and dressed" there wasn't any money left to pay for trolley fare. "Now no matter how [the children] look, we just poke 'em in the car and take 'em along."

1920s gas pump

After World War I, the American economy experienced problems readjusting to peacetime. Millions of soldiers returned, entering the labor force and competing for jobs. Government orders for wartime goods came to a halt, forcing many companies to lay off workers. Other companies went bankrupt. Prices rose, making it hard for workers to make ends meet.

This economic downturn, or recession, lasted about 2 years. Then the economy began a steady growth that lasted most of the decade. In 1922 the nation's gross national product (GNP)—the total value of all goods and services produced—was $70 billion. By 1929 it had risen to $100 billion!

Growth in the 1920s

★ Technology made rapid industrial growth possible, and electricity powered American industry. Before World War I, only 30 percent of factories were run by electricity. By 1929 this figure had risen to 70 percent. Electricity was cheaper than steam power. By cutting costs, businesses could lower prices and increase profits.

Scientific Management

New ways of managing operations contributed to economic growth as well. Many employers used **scientific management**—hiring experts to study how goods could be produced more quickly. By adopting new work methods, businesses sought to lower costs and increase productivity—how much work each worker could do.

Many businesses adopted mass production techniques using the **assembly line,** first introduced in Henry Ford's automobile factories. Assembly line methods increased productivity and cut production costs.

Worker Relations

Businesses tried to build better relations with workers. Many companies set up safety programs that lowered the risk of death or injury on the job. Some began to provide health and accident insurance. Many companies encouraged workers to buy stock in the company. These steps—known as **welfare capitalism**—were designed to link workers more closely to the company they worked for. Business also adopted these steps to discourage workers from joining independent unions.

The Consumer Economy

American industry changed in another way as well. As electricity became more available, demand grew for appliances using electric power. By the 1920s, more than 60 percent of American households had electricity. Consumers eagerly acquired refrigerators, stoves, vacuum cleaners, fans, and radios. As demand for these items grew, more and more of them were produced, leading to reduced production costs and lower prices. Between 1920 and 1929, for example, the cost of a refrigerator dropped from $600 to $300.

These appliances transformed daily life. People did not have to spend as much time on household chores. Now they had more leisure time.

National Brands and Advertising

In the 1920s successful companies joined with or purchased competitors. Three companies—Ford, General Motors, and Chrysler—dominated the auto industry. One grocery chain—the Great Atlantic and Pacific Tea Company (A&P)—had more than 15,000 stores across the country. Businesses became national as many products of local companies were replaced by national brands.

To market those national brands, businesses spent more and more money on advertising. Propaganda techniques learned during World War I now persuaded consumers to buy a particular brand of toothpaste, clothing, or soap. Newspapers and magazines were filled with ads, and with the spread of radio a new advertising form—the commercial announcement—was born.

Buy Now, Pay Later

Spurred by ads to buy more and more, consumers gained a new way to make those purchases—installment buying. Consumers could now buy products by promising to pay small, regular amounts over a period of time. One critic of installment buying called the system "a dollar down and a dollar a week forever." The plan boosted consumer spending.

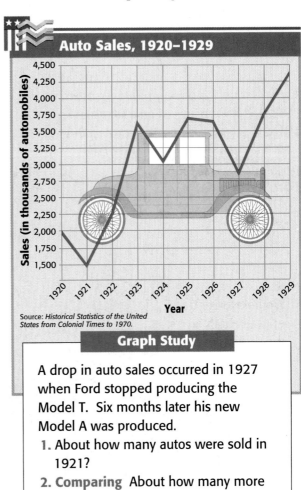

Auto Sales, 1920–1929

Source: *Historical Statistics of the United States from Colonial Times to 1970.*

Graph Study

A drop in auto sales occurred in 1927 when Ford stopped producing the Model T. Six months later his new Model A was produced.

1. About how many autos were sold in 1921?
2. **Comparing** About how many more autos were sold in 1928 than in 1924?

The Automobile Age

★ More often than not, people used the installment plan to buy a new car. During the 1920s, automobile registrations jumped from 8 million to 23 million. America quickly became a "car culture," in which people's lives revolved around the automobile. The nation's economy, too, revolved around the automobile. Almost 4 million Americans worked for auto companies or in related jobs. **Detroit, Michigan,** became the automobile manufacturing center of the world.

Cheaper Cars

Henry Ford was a pioneer in the manufacture of affordable automobiles with his **Model T,** built using assembly line methods. The car was sturdy, reliable, inexpensive, and available only in black. In 1914 Ford had stunned the auto industry—and all corporate leaders, for that matter—by announcing that he would pay his workers the high wage of $5 per day. Workers were happy, and Ford had more potential customers as he steadily dropped the price of his Model T. By 1924 the car sold for less than $300. With the average industrial worker earning about $1,300 a year, many families could afford to buy a Model T.

By the mid-1920s, other automobile models challenged the Model T. General Motors cut into Ford's sales by offering a line of cars in a range of colors and with features to improve passenger comfort. In 1927 Ford responded with the **Model A,** which had better engineering and came in several colors. Out of this competition came the practice of introducing new car models each year.

TECHNOLOGY AND HISTORY

Henry Ford's Assembly Line

The industrial boom of the 1920s owed much to the assembly line Henry Ford first used in 1913–1914. Parts moved on a conveyor belt. Workers attached the parts to cars moving past them at a steady speed of six feet per minute. **How large was Ford's plant?**

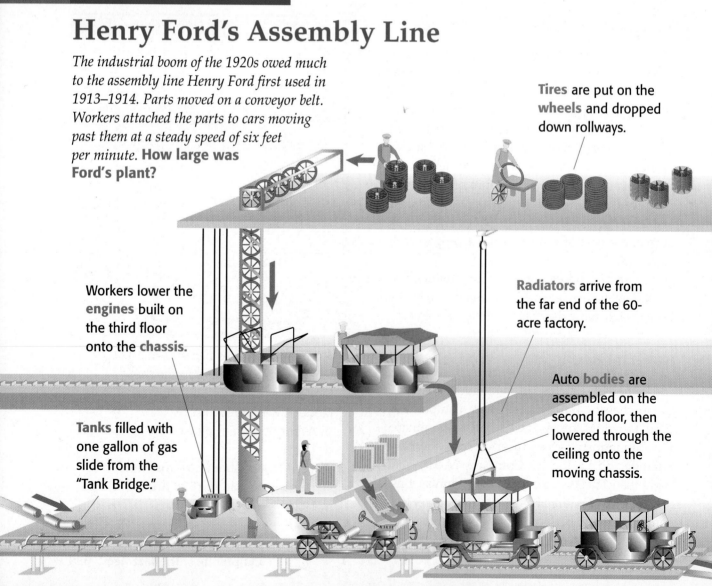

Tires are put on the **wheels** and dropped down rollways.

Workers lower the **engines** built on the third floor onto the **chassis.**

Radiators arrive from the far end of the 60-acre factory.

Tanks filled with one gallon of gas slide from the "Tank Bridge."

Auto **bodies** are assembled on the second floor, then lowered through the ceiling onto the moving chassis.

Effect on Other Industries

The automobile had a tremendous impact on other American industries. Americans' love of driving called for new roads and highways. Highways, in turn, needed gas stations and rest stops. Businesses along major roads profited from the millions of people now traveling around the country by car. Tourism grew dramatically.

The car boom affected industries that made products used in cars. The steel, rubber, and glass industries grew. During the 1920s the oil industry shifted from producing lubricants to refining gasoline for automobiles.

Car Culture

The automobile dramatically changed the lives of many Americans. Travel for pleasure became a regular part of American life. People could now get into their cars and go wherever they wished. Cars also contributed to the spread of suburbs. Because people could now drive to work, they could live in a suburb and still hold a job in the city.

Those Left Behind

Despite all the signs of prosperity and the mood of optimism, many Americans did not share in the boom of the 1920s. Farmers had an especially difficult time. During the war, the federal government had purchased wheat, corn, and other

Picturing HISTORY During the 1920s, an increasing number of Americans used their automobiles to take trips away from home. **How did the automobile affect where people lived?**

products, and farmers had prospered from higher prices. When the war ended, farmers had to compete with European agriculture again. Food prices fell, and farm income plummeted. Unable to pay their debts, many farmers lost their farms.

Not all industrial workers shared in the prosperity of the 1920s. Those who worked in the coal mining and railroad industries had a difficult time as trucks took business from railroads and electricity replaced coal as a power source. Wages rose slightly for most workers, but the cost of living rose more. By 1929 nearly three-fourths of families had incomes below $2,500, the accepted level necessary for a comfortable life.

Section 3 Assessment

Checking for Understanding
1. **Identify** scientific management, assembly line, welfare capitalism, Henry Ford.
2. **Define** recession, gross national product, productivity, installment buying.
3. **Describe** the economic problems that existed in America after World War I.

Reviewing Themes
4. **Economic Factors** How did the auto industry help boost other industries?

Critical Thinking
5. **Drawing Conclusions** How did welfare capitalism discourage people from joining unions?

Activity

Tracking Progress Compare a photograph or drawing of Ford's Model T to a modern car and describe the major differences you see.

1920
Nineteenth
Amendment grants
woman suffrage

1924
Crossword puzzles
are a popular
activity

1927
Charles Lindbergh flies
solo across the Atlantic;
Babe Ruth hits 60
home runs

Section 4

The Roaring Twenties

READ TO DISCOVER . . .
- how lifestyles in America changed in the 1920s.
- what features characterized the music and literature of the Jazz Age.

TERMS TO LEARN
flapper   expatriate
mass media

The Storyteller

On the evening of May 19, 1927, a young pilot named Charles Lindbergh learned that, although it was drizzling on Long Island, the weather reports predicted fair skies for his miraculous trip. He decided to get ready. Throughout a sleepless night, Lindbergh made the final preparations for takeoff. Shortly before 8:00 A.M., Lindbergh climbed into his aircraft and took off for Paris. With the news of his departure "flashing along the wires," the American people were united in "the exaltation of a common emotion." All minds and hearts were focused on the brave pilot who was crossing the vast Atlantic Ocean.

Song sheet honoring Lindbergh

In May 1927, aviator **Charles Lindbergh** became the first person to fly alone across the Atlantic Ocean. He did so in a tiny, single-engine plane, the *Spirit of St. Louis*. Americans went wild and hailed a new hero. Cities across the nation held parades to honor Lindbergh—in New York City well-wishers threw 1,800 tons of paper streamers—and newspapers reported on his every move. The national embrace of Lindbergh showed what one historian called a "delighted concern over things that were exciting but didn't matter profoundly."

Changes for Women

The 1920s did bring profound changes for women. One important change took place with the ratification of the **Nineteenth Amendment** in 1920. The amendment guaranteed women in all states the right to vote. Women also ran for election to political offices.

In the Workplace

Throughout the 1920s the number of women holding jobs outside the home continued to grow. Most women had to take jobs considered "women's" work, such as teaching and working in offices as clerks and typists. At the same time, increasing numbers of college-educated women started professional careers, and more women worked after marriage. But the vast majority of married women remained within the home, working as homemakers and mothers.

The Flapper

Symbolizing the new "liberated" woman of the 1920s was the flapper. Pictures of flappers—carefree young women with short, "bobbed" hair, heavy makeup, and short skirts—appeared in magazines. Many people saw the bold, boyish look and shocking behavior of flappers as a sign of changing morals. Though hardly typical of American women, the flapper image reinforced the idea that women now had more freedom. Prewar values had shifted, and many people were beginning to challenge traditional ways.

Entertainment

★ Changes in attitudes spread quickly because of the growth of mass media—forms of communication, such as newspapers and radio, that reach millions of people. Laborsaving devices and fewer working hours gave Americans more leisure time. In those nonworking hours, they enjoyed tabloid-style newspapers, large-circulation magazines, phonograph records, the radio, and the movies.

The Movies

In the 1920s the motion picture industry in **Hollywood,** California, became one of the country's leading businesses. For millions of Americans, the movies offered entertainment and escape.

The first movies were black and white and silent, with the actors' dialog printed on the screen and a pianist playing music to accompany the action. In 1927 Hollywood introduced movies with sound. The first "talkie," *The Jazz Singer,* created a sensation.

As the popularity of movies increased, Americans became fascinated with the people who appeared in them. Adoring fans idolized stars such as Douglas Fairbanks, Gloria Swanson, Clara Bow, Charlie Chaplin, and Rudolph Valentino. Enthusiastic fans read movie magazines filled with stories about the stars' personal lives. Scandals revealed some of those lives to be less than ideal. Many Americans worried about the impact

Flappers

***Poster for a
Valentino movie***

of movies on the nation's morality. The movie industry responded by creating an office to inspect the content of films and to keep out material that might offend people.

Radio

The radio brought entertainment to people's homes in the 1920s. In 1920 the first commercial radio broadcast, which carried the presidential election returns, was transmitted by station KDKA in Pittsburgh. In the next 3 years nearly 600 stations joined the airwaves. Soon stations began to combine into powerful national networks.

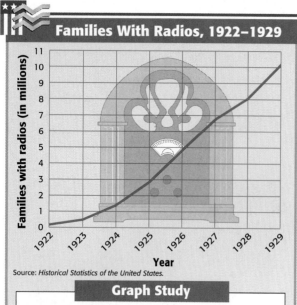

Families With Radios, 1922–1929

Families with radios (in millions) vs **Year**

Source: *Historical Statistics of the United States.*

Graph Study

In their newfound leisure time, Americans in the 1920s listened to the radio or their phonographs.

1. About how many families had radios in 1923?
2. **Comparing** About how many more families had radios in 1929 than in 1928?

The networks broadcast popular programs across the nation. The evening lineup of programs included something for everyone—news, concerts, sporting events, and comedies. Radio offered listeners a wide range of music—opera, classical, country and western, blues, and jazz. *Amos 'n' Andy* and the *Grand Ole Opry* were among the hit shows of the 1920s. Families sat down to listen to the radio together.

Businesses soon realized that the radio offered an enormous audience for messages about their products, so they began to help finance radio programs. Radio stations sold spot advertisements, or commercials, to companies.

Sports and Fads

Among the favorite radio broadcasts of the 1920s were athletic events. Americans became fascinated with sports and sports figures. Baseball, football, and boxing soared in popularity. Americans flocked to sporting events, and more people participated in sports activities as well.

Sports stars became larger-than-life heroes. Baseball fans idolized **Babe Ruth,** the great outfielder, who hit 60 home runs in 1927—a record that would stand for 34 years. Football star Red Grange, who once scored 4 touchdowns in 12 minutes, became a national hero, too, as did boxer Jack Dempsey. Golfer Bobby Jones and Gertrude Ederle, the first woman to swim the English Channel, became household names.

In the 1920s Americans took up new activities with enthusiasm, turning them into fads. A craze for the Chinese board game mah-jongg (mah•ZHAHNG) swept the country in 1922, and in 1924 crossword puzzles were all the rage. Contests such as flagpole sitting—Alvin "Shipwreck" Kelly set the record of 23 days, 7 hours—and dance marathons—often lasting 3 or 4 days—made headlines. Americans also loved the Miss America Pageant, first held in 1921.

The Jazz Age

During the 1920s people danced to the beat of a new kind of music called jazz. Jazz captured the spirit of the era so well that the 1920s is often referred to as the **Jazz Age.**

Jazz had its roots in the South in African American work songs and in African music. A blend of ragtime and blues, it used dynamic rhythms and **improvisation**—new rhythms and melodies created during a performance. Among the best-known African American jazz musicians were trumpeter **Louis Armstrong,** pianist and composer **Duke Ellington,** and singer **Bessie Smith.** White musicians such as Paul Whiteman and Bix Biederbecke also played jazz and helped bring it to a wider audience.

Interest in jazz spread via radio and phonograph records. Jazz helped

Babe Ruth

Clarinet

Jazz record label

Trumpet

What Was It Like? Jazz music probably began in New Orleans in the early 1900s and soon spread to Chicago, New York, and other cities. What instruments are associated with jazz music?

create a unique African American recording industry. Equally important, jazz gave America one of its most distinctive art forms.

Harlem Renaissance

The rhythm and themes of jazz inspired the poetry of **Langston Hughes,** an African American writer. In the 1920s, Hughes joined the growing number of African American writers and artists who gathered in **Harlem,** an African American section of New York City. Hughes described his arrival in Harlem:

> ❝ I can never put on paper the thrill of the underground ride to Harlem. I went up the steps and out into the bright September sunlight. Harlem! I stood there, dropped my bags, took a deep breath and felt happy again. ❞

Harlem witnessed a burst of creativity in the 1920s—a flowering of African American culture called the **Harlem Renaissance.** This movement instilled an interest in African culture and pride in being African American.

During the Harlem Renaissance, a number of important writers explored the African American experience in novels, poems, and short stories. Along with Hughes were poets **James Weldon Johnson, Claude McKay, Countee Cullen,** and the short story writer **Zora Neale Hurston.** African American theater also blossomed during the Harlem Renaissance. Stars included actor and singer **Paul Robeson** and one of the first women in musical comedy, **Florence Mills.**

Langston Hughes

Zora Neale Hurston

The Harlem Renaissance faded in the 1930s with the Great Depression. Its influence, however, lived on and affected the work of later generations of African American artists.

A Lost Generation of Writers

At the same time the Harlem Renaissance blossomed, other writers were questioning American ideals. Disappointed with American values and in search of inspiration, they settled in Paris. These writers were called expatriates—people who choose to live in another country. Writer **Gertrude Stein** called these rootless Americans "the lost generation."

Novelist **F. Scott Fitzgerald** and his wife, Zelda, joined the expatriates in Europe. In *Tender Is the Night,*

Fitzgerald wrote of people who had been damaged emotionally by World War I. They were dedicated, he said, "to the fear of poverty and the worship of success." Another famous American expatriate was novelist **Ernest Hemingway,** whose books *The Sun Also Rises* and *A Farewell to Arms* reflected the mood of Americans in postwar Europe.

While some artists fled the United States, others stayed home and wrote about life in America. Novelist **Sinclair Lewis** presented a critical view of American culture in such books as *Main Street* and *Babbitt*. Another influential American writer was **Sherwood Anderson.** In his most famous book, *Winesburg, Ohio,* Anderson explored small-town life in the Midwest.

Throughout the 1920s America's writers and intellectuals continued to examine and criticize the changing culture of the United States. Their work revealed the underlying clashes in American society during this time of great upheaval.

Ernest Hemingway

Section 4 Assessment

Checking for Understanding
1. *Identify* Charles Lindbergh, Nineteenth Amendment, Jazz Age, Langston Hughes, Harlem Renaissance, F. Scott Fitzgerald.
2. *Define* flapper, mass media, expatriate.
3. *Summarize* the changes in women's personal and economic status during the 1920s.

Reviewing Themes
4. **Science and Technology** How did the growth of mass media affect society?

Critical Thinking
5. **Making Generalizations** Why do you think Gertrude Stein referred to many American writers as "the lost generation"?

Activity

Illustrating a Poem Read a poem by one of the writers associated with the Harlem Renaissance. Find illustrations and photographs that help to communicate the meaning of the poem. Display the poem and illustrations on a piece of poster board.

All That Jazz

Almost 80 years after the Jazz Age, its music and moods are still at the heart of American culture. Read about the changes that people experienced as they moved to cities and experimented with new forms of art, music, and literature. Then become part of the Jazz Age yourself as you complete these activities.

Language Arts

Staging a Play Imagine that you have been asked to produce a play or musical set in the Roaring Twenties. Research the background of the 1920s, then design a series of costumes for men and women or make sketches for several different scenes. These may include a city street or a night-club. If possible, make costumes for your class-mates who perform the music of the Jazz Age.

Science

Writing a '20s Musical Listen to recordings of jazz and performances by popular musicians from the 1920s, such as Duke Ellington and George Gershwin. Choose a selection of songs you like and write a script that brings them together in a one-act musical comedy. Use the songs' original words or write new ones and add them to your script. With a group of classmates, memorize the songs and script to put on a performance for the class.

Art

Painting a Mural With a group, make a list of people and events that represent the Jazz Age. In-clude musicians, writers, sports figures, and other entertainers. Use a roll of brown paper to make a wall mural in the classroom. First make small sketches on a sheet of paper. Then transfer the sketches to the mural paper using chalk or pencil. Fill in color and patterns with markers or acrylics.

Mathematics

Designing a Skyscraper By the 1920s skyscrap-ers were becoming part of the skyline of American cities. Research a well-known building of this period, such as the Chrysler Building in New York City. Construct a cardboard or wooden model of or sketch your own plans for a 1920s skyscraper.

Duke Ellington song sheet (left) and blues singer Bessie Smith (right)

1915	1920	1925	1930

1915
Second
Ku Klux Klan
is organized

1920
Eighteenth
Amendment
establishes
Prohibition

1924
Congress
passes
National
Origins Act

1925
Scopes trial
tests teaching
of evolution

1928
Herbert
Hoover
is elected
president

Section 5

Clashing Cultures

READ TO DISCOVER . . .
- how Prohibition affected American society.
- what cultural clashes occurred in the United States in the 1920s.
- why Americans closed the door to new immigrants.

TERMS TO LEARN
Prohibition
nativism
quota system
evolution

The Storyteller

During the 1920s many Americans called for limits on immigration. "Refuse the refuse!" was the popular cry of those who cherished "100 percent Americanism." The secretary of the St. Petersburg, Florida, Chamber of Commerce spoke for many uninformed citizens when he declared: "The time has come to make this a hundred percent American . . . city as free from foreigners as from slums."

Anti-immigrant song sheet

During the 1920s the number of people living in cities swelled, and a modern industrial society came of age. Outside of the cities, many Americans identified this new, urban society with crime, corruption, immoral behavior, and foreign influences. They felt that the America they knew and valued—based on family, church, and tradition—was under attack.

Those most distressed by the changing society reacted with fear and anger. A series of battles erupted between two clashing cultures, between those who defended traditional beliefs and those who welcomed new ideas and lifestyles.

Prohibition

The clash of cultures during the 1920s affected many aspects of American life, particularly the use of alcoholic beverages. The temperance movement, the campaign against alcohol use, had begun in the 1800s. The movement was rooted both in religious objections to drinking alcohol and in the belief that society would benefit if alcohol were unavailable.

The movement finally achieved its goal in 1920 with the ratification of the **Eighteenth Amendment** to the Constitution. This amendment established Prohibition—a total ban on the manufacture, sale, and transportation of liquor throughout the United States. Congress passed the **Volstead Act** to provide the means of enforcing the ban.

Much of the support for Prohibition came from middle-class women, who considered it a progressive social reform, and from rural Protestants, who saw it as a moral crusade. Its supporters hailed Prohibition as a "noble experiment" that would help solve such problems as poverty, unemployment, and domestic violence.

Prohibition Breaks Down

In rural areas in the South and the Midwest, where the temperance movement was strong, Prohibition generally succeeded. In the cities, however, Prohibition had little support. The nation divided into two camps: the "drys"—those who supported Prohibition—and the "wets"—those who opposed it.

A continuing demand for alcohol led to widespread lawbreaking. Some people began making wine or "bathtub gin" in their homes. Illegal bars and clubs, known as speakeasies, sprang up in cities. Hidden from view, these clubs could be entered only by saying a secret password.

With only about 1,500 agents to cover the whole country, the federal government could do little to enforce the Prohibition laws. By the early 1920s, many states in the East stopped trying to enforce the law.

Organized Crime

Prohibition contributed to the rise of organized crime. Recognizing that millions of dollars could be made from **bootlegging**—making and selling illegal alcohol—members of organized crime moved in quickly and took control. They used their profits to gain influence in businesses, labor unions, and governments.

Al "Scarface" Capone, a famous crime lord of the day, controlled organized crime and local politics in Chicago. Defending his involvement in illegal alcohol, Capone said, "I make my money by supplying a popular demand. If I break the law, my customers are as guilty as I am." Eventually, Capone was arrested and sent to prison—for income tax evasion.

Over time many Americans realized that the "noble experiment" had failed. Prohibition was repealed in 1933 with the passage of the **Twenty-first Amendment.**

Nativism

The anxieties many native-born Americans felt about the rapid changes in society contributed to an upsurge of nativism—the belief that native-born Americans are superior to foreigners. With this renewed nativism came a revival of the **Ku Klux Klan.**

As you read in Chapter 17, the first Klan had been founded in the 1860s in the South to control newly freed African Americans by the use of threats and violence. The second Klan, organized in 1915, still preyed on African Americans, but it had other targets as well—Catholics, Jews, immigrants, and other groups believed to represent "un-American" values.

In the 1920s the new Klan spread from the South to other areas of the country, gaining considerable power in such states as Indiana and Oregon and in many large cities. For the most part, the Klan used pressure and scare tactics to get its way, but sometimes Klan members whipped or lynched people or burned property. By 1924 the Klan claimed more than 4 million members— about 3.5 percent of the nation's population.

The Klan began to decline in the late 1920s, however, largely as a result of scandals and power struggles involving Klan leaders. Membership shrank, and politicians who had been supported by the Klan were voted out of office.

Fear of Foreigners

The concerns of the Red Scare days had not completely disappeared. Some Americans feared foreign radicals would overthrow the government. Others believed foreigners would take away their jobs. This anti-immigrant prejudice was directed mainly at southern and eastern Europeans and Asians.

New Laws

In 1921 Congress responded to nativist fears by passing the **Emergency Quota Act.** This law established a quota system, an arrangement placing a limit on the number of immigrants from each country. According to the act, only 3 percent of the total number of people in any national group already living in the United States would be admitted during a single year. Because there had been fewer immigrants from southern and eastern Europe than from northern and western Europe at that time, the law favored northern and western European immigrants.

Congress revised the immigration law in 1924. The **National Origins Act** reduced the annual country quota from 3 to 2 percent and based it on the census of 1890—when even fewer people from southern or eastern Europe lived in America. The law excluded Japanese immigrants completely. An earlier law, passed in 1890, had already excluded the Chinese.

These quota laws did not apply to countries in the Western Hemisphere. As a result, immigration of Canadians and Mexicans increased. By 1930 more than 1 million Mexicans had come to live in the United States.

The Scopes Trial

★ Another cultural clash in the 1920s involved the role of religion in society. This conflict gained national attention in 1925 in one of the most famous trials of the era.

★ Picturing HISTORY Opposing attorneys Clarence Darrow (left) and William Jennings Bryan pose during the Scopes trial. **What basic clash of values in 1920s society did the trial represent?**

Opposing Evolution

In 1925 the state of **Tennessee** passed a law making it illegal to teach evolution—the scientific theory that humans evolved over vast periods of time. The law was supported by Christian fundamentalists, who accepted the biblical story of creation. The fundamentalists saw evolution as a challenge to their values and their religious beliefs.

A young high school teacher named **John Scopes** deliberately broke the law against teaching evolution so that a trial could test its legality. Scopes acted with the support of the American Civil Liberties Union (ACLU). During the sweltering summer of 1925, the nation followed day-to-day developments in the **Scopes trial** with great interest. More than a hundred journalists from around the country descended on Dayton, Tennessee, to report on the trial.

Darrow Versus Bryan

Two famous lawyers took opposing sides in the trial. **William Jennings Bryan,** Democratic candidate for president in 1896, 1900, and 1908 and a strong opponent of evolution, led the prosecution. **Clarence Darrow,** who had defended many radicals and labor union members, spoke for Scopes. The turning point of the Scopes trial came when Darrow called Bryan to the stand as an expert on the Bible. Darrow's clever questions confused Bryan, and the press ridiculed him.

Although Scopes was convicted of breaking the law and fined $100, the fundamentalists lost the larger battle. Darrow's defense made it appear that Bryan wanted to impose his religious beliefs on the entire nation. The Tennessee Supreme Court overturned Scopes's conviction, and other states decided not to prosecute similar cases.

The Scopes case may have dealt a blow to fundamentalism, but the movement continued to thrive. Rural people, especially in the South and Midwest, remained faithful to their religious beliefs. When large numbers of farmers migrated to cities during the 1920s, they brought fundamentalism with them.

The Election of 1928

⭐ The cultural clashes of the 1920s were played out in the 1928 presidential election. The election featured two candidates who represented very different views of American life.

Al Smith campaign button

Hoover campaign poster

📖 **Biography**

Herbert Hoover

In 1927 President Coolidge shocked everyone by announcing that he would not run for a second full term. **Herbert Hoover** declared his candidacy for the Republican nomination.

Born in Iowa and trained as a mining engineer, Hoover had made millions of dollars in private business and then turned to public service. During World War I, Hoover had won respect as the head of a committee providing food relief for Europe. He showed such a gift in the role that "to Hooverize" came to mean "to economize, to save and share." Later, Hoover ably served Presidents Harding and Coolidge as secretary of commerce.

Hoover worked tirelessly to promote cooperation between government and business. A symbol of the forward-looking middle class, he easily won the Republican nomination. 📖

The Democratic Candidate

The Democrats chose a far different kind of candidate—**Alfred E. Smith,** governor of New York. The son of immigrants and a man of the city, Smith opposed Prohibition and championed the poor and the working class. Many Americans found his strong New York accent jarring. As the first Roman Catholic nominee for president, Smith was the target of anti-Catholic feeling. Hoover won the election by a landslide due to both the Republican prosperity of the 1920s and the prejudice against Smith. The contest reflected many of the tensions in American society—rural versus urban life, nativism versus foreign influences, "wets" versus "drys," Protestants versus Catholics, traditional values versus modern values.

⭐ ⭐ ⭐ ⭐ ⭐ **Section 5 Assessment** ⭐ ⭐ ⭐ ⭐ ⭐

Checking for Understanding
1. *Identify* Eighteenth Amendment, Twenty-first Amendment, Ku Klux Klan, National Origins Act, Scopes trial, William Jennings Bryan, Clarence Darrow, Herbert Hoover, Alfred E. Smith.
2. *Define* Prohibition, nativism, quota system, evolution.
3. *Discuss* how Prohibition led to a rise in organized crime.

Reviewing Themes
4. **Culture and Traditions** How did the Scopes trial reflect the desire of many Americans to return to traditional values?

Critical Thinking
5. **Making Inferences** If a presidential election were held today, do you think Herbert Hoover or Alfred E. Smith would be most likely to win? Explain.

Activity

Composing a Song Write a humorous song that someone might have written during the 1920s that pokes fun at the fads of the era.

Assessment and Activities

⭐ Reviewing Key Terms

On a sheet of paper, use the following vocabulary words to write two paragraphs about the "turbulent decade" of the 1920s.

anarchist

deport

lease

isolationism

recession

gross national product

productivity

installment buying

flapper

mass media

expatriate

Prohibition

nativism

quota system

evolution

⭐ Reviewing Key Facts

1. Describe the attitude of many Americans toward foreigners and radicals after the war.
2. What role did Presidents Harding and Coolidge think that the United States should play in world affairs?
3. How did electricity change the lives of American consumers?
4. How did African Americans benefit from the Harlem Renaissance?
5. What two laws did Congress pass to control immigration?

⭐ Critical Thinking

Making Inferences

Although the 1920s was a prosperous time for many Americans, corruption and scandal were widespread.

1. Why do you think the new prosperity made corruption more tempting?
2. Novelist F. Scott Fitzgerald said that after World War I many people were dedicated "to the fear of poverty and the worship of success." What do you think he meant?

⭐ Time Line Activity

Create a time line on which you place the following events in chronological order.

- First movie with sound is released
- Thousands arrested in Red Scare
- Prohibition repealed
- Teapot Dome scandal
- Scopes trial
- Herbert Hoover takes office as president

⭐ Reviewing Themes

1. **Groups and Institutions** How did some companies use the Red Scare to turn the public against unions?
2. **Global Connections** How did Presidents Harding and Coolidge feel about the League of Nations?
3. **Economic Factors** What were the advantages of scientific management? Can you think of any disadvantages? What are they?
4. **Science and Technology** What new forms of entertainment were available to the American people in the 1920s as a result of new technology?
5. **Culture and Traditions** Discuss the cultural and political differences between the two major-party candidates in the presidential election of 1928.

⭐ Cooperative Activity

History and the Arts With a partner select an American writer or artist of the 1920s. Find and copy examples of his or her work that illustrate some of the turmoil in the United States during this period. Combine your examples with those of your classmates in a booklet entitled "The 1920s through the Eyes of Its Artists and Writers."

★ Geography Activity

Study the chart below, then answer the questions that follow.

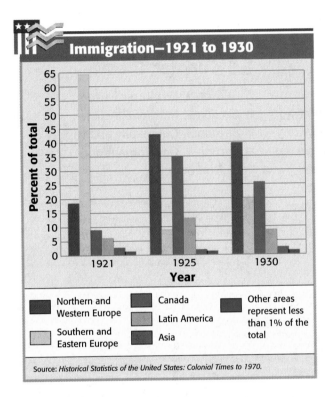

Immigration—1921 to 1930

Percent of total / Year

Source: *Historical Statistics of the United States: Colonial Times to 1970.*

Legend:
- Northern and Western Europe
- Southern and Eastern Europe
- Canada
- Latin America
- Asia
- Other areas represent less than 1% of the total

1. **Movement** What percentage of immigrants came from Asia in 1925?
2. **Movement** During which year shown was immigration from Canada the highest?
3. **Place** From what region was immigration the highest in 1921?

★ Technology Activity

Using a Word Processor The 1920s was a time of fads. Look through current store catalogs and magazines for fads of today. Choose one that you think is particularly interesting. On your word processor, write a one-paragraph explanation of why you think this fad developed.

★ Skill Practice Activity

Making Generalizations

Read the two paragraphs that follow. Then write a generalization about each paragraph that is supported by statements in the passage.

A. Before World War I, women had been arrested for smoking or using profanity in public. Appearing at the beach without stockings was considered indecent exposure, even in cities as large and sophisticated as Chicago.

B. Singing of joy in the face of oppression, jazz contains strands of music from many European countries. Nevertheless, jazz is above all an African American creation, and it could have developed only in the United States. Jazz drew upon field work songs, spirituals, and special funeral music. Other influences were the blues and ragtime. In 1925 J.A. Rogers wrote, "With its cowbells, auto horns, calliopes, rattles, dinner gongs, kitchen utensils, cymbals, screams, crashes, clankings and monotonous rhythm [jazz] bears all the marks of a [noisy, excitable] civilization."

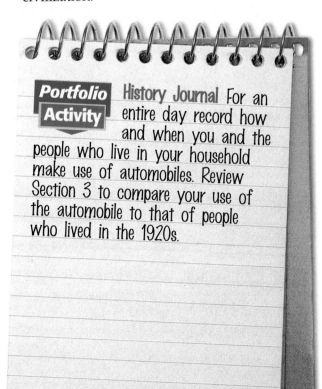

Portfolio Activity **History Journal** For an entire day record how and when you and the people who live in your household make use of automobiles. Review Section 3 to compare your use of the automobile to that of people who lived in the 1920s.

1929–1941

The Depression and FDR

★ Why It's Important

The boom years of the 1920s had hidden problems. Those problems became visible in 1929, when the nation's economy shifted into a downward slide. The New Deal, created in the midst of the Depression, changed the way Americans viewed government. Before the New Deal, the government usually took little responsibility for the economy's health. The New Deal actively involved the government in social and economic concerns and created the Social Security system, which still affects us all.

★ Chapter Themes

■ *Section 1,* Economic Factors
■ *Section 2,* Individual Action
■ *Section 3,* Geography and History
■ *Section 4,* Government and Democracy

PRIMARY SOURCES
Library *See pages 984–985 for primary source readings to accompany Chapter 25*

 HISTORY AND ART *Private Cars* **by LeConte Stewart** During the Depression, many unemployed workers in search of jobs traveled around the country by hitchhiking on trains.

1928 • 1930 • 1932

1928
Herbert Hoover is
elected president

1929
Stock market
crashes

1930s
The Great Depression
engulfs country

1932
Bonus Army
marches on
Washington, D.C.

Section 1

The Great Depression

READ TO DISCOVER . . .

- what caused the stock market crash.
- how the Great Depression plunged many Americans into poverty and misery.
- how Hoover reacted to the Depression.

TERMS TO LEARN

stock exchange   relief
on margin   public works
default

The Storyteller

The bubble of American prosperity burst when the New York stock market collapsed in October 1929. Thousands of investors lost all their savings. Wall Street—the nation's financial center—was in a state of shock. Many Americans suddenly found themselves out of work. In 1932 the popular actor and humorist Will Rogers remarked: "We'll hold the distinction of being the only nation in the history of the world that ever went to the poorhouse in an automobile."

Stock market crash headline

In the booming economy of the 1920s confident business and government leaders said the nation had entered a new era of prosperity for all. The chairman of General Motors advised people to invest money in the stock market every month—and many followed his advice. "Grocers, motormen, plumbers, seamstresses, and . . . waiters were in the market," reported writer Frederick Lewis Allen. The "market had become a national mania."

Suddenly, in October 1929, the picture changed. Almost overnight the value of stocks plunged. Millionaires lost fortunes, and thousands of less wealthy investors lost their savings. The United States was about to enter its worst domestic crisis since the Civil War.

The Stock Market Boom

A **stock exchange** is an organized system for buying and selling shares, or blocks of investments, in corporations. In the late 1920s, the value of stocks on the New York Stock Exchange climbed to dizzying heights, reaching record levels in September 1929. Because many investors lacked the money to continue purchasing stock, they bought **on margin**. This means they paid only a fraction of the stock price and borrowed the rest from their brokers. Brokers, in turn, borrowed their money from banks. As long as the value of stocks continued to rise, the buyer could sell later, pay back what had been borrowed, and make a profit. If that value fell, though, investors and brokers would not have enough cash to pay off the loans.

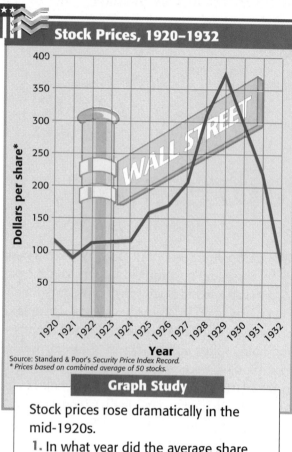

Stock Prices, 1920–1932

Dollars per share*

400
350
300
250
200
150
100
50

1920 1921 1922 1923 1924 1925 1926 1927 1928 1929 1930 1931 1932

Year

Source: Standard & Poor's *Security Price Index Record.*
* Prices based on combined average of 50 stocks.

Graph Study

Stock prices rose dramatically in the mid-1920s.

1. In what year did the average share of stock reach its highest price?
2. **Comparing** During what years did stock prices pass $200 per share?

Eyewitness to HISTORY

The Crash

Fearing that the boom market would end, some investors began selling their stocks in late September. Their selling made stock prices fall. Brokers began to demand repayment of loans, forcing investors who had bought on margin to sell their stock.

Prices declined steadily until October 21, but most financial experts thought the market was experiencing nothing more than a "period of readjustment." Then, for 3 straight days, stock prices plunged as investors sold millions of shares a day. Panicked traders sold almost 13 million shares on **"Black Thursday,"** October 24.

Following a few days of calm, the decline and confusion continued on Monday. On Tuesday,

October 29, the crisis worsened. By the end of the day, more than 16 million shares had changed hands and stock prices had plummeted. Journalist Jonathan Norton Leonard described the scene:

66 The selling pressure was . . . coming from everywhere. The wires to other cities were jammed with frantic orders to sell. So were the cables, radio, and telephones to Europe and the rest of the world. Buyers were few, sometimes wholly absent. 99

The New York Stock Exchange closed for a few days to prevent more panic selling. Shock spread across the country.

The Great Depression

During the next two years, the United States slid into a severe economic crisis called the **Great Depression.** The nation's total economic output dropped 43 percent in 3 years, from $104 billion in 1929 to $58 billion in 1932.

While the stock market crash shook people's confidence in the economy, it did not cause the Depression. Other factors, working together, sent the economy into a long tailspin.

An Unbalanced Economy

The problems that led to the Great Depression began to give out warning signals in the early 1920s. Farm income shrank throughout the decade. The textile, lumber, mining, and railroad industries also declined. In the months before the stock market crash, the automobile and construction industries suffered from lagging orders. As a result, employers cut wages and laid off workers. With their incomes slashed, many Americans could no longer afford the consumer goods that the nation's industries had been churning out.

Another factor that fueled the Depression was the growing gap in wealth between rich people and most Americans. The prosperity of the 1920s did not help all Americans equally. In 1929

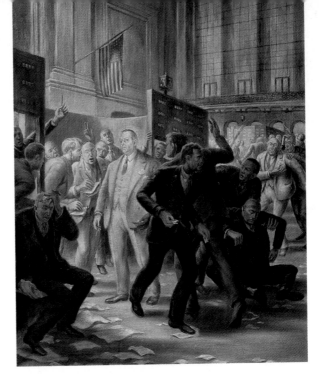

Panic hits the stock market

less than 1 percent of the population owned nearly one-third of the country's wealth. At the same time, about 75 percent of American families lived in poverty or on the very edge of it.

Credit Crisis

Borrowed money fueled much of the economy in the 1920s. Farmers, plagued by low prices since the end of World War I, bought land, equipment, and supplies on credit. Consumers used credit to buy cars. Investors borrowed to buy stocks. Many small banks suffered when farmers *defaulted,* or failed to meet loan payments. Large banks, which had bought stocks as an investment, suffered huge losses in the stock market crash. These losses forced 9,000 banks across the nation to close between 1930 and 1933, and millions of depositors lost their money.

International Depression

Weaknesses in the American economy also sapped the strength of foreign economies. European countries needed to borrow money from American banks and to sell goods to American consumers in order to repay their World War I debts to the United States. During the late 1920s, bank funds for loans dried up. International trade slowed down because, without American loans, other nations had less money to spend.

Joblessness and Poverty

As the Depression tightened its grip on the United States, millions lost their jobs. By 1932, 25 percent of American workers were out of work. The unemployment rate remained near 20 percent throughout the decade. Industrial cities were hardest hit. Workers who managed to keep their jobs worked only part-time or for reduced wages.

The newly unemployed felt devastated. New Yorker Sidney Lens, who lost his job, wrote about developing "a feeling of worthlessness—and loneliness; I began to think of myself as a freak and misfit." Long lines of hungry people snaked through the streets of the nation's cities. They waited for hours to receive a slice of bread, a cup

of coffee, or a bowl of soup from soup kitchens run by local government or charities.

Unemployed people tried to earn a few cents by shining shoes or selling apples on street corners. Those who had lost their homes built shelters out of old boxes and other debris, sometimes grouped together in pitiful shantytowns. Some referred bitterly to the shantytowns as **Hoovervilles** because of President Hoover's failure to act. Across the country Americans wondered why the president did nothing to end the suffering.

Hoover and the Crisis

President Hoover thought the economic crisis was only temporary, that prosperity was "just around the corner." He also believed that the "depression cannot be cured by legislative action or executive pronouncement." Instead, Hoover called on business leaders not to cut wages or production of goods and on charities to do their best for the needy. Voluntary action by private citizens and local governments, Hoover said, would pull the nation through tough times.

Charities, churches, and volunteers worked heroically to provide relief—aid for the needy. So did state and local governments. Some cities

Bonus Army camp, June 1932

withheld part of city workers' wages—already reduced—to fund soup kitchens. But the masses who needed help were simply overwhelming.

Government Action

Eventually Hoover recognized that the federal government had to take steps to combat the Depression. In 1931 he authorized additional federal spending on public works—projects such as highways, parks, and libraries—to create new jobs. State and local governments ran out of money, however, and the combined spending by all three levels of government declined.

Hoover tried a different measure in January 1932, when he asked Congress to create the **Reconstruction Finance Corporation** (RFC). The RFC lent money to businesses. It also provided funds for state and local programs providing relief. However, the RFC's directors were reluctant to make risky loans, and much of its budget remained unspent.

★ ★ ★ ★ ★ ★ ★ ★ ★ ★ ★ ★ ★ ★ ★ ★ ★

The Bonus Army

The march on Washington by the **Bonus Army** turned many Americans, who were already blaming Hoover for the Depression, firmly against the president. Congress had agreed to give each veteran of World War I a $1,000 bonus in 1945. Jobless veterans wanted the bonuses right away. In June 1932, they formed the Bonus Army and marched to **Washington, D.C.,** to demand their money. At its peak the Bonus Army included about 20,000 veterans. Congress and the president turned the veterans down. Most of the veterans left, but about 2,000, joined by their families, vowed to remain until the bonuses were paid. When the police tried to disband the veterans' camp, conflict broke out and two people were killed.

Hoover responded by calling in the army. With tanks, machine guns, and cavalry, troops led by Army chief of staff General **Douglas MacArthur** and his aide **Dwight D. Eisenhower** entered the protesters' camp. Veterans and their families fled in terror as the troops burned their camp.

Hoover announced that "a challenge to the authority of the United States government has been met." Many Americans were horrified that the government had attacked its own citizens, particularly war veterans. Hoover seemed cold, distant, and out of touch with ordinary people. Many people thought the time had come for a change in government.

★ ★ ★ ★ ★ **Section 1 Assessment** ★ ★ ★ ★ ★

Checking for Understanding

1. **Identify** Great Depression, Bonus Army.
2. **Define** stock exchange, on margin, default, relief, public works.
3. **List** four factors that led to the Depression.

Reviewing Themes

4. **Economic Factors** How did buying stocks on margin contribute to the stock market crash?

Critical Thinking

5. **Making Critical Judgments** Do you think President Hoover followed the proper course in his handling of the Depression?

Activity

Tracking the Economy For one week keep track of references in the media to unemployment. Indicate whether the information was, in your view, positive or negative.

Brother Can You Spare a Dime?

The Great Depression saw "Hoovervilles," such as this one in New York City, and unemployed workers standing on street corners pleading for jobs.

Listed below are Depression-era prices for selected foods. Read the list to see how far that "dime" from your "brother" would last.

Brother Can You Spare a Dime?" was a popular song in the 1930s during the Great Depression. In those days, prices were so low that if you were lucky enough to have a dime, you could actually buy something with it.

When the stock market crashed in 1929, the economy fell sharply. One quarter of the workforce was unemployed, and those who kept their jobs faced salary cuts. Hourly wages dropped as much as 60 percent. This meant that someone who previously earned 1 dollar an hour was now making only 40 cents an hour.

Few people could afford meat or fresh vegetables, so they lived on beans and soup. To cut down on heating bills, many families heated only one room of their homes. They stopped going to doctors and dentists, and patched their shoes with rubber from tires. People in one Iowa county burned corn to heat the courthouse because corn was cheaper than coal.

Prices During 1932–1934	
Sirloin steak (per pound)	$0.29
Chicken (per pound)	.22
Bread (20-ounce loaf)	.05
Potatoes (per pound)	.02
Bananas (per pound)	.07
Milk (per quart)	.10
Cheese (per pound)	.29
Tomatoes (16-ounce can)	.09
Oranges (per dozen)	.27
Cornflakes (8 ounces)	.08

Activity

Budgeting Using the food prices from 1932 to 1934, make a grocery list of what you could buy on a budget of $3.00 a week. Make another list of what you could buy today if you only had $3.00 a week.

1932
Franklin Roosevelt
is elected president

1933
Programs during
the Hundred Days
improve the economy

1934
Securities
and Exchange
Commission
is created

Section 2

Roosevelt's New Deal

READ TO DISCOVER . . .
- how Roosevelt reassured the American people.
- what New Deal programs were created in Roosevelt's first 100 days.

TERMS TO LEARN
Hundred Days   work relief
New Deal   subsidy

Storyteller

Washington, D.C., was dark and dreary on March 4, 1933. President Franklin D. Roosevelt stood bareheaded in the chilly wind, tightly gripping the sides of the reading stand in front of him. His face was stern as he began his Inaugural Address. "This nation asks for action and action now!" he cried.

As Roosevelt spoke, his voice had an electric effect on the masses of people before him. The crowd shouted back its approval. To millions of despairing Americans, Roosevelt's voice was the symbol of hope. It seemed that the gloom was starting to lift.

Roosevelt inaugural button, 1933

With the nation's economy crumbling, the Democrats believed they had a good chance of winning the presidency. Meeting in Chicago in June 1932, the Democrats chose Governor **Franklin D. Roosevelt** of New York as their candidate. Roosevelt—or FDR, as he was called—seemed to bring a fresh approach to politics.

When Roosevelt learned that he had been nominated, he flew to Chicago to deliver the first acceptance speech ever made at a convention. He told the Democrats—and the nation—"I pledge you, I pledge myself, to a new deal for the American people."

Biography

Franklin D. Roosevelt

★ As the Republicans and Democrats held their conventions in 1932, the Depression grew worse. The Republicans met in Chicago and nominated President Hoover for reelection. With the country's economy in trouble, Hoover's chances for winning reelection looked poor.

Early Years of Promise

Franklin D. Roosevelt, a distant cousin of former president Theodore Roosevelt, came from a wealthy family. Ambitious and charming, FDR decided on a career in politics. In 1904 he married Theodore Roosevelt's niece, **Eleanor Roosevelt,** and she became a tireless partner in his public life.

Picturing HISTORY President Roosevelt explained his policies directly to the people in his "fireside chats" over the radio. **What effect did Roosevelt's radio talks have on the American people?**

FDR's political career began with his election to the New York state senate in 1910. In 1913 he became assistant secretary of the navy, and in 1920 the Democrats chose him as their candidate for vice president. The Democrats lost the election to Warren G. Harding, but Franklin Roosevelt's political future seemed bright.

Then in 1921 polio struck Roosevelt, paralyzing both his legs. Yet FDR's will remained strong. "Once I spent two years lying in bed trying to move my big toe," he said later. "After that, anything else seems easy."

Return to Politics

After a few years, FDR decided to return to politics. He never publicly mentioned his paralyzed legs, and he asked journalists not to photograph his leg braces or wheelchair. Elected governor of New York in 1928 and reelected in 1930, Roosevelt won a national reputation as a reformer. He drew on the advice of a group of progressive lawyers, economists, and social workers—known as the **Brain Trust**—to develop relief programs for the state. When he decided to run for president, he counted on the Brain Trust to help him guide the nation to recovery.

During the 1932 campaign, Roosevelt declared that "the country needs and . . . demands bold, persistent experimentation." He also spoke of trying to help "the forgotten man at the bottom of the economic pyramid."

FDR Takes Charge

The American people were charmed by Roosevelt's confidence and his promise of action. On November 8, they went to the polls and elected Roosevelt in a landslide. He captured all but 6 states and received 472 of the 531 electoral votes. Democrats won important victories in Congress, also. People clearly wanted a change.

In the months before Roosevelt took office, the economy worsened. Protests in some cities erupted into violence. Meanwhile the banking system was collapsing. As more people rushed to withdraw their deposits, more and more banks went out of business. People became desperately afraid.

At his inauguration on March 4, 1933, Roosevelt told the nation that "the only thing we have to fear is fear itself—nameless, unreasoning, unjustified terror." He reassured people and pointed

Footnotes to History

A Presidential Family Theodore Roosevelt was Franklin Roosevelt's fifth cousin. Franklin was also distantly related to 10 other presidents: Washington, both Adamses, Madison, Van Buren, both Harrisons, Taylor, Grant, and Taft.

out that the "greatest primary task is to put people to work." He also promised immediate action on the banking crisis.

Restoring Confidence in Banks

Two days after the inauguration, Roosevelt ordered all banks closed for four days. He also called Congress to a special session, at which he presented the administration's plan for handling the banking problem. About seven hours later, Congress had passed and Roosevelt had signed the **Emergency Banking Relief Act.** The act proposed a wide range of presidential powers over banking and set up a system by which banks would open again or be reorganized. By mid-March half of the nation's banks had reopened.

At the end of his first week in office, FDR assured Americans "that it is safer to keep your money in a reopened bank than under the mattress." The next day deposits far exceeded withdrawals. The banking crisis had ended.

The New Deal

Program	Initials	Begun	Purpose
Civilian Conservation Corps	CCC	1933	Provided jobs for young men to plant trees, build bridges and parks, and set up flood control projects
Tennessee Valley Authority	TVA	1933	Built dams to provide cheap electric power to seven Southern states; set up schools and health centers
Federal Emergency Relief Administration	FERA	1933	Gave relief to unemployed and needy
Agricultural Adjustment Administration	AAA	1933	Paid farmers not to grow certain crops
National Recovery Administration	NRA	1933	Helped devise standards for production, prices, and wages
Public Works Administration	PWA	1933	Built ports, schools, and aircraft carriers
Federal Deposit Insurance Corporation	FDIC	1933	Insured savings accounts in banks approved by the government
Rural Electrification Administration	REA	1935	Loaned money to extend electricity to rural areas
Works Progress Administration	WPA	1935	Employed men and women to build hospitals, schools, parks, and airports; employed artists, writers, and musicians
Social Security Act	SSA	1935	Set up a system of pensions for the elderly, unemployed, and people with disabilities
Farm Security Administration	FSA	1937	Lent money to sharecroppers; set up camps for migrant workers
Fair Labor Standards Act	FLSA	1938	Established minimum wages and maximum hours for all businesses engaged in interstate commerce

Chart Study

Under the Roosevelt New Deal during the 1930s, the federal government assumed responsibility for the welfare of many citizens.

1. Which programs listed above improved the lives of farmers?
2. **Analyzing Information** Why did setting up the FDIC help all Americans?

A 1930s Kitchen

Teapot

Cookbook, 1930s

Coal bucket

What Was It Like? In 1939 President Roosevelt set the next-to-last Thursday in November as Thanksgiving Day. **How do you think Americans celebrated Thanksgiving during the 1930s?**

The president's radio talk was the first of many. He called these informal talks **fireside chats** because he sat next to a fireplace in the White House as he spoke. These fireside chats, which often began with "My friends," helped FDR gain the public's confidence.

The Hundred Days

After solving the banking crisis, FDR quickly tackled other areas of concern. He sent Congress a stack of proposals for new programs to deal with the nation's economic problems. In all Roosevelt sent 15 proposals to Congress, and Congress approved every one of them.

Lasting about three months, the special session of Congress came to be called the Hundred Days. It was an amazingly productive time. Optimism swept through the capital. Journalist Thomas Stokes recalled, "The gloom, the tenseness, the fear of the closing months of the Hoover administration had vanished."

The New Deal Takes Shape

The new laws that Congress passed during the Hundred Days—and in the months and years that followed—came to be called the New Deal. New Deal laws and regulations affected banking, the stock market, industry, agriculture, public works, relief for the poor, and conservation of resources. These laws changed the face of America dramatically.

Frances Perkins, Roosevelt's secretary of labor, later recalled those early, exciting days of the New Deal:

“ In March 1933, the New Deal was not a plan. . . . It was a happy phrase [FDR] had coined during the campaign. . . . It made people feel better, and in that terrible period of depression they needed to feel better. ”

Chapter 25 The Depression and FDR **723**

Electrification by David Stone Martin Workers install power lines that will bring electricity to an area of Tennessee. What other activities were carried out by the Tennessee Valley Authority (TVA)?

💲 Economics

Jobs and Relief

Roosevelt gave high priority to creating jobs. He planned to help the unemployed with work relief programs, giving needy people government jobs. During his first month in office, FDR asked Congress to create the **Civilian Conservation Corps** (CCC). Over the next 10 years, the CCC employed about 2.5 million young men to work on projects that benefited the public, planting trees to reforest areas, building levees for flood control, and improving national parks.

Roosevelt made aid to the poor and suffering another priority. FDR established the **Federal Emergency Relief Administration** (FERA) to give money to the states for use in helping people in need. Roosevelt appointed **Harry Hopkins,** a New York social worker, to lead the FERA. Hopkins became one of FDR's closest advisers and got involved in several other New Deal programs.

Roosevelt did not forget agriculture. On May 12, Congress passed the **Agricultural Adjustment Act** (AAA). The act had two goals—to raise farm prices quickly and to control production so that farm prices would stay up over the long term.

In the AAA's first year, though, the supply of food outstripped demand. The AAA could raise prices only by paying farmers to destroy crops, milk, and livestock. To many it seemed shocking to throw food away when millions of people went hungry. The New Dealers claimed the action was necessary to bring prices up.

To control production and farm prices, the AAA paid farmers to leave some of their land uncultivated. If market prices of key farm products such as wheat and cotton fell below a certain level, the AAA would pay farmers subsidies—grants of money—to make up the difference. In the first three years of the New Deal, farmers' incomes rose by about 50 percent. The Supreme Court ruled that the AAA was unconstitutional in *United States* v. *Butler* (1936).

Rebuilding a Region

One of the boldest programs launched during the Hundred Days was the **Tennessee Valley Authority** (TVA), an experiment in regional planning. The TVA aimed to control flooding, promote conservation and development, and bring electricity to rural areas along the **Tennessee River.** By building 5 dams and improving 20 others, the TVA ended the region's disastrous floods. And with hydroelectric power generating affordable electricity, thousands of farms and homes in 6 Southern states were wired for electricity for the first time.

Some critics charged that funds for the TVA should be used to support programs nationwide. Power companies also attacked the program as unfair and communistic. When the spring rains came in 1937, however, the system worked—the dams prevented the Tennessee River from flooding. In the end, most observers agreed that the TVA was an example of successful social and economic planning.

Quilt displaying NRA emblem

Helping Business and Labor

On the last day of the Hundred Days, Congress passed the **National Industrial Recovery Act** (NIRA), which Roosevelt called "the most important and far-reaching legislation" ever passed in the United States. The NIRA aimed to boost the economy by helping business regulate itself.

The NIRA created the **National Recovery Administration** (NRA), which encouraged businesses to set a minimum wage and abolish child labor. In addition the NRA tried to set up codes governing pricing and other practices for every industry. **Hugh Johnson,** a former general named to head the NRA, launched a campaign to promote the agency. Before long, the agency's blue eagle symbol and slogan—"We Do Our Part"—appeared everywhere.

Another program that the NIRA launched was the **Public Works Administration** (PWA). Its goal was to stimulate the economy through the building of huge public works projects that needed large numbers of workers. The agency employed people to work on the construction of roads, shipyards, hospitals, city halls, and schools. Many PWA projects—such as New York City's Lincoln Tunnel and Kentucky's Fort Knox—still stand. The PWA spent its funds slowly, though, and did not have much immediate impact on unemployment.

To avoid future banking crises, Roosevelt called for reform of the nation's financial system. Congress established the **Federal Deposit Insurance Corporation** (FDIC) to insure bank deposits. The government guaranteed that money placed in a bank insured by the FDIC would not be lost if the bank failed.

Congress also passed a law regulating the sale of stocks and bonds and created the **Securities and Exchange Commission** (SEC). This 1934 law gave the SEC the power to punish dishonest stockbrokers and speculators.

Assessing the Early New Deal

The New Deal did not cure the nation's ills. The Depression dragged on, bringing continued hardship. Farmers continued to lose their land. Unemployment remained at high levels. Many people still struggled to survive and to make ends meet.

Yet the darkest days had passed. The panic of 1932 and 1933 had receded, and the flurry of activity from the nation's capital had restored some measure of confidence.

★ ★ ★ ★ ★ ★ ★ ★ Section 2 Assessment ★ ★ ★ ★ ★ ★

Checking for Understanding

1. **Identify** Franklin D. Roosevelt, Civilian Conservation Corps, Harry Hopkins, Tennessee Valley Authority, National Recovery Administration.

2. **Define** Hundred Days, New Deal, work relief, subsidy.

3. **Discuss** actions that President Roosevelt took to restore public confidence in banks and in the stock exchange.

Reviewing Themes

4. **Individual Action** What programs did Roosevelt create to provide work relief?

Critical Thinking

5. **Making Comparisons** Compare Hoover's and Roosevelt's programs to combat the Depression.

Making a Table Create a table that lists the positive and negative aspects of the New Deal farm program.

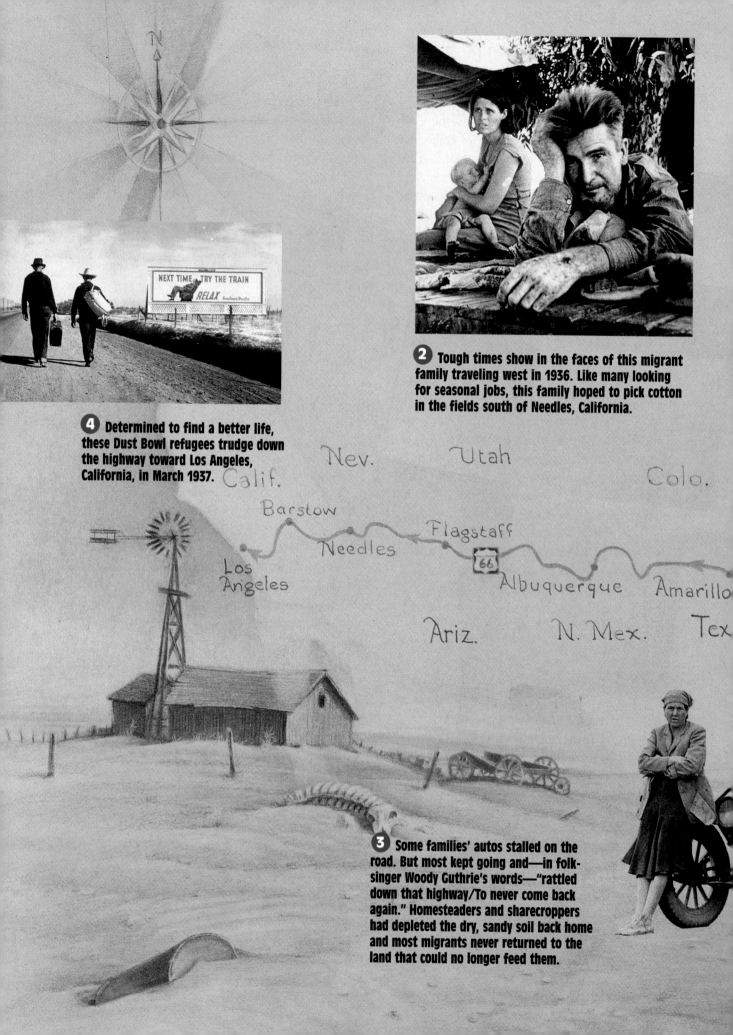

2 Tough times show in the faces of this migrant family traveling west in 1936. Like many looking for seasonal jobs, this family hoped to pick cotton in the fields south of Needles, California.

4 Determined to find a better life, these Dust Bowl refugees trudge down the highway toward Los Angeles, California, in March 1937.

Nev. Utah Colo.

Calif.

Barstow

Needles Flagstaff

66

Los Angeles Albuquerque Amarillo

Ariz. N. Mex. Tex

3 Some families' autos stalled on the road. But most kept going and—in folk-singer Woody Guthrie's words—"rattled down that highway/To never come back again." Homesteaders and sharecroppers had depleted the dry, sandy soil back home and most migrants never returned to the land that could no longer feed them.

NEXT TIME TRY THE TRAIN
RELAX
Southern Pacific

1 Depression and drought drove half a million migrants west during the 1930s. Abandoning the Dust Bowl states of the Great Plains, many of the migrants headed across Route 66 bound for California, the land of opportunity and hope.

A Hard Times Road

66 Highway 66 is the path of a people in flight, refugees from the dust and shrinking land, from the thunder of tractors and shrinking ownership... from the twisting winds that howl up out of Texas, from the floods that ... steal what richness is there.... They come into 66 from the tributary side roads, from the wagon tracks and the rutted country roads. 66 is the mother road, the road of flight. 99

—*From* The Grapes of Wrath *by John Steinbeck, published in 1939.*

1932
Hattie Caraway
is elected first
woman senator

1934
Indian
Reorganization
Act is passed

1939
Gone With the Wind
film is released

Section 3

Life During the Depression

READ TO DISCOVER . . .

■ how the Depression affected minority groups.

■ what radical political movements gained influence during the Depression.

TERMS TO LEARN

Dust Bowl   migrant worker

The Storyteller

"They hung around street corners and in groups. . . . They felt despised, they were ashamed of themselves. They cringed, they comforted one another. They avoided home." With these words, a social worker described unemployed Pennsylvania coal miners. Their pain was echoed across America by countless men, women, and children whose hopes were being crushed by the Depression.

Soup kitchen

Not every worker lost a job during the Depression. Not every family needed aid. Most Americans, however, had to make do with less—less income, less food, and less security.

Hard Times in America

⭐ Some families survived the Depression by pulling together. Parents and children shared homes with grandparents or other relatives to save money. Although the birthrate had decreased, school enrollment actually increased; because fewer young people could find work, they remained in school.

The strain shattered other families, however. Nearly 2 million men—and a much smaller number of women—abandoned their homes. They took to the road, drifting to warm places such as Florida and California.

Women Go to Work

Many people thought that women should not hold jobs as long as men were unemployed. Despite such prejudices, desperation drove a large number of women into the workforce. Many families survived on a woman's income—even though American women earned less than men.

Women also worked harder at home to make ends meet. Instead of buying clothes or groceries, they sewed their own clothing, baked their own bread, and canned their own vegetables. Some women started home businesses such as laundries or boardinghouses.

The New Deal era opened doors for women in public life. President Roosevelt appointed the first woman ever to serve in the cabinet, **Frances Perkins.** He also named more than 100 other women to federal posts. One—Ellen Sullivan Woodward—started a program to give jobs to women. In 1932 **Hattie Caraway** of Arkansas became the first woman to be elected to the United States Senate.

The best-known woman in American public life was **Eleanor Roosevelt,** who often acted as her husband's "eyes and ears." She made many fact-finding trips for the president because polio had limited his mobility. Mrs. Roosevelt campaigned vigorously for women and minorities and other humanitarian concerns. She wrote a daily newspaper column and used her boundless energy to meet people all over the country.

Eyewitness to HISTORY

The Dust Bowl

★ The southern Great Plains suffered an environmental disaster during the 1930s. Hardest hit were western Kansas and Oklahoma, northern Texas, and eastern Colorado and New Mexico—the region dubbed the Dust Bowl.

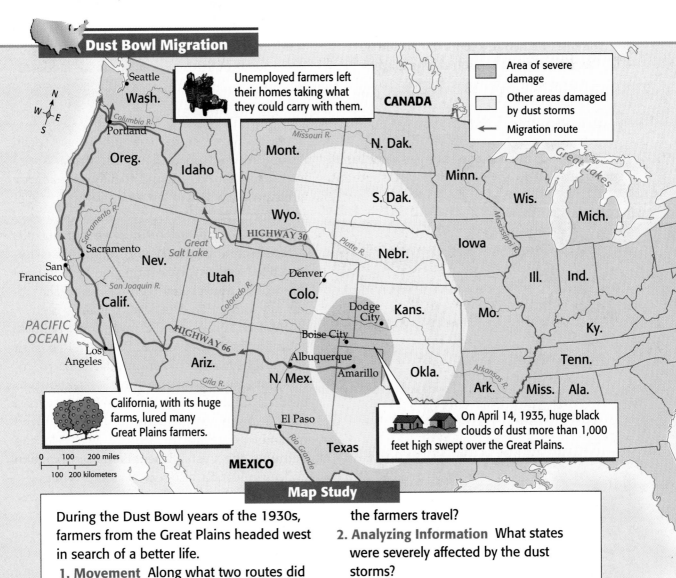

Dust Bowl Migration

Unemployed farmers left their homes taking what they could carry with them.

California, with its huge farms, lured many Great Plains farmers.

On April 14, 1935, huge black clouds of dust more than 1,000 feet high swept over the Great Plains.

Area of severe damage

Other areas damaged by dust storms

Migration route

0 100 200 miles
100 200 kilometers

Map Study

During the Dust Bowl years of the 1930s, farmers from the Great Plains headed west in search of a better life.

1. **Movement** Along what two routes did the farmers travel?

2. **Analyzing Information** What states were severely affected by the dust storms?

What Caused the Dust Bowl?

Using new technology such as tractors and disc plows, farmers had cleared millions of acres of sod for wheat farming. They did not realize that the roots of the grass had held the soil in place. When a severe drought struck in 1931, crops died and the soil dried out. Strong prairie winds simply blew the soil away.

Each storm stripped away more soil. One storm in 1934 carried about 300 million tons of soil, depositing some of it on ships 300 miles out in the Atlantic Ocean. The drought—and the storms—continued for years.

People called the storms "black blizzards." A Texas boy wrote:

66 These storms were like rolling black smoke. We had to keep the lights on all day. We went to school with headlights on, and with dust masks on. 99

Leaving Home

Thousands of Dust Bowl farmers went bankrupt and had to give up their farms. About 300,000 farmers migrated to California and became migrant workers, moving from place to place to harvest fruits and vegetables. So many came from Oklahoma that people called them "Okies." One observer described their arrival:

66 They came in decrepit [broken-down], square-shouldered [cars] . . . that looked like relics of some antique culture . . . piled high with mattresses and cooking utensils and children, with suitcases, jugs and sacks strapped to the running boards. 99 🔍

The Plight of Minorities

⭐ The Depression fell especially hard on the minority groups who were already on the lower rungs of the American economic ladder.

African Americans

In the South more than half of the African American population had no jobs. African American urban workers found their jobs taken by white people who had lost theirs. The collapse of farm prices crushed African American farmers.

Seeking more opportunity, about 400,000 African American men, women, and children migrated to Northern cities during the decade. They did not fare much better there, however. The jobless rate for African Americans remained high.

African Americans did make some political gains during the Depression. President Roosevelt appointed a number of African Americans to federal posts. He had a group of advisers, known as the Black Cabinet, that included Robert Weaver, a college professor, and **Ralph Bunche,** who worked for the State Department. **Mary McLeod Bethune,** who established Bethune-Cookman College in Florida, also served as an adviser.

African Americans continued to fight against prejudice. In 1939 opera singer Marian Anderson was denied permission to sing in Constitution Hall because she was black. Mrs. Roosevelt helped arrange for Anderson to give a historic concert at the Lincoln Memorial.

⭐ **Picturing HISTORY** Dorothea Lange photographed a homeless Oklahoma family during Dust Bowl days. **How did Dust Bowl farmers survive?**

Native Americans

The 1930s did bring some benefits to Native Americans. The new head of the Bureau of Indian Affairs, **John Collier,** introduced a set of reforms known as the Indian New Deal.

Collier halted the sale of reservation land, got jobs for 77,000 Native Americans in the Civilian Conservation Corps, and obtained Public Works Administration funds to build new reservation schools. Most important, he pushed Congress to pass the Indian Reorganization Act of 1934. This law restored traditional tribal government and provided money for land purchases to enlarge some reservations.

Hispanics

At the beginning of the 1930s, about 2 million people of Hispanic descent lived in the United States, mostly in California and the Southwest. Many had emigrated from Mexico. They worked as farmers, migrant workers, and laborers. As the Great Depression deepened, resentment against Mexican Americans grew. Many lost their jobs. Politicians and labor unions demanded that Mexicans be forced to leave the United States.

The government encouraged Mexican immigrants to return to Mexico. Authorities gave them one-way train tickets to Mexico or simply rounded them up and shipped them south across the border. More than 500,000 Mexican Americans left the United States during the early years of the Depression, often involuntarily.

Radical Political Movements

Hard times helped **radical** political groups gain ground in the United States during the 1930s. Radical groups advocate extreme and immediate change. Socialists and Communists viewed the Depression not as a temporary economic problem but as the death of a failed system. They proposed sweeping changes.

★ **Picturing HISTORY** Mary McLeod Bethune worked to improve educational opportunities for African Americans. **What other African Americans advised President Roosevelt?**

Communism attracted workers, minority-rights activists, and intellectuals with promises to end economic and racial injustice. Although both socialism and communism had significant influence, neither became a major political force in the United States.

Another political development that caught the attention of many Americans was the rise of **fascists** in Germany and Italy. Fascism is a political philosophy that holds the individual second to the nation and advocates government by dictatorship. In 1936 the **Spanish Civil War** began. Germany and Italy supported fascists who were trying to take over the Spanish government. Although the United States remained neutral, more than 3,000 Americans went to Spain to fight the fascists.

---

*F*ootnotes to History

Monopoly Each player's goal in the board game Monopoly is to make money while forcing opponents into bankruptcy. Oddly enough, the game was invented during the height of the Great Depression. Charles Darrow was an unemployed Philadelphia engineer when he designed the game in 1931.

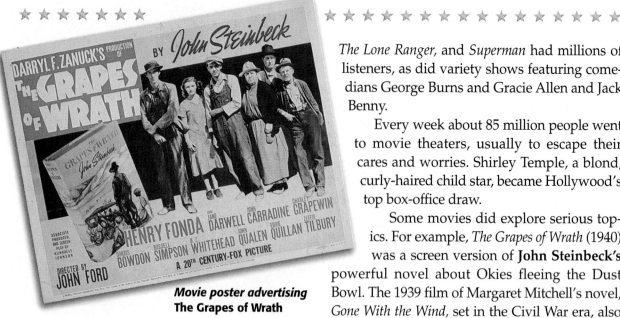

Movie poster advertising
The Grapes of Wrath

The Lone Ranger, and Superman had millions of listeners, as did variety shows featuring comedians George Burns and Gracie Allen and Jack Benny.

Every week about 85 million people went to movie theaters, usually to escape their cares and worries. Shirley Temple, a blond, curly-haired child star, became Hollywood's top box-office draw.

Some movies did explore serious topics. For example, The Grapes of Wrath (1940) was a screen version of **John Steinbeck's** powerful novel about Okies fleeing the Dust Bowl. The 1939 film of Margaret Mitchell's novel, Gone With the Wind, set in the Civil War era, also portrayed people coping with hard times.

Entertainment and the Arts

The Depression produced two separate trends in entertainment and the arts. One was escapism—light or romantic entertainment that helped people forget about their problems. The other was social criticism—portraits of the suffering and injustice of Depression America.

Escaping Troubled Times

Radio became enormously popular during the 1930s. Daytime dramas sponsored by laundry detergents earned the nickname "soap operas." Adventure programs such as Dick Tracy,

Images of Despair

Many writers and painters portrayed the grim realities of Depression life. **Richard Wright's** novel Native Son told the story of an African American man growing up in Chicago. Writer **James Agee** and photographer **Walker Evans** depicted poor Southern farm families in Let Us Now Praise Famous Men.

Photographer **Margaret Bourke-White** also recorded the plight of American farmers, and **Dorothea Lange** took gripping photographs of migrant workers. Painters such as **Grant Wood** and **Thomas Hart Benton** showed ordinary people confronting the hardships of Depression life.

★ ★ ★ ★ ★ Section 3 Assessment ★ ★ ★ ★ ★

Checking for Understanding
1. **Identify** Frances Perkins, Eleanor Roosevelt, Ralph Bunche, Mary McLeod Bethune, John Collier.
2. **Define** Dust Bowl, migrant worker.
3. **List** three benefits that Native Americans received from the Indian New Deal.

Reviewing Themes
4. **Geography and History** What caused the Dust Bowl?

Critical Thinking
5. **Determining Cause and Effect** Why did radical political movements gain popularity during the 1930s?

Writing a Screenplay Think of a modern story idea that would be considered social criticism. Using the outline of the story, write a play in which the characters point out a flaw in their society.

1934	1935	1936	1937
1934 John L. Lewis forms the CIO	**1935** FDR launches the Second New Deal	**1936** FDR wins reelection	**1937** Sit-down strike occurs in Flint, Michigan

Section 4

Effects of the New Deal

READ TO DISCOVER . . .

■ why people criticized Roosevelt and the New Deal.
■ how the Second New Deal created new economic and social roles for government.

TERMS TO LEARN

pension
Second New Deal
Social Security Act
unemployment insurance

The Storyteller

Support for Franklin D. Roosevelt's efforts to end the Great Depression was far from unanimous. Many wealthy and conservative people attacked the president's "radical" policies. A political cartoon of the 1930s showed a boy writing the word *ROOSEVELT* on the sidewalk in front of his rich family's house. His sister calls out, "Mother, Wilfred wrote a bad word!"

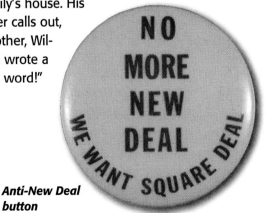

Anti-New Deal button

In the early days of his presidency, FDR counted on big business to support his efforts to revive the economy. The National Recovery Administration, for example, invited participation from the business community. In general, however, the business world opposed the New Deal.

New Deal Opponents

Business leaders accused Roosevelt of spending too much government money and of trying to destroy free enterprise. In 1934 some of these conservative critics formed the Liberty League. The League wanted government to let business alone and play a less active role in the economy. Although the Liberty League did not win widespread support, its existence convinced FDR that big business was against him.

Demanding More Reform

At the same time, Roosevelt drew fire from liberal and radical critics. They wanted a more active government. Three men gained wide popularity with schemes to help the average American.

One of Roosevelt's critics was Father **Charles Coughlin,** a Detroit priest who reached millions of listeners through his weekly radio program. Coughlin, once a Roosevelt supporter, attacked FDR for not dealing firmly enough with big business, calling him "Franklin Double-Crossing Roosevelt." Coughlin used his radio show to attack bankers, Jews, Communists, and labor unions, as well as the New Deal. In time Coughlin lost support because of his extreme views.

Francis Townsend, a California doctor, rose to fame with his plan for a monthly pension, or payment, for older people. Older workers who quit their jobs, making them available to younger people, would receive a pension. Townsend's plan received little support from Congress. It did, however, force many Americans to think about the plight of the elderly poor and the needs of retired people.

Of greatest concern to Roosevelt, however, was Senator **Huey Long** of Louisiana. Long had won wide support when he was governor of Louisiana with public works projects and attacks on big businesses.

In 1932 Long supported FDR, but within a year, the two men had split. One of Long's major complaints against the president was that he had not taken steps to redistribute wealth in the United States. By 1934 Long had developed his own plan for doing so. His "Share Our Wealth Plan" called for taxing the rich heavily, then using that money to give every American a home and $2,500 a year. As his appeal spread, Long became a threat to Roosevelt. Polls indicated that he might receive as many as 4 million votes on a third-party ticket in 1936. But in 1935 he was assassinated.

Father Coughlin emblem

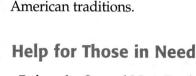

The Second New Deal

⭐ By the mid-1930s the economy had improved slightly, but the Depression was far from over. FDR took bolder steps.

To bring in more government funds, Roosevelt pushed Congress to pass the **Revenue Act** of 1935. The act raised taxes on wealthy people and corporations. Critics accused him of "soaking the rich" to pay for his programs, but many Americans cheered.

In 1935 President Roosevelt launched a new set of programs and reforms, often called the Second New Deal. The laws passed at this time changed American life even more than the Hundred Days had done.

Creating Jobs

Millions of people—20 percent of the workforce—were still unemployed in 1935. In April Congress created the **Works Progress Administration** (WPA). Led by Harry Hopkins, the WPA kept about 2 million people employed between 1935 and 1941. WPA workers built or repaired about 600 airports, 110,000 public buildings, 100,000 bridges, and 500,000 miles of roads.

The WPA also found work for unemployed writers, artists, and musicians. WPA painters decorated the new public buildings with murals. Writers and photographers documented life throughout America. The writers produced *Life in America,* 150 volumes that recorded folktales and songs, African American narratives, and Native American traditions.

Help for Those in Need

Before the Second New Deal, America was the only advanced industrial nation without a national government program to help the needy. In August 1935 Congress passed the Social Security Act.

The Social Security Act created a tax on workers and employers. That money provided monthly pensions for retired people. Another tax, on employers alone, funded unemployment insurance payments to people who lost their jobs. In addition, Social Security helped people with disabilities, the elderly poor, and children of parents who could not support them.

With the Social Security Act, the federal government took responsibility for the welfare of all citizens. It launched the American welfare system. 💲

The Labor Movement

★ Labor unions grew stronger as workers battled the Depression. In 1937 workers at the General Motors plant in **Flint, Michigan,** used a new technique—the sit-down strike. Strikers occupied the plant and refused to work until management agreed to negotiate their demands. For 44 days families and friends of the Flint strikers brought them food. Finally, the strikers won the right to organize their union.

The most influential labor leader during the 1930s was **John L. Lewis,** head of the United Mine Workers. To increase labor's power, Lewis strived to unite workers in every industry in a single union. Most unions in the American Federation of Labor (AFL) represented only skilled workers. Lewis called for industrial unions to include unskilled workers—the largest group in the labor force—as well as skilled workers.

In 1935 Lewis formed a new union called the **Congress of Industrial Organizations** (CIO), which helped create industrial unions. By 1938 the CIO had 4 million members, including large numbers of women and African Americans.

Unions found support in the New Deal. The 1935 **National Labor Relations Act**—also called the **Wagner Act** after its sponsor, Senator Robert Wagner of New York—guaranteed workers the right to form unions to bargain collectively with employers. The act also created the National Labor Relations Board to enforce its provisions. In 1938 Congress passed the **Fair Labor Standards Act** (FLSA), which banned child labor and set a minimum wage of 40 cents an hour. The FLSA and the Wagner Act form the basis of American labor rights today.

The Supreme Court

★ Those who opposed the New Deal challenged many of its laws in the courts, claiming that they were unconstitutional. Several important cases reached the Supreme Court.

In May 1935, the Supreme Court ruled that the National Industrial Recovery Act was unconstitutional. In the opinion of the Court, Congress

★ **Picturing HISTORY** This glass sign was hand-painted by a member of the United Mine Workers union. **How did workers benefit from the New Deal?**

had exceeded its lawful power to regulate interstate commerce. In January 1936, the Supreme Court struck down the Agricultural Adjustment Act. Cases were also pending against the Wagner Act, the Social Security Act, and the Tennessee Valley Authority. It seemed as though the Supreme Court might destroy the New Deal.

A Second Term

The presidential campaign of 1936 was based on a single issue: Did the American people support FDR and the New Deal?

To run against Roosevelt, the Republicans nominated **Alfred M. Landon,** governor of Kansas. Landon attracted dissatisfied Democrats as well as Republicans. FDR campaigned as the champion of the average American. He denounced big business and the rich, who "are unanimous in their hate for me—and I welcome their hatred."

On Election Day FDR received 61 percent of the popular vote, the biggest landslide in an American presidential election to that time. Roosevelt's support came from progressives and liberals, the poor and unemployed, urban workers, and African Americans. These groups would form the core of the Democratic Party for decades to come.

Packing the Court cartoon, 1937

Roosevelt's "Court-Packing" Plan

Soon after his reelection, FDR took action to prevent the Supreme Court from undoing the New Deal. He asked Congress to increase the number of justices on the Court from 9 to 15, saying that the 9 justices were overworked and needed additional help. FDR would appoint the 6 new justices—selecting, of course, justices who would uphold the New Deal.

The proposal aroused bitter opposition. Critics accused the president of trying to "pack" the Court and ruin the system of checks and balances set up in the Constitution. The issue died when the Court ruled in favor of the Wagner Act and the Social Security Act. The New Deal was no longer in serious danger from the Court. The unpopularity of the court-packing plan, however, cost Roosevelt a great deal of support and triggered a split in the Democratic Party.

The Roosevelt Recession

By the summer of 1937, the national income had nearly returned to its 1929 level. Believing that the Depression was finally over, Roosevelt tried to reduce the government's debt by cutting spending on relief and job programs.

The economy faltered immediately. Farm prices dropped. Four million people lost their jobs. Times nearly as hard as 1932–1933 returned. The new economic downturn, known to some as the **Roosevelt Recession,** lasted into 1938. Roosevelt helped to reverse it with a flood of government spending on public works.

The End of the New Deal

The court-packing fight and the Roosevelt Recession cost FDR support in Congress. The economy had not fully recovered, in spite of the wide-ranging New Deal programs. As the 1930s drew to a close, however, world events caused Americans to turn their attention from domestic to foreign affairs. Dangerous forces were on the rise in Asia and Europe.

Section 4 Assessment

Checking for Understanding

1. **Identify** Charles Coughlin, Huey Long, Works Progress Administration, John L. Lewis, Wagner Act, Roosevelt Recession.
2. **Define** pension, Second New Deal, Social Security Act, unemployment insurance.
3. **Summarize** the economic plans of Huey Long and Francis Townsend.

Reviewing Themes

4. **Government and Democracy** What was the aim of Social Security?

Critical Thinking

5. **Identifying Central Issues** Why did many business leaders oppose Roosevelt's New Deal programs?

Activity

Doing Community Research Research the effect of the New Deal in your community. Find out if the federal government in the 1930s supported any local projects in conservation, construction, or the arts.

Analyzing News Media

Every citizen needs to be aware of current issues and events to make good decisions when exercising citizenship rights. To stay informed, people use a variety of news sources—including print media, broadcast media, and electronic media.

Learning the Skill

To get an accurate profile of current events, you must learn to think critically about the news. The steps below will help you think critically.

- First, think about the source of the news story. Reports that reveal sources are more reliable than those that do not. If you know the sources, you can evaluate them. Can all facts be verified?
- Many news stories also analyze and interpret events. Such analyses may be more detailed than other reports, but they also reflect a reporter's biases. Look for biases as you read or listen to news stories.
- Ask yourself whether the news is even-handed and thorough. Is it reported on the scene or secondhand? Does it represent both sides of an issue? How many sources are used? The more sources cited for a fact, the more reliable it usually is.

Practicing the Skill

On this page is an excerpt from the *New York Times* newspaper of February 6, 1937. Read the excerpt, then answer the following questions.

1. What point is the article trying to make?
2. Is the article reported on the scene or secondhand?
3. Does the article reflect bias?
4. Is only one side of the issue presented?

AIM TO PACK COURT, DECLARES HOOVER

President Roosevelt's message to Congress asking for authority to appoint new Federal judges whenever existing ones were over 70 years old was characterized last night by Herbert Hoover, his predecessor in the White House, as a proposal for "packing" the Supreme Court to get through New Deal measures. . . .

"The Supreme Court has proved many of the New Deal proposals as unconstitutional. Instead of the ample alternatives of the Constitution by which these proposals could be submitted to the people through constitutional amendment, it is now proposed to make changes by 'packing' the Supreme Court. It has the implication of subordination of the court to the personal power of the Executive."

▶ Applying the Skill ◀

Analyzing News Media Think of an issue in your community on which public opinion is divided. Read newspaper features and editorials about the issue and listen to television reports. Can you identify biases? Which reports more fairly represent the issue and the solutions? Which reports are the most reliable?

GO TO

Glencoe's **Skillbuilder Interactive Workbook, Level 1** provides instruction and practice in key social studies skills.

Assessment and Activities

★ Reviewing Key Terms

On a sheet of paper, use at least six of the following terms to write a paragraph on the Great Depression or New Deal.

on margin	migrant worker
default	pension
relief	Second New Deal
public works	Social Security Act
Hundred Days	subsidy
New Deal	unemployment
Dust Bowl	insurance

★ Reviewing Key Facts

1. Why did a rise in unemployment during the Depression cause a decrease in consumer spending?
2. How did the CCC benefit the unemployed as well as the nation?
3. What was the purpose of the Tennessee Valley Authority project?
4. Summarize the advances made by African Americans and women during the Great Depression.
5. Describe the two laws passed during the Second New Deal that helped workers and unions.

★ Critical Thinking

Making Generalizations

President Roosevelt's leadership abilities and personality helped him push through his New Deal policies and made him popular with the public.

1. What personality traits and leadership abilities helped Roosevelt manage the country during the Great Depression?
2. How did Hoover's and Roosevelt's personalities and styles of leadership differ?

★ Time Line Activity

Create a time line on which you place the following events in chronological order.

- Roosevelt wins second term
- Stock market crashes
- Congress passes Social Security Act
- President Hoover loses reelection bid
- Indian Reorganization Act passed

★ Reviewing Themes

1. **Economic Factors** How did the trend of buying on credit in the 1920s affect banks during the Depression?
2. **Individual Action** In what way did FDR's fireside chats raise public confidence?
3. **Geography and History** How did new technology help cause the Dust Bowl disaster?
4. **Government and Democracy** How did the role of the federal government change during Roosevelt's administration?

★ Skill Practice Activity

Analyzing News Media

Find two articles, one in a current newspaper and the other in a newsmagazine, on a topic involving welfare reform. Read the articles, then answer the following questions.

1. Which article provided more in-depth coverage?
2. What points were the articles trying to make? Were the articles successful? Can the facts be verified?
3. Did either of the articles reflect bias? List any unsupported statements.
4. Was the news reported on the scene or secondhand? Do the articles seem to represent both sides fairly?

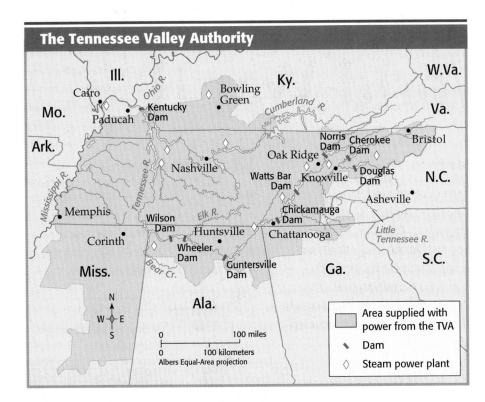

The Tennessee Valley Authority

Cooperative Activity

History and Art Work with members of your group to prepare a photo essay to document the hardships of the Depression. Research to find out the names of photographers who documented the plight of Americans during this time. Photocopy some of their photos and display them in an interesting way on a sheet of cardboard. Write captions for each photo, provide photo credits, and write a title for your essay. Then with the rest of the class, create a walk-through gallery to display all the photo essays.

★ Geography Activity

Study the map above and answer these questions.
1. **Place** What physical feature made Tennessee particularly suited for the Tennessee Valley Authority project?
2. **Region** Which states were supplied with power from the TVA?
3. **Location** On the map, what seven dams are located along the Tennessee River?

★ Technology Activity

Using an Electronic Card Catalog Use the electronic card catalog at your school or community library to find information about the current Social Security Administration and its activities. Type in the words *Social Security* at the "subject" prompt. Note the call numbers of the books listed, and find these books in the library. Prepare a list of benefits and services that this organization provides to Americans today.

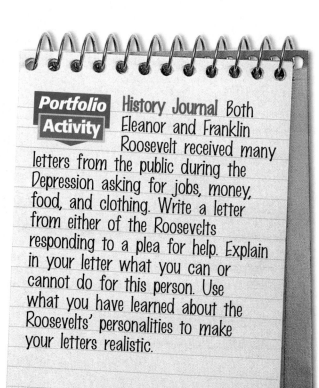

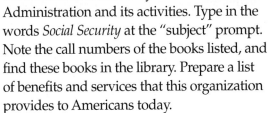

Portfolio Activity **History Journal** Both Eleanor and Franklin Roosevelt received many letters from the public during the Depression asking for jobs, money, food, and clothing. Write a letter from either of the Roosevelts responding to a plea for help. Explain in your letter what you can or cannot do for this person. Use what you have learned about the Roosevelts' personalities to make your letters realistic.

1939–1945

World War II

★ Why It's Important

World War II, the most destructive war in history, resulted in the deaths of more than 40 million people. More than half of them were civilians, including about 6 million Jews and many others killed in the Holocaust. At the end of the war, the United States emerged as the strongest nation in the world and the sole possessor of a powerful weapon—the atomic bomb. This marked the beginning of the nation's role as a superpower. It brought the United States new responsibilities in almost every area of the world.

★ Chapter Themes

■ *Section 1,* Continuity and Change
■ *Section 2,* Global Connections
■ *Section 3,* Economic Factors
■ *Section 4,* Geography and History
■ *Section 5,* Individual Action

PRIMARY SOURCES
Library

See pages 986–987 for primary source readings to accompany Chapter 26

★ **HISTORY AND ART** *Embarkation, San Francisco, California* **by Barse Miller** World War II American soldiers believed they were fighting for what President Roosevelt called the Four Freedoms: freedom of speech and expression, freedom of worship, freedom from want, and freedom from fear.

1930　　　　　　　　　　1935　　　　　　　　　　1940

1931
Japan invades
Manchuria

1933
Hitler becomes
chancellor of
Germany

1935
Italian forces
invade Ethiopia

1939
Germany seizes
Czechoslovakia

Section 1

Road to War

READ TO DISCOVER . . .
- why dictators came to power around the world.
- what foreign policy the United States pursued in the 1930s.
- what actions led to the outbreak of World War II.

TERMS TO LEARN
dictator　　　　　　totalitarian
fascism　　　　　　appeasement
anti-Semitism

The Storyteller

Many people underestimated Adolf Hitler's influence, but not American journalist William Shirer. He described a rally for Hitler at Nuremberg in September 1934: "Like a Roman emperor Hitler rode into this medieval town. . . . The streets, hardly wider than alleys, are a sea of brown and black uniforms. . . . [W]hen Hitler finally appeared on the balcony for a moment . . . [people] looked up at him as if he were a Messiah, their faces transformed into something positively inhuman." The passion of the Nazis shocked Shirer, and soon it would shock the rest of the world.

Hitler's _Mein Kampf_

In the late 1920s, **Adolf Hitler** achieved wide popularity in Germany. In his book _Mein Kampf_ (My Struggle), Hitler set forth his political views.

66 He who wants to live must fight, and he who does not want to fight in this world, where eternal struggle is the law of life, has no right to exist. 99

When Hitler became the leader of Germany, he put his strong words into action.

The Rise of Dictators

★ A number of ruthless men—such as Adolf Hitler—rose to power in the 1920s and 1930s by taking advantage of people's anger and suffering. Some Europeans resented the terms of the Treaty of Versailles, signed in 1919, which ended World War I. When a worldwide depression hit in the 1930s, frustration and fear added to this anger.

Hitler and other leaders promised a better life. They described a glorious future to people humiliated by losing a war. Once they gained political power, these men became dictators, leaders who control their nations by force.

Italy

Benito Mussolini rose to power by appealing to the resentment of many Italians who felt they had not won enough in the Versailles treaty.

Chapter 26　World War II　741

American cartoon of Mussolini

Mussolini made fascism—extreme nationalism and racism—popular in Italy. By 1922 his **Fascist Party** had gained enough strength to force the king of Italy to declare Mussolini the head of the government. Within a few years, Mussolini had banned all political parties except his Fascist Party.

Known as *Il Duce*—the leader—Mussolini quickly put an end to democratic rule in Italy. Civil liberties and the free press ceased to exist. Boys and girls of all ages were enrolled in military organizations that taught them loyalty to the regime. Mussolini built up Italy's military and vowed to recapture the glory of the ancient Romans.

In 1935 Mussolini sent Italian forces to invade the African nation of **Ethiopia,** which it annexed—took over as its own territory. Ethiopian emperor Haile Selassie appealed to the League of Nations for help: "God and history will remember your judgment. It is us today. It will be you tomorrow." The League responded by banning trade in weapons and certain other materials with Italy, but it lacked the power to enforce the ban. Italy withdrew from the League and continued its aggressive policies, attacking and annexing its neighbor Albania in 1939.

Germany

The Great Depression had hit Germany extremely hard. Millions of people had lost their jobs, and its economy teetered on the edge of collapse. Germans rallied around Adolf Hitler, a shrewd

politician and a spellbinding speaker. Hitler gained popularity by exploiting people's concern about unchecked inflation and severe unemployment. Hitler also played upon bitterness over the Versailles treaty. The treaty had forced Germany to give up some of its territory and to make heavy payments to the victors for war damages.

In 1921 Hitler became chairman of the National Socialist German Workers' Party, or the **Nazi Party.** Openly racist, Hitler and the Nazis portrayed the German people as superior to all others. They directed much of their anger against Jews, whom Hitler blamed for Germany's problems. His extreme anti-Semitism—hatred of the Jews—would later lead to unspeakable horrors.

Soon after he became chancellor, or chief minister, of Germany in 1933, Hitler ended all democracy and established totalitarian rule. In a totalitarian state, a single party and its leader suppress all opposition and control all aspects of people's lives.

Hitler claimed that Germany had a right to expand its territory. The country needed *lebensraum*—living space—he said. Germany's neighbors watched uneasily as he rebuilt Germany's military strength in defiance of the Versailles treaty. To gain support in his expansion plans, Hitler formed an alliance with Italy in 1936.

★ **Picturing HISTORY** Hitler salutes German troops at a Nazi rally in 1938. **What group especially suffered from the Nazis?**

★ ★

Japan

During the Depression many Japanese grew frustrated with their government's failure to solve economic problems. As a result, military leaders rose to power in the early 1930s. These leaders thought they would solve Japan's problems by expanding Japanese power in Asia.

In September 1931, Japan launched an attack on the province of **Manchuria** in northeastern China. Henry Stimson, the American secretary of state, and the League of Nations condemned the attack—but took no action to halt the aggression.

Left unchallenged, Japan set up a government in Manchuria. In 1937 Japan took further steps to expand its power, invading northern China and moving southward until it occupied most of the country. Three years later Japan signed a pact of alliance, known as the "Axis," with Germany and Italy.

Soviet Union

In the late 1920s, **Joseph Stalin** rose to power as the Communist leader of the Soviet Union. Stalin demanded complete obedience from the people he ruled and got it through the use of force. Stalin executed his rivals, ordered the death of thousands suspected of supporting his rivals, and sent millions of Russians to labor camps. He also reorganized the nation's economy, forcing millions onto government-owned farms.

American Neutrality

★ While dramatic changes were taking place in the world in the 1920s and the 1930s, most Americans wanted to avoid involvement in international crises and conflicts. To keep the nation out of future wars, Congress passed a series of **Neutrality Acts** between 1935 and 1937 that banned the sale of weapons to nations at war. The laws also restricted trade to nations that could pay cash for goods and transport the goods in their own ships. Many American loans to European countries from World War I remained unpaid, and Congress wanted to prevent more debts.

★ Picturing HISTORY Victorious Japanese soldiers celebrate their capture of the Chinese port of Hankou in October 1938. **Why did military leaders rise to power in Japan during the 1930s?**

Germany on the March

★ In Germany, Hitler began moving forward with his plans for expansion. In March 1936, he ordered troops into the **Rhineland.** The Treaty of Versailles had declared the Rhineland, a German territory west of the Rhine River, a neutral zone and had prohibited German soldiers in the area. France and Britain protested the German action—but did little else.

Hitler's next victim was **Austria.** Hitler insisted that Germany should be unified with Austria, a German-speaking nation. In March 1938, he sent troops into Austria and annexed it.

Hitler turned next to the **Sudetenland,** an area of Czechoslovakia where many German-speaking people lived. Falsely claiming that these people were being persecuted, Hitler announced Germany's right to annex the Sudetenland.

Czechoslovakia was prepared to fight to keep the Sudetenland. Britain and France, fearing a full-fledged war in the region, sought a peaceful solution to the crisis. In September 1938, the leaders of Germany, Italy, France, and Great Britain met in Munich, Germany, to discuss the Sudetenland.

A deeply saddened woman (left) gives a forced Nazi salute as German troops enter the Sudetenland. Neville Chamberlain greets Hitler at the Munich Conference (right). **What happened to the Sudetenland as a result of the Munich agreement?**

The Munich Pact

Britain and France thought that they could avoid war by accepting Germany's demands—a policy later known as appeasement. At the **Munich Conference,** the leaders agreed to turn the Sudetenland over to Germany. Hitler, in turn, promised not to expand Germany's territory further. The British prime minister, **Neville Chamberlain,** returned home to cheering crowds, declaring that the agreement had preserved "peace for our time."

Hopes for peace were shattered the following spring. In March 1939, Hitler's army seized the rest of Czechoslovakia. Now even Chamberlain realized that Hitler could not be trusted.

The Nazi-Soviet Pact

Meanwhile, Hitler was making plans to invade **Poland.** He worried, however, that such an attack would anger Stalin because Poland bordered the Soviet Union. Though bitter enemies, Hitler and Stalin signed a treaty called the **Soviet-German Non-Aggression Pact** in August 1939.

The two leaders pledged not to attack one another. They also secretly agreed to divide Poland and other eastern European countries between them. The pact freed Hitler to use force against Poland without fear of Soviet intervention. Stalin wanted to delay the day the Soviet Union would have to fight Germany. The Nazi-Soviet pact shocked the leaders of Europe.

★ ★ ★ ★ ★ Section 1 Assessment ★ ★ ★ ★ ★

Checking for Understanding

1. **Identify** Adolf Hitler, Benito Mussolini, Joseph Stalin, Neutrality Acts, Rhineland.
2. **Define** dictator, fascism, anti-Semitism, totalitarian, appeasement.
3. **Explain** how Hitler gained popularity in Germany.

Reviewing Themes

4. **Continuity and Change** What was the aim of U.S. foreign policy in the 1930s?

Critical Thinking

5. **Making Comparisons** What goals did the dictators and military leaders of the nations of Germany, Italy, and Japan share in the 1930s?

Making a Time Line Create a time line tracing the major events in Hitler's rise to power in Germany before World War II.

1939	1940	1941	1942

September 1939
Germany invades
Poland

August 1940
Britain is
bombed by
Germany

June 1941
Hitler attacks
the Soviet Union

December 1941
Japan bombs
Pearl Harbor

Section 2

War Begins

READ TO DISCOVER . . .
- which European countries fell to Germany in 1939 and 1940.
- how America responded to the war in Europe.
- what effect Japan's actions had on America.

TERMS TO LEARN
blitzkrieg   disarmament
lend-lease

The Storyteller

Sixteen-year-old John Garcia, like others who witnessed the attack on Pearl Harbor, never forgot it: "My grandmother . . . informed me that the Japanese were bombing Pearl Harbor. I said, 'They're just practicing.' She said, no, it was real and the announcer is requesting that all Pearl Harbor workers report to work. . . . I was asked . . . to go into the water and get sailors out that had been blown off the ships. Some were unconscious, some were dead. So I spent the rest of the day swimming inside the harbor, along with some other Hawaiians. . . . We worked all day at that."

United States poster after Pearl Harbor bombing

In a speech in 1937, President Franklin Roosevelt expressed the feeling of many Americans toward the growing "epidemic of world lawlessness":

66 We are determined to keep out of war, yet we cannot insure ourselves against the disastrous effects of war and the dangers of involvement. 99

Within two years the nations of Europe were at war again. Two years after that, a surprise attack by Japan on Pearl Harbor plunged America deep into the terrible conflict.

War in Europe

On September 1, 1939, Hitler sent his armies into **Poland.** Two days later Great Britain and France declared war on Germany. World War II had begun.

The German attack on Poland was swift and fierce. German planes bombed and machine-gunned targets, German tanks blasted holes in Polish defenses, and thousands of soldiers poured into Poland. The Germans called the offensive a blitzkrieg, or "lightning war." Then Soviet troops moved into and occupied eastern Poland, acting on the Soviet agreement with Germany to divide Poland.

Great Britain and France could do little to help Poland because its defeat came so quickly. In late September 1939, the conquered country was split in half by Hitler and Stalin. Stalin also forced the **Baltic** republics of Latvia, Lithuania, and Estonia to accept Soviet military bases. When he tried to do the same with **Finland,** war broke out. The Finns held out heroically until March 1940 before the Soviets forced them to surrender.

The War Expands

All through the winter of 1939–40, the western front was quiet. British and French forces settled in at the **Maginot Line,** a string of steel-and-concrete bunkers along the German border from Belgium to Switzerland. In the spring the fighting began again. Hitler attacked **Denmark** and **Norway** to the north in April, and the following month he turned west to invade the **Netherlands** and **Belgium.** The Netherlands and Belgium immediately asked for help from Great Britain and France—the **Allies.** After terrible bombing raids, the Dutch surrendered. The Belgians fought courageously, but they too were overwhelmed.

With the collapse of Belgium, Allied troops retreated to the port of **Dunkirk** in the northwest corner of France on the **English Channel.** They were now trapped between the advancing Germans and the French coast. In a daring move, more than 800 British ships—warships, ferries, and fishing boats—joined an operation to rescue the troops. Crossing the Channel again and again, the boats evacuated more than 300,000 French and British troops to safety.

In June the Germans crossed the Somme River and continued their sweep into France. Italy joined the war on the side of Germany and attacked France from the southeast. Germany and Italy—and later Japan—formed the **Axis Powers.** On June 14, 1940, German troops marched victoriously into Paris. The French surrendered a week later, stunned by the German blitzkrieg.

The Battle of Britain

All that stood between Hitler's domination of western Europe was Great Britain. In August 1940, the Germans bombed British shipyards, industries, and cities, destroying entire neighborhoods of London and killing many civilians. Hitler's goal was to break British morale before invading Britain. The British people endured, however, in part because of the inspiration of Prime Minister **Winston Churchill.** When Hitler called for Britain to surrender, Churchill responded defiantly:

> **66** We shall defend our island, whatever the cost may be. We shall fight on the beaches, we shall fight on the landing grounds, we shall fight in the fields and in the streets, we shall fight in the hills; we shall never surrender. **99**

Although the **Battle of Britain** continued until October, the Germans never gained control

HISTORY AND ART

The Withdrawal from Dunkirk, June 1940 by Charles R.A. Cundall Boats of every size crossed the English Channel to bring Allied troops from France to safety in England. **Why did Allied forces retreat?**

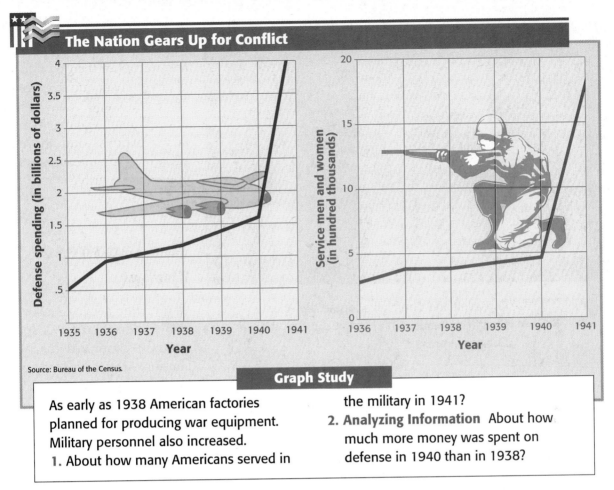

Source: Bureau of the Census.

Graph Study

As early as 1938 American factories planned for producing war equipment. Military personnel also increased.

1. About how many Americans served in the military in 1941?

2. **Analyzing Information** About how much more money was spent on defense in 1940 than in 1938?

---

of the skies over Britain. The British Royal Air Force (RAF) mounted a heroic defense and inflicted heavy losses on the German air force. Finally, Hitler ended the air attacks and called off the invasion of Britain.

Germany Turns East

Frustrated by his failure in Britain, Hitler decided to realize one of his oldest dreams—to destroy the Soviet Union. Ignoring the pact he had made with Stalin, Hitler launched an attack on the Soviet Union in June 1941. Within months German armies had moved into Soviet territory.

America and the War

★ The United States watched the war in Europe with growing concern. Although most Americans sympathized with the Allies, they were determined to avoid war. Isolationists banded together to form the **America First Committee.** Its members thought the United States

should keep out of Europe's business. Among those who led this group were aviation hero Charles Lindbergh and automaker Henry Ford.

While vowing to remain neutral, Roosevelt took steps to prepare for war. In 1938, at his request, Congress voted to strengthen the navy. In 1939 the president asked Congress to pass a new Neutrality Act that allowed the United States to sell weapons to other countries on a "cash and carry" basis. In 1940 FDR signed the Selective Training and Service Act, the first peacetime draft in United States history. The law applied to American men between the ages of 21 and 35.

The 1940 Election

With the world in crisis, President Roosevelt decided to run for a third term, breaking the tradition set by George Washington. His Republican opponent was **Wendell Willkie.** Public sentiment to stay out of the war was so strong that Roosevelt promised the American people, "Your boys are not going to be sent into any foreign wars." Roosevelt won an easy victory.

Roosevelt and Churchill adopted the Atlantic Charter in August 1941. **What did the Atlantic Charter express?**

free to choose their own form of government and live free of "fear and want." They urged disarmament—giving up military weapons—and the creation of a "permanent system of general security."

Growing Involvement

With the election won, Roosevelt moved to support the Allies openly. At Roosevelt's urging, Congress approved the Lend-Lease Act in March 1941. The Lend-Lease Act allowed America to sell, lend, or lease arms or other war supplies to any nation considered "vital to the defense of the United States." Britain, which was running out of cash, was the first to use lend-lease. Isolationists opposed the Lend-Lease Act, arguing that it would increase American involvement in the war.

German submarines in the Atlantic Ocean had been sinking British ships, including those carrying supplies from the United States. In April 1941, American ships began escorting convoys of British merchant ships. After the Germans began firing on American destroyers, Roosevelt issued a "shoot-on-sight" order to American naval vessels that found German and Italian ships in certain areas.

The Atlantic Charter

In August 1941, President Roosevelt and British prime minister Churchill met and drew up the **Atlantic Charter.** While Roosevelt made no military commitments, he joined Churchill in setting goals for a world after "the final destruction of the Nazi tyranny." The two nations pledged that the people of every nation would be

The Japanese Threat

★ After seizing much of China in the 1930s, the Japanese continued their expansion. After the fall of France in 1940, they seized the French colony of **Indochina** in Southeast Asia. Japan also planned to take the Dutch East Indies, British Malaya, and the American territory of the Philippines, primarily to acquire badly needed rubber and oil.

The United States Responds

The United States responded to Japan's aggression by applying economic pressure. Roosevelt froze all Japanese assets in American banks, preventing the Japanese from obtaining funds they had in the United States. He also stopped the sale of oil, gasoline, and other natural resources that Japan lacked. The action outraged the Japanese.

In September 1941, General **Hideki Tōjō** became prime minister of Japan. Desperate for resources and confident of Japan's military might, the Tōjō government began planning an attack on the United States.

⦿ Eyewitness to HISTORY

Attack on Pearl Harbor

At 7:55 A.M. on Sunday, December 7, 1941, Japanese warplanes attacked the American military base at **Pearl Harbor,** Hawaii, putting an end to American neutrality. Rear Admiral William R. Furlong reported:

❝I was on the deck of my flagship and saw the first enemy bomb fall. . . . Plumes over one hundred feet high went up from bombs that hit close alongside of battleships.❞

The attack devastated the American fleet, destroying 8 battleships, 3 cruisers, and 4 other vessels. Hundreds of planes were destroyed on the ground. More than 2,400 soldiers, sailors, and civilians were killed.

Fortunately, at the time of the attack, the navy's three aircraft carriers were at sea. Their escape from destruction provided the only good news that day.

Grace Tully, one of the president's secretaries, received an urgent call to report to the White House. She later recalled:

❝Most of the news on the . . . attack was then coming to the White House by telephone from Admiral Stark, Chief of Naval Operations, at the Navy Department . . . each report more terrible than the last, and I could hear the shocked unbelief in Admiral Stark's voice.❞

Pearl Harbor was the worst defeat in United States military history. Yet Pearl Harbor also united Americans. All debate about involvement in the war ended. On the day after Pearl Harbor, President Roosevelt asked Congress for a

★ **Picturing HISTORY** Japan's surprise attack on Pearl Harbor severely damaged the United States Pacific Fleet. **How did the attack affect American neutrality?**

declaration of war, calling December 7 "a date which will live in infamy [shame]." Congress quickly approved the president's request to declare war on Japan.

Three days later Germany and Italy, Japan's allies, declared war on the United States. Congress then declared war on them as well. The United States had joined the Allied nations—including Great Britain, France, and the Soviet Union—against the Axis Powers—Germany, Italy, and Japan—in World War II.

★ ★ ★ ★ ★ **Section 2 Assessment** ★ ★ ★ ★ ★

Checking for Understanding

1. **Identify** Allies, Axis Powers, Winston Churchill, Atlantic Charter, Pearl Harbor.
2. **Define** blitzkrieg, lend-lease, disarmament.
3. **Describe** the action that started World War II.

Reviewing Themes

4. **Global Connections** What actions did the United States take to prevent Japan from taking over nations in Asia?

Critical Thinking

5. **Predicting Consequences** Do you think the United States would have eventually joined the war even if the Japanese had not bombed Pearl Harbor? Explain.

Activity

Media Literacy Write and record a 15-second radio news bulletin announcing the Japanese bombing of Pearl Harbor.

1941
FDR establishes
Fair Employment
Practices Commission

1942
Revenue Act raises taxes
to finance the war;
Office of War Information
promotes patriotism

1943
Navajo soldiers
develop unbreakable
radio code

Section 3

On the Home Front

READ TO DISCOVER . . .

■ what steps the United States took to
prepare for fighting World War II.
■ how the war affected the American people.

TERMS TO LEARN

mobilization   internment camp
ration

The Storyteller

Despite the serious nature of war,
Americans tried to keep their morale high
during World War II through cooperation and
humor. People bought war bonds, ate less butter, made war jokes, and became air raid war-
dens. In *Yank,* the
Army weekly maga-
zine, one writer had
this to say about the
rationing of foods
such as butter and
sugar:

"Roses are red,
Violets are blue,
Sugar is sweet—
remember?"

U.S. sailor,
World War II

World War II required commitment and
sacrifice from all Americans. While
American soldiers risked their lives in
combat overseas, people at home worked hard
and learned to do without goods and services
they had taken for granted.

America Prepares

★ The Japanese attack on Pearl Harbor united the American people as nothing else
could. With astonishing speed the nation's economy and its people prepared to fight the war.

Raising an Army

Even before Pearl Harbor, the United States
had begun raising an army under the Selective
Service acts of 1940 and 1941. More than 15 million Americans joined the armed forces during
the war, both as draftees and as volunteers.

For the first time, large numbers of women
served in the military. About 350,000 women
served in the **WACs** (Women's Army Corps), the
WAVES (Women Appointed for Volunteer Emergency Service in the Navy), and women's units in
the marines, Coast Guard, and army air corps.
These women did not fight in combat—most performed clerical tasks or worked as nurses—but
they played important roles in the war effort.

Equipping the troops and providing arms
and other war materials required changes in the
nation's economy. To speed up mobilization—
military and civilian preparations for war—the

American government created a number of new government agencies.

The **War Production Board** supervised the conversion of industries to war production. Under its guidance, automakers shifted from building cars to producing trucks and tanks. The **Office of Price Administration** set limits on consumer prices and rents to prevent inflation. The **National War Labor Board** helped resolve labor disputes that might slow down war production. Later, the **Office of War Mobilization** was established to help these agencies operate efficiently.

Financing the War

From 1941 to the end of World War II, the United States spent more than $320 billion on the war effort—10 times the amount spent in World War I. Much of this money was raised through taxes. The Revenue Act of 1942 raised corporate taxes and required nearly all Americans to pay income taxes. Congress approved a system for withholding taxes from workers' paychecks—a practice still in effect.

The government also borrowed money to finance the war. As in World War I, the government sold war bonds. Movie stars and other celebrities urged people to buy bonds to support the war.

Wartime America

⭐ During the war, industry soared. Factories produced more than 70,000 ships, almost 100,000 tanks and airplanes, and millions of guns. Production speed increased as well. Some cargo ships were built in only 17 days.

Wartime production helped restore prosperity to the nation after the long years of the Depression. Incomes rose and prices remained fairly stable.

WAC hat

⭐ **Picturing HISTORY** More than 25,000 women applied to become members of the Women's Airforce Service Pilots (WASPs). About 2,000 were accepted, and 1,074 won their wings. **What were the responsibilities of women in the service?**

Making Sacrifices

With the war effort came sacrifices. For millions of American families, the war meant separation from loved ones serving overseas. Those at home lived in dread of receiving a telegram announcing that a family member had been killed, wounded, or captured.

With industries making war materials, Americans faced shortages of many consumer goods. After 1942, for example, automakers stopped making new cars and turned instead to making tanks, planes, and trucks. Women could not buy stockings—silk imports from war-torn Asia had halted, and nylon was needed to make parachutes.

In addition many resources and goods needed for the war effort were rationed—consumers could buy only limited numbers of them. Americans used government-issued books of ration coupons to purchase certain items, such as shoes, gasoline, tires, sugar, and meat. When people ran out of coupons, they did without the rationed items. But because Americans overwhelmingly supported the war effort, they generally accepted inconveniences and shortages with good spirits.

Ration coupons

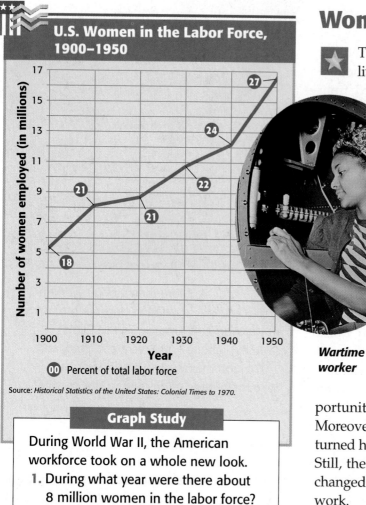

U.S. Women in the Labor Force, 1900–1950

Number of women employed (in millions) (y-axis: 1, 3, 5, 7, 9, 11, 13, 15, 17)

Data points (Percent of total labor force):
- 1900: 18
- 1910: 21
- 1920: 21
- 1930: 22
- 1940: 24
- 1950: 27

Year (x-axis: 1900, 1910, 1920, 1930, 1940, 1950)

00 Percent of total labor force

Source: *Historical Statistics of the United States: Colonial Times to 1970.*

Graph Study

During World War II, the American workforce took on a whole new look.

1. During what year were there about 8 million women in the labor force?

2. **Analyzing Information** In 1940 what percent of the labor force was made up of women?

Helping the War Effort

People found other ways to help the war effort. Many planted "victory gardens" to grow vegetables, which were in short supply. Children collected scrap metal for use in industry.

Many people joined in **civil defense**—protective measures in case of attack. For example, volunteer spotters scanned the skies for enemy aircraft that might try to approach America. Coastal cities enforced blackouts at night so that lights could not serve as beacons for enemy pilots.

The **Office of War Information,** established by the government, promoted patriotism and helped keep Americans united behind the war effort. It also broadcast messages all over the world.

Women and Minorities

★ The war had a tremendous impact on the lives of women and minorities. It brought opportunity for new jobs and a new role in society. Yet for some, unfair treatment left lasting scars.

As millions of men joined the armed forces, more women than ever before entered the labor force. In factories women worked as welders and riveters and in other jobs held previously by men. An advertising campaign featuring a character called **Rosie the Riveter** encouraged women to take factory jobs. For many women it was their first opportunity to work outside the home.

Wartime worker

Although women had new job opportunities, they usually earned less than men. Moreover, when the war ended and the troops returned home, most women would lose their jobs. Still, the war opened new fields to women and changed public opinion about women's right to work.

African Americans During the War

About 700,000 African Americans served in the armed forces during the war. At first most were given low-level assignments and kept in segregated units. Gradually, military leaders assigned them to integrated units. In 1942 the army began training whites and African Americans together in officer candidate school. Finally, African Americans were allowed to take combat assignments. The 332nd Fighter Group, known as the **Tuskegee Airmen,** shot down more than 200 enemy planes. **Benjamin Davis, Jr.,** who trained at the Tuskegee flying school, became the first African American general in the United States Air Force. His father, Benjamin Davis, Sr., had been the first African American general in the army.

In civilian life African Americans sought change. In the summer of 1941, labor leader **A. Philip Randolph** demanded that the government ban discrimination against African Americans in defense industries. He planned a large demonstration in Washington in support of his demands. President Roosevelt persuaded Randolph to call off the march by establishing the Fair Employment Practices Commission to combat discrimination in industries that held government contracts. The president announced that

66 . . . there shall be no discrimination in the employment of workers in defense industries or government because of race, creed, color, or national origin. 99

The war accelerated the population shift that had begun during World War I. Large numbers of African Americans moved from the rural South to industrialized cities in the North and the West in search of work. In some cities, racial tensions erupted in violence. The violence sometimes resulted in death. The riots inspired the African American poet **Langston Hughes** to write:

Picturing HISTORY Doris Miller, World War II's first recognized African American hero, won the Navy Cross for bravery for defending a battleship during the Japanese attack at Pearl Harbor. **How did the position of African Americans in the armed forces change during World War II?**

66 Yet you say we're fightin'
for democracy.
Then why don't democracy
Include me? 99

Native Americans

Thousands of Native Americans served in the armed forces. **Ira Hayes** became a hero in the battle for Iwo Jima in the Pacific. Navajo soldiers worked as radio operators, using their own language as a code. Many Native Americans left reservations to work in defense industries.

Hispanic Americans

Approximately 500,000 Hispanic Americans served in the armed forces. The Congressional Medal of Honor, the nation's highest military medal, was awarded to 17 Mexican Americans. **Mercedes Cubría** of Cuba became the first Hispanic woman officer in the Women's Army Corps. **Horacio Rivero** of Puerto Rico became the first Hispanic four-star admiral since David Farragut to serve in the United States Navy.

Prompted by the wartime need for labor, United States labor agents recruited thousands of farm and railroad workers from Mexico. This program, called the **bracero** program, stimulated emigration from Mexico during the war years.

Like African Americans, Mexican Americans suffered from discrimination, and their presence

Picturing HISTORY In 1943 the United States Marines recruited Navajo soldiers to develop a military code that the Japanese could not break. **In what other ways did Native Americans contribute to the war effort?**

Picturing HISTORY A distressed Japanese American family watches an FBI agent search their family albums for evidence of disloyalty to the United States. **What major hardship did West Coast Japanese Americans face during World War II?**

created tensions in some cities. In 1943, for example, a four-day riot started in **Los Angeles** when white sailors attacked Mexican American teens.

Japanese Americans

After the Japanese bombed Pearl Harbor, Japanese Americans were feared and hated by many other Americans. About two-thirds of Japanese Americans were **Nisei**—American citizens who had been born in the United States. But this fact made little difference to some who questioned the loyalty of Japanese Americans.

Japanese Americans Relocated

Military and political leaders worried about the loyalty of Japanese Americans if Japanese forces invaded the United States. The president directed the army to relocate more than 100,000 West Coast Japanese Americans to detention centers. Located mostly in desert areas, these internment camps were crowded and uncomfortable. Conditions were harsh.

With only days to prepare for the move, most Japanese Americans left valuable possessions behind. Many abandoned their homes and businesses or sold them at a loss. Most had to stay in internment camps for the next three years.

Peter Ota and his family were sent to a camp in Colorado. His father had come to California in 1904 and built up a successful fruit and vegetable business. After the war Ota remembered how his father had suffered.

❝ After all those years, having worked his whole life to build a dream—having it all taken away. . . . He died a broken man. ❞

In 1988 Americans acknowledged the injustice of relocation. Congress issued a formal apology and agreed to give each survivor $20,000, a token of the nation's regret.

★ ★ ★ ★ ★ Section 3 Assessment ★ ★ ★ ★ ★

Checking for Understanding

1. **Identify** WACs, WAVES, Benjamin Davis, Jr., A. Philip Randolph.
2. **Define** mobilization, ration, internment camp.
3. **List** two ways the United States financed the war effort.

Reviewing Themes

4. **Economic Factors** How did wartime industrial production help the American economy recover from the Depression?

Critical Thinking

5. **Making Critical Judgments** Do you think the United States government was justified in sending Japanese Americans to internment camps? Explain.

Activity

Writing a Journal Entry Imagine you are a woman working in a defense factory during the war. This is the first job you have ever had away from home. Write a journal entry describing your first day on the job.

January 1942
U.S. joins Allies

June 1944
Allied ships land
at Normandy

December 1944
Battle of the Bulge
takes 75,000 lives

May 1945
Germany
surrenders

Section 4

War in Europe and Africa

READ TO DISCOVER . . .

■ what important battles took place in North Africa, Italy, and the Soviet Union between 1942 and 1944.

■ what factors contributed to the Allied victory in Europe.

TERMS TO LEARN

genocide   Holocaust

The Storyteller

Ernie Pyle, a war correspondent, described the life of the World War II American soldier: "In the magazines war seemed romantic and exciting, full of heroics and vitality. . . . I saw instead men suffering and wishing they were somewhere else. . . . All of them desperately hungry for somebody to talk to besides themselves . . . cold and fairly dirty, just toiling from day to day in a world full of insecurity, discomfort, homesickness and a dulled sense of danger."

World War II GI work uniform

On January 1, 1942—three weeks after Pearl Harbor—the United States joined Britain, the Soviet Union, and 23 other Allied nations in vowing to defeat the Axis Powers. Although the Japanese were conquering vast areas in the Pacific, the Allied leaders decided to concentrate first on defeating Hitler before dealing with Japan. The situation in Europe was desperate. German forces occupied almost all of Europe and much of **North Africa.** If the Germans defeated the Soviets, Germany might prove unstoppable.

North African Campaign

★ Stalin and many American military leaders wanted the Allies to launch a major attack on continental Europe across the English Channel. Such an attack would force the Germans to defend the heart of their own empire. Churchill, however, argued that such an assault would be too difficult because of the German military presence in the area. FDR concluded that Churchill was right. The Allies made plans to attack North Africa instead. The Axis forces there were under the command of German general **Erwin Rommel,** known as the "Desert Fox" because of his success in desert warfare.

In November 1942, the British turned Rommel back at El Alamein in Egypt. The victory prevented the Germans from capturing the **Suez Canal,** a vital sea link between Europe and Asia.

Landing in Algeria and Morocco on November 8, American, British, and Canadian troops under American general **Dwight D. Eisenhower** advanced eastward swiftly. The inexperienced Americans met defeat in Tunisia. With the backing of British air and naval power, however, American general **George Patton** closed in on Rommel. The Allies drove the Germans out of North Africa in May 1943.

The Invasion of Italy

The Allies used bases in North Africa to launch an invasion of southern Europe. They took the island of **Sicily** in the summer of 1943 and landed on the Italian mainland in September. As the Allies advanced, the Italians overthrew dictator Benito Mussolini and surrendered. However, German forces in Italy continued to fight.

In the winter of 1943, the Allies met fierce resistance at the monastery town of **Monte Cassino** in central Italy, and their advance faltered. The next January the Allies landed farther north at **Anzio,** a seaport near Rome. German forces kept the Allies pinned down on the beaches at Anzio for four months. The Allies finally broke through the German lines in May and advanced toward **Rome.** They liberated Rome in June 1944.

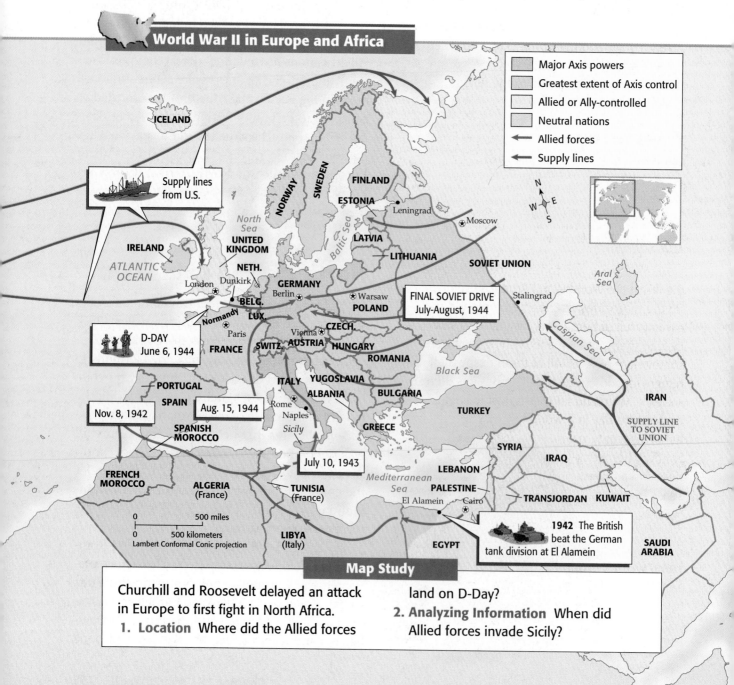

World War II in Europe and Africa

Map Study

Churchill and Roosevelt delayed an attack in Europe to first fight in North Africa.
1. **Location** Where did the Allied forces land on D-Day?
2. **Analyzing Information** When did Allied forces invade Sicily?

Homeless woman in Cologne, Germany

Air War over Germany

While fighting raged in North Africa and Italy, the Allies launched an air war against Germany. In the summer of 1942, British and American air forces began a massive bombing campaign against Germany. Each day hundreds of American bombers pounded German factories and cities. Each night British bombers battered the same targets. The bombing caused massive destruction in many German cities and killed thousands of German civilians. Yet the attacks failed to crack Germany's determination to win the war.

The Tide Turns in Europe

Meanwhile, the Soviets and the Germans were locked in ferocious combat. For months the Soviet Union bore the main force of Germany's European war effort.

The Eastern Front

After invading the Soviet Union in June 1941, German troops had moved quickly into the nation's interior. By September the Germans surrounded **Leningrad** and began a **siege,** or military blockade, that lasted nearly 900 days. The German attack continued, but Leningrad did not fall. As food ran out, the people of the city ate horses, cats, and dogs—even bread made from wallpaper paste. Thousands died. The Germans could not take the city, however, and in early 1944 the siege was broken.

German forces also attacked other Soviet cities. In 1941 the Germans tried to capture the Soviet capital of **Moscow.** Heavy losses and bad weather slowed their advance, but the Germans reached Moscow's outskirts by December. When all seemed lost, the Soviets staged a counterattack and forced a German retreat.

In the spring of 1942, Germany launched another powerful offensive. A major German target was the city of **Stalingrad,** key to oil-rich lands to the south. To take the city, the Germans had to fight street by street and house by house. No sooner had the Germans won Stalingrad than

Soviet forces surrounded the city, cutting off the German supply lines. Cold and starving, the German troops fought on until February 2, 1943, when the tattered remains of their army finally surrendered. German losses exceeded 300,000.

After Stalingrad, a major Soviet offensive drove the Germans back hundreds of miles. The Germans mounted a counteroffensive in the summer of 1943, but their defeat at Stalingrad marked a major turning point in the war.

Invasion of France

As the Soviets pushed toward Germany from the east, the Allies were planning a massive invasion of France from the west. General Eisenhower, the commander of Allied forces in Europe, directed this invasion, known as **Operation Overlord.**

Eisenhower planned to land his troops on the French coast of **Normandy** on June 5, but rough seas forced him to delay the landing. Finally, on June 6, 1944—**D-Day**—the Allied ships landed on the coast of Normandy. After wading ashore the troops faced land mines and fierce fire from the Germans. Many Allied troops were hit as they stormed across the beaches to establish a foothold on high ground. Within a few weeks, the Allies had landed a million troops, 566,648 tons of supplies, and 171,532 vehicles in France.

From Normandy the Allies pushed across France. On August 25 French and American soldiers marched through joyful crowds and liberated Paris.

★ ★ ★ ★ ★ ★ ★

General Dwight D. Eisenhower

Picturing HISTORY American, British, Canadian, and French troops took part in the D-Day invasion, making it the largest invasion force ever assembled. **What dangers did the Allied soldiers face when landing on the Normandy beaches?**

Victory in Europe

★ Germany fought for survival on two fronts. In the east the Soviets pushed the Germans out of eastern Europe. In the west the British and Americans approached the German border.

The Advance on Germany

The Allied advance across France moved so rapidly that some people thought the war would be over by the end of the year. In late 1944, however, the drive came to a halt at the Rhine River, stalled by German defenses and cold weather.

In mid-December the Germans mounted a last, desperate offensive. On December 16, 1944, they launched a surprise attack along a 50-mile front in Belgium. In the **Battle of the Bulge,** the Germans at first drove troops and artillery deep into a bulge in the Allied lines. After several weeks, however, the Allies pushed the Germans back. The battle, which resulted in more than 75,000 casualties, marked the end of serious German resistance.

The final phase of the war in Europe now began. By mid-April 1945, the Soviets had surrounded **Berlin,** the German capital. Hitler, who had spent the final months of the war in an underground bunker there, realized that the situation was hopeless and committed suicide on April 30. Germany signed an unconditional surrender on May 7, ending the war in Europe. The Allies declared May 8 **V-E Day** for "Victory in Europe."

Death of a President

President Roosevelt did not share in the Allied victory celebration. In February 1945, he had traveled to Yalta in the Soviet Union to meet with Churchill and Stalin. After returning home Roosevelt had gone to Warm Springs, Georgia, for a vacation. He died there suddenly on April 12, 1945.

Americans were saddened by the death of the man who had led them for 12 difficult years. When Vice President **Harry S Truman** heard the news, he asked Eleanor Roosevelt if there was anything he could do for her. She replied, "Is there anything *we* can do for *you*? You are the one in trouble now."

🔍 **Eyewitness to HISTORY**

The Holocaust

★ As the Allies liberated areas that had been under German control, they found horrifying evidence of Nazi brutality. Hitler had warned in 1939 that another war would result in "the destruction of the Jews in Europe." Nazi leaders developed what they called "the final solution of the Jewish question." Their "solution" was geno-cide—wiping out an entire group of people.

Ever since Hitler had gained power in 1933, the Nazis persecuted Jews. This persecution became more deadly as German power spread through Europe. Once the war began, Nazis rounded up thousands of Jews, shooting them and throwing them into mass graves. One man who witnessed a massacre of Russian Jews wrote:

> 66 I watched a family of about eight persons. . . . [A soldier] instructed them to go behind the earth mound. . . . They went down into the pit, lined themselves up against the previous victims and were shot. 99

Nazi troops crammed thousands more into railroad cars like cattle, depositing them in **concentration camp**s—prison camps for civilians. Guards took the prisoners' belongings, shaved their heads, and tattooed camp numbers on their arms. Forced to live in horrible conditions, the prisoners often had only a crust of bread or watery soup to eat. Thousands became sick and died.

In the early 1940s, the Nazis embarked on their "final solution" to destroy the Jews. They built death camps where they killed thousands of people a day in gas chambers, then burned their bodies in ovens. At the largest camp—**Auschwitz** in Poland—the Nazis killed between 1 and 2 million people. As many as 6 million Jews died in what has become known as the Holocaust. Millions of others—Soviet prisoners of war, Poles, Gypsies, and people with handicaps—were also ruthlessly killed.

As Allied forces moved through Germany and Poland after V-E Day, they saw firsthand the

Starved survivors at the concentration camp at Evensee, Austria

unspeakable horrors of the camps. R.W. Thompson, a British reporter, wrote about one such camp:

> 66 Across the sandy clearing is the incinerator, but it ran out of [fuel]. A rough record by the chief burner of bodies records 17,000 burned last month. They say each body was roughly clubbed as it went in. 99

People around the world were stunned by this terrible result of Nazi tyranny.

Section 4 Assessment

Checking for Understanding

1. *Identify* Erwin Rommel, Dwight D. Eisenhower, George Patton, D-Day, V-E Day.
2. *Define* genocide, Holocaust.
3. *Trace* the path of Allied forces through Africa and Europe from 1942 to D-Day.

Reviewing Themes

4. **Geography and History** Which large Allied countries defended the eastern front in Europe in 1944? The western front?

Critical Thinking

5. **Drawing Conclusions** Why do you think Hitler felt threatened by Jews and other minorities?

Activity

Making a Map Make a map of the former Soviet Union and use symbols to show the outcome of battles between the Germans and the Soviets during World War II.

Multimedia Activities

Historic America Electronic Field Trips

Field Trip to the U.S.S. *Arizona* Memorial

Setting up the Video

Work with a group of your classmates to view the videodisc "The U.S.S. *Arizona* Memorial" on the videodisc *Historic America: Electronic Field Trips*. This program gives detailed accounts of the December 7, 1941, bombing of Pearl Harbor, which caused the United States to join the Allied cause in World War II. The program ends with scenes of the U.S.S. *Arizona* Memorial.

Side 2, Chapter 8

View the video by scanning the bar code or by entering the chapter number on your keypad and pressing Search.

Hands-On Activity

As a nation we have built many memorials to Americans who have lost their lives during war. On large drawing paper, create a sketch of a monument for a patriotic cause. Then use your sketch to make a three-dimensional monument out of papier-mâché or modeling clay.

Surfing the "Net"

The Holocaust

During World War II the Nazis murdered 12 million people, 6 million of whom were Jews. This mass murder of Jewish people has come to be known as the Holocaust. As Allied forces moved through Germany and Poland after V-E Day, they saw the horrors of the concentration camps. To learn more about the Holocaust, use the Internet.

Getting There

Follow these steps to gather information about the Holocaust experience.

1. Use a search engine. Type in the phrase *Holocaust Survivors.*
2. After typing in this phrase, enter words such as the following to focus your search: *stories, experiences, oral history.*

3. The search engine should provide you with a number of links to follow. Links are "pointers" to different sites on the Internet.

What to Do When You Are There

Click on the links to navigate through the pages of information. Print your findings. Work with a partner or group to create a booklet of Holocaust survivors' memoirs. Design each memoir as a separate page of your book. Show your booklet to your parents or older adults and discuss the experiences of the Holocaust survivors. If possible, interview a person who lived during the World War II era. Ask what he or she remembers about the public's response when the existence of concentration camps became known.

April 1942
Allies surrender Bataan

March 1945
Americans seize Iwo Jima

August 1945
Atomic bomb is dropped on Hiroshima

September 1945
Japan surrenders; World War II ends

Section 5

War in the Pacific

READ TO DISCOVER . . .

- how the United States planned to gain control in the Pacific region.
- what role the atomic bomb played in ending the war.

TERMS TO LEARN

island hopping   kamikaze

The Storyteller

Bob Krell, a soldier in World War II, felt a need to describe his life in the war: "At night before a big airborne operation you crawl deeper in your sack, but you can't get away from the noise. Over the roar of engines, somebody is shouting a bunch of names. . . . [W]e will climb into our parachutes as dawn breaks. We will trudge out to the planes and climb in, not saying much of anything about anything. . . ." Bob Krell was killed in action 12 hours after he wrote these words.

Silver Star, awarded for gallantry in action

On December 7, 1941, the same day the Japanese attacked Pearl Harbor, Japanese bombers struck American airfields in the **Philippines** and on the islands of **Wake** and **Guam**—key American bases in the Pacific. In the following days, the Japanese intensified their campaign in the Pacific. They invaded Thailand and Malaya and captured Guam, Wake Island, and the British colony of Hong Kong.

The Pacific Front

★ Japanese troops had landed in the Philippines in mid-December and quickly taken the capital of Manila. The defending forces—Filipino and American troops commanded by American general **Douglas MacArthur**—were forced to retreat to the rugged **Bataan** Peninsula west of Manila and the small island fortress of **Corregidor.**

Eyewitness to HISTORY

The Philippines Fall

After months of fierce fighting, the exhausted Allied troops defending Bataan surrendered on April 9, 1942. The forces on Corregidor held out for another month. The Japanese forced their Bataan prisoners—many sick and near starvation—to march to a prison camp more than 60 miles away. Only much later did the public learn what these prisoners endured. About 76,000 prisoners started out, but only about 54,000 of those on the **Bataan Death March** reached the camp. As one survivor recalled:

❝ Anybody that could walk, they forced 'em into line. . . . If you fell out to the side, you were either shot by the guards or you were bayoneted [stabbed] and left there. ❞

Two months before the surrender, General MacArthur had left for Australia to take command of Allied forces in the Pacific. MacArthur promised the Filipinos, "I shall return." 🔍

General Douglas MacArthur

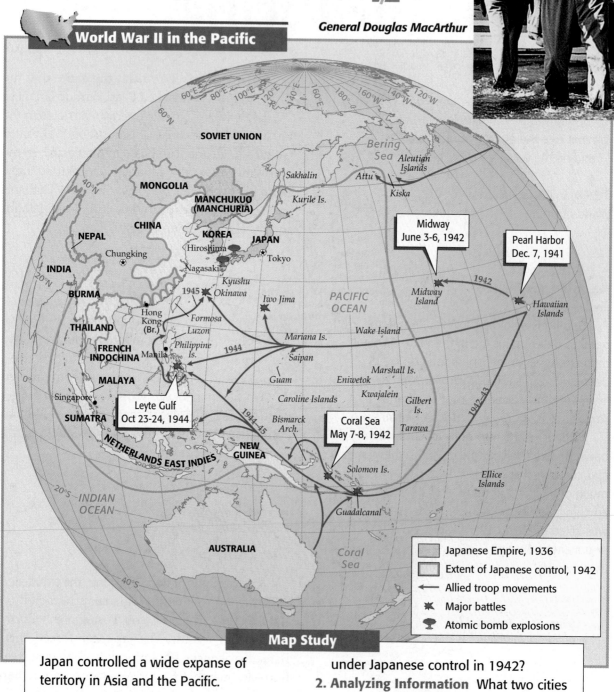

World War II in the Pacific

Map Study

Japan controlled a wide expanse of territory in Asia and the Pacific.
1. **Location** What parts of China were under Japanese control in 1942?
2. **Analyzing Information** What two cities were destroyed by atomic bombs?

Island Hopping

With Japan's string of quick victories, American morale was low. Then in mid-April, 16 American B-25 twin-engine bombers, launched from an aircraft carrier in the Pacific, bombed **Tokyo.** This daring raid led by James Doolittle had little military importance, but it lifted Americans' spirits.

In May, American and Japanese fleets clashed in the Coral Sea northeast of Australia. American ships were heavily damaged, but the Japanese suffered crippling losses. The **Battle of the Coral Sea** was a strategic victory because it halted the Japanese advance on Australia.

An even greater victory followed in June 1942. In the **Battle of Midway,** northwest of Hawaii, the navy destroyed four Japanese aircraft carriers and hundreds of airplanes. This was the first major Japanese defeat.

The United States was now ready to go on the offensive against Japan. The commanders—General MacArthur and Admiral **Chester Nimitz**—adopted a strategy known as island hopping. This called for attacking and capturing certain key islands. The United States then used these islands as bases for leapfrogging to others, moving ever closer to the Philippines—and to Japan.

Between August 1942 and February 1943, American forces engaged in one of the most vicious campaigns of the war for the control of **Guadalcanal,** one of the Solomon Islands. The Japanese put up fierce resistance; however, with superior air and naval power, the Americans finally secured the island.

In June 1944, American forces captured Guam and other islands nearby. Guam provided a base for launching bombing strikes on Japan. In October, American ships destroyed most of the Japanese fleet at the **Battle of Leyte Gulf** in the Philippines, the biggest naval battle in history—in all, 282 ships took part. MacArthur had fulfilled his promise to return to the Philippines.

The Advance on Japan

American forces now closed in on Japan itself. In March 1945, they seized the island of **Iwo Jima** and in June the island of **Okinawa.** The Japanese

Linking PAST & PRESENT

Aerial Warfare

Germany introduced jet planes late in World War II. The German jets could fly almost 550 miles per hour. By the 1960s American and Soviet jets roared through the skies at 1,000 miles per hour. Today United States military aircraft includes the F-117 stealth fighter. A winglike shape and flat surfaces that absorb radar energy make it difficult for enemy radar to detect it. **How do World War II planes differ from modern stealth bombers?**

Flying Grumman Wildcat Fighter, 1942

Past

Present · **Stealth bomber**

fought fiercely to defend these islands so near to Japan. Thousands of Americans died in the battles, and many thousands more were wounded.

With most of Japan's air force and navy destroyed, American B-29 bombers pounded Tokyo and other Japanese cities. The raids killed thousands of civilians and crippled Japan's economy.

In desperation, the Japanese unleashed a corps of suicide pilots known as kamikazes. They crashed planes loaded with explosives into American ships. Kamikaze pilots sank several destroyers during the battle for Okinawa.

The Atomic Bomb

Although the Japanese faced certain defeat, they continued to fight. Their refusal to surrender led the United States to use a powerful new weapon: the atomic bomb.

In 1939 the German-born physicist **Albert Einstein** had written to President Roosevelt warning him that the Nazis might try to use the energy of the atom to build "extremely powerful bombs of a new type." Wanting to develop such weapons first, Roosevelt created a top-secret operation, the **Manhattan Project.** After years of work, scientists tested the atomic bomb in the New Mexico desert on July 16, 1945. Truman now had to decide whether to use the bomb against Japan.

The Allies issued the **Potsdam Declaration,** warning that if Japan did not surrender, it faced "prompt and utter destruction." The Japanese leaders did not surrender, and Truman ordered the use of the bomb.

On August 6, 1945, an American B-29 bomber, the *Enola Gay,* dropped an atomic bomb on the Japanese city of **Hiroshima.** Three days later, a second bomb was dropped on the city of **Nagasaki.** The atomic bombs caused unimaginable destruction. The first bomb leveled Hiroshima and killed about 70,000 people; the Nagasaki bomb killed about 40,000. Thousands more were injured, and many died later from radiation.

The War Ends

After the bombings, the Japanese government agreed to surrender. August 15, 1945, was proclaimed **V-J Day,** for "Victory over Japan." All around America, people expressed happiness and relief. Japan signed the formal surrender on September 2 aboard the battleship the

Raising the U.S. flag at Iwo Jima

U.S.S. *Missouri.* World War II had finally ended.

The War Trials

In the years immediately after the war, Allied authorities put the top Nazi and Japanese leaders on trial. Those brought to trial were accused of war crimes and crimes against humanity. The Allies held the trials in Nuremberg, Germany, and in Tokyo, eventually convicting and executing 24 Nazis and 7 Japanese for their crimes. Hundreds more were imprisoned.

The Cost of the War

World War II was the most destructive conflict in history. More than 40 million people died during the war; more than half of these were civilians killed by bombing, starvation, disease, torture, and murder. American casualties—about 322,000 dead and 800,000 injured—were high, but light compared with those of other nations. The Soviet Union suffered more than 20 million deaths. Those who survived faced the daunting task of trying to rebuild their lives and their countries. Nationalist movements grew, particularly in colonial nations that had suffered invasions by the warring powers. Many colonies began to seek independence in the postwar years.

★ ★ ★ ★ ★ Section 5 Assessment ★ ★ ★ ★ ★

Checking for Understanding
1. **Identify** Douglas MacArthur, Chester Nimitz, Manhattan Project, V-J Day.
2. **Define** island hopping, kamikaze.
3. **Explain** the significance of the Battle of Leyte Gulf.

Reviewing Themes
4. **Individual Action** What did Japan's use of kamikazes illustrate about its desire to win the war?

Critical Thinking
5. **Identifying Central Issues** If you had been President Truman, would you have allowed the United States to drop the atomic bomb on Japan? Why or why not?

Activity

Creating a Graph Make a line graph that compares the number of people killed during the war in the major Axis and Allied countries.

Writing a Paragraph

Paragraphs are the building blocks of an essay or other composition. Each paragraph is a unit, a group of sentences about a single topic or idea.

Learning the Skill

Most well-written paragraphs share four characteristics.

- First, a paragraph expresses one main idea or is about one subject. A topic sentence states that main idea. The topic sentence may be located at the beginning, the middle, or the end of a paragraph.
- Second, the rest of the sentences in a paragraph support the main idea. The main idea may be developed by facts, examples, or reasons.
- Third, the sentences are arranged in a logical order.
- Fourth, transitional words link sentences within the paragraph. These words can also link one paragraph with the next. Examples include *next, then, finally, also, because, however,* and *as a result.*

Practicing the Skill

Use the following sentences to build a paragraph containing a topic sentence and other sentences that give supporting details. Put the sentences in a logical order and add transitional words if you need to. Underline your topic sentence.

1. Three days later an American plane dropped another bomb on Nagasaki.
2. The bomb killed between 70,000 and 100,000 people.
3. This second bomb killed nearly 40,000 people instantly and many more later.

Hiroshima after the atomic bomb

4. On August 6, 1945, the United States dropped an atomic bomb on Hiroshima, Japan.
5. About 100,000 others died later from the effects of radiation.
6. When the bomb exploded, a sheet of flame spread over the city.

Applying the Skill

Writing a Paragraph Choose a topic from the World War II era and write a paragraph about it. Then rewrite the paragraph with its sentences out of order. Exchange papers with a classmate. Can he or she find the topic sentence? Does it work logically?

GO TO

Glencoe's **Skillbuilder Interactive Workbook, Level 1** provides instruction and practice in key social studies skills.

Assessment and Activities

★ Reviewing Key Terms

On a sheet of paper, use each of the following terms in a sentence:

dictator
fascism
anti-Semitism
appeasement
blitzkrieg
lend-lease
ration
internment camp
genocide
Holocaust
island hopping
kamikaze

★ Reviewing Key Facts

1. How did Britain and France try to prevent war with Germany?
2. What steps did President Roosevelt take to prepare for war even though he vowed to remain neutral?
3. What did the government do to keep the American economy stable and to ensure that industries produced enough war materials?
4. What was Operation Overlord?
5. What actions by the Japanese convinced the United States to use the atomic bomb?

★ Critical Thinking

Analyzing Information

Despite having to deal with continuing racial tension, African Americans gained new opportunities during the war.

1. What advances did African Americans make in the military?
2. What rights did A. Philip Randolph win for civilian African Americans?

★ Time Line Activity

Create a time line on which you place the following events in chronological order.

- Congress passes Lend-Lease Act
- World War II begins
- Hitler and Stalin sign nonaggression pact
- V-E Day
- Hitler becomes German chancellor
- Japan bombs Pearl Harbor

★ Reviewing Themes

1. **Continuity and Change** Why did most Americans want to avoid involvement in international conflicts after World War I?
2. **Global Connections** What was Japan's main reason for wanting to take over the Dutch East Indies, British Malaya, and the Philippines?
3. **Economic Factors** Why did the government require rationing during the war?
4. **Geography and History** Despite the fact that Japan was conquering areas in the Pacific, why did the Allies focus first on the war in Europe?
5. **Individual Action** What was the significance of the bombing raid on Tokyo led by American James Doolittle?

★ Technology Activity

Using the Internet Search the Internet for a World War II site that includes memoirs or excerpts from veterans and/or civilians. Copy or print a part of the memoirs that you find interesting. Post the excerpts on the classroom bulletin board under the heading "Voices of World War II."

★ Geography Activity

The map below shows the Allied invasion routes from Great Britain to Normandy beginning on June 6, 1944. Utah, Omaha, Gold, Juno, and Sword were code names for the Normandy beaches. Study the map below, then answer the questions that follow.

D-Day Invasion, June 6, 1944

1. **Location** From where did the United States forces leave Great Britain?
2. **Movement** Why do you think the invasion was launched from five sites?
3. **Location** The Nazis were fooled into thinking the invasion would come near Calais. Why do you think the Allies chose to land on the Normandy peninsula instead?

★ Skill Practice Activity

Writing a Paragraph

Write a short paragraph for each of the topic sentences that follow. Each paragraph must have at least three sentences supporting the topic and arranged in a logical way. Use transitional words or phrases to connect your ideas smoothly.

1. The leaders of Italy, Germany, and Japan attempted to restore their nations to their former greatness through the use of the military.
2. Minority groups played vital roles in World War II, both in the armed forces and at home.
3. During World War II, Americans at home made many sacrifices.

★ Cooperative Activity

History and Law As a class create a courtroom with students role-playing a panel of judges, a three-member prosecution team, three defense attorneys, a jury, three defendants, and an audience. Put the following people on trial for crimes against humanity: Adolf Hitler—for beginning World War II and establishing the Nazi death camps; a German military officer—for carrying out orders to execute Jews in a death camp; General Hideki Tōjō—for ordering kamikaze attacks against Allied forces in the Pacific. Try each case separately, decide on a verdict, and recommend a punishment.

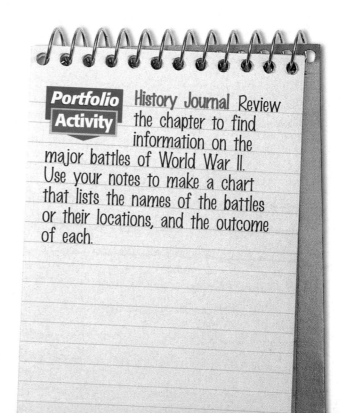

Portfolio Activity History Journal Review the chapter to find information on the major battles of World War II. Use your notes to make a chart that lists the names of the battles or their locations, and the outcome of each.

Unit 10

Turning Points

1945–1975

"Justice too long delayed is justice denied."

—MARTIN LUTHER KING, JR., 1963

interNET CONNECTION

To learn more about this period in history, visit the Glencoe Social Studies Web Site at **www.glencoe.com** for information, activities, and links to other sites.

MAPPING *America*

Portfolio Activity Draw a freehand outline map of China, Korea, and the former Soviet Union. As you read this unit about turning points in postwar America, note major events. Plot the location of these events on your map and label them.

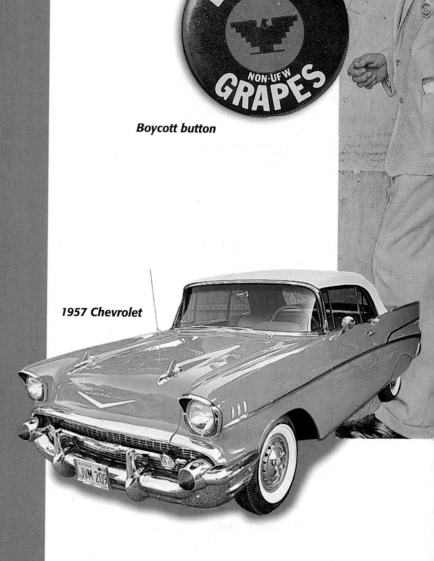

Boycott button

1957 Chevrolet

United States

1947 Jackie Robinson first plays for Brooklyn Dodgers

1953 McCarthyism stirs nation

1940

1950

World

1947 Truman Doctrine is announced

1949 Communist forces take China

1950 North Korea invades South Korea

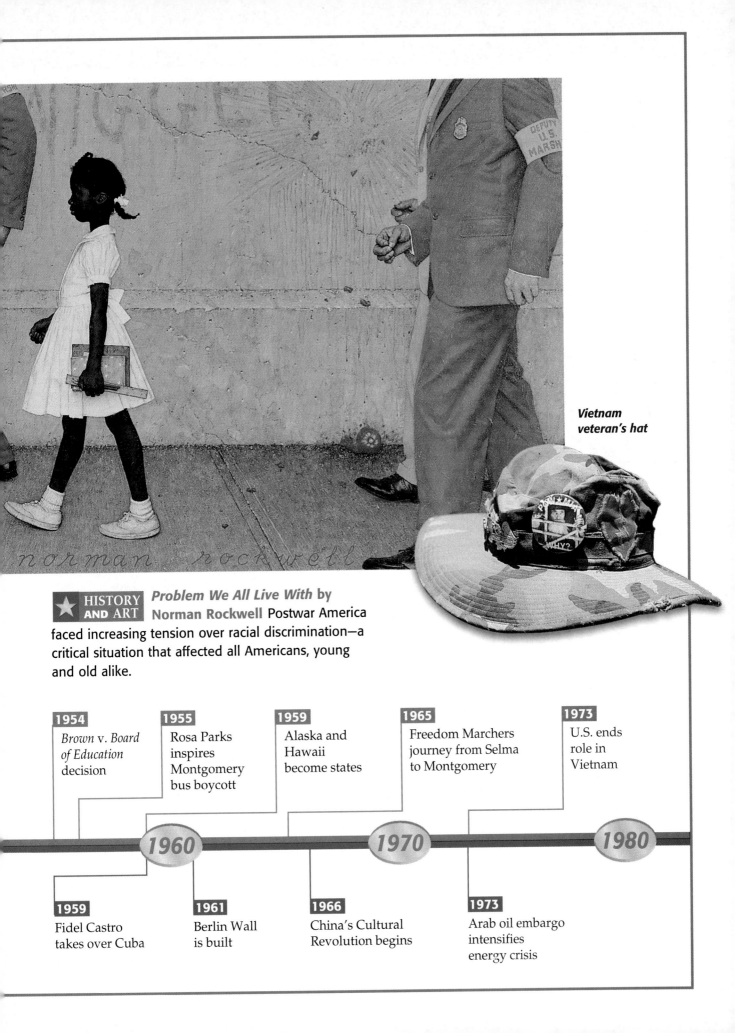

Vietnam veteran's hat

★ HISTORY AND ART **Problem We All Live With** by **Norman Rockwell** Postwar America faced increasing tension over racial discrimination—a critical situation that affected all Americans, young and old alike.

1954
Brown v. *Board of Education* decision

1955
Rosa Parks inspires Montgomery bus boycott

1959
Alaska and Hawaii become states

1965
Freedom Marchers journey from Selma to Montgomery

1973
U.S. ends role in Vietnam

1960

1970

1980

1959
Fidel Castro takes over Cuba

1961
Berlin Wall is built

1966
China's Cultural Revolution begins

1973
Arab oil embargo intensifies energy crisis

America's LITERATURE

I Know Why the Caged Bird Sings

by Maya Angelou

Maya Angelou (1928–) has written poetry, fiction, and plays. She worked on a newspaper in Egypt, lectured at the University of Ghana, and directed a film in Hollywood. Born Marguerite Johnson, Angelou and her brother, Bailey, were raised by their grandmother, Annie Henderson (whom they called "Momma"), the owner of a general store in the black area of Stamps, Arkansas.

■ READ TO DISCOVER

In the following excerpt from Angelou's autobiography, she is about 10 years old. Bright but painfully self-conscious, she has become withdrawn and refuses to speak to anyone. As you read, notice the influence that Mrs. Flowers has on Marguerite.

■ READER'S DICTIONARY

voile: lightweight, sheer fabric
benign: showing kindness and gentleness
bungalow: one-story house with a low roof
moors: also called "heath"; open, wild land
scones: pastries
crumpets: muffins
morocco: soft leather

For nearly a year, I sopped around the house, the store, the school and the church, like an old biscuit, dirty and inedible. Then I met, or rather got to know, the lady who threw me my first life line.

Mrs. Bertha Flowers was the aristocrat of Black Stamps. She had the grace of control to appear warm in the coldest weather, and on the Arkansas summer days it seemed she had a private breeze which swirled around, cooling her. She was thin without the taut look of wiry people, and her printed voile dresses and flowered hat were as right for her as denim overalls for a farmer. She was our side's answer to the richest white women in town.

Her skin was a rich black that would have peeled like a plum if snagged, but then no one would have thought of getting close enough to Mrs. Flowers to ruffle her dress, let alone snag her skin. She didn't encourage familiarity. She wore gloves too.

I don't think I ever saw Mrs. Flowers laugh, but she smiled often. A slow widening of her thin black lips to show even, small white teeth, then the slow effortless closing. When she chose to smile on me, I always wanted to thank her. The action was so graceful and inclusively benign.

She was one of the few gentlewomen I have ever known, and has remained throughout my life the measure of what a human being can be.

Momma had a strange relationship with her. Most often when she passed on the road in front of the Store, she spoke to Momma in that soft yet carrying voice, "Good day, Mrs. Henderson." Momma responded with "How you, Sister Flowers?"

Mrs. Flowers didn't belong to our church, nor was she Momma's familiar.

Why on earth did she insist on calling her Sister Flowers? Shame made me want to hide my face. Mrs. Flowers deserved better than to be called Sister. Then, Momma left out the verb. Why not ask, "How *are* you, *Mrs.* Flowers?" With the unbalanced passion of the young, I hated her for showing her ignorance to Mrs. Flowers. It didn't occur to me for many years that they were as alike as sisters, separated only by formal education.

Although I was upset, neither of the women was in the least shaken by what I thought an unceremonious greeting. Mrs. Flowers would continue her easy gait up the hill to her little bungalow, and Momma kept on shelling peas or doing whatever had brought her to the front porch.

Occasionally, though, Mrs. Flowers would drift off the road and down to the Store and Momma would say to me, "Sister, you go on and play." As I left I would hear the beginning of an intimate conversation. Momma persistently using the wrong verb, or none at all.

"Brother and Sister Wilcox is sho'ly the meanest—" "Is," Momma? "Is"? Oh, please, not "is," Momma, for two or more. But they talked, and from the side of the building where I waited for the ground to open up and swallow me, I heard the soft-voiced Mrs. Flowers and the textured voice of my grandmother merging and melting. They were interrupted from time to time by giggles that must have come from Mrs. Flowers (Momma never giggled in her life). Then she was gone.

She appealed to me because she was like people I had never met personally. Like women in English novels who walked the moors

Her World *by Philip Evergood*

(whatever they were) with their loyal dogs racing at a respectful distance. Like the women who sat in front of roaring fireplaces, drinking tea incessantly from silver trays full of scones and crumpets. Women who walked over the "heath" and read morocco-bound books and had two last names divided by a hyphen. It would be safe to say that she made me proud to be Negro, just by being herself.

She acted just as refined as whitefolks in the movies and books and she was more beautiful, for none of them could have come near that warm color without looking gray by comparison.

From *I Know Why the Caged Bird Sings,* by Maya Angelou. Copyright © 1969 by Maya Angelou. Reprinted by permission of Random House, Inc.

■ RESPONDING TO LITERATURE

1. How does the author describe Mrs. Flowers's attitude toward familiarity?
2. Does this attitude make you like or dislike Mrs. Flowers? Explain.
3. In what way does Marguerite think her grandmother's relationship with Mrs. Flowers is strange?

Activity

Writing a Sketch Write a one-page sketch describing an encounter you had with a person who influenced your life in a positive way. Explain the changes that occurred as a result of the encounter.

1945–1954

The Cold War Era

★ Why It's Important

The bitter rivalry between the United States and the Soviet Union after World War II shaped much of the modern world. Each side sought to gain allies and to prove that its system—democracy and free enterprise or communism—was better. At times their rivalry and hostile relations threatened to turn into open warfare. The collapse of the Soviet Union in 1991 marked the end of the cold war era.

★ Chapter Themes

- *Section 1*, Global Connections
- *Section 2*, Economic Factors
- *Section 3*, Government and Democracy
- *Section 4*, Individual Action

PRIMARY SOURCES
Library

See pages 988–989 for primary source readings to accompany Chapter 27

★ HISTORY AND ART *Korea* by T.H. Jackson The Korean War began in June 1950 when North Korean forces invaded South Korea. For three years UN troops and Communist forces battled up and down the Korean peninsula.

1945	1947	1949

February 1945
Conference at Yalta is held

April 1945
Harry S Truman succeeds FDR

May 1948
Jewish leaders proclaim new state of Israel

June 1948
Soviets blockade West Berlin

October 1949
Mao Zedong forms Communist China

Section 1

Cold War Origins

READ TO DISCOVER . . .

- how the United States attempted to stop the spread of communism.
- how postwar foreign policy changed as a result of the cold war.

TERMS TO LEARN

iron curtain
containment

airlift
cold war

The Storyteller

The three most powerful men in the world met around a conference table in Yalta to discuss the fate of the postwar world. President Roosevelt hoped to promote his vision of post-war cooperation. Prime Minister Churchill spoke elegantly and forcefully. Soviet leader Stalin remained stubbornly opposed to much of what was proposed. Stalin stated to his aides: "They want to force us to accept their plans on Europe and the world. Well, that's not going to happen." As the Allies discovered, Stalin had his own plans.

The Big Three at Yalta

As the Allies moved toward victory in 1945, questions about the organization of the postwar world arose. Soviet forces had pushed back German armies and occupied much of Eastern and Central Europe. Should these areas—including Poland, Hungary, and Czechoslovakia—remain in Soviet hands?

Wartime Diplomacy

★ In February 1945, the "Big Three" Allied leaders—**Franklin D. Roosevelt, Winston Churchill,** and **Joseph Stalin**—met at **Yalta,** a Soviet port on the Black Sea. They came to discuss issues affecting the postwar world. Out of this meeting came the Yalta agreement, in which the Soviet Union agreed to enter the war against Japan. In return, the Soviets received some territories in Asia.

Reaching an agreement on postwar arrangements proved more difficult. Roosevelt and Churchill feared the Soviet domination of Eastern Europe and the spread of communism. Stalin, on the other hand, wanted to keep a large area of land between the Soviet Union and its potential enemies in the West.

Germany presented a special problem. The Allies finally agreed to divide Germany into four zones until elections could be held to determine its future. The Soviet Union, the United States, Britain, and France would each control a zone.

Stalin agreed to allow free elections in occupied Eastern Europe and to cooperate in planning for the new international organization proposed

Chapter 27 The Cold War Era **773**

by the United States and Britain. Roosevelt and Churchill felt encouraged about a peaceful postwar world. Their hopes went unfulfilled.

The United Nations

President Roosevelt died suddenly on April 12, 1945. Vice President **Harry S Truman** succeeded him. Facing the enormous responsibilities of the presidency, Truman told reporters, "When they told me yesterday [of Roosevelt's death], I felt like the moon, the stars, and all the planets had fallen on me."

One of Truman's first decisions as president was to go ahead with the meeting to form the new international organization discussed at Yalta. On June 26, in San Francisco, California, 50 nations—including the Soviet Union—signed the charter creating the **United Nations** (UN). The members hoped the UN could settle disputes between nations and prevent future wars.

UN flag

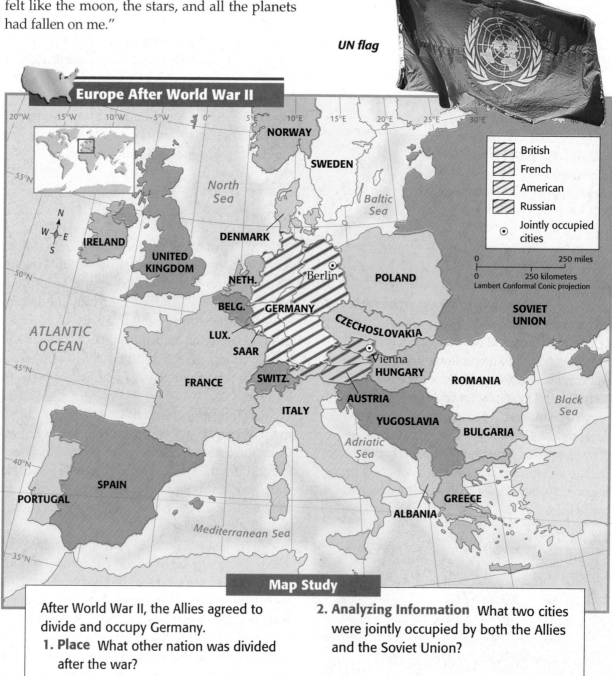

Europe After World War II

Legend:
- British
- French
- American
- Russian
- ⊙ Jointly occupied cities

0 — 250 miles
0 — 250 kilometers
Lambert Conformal Conic projection

Map Study

After World War II, the Allies agreed to divide and occupy Germany.

1. **Place** What other nation was divided after the war?

2. **Analyzing Information** What two cities were jointly occupied by both the Allies and the Soviet Union?

★ ★ ★ ★ ★ ★ ★ ★ ★ ★ ★ ★ ★ ★ ★ ★

🌐 Geography

Soviet Expansion in Europe

★ The uneasy wartime alliance between the Western nations and the Soviet Union did not last. Stalin did not keep his promise to hold free elections in Eastern Europe. Instead the Soviets set up Communist governments in these countries, and Soviet forces remained in the region.

Developments in Eastern Europe led to a growing distrust between the Soviet Union and Western nations. Europe split into two camps— the Soviet-controlled Communist governments of the East and the capitalist democracies.

The Iron Curtain

Winston Churchill believed that the division between East and West was permanent. In 1946 he declared in a speech in Fulton, Missouri, that an "iron curtain" had descended on Europe. Churchill meant that the Soviets had cut off Eastern Europe from the West. Behind this iron curtain, he said, lay the countries of Eastern Europe "in what I must call the Soviet sphere, and all are subject to a very high . . . measure of control from Moscow."

Churchill warned that the Soviets would eventually look beyond Eastern Europe and try to gain control of other parts of the world. This idea alarmed Americans, who had feared the spread of communism ever since the Russian Revolution in 1917.

In **Greece,** as Communist rebels armed by the Soviet Union attempted to overthrow the Greek king and his pro-Western government, civil war raged in the country. At the same time, the Soviets put enormous pressure on **Turkey** to give them naval bases on the straits leading to the Mediterranean Sea.

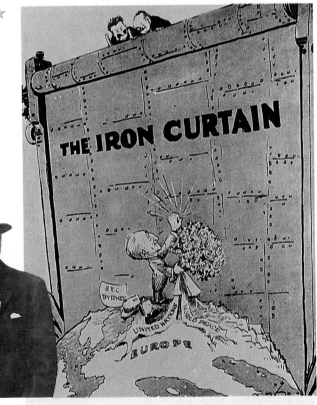

★ **Picturing HISTORY** James Byrne, President Truman's secretary of state, tried to get along with the Soviets. But Winston Churchill (left), who coined the phrase "iron curtain," foresaw troubles with the Soviet Union. **What did Churchill mean by this phrase?**

Containing the Soviets

★ Seeking ways to counter Soviet expansion, President Truman drew from the ideas of **George F. Kennan,** an American diplomat and an expert on Soviet history and culture. Kennan argued that the United States and the Soviet Union could not cooperate and that the United States must take forceful steps to stop Soviet expansion. His ideas led to the policy of containment. The United States would try to "contain" Soviet expansion through limited military means and nonmilitary means in areas of the world that were of strategic importance to the United States. Kennan defined these areas narrowly—mostly Western Europe and Japan. But other United States officials gradually expanded their view of what was of strategic importance to the country and its future.

The Truman Doctrine

The policy of containment soon went into effect. Speaking to Congress in March 1947, the president proposed a policy that became known as the **Truman Doctrine,** a commitment to help nations threatened by communism and Soviet expansion.

> **❝**I believe that it must be the policy of the United States to support free peoples who are resisting attempted subjugation [conquest] by armed minorities or by outside pressures. **❞**

Congress voted to give military and economic assistance to Greece and Turkey to hold back the Soviets.

The Marshall Plan

At the end of World War II, much of Europe lay in ruins. Bombing had destroyed countless houses, factories, bridges, and roads. Many people lacked homes, jobs, and often enough food to eat. Their war-ravaged societies provided fertile ground for communism with its promises of housing and employment for all.

George Marshall, the United States secretary of state, saw Western Europe as strategically important to the United States. He believed that the best way to keep the countries of Western Europe free of communism would be to help restore their economies. In June 1947, Marshall proposed a plan to provide massive economic aid to Europe. At first his plan met some resistance in Congress. After Soviet-supported Communists took over the government of **Czechoslovakia** in February 1948, however, this resistance disappeared.

Congress approved the program of economic aid for Europe, the **Marshall Plan,** which became a vital part of the policy of containment. Between 1948 and 1951, the Marshall Plan contributed nearly $13 billion to the rebuilding of the countries of Western Europe. As Marshall had predicted, no Western government in the region fell to a Communist revolution.

Crisis in Berlin

★ The Allied leaders at Yalta had divided Germany into four occupation zones. The Soviet Union controlled the eastern part of the country, while the United States, Britain, and France divided the western part. The German capital of **Berlin,** located deep within Soviet-controlled East Germany, was also divided among the four nations.

President Truman believed that a reunited Germany was essential to the future of Europe. Stalin, on the other hand, feared that a reunited Germany would once again pose a threat to the Soviet Union. He sought to maintain Soviet influence in a divided Germany. Tensions over the German issue led to a serious crisis in 1948.

The Berlin Blockade

On June 7, 1948, the United States, Britain, and France announced that they were uniting their zones to form a new West German republic. Each nation's section of Berlin would be included in this republic as well, even though the city lay within Soviet-held East Germany.

The **Berlin blockade** was Stalin's answer to the West's plans for West Germany. On June 24, 1948, Soviet troops rushed into position around the

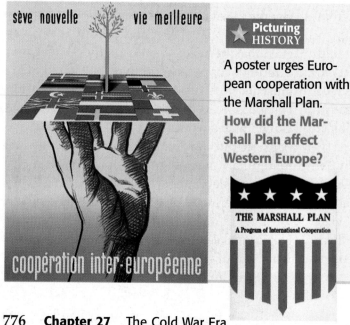

sève nouvelle vie meilleure
coopération inter·européenne

★ Picturing HISTORY
A poster urges European cooperation with the Marshall Plan. **How did the Marshall Plan affect Western Europe?**

THE MARSHALL PLAN
A Program of International Cooperation

Picturing HISTORY During the 1948 blockade, Berlin children, standing in the rubble of their shattered city, watch an American bomber fly in with supplies. **What effect did the airlift have on the Soviet blockade?**

edge of West Berlin. Almost overnight they created a blockade, stopping traffic on all highway, railroad, and water routes through East Germany to West Berlin. As a result, West Berlin and its 2 million citizens were cut off from vital supplies. The Soviets hoped this blockade would drive the West out of Berlin.

The Berlin Airlift

President Truman refused to give in to the Soviets. "We stay in Berlin, period," he declared, but he did not want to risk war by using military force to end the blockade. Instead he organized a massive airlift to save the city.

American and British cargo planes began flying food, fuel, and other supplies into West Berlin. The **Berlin airlift** continued day and night for more than 10 months, delivering about 2.5 million tons of supplies to West Berlin. A West Berlin taxi driver told a visiting journalist about how the airlift boosted Berliners' morale:

❝We lost all our faith at first. . . . We thought the West would pull out. Now we have it back. There. You hear? There is another plane. And there's another. Our faith doesn't come from our hearts or our brains any more. It comes through the ears.❞

Realizing that the Western powers intended to stay in the city, Stalin ended the Berlin blockade in May 1949.

Despite the success of the airlift, Berlin and Germany remained divided. In October 1949, the division of Germany into two nations—the **Federal Republic of Germany,** or West Germany, and the **German Democratic Republic,** or East Germany—became official.

Two Armed Camps

The crisis in Berlin confirmed that the United States and the Soviet Union were locked in a cold war—a war in which the two enemies

Linking PAST & PRESENT

German Reunification

On October 3, 1990, the two parts of Germany finally reunited, and Berlin—rejoined as one city—again became the nation's official capital. The German government's move to Berlin from the West German capital of Bonn is scheduled to be completed in the year 2003.

Picturing HISTORY

After World War II, many Jewish refugees from the Holocaust settled in Palestine. In 1948 part of Palestine became the Jewish state of Israel. **What major challenge did Israel face?**

Declaration of the State of Israel

did not actually fight each other. Instead each nation began building up its military forces and arms in an attempt to intimidate the other. European nations began to take sides in this mounting cold war.

NATO

The United States and the countries of Western Europe agreed that the best way to contain the Soviets was through mutual defense. In April 1949, the United States, Canada, and 10 Western European nations signed a pact establishing the **North Atlantic Treaty Organization** (NATO). The agreement stated that "an armed attack against one or more of [the member nations] shall be considered an attack against all." To defend against a possible Soviet invasion of Western Europe, the NATO countries created a large military force composed of troops from all the member nations.

The Warsaw Pact

In response to NATO, the Soviet Union created an alliance of its own with the Communist governments of Eastern Europe. The alliance,

established in 1955 by mutual defense treaties known as the **Warsaw Pact,** had a military force that the Soviet Union controlled. The formation of NATO and the Warsaw Pact divided Europe into two armed camps.

The United States Rearms

After World War II, some of President Truman's foreign policy advisers in the **National Security Council** (NSC) argued that America could not rely on other nations to contain the Soviets and resist the spread of communism. Unlike George Kennan and the supporters of the containment policy, the NSC advisers believed the United States needed to take a more active stand against communism everywhere—not just in strategic locations.

In 1950 the NSC released a report, known as **NSC-68,** which said that the United States must actively "foster the seeds of destruction within the Soviet Union" and fight Communist movements wherever they arose. Within several years of this report, the United States had built the largest military force in history and was committed to combating Communist expansion everywhere in the world.

★ ★

Postwar Developments

★ As the cold war grew more bitter in Europe, nations in other parts of the world were undergoing dramatic changes. Many states broke free of colonial rule and established independence. Others suffered strife.

Independence Movements

The Philippines gained independence from the United States in 1946. For years afterward Filipinos struggled with terrible poverty, government corruption, and civil war. In the late 1940s, Asian countries such as India, Pakistan, and Burma broke away from the British Empire to form new nations. During the 1950s and the early 1960s, more than 25 African nations gained independence from European colonial powers. As these new nations struggled with political and economic problems, the United States and the Soviet Union competed for influence in Africa and Asia.

In the Middle East, Jews and Arabs both claimed the region of **Palestine,** an area the British had controlled. In 1947 the United Nations proposed dividing Palestine into independent Jewish and Arab states with Jerusalem as

Mao Zedong

an international city. The Jews accepted the plan, but the Arab states did not. After Israel declared its independence Arab armies attacked the new Jewish state of **Israel** in the first of six major wars in the region between the Arabs and Israel.

Communism in China

Perhaps the most threatening change of the postwar period occurred in **China,** the largest country in Asia. In 1949 a long civil war ended with the victory of Chinese Communist forces led by **Mao Zedong** (MAU ZUH•DUNG) over the armies commanded by **Chiang Kai-shek** (JEE•AHNG KY•SHEHK), the head of the Chinese government. Mao Zedong formed a new Communist state, the People's Republic of China, while Chiang Kai-shek retreated with his forces to the island of **Taiwan** off the southeastern coast of China. The United States recognized the government in Taiwan as the legitimate government of all China.

With Communists in control of mainland China, the Soviet Union had a powerful ally in Asia. It appeared to many people that the entire continent of Asia was in danger of turning to communism.

★ ★ ★ ★ ★   **Section 1 Assessment**   ★ ★ ★ ★ ★ ★

Checking for Understanding

1. *Identify* Winston Churchill, Joseph Stalin, Harry S Truman, Mao Zedong, Chiang Kai-shek.
2. *Define* iron curtain, containment, airlift, cold war.
3. *Explain* how the Marshall Plan helped to contain the spread of communism in Western Europe.

Reviewing Themes

4. **Global Connections** Summarize Truman's postwar foreign policy.

Critical Thinking

5. **Synthesizing Information** Explain why the United States's actions against the Soviet Union in the Berlin blockade were considered part of a "cold war."

Activity

Comparing Maps Compare a map of Africa after World War II to a map of Africa today. Photocopy or draw a modern map and indicate five countries that have changed their names or boundaries during this 50-year period.

1944
Congress approves
the GI Bill of Rights

1946
Miners and railroad
workers strike

1947
Taft-Hartley Act
limits unions

1948
Truman
wins the
presidency

Section 2

Postwar Politics

READ TO DISCOVER . . .
- what economic problems Americans faced in the immediate postwar years.
- how President Truman and the Republican-controlled Congress proposed to deal with the nation's problems.

TERMS TO LEARN
inflation   closed shop

Storyteller

When soldiers returned home after World War II, they came back to a nation facing the difficult task of changing from wartime to peacetime. Would the economy collapse again and another depression sweep the country? President Truman was optimistic: "We are having our little troubles now. Just a blowup after a little let-down from war." Public concern, however, forced the nation's political leaders into a heated debate over the best way to deal with America's economic problems.

Truman campaign button

After World War II, the nation and its economy had to adjust to peacetime life. Industries had to shift from producing war materials to making **consumer goods.** Defense workers had to be retrained to work in consumer industries, and returning soldiers needed jobs.

💲 Economics

The Postwar Economy

In 1944 Congress passed the Servicemen's Readjustment Act, better known as the **GI Bill of Rights.** This law provided billions of dollars in loans to help returning GIs—soldiers, sailors, and marines—attend college, receive special training, set up businesses, or buy homes. It also provided unemployment and health benefits for the GIs as they looked for jobs.

This flood of money to GIs helped reduce unemployment in the postwar years and boosted the economy. At the same time, though, it contributed to one of the major problems of the period—rapidly increasing prices.

Threat of Inflation

During the war, government price controls had kept the cost of consumer goods such as food and clothing quite stable. When the government removed these controls, prices began to surge. This rise in prices, or *inflation,* also resulted from a huge increase in consumer demand and spending. During the war years, Americans had saved their money because many consumer goods were unavailable or rationed. Now they were eager to spend this money on new consumer products and services.

Workers Seek Higher Wages

As a result of inflation, consumer prices rose at a much faster rate than wages. During the war, workers had accepted government controls on wages and agreed not to strike. Now they would no longer be put off. When employers refused to raise wages, labor unions called strikes. In 1945 and 1946, millions of steelworkers, railroad workers, and others walked off their jobs, demanding higher wages and better conditions.

Labor unrest and strikes disrupted the nation's economy. When miners went on strike in 1946, many Americans feared that dwindling coal supplies would cause the economy to grind to a halt. At about the same time, a strike by railroad workers caused a total shutdown of the nation's railroads, which were vital to the economy.

Truman Takes Action

Alarmed by the labor unrest, President Truman pressured the striking miners and railroad workers to go back to their jobs. In May 1946, he threatened to draft them into the army if they did not return to work. The president insisted he had the right to take such steps to keep vital industries operating.

President Truman finally forced striking miners back on the job by having the government take over the mines. At the same time, however, he persuaded the mine owners to grant many of the workers' demands. Truman also pressured railroad workers to return to work.

★ **Picturing HISTORY** Enthusiastic military veterans at Indiana University clutch admission papers. **What benefits did the GI Bill of Rights provide to veterans?**

Truman Faces the Republicans

★ In September 1945, President Truman, a Democrat, presented Congress with a plan of domestic reforms aimed at solving some of the nation's economic problems. Truman later called this program the **Fair Deal.**

Truman proposed to raise the minimum wage, expand Social Security benefits, increase federal spending to create jobs, build new public housing, and create a system of national health insurance. But because of opposition by a coalition of Republicans and Southern Democrats, these measures failed to pass in Congress.

---

*F*ootnotes to History

A Young Scholar By the time Harry Truman was 8 years old, he had to wear glasses. Afraid that he might break them, he spent his time reading instead of playing sports. Truman did not go to college, but by the time he was 14 he had read every book in the Independence, Missouri, library.

Republicans Control Congress

Many Americans blamed Truman and the Democratic Party for the nation's economic problems. In the congressional elections of 1946, the slogan "Had Enough?" helped Republicans win control of both houses of Congress.

The new Republican Congress moved quickly to create its own plans for the nation. Having rejected Truman's program for reform, the Republicans now set up proposals to enact a program that would limit government spending, control labor unions, reduce government regulation of the economy, and reverse policies adopted in the 1930s under FDR's New Deal.

For many Republicans in Congress, the most important problem facing the nation was labor unrest and the growing power of labor unions. Conservative Republicans favored big business and wanted to limit the power of unions. In the spring of 1947, Congress introduced the

Taft-Hartley bill. This bill limited the actions workers could take against their employers. It outlawed the closed shop, a workplace that hires only union members. It also allowed the government to temporarily stop any strike that endangered public health or safety. This provision aimed to prevent any future strikes like those of the miners and the railroad workers the year before. Union members and their leaders sharply criticized the Taft-Hartley Act, calling it a "slave labor bill." Although President Truman opposed recent strikes, he also knew that the Democrats needed the support of labor. Truman vetoed the act, but the Republican-controlled Congress overrode his veto.

The Election of 1948

As the 1948 presidential election approached, Truman appeared to be the underdog. Continuing economic problems made the president unpopular with many Americans, and his lack of success in winning passage of domestic reforms made his administration look weak and ineffective.

Divisions within the Democratic Party also increased the chances of an easy Republican victory. At the party's national convention, a group of Southern Democrats walked out to protest Truman's support for civil rights legislation. The Southern Democrats formed the States' Rights Democratic Party, or Dixiecrats, and nominated Governor **Strom Thurmond** of South Carolina for president. At the same time, some liberal members of the Democratic Party left to form the Progressive Party, with **Henry Wallace** as their nominee for president. Wallace opposed Truman's foreign policy and called for closer ties between the United States and the Soviet Union.

The Election of 1948

	Popular vote:	Electoral vote:
Truman	24,105,812	303
Dewey	21,970,065	189
Thurmond	1,169,063	39

Lambert Conformal Conic projection

Map Study

The Democrats split in 1948, supporting both Truman and Thurmond.

1. **Region** From which region did Thurmond receive support?
2. **Analyzing Information** By how many electoral votes did Truman win over Dewey?

Dewey Leads Polls

With the Democrats badly divided, it looked as though Governor **Thomas Dewey** of New York, the Republican nominee, would surely win the election. Opinion polls showed Dewey with a huge lead. One pollster remarked: "Mr. Dewey is still so clearly ahead that we might just as well get ready to listen to his inaugural."

President Truman displays a newspaper headline that wrongly declared Thomas E. Dewey as the winner of the 1948 presidential race. **Why was Truman expected to lose the election?**

Truman campaigned aggressively. Traveling more than 30,000 miles by train on a "whistle-stop" tour of the country, he gave some 350 speeches along the way. In town after town, he sharply attacked what he called "that do-nothing, good-for-nothing, worst Congress" for rejecting his Fair Deal legislation.

Truman Stages an Upset

On Election Day experts still expected Dewey to win. Expectations for a Republican victory were so great that on the evening of the election—before many votes were counted—the *Chicago Daily Tribune* newspaper issued a special edition announcing "Dewey Defeats Truman."

The nation was in for a great surprise. When all the ballots were counted, Truman had edged out Dewey by more than 2 million votes in a narrow upset victory. Democrats also regained control of both the House of Representatives and the Senate in the election.

A Fair Deal for Americans

★ Truman took the election results as a sign that Americans wanted reform. He quickly reintroduced the **Fair Deal** legislation he had presented to Congress in 1945. Some of these reform measures passed, but his plan lacked broad support among the American people, and Congress responded by defeating most of the measures. Congress did pass laws to raise the minimum wage, expand Social Security benefits for senior citizens, and provide funds for housing for low-income families.

🕊 Citizenship

A Stand on Civil Rights

In a message to Congress in 1948, President Truman declared:

> ❝We shall not, however, finally achieve the ideals for which this nation was founded so long as any American suffers discrimination as a result of his race, or religion, or color, or the land of origin of his forefathers. ❞

Although Truman championed ending such discrimination, he was unable to persuade Congress to pass legislation that would protect the voting rights of African Americans, abolish the poll tax, and make lynching a federal crime. Still, President Truman did take serious steps to

1948 civil rights button

★ ★ ★ ★ ★ ★ ★

★ **Picturing HISTORY** African Americans welcome Truman to Harlem during his 1948 presidential campaign. **How was Truman successful in advancing civil rights?**

advance the civil rights of African Americans. He ordered federal departments and agencies to end job discrimination against African Americans and ordered the armed forces to **desegregate**—to end the separation of races. The president also instructed the Justice Department to actively enforce existing civil rights laws.

When Truman proposed his domestic agenda to Congress in 1949, he proclaimed that "every segment of our population and every individual has a right to expect from our government a fair deal." Truman asked for the clearance of slums, government-backed medical insurance, higher minimum wages, and more federal money for public schools. Although much of the president's Fair Deal vision went unfulfilled, he made an important start toward improving the lives of millions of Americans.

★ ★ ★ ★ ★ **Section 2 Assessment** ★ ★ ★ ★ ★

Checking for Understanding

1. **Identify** GI Bill of Rights, Taft-Hartley bill, Strom Thurmond, Henry Wallace, Thomas Dewey.
2. **Define** inflation, closed shop.
3. **Describe** the adjustments made in the United States after World War II to convert from a wartime to a peacetime economy.

Reviewing Themes

4. **Economic Factors** What caused inflation after World War II?

Critical Thinking

5. **Determining Cause and Effect** How was the Republican Congress's view of big business reflected in the Taft-Hartley bill?

Activity

Tracking Inflation At your school or public library, ask to see copies of newspapers published 5–10 years ago. Compare the prices of items advertised at that time to the same items today. Calculate the percent of increase in price for each of the products to determine an inflation rate.

1950   1952   1954

June 1950
North Korea invades
South Korea; Truman
sends "police action"
to help South Korea

April 1951
Truman fires
General MacArthur

July 1953
Cease-fire
agreement
is signed

Section 3

The Korean War

READ TO DISCOVER . . .
- what events led to the Korean War.
- how America's war aims changed during the course of the Korean War.
- how the war ended.

TERMS TO LEARN
stalemate   demilitarized zone

The Storyteller

The bitter wind stung the raw faces of 12 U.S. Marine officers. They had just fought for 5 bloody days to lead their troops out of a Chinese trap in the icy wastes of northeast Korea. Now they listened to the words of their commander: "We are going to come out of this as Marines, not as stragglers. We're going to bring out our wounded and our equipment. We're coming out . . . as Marines or not at all." Two more days of fighting followed, as the tired but determined Marines held off fierce enemy attacks. With the arrival of air cover on the third day, the Marines were able to push back the Chinese and make their escape.

Korean service medal

On June 24, 1950, President Truman flew to his home in Independence, Missouri, for a brief vacation. While sitting on his porch on a hot summer night, the president received a telephone call from Secretary of State Dean Acheson. "Mr. President," Acheson said in a grim tone, "I have very serious news. The North Koreans have invaded South Korea." Truman knew this meant only one thing: the United States soon would be involved in military action in Asia.

The Conflict Begins

Before June 1950, few Americans knew much about **Korea,** a small east Asian country located on the Korean Peninsula west of Japan. In 1945 the country was a colony of Japan. At the end of World War II, the United States and the Soviet Union both sent troops into Korea and agreed to occupy it temporarily. They divided the peninsula in half along the **38th parallel** of latitude, with the Soviets controlling North Korea and the Americans controlling South Korea.

The Soviet Union and the United States could not agree on how to unify Korea. When these two nations removed their forces in 1949, Korea remained divided. Tensions between the two Koreas were high.

The Invasion of South Korea

After the American troops pulled out of South Korea, North Korea decided to unify the country by force. On June 25, 1950, the armies of North

Korea crossed the 38th parallel into South Korea. Poorly armed, the South Koreans were no match for the North. Within days the Communist forces had gained control over much of South Korea, including **Seoul,** the capital city.

President Truman reacted quickly to the Korean invasion, which he believed was supported by the Soviet Union. Without asking Congress to actually declare war, Truman ordered the use of limited American air and sea forces in Korea. He called this "police action" necessary to carry out America's policy of containment. Truman said:

> 66 Korea is the Greece of the Far East. If we are tough enough now, if we stand up to them like we did in Greece three years ago, they won't take any next steps. 99

United Nations Responds

At the same time, President Truman asked the UN to send forces to defend the South Koreans. The United Nations condemned the invasion of South Korea and agreed to send a special force to the region under the United States's direction. President Truman quickly appointed General **Douglas MacArthur,** a hero of World War II, to command the UN forces.

On June 30, just days after the North Korean invasion, General MacArthur led American troops into Korea to stop the Communist advance. By the end of 1950, 20 nations were supplying troops or other assistance to the American-led war effort. Even so, Americans made up the majority of troops throughout the Korean War.

The Korean War

⭐ The United Nations had a clear but difficult goal: push the North Koreans back across the 38th parallel. During the course of the war, this goal changed as China intervened in the conflict, and Truman and MacArthur clashed over military strategy.

Early Phases of the War

By September 1950, North Korean forces had pushed all the way to the southern tip of the Korean Peninsula. Only a small area in the southeast around the port city of **Pusan** was still held by the South Korean army.

After joining the South Koreans, General MacArthur designed a bold counterattack against North Korea. In September, United Nations forces

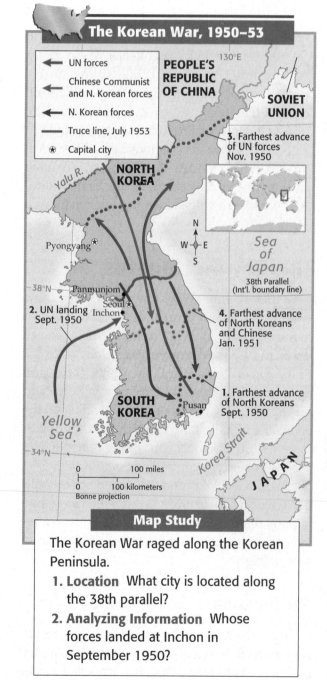

The Korean War, 1950–53

Legend:
- ← UN forces
- ← Chinese Communist and N. Korean forces
- ← N. Korean forces
- — Truce line, July 1953
- ⊛ Capital city

PEOPLE'S REPUBLIC OF CHINA

SOVIET UNION

130°E

Yalu R.

NORTH KOREA

3. Farthest advance of UN forces Nov. 1950

Pyongyang ⊛

Sea of Japan

38°N

Panmunjom

38th Parallel (Int'l. boundary line)

Seoul ⊛

2. UN landing Sept. 1950   Inchon

4. Farthest advance of North Koreans and Chinese Jan. 1951

SOUTH KOREA   Pusan

1. Farthest advance of North Koreans Sept. 1950

Yellow Sea

34°N

Korea Strait

JAPAN

0   100 miles
0   100 kilometers
Bonne projection

Map Study

The Korean War raged along the Korean Peninsula.

1. **Location** What city is located along the 38th parallel?
2. **Analyzing Information** Whose forces landed at Inchon in September 1950?

made a daring landing midway on the Korean Peninsula near the port of **Inchon.** They took that strategic city and moved on to recapture Seoul.

Meanwhile American and UN troops began pushing north from Pusan. By October 1 the North Koreans, caught between UN forces advancing from both Seoul and Pusan, were forced to retreat north across the 38th parallel. South Korea now came under the control of the United Nations forces.

Taking the Offensive

Encouraged by this success, General Mac-Arthur urged President Truman to order an invasion of North Korea. He assured Truman that neither **China** nor the Soviet Union would enter the war to help North Korea, and he promised to have troops "home by Christmas." Truman sought and received approval from the United Nations to cross the 38th parallel, invade the North, and create "a unified, independent and democratic Korea"—a new goal for the war.

After receiving the new orders from Truman, MacArthur moved his forces swiftly northward. The UN forces captured **Pyongyang,** the North Korean capital, on October 19, and then moved north toward the **Yalu River,** part of North Korea's border with China. Total victory seemed just days away.

As the United Nations forces advanced northward, the United States Department of State received a serious warning from the Chinese. If the invasion of North Korea continued, China would send in its army to support the North Koreans. Believing the Chinese warning was a bluff, President Truman allowed MacArthur to continue moving north.

★ **Picturing HISTORY** American troops move forward to the battlefield, while South Korean women and children flee from the Communists. **What was the state of the Korean conflict in 1951?**

The Chinese were not bluffing, however. By late October, thousands of Chinese troops began massing along the border, and some crossed the Yalu River southward into North Korea. On November 26, huge numbers of Chinese troops launched an attack on United Nations forces. Badly outnumbered, the UN forces retreated south back across the 38th parallel. Within weeks, the Communists had recaptured Seoul.

American Leadership Divided

★ By January 1951, United Nations forces managed to stop their retreat. Launching a counteroffensive, they retook Seoul and pushed the Communists back across the 38th parallel. The war now became a **stalemate,** a situation in which neither side was able to gain much ground or achieve a decisive victory. The stalemate lasted for almost two years, with much bitter fighting along the 38th parallel.

F **ootnotes to History**

Like Father, Like Son Douglas MacArthur and his father are the only father and son to have both received the Congressional Medal of Honor. This medal is given only to people who perform extraordinary acts of heroism.

Truman and MacArthur Disagree

As the stalemate dragged on, President Truman began to consider negotiating an end to the fighting. General MacArthur, however, argued that the UN forces should now attack China, either by invading the country or by bombing Chinese troops stationed in North Korea. Truman opposed MacArthur's plan, fearing that such actions would lead to a larger war with China or escalate into another world war.

In a letter to a member of Congress, MacArthur complained that he was being kept from doing his job. "We must win," he wrote. "There is no substitute for victory."

MacArthur Fired

On April 12, 1951, President Truman relieved General MacArthur of his command in Korea. "I could do nothing else and still be president of the United States," Truman concluded. He later wrote:

❝ If I allowed him to defy the civil authorities in this manner, I myself would be violating my oath to uphold and defend the Constitution. ❞

MacArthur's firing created a storm of protest in the United States. The general was extremely popular, and polls showed that a majority of Americans supported him against the president. Moreover, MacArthur did not go quietly. After receiving a hero's welcome on his return to the United States, he delivered a farewell speech to Congress. "Old soldiers never die," he said, "they just fade away."

Ending the Conflict

The two sides in the Korean War began negotiations in July 1951. The talks lasted for two years before a cease-fire agreement was signed on July 27, 1953, during the presidency of Dwight Eisenhower. This agreement ending the war created a demilitarized zone—a region where military forces could not enter—between North and South Korea. The zone extended roughly a mile and a half on either side of the 38th parallel.

The Korean War ended with neither side achieving victory and almost no change in territory. Losses had been great. More than 54,000 Americans died in the war, and another 103,000 were wounded. Nearly 2 million Koreans and Chinese lost their lives, and large portions of North and South Korea were devastated.

America's involvement in the Korean War sent a clear message to the Soviet Union: The United States was committed to fighting Communist expansion with money, arms, and even lives.

Section 3 Assessment

Checking for Understanding
1. **Identify** 38th parallel, Seoul, Douglas MacArthur, Pyongyang.
2. **Define** stalemate, demilitarized zone.
3. **Summarize** Truman's actions after he heard that South Korea had been invaded.

Reviewing Themes
4. **Government and Democracy** How did American goals change during the course of the Korean War?

Critical Thinking
5. **Making Critical Judgments** Do you think Truman should have allowed MacArthur to attack China? Why or why not?

Writing an Editorial Write a one-page editorial in which you argue whether a United States military leader should or should not be able to override a president's decision.

1947
House Un-American Activities Committee holds hearings

1950
Congress passes the McCarran Act

1953
The Rosenbergs are executed as spies

1954
McCarthy is censured

Section 4

The Red Scare

READ TO DISCOVER . . .
■ what effect cold war fears had on domestic politics.
■ how McCarthyism affected the country.

TERMS TO LEARN
subversion   allege
blacklist   censure
perjury

The Storyteller

In 1947, a congressional committee held public hearings on the alleged Communist influence in the Hollywood film industry. Many witnesses called before the committee were asked the same questions: "Are you now or have you ever been a member of the Communist Party?" Two witnesses denied having Communist ties, but 10 others refused to give a straight "yes" or "no" answer. In dramatic moments worthy of the movies, these "Hollywood Ten" challenged the committee's right to ask about their political beliefs. One of the accused yelled, "This is the beginning of an American concentration camp!"

"Red Scare" literature

The cold war intensified Americans' fears of Communist subversion, or sabotage. Stories of stolen government documents and spy rings gripped the country in the late 1940s. Then in 1949 Americans learned that the Soviet Union had built its own atomic bomb.

Many Americans worried that Communist spies and sympathizers—people friendly to Communists, or "Reds" as they were known—had penetrated all levels of American society and were attempting to weaken the government. This **Red Scare** dominated the nation's politics for years and led to a massive hunt to uncover Communists across the country. In this climate of fear, few Americans were safe from accusations of disloyalty—not even the president.

Cold War Fears

★ Republican critics began accusing President Truman of being too easy on Communists. In 1947 Truman responded by ordering an investigation into the loyalty of all federal employees. More than 6 million government workers had to undergo security checks, and 14,000 were investigated by the FBI. Although the investigations found little evidence of espionage, many federal employees lost their jobs.

Loyalty Oaths

Many state and local governments, colleges and universities, businesses, and other institutions began similar campaigns to uncover Communist

★ **Picturing HISTORY** On April 5, 1951, Ethel and Julius Rosenberg were convicted of spying for the Soviet Union. **How did the government, universities, and businesses try to uncover Communist subversion?**

subversion. Some organizations required individuals to sign oaths swearing their loyalty to the United States. Those who refused risked losing their jobs.

In 1950 Congress passed the **McCarran Act,** which required all Communist organizations to register with the government and to provide lists of members. President Truman vetoed the act. "In a free country, we punish men for crimes they commit," he said, "but never for the opinions they hold." Congress overrode his veto.

Un-American Activities

In 1947 a congressional committee, the **House Un-American Activities Committee** (HUAC), began investigating Communist subversion in the nation. In widely publicized hearings, the committee questioned people about their knowledge of Communists or Communist sympathizers. Individuals came under suspicion because of the beliefs of their friends or coworkers—guilt by association. The committee's activities fueled an anti-Communist hysteria in the nation.

Footnotes to History

"Witch" Trials In his 1953 play *The Crucible*, playwright Arthur Miller wrote about the witch trials in Salem, Massachusetts, in the 1600s. Despite its seventeenth-century setting, the play was widely recognized as referring to the anti-Communist fervor of the McCarthy era.

HUAC launched a sensational investigation of the Hollywood film industry, rumored to be full of Communists. A number of those who were summoned refused to testify, and several screenwriters and directors—the "Hollywood Ten"—went to jail for refusing to answer questions about their political beliefs or those of their colleagues. Reacting to public and government pressure, film companies created blacklists—lists of individuals whose loyalty was suspicious—that barred people from working in Hollywood.

American Spies Revealed

In 1948 **Whittaker Chambers,** a magazine editor, volunteered to testify before HUAC. After admitting that he had spied for the Soviet Union in the 1930s, Chambers accused **Alger Hiss,** a former State Department official, of giving him secret government documents in 1937 and 1938 to pass on to the Soviets.

Hiss denied the charges. Chambers produced secret State Department papers he claimed were written by Hiss and microfilm of other secret documents. Chambers swore that he had received the microfilm (which was hidden in a pumpkin in his garden) from Hiss. Investigators could not prosecute Hiss for spying because too much time had passed since the events in the case had occurred. However, he was found guilty of perjury, or lying, and sent to prison.

The most dramatic spy case to come before HUAC involved the atomic bomb. **Julius and Ethel Rosenberg,** a New York couple who were members of the Communist Party, were accused of plotting to pass secret information about the atomic bomb to the Soviet Union. Brought to trial in 1951, the Rosenbergs were convicted and sentenced to death. The judge in the case declared their crime "worse than murder."

Groups around the world protested the sentence as a gross injustice, but higher courts upheld the death sentence decision. Executed in 1953, the Rosenbergs maintained their innocence to the end and claimed that they were persecuted because of their political beliefs.

McCarthyism

From 1950 to 1954, the hunt for Communists in America was dominated by Senator **Joseph McCarthy** of Wisconsin. During those years, McCarthy publicly attacked many people alleged—declared without proof—to be Communists. His unfounded accusations destroyed the careers of numerous innocent Americans and heightened the atmosphere of anti-Communist hysteria in the country. A new word was coined, *McCarthyism,* which meant the use of unproved accusations against political opponents.

Biography

The Rise of McCarthy

Joseph McCarthy rose to national attention almost overnight. In a speech in Wheeling, West Virginia, in February 1950, he announced that America had been betrayed by the "traitorous actions" of certain individuals. Raising a sheet of paper, he claimed to have in his hand "a list of 205 State Department employees who were members of the Communist Party." Millions of Americans believed McCarthy's charges.

Over the next four years, McCarthy continued to accuse government officials and others of being Communists. His congressional subcommittee attacked and bullied the people it called to testify. Many federal employees resigned or were dismissed as a result of McCarthy's investigations. Even the most powerful government

Causes and Effects

CAUSES

★ The Soviet Union expands into Eastern Europe.
★ Communism extends into Western Europe, the Middle East, and Asia.
★ Western governments fear Soviet aggression.

The Cold War

EFFECTS

★ United States aids anti-Communist forces in Greece, Turkey, and Western Europe.
★ Berlin airlift ends Soviet blockade.
★ Western powers form NATO. Communist nations form the Warsaw Pact.
★ Korean War erupts.
★ Americans fear Communist influence at home.
★ U.S.–Soviet arms race develops.

Chart Study

The cold war pitted the Soviet Union and its satellites against the United States and its allies.
Analyzing Information What organization did Western powers form?

officials hesitated to oppose him. Senator **Margaret Chase Smith** of Maine did speak up, however. In an attack on McCarthy's tactics in June 1950, she declared:

❝ Those of us who shout the loudest about Americanism in making character assassinations are all too frequently those who . . . ignore some of the basic principles of Americanism: the right to criticize, the right to hold unpopular beliefs, the right to protest, the right of independent thought. ❞

McCarthy often targeted Democrats. He and his Republican colleagues in Congress saw anti-communism as an important issue to use against the Democratic Party. Some Republican candidates for Congress, including **Richard Nixon,** successfully smeared their opponents with charges of being soft on communism. Such tactics worked because so many Americans were terrified of the Soviet Union and the threat of communism.

McCarthy's Downfall

In 1954 McCarthy launched an investigation of the United States Army. He made alarming claims that Communists had infiltrated the military. In a series of televised hearings, watched by millions of Americans, McCarthy hurled wild accusations at highly respected army officials.

The televised Army-McCarthy Hearings proved the turning point in the McCarthy investigations. For weeks Americans witnessed McCarthy's sneering and cruel attacks. Toward the end of the hearings, **Joseph Welch,** an attorney for the army, said to McCarthy:

❝ Until this moment, Senator, I think I never really gauged your cruelty or your recklessness. . . . Have you left no sense of decency? ❞

Many Americans now came to view McCarthy as a cruel bully who had little basis for his

★ **Picturing HISTORY** This 1950 political cartoon shows McCarthy spreading charges of disloyalty and damaging American ideals. **What event brought about McCarthy's downfall?**

accusations. Congress also turned against McCarthy. In December 1954, the Senate voted to censure, or formally criticize, him for "conduct unbecoming a senator." Censure and the loss of public support ended McCarthy's influence. Yet during the years when fears of communism had raged in the country, McCarthyism had damaged the lives of many innocent people.

Section 4 Assessment

★ ★ ★ ★ ★ ★ ★ ★ ★ ★

Checking for Understanding
1. *Identify* Red Scare, Whittaker Chambers, Alger Hiss, Julius and Ethel Rosenberg, Joseph McCarthy, Richard Nixon.
2. *Define* subversion, blacklist, perjury, allege, censure.
3. *Describe* the aim of loyalty oaths.

Reviewing Themes
4. **Individual Action** What negative effects did McCarthy's anti-Communist

actions have on American society?

Critical Thinking
5. **Drawing Conclusions** What part of the Constitution is supposed to protect Americans from laws such as the McCarran Act?

Drawing a Political Cartoon Draw a political cartoon that focuses on the effect Senator Joseph McCarthy had on the American people.

Using E-Mail

When people share information, thoughts, and feelings with others, they are communicating. *Telecommunication* refers to communicating at a distance through the use of a telephone, video, or computer. How can you get your own computer to "talk" with other computers?

Learning the Skill

A computer is ready for telecommunication after two parts are added to it. The first is a piece of hardware called a *modem*. A modem is a device that enables computers to communicate with each other through telephone lines.

The second part is *communications software*, which lets your computer prepare and send information to the modem. It also lets your computer receive and understand the information it receives from the modem.

Electronic mail, or "E-mail" for short, is one way of sending and receiving messages electronically. Anyone who is part of an E-mail network can send and receive private messages.

If you are on an E-mail network you have a specific address. This address identifies the location of your electronic "mailbox"—the place where you receive your E-mail. To send an E-mail message to another person you must include that person's E-mail address, just as you might address an envelope.

Many corporations are using E-mail communications, which makes some environmentalists happier. More electronic communication means less use of paper and more saved trees.

Practicing the Skill

To send a message to a friend on an E-mail network, complete the following steps.
- Select the "message" function from your communications software.
- Type in your message—and proofread it for errors.
- Type in an E-mail address and select the "send" button.

The E-mail system places the message in the receiver's "mailbox." He or she can read the message at any time—and then send you a return message.

Applying the Skill

Using E-Mail Many intriguing spy novels were written during the Red Scare. Use E-mail to contact a librarian. Ask for recommendations of young adult books related to the Red Scare or the cold war era.

Assessment and Activities

⭐ Reviewing Key Terms

On graph paper, create a word search puzzle using the following terms. Crisscross the terms vertically and horizontally, then fill in the remaining squares with extra letters. Use the terms' definitions as clues to find the words in the puzzle. Share your puzzle with a classmate.

iron curtain   stalemate

containment   subversion

airlift   blacklist

cold war   perjury

inflation   allege

closed shop   censure

demilitarized zone

⭐ Reviewing Key Facts

1. Why was communism attractive to some European countries after the war?
2. Why did many labor unions strike after the war?
3. Which of Truman's Fair Deal reforms were approved by Congress?
4. What was the outcome of the conflict in Korea?
5. What was the purpose of the House Un-American Activities Committee?

⭐ Critical Thinking

Identifying Central Issues

After World War II, Joseph Stalin, leader of the Soviet Union, began to cut his ties with the West.

1. What was the first sign that Stalin was not going to cooperate with Western nations after the war?
2. According to most Americans, what was the Soviet Union's main ambition after the war?

⭐ Time Line Activity

Create a time line on which you place the following events in chronological order.

- The Taft-Hartley bill is passed
- Berlin blockade stops traffic through East Germany to West Berlin
- United Nations is established
- Communists take control of China
- Korean War begins
- Senate censures Joseph McCarthy

⭐ Reviewing Themes

1. **Global Connections** What was the purpose of the Truman Doctrine?
2. **Economic Factors** How did the GI Bill of Rights affect inflation?
3. **Government and Democracy** How did Truman exercise his power as commander in chief of the United States military during the Korean War?
4. **Individual Action** In addition to a fear of communism, what other motivation did Senator McCarthy have for his actions?

⭐ Skill Practice Activity

Using E-Mail

Using your communications software, type a message asking people who grew up during the 1950s for their memories of Harry S Truman, Douglas MacArthur, or the Korean War.

1. What do the people remember?
2. How did people feel about American involvement in the war between North and South Korea?
3. How did civilians feel about Truman firing MacArthur?
4. How did soldiers feel about it? Share your responses with the rest of the class.

★ Geography Activity

Study the map below, then answer the questions that follow.

The Occupation of Berlin

EAST BERLIN

WEST BERLIN

Tegel

Spree R.

Gatow

Tempelhof

Allied Sectors in Berlin

- British
- American
- French
- Russian
- ✈ Airports

0 — 5 miles
0 — 5 kilometers
Miller projection

1. **Region** Among what four countries was Berlin divided?
2. **Place** What country or countries occupied East Berlin?
3. **Place** What country or countries occupied West Berlin?
4. **Location** What is unusual about the location of the airports in Berlin? Explain your reasoning.

★ Technology Activity

Using the Internet Search the Internet for information about how the United Nations is organized. Design a flowchart or graphic organizer that shows the names of each of the main bodies of the UN and how they are related to each other.

★ Cooperative Activity

History and Citizenship The GI Bill provided many benefits to soldiers returning from World War II. Through these benefits Americans who thought they could never go to college or own their own homes could now achieve these goals. Organize into four groups to explore the incentives offered today for people who join the United States Army, Navy, Marines, and Coast Guard. Use the list of questions that follow to guide your group's research.

- Is attending college or another institution of extended learning still an option?
- What kinds of economic incentives are offered to recruits?
- What advantages are awarded to those joining the armed services today that were not available at the end of World War II?

Use your information to design a recruitment plan to attract people to a particular branch of the service. Include all forms of media in your plan such as billboards, newspaper ads, radio, and television.

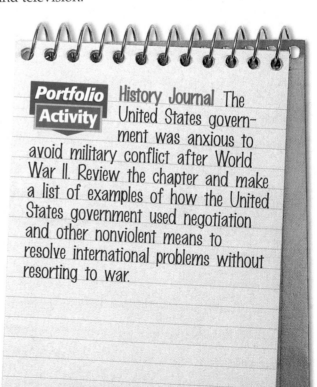

Portfolio Activity History Journal The United States government was anxious to avoid military conflict after World War II. Review the chapter and make a list of examples of how the United States government used negotiation and other nonviolent means to resolve international problems without resorting to war.

1953–1960

America in the Fifties

★ Why It's Important

The prosperity of the 1950s raised questions that remain important in American society today. First, can a period of economic growth bring benefits to all Americans—or are some groups likely to be excluded? Second, can the nation's economic growth be guided by cultural and social values—or does growth occur at the expense of those values? Americans in the 1950s discussed these issues and still debate them today.

★ Chapter Themes

- *Section 1,* Economic Factors
- *Section 2,* Science and Technology
- *Section 3,* Continuity and Change
- *Section 4,* Groups and Institutions

PRIMARY SOURCES
Library   *See pages 990–991 for primary source readings to accompany Chapter 28*

★ **HISTORY AND ART**   *Happy New Year* **by Ben Prins** The 1950s was a unique period in American life. Steady economic growth and new technology gave birth to new forms of leisure for many Americans.

1950	1955	1960

1952
Eisenhower is
elected president

1953
Oveta Culp Hobby
heads HEW

1956
Congress passes
the Federal
Highway Act

1959
Alaska and
Hawaii enter
the Union

Section 1

Eisenhower's Domestic Policy

READ TO DISCOVER . . .

- why Republicans won the election of 1952.
- what beliefs and policies characterized Eisenhower Republicanism.

TERMS TO LEARN

moderate   surplus

Storyteller

"He merely has to smile at you, and you trust him at once." These words were used to describe Dwight D. Eisenhower, Republican presidential candidate in 1952. Eisenhower had an appeal that went far beyond his party label. His performance in World War II had made him an unquestioned hero in the eyes of almost every American. Above all, his personality and political style made many people feel safe, comfortable, and confident.

MAMIE
FOR
FIRST LADY

*Campaign button
and woman's compact*

By 1952 Harry S Truman faced widespread dissatisfaction with his presidency. Many Americans were frustrated over the stalemated war in Korea and worried about reports of Communist subversion in government. As Truman's popularity sank, Republicans saw a chance to recapture the White House.

Republican Revival

⭐ To the Democrats' relief, Truman decided not to run for reelection. The Democrats nominated the respected governor of Illinois, **Adlai E. Stevenson,** for president and Senator John J. Sparkman of Alabama as his running mate.

To head their presidential ticket, the Republicans chose General **Dwight D. Eisenhower**—the popular World War II hero. For vice president, the Republicans selected **Richard M. Nixon,** a young senator from California who had won fame as a tough opponent of communism.

📖 Biography

Soldier Turned Politician

Born in Texas and raised in rural Kansas, Dwight D. Eisenhower graduated from the United States Military Academy at West Point. He rose steadily through the army to become supreme

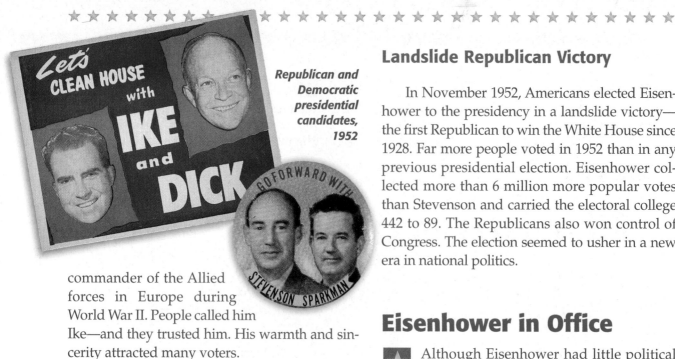

Republican and Democratic presidential candidates, 1952

commander of the Allied forces in Europe during World War II. People called him Ike—and they trusted him. His warmth and sincerity attracted many voters.

Eisenhower's steadiness made Americans feel secure. He won wide support with his pledge to "bring the Korean War to an early and honorable end. If that job requires a personal trip to Korea," he declared, "I shall make that trip."

A Brief Crisis

The Republicans faced a brief crisis during the presidential campaign when the story broke that Richard Nixon had accepted political gifts from supporters. Nixon went on television to defend himself in what came to be known as the "Checkers" speech. He proclaimed that he had done nothing wrong and had kept only one gift—his family dog, Checkers. The speech won broad support for Nixon, persuading Eisenhower to keep him on the ticket.

The Democratic Candidate

Intelligent and often witty, Adlai Stevenson became a target of the Republican Party. Nixon unleashed harsh attacks on Stevenson, charging him with being "soft" on communism. Republicans claimed Stevenson was more concerned with intellectual matters than with practical matters. They said that he questioned too many things and lacked the decisiveness needed to combat communism.

Landslide Republican Victory

In November 1952, Americans elected Eisenhower to the presidency in a landslide victory—the first Republican to win the White House since 1928. Far more people voted in 1952 than in any previous presidential election. Eisenhower collected more than 6 million more popular votes than Stevenson and carried the electoral college 442 to 89. The Republicans also won control of Congress. The election seemed to usher in a new era in national politics.

Eisenhower in Office

★ Although Eisenhower had little political experience, he proved to be an effective politician. During his two terms in office, Eisenhower followed a moderate, or middle-of-the-road, approach to domestic policy. He described himself as "conservative when it comes to money and liberal when it comes to human beings."

Eisenhower helped steer the country on a steady course. He avoided ambitious new government programs but resisted the pressure to abolish popular older ones and sometimes even expanded them. As he once told reporters:

> 66 I feel pretty good when I'm attacked from both sides. It makes me more certain I'm on the right track. 99

Economic Policy

President Eisenhower wanted to make the federal government "smaller rather than bigger." He supported economic policies aimed at limiting government spending and encouraging private enterprise. With the support of Republicans and conservative Democrats in Congress, the president removed the wage and price controls that the Truman administration had established during the Korean War. He also managed to transfer some authority in financial matters to the states and to make some cuts in government spending. When he left office in 1961, the federal budget had a surplus, or excess, of $300 million.

The Nation Expands

The greatest domestic program of the Eisenhower presidency involved building a network of interstate highways. In June 1956 Congress passed the **Federal Highway Act** to provide easy transportation for military forces in case of an attack. The law funded the construction of more than 40,000 miles (64,000 km) of highways that tied the nation together. The highway program—the largest public works program in the nation's history—also spurred growth in many areas of the nation's economy, including the automobile and oil industries.

The nation itself also grew during Eisenhower's presidency. In 1959 **Alaska** and **Hawaii** entered the Union, bringing the number of states to 50. Alaska and Hawaii became the only states not bordering on the other states.

Social Programs

Eisenhower believed that government should protect the basic welfare of Americans. He refused to tamper with Social Security and other New Deal social programs. During his presidency, Eisenhower agreed to extend Social Security benefits to 10 million more people and to provide unemployment insurance to 4 million more Americans. He also approved greater funding for

Stars and Stripes Today Statehood for **Alaska and Hawaii brought the number of stars to 50 (its current number) in the flag of 1960.**

public housing and, in 1955, Eisenhower agreed to an increase in the minimum wage from 75 cents an hour to $1.00.

The creation of the **Department of Health, Education, and Welfare** (HEW) in 1953 confirmed the government's role in helping Americans meet their basic social needs. Eisenhower named **Oveta Culp Hobby** as the first secretary of the new department. Hobby was only the second woman in American history to hold a cabinet post.

Eisenhower's moderation and leadership won the approval of a majority of Americans. In the 1956 presidential election, he ran against Democrat Adlai Stevenson again. This time Eisenhower won by an even bigger margin, receiving more than 57 percent of the popular vote.

★ ★ ★ ★ ★ Section 1 Assessment ★ ★ ★ ★ ★

Checking for Understanding

1. ***Identify*** Adlai E. Stevenson, Dwight D. Eisenhower, Richard M. Nixon, Federal Highway Act, Oveta Culp Hobby.
2. ***Define*** moderate, surplus.
3. ***Name*** the two states added to the Union while Eisenhower was president.

Reviewing Themes

4. **Economic Factors** What public works program spurred growth in the automotive and oil industries?

Critical Thinking

5. **Analyzing Primary Sources** How did Eisenhower's domestic policy reflect his belief that he was "conservative when it comes to money and liberal when it comes to human beings"?

Activity

Drawing a Cartoon Draw a cartoon describing the phrase *middle-of-the-road* as it applies to politics.

1957	1958	1959	1960

1957
The Soviets launch *Sputnik*

1958
NASA launches the *Explorer*

1959
Fidel Castro takes over Cuba

1960
Soviets shoot down U.S. U-2 plane

Section 2

Eisenhower and the Cold War

READ TO DISCOVER . . .

- what characterized American foreign policy under President Eisenhower.
- what foreign policy challenges the Eisenhower administration faced.

TERMS TO LEARN

arms race
domino theory

summit
peaceful coexistence

The Storyteller

On October 4, 1957, millions of Americans heard startling news: the Soviets had launched a satellite known as *Sputnik.* That evening, Lyndon B. Johnson took a walk on his Texas ranch. His eyes focused on the clear night sky for any sign of the Soviet spacecraft. "In the Open West you learn to live closely with the sky," Johnson wrote later. "It is a part of your life. But now, somehow, in some new way, the sky seemed almost alien. . . ."

Card game

On October 4, 1957, the Soviet Union stunned the world with an announcement that it had sent into space the world's first artificial satellite—called *Sputnik.* A month later, the Soviets successfully launched a second satellite.

Americans read the news with horror and awe. They feared that the United States was lagging behind the Soviets in scientific knowledge. They also feared that the Soviets could launch atomic weapons against America from space.

Worry turned to embarrassment in December 1957, when the United States tried to launch its own space satellite—*Vanguard.* Hundreds of reporters and spectators watched the rocket rise a few feet off the launching pad—and then explode. The foreign press made fun of the launch, calling it "Flopnik" and "Stayputnik." American prestige declined.

United States–Soviet Rivalry

⭐ During the 1950s the United States–Soviet rivalry kept the cold war at the center of American foreign policy. The Eisenhower administration continued to oppose the spread of communism. At the same time, the president looked for ways to keep American-Soviet tensions from erupting into open conflict.

New Foreign Policy

Secretary of State **John Foster Dulles** became Eisenhower's most important foreign policy adviser. Dulles condemned the containment policy of the Truman administration. Eisenhower and Dulles proposed a new, bolder policy. If the Soviet Union attacked any nation, the United States would launch **massive retaliation**—an instant nuclear attack. Vice President Nixon explained:

> 66 Rather than let the Communists nibble us to death all over the world in little wars, we will rely in the future on massive mobile retaliatory [attacking] powers. 99

Dulles believed that the United States had to use threats to push the Soviets to the brink of war before they would agree to anything. Critics called this tough stance "brinkmanship." The more cautious Eisenhower, however, almost always avoided taking crises to "the brink."

By relying more on nuclear weapons, the Eisenhower administration could reduce other areas of defense, such as the size of the army and the arsenal of **conventional,** or non-nuclear, weapons. These reductions would allow Eisenhower to cut the military budget. As Secretary of Defense Charles Wilson explained, nuclear weapons gave the United States "more bang for the buck."

The Arms Race

Despite Eisenhower's intentions, defense spending increased again. The policy of massive retaliation—and Soviet efforts to counter it—produced a nuclear arms race. Both the United States and the Soviet Union built more and more weapons in an effort to surpass the other's military strength.

The superpowers built immensely destructive hydrogen bombs—nuclear weapons that were many times more powerful than atomic bombs. They developed a variety of guided missiles capable of delivering nuclear warheads. The **intermediate-range ballistic missile** (IRBM) could

★ **Picturing HISTORY** During the 1950s, the intercontinental ballistic missile (ICBM) became part of the arsenals of the United States and the Soviet Union. **Why were missiles developed?**

reach targets up to 1,500 miles (2,414 km) away. The **intercontinental ballistic missile** (ICBM) had a range of many thousands of miles. Soon both sides had massive nuclear arsenals capable of destroying the other side many times over.

As the arms race continued, Americans began preparing for a nuclear attack. The federal **Civil Defense Administration** educated the public with pamphlets and radio and television messages. Some families built air-raid shelters in their basements or backyards. Schools held air-raid drills. One student described his school's air-raid drill: "Students lie on the floor and stick their heads under the lockers." He later recalled that he believed this would make him safe during a nuclear attack.

Competing in Space

The Soviet launch of *Sputnik* and the *Vanguard* failure led America to develop its own space program. Federal money poured into the **National Aeronautics and Space Administration (NASA),** the new government agency in charge of the space program. When the United States succeeded in launching the *Explorer* satellite in January 1958, the Associated Press reported:

66 The missile took off in a beautiful launching. It rose slowly at first in a huge splash of flame with a roar that could be heard for miles. . . . 99

The **space race** had begun, and the United States soon began pulling ahead. **Project Mercury** was the nation's first program to put an astronaut in space. Along with its commitment to space exploration and scientific research, the government also encouraged science education by providing more funds for the teaching of science and technology in the nation's schools.

Foreign Policy Challenges

★ With the stakes in the nuclear arms race so high, the United States and the Soviet Union had to act carefully. A minor crisis, badly managed, could lead to all-out war.

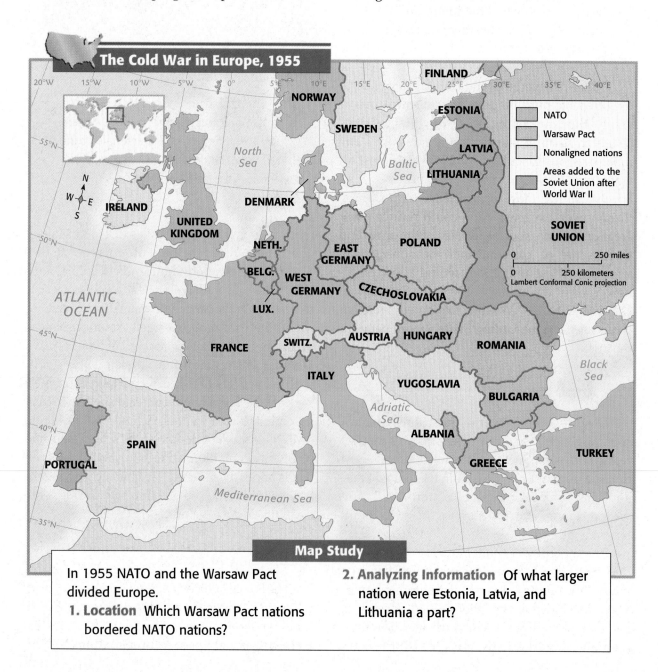

The Cold War in Europe, 1955

	NATO
	Warsaw Pact
	Nonaligned nations
	Areas added to the Soviet Union after World War II

Map Study

In 1955 NATO and the Warsaw Pact divided Europe.

1. Location Which Warsaw Pact nations bordered NATO nations?

2. Analyzing Information Of what larger nation were Estonia, Latvia, and Lithuania a part?

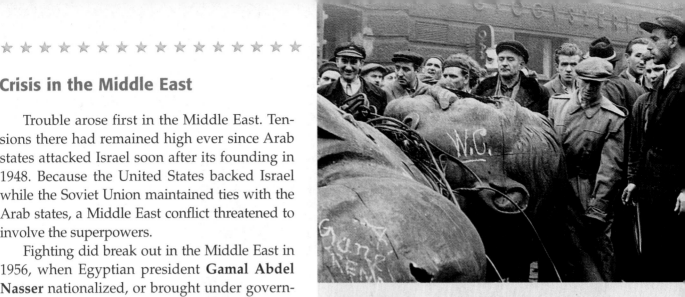

Crisis in the Middle East

Trouble arose first in the Middle East. Tensions there had remained high ever since Arab states attacked Israel soon after its founding in 1948. Because the United States backed Israel while the Soviet Union maintained ties with the Arab states, a Middle East conflict threatened to involve the superpowers.

Fighting did break out in the Middle East in 1956, when Egyptian president **Gamal Abdel Nasser** nationalized, or brought under government control, the **Suez Canal** from British control. Great Britain and France feared that Nasser might close the canal and cut off shipments of oil between the Middle East and Western Europe. In October, the two European powers invaded Egypt. Great Britain and France hoped to overthrow Nasser and seize the canal. Israel, angered by repeated Arab attacks along its borders, agreed to help by invading Egypt.

The United States immediately sponsored a United Nations resolution calling for British and French withdrawal from Egypt. The Soviets threatened rocket attacks on British and French cities. In the face of this pressure, the three nations pulled out of Egypt. United Nations forces were sent to patrol the Egyptian-Israeli border.

Uprising in Hungary

Another crisis erupted that fall in Europe. In October 1956, students and workers demonstrated in **Budapest,** the capital of **Hungary,** for changes in the government. Strikes and riots soon spread throughout the country. A new government came to power and demanded withdrawal of all Soviet troops from Hungary. Early in

★ **Picturing HISTORY** Hungarians topple a statue of Soviet dictator Joseph Stalin during demonstrations in 1956. **How did the Hungarian uprising end?**

November, Soviet tanks and troops poured into Hungary and crushed the revolt. Hungarian rebels appealed to the United States for help. President Eisenhower condemned the Soviet crackdown and aided Hungarian refugees but did not intervene.

War in Southeast Asia

Another trouble spot appeared in Southeast Asia, in France's former colony of **Vietnam.** In the early 1950s, the United States gave France billions of dollars in military aid to help it fight the **Vietminh,** nationalist rebels led by Communist leader **Ho Chi Minh.**

In spite of American aid, the French soon faced defeat. In March 1954, Vietminh forces trapped 25,000 French troops at the French base of **Dien Bien Phu.** The French pleaded with the United States to send American forces, but Eisenhower refused. The Korean War was still fresh in his memory. "I can conceive of no greater tragedy," he said, "than for the United States to become engaged in all-out war in Indochina."

Without American troops, the French were forced to surrender in May. Soon after, French and Vietminh representatives in **Geneva,** Switzerland, negotiated a cease-fire agreement. The agreement, known as the **Geneva Accords,** temporarily divided Vietnam. The Vietminh

---

*F*ootnotes to History

Bomb Goes Airborne On May 21, 1956, the world's first airborne hydrogen bomb was exploded. This explosion was part of a new series of nuclear tests in the Pacific conducted by the U.S. Atomic Energy Commission.

During a 1959 visit to the Soviet Union, Vice President Nixon (center) debates issues with Soviet premier Khrushchev (left front) at the American Exhibition in Moscow. **What incident in 1960 ended hopes for a "thaw" between the two superpowers?**

controlled the north, while other Vietnamese—more friendly to the French—held the south. The accords also arranged for the withdrawal of all French troops and called for free elections in a reunited Vietnam in 1956.

Eisenhower believed that if one nation in Asia fell to the Communists, others would also fall, one after the other. He described the danger in what came to be called the domino theory:

❝ You have a row of dominoes set up. You knock over the first one, and what will happen to the last one is that it will go over very quickly. ❞

To keep South Vietnam from becoming the first domino, the United States aided its anti-Communist government, even though the rulers had little support among the people. In another step to defend against Communist aggression, the United States helped to create the **Southeast Asia Treaty Organization** (SEATO) in 1954. The United States, Great Britain, France, New Zealand, Australia, the Philippines, Pakistan, and Thailand made up the alliance. The nations pledged joint action against any aggressor.

Troubles in Latin America

The Eisenhower administration also faced Communist challenges in Latin America. In 1954 the **Central Intelligence Agency** (CIA) helped overthrow the government of Jacobo Arbenz in **Guatemala,** which some American leaders feared was leaning toward communism. Latin Americans resented the intervention in Guatemala, criticizing what they considered "Yankee imperialism." Growing anti-American feelings began to erode the Good Neighbor Policy established in the 1930s.

Anti-American feeling became a part of the growing revolutionary movement in **Cuba.** Following the overthrow of dictator Fulgencio Batista (buh•TEES•tuh), rebel leader **Fidel Castro** formed a new government in January 1959. The United States supported Castro at first and welcomed his promise of democratic reforms. But Castro angered Americans when he seized foreign-owned property. His government became a dictatorship and formed close ties with the Soviet Union. During the last days of his presidency in 1961, Eisenhower cut diplomatic ties with Cuba. Relations between the two nations have remained strained ever since.

Cold War "Thaws"

★ When Soviet dictator Joseph Stalin died in 1953, **Nikita Khrushchev** (krush•CHAWF) emerged as the dominant leader. By the mid-1950s, both American and Soviet leaders were interested in easing cold war tensions and improving relations.

The Geneva Summit

In July 1955, Eisenhower, NATO leaders, and Soviet officials met at a summit conference in Geneva, Switzerland. A summit is a meeting of heads of government. The leaders discussed disarmament and German reunification. The meeting produced no specific agreements, but the friendly atmosphere, promptly called the "Spirit of Geneva," renewed hopes for peace.

Peaceful Coexistence

After the Geneva summit, a policy of peaceful coexistence began to emerge. This meant that the two superpowers would compete with one another but would avoid war. Khrushchev proposed to Eisenhower that the two leaders visit each other's country and attend another summit in Paris in 1960. Eisenhower agreed.

Khrushchev's 10-day trip to the United States in 1959 captured world headlines. As the leaders made plans for their next meeting in Paris, Eisenhower hoped to reach agreements on arms control and nuclear test bans.

The U-2 Incident

Hopes of peace fell to earth with an American plane. For years American pilots had flown high-altitude spy planes—U-2s—over Soviet territory to photograph Soviet nuclear sites and military bases. As the Paris summit approached, Eisenhower ordered a final U-2 flight over an area of the Soviet Union that had not been inspected for missile sites.

The Soviets shot down the plane on May 1, 1960 and captured its pilot, Francis Gary Powers. Khrushchev denounced the United States for invading Soviet airspace. Although the Paris summit began as scheduled on May 16, the mood had changed. Hauling along part of the wreckage of the U-2 plane, Khrushchev attacked the United States for the spy flights and called off Eisenhower's trip to the Soviet Union. The summit broke up the next day. The brief "thaw" in the cold war had ended.

Eisenhower's Warning

In his January 1961 Farewell Address to the nation, President Eisenhower issued a warning about the growing influence of the military. The military budget had grown dramatically, he said, and military leaders had allied with business to seek bigger and more expensive weapons. Eisenhower feared that this alliance—a **"military-industrial complex"**—heated the arms race and could "endanger our liberties or democratic processes." In a twist of history, this former army general warned the nation of the growing influence of the military.

★ ★ ★ ★ ★ Section 2 Assessment ★ ★ ★ ★ ★

Checking for Understanding
1. *Identify* Gamal Abdel Nasser, Ho Chi Minh, Dien Bien Phu, Geneva Accords, Fidel Castro, Nikita Khrushchev.
2. *Define* arms race, domino theory, summit, peaceful coexistence.
3. *Explain* why President Eisenhower was willing to send massive aid to Vietnam.

Reviewing Themes
4. **Science and Technology** How did the Soviet launch of *Sputnik* affect science and technology in the United States?

Critical Thinking
5. **Making Comparisons** How did the Eisenhower administration differ with Truman's view of foreign policy?

Activity

Making a Time Line Make a two-level time line tracking the achievements of the United States and Soviet Union in space from 1957 to 1967.

INTERDISCIPLINARY
Activities

The Space Race

When the first humans stood on the moon in 1969, it was a high point in the exploration of space and in the space race between the United States and the Soviet Union. Learn more about the early days of space flight as you complete these out-of-the-world activities.

Art

Picturing Other Worlds Movies and television have given us many pictures of space journeys and alien worlds. Use your imagination to paint a scene from outer space—the sun (or suns) rising on the surface of a distant planet, an alien civilization, or a space station. Use any medium you like—acrylics, watercolor, markers. Give your painting a title and display it in class.

Science

Designing a Science Experiment Most space flights today carry various experiments that test how organisms or machines work in space. Design a biology experiment for astronauts to take into space. Specify the kinds of organisms—plant or animal—that the experiment will involve and the information you hope to gain from it. How will these results be important on Earth? Write a description of your experiment to share with the rest of the class.

Language Arts

Writing Science Fiction Write a science fiction story whose central figure is traveling in space. Your story should focus on this character, not on space aliens or monsters, and explain the purpose of his or her space voyage. Remember to set your story in a specific location and time. Read your story to the class.

School-to-Work

Showing How Rockets Work What propels a rocket? You can demonstrate rocket propulsion with a balloon, a drinking straw, and a long cord. Push the cord through the straw, then anchor both ends of the cord on either side of the room. Blow up the balloon part way, holding the end tightly so air does not escape. Have another person use two pieces of tape to hang the balloon securely from the straw. Blow the balloon up all the way, then let go. Notice how far and how fast it travels along the cord.

Astronaut in space

1947
William Levitt
starts first suburban
development

1955
Polio vaccine
given to
school children

1956
Elvis Presley
gains national
popularity

Section 3

1950s Prosperity

READ TO DISCOVER . . .

- what factors contributed to the booming economy of the 1950s.
- what effect the prosperity of the 1950s had on American society and culture.

TERMS TO LEARN

productivity
standard of living
per capita income

affluence
baby boom

The Storyteller

During the prosperous 1950s, many Americans left the cities to settle in the suburbs, hoping for a better life for themselves and their children. "Suburbia"—with its great distances between home, school, shopping area, and downtown—gradually became not only a place but also a lifestyle. One suburban resident observed: "Before we came here, we used to live pretty much to ourselves. . . . Now we stop around and visit people or they visit us. I really think [suburban living] has broadened us."

1950s children's board game

After World War II, many experts predicted America's economy would level off or decline as production of war goods decreased. Instead, after a few years of adjustment, the economy began to grow rapidly and steadily.

A Booming Economy

From 1945 to 1960, the total value of goods and services produced each year in the United States increased about 250 percent. Some of this amazing growth resulted from the burst of military spending during the Korean War. Government spending on housing, schools, welfare, highways, and veteran benefits also spurred the rapid economic expansion.

Technological advances contributed to economic growth as well. Business, industry, and agriculture adopted new technology and new production methods, resulting in greater productivity—the ability to produce more goods with the same amount of labor. The demand for new technology led to greater investment in research and in the education and training of scientists, engineers, and technicians.

The **computer** represented one of the 1950s' important technological advances. Unlike today's small personal computers, early computers were immense, weighing tons and filling whole rooms. Although first used only by the military and the government, computers soon appeared in large corporations. By 1955 International Business Machines (IBM) was the leader in the field, with orders for 129 of its big computers.

Chapter 28   America in the Fifties   **807**

Higher Incomes

The economic boom of the 1950s raised the standard of living—a measure of people's overall wealth and quality of life—of millions of Americans. Between 1945 and 1960, per capita income—the average income of every individual in the nation—increased 46 percent, from $1,515 to $2,219. By the end of the 1950s, Americans had the highest standard of living in the world.

A Rosy Future

Prosperity and steady economic growth also led to new optimism. Economists began to think it was possible to maintain prosperity and growth permanently. Americans felt confident that the government could, when necessary, take steps to avoid serious recessions, or downturns in the economy.

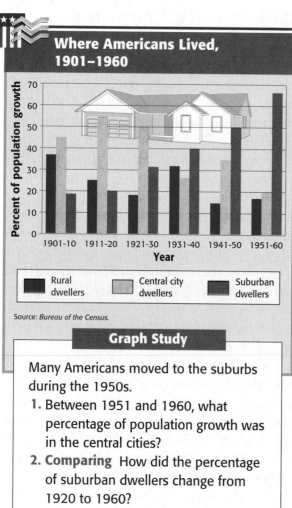

Where Americans Lived, 1901–1960

Source: *Bureau of the Census.*

Graph Study

Many Americans moved to the suburbs during the 1950s.

1. Between 1951 and 1960, what percentage of population growth was in the central cities?
2. **Comparing** How did the percentage of suburban dwellers change from 1920 to 1960?

A Changing Nation

Economic growth and prosperity brought many changes to America. These included a growth in population, increased affluence, or wealth, suburban expansion, and a greater demand for consumer goods.

The Baby Boom

Like the economy, the family enjoyed great growth during the postwar years. During the 1950s the nation's population rose from 150 million to 179 million, an increase of nearly 20 percent. People called the nation's soaring birthrate a baby boom.

Several factors encouraged the baby boom. Couples who had postponed having children during the Depression and World War II started having families. With higher incomes, couples felt they could afford to have more children. In addition, better health care for women and babies, improved nutrition, and medical advances against disease helped reduce the infant death rate.

The baby boom had a powerful impact on society. Many women left the workforce to stay home and raise their children. The demand for baby products and services grew, stimulating the economy. School enrollment soared as the "baby boomers" reached school age, putting a great strain on the educational system.

Medical Advances

By the early 1950s, medical science had made great strides toward combating childhood diseases. Antibiotics and vaccines helped control diseases such as diphtheria, influenza, and typhoid fever. **Polio,** however, continued to baffle the medical profession. Polio became the most feared disease of the postwar period because the disease left many of its victims paralyzed for life. In the mid-1950s, Dr. **Jonas Salk,** an American physician, developed an effective vaccine against polio. After the vaccine was tested, the Salk vaccine was administered to school children beginning in 1955. The threat of polio was almost completely eliminated.

What Was It Like? With greater affluence, everyday life in the 1950s became easier and more comfortable for Americans living in the suburbs. **What leisure activities do you think were popular in 1950s suburban America?**

Expanding Suburbs

During the 1950s, 85 percent of new home construction took place in the **suburbs.** The new suburbs were usually located on the fringes of major cities.

William Levitt introduced mass-produced housing, based on experience he had gained building houses for the navy. He started his first suburban development, called **Levittown,** on Long Island, New York, in 1947. Levittown included more than 17,000 identical houses, built from materials precut and preassembled at a factory and then erected quickly on designated lots. Other builders adopted Levitt's methods or used their own techniques for rapid construction, creating a massive house-building boom.

Suburban housing developments appealed to many Americans. In addition to affordable homes, they offered privacy, isolation from urban problems, space for cars, and a sense of belonging to a community formed by people similar in age, social background, and race.

Though affordable, the suburbs did not offer opportunities for home ownership to everyone. Many American cities had growing populations of middle-class minorities, particularly African American and Hispanic American, who longed to escape the noise and the crime of the cities. However, the developers of the nation's postwar suburbs often refused to sell homes to minorities.

A Nation on Wheels

The car made suburban escape possible. People needed cars to get to work, to go shopping, and to run errands. For suburban families cars were not a luxury but a necessity.

The construction of thousands of miles of new highways in the 1950s encouraged the spread of suburbs. Suburban America became a "car culture" in which life centered on the automobile. Southern California came to symbolize suburban life and this car culture. In California, the drive-in capital of the nation, a person could go to the movies, eat fast food, do banking,

This fleet of diaper service trucks in front of new homes represents two major social trends of the period: the baby boom and the growth of the suburbs. **What factors encouraged the baby boom?**

and even attend religious services without leaving the car. One suburban California woman explained the need for a car:

> 66 I live in Garden Grove, work in Irvine, shop in Santa Ana, go to the dentist in Anaheim, my husband works in Long Beach, and I used to be the president of the League of Women Voters in Fullerton. 99

Air Travel

Americans were also finding it easier to travel by air. The jet engine was perfected in the 1950s, and the first jet-powered commercial aircraft began operation. By the early 1950s, the airliner was on the way to replacing the railroad train and the ocean liner as the preferred transportation for long-distance travel.

A Consumer Society

Americans of the 1950s went on a buying spree. Affluence, the growing variety and quantity of products available, and expanded advertising all played a role in the increased demand for consumer goods. Buying goods became easier, too, with the use of credit cards, charge accounts, and easy-payment plans.

Consumers eagerly sought the latest products—dishwashers, washing machines, television sets, stereos, and clothes made from synthetic fabrics. The growing market for bigger and better cars prompted automakers to outdo one another by manufacturing bigger,

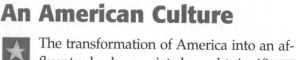

Cereal ad, 1950s

faster, and flashier cars. They came out with new models every year, adding stylish features such as chrome-plated bumpers and soaring tail fins.

The advertising and marketing of products on television, on radio, and in magazines created consumer fads and crazes that swept the nation. In the late 1950s, Americans bought millions of hula hoops—large plastic rings they twirled around their waists. Other popular fads included crew cuts for boys, poodle skirts for girls, and a new snack—pizza.

An American Culture

★ The transformation of America into an affluent suburban society brought significant changes in popular culture. Television came to dominate entertainment, and a new form of popular music burst on the American scene.

Television

In the late 1940s, about 17,000 Americans owned television sets. These large wooden cabinets had small screens that displayed grainy black-and-white images. During the 1950s Americans bought 6 or 7 million sets a year. By the end of the decade, nearly 90 percent of American families had television.

Television profoundly changed American life. It became the main form of entertainment for many people as well as an important source of news and information.

Millions of Americans watched the same programs. Families gathered to watch quiz shows such as *The $64,000 Question*. Children tuned in to programs such as *The Mickey Mouse Club* and *Howdy Doody*. Teens kept up with the latest hit songs on *American Bandstand*. Families followed weekly episodes of *I Love Lucy, Leave It to Beaver*, and *Father Knows Best*. The images shown in many programs—of happy middle-class families in neat middle-class homes—helped shape Americans' expectations for their own lives.

Finally, television had an important effect on the consumer culture. The Davy Crockett stories shown on television led to a national craze for Davy Crockett hats, lunch boxes, and other goods. Television advertising helped create a vast national market for new products and fashions. Some shows—such as the *Philco Television Playhouse*—adopted the names of their sponsors, which brought the sponsors prestige.

Rock 'n' Roll

A new form of music—rock 'n' roll—achieved great popularity in the 1950s. A blending of African American rhythm and blues with country,

TECHNOLOGY AND HISTORY

Jet Travel

The first commercial jet transport, the Boeing 707, made aviation history with its maiden flight July 15, 1954. It could carry more passengers for longer distances than any previous aircraft. **In what ways do you think jet aircraft affected the American economy?**

Fuel tanks held up to 21,000 gallons, allowing the 707 to fly for nearly 5,000 miles before stopping to refuel.

The Boeing 707 could carry up to 179 people in passenger seating.

Rudder

Elevator

On October 26, 1958, Pan American World Airways started the first 707 jet service between New York and Paris.

Flight deck

Aileron

Landing gear

Cargo hold

Flaps

The 4 turbofan **jet engines** powered a cruising speed of 568 mph. (Earlier transports had carried 21 passengers at a speed of 170 mph.)

gospel, and other forms of popular music, rock 'n' roll found a ready audience among teenagers.

Rock 'n' roll grew from the rhythm and blues music that African American musicians had created years before. It often had some elements of country music. In rock 'n' roll, the tempo was quicker and electrically amplified instruments—mostly guitars—were used.

One of the first rock hits, recorded in 1955, was Bill Haley and the Comets' *Rock Around the Clock,* which sold 17 million copies. Adapting the style of African American performers such as Chuck Berry and Little Richard, **Elvis Presley** burst on the national scene in 1956. Presley quickly became known as the king of rock 'n' roll and an idol to millions of young Americans. Many young men copied his ducktail haircut and swaggering manner.

1950s TV

For teenagers, the shared experience of listening to the music helped forge a common identity and bond. The differing attitudes of the older and younger generations toward music, as well as other forms of popular culture, later came to be known as the **generation gap.**

Homes With Television Sets

Source: *Statistical Abstract of the United States.*

Graph Study

During the 1950s electricity consumption more than doubled as Americans purchased more electrical appliances.
1. About how many homes had television sets in 1950?
2. **Comparing** How many more homes had sets in 1960 than in 1954?

Section 3 Assessment

Checking for Understanding
1. *Identify* William Levitt, Elvis Presley.
2. *Define* productivity, standard of living, per capita income, affluence, baby boom.
3. *Describe* two major changes in the United States that resulted from the economic growth and prosperity of the 1950s.

Reviewing Themes
4. **Continuity and Change** Why did suburban life appeal to many Americans?

Critical Thinking
5. **Determining Cause and Effect** Describe the link between television and consumer spending in the 1950s.

Activity

Defining Rock 'n' Roll Paste photographs or drawings on poster board of the musician or musical group that you think represents the best of modern rock 'n' roll. Write captions that include your definition of rock 'n' roll.

1950s

More than 20 percent
of Americans live in
poverty

1950s

"Beat" writers
influence
nonconformists

1950s

Women and African
Americans question
their roles in society

Section 4

Problems in a Time of Plenty

READ TO DISCOVER . . .

■ what groups of Americans did not share in the prosperity of the 1950s.

■ why some people criticized American values of the 1950s.

TERMS TO LEARN

ghetto

automation

materialism

The Storyteller

Picture postcards of New York City in the 1950s showed soaring skyscrapers, sleek passenger jets, and the Statue of Liberty offering promises of a good life. Hidden behind the tall buildings was a very different United States, however. It was a nation of crumbling streets and rat-infested tenements, hungry and, sometimes, homeless people. The "invisible poor" lived in a nation not of affluence and plenty but of desperate need.

THE AFFLUENT SOCIETY

GALBRAITH

*Study of the changing
American society*

In the 1950s more than 20 percent of Americans lived in poverty. Millions more struggled to survive on incomes only slightly above the poverty level. Such poverty marred the landscape of the affluent society.

Rural Poverty

Many farmers did not share in the prosperity of the 1950s. Huge crop surpluses during those years caused the prices of farm products—and thus farm income—to decline dramatically.

Large business enterprises bought vast areas of available farmland. They used large sums of money to transform agriculture into a thriving business. New machines and chemicals helped produce an abundance of food for American and foreign consumers.

While some farmers benefited from these changes, others suffered. Because small farms could not compete with large farms, many small-farm families sold their land and migrated to urban areas. Thousands of small farmers who remained in agriculture struggled to stay out of poverty.

Farmworkers suffered as well. In the South, African American sharecroppers and tenant farmers had always struggled to survive. Their problems increased when mechanized cotton pickers replaced workers. The popularity of synthetic

★ Picturing HISTORY
Poverty affected families in urban and rural America. Families like the Sturgills of Mayking, Kentucky, (right) worked hard but struggled to make ends meet. Children play in the streets of a Washington, D.C., ghetto, not far from the Capitol (far left). **About what percentage of Americans in the 1950s lived in poverty?**

fibers reduced the demand for cotton. Southern farmworkers lost their jobs, cotton production fell, and thousands of farmers lost their land. Migrant farmworkers in the West and the Southwest—mostly Mexican Americans and Asian Americans—also suffered. They toiled long hours for very low wages and lived in substandard housing.

Rural poverty did not always come from agricultural problems. In **Appalachia,** a region stretching along the Appalachian Mountains through several states, the decline of the coal industry plunged thousands of rural mountain people into desperate poverty.

Urban Poverty

As increasing numbers of middle-class Americans moved to the suburbs in the 1950s, they left the poor behind. The inner cities became islands of poverty. To these islands people still came looking for work. Continuing their migration from rural areas of the South, more than 3 million African Americans moved to cities in the North and the Midwest between 1940 and 1960. Many poor Hispanics—Puerto Ricans in the East and Mexicans in the Southwest and the West—also moved to American cities.

The migration of poor African Americans and Hispanics to Northern cities hastened the departure of whites to the suburbs. This "white flight" turned some areas of cities into ghettos—neighborhoods inhabited mainly by poor minority groups.

Urban Unemployment

Few good job opportunities existed for the growing numbers of urban poor. As whites fled cities, factories and businesses also relocated in suburban areas. With a declining population, cities faced growing financial problems. Taxes could no longer keep up with the demands for such services as public transportation and police protection. Moreover, automation—producing goods using mechanical and electronic devices—reduced jobs in the industries that remained. It became more and more difficult for the urban poor to rise from poverty and improve their lives.

The urban poor struggled not only with poverty but also with racial discrimination in employment, housing, and education. Crime and violence often grew out of inner-city poverty, especially among young people who saw no hope for escape from life in the ghetto.

Voices of Dissent

⭐ Changes in American society in the 1950s caused some people to question the values that were emerging. Some critics charged that the sameness of suburban and corporate life had a cost—the loss of individuality. Others condemned American materialism—a focus on accumulating money and possessions rather than an interest in spiritual matters.

Social Critics

During the 1950s, leading social critics examined the complexity of modern society. Many wrote about its effects on individual behavior. **William H. Whyte, Jr.,** in *The Organization Man,* studied American business life. He concluded that young executives who abandoned their own views to "get along" were the most likely to succeed. He drew a somber picture of "organization men" who "have left home spiritually as well as physically."

In his book *The Affluent Society,* economist **John Kenneth Galbraith** wrote of the prosperous American society of the 1950s. Not all Americans shared in this prosperity, however. Galbraith described a suburban family, comfortably installed in an "air-conditioned, power-steered and power-braked automobile," driving "through cities that are badly paved, made hideous by litter, blighted buildings, billboards." Prosperous Americans, he claimed, often ignored the problems and hardships faced by other Americans.

The Beat Generation

A group of writers called the Beats had even sharper criticism of American society. The term *Beat,* invented by novelist **Jack Kerouac** in 1948, meant "weariness with all forms of the modern industrial state." Kerouac, poet **Allen Ginsberg,** and other Beats rebelled against American culture for its conformity, blind faith in technology, and materialism.

Kerouac's novel *On the Road,* the most influential book of the Beats, described the wild adventures of friends who drove aimlessly around the country. Its main character was "mad to live, mad to talk, mad to be saved, desirous of everything at the same time." The novel made Kerouac an instant celebrity.

Millions of young Americans read the works of Beat writers. Some adopted Beat attitudes of rebellion and isolation from society. Dressed in black and wearing sunglasses and berets, they were called **beatniks.** The Beat writers and their followers put forth ideas and attitudes that contributed to the youth rebellion of the 1960s.

Writer Jack Kerouac

⭐ **Picturing HISTORY** A crowd of similarly dressed suburban residents returns home from working in the city. **What criticisms did writers such as Jack Kerouac make about American middle-class society of the 1950s?**

Linking PAST & PRESENT

Political Power

The growing African American population in the cities laid the foundation for political power in the 1950s and beyond. In 1950 no American city had an African American mayor. By the early 1990s, African Americans served as mayors of 30 major cities and held more than 10,000 other city and county offices across the nation.

Questioning Roles

★ With society changing, women and African Americans began questioning their roles. In the 1950s African Americans fought to end segregation and to gain greater freedom and equality.

The Suburban Housewife

"The suburban housewife was the dream image of the young American woman," wrote **Betty Friedan,** herself a suburban wife and mother. "She was healthy, beautiful, educated, [and] concerned only about her husband, her children, and her home." Television, advertising, and magazines reinforced this image of women as perfect wives and mothers and suburban life as the path to a full and happy life.

As Friedan discovered, however, many suburban housewives were dissatisfied with this role. Her book, *The Feminine Mystique,* became one of the first works to describe the frustration and unhappiness of these women.

African Americans

African Americans also questioned their place in society in the 1950s. After years of struggling for their rights, African Americans became increasingly impatient for change and less willing to accept their status as second-class citizens. They launched a new campaign for full civil rights.

Three events in the 1950s proved especially important for African Americans. First came the Supreme Court decision in *Brown v. Topeka Board of Education* (1954), which declared racial segregation in public schools to be unconstitutional. Second, African Americans staged a successful boycott of segregated public buses in **Montgomery, Alabama.** Third, President Eisenhower sent federal troops to **Little Rock, Arkansas,** to enforce a court order to integrate a high school. These three events, which you will learn more about in Chapter 29, helped pave the way for the successes of the civil rights movement in the 1960s.

Section 4 Assessment

Checking for Understanding
1. *Identify* Jack Kerouac, Allen Ginsberg, Betty Friedan.
2. *Define* ghetto, automation, materialism.
3. *Summarize* the reasons most farmers did not share in the prosperity of the 1950s.

Reviewing Themes
4. **Groups and Institutions** What did the Beats dislike about American society?

Critical Thinking
5. **Drawing Conclusions** Why do you think some suburban housewives were dissatisfied with their roles in life during the 1950s?

Activity

Writing a Poem Write a poem at least 12 lines long that might have been written by a social critic of the 1950s.

Using the Internet

Are you one of the many people world-wide who would like to surf the Net? Using the Internet can give you the chance to find information on many subjects.

Learning the Skill

The Internet is a global computer network that offers many features, including electronic mail, information, and on-line shopping. Before you can connect to the Internet and use the services it offers, however, you must have three things: a computer, a modem (the device that lets your computer send and receive data over a telephone line), and a service provider. A service provider is a company that, for a fee, gives you entry to the Internet.

Once you are connected, the easiest and fastest way to access sites and information is to use a "Web browser," a program that lets you view and explore information on the World Wide Web. The Web consists of many documents called "Web pages," each of which has its own address, or Uniform Resource Locator (URL). Many URLs start with the keystrokes *http://*

Practicing the Skill

This chapter focuses on the 1950s, when Elvis Presley became popular. Surf the Internet to learn about the king of rock 'n' roll.

1. Log on to the Internet and access one of the World Wide Web search tools, such as Yahoo, Lycos, or WebCrawler.
2. Search by category or by name. If you search by category in Yahoo, for example, click on *Entertainment* or *Business and Economy*. To search by name, type in *Elvis* or *Elvis Presley*.

3. Scroll the list of Web pages that appears when the search is complete. Select a page to bring up and read or print. Repeat the process until you have enough information you can use to develop a short report on Elvis and his music during the 1950s.

Elvis Presley

◄ Applying the Skill ►

Using the Internet Go through the steps just described to search the Internet for information on automobiles of the 1950s or baseball in the 1950s. Based on the information, write an article for your school newspaper or magazine about your topic.

Assessment and Activities

★ Reviewing Key Terms

On a sheet of paper, use the following words in two paragraphs that describe life in America in the 1950s.

moderate
arms race
domino theory
summit
peaceful coexistence
productivity
standard of living
per capita income
affluence
baby boom
ghetto
automation
materialism

★ Reviewing Key Facts

1. Summarize President Eisenhower's domestic policy.
2. Name three foreign policy challenges the Eisenhower administration faced.
3. How did the Geneva summit help to ease cold war tensions?
4. Identify technological advances of the 1950s.
5. How did the mass movement to the suburbs affect inner cities?

★ Critical Thinking

Making Inferences

The social critics of the 1950s criticized American culture for its conformity, blind faith in technology, and materialism.

1. Give an example of the conformity that these critics might have been referring to.
2. Why do you think a blind faith in technology might be harmful?

★ Time Line Activity

Create a time line on which you place the following events in chronological order.

- SEATO formed
- Alaska and Hawaii enter Union
- Federal Highway Act passed
- Nixon gives "Checkers" speech
- Soviets launch *Sputnik*
- President Eisenhower is elected to first term
- Strikes spread through Hungary
- *Explorer* satellite is launched
- Salk vaccine first given to school children

★ Reviewing Themes

1. **Economic Factors** What general economic policies did the Eisenhower administration support?
2. **Science and Technology** Why did the development of nuclear weapons allow Eisenhower to cut the military budget?
3. **Continuity and Change** Why was there such a great demand for automobiles in the 1950s?
4. **Groups and Institutions** Discuss two problems farmers faced in the 1950s.

★ Skill Practice Activity

Using the Internet

Go through the steps described on page 817 to search the Internet for information on the beatniks or fads—such as telephone booth stuffing or the hula hoop—of the 1950s. Write an article for the school newspaper or magazine based on the information you retrieve about your topic.

★ Geography Activity

Coal mining is a crucial part of Appalachia's economy. The introduction of new machine technology after World War II had a drastic effect on employment. Study the map below, then answer the questions that follow.

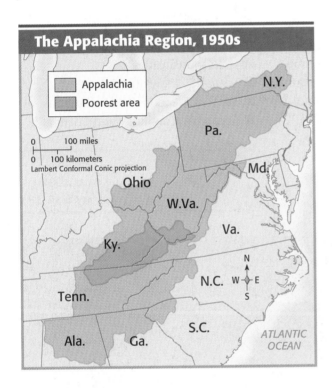

The Appalachia Region, 1950s

1. **Region** How many states are included in the Appalachia region?
2. **Location** In what states did poverty strike the hardest?
3. **Human/Environment Interaction** Why do you think unemployed miners did not turn to farming or ranching to make a living?

★ Cooperative Activity

History and Literature Throughout history social critics have tried to draw attention to the ills of society. With members of your group, research to find three poems written by modern poets that deal with current social problems. Social problems might include, for example, poverty, prejudice, and the prevalence of violence. Mount each of your poems on an 8 ½" x 11" sheet of paper and use photographs or drawings to illustrate each. Your group might also want to include short descriptions or captions to identify your photographs or drawings. Combine your poems with those of other groups to create a poetry collection book titled "A Decade of Dissent."

★ Technology Activity

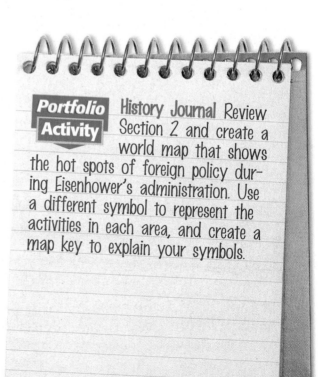

Using E-Mail In the 1950s it would have been hard to imagine the role computers would play in our lives today. One by-product of the computer revolution is the hundreds of new computer-related words we have added to our language. Words such as *surfing* and *megabyte* describe computers and how we use them. Using E-mail, send a message asking for a list of words that probably did not exist before computers were invented in the 1950s. Share your findings with the class.

Portfolio Activity History Journal Review Section 2 and create a world map that shows the hot spots of foreign policy during Eisenhower's administration. Use a different symbol to represent the activities in each area, and create a map key to explain your symbols.

1954–1973

The Civil Rights Era

★ Why It's Important

In the 1950s a tide of protest began to rise in America against deeply rooted attitudes of racism and discrimination. The campaign for equality expanded and gained momentum in the 1960s. Although the civil rights movement could not overcome all the obstacles that stood in the way of full citizenship, it achieved some stunning successes. Inspired by those victories, women, Hispanics, Native Americans, and others intensified their efforts to secure their full rights as citizens.

★ Chapter Themes

- *Section 1,* Civic Rights and Responsibilities
- *Section 2,* Individual Action
- *Section 3,* Groups and Institutions
- *Section 4,* Continuity and Change

PRIMARY SOURCES Library *See pages 992–993 for primary source readings to accompany Chapter 29*

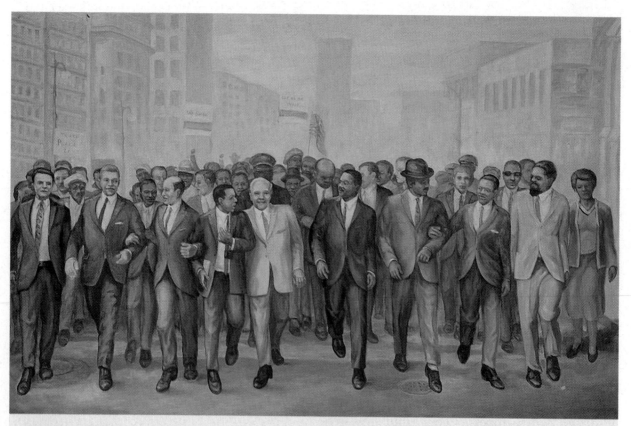

 March on Detroit **by Stephen Hall** Demonstrations brought thousands together in the demand for social justice and equal opportunity.

1954
Supreme Court strikes down segregation in education

1955
Rosa Parks is arrested; Montgomery bus boycott begins

1957
Martin Luther King, Jr., heads SCLC; Federal troops help integrate a Little Rock high school

Section 1

The Civil Rights Movement

READ TO DISCOVER . . .

- how a Supreme Court decision helped African Americans in their struggle for equal rights.
- why Martin Luther King, Jr., emerged as a leader of the civil rights movement.

TERMS TO LEARN

segregation
integrate

boycott
civil disobedience

Storyteller

Jackie Robinson could do everything on a baseball field—hit singles, slam home runs, and speed from base to base. Robinson was the first African American to play major league baseball. When his team, the Brooklyn Dodgers, reached the World Series in 1947, Robinson recalled: "I experienced a completely new emotion when the National Anthem was played. This time, I thought, it is being played for me, as much as for anyone else. . . . I am standing here with all the others; and everything that takes place includes me."

JACKIE ROBINSON
third base BROOKLYN DODGERS

Jackie Robinson baseball card

African Americans had suffered from racism and discrimination in the United States since colonial times. As the nation entered the second half of the twentieth century, many African Americans believed that the time had come for them to enjoy an equal place in American life. They fought for equal opportunities in jobs, housing, and education. They also fought against segregation—the separation of people of different races.

Equality in Education

During the 1950s and the early 1960s, African Americans boldly rejected the humiliating practice of forced separation. The **NAACP** (National Association for the Advancement of Colored People) had worked on behalf of African Americans since its founding in 1909, attacking discrimination and segregation. In the 1950s, NAACP lawyers searched for cases they could use to challenge the laws allowing the segregation of public education.

The Supreme Court had upheld segregation laws in the past. In 1896 in *Plessy* v. *Ferguson,* it had ruled that "separate but equal" public facilities were legal. **Thurgood Marshall,** the chief lawyer for the NAACP, decided to challenge the idea of "separate but equal." Then the NAACP began to decide which among the nation's segregated school districts to bring before the Court.

The *Brown* Decision

Seven-year-old African American Linda Brown was not permitted to attend an all-white elementary school just blocks from her house. To get to the segregated elementary school she was assigned to, Brown had to cross railroad tracks and take a bus for several miles. The Brown family sued the school system but lost. Marshall and the NAACP appealed the case all the way to the Supreme Court.

The case of **Brown v. Board of Education of Topeka, Kansas,** combined with several similar cases, reached the Supreme Court in December 1952. Thurgood Marshall argued that segregated schools were not and could not be equal to white schools. For that reason segregated schools violated the Fourteenth Amendment to the Constitution.

On May 17, 1954, the Court delivered its opinion. Quiet filled the Supreme Court chamber when the ruling was announced. All nine justices sat at the long bench. Nobody knew what the Court would say. Contrary to its usual practice, the Court had not released the text of the decision beforehand.

The Supreme Court ruled in *Brown* v. *Board of Education of Topeka, Kansas* that it was unconstitutional to separate schoolchildren by race. The *Brown* decision reversed the Court's decision in *Plessy* v. *Ferguson.*

Integrating the Schools

The Court's decision in *Brown* v. *Board of Education* called on school authorities to make plans for integrating—bringing races together in—public schools. The Court also ordered that

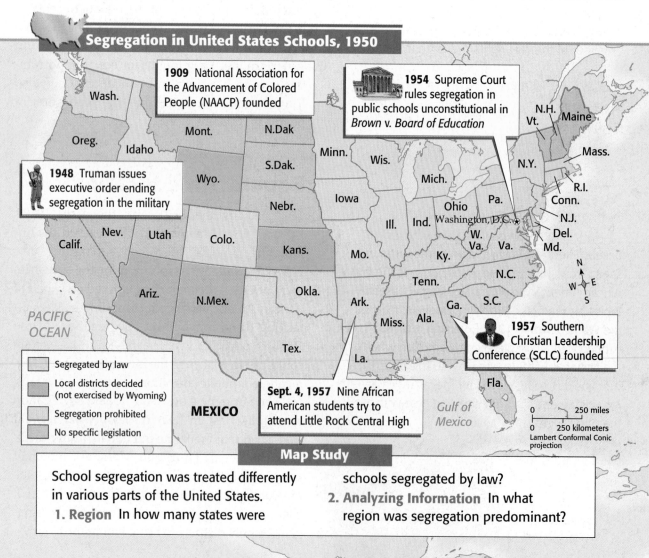

Segregation in United States Schools, 1950

1909 National Association for the Advancement of Colored People (NAACP) founded

1954 Supreme Court rules segregation in public schools unconstitutional in *Brown v. Board of Education*

1948 Truman issues executive order ending segregation in the military

1957 Southern Christian Leadership Conference (SCLC) founded

Sept. 4, 1957 Nine African American students try to attend Little Rock Central High

Wash. Oreg. Idaho Mont. N.Dak. Minn. Wis. Mich. N.Y. N.H. Vt. Maine Mass. R.I. Conn. N.J. Del. Md. Pa. Ohio Ind. W.Va. Va. Ky. Tenn. N.C. S.C. Ga. Ala. Miss. La. Ark. Okla. Tex. Kans. Nebr. Iowa Mo. S.Dak. Wyo. Colo. Utah Nev. Calif. Ariz. N.Mex. Washington, D.C. Ill. Fla.

PACIFIC OCEAN

MEXICO

Gulf of Mexico

N W E S

- Segregated by law
- Local districts decided (not exercised by Wyoming)
- Segregation prohibited
- No specific legislation

0 250 miles
0 250 kilometers
Lambert Conformal Conic projection

Map Study

School segregation was treated differently in various parts of the United States.
1. Region In how many states were schools segregated by law?
2. Analyzing Information In what region was segregation predominant?

Picturing HISTORY Elizabeth Eckford (center) braves the insults of white citizens to enter Central High School in Little Rock, Arkansas. **NAACP button**

How did President Eisenhower respond to the crisis in Little Rock?

integration was to be carried out "with all deliberate speed"—as fast as reasonably possible.

Some school systems across the country integrated quickly. However, in parts of the South, local leaders vowed to keep African American children out of white schools. Some people formed organizations to fight integration. A clash between the federal government and these states seemed unavoidable.

Confrontation in Little Rock

In 1957 a federal judge ordered Central High School in **Little Rock, Arkansas,** an all-white school, to admit African American students. Arkansas governor **Orval Faubus** opposed integration. He called out the state's National Guard to prevent African Americans from entering the high school.

On the day the students were scheduled to begin school, armed members of the National Guard blocked the school's entrance and turned away nine African American students. One of them, 15-year-old **Elizabeth Eckford,** recalled that when she tried to squeeze past a member of the guard, "He raised his bayonet, and then the other guards moved in and raised their bayonets."

For the first time since the Civil War, a Southern state had defied the authority of the federal government. Although Eisenhower had some doubts about the *Brown* decision, he believed it was his duty to enforce the law. The president warned Faubus that if the governor did not admit the students, the federal government would act.

When a federal judge ruled that the governor had violated federal law, Faubus finally removed the National Guard. Eisenhower sent hundreds of soldiers to Little Rock to protect the students. Shielded by the federal troops, the nine African American students finally entered the school.

Gains on Other Fronts

While school integration continued, African Americans made other advances in securing their rights. More and more took part in a movement dedicated to securing fair and equal treatment.

Footnotes to History

Thurgood Marshall In 1967 Thurgood Marshall—the great-grandson of an enslaved person—became the first African American justice on the Supreme Court.

Eyewitness to HISTORY

The Montgomery Bus Boycott

On the evening of December 1, 1955, **Rosa Parks** boarded a bus in downtown **Montgomery, Alabama.** Parks, a seamstress, was secretary of the local chapter of the NAACP. She found an empty seat in the section reserved for whites.

When white passengers entered the bus, the driver told Parks, an African American, to move to the rear of the bus. Parks refused. At the next bus stop, she was taken off the bus by police, arrested for breaking the law, and fined $10. The episode could have ended there—but it did not.

Causes and Effects

CAUSES

★ 1955 Rosa Parks is arrested
★ 1955 Montgomery bus boycott begins
★ 1957 Conflict at Little Rock
★ 1957 SCLC is organized
★ 1960 Students stage sit-ins
★ 1963 March on Washington, D.C.

Move Toward Equality

EFFECTS

★ 1962 James Meredith enrolls at University of Mississippi
★ 1967 Thurgood Marshall appointed to Supreme Court
★ 1968 Shirley Chisholm elected to House
★ 1972 Barbara Jordan first African American woman from a Southern state to serve in Congress

Chart Study

African Americans faced many obstacles in their struggle for equal rights. **Analyzing Information** What protest followed the arrest of Rosa Parks?

Rosa Parks's arrest led African Americans in Montgomery to put into effect plans to boycott— refuse to use—the city's buses. The boycott organizers hoped to hurt the city financially and force it to alter its policies. They had strength in numbers—almost 75 percent of the bus company's riders were African American.

At a boycott meeting, a young Baptist minister came forward to speak. Not widely known at the time, **Martin Luther King, Jr.,** made an impact on the crowd. He declared:

> ❝We're here because first and foremost, we are American citizens, and we are determined to acquire our citizenship to the fullness of its meaning. We are tired—tired of being segregated and humiliated, tired of being kicked about by the brutal feet of oppression. ❞

The boycott upset many people's daily lives, but the African Americans of Montgomery pulled together to make it work. Students hitchhiked to school; workers walked or rode bikes to their jobs. King helped organize car pools to shuttle people from place to place.

Rosa Parks on the Montgomery bus

Some white people in Montgomery struck back. Old laws were dug up to arrest the boycott's leaders. In January 1956, extremists exploded a bomb at King's house, causing damage but no injuries. The attack was only one of several violent incidents.

The bus boycott lasted for more than a year. City officials arrested King and other leaders at different times, but African Americans held firm. The local bus company lost thousands of dollars in fares, and downtown businesses lost many of their African American customers. Finally, the Supreme Court settled the matter by ruling that the Montgomery bus segregation law was unconstitutional. In December, the boycott ended.

Biography
Martin Luther King, Jr.

★ With the victory in Montgomery, King became a leader of the civil rights movement. He followed the tactics of **A. Philip Randolph,** the nation's most prominent African American labor leader. King was also strongly influenced by **Mohandas Gandhi,** who had used nonviolent protest to help free the nation of India from Great Britain. In keeping with his beliefs, Gandhi used protest methods based on civil disobedience, or the refusal to obey laws that are considered unjust. King applied the same techniques to the struggle for African American rights in the United States.

In January 1957, King and 60 other ministers started a new organization called the **Southern Christian Leadership Conference** (SCLC). The SCLC elected King as president.

The SCLC leaders emphasized nonviolent protest. They suggested ways to react to taunts and jeers and showed civil rights workers how to protect themselves from violent attacks. The SCLC also discussed how to identify targets for protests and how to organize people for support. In taking these steps, the SCLC prepared African Americans for the struggle for equal rights.

★ **Picturing HISTORY** Martin Luther King, Jr., stands in his office near a portrait of the Indian independence leader, Mohandas Gandhi. **How was King influenced by Gandhi?**

★ ★ ★ ★ ★ Section 1 Assessment ★ ★ ★ ★ ★

Checking for Understanding
1. **Identify** NAACP, *Brown* v. *Board of Education,* Rosa Parks, Martin Luther King, Jr., SCLC.
2. **Define** segregation, integrate, boycott, civil disobedience.
3. **Name** the Supreme Court decision that banned segregation in education.

Reviewing Themes
4. **Civic Rights and Responsibilities** How did the Montgomery bus boycott end?

Critical Thinking
5. **Demonstrating Reasoned Judgment** Why do you suppose Martin Luther King, Jr., thought nonviolent protest would be the most effective way to work toward civil rights?

Composing Lyrics Write song lyrics to be sung at a civil rights march. Base your lyrics on the story of Rosa Parks and her courage the night of her arrest.

1961
John F. Kennedy
takes office as
president

1963
Kennedy is
assassinated

1964
President Johnson
announces war
on poverty

July 1964
Civil Rights Act
of 1964 is passed

Section 2

Kennedy and Johnson

READ TO DISCOVER . . .
- what John F. Kennedy planned for America.
- how the nation responded to Kennedy's assassination.
- what new programs were created as part of the "Great Society."

TERMS TO LEARN
poverty line   Medicaid
Medicare

Storyteller

They stood together on the inaugural platform: 43-year-old John F. Kennedy, tanned, vigorous, and coatless despite the subfreezing weather, and 70-year-old Dwight D. Eisenhower, wearing a muffler, looking like a tired general. The appearances of the two men, a generation apart in age, symbolized the change of leadership.

Kennedy's speech promised so much: "Let every nation know . . . that we shall pay any price, bear any burden, meet any hardship, support any friend, oppose any foe to assure the survival and the success of liberty. . . ."

1960 presidential campaign items

By 1960, the crusade for civil rights had become a national movement. Against this background, the nation prepared for a presidential election.

The Republican candidate, Vice President **Richard M. Nixon,** pledged to continue the policies of President Eisenhower. The Democratic candidate, **John F. Kennedy,** promised new programs to help the poor and the elderly. He vowed to "get the country moving again."

Election of 1960

For much of the campaign, polls showed Nixon in the lead. One reason for this was the fact that Kennedy was Roman Catholic. No Catholic had ever been president, and many Americans feared that if Kennedy won he might show more loyalty to his church than to his country. Kennedy answered by stressing his belief in the separation of church and state.

Biography

John F. Kennedy

Kennedy came from one of the country's wealthiest and most powerful families. His father, Joseph P. Kennedy, was a successful business leader and the American ambassador to Britain during World War II.

John Kennedy joined the United States Navy during World War II and was assigned to active duty in the Pacific. When the Japanese sank the PT (patrol torpedo) boat he commanded, Kennedy saved the life of a crew member by swimming to shore with the injured man on his back. The rescue effort led to navy and marine medals for Kennedy but also aggravated an old back injury he had. The story of the rescue was later described in Robert Donovan's book *PT 109.*

Kennedy's political career began in 1946 when he won a seat in Congress from Massachusetts. Six years later, he was elected to the United States Senate. The young senator wrote a book, *Profiles in Courage,* which described difficult political decisions made by past United States senators. The book became a best-seller and received a Pulitzer Prize. After easily winning reelection to the Senate in 1958, Kennedy began campaigning for the presidency in 1960.

A New President

The turning point in the 1960 election came when the candidates took part in the first televised presidential debates. Kennedy appeared handsome and youthful. Nixon, who was recovering from an illness, looked tired and sick. Kennedy spoke with confidence about the future. Many viewers thought that Kennedy made a better impression.

In November, nearly 70 million voters turned out to choose between Nixon and Kennedy. For the first time, the people of Alaska and Hawaii took part in a presidential election. The results were extremely close. In the popular vote, Kennedy won 49.9 percent, while Nixon received 49.6 percent. In the electoral vote, Kennedy gained a greater margin over Nixon—303 to 219 votes.

The New Frontier

On January 20, 1961, snow covered Washington, D.C., and icy winds whipped through the city. Still, thousands of people streamed to the Capitol to see John Fitzgerald Kennedy become the thirty-fifth president of the United States. He offered the nation youth,

President John F. Kennedy

energy, and hope. In his Inaugural Address, Kennedy spoke of a new era:

> 66 Let the word go forth from this time and place . . . that the torch has been passed to a new generation of Americans. 99

The young president promised to face the nation's challenges with determination. In closing, Kennedy roused the American people to action:

> 66 And so, my fellow Americans: ask not what your country can do for you—ask what you can do for your country. 99

Domestic Policies

Kennedy drew up plans for the **New Frontier,** a group of proposals involving increased government spending on social programs. One bill he sent to Congress called for more federal funds for education. Another bill aimed to help poor people get jobs. Reluctant to commit to Kennedy's expensive, untried programs, Congress failed to pass most of these bills.

Another area of concern for Kennedy was civil rights. The president wished to help African Americans in their fight for equal rights. At the same time, he worried that moving too quickly would anger Southern Democrats in Congress whose support he needed to enact legislation.

In 1963 Kennedy decided to ask Congress to pass a bill guaranteeing civil rights. The House approved the measure, but it stalled in the Senate. Meanwhile, the president left on a campaign trip for **Dallas, Texas.**

Kennedy Assassinated

On November 22, 1963, Kennedy arrived in Dallas with his wife, Jacqueline. As the president and the First Lady rode through the streets in an open car, several shots rang out. Kennedy slumped against his wife. The car sped to a hospital, but the president was dead. Shortly afterward, Vice President **Lyndon B. Johnson** took the oath of office as president.

The assassination stunned the nation. Television networks broadcast the news almost without interruption for the next few days. Millions of Americans numbly watched the funeral.

In the midst of the grief came another shock. The day of Kennedy's shooting, Dallas police had arrested **Lee Harvey Oswald** and charged him with killing the president. Two days later, as

Lyndon Johnson takes the oath of office after the assassination of President Kennedy

police moved Oswald from one jail to another, Jack Ruby jumped through the circle of police officers and journalists and shot and killed Oswald.

Rumors that a group of enemies had plotted the assassination swirled around the country. Soon afterward, President Johnson appointed **Earl Warren,** chief justice of the United States, to head a commission to investigate the Kennedy shooting. After months of study, the **Warren Commission** issued its report. Oswald had acted on his own, it said. The report did not satisfy everyone, however. Many people believed the assassination was a conspiracy, or secret plot.

The "Great Society"

Soon after becoming president, Lyndon B. Johnson outlined a set of programs even more ambitious than Kennedy's New Frontier. He called his proposals the **"Great Society."** In a speech he explained his vision of America:

❝In a land of great wealth, families must not live in hopeless poverty. In a land rich in harvest, children must not go hungry. . . . In a great land of learning and scholars, young people must be taught to read and write.❞

Johnson had acquired great skill as a legislator during his 22 years in Congress. He used this skill to persuade Congress to launch programs that would make the Great Society real.

The War on Poverty

In January 1964, President Johnson declared "an unconditional war on poverty in America." The first part of his plan for a Great Society consisted of programs to help Americans who lived below the poverty line—the minimum income needed to survive. A program called **Head Start** provided preschool education for the children of poor families. **Upward Bound** helped poor students attend college. The **Job Corps** offered training to young people who wanted to work. **Volunteers in Service to America** (VISTA) was a kind of domestic peace corps of citizens working in poor neighborhoods.

Among the most important laws passed under Johnson were those establishing Medicare and Medicaid. Medicare helped pay for medical care for senior citizens. Medicaid helped poor people pay their hospital bills.

Helping Cities and Schools

Other parts of the Great Society targeted the nation's crumbling cities. In 1966 President Johnson established the **Department of Housing and Urban Development** (HUD), which helped fund public housing projects. Another program, Model Cities, provided money to help rebuild cities.

Schools received a boost from the Elementary and Secondary Education Act of 1965, which greatly increased spending for education. Under Johnson, the amount of federal money spent on education more than doubled.

Civil Rights

Although raised in the South, Lyndon Johnson was not a segregationist. He believed that the nation must protect the rights of all American citizens.

When Johnson took office, he vowed to turn the civil rights bill Kennedy had proposed into law. In early 1964 he warned Congress that he

★ **Picturing HISTORY** President Johnson passes out Medicare checks to senior citizens in Beaumont, Texas. **What was the purpose of Medicare?**

"Thank you" gift to LBJ for Medicare

would accept nothing but success: "We are going to pass a civil rights bill if it takes all summer."

Congress passed the **Civil Rights Act of 1964** in July. The act prohibited discrimination against African Americans in employment, voting, and public accommodations. It banned discrimination not only by race and color, but also by sex, religion, or national origin.

A major force leading to its passage came from outside the nation's capital in the form of growing support for the goals of the civil rights movement.

★ ★ ★ ★ ★ Section 2 Assessment ★ ★ ★ ★ ★

Checking for Understanding

1. **Identify** John F. Kennedy, New Frontier, Lyndon B. Johnson.
2. **Define** poverty line, Medicare, Medicaid.
3. **List** the new government programs that Johnson created in his "War on Poverty."

Reviewing Themes

4. **Individual Action** Describe Johnson's policies regarding equal rights.

Critical Thinking

5. **Making Comparisons** If Nixon had won the 1960 presidential election, do you think he would have created his own Great Society? Explain.

◆ **Activity** ◆

Creating a Poster Choose one of President Kennedy's or Johnson's programs and make a poster supporting or opposing it.

1961
Freedom Riders move through the South

1962
James Meredith enrolls at University of Mississippi

1963
More than 200,000 people march in Washington, D.C.

1968
Martin Luther King, Jr., is assassinated

Section 3

The Struggle Continues

READ TO DISCOVER . . .

- what actions African Americans took in the early 1960s to secure their rights.
- how radical voices emerged in the civil rights movement.
- why riots erupted in some cities.

TERMS TO LEARN

sit-in   interstate

Storyteller

On February 1, 1960, four African American students walked into a store in Greensboro, North Carolina. After buying a few items, they sat down at a "whites-only" lunch counter. When a waitress questioned what they were doing, one of the students replied, "We believe since we buy books and papers in the other part of the store, we should get served in this part." They were refused service, and the four sat at the counter until the store closed. By the end of the week, hundreds of students had joined the protest. Angry whites jeered at the students and dumped food on them. The protesters refused to leave or strike back.

Supporting the sit-ins

A new wave of civil rights activity swept across the nation in the 1960s. Early actions targeted segregation in the South. Segregation existed in the North as well, but social patterns rather than laws provided the main obstacle to integration there. In Northern cities and suburbs, African Americans and whites often lived in different neighborhoods; as a result, their children often attended different schools. Soon African Americans expanded their goal to fighting discrimination and racism in the North as well as in the South.

Growing Protests

⭐ What four students began in Greensboro in February 1960 quickly spread. High school and college students staged sit-ins in nearly 80 cities. A sit-in is the act of protesting by sitting down. By the summer of 1961, more than 70,000 activists—African American and white—had taken part in sit-ins. Sit-ins were staged throughout the nation against stores that practiced segregation. Store managers wanted to end the disturbances and the loss of business. Gradually many stores agreed to desegregate.

The sit-ins helped launch a new civil rights group, the **Student Nonviolent Coordinating Committee** (SNCC). Civil rights activist **Ella Baker** was a guiding spirit behind SNCC and one of its organizers. Earlier, Baker had played important roles in both the NAACP and the SCLC. SNCC was a key player in the civil rights movement for several years.

Freedom Rides

The Supreme Court had ruled in 1960 against segregated bus facilities. Another civil rights group, the **Congress of Racial Equality** (CORE), decided to see whether the ruling was being enforced.

On May 4, 1961, a group of African American and white CORE members left Washington, D.C., on two buses bound for New Orleans. They called themselves **Freedom Riders.** The bus trip went smoothly until it reached Alabama, where angry whites stoned and beat the Freedom Riders.

Television and newspapers broadcast reports of the beatings. **Robert Kennedy**, the United States attorney general, asked CORE to stop the Freedom Rides for a "cooling-off period." CORE leader **James Farmer** responded: "We have been cooling off for 350 years. If we cool off any more, we will be in a deep freeze."

Violence and Arrests

The Freedom Riders pressed on, only to meet more violence in Birmingham and Montgomery, Alabama. There were no mobs waiting for the Freedom Riders in Jackson, Mississippi. However, police, state troopers, and Mississippi National Guard units were everywhere. As the Riders stepped off the bus and tried to enter the whites-only waiting room at the bus station, they were arrested for trespassing and jailed.

Despite the violence and the jail sentences, more Freedom Riders kept coming all summer. In the fall the Interstate Commerce Commission took steps to enforce the Supreme Court ruling, issuing new regulations that banned segregation on interstate buses—those that crossed state lines—and in bus stations.

Gaining Momentum

African Americans continued to apply pressure to secure their civil rights. Their actions came during John Kennedy's presidency. They spurred the president to take a more active role in the civil rights struggle.

Integrating Universities

In 1962 a federal court ordered the University of Mississippi to enroll its first African American student, **James Meredith.** However, Mississippi governor **Ross Barnett,** with the aid of state police, prevented Meredith from registering. When President Kennedy sent federal marshals to escort Meredith to the campus, riots erupted. A mob stormed the administration building armed with guns and rocks. The marshals fought back with tear gas and nightsticks. Two people were killed, but Meredith succeeded in registering. Federal troops were stationed at the university to protect him until he graduated in 1963.

Another confrontation between state and federal power took place in June 1963—this time in Alabama. Governor **George Wallace** vowed he would "stand in the schoolhouse door" to block the integration of the University of Alabama in Tuscaloosa. President Kennedy, acting on the advice of his brother, sent the Alabama National Guard to ensure the entry of African Americans to the university. As a result, Wallace backed down.

★ **Picturing HISTORY** James Meredith (center) became the first African American to attend the University of Mississippi. **What action did the federal government take to make sure that Meredith could enroll?**

Police in Birmingham, Alabama, used high-pressure water hoses against civil rights marchers. **What role did television have in advancing the civil rights cause?**

Poster advertising 1963 March on Washington

Birmingham

In the spring of 1963, Martin Luther King, Jr., and the SCLC targeted **Birmingham, Alabama,** for a desegregation protest. Police arrested hundreds of demonstrators, including King, but the demonstrations continued. National television carried vivid pictures of police setting snarling police dogs on unarmed demonstrators and washing small children across streets with the powerful impact of fire hoses. President Kennedy sent 3,000 troops to restore peace. Then, in June, he proposed a new civil rights bill that would outlaw segregation throughout the nation.

March on Washington

To rally support for the civil rights bill, Martin Luther King, Jr., and the SCLC organized a massive march in Washington, D.C., on August 28, 1963. More than 200,000 people, of all colors and from all over the country, arrived to take part.

Emily Rock, a 15-year-old African American, described how she felt at the march:

❝There was this sense of hope for the future—the belief that this march was the big step in the right direction. It could be heard in the voices of the people singing and seen in the way they walked. It poured out into smiles. ❞

About 6,000 police officers stood nearby, but they had nothing to do but direct traffic. There was no trouble. Proceeding with great dignity and joy, the marchers carried signs urging Congress to act. They sang songs, including one that was becoming the anthem of the civil rights movement: "We Shall Overcome."

Late in the afternoon, Martin Luther King, Jr., spoke to the crowd in ringing words of his desire to see America transformed:

❝I have a dream that one day this nation will rise up and live out the true meaning of its creed: 'We hold these truths to be self-evident; that all men are created equal.' . . . When we let freedom ring, . . . we will be able to speed up that day when all of God's children . . . [will] join hands and sing in the words of the old . . . spiritual, 'Free at last! Free at last! Thank God Almighty, we are free at last!' ❞

*F*ootnotes to History

The Prize For his nonviolent pursuit of equal rights, Martin Luther King, Jr., won the Nobel Peace Prize in 1964.

Freedom Summer

Congress did not pass Kennedy's civil rights bill until after his death. President **Lyndon B. Johnson,** who succeeded Kennedy, finally persuaded Congress to pass the bill. The **Civil Rights Act of 1964** outlawed discrimination in hiring and ended segregation in stores, restaurants, theaters, and hotels. Yet in many states, African Americans still could not vote. Poll taxes and other discriminatory laws prevented them from exercising this right.

During the summer of 1964, thousands of civil rights workers spread throughout the South to help African Americans register to vote. They called the campaign **Freedom Summer,** but the workers faced strong, sometimes violent, opposition.

The Right to Vote

The next year SNCC organized a major demonstration in **Selma, Alabama,** to protest the continued denial of African Americans' right to vote. Police attacks on the marchers again dramatized the cause.

President Johnson stepped in. On March 15, 1965, in a televised speech, the president urged passage of a voting rights bill. "About this there can be no argument," he said. "Every American citizen must have an equal right to vote." Three months later Johnson signed the **Voting Rights Act of 1965** into law. The act gave the federal government the power to force local officials to allow African Americans to register to vote.

The act led to dramatic changes in political life in the South. In 1966 about 100 African Americans held elective office in the South. By 1972 that number had increased 10 times.

Other Voices

By the mid-1960s, the civil rights movement had won numerous victories. Yet a growing number of African Americans grew tired of the slow pace of change and bitter over white attacks.

American Memories

March on Washington, 1963

Button celebrating the March on Washington

What Was It Like? On August 28, 1963, more than 200,000 gathered at the Lincoln Memorial to call for civil rights reform. **What was the theme of Martin Luther King, Jr.'s, address?**

Button honoring the march

NAACP hat

★ Picturing HISTORY In 1964, after a lengthy trip to Africa and the Middle East, Malcolm X called for closer ties between African Americans and African people in other parts of the world. **How did Malcolm X's ideas change during the early 1960s?**

Separatism

Malcolm X, a leader in the Nation of Islam (or Black Muslims), emerged as an important new voice for some African Americans. Malcolm X criticized the civil rights goal of integration, declaring that the best way for African Americans to achieve justice was to separate themselves from whites.

Malcolm X gained increasing support. By 1965, however, he had begun to change his ideas. Instead of racial separation, he called for "a society in which there could exist honest white-black brotherhood." Soon afterwards, he was killed by an assassin from a rival group among the Black Muslims.

His fiery words and passionate ideas, contained in his autobiography and other writings, continued to influence the civil rights movement after his death.

Black Power

Other African American leaders embraced more radical approaches. **Stokely Carmichael,** who became the leader of SNCC, advanced the idea of **Black Power.** This was a philosophy of racial pride that said African Americans should create their own culture and political institutions. Carmichael and other radicals called at times for revolution, a complete transformation of society. Although rejected by such groups as the NAACP, which saw it as a threat to law and order, the idea of Black Power had a great impact on the civil rights movement.

Violence Erupts

★ In Oakland, California, a group of young radicals formed the **Black Panther Party.** A chief goal of the group was to protect the African American community from police actions that Panther leaders considered brutality.

The Black Panthers symbolized a growing tension between African Americans and urban police. Large numbers of African Americans in urban areas felt frustrated over poverty and unemployment. The Panthers demanded reforms and armed themselves in opposition to the police. Several armed clashes with the police occurred.

Cities Burn

The first major urban riots since the 1940s took place in the summer of 1965 in the **Watts** section of **Los Angeles.** In a week of rioting, 34 people died and much of Watts burned to the ground. National Guard troops were called in to end the

★★★ Linking PAST & PRESENT

Honoring King

In 1983 Congress made the birthday of Martin Luther King, Jr., a national holiday. It is celebrated on the third Monday in January.

uprising. The Watts riot was the first of a series of racial disorders that hit cities in the summers of 1965, 1966, and 1967.

In 1966 rioting broke out in more than 40 Northern cities, including San Francisco, Chicago, and Cleveland. In July 1967, 5 days of protests, looting, and burning of buildings in Newark, New Jersey, ended with the deaths of 23 people and more than $10 million in damage. The next week, a massive uprising in **Detroit** shut the city down for several days until the National Guard and the army could restore order.

President Johnson named a commission of officials and scholars to study the causes of the riots and to suggest steps to improve conditions. The report of this group, the Kerner Commission, warned that "our nation is moving toward two societies, one black, one white—separate and unequal."

The wave of urban riots devastated many African American neighborhoods. The riots ended—but not before one last burst of rage.

Family and friends mourn at the funeral of Martin Luther King, Jr.

King Is Assassinated

On April 4, 1968, racial tension in the United States took another tragic turn. On that night in Memphis, Tennessee, an assassin shot and killed Dr. Martin Luther King, Jr. King's assassination set off angry rioting in more than 100 cities. Fires burned in the nation's capital, just blocks from the Capitol and the White House.

Thousands of people attended King's funeral in Atlanta. Millions more watched on television. All mourned the death of an American hero who, the night before his death, had said God "has allowed me to go up to the mountain, and I've seen the promised land. I may not get there with you. But I want you to know tonight, that we, as a people, will get to the promised land!"

Section 3 Assessment

Checking for Understanding
1. **Identify** Freedom Riders, James Meredith, Civil Rights Act of 1964, Voting Rights Act of 1965, Malcolm X, Stokely Carmichael.
2. **Define** sit-in, interstate.
3. **Describe** actions taken by African Americans to secure the right to vote.

Reviewing Themes
4. **Groups and Institutions** How did the philosophy of radical groups such as the Black Panthers differ from that of Martin Luther King, Jr.?

Critical Thinking
5. **Drawing Conclusions** Why did riots take place in so many of the nation's cities during the 1960s?

Activity

Creating a Visual Biography Use photographs and drawings to illustrate a poster on the life and accomplishments of Martin Luther King, Jr.

2 On May 14th, a white mob ambushed the bus in Anniston, Alabama. They stoned the bus, slashed tires, ripped luggage, and threw a firebomb into the bus. The angry whites tried to block the doors, but officers waved their guns and finally dispersed the mob, allowing the Freedom Riders to stumble out.

4 The eyes of the nation focused on James Farmer, a principal organizer, and other Freedom Riders as they filed into police vehicles in Jackson, Mississippi. The Freedom Riders were arrested for "disobeying an officer" when they refused to leave the whites-only waiting room in the bus station. Busloads of black and white civil rights workers continued to pour into Jackson until the facilities were finally desegregated.

5 Tired of violence and fearing more delays, the original group of Freedom Riders completed the last leg of the journey—from Jackson to New Orleans—by plane.

Tenn.

Ala.

Miss.

Atlanta

Anniston

Birmingham

Montgomery

Jackson

La.

3 Attorney General Robert Kennedy struggled to stop the racial violence when mobs attacked the Freedom Riders in Birmingham and Montgomery, Alabama. To restore order, Kennedy sent out hundreds of federal marshals, and the governor of Alabama called out the National Guard.

New Orleans

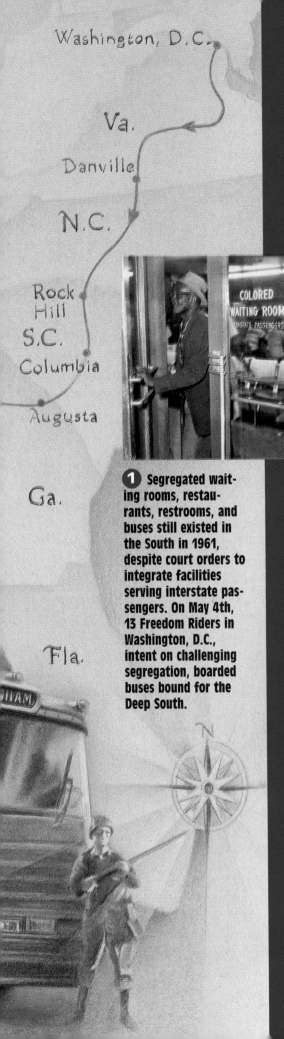

The Freedom Riders

1 Segregated waiting rooms, restaurants, restrooms, and buses still existed in the South in 1961, despite court orders to integrate facilities serving interstate passengers. On May 4th, 13 Freedom Riders in Washington, D.C., intent on challenging segregation, boarded buses bound for the Deep South.

66 [Martin Luther] King emerged from the office looking very weary. He called me to him and said, 'Jim, the attorney general asks that you halt the Freedom Rides and have a cooling-off period to give him time to work things out.'

'No, Martin,' I replied. 'I won't stop it now.... We will continue the Ride until people can sit wherever they wish on buses and use the facilities in any waiting room available to the public. Please tell the attorney general that we have been cooling off for 350 years. If we cool off any more, we will be in a deep freeze. The Freedom Ride will go on.' 99

—*From James Farmer in* Lay Bare the Heart: An Autobiography of the Civil Rights Movement, *published 1985.*

1963
Congress passes
Equal Pay Act;
*The Feminine
Mystique* is
published

1966
National
Organization
for Women
is created

1973
American Indian
Movement protests
at Wounded Knee,
South Dakota

Section 4

Other Groups Seek Rights

READ TO DISCOVER . . .

- what steps women took to claim their civil rights.
- how Hispanic American groups organized in the 1960s and the 1970s.
- why Native Americans took action to improve their lives.

TERMS TO LEARN

feminist   Hispanic

The Storyteller

Mexican American farmworker Jesse Lopez de la Cruz had labored for decades in the grape and cotton fields of the Southwest. In 1972 she began working for the United Farm Workers Union. Cruz made speaking tours, trying to bring women into the union. "Women can no longer be taken for granted—that we're just going to stay home and do the cooking and cleaning," she told her listeners. "It's way past the time when our husbands could say, 'You stay home! You have to take care of the children! You have to do as I say!'"

*Women's
rights button*

The effects of the civil rights movement reached well beyond the African American community. Women, Hispanics, Native Americans, and people with disabilities all found inspiration in the struggles of African Americans.

Women's Rights

In 1961 President John F. Kennedy created the Commission on the Status of Women. It reported that women—an ever growing part of the workforce—received lower pay than men, even for performing the same jobs. In 1963 Kennedy convinced Congress to pass the **Equal Pay Act,** which prohibited employers from paying women less than men for the same work.

Voices of Change

In a book called *The Feminine Mystique,* **Betty Friedan** gave voice to the frustration that a growing number of women experienced. Friedan's book described how many women felt disappointed in a society that expected them to be wives and mothers but did not support women in other roles.

Uniting for Action

In 1966 Friedan and other feminists—activists for women's rights—created the **National Organization for Women** (NOW). NOW fought for equal rights for women in all aspects of life—in jobs, education, and marriage.

★ ★

NOW launched a campaign for an **Equal Rights Amendment** (ERA) to the Constitution. The amendment stated that "equality of rights under the law shall not be denied or abridged by the United States or by any state on account of sex." **Phyllis Schlafly** and other opponents of the ERA warned that the amendment would upset the traditional roles of society and lead to the breakdown of the family. Some people argued that the amendment was unnecessary because the Constitution already provided women with adequate protection. In the end, not enough states ratified the amendment to make it law.

Women Gain Opportunities

Despite the defeat of the Equal Rights Amendment, women progressed in a number of areas in the 1970s. In 1971 the federal government outlawed discrimination against women in the workplace. This law, along with the efforts of many businesses, helped women begin to make advances in the world of work. Women gained more job opportunities, and more women rose to higher-level jobs in their companies.

Changes in education benefited women as well. Most of the nation's all-male colleges and universities began admitting women. More women than ever before entered medical school and law school to become doctors and lawyers.

Women also made progress in the political arena. Many women gained local and state

ERA opponent Phyllis Schlafly

Women march for equal rights

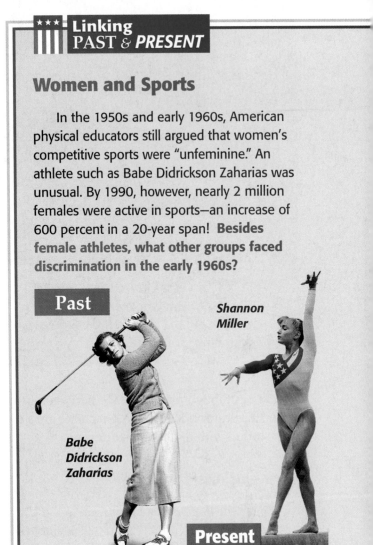
offices. Several women won seats in the Senate and the House of Representatives and appointments to the president's cabinet. In 1981 President Ronald Reagan appointed **Sandra Day O'Connor** as the first female justice of the Supreme Court.

Hispanic Americans

In the 1960s the rapidly growing Hispanic population sought equal rights. The term *Hispanic American* refers to those Americans who have come, or are descended from others who have come to the United States, from the countries of Latin America and Spain. From 3 million in 1960, the Hispanic population in the United States rose to 9 million in 1970 and to 15 million

César Chávez led the United Farm Workers during the 1960s. **How did the UFW help Mexican American migrant farmworkers?**

by 1980. Although they share the heritage of the Spanish culture and language, Hispanics are a diverse group with different histories.

Farmworkers Organize

By far, the largest Hispanic group in the United States comes from the country of Mexico. By 1980 more than 8 million Mexican Americans were living in the United States.

The fight for rights started among Mexican American migrant farmworkers. These people, who planted and harvested a large share of the nation's food supply, faced great hardships. The migrant farmers did backbreaking work, laboring from dawn until dusk for low wages. When one job ended, they had to travel from farm to farm in search of the next job.

In the early 1960s, migrant workers formed unions to fight for better wages and working conditions. Their leader, **César Chávez,** organized thousands of farmworkers into the United Farm Workers (UFW).

The union went on strike and organized nationwide boycotts. Consumers across the country supported the UFW by refusing to buy grapes, lettuce, and other farm produce under boycott. The success of the boycotts enabled the UFW to win higher wages and shorter work hours for many farmworkers.

The union boycott was followed by emerging political power among Hispanic Americans. In the years that followed, Hispanic Americans would join together in an organization called **La Raza Unida** to fight discrimination and to elect Hispanics to government posts. **The League of United Latin American Citizens** (LULAC) won suits in federal court to guarantee Hispanic Americans the right to serve on juries and to send their children to unsegregated schools.

Puerto Ricans

Puerto Ricans, another major group of Hispanics, come from the island of Puerto Rico, a commonwealth of the United States. They are American citizens who have made major contributions to the United States.

In 1970 the first representative to Congress of Puerto Rican origin, **Herman Badillo,** was elected from New York City. After four terms, Badillo served as the city's deputy mayor. Baseball all-time great **Roberto Clemente** performed heroically both on and off the baseball diamond. In 1972 Clemente died in a plane crash while delivering relief supplies to earthquake victims in Nicaragua.

Because Puerto Rico is not a wealthy island, many Puerto Ricans have migrated to American cities in search of jobs. By 1970 they made up 10 percent of the population of New York City. As with African Americans, though, they often faced discrimination in their job search, leading to no work or work for low pay. Many of the children and grandchildren of the Puerto Ricans who arrived in New York in the 1960s migrated to neighboring states, but many Puerto Ricans remained centered in New York City.

Cubans Arrive

After the Cuban Revolution of 1959, dictator Fidel Castro established a Communist government and seized the property of many Cubans. More than 200,000 people opposed to Castro fled to the United States in the 1960s. Thousands more came in the 1980s.

These immigrants settled all over the United States. The largest number of Cubans settled in south Florida, where they have established a thriving community.

In 1975 Hispanic people and other groups won a victory with the extension of voting rights. The new law required that registration and voting be carried out in other languages as well as in English. This was designed to help those citizens who might not read or speak English. Election materials, for example, are available in Spanish and English in many states.

Native Americans

⭐ The years after World War II were a time of transition for Native Americans. Starting in the early 1950s, the federal government urged Native Americans to leave the reservations for work in cities. Federal policy also tried to weaken the power of tribal government.

This policy did not improve the lives of Native Americans. Many could not find jobs in the cities. Those still crowded on reservations enjoyed few jobs or other opportunities. More than one-third of Native Americans lived below the poverty line. Unemployment was widespread— as high as 50 percent in some areas. A 1966 study revealed that Native Americans suffered so much from malnutrition and disease that their life expectancy was only 46 years.

Efforts to Organize

In the 1960s Native Americans organized to combat these problems. They demanded political power and independence from the United States government. Native Americans also increasingly emphasized their own history, language, and culture in their schools. The **National Congress of American Indians** (NCAI) sought more control over Native American affairs.

In 1961 more than 400 members of 67 Native American nations gathered in Chicago. In a Declaration of Indian Purpose, these delegates asserted that Native Americans have the "right to choose our own way of life."

The federal government recognized the Native Americans' issues. Congress passed the **Indian Civil Rights Act of 1968,** which formally protected the constitutional rights of all Native Americans. At the same time, the new law recognized the right of Native American nations to make laws on their reservations.

A Supreme Court decision in the 1970s reaffirmed the independence of tribal governments. Other court decisions confirmed Native Americans' rights to land granted in treaties.

American Indian Movement

Believing the process of change too slow, some younger Native Americans began taking stronger actions. In 1968 a group established the

Picturing HISTORY In the 1973 AIM takeover of Wounded Knee, Native American leaders Russell Means (left) and Dennis Banks (right) protested broken treaties and civil rights violations. **Why was Wounded Knee chosen as the place for the AIM protest?**

Wounded Knee button

WOUNDED KNEE 1890 1973

American Indian Movement (AIM), which worked for equal rights and improvement of living conditions. AIM was founded by Clyde Bellecourt, Dennis Banks, and others. Later, Russell Means became a leader.

AIM carried out several protests. In November 1969, for example, AIM was one of the Native American groups that took over Alcatraz Island, a former federal prison in San Francisco Bay. AIM wanted the island to serve as a cultural center. The incident ended in June 1971 when the groups surrendered to United States marshals.

In the fall of 1972, AIM members occupied the Bureau of Indian Affairs in Washington, D.C. They demanded the lands and rights guaranteed Indians under treaties with the United States. They surrendered the building after the government agreed to review their complaints.

In February 1973, AIM seized the town of **Wounded Knee, South Dakota,** the site of the 1890 massacre of Sioux by federal troops. In the early 1970s, Wounded Knee was part of a large Sioux reservation. The people there suffered from terrible poverty and ill health.

AIM leaders vowed to stay until the government met demands for change and investigated the treatment of Native Americans. The siege ended on May 8, but it focused national attention on the terrible conditions of Native Americans.

★ **Picturing HISTORY** Since the 1960s, people with physical disabilities have demanded better access to stadiums, restaurants, and other public buildings. **How has Congress responded to their protests?**

Americans With Disabilities

★ People with physical disabilities also sought equal treatment in the 1960s and the 1970s. Congress responded by passing a number of laws.

One law concerned the removal of barriers that prevented some people from gaining access to public facilities. Another required employers to offer more opportunities for disabled people in the workplace. Yet another asserted the right of children with disabilities to equal educational opportunities. As a result of these actions, people with disabilities enjoyed more job opportunities, better access to public facilities, and a greater role in society.

Section 4 Assessment

Checking for Understanding

1. *Identify* Betty Friedan, National Organization for Women, Equal Rights Amendment, César Chávez.
2. *Define* feminist, Hispanic.
3. *Explain* what migrant farmworkers did to earn more rights.

Reviewing Themes

4. **Continuity and Change** What rights did Native Americans gain in the 1960s?

Critical Thinking

5. **Stating Problems Clearly** Why do you think people with disabilities felt the need to work for equal treatment in the 1960s and 1970s?

Making a Protest Sign Create a sign that you might carry in a protest march to either support or oppose the ERA.

Drawing Conclusions

"Elementary, my dear Watson." Detective Sherlock Holmes often said these words to his assistant when he unlocked the key to a mystery. Holmes would examine all the available evidence, or facts, and draw conclusions to solve the case.

Learning the Skill

Drawing conclusions allows you to understand ideas that are not stated directly. Follow these steps in learning to draw conclusions:
- Review the facts that are stated directly.
- Use your knowledge and insight to develop some conclusions about these facts.
- Look for information to check the accuracy of your conclusions.

Practicing the Skill

The excerpt on this page was written by Martin Luther King, Jr., after he was arrested in Birmingham, Alabama, for peaceably demonstrating against segregation. King began writing this letter in response to a newspaper ad in which a group of white ministers called for an end to the demonstrations. King's words attempt to explain to the white ministers his use of civil disobedience.

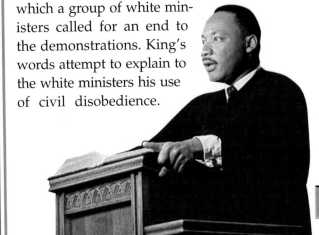

Martin Luther King, Jr.

After reading the excerpt, answer the questions, which require you to draw conclusions.

> " We know through painful experience that freedom is never voluntarily given by the oppressor; it must be demanded by the oppressed. . . . For years now I have heard the word 'Wait!' It rings in the ear of every Negro with piercing familiarity. This 'Wait' has almost always meant 'Never.' We must come to see, with one of our distinguished jurists, that 'justice too long delayed is justice denied.' "

—Martin Luther King, Jr.
"Letter from Birmingham Jail," 1963

1. How does King say that freedom is earned?
2. What were the African Americans "waiting" for?
3. What happens to justice if it is delayed?
4. What conclusions can you draw from King's overall tone in his letter?
5. What evidence could help prove your conclusions?

Applying the Skill

Drawing Conclusions Read a newspaper article about a criminal court case. Use the facts in the article to draw a conclusion about the innocence or guilt of the accused.

GO TO Glencoe's **Skillbuilder Interactive Workbook, Level 1** provides instruction and practice in key social studies skills.

Assessment and Activities

★ Reviewing Key Terms

On graph paper, create a word search puzzle using the following terms. Crisscross the terms vertically and horizontally, then fill in the remaining squares with extra letters. Use the terms' definitions as clues to find the words in the puzzle. Share your puzzle with a classmate.

poverty line	integrate
Medicare	boycott
Medicaid	sit-in
segregation	Hispanic

★ Reviewing Key Facts

1. What Supreme Court case abolished segregation in schools?
2. What was the main goal of President Kennedy's New Frontier program?
3. Summarize the philosophy and goals of Martin Luther King, Jr.

★ Critical Thinking

Making Generalizations

During the 1950s and 1960s, many African Americans worked for equal rights.

1. Why do you think the civil rights movement gained momentum during this era?
2. How did television affect the struggle for civil rights?

★ Time Line Activity

Create a time line on which you place the following events in chronological order.

- President Johnson signs Civil Rights Act
- Supreme Court bans segregation in schools
- President Kennedy is assassinated
- Montgomery bus boycott begins

★ Reviewing Themes

1. **Civic Rights and Responsibilities** According to Thurgood Marshall, what constitutional amendment was violated by allowing segregation in schools?
2. **Individual Action** Summarize the goals of Johnson's Great Society.
3. **Groups and Institutions** How did the idea of Black Power differ from Martin Luther King's goals for the civil rights movement?
4. **Continuity and Change** Summarize the impact that the African American civil rights movement had on other minorities.

★ Skill Practice Activity

Drawing Conclusions

Read the passage below and answer the questions that follow. Remember to review the information and add your own knowledge before drawing any conclusions.

Malcolm X, a strong African American leader, bitterly and regretfully recalled his youthful efforts at straightening his hair in order to look more like a white person:

66 This was my first big step toward self-degradation: when I endured all of that pain, literally burning my flesh to have it look like a white man's hair. I had joined that multitude of Negro men and women in America who are brainwashed into believing that the black people are 'inferior'—and white people 'superior.' 99

—Malcolm X, *Autobiography of Malcolm X*, 1965

1. What reason does Malcolm X give for straightening his hair?
2. As an adult, how did he view his youthful actions?

3. What conclusion can you draw about the views of many African American people toward white people at that time?
4. What statement from the passage supports your conclusion?

★ Geography Activity

The map below shows the route that the Freedom Riders took in 1961. Study the map, then answer the questions that follow.

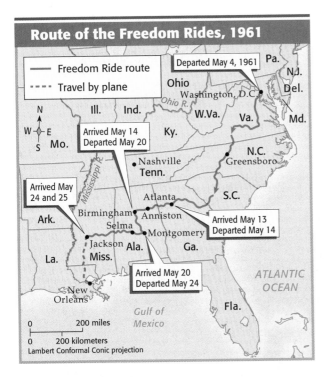

Route of the Freedom Rides, 1961

— Freedom Ride route
---- Travel by plane

Departed May 4, 1961
Washington, D.C.
Arrived May 14 Departed May 20
Nashville Tenn.
Arrived May 24 and 25
Greensboro
Atlanta
Birmingham Anniston
Selma
Montgomery
Arrived May 13 Departed May 14
Jackson
Arrived May 20 Departed May 24
New Orleans
ATLANTIC OCEAN
Gulf of Mexico

0   200 miles
0   200 kilometers
Lambert Conformal Conic projection

1. **Movement** What direction did the route follow from Atlanta to Montgomery?
2. **Location** Where did the Freedom Rides begin?
3. **Location** In what city did the entire route end?
4. **Movement** About how many miles did the Freedom Riders go by bus?
5. **Movement** About how many miles did the Freedom Riders travel by airplane?
6. **Region** Through what states did the Freedom Riders journey?

★ Cooperative Activity

History and Citizenship With members of your group research to find out how many people of different ethnic backgrounds live in your county. Make a graph to illustrate your findings. Then choose one of the minority ethnic groups to research. Prepare a written report with illustrations to provide more information about this particular ethnic group in your county. You may want to find out if members of this ethnic group have settled in one particular area of the county, if they have formed special clubs or organizations, or if they observe any special holidays.

★ Technology Activity

Using the Internet The United Farm Workers are still active today. Search the Internet for information about this organization and create a brochure that explains its goals.

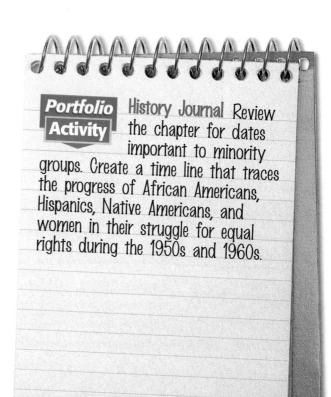

Portfolio Activity | **History Journal** Review the chapter for dates important to minority groups. Create a time line that traces the progress of African Americans, Hispanics, Native Americans, and women in their struggle for equal rights during the 1950s and 1960s.

1960–1975

The Vietnam Era

★ Why It's Important

The Vietnam era left scars on America. More than 58,000 United States troops died in Vietnam, and thousands more were wounded. The war damaged people's confidence in their government. The American people became more willing to challenge the president on military and foreign policy issues after Vietnam. The war also became a yardstick to gauge whether to involve American troops in later crises in other countries.

★ Chapter Themes

- *Section 1,* Geography and History
- *Section 2,* Government and Democracy
- *Section 3,* Continuity and Change
- *Section 4,* Civic Rights and Responsibilities
- *Section 5,* Individual Action

PRIMARY SOURCES Library

See pages 994–995 for primary source readings to accompany Chapter 30

★ HISTORY AND ART

***Chopper Pick-Up* by Brian H. Clark** Helicopters in combat were first used on a large scale by United States forces during the Vietnam War. Helicopters served on rescue missions and for aerial observation.

1961
Bay of Pigs
invasion fails

1962
Cuban missile
crisis occurs

1963
Telephone hot line
links U.S., Soviet leaders

1969
Neil Armstrong
walks on the moon

Section 1

Kennedy's Foreign Policy

READ TO DISCOVER . . .
- what course President Kennedy planned to follow in foreign policy.
- how the Kennedy administration handled foreign policy crises in its first year.
- what happened in the Cuban missile crisis.

TERMS TO LEARN

guerrilla warfare
flexible response
executive order

exile
blockade
hot line

The Storyteller

"In the long history of the world, only a few generations have been granted the role of defending freedom in its hour of maximum danger. I do not shrink from this responsibility—I welcome it." So spoke John F. Kennedy in his Inaugural Address. Although Kennedy talked of approaching this responsibility with "energy" and "devotion," events unfolding around the world—in Cuba, Eastern Europe, and Vietnam—would challenge his determination. The new president and nation soon faced a series of crises.

Kennedy inaugural ribbon

President Kennedy continued the anti-Communist foreign policy begun under Presidents Truman and Eisenhower. In pursuing that policy, though, Kennedy tried some new approaches.

New Directions

During the presidential campaign, Kennedy led Americans to believe that the nation had fewer nuclear missiles than the Soviet Union. As president, Kennedy increased spending on nuclear arms. At the same time, he tried to convince **Nikita Khrushchev,** the Soviet leader, to agree to a ban on nuclear testing.

Strength Through Flexibility

Kennedy also worked to improve America's ability to respond to threats abroad. In certain areas of the world, Communist groups fought to take control of their nation's government. Many of these groups received aid from the Soviet Union. They employed guerrilla warfare, or fighting by small bands using tactics such as sudden ambushes.

The United States needed a new approach for fighting guerrilla wars. Kennedy introduced a plan called flexible response, which relied on special military units trained to fight guerrilla wars. One of these units was the Special Forces, known as the **Green Berets.** The Special Forces provided the president with troops ready to fight guerrilla wars anywhere around the world.

Chapter 30 The Vietnam Era **847**

Strength Through Aid

President Kennedy understood that the poverty in Latin America, Asia, and Africa made the Communist promises of economic equality seem attractive. He decided to provide aid to countries in those areas to counteract the appeal of communism. On March 1, 1961, the president signed an executive order creating the **Peace Corps.** An executive order is a rule issued by the Chief Executive.

Americans who volunteered for the Peace Corps worked in other countries as teachers, health workers, and advisers in farming, industry, and government. By 1963 some 5,000 Peace Corps volunteers worked in more than 40 countries.

To promote Latin America's growth, Kennedy proposed a 10-year development plan for the region called the **Alliance for Progress.** In his Inaugural Address, Kennedy promised Latin American leaders that the United States would "assist free men and free governments in casting off the chains of poverty." He hoped as well to prevent the rise of Communist states in the region.

Cold War Confrontations

★ In 1961, just a few months after taking office, President Kennedy faced a foreign policy crisis in **Cuba.** That same year, the United States and the Soviet Union clashed in Europe.

The Bay of Pigs

As you read in Chapter 28, **Fidel Castro** had seized power in Cuba in 1959. When Castro formed an alliance with the Soviet Union, Americans felt threatened because Cuba lay only 90 miles (144 km) south of Florida. In the final months of Eisenhower's presidency, officials in the Central Intelligence Agency (CIA) forged a plan to overthrow Castro.

The CIA recruited a military force from the refugees who had fled Castro's Cuba and settled in the United States. The plan called for these exiles, or persons forced from their homes, to land in Cuba, spark an uprising, and overthrow Castro. Although Kennedy had doubts about the plan, he accepted the advice of military advisers and the CIA and allowed it to go forward.

On April 17, 1961, 1,500 CIA-trained Cuban exiles landed at the **Bay of Pigs** in southern Cuba. Many blunders occurred, and at a crucial moment, Kennedy refused to provide American air support. Within days Cuban forces crushed the invasion and captured the survivors.

The Bay of Pigs embarrassed Kennedy, who took the blame for the failure. The disaster had three consequences. First, Kennedy never again completely trusted military and intelligence advice. Second, other nations in Latin America lost trust in Kennedy. Third, Soviet premier Khrushchev concluded that Kennedy was not a strong leader and could be bullied.

 **HISTORY AND ART**

***The Peace Corps in Ethiopia, 1966* by Norman Rockwell** Volunteers worked in many developing countries. **Which Kennedy program dealt with Latin America's economy?**

Picturing HISTORY In the early 1960s, some East Germans tried to escape their Communist-ruled homeland by building tunnels (shown below) under the Berlin Wall. **What did the Berlin Wall come to symbolize?**

The Berlin Wall

Though 16 years had passed since the end of World War II, the wartime Allies had still not settled the status of Germany. West Germany gained complete independence in 1949, but the Soviet Union continued to control East Germany.

The location of **Berlin**—fully within Soviet-controlled East Germany—posed special problems. American, British, and French troops still remained in the western part of the city, and they sometimes had difficulty getting into West Berlin and maintaining control there. Meanwhile a steady flow of people fled to West Berlin from Communist East Berlin, hoping to escape economic hardship and find freedom.

At a June 1961 summit conference in **Vienna, Austria,** Premier Khrushchev told President Kennedy that the West must move out of Berlin, and he insisted on an agreement by the end of the year. Kennedy rejected Khrushchev's demand. To emphasize the West's right to stay in West Berlin, the United States later sent more troops to protect the city.

Later that summer, a large number of East Germans fled to the West. On August 13, the East German government, with Soviet backing, closed the border between East and West Berlin and built a wall of concrete blocks and barbed wire along it. The Soviets posted armed guards along the wall to stop more East Germans from fleeing to the West. The **Berlin Wall** cut communications between the two parts of the city.

The Western Allies continued to support the freedom and independence of West Berlin. They could do little, however, to stop the building of the wall, which came to symbolize Communist repression.

The Cuban Missile Crisis

The most dangerous cold war dispute between the Americans and Soviets came in 1962. Once again the dispute involved Cuba.

Missiles in Cuba

In mid-October 1962, an American spy plane flying over Cuba made a disturbing discovery. Photographs revealed that the Soviets were building launching sites for nuclear missiles. These missiles could easily reach the United States in a matter of minutes.

The Cuban Missile Crisis: October 14–28, 1962

Thousands of U.S. troops, including reserve units, were placed on alert and moved to Florida.

This map shows the range of the Soviet missiles in Cuba. Their accuracy fell off as range increased.

	MRBM range
	IRBM range

0   250 miles
0   250 kilometers
Mercator projection

Fla.

CUBA

DOMINICAN REPUBLIC

Puerto Rico

HAITI

N
W — E
S

The U.S. naval base at Guantanamo Bay was strengthened. All civilians were evacuated.

↓ Soviet missile		✈ U.S. base	
⚔ Soviet troops		🧍 U.S. troops	
		⚓ U.S. aircraft carrier	

Map Study

Medium Range and Intermediate Range Ballistic Missiles (MRBMs and IRBMs) in Cuba posed an immediate danger to the United States.

1. **Location** Where was the major U.S. naval base on Cuba located?
2. **Analyzing Information** What military equipment did the United States use to answer the Soviet threat in Cuba?

For the next week, President Kennedy met secretly with advisers to determine how to deal with the **Cuban missile crisis.** They explored several options, including invading Cuba and bombing the missile sites. New spy photographs showed the bases nearing completion faster than expected. A decision had to be made.

Eyewitness to HISTORY

"Eyeball to Eyeball"

On October 22, President Kennedy, speaking on national television, revealed the "secret, swift, and extraordinary buildup" of missiles in Cuba. Kennedy ordered the navy to blockade, or close

off, Cuba until the Soviets removed the missiles. He promised to destroy any Soviet ship that tried to break through the blockade. The president also declared:

> ❝ It shall be the policy of this nation to regard any nuclear missile launched from Cuba against any nation in the Western Hemisphere as an attack by the Soviet Union on the United States. ❞

The United States would respond, he warned, with a nuclear attack against the Soviet Union.

As the two superpowers neared the brink of nuclear war, people all over the world waited nervously. However, Khrushchev was not ready to back down, and Soviet ships—some carrying missiles—continued to approach Cuba.

Two days after Kennedy's announcement, a breakthrough occurred. Some Soviet ships nearing the blockade turned back. One American official announced, "We're eyeball to eyeball, and I think the other fellow just blinked."

Khrushchev sent a message, saying that the two countries

> ❝ ... ought not to pull on the ends of the rope in which you have tied the knot of war. ... Let us take measures to untie that knot. ❞

However, some Soviet ships still headed toward Cuba, and work on the missile bases continued. The president's advisers worked on plans for an air attack on the missile sites—just in case.

Fears grew on the fifth day, when Cuba shot down an American spy plane. At the same time, Kennedy and Khrushchev neared an agreement. Finally, after a week of tension, the Soviets announced they would "dismantle the arms which you describe as offensive, and ... crate and return them to the Soviet Union." In return, Kennedy agreed not to invade Cuba. He also gave private assurances that the United States would remove some missiles—aimed at the Soviet Union—from Turkey and Italy after the Soviet Union removed the missiles from Cuba.

The Aftermath

Having come so close to nuclear disaster, the superpowers worked to establish a better relationship. In the summer of 1963, Kennedy and Khrushchev created a direct telephone link, called the hot line, between Moscow and Washington to allow the leaders to communicate instantly in times of crisis.

That same summer, the two nations signed a treaty banning nuclear tests above ground and underwater.

Rivalry in Space

★ The United States competed with the Soviet Union in another area during the Kennedy administration—outer space. The space race began when the Soviet Union launched *Sputnik*, the world's first successful satellite, in 1957. In April 1961, Soviet cosmonaut **Yuri Gagarin** (guh•GAHR•uhn) became the first person to orbit the earth. One month later, **Alan Shepard, Jr.,** became the first American to make a spaceflight.

Shortly after Shepard's flight, Kennedy challenged the nation to a great undertaking. In a speech to Congress, he said:

Apollo *button*

❝I believe that this nation should commit itself to achieving the goal, before this decade is out, of landing a man on the moon and returning him safely to the earth.❞

The president asked Congress for more money for **NASA** (the National Aeronautics and Space Administration), which ran the space program. NASA expanded its launching facility in Florida and built a control center in Houston, Texas.

Astronaut **John Glenn** thrilled the country in February 1962 when he orbited the earth in a spacecraft, the first American to do so. An even greater triumph for the space program came on July 20, 1969, with the **Apollo project.** Awestruck television viewers around the world watched the spacecraft *Eagle* land on the surface of the moon. Hours later, with millions still watching, astronaut **Neil Armstrong** took the first human step on the moon and announced: "That's one small step for man, one giant leap for mankind." By the end of the Apollo project in 1972, 10 more Americans had landed on the moon.

★ ★ ★ ★ ★ **Section 1 Assessment** ★ ★ ★ ★ ★

Checking for Understanding
1. *Identify* John F. Kennedy, Nikita Khrushchev, Alliance for Progress, Fidel Castro, Bay of Pigs, Berlin, Cuban missile crisis, Apollo project.
2. *Define* guerrilla warfare, flexible response, executive order, exile, blockade, hot line.
3. *Cite* three consequences that President Kennedy faced as a result of the failure of the Bay of Pigs invasion.

Reviewing Themes
4. **Geography and History** Why did West Berlin's location make it difficult for the United States and its allies to defend it?

Critical Thinking
5. **Making Inferences** Why do you think Khrushchev sent missiles to Cuba?

Writing a Speech Write a speech that President Kennedy might have written to defend his actions during the Cuban missile crisis.

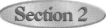

1950   1960   1970

1954
Geneva Accords
divide Vietnam

1959
Civil war in
Vietnam begins

1964
Gulf of Tonkin
Resolution passed

1967
More than 500,000
U.S. troops are in
Vietnam

Section 2

War in Vietnam

READ TO DISCOVER . . .

- how Vietnam became a divided country.
- how the United States first became involved in Vietnam.
- why America increased its involvement in the Vietnam War.

TERMS TO LEARN

Vietcong
domino theory
coup

escalate
search-and-destroy
   mission

The **S**toryteller

In March 1967 David Parks, an African American soldier serving in Vietnam, described an enemy attack on his camp: "I was asleep when the first shell exploded. The earth shook and I rolled to the ground as someone hollered, 'Incoming!' . . . I shook like jelly as the shrapnel burst all around our bunker. . . . All we could do was open up with our 50-caliber and small arms. . . . I'm not sure the native people are with us.

They smile at us in the daytime and their sons shoot at us at night. It's hard to spot the real enemy."

***Soldier's boots,
Vietnam War***

In the early 1960s, the United States became involved in a fight against communism in Southeast Asia. The war in **Vietnam** did not unfold as Americans had hoped, however. General Maxwell Taylor, who served as American ambassador to Vietnam, reflected on the war in Vietnam years after it had ended:

❝ First, we didn't know ourselves. We thought we were going into another Korean war, but this was a different country. Secondly, we didn't know our South Vietnamese allies. We never understood them, and that was another surprise. And we knew even less about North Vietnam. ❞

Origins of the War

⭐ The roots of the Vietnam conflict can be traced back to World War II, when Japanese forces captured the French colony of Indochina in Southeast Asia. Vietnamese forces led by Communist **Ho Chi Minh** (HOH CHEE MIHN) fought against the Japanese.

When Japan surrendered at the end of World War II, Ho declared Vietnam's independence. The French, however, were unwilling to give up their empire. Their Indochina colony—the present-day nations of Cambodia, Laos, and Vietnam—was among the richest of France's colonies, supplying such valuable resources as rice, rubber, and tin. Ho and his forces fought the French in a long, bloody war, finally defeating the French in 1954.

The Geneva Accords

That same year, diplomats from the United States, France, Great Britain, the Soviet Union, Communist China, and Vietnam met in Geneva, Switzerland, to hammer out a peace agreement. According to the **Geneva Accords,** Vietnam would be divided temporarily. Ho Chi Minh's Communist nationalists would control the North. Non-Communist forces—supported by the United States—would control the South. Vietnam would be unified in 1956 after national elections.

Neither the United States nor South Vietnam signed the agreement, but they did not oppose its provisions. At the same time, an American representative warned that the United States reserved the right to step in if Communist North Vietnam moved aggressively against the South.

Renewed Conflict

In 1955 **Ngo Dinh Diem** (NOH DIHN deh •EHM), French-educated Vietnamese leader, gained control of the government of South Vietnam. The following year, Diem, with American support, refused to hold the elections promised by the Geneva Accords. Diem's brutal policies and his refusal to hold elections angered many Vietnamese.

Communist supporters of Ho Chi Minh remained in the South after Vietnam was divided. They challenged Diem's efforts to gain control of the country. In the late 1950s, Diem launched a campaign to destroy the power of the Communists. In response, the Communists organized themselves as the **National Liberation Front** (NLF)— better known to Americans as the Vietcong. In 1959 the Vietcong, on orders from Ho Chi Minh, began a war against the Diem regime.

A Growing American Role

The United States had replaced the French as the dominant foreign power in the South in 1955. If Communists took South Vietnam, President Eisenhower once said, the other countries of Southeast Asia would fall to communism like a row of dominoes—one right after the other. This domino theory helped shape American policy in Vietnam for the next 20 years.

To support South Vietnam, the Eisenhower administration sent the country billions of dollars in aid. It also dispatched a few hundred soldiers, who acted as advisers to the South Vietnamese government and army.

The Kennedy Years

Like Eisenhower, President Kennedy saw Vietnam as part of the global struggle in the fight against communism. Kennedy sent more Special Forces troops— the Green Berets—to train and advise South Vietnamese troops. Kennedy also pressured Diem to make political and economic reforms to

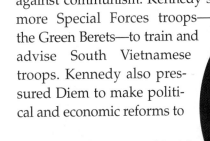

Ho Chi Minh

★ **Picturing HISTORY** Buddhist monks often led protests against unpopular South Vietnamese governments. **Why did Vietnam's Buddhists protest against the Diem government?**

American soldiers leap from a helicopter during a mission in South Vietnam. **When did President Johnson begin to escalate American involvement in Vietnam?**

eliminate the conditions that had allowed communism to take root in the first place. But Diem refused to comply. Instead of paying for new schools, health clinics, or land reform, American funds often ended up in the pockets of corrupt South Vietnamese officials. At the same time, North Vietnam sent aid and troops to the South to help the Vietcong in a guerrilla war against Diem that began in 1959.

The Diem government lost support throughout the country. His government took rights away from **Buddhists**—the majority of the people in South Vietnam—and favored Catholics, like himself. Buddhists responded with protests, some of which ended in bloodshed when government troops fired into the crowds.

In early 1963 Buddhist monks showed their opposition to Diem's rule by setting themselves on fire on busy streets. Horrifying photographs of monks engulfed in flames appeared in newspapers and on television screens around the world. The Kennedy administration found it difficult to continue to support Diem.

On November 1, 1963, a group of South Vietnamese army officers staged a coup—overthrew the government—and assassinated Diem. The Kennedy administration had supported the coup, but not the assassination. After President Kennedy was assassinated later that same month, the question of what to do in Vietnam fell on the shoulders of President **Lyndon B. Johnson.**

The Conflict Deepens

★ At the time of Kennedy's death, the United States had nearly 15,000 American troops in Vietnam as advisers. President Johnson sent Secretary of Defense **Robert McNamara** to Vietnam on a fact-finding mission.

McNamara told the president that South Vietnam could not resist the Vietcong rebels without more help from the United States. In a May 1964 conversation, taped but not made public until 1997, Johnson himself expressed doubts about American commitment. "I don't think it's worth

Linking
PAST & PRESENT

From War to Tourism

Ho Chi Minh City (formerly Saigon) proclaimed 1990 its "Year of Tourism." Tunnels once used by the Vietcong guerrillas—a network of 200 miles—were one of the featured tourist attractions.

fighting for," he said, "but I don't think we can get out." Nevertheless, as Vietcong attacks continued, the United States moved toward deeper involvement.

Gulf of Tonkin Resolution

President Johnson wanted congressional support for expanding the American role in Vietnam. The opportunity to get that support came in August 1964, when North Vietnamese patrol boats allegedly attacked American destroyers in the **Gulf of Tonkin** near North Vietnam. Congress quickly passed a resolution that allowed the president to "take all necessary measures to repel any armed attack against the forces of the United States." The **Gulf of Tonkin Resolution** gave Johnson broad authority to use American forces in Vietnam.

Military Buildup

In 1965 Johnson began to escalate—gradually increase—United States involvement in Vietnam. The buildup included both ground troops and an air campaign.

United States Marines landed near **Da Nang,** South Vietnam, on March 8, 1965. During the next three years, the number of American troops in Vietnam increased sharply. About 180,000 soldiers were in Vietnam by the end of 1965, almost 400,000 by the end of 1966, and more than 500,000 by late 1967.

The United States also unleashed an intense bombing campaign called Operation Rolling Thunder. Some planes attacked the **Ho Chi Minh**

Trail, a network of roads, paths, and bridges that snaked from North Vietnam through **Cambodia** and **Laos** into South Vietnam. North Vietnamese troops used this route to bring equipment south. Other planes targeted bridges, docks, factories, and military bases in the North.

The bombing increased in intensity from 1965 through 1968. By then American planes had dropped more bombs on North Vietnam than they had dropped on Germany, Italy, and Japan during World War II.

Fighting the War

★ The American troops found fighting a ground war in Vietnam difficult. Dense jungles, muddy trails, and swampy rice paddies

★ **Picturing HISTORY** Villagers believed to be Vietcong supporters are watched by South Vietnamese soldiers. **How did the North Vietnamese send supplies to the Vietcong in South Vietnam?**

Chapter 30 The Vietnam Era 855

hampered troop movement. The South Vietnamese army did not always fight effectively. As the Vietcong guerrillas blended with the population, American soldiers found it hard to tell friends and enemies apart.

On the Ground

The American forces began to conduct search-and-destroy missions. The goal was to seek out Vietcong or North Vietnamese units and destroy them. The Americans hoped to eventually defeat the Communists or force them to negotiate.

Ground troops coordinated their moves with air support. Patrols on the ground radioed their location, and helicopter gunships roared to the scene to blast the enemy with cannon and machine-gun fire.

Planes bombed areas of South Vietnam in an effort to drive guerrillas from their jungle cover. Both sides used planes to drop **napalm,** an explosive that burned intensely, to destroy jungle growth. North Vietnamese and Vietcong forces also used napalm in flamethrowers, devices that expel fuel or a burning stream of liquids. To improve visibility, chemical herbicides were sprayed in Vietnam to clear out forests and tall

grasses. One herbicide, **Agent Orange,** is believed to have contaminated many Americans and Vietnamese, causing serious health problems.

Frustration Grows

The bombing of the Ho Chi Minh Trail and the North did not stop the constant flow of troops and equipment south. Neither did it break the morale of the North Vietnamese. As one of their leaders later said,

> ❝ The Americans thought that the more bombs they dropped, the quicker we would fall to our knees and surrender. But the bombs heightened, rather than dampened, our spirit. ❞

The search-and-destroy missions killed thousands of North Vietnamese and Vietcong

More than 7,500 American nurses (below) served during the Vietnam conflict.

★ **Picturing HISTORY** A wounded American soldier reaches for a fallen comrade (above). **How many American troops were in Vietnam by the end of 1967?**

troops—but the troops always seemed to be replaced. What Ho Chi Minh had said to the French became true again:

> 66 You can kill ten of my men for every one I kill of yours. But even at those odds, you will lose and I will win. 99

American troops advanced into rice paddies, jungles, and small villages and killed scores of Vietcong. Yet the next day, the same area had to be attacked again.

American soldiers grew frustrated. Philip Caputo, a young marine lieutenant, recalled the changing attitude:

> 66 When we marched into the rice paddies on that damp March afternoon, we carried, along with our packs and rifles, the implicit convictions that the Vietcong could be quickly beaten. We kept the packs and rifles; the convictions, we lost. 99 🔍

Debate in the White House

Officials in the Johnson administration saw the mounting Communist losses and believed at first that the United States could succeed. As the

American soldiers on patrol

war dragged on, however, some government officials saw a gloomier situation. Secretary of Defense McNamara began to argue that the ground war and the air attacks had failed and that the war could not be won. Outside the nation's capital, opposition to the war grew. Soon it swelled to anger.

★ ★ ★ ★ ★ **Section 2 Assessment** ★ ★ ★ ★ ★

Checking for Understanding
1. *Identify* Ho Chi Minh, Ngo Dinh Diem, Lyndon B. Johnson, Gulf of Tonkin Resolution.
2. *Define* Vietcong, domino theory, coup, escalate, search-and-destroy mission.
3. *Describe* the agreement reached at the Geneva Accords.

Reviewing Themes
4. **Government and Democracy** How did President Johnson gain the approval from Congress to use American forces in Vietnam?

Critical Thinking
5. **Analyzing Information** What signs existed during the mid-1960s that indicated the United States would have a difficult time winning the Vietnam War?

◆ **Activity** ◆

Creating a Cartoon Draw a cartoon illustrating the domino theory as it applied to the spread of communism in Southeast Asia.

| 1962 | 1964 | 1966 | 1968 |

1962
Students for a Democratic Society organize

1964
Free Speech Movement protests at Berkeley

1967
War protesters march on Pentagon

Section 3

The Vietnam Years at Home

READ TO DISCOVER . . .

■ what factors contributed to the rise of the counterculture.

■ how Americans at home responded to the war in Vietnam.

TERMS TO LEARN

radical
counterculture
deferment

dove
hawk

The Storyteller

As the Vietnam War dragged on, Americans became divided—usually by age—over the U.S. presence in that country. Even reporters showed their biases when they covered the antiwar demonstrations at the Pentagon in 1967. On one hand, older reporters who stood behind the police wrote about radicals storming the Pentagon. On the other side of the police barricade, younger reporters wrote about the brutality of the U.S. marshals. Each side of the generation gap firmly believed that its version of the story was correct.

Antiwar button

While fighting raged in Vietnam, the American people disagreed sharply over the war. Prowar and antiwar groups attacked each other with mounting anger. Antiwar demonstrators called President Johnson and his supporters "killers." Supporters of the war referred to the protesters as "traitors."

Americans watched these deep divisions with increasing alarm. The war seemed to split America—and much of the division resulted from what people called the **generation gap.**

The Youth Protest

The protest movement against the Vietnam War grew in part out of a broader dissatisfaction with American society. Inspired by the ideals of the civil rights movement, many high school and college students criticized the United States for its racial discrimination and its overemphasis on material values. The desire of these young people to change society came to be focused on the war in Vietnam. The Students for a Democratic Society and the Free Speech Movement were two influential groups.

The New Left

In 1962, at a meeting in Port Huron, Michigan, students from across the country organized **Students for a Democratic Society** (SDS). The group had broad goals and "an agenda for a generation," which condemned racism, poverty, and nuclear weapons. Rejecting efforts at reform, the students in SDS called for a radical transformation of American society.

Another movement emerged in California two years later. Officials of the University of California at Berkeley had taken steps to limit the recruiting efforts of protest groups on campus. Angered by the restrictions, students launched what they called the **Free Speech Movement,** staging a protest that paralyzed the university for several days.

These new ideas and protests spread to other campuses around the country. Although not part of a single movement, the activists who shared these ideas came to be called the **New Left.**

The Counterculture

The radical ideas of the New Left, which challenged the values and institutions of American society, reached only a minority of students. Yet many young people did rebel against their parents' world, and they expressed their opposition in colorful ways.

In the counterculture, a movement that rejected traditional American values, the students sought to create a new lifestyle. Some common symbols of the counterculture—torn blue jeans and long hair for males—aroused opposition from parents. Popular music played a role in communicating the ideas of the counterculture. Many 1960s songs, such as this one by Bob Dylan, expressed a longing for peace and justice:

> 66 Yes, 'n' how many times must the cannon balls fly
> Before they're forever banned?
> The answer, my friend, is blowin' in the wind,
> The answer is blowin' in the wind. 99

Other parts of the counterculture represented a more serious challenge to traditional middle-class values. Some young people refused to follow customary social roles of study, work, and family. They aimed to reject aspects of American society they criticized—the competition for material goods and personal success.

As the 1960s progressed, the New Left, the counterculture, and other movements shared one common element. They all expressed growing opposition to the war in Vietnam.

Opposition to the Draft

Student protests targeted the selective service system—the **draft** that supplied soldiers for the war. The law required all men to register for the

★ Picturing HISTORY An antiwar protester places flowers in the rifles of soldiers guarding the Pentagon near Washington, D.C. **What were common symbols of the counterculture?**

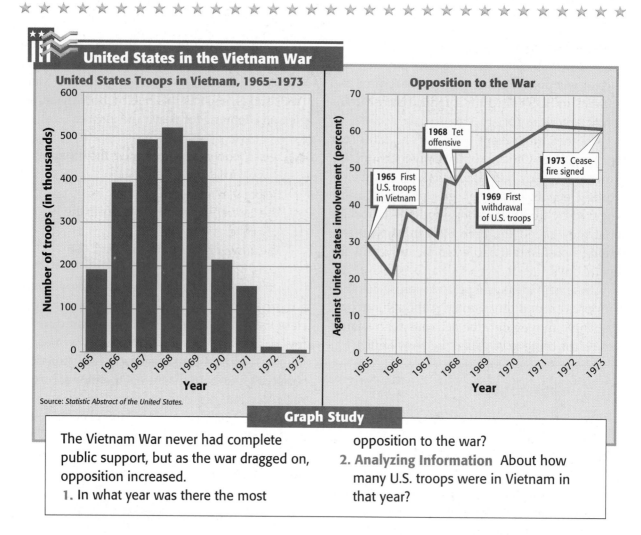

United States in the Vietnam War

United States Troops in Vietnam, 1965–1973

Number of troops (in thousands) vs. *Year (1965–1973)*

Source: *Statistic Abstract of the United States.*

Opposition to the War

Against United States involvement (percent) vs. *Year*

- **1965** First U.S. troops in Vietnam
- **1968** Tet offensive
- **1969** First withdrawal of U.S. troops
- **1973** Cease-fire signed

Graph Study

The Vietnam War never had complete public support, but as the war dragged on, opposition increased.

1. In what year was there the most opposition to the war?
2. **Analyzing Information** About how many U.S. troops were in Vietnam in that year?

draft when they reached age 18. Opposition to the draft had two sources.

Those strongly opposed to American involvement in Vietnam believed that by forcing an end to the draft they could halt the supply of soldiers needed to fight there. Others called the draft unfair. Draft boards could give people deferments that excused them from the draft for various reasons. Full-time college students—mostly from the middle class—received such deferments. As a result an increasing percentage of soldiers came from poor or working-class families. Many who opposed the draft argued that deferments discriminated against the poor.

Some protesters became **conscientious objectors,** claiming that their moral or religious beliefs prevented them from fighting in the war. Other protesters showed their opposition by burning their draft cards, their military registration forms. Congress responded with a law making draft-card burning a crime.

Debating the War

Students and other opponents of the Vietnam War came to be called doves. Supporters of the war became known as hawks.

Doves and Hawks

Opposition to the war grew within the government. Two sets of Senate hearings intensified the debate between the doves and hawks.

In 1966 Senator **J. William Fulbright,** head of the Senate Foreign Relations Committee, held hearings on the war in Vietnam. Some of the government officials who testified thought the war was a mistake. The televised hearings brought the debate into Americans' homes. Fulbright, who had once supported the war, now doubted "the ability of the United States to achieve [its] aims."

Senator **John C. Stennis** of Mississippi held another round of hearings in 1967. At these hearings of the Senate Armed Services Committee, officials made a case for continuing the war. A report from the Stennis hearings concluded that the United States should "do whatever is necessary . . . and apply the force that is required to see the job through."

Congress was of two minds on the Vietnam War. The same could be said of the American people.

America Divided

Across the nation more and more Americans came to view the war unfavorably. Some thought the United States should not be fighting in Vietnam. Others opposed the way the government conducted the war. Both hawks and doves criticized President Johnson for his handling of the war in Vietnam, and his approval rating declined dramatically.

The War Loses Support

As opposition to the war mounted, the opponents staged larger demonstrations. In October 1967, more than 50,000 people marched to the **Pentagon**—headquarters of the Defense Department—to protest the war.

Attacks by opponents of the war grew sharper and more bitter. The Secret Service, charged

★ **Picturing HISTORY** Antiwar demonstrations, such as this gathering in Washington, D.C., were held throughout the nation in the late 1960s. **What government practice affecting young men was often targeted by antiwar protesters?**

with guarding President Johnson, feared for his safety and urged him not to speak in public. He began to appear only before crowds known to be sympathetic.

The president had often urged people to come together to discuss issues calmly. "Let us reason together," he had said. By 1968 Americans showed less willingness to talk reasonably, and violent events often overtook discussion.

★ ★ ★ ★ ★ **Section 3 Assessment** ★ ★ ★ ★ ★

Checking for Understanding
1. *Identify* New Left, J. William Fulbright, John C. Stennis, Pentagon.
2. *Define* radical, counterculture, deferment, dove, hawk.
3. *List* two reasons some Americans began to oppose involvement in Vietnam.

Reviewing Themes
4. **Continuity and Change** Besides the Vietnam War, what other parts of American society did the counterculture of the 1960s condemn?

Critical Thinking
5. **Synthesizing Information** How would you define the "generation gap"?

Conducting an Interview Interview friends and relatives who lived during the Vietnam War era to see how people in your community reacted to the conflict. Present an oral report of your findings.

January
North Korea captures U.S.S. *Pueblo*

April
Martin Luther King, Jr., is assassinated

June
Robert Kennedy is assassinated

August
Violence erupts at Democratic convention in Chicago

November
Richard Nixon wins presidency

Section 4

1968–Year of Crises

READ TO DISCOVER . . .

- how the Tet offensive affected the war in Vietnam and politics in the United States.
- which political leaders ran for president in 1968 and what they stood for.

TERMS TO LEARN

credibility gap   silent majority

The Storyteller

In January 1968, about 10,000 U.S. Marines fought fiercely to hold their position in the hills at Khe Sanh, Vietnam, north of Saigon. North Vietnamese troops had surrounded Khe Sanh and opened fire on the Americans. The marines held Khe Sanh. Corporal James Hebron later explained what it was like to be there for 77 days: "All you saw was the air being ripped apart and the ground shaking underneath you—and you bouncing into the air. . . . [T]he trenches would shake."

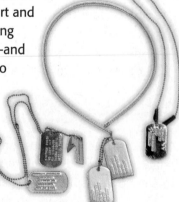

Dog tags—military identification tags

The year 1968 opened with a shock for the American people. On January 23, North Korean boats seized the **U.S.S. *Pueblo***, a navy spy ship cruising in international waters off the coast of Korea. The news that a foreign country had captured an American ship and its crew shocked the nation.

The next week brought another staggering blow as North Vietnam launched a major series of attacks in South Vietnam. As Americans soon learned, 1968 would be a long, dramatic, and very difficult year.

The Tet Offensive

On January 31, 1968, the North Vietnamese and Vietcong launched a series of attacks throughout South Vietnam. The attacks, which began on the Vietnamese new year—Tet—became known as the **Tet offensive.** Tet marked a turning point in the Vietnam War.

Attacks in South Vietnam

The Tet offensive targeted American military bases and South Vietnam's major cities. Vietcong troops raided the United States embassy in **Saigon,** the capital. The Vietcong also struck in **Hue,** the ancient capital of Vietnam, and fought for almost a month.

All across South Vietnam, Americans and South Vietnamese troops fought bravely to retake the cities. They finally drove the Vietcong back and inflicted thousands of casualties. The enormous losses that the Vietcong suffered forced North Vietnam to take over a larger share of the fighting. In military terms, the Americans and the South Vietnamese won the battle.

Impact Back Home

In the United States, however, the Tet offensive turned many more Americans against the war—and against President Johnson. The sight of Vietcong guerrillas killing Americans in the embassy shocked television viewers. The many days needed to defeat the assault on Hue undermined the army's statements about the United States winning the war.

Major newspapers and magazines openly criticized the Johnson administration's conduct of the war. The *Wall Street Journal* wrote, "The American people should be getting ready to accept . . . the prospect that the whole Vietnam effort may be doomed."

Most Americans seemed to agree. Fewer people believed that the army was making progress in the war. More people believed that the army was losing ground. The Johnson administration developed a credibility gap—fewer people trusted its statements about the war.

★ Picturing HISTORY During the Tet offensive, United States Marines climb a mound of rubble that was once a tower of the fortress of Hue. **Why was the Tet offensive a turning point in the Vietnam War?**

President Lyndon Johnson

Challenges to the President

As opposition to the war grew, President Johnson faced challenges in his own party. In late 1967, Democratic senator **Eugene McCarthy** of Minnesota had announced that he would run for the party's nomination for the presidency as a protest against the war. Not well known, McCarthy seemed to have little chance of winning. In the March 12 primary in New Hampshire, however, McCarthy surprised everyone by taking 42 percent of the popular vote. Although Johnson won the primary, McCarthy's strong showing indicated widespread opposition to the war.

Later, another antiwar candidate entered the race. **Robert F. Kennedy,** attorney general during his brother's presidency and now a senator from New York, announced that he, too, would seek the Democratic nomination.

The President Responds

Events in Vietnam and the growing antiwar movement disturbed President Johnson. Following the Tet offensive, the American commander in Vietnam, General **William Westmoreland,** had requested still more troops. Instead of agreeing, the president ordered a reevaluation of the war. He also reevaluated his own campaign for reelection in 1968.

On March 31, 1968, after consulting advisers, President Johnson appeared on television to announce a "new step toward peace"—he would halt the bombing of North Vietnam's cities. He asked North Vietnam for a comparable action so that peace negotiations could begin.

The president concluded his speech with a startling announcement. He said, "I shall not seek, and I will not accept, the nomination of my party for another term as your president."

Picturing HISTORY After Robert Kennedy's death in June 1968, a divided Democratic convention met in Chicago. Chicago mayor Richard Daley had barbed wire set up at the convention hall to keep out antiwar protesters. **How did most Americans react to the violence in Chicago?**

Violence Erupts

A few days after Johnson's withdrawal from the presidential race, tragedy struck the nation. A sniper in Memphis, Tennessee, shot and killed **Martin Luther King, Jr.,** the leading activist in the civil rights movement.

The King assassination triggered a rash of riots across the country. Army troops were called on to control unruly crowds in various cities. Already saddened by King's death, Americans worried about the renewed urban violence.

Another Kennedy Assassination

While the nation agonized over unrest at home and war abroad, the presidential race picked up speed. Vice President **Hubert H. Humphrey** joined Eugene McCarthy and Robert Kennedy in seeking the Democratic nomination. Kennedy edged out McCarthy in a number of primary elections, but McCarthy rebounded and scored a primary victory in Oregon. Humphrey, meanwhile, avoided the primaries. He gathered support among Democratic Party leaders, who in some states chose the delegates.

In early June 1968, Kennedy and McCarthy faced each other in the primary election in California, the state with the most delegates. That night, after Kennedy won, an assassin shot and killed him—and the nation reeled with the shock of yet another assassination.

The Democratic Convention

By the time the Democrats held their convention in **Chicago,** Humphrey appeared to have enough votes to win the nomination. As a longtime supporter of civil rights and labor causes, Humphrey had considerable backing in his party. As a supporter of Johnson's Vietnam policy, however, Humphrey was linked to the prowar faction of the party.

Antiwar Democrats felt angry and excluded from the convention. Tension filled the air. When trouble broke out, though, it did not occur as much in the convention hall as in the city's streets.

Frustrated by the almost certain victory of Humphrey, thousands of antiwar activists flocked to Chicago to protest. Chicago's mayor, **Richard J. Daley,** feared violence from the demonstrators and had the police out in force. The police made some arrests the first two nights, but no major problems developed.

On the third day, the antiwar protesters planned to march to the convention site to protest Humphrey's nomination. Police blocked the marchers at the hall. When the marchers headed in another direction, the police stopped them again. The protesters began to pelt the police with sticks and bottles. The police threw tear gas and charged in, wielding nightsticks. They pursued those who fled, beating some and arresting many.

Humphrey won the Democratic nomination, but the violence outside and the anger within the hall—all shown on television—had damaged his candidacy. The Democrats appeared unable to control their own convention. Humphrey admitted, "Chicago was a catastrophe."

Election of 1968

★ A majority of Americans disapproved of the police action in Chicago but, at the same time, strongly opposed the actions of the protesters. The years of protest and dissent had taken their toll, and a backlash had set in. Most Americans fervently wished for a return to "law and order."

The Wallace Candidacy

One presidential candidate who used the "law and order" theme was Governor **George C. Wallace** of Alabama. Running as a third-party candidate, Wallace promised to crack down on "long-hair . . . draft card-burning youth." In addition, he criticized efforts to integrate schools by busing students and ridiculed "pointy-headed" bureaucrats in Washington for telling people how to run their lives.

Wallace's tough stand on law and order and his appeal to racial fears attracted many voters. Some political reporters predicted Wallace could win as much as 20 percent of the vote.

The "Silent Majority"

The Republican presidential nominee, former vice president **Richard M. Nixon,** also tried to tap into voters' growing conservative sentiment. Nixon pledged to represent the "quiet voice" of the "great majority of Americans, the non-shouters, the nondemonstrators." He called these people the "silent majority." Declaring that the "first civil right of every American is to be free from domestic violence," Nixon promised a return to law and order.

On Vietnam Nixon remained vague. He promised that he would achieve "peace with honor," but he would not provide details of his plan.

During the election campaign, Nixon sought to win some of the traditionally Democratic Southern states with the law-and-order issue. This "Southern strategy" paid off. Although Wallace did take 5 Southern states, Nixon won 7 Southern states and their 78 electoral votes.

Nixon Wins

The popular vote was close. Nixon edged out Humphrey by about 500,000 votes—a difference of less than 1 percent. In the electoral vote, however, Nixon won a solid majority—301 votes to Humphrey's 191.

Nixon entered the presidency with the votes of only 43.4 percent of the people. Nixon and Wallace together, however, had won almost 57 percent of the vote. It seemed that a substantial majority of Americans wanted the government to restore order.

★ ★ ★ ★ ★ ★ **Section 4 Assessment** ★ ★ ★ ★ ★ ★

Checking for Understanding
1. *Identify* Tet offensive, Eugene McCarthy, Robert F. Kennedy, William Westmoreland, Hubert H. Humphrey, Richard M. Nixon.
2. *Define* credibility gap, silent majority.
3. *Discuss* the effect of the Tet offensive.

Reviewing Themes
4. **Civic Rights and Responsibilities** What was the result of the 1968 election?

Critical Thinking
5. **Making Inferences** How did a credibility gap affect Johnson's effectiveness as president?

Activity

Making Headlines Write a headline that might have appeared in a January 1, 1969, newspaper article summing up the mood of the country after surviving the turmoil of 1968.

Building a Database

Have you ever collected baseball cards or cataloged the CDs in your collection? Have you ever kept a list of the names and addresses of your friends and relatives? If you have collected information and kept some sort of list or file, then you have created a database.

Nixon greets well-wishers at a campaign rally

Learning the Skill

An electronic database is a collection of facts that are stored in files on the computer. The information is organized in fields.

A database can be organized and reorganized in any way that is useful to you. By using a database management system (DBMS)—special software developed for record keeping—you can easily add, delete, change, or update information. You give commands to the computer telling it what to do with the information, and it follows your commands. When you want to retrieve information, the computer searches through the files, finds the information, and displays it on the screen.

Practicing the Skill

Richard M. Nixon is one of the presidents discussed in this chapter. Follow these steps to build a database of the political and cultural events that took place during his presidency.

1. Determine what facts you want to include in your database.
2. Follow instructions in the DBMS you are using to set up fields. Then enter each item of data in its assigned field.
3. Determine how you want to organize the facts in the database—chronologically by the date of the event, or alphabetically by the name of the event.
4. Follow the instructions in your computer program to place the information in order of importance.
5. Check that the information in your database is all correct. If necessary, add, delete, or change information or fields.

Applying the Skill

Building a Database Bring to class current newspapers. Using the steps just described, build a database of political figures mentioned in the newspapers. Explain to a partner why the database is organized the way it is and how it might be used in this class.

June 1969
Nixon begins to
withdraw troops
from Vietnam

April 1970
Nixon sends
troops to
Cambodia

May 1970
Six students killed
at Kent State and
Jackson State

January 1973
Paris peace accords
end U.S. involvement
in Vietnam

Section 5

Nixon and Vietnam

READ TO DISCOVER . . .

- what new strategy President Nixon
  followed in Vietnam.
- how protests against the war continued.
- how the fighting in Vietnam ended.

TERMS TO LEARN

Vietnamization   MIAs
martial law

The Storyteller

President Nixon's inauguration in January
1969 took place on a cold, gloomy day. Along
Pennsylvania Avenue in Washington, D.C.,
stood hundreds of demonstrators chanting
antiwar slogans and holding anti-Nixon
posters. At one point Nixon's limousine was
pelted with sticks, stones, and bottles. Offended by this behavior, World War II veterans
shouted at the demonstrators, labeling the
protesters "Communists"
and "traitors." This
marked the first
time an inaugur-
al parade was
disrupted in the
180 years of the
presidency.

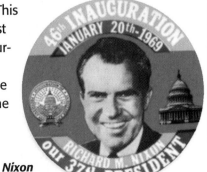

*Nixon
inaugural
button*

In his Inaugural Address in January 1969,
Richard M. Nixon appealed to the American
people for calm:

> ❝We cannot learn from one another until
> we stop shouting at one another—until
> we speak quietly enough so that our
> words can be heard as well as our
> voices.❞

In the early days of Nixon's presidency, the
level of anger and confrontation decreased. Still,
as Nixon said, Vietnam remained a "bone in the
nation's throat." The war created divisions
among Americans, and those divisions could rise
to the surface at any time.

A New Strategy

The new president had campaigned on a
pledge of "peace with honor" in Vietnam.
He wanted to pull American forces out of Vietnam, but he did not want American withdrawal
to be seen as a sign of defeat. Nixon's strategy of
peace with honor had three parts—reform of the
selective service system, giving South Vietnam
more responsibility in fighting the war, and
intense bombing.

Draft Reform

Under President Nixon the selective service
system changed. College students could no longer
obtain draft deferments; only 19-year-olds could

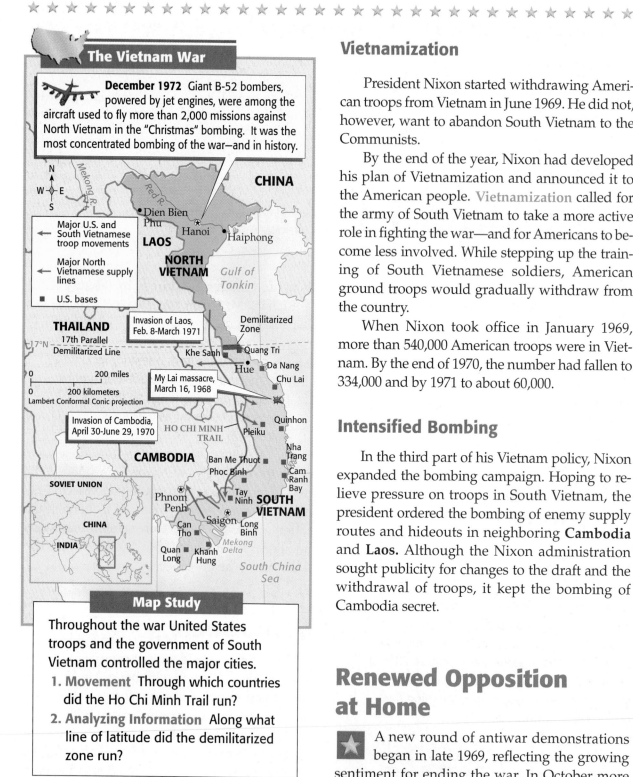

The Vietnam War

December 1972 Giant B-52 bombers, powered by jet engines, were among the aircraft used to fly more than 2,000 missions against North Vietnam in the "Christmas" bombing. It was the most concentrated bombing of the war—and in history.

CHINA

Red R.

Mekong R.

• Dien Bien Phu

★ Hanoi • Haiphong

LAOS

NORTH VIETNAM

Gulf of Tonkin

Major U.S. and South Vietnamese troop movements

Major North Vietnamese supply lines

U.S. bases

THAILAND

17th Parallel Demilitarized Line

0   200 miles

0   200 kilometers
Lambert Conformal Conic projection

Invasion of Laos, Feb. 8–March 1971

Demilitarized Zone

Khe Sanh ■ Quang Tri

Hue • ■ Da Nang
■ Chu Lai

My Lai massacre, March 16, 1968

Invasion of Cambodia, April 30–June 29, 1970

HO CHI MINH TRAIL

Pleiku ■

Quinhon ■

Nha Trang

CAMBODIA   Ban Me Thuot ■

Phoc Binh •

Cam Ranh Bay

SOVIET UNION

Phnom Penh ★

Tay Ninh SOUTH VIETNAM

CHINA

Can Tho •

Saigon ★ Long Binh

INDIA

Quan Long ■ Khanh Hung ■

Mekong Delta

South China Sea

Map Study

Throughout the war United States troops and the government of South Vietnam controlled the major cities.

1. **Movement** Through which countries did the Ho Chi Minh Trail run?

2. **Analyzing Information** Along what line of latitude did the demilitarized zone run?

Vietnamization

President Nixon started withdrawing American troops from Vietnam in June 1969. He did not, however, want to abandon South Vietnam to the Communists.

By the end of the year, Nixon had developed his plan of Vietnamization and announced it to the American people. Vietnamization called for the army of South Vietnam to take a more active role in fighting the war—and for Americans to become less involved. While stepping up the training of South Vietnamese soldiers, American ground troops would gradually withdraw from the country.

When Nixon took office in January 1969, more than 540,000 American troops were in Vietnam. By the end of 1970, the number had fallen to 334,000 and by 1971 to about 60,000.

Intensified Bombing

In the third part of his Vietnam policy, Nixon expanded the bombing campaign. Hoping to relieve pressure on troops in South Vietnam, the president ordered the bombing of enemy supply routes and hideouts in neighboring **Cambodia** and **Laos.** Although the Nixon administration sought publicity for changes to the draft and the withdrawal of troops, it kept the bombing of Cambodia secret.

Renewed Opposition at Home

A new round of antiwar demonstrations began in late 1969, reflecting the growing sentiment for ending the war. In October more than 300,000 people took part in an antiwar protest in Washington, D.C.

Appeal for Support

The government also tried to end the war through peace talks with North Vietnam. **Henry Kissinger,** the president's national security

be called for service in Vietnam; and draftees would be chosen by lottery on the basis of their birth date. Protests against the draft faded because of these reforms, because the government began calling up fewer young men, and because President Nixon promised to eliminate the selective service in the future.

★ ★

adviser, represented the United States in the Paris talks. The United States had launched the bombing campaign to persuade the North Vietnamese to agree to settlement terms, but the North Vietnamese adopted a wait-and-see attitude. They believed that the strength of the antiwar movement in the United States would force the Americans to withdraw.

The new antiwar protests and North Vietnam's unyielding attitude alarmed President Nixon. In his speech on Vietnamization in November, he appealed to the "silent majority" of Americans for support for his policy. "North Vietnam cannot defeat or humiliate the United States," he said. "Only Americans can do that."

Expanding the War

Further conflict gripped Southeast Asia when Cambodia plunged into a civil war between Communist and non-Communist forces. Nixon decided in April 1970 to send American troops to destroy Communist bases in Cambodia.

On April 30, President Nixon told the nation of the attack on Cambodia, saying, "We shall not be defeated in Vietnam. . . . The world's most powerful nation [will not act] like a pitiful helpless giant." Yet the attack aroused outrage in Congress and elsewhere. By sending American troops

to Cambodia, critics charged, Nixon invaded a neutral country and overstepped his constitutional authority as president.

Kent State

The Cambodian invasion provoked a storm of antiwar protests on campuses across the nation. Most proceeded peacefully. But two protests ended in tragedy.

At a protest at Kent State University in **Kent, Ohio,** students burned a military building on campus. Ohio's governor declared martial law—emergency military rule—on the campus and ordered 3,000 National Guard troops to Kent.

On May 4 armed troops arrived on campus. Eighteen-year-old Leone Keegan, a freshman, remembered going to class that morning:

> 66 I saw all these young men in uniforms standing on the street corners with their rifles, and I was thinking, What is this? 99

At noon students gathered for a protest rally on the campus lawn. The National Guard members—young, inexperienced, and nervous—told

★ **Picturing HISTORY** President Nixon (left) and national security adviser Henry Kissinger discuss foreign policy strategy. **In what three ways did Nixon plan to achieve "peace with honor" in Vietnam?**

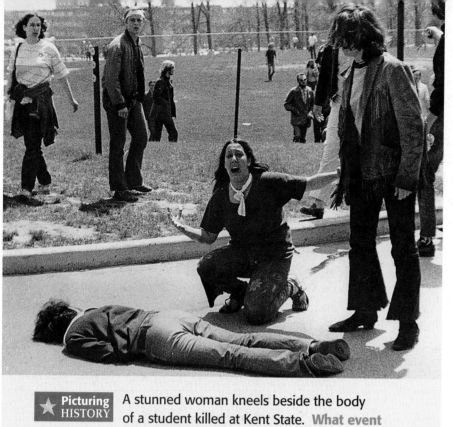

A stunned woman kneels beside the body of a student killed at Kent State. **What event sparked the student unrest at Kent State?**

the protesting students to leave. "Evacuate the area. You have no right to assemble," they shouted through bullhorns. The students shouted back, "We don't want your war." Some students threw stones.

The troops shot tear gas toward the students; many students ran. One National Guard unit chased some students between two buildings. Then—for reasons that are unclear—the troops opened fire. ". . . [T]hey're killing us," screamed one student in disbelief. Four students were dead and nine more were wounded.

Jackson State

Violence flared again on May 14 at the nearly all-African American college of **Jackson State** in Mississippi. Following a night of campus vio-

lence, two students were shot and killed. Witnesses charged that the police had recklessly blasted the residence hall with shotguns. The police claimed they were protecting themselves from sniper fire.

Reactions

A wave of student strikes followed the tragedies at Kent State and Jackson State. Hundreds of colleges and universities suspended classes or closed down completely.

The president took a hard line. The Kent State shootings, he said, "should remind us once again that when dissent turns to violence it invites tragedy." A commission that investigated events at Kent State found that the shootings were unjustified. A majority of Americans, however, seemed to agree with the president.

"Peace Is at Hand"

★ Meanwhile, the Nixon administration continued to negotiate with representatives of the North Vietnamese government. These talks stalled, however.

A Peace Agreement Fails

In March 1972, the North Vietnamese launched another major offensive in the south. Because the United States had few troops left in Vietnam, Nixon responded to the attacks with renewed bombing. He also ordered the navy to plant mines in North Vietnamese harbors.

The president stopped insisting that North Vietnam remove all its troops from South Vietnam before a full American withdrawal. Nixon sent Henry Kissinger to meet in private with the North Vietnamese foreign minister. In the fall of 1972—just before the presidential

---

*F*ootnotes to History

Peace Prize In 1973 Henry Kissinger of the United States shared the Nobel Peace Prize with Le Duc Tho of North Vietnam for negotiating a cease-fire in the Vietnam War.

election in the United States—they reached a tentative agreement. "Peace is at hand," Kissinger announced.

His statement came too soon. The agreement collapsed because the South Vietnamese president objected to allowing North Vietnamese forces to remain in South Vietnam.

Peace Finally Comes

After his reelection, Nixon unleashed American airpower against North Vietnam. In December 1972, the heaviest bombardment of the war fell on North Vietnam's cities, provoking outrage in the United States and abroad.

Nixon stood firm, and North Vietnam returned to the peace talks. The Americans pressured the South Vietnamese to accept the peace terms. On January 27, 1973, the negotiators signed the peace agreement.

The United States agreed to pull its remaining troops out of the country. The North Vietnamese agreed to return all American prisoners of war. While the Paris peace accords ended American involvement in Vietnam, they did not end the conflict.

The War Ends

The North Vietnamese never abandoned their goal of unifying Vietnam under their control. In early 1975 they launched a final major offensive. The weakened South Vietnamese army collapsed suddenly on all fronts. Within a few weeks, North Vietnamese tanks reached the outskirts of Saigon.

The Fall of Saigon

As North Vietnamese forces closed in on Saigon, the last Americans scrambled to escape the country, some by helicopter from the roof of the American embassy. Thousands of Vietnamese citizens who had supported or worked for the Americans also fled to the United States. Many more could not escape. In the early hours of April 30, 1975, Saigon fell to the Communists. Soon after, South Vietnam surrendered. The long war was over.

Legacy of the War

⭐ The Vietnam War took a staggering toll of life and suffering. An estimated 1.4 million Vietnamese—civilians as well as soldiers on one side or the other—died between 1965 and 1975. Vietnam lay in ruins, with many villages destroyed.

More than 58,000 Americans were dead; 300,000 were wounded, many of them permanently disabled. The United States had poured more than $150 billion into the war.

About 2.7 million Americans had served in Vietnam. Unlike the veterans of World War II, they found no hero's welcome when they returned home. Many Americans simply wanted to forget the war. They paid little attention to those who had fought and sacrificed in Vietnam.

The relatives of the American soldiers who had been classified as missing in action, or as MIAs, continued to demand that the government press the Vietnamese for information. The Vietnamese did allow a number of American groups to scour the countryside looking for MIAs. As the years passed, however, the likelihood of finding anyone alive faded.

⭐ **Picturing HISTORY** On April 29, 1975, an American helicopter evacuated Americans and South Vietnamese from the roof of the American embassy in Saigon. **Why were these people fleeing the city?**

Healing the Wounds

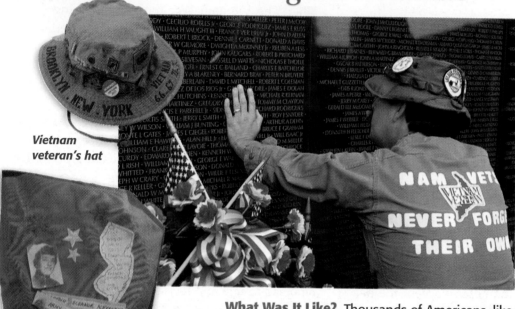

Vietnam veteran's hat

Item in remembrance of member of Army Nurses Corps

Wreath left on Memorial Day, 1989

What Was It Like? Thousands of Americans, like this Vietnam veteran visiting the wall, are still dealing with the painful legacy of the Vietnam War. **Why do you think the items shown here would have an effect on Americans when they remember the war?**

A Step Toward Healing

The construction of the **Vietnam Veterans Memorial** in Washington, D.C., provided a step toward healing the country's wounds. Designed by **Maya Ying Lin,** the striking memorial is a polished black granite wall in the shape of a private's stripes. It bears the names of all the Americans who died or were missing in action in the conflict.

When they visit the wall, families, friends, and comrades in war seek out the names of those who fought in Vietnam and did not return. Since the memorial was dedicated in 1982, visitors have left thousands of keepsakes and remembrances there. The flowers, letters, poems, and pictures left at the wall pay a proud and moving tribute to the Americans who died in the service of their country.

★ ★ ★ ★ ★ Section 5 Assessment ★ ★ ★ ★ ★

Checking for Understanding

1. ***Identify*** Richard M. Nixon, Henry Kissinger.
2. ***Define*** Vietnamization, martial law, MIAs.
3. ***Describe*** Nixon's three-part strategy for ending the war.

Reviewing Themes

4. **Individual Action** Why did Nixon's actions in Cambodia anger many people?

Critical Thinking

5. **Demonstrating Reasoned Judgment** Do you think Nixon succeeded in attaining "peace with honor"? Explain.

Activity

Creating a Memorial Design a memorial to the students who died at Kent State in Ohio.

Multimedia Activities

ABCNEWS INTERACTIVE™ Historic America Electronic Field Trips

Field Trip to the Vietnam Veterans War Memorial

Setting up the Video

With a group of your classmates, view "The Vietnam Veterans War Memorial" on the videodisc *Historic America: Electronic Field Trips*. On November 13, 1982, a monument for Americans who served during the Vietnam War was dedicated in Washington, D.C. This program gives a short overview of United States involvement in the Vietnam War, and the conflict it created among the American people.

Side 2, Chapter 8

View the video by scanning the bar code or by entering the chapter number on your keypad and pressing Search.

Hands-On Activity

After the Vietnam War, many veterans suffered from what is today called post-traumatic stress disorder. This is a condition in which a person who has experienced a traumatic event feels severe and long-lasting aftereffects. Using your school or local library, write a minireport on how this disorder is treated.

 ## Surfing the "Net"

The Vietnam War

The Vietnam War left a profound mark on many Americans. Most deeply affected were the 2.7 million men and women who fought in the war and their families. Veterans who returned home did not receive a hero's welcome. Bitter memories of the war still remain with many veterans today. The war left many with physical and psychological problems. To learn more about experiences of soldiers of the Vietnam War, look on the Internet.

Getting There

Follow these steps to gather information about the Vietnam experience for American military veterans.

1. Go to a search engine.
2. Type in the word *Vietnam*. Following this word, enter words like these to focus your search: *oral history, stories, history.*
3. The search engine should provide you with a number of links to follow. Links are "pointers" to different sites on the Internet.

What to Do When You Are There

Click on the links to navigate through the pages of information. Gather your findings. Using the information from the Internet, interview a Vietnam veteran about his or her experiences during the war. Record your interview and share your findings with the class.

Assessment and Activities

⭐ Reviewing Key Terms

On a sheet of paper, define the following terms:

flexible response	escalate
hot line	deferment
Vietcong	Vietnamization
domino theory	MIAs

⭐ Reviewing Key Facts

1. What was the main purpose of the Bay of Pigs invasion?
2. How did the Geneva Accords plan to unite North and South Vietnam?
3. Why were the American people divided over the Vietnam War?
4. How did the Tet offensive affect the war?
5. What happened in Vietnam after the United States withdrew?

⭐ Critical Thinking

Making Comparisons

World War II and the Vietnam War had very different outcomes.

1. Why do you think most Americans supported World War II but did not support the Vietnam War?
2. How did the American people's attitudes toward both wars affect the way Americans treated returning soldiers?

⭐ Time Line Activity

Create a time line on which you place the following events in chronological order.

- Neil Armstrong walks on moon
- Berlin Wall constructed
- United States pulls out of Vietnam
- Cuban missile crisis erupts

⭐ Reviewing Themes

1. **Geography and History** Why was the Berlin Wall built?
2. **Government and Democracy** What actions did President Eisenhower take regarding the conflict in Vietnam?
3. **Continuity and Change** How did members of the antiwar movement demonstrate against the war?
4. **Civic Rights and Responsibilities** How did American voters express their discontent with the direction the country was taking in the election of 1968?
5. **Individual Action** Why did Nixon order the bombing of Cambodia and Laos?

⭐ Skill Practice Activity

Using a Database Prepare a database of the major battles of the Vietnam War involving United States troops. At your local library, research to find information about the sites of the battles, who the commanding officer was, how many American soldiers were killed or wounded at the sites, and how many North Vietnamese were killed or wounded. Share your database with the rest of your class.

⭐ Cooperative Activity

History and Global Issues One of the hardest decisions a president has to make is when to intervene in an international crisis. With members of your group brainstorm to create a list of international situations in which you think the United States would be justified in intervening and using military force if necessary. Combine your list with those of the other groups and then have all the groups vote to narrow your list down to three situations.

★ Geography Activity

Study the two maps on this page, then answer the questions that follow.

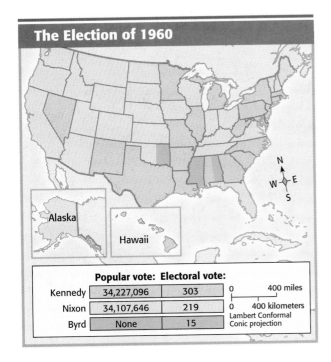

The Election of 1960

Popular vote:		Electoral vote:
Kennedy	34,227,096	303
Nixon	34,107,646	219
Byrd	None	15

0 — 400 miles
0 — 400 kilometers
Lambert Conformal
Conic projection

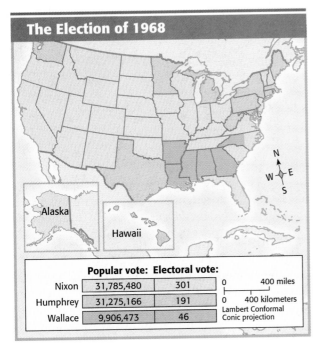

The Election of 1968

Popular vote:		Electoral vote:
Nixon	31,785,480	301
Humphrey	31,275,166	191
Wallace	9,906,473	46

0 — 400 miles
0 — 400 kilometers
Lambert Conformal
Conic projection

1. **Place** Which candidate won Florida's electoral votes in 1960? In 1968?

2. **Place** Which candidate won Alaska's electoral votes in 1968?

3. **Location** How many states voted for Nixon in 1960?

4. **Region** In what regions of the country did Kennedy receive the strongest support in the 1960 election? In which regions was support for Kennedy weakest?

5. **Region** What regions supported Nixon in 1960? In 1968?

6. **Region** Explain why you agree or disagree with the following: The Northeast was Nixon's strongest region in 1968.

★ Technology Activity

Using a Word Processor Complete research at your school or local library for information about the assassinations of John F. Kennedy, Martin Luther King, Jr., and Robert Kennedy. Use the information you find and your word processor to compose a ballad-type song honoring their memory. Add graphics and a border around your printed song sheet.

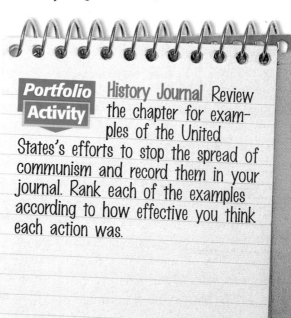

Portfolio Activity

History Journal Review the chapter for examples of the United States's efforts to stop the spread of communism and record them in your journal. Rank each of the examples according to how effective you think each action was.

Unit 11

Modern America

1968–present

"Let us set our sights upon a land of new promise."

—PRESIDENT BILL CLINTON,
1997 INAUGURAL ADDRESS

inteNET CONNECTION

To learn more about the United States today, visit the Glencoe Social Studies Web Site at **www.glencoe.com** for information, activities, and links to other sites.

 **MAPPING** *America*

Portfolio Activity Trace an outline map of the world. As you read this unit about modern America, note the countries involved in U.S. foreign policy issues during the 1970s, 1980s, and 1990s. Mark the location of these countries on your map, with a short caption explaining the reasons for their involvement with the United States.

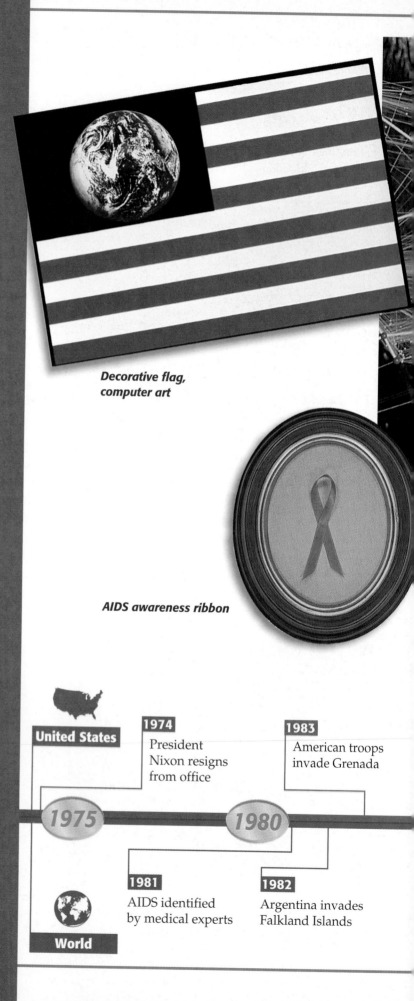

Decorative flag, computer art

AIDS awareness ribbon

United States

1974 President Nixon resigns from office

1983 American troops invade Grenada

1975

1980

1981 AIDS identified by medical experts

1982 Argentina invades Falkland Islands

World

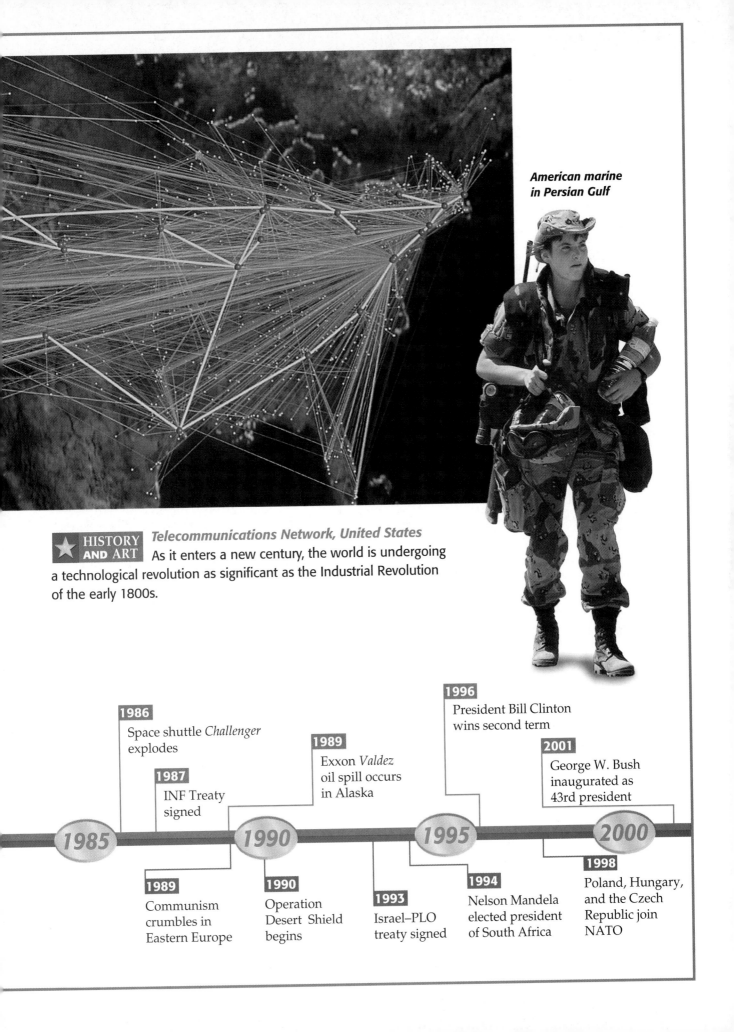

American marine in Persian Gulf

★ HISTORY AND ART

Telecommunications Network, United States
As it enters a new century, the world is undergoing a technological revolution as significant as the Industrial Revolution of the early 1800s.

1986
Space shuttle *Challenger* explodes

1987
INF Treaty signed

1989
Exxon *Valdez* oil spill occurs in Alaska

1996
President Bill Clinton wins second term

2001
George W. Bush inaugurated as 43rd president

1985

1990

1995

2000

1989
Communism crumbles in Eastern Europe

1990
Operation Desert Shield begins

1993
Israel–PLO treaty signed

1994
Nelson Mandela elected president of South Africa

1998
Poland, Hungary, and the Czech Republic join NATO

Barrio Boy

by Ernesto Galarza

Like many immigrants who come continually to the United States, Ernesto Galarza (1905–1984) arrived facing the challenge of adjusting to his adopted country. This excerpt from his autobiography, Barrio Boy, *tells the story of how Galarza and his mother traveled from Mexico to Sacramento, California, to meet his uncles, Gustavo and José. His story describes common experiences of those arriving in the United States then and now.*

■ READ TO DISCOVER

Unable to speak English and unfamiliar with the customs in the United States, 6-year-old Galarza and his mother embarked on a new life. Their trip was a journey into another world for young Ernesto. As you read, notice what is frightening and what is amusing about moving to a new community.

■ READER'S DICTIONARY

barrio: Spanish word for "neighborhood"
Jalcocotán: a mountain village in western Mexico
mesón: Spanish word for "inn"
Mazatlán: a city on the west coast of central Mexico
Sacramento: a city in central California; the capital of the state
Tucson: a city in southeastern Arizona
centavo, tostón, peso: Mexican money; the peso is the monetary unit and contains 100 centavos; a tostón is a 50-centavo piece

In the sunny morning of the next day we walked back to the station. Our train was still there, the flats and box-cars and coaches deserted, Mexican and American soldiers walking back and forth. "Look, the American flag," my mother said. It was flying over a building near us. Down the street, beyond the depot, there was a Mexican flag on a staff. "We are in the United States. Mexico is over there."

It took further explaining to clear up certain points to my satisfaction. The North was the same place as the United States, and we had finally arrived. The Americans never drew an eagle on their flag. The red and white were the same as on ours but why they liked blue better than green was just one of those peculiar things about Americans. Where did Mexico begin? Just beyond the railway station. How far did it go? "A long way," said Doña Henriqueta, "far down the track, farther than Jalcocotán." It was the closest thing we did to saying good-bye to our country.

That evening at the mesón, José and my mother and I reread Gustavo's letter, the last we had received in Mazatlán. José was to work his way on the railroad to a place called Sacramento. My mother and I were to go to another city called Tucson and wait there until another pass and money could be obtained.

José then explained a remarkable thing about our money. Mexican centavos and tostones and pesos were good for nothing in the United States. He had already exchanged some of our Mexican currency for dollars. "Listen carefully," he told us. "You have to give two pesos for one dollar. For one tostón you get one quarter. For ten centavos you get one nickel." On the table he laid out the coins in rows two for one.

. . . In Tucson we found our way to the address Gustavo had sent. It was a small hotel where the clerk spoke Spanish. He took us down a long, dark hall to a room, where I immediately began to explore the remarkable inventions of the Americans.

Hanging from a cord attached to the middle of the ceiling there was an electric bulb, low enough for an adult to reach and turn the black switch. I realized that this was our own electric light for us to turn on and off as we pleased. I pushed a chair under it and after some instruction from my mother proceeded to create lightening in the room by turning the switch as fast as I could.

. . . Regularly we went to the hotel to ask for mail from Gustavo. Almost always there was a letter with money, but it was many weeks before we received the most important one of all, the one that had the pass and the instructions for the trip. We were to take the train to Sacramento, go to the Hotel Español and stay there until Gustavo and José came for us.

. . . And from what I saw in the coach on that long ride, the Americans were indeed different. They ate the repulsive sandwiches with relish. They put their feet, shoes and all, on the seats in front of them. When the men laughed it seemed more like a roar, and if they were close by it scared me. Doña Henriqueta frowned and admonished me. "Be careful I never hear you braying like that." Many of them kept their hats on as if they didn't know that the inside of a

Young Hispanic dancers perform at a festival

coach was like the inside of a house, and wearing your hat in either a sure sign of being *mal educado* [ill-mannered].

From *Barrio Boy* by Ernesto Galarza. © 1971 by the University of Notre Dame Press. Used by permission of the publisher.

■ RESPONDING TO LITERATURE

1. What does Ernesto do with the electric light switch? Why do you think he is so excited about it?
2. What observations do Ernesto and his mother make about Americans?
3. What parts of Ernesto's story are probably shared by all people coming to a new place?

Activity

Writing a Postcard Imagine that you are Ernesto writing a postcard to a friend in Mazatlán. Describe the "modern" conveniences that you have seen, and explain their functions in a comical way.

Chapter 31

1968–1981

Search for Stability

★ Why It's Important

During the 1960s and 1970s, the American people's view of the nation and the government changed. Some believed that the United States had lost its position as the economic and political leader of the free world. Many grew distrustful of politics and political leaders. Today many Americans continue to express doubts about the political system. Mistrust of politicians, especially "Washington insiders," has reduced voter turnout in elections. It has also spurred the creation of political movements outside the two major parties.

★ Chapter Themes

- *Section 1,* Global Connections
- *Section 2,* Economic Factors
- *Section 3,* Continuity and Change
- *Section 4,* Civic Rights and Responsibilities

 HISTORY AND ART *America's Bicentennial, 1976* On July 4, 1976, Americans celebrated the Bicentennial, the nation's 200th birthday. These Bicentennial fireworks explode over New York Harbor and the Statue of Liberty.

April 1971
American ping-pong team visits Communist China

February 1972
President Nixon visits Beijing

May 1972
Nixon and Brezhnev sign the first Strategic Arms Limitation Treaty

October 1973
Arab countries impose oil embargo on the U.S.

Section 1

Nixon's Foreign Policy

READ TO DISCOVER . . .
- how Nixon attempted to ease cold war tensions.
- what policies the United States pursued in the Middle East and Latin America.

TERMS TO LEARN
détente
balance of power
embargo
shuttle diplomacy

The Storyteller

To improve relations with the Communist world, President Richard Nixon made a historic visit to China in February 1972. Nixon later described how he felt upon his arrival in Beijing, the Chinese capital: ". . . 'The Star Spangled Banner' had never sounded so stirring to me as on that windswept runway in the heart of Communist China. . . . As we left the airport, [Chinese leader Chou En-lai] said, 'Your handshake came over the vastest ocean in the world— twenty-five years of no communication.'"

1972 button

In his Inaugural Address on January 20, 1969, President Richard M. Nixon told the American people, "The greatest honor . . . is the title of peacemaker." Many Americans wondered whether Nixon fit the role of peacemaker. During his years in Congress, he had gained a reputation as a fierce enemy of communism. Few people imagined that Nixon, the anti-Communist crusader, would introduce policies to improve America's relations with the Communist world.

Easing the Cold War

President Nixon intended to leave his mark on foreign policy. He hoped to build a more stable, peaceful world by reaching out to the Soviet Union and the People's Republic of China. In the summer of 1969, Nixon visited several countries, including Romania—the first time an American president had gone behind the iron curtain. Nixon wanted to find areas of common interest and cooperation with these cold war opponents.

Changes in Foreign Policy

To help him in this ambitious task, Nixon appointed **Henry Kissinger,** a Harvard University professor, as his national security adviser. Kissinger and Nixon shared a belief in *realpolitik*—policies based on national interests rather than political ideology. They believed that peace among nations would come through negotiation rather than through threats or force.

Secretary of State Henry Kissinger (center) and Chinese officials walk across part of the Great Wall, one of China's historic structures. **Why did President Nixon seek to improve relations with China?**

Détente

President Nixon formulated a foreign policy plan of détente—attempts at relaxing, or easing, international tensions. As détente replaced confrontation, the United States and Communist states could begin working together to resolve issues that divided them.

Nixon realized that détente would work only if a balance of power existed. A balance of power is a distribution of power among nations to prevent any one nation from becoming too powerful. "It will be a safer world and a better world," he declared, "if we have a strong, healthy United States, Europe, Soviet Union, China, Japan—each balancing the other, not playing one against the other."

China

The **People's Republic of China** played a key role in Nixon's plan for achieving a balance of power. Diplomatic relations and trade between the United States and China had been severed after the Communists took control of mainland China in 1949.

If the United States could improve relations with the People's Republic, Nixon reasoned, the Soviets might become more cooperative. Nixon knew that the Soviets would fear a Chinese-American alliance.

In the fall of 1970, Nixon hinted at a new China policy. "If there is anything I want to do before I die," he told a reporter, "it is to go to China."

He also stopped referring to China as "Red China," a negative term used by U.S. presidents since Truman. Noting this change in tone, the Chinese responded by inviting an American table-tennis team to visit the country in April 1971. A week later the United States announced the opening of trade with China.

"Ping-pong diplomacy" was accompanied by secret talks between U.S. and Chinese officials about forging closer ties between the two nations. After Kissinger made a secret trip to China in June 1971, President Nixon announced that he would visit **Beijing,** the Chinese capital, "to seek the normalization of relations."

Accompanied by his wife, Pat, government officials, and reporters, Nixon arrived in Beijing in February 1972. "While we cannot close the gulf between us," Nixon told the Chinese leaders, "we can try to bridge it so that we may be able to talk across it." Pictures of the American president visiting the Great Wall of China and toasting Chinese Communist leaders at lavish banquets made news all over the world.

Another seven years passed, however, before China and the United States established full diplomatic relations. In the meantime, trade

*F*ootnotes to History

No More Red The term *Red,* referring to communism, came from the main color in the Communist flag—red.

relations and cultural exchanges between the two countries increased. The Nixon visit signaled a relaxation of tensions between China and the United States.

The Soviet Union

Nixon followed his history-making trip to China with a visit to **Moscow,** the Soviet capital, in May 1972. The Soviets eagerly welcomed the thaw in cold-war politics. They wanted to prevent a Chinese-American alliance and to slow the costly arms race. They also hoped to gain access to United States technology and to buy badly needed American grain. Soviet leader **Leonid Brezhnev** remarked, "There must be room in this world for two great nations with different systems to live together and work together."

Pictures of Nixon in Moscow, talking and smiling with Brezhnev in the halls of the Kremlin, gave the impression of a new era in Soviet-American relations. While in Moscow, President Nixon signed the Strategic Arms Limitation Treaty, or **SALT I.** This landmark treaty, the result of talks begun in 1969, restricted the number of certain types of nuclear missiles in U.S. and Soviet arsenals. Although SALT I did not end the arms race, it greatly reduced tensions between the United States and the Soviet Union.

The United States and the Soviet Union also agreed to work together in trade and science. Nixon—and the world—hoped that a new era of

Picturing HISTORY Soviet leader Brezhnev and President Nixon sign the SALT I agreement during Nixon's visit to Moscow in 1972. **What was the goal of the SALT I treaty?**

cooperation between the United States and the Soviet Union would bring greater stability to world affairs.

The Middle East

★ President Nixon's foreign policy aimed to maintain world stability without being drawn into regional disputes. The president wanted to avoid any involvement that might lead to another situation like Vietnam. Nixon stated that the United States would help in "the defense and development of allies and friends" but not take "basic responsibility" for the future of those nations. A crisis soon arose in the Middle East that tested this policy.

Arab-Israeli Tensions

Since the founding of the Jewish state of Israel in 1948, the United States had supported Israel in its struggles against its Arab neighbors. Tensions between Israel and the Arab states had erupted in war in 1948, 1956, and 1967. The Six-Day War of 1967 left Israel in control of east Jerusalem, the **West Bank,** the **Golan Heights** of Syria, and the

Linking
PAST & PRESENT

China's Leaders

China under Mao Zedong underwent dramatic changes. After Mao's death in 1976, new Communist leaders, led by Deng Xiaoping, allowed Western-style economic reforms while maintaining tight political control over the country. With Deng's death in 1997 came political change. A group of leaders—rather than one individual like Mao or Deng—is expected to hold governing authority.

★ **Picturing HISTORY** Many Palestinians lived in exile, scattered throughout the Middle East, North Africa, and Europe. **What was the cause of the Yom Kippur War?**

Gaza Strip and **Sinai Peninsula** of Egypt. The 1967 war also increased the number of Arab refugees. Thousands of Palestinians now lived in Israeli-held territory, and thousands more lived in neighboring Arab states. The Palestinians' demand for their own homeland became another source of instability in the region.

Yom Kippur War

War erupted again on October 6, 1973. Egypt and Syria attacked Israel in an attempt to regain territory lost in the Six-Day War. Because the attack occurred on Yom Kippur, a major Jewish holiday, the conflict became known as the **Yom Kippur War.**

Caught off guard, the Israelis struggled at first to stop the Arab advance before launching a counteroffensive. The United States helped by rushing ammunition to Israel. Meanwhile, the Soviets supplied arms to Egypt and Syria.

The war tested the United States–Soviet détente. The Soviet Union threatened to send air-borne troops to the Middle East. The United States responded by putting its nuclear forces on global alert for the first time since the Cuban missile crisis in 1962. Both sides backed down.

In the end the United States pressured Israel to accept a cease-fire. But not before the Israelis had regained most of the territory lost in the initial Arab advance and had taken additional territory from Syria and Egypt.

Angry at the United States for supporting Israel, Arab oil-producing states imposed an embargo—a ban on shipments—of oil to the United States and to other nations not seen as "friendly." The embargo caused an oil shortage in the United States. Long lines of cars formed at gas pumps, and Americans became angry as gas prices skyrocketed.

Shuttle Diplomacy

President Nixon sent Kissinger, now secretary of state, to the region to gain the trust of Arab leaders and to negotiate some type of agreement between Israel and its Arab neighbors. During the next two years, Kissinger engaged in shuttle diplomacy—traveling back and forth between the capitals of Israel, Egypt, and Syria trying to resolve the oil crisis and forge a lasting peace.

Early in 1974, **Golda Meir,** the prime minister of Israel, and **Anwar el-Sadat,** the president of Egypt, reached agreements that separated Israeli and Arab forces in the Sinai Peninsula and Golan Heights. Then in March 1974, Kissinger persuaded the Arab nations to end the oil embargo. Kissinger also improved U.S. relations with Egypt, the largest and most powerful Arab state, by promising large amounts of foreign aid.

Golda Meir

Latin America

⭐ The Nixon administration sought to protect U.S. interests in Latin America and to prevent the spread of communism. In 1970 the South American country of **Chile** elected **Salvador Allende** president. Allende was a follower of **Karl Marx,** the founder of communism. When the new Chilean government took over U.S. businesses in Chile, the United States protested. Nixon and his foreign-policy advisers feared an increase in Soviet influence in Chile and the spread of communism in Latin America.

With the backing of the CIA (Central Intelligence Agency), a small group of Chilean military leaders under General **Augusto Pinochet** overthrew the government and killed Allende. The United States immediately recognized the new military dictatorship and restored foreign aid to Chile.

The situation in Chile reflected another aspect of Nixon's foreign policy. Although willing to pursue détente with China and the Soviet Union, the president was still determined to contain the spread of communism—and Soviet influence—in the world.

*F*ootnotes to History

Young Leader Golda Meir showed remarkable leadership while growing up in Milwaukee, Wisconsin. Realizing that many of the students in her school could not afford the fees for books, Meir rented a large hall for a fund-raiser featuring refreshments and speeches. Eleven-year-old Golda herself presented the main speech.

Section 1 Assessment

Checking for Understanding
1. *Identify* Henry Kissinger, Leonid Brezhnev, SALT I, Yom Kippur War, Golda Meir, Anwar el-Sadat, Salvador Allende.
2. *Define* détente, balance of power, embargo, shuttle diplomacy.
3. *Summarize* Nixon's main foreign policy goal.

Reviewing Themes
4. **Global Connections** Why did Nixon think that improving relations with China would make the Soviet Union more cooperative?

Critical Thinking
5. **Identifying Central Issues** How did Nixon show that he was still devoted to containing the spread of communism?

Activity

Studying Current Events Find a newspaper article that discusses the Israeli-Arab relationship today and compare it to the relationship that existed in the 1960s and 1970s.

June 1972
Break-in at
Watergate
occurs

November 1972
Nixon wins
reelection

1973
OPEC oil embargo
reduces U.S. supplies

August 1974
Nixon resigns
the presidency

Section 2

Nixon and Watergate

READ TO DISCOVER . . .
- why Nixon called for a "New Federalism."
- how Nixon dealt with the nation's economic problems.
- how the Watergate scandal affected the nation.

TERMS TO LEARN
revenue sharing   deficit
affirmative action   impeachment
stagflation

Storyteller

President Nixon had grave concerns about the state of American society. "We live in a deeply troubled and profoundly unsettled time. Drugs, crime, campus revolts, racial discord, draft resistance—on every hand we find old standards violated, old values discarded." Nixon believed that a "silent majority" of middle-class Americans shared his concerns about increasing crime and social disorder. In an ironic twist of events, however, the Nixon administration itself would get caught up in a web of illegal activities.

1968 Republican campaign button

In his 1968 presidential campaign, Nixon had pledged to bring "law and order" back to American society. He also vowed to reduce government's role in people's lives.

Domestic Goals

Nixon's drive to restore law and order involved "cracking down on crime" and imposing stiffer penalties on lawbreakers. To strengthen the power of the police Nixon used federal funds to help state and city police forces.

The Courts

Nixon thought the federal courts should be tougher on criminals. "As a judicial conservative," he said, "I believe some Court decisions have gone too far in weakening the peace forces against the criminal forces in our society." During his presidency, four vacancies arose on the Supreme Court. Nixon hoped that the justices he appointed—**Warren Burger** as chief justice, and **Harry Blackmun, Lewis Powell,** and **William Rehnquist**—would shift the Court to a more conservative position. The decisions of the new justices did not fully meet the president's conservative goals, however.

New Federalism

Nixon wanted to reduce federal involvement in people's lives and to cut federal spending. He pledged to "reverse the flow of power and resources from the states and communities to

Washington and start power and resources flowing back . . . to the people." To accomplish this goal, he introduced a program called the **New Federalism.**

One part of the New Federalism called for giving the states some of the revenue earned from federal taxes for use at the state and local levels. This revenue sharing became law in 1972.

Nixon also sought to end or scale back many Great Society programs begun under President Johnson. He promised to "quit pouring billions of dollars into programs that have failed." He abolished the Office of Economic Opportunity, the agency that had led Johnson's War on Poverty.

On civil rights issues, Nixon took a conservative position aimed at appealing to white voters. For example, Nixon opposed **busing.** Busing was used to promote racial integration by transporting students from mostly white or African American neighborhoods to racially mixed schools. At the same time, however, his administration worked to carry out federal court orders to integrate schools. The Nixon administration also promoted affirmative action, or preference to minorities in jobs where they had previously been excluded.

A practical politician, President Nixon did accept new government programs that had popular support. He approved the creation of two new agencies—the **Occupational Safety and Health Administration** (OSHA) to ensure workers' safety and the **Environmental Protection Agency** (EPA) to protect the environment.

$ Economics

Economic Problems

★ While attempting to change the direction of government, President Nixon had to deal with serious economic problems. Industry and manufacturing were declining because of foreign competition. Businesses and consumers struggled with **inflation**—a general rise in the prices of goods and services—fueled by international competition for raw materials and the increasing cost of oil. The United States also faced slow economic growth and high unemployment.

Seeking Economic Stability

President Nixon tried a number of approaches to reduce inflation. He began by cutting federal spending. At the same time, he called for a **tight money policy.** Interest rates were raised so that people would borrow less and spend less. With less money in circulation, prices dropped. However, as demand slowed, business began to cut back and output fell. These steps slowed economic growth and brought on stagflation—a combination of rising prices and a sluggish economy.

Nixon then switched tactics. He temporarily froze wages and prices and issued guidelines for any future increases. This put a brake on inflation, but the economy remained in a recession.

Late in 1971, Nixon tried a third approach—increasing federal spending to stimulate the economy. Although this policy helped revive the economy for a short time, it also created a budget

★ **Picturing HISTORY** This cartoon reflects how the value of the American dollar declined during the early 1970s. **What other economic problems did Americans face during this period?**

deficit in which government spending was greater than government revenue. None of Nixon's policies managed to restore the economy to its previous strength, and economic problems continued to trouble his administration. 💲

The Election of 1972

⭐ Looking ahead in 1971 to the presidential campaign of 1972, Nixon had doubts about his chances for reelection. The war in Vietnam had not yet ended, and the easing of tensions with China had not yet occurred. Businesses and consumers had to struggle with the effects of inflation. The president and his supporters wanted to ensure his reelection.

A Campaign Against Enemies

To help plan campaign strategy, Nixon relied on a small group of loyal aides. The aides closest to the president were **John Ehrlichman,** his chief domestic adviser, and **H.R. Haldeman,** his chief of staff.

In their drive to win reelection, the president and his closest advisers, it was later revealed, stretched, and sometimes crossed, the boundaries of the law. In 1971, for example, Nixon asked his aides for an "enemies list" of people considered unfriendly to the administration. He then ordered the FBI and the Internal Revenue Service (IRS) to investigate some of these people. Nixon justified such actions as necessary to maintain national security, arguing that those who challenged government policies posed a serious danger to the nation.

Nixon's campaign committee collected millions of dollars. It used

Nixon button and McGovern tie

some of this money to create a secret group—nicknamed "the plumbers"—to stop leaks of information that might hurt the administration. Some campaign money also went to pay for dirty tricks against Nixon's Democratic foes, but that party had many problems of its own.

Democratic Disunity

The Democratic Party was split. Four candidates competed for the nomination: former vice president **Hubert Humphrey,** Senators **Edmund Muskie** of Maine and **George Mc-Govern** of South Dakota, and former governor of Alabama **George Wallace.** Muskie and Humphrey could not gain enough support. Wallace's campaign was cut short in May 1972 by a would-be assassin's bullet that left him paralyzed.

McGovern, the most liberal of the four candidates, won the nomination. Many voters found some of his views disturbing.

A Landslide Victory

The Democrats' lack of unity as well as an upsurge in the economy and the prospect of peace in Vietnam led to a landslide victory for Nixon. He won 60.7 percent of the popular vote. The Republican victory in the electoral college was even more lopsided—520 to 17.

The Energy Crisis

⭐ During Nixon's second term as president, severe economic problems confronted the nation. One of the most critical problems was the cost of fuel, especially imported oil.

The U.S. economy depended heavily on oil. Much of this oil came from the Middle East. Arab oil-producing countries belonged to **OPEC,** the Organization of Petroleum Exporting Countries. In 1973 these countries placed an embargo on all oil shipments to the United States. At the same time, they raised their prices. Between 1971 and 1974, the price of light crude oil jumped from $1.80 to $11.65 a barrel (42 gallons).

The sharp price increases and the six-month embargo damaged the nation's economy. Many companies had to lay off workers, while others raised their prices. Angry consumers complained about the high prices and the long lines at gas stations.

Sign of the times

The president imposed emergency measures to conserve oil. Nixon also urged Americans to conserve energy voluntarily. Congress reduced speed limits on highways because a vehicle burns less fuel at lower speeds.

To deal with the long-range problem of dependence on imported oil, Nixon urged development of domestic oil, especially in **Alaska,** which possessed vast, untapped oil reserves.

★ **Picturing HISTORY** Motorists line up outside a Virginia gas station. **Why did Americans face higher fuel prices and gas shortages?**

The Watergate Crisis

★ During Nixon's second term, what seemed like a small scandal turned into a presidential crisis. The scandal began with the president's reelection campaign. In June 1972, his reelection committee had wanted information about the Democrats' campaign plans. Members of the Nixon campaign ordered "the plumbers" to break into the headquarters of the Democratic National Committee to install telephone listening devices—bugs. This break-in set in motion events that would rock the presidency and the nation.

A Third-Rate Burglary

Sometime after midnight on June 17, 1972, Frank Wills, a security guard at the **Watergate** office-apartment complex in Washington, D.C., noticed tape covering the locks on doors leading to an underground parking garage. "I took the tape off," he later recalled, "but I didn't think anything of it." About an hour later, he found that someone had retaped the locks. Wills decided to call the police.

Frank Wills's discovery led to the arrest of five men who had broken into Democratic Committee headquarters in the Watergate complex. The arrests of "plumbers" Gordon Liddy and E. Howard Hunt followed soon afterward. Investigations revealed that Liddy and Hunt were connected to the Nixon campaign and were paid from White House funds.

The White House denied any involvement. Nixon's press secretary, Ronald Ziegler, dismissed the break-in as a "third-rate burglary." The president declared that "no one in the White House staff, no one in the administration . . . was involved in this bizarre incident."

A Scandal Unravels

Meanwhile, two newspaper reporters for the *Washington Post,* **Bob Woodward** and **Carl Bernstein,** began publishing a series of articles that linked the burglary to the Nixon campaign. As the election approached, however, fewer than half of the American people had even heard of the Watergate break-in.

John Sirica, the federal district court judge presiding over the trial of the Watergate burglars, resolved to uncover the truth. Eventually, one of the burglars, James McCord, admitted that White House aides had lied about their involvement and had pressured the burglars "to plead guilty and remain silent."

The Senate Watergate Committee hears testimony.
What evidence later revealed that President Nixon had been involved in a cover-up?

Early in 1973 the Senate voted to hold hearings on Watergate. As pressures mounted, Nixon shook up the White House staff. He fired the White House counsel, **John Dean,** and forced aides H.R. Haldeman and John Ehrlichman to resign. He also declared that he would take responsibility for the mistakes of others because "there can be no whitewash at the White House." Nixon also agreed to Senate demands to appoint a special prosecutor—someone independent of the Justice Department—to investigate Watergate. **Archibald Cox** took the job.

The Senate Watergate hearings began in May 1973. Chaired by Senator **Sam Ervin** of North Carolina, the hearings slowly revealed the inner workings of the Nixon White House. The most damaging testimony came from John Dean. Dean testified that there had been a cover-up and that Nixon himself directed it, but he produced no evidence to confirm his account.

Then in July investigators learned that a secret taping system had recorded all conversations in the president's office. Ervin and Cox demanded the tapes. President Nixon refused and claimed **executive privilege,** insisting that release of the tapes would endanger national security.

When Cox requested a court order to get the tapes in October, Nixon ordered his attorney general, Elliot Richardson, to fire Cox. Richardson

refused—and then resigned. Deputy Attorney General William Ruckelshaus also refused to carry out the order and resigned. Finally, Nixon found a Justice Department official willing to fire Cox. This **Saturday Night Massacre,** as the resignations and firing became known, resulted in a storm of public protest.

A New Vice President

In the middle of this turmoil, another scandal struck the administration. The Justice Department charged Vice President **Spiro Agnew** with taking bribes while governor of Maryland. On October 10, 1973, he resigned. Nixon appointed Representative **Gerald R. Ford** of Michigan, the Republican leader of the House, to succeed Agnew. Congress quickly confirmed the nomination.

The Crisis Deepens

Public outrage over the Saturday Night Massacre forced Nixon to appoint a new special prosecutor, **Leon Jaworski.** Meanwhile, the House of Representatives began considering impeachment—the constitutional provision to remove a president from office. If the House charged Nixon with committing "high crimes and misdemeanors," he would then be tried in the Senate. If a two-thirds majority of senators found him guilty, he would no longer be president.

In April 1974, Nixon decided to release printed copies of some of the tapes. These transcripts, heavily edited and missing significant portions, led to new protests. Nixon refused court orders to hand over the unedited tapes. Appeals reached the Supreme Court, which ruled on July 24 that the president had to surrender the tapes.

*F*ootnotes to History

Watergate Statistics A total of 56 men were convicted of Watergate-related offenses, including 20 members of the cabinet, the White House staff, and the Committee to Re-Elect the President (CREEP).

At the end of July, after weeks of closed hearings, the House Judiciary Committee adopted three articles of impeachment, charging the president with obstruction of justice, abuse of power, and contempt of Congress. Nixon released the tapes on August 5. A conversation on one tape revealed that the president had ordered a cover-up of the Watergate break-in just a few days after it happened. The conversation provided the crucial piece of evidence that linked Nixon to Watergate.

Nixon Resigns

Public reaction and the prospect of an impeachment trial forced Nixon to resign. On the evening of August 8, 1974, he went on national television to announce his decision.

The next morning a tearful Richard Nixon said good-bye to his staff and then left the White House by helicopter. He was succeeded by Gerald Ford, who became the first U.S. president never elected to the office of president or vice president.

President Nixon leaves the White House

Impact of Watergate

⭐ The Watergate crisis revealed that a powerful president could abuse his power and violate the Constitution. Yet the system of checks and balances had worked, and the president who had abused his oath of office lost his power.

Congress passed laws to correct abuses, including a law limiting campaign spending. Congress also strengthened the **Freedom of Information Act** of 1972, giving citizens more access to government files containing information about them and others.

The Watergate scandal damaged the public's faith in their political institutions and leaders and tarnished the image of the presidency. It would take time for this faith to be restored.

★ ★ ★ ★ ★ **Section 2 Assessment** ★ ★ ★ ★ ★ ★

Checking for Understanding
1. **Identify** John Ehrlichman, H.R. Haldeman, Watergate, Spiro Agnew, Gerald R. Ford.
2. **Define** revenue sharing, affirmative action, stagflation, deficit, impeachment.
3. **List** three actions that Nixon took to restore law and order.

Reviewing Themes
4. **Economic Factors** What role did the oil embargo play in America's economic crisis?

Critical Thinking
5. **Synthesizing Information** Explain how the government's checks and balances system worked when Nixon abused his power as president.

▶ **Activity** ◀

Preparing a Résumé Research one of the persons involved in the Watergate scandal. Prepare a résumé of that person's career since Watergate.

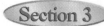
August 1974
Gerald Ford
becomes president

September 1974
Ford pardons
Nixon

December 1974
CIA's secret files
revealed

July 1975
Helsinki
Accords
signed

Section 3

A Time for Healing

READ TO DISCOVER . . .
- what controversies arose during Ford's presidency.
- what policies Ford followed in foreign affairs.
- how Ford tried to solve economic problems.

TERMS TO LEARN
amnesty   underemployment

The Storyteller

Millions watched on television as the helicopter carrying Richard Nixon rose into the sky. Vice President Gerald Ford and his wife, Betty, turned and walked back to the White House. There, in the East Room, 61-year-old Ford took the oath to become the thirty-eighth president of the United States. Ford assured Americans, "Our long national nightmare is over." Relieved to put the Watergate crisis behind them, most Americans welcomed the new president and a fresh start for the nation.

Time magazine,
August 19, 1974

President Gerald Ford promised the American people that he would be open and honest as president and would work with Congress to solve the nation's problems. To fill the office of vice president, Ford selected **Nelson Rockefeller,** a highly respected Republican and former governor of New York. *Time* magazine remarked on "a mood of good feeling and even exhilaration in Washington that the city has not experienced for many years."

Ford Faces Controversy

Ford's reputation for honesty and his sincere desire to put the Watergate crisis behind brought the promise of stability to the American nation. One of Ford's first acts, however, destroyed much of this confidence. On September 8, 1974, only a month after taking office, Ford granted Richard Nixon a **pardon** for any crimes he may have committed as president.

This meant that the former president could not be prosecuted for his part in the cover-up. Ford hoped that the pardon would help heal the wounds of Watergate. Instead, the pardon stirred controversy. Many Americans questioned why Nixon should escape punishment when others involved in the Watergate scandal went to jail. Some even accused Ford of striking a bargain with Nixon in advance—the promise of a pardon in exchange for Nixon's resignation. Although Ford defended his action, the new president never fully regained the trust and popularity he had enjoyed in his first weeks in office.

★ ★ ★ ★ ★ ★ ★ ★ ★ ★ ★ ★ ★ ★ ★ ★

Spying on American Citizens

In December 1974, Americans were startled to learn that the CIA had spied and kept secret files on some U.S. citizens. A few months later, they discovered that the FBI also had secret files. President Ford appointed a special commission to investigate CIA and FBI misconduct. He and Congress began working on new laws to regulate the activities of the two agencies.

Vietnam Amnesty

Yet another controversy arose when President Ford offered amnesty, or protection from prosecution, to men who had illegally avoided military service during the Vietnam War. Ford promised that these people would not be punished if they pledged loyalty to the United States and performed some type of national service. While many people approved of amnesty, others thought it was too lenient. Supporters of the Vietnam War argued that draft dodgers and deserters should be punished.

Ford and Foreign Affairs

★ With little experience in foreign affairs, Ford relied on Henry Kissinger, his secretary of state, and continued the policies of the Nixon administration. Ford extended the policy of détente with the Soviet Union. In late 1974, he met with Soviet leader **Leonid Brezhnev** to discuss arms control. The two leaders reached a preliminary agreement on limiting nuclear weapons.

In July 1975, Ford traveled to Helsinki, Finland, where he signed the **Helsinki Accords** with

★ **Picturing HISTORY** The changing of presidents on August 9, 1974, is symbolized in this replacement of former president Nixon's official portrait by one of the new president, Gerald Ford. **What position did Ford hold before becoming president?**

the Soviet Union and various Western nations. The countries pledged to respect the human rights and civil liberties of their citizens.

The Ford administration also worked to improve relations with China. When Chinese premier **Mao Zedong** died in 1976, a more moderate government came to power. The new Chinese leaders wanted to expand economic and political ties to the United States, and the two nations moved a little closer.

*F*ootnotes to History

Twenty-fifth Amendment Ratified in 1967, the Twenty-fifth Amendment deals with presidential succession if the president dies, becomes disabled, or leaves office. It also establishes a procedure for selecting a new vice president.

Domestic Affairs

★ The economic problems that the Nixon administration faced continued to plague President Ford. Inflation remained high and unemployment rose.

A Troubled Economy

By the 1970s Europe and Japan challenged America's world economic supremacy. Inexpensive and efficient Japanese cars flooded the American market. European products also provided strong competition to American-made goods.

This foreign competition led to factory closings in the United States and massive layoffs of U.S. workers. America began to suffer from underemployment; that is, people worked in jobs for which they were overqualified or that did not use their skills. Underemployment resulted, in part, from the loss of jobs to foreign competition.

The actions of OPEC continued to influence the American economy, also. Although the oil shortage caused by the embargo of 1973–1974 had eased, OPEC kept oil prices high, and the high prices contributed to inflation. The American economy seemed to be crumbling, and Ford struggled for a solution.

Ford's Response

To fight inflation Ford launched a campaign called Whip Inflation Now (WIN), a voluntary program of wage and price controls. He called on Americans to save their money rather than spend it and to plant their own gardens to counter rising food prices. Although the effort led to a small drop in inflation, the economy declined and the nation headed into recession.

Another approach Ford urged for controlling inflation was to cut government spending. However, the Democratic-controlled Congress wanted to maintain or increase spending for social programs. Ford vetoed several congressional spending bills in an attempt to control spending, but his actions did not curb inflation.

To stimulate the economy and encourage economic growth, Ford persuaded Congress to pass a tax cut. Although the cut did bring some improvement in the economy, it led to larger budget

American Memories

Teens of the '70s

Popular album, 1972

Acoustic guitar

Bell-bottom jeans

What Was It Like? Teenagers of the 1970s had a lifestyle that set them apart from older generations. How do teenagers today differ from teens of the 1970s in dress and style?

deficits as government revenue declined and spending remained the same or increased. Despite his efforts, President Ford was unable to solve the nation's economic problems.

Caricature of Gerald Ford

The Election of 1976

★ As the 1976 elections approached, President Ford hoped to win the election outright. But Ford's prospects did not look particularly good. Although he had helped to restore confidence in government, Watergate was still fresh in the minds of the American people.

In early 1976, **Jimmy Carter** ran as a Democratic candidate in the presidential primary election in New Hampshire. Few voters knew who Carter was. Then Carter began winning key primary elections. Stressing his integrity, religious faith, and his standing as an outsider, Carter gathered enough delegates to win the Democratic nomination. Senator **Walter Mondale** of Minnesota ran as vice president.

Meanwhile President Ford had struggled to gain the Republican nomination. He faced a strong challenge from the former governor of California, **Ronald Reagan,** who was favored by party conservatives. Ford chose Senator **Robert Dole** of Kansas as his running mate.

During the campaign, Ford tried to stress his achievements as president. Carter promised to

Jimmy Carter/Walter Mondale
To Bring America Together Again

En el Espíritu de
Por Empleo Pleno y
Plenitud de Vida

★ **Picturing HISTORY** Gerald Ford and Jimmy Carter were the major party candidates for president in 1976. **Who won the election?**

clean up the government and ran as much against the memory of Nixon and government corruption as against Ford. Carter won in a very close election, gaining 50 percent of the popular vote to Ford's 47.9 percent. To a great extent, Carter owed his margin of victory to support from African American Southern voters.

Section 3 Assessment

Checking for Understanding
1. **Identify** Leonid Brezhnev, Helsinki Accords, Mao Zedong, Jimmy Carter.
2. **Define** amnesty, underemployment.
3. **Cite** two of Ford's actions early in his presidency that angered many citizens.

Reviewing Themes
4. **Continuity and Change** Explain why the Democrats regained the presidency in 1976.

Critical Thinking
5. **Determining Cause and Effect** How did strong competition from Europe and Japan in the 1970s affect the economy of the United States?

Activity

Creating a Bumper Sticker Create a bumper sticker that supports or opposes Ford's pardon of President Nixon in the Watergate scandal.

INTERDISCIPLINARY

Activities

Our Fragile Planet

In the 1970s, people around the world became increasingly aware that Planet Earth's environment might be in danger. Increase your environmental awareness by completing these activities.

Science

Testing for Acid Rain Acid rain, caused by pollution in the air, damages forests and kills wildlife. This experiment demonstrates that damage. Label one glass jar "Water," another, "Vinegar." Dig up two clumps of sod and grass; put one clump in each jar. Add 1/4 cup of water to one jar and 1/4 cup of vinegar to the other. Observe the two clumps of grass for 4 to 6 days. Keep a record of the changes you see. If the jars dry out, add water to both. Explain the results of your experiment to the class.

Mathematics

Measuring Wasted Water Water shortages threaten the environment in many places. How much water do people waste? Take a survey based on the following figures. If you leave the faucet running (as most people do), you use these amounts of water: 15-25 gallons per shower, 36 gallons for a tub bath, 2 gallons for washing hands, 10 gallons for brushing teeth. How much water does your family use on an average morning? How much water does your class use every morning? Chart your results.

School-to-Work

Planning a Recycling Program Plan a program in which students and teachers in your school recycle paper, glass, and plastic. Before starting, check with local community programs to see what materials are being collected. Then, with your school administrator, prepare a plan that explains where to place bins in the collection areas of your school, who will collect the materials, and how often recyclable materials will be collected.

Art

Making an Earth Day Poster Since 1970 people have observed Earth Day as a reminder to take care of the environment. Design a poster with original artwork or a collage encouraging people to observe this environmental holiday and respect the earth and its ecology. Hang your posters in the classroom.

Celebrating Earth Day

Section 4

The Carter Presidency

READ TO DISCOVER . . .
■ how Carter differed from Nixon and Ford.
■ how Carter dealt with economic problems.
■ how Carter changed the nation's foreign policy.
■ why Carter failed to win reelection.

TERMS TO LEARN
trade deficit
human rights
apartheid
fundamentalist

The Storyteller

Jimmy Carter brought a simple lifestyle to the White House. For example, to save money President Carter once planned to visit his hometown of Plains, Georgia, by car instead of by helicopter. He soon discovered that it was much less expensive to go by helicopter. Carter later stated about going by car: "A good portion of the Georgia State Patrol had been marshaled to block every country crossroads for more than 60 miles! It was obvious that I was not simply one of the people anymore."

Papier-mâché peanut with Jimmy Carter grin

"A Tribute to Jimmy"

Carter, an "outsider" with no experience in national politics, did not fit the image of a typical politician. A former governor of Georgia, Carter liked to say he was just a peanut farmer from a small town called Plains who wanted to serve his country.

An Informal Presidency

★ From the beginning, Carter set a down-to-earth tone. At his inauguration he wore an ordinary business suit rather than formal clothing. After the ceremony, Carter and his family walked up Pennsylvania Avenue from the Capitol to the White House instead of riding in the traditional limousine. These gestures symbolized Carter's desire to create a more informal presidency. Carter wanted to be seen as an average American.

Struggling with the Economy

When Carter took office, the nation still suffered from high inflation and unemployment. Carter tried to jolt the economy out of recession by increasing federal spending and cutting taxes. Both measures were meant to stimulate economic growth. Unemployment came down, but inflation took off. Carter then reversed course and proposed spending cuts and a delayed tax cut.

Carter's reversals on economic policies made him seem weak and uncertain. As an outsider, the president had trouble gaining support for his programs in Congress. Although Carter needed the backing of congressional Democrats, his administration made little effort to work with them.

Energy Crisis

Carter made energy policy a priority. The high costs of energy added to inflation. In addition, as American money flowed overseas to purchase oil, the nation faced a growing trade deficit—the value of foreign imports exceeded the value of American exports.

In April 1977, Carter presented the **National Energy Plan,** aimed at resolving the energy crisis. To stress the need to reduce energy use, for example, the president turned down the thermostat in the White House.

Carter's plan included the creation of a Department of Energy to coordinate energy policy, research funds to explore alternative sources of energy, and tax policies to encourage domestic oil production and energy conservation. Congress enacted a weakened version of the plan in 1978.

Nuclear Power

In the late 1970s, Americans became more concerned about the threats of nuclear power. In March 1979 a major accident occurred at the **Three Mile Island** nuclear power plant near Harrisburg, Pennsylvania.

An anti-nuclear protest movement soon spread. President Carter, however, was unwilling to halt the nuclear energy program, which provided more than 10 percent of the nation's energy needs. At the same time, supporters of nuclear power argued that, with proper safeguards, there was no danger to the environment.

Foreign Affairs

★ Carter based his foreign policy on human rights—a concern that governments around the world grant greater freedom and opportunity without the threat of persecution or violence. He proposed that any nation that violated human rights should not receive U.S. aid and support.

Carter withdrew economic and military aid from such countries as Argentina, Uruguay, and Ethiopia because of human rights violations. He condemned South Africa for its policy of apartheid, racial separation and economic and political discrimination against non-whites.

Carter's human rights diplomacy sometimes caused problems in the United States. In 1980 Cuban dictator Fidel Castro allowed thousands of Cubans, including criminals and political prisoners, to leave Cuba.

Beginning in April, Cuban refugees began leaving from **Mariel Harbor;** most were en route to Florida. The United States, however, had trouble absorbing such large numbers of people. Some of the emigrants were detained in refugee camps. In June, President Carter ordered other Cubans be moved to federal prisons to await removal hearings. Then, in September, Castro sealed off the boatlift. About 125,000 Cuban refugees had entered the United States.

★ Picturing HISTORY Jimmy Carter and his wife, Rosalynn, worship with African American leaders, including Coretta Scott King, widow of Martin Luther King, Jr. **What stand did Carter take against South Africa once he became president?**

Carter had learned that a foreign policy based on a single issue, human rights, had many limitations. Even so, the president continued to speak out on the issue.

The Panama Canal

Carter also acted to end Latin American bitterness over the Panama Canal. Over the years, U.S. ownership of the canal and its control of the Canal Zone had caused friction between the United States and **Panama.** Carter signed two treaties with Panama in 1977. The treaties turned the U.S.-controlled Panama Canal over to Panama by the year 2000 but guaranteed that the canal would remain a neutral waterway open to all shipping. Some Republicans in the Senate tried to block ratification of the treaties, charging that Carter was giving away U.S. property. The Senate approved the treaties in 1978, however.

The Middle East

President Carter sought to bring peace to the Middle East. When peace talks between Israel and Egypt stalled in 1978, Carter invited Israeli prime minister **Menachem Begin** and Egyptian president **Anwar el-Sadat** to Camp David, Maryland, for a summit meeting.

For two weeks, the three leaders discussed issues dividing Israel and Egypt. On September 17, 1978, they announced an agreement to work toward peace. Known as the **Camp David Accords,** the agreement led to an Egyptian-Israeli peace treaty signed at the White House in March 1979. The treaty marked the first time that Israel and an Arab nation had reached a peace agreement.

The Soviet Union

Carter hoped to continue détente with the Soviet Union. At the same time, he strongly criticized Soviet human-rights violations—which broke promises Soviet leaders had made in the Helsinki Accords. At the same time, he continued negotiations on arms control. In June 1979, the president signed a second Strategic Arms Limitation Treaty, or **SALT II.** Critics in the Senate

Picturing HISTORY President Carter meets with Egyptian president Anwar el-Sadat (left) and Israeli prime minister Menachem Begin (right). **Why were the Camp David Accords important?**

charged that the treaty gave the Soviets an advantage, and the Senate delayed ratification.

Any hope of the Senate approving SALT II disappeared in December 1979, when Soviet troops invaded **Afghanistan,** a country in southwestern Asia bordering the Soviet Union. Responding to the invasion, Carter imposed an embargo on U.S. grain exports to the Soviet Union. In addition, the United States and 61 other nations refused to send athletes to the 1980 summer Olympic Games in Moscow. Soviet actions cast a dark cloud over Soviet-U.S. relations, and the cold war began to heat up again.

Crisis in Iran

In the 1970s, **Iran** was one of the strongest U.S. allies in the Persian Gulf region, an area vital to Western oil needs. Shah Mohammed Reza Pahlavi, the ruler of Iran, used U.S. aid to build up a powerful military force. Many Iranians, however, complained about corruption in the government. Others objected to Western influence in the country, which they felt weakened traditional Muslim values.

Iranians present blindfolded and handcuffed American hostages. **How did the hostage crisis affect Carter's presidency?**

In January 1979, Islamic fundamentalists—people who believe in strict obedience to religious laws—forced the shah to flee Iran. The new ruler, Muslim leader **Ayatollah Khomeini,** was hostile to the United States because of its support of the shah.

In November 1979, Iranian students, with the support of fundamentalists in the government, stormed the American embassy in **Tehran,** the capital of Iran, and took 52 Americans hostage. The United States was outraged. Attempts to negotiate the release of the hostages failed, and a daring desert rescue attempt ended in tragedy with the death of 8 American soldiers. The hostage crisis dragged on and became a major issue in the presidential election of 1980.

The Election of 1980

The Iranian crisis, together with increased cold war tensions and continuing economic problems, damaged the president politically. By the time the election campaign began, Carter's popularity among the public had declined dramatically.

The Republicans nominated **Ronald Reagan** for president in 1980. In marked contrast to Carter, Reagan radiated charm, confidence, and optimism. His conservative message of lower taxes, reduced spending, stronger defense, and a restoration of American pride found an eager reception among Americans weary of government and economic problems. When Reagan asked, "Are you better off now than you were four years ago?" most Americans answered, "No!"

Reagan swept to victory, with 51 percent of the popular vote and an electoral vote margin of 489 to 49. Republicans also gained control of the Senate for the first time since 1952. The election resulted in a bitter defeat for Jimmy Carter, who only 4 years earlier had promised a new era in American politics.

A final disappointment for Carter came in January 1981. During the closing weeks of his administration, he worked tirelessly to obtain the release of the hostages. The Iranians finally did release them—after Ronald Reagan took the oath of office.

Section 4 Assessment

Checking for Understanding

1. **Identify** Menachem Begin, Anwar el-Sadat, Ayatollah Khomeini.
2. **Define** trade deficit, human rights, apartheid, fundamentalist.
3. **Explain** how Jimmy Carter's manner differed from many other president's.

Reviewing Themes

4. **Civic Rights and Responsibilities** What issue guided Carter's foreign policy?

Critical Thinking

5. **Drawing Conclusions** Which of Carter's actions do you think did the greatest damage to his chances for reelection? Explain.

Creating a Poster Divide a sheet of paper into two vertical columns. Label one column "Successes" and the other "Failures." Create a poster that lists each of President Carter's domestic and foreign policy efforts in the appropriate column.

Predicting Consequences

Did you ever wish you could see into the future? Predicting future events is very difficult. You can, however, develop skills that will help you identify the logical consequences of decisions or actions.

Learning the Skill

Follow these steps to help you accurately predict consequences.

- Review what you already know about a situation by listing facts, events, and people's responses. The list will help you recall events and how they affected people.
- Analyze patterns. Try to determine what the patterns show.
- Use your knowledge and observations of similar situations. In other words, ask yourself, "What were the consequences of a similar decision or action that occured in the past?"
- Analyze each of the potential consequences by asking, "How likely is it that this will occur?"
- Make a prediction.

Practicing the Skill

Candidates for public office often make campaign promises based on how they think voters will respond. Use the information in the chart below to help you predict what type of candidate would be elected president in 1980. Answer the questions that follow.

1. Review the facts and events listed on the chart. Do you notice any patterns? What do the facts tell you about the 1970s?
2. Recall similar situations in which voters faced hard times. What kind of president do you think Americans would want?

Applying the Skill

Predicting Consequences Read newspapers for articles about an event that affects your community. Make an educated prediction about what will happen. Explain your reasoning.

Glencoe's **Skillbuilder Interactive Workbook, Level 1** provides instruction and practice in key social studies skills.

Events of the 1970s	Results and Reactions
OPEC oil embargo causes a shortage of fuel.	Americans feel helpless and angry.
President Ford vetoes programs in health, housing, and education to reduce government spending.	Many people lose jobs, and the nation suffers the worst recession in 40 years.
President Carter asks the public to conserve energy.	Americans feel frustrated.
To conserve energy, Americans buy smaller, imported cars.	American workers suffer unemployment as several automobile plants close.
U.S. citizens are taken hostage by Iranians. The hostages are released after 14 months.	Americans see their leaders forced to give in to terrorists' demands.

Assessment and Activities

★ Reviewing Key Terms

On graph paper, create a word search puzzle using the following terms. Crisscross the terms vertically and horizontally, then fill in the remaining squares with extra letters. Use the terms' definitions as clues to find the words in the puzzle. Share your puzzle with a classmate.

détente	amnesty
embargo	underemployment
shuttle diplomacy	trade deficit
revenue sharing	human rights
stagflation	apartheid
deficit	fundamentalist
impeachment	

★ Reviewing Key Facts

1. Which two nations were the focus of Nixon's attempt to ease cold war tensions?
2. Explain why President Nixon was forced to resign.
3. Why did the United States lose its place as a world economic leader in the 1970s?
4. What did President Carter do to resolve the energy crisis?
5. How did Carter bring temporary peace to the Middle East?

★ Critical Thinking

Drawing Conclusions

Using human rights as the primary basis for foreign policy caused many problems for President Carter.

1. How did Carter's support of the shah of Iran ignore the interest of Islamic fundamentalists in that country?
2. Do you think our government can fairly judge when other nations are violating human rights? Explain.

★ Time Line Activity

Create a time line on which you place the following events in chronological order.
- Camp David Accords are signed
- Yom Kippur War occurs
- Nixon resigns
- Carter is elected president
- Nixon signs SALT I
- Iranians seize 52 U.S. hostages
- Watergate hearings begin
- Ford meets with Brezhnev
- Carter proposes National Energy Plan

★ Reviewing Themes

1. **Global Connections** What was Nixon's main reason for establishing friendly relations with the Soviet Union?
2. **Economic Factors** What did Nixon do to create a New Federalism?
3. **Continuity and Change** How were the foreign policies of Ford and Nixon alike?
4. **Civic Rights and Responsibilities** What did Carter think the United States should do to any nation that violated human rights?

★ Skill Practice Activity

Predicting Consequences
Review the skill on predicting consequences on page 901. Then read the following statements and predict three consequences for each. Rank the three consequences in order of most likely to occur to least likely to occur.

1. If a person in a public office, including the president, commits a crime, he or she should not be pardoned.
2. Engineers develop an effective, efficient electric-powered automobile.
3. The school year is lengthened by 30 days.

★ Geography Activity

In 1973 Saudi Arabia imposed an embargo, or a restriction of trade, on oil shipped to Israel's allies including the United States. At the same time, other OPEC countries raised their prices. Although the embargo was lifted in 1974, its economic effects continued through the end of the decade. Study the chart below, then answer the questions that follow.

Gasoline Consumption and Prices

Year	Consumption (billions of gallons)	Cost per Gallon		
		Reg.	Prem.	No lead
1973	110.5	$.40	.45	NA
1974	106.3	.53	.57	.55
1975	109.0	.57	.61	.60
1976	115.7	.59	.64	.61
1977	119.6	.62	.67	.66
1978	125.1	.63	.69	.67
1979	122.1	.86	.92	.90
1980	115.0	1.19	1.28	1.25

Source: *Statistical Abstract of the United States.*

1. **Movement** In what year did consumption first exceed 120 billion gallons?
2. **Movement** How much more did a gallon of regular gasoline cost in 1980 than in 1973?
3. **Human/Environment Interaction** Based on billions of gallons consumed, in which year shown on the chart was the environment most polluted with automobile fumes?

★ Cooperative Activity

History and Economics Since the 1930s the United States has had deficit, or unbalanced, federal budgets most of the time. This policy of deficit spending led to increasingly large budgets and a growing national debt. The United States entered World War II with a national debt of about $40 billion. The government emerged from the war owing nearly $259 billion. By 1996 the national debt surpassed $5 trillion. With a partner, research to find the dollar figure of the national debt from 1950 to today. Use the figures to construct a line graph. Then answer these questions: What definite patterns or directions can be seen on the graph? What could be some underlying causes of the trends shown on the graph?

★ Technology Activity

Using a Word Processor The Freedom of Information Act of 1974 allowed public access to many government records. Before 1974 and prior to the abuses of the CIA and FBI in the 1970s, those records were kept secret. Research information on how to use the Freedom of Information Act to get government records. Then using your word processor, write a step-by-step guide explaining the procedure.

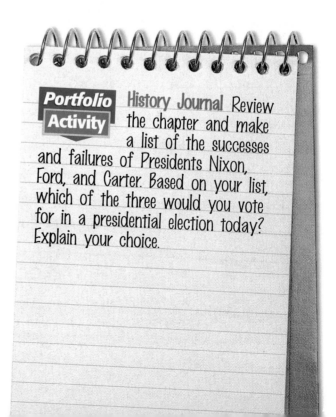

Portfolio Activity **History Journal** Review the chapter and make a list of the successes and failures of Presidents Nixon, Ford, and Carter. Based on your list, which of the three would you vote for in a presidential election today? Explain your choice.

1981–Present

New Challenges

★ Why It's Important

The 1980s and 1990s ushered in a period of great change. With the collapse of communism in Europe, relations between East and West changed dramatically. Former foes sought closer ties. At home, new advances in technology, medicine, and industry helped the nation move forward.

★ Chapter Themes

- *Section 1,* Economic Factors
- *Section 2,* Global Connections
- *Section 3,* Groups and Institutions
- *Section 4,* Science and Technology

PRIMARY SOURCES
Library

See pages 996–997 for primary source readings to accompany Chapter 32

 Picturing HISTORY **A Bill-Signing Ceremony** Members of Congress, cabinet members, and private citizens attend the signing of a 1996 health care bill by President Bill Clinton.

904

1981
Sandra Day O'Connor appointed to Supreme Court

1985
Mikhail Gorbachev becomes leader of Soviet Union

1987
Reagan and Gorbachev sign INF Treaty

Section 1

The Reagan Presidency

READ TO DISCOVER . . .
- what factors contributed to the growth of conservatism.
- what economic policies Ronald Reagan followed.
- what approach President Reagan took toward communism.

TERMS TO LEARN

deregulation   glasnost
federal debt   perestroika

Storyteller

On March 30, 1981, President Reagan gave a speech at the Washington Hilton. As he walked to his car, gunshots rang out. The president was hit in the chest. Also injured were two security officers and the president's press secretary, James Brady. The assassin, John Hinckley, Jr., was quickly subdued. Despite the attempt on his life, the president never lost his sense of humor. In the operating room, he told the surgeons, "Please tell me you're Republicans."

1980 Reagan campaign poster

★REAGAN

FOR PRESIDENT
Let's make America great again.

Ronald Reagan's election to the presidency in 1980 marked a significant conservative shift in America. The conservative movement grew across the country, particularly in the South and Southwest, a region known as the **Sunbelt.** When the Sunbelt's population increased during the 1970s, the conservative movement gained political power.

The Reagan Revolution

Many Americans wanted a return to what President Ronald Reagan called "traditional American values"—an emphasis on family life, hard work, respect for law, and patriotism. They shared the conservative view that the federal government made too many rules, collected too much in taxes, and spent too much money on social programs.

Air Traffic Controllers' Strike

A few months after Ronald Reagan became president, the nation's air traffic controllers went on strike. They refused to go back to work despite the president's orders to do so. President Reagan acted at once, firing the controllers and ordering military staff to oversee air traffic while new controllers were trained to do the work.

President Carter had been criticized for his lack of leadership and indecision. With this action, Ronald Reagan showed that he would stand firm and use his position as president to carry out the policies in which he believed.

Chapter 32 New Challenges **905**

Sandra Day O'Connor appears with Supreme Court Chief Justice Warren Burger on the steps of the Supreme Court building. **Why was O'Connor's appointment significant?**

Deregulation

As part of his promise to reduce government and "get the government off the backs of the American people," President Reagan pursued a policy of deregulation. This meant cutting the rules and regulations government agencies placed on businesses. Under President Reagan, for example, the Department of Transportation wrote new rules for automobile exhaust systems and safety measures that were easier for car manufacturers to meet.

Footnotes to History

Oldest President Ronald Reagan was 69 years old when he was elected—the oldest man to be elected president. A professional actor most of his life, Reagan made such convincing speeches that the media called him the "Great Communicator."

★ ★ ★ ★ ★ ★ ★ ★ ★ ★ ★ ★ ★ ★ ★ ★ ★ ★

The Supreme Court

Reagan also put a conservative stamp on the Supreme Court by naming justices to the Court who shared his views. He appointed **Sandra Day O'Connor** in 1981, the first woman ever appointed to the Supreme Court. He later appointed **Antonin Scalia** and **Anthony Kennedy.**

Reaganomics

Deregulation and his court appointments showed President Reagan's commitment to a conservative view of government. It was his economic policies, however, that formed the core of the "Reagan Revolution." Reagan believed that lower taxes would allow individuals and corporations to invest in new businesses. Because a tax cut would mean less income, Reagan also called for less government spending. Supporters called Reagan's economic policy **supply-side economics** because it proposed to stimulate the economy by increasing the supply of goods and services. The president's critics ridiculed the policy as "Reaganomics."

In 1981 Congress lowered taxes and slashed nearly $40 billion from federal programs such as school lunches, student aid, welfare, low-income housing, and food stamps. Critics charged that these cuts hurt both the working poor and unemployed people. Supporters argued that Reaganomics would boost the economy, helping everybody in the long run.

While Reagan cut domestic programs, he pushed for sharp increases in military spending. The president declared that the Soviet threat made it necessary to build up the military.

Government Debt

With higher defense spending and lower taxes, the government spent more money than it collected in revenue. It had to borrow money to make up the difference. This borrowing increased the federal debt—the amount of money owed by the government. Between 1970 and 1980, the federal debt had grown from $381 to $909 billion. By 1990 the debt had jumped to $3.2 trillion.

★ ★

Recession and Recovery

President Reagan's new economic policies seemed to falter when a serious recession began early in his first term. However, the economy recovered a year later and began to boom.

In 1983 the economy began a long, steady rise. Businesses expanded, and the high jobless rate of 1982 declined. Investors showed confidence in the economy with a boom in stock trading.

The federal debt continued to grow as well. In 1985 Congress tried to halt growth of the debt by passing the **Gramm-Rudman-Hollings Act.** The act set a series of targets for eliminating the federal budget deficit by October 1990. If Congress and the president could not agree on *voluntary* spending cuts, the law called for *automatic* spending cuts to balance the budget. The provision for automatic cuts did not apply to all areas of the budget, however, so it had limited success. **$**

Reagan's Foreign Policy

Ronald Reagan pledged in his campaign to wage a tough fight against communism. To carry out his policy, President Reagan launched a massive buildup of the military. He expanded the American arsenal of tanks, ships, aircraft, and nuclear missiles. He defended these actions by quoting George Washington's advice: "To be prepared for war is one of the most effective means of preserving peace."

Reagan also proposed a new antimissile defense system, the **Strategic Defense Initiative** (SDI). Nicknamed "Star Wars," the SDI would consist of a land- and space-based defensive shield against enemy missiles. However, scientists were unable to develop the necessary technology.

Latin America

Besides building up the nation's military strength, Reagan also committed American forces and aid to the fight against communism, especially in nearby Latin America.

Late in the Carter presidency, Communist rebels in **Nicaragua**—called **Sandinistas**—had overthrown the government. After becoming president, Reagan sent aid to the **contras,** a group battling the Sandinistas. The fighting in Nicaragua continued for many years and became a source of disagreement between President Reagan and Congress.

In October 1983, President Reagan took direct military action in the Caribbean. Rebels on the tiny Caribbean island of Grenada staged an uprising. Concerned about the fate of 800 American medical students on the island, Reagan dispatched troops to rescue the Americans and establish a prodemocracy government. Reagan's action won widespread approval at home.

The Middle East

President Reagan was less successful with peace efforts in the Middle East. In 1982, he sent a force of marines to help keep the peace in the war-

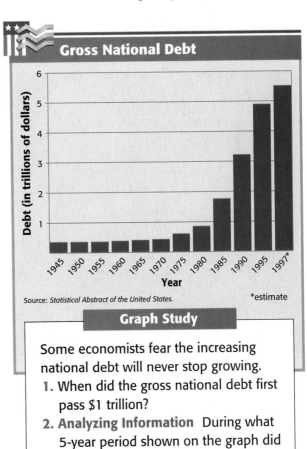

Gross National Debt

Debt (in trillions of dollars) vs. Year (1945–1997*)

Source: *Statistical Abstract of the United States.*   *estimate

Graph Study

Some economists fear the increasing national debt will never stop growing.
1. When did the gross national debt first pass $1 trillion?
2. **Analyzing Information** During what 5-year period shown on the graph did the national debt increase the most?

torn nation of Lebanon. The Americans soon were caught in a web of violence. A car bomb blast killed more than 50 people at the U.S. embassy in Beirut in April 1983. Then in October, 241 Americans and 58 French died in attacks on U.S. and French military headquarters. Rather than become more deeply involved in the struggle, the president withdrew all U.S. forces from Lebanon.

Reagan's Second Term

By 1984 the American economy was booming. In his State of the Union Address, President Reagan declared: "America is back—standing tall, looking [toward the future] with courage, confidence and hope."

President Reagan and Vice President **George Bush** continued using this optimistic theme in their campaign for reelection. The Democrats chose **Walter Mondale,** vice president under Jimmy Carter, and **Geraldine Ferraro,** a member of Congress from New York. Ferraro became the first woman to run for vice president on a major political party ticket.

Picturing HISTORY Marine lieutenant colonel Oliver North (center) takes the oath before the joint congressional committee investigating the Iran-Contra affair. **Why did the Iran-Contra dealings create an uproar?**

Reagan won the electoral votes of 49 out of 50 states. It was one of the most lopsided presidential elections in American history. Spurred on by high employment, a strong economy, and low interest rates, Reagan enjoyed high popularity ratings early in his second term.

The Iran-Contra Scandal

Despite his popularity, a scandal cast a shadow over part of President Reagan's second term. Terrorists, with ties to the Iranian government, held U.S. citizens hostage in Lebanon. Hoping to secure the release of the hostages, Reagan officials made a deal with Iran.

Marine lieutenant colonel **Oliver North** and Navy vice admiral John Poindexter, both assigned to the White House National Security Council, arranged for the sale of weapons to Iran in return for help in freeing American hostages. North and Poindexter decided to funnel money from this secret arms sale to help the Nicaraguan contras.

News of these secret deals—which came to be known as the **Iran-Contra scandal**—created an uproar in the United States. Critics charged that these activities violated federal laws barring officials from aiding the contras. They also said that the deals violated the Constitution by interfering with Congress's role in making foreign policy. Congress held hearings to determine whether President Reagan had participated in breaking the law. But there was never any proof of the president's involvement.

A Changing Soviet Policy

A remarkable shift in Soviet-American relations began to take shape at the beginning of Reagan's second term as president. Changes in Soviet leadership helped trigger the change. In 1985 Communist Party leaders of the Soviet Union chose a new general secretary, or leader—**Mikhail Gorbachev.** To the surprise of people all around the world, Gorbachev was committed to reforming the Soviet government. He called for a policy of glasnost—opening Soviet society to new ideas.

President Reagan and Soviet leader Gorbachev shake hands at their June 1988 summit meeting in Moscow. **What major step did both leaders take earlier toward ending the threat of nuclear war?**

Soviet button celebrating summit

Gorbachev also tried to change the way his country was governed. Moving away from the government's near-total control of the economy, he allowed more democracy and local economic planning. This new policy, perestroika, encouraged the Soviets to seek even greater changes.

Gorbachev also wanted to establish productive ties with the United States. With the Soviet economy in shambles, Gorbachev knew that the Soviet Union could not afford to build nuclear weapons. At several meetings he tried to convince President Reagan that he wanted to end the nuclear arms race. These early meetings accomplished little.

In 1987, however, President Reagan and Premier Gorbachev signed an agreement, the **Intermediate-Range Nuclear Forces (INF) Treaty.** The treaty aimed to reduce the number of nuclear missiles in each superpower's arsenal. Reagan explained the agreement by quoting what he said was a Russian proverb: "Trust, but verify." While both nations still held vast nuclear arsenals, they had taken a major step toward reducing the threat of nuclear war.

Section 1 Assessment

Checking for Understanding

1. *Identify* Sandra Day O'Connor, George Bush, Geraldine Ferraro, Oliver North, Mikhail Gorbachev.
2. *Define* deregulation, federal debt, glasnost, perestroika.
3. *List* two of President Reagan's actions that proved he was committed to creating a more conservative government.

Reviewing Themes

4. **Economic Factors** Why did Reagan think that lower taxes would aid the economy?

Critical Thinking

5. **Demonstrating Reasoned Judgment** Do you think Reagan administration officials were justified in violating policies and laws in the Iran-Contra incident? Explain.

Activity

Analyzing Language Research to find the literal meaning of the terms *contras* (Spanish) and *perestroika* (Russian). Then find an English word or phrase that has the same meaning.

1988	1990	1992

1988
George Bush is elected president

June 1989
Chinese students protest in Tiananmen Square

November 1989
The Berlin Wall is torn down

January 1991
Allies launch Operation Desert Storm

December 1991
The Soviet Union is dismantled

Section 2

The Bush Presidency

READ TO DISCOVER . . .

- how the cold war ended.
- why the Soviet Union broke apart.
- what President Bush's foreign policy was.
- why President Bush began few new domestic programs.

TERMS TO LEARN

coup   bankruptcy

The Storyteller

On September 2, 1944, a young pilot took part in a bombing mission against Japanese bases. World War II was raging. His plane—launched from an aircraft carrier—suffered a direct hit from a Japanese anti-aircraft gun. The pilot and his two crew members bailed out into the Pacific Ocean. A U.S. submarine rescued the pilot from a life raft, but the other two men were never found. For his heroism, the pilot—George Bush—was awarded the Distinguished Flying Cross. More than 40 years later, Bush would become the forty-first president of the United States.

1992 Bush campaign button

As Ronald Reagan's second term drew to a close, the election campaign for his successor heated up. Vice President **George Bush** swept through the 1988 primaries to win the Republican presidential nomination. Bush chose Indiana senator **Dan Quayle** as his running mate.

Election of 1988

★ Many Democrats vied for their party's nomination, but the field quickly narrowed to two candidates—civil rights leader **Jesse Jackson** and Massachusetts governor **Michael Dukakis.** Dukakis, who ran the most effective primary campaign, won the nomination and chose Senator **Lloyd Bentsen** of Texas as his running mate.

On Election Day, Bush carried 40 states, giving him 426 electoral votes to 112 for Dukakis. However, Bush's victory did not extend to Congress. The Democrats retained control of the House and the Senate.

With much experience in foreign affairs, newly elected president George Bush was called upon to steer the United States through a time of sweeping change facing the world. Many important changes dealt with the Soviet Union.

A New World Order

★ In December 1988, Soviet leader Mikhail Gorbachev stood before the United Nations to describe the "new world order" to come.

Gorbachev stressed that people throughout the world wanted "independence, democracy, and social justice."

Achieving Arms Cuts

Gorbachev wanted to end the arms race so he could focus on reforms within the Soviet Union. He sought to continue the progress on arms control begun with President Reagan.

In 1990 Gorbachev and President Bush agreed with European leaders to destroy tanks and other conventional weapons deployed in Europe. In 1991, with the **Strategic Arms Reduction Treaty** (START), they achieved a breakthrough. For the first time, two nuclear powers agreed to destroy existing nuclear weapons.

Unrest in the Soviet Union

Most Soviet citizens, however, were more concerned about their own problems than about arms control. For years they had endured shortages of food and basic items such as shoes and soap because of government mismanagement and heavy defense spending.

Gorbachev's policies aimed to solve the economic problems, but changes came slowly. The shortages continued, and people grew impatient with the conditions.

With Gorbachev's policy of glasnost, Soviet citizens began to express their dissatisfaction openly. Thousands of people marched through Moscow in February 1990, demanding an end to Communist rule. Unrest and calls for democracy had also spread throughout the Soviet Union. Many of the republics that made up the Soviet Union demanded independence.

Eastern Europe

★ While events were unfolding in the Soviet Union, the people of Eastern Europe also grew restless. Many people sensing change occurring in the Soviet Union under Gorbachev's leadership felt freer to demand change in their countries as well.

A Rising Tide of Freedom

The first democratic moves outside of the Soviet Union occurred in **Poland,** where shipyard workers had won the right to form an independent labor union—called **Solidarity**—in October 1980. **Lech Walesa,** the leader of Solidarity, emerged as a symbol of resistance to Communist rule. He led the Poles in calling for reforms. Although the government cracked down on the democratic movement in the mid-1980s, the movement gained strength and forced the government to hold open elections in June 1989.

The democratic cause spread to neighboring countries. Across Eastern Europe, demonstrators filled the streets of major cities. As a result of a relaxation of Soviet control and public pressure, long-sealed national borders were opened and Communist governments toppled. In the last 3 months of 1989, the Iron Curtain that had separated Eastern and Western Europe for more than 40 years began to crumble. Throughout 1989, Gorbachev not only refused to intervene, but he encouraged reform.

★ Picturing HISTORY Lech Walesa served as Poland's president from 1990 to 1995. **What role did Walesa have in Polish affairs during the 1980s?**

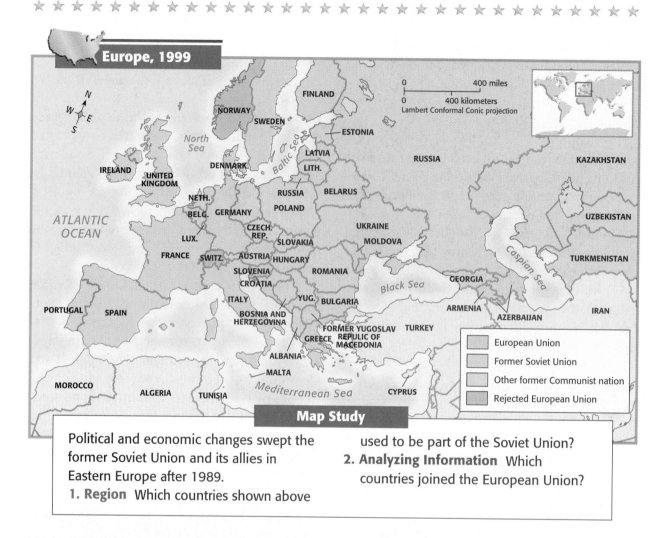

Europe, 1999

FINLAND · NORWAY · SWEDEN · ESTONIA · North Sea · Baltic Sea · LATVIA · LITH. · RUSSIA · KAZAKHSTAN · IRELAND · UNITED KINGDOM · DENMARK · RUSSIA · BELARUS · UZBEKISTAN · NETH. · BELG. · GERMANY · POLAND · ATLANTIC OCEAN · LUX. · CZECH. REP. · UKRAINE · MOLDOVA · Caspian Sea · TURKMENISTAN · FRANCE · SWITZ. · AUSTRIA · HUNGARY · SLOVAKIA · SLOVENIA · ROMANIA · GEORGIA · PORTUGAL · SPAIN · CROATIA · ITALY · YUG. · BULGARIA · Black Sea · ARMENIA · AZERBAIJAN · IRAN · BOSNIA AND HERZEGOVINA · FORMER YUGOSLAV REPUBLIC OF MACEDONIA · TURKEY · GREECE · ALBANIA · MOROCCO · ALGERIA · TUNISIA · MALTA · Mediterranean Sea · CYPRUS

0 — 400 miles
0 — 400 kilometers
Lambert Conformal Conic projection

European Union
Former Soviet Union
Other former Communist nation
Rejected European Union

Map Study

Political and economic changes swept the former Soviet Union and its allies in Eastern Europe after 1989.

1. Region Which countries shown above used to be part of the Soviet Union?

2. Analyzing Information Which countries joined the European Union?

The Wall Comes Tumbling Down

Freedom also came to East Germany—the focus of so much cold war tension. With protests raging and thousands of citizens fleeing to West Germany, the Communist government opened the Berlin Wall on November 9, 1989.

Germans brought hammers and chisels to chop away at the Berlin Wall, long the symbol of the barrier to the West. In 1990 East Germany voted to reunite with West Germany.

Collapse of the Soviet Union

As Europe was changing, Gorbachev faced mounting opposition from political rivals within the Soviet Union. Some

Russian soldier after coup failed

reformers demanded that he move more quickly. Hard-line Communists in the military and secret police resisted his changes and feared the collapse of the Soviet empire.

In August 1991, the hard-liners struck back. A group of Communist officials and army generals staged a coup, an overthrow of the government. They held Gorbachev captive and ordered soldiers to seize the parliament building.

As the world waited anxiously, about 50,000 Russians surrounded the parliament building to protect it from the soldiers. **Boris Yeltsin,** president of the Russian Republic and a reformer, stood on top of a tank and declared, "Democracy will win!" President Bush telephoned Yeltsin to express America's support. On August 22 the coup collapsed. Freed, Gorbachev returned to Moscow.

The defeat of the coup turned the tide of democracy into a tidal wave. Soon all 15 republics had declared their independence from the Soviet Union. Yeltsin outlawed the Communist Party in Russia. On December 25, 1991, Gorbachev announced the end of the Soviet Union, and the Soviet flag that flew over the Kremlin was lowered for the last time.

The End of the Cold War

President Bush responded quickly to the new situation. In the spring of 1992, Bush and other world leaders pledged $24 billion in assistance to the former Soviet republics. President Bush declared:

> 66 For over 40 years, the United States led the West in the struggle against communism and the threat it posed to our most precious values. That confrontation is over. 99

A New Foreign Policy

★ With the end of the cold war came both renewed hope and new challenges to maintaining world peace. While trying to redefine the goals of American foreign policy, President Bush had to deal with crises in Central America, China, the Middle East, and the Balkans.

Panama

In the eyes of the United States, **Manuel Noriega,** the military dictator of Panama, had two strikes against him. First, Noriega had been charged with drug trafficking by an American court. Second, he had refused to yield power to the newly elected president of Panama, Guillermo Endara. In December 1989, Bush ordered U.S. troops to the Central American nation to overthrow Noriega. When the troops gained control of the country, Noriega surrendered. Endara became Panama's new president, and the U.S. troops left Panama. In 1992 Noriega was tried and convicted in the United States.

China

George Bush had served as the first U.S. **envoy**—diplomatic representative—to China, when the two countries reopened relations in 1974. He took a special interest in China, claiming, "I know the Chinese." During the 1980s, China's Communist government began to reform the economy, but it refused to make political reforms. In May 1989, students and workers in China held demonstrations calling for more democracy. As the protests spread, the country seemed on the verge of revolution.

The Chinese government sent troops to crush the uprising. On June 3, 1989, soldiers and tanks killed several thousand protesters gathered in

★ **Picturing HISTORY** In the spring of 1989, about 100,000 students demanding democratic reform gathered in the main square of Beijing, China's capital. **How did the Chinese government respond to the demonstrations?**

Tiananmen Square in the center of Beijing. World leaders condemned the slaughter. Although President Bush disapproved of the Chinese leaders' use of force, he carefully avoided words or actions that might lead the Chinese to break off relations with the United States. He did not believe that international pressure or trade sanctions would result in a change in Chinese policies. Although Bush's policy met opposition, it permitted U.S. trade with China to continue to grow.

Eyewitness to HISTORY

The Persian Gulf War

The Bush administration—and the world—faced a serious challenge to stability in 1990. On August 2 Iraq's dictator, **Saddam Hussein** (hoo•SAYN), sent his army into **Kuwait,** a small neighboring country rich in oil. Kuwait was quickly overwhelmed. Nations around the world feared that Iraq would also invade Saudi Arabia.

Vowing to "draw a line in the sand," President Bush persuaded other nations to join what he called **Operation Desert Shield.** Hundreds of thousands of troops moved to Saudi Arabia to prevent an invasion of that country. The coalition forces were under the command of United States general **Norman Schwarzkopf.** Hussein was ordered to withdraw his troops from Kuwait—but the Iraqi troops did not leave and tension mounted. The United Nations set a deadline. Iraq must withdraw by January 15, 1991, or the allies would use force to remove them. Congress voted to support military action if Iraq did not withdraw.

Operation Desert Storm

Iraq refused to budge, and on January 16 the allies launched **Operation Desert Storm.** Laser-guided missiles and thousands of tons of bombs fell on Iraq, destroying its air defenses and other military targets, and damaging many civilian sites as well. President Bush explained the attack:

> 66 The world could wait no longer. . . . While the world waited, Saddam Hussein met every overture of peace with open contempt. 99

After six weeks of round-the-clock bombardment, Hussein's forces still refused to leave Kuwait. In late February the allies opened the second phase of Desert Storm—a ground war in which they attacked Iraqi troops from the side and rear. At the same time, planes bombarded Iraqi positions.

Kuwait is Liberated

Thousands of Iraqi soldiers died. Thousands more surrendered. Just 100 hours after the ground war began, President Bush suspended military action. "Kuwait is liberated," he announced. "America and the world have kept their word."

★ **Picturing HISTORY** Customers in an Illinois cafe eagerly search newspapers for details about allied air strikes in Iraq. **Why did the United States go to war?**

Iraq accepted the allied cease-fire terms, and Saddam Hussein's troops finally left Kuwait.

Americans celebrated the sudden victory. They hailed the leaders of Desert Storm, Norman Schwarzkopf and General **Colin Powell,** chairman of the Joint Chiefs of Staff, and held parades for the troops. President Bush's approval rating in opinion polls soared above 90 percent. After the war, the United States helped rebuild Kuwait. It took 9 months to extinguish the hundreds of oil well fires set by fleeing Iraqi troops. 🔍

⭐ **Picturing HISTORY** Women serving in the military made up about 10 percent of the U.S. forces involved in the Persian Gulf War. **What was the outcome of the Persian Gulf War?**

War in the Balkans

Another challenge to world peace arose in Yugoslavia. Yugoslavia had been composed of several republics. After the collapse of Yugoslavia's government, the republics of **Slovenia, Croatia,** and **Bosnia-Herzegovina** declared independence in 1991. The population of Croatia and Bosnia included many Serbs—people from the Yugoslav republic of Serbia. These Serbs, backed by the Serbian republic, fought to hold on to certain areas of Croatia and Bosnia. In the terrible civil war that followed, thousands died.

Reports of atrocities committed by the Serbs outraged world leaders. In 1992 the UN passed a resolution that placed a boycott on trade with Serbia until the fighting stopped.

💲 **Economics**

Domestic Issues

⭐ At home the Bush administration faced great difficulties. Like Reagan, Bush opposed an active government role in domestic affairs. The few proposals Bush did introduce faced determined opposition in the Democratic Congress. Most important, though, the federal debt and a banking crisis required substantial government funds, leaving little money for new programs.

Banking Crisis

Early in his presidency, Bush faced a banking crisis. During the 1980s, the Reagan administration had cut regulations in many industries. New laws eased restrictions on savings and loan associations (S&Ls)—financial institutions that specialized in making loans to buy homes.

The new laws allowed managers of S&Ls to become more aggressive in offering attractive returns to savers—and in making far more risky loans. When many borrowers could not repay their loans and real estate values declined, S&Ls began to lose millions of dollars. Many failed completely and closed their doors. Individual deposits in S&Ls were insured by the government, which now had to pay out billions of dollars to the customers of the failed institutions. To prevent the crisis from spreading, the government bailed out other struggling S&Ls. This policy eventually cost taxpayers almost $500 billion.

Economic Downturn

The heavy borrowing of the 1980s loomed as another source of trouble for the economy. As the federal debt continued to reach new highs, business and personal debt grew as well. In 1991, when the economy slowed to a recession, many

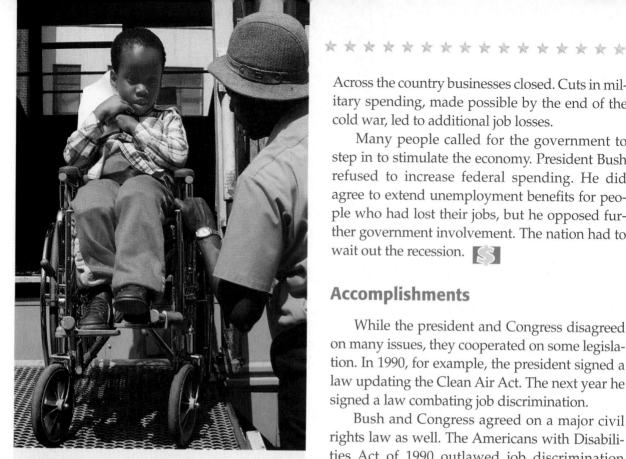

★ Picturing HISTORY The Americans with Disabilities Act of 1990 requires institutions to provide disabled people with easier access to public transportation. **What other protection does the act provide?**

Across the country businesses closed. Cuts in military spending, made possible by the end of the cold war, led to additional job losses.

Many people called for the government to step in to stimulate the economy. President Bush refused to increase federal spending. He did agree to extend unemployment benefits for people who had lost their jobs, but he opposed further government involvement. The nation had to wait out the recession.

Accomplishments

While the president and Congress disagreed on many issues, they cooperated on some legislation. In 1990, for example, the president signed a law updating the Clean Air Act. The next year he signed a law combating job discrimination.

Bush and Congress agreed on a major civil rights law as well. The Americans with Disabilities Act of 1990 outlawed job discrimination against people with disabilities. It also required institutions to provide disabled people with easier access to workplaces, communications, transportation, and housing.

Another important part of the president's domestic agenda was the war on illegal drugs. In 1989 President Bush created the Office of National Drug Control Policy. This department coordinates the activities of more than 50 federal agencies involved in the war on drugs.

people and businesses could not meet loan payments. Some had to declare bankruptcy, selling off everything they owned to pay debts.

Section 2 Assessment

Checking for Understanding

1. *Identify* George Bush, Jesse Jackson, Lech Walesa, Boris Yeltsin, Saddam Hussein.
2. *Define* coup, bankruptcy.
3. *Explain* why the people of Eastern Europe abandoned communism.

Reviewing Themes

4. **Global Connections** Compare President Bush's handling of the Tiananmen Square incident in China to his handling of Iraq's invasion of Kuwait.

Critical Thinking

5. **Determining Cause and Effect** What economic issues reduced Bush's popularity?

Activity

Drawing a Map Illustrate a world map showing the cities and regions discussed in the section.

The Berlin Wall

On the night of August 12, 1961, all of the trains between East Berlin and West Berlin screeched to a halt. The passengers were told to get off and walk home. As people watched in disbelief, Soviet troops unloaded trucks filled with barbed wire, cement, and steel posts. The sound of jackhammers rang throughout the night as the army began building a wall that would separate East and West Berlin.

Built to prevent East Germans from escaping to West Berlin, the "Wall of Shame" cut through back-yards and neighborhoods,

A joyful crowd celebrates the destruction of the Berlin Wall in November 1989.

dividing families in its wake. About 13 feet high and 97 miles long, the wall looped around West Berlin and cut the city off from East Berlin and East Germany.

Hundreds of people died trying to escape across the wall to West Berlin. Guards with searchlights and machine guns were stationed along the wall in its 300 towers. Some people who tried to escape hid under cars or in coffins. Others swam canals or scaled the wall with grappling hooks. One person even built a sub-marine and made his escape underwater. About 5,000 people escaped to West Berlin.

For 28 years the wall divided Berlin and its people. With the reunification of the two Germanys in 1990, the wall was destroyed. Today only one section remains as a memorial to its history and the people who died in their at-tempts to escape.

Activity

"Walling" Your State Make a photocopy of your state map. Draw a line that runs from north to south down the middle of your state to represent a wall. If you were prevented from crossing this wall, which large cities would you be cut off from? What friends and relatives would you never see again? What parks, recreation areas, and bodies of water would be off-limits?

1992
Bill Clinton is elected president

1993
Congress passes the Brady Bill; NAFTA eliminates trade barriers

1995
Serbs, Croats, and Bosnian Muslims sign a peace plan

1996
Legislation reverses New Deal social welfare

Section 3

The Clinton Presidency

READ TO DISCOVER...

- what policies Clinton pursued as president.
- what happened after the Republicans gained control of Congress in 1994.

TERMS TO LEARN

grassroots   line-item veto
budget deficit

Storyteller

A president appears on MTV. Politicians perform rock music on talk shows. What would George Washington have thought about such events? In 1991, polls showed that voters were turned off by politics. So the 1992 presidential candidates found new ways to reach the public—especially young people. President Bush and challenger Bill Clinton appeared on TV and radio talk shows. On the late evening Arsenio Hall show, Clinton put on sunglasses, and played saxophone. Both he and running mate Al Gore appeared on MTV. By the end of the campaign, even President Bush wanted his time on the music network—and got it!

Clinton inaugural button

After the Gulf War victory, President Bush's reelection seemed assured. A lingering recession, however, raised doubts about his leadership and encouraged challengers to enter the race.

The 1992 Election

★ In 1992, the Democrats nominated Arkansas governor **Bill Clinton** to run against President Bush. Clinton chose Tennessee Senator **Al Gore** as his running mate. Clinton made the economy the major campaign issue. Calling himself a New Democrat, Clinton promised to cut taxes and spending, and to reform welfare and the health-care system.

Unhappy with "politics as usual," many Americans did not want to vote for either major party. A grassroots movement—people organizing at the local level around the nation—put billionaire Texas businessman **H. Ross Perot** on the ballot as a third-party candidate. Perot stressed the need to end the government's deficit spending, or spending more money than it takes in.

Although Clinton received only 43 percent of the popular vote, he won a majority of electoral votes and the election. Bush won 38 percent of the popular vote, and Perot received 19 percent—the best showing for a third-party candidate since 1912.

Clinton's Agenda

★ The new president put forth an ambitious domestic program. President Clinton also tried to reduce the budget deficit—the amount

President George Bush, H. Ross Perot, and Bill Clinton debate during the 1992 campaign.

by which spending exceeds revenue—while ending the recession. His first budget cut government spending, increased taxes on the wealthiest Americans, and gave tax credits to the poorest.

Health Care

During the election campaign, Clinton had promised to reform America's health-care system. His goal was to control rising health-care costs and provide adequate health insurance for every American. To prepare the plan, the president appointed a task force headed by his wife, **Hillary Rodham Clinton**—an unprecedented role for a first lady.

Critics soon attacked the Clinton plan. They called it too complex, too expensive, and too reliant on government control. In the end, Congress never voted on the plan, and the Clintons' health-care reform effort died.

Domestic Legislation

During his first term, President Clinton achieved some success. Despite strong opposition, the president succeeded in passing the **Brady Bill** of 1993. The bill required a waiting period before people could buy handguns. The 1994 crime bill banned 19 kinds of assault weapons and provided for 100,000 new police officers.

Another bill on the Clinton agenda to pass Congress was the Family Medical Leave Act of 1993. It permitted workers to take time off from their jobs for special family situations. The National Service Act created AmeriCorps, which enabled college students to repay government education loans by performing community service. The "Motor Voter Law" of 1993 allowed citizens to register to vote when getting a driver's license.

Foreign Policy

President Clinton took office at a time when the nation's attention had shifted from foreign to domestic affairs. With the Soviet Union gone, Clinton's foreign policy focused on expanding trade and resolving regional conflicts around the world.

NAFTA

In 1993 Clinton persuaded Congress to ratify the North American Free Trade Agreement, or **NAFTA**. In NAFTA the United States, Canada, and Mexico agreed to eliminate trade barriers among the three nations. NAFTA opponents feared a loss of U.S. jobs, but supporters argued that it would lower prices for American consumers and expand markets.

Middle East Peace Accords

In September 1993, President Clinton invited Israeli prime minister **Yitzhak Rabin** and **Yassir Arafat,** head of the Palestine Liberation Organization (PLO), to the White House for the signing of a historic agreement between the two leaders. Israel recognized the PLO as the representative of the Palestinian people, and the PLO recognized Israel's right to exist. The agreement created a plan for limited Palestinian self-government over certain areas in Israel.

Some Arabs and Israelis opposed the agreement. Militant Arabs exploded bombs in Israel. In 1995, an Israeli extremist assassinated Prime Minister Rabin. Concerned about the violence, Israelis elected **Benjamin Netanyahu**, a leader who emphasized security and wanted to slow the peace process. After months of stalemate, President

Clinton arranged a meeting in late 1998 between Netanyahu and Arafat in Wye Mills, Maryland. There, both leaders agreed to compromises that pushed the peace process forward.

Civil War in Bosnia

As you read earlier, in 1991 civil war had erupted in the former Yugoslavia. In the small nation of **Bosnia-Herzegovina**, Bosnian Serbs waged an especially cruel war against Bosnian Muslims and Croats. After nearly four years of fighting, the United States convinced NATO to launch air attacks against the Serbs to force them to negotiate. The Clinton administration then brought the three sides together for peace talks in Dayton, Ohio, where they accepted a peace plan and signed an agreement in December 1995.

A Republican Congress

President Clinton's achievements in foreign policy did not increase his popularity at home. With scandals that touched the Clintons further weakening the president, Republicans hoped to gain ground in the 1994 elections.

The "Contract With America"

To increase their support, the Republicans created a document called the Contract With America. Representative **Newt Gingrich** of Georgia hailed the contract as "a first step toward renewing American civilization." In the contract, Republicans promised to cut back the size of the federal government, balance the budget, lower taxes, and reform how Congress operates. They also pledged to pass laws to reduce crime, reform welfare, and strengthen the family.

Following the election, the Republicans gained control of both houses of Congress for the first time in 40 years. Newt Gingrich was chosen Speaker of the

Rep. Newt Gingrich leads a campaign rally.

House. In their first hundred days in office, the House Republicans passed every point in the Contract With America.

The Republican program gradually lost momentum, however. Some proposals stalled in the Senate, and President Clinton used his veto to kill several Republican bills on welfare reform and the budget. Clinton argued that Republican budget cuts would hurt elderly people on Medicare, damage the environment, and undermine education.

Disputes between the president and congressional Republicans blocked passage of the 1996 budget, causing the federal government to run out of money. The government shut down nonessential services twice for a total of 27 days. Finally, in April 1996, President Clinton and Congress reached a compromise. They also agreed to balance the budget by 2002.

Bipartisan Action

In the months before the 1996 election, Democrats and Republicans came together to pass sweeping legislation. Congress passed and the president signed a line-item veto bill. Intended as a way to reduce wasteful spending, the line-item veto allowed the president to cancel any individual items within a spending bill. However, the Supreme Court later overturned the law. It ruled that such an increase in the president's powers could be granted only through a constitutional amendment.

In August 1996, the president signed a bill that reversed social welfare policy introduced during the New Deal. This welfare reform law established a work requirement for people receiving benefits and set a five-year time limit on benefits.

Congress also approved a bill to protect health insurance. While not the major health-care reform the president wanted, the bill assured health coverage for people who changed or lost jobs. Both Democrats and Republicans claimed credit for the legislation as they prepared to campaign to win the White House and Congress.

The 1996 Elections

★ Early in 1995, the Republicans had high hopes of winning the White House. However, the political climate changed during the budget battles of 1995–1996. Polls showed that most Americans blamed Republicans in Congress for the government shutdowns. Clinton gained support by claiming to defend the elderly, education, and the environment against Republican budget cuts. He also gained strength by moving towards the political center on such issues as welfare reform.

As the 1996 campaign began, Clinton also took credit for the strong economy. Unemployment and inflation were the lowest they had been in 40 years. Wages were up, the crime rate was down, and the number of people on welfare was declining.

The Republicans nominated Senator **Bob Dole** of Kansas, the Senate majority leader, to run against Clinton. Dole chose as his running mate **Jack Kemp**, a popular conservative and former New York congressman. Dole promised a 15 percent tax cut if elected. Ross Perot entered the presidential race again, this time as the candidate of the new Reform Party. As before, Perot tried to make the budget deficit the main campaign issue.

President Clinton won reelection, winning 49 percent of the popular vote. Dole received 41 percent and Perot 9 percent—less than half of what he had received in 1992.

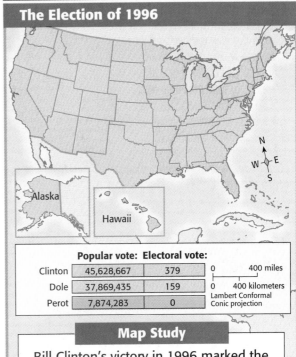

The Election of 1996

	Popular vote:	Electoral vote:
Clinton	45,628,667	379
Dole	37,869,435	159
Perot	7,874,283	0

0   400 miles
0   400 kilometers
Lambert Conformal
Conic projection

Map Study

Bill Clinton's victory in 1996 marked the first time a Democratic president had won reelection in more than 50 years.

1. **Place** Which candidate won the electoral votes in your state?
2. **Analyzing Information** How many electoral votes did Clinton receive?

Despite Clinton's victory in the presidential race, Republicans maintained control of both houses of Congress. Overall, the 1996 election results suggested that voters were pleased with the economy and direction of the country.

★ ★ ★ ★ ★ Section 3 Assessment ★ ★ ★ ★ ★

Checking for Understanding

1. *Identify* Bill Clinton, Al Gore, H. Ross Perot, Hillary Rodham Clinton, Brady Bill.
2. *Define* grassroots, budget deficit, line-item veto.
3. *Summarize* Bill Clinton's foreign policy.

Reviewing Themes

4. **Groups and Institutions** How did the 1994 election affect the balance of parties in Congress?

Critical Thinking

5. **Drawing Conclusions** Why do you think the Republicans and Democrats agreed to cooperate on budget issues in the final months before the 1996 election?

Activity

Prioritizing Events Make a list of Clinton's foreign policy achievements. Then use your own judgment to rank them in order, with the most important achievement as number one. Explain your reasons for your first and last choices.

Computer chips and fiber-optic cables (in background) have changed the way we live and work. Introduced in the 1970s, the computer chip went inside machines, cars, and appliances. Fiber-optic cables—sending messages as pulses of light through glass in the cables—enabled computers to communicate at lightning speeds. Everywhere, people hooked up computers and shared information.

2 In 1903 the Wright brothers coaxed an airplane (above left) into the air for a 12-second flight. Today the space shuttle (above), guided by scientists and computers, carries people and experiments hundreds of miles beyond the planet.

1 Invented in 1876, the telephone quickly gained popularity. By the mid-20th century, the world was using it for business and pleasure. Today a computer chip in a portable cellular phone (above right) processes radio signals so that a caller can make a call from virtually anywhere.

3 Surgeons once operated with crude equipment, such as the implements at left, with no idea that germs cause infection. Today's doctors are armed with greater knowledge and sophisticated machinery. The patient above gets a CT (computer tomography) scan, which will give her doctor a 3-D image of her brain before—or perhaps even instead of—an operation.

Technology's Journey

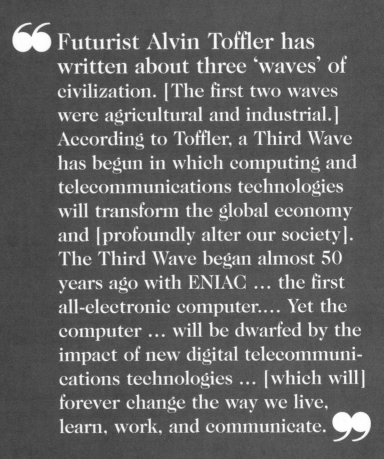

4 A century ago students learned to read and write in one-room schoolhouses. Today students can sit in class and roam the planet. Computers and telephones collaborate to bring information, images, and sound from all corners of the world. In the photo above, a student, using a computer at National Geographic Society headquarters in Washington, D.C., interacts with members of a scientific expedition in Hawaii.

❝ Futurist Alvin Toffler has written about three 'waves' of civilization. [The first two waves were agricultural and industrial.] According to Toffler, a Third Wave has begun in which computing and telecommunications technologies will transform the global economy and [profoundly alter our society]. The Third Wave began almost 50 years ago with ENIAC ... the first all-electronic computer.... Yet the computer ... will be dwarfed by the impact of new digital telecommunications technologies ... [which will] forever change the way we live, learn, work, and communicate. ❞

—From "The Information Superhighway: What It Will Mean" by Vice President Al Gore, Jr., published in The World Almanac, 1995.

1994	1996	1998	2000

1995
Computers are an essential part of American life

1996
Bill Clinton wins reelection

1998
Bill Clinton is impeached

2001
George W. Bush inaugurated as 43rd president

Section 4

Toward the 21st Century

READ TO DISCOVER . . .

- what domestic and foreign challenges President Clinton faced in his second term.
- how American society is changing.

TERMS TO LEARN

gross domestic product
impeach
incumbent
Internet
ozone
global warming

The Storyteller

Poet Robert Frost wrote "The Road Not Taken" in 1915. As the 21st century dawns, what will your own journey be like?

Two roads diverged in a yellow wood,
And sorry I could not travel both
And be one traveler, long I stood
And looked down one as far as I could
To where it bent in the undergrowth; . . .

I shall be telling this with a sigh
Somewhere ages and
   ages hence;
Two roads diverged in a
   wood, and I—
I took the one less
   traveled by,
And that has made all
   the difference.

***Space Shuttle* Discovery**

In his second inaugural address, President Clinton sounded a hopeful note as he described the challenges and opportunities that lay ahead:

❝ At the dawn of the twenty-first century a free people must now choose to shape the forces of the Information Age and the global society, to unleash the limitless potential of all our people, and, yes, to form a more perfect union. ❞

Clinton's Second Term

⭐ During his second term in office, President Clinton focused on many of the same issues—families, education, and health care—that had been on his first-term agenda. He also dealt with crises in the Middle East and the Balkans.

Domestic Issues

Education was a major focus of President Clinton's second term. He expanded the Head Start program and introduced a new college scholarship fund. The president then established the Technology Literacy Challenge Fund to help connect every school to the Internet. He also introduced GEAR UP—a mentoring program for middle school students.

To promote the health of America's young people, President Clinton convinced Congress to ban cigarette advertising aimed at children. At the president's urging, Congress also approved a program that provided health insurance for children whose parents could not afford it.

Foreign Policy

Achieving stability in the post-cold war world proved to be very difficult. After the Persian Gulf War, Iraq's dictator, **Saddam Hussein**, tried to prevent UN inspectors from checking that Iraq had eliminated its chemical, biological, and nuclear weapons. In December 1998, after repeated warnings, the United States and Great Britain bombed Iraq for several days. The goal of the mission—named Operation Desert Fox—was to destroy Iraq's weapons of mass destruction.

While dealing with Iraq, the United States also was worried about a crisis in Serbia, the largest republic in Yugoslavia. The Serbian province of Kosovo has two major ethnic groups—Serbs and Albanians. Many of the Albanians wanted Kosovo to separate from Serbia. To keep Kosovo in Serbia, the Serbian leader **Slobodan Milosevic** ordered a crackdown. The Albanians then organized the Kosovo Liberation Army (KLA). By the late 1990s, fighting between the KLA and Serbian troops had caused hundreds of thousands of refugees to flee Kosovo.

The Serbian treatment of the Kosovo Albanians enraged people around the world. President Clinton and European leaders tried unsuccessfully to bring the two sides together. Worried by reports of Serbian violence, President Clinton convinced European leaders that NATO should use force to stop the fighting.

In March 1999, NATO began bombing Serbia. The bombing convinced Serbia to pull its troops out of Kosovo. Several weeks later, an international force led by American, British, French, German, and Russian troops entered Kosovo to maintain the peace.

At the same time, Israeli and Palestinian leaders continued their negotiations. They disagreed about the territory the Palestinians would be allowed to control. In July 2000, President Clinton invited Yassir Arafat, head of the Palestinian Authority, and the new Israeli prime minister, Ehud Barak, to Camp David for an intensive round of peace negotiations. No agreement was reached.

A few weeks later, fighting began between Palestinians and Israelis in the disputed territories. President Clinton then arranged an emergency meeting between Arafat and Barak in Egypt. Although both men agreed to a cease-fire, the fighting continued.

$ Economics

Economic Boom

During President Clinton's two terms, the American economy grew at an extraordinary rate. The measure of this growth is the gross domestic product (GDP), which is the value of all the goods and services produced in a nation in a year. In 1996 and 1997, the GDP grew by about 4 percent a year—the highest rate of growth since the post-World War II boom. The rapid growth of the economy continued through the year 2000, making the economic expansion the longest in American history.

The economy's growth increased the amount of money the government received. At the same time, the president and Congress cut back the size of the federal budget. As a result, in 1997, for the first time in 24 years, the president was able to submit a balanced budget to Congress. Beginning in 1998, the government also began to run a surplus—that is, it collected more money than it spent. The surplus in 2000 was expected to be the largest since 1948. **$**

A Troubled Presidency

★ Although the American economy was doing very well in the late 1990s, President Clinton faced a serious personal crisis. In 1998, a scandal erupted that endangered his presidency.

Under Investigation

President Clinton's problems began in 1994, when legal questions arose relating to real estate investments he had made while governor of Arkansas. Attorney General **Janet Reno** decided that an independent counsel should investigate the president. A special panel appointed **Kenneth Starr**, a former federal judge, to this position.

In early 1998, a new scandal emerged involving a personal relationship between the president and a White House intern. Some evidence suggested that the president had committed perjury, or lied under oath, about the relationship. After examining the evidence, Ken Starr reported to Congress in September 1998 that President Clinton had committed perjury, obstructed justice, and abused his power in order to conceal the personal relationship.

In response to Starr's report, the House of Representatives voted to hold hearings to decide whether or not to impeach the president. To impeach is to make a formal accusation of wrongdoing against a public official.

The Republicans hoped the scandal would help them in the 1998 elections. Instead, the Democrats gained five seats in the House, and the Senate remained unchanged. Incumbents—current officeholders—did very well in the 1998 elections. The Republican failure to gain seats led House Speaker Newt Gingrich to resign from Congress. In 1999, Republican **Dennis Hastert** of Illinois became the new speaker.

Impeachment

After the 1998 elections the House began impeachment hearings. Clinton's supporters argued very strongly that his offenses did not qualify as "high crimes and misdemeanors," as stated in the Constitution. Clinton's accusers insisted that the president should be held accountable if his actions were illegal. The debate divided Congress along party lines. Democrats supported President Clinton, while most Republicans favored impeachment.

On December 19, 1998, the House of Representatives passed two articles of impeachment, one for perjury and one for obstruction of justice. No Democrats voted for impeachment. This made President Clinton only the second president ever to be impeached. The case moved to the Senate for trial, where a two-thirds majority was necessary for conviction. On February 12, 1999, the senators cast their votes. The result was 45 guilty to 55 not guilty of perjury, and 50 guilty to 50 not guilty of obstruction of justice. Acquitted of both charges, Bill Clinton had survived the biggest possible challenge to his presidency.

Looking to the Future

As Americans entered a new century, they faced many uncertainties—and opportunities. New technologies and a changing society had begun to transform America in new ways.

The Impeachment Process

The Constitution gives Congress the power to remove a president from office. Article II, Section 4, says that a president "shall be removed from office upon impeachment for and Conviction of, Treason, Bribery, or other High Crimes and Misdemeanors."

The House of Representatives has the sole power over impeachment—the formal accusation of wrongdoing in office. If a majority of the House votes to impeach the president, the Senate conducts a trial. A two-thirds majority Senate vote is needed to convict and remove the president from office. The Chief Justice of the United States presides over the trial.

President Clinton prepares to address the nation hours after his impeachment.

$ Economics

The Global Economy

During the 1990s, many American businesses benefited from more free trade among nations. To promote trade, 132 countries, including the United States, signed a new General Agreement on Tariffs and Trade (GATT). The agreement created the World Trade Organization (WTO) to monitor GATT.

Another reason the economy did so well in the 1990s was the growth of technology industries. Telecommunications grew rapidly as Americans watched television by cable or satellite, spoke on cell phones, and exchanged messages by fax. Even more dramatic was the increasing use of personal computers in homes, schools, and businesses and the rise of the Internet—a worldwide linking of computer networks. **$**

A Changing Society

As America entered the twenty-first century, its population had changed. Because Americans were living longer, elderly people formed a larger part of the population. The Census Bureau reported that nearly 14 percent of the population was over 65 in the year 2000. As the baby boom generation ages, this percentage will grow even larger. This will require greater government payments for Social Security and Medicare.

Immigration also changed the composition of American society. In the late 1990s about 9 percent of the population were immigrants—the highest level since the 1920s. Latin America and Asia provided the most immigrants. In 1995, Hispanic Americans made up more than 10 percent of the population. By 2000, more than four percent of the population were Asian Americans and nearly 12 percent were Hispanic Americans. If the trends continue, Hispanic Americans will soon become the largest minority in the United States.

Global Challenges

Today, more than ever, the peoples of the world depend on each other. Beginning in the 1980s, scientists noticed that the atmosphere was losing ozone. This layer of gas protects life on Earth from cancer-causing rays of the sun. In 1987, the United States and 22 other nations agreed to stop making chemicals that might be weakening the ozone layer.

Some scientists have also found evidence of global warming—an increase in average world temperatures over time. Several theories about it exist. No one is sure what causes global warming, but a UN report warned that air pollution could be a factor. In 1997, 39 nations signed the Kyoto Protocol agreeing to reduce their air pollution by the year 2008.

Preserving peace remains the most pressing global issue. Throughout the 1990s, the United States worked with other nations to reduce the danger from nuclear, chemical, and biological weapons. In 1996, President Clinton signed a worldwide Comprehensive Test Ban Treaty. In 1997, the Senate ratified an international agreement to ban chemical weapons.

The Election of 2000

President Clinton's years in power had left the country divided. Many people were pleased with the economy, but were disappointed with the president's personal behavior. As the 2000 election approached, both the Republicans and the Democrats tried to find candidates that would appeal to a broad cross-section of society.

Gore vs. Bush

The Democrats nominated Vice President **Al Gore** for president in 2000, hoping that the popularity of Clinton's policies would convince Americans to vote for Gore. The Republican contest came down to two men: Governor **George W. Bush** of Texas, and Senator John McCain of Arizona. Ultimately, the Republicans chose George W. Bush, the son of former President Bush, as their nominee.

As his vice-presidential running mate, Al Gore chose Senator Joseph Lieberman from Connecticut. Lieberman was the first Jewish American ever to run for vice president. George W. Bush chose Richard Cheney as his running mate.

Picturing HISTORY George W. Bush narrowly won the extremely close 2000 presidential election. **Which state was key to the outcome of this race?**

Cheney had served as Secretary of Defense in the Bush administration.

The campaign of 2000 revolved around the question of what to do with the surplus—the extra money the federal government was collecting. Both presidential candidates agreed that Social Security and Medicare needed reform, but disagreed on the details. Both also supported tax cuts and plans to help seniors pay for prescription drugs. Frustrated by the similarities between Bush and Gore, Ralph Nader entered the race as the nominee of the Green Party.

A Close Vote

The 2000 election was one of the closest in history. On election night, no one knew the winner. Although Bush had a slim lead in Florida, the results were so close, an automatic recount was required by state law. Without Florida's 25 electoral votes, neither Bush nor Gore had the 270 electoral votes needed to win.

Gore also asked for manual recounts in several counties, and a battle began over whether and how to conduct them. Lawsuits were filed in state and federal courts. The issue ultimately reached the United States Supreme Court. On December 12, five weeks after the election, the Court issued its decision. In *Bush* v. *Gore*, the Court ruled that a hand recount of selected votes in Florida ordered by the Florida Supreme Court violated the equal protection clause of the Constitution. It further held that there was not enough time to conduct a recount that would pass constitutional standards.

In a televised speech the following day, Gore conceded. On January 20, 2001, Bush became the 43rd president of the United States.

Section 4 Assessment

★ ★ ★ ★ ★ ★ ★ ★ ★ ★ ★

Checking for Understanding
1. **Identify** Saddam Hussein, Slobodan Milosevic, Janet Reno, Kenneth Starr, Dennis Hastert.
2. **Define** gross domestic product, impeach, incumbent, Internet, ozone, global warming.
3. **Summarize** Clinton's impeachment.

Reviewing Themes
4. **Global Connections** What foreign policy challenges did the second-term Clinton administration face?

Critical Thinking
5. **Predicting Consequences** How might an aging population place a burden on younger people in the workforce?

Activity

Creating a Diagram Draw a diagram that illustrates the process of global warming.

SKILL BUILDER

Using an Electronic Spreadsheet

People use electronic spreadsheets to manage numbers quickly and easily. You can use a spreadsheet any time a problem involves numbers that you can arrange in rows and columns.

Students working on a computer spreadsheet

Learning the Skill

A spreadsheet is an electronic worksheet. All spreadsheets follow a basic design of rows and columns. Each column (vertical) is assigned a letter or a number. Each row (horizontal) is assigned a number. Each point where a column and row intersect is called a *cell*. The cell's position on the spreadsheet is labeled according to its corresponding column and row—Column A, Row 1 (A1); Column B, Row 2 (B2), etc.

Spreadsheets use *standard formulas* to calculate the numbers. You create a simple mathematical equation that uses these standard formulas and the computer does the calculations for you.

Practicing the Skill

Suppose you want to know how many votes the Republican, Democratic, and Independent candidates received across six states in the 1996 presidential election. Use these steps to create a spreadsheet that will provide this information:

1. In cells B1, C1, and D1 respectively, type a candidate's name or political party. In cell E1, type the term *total*.
2. In cells A2–A7, type the name of a state. In cell A8, type the word *total*.

3. In row 2, enter the number of votes each candidate received in the state named in cell A2. Repeat this process in rows 3–7.
4. Create a formula to calculate the votes. The formula for the equation tells what cells (2B + 2C + 2D) to add together.
5. Copy the formula down in the cells for the other five states.
6. Use the process in steps 4 and 5 to create and copy a formula to calculate the total number of votes each candidate received.

Applying the Skill

Using a Spreadsheet Use a spreadsheet to enter your test scores and your homework grades. At the end of the grading period, the spreadsheet will calculate your average grade.

Chapter 32

Assessment and Activities

★ Reviewing Key Terms

On a sheet of paper, define the following terms:

deregulation
federal debt
glasnost
perestroika
coup
bankruptcy
grassroots

budget deficit
incumbent
gross domestic product
Internet
ozone
global warming
line-item veto

★ Reviewing Key Facts

1. What is supply-side economics?
2. How did Mikhail Gorbachev try to reform the Soviet government?
3. How did Poland lead the way in toppling communism in Eastern Europe?
4. What event triggered the Persian Gulf War?
5. Why was health care an important issue in the 1990s?
6. What was the significance of the Middle East Peace Accords?
7. How did the growth rate of the gross domestic product in 1996 and 1997 compare to the rate after World War II?
8. What world regions contributed the largest number of immigrants during the 1990s?

★ Critical Thinking

Making Inferences

Republicans gained control of both houses of Congress in the 1994 election.

1. How did this affect Clinton's effectiveness as president?
2. What message do you think voters were trying to convey by electing a majority of Republicans to both houses of Congress?

★ Time Line Activity

Create a time line on which you place the following events in chronological order.

- Serbs, Croats, and Bosnian Muslims sign peace agreement to end civil war
- Soviet Union dissolves
- Bill Clinton is elected to first term as president
- Geraldine Ferraro is first woman from a major party to run for vice president
- Iraq invades Kuwait
- Sandra Day O'Connor named to Supreme Court
- Ronald Reagan is reelected president

★ Reviewing Themes

1. **Economic Factors** What was the goal of President Reagan's policy of deregulation?
2. **Global Connections** What event marked the end of the cold war?
3. **Groups and Institutions** Why did the federal government run out of money in 1995?
4. **Science and Technology** What is the connection between technology and global warming?

★ Skill Practice Activity

Using an Electronic Spreadsheet

Use a spreadsheet to enter the daily high, average, and low temperatures for your community for four weeks. At the end of this period, calculate your average local temperature. Then use the spreadsheet to make line graphs showing the monthly high temperatures, average temperatures, and low temperatures for your community.

Persian Gulf War, 1991

Iraq and occupied territory

Nations sympathetic to Iraq

Nations contributing forces against Iraq

● Oil fields

← Allied ground attack

⬥ U.S. warships

0   300 miles
0   300 kilometers
Lambert Equal-Area projection

Cooperative Activity

History and Music

What do you think the United States will be like in 100 years? Will everyday life be vastly different or much like it is today? What challenges will the nation face? Work with a group of classmates to write lyrics for a song about the future. You may want to focus on one specific issue such as the environment, or you might fashion your lyrics to express your thoughts about several issues. Use the music from an existing song to accompany your lyrics. Type or write down your lyrics and share them with the other students.

★ Geography Activity

Study the map on this page, then answer the questions that follow.

1. **Region** Which countries were sympathetic to Iraq?
2. **Location** In what countries did the allied ground attack take place?
3. **Movement** Which nations helped in the allied invasion?
4. **Location** In what three bodies of water did U.S. warships show their presence?

★ Technology Activity

Using the Internet

Use a browser to search the Internet for information about Kuwait. Write a short description of what a traveler visiting this nation might expect to find.

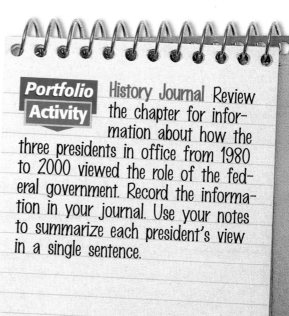

Portfolio Activity   History Journal Review the chapter for information about how the three presidents in office from 1980 to 2000 viewed the role of the federal government. Record the information in your journal. Use your notes to summarize each president's view in a single sentence.

Hands-On HISTORY Lab Activity

Recycling Your Own Paper

One of the challenges facing the United States today is TRASH. Americans generate about four pounds of trash per person per day. One way to reduce the amount of trash is to recycle. Try making your own paper—and recycle it at the same time!

The Way It Was

People have been writing for centuries. But what did they write *on* throughout history? Ancient Egyptians learned how to make paper from papyrus reeds, which they flattened and pressed together. The American colonists wrote government documents on parchment; newspapers, pamphlets, and personal letters were written on paper of lesser quality. Fibers from linen and cotton rags were pounded and pressed together to make this paper. Modern paper is made from wood pulp.

1 Materials

- wire clothes hanger
- 1 woman's nylon stocking
- 2 full pages of newspaper torn into small pieces
- 2-3 cups of water
- a blender (a kitchen mixer or similar hand tool will also work)
- dishpan
- 2 tablespoons of school glue

Believe It Or Not!

The garbage thrown away each year in the United States could fill garbage trucks lined up bumper-to-bumper on a four-lane highway circling the earth.

2 What To Do

1. Untwist the clothes hanger and form it into a 6-inch square.

2. Carefully slip the nylon stocking around the wire square. Pull the nylon tight so it fits snugly. Tie a knot on both sides to keep it in place.

3. Put some torn newspaper into the blender. Close the lid and turn the blender on high. Slowly add the rest of the paper and small amounts of water until the paper disappears and the mixture turns into a large ball of pulp. Put 4 inches of water into the dishpan. Add the glue and pulp mixture and stir.

4. While stirring the mixture, quickly slip the wire frame under the pulp and rest it on the bottom of the dishpan. Then lift the frame slowly as you count to 20. Your wire frame should be covered with pulp mixture.

5. Place the wire frame on paper towels or another flat surface to dry completely. When the paper is completely dry, gently peel it off the frame.

6. If possible, use a hot iron to steam your paper as flat as possible. Your paper is ready to use!

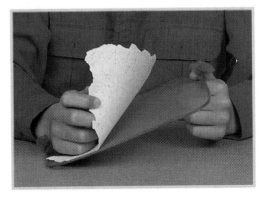

Step 5

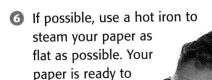

Step 3

3 Lab Report

1. About how long did you have to mix the paper and water for it to form a ball of pulp?

2. Describe the texture of the pulp before you added it to the dishpan.

3. How easy or difficult was it to write on your paper?

4. **Drawing Conclusions** How do you think your paper compares to the paper made out of cloth rags by the colonists? Which type of paper would be easier to use?

Go a Step Further

A ton of recycled paper saves more than 4,000 kilowatt-hours of energy, 7,000 gallons of water, and 17 trees. Research solutions to the trash crisis facing the United States that you can support or implement.

WORKING WITH PRIMARY SOURCES

Suppose that you have been asked to write a report on changes in your community over the past 25 years. Where would you get the information you need to begin writing? You would draw upon two types of information—primary sources and secondary sources.

Definitions

Primary sources are often first-person accounts by someone who actually saw or lived through what is being described. In other words, if you see a fire or live through a great storm and then write about your experiences, you are creating a primary source. Diaries, journals, photographs, and eyewitness reports are examples of primary sources. **Secondary sources** are second-hand accounts. For instance, if your friend experiences the fire or storm and tells you about it, or if you read about the fire or storm in the newspaper, and then you write about it, you are creating a secondary source. Textbooks, biographies, and histories are secondary sources.

Checking Your Sources

When you read primary or secondary sources, you should analyze them to figure out if they are dependable or reliable. Historians usually prefer primary sources to secondary sources, but both can be reliable or unreliable, depending on the following factors.

Time Span

With primary sources, it is important to consider how long after the event occurred the primary source was written. Chances are the longer the time span between the event and the account, the less reliable the account is. As time passes, people often forget details and fill in gaps with events that never took place. Although we like to think we remember things exactly as they happened, the fact is we often remember them as we wanted them to occur.

Reliability

Another factor to consider when evaluating a primary source is the writer's background and reliability. First, try to determine how this person knows about what he or she is writing. How much does he or she know? Is the writer being truthful? Is the account convincing?

Opinions

When evaluating a primary source, you should also decide whether the account has been

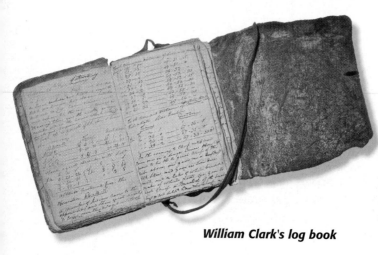

William Clark's log book

Opera glasses, late 1800s

influenced by emotion, opinion, or exaggeration. Writers can have reasons to distort the truth to suit their personal purposes. Ask yourself: Why did the person write the account? Do any key words or expressions reveal the author's emotions or opinions? You may wish to compare the account with one written by another witness to the event. If the two accounts differ, ask yourself why they differ and which is more accurate.

Interpreting Primary Sources

To help you analyze a primary source, use the following steps:

- **Examine the origins of the document.**
  You need to determine if it is a primary source.

- **Find the main ideas.**
  Read the document and summarize the main ideas in your own words. These ideas may be fairly easy to identify in newspapers and journals, for example, but are much more difficult to find in poetry.

- **Reread the document.**
  Difficult ideas are not always easily understood on the first reading.

- **Use a variety of resources.**
  Form the habit of using the dictionary, the encyclopedia, and maps. These resources are tools to help you discover new ideas and knowledge and check the validity of sources.

Classifying Primary Sources

Primary sources fall into different categories:

 Printed Publications

Printed Publications include books such as autobiographies. Printed publications also include newspapers and magazines.

 **Personal Records**

Personal Records are accounts of events kept by an individual who is a participant in or witness to these events. Personal records include diaries, journals, and letters.

 **Visual Materials**

Visual Materials include a wide range of forms: original paintings, drawings, and sculpture; photographs; film; and maps.

 **Oral Histories**

Oral Histories are chronicles, memoirs, myths, and legends that are passed along from one generation to another by word of mouth. Interviews are another form of oral history.

 **Songs and Poems**

Songs and Poems include works that express the personal thoughts and feelings, or political or religious beliefs of the writer, usually using rhyming and rhythmic language.

Artifacts

Artifacts are objects such as tools or ornaments. Artifacts present information about a particular culture or a stage of technological development.

NATIVE AMERICAN LEGENDS

Generation after generation Native Americans told stories, sang songs, and recited tales that recounted their past and told of their close relationship with the natural world. Although their stories and songs were rarely written down, these works survived through the oral tradition. This means that each generation passed down its stories and songs to its young people by word of mouth. As you read, think about how oral history, folklore, and tradition connect us to the past.

■ READER'S DICTIONARY

Lakota: a member of the Sioux people of central and eastern North America

prophecy: a prediction about the future

Black Hills: mountains in the western Dakotas and northeast Wyoming

elder: a person who is honored for his or her age and experience

White Buffalo Calf Woman Brings the First Pipe

 **Oral Histories**

Joseph Chasing Horse of the Lakota people tells the story of the White Buffalo Calf Woman.

We Lakota people have a prophecy about the white buffalo calf. How that prophecy originated was that we have a sacred bundle, a sacred pipe, that was brought to us about 2,000 years ago by what we know as the White Buffalo Calf Woman.

The story goes that she appeared to two warriors at that time. These two warriors were out hunting buffalo . . . in the sacred Black Hills of South Dakota, and they saw a big body coming toward them. And they saw that it was a white buffalo calf. As it came closer to them, it turned into a beautiful young Indian girl.

[At] that time one of the warriors [had bad thoughts] and so the young girl told him to step forward. And when he did step forward, a black cloud came over his body, and when the black cloud disappeared, the warrior who had bad thoughts was left with no flesh or blood on his bones. The other warrior kneeled and began to pray.

And when he prayed, the white buffalo calf, who was now an Indian girl told him to go back to his people and warn

*Kiowa Animal
hide calendar*

them that in four days she was going to bring a sacred bundle.

So the warrior did as he was told. He went back to his people, and he gathered all the elders, and all the leaders, and all the people in a circle and told them what she had instructed him to do. And sure enough, just as she said she would, on the fourth day, she came.

They say a cloud came down from the sky, and off of the cloud stepped the white buffalo calf. As it rolled onto the earth, the calf stood up and became this beautiful young woman who was carrying the sacred bundle in her hand.

As she entered into the circle of the nation, she sang a sacred song and took the sacred bundle to the people who were there to take [it from] her.

. . . And she instructed our people that as long as we performed these ceremonies we would always remain caretakers and guardians of sacred land. She told us that as long as we took care of it and respected it that our people would never die and would always live.

The sacred bundle is known as the White Buffalo Calf Pipe because it was brought by the White Buffalo Calf Woman. . . .

When White Buffalo Calf Woman promised to return again, she made some prophecies at that time. One of those prophecies was that the birth of a white buffalo calf would be a sign that it would be near the time when she would return again to purify the world. What she meant by that was that she would bring back [spiritual] harmony. . . .

Listen! Rain Approaches!

Songs and Poems

The Navaho of the American Southwest composed songs to celebrate the growth of crops and to control the coming of the rain.

Truly in the East
The white bean
And the great corn plant
Are tied with the white lightning.
Listen! It approaches!
The voice of the bluebird is heard.

Truly in the East
The white bean
And the great squash
Are tied with the rainbow.
Listen! It approaches!
The voice of the bluebird is heard.

■ INTERPRETING PRIMARY SOURCES

1. What did the Indian woman tell the Lakota warriors?
2. What prophecy did the White Buffalo Calf Woman make to the people?
3. Is the rain viewed as a good thing in the poem? Explain.
4. What does the use of the animal hide tell you about the people who made the calendar?

> **Activity** ▷

Creating Art Make a painting or drawing that portrays your image of the White Buffalo Calf Woman.

EUROPE AND THE AMERICAS

Prior to the 1400s, Native Americans had little contact with people from any other continent. But the desire for goods and improved ways of sea travel led to the growth of overseas trade in the 1400s and 1500s. During this time, the people of Europe, Asia, and Africa came into direct contact with the Native Americans. As you read these primary source selections, think about how the people who lived in the Americas reacted toward the newcomers.

■ READER'S DICTIONARY

Pinta: one of the three ships under Columbus's command during his first trip to the Americas

dexterous: skillful

subsist: survive or live on

compelled: forced

league: unit of distance from 2.4 to 4.6 statute miles (3.9 to 7.4 kilometers)

victuals: food

maize: corn

Castilla: a region of Spain

Columbus Crosses the Atlantic

Personal Records

Christopher Columbus left Spain in August 1492 with about 90 sailors. On October 11 Columbus wrote in his log:

The crew of the Pinta spotted some . . . reeds and some other plants; they also saw what looked like a small board or plank. A stick was recovered that looks man-made, perhaps carved with an iron tool . . . but even these few [things] made the crew breathe easier; in fact the men have even become cheerful.

The next day at dawn, Columbus went ashore on a small island in the Bahamas and claimed it for Spain. Believing he had reached the East Indies off the coast of Asia, he called the native people Indians.

The islanders came to the ships' boats, swimming and bringing us parrots and balls of cotton thread . . . which they exchanged for . . . glass beads and hawk bells . . . they took and gave of what they had very willingly, but it seemed to me that they were poor in every way. They bore no weapons, nor were they acquainted with them, because when I showed them swords they seized them by the edge and so cut themselves from ignorance.

Astrolabe

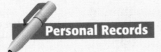

The Journey of Àlvar Núñez Cabeza de Vaca

Personal Records

Cabeza de Vaca was a member of a failed expedition sent to conquer the area between Florida and Mexico in 1528. For years, Cabeza de Vaca lived as a trader among the Native Americans of East Texas.

To this island we gave the name of the Island of Ill-Fate. The people on it are tall and well-formed; they have no other weapons than bows and arrows with which they are most dexterous. . . . The women do the hard work. People stay on this island from October till the end of February, feeding on the roots . . . taken from under the water in November and December. They have channels made of reeds and get fish only during that time; afterwards they subsist on roots. At the end of February they remove to other parts in search of food, because the roots begin to sprout and are not good anymore. . . .

I could not long stand the life I was compelled to lead. Among many other troubles I had to pull the eatable roots out of the water and from among the canes where they were buried in the ground, and from this my fingers had become so tender that the mere touch of a straw caused them to bleed. . . . This is why I went to work and joined the other Indians. Among these I improved my condition a little by becoming a trader, doing the best in it I could, and they gave me food and treated me well. . . .

Nearly six years I spent thus in the country, alone among them and naked, as they all were themselves. . . .

We believe that, near the coast, in a line with the villages which we followed, there are more than a thousand leagues of inhabited land, where they have plenty of victuals, since they raise three crops of beans and maize in the year. There are three kinds of deer, one kind as large as calves are in Castilla. The houses in which they live are huts. They have a poison, from certain trees of the size of our apple trees. They need but pick the fruit and rub their arrows with it; and if there is no fruit they take a branch and with its milky sap do the same. . . . In this village we stayed three days, and at a day's journey from it was another one, where such a rain overtook us that, as the river rose high, we could not cross it, and remained there fifteen days. . . .

■ INTERPRETING PRIMARY SOURCES

1. Why were the members of Columbus's crew cheerful when they spied the objects at sea?
2. What difficulties did Cabeza de Vaca encounter?
3. An astrolabe is an instrument used to calculate the position of the planets, sun, and stars. Why was the astrolabe important to sailors?

Activity

Journal Writing   Imagine you are one of the Native Americans who first met Columbus's crew. Write a journal entry describing how you communicated with the newcomers over the first three days.

A NEW WAY OF LIFE

After arriving in the Caribbean, the Spanish continued their exploration of North and South America. In the early 1600s, the French, Dutch, and English also started American colonies. As you read these primary source selections, think about how life during the colonial period differs from life today.

■ READER'S DICTIONARY

enlightened: informed

haughty: proud, vain

indigence: poverty

habitation: home

appellation: title

contention: struggle

El Paso: city in present-day West Texas

presidio: military post

patron: protector or champion

Rio del Norte: Rio Grande

What is an American?

Printed Publications

J. Hector St. John Crevecoeur of France traveled widely in the American colonies and farmed in New York. His Letters from an American Farmer *was published in 1782.*

I wish I could be acquainted with the feelings and thoughts which must . . . present themselves to the mind of an enlightened Englishman, when he first lands on the continent. . . . If he travels through our rural districts he views not the hostile castle, and the haughty mansion, contrasted with the clay-built hut and miserable cabin, where cattle and men help to keep each other warm, and dwell in meanness, smoke, and indigence. A pleasing uniformity of decent competence appears throughout our habitations. The meanest of our log-houses is dry and comfortable. . . . Lawyer or merchant are the fairest titles our towns afford; that of a farmer is the only appellation of the rural inhabitants of our country. It must take some time [before] he can reconcile himself to our dictionary, which is but short in words of dignity, and names of honour. . . . What then is the American, this new man? He is either a European, or the descendant of a European, hence that strange mixture of blood, which you will find in no other country. I could point out to you a family whose grandfather was an Englishman, whose wife was Dutch, and whose son

Butter churn

married a French woman, and whose present four sons have now four wives of different nations. . . . He does not find, as in Europe, a crowded society, where every place is over-stocked; he does not feel that perpetual collision of parties, that difficulty of beginning, that contention which oversets so many. There is room for everybody in America; has he particular talent, or industry? He exerts it in order to produce a livelihood, and it succeeds. . . .

Health Tips

The colonists developed their own remedies for various ailments. Note the different spellings for words like "ear," "wool," and "eat."

For Deafness

The fat of a Hedg-hog roasted drip it into the Eare, is an excellent remedy against deafness. Also a Clove of Garlick, make holes in it, dip it into Honey, & put it into the Eare at night going to bed, first on one side, then on the other for 8 or 9 dayes together, keeping in ye Eares black wooll.

For Hoarseness

Take 3 or 4 figs, cleave them in two, put in a pretty quantity of Ginger in powder, roast them & Eate them often.

New Mexico in 1760

Personal Records

Church official Pedro Tamaron y Romeral visited many settlements in New Mexico and wrote his impressions in his diary.

El Paso

This town's population is made up of Spaniards, Europeanized mixtures, and Indians. Its patron saints are Our Lady of the Pillar and St. Joseph. There is a royal presidio with a captain and fifty soldiers in the pay of the king. . . .

El Paso has 354 families of Spanish and Europeanized citizens, with 2,479 persons. There are 72 Indian families with 249 persons. . . .

El Paso is in latitude 32°9′, longitude 261°40′. There is a large irrigation ditch with which they bleed the Rio del Norte. . . . By this means they maintain a large number of vineyards,. . . . They grow wheat, maize, and other grains of the region, as well as fruit trees, apples, pears, peaches, figs. It is delightful country in the summer.

■ INTERPRETING PRIMARY SOURCES

1. How does de Crevecoeur describe the typical home in the colonies?
2. Do you think Pedro Tamaron y Romeral was a careful observer? Explain.

Activity

Creating a Graph Use the figures Tamaron y Romeral provides in the excerpt on New Mexico to make a bar graph showing the population of Spanish or European residents and Native American residents in El Paso in 1760.

LIFE IN THE ENGLISH COLONIES

In the 1600s and early 1700s, the English established 13 colonies along the Atlantic coast of North America. People came to the American colonies for various reasons—including the pursuit of wealth, land, or religious freedom. Settlers also brought with them new ideas about self–government. As you read these selections, think how different ways of life and new notions of liberty took root and grew in the colonies.

■ READER'S DICTIONARY

tolerable: satisfactory

conceive: imagine

descent: birth

phial: small bottle

blunder: mistake

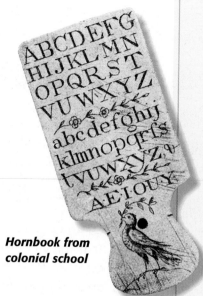

Hornbook from colonial school

Penn's Colony

Personal Records

In a letter written in 1683, William Penn describes the growth of his colony.

Our capital town is advanced to about 150 very tolerable houses for wooden ones; they are chiefly on both the navigable rivers that bound the ends or sides of the town. The farmers have got their winter corn in the ground. I suppose we may be 500 farmers strong. I settle them in villages, dividing 5,000 acres among ten, fifteen, or twenty families, as their ability is to plant it. . . .

Against Slavery

Printed Publications

One of the earliest known protests against slavery was this statement written in 1688 by a religious group known as the Mennonites.

Now, though, they are black, we cannot conceive there is more liberty to have them slaves, than to have other white ones. There is a saying, that we should do to all men as we will be done ourselves, making no difference of what generation, descent, or color they are.

Ben Franklin

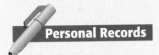
Personal Records

We often think of Benjamin Franklin as a successful diplomat and inventor. In 1750, Franklin wrote to a friend about an experiment that did not go as well as he had planned.

I have lately made an experiment in electricity, that I desire never to repeat. Two nights ago, being about to kill a turkey by the shock from two large glass jars, containing as much electrical fire as forty common phials, I . . . took the whole [charge] through my own arms and body, by receiving the fire from the united top wires with one hand, while the other held a chain connected with the outsides of both jars. The company present (whose talking to me, and to one another, I supposed occasioned my inattention to what I was about) say, that the flash was very great, and the crack as loud as a pistol; yet, my senses being instantly gone, I neither saw the one nor heard the other. . . . Nothing remains now of this shock, but a soreness in my breast-bone, which feels as if it had been bruised. I did not fall, but suppose I should have been knocked down, if I had received the stroke in my head. The whole was over in less than a minute.

You may communicate this to Mr. Bowdoin, as a caution to him, but do not make it more public, for I am ashamed to have been guilty of so notorious a blunder;. . . . I am yours . . .

B. Franklin

P.S. The jars hold six gallons each.

Poor Richard's Almanack

Printed Publications

Ben Franklin published Poor Richard's Almanack *every year for 25 years. An almanac is an annual collection of statistics and other useful or entertaining information. Franklin also included proverbs, or short witty sayings like those that follow. See if you recognize any of them.*

God helps them that help themselves.

No gains without pain.

He that falls in love with himself, will have no rivals.

Love your Neighbor; yet don't pull down your Hedge.

Keep thy shop, and thy shop will keep thee.

The Cat in Gloves catches no Mice.

INTERPRETING PRIMARY SOURCES

1. During what season of the year did Penn write this letter? How can you tell?
2. Which of Franklin's proverbs stress the importance of hard work?

Activity

Writing Proverbs Write a proverb about studying for school. Ask a friend to read it to see if he or she easily understands the point you are making.

TOWARD FREEDOM

In settling North America, the colonists developed a sense that they were taking part in the birth of a new society, different from Europe, where people had the opportunity to better themselves. When Great Britain tried to tighten its control over its American territories, the colonists expressed their dislike for British policy in printed publications, in religious services, and in their own personal letters and diaries. As you read these primary source selections, think about how the colonists' feelings about Great Britain were changing.

▣ READER'S DICTIONARY

pulpit: platform or reading desk used in worship services

crown officer: official of the king of England

reap: to harvest or gain

independency: a free nation

tyrant: a ruler who exercises power harshly

foment: start

sovereign: king or leader

The People and Liberty

John Adams, a colonial leader from Massachusetts, wrote in his diary:

The people have become more attentive to their liberties, . . . and more determined to defend them. . . . Our presses have groaned, our pulpits have thundered, our legislatures have resolved, our towns have voted; the crown officers have everywhere trembled, and all their little tools and creatures been afraid to speak and ashamed to be seen.

Common Sense

In Common Sense, *written in January 1776, patriot Thomas Paine called upon the colonists to break away from Great Britain.*

Every thing that is right begs for separation from [Great] Britain. The Americans who have been killed seem to say, 'TIS TIME TO PART. England and America are located a great distance apart. That is itself strong and natural proof that God never expected one to rule over the other.

Remember the Ladies

Personal Records

Abigail Adams wrote this letter to her husband, John Adams, at the Continental Congress.

March 31, 1776

. . . I feel very differently at the approach of spring to what I did a month ago. We knew not then whether we could plant or sow with safety, whether when we had toild we could reap the fruits of our own industry, whether we could rest in our own Cottages, or whether we should not be driven from the sea coast to seek shelter in the wilderness, but now we feel as if we might sit under our own vine and eat the good of the land.

. . . I long to hear that you have declared an independency—and by the way in the new Code of Laws which I suppose it will be necessary for you to make I desire you would Remember the Ladies, and be more generous and favourable to them than your ancestors. Do not put such unlimited powers into the hands of the Husbands. Remember all Men would be tyrants if they could. If perticular care and attention is not paid to the Ladies we are determined to foment a Rebellion, and will not hold ourselves bound by any Laws in which we have no voice or Representation.

Powderhorn

The Bold Americans

Songs and Poems

Broadside ballads—emotionally-charged story poems printed on a single sheet of paper— were distributed widely and helped fuel colonists' passion for freedom.

Come all you bold young Bostonians, come
    listen unto me:
I will sing you a song concerning liberty.
Concerning liberty, my boys, the truth I will
    unfold,
Of the bold Americans, who scorn to be
    controlled.
We'll honor George, our sovereign, on any
    reasonable terms,
But if he don't grant us liberty, we'll all lay
    down our arms.
But if he will grant us liberty, so plainly shall
    you see,
We are the boys that fear no noise! Success to
    liberty!

■ INTERPRETING PRIMARY SOURCES

1. What is the main point that each of the writers makes?
2. What do the bold Americans scorn?

Activity

Writing a Letter Assume that you are writing a letter to the editor of your local newspaper. Using the Declaration of Independence as a basis, address the people of your community. First, list three things that the Declaration means to you and then what it can continue to mean for your community.

THE STRUGGLE FOR INDEPENDENCE

The signing of the Declaration of Independence made war a certainty. The Americans had taken a step that made peaceful reconciliation with Great Britain impossible. The American Revolution and the thirteen colonies' final break with Britain soon followed. As you read these primary source selections, identify problems that the British and Americans faced in continuing the war effort.

■ READER'S DICTIONARY

incessant: never-ending

refulgent: brightly shining

destitute: lacking

procure: gain or obtain

gall: to become sore by rubbing

celestial: honored or sacred

Columbia: goddess personifying America

The British Retreat

Personal Records

A British soldier described the retreat from Concord.

[The countryside was] lined with people who kept an incessant fire upon us, as we did upon them, but not with the same advantage, for they were so concealed there was hardly any seeing them. In this way we marched between nine and ten miles, their number increasing from all parts while ours was reducing by deaths, wounds, and fatigue. . . .

Flight from War

Personal Records

Mercy Otis Warren was a witty and skillful writer who supported the American Revolution. In the following passage, she describes citizens fleeing from the horrors of the war.

The roads [were] filled with frightened women and children; some in carts with their tattered furniture, others on foot fleeing into the woods. But what added greatly to the horrors of the scene, was our passing through the bloody field of Monotong, which was strewed with mangled bodies. We met one affectionate father with a cart, looking for his murdered son. . . .

*Military Drum
of the American
Revolution*

Surviving at Valley Forge

Personal Records

Below are excerpts from the personal records of two different people who served at Valley Forge. The first selection is by Albigence Waldo, a surgeon who tended the sick and injured.

I am sick—discontented . . . Poor food—hard lodging—cold weather—fatigue—nasty cloathes—nasty cookery. . . . I can't endure it—Why are we sent here to starve and freeze? . . .

In this selection, soldier Joseph Plumb Martin remembers the hardships on the way to Valley Forge.

The army was not only starved but naked. The greatest part were not only shirtless and barefoot, but destitute of all other clothing, especially blankets. I procured a small piece of rawhide and made myself a pair of moccasins, which kept my feet (while they lasted) from the frozen ground, although, as I well remember, the hard edges so galled my ankles, while on a march, that it was with much difficulty and pain that I could wear them afterwards; but the only alternative I had was to endure this inconvenience or to go barefoot, as hundreds of my companions had to, till they might be tracked by their bloods upon the rough frozen ground.

To His Excellency, General Washington

Songs and Poems

The heroic words that follow were penned by an enslaved woman who also happened to be a gifted poet. Her name was Phillis Wheatley, and in 1770, at age 20, she became the first published African American woman poet.

Celestial choir! Enthron'd in realms of light,
Columbia's scenes of glorious toils I write.
While freedom's cause her anxious breast
   alarms,
She flashes dreadful in refulgent arms.
See mother earth her offspring's fate bemoan,
And nation's gaze at scenes before unknown!
See the bright beams of heaven's revolving light
Involved in sorrows and the veil of night!

■ INTERPRETING PRIMARY SOURCES

1. Why did the British soldier find it difficult to fight the colonists?
2. Both Waldo and Martin's writings are about Valley Forge. How do these passages differ in the way the writers express themselves?

Activity

Writing Interview Questions Imagine that you could ask Mercy Otis Warren or Phillis Wheatley five questions about what life was like during the American Revolution. Write these questions, and use them to do more research about this historic period. Present the results of your research to the other students.

A NATION IN TRANSITION

After the Revolutionary War, the United States briefly functioned as a loose union of states. In 1788 the nation ratified the United States Constitution. This framework of law served as a model for people in other countries who wanted republican governments. As you read these primary source selections, think about the adjustments Native Americans and the settlers in a new land would have to make.

▮ READER'S DICTIONARY

husbandry: farming

ally: supporter or partner

late wars: the American Revolution

Ben Franklin on Coming to America

Printed Publications

This advertisement about coming to America, written by Ben Franklin, was translated and widely reprinted in Europe.

. . . Hearty young laboring men, who understand the husbandry of corn and cattle, which is nearly the same in that country as in Europe, may establish themselves there. A little money saved of the good wages they receive there, while working for others, enables them to buy the land and begin their plantation. . . . [Many] poor people from England, Ireland, Scotland, and Germany, have, by this means, in a few years become wealthy farmers, who, in their own countries, where all the lands are fully occupied, and the wages of labor low, could never have emerged from the poor condition wherein they were born.

Mother and daughter, 1790s

Immigrant Life in America

Personal Records

A German immigrant wrote this account of his experiences.

But during the voyage there is on board these ships terrible misery, stench, fumes, horror, vomiting, many kinds of seasickness, fever . . . all of which comes from old and sharply salted food and meat, also from very bad and foul water, so that many die miserably. . . .

Many parents must sell and trade away their children like so many head of cattle. . . . [I]t often happens that such parents and children, after leaving the ship, do not see each other again for many years, perhaps no more in all their lives.

The Oneida and the Use of Land

Personal Records

In March 1788 leaders of the Oneida people sent this message to the New York state legislature.

Brothers, we are your allies: we are a free people: our chiefs have directed us to speak to you, as such therefore, open your ears, and hear our words.

Brothers, in your late wars with the people on the other side of the great water,. . . . We fought by your side. Our blood flowed together: and the bones of our warriors mingled with yours. . . . [W]e received an invitation to meet some of your chiefs, . . . Those chiefs, who then met us, will doubtless remember, how much we were disappointed, when they told us, they were only sent to buy our lands. . . .

Brothers, we are determined, then, never to sell any more. The experience of all the Indian nations to the east and south, has fully convinced us, that if we follow their example, we shall soon share their fate. We wish that our children and grandchildren may derive a comfortable living from the lands which the Great Spirit has given us and our forefathers. . . .

Brothers, we wish you to consider this matter well, and to do us justice. . . .

■ INTERPRETING PRIMARY SOURCES

1. Why do you think Ben Franklin wrote this advertisement?
2. Do you think the German immigrant would agree or disagree with Ben Franklin? Why or why not?
3. Who are the "Brothers" that the Oneida leaders address? What are the Oneida asking?
4. What adjective would you use to describe the mother and the daughter in the painting? Explain.

Activity

Making a Poster Make a poster advertising the new nation. Include reasons why people would want to settle in the United States.

THE AGE OF WASHINGTON

The Constitution set up a completely new framework of government that was meant to be flexible and lasting. Along with the excitement of starting a new nation came challenges and growing pains. Many people, both American-born and foreign-born, wondered: Could this new kind of government last? As you read this primary source selection, think about how people's beliefs and ideas can influence the development of their government.

READER'S DICTIONARY

gallery: outdoor balcony

proclamation: announcement

ungainly: awkward, clumsy

agitated: upset and nervous

plainest manner: in a simple way

procession: parade

militia: soldiers

Washington's First Inaugural

Pennsylvania Senator William Maclay was one of the many witnesses to the nation's first presidential inauguration.

The President was conducted out of the middle window into the gallery [overlooking Wall Street], and the oath was administered by the Chancellor [the highest judicial officer in the state of New York]. Notice that the business done was communicated to the crowd by proclamation . . . who gave three cheers, and repeated it on the President's bowing to them.

As the company returned into the Senate chamber, the President took the chair and the Senators and Representatives their seats. He rose, and all arose also, and [he] addressed them. This great man was agitated and embarrassed more than ever he was by the leveled cannon or pointed musket. He trembled, and several times could scarce make out to read, though it must be supposed he had often read it before. . . . When he came to the words *all the world*, he made a flourish with his right hand, which left rather an ungainly impression. I sincerely, for my part, wished all set ceremony in the hands of the dancing-masters, and that this first of men had read off his address in the plainest manner, without ever taking his eyes from the paper, for I felt hurt that he was not first in everything.

Hats

Artifacts

No one knows when people first wore hats. Hundreds of thousands of years ago, people may have worn fur hoods as protection against the weather. By 1800, more and more manufacturers began to make hats to order in all shapes and sizes. They made them of fur, straw, felt, and fabric. They also provided elegantly decorated boxes and holders to protect the hats.

■ INTERPRETING PRIMARY SOURCES

1. What events at Washington's inaugural did Maclay seem to like?
2. What was it about Washington's public speaking manner that Maclay criticized?
3. What are the functions of headwear today? Do you often wear a hat or a cap? Does your headwear serve a decorative or functional purpose? Explain.

Activity

Writing a Poem   Write a short poem describing Washington's inauguration.

LOOKING WESTWARD

The election of Thomas Jefferson to the presidency in 1800 was one of the turning points in American history. For the first time in modern history, the political power of a country transferred peacefully from one political party to another. Jefferson's election also marked a time of great expansion and change for the United States. As you read these primary source selections, think about why this was a time of such rapid growth for the nation.

▌ READER'S DICTIONARY

discord: disagreement, conflict

rapture: joy

sprightly: quick and alert

maritime: oceanic

Song of Liberty

Songs and Poems

The following song is one of the hundreds of anonymous patriotic songs written, printed, and distributed in little song books during the early 1800s.

The fruits of our country, our flocks and
    our fleeces,
What treasures immense, in our moun-
    tains that lie,
While discord is tearing Old Europe to
    pieces,
Shall amply the wants of the people
    supply;
New roads and canals, on their bosoms
    conveying,
Refinement and wealth through our
    forests shall roam,
And millions of freemen, with rapture
    surveying,
Shall shout out "O Liberty! this is thy
    home!

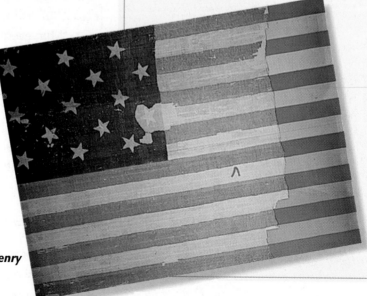

**Flag flown at Fort McHenry
during War of 1812**

California in 1804

Personal Records

Sea captain William Shaler visited the coast of California while engaged in trade with China and recorded his observations.

The Indians that inhabit the shores and islands of the canal of Santa Barbara seem to be a race of people quite distinct from the other [native people] of the country. They are a handsome people, remarkably sprightly, courteous, and intelligent, and display great ingenuity in all their arts. They make fine canoes of small pine boards, sewed together in a very curious manner; these are generally capable of carrying from six to fourteen people, and are in form not unlike a whale boat; they are managed with paddles, and go with surprising velocity: they besides make a great variety of curious and useful articles of wicker work, and excellent pots and mortars of stone. . . .

. . . At present Lower California is nearly depopulated: no mission there numbers above 350 Indians; not more than three exceed 250; and the greater part have less than fifty persons. It is difficult to imagine what can have been the cause of this extraordinary depopulation, . . .

The Spanish population of the Californias is [small]; by the best information I could obtain, it hardly exceeds 3,000 souls. . . .

The plan of civilization in the missions is to instruct the Indians in the Catholic religion, the Spanish language, the necessary arts, agriculture. . . .

The Spaniards have complete possession of the peninsula of California; but that is not the case above: there their domination is bounded by the Sierra Madre, which in no part is far removed from the coast; so that in reality they are masters of the maritime part of the country only. Beyond that range of mountains the country is remarkably fine, well watered, and covered with forests: these they have not as yet been able to penetrate, on account of their being thickly inhabited by warlike tribes of Indians. I am informed that the government [aims] to establish lines of missions and garrisons from San Francisco to New Mexico, and by the country of the Colorado Indians to the same place, and by these means to complete the conquest of the country. But that is a project that does not seem likely to be very soon realized.

■ INTERPRETING PRIMARY SOURCES

1. In the song, what does the phrase "treasures immense" mean?
2. Does William Shaler view the Native Americans he meets in a positive light? Explain.
3. Why does Shaler think it will take a long time for the Spanish to settle California?
4. How does the flag on page 952 differ from the United States flag today?

Activity

Creating an Advertisement Create a want ad to hire missionaries to help teach Native Americans. A missionary is a religious person who travels to foreign lands to educate and help people. Your ad should include the skills and abilities that the people would need for missionary work.

SOCIAL CHANGE

The Industrial Revolution brought new kinds of jobs and leisure activities to many people. It also brought challenges. Cities became overcrowded and the gap between rich and poor widened. Change came for Native Americans as well as a tide of settlers streamed west, threatening their way of life. As you read these primary source selections, think about how people's values and daily lives changed during this period of time.

■ READER'S DICTIONARY

obliged: forced

lock-jaw: an infectious disease that affects the ability to open the jaws

sage: a mint used to flavor foods

rind: outer layer

marsh: soft, wet land

corduroy-road: a road made of logs laid side by side

Working in the Mills

Personal Records

Time ruled the lives of the industry workers down to the second. A woman who worked in a Lowell, Massachusetts, textile mill wrote about her frustration in 1841.

I am going home, where I shall not be obliged to rise so early in the morning, nor be dragged about by the factory bell, nor confined in a close noisy room from morning to night. I shall not stay here. . . . Up before day, at the clang of the bell—and out of the mill by the clang of the bell—into the mill, and at work in obedience to that ding-dong of a bell—just as though we were so many living machines.

Remedies

Printed Publications

Lydia Maria Child wrote about many subjects. Here she describes some simple remedies popular in the 1820s.

A good quantity of old cheese is the best thing to eat, when distressed by eating too much fruit, or oppressed with any kind of food. Physicians have given it in cases of extreme danger.

Honey and milk is very good for worms; so is strong salt water; likewise powdered sage and molasses taken freely.

A rind of pork bound upon a wound occasioned by a needle, pin, or nail, prevents the lock-jaw.

On the Road

Printed Publications

David Stevenson described a journey by stagecoach along a typical route of the time.

Sometimes our way lay for miles through extensive marshes, which we crossed by corduroy-roads. . . . At others the coach stuck fast in mud, from which it could be [moved] only by the combined efforts of the coachman and passengers; at one place we traveled . . . through a forest flooded with water, which stood to a height of several feet. . . . The distance of the route from Pittsburgh to Erie is 128 miles, which was accomplished in forty-six hours . . . although the [stagecoach] by which I traveled carried the mail, and stopped only for breakfast, dinner and tea, but there was considerable delay by the coach being once upset and several times "mired."

A woman named Elizabeth Smith Geer wrote about winter travel in her diary:

My children gave out with cold and fatigue and could not travel, and the boys had to unhitch the oxen and bring them and carry the children on to camp. It was so cold and numb I could not tell by feeling that I had any feet at all. . . . I have not told you half we suffered.

Horse-drawn coaches carried passengers between towns and cities. Many journeys lasted two days or more. The coaches stopped at inns at night and completed trips in stages. As a result, people called the coaches "stagecoaches."

■ INTERPRETING PRIMARY SOURCES

1. What does the factory worker dislike about her job?
2. How many miles was it from Pittsburgh to Erie? How long did the trip take?
3. What were some of the hardships the travelers encountered on the road?

Activity

Mapping a Route Imagine you are going on a stagecoach trip. Choose a city or town that will be your destination. Map a route from your community to that city. Find out how long your trip will take if the stagecoach averages 6 miles per day.

For use with Chapter 11
"The Jackson Era"

NATIVE AMERICAN STRUGGLES

Andrew Jackson's election to the presidency in 1828 marked the beginning of a new era. Jackson's supporters were farmers in the south, western settlers, and laborers in the eastern cities. They believed that he represented the "common man," and so Jackson became a symbol of the growing power of democracy. Not all people in the United States benefited from the new democracy, however. As you read, think about the difficulties of life for those who were not given equal rights.

▮ READER'S DICTIONARY

detachment: group or body of people

inclemency: harsh conditions

multitude: a large number

exile: person forced to leave his country or home

expel: drive away

Trail of Tears

Printed Publications

Although recognized as a separate nation by several U.S. treaties, the Cherokee people were forced to leave their lands because white people wanted it for farming. Thousands died before they reached Indian Territory, the present-day state of Oklahoma. This forced journey became known as the "Trail of Tears." A newspaper published this account.

On Tuesday evening we fell in with a detachment of the poor Cherokee Indians . . . about eleven hundred Indians—sixty wagons—six hundred horses, and perhaps forty pairs of oxen. We found them in the forest camped for the night by the road side . . . under a severe fall of rain accompanied by heavy wind. With their canvas for a shield from the inclemency of the weather, and the cold wet ground for a resting place, after the fatigue of the day, they spent the night . . . many of the aged Indians were suffering extremely from the fatigue of the journey, and the ill health consequent upon it . . . several were then quite ill, and one aged man we were informed was then in the last struggles of death.

. . . The forward part of the train we found just pitching their tents for the night, and notwithstanding some thirty or forty wagons were already stationed, we found the road literally filled with the procession for about three miles in length.

The Cherokee called the forced march from their land the "Trail of Tears"

The sick and feeble were carried in wagons—about as comfortable for traveling as a New England ox cart with a covering over it—a great many ride on horseback and multitudes go on foot . . . on the sometimes frozen ground, and sometimes muddy streets, with no covering for the feet except what nature had given them. . . .

We learned from the [settlers along] the road where the Indians passed, that they buried fourteen or fifteen at every stopping place, and they made a journey of ten miles per day on an average . . . When I past the last detachment of those suffering exiles and thought that my native countrymen had thus expelled them from their native soil and their much loved homes, and that too in this inclement season of the year in all their suffering, I turned from the sight with feelings which language cannot express. . . .

When I read in the President's Message that he was happy to inform the Senate that the Cherokees were peaceably and without reluctance removed—and remember that it was on the third day of December when not one of the detachments had reached their destination; and that a large majority had not made even half

their journey when he made that declaration, I thought I wished the President could have been there that very day in Kentucky with myself, and have seen the comfort and the willingness with which the Cherokees were making their journey.

■ INTERPRETING PRIMARY SOURCES

1. How did the Cherokee travel from Georgia to the Indian Territory?
2. List three hardships the Cherokee faced along the "Trail of Tears."
3. Do you think the writer feels sympathy toward the Cherokee? Explain.
4. What scenes in the painting do you think capture the sadness of the Cherokee people?

◆ Activity ◆

Creating a Time Line Research information to help you make a time line of the Cherokee people from 1800 to the present day.

THE THIRST FOR NEW LANDS

During the 1800s, the United States grew in size, wealth, and power. The vast area of forests and plains west of the original colonies lured American settlers by the thousands. The drive to expand the boundaries of the United States across North America became a goal for many Americans in the 1830s and 1840s. As you read these, think about the hardships settlers faced on the frontier.

▨ READER'S DICTIONARY

Promised Land: nickname for California

powwow: meeting

grub: food

Humboldt Desert: arid region in Nevada

cholera: disease affecting the stomach and intestines

shanty: shack or crude dwelling

Doll made of cornhusks

Settling in Texas

Mary Crownover Rabb moved to Texas with her family in 1823. She recalls what her first home in Texas was like:

The house was made of logs. They made a chimney to it. The door shutter was made of thick slabs split out of thick pieces of timber, and [to fasten the door] we had a large pin or peg that was drove in hard and fast [at night], and then the Indians could not get in. We had an earthen floor. . . .

I was in my first Texas house and . . . I was very much pleased, and I soon got to work to make clothing for my family.

West to California

Lured by the discovery of gold, thousands migrated to California. Traveler Andrew Gordon described life on the trail to California in 1849.

May 8
We met two wagons coming back from the Promised Land today. The men with them looked pretty well down in the mouth. . . . They stopped and we had a long powwow. We gave them some liquor

and grub. They had not been to California—never got there. It seemed that the Humboldt Desert had almost ruined them, and they turned back. Two of their men died of cholera; they had three left, and these survivors had hollow eyes and caved-in cheeks, and looked like they were about done for.

They had painted on the white cover of the wagon the words, " Going for Gold." It was not funny, but sad.

June 12

As the trail gets rougher we encounter piles of things that people have thrown away to lighten their loads. This was a day of scenes of abandoned property; stoves, blacksmith tools, mattresses, cooking utensils, and provisions of every kind strung along the road. There was also an abandoned wagon with broken axles. We have been seeing dead animals from the first day, but today we saw three dead mules and an ox lying by the side of the road. . . .

August 20

I hardly know whether I am alive or dead. All day in a blazing heat, with the air so hot that in moving my hand through it I feel as if I were thrusting it into the hot air over a bed of coals. The oxen stagger along, with their tongues hanging out. . . . Our barrel of water helps. The river can be drunk when it is flowing—in small quantities—but is dangerous (I may say deadly) after it stands a while. Why, I cannot say. . . .

September 24

We got to San Francisco yesterday, and have been on the go ever since. . . . This town was built for 800 people and now it has 10,000. We stayed last night at the Parker House, which is called a hotel, but I would call it a shanty. It is small, having room for about a dozen people, if all the space is used. Last night four men slept in the small room we occupied on bunks put up one above the other. We paid ten dollars apiece. That means the proprietor got forty dollars for the rent of that room for one night. . . . Are we crazy?

The inside of a Conestoga wagon

■ INTERPRETING PRIMARY SOURCES

1. Is Mary Crownover Rabb happy or disapointed with her new home? Explain.
2. What hardships did Gordon face?

Activity

Writing Dialogue Write a conversation between two settlers on their way to California during the Gold Rush of 1849. Have them express their hopes as well as their fears.

SECTIONAL ISSUES

The North and South were developing different ways of life. By the mid-1800s, the North had developed a manufacturing economy that rivaled industrial Europe. The South experienced remarkable growth, too, but mainly in agriculture. Southerners increased cotton production dramatically and spread their plantations to the south and west. As you read the following primary source selection, think about the lives of people under slavery.

▮ READER'S DICTIONARY

auction block: site where enslaved people were bought and sold

Delicia Patterson

Oral Histories

Delicia Patterson provided this look at life under slavery. She was 92 years old when she was interviewed.

I was born in Boonville, Missouri, January 2, 1845. My mother's name was Maria and my father's was Jack Wiley. Mother had five children but raised only two of us. I was owned by Charles Mitchell until I was fifteen years old. They were fairly nice to all of their slaves and they had several of us. . . .

When I was fifteen years old, I was brought to the courthouse, put up on the auction block to be sold. Old Judge Miller from my county was there. I knew him well because he was one of the wealthiest slave owners in the county, and the meanest one. He was so cruel all the slaves and many owners hated him because of it. He saw me on the block for sale, and he knew I was a good worker. So, when he bid for me, I spoke right out on the auction block and told him: "Old Judge Miller, don't you bid for me, 'cause if you do, I would not live on your plantation. I will take a knife and cut my own throat from ear to ear before I would be owned by you."

So he stepped back and let someone else bid for me. . . . So I was sold to a Southern Englishman named Thomas Steele for fifteen hundred dollars. . . .

Travel and Transportation

Visual Materials

Steamboats proved their ability to carry passengers and goods quickly and efficiently. By 1850 nearly 800 steamboats regularly traveled the Mississippi and its tributaries. The benefits of steamboat travel were great, but risks were high. The average life of a river steamboat was three to six years—not surprising considering the dangers presented by snags, ice, bursting boilers, collisions, fires, and sand bars.

Conestoga wagons, developed by Pennsylvania's German Americans during the colonial era, carried settlers westward. These sturdy wagons, pulled by yoked oxen, had canvas tops.

■ INTERPRETING PRIMARY SOURCES

1. Why did Delicia not want to serve on Judge Miller's plantation?
2. What were some of the advantages of steamboat transportation? What were the disadvantages?

Activity

Making Illustrations   Draw sketches illustrating the major means of transportation that helped the United States grow. Write a caption under each sketch explaining how this mode of transportation helped the country develop.

A NATIONAL SPIRIT

During the 1800s, many Americans were interested in improving themselves and their society. The result was an age of social reform, which was strengthened by the religious revivals of the Second Great Awakening. Reformers banded together in voluntary organizations to work toward their goals. As you read these primary source selections, think about the goals of reformers then and the goals of reformers today.

▮ READER'S DICTIONARY

fathom: understand

diffusion: spread or widening

degrading: embarrassing or shameful

piteous: sad, distressed

vociferously: loudly

battery: a grouping of weapons

rent: open or part

The Country School by Winslow Homer, 1871

Women and Education

Personal Records

An anonymous writer, named "Matilda," wrote to the Freedom's Journal, the first African American newspaper in America, regarding the education of women.

August 10, 1827
Messrs. Editors:

Will you allow a female to offer a few remarks upon a subject that you must allow to be all-important? I don't know that in any of your papers you have said [enough about] the education of females. I hope you are not to be classed with those who think that our mathematical knowledge should be limited to "fathoming the dish-kettle,"and that we have acquired enough of history if we know that our grandfather's father lived and died. It is true the time has been when to darn a stocking and cook a pudding well was considered the end aim of a woman's being. But those were days when ignorance blinded men's eyes. The diffusion of knowledge has destroyed those degrading opinions, and men of the present age allow that we have minds that are capable and deserving of culture.

There are difficulties, and great difficulties, in the way of our advancement; but that should only stir us to greater efforts. We possess not the advantages with those of our sex whose skins are not colored like our own, but we can improve what little we have and make our one talent produce twofold. The influence that we have over the male sex demands that our minds should be instructed and improved with the principles of education and religion, in order that this influence should be properly directed. Ignorant ourselves, how can we be expected to form the minds of our youth and conduct them in the paths of knowledge? How can we "teach the young idea how to shoot" if we have none ourselves? There is a great responsibility resting somewhere, and it is time for us to be up and doing.

I would address myself to all mothers, and say to them that while it is necessary to possess a knowledge of cookery and the various mysteries of pudding making, something more is [needed]. It is their . . . duty to store their daughters' minds with useful learning. They should be made to devote their leisure time to reading books, when they would derive valuable information which could never be taken from them.

I will not longer trespass on your time and patience. I merely throw out these hints in order that some more able pen will take up the subject.

MATILDA

Religious Camp Meeting

Personal Records

The desire for self-improvement was closely connected to a renewed interest in religion. By the 1830s, the Second Great Awakening, the second great period of religious revival in the United States, was in full swing. The camp meeting was especially important to isolated frontier families. One preacher, James Finley, described a revival meeting:

The noise was like the roar of Niagara. . . . Some of the people were singing, others praying, some crying for mercy in the most piteous accents, while others were shouting most vociferously. . . . At one time I saw at least five hundred swept down in a moment, as if a battery of a thousand guns had been opened upon them, and then immediately followed shrieks and shouts that rent the very heavens.

INTERPRETING PRIMARY SOURCES

1. What changes does Matilda propose?
2. What scene is James Finley describing?
3. Artist Winslow Homer often painted scenes of everyday life. What ideas do you think Homer is expressing in "The Country School"?

Activity

Writing a Song Compose lyrics designed to win supporters for a reform.

DRIFTING TOWARD WAR

As new states entered the Union, the slavery issue began to divide public opinion. The South favored the protection and expansion of slavery. The North argued for either limiting slavery to the South or abolishing it altogether. Compromise worked in 1850, but by 1860 compromise was no longer possible. With the election of Abraham Lincoln in 1860, the South believed it had no choice but to leave the Union. As you read these primary source selections, be alert to the writers' attitudes toward life before the Civil War.

■ READER'S DICTIONARY

severity: harshness and anger

uncompromising: firm or unbending

moderation: restraint; avoiding extreme behavior

equivocate: avoid

secede: withdraw from the United States

coercion: control or domination

Swing Low, Sweet Chariot

Songs and Poems

Spirituals—songs of salvation— provided the enslaved African Americans who wrote and sang them with not only a measure of comfort in bleak times but with a means for communicating secretly among themselves.

Swing low, sweet chariot,
Coming for to carry me home,
Swing low, sweet chariot,
Coming to carry me home.

I looked over Jordan and what
did I see
Coming for to carry me home,
A band of angels coming after me.
Coming to carry me home.

If you get there before I do,
Coming for to carry me home,
Tell all my friends I'm coming too,
Coming to carry me home.

Swing low, sweet chariot,
Coming for to carry me home,
Swing low, sweet chariot,
Coming to carry me home.

The Liberator

 **Printed Publications**

Through his newspaper, the Liberator, *William Lloyd Garrison demanded slavery's immediate and total abolition.*

I am aware that many object to the severity of my language; but is there not cause for severity? I *will be* harsh as truth and as uncompromising as justice. On this subject I do not wish to think or speak, or write with moderation. No! No! Tell a [person] whose house is on fire to give a moderate alarm; tell him to moderately rescue his [spouse] from the hands of a ravisher; tell the [parent] to gradually extricate [a] babe from the fire into which it has fallen;—but urge me not to use moderation in a cause like the present. I am in earnest; I will not equivocate; I will not excuse; I will not retreat a single inch—AND I WILL BE HEARD. . . .

American slave market

On the Eve of War

 **Personal Records**

Augusta, a young woman living in Chatham County, Georgia, wrote this letter in January 1861, to her brother, George, a student at Virginia Military Institute.

Dear Brother, I suppose you have seen by the papers that our good State has seceded, and that now we are a *free & independent people.* . . . The whole city has been wild with excitement ever since Sumter was taken, & has just begun to get a little quiet, but I suppose we must prepare for hot times now, that is if the Federal Government persists in the insane policy of coercion. It is the most absurd thing I ever heard of. . . .

■ INTERPRETING PRIMARY SOURCES

1. What does "Swing Low, Sweet Chariot" show about the condition and faith of the people who sang it?
2. With what does Garrison compare the danger of slavery?
3. What is Augusta's mood regarding the coming civil war? Why do you think she feels the way she does?

Activity

Analyzing Write a one-page paper that answers these questions: What songs of today give people hope for the future? Would you call these songs spirituals? Why or why not?

THE UNION IN DANGER

*The American Civil War, or the War
Between the States, was a major turning
point for the American people. When the
fighting ended, 600,000 Americans had lost
their lives, slavery had been abolished, and
much of the South lay in ruins. As you read
these primary source selections, think about
how war affects civilians as well as soldiers.*

■ READER'S DICTIONARY

enlist: sign up to serve in the military

bluffer: one who misleads or deceives

musket: soldier's rifle

melancholy: sad

regiment: a military unit

Early Days of the War

Printed Publications

*Seventeen-year-old Theodore Upson
wrote about his feelings during the
first days of the Civil War in his
Indiana village.*

We had another meeting at the
school house last night; we are
raising money to take care of
the families of those who enlist. . . . I said I
would go but they laughed at me and said
they wanted men not boys for this job;
that it would all be over soon; that those
fellows down South are big bluffers and
would rather talk than fight. I am not so
sure about that. . . . Mother had a letter
from the Hales. Charlie and his Father are
in their army and Dayton wanted to go
but was too young. I wonder if I were in
our army and they should meet me would
they shoot me. I suppose they would.

Soldier's canteen

The Fire of Battle

Personal Records

Union soldier George Sargent served in the area west of Washington, D.C., throughout the Shenandoah Valley. He wrote his impressions of how soldiers react in battle.

Can you imagine a fellow's feelings about that time, to have to face thousands of muskets with a prospect of having a bullet put through you? If you can, all right; I can't describe it. I've heard some say that they were not scared going into a fight, but I think it's all nonsense. I don't believe there was ever a man who went into battle but was scared, more or less. Some will turn pale as a sheet, look wild and ferocious, some will be so excited that they don't know what they are about while others will be as cool and collected as on other occasions.

Retreat

Personal Records

After the Confederate victory at the Battle of Chickamauga in September 1863, a Union officer described his army's retreat:

The march was a melancholy one. All along the road for miles, wounded men were lying. They had crawled or hobbled slowly away from the fury of the battle, become exhausted, and lain down by the roadside to die. Some were calling the names and numbers of their regiments, but many had become too weak to do this . . . the army is simply a mob. There appears to be neither organization nor discipline. Were a division of the enemy to pounce down upon us . . . I fear the Army of the Cumberland would be blotted out.

Confederate soldier's cap (left) and Union soldier's cap (right)

■ INTERPRETING PRIMARY SOURCES

1. Why was Theodore Upson not allowed to enlist?
2. What does George Sargent say happens to all soldiers in battle?
3. How does the writer describe the Union forces after the Battle of Chickamauga?
4. What tools and utensils might a Civil War soldier carry?

Activity

Creating a Scrapbook Put together a scrapbook on the Civil War. Use your own original drawings and photocopies of maps, pictures, and other illustrations. Arrange your collection around different subjects and write a short explanation of each subject.

AFTER THE CIVIL WAR

The Civil War had ended. Readmitting the Southern states to the Union became the first order of business. Leaders agonized and argued over how to reunite the shattered nation. And even though slavery had been abolished, African Americans quickly discovered that freedom did not mean equality. As you read these primary source selections, think about the changes that took place after the Civil War.

■ READER'S DICTIONARY

exterminating: destructive

bondage: slavery

suffrage: the right to vote

The South in Ruins

Newspaper reporter Sidney Andrews toured the ruins of the major Southern cities in the fall of 1865 and wrote this account.

[Columbia, South Carolina] is now a wilderness of ruins. Its heart is but a mass of blackened chimneys and crumbling walls. Two thirds of the buildings in the place were burned, including, without exception, everything in the business portion. Not a store, office, or shop escaped; and for a distance of three fourths of a mile on each of twelve streets there was not a building left.

Looking for Relatives

Families that had been separated during slavery were now trying to reunite. Newspapers carried advertisements like the one below from African Americans seeking information about missing relatives:

$200 reward. During the year 1849, Thomas Sample carried away from this city, as his slaves, our daughter Polly, and son, Geo. Washington, to the State of Mississippi, and [later] to Texas. . . . We will give $100 each for them, to any person who assists them, or either of them, to get to Nashville, or get word to us [about where to find them], if they are alive.

On the Plight of African Americans

Personal Records

In 1867 Frederick Douglass appealed eloquently to Congress on behalf of African Americans.

. . . Yet the Negroes have marvelously survived all the exterminating forces of slavery, and have emerged at the end of 250 years of bondage, not [sad and hateful], but cheerful, hopeful, and forgiving. They now stand before Congress and the country, not complaining of the past, but simply asking for a better future.

. . . It is true that a strong plea for equal suffrage might be addressed to the national sense of honor. Something, too, might be said of national gratitude. A nation might well hesitate before the temptation to betray its allies. There is something . . . mean, to say nothing of the cruelty, in placing the loyal Negroes of the South under the political power of their rebel masters. . . . We asked the Negroes to [support] our cause, to be our friends, to fight for us and against their masters; and now, after they have done all that we asked them to do . . . it is proposed in some quarters to turn them over to the

The Fisk Jubilee Singers

political control of the common enemy of the government and of the Negro. . . .

What, then, is the work before Congress? . . . In a word, it must [allow African Americans to vote], and by means of the loyal Negroes and the loyal white men of the South build up a national party there, and in time bridge the [gap] between North and South, so that our country may have a common liberty and a common civilization. . . .

■ INTERPRETING PRIMARY SOURCES

1. What is the aim of the advertisement?
2. What did Frederick Douglass urge Congress to do?
3. Why do you think musical groups such as the Fisk Jubilee Singers traveled throughout the country to perform spirituals?

Activity

Create a Book Jacket Create a book jacket for an imaginary novel about life in your community after the Civil War. On the front, draw a scene from the book. On the back, write a story summary.

LIFE IN THE WEST

The settlement of the West was filled with hardships and tragedy as well as adventure. For Native Americans, expanding white settlement meant vast changes in their own way of life. For miners, ranchers, and farmers, life on the Great Plains meant long hours of work, a harsh climate, and isolation. As you read these primary source selections, think about how people adapted to the environment and to a new way of life.

▇ READER'S DICTIONARY

stampede: run away in panic

reservation: land set aside for Native Americans

abide: follow

On the Cattle Trail

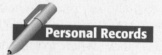

Personal Records

Cowhand George Duffield describes the troubles along a four-month trek from mid-Texas to Iowa in 1866.

April 29
. . . Started in evening from Salt Creek & traveled 5 miles to Alexanders Gap between Colorado & Brazos.

May 1
. . . Big Stampede   lost 200 head of cattle.

May 4
Continued the hunt   found 40 head day pleasant   Sun shone once more. Heard that the other herd has stampeded & lost over 200.

May 13
Big Thunder Storm last night Stampede lost 100 Beeves [head of cattle] hunted all day found 50 all tired. Everything discouraging.

June 12
Hard Rain & Wind   Big stampede & here we are among the Indians with 150 head of Cattle gone   hunted all day & the Rain pouring down with but poor success   Dark days are these to me   Nothing but Bread & Coffee   Hands all Growling & Swearing—everything wet and cold Beeves gone   rode all day & gathered all but 35. . . .

Sioux ghost dance shirt

Christmas in Kansas

Personal Records

Soon after Christmas in 1871, Kansas settler Ida Lingdren wrote to her mother in Sweden.

Dear, beloved Mamma,

I must tell you about our Christmas! [Magnus and his family] had everything so fine and cozy, three rooms downstairs and the attic all in order, and a Christmas tree of green cedar with candles and bonbons and apples on it, and the coffee table set, so it was really Christmas-like, and because of that I could not tear my thoughts away from you and from my old home and the tears kept welling up! Magnus played and we were to sing, but it didn't go too well. Then we had a few Christmas presents, the finest was a rocking chair which Magnus and his family gave us. From Gustaf I got two serving dishes, since we had none before. . . .

After we had eaten our rice pudding and Christmas cookies, we sang a few hymns and "Hosianna," and then we broke up, though we all slept there. . . .

Indian School

Oral Histories

Ah-nen-la-de-ni of the Mohawk people describes his first experience in school.

After the almost complete freedom of reservation life the cramped quarters and the dull routine of the school were maddening to all us strangers. There were endless rules for us to study and abide by, and hardest of all was the rule against speaking to each other in our own language. We must speak English or remain silent, and those who knew no English were forced to be dumb or else break the rules in secret. This last we did quite frequently, and were punished, when detected, by being made to stand in the "public hall" for a long time or to march about the yard while the other boys were at play.

■ INTERPRETING PRIMARY SOURCES

1. What crises did George Duffield face on the trail?
2. Do you think the holidays are a happy time for Ida Lindgren? Explain.
3. How does the boy at the Indian school compare life there with life on the reservation?

Activity

Constructing a Plan Make a plan for a late-1800s western town. Ask yourself: What buildings will you include? Where should they be located? What building materials would you use? Draw a map of your town.

INDUSTRY TAKES HOLD

The period from the end of the Civil War to 1900 was an era of unmatched economic growth in the United States. The key to this growth was industrialization. Because of the trend toward large-scale industrial operations, the late 1800s has often been called the Age of Big Business. As you read these primary source selections, consider how industry greatly influenced new ways of life.

■ READER'S DICTIONARY

pious: religious

multitude: crowd

sinew: strength

phalanx: a body of troops

disperse: scatter

You Ought to Get Rich

Oral Histories

Many religious leaders supported a pro-business philosophy. Baptist preacher Russell H. Conwell expressed his views in a sermon called "Acres of Diamonds."

I say that you ought to get rich, and it is your duty to get rich. How many of my pious brethren say to me, "Do you, a Christian minister, spend your time going up and down the country advising young people to get rich, to get money?" "Yes, of course I do." They say, "Isn't that awful! Why don't you preach the gospel instead of preaching about man's making money?" Because to make money honestly is to preach the gospel."

Factory Chimneys
by Maximillian Luce

Protests and Violence

Printed Publications

*Chicago was the center of violence relating
to a strike between workers and management
of the McCormick Harvester Company.
A Chicago newspaper reports on a
confrontation between police and strikers
on May 3, 1886.*

. . . At 2 o'clock a man, coatless and hatless,
climbed upon an empty freight train standing
near the multitude. He stepped to the edge of
the roof and then waved his hands about his
head. "Stand firm," he shouted in German. "Let
every man stand shoulder to shoulder and we
will win this fight. We must have our rights. . . .
Drive the 'scabs' [non-union labor] out of the
yards and let us show McCormick that he cannot hire non-union men and keep them at work
while we, the bone and sinew of Chicago, are
forced to have our wives and our children crying for bread." . . .

"Now for the scabs," shouted a man with a
red handkerchief knotted about his neck.

"Let's drive 'em out of the building and
kill 'em," roared a broad-breasted [striker] as he
took after the heels of the man with a red
handkerchief.

The excitement was electric. It spread from
man to man in the twinkling of a star, there
were cheers from a thousand throats, and then
the noise grew into a mighty roar.

"Off to McCormicks!" was the cry. Blue
Island Avenue was choked with hurrying men
and boys. They rushed down the car-tracks in
a resistless body, and swept over the vacant
lots in solid phalanxes. The roar grew mightier
in volume as the mob poured down upon
the huge, gray somber building at Western
Avenue. . . .

The mob pressed forward with a yell. Just
as it was about to burst into the yard the Hin-
man Street patrol wagon dashed down the
dusty road. . . .

"Disperse or we'll fire," shouted Sergeant
Enright. His reply was a shower of stones that
whistled unpleasantly about the little band of
blue-coats [police]. The officers wavered for a
moment before the onslaught, and then leveled
their revolvers at the crowd. The barrels of the
weapons glistened in the sunlight, there was a
flash, and then an explosion followed that startled the horses in the car barns, two blocks
away. The first shot of the strike had been fired.

■ INTERPRETING PRIMARY SOURCES

1. What is Conwell's main point? Do you
   agree or disagree? Explain.
2. What is the mood of the strikers? What
   words does the writer use to describe
   the strikers?
3. Mass production—production of large
   quantities of goods at low cost—was
   the heart of the new industrial system.
   What idea about industry does artist
   Maximillian Luce capture in *Factory
   Chimneys*?

Activity

Making Inventions   Develop an idea
for a game, a household device, vehicle,
or other invention. Sketch a design for it,
and diagram all the pieces and parts.
Name your invention and write a brief
description of its purpose and unique
qualities.

A NATION OF CITIES

*With the growth of industry, the landscape
of the United States changed. Railroads
crisscrossed the continent. Where farms once
stood, factories spewed forth black smoke.
Thousands of Americans left their farms
hoping to make their fortunes in the city.
Millions of immigrants came hoping to share
in the benefits of the new industrial age. As
you read the primary source selections, think
about what problems as well as what benefits
resulted from the Industrial Revolution.*

◼ READER'S DICTIONARY

inclined: slanted or leaning

poultice: dressing applied to the body

repose: rest

kosher: approved by Jewish law

babel: a scene of noise and confusion

The Sweat Shop

Oral Histories

*In factories, people had to work at an
inhuman pace. Following is the account
of a young woman employed in New York
City's garment industry.*

At seven o'clock we all sit down to
our machines and the boss brings
to each one the pile of work that
he or she is to finish during the day. . . .
This pile is put down beside the machine
and as soon as a skirt is done it is laid on
the other side of the machine. . . . The machines go like mad all day, because the
faster you work, the more money you get.
Sometimes in my haste I get my finger
caught and the needle goes right through
it. . . . We all have accidents like that. . . .
Sometimes a finger has to come off. . . . All
the time we are working the boss walks
about examining the finished garments
and making us do them over again if they
are not just right. So we have to be careful
as well as swift. . . .

*Young coal miners in
Kingston, Pennsylvania*

Child Labor

Printed Publications

Children as well as adults suffered in unhealthy work conditions, as the following description shows:

In a little room in this big, block shed—a room not twenty feet square—forty boys are picking their lives away. The floor of this room is an inclined plane, and a stream of coal pours constantly in. They work here, in this little black hole, all day and every day . . . picking away among the black coals, bending over till their little spines are curved. . . . Not three boys in this roomful could read or write. Shut in from everything that is pleasant, with no chance to learn, with no knowledge of what is going on about them. . . . They know nothing but the difference between slate and coal.

Advice

Printed Publications

This selection from the 1890s offers some interesting tips.

Lemon-juice will sometimes cure freckles. Dip your finger-tip in the acid and touch the freckles with it. Buttermilk may be used in the same way.

The best plan for keeping free of wrinkles is to avoid tricks of grimacing, raising the eyebrows, frowning, etc. A few minutes' absolute facial repose during the day is said to [slow] the approach of wrinkles.

An Emigrant's Story

Printed Publications

In her book The Promised Land, *Mary Antin tells of leaving her native country Poland to come to America when she was 13 years old.*

What did they not ask, the eager, foolish, friendly people? They wanted to handle the ticket, and mother must read them what is written on it. How much did it cost? Was it all paid for? Were we going to have a foreign passport or did we intend to steal across the border? Were we not going to have new dresses to travel in? Was it sure that we could get kosher food on the ship?

[After we boarded the train] when the warning bell rang out, it was drowned in a confounding babel of voices—fragments of oft-repeated messages . . . [of] blessings, farewells— "Don't forget!"—"Take care of—" "Keep your tickets—" "Moshele—newspapers!—" "Garlick is best!" "Happy journey!" "God help you!" "Good-bye!" "Remember—"

■ **INTERPRETING PRIMARY SOURCES**

1. Why did the workers in the sweat shop work quickly?
2. What words does Mary Antin use to describe the townspeople?

◤ **Activity** ▶

Researching Identify one ethnic group in your community. Research their music, food, and other customs. Think about this group's effect on everyday life in your community.

SEEKING A BETTER LIFE

As city populations grew, people's living and working conditions became worse and worse. Many people began to call for improvements in the quality of life. As you read these primary source selections, think about what were the most important concerns for reformers in the late 1800s and early 1900s.

■ READER'S DICTIONARY

bewildered: confused

damages: money

outrage: insult

ballot: right to vote

harassing: disturbing

The Jungle, *a novel about the meat packing industry*

The Farmer

Songs and Poems

Farmers joined with representatives of labor and other reform movements to form the Populist party in 1892. The party's song was "The Farmer is the Man."

When the banker says he's broke,
And the merchant's up in smoke,
They forget that it's the farmer feeds
    them all.
It would put them to the test
If the farmer took a rest,
Then they'd know that it's the farmer
    feeds them all.

Hull House

Printed Publications

Social workers established settlement houses in the slums of the large cities. One of the more famous was Hull House, founded in Chicago by Jane Addams. This excerpt explains how settlement houses helped poor and disadvantaged people living in the city.

We early found ourselves spending many hours in efforts to secure support for deserted women, insurance for bewildered widows, damages for injured operators, furniture from the clutches of the installment store. The Settlement is valuable as an information and interpretation bureau. It constantly acts between the various institutions of the city and the people for whose benefit these were erected. The hospitals, county agencies, and State asylums are often but vague rumors to the people who need them most. Another function of the Settlement to its neighborhood resembles that of the big brother whose mere presence on the playground protects the little one from bullies.

Woman Suffrage

 **Oral Histories**

Ernestine Hara Kettler picketed the White House in 1912 for the right to vote. She was 21 years old.

. . . It was very just for women to vote and it was highly undemocratic and an outrage that so much opposition had been placed against their getting the ballot. There were, after all, as many women in the country as men. What is this business? Is a woman so far below a man intellectually that she's not fit to vote? When I think of it, it's just incredible! I can't believe it! I condemned it. I was actually outraged that women didn't have the vote! That's why I went down to Washington.

. . . A pretty big crowd would gather every day—at least it seemed pretty big to me. There were always men and women standing there harassing us and throwing some pretty bad insults—and pretty obscene ones. The women

weren't obscene, but the men were. Our instructions were to pay absolutely no attention to them. I ignored them. I was brave. My goodness, I was fighting for a cause.

We had some support, but they took their lives in their hands. If any of the bystanders supported us, they could be beaten by the rest of the crowd. Towards the end, they started throwing stuff at the women. In fact, during this period somebody fired a shot through the windows of the Little White House, the headquarters. Any woman that happened to be in the right position for it could have been killed. And we couldn't get police protection. We just couldn't get it. The only protection we had was when we were arrested. Then we were protected!

Suffrage marcher

■ INTERPRETING PRIMARY SOURCES

1. According to Jane Addams, what is the role of the settlement house?
2. Why did Ernestine Kettler go to Washington, D.C.?

Activity

Making a Time Line Make a time line of the woman suffrage movement. Include important marches, demonstrations, and people. Write a paragraph on the importance of women's clubs in the suffrage movement.

For use with Chapter 22
"Overseas Expansion"

AMERICA LOOKS ABROAD

Like the European powers, the United States in the late 1800s and early 1900s wanted to exercise influence on world affairs. During these decades the United States used the Monroe Doctrine to oppose European involvement in Latin America. At the same time, the United States government and businesses became more involved in the affairs of Latin American nations. As you read these primary source selections, think about how other nations might have viewed growing U.S. involvement in other nations' affairs.

▧ READER'S DICTIONARY

score: twenty

hatch: opening in the deck of a ship

aft: back

port: left side of a ship looking foward

turret: tower

detonation: explosion

calamity: tragedy

Havana: city and port of Cuba on Gulf of Mexico

The United States and Cuba

Printed Publications

Sympathy for Cubans under Spanish rule grew as newspapers competed with each other in reporting stories of Spanish atrocities. An editorial in Joseph Pulitzer's New York World *is a case in point:*

How long are the Spaniards to drench Cuba with the blood and tears of her people?
. . . How long shall old men and women and children be murdered by the score, the innocent victims of Spanish rage against the patriot armies they cannot conquer?
. . . How long shall the United States sit idle and indifferent . . . ?

Destruction of the *Maine*

Oral Histories

The following is an account of the sinking of the battleship Maine, *told by a U.S. naval officer.*

I was on watch, and when the men had been [signaled] below I looked down the main hatches and over the side of the ship. Everything was absolutely normal. I walked aft to the quarter deck

behind the rear turret . . . and sat down on the port side, where I remained for a few minutes. . . . I was feeling a bit glum, and in fact was so quiet that Lieutenant J. Hood came up and asked laughingly if I was asleep. I said, "No, I am on watch."

Scarcely had I spoken when there came a dull, sullen roar. Would to God that I could blot out the sound and the scenes that followed. Then came a sharp explosion—some say numerous detonations. I remember only one. It seemed to me that the sound came from the port side forward. Then came a perfect rain of missiles of all descriptions, from huge pieces of cement to blocks of wood, steel railings, fragments of gratings. . . .

I was struck on the head by a piece of cement and knocked down, but I was not hurt, and got to my feet in a moment. . . .

Lieutenant Commander Wainwright on his return reported the total and awful character of the calamity, and Captain Sigsbee gave the . . . order, "Abandon ship," to men overwhelmed with grief indeed, but calm and apparently unexcited. . . .

I have no theories as to the cause of the explosion. I cannot form any. I, with others, had heard that the Havana harbor was full of torpedoes, but the officers whose duty it was to examine into that reported that they found no signs of any. Personally, I do not believe that the Spanish had anything to do with the disaster. Time may tell. I hope so.

The Return of the Conquerors *by Edward Moran*

I Cultivate the White Rose

Songs and Poems

José Martí was a Cuban political activist, journalist, and writer. Forced to flee Cuba because of his opposition to Spanish rule, Martí lived in exile in many countries, including the United States. Martí was killed fighting for Cuban independence.

I cultivate the white rose
In June as in January
For the sincere friend
Who gives me his hand frankly.

And for the cruel person who tears out
    the heart with which I live,
I cultivate neither snails nor thorns:
I cultivate the white rose.

■ INTERPRETING PRIMARY SOURCES

1. What action do you think the newspaper editorial wants the United States to take? Explain.
2. Does the naval officer's account seem factual to you? Why or why not?
3. The artist painted *The Return of the Conquerors* after the Spanish American War. What image does it portray about the United States?

Activity

Making a Map Make an outline map of the United States in 1900. Label the states and territories.

VOICES OF WAR

People had never known a war as terrible as World War I. As old empires fell, a quieter way of life came to an end. Hoping they would never see such destruction again, they called it "the war to end wars." As you read these selections, think about what these events meant for the decades to come.

■ READER'S DICTIONARY

ruefully: regretfully

starboard: the right side of a ship

periscope: a viewing device for submarines to see above the ocean surface

stern: the rear of a ship

Flanders: area on the French-Belgian border where fighting was heavy

foe: enemy

Propaganda poster

Aboard the *Lusitania*

Personal Records

Despite the threat of German U-boat, or submarine, attacks, American architect Theodate Pope boarded the Lusitania *to sail home from Europe. On May 7, 1915, a German torpedo sank the British luxury liner. After being rescued, Pope wrote this letter home.*

Friday morning we came slowly through fog, blowing our fog horn. It cleared off about an hour before we went below for lunch. A young Englishman at our table had been served with his ice cream, and was waiting for the steward to bring him a spoon to eat it with. He looked ruefully at it and said he would hate to have a torpedo get him before he ate it. We all laughed, and then commented on how slowly we were running. We thought the engines had stopped.

Mr. Friend [another passenger] and I went up on deck B on the starboard side and leaned over the railing, looking at the sea, which was a marvellous blue and very dazzling in the sunlight. I said, "How could the officers ever see a periscope there?" The torpedo was on its way to us at that moment, for we went a short distance farther toward the stern, turning the corner by the smoking-room, when the ship was struck on the starboard side. The sound was like that of an arrow entering the canvas and straw of a target, magnified a thousand times, and I imagined I heard a dull explosion follow. The water and timbers flew past the deck. Mr. Friend struck his fist in his hand and said, "By Jove! they've got us." The ship steadied herself a few seconds and then listed [tilted] heavily to starboard, throwing us against the wall of a small corridor. . . .

. . . [The] deck suddenly looked very strange, crowded with people, and I remember that two women were crying in a pitifully weak way. An officer was shouting orders to stop lowering the boats, and we were told to go down to deck B. We first looked over the rail and watched a boat filled with men and women being lowered. The stern was lowered too quickly and half the boatload were spilled backwards into the water. We looked at each other, sickened by the sight. . . .

Daily Rigors

Songs and Poems

Soldiers use short marching songs to step in time. This marching song expresses the daily misery of the soldiers in World War I.

Nobody knows how tired we are,
Tired we are, Tired we are, Tired we are,
Nobody knows how tired we are,
And nobody seems to care.

In Flanders Fields

Songs and Poems

John McCrae, a Canadian doctor serving in World War I, wrote this poem early in 1918, shortly before he was killed.

In Flanders fields the poppies blow
Between the crosses, row on row,
    That mark our place, and in the sky,
    The larks, still bravely singing, fly,
Scarce heard amid the guns below.

We are the dead; short days ago
We lived, felt dawn, saw sunset glow,
    Loved and were loved, and now we lie
    In Flanders fields.

Take up our quarrel with the foe!
To you from failing hands we throw
    The torch; be yours to hold it high!
    If ye break faith with us who die
We shall not sleep, though poppies grow
    In Flanders fields.

▮ INTERPRETING PRIMARY SOURCES

1. The *Lusitania* passengers were aware that Germany had threatened to attack British ships. From Theodate Pope's account, do you think they took the threat seriously?
2. What emotions are expressed in the soldiers' marching song?
3. To whom is the poet speaking in the last verse of "In Flanders Fields"?

Activity

Conducting an Interview Imagine you are a journalist. Make a list of five questions you would ask a passenger surviving the sinking of the *Lusitania*.

**For use with Chapter 24
"The Jazz Age"**

A RESTLESS TIME

World War I had swept away many traditional ideas. Young people, especially, were restless in the 1920s. They wanted to forget the horrors of war and have a good time. In the big cities, African Americans found a new voice in the sounds of jazz and blues. The new music was just one sign of the changing times. As you read these primary source selections, think about how the Jazz Age was like and unlike the era you live in.

■ READER'S DICTIONARY

rookie: first-year player on a professional sports team

transatlantic: across the Atlantic Ocean

Harlem: New York neighborhood where many African Americans lived

treble: high-pitched musical notes

bass: low-pitched musical notes

Baseball autographed by Babe Ruth

Making It in the Big Leagues

In 1927 Dick Bartell was a scared young rookie shortstop with the Pittsburgh Pirates. He remembers how a superstar—Babe Ruth—had time for a newcomer.

We were playing a spring training game against the Yankees and I guess Babe Ruth was watching me try to get my grounders at short and second [base] and getting pushed around by the [veteran players]. I looked at him; he waved a finger and called me over. Here's a nineteen-year-old being called over by the greatest player in baseball.

I went over to him and stuttered, "D-d-do you want me, Mr. Ruth?"

He just smiled and looked at me and said, "I know you're a rookie and the old guys are giving you a hard time. Put up with it. Work hard and don't worry about other guys. Don't say too much and just let your play do the talking. I've watched you, kid, and I think you're gonna make it big in the Big Leagues. Just be careful and let those old guys do what they want. Soon it'll be your turn."

I never forgot the advice and whenever I was down or in a slump or was mistreated by other ballplayers or owners, Babe's advice kept me going and kept me in baseball. . . .

"Lucky Lindy"

Oral Histories

In May 1927, Charles Lindbergh fulfilled a dream. Lifting off from United States soil, he flew his airplane solo across the Atlantic Ocean to France. The following is an excerpt from a newspaper interview he gave the day after he landed.

There's one thing I wish to get straight about this flight. They call me "Lucky," but luck isn't enough. As a matter of fact, I had what I regarded and still regard as the best existing plane to make the flight from New York to Paris. . . .

That I landed with considerable gasoline left means that I had recalled the fact that so many flights had failed because of lack of fuel, and that was one mistake I tried to avoid. . . .

I look forward to the day when transatlantic flying will be a regular thing. It is a question largely of money. If people can be found willing to spend enough to make proper preparations, there is no reason why it can't be made very practical. . . .

I didn't bring any extra clothes with me. I am wearing a borrowed suit now. It was a case of clothes or gasoline, and I took the gasoline. I have a check on a Paris bank and am going to cash it tomorrow morning, buy shirts, socks, and other things. I expect to have a good time in Paris.

But I do want to do a little flying over here.

Dream Boogie: Variation

Songs and Poems

Langston Hughes, a leading writer of the Harlem Renaissance, often drew inspiration for his poetry from jazz music and from his Harlem neighborhood.

Tinkling treble,
Rolling bass,
High noon teeth
In a midnight face,
Great long fingers
On great big hands,
Screaming pedals
Where his twelve-shoe lands,
Looks like his eyes
Are teasing pain,
A few minutes late
For the Freedom Train.

■ INTERPRETING PRIMARY SOURCES

1. What advice did Babe Ruth offer to Dick Bartell? Do you think the same advice could be given to a young ballplayer today?
2. What did Lindbergh mean when he said "luck isn't enough"?
3. What musical instrument is being played in Hughes' poem?

Activity

Writing a poem   Poetry often reflects the beat, or rhythm, of music and dance. Write a short poem that uses the rhythms of a kind of music you enjoy.

BOOM AND BUST

The collapse of the American stock market in October 1929 signaled an end to the carefree spirit of the Jazz Age. The crash was followed by the Great Depression of the 1930s, an economic slump that shook the rich and made life harder for those who were already poor. Then a new president, Franklin D. Roosevelt, vowed to use the power of the government to help Americans recover. As you examine these selections, think about how people responded to the hardships of the Depression.

▮ READER'S DICTIONARY

soup line: outdoor kitchen set up to distribute free food to needy people

contemptuous: scornful

The Long Wait

Visual Materials

Dorothea Lange was an American photographer who captured many powerful images of the Great Depression. The photograph below, "White Angel Bread Line," shows people waiting for food in San Francisco in 1933. Lange considered this her most famous photograph.

At the time, Lange made her living as a portrait photographer. She began to shoot street scenes such as this and hang them in her studio. As she told an interviewer: "The only comment I ever got was, 'What are you going to do with this kind of thing?' I didn't know. But I knew that picture was on my wall, and I knew that it was worth doing."

A fruit seller

Standing in the Soup Line

Oral Histories

Peggy Terry came from the hills of Kentucky, but her family spent the hard years of the Depression in Oklahoma City. She describes how the family managed to eat during the tough times.

I first noticed the difference when we'd come home from school in the evening. My mother'd send us to the soup line. . . . If you happened to be one of the first ones in line, you didn't get anything but water that was on top. So we'd ask the guy that was ladling out the soup into the buckets—everybody had to bring their own bucket to get the soup—he'd dip the greasy, watery stuff off the top. So we'd ask him to please dip down to get some meat and potatoes from the bottom of the kettle. . . .

Then we'd go across the street. One place had bread, large loaves of bread. Down the road just a little piece was a big shed, and they gave milk. My sister and me would take two buckets each. And that's what we lived off for the longest time.

I can remember one time, the only thing in the house to eat was mustard. My sister and I put so much mustard on biscuits that we got sick. And we can't stand mustard till today. . . .

When they had food to give to people, you'd get a notice and you'd go down. So Daddy went down that day and he took my sister and me. They were giving away potatoes and things like that. But they had a truck of oranges parked in the alley. Somebody asked them who the oranges were for, and they wouldn't tell 'em. So they said, well, we're gonna take those oranges. And they did. My dad was one of the ones that got up on the truck. They called the police, and the police chased us all away. But we got the oranges.

It's different today. People are made to feel ashamed now if they don't have anything. Back then, I'm not sure how the rich felt. I think the rich were as contemptuous of the poor then as they are now. But among the people that I knew, we all had an understanding that it wasn't our fault. It was something that had happened to the machinery. . . .

I remember it was fun. It was fun going to the soup line. 'Cause we all went down the road, and we laughed and we played. The only thing we felt is that we were hungry and we were going to get food. Nobody made us feel ashamed. There just wasn't any of that.

■ INTERPRETING PRIMARY SOURCES

1. What do you think is the mood of the people in the Lange photograph? How does the mood of this scene compare with Peggy Terry's memories of the soup line?
2. What does Peggy Terry mean when she says that the hard times were due to "something that had happened to the machinery"?

Activity

Researching Music   Research to find songs of the 1930s that reflect the mood of the Depression. Present the lyrics and/or melodies to the class.

A WORLD AT WAR

Two decades after World War I had ended, power-hungry and ruthless leaders dragged the world into war again. World War II was even more widespread and destructive than the first. It involved many nations and billions of people around the world. As you read these selections, think about how the turmoil of war affected different groups of people.

■ READER'S DICTIONARY

disembark: to go ashore from a ship

femoral: relating to the thigh

sulfa: a drug that prevents decay

morphine: a drug that calms or numbs pain

Bronze Star, awarded for heroism

The Longest Day

Personal Records

At fifteen minutes past midnight on June 6, 1944, European and American troops landed off the beaches of Normandy, France. The day's battle cost many lives. Cornelius Ryan, a war correspondent, covered the D-Day landings.

The great square-faced ramps of the assault craft butted into every wave, and chilling, frothing green water sloshed over everyone. There were no heroes in these boats—just cold, miserable, anxious men, so jam-packed together, so weighed down by equipment, that often there was no place to be seasick except over one another. . . .

In an instant the war had become personal. Troops heading for Utah Beach saw a control boat . . . suddenly rear up out of the water and explode. . . .

Scores of Utah-bound men saw the dead bodies and heard the yells and screams of the drowning. One man, Lieutenant (j. g.) Francis X. Riley of the Coast Guard, remembers the scene vividly. The twenty-four-year-old officer . . . could only listen "to the anguished cries for help from the wounded and shocked soldiers and sailors as they pleaded with us to pull them out of the water." But Riley's orders were to "disembark the troops on time regardless of casualties." . . .

Small islands of wounded men dotted the sand. . . . In his first few minutes on the beach, [Staff Sergeant Aflred] Eigenberg found so many wounded that he did not know "where to start or with whom." On Dog Red he came across a young soldier sitting in the sand with his leg "laid open from the knee to the pelvis as neatly as though a surgeon had done it with a scalpel." The wound was so deep that Eigenberg could clearly see the femoral artery pulsing. The soldier was in deep shock. Calmly he informed Eigenberg, "I've taken my sulfa pills and I've shaken all my sulfa powder into the wound. I'll be all right, won't I?" The nineteen-year-old Eigenberg didn't quite know what to say. He gave the soldier a shot of morphine and told him, "Sure, you'll be all right." Then, folding the neatly sliced halves of the man's leg together, Eigenberg did the only thing he could think of—he carefully closed the wound with safety pins.

Wartime conservation poster

On the Home Front

 **Printed Publications**

The U. S. government appealed to civilians to support the war effort in many ways. This bulletin was posted in meat markets.

1] THE NEED IS URGENT—War in the Pacific has greatly reduced our supply of vegetable fats from the Far East. It is necessary to find substitutes for them. Fat makes glycerine. And glycerine makes explosives for us and our Allies—explosives to down Axis planes, stop their tanks, and sink their ships. We need millions of pounds of glycerine and you housewives can help supply it.

2] DON'T throw away a single drop of used cooking fat, bacon fat, meat drippings, fry fats—every kind you use. After you've got all the cooking good from them, pour them through a kitchen strainer into a clean, wide-mouthed can. Keep it in a cool dark place. . . .

3] TAKE THEM to your meat dealer when you've saved a pound or more. He is cooperating patriotically. He will pay you for your waste fats and get them started on their way to war industries. . . .

■ INTERPRETING PRIMARY SOURCES

1. What happened to the control boat landing at Utah Beach?
2. For what purpose did the government ask people to save fats?

 Activity

Making a Poster Find out what items the government rationed or asked Americans to conserve during World War II. Design a poster that encourages people to conserve one of these items.

LIVING ON THE EDGE

During the cold war era, the world lingered on the edge of nuclear disaster as the superpowers—the United States and the Soviet Union—both tried to extend their influence around the world. As you read the selections, consider the atmosphere of fear that hung over American society. What do Americans fear today?

■ READER'S DICTIONARY

fallout: particles of radioactive material that drift through the atmosphere after a nuclear explosion

Conelrad: (from "<u>Con</u>trol of <u>El</u>ectromagnetic <u>Rad</u>iation") an emergency radio broadcasting system that would replace normal broadcasts

GI: member of the U.S. armed forces

shrapnel: bomb, mine, or shell fragments

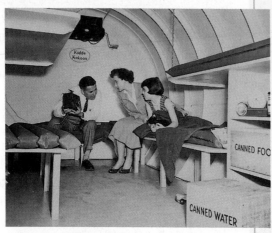

A family's fallout shelter

Fallout Fears

Printed Publications

By 1961 fears of nuclear war were so great that the government urged people to be prepared for a nuclear attack. LIFE magazine reminded Americans what to do during such an attack.

The standard Civil Defense signal for an alert is a steady 3- to 5-minute blast of a siren or whistle. The warning to take cover is a 3-minute period of short blasts or a wailing siren. If an attack should come, however, the first warning you may get could be the flash itself. Your first move should be to close your eyes and bury your head in your arms or clothing to block out the light. The flash may last for several seconds, so keep covered until it begins to dim.

The shockwave will come next. Take cover so you will not be knocked down. If you are in a car, roll down windows to avoid flying glass and lie on the floor. Try to count the seconds between the flash and shockwave. This will help you estimate how far away the bomb has hit and how long you have to find better cover before the fallout can reach you. . . .

Wherever you are, try to reach a radio—preferably a battery radio since the electricity may be out—and tune it to 640 or 1240 on your dial, which are the Conelrad frequencies for emergency instructions. If you have a shelter, go to it immediately. . . .

If you have no shelter and there is an hour or so left before the fallout is due to reach your area, you can block up the windows of your basement with one foot of earth, and take shelter there under tables on which you have piled books and magazines for extra shielding. You should also get together a supply of food and water and take it to the basement with you. . . .

Left Behind

Personal Records

Writer Henry Berry asked Joe Saluzzi, a Marine, to recall a battle during the Korean War.

There is a tradition in the Marine Corps that you do not leave your dead, and above all, you do not abandon your wounded. There are times, however, when the . . . rule has to be violated. . . .

. . . I had never met a Marine who knew of any wounded being left behind in Korea until I met Joe Saluzzi. . . .

"We were near Seoul," says Joe, "probably in a suburb. It was the morning of the twenty-sixth of September. . . ."

What Joe and the rest of Dog Company didn't know was that there was a unit of North Korean troops lying in ambush for them. . . . They were sitting ducks.

The North Koreans opened up. . . . Platoon Sergeant John O'Neill was killed.

"John was a real good man," said Joe. "He had a wife and children back in the States.

When I saw O'Neill riddled with bullets, it was a tremendous shock. . . .

. . . Right after that, it was my turn.

My God, it felt like someone had hit me in the chest with a baseball bat. The bullet cracked one of my ribs and was painful. . . . "

At this point, Joe is not sure of many things. He thinks he saw several North Korean soldiers and he knows that he heard very heavy shellings. His company . . . called in artillery. Miraculously, Joe wasn't touched. The next morning he did see several Communist soldiers who had not been so fortunate. They were all dead.

"Shortly after dawn the next morning," says Joe, "I looked up to see four Korean kids grinning at me. There was an old man jabbering away to the kids. Then the kids took off.

A little later the youngsters returned with some kind of a mat and, as gently as they could, lifted me onto it. They picked me up and started off. There must have been some [North Korean] snipers around because someone was shooting at us, but it didn't bother my saviors. . . . "

■ **INTERPRETING PRIMARY SOURCES**

1. According to the *LIFE* magazine article, in what order would someone probably experience the effects of a nuclear attack some distance away?
2. Why did Joe's platoon leave him on the battlefield?

Activity

Analyzing Create a fictional account of a day in the life of a teenager at this time. Your account may take the form of a diary, story, or play.

For use with Chapter 28
"America in the Fifties"

A NEW LIFESTYLE

Turquoise refrigerators, ranch houses, shiny new cars—Americans in the 1950s could buy things they had gone without during the Depression and war years. Some trends of the 1950s—television, the baby boom, suburbia, and rock 'n' roll—changed the way Americans lived. As you read these selections, consider how life in the 1950s is similar to life today.

■ **READER'S DICTIONARY**

frugal: thrifty, careful in spending money

crinoline: stiff cotton fabric

Rock 'N' Roll

Printed Publications

A sensation hit the sound waves in the mid-1950s—Elvis Presley. The following report from the La Crosse [Wisconsin] Register *describes the scene at one of his performances in 1956.*

Elvis Presley stepped on to the stage and immediately the soft-spoken kid with the nervous laugh disappeared and turned into a purple-coated musical demon who belted out songs as if his young life depended on it. The results were unbelievable. This kid, with jet-black hair, gleaming, darting eyes and dressed in New York clothes, stood for a moment and then let them have it. At the first tap of his leg the auditorium almost exploded. The listeners could not sit still. Every time he moved a muscle fifteen or twenty youngsters rushed forward and tried to break through the line of police to get to him. From then on, it was an even match to see who would entertain whom. . . . Elvis has somehow picked out a bit of teenage spirit and tucked it into his whanging geetar. You don't have to understand it. Just listen to it and the kids will tell you: This boy is crazy, man . . . crazy. . . .

Teenage Styles

Oral Histories

Social pressure and the new prosperity of the time led to the rise of the teenager as a consumer. Conformity was important in the 1950s. In these selections, two female teenagers remember how important it was to "fit in."

Refresh...Add Zest to the Hour

1950s advertisement

You had to have lots and lots of clothes. What mattered was variety; the more you had the better. The things that were very 'in' were just what poorer parents couldn't come up with, like cashmere sweaters. My family still didn't have much money; they were also very frugal. I was put on a clothing allowance when I started high school. It had to pay for everything except a winter coat and formal [evening dress]. So I did a lot of babysitting and sewing because I wanted a big wardrobe more than anything.

We wore full corduroy skirts with layers of crinoline petticoats underneath; wide elastic cinch belts and short-sleeved Ship'N Shore blouses. They cost $2.98, so they were one of the few things I could afford to buy. We wore them with little scarves knotted at the neck; you had to have lots and lots of little scarves.

■ INTERPRETING PRIMARY SOURCES

1. Why do you think Elvis appealed to the teenagers of the 1950s?
2. What characteristics of the 1950s can you identify from the teenagers' comments?

Activity

Making Comparisons Create a picture comparing teenagers of the 1950s and today. You may use original art or magazine photos to compare the clothing styles, music, or lifestyles of the two eras.

For use with Chapter 29
"The Civil Rights Era"

STRUGGLING FOR EQUALITY

For the most part, African Americans and other minority groups did not share in the prosperity and promise that followed World War II. During the 1950s and 1960s, however, the civil rights movement made great gains in voting rights, education, and other opportunities. As you read these selections, think of the various groups that are still working to gain an equal place in society.

■ READER'S DICTIONARY

Jim Crow laws: laws passed in the South in the late 1800s that enforced segregation and kept African Americans out of many public places

intolerable: not bearable

oppression: unjust or cruel exercise of authority or power

A Tired Woman's Fight

Personal Records

Rosa Parks's refusal to give up her seat on a bus helped spark the civil rights movement. In this selection, she answered a letter that asked, "How did you feel when you were on the bus?"

The custom of getting on the bus for black people in Montgomery in the 1950s was to pay at the front door, get off the bus, and then reenter through the back door to find a seat. Black people could not sit in the same rows with white people. This custom was humiliating.

When I sat down on the bus on the day I was arrested, I decided I must do what was right to do. People have said over the years that the reason I did not give up my seat was because I was tired. I did not think of being physically tired. My feet were not hurting. I was tired in a different way. I was tired of seeing so many men treated as boys and not called by their proper names or titles. I was tired of seeing children and women mistreated and disrespected because of the color of their skin. I was tired of Jim Crow laws, of legally enforced racial segregation.

I thought of the pain and the years of oppression and mistreatment that my people had suffered. I felt that way every day. December 1, 1955, was no different. Fear was the last thing I thought of that day. I put my trust in the Lord for guidance and help to endure whatever I had to face. I knew I was sitting in the right seat.

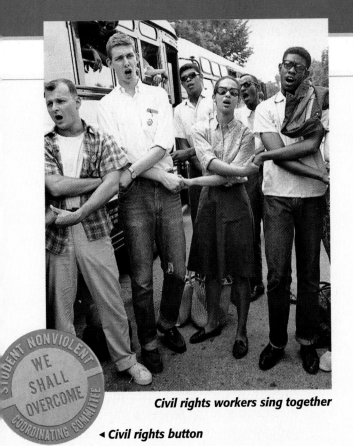

Civil rights workers sing together

◄ **Civil rights button**

We Shall Overcome

Songs and Poems

*As civil rights supporters marched in protest,
they often raised their voices in unison
to drown out their fears and bolster
their hopes. Many considered this song
the civil rights anthem.*

We shall overcome, we shall overcome
We shall overcome someday
Oh deep in my heart, I do believe
That we shall overcome someday

We'll walk hand in hand, we'll walk hand in
hand
We'll walk hand in hand someday
Oh deep in my heart, I do believe
We shall overcome someday

We shall live in peace, we shall live in peace
We shall live in peace someday
Oh deep in my heart, I do believe
That we shall overcome someday

Working Women

Oral Histories

*During the 1960s and 1970s, women began
demanding equal pay for equal work. Women
such as Joanne Gus, a warehouse worker, filed
lawsuits to get back pay from their employers.
In this excerpt, Gus describes the difficulties
she and her coworkers faced after receiving a
disappointing $500 offer to settle their lawsuit.*

. . . I was ready to cry. You can't realize all
the aggravation and amount of work that had
been done so far. The really sad part about it
was that most of the women were willing to settle. They were afraid to take it any further. Well,
I can be very stubborn, especially if I know I'm
right about an issue. So I refused the offer for
them all. Well, the next few days were really
[awful] at work. Still, I knew I was worth more.

*The case made it to federal court. A settlement of
$548,000 in back pay for 246 women was reached.*

■ INTERPRETING PRIMARY SOURCES

1. In what way was Rosa Parks "tired" when
   she boarded the Montgomery bus?
2. What things did workers in the civil
   rights movement want to "overcome"?
3. How did Joanne Gus's attitude differ
   from those of her coworkers?

Activity

Writing a Song Lyric Crowds at civil
rights rallies often made up their own
verses for "We Shall Overcome." Write
your own verse for the song, expressing
the same spirit and your own beliefs.

VOICES OF THE SIXTIES

While a war fought by soldiers exploded in Vietnam, Americans waged their own war at home. Deep and bitter divisions among Americans occurred during the 1960s, as Americans questioned both the wisdom and justice of the United States's actions abroad and the values of the traditional culture. As you read the selections, think about how the battles that took place during the 1960s impact Americans even today.

■ READER'S DICTIONARY

Viet Cong: Communist guerrilla forces in South Vietnam

colossal: huge

cadremen: trained Viet Cong members

kangaroo court: a court set up outside the legal system that follows irregular or unfair procedures

Republicans: in Vietnam, forces of the U.S.-backed government of South Vietnam

interrogation: a formal and systematic questioning

Pop Art

Rebellion in the 1960s took many forms. Young people marched in the streets for social reform, protested on college campuses against the Vietnam War, and rejected the social rules of their parents' generation. Artists of the 1960s challenged traditional ideas about fine art. Andy Warhol's painting *One Hundred Cans* uses the repeated image of an ordinary object—a soup can—to comment on art, society, and values.

A Vietnamese Village

Personal Records

Many Vietnamese people felt trapped between the forces fighting over their country. Writer Le Ly Hayslip, who grew up in South Vietnam, describes what happened in her village, Ky La, during the war.

Washington Monument reflected in the Vietnam Veterans Memorial

. . . The Republicans and Americans poured troops and firepower into the jungle around Ky La. . . . The Viet Cong had planned a three-day battle, but they had underestimated the colossal numbers of men and arms the enemy was willing to commit to prevent Ky La from falling into their hands. Inside the village, soldiers went from house to house, tearing everything apart to find the Viet Cong hideouts. Where anything suspicious was found, the house was burned and its occupants tied up and taken away for interrogation. Two thirds of my village disappeared this way. . . . So little was left that even the Viet Cong soon lost interest in Ky La as a prize of war. Instead, they turned their attention to the one thing they knew they could gain no matter what: a grip of terror on the survivors.

Despite—or perhaps because of—the terrible battle, the Viet Cong cadremen took even harsher steps to control us. They began by killing those they suspected of spying for the enemy, usually by taking the accused from their houses in the middle of the night and shooting them in the street—leaving the bodies for relatives to discover. Later, when government forces weren't around, the Viet Cong called villagers to special justice meetings . . . during which they held kangaroo courts for the accused and shot them afterward. . . .

Naturally, these trials made us stay on our toes. . . . After a while, our fear of the Viet Cong—of false accusation by jealous neighbors or headstrong kids—was almost as strong as our fear of the Republicans.

■ INTERPRETING PRIMARY SOURCES

1. What effect do you think Warhol was trying to create by using repeated, commercial images, like the soup cans?
2. Do you think the people in Hayslip's village feared the government troops or the Viet Cong more? Explain.

Activity

Writing a Speech Investigate the history of the Vietnam Veterans Memorial in Washington, D.C. Imagine that you were a speaker at the ceremony when it was unveiled. Write a brief dedication speech that justifies the memorial and its design.

For use with Chapter 32
"New Challenges"

ELECTION 2000

The presidential election of 2000 was one of the closest elections in American history. Although Americans voted on November 7, the winner was not known until December 13, because recounts in Florida were challenged in court. Eventually, the United States Supreme Court resolved the dispute. On December 13, Vice President Al Gore gave his concession speech. Shortly afterward, George W. Bush spoke, accepting his election as forty-third president of the United States.

■ READER'S DICTIONARY

partisan: strongly supporting one party
rancor: bitter feelings
stewardship: the managing or supervising of something
consensus: agreement
beacon: a sign or signal

Al Gore Concedes

Oral Histories

Just moments ago, I spoke with George W. Bush and congratulated him on becoming the 43rd president of the United States. . . . I offered to meet with him as soon as possible so that we can start to heal the divisions of the campaign and the contest through which we just passed.

Almost a century and a half ago, Senator Stephen Douglas told Abraham Lincoln, who had just defeated him for the presidency, "Partisan feeling must yield to patriotism. I'm with you, Mr. President, and God bless you." Well, in that same spirit, I say to President-elect Bush that what remains of partisan rancor must now be put aside, and may God bless his stewardship of this country. . . .

Now the U.S. Supreme Court has spoken. Let there be no doubt, while I strongly disagree with the court's decision, I accept it. . . . And tonight, for the sake of our unity of the people and the strength of our democracy, I offer my concession. I also accept my responsibility. . . . to honor the new president elect and do everything possible to help him bring Americans together. . . .

Al Gore with supporters

Now the political struggle is over and we turn again to the unending struggle for the common good of all Americans. . . . In the words of our great hymn, "America, America": "Let us crown thy good with brotherhood, from sea to shining sea." . . .

George W. Bush Accepts

Oral Histories

Tonight I chose to speak from the chamber of the Texas House of Representatives because it has been a home to bipartisan cooperation. Here in a place where Democrats have the majority, Republicans and Democrats have worked together to do what is right for the people we represent. . . .

The spirit of cooperation I have seen in this hall is what is needed in Washington, D.C. It is the challenge of our moment. . . . I believe things happen for a reason, and I hope the long wait of the last five weeks will heighten a desire to move beyond the bitterness and partisanship of the recent past.

Our nation must rise above a house divided. Americans share hopes and goals and values far more important than any political disagreements. Republicans want the best for our nation, and so do Democrats. Our votes may differ, but not our hopes. . . . Together, guided by a spirit of common sense, common courtesy and common goals, we can unite and inspire the American citizens. . . .

We have discussed our differences. Now it is time to find common ground and build consensus to make America a beacon of opportunity in the 21st century. . . .

George W. Bush and his wife, Laura

I have something else to ask you, to ask every American. I ask for you to pray for this great nation. . . . I have faith that with God's help we as a nation will move forward together as one nation, indivisible. And together we will create an America that is open, so every citizen has access to the American dream; an America that is educated, so every child has the keys to realize that dream; and an America that is united in our diversity and our shared American values that are larger than race or party. . . .

INTERPRETING PRIMARY SOURCES

1. What are Al Gore's feelings about the Supreme Court's decision?
2. What is the significance of the setting for George W. Bush's speech?

Activity

Planning a Time Capsule Imagine that you are in charge of making a time capsule to be opened 100 years from now. List 10-12 items you would include and explain your choices.

Appendix Contents

Flag Etiquette

Over the years, Americans have developed rules and customs concerning the use and display of the flag. One of the most important things every American should remember is to treat the flag with respect:

★ The flag should be raised and lowered by hand and displayed only from sunrise to sunset. On special occasions, it may be displayed at night.

★ The flag may be displayed on all days, weather permitting, particularly on national and state holidays and on historic and special occasions.

★ No flag should be flown above the American flag or to the right of it at the same height.

★ The flag may be flown at half-mast to mourn the death of public officials.

★ The flag should never touch the ground or floor beneath it.

★ The flag may be flown upside down only to signal distress.

★ When the flag becomes old and tattered, it should be destroyed by burning. According to an approved custom, the Union (the white stars on the blue field) is first cut from the flag; then the two pieces, which no longer form a flag, are burned.

Presidents
of the
United States

George Washington

1

1789–1797

Born: 1732
Died: 1799
Born in: Virginia
Elected from: Virginia
Age when elected: 56
Occupations: Planter, Soldier
Party: None
Vice President: John Adams

John Adams

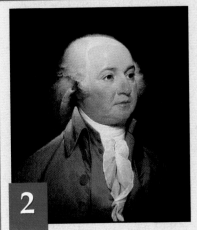

2

1797–1801

Born: 1735
Died: 1826
Born in: Massachusetts
Elected from: Massachusetts
Age when elected: 61
Occupations: Teacher, Lawyer
Party: Federalist
Vice President: Thomas Jefferson

Thomas Jefferson

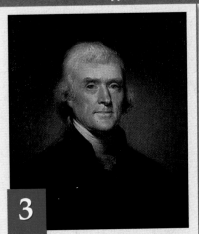

3

1801–1809

Born: 1743
Died: 1826
Born in: Virginia
Elected from: Virginia
Age when elected: 57
Occupations: Planter, Lawyer
Party: Republican**
Vice Presidents: Aaron Burr,
George Clinton

James Madison

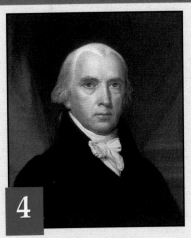

4

1809–1817

Born: 1751
Died: 1836
Born in: Virginia
Elected from: Virginia
Age when elected: 57
Occupation: Planter
Party: Republican**
Vice Presidents: George Clinton,
Elbridge Gerry

James Monroe

5

1817–1825

Born: 1758
Died: 1831
Born in: Virginia
Elected from: Virginia
Age when elected: 58
Occupation: Lawyer
Party: Republican**
Vice President: Daniel D. Tompkins

John Quincy Adams

6

1825–1829

Born: 1767
Died: 1848
Born in: Massachusetts
Elected from: Massachusetts
Age when elected: 57
Occupation: Lawyer
Party: Republican**
Vice President: John C. Calhoun

Andrew Jackson

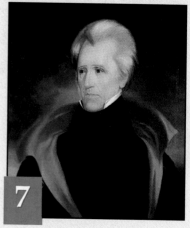

7

1829–1837

Born: 1767
Died: 1845
Born in: South Carolina
Elected from: Tennessee
Age when elected: 61
Occupations: Lawyer, Soldier
Party: Democratic
Vice Presidents: John C. Calhoun,
Martin Van Buren

Martin Van Buren

8

1837–1841

Born: 1782
Died: 1862
Born in: New York
Elected from: New York
Age when elected: 54
Occupation: Lawyer
Party: Democratic
Vice President: Richard M. Johnson

William H. Harrison

9

1841

Born: 1773
Died: 1841
Born in: Virginia
Elected from: Ohio
Age when elected: 67
Occupations: Soldier, Planter
Party: Whig
Vice President: John Tyler

John Tyler

10

1841–1845

Born: 1790
Died: 1862
Born in: Virginia
Elected as V.P. from: Virginia
Succeeded Harrison
Age when became President: 51
Occupation: Lawyer
Party: Whig
Vice President: None

James K. Polk

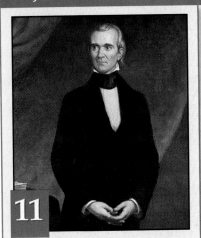

11

1845–1849

Born: 1795
Died: 1849
Born in: North Carolina
Elected from: Tennessee
Age when elected: 49
Occupation: Lawyer
Party: Democratic
Vice President: George M. Dallas

Zachary Taylor

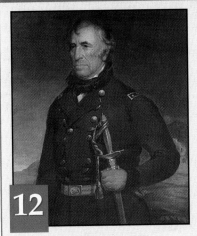

12

1849–1850

Born: 1784
Died: 1850
Born in: Virginia
Elected from: Louisiana
Age when elected: 63
Occupation: Soldier
Party: Whig
Vice President: Millard Fillmore

Millard Fillmore

13

1850–1853

Born: 1800
Died: 1874
Born in: New York
Elected as V.P. from: New York
Succeeded Taylor
Age when became President: 50
Occupation: Lawyer
Party: Whig
Vice President: None

Franklin Pierce

14

1853–1857

Born: 1804
Died: 1869
Born in: New Hampshire
Elected from: New Hampshire
Age when elected: 47
Occupation: Lawyer
Party: Democratic
Vice President: William R. King

James Buchanan

15

1857–1861

Born: 1791
Died: 1868
Born in: Pennsylvania
Elected from: Pennsylvania
Age when elected: 65
Occupation: Lawyer
Party: Democratic
Vice President: John C. Breckinridge

Abraham Lincoln

16

1861–1865

Born: 1809
Died: 1865
Born in: Kentucky
Elected from: Illinois
Age when elected: 51
Occupation: Lawyer
Party: Republican
Vice Presidents: Hannibal Hamlin,
Andrew Johnson

Andrew Johnson

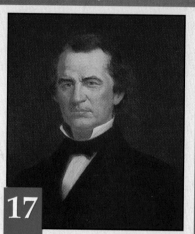

17

1865–1869

Born: 1808
Died: 1875
Born in: North Carolina
Elected as V.P. from: Tennessee
Age when became President: 55
Succeeded Lincoln
Occupation: Tailor
Party: Republican
Vice President: None

Ulysses S. Grant

18

1869–1877

Born: 1822
Died: 1885
Born in: Ohio
Elected from: Illinois
Age when elected: 46
Occupations: Farmer, Soldier
Party: Republican
Vice Presidents: Schuyler Colfax,
Henry Wilson

Rutherford B. Hayes

19

1877–1881

Born: 1822
Died: 1893
Born in: Ohio
Elected from: Ohio
Age when elected: 54
Occupation: Lawyer
Party: Republican
Vice President: William A. Wheeler

James A. Garfield

20

1881

Born: 1831
Died: 1881
Born in: Ohio
Elected from: Ohio
Age when elected: 48
Occupations: Laborer, Professor
Party: Republican
Vice President: Chester A. Arthur

Chester A. Arthur

21

1881–1885

Born: 1830
Died: 1886
Born in: Vermont
Elected as V.P. from: New York
Succeeded Garfield
Age when became President: 50
Occupations: Teacher, Lawyer
Party: Republican
Vice President: None

Grover Cleveland

22   **24**

1885–89, 1893–97

Born: 1837
Died: 1908
Born in: New Jersey
Elected from: New York
Age when elected: 47; 55
Occupation: Lawyer
Party: Democratic
Vice Presidents: Thomas A.
Hendricks, Adlai E. Stevenson

Benjamin Harrison

23

1889–1893

Born: 1833
Died: 1901
Born in: Ohio
Elected from: Indiana
Age when elected: 55
Occupation: Lawyer
Party: Republican
Vice President: Levi P. Morton

William McKinley

25

1897–1901

Born: 1843
Died: 1901
Born in: Ohio
Elected from: Ohio
Age when elected: 53
Occupations: Teacher, Lawyer
Party: Republican
Vice Presidents: Garret Hobart,
Theodore Roosevelt

Theodore Roosevelt

26

1901–1909

Born: 1858
Died: 1919
Born in: New York
Elected as V.P. from: New York
Succeeded McKinley
Age when became President: 42
Occupations: Historian, Rancher
Party: Republican
Vice President: Charles W. Fairbanks

William H. Taft

27

1909–1913

Born: 1857
Died: 1930
Born in: Ohio
Elected from: Ohio
Age when elected: 51
Occupation: Lawyer
Party: Republican
Vice President: James S. Sherman

Woodrow Wilson

28

1913–1921

Born: 1856
Died: 1924
Born in: Virginia
Elected from: New Jersey
Age when elected: 55
Occupation: College Professor
Party: Democratic
Vice President: Thomas R. Marshall

Warren G. Harding

29

1921–1923

Born: 1865
Died: 1923
Born in: Ohio
Elected from: Ohio
Age when elected: 55
Occupations: Newspaper Editor,
Publisher
Party: Republican
Vice President: Calvin Coolidge

Calvin Coolidge

30

1923–1929

Born: 1872
Died: 1933
Born in: Vermont
Elected as V.P. from: Massachusetts
Succeeded Harding
Age when became President: 51
Occupation: Lawyer
Party: Republican
Vice President: Charles G. Dawes

Herbert C. Hoover

31

1929–1933

Born: 1874
Died: 1964
Born in: Iowa
Elected from: California
Age when elected: 54
Occupation: Engineer
Party: Republican
Vice President: Charles Curtis

Franklin D. Roosevelt

32

1933–1945

Born: 1882
Died: 1945
Born in: New York
Elected from: New York
Age when elected: 50
Occupation: Lawyer
Party: Democratic
Vice Presidents: John N. Garner,
    Henry A. Wallace, Harry S Truman

Harry S Truman

33

1945–1953

Born: 1884
Died: 1972
Born in: Missouri
Elected as V.P. from: Missouri
Succeeded Roosevelt
Age when became President: 60
Occupations: Clerk, Farmer
Party: Democratic
Vice President: Alben W. Barkley

Dwight D. Eisenhower

34

1953–1961

Born: 1890
Died: 1969
Born in: Texas
Elected from: New York
Age when elected: 62
Occupation: Soldier
Party: Republican
Vice President: Richard M. Nixon

John F. Kennedy

35

1961–1963

Born: 1917
Died: 1963
Born in: Massachusetts
Elected from: Massachusetts
Age when elected: 43
Occupations: Author, Reporter
Party: Democratic
Vice President: Lyndon B. Johnson

Lyndon B. Johnson

36

1963–1969

Born: 1908
Died: 1973
Born in: Texas
Elected as V.P. from: Texas
Succeeded Kennedy
Age when became President: 55
Occupation: Teacher
Party: Democratic
Vice President: Hubert H. Humphrey

Richard M. Nixon

37

1969–1974

Born: 1913
Died: 1994
Born in: California
Elected from: New York
Age when elected: 55
Occupation: Lawyer
Party: Republican
Vice Presidents: Spiro T. Agnew,
Gerald R. Ford

Gerald R. Ford

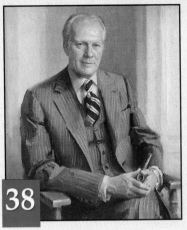

38

1974–1977

Born: 1913
Born in: Nebraska
Appointed by Nixon as V.P. upon
Agnew's resignation; assumed presidency upon Nixon's resignation
Age when became President: 61
Occupation: Lawyer
Party: Republican
Vice President: Nelson A. Rockefeller

James E. Carter, Jr.

39

1977–1981

Born: 1924
Born in: Georgia
Elected from: Georgia
Age when elected: 52
Occupations: Business, Farmer
Party: Democratic
Vice President: Walter F. Mondale

Ronald W. Reagan

40

1981–1989

Born: 1911
Born in: Illinois
Elected from: California
Age when elected: 69
Occupations: Actor, Lecturer
Party: Republican
Vice President: George H.W. Bush

George H.W. Bush

41

1989–1993

Born: 1924
Born in: Massachusetts
Elected from: Texas
Age when elected: 64
Occupation: Business
Party: Republican
Vice President: J. Danforth Quayle

William J. Clinton

42

1993–2001

Born: 1946
Born in: Arkansas
Elected from: Arkansas
Age when elected: 46
Occupation: Lawyer
Party: Democratic
Vice President: Albert Gore, Jr.

George W. Bush

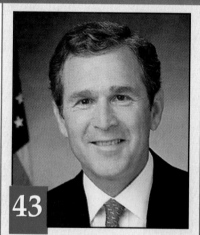

43

2001–

Born: 1946
Born in: Connecticut
Elected from: Texas
Age when elected: 54
Occupation: Business, Politician
Party: Republican
Vice President: Richard B. Cheney

THE WHITE HOUSE . . .
The President's Home

White House Statistics

3 Elevators
5 Major Floors with:
2 Basements
7 Staircases
12 Chimneys
32 Bathrooms
132 Rooms
160 Windows
412 Doors

White House Technology Firsts

1834	Indoor Plumbing
1845	Central Heating
1848	Gas Lighting
1866	Telegraph
1877	Telephone
1891	Electricity
1921	Radio
1926	Electric Refrigerator
1933	Air Conditioning
1942	Bomb Shelter
1947	Television
1979	Computer

Did You Know?

- *The first baby born in the White House* was Thomas Jefferson's grandson in 1806.
- *The first White House wedding held* was for Dolley Madison's sister in 1812.
- *General Lafayette visited the White House in 1825 with his pet alligator,* which he kept in the East Room.
- *Cows grazed on the front lawn of the White House* up until 1913.
- *The only president married in the White House* was Grover Cleveland, in 1886.

Documents of America's Heritage

★ ★

The Magna Carta

The Magna Carta, signed by King John in 1215, marked a decisive step forward in the development of constitutional government in England. Later, it became a model for colonists who carried the Magna Carta's guarantees of legal and political rights to America.

1. That the English church shall be free, and shall have her rights entire, and her liberties inviolate; . . .

2. We also have granted to all the freemen of our kingdom, for us and for our heirs forever, all the underwritten liberties, to be had and holden by them and their heirs, of us and our heirs forever. . . .

39. No freeman shall be taken or imprisoned, or diseased, or outlawed, or banished, or in any way destroyed, nor will we pass upon him, nor will we send upon him, unless by the lawful judgment of his peers, or by the law of the land.

40. We will sell to no man, we will not deny to any man, either justice or right.

41. All merchants shall have safe and secure conduct to go out of, and to come into, England, and to stay there and to pass as well by land as by water, for buying and selling by the ancient and allowed customs, without any unjust tolls, except in time of war, or when they are of any nation at war with us. . . .

42. It shall be lawful, for the time to come, for any one to go out of our kingdom and return safely and securely by land or by water, saving his allegiance to us (unless in time of war, by some short space, for the common benefit of the realm).

60. All the aforesaid customs and liberties, which we have granted to be holden in our kingdom, as much as it belongs to us, all people of our kingdom, as well clergy as laity, shall observe, as far as they are concerned, towards their dependents.

63. . . . It is also sworn, as well on our part as on the part of the barons, that all the things aforesaid shall be observed in good faith, and without evil duplicity. Given under our hand, in the presence of the witnesses above named, and many others, in the meadow called Runnymede, between Windsor and Staines, the 15th day of June, in the 17th year of our reign.

Illuminated manuscript, Middle Ages

The Mayflower Compact

On November 21, 1620, 41 colonists aboard the Mayflower drafted this agreement. The Mayflower Compact was the first plan of self-government ever put in force in the English colonies.

In ye name of God Amen. We whose names are underwritten, the loyall subjects of our dread soveraigne Lord King James, by ye grace of God, of Great Britaine, Franc, & Ireland king, defender of ye faith, &c. Haveing undertaken, for ye glorie of God, and advancemente of ye Christian faith and honour of our king & countrie, a voyage to plant ye first colonie in ye Northerne parts of Virginia, doe by these presents solemnly & mutualy in ye presence of God, and one of another, covenant, & combine ourselves togeather into a Civill body politick; for our better ordering, & preservation & furtherance of ye ends aforesaid; and by vertue hereof to enacte, constitute, and frame such just & equall Lawes, ordinances, Acts, constitutions, & offices, from time to time, as shall be thought most meete & convenient for ye generall good of ye colonie: unto which we promise all due submission and obedience. In witnes whereof we have hereunder subscribed our names at Cap-Codd ye -11- of November, in ye year of ye raigne of our soveraigne Lord King James of England, Franc, & Ireland ye eighteenth, and of Scotland ye fiftie fourth. Ano Dom. 1620.

The Federalist, No. 10

James Madison wrote several articles supporting ratification of the Constitution for a New York newspaper. In the excerpt below, Madison argues for the idea of a federal republic.

By a faction, I understand a number of citizens . . . who are united and actuated by some common impulse . . . adverse to the rights of other citizens. . . .

The inference to which we are brought is that the causes of faction cannot be removed and that relief is only to be sought in the means of controlling its effects. . . .

A republic, by which I mean a government in which the scheme of representation takes place . . . promises the cure for which we are seeking. . . .

The two great points of difference between a democracy and a republic are: first, the delegation of the government, in the latter, to a small number of citizens elected by the rest; secondly, the greater number of citizens, and greater sphere of country, over which the latter may be extended.

The effect of the first difference is . . . to refine and enlarge the public views by passing them through the medium of a chosen body of citizens, whose wisdom may best discern the true interest of their country, and whose patriotism and love of justice will be least likely to sacrifice it to temporary or partial considerations. . . .

James Madison

Washington's Farewell Address

At the end of his second term as president, George Washington spoke of the dangers facing the young nation. He warned against the dangers of political parties and sectionalism, and he advised the nation against permanent alliances with other nations.

Citizens by birth or choice of a common country, that country has a right to concentrate your affections. The name of American, which belongs to you, in your national capacity, must always exalt the just pride of patriotism more than any appellation derived from local discriminations. With slight shades of difference, you have the same religion, manners, habits, and political principles. You have in a common cause fought and triumphed together. . . .

In contemplating the causes which may disturb our Union, it occurs as matter of serious concern that any ground should have been furnished for characterizing parties by geographical discriminations. . . .

No alliances, however strict between the parts, can be an adequate substitute. They must inevitably experience the infractions and interruptions which all alliances in all times have experienced. . . .

George Washington

The great rule of conduct for us, in regard to foreign nations, is in extending our commercial relations to have with them as little political connection as possible. . . .

. . . I anticipate with pleasing expectations that retreat in which I promise myself to realize . . . the sweet enjoyment of partaking, in the midst of my fellow citizens, the benign influence of good laws under a free government, the ever favorite object of my heart, and the happy reward, as I trust, of our mutual cares, labors, and dangers.

The Star-Spangled Banner

During the British bombardment of Fort McHenry during the War of 1812, a young Baltimore lawyer named Francis Scott Key was inspired to write the words to "The Star-Spangled Banner." Although it became popular immediately, it was not until 1931 that Congress officially declared "The Star-Spangled Banner" as our national anthem.

O! say can you see, by the dawn's early light,
What so proudly we hail'd at the twilight's last gleaming,
Whose broad stripes and bright stars through the perilous fight,
O'er the ramparts we watched, were so gallantly streaming?
And the Rockets' red glare, the Bombs bursting in air,
Gave proof through the night that our Flag was still there;
O! say, does that star-spangled banner yet wave
O'er the Land of the free and the home of the brave!

The Monroe Doctrine

In an 1823 address to Congress, President James Monroe proclaimed the Monroe Doctrine. Designed to end European influence in the Western Hemisphere, it became a cornerstone of United States foreign policy.

. . . With the existing colonies or dependencies of any European power we have not interfered and shall not interfere. But with the governments who have declared their independence and maintained it, and whose independence we have, on great consideration and on just principles, acknowledged, we could not view any interposition for the purpose of oppressing them, or controlling in any other manner their destiny, by any European power in any other light than as the manifestation of any unfriendly disposition toward the United States. . . .

Our policy in regard to Europe, which was adopted at an early stage of the wars which have so long agitated that quarter of the globe, nevertheless remains the same, which is not to interfere in the internal concerns of any of its powers; to consider the government de facto as the legitimate government for us; to cultivate friendly relations with it, and to preserve those relations by a frank, firm, and manly policy, meeting in all instances the just claims of every power, submitting to injuries from none. . . .

James Monroe

Memorial and Protest of the Cherokee Nation

While Native Americans were being forced from their homeland, Cherokee leaders put their protest before the United States Senate. Their call for justice went unheard.

It cannot be concealed that the situation of the Cherokees is peculiarly distressing. In adverting to that situation it is not done to arouse, at this late day, a useless sympathy, but only as matter of history, and from necessity in giving a fair and impartial illustration of their difficulties. It is well known to those who have paid any attention to their history for the last five years, that they have been contending for the faithful execution of treaties between their nation and the United States, and that their distresses have not been mitigated; their efforts seem to have increased their difficulties. It remains for them to seek an adjustment by treaty, and an equitable acknowledge-ment of their rights and claims, so far as circumstances will permit.

For this purpose, this delegation has been deputed, as the proper organ of the Cherokee people, to settle, by treaty, their difficulties; and they wish, in sincerity, to have them settled, for the good, peace, and harmony of the whole nation.

Beaded shoulder bag, Cherokee people

The Seneca Falls Declaration

One of the first documents to express the desire for equal rights for women is the Declaration of Sentiments and Resolutions, issued in 1848 at the Seneca Falls Convention in Seneca Falls, New York. Led by Lucretia Mott and Elizabeth Cady Stanton, the delegates adopted a set of resolutions that called for woman suffrage and opportunities for women in employment and education. Excerpts from the Declaration follow.

When, in the course of human events, it becomes necessary for one portion of the family of man to assume among the people of the earth a position different from that which they have hitherto occupied, but one to which the laws of nature and of nature's God entitle them, a decent respect to the opinions of mankind requires that they should declare the causes that impel them to such a course.

We hold these truths to be self-evident: that all men and women are created equal; that they are endowed by their Creator with certain inalienable rights; that among these are life, liberty, and the pursuit of happiness; that to secure these rights governments are instituted, deriving their just powers from the consent of the governed. Whenever any form of government becomes destructive of these ends, it is the right of those who suffer from it to refuse allegiance to it, and to insist upon the institution of a new government, laying its foundation on such principles, and organizing its powers in such form, as to them shall seem most likely to effect their safety and happiness. Prudence, indeed, will dictate that governments long established should not be changed for light and transient causes; . . . But when a long train of abuses and usurpations, pursuing invariably the same object, evinces a design to reduce them under absolute despotism, it is their duty to throw off such government and to provide new guards for their future security. . . .

The history of mankind is a history of repeated injuries and usurpations on the part of man toward woman, having in direct object the establishment of an absolute tyranny over her. To prove this, let facts be submitted to a candid world. . . .

Now, in view of the entire disfranchisement of one-half the people of this country, their social and religious degradation, in view of the unjust laws above mentioned, and because women do feel themselves aggrieved, oppressed, and fraudulently deprived of their most sacred rights, we insist that they have immediate admission to all the rights and privileges which belong to them as citizens of the United States. . . .

Elizabeth Cady Stanton

The Emancipation Proclamation

On January 1, 1863, President Abraham Lincoln issued the Emancipation Proclamation, which freed all slaves in states under Confederate control. The Proclamation was a significant step toward the Thirteenth Amendment (1865) that ended slavery in all of the United States.

. . . That on the 1st day of January, in the year of our Lord 1863, all persons held as slaves within any state or designated part of a state, the people whereof shall then be in rebellion against the United States, shall be then, thenceforward, and forever free; and the executive government of the United States, including the military and naval authority thereof, will recognize and maintain the freedom of such persons and will do no act or acts to repress such persons, or any of them, in any efforts they may make for their actual freedom.

That the executive will, on the 1st day of January aforesaid, by proclamation, designate the states and parts of states, if any, in which the people thereof, respectively, shall then be in rebellion against the United States; and the fact that any state or the people thereof shall on that day be in good faith represented in the Congress of the United States by members chosen thereto at elections wherein a majority of the qualified voters of such states shall have participated shall, in the absence of strong countervailing testimony, be deemed conclusive evidence that such state and the people thereof are not then in rebellion against the United States. . . .

And, by virtue of the power and for the purpose aforesaid, I do order and declare that all persons held as slaves within said designated states and parts of states are, and henceforward shall be, free; and that the executive government of the United States, including the military and naval authorities thereof, will recognize and maintain the freedom of said persons.

And I hereby enjoin upon the people so declared to be free to abstain from all violence, unless in necessary self-defense; and I recommend to them that, in all cases when allowed, they labor faithfully for reasonable wages.

And I further declare and make known that such persons of suitable condition will be received into the armed service of the United States. . . .

Abraham Lincoln

Members of 4th U.S. Infantry

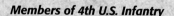

The Gettysburg Address

On November 19, 1863, President Abraham Lincoln gave a short speech at the dedication of a national cemetery on the battlefield of Gettysburg. His simple yet eloquent words expressed his hopes for a nation divided by civil war.

Four score and seven years ago our fathers brought forth on this continent a new nation, conceived in liberty, and dedicated to the proposition that all men are created equal.

Now we are engaged in a great civil war, testing whether that nation or any nation so conceived and so dedicated can long endure. We are met on a great battlefield of that war. We have come to dedicate a portion of that field as a final resting place for those who here gave their lives that that nation might live. It is altogether fitting and proper that we should do this.

But, in a larger sense, we can not dedicate—we can not consecrate—we can not hallow—this ground. The brave men, living and dead, who struggled here have consecrated it far beyond our poor power to add or detract. The world will little note nor long remember what we say here, but it can never forget what they did here. It is for us, the living, rather, to be dedicated here to the unfinished work which they who fought here have thus far so nobly advanced.

It is rather for us to be here dedicated to the great task remaining before us—that from these honored dead we take increased devotion to that cause for which they gave the last full measure of devotion; that we here highly resolve that these dead shall not have died in vain; that this nation, under God, shall have a new birth of freedom; and that government of the people, by the people, and for the people, shall not perish from the earth.

Soldier's kit, Civil War

Gettysburg Memorial

I Will Fight No More

In 1877 the Nez Perce fought the government's attempt to move them to a smaller reservation. After a remarkable attempt to escape to Canada, Chief Joseph realized that resistance was hopeless and advised his people to surrender.

Tell General Howard I know his heart. What he told me before I have in my heart. I am tired of fighting. Our chiefs are killed. Looking Glass is dead. It is the young men who say yes or no. He who led the young men is dead. It is cold and we have no blankets. The little children are freezing to death. My people, some of them have run away to the hills and have no blankets, no food; no one knows where they are—perhaps freezing to death. I want to have time to look for my children and see how many I can find. Maybe I shall find them among the dead. Hear me my chiefs. I am tired; my heart is sick and sad. From where the sun now stands, I will fight no more forever.

Shield made of buffalo hide

The Pledge of Allegiance

In 1892 the nation celebrated the 400th anniversary of Columbus's landing in America. In connection with this celebration, Francis Bellamy, a magazine editor, wrote and published the Pledge of Allegiance. The words "under God" were added by Congress in 1954 at the urging of President Dwight D. Eisenhower.

I pledge allegiance to the Flag of the United States of America and to the Republic for which it stands, one Nation under God, indivisible, with liberty and justice for all.

Students in a New York City school recite the Pledge of Allegiance

The Fourteen Points

On January 8, 1918, President Woodrow Wilson went before Congress to offer a statement of aims called the Fourteen Points. Wilson's plan called for freedom of the seas in peace and war, an end to secret alliances, and equal trading rights for all countries. The excerpt that follows is taken from the President's message.

. . . We entered this war because violations of right had occurred which touched us to the quick and made the life of our own people impossible unless they were corrected and the world secured once for all against their recurrence. What we demand in this war, therefore, is nothing peculiar to ourselves. It is that the world be made fit and safe to live in; and particularly that it be made safe for every peace-loving nation which, like our own, wishes to live its own life, determine its own institutions, be assured of justice and fair dealings by the other peoples of the world, as against force and selfish aggression. All the peoples of the world are in effect partners in this interest, and for our own part we see very clearly that unless justice be done to others it will not be done to us.

The program of the world's peace, therefore, is our program, and that program, the only possible program, as we see it, is this:

I. Open covenants of peace, openly arrived at, after which there shall be no private international understandings of any kind, but diplomacy shall proceed always frankly and in the public view.

II. Absolute freedom of navigation upon the seas, outside territorial waters, alike in peace and in war, except as the seas may be closed in whole or in part by international action for the enforcement of international covenants.

III. The removal, so far as possible, of all economic barriers and the establishment of an equality of trade conditions among all the nations consenting to the peace and associating themselves for its maintenance.

IV. Adequate guarantees given and taken that national armaments will be reduced to the lowest point consistent with domestic safety.

V. Free, open-minded, and absolutely impartial adjustment of all colonial claims, based upon a strict observance of the principle that in determining all such questions of sovereignty the interests of the population concerned must have equal weight with the equitable claims of the Government whose title is to be determined. . . .

XIV. A general association of nations must be formed under specific covenants for the purpose of affording mutual guarantees of political independence and territorial integrity to great and small states alike. . . .

Leaders (left to right) David Lloyd George of Great Britain, Vittorio Orlando of Italy, Georges Clemenceau of France, and Woodrow Wilson of the United States

Brown v. Board of Education

On May 17, 1954, the Supreme Court ruled in Brown *v.* Board of Education *that racial segregation in public schools was unconstitutional. This decision provided the legal basis for court challenges to segregation in every aspect of American life.*

The plaintiffs contend that segregated public schools are not "equal" and cannot be made "equal," and that hence they are deprived of the equal protection of the laws. Because of the obvious importance of the question presented, the Court took jurisdiction. . . .

Our decision . . . cannot turn on merely a comparison of these tangible factors in the Negro and white schools involved in each of the cases. We must look instead to the effect of segregation itself on public education.

In approaching this problem, we cannot turn the clock back to 1868 when the Amendment was adopted, or even to 1896 when *Plessy* v. *Ferguson* was written. We must consider public education in the light of its full development and its present place in American life throughout the nation. Only in this way can it be determined if segregation in public schools deprives these plaintiffs of the equal protection of the laws.

Today, education is perhaps the most important function of state and local governments. Compulsory school attendance laws and the great expenditures for education both demonstrate our recognition of the importance of education to our democratic society. . . . In these days, it is doubtful that any child may reasonably be expected to succeed in life if he is denied the opportunity of an education. Such an opportunity, where the state has undertaken to provide it, is a right which must be made available to all on equal terms.

Troops escort students to newly integrated school.

We come then to the question presented: Does segregation of children in public schools solely on the basis of race, even though the physical facilities and other "tangible" factors may be equal, deprive the children of the minority group of equal educational opportunities? We believe that it does.

. . . We conclude that in the field of public education the doctrine of "separate but equal" has no place. Separate educational facilities are inherently unequal. Therefore, we hold that the plaintiffs and others similarly situated for whom the actions have been brought are, by reason of the segregation complained of, deprived of the equal protection of the laws guaranteed by the Fourteenth Amendment. . . .

John F. Kennedy's Inaugural Address

President Kennedy's Inaugural Address on January 20, 1961, set the tone for his administration. In his address Kennedy stirred the nation by calling for "a grand and global alliance" to fight tyranny, poverty, disease, and war.

We observe today not a victory of party but a celebration of freedom—symbolizing an end as well as a beginning—signifying renewal as well as change. For I have sworn before you and Almighty God the same solemn oath our forebears prescribed nearly a century and three-quarters ago.

The world is very different now. For man holds in his mortal hands the power to abolish all forms of human poverty and all forms of human life. And yet the same revolutionary beliefs for which our forebears fought are still at issue around the globe—the belief that the rights of man come not from the generosity of the state but from the hand of God.

We dare not forget today that we are the heirs of that first revolution. Let the word go forth from this time and place, to friend and foe alike, that the torch has been passed to a new generation of Americans born in this century, tempered by war, disciplined by a hard and bitter peace, proud of our ancient heritage—and unwilling to witness or permit the slow undoing of those human rights to which this nation has always been committed, and to which we are committed today at home and around the world.

Let every nation know, whether it wishes us well or ill, that we shall pay any price, bear any burden, meet any hardship, support any friend, oppose any foe to assure the survival and the success of liberty.

This much we pledge—and more.

To those old allies whose cultural and spiritual origins we share, we pledge the loyalty of faithful friends. United, there is little we cannot do in a host of cooperative ventures. Divided, there is little we can do. . . .

Let us never negotiate out of fear. But let us never fear to negotiate. . . . Let both sides explore what problems unite us instead of belaboring those problems which divide us. . . . Let both sides seek to invoke the wonders of science instead of its terrors. Together let us explore the stars, conquer the deserts, eradicate disease, tap the ocean depths, and encourage the arts and commerce. . . .

And so, my fellow Americans—ask not what your country can do for you—ask what you can do for your country.

My fellow citizens of the world—ask not what America will do for you but what together we can do for the freedom of man.

President Kennedy speaking at his inauguration

I Have a Dream

On August 28, 1963, while Congress debated wide-ranging civil rights legislation, Martin Luther King, Jr., led more than 200,000 people in a march on Washington, D.C. On the steps of the Lincoln Memorial he gave a stirring speech in which he eloquently spoke of his dreams for African Americans and for the United States. Excerpts of the speech follow.

. . . There are those who are asking the devotees of civil rights, "When will you be satisfied?"

We can never be satisfied as long as the Negro is the victim of the unspeakable horrors of police brutality. . . .We cannot be satisfied as long as the Negro's basic mobility is from a smaller ghetto to a larger one. We can never be satisfied as long as a Negro in Mississippi cannot vote and a Negro in New York believes he has nothing for which to vote. . . .

I say to you today, my friends, that in spite of the difficulties and frustrations of the moment I still have a dream. It is a dream deeply rooted in the American dream.

I have a dream that one day this nation will rise up and live out the true meaning of its creed, "We hold these truths to be self-evident, that all men are created equal."

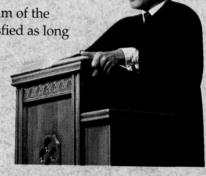

Martin Luther King, Jr.

I have a dream that one day on the red hills of Georgia the sons of former slaves and the sons of former slaveowners will be able to sit down together at the table of brotherhood.

I have a dream that one day even the state of Mississippi, a desert state sweltering with the heat of injustice and oppression, will be transformed into an oasis of freedom and justice.

I have a dream that my four little children will one day live in a nation where they will not be judged by the color of their skin, but by the content of their character. . . .

. . . When we let freedom ring, when we let it ring from every village and every hamlet, from every state and every city, we will be able to speed up that day when all of God's children, black men and white men, Jews and Gentiles, Protestants and Catholics, will be able to join hands and sing in the words of the old Negro spiritual: "Free at last! Free at last! Thank God Almighty, we are free at last!"

The March on Washington

The gazetteer is a geographical dictionary that lists political divisions, natural features, and other places and locations. Following each entry is a description, its latitude and longitude, and a page reference that indicates where each entry may be found in this text.

A

Abilene city in Kansas (39°N/97°W) 531

Africa continent of the Eastern Hemisphere south of the Mediterranean Sea and adjoining Asia on its northeastern border (10°N/22°E) 40

Alabama state in the southeastern United States; 22nd state to enter the Union (33°N/87°W) 314

Alamo Texas mission captured by Mexican forces in 1836 (29°N/98°W) 364

Alaska state in the United States, located in northwestern North America (64°N/150°W) 633

Albany capital of New York State located in the Hudson Valley; site where Albany Congress proposed first formal plan to unite the 13 colonies (42°N/74°W) 85

Allegheny River river in western Pennsylvania uniting with the Monongahela River at Pittsburgh to form the Ohio River (41°N/79°W) 122

Andes Mountains mountain system extending along western coast of South America (13°S/75°W) 26

Antietam Civil War battle site in western Maryland (40°N/77°W) 471

Appalachian Mountains chief mountain system in eastern North America extending from Quebec and New Brunswick to central Alabama (37°N/82°W) 60

Appomattox Court House site in central Virginia where Confederate forces surrendered ending the Civil War (37°N/78°W) 488

Arizona state in the southwestern United States; 48th state to enter the Union (34°N/113°W) 27

Arkansas state in the south central U.S.; acquired as part of Louisiana Purchase (35°N/94°W) 314

Asia continent of the Eastern Hemisphere forming a single landmass with Europe (50°N/100°E) 42

Atlanta capital of Georgia located in the northwest central part of the state (34°N/84°W) 419

Atlantic Ocean ocean separating North and South America from Europe and Africa (5°S/25°W) RA14

Australia continent and country southeast of Asia (25°S/125°E) 42

Austria-Hungary former monarchy in central Europe (47°N/12°E) 656

B

Baltimore city on the Chesapeake Bay in central Maryland (39°N/77°W) 89

Barbary Coast north coast of Africa between Morocco and Tunisia (35°N/3°E) 289

Bay of Pigs site of 1961 invasion of Cuba by U.S.-trained Cuban exiles (22°N/79°W) 848

Beijing capital of China located in the northeastern part of the country (40°N/116°E) 638

Belgium country in northwest Europe (51°N/3°E) 657

Bering Strait waterway between North America and Asia where a land bridge once existed (65°N/170°W) 18

Beringia land bridge that linked Asia and North America during the last Ice Age (65°N/170°W) 17

Berlin city in east central Germany; former capital divided into sectors after World War II (53°N/13°E) 758

Birmingham city in north central Alabama; scene of several civil rights protests (33°N/86°W) 832

Black Hills mountains in southwestern South Dakota; site of conflict between the Sioux and white settlers during 1870s (44°N/104°W) 541

Boston capital of Massachusetts located in the eastern part of the state; founded by English Puritans in 1630 (42°N/71°W) 80

Brazil country in eastern South America (9°S/53°W) 47

Breed's Hill site near Boston where the Battle of Bunker Hill took place (42°N/71°W) 146

Buffalo industrial city and rail center in New York State (43°N/79°W) 313

Bull Run site of two Civil War battles in northern Virginia; also called Manassas (39°N/77°W) 466

C

Cahokia fur trading post in Illinois during the Revolution (39°N/90°W) 29

California state in the western United States; attracted thousands of miners during gold rush of 1849 (38°N/121°W) 369

Cambodia country in Southeastern Asia bordering Gulf of Siam; official name Democratic Kampuchea (12°N/105°E) 855

Canada country in northern North America (50°N/100°W) 62

Cape of Good Hope southern tip of Africa (34°S/18°E) 44

Caribbean Sea tropical sea in the Western Hemisphere (15°N/75°W) 19

Central America area of North America between Mexico and South America (11°N/86°W) 19

Chancellorsville site of 1863 Confederate victory (38°N/78°W) 483

Charleston city in South Carolina on the Atlantic coast; original name Charles Town (33°N/80°W) 90

Chesapeake Bay inlet of the Atlantic Ocean in Virginia and Maryland (38°N/76°W) 72

Chicago largest city in Illinois; located in northeastern part of the state along Lake Michigan (42°N/88°W) 314

Chile South American country (35°S/72°W) 885

China country in eastern Asia; mainland (People's Republic of China) under communist control since 1949 (37°N/93°E) 638

Chisholm Trail pioneer cattle trail from Texas to Kansas (34°N/98°W) 532

Cincinnati city in southern Ohio on the Ohio River; grew as a result of increasing steamship traffic during the mid-1800s (39°N/84°W) 264

Cleveland city in northern Ohio on Lake Erie (41°N/82°W) 419

Colombia country in South America (4°N/73°W) 24

Colorado state in the western United States (39°N/107°W) 510

Colorado River river that flows from the Colorado Rockies to the Gulf of California (36°N/113°W) 52

Columbia River river flowing through southwest Canada and northwestern United States into the Pacific Ocean (46°N/120°W) 284

Concord village northwest of Boston, Massachusetts; site of early battle of the American Revolution (42°N/71°W) 144

Connecticut state in the northeastern United States; one of the original 13 states (42°N/73°W) 81

Cuba country in the West Indies, North America (22°N/79°W) 52

Czechoslovakia former country in central Europe; now two countries, the Czech Republic and Slovakia (49°N/16°E) 676

Gazetteer

Dallas a leading city in Texas (33°N/97°W) 828

Delaware state in the northeastern United States; one of the original 13 states (39°N/75°W) 85

Detroit city in southeastern Michigan; site of significant battles during the French and Indian War and the War of 1812; center of automobile industry (42°N/83°W) 296

Dien Bien Phu site in northwestern Vietnam where French troops were defeated by Vietminh troops in 1954 (21°N/102°E) 868

Dodge City Kansas cattle town during the 19th century (37°N/100°W) 531

Dominican Republic country in the West Indies on the eastern part of Hispaniola Island (19°N/71°W) 47

Dust Bowl area of the Great Plains where the drought of the 1930s turned the soil to wind-borne dust (37°N/98°W) 729

East Germany country in central Europe; reunified with West Germany in 1990 (52°N/12°E) 776

Egypt country in northeastern Africa (27°N/27°E) 756

England division of the United Kingdom of Great Britain and Northern Ireland (52°N/2°W) 48

Erie Canal the waterway connecting the Hudson River with Lake Erie through New York State (43°N/76°W) 316

Ethiopia country in eastern Africa, north of Somalia and Kenya (8°N/38°E) 742

Europe continent of the northern part of the Eastern Hemisphere between Asia and the Atlantic Ocean (50°N/15°E) 48

Florida state in the southeastern United States (30°N/85°W) 322

Fort McHenry fort in Baltimore harbor; inspired poem that later became "The Star-Spangled Banner" (39°N/76°W) 298

Fort Necessity Pennsylvania fort built by George Washington's troops in 1754 (40°N/80°W) 119

Fort Sumter Union fort during the Civil War located on island near Charleston, South Carolina; site of first military engagement of Civil War (33°N/80°W) 457

Fort Ticonderoga British fort on Lake Champlain (44°N/73°W) 147, 166

France country in western Europe (50°N/1°E) 48

Fredericksburg city and Civil War battle site in northeast Virginia (38°N/77°W) 482

Freeport city in northern Illinois; site of 1858 Lincoln-Douglas campaign debate (42°N/89°W) 451

Gadsden Purchase portion of present-day Arizona and New Mexico; area purchased from Mexico in 1853 (32°N/111°W) 375

Galveston city on the Gulf of Mexico coast in Texas; created nation's first commission form of city government (29°N/95°W) 604

Gaza Strip narrow coastal strip along the Mediterranean (31°N/34°E) 884

Georgia state in the southeastern United States (33°N/84°W) 92

Germany country in central Europe; divided after World War II into East Germany and West Germany; unified in 1990 (50°N/10°E) 655

Gettysburg city and Civil War battle site in south central Pennsylvania; site where Lincoln delivered the Gettysburg Address (40°N/77°W) 483

Great Britain commonwealth comprising England, Scotland, and Wales (56°N/2°W) 655

Great Lakes chain of five lakes, Superior, Erie, Michigan, Ontario, and Huron, in central North America (45°N/87°W) 61

Great Plains flat grassland in the central United States (45°N/104°W) 389

Great Salt Lake lake in northern Utah with no outlet and strongly saline waters (41°N/113°W) 379

Greece country in southeastern Europe (39°N/21°E) 775

Greensboro northern North Carolina city; scene of sit-ins to protest segregation (36°N/80°W) 830

Grenada country in the Caribbean (12°N/61°W) 907

Guadalcanal island in the Solomons east of Australia (10°S/159°E) 763

Guam U.S. possession in the western Pacific Ocean (14°N/143°E) 643

Guatemala country in Central America, south of Mexico (16°N/92°W) 21

Gulf of Mexico gulf on the southeast coast of North America (25°N/94°W) 26

Gulf of Tonkin gulf in South China Sea east of northern Vietnam (20°N/108°E) 855

Haiti country on Hispaniola Island in the West Indies (19°N/72°W) 47

Hanoi capital of Vietnam (21°N/106°E) 868

Harlem northern section of Manhattan in New York City; cultural center of African Americans in the early and mid-1900s (41°N/74°W) 705

Harpers Ferry town in northern West Virginia on the Potomac River (39°N/78°W) 452

Hartford capital of Connecticut located along the Connecticut River (42°N/73°W) 81

Hawaii state in the United States located in the Pacific Ocean (20°N/157°W) 635

Hiroshima city in southern Japan; site of first military use of atomic bomb, August 6, 1945 (34°N/132°E) 764

Hispaniola island in the West Indies in North America (17°N/73°W) 52

Horseshoe Bend Alabama site where Creek-U.S. battled in 1814 (33°N/86°W) 297

Hudson Bay large bay in northern Canada (60°N/86°W) 62

Hudson River river flowing through New York State (53°N/74°W) 315

Hungary country in central Europe (47°N/20°E) 676

Idaho state in the northwestern U.S.; ranks among top states in silver production (44°N/115°W) 537

Illinois state in the north central United States; one of the states formed in the Northwest Territory (40°N/91°W) 193

Indian Territory land reserved by the United States government for Native Americans, now the state of Oklahoma (36°N/98°W) 342

Indiana state in the north central United States; one of the states formed in the Northwest Territory (40°N/87°W) 193

Indochina region in Southeast Asia (17°N/105°E) 748

Iowa state in the north central U.S. acquired as part of the Louisiana Purchase (42°N/94°W) 419

Iran country in southwestern Asia (31°N/53°E) 756

Iraq country in southwestern Asia (32°N/42°E) 756

Ireland island west of England, occupied by the Republic of Ireland and by Northern Ireland (54°N/8°W) 756

Israel country of the Middle East in southwestern Asia along the Mediterranean Sea (33°N/34°E) 779

Italy country in southern Europe along the Mediterranean (44°N/11°E) 655

Jackson Mississippi capital (32°N/90°W) 831

Jamestown first permanent English settlement in North America; located in southeastern Virginia (37°N/77°W) 72

Japan island country in eastern Asia (36°N/133°E) 632

Kansas state in the central United States; fighting over slavery issue in 1850s gave territory the name "Bleeding Kansas" (38°N/99°W) 400

Kentucky state in the south central United States; border state that sided with the Union during the Civil War (37°N/87°W) 283

Korea peninsula in eastern Asia between China, Russia, and the Sea of Japan, on which are located the countries North Korea and South Korea (38°N/127°E) 785

Kuwait country of the Middle East in southwestern Asia between Iraq and Saudi Arabia (29°N/49°E) 916

Lake Erie one of the five Great Lakes between Canada and the U.S. (42°N/81°W) 60

Lake Huron one of the five Great Lakes between Canada and the U.S. (45°N/83°W) 60

Lake Michigan one of the five Great Lakes between Canada and the U.S. (43°N/87°W) 60

Lake Ontario the smallest of the five Great Lakes (43°N/79°W) 60

Lake Superior the largest of the five Great Lakes (48°N/89°W) 60

Laos southeast Asian country, south of China and west of Vietnam (20°N/102°E) 852

Latin America Central and South America; settled by Spain and Portugal (14°N/90°W) 848

Lexington Revolutionary War battle site in eastern Massachusetts; site of first clash between colonists and British, April 19, 1775 (42°N/71°W) 144

Leyte island of the east central Philippines, north of Mindanao (10°N/125°E) 763

Little Rock capital of Arkansas located in the center of the state; site of 1957 conflict over public school integration (35°N/92°W) 419

London capital of United Kingdom located in the southeastern part of England (51°N/0°) 72

Los Angeles city along Pacific coast in southern California; industrial, financial, and trade center of western United States (34°N/118°W) 358

Louisiana state in the south central United States (31°N/93°W) 298

Louisiana Territory region of west central United States between the Mississippi River and the Rocky Mountains purchased from France in 1803 (40°N/95°W) 134

Lowell city in Massachusetts (43°N/83°W) 390

Maine state in the northeastern United States; 23rd state to enter the Union (45°N/70°W) 320

Mali country in Western Africa (16°N/0°) 40

Manchuria region of northeast China; invaded by Japan in 1931 (48°N/125°E) 743

Manila capital and largest city of the Philippines located on southwest Luzon Island and Manila Bay (14°N/121°E) 642

Maryland state in the eastern United States; one of the original 13 states (39°N/76°W) 88

Massachusetts state in the northeastern United States; one of the original 13 states (42°N/72°W) 73

Massachusetts Bay Colony Pilgrim settlements along the Charles River (42°N/71°W) 80

Mediterranean Sea sea between Europe and Africa (36°N/13°E) 38

Memphis Tennessee city on the Mississippi River near the Mississippi border (35°N/90°W) 484

Mexican Cession territory gained by the United States after war with Mexico in 1848 (37°N/111°W) 375

Mexico country in North America south of the United States (24°N/104°W) 21

Mexico City capital and most populous city of Mexico (19°N/99°W) 23

Michigan state in the north central United States; one of the states formed in the Northwest Territory (45°N/85°W) 193

Midway Islands U.S. possession in the central Pacific Ocean (28°N/179°W) 763

Milwaukee city in eastern Wisconsin (43°N/88°W) 597

Minnesota state in the north central United States; fur trade, good soil, and lumber attracted early settlers (46°N/96°W) 408

Mississippi state in the southeastern United States; became English territory after French and Indian War (32°N/90°W) 314

Mississippi River river flowing through the United States from Minnesota to the Gulf of Mexico; explored by French in 1600s (29°N/89°W) 53

Missouri state in the south central U.S.; petition for statehood resulted in sectional conflict and the Missouri Compromise (41°N/93°W) 314

Missouri River river flowing through the United States from the Rocky Mountains to the Mississippi River near St. Louis (39°N/90°W) 117

Montana state in the northwestern United States; cattle industry grew during 1850s (47°N/112°W) 527

Montgomery capital of Alabama located in the central part of the state; site of 1955 bus boycott to protest segregation (32°N/86°W) 824

Montreal city along the St. Lawrence River in southern Quebec, Canada (45°N/73°W) 60

Moscow capital of former Soviet Union and capital of Russia (56°N/37°E) 757

Nagasaki Japanese city; site of the second atom-bombing in 1945, ending World War II (32°N/130°E) 764

Nashville capital of Tennessee located in the north central part of the state (36°N/87°W) 419

Natchez city in western Mississippi along the Mississippi River (32°N/91°W) 314

National Road road from Baltimore, Maryland, to Vandalia, Illinois (40°N/81°W) 314

Nebraska state in the central United States (42°N/101°W) 400

Netherlands country in northwestern Europe (53°N/4°E) 48

Nevada state in the western United States (39°N/117°W) 510

New Amsterdam town founded on Manhattan Island by Dutch settlers in 1625; renamed New York by British settlers (41°N/74°W) 84

New England region in northeastern United States (42°N/72°W) 79

New France French land claims stretching from Quebec to Louisiana (39°N/85°W) 94

Gazetteer

New Hampshire state in the northeastern United States; one of the original 13 states (44°N/72°W) 81

New Jersey state in the northeastern United States; one of the original 13 states (40°N/75°W) 86

New Mexico state in the southwestern United States; ceded to the United States by Mexico in 1848 (34°N/107°W) 368

New Netherland Dutch Hudson River colony (42°N/72°W) 84

New Orleans city in Louisiana in the Mississippi Delta (30°N/90°W) 95

New Spain part of Spain's empire in the Western Hemisphere (35°N/110°W) 95

New York state in the northeastern United States; one of the original 13 states (43°N/78°W) 85

New York City city in southeastern New York State at the mouth of the Hudson River; first capital of nation (41°N/74°W) 86

Newfoundland province in eastern Canada (48°N/56°W) 46

Nicaragua country in Central America (13°N/86°W) 696

Normandy region along French coast and site of D-Day invasion, June 6, 1944 (48°N/2°W) 757

North America continent in the northern part of the Western Hemisphere between the Atlantic and Pacific oceans (45°N/100°W) 19

North Carolina state in the southeastern United States; one of the original 13 states (36°N/81°W) 89

North Dakota state in the north central U.S.; Congress created Dakota Territory in 1861 (47°N/102°W) 284

North Korea Asian country on the northern Korean Peninsula (40°N/127°E) 785

North Vietnam communist nation in Southeast Asia; unified with South Vietnam (21°N/106°E) 853

Northwest Territory territory north of the Ohio River and east of the Mississippi River (47°N/87°W) 193

Ohio state in the north central United States; first state in the Northwest Territory (40°N/83°W) 193

Ohio River river flowing from Allegheny and Monongahela rivers in western Pennsylvania into the Mississippi River (37°N/85°W) 117

Oklahoma state in the south central United States; Five Civilized Tribes moved to territory in the period 1830–1842 (36°N/98°W) 400

Oregon state in the northwestern United States; adopted woman suffrage in 1912 (44°N/124°W) 355

Oregon Trail pioneer trail from Independence, Missouri, to the Oregon Territory (42°N/110°W) 357

Pacific Ocean world's largest ocean located between Asia and the Americas (0°/175°W) 19

Palestine region or country in southwest Asia between the Mediterranean Sea and the Jordan River; area sometimes called the Holy Land (32°N/35°E) 779

Panama country in the southern part of Central America, occupying the Isthmus of Panama (8°N/81°W) 646

Panama Canal canal built across the Isthmus of Panama through Panama to connect the Caribbean Sea and the Pacific Ocean (9°N/80°W) 647

Pearl Harbor naval base at Honolulu, Hawaii; site of 1941 Japanese attack, leading to United States entry into World War II (21°N/158°W) 636

Pennsylvania state in the northeastern United States (41°N/78°W) 85

Persian Gulf gulf in southwestern Asia between Iran and the Arabian Peninsula (28°N/50°E) 916

Peru country in South America, south of Ecuador and Colombia (10°S/75°W) 26

Philadelphia city in eastern Pennsylvania on the Delaware River; Declaration of Independence and the Constitution both adopted in city's Independence Hall (40°N/75°W) 85

Philippines island country in southeast Asia (14°N/125°E) 641

Pikes Peak mountain in Rocky Mountains in central Colorado (38°N/105°W) 283

Pittsburgh city in western Pennsylvania; one of the great steelmaking centers of the world (40°N/80°W) 563

Plymouth town in eastern Massachusetts, first successful English colony in New England (42°N/71°W) 78

Poland country on the Baltic Sea in Eastern Europe (52°N/18°E) 744

Portugal country in southwestern Europe (38°N/8°W) 48

Potomac River river flowing from West Virginia into Chesapeake Bay (38°N/77°W) 89

Providence capital of Rhode Island; site of first English settlement in Rhode Island (42°N/71°W) 81

Puerto Rico United States possession in the West Indies (18°N/67°W) 52

Pullman a company town south of Chicago; site of 1897 railroad strike (42°N/87°W) 568

Quebec city in Canada, capital of Quebec Province, on the St. Lawrence River; first settlement in New France (47°N/71°W) 94

Rhode Island state in the northeastern United States; one of the original 13 states (41°N/72°W) 81

Richmond capital of Virginia located in the central part of the state; capital of the Confederacy during the Civil War (37°N/77°W) 406

Rio Grande river between the United States and Mexico in north America; forms the boundary between Texas and Mexico (26°N/97°W) 52

Roanoke island off the coast of present-day North Carolina that was site of early British colonizing efforts (35°N/76°W) 72

Rocky Mountains mountain range in western United States and Canada in North America (50°N/114°W) 284

Russia name of republic; former empire of eastern Europe and northern Asia-coinciding with Soviet Union (60°N/64°E) 633

S

Sacramento capital of California located in the north central part of the state (38°N/121°W) 358

Saigon present-day Ho Chi Minh City; former capital of South Vietnam (11°N/106°E) 862

Salt Lake City capital of Utah located in the northern part of the state; founded by Mormons in 1847 (41°N/112°W) 379

San Antonio city in south central Texas (29°N/98°W) 365

San Diego city in southern California (33°N/117°W) 96

San Francisco city in northern California on the Pacific coast (38°N/122°W) 358

Santa Fe capital of New Mexico located in the north central part of the state (36°N/106°W) 358

Santa Fe Trail cattle trail from Independence, Missouri, to Santa Fe, New Mexico (36°N/106°W) 358

Saratoga Revolutionary War battle site in the Hudson Valley of eastern New York State (43°N/74°W) 169

Savannah city in far eastern Georgia (32°N/81°W) 89

Seattle Washington city bordered by Puget Sound and Lake Washington (47°N/122°W) RA6

Selma Alabama city; site of a 1965 voter-registration drive (32°N/87°W) 833

Seneca Falls town in New York State; site of women's rights convention in 1848 (43°N/77°W) 425

Shiloh site of 1862 Union victory in Tennessee (35°N/88°W) 469

Sicily Italian island in the Mediterranean (37°N/13°E) 756

Sierra Nevada mountain range in eastern California (39°N/120°W) 358

Sinai Peninsula peninsula in the Middle East separating Egypt from Israel (29°N/34°E) 884

South America continent in the southern part of the Western Hemisphere lying between the Atlantic and Pacific oceans (15°S/60°W) 19

South Carolina state in the southeastern United States; one of the original 13 states (34°N/81°W) 89

South Dakota state in the north central United States; acquired through the Louisiana Purchase (44°N/102°W) 527

South Korea country in Asia on the Korean Peninsula (36°N/128°E) 785

South Vietnam country in Southeast Asia united in 1976 with North Vietnam to form Vietnam (11°N/107°E) 853

Soviet Union former country in northern Europe and Asia (60°N/64°E) 743

Spain country in southwestern Europe (40°N/4°W) 48

St. Augustine city in northeastern Florida on the Atlantic coast; oldest permanent existing European settlement in North America, founded in 1565 (30°N/81°W) 52

St. Lawrence River river flowing from Lake Ontario, between Canada and the United States, through parts of Canada to the Atlantic Ocean (48°N/69°W) 60

Stalingrad city in the former Soviet Union on the Volga River; present name Volgograd (49°N/42°E) 757

Sudetenland region in northwest Czechoslovakia; taken by Hitler's forces in 1938 (50°N/18°E) 743

Suez Canal canal built between the Mediterranean Sea and the Red Sea through northeastern Egypt (31°N/32°E) 755

Switzerland European country in the Alps (47°N/8°E) 93

Taiwan island country off the southeast coast of China; seat of the Chinese Nationalist government (24°N/122°E) 779

Tehran capital of Iran (36°N/52°E) 900

Tennessee state in the south central United States; first state readmitted to the Union after the Civil War (36°N/88°W) 283

Tenochtitlán Aztec capital on the site of present-day Mexico City (19°N/99°W) 23

Texas state in the south central United States; Mexican colony that became a republic before joining the United States (31°N/101°W) 365

Tokyo capital of Japan located on the eastern coast of Honshu Island (36°N/140°E) 763

Toronto city in Canada on Lake Ontario; capital of the province of Ontario (44°N/79°W) RA12

Trenton capital of New Jersey located on the Delaware River in the central part of the state; site of Revolutionary War battle in December 1776 (40°N/75°W) 167

Union of Soviet Socialist Republics *See* Soviet Union.

United Kingdom country in northwestern Europe made up of England, Scotland, Wales, and Northern Ireland (56°N/2°W) 774

United States country in central North America; fourth largest country in the world in both area and population (38°N/110°W) RA6

Utah state in the western United States; settled by Mormons in 1840s (39°N/113°W) 379

Valley Forge Revolutionary War winter camp northwest of Philadelphia (40°N/75°W) 172

Venezuela South American country on the Caribbean Sea (8°N/65°W) 648

Vermont state in the northeastern United States; 14th state to enter the Union (44°N/73°W) 191

Vicksburg city and Civil War battle site in western Mississippi on the Mississippi River (42°N/85°W) 484

Vietnam country in southeastern Asia (16°N/108°E) 852

Virginia state in the eastern United States; colony of first permanent English settlement in the Americas (37°N/80°W) 73

Wake Island island in the central Pacific Ocean; annexed by United States in 1898 (19°N/167°E) 761

Washington state in the northwestern United States; territory reached by Lewis and Clark in 1805 (47°N/121°W) 527

Washington, D.C. capital of the United States located on the Potomac River at its confluence with the Anacostia River, between Maryland and Virginia coinciding with the District of Columbia (39°N/77°W) 260

West Indies islands in the Caribbean Sea, between North America and South America (19°N/79°W) 47

West Virginia state in the east central United States (39°N/81°W) 462

Willamette Valley valley of the Willamette River in western Oregon (45°N/123°W) 359

Wisconsin state in the north central United States; passed first state unemployment compensation act, 1932 (44°N/91°W) 193

Wounded Knee site of battle between settlers and Native Americans in southern South Dakota in 1890 and of Native American movement protest in 1973 (43°N/102°W) 543

Wyoming state in the western United States; territory provided women the right to vote, 1869 (43°N/108°W) 531

Yalu River river in eastern Asia, between China and North Korea (41°N/126°E) 787

Yorktown town in southeastern Virginia and site of final battle of Revolutionary War (37°N/76°W) 182

Yugoslavia country in southeast Europe, on the Adriatic Sea (44°N/20°E) 677

Glossary

—————————— **A** ——————————

abolitionist a person who strongly favors doing away with slavery (p. 416)

abstain to not take part in some activity, such as voting (p. 440)

adobe a sun-dried mud brick used to build the homes of Native Americans (p. 31)

affirmative action an active effort to improve educational and employment opportunities for minority groups and women (p. 887)

affluence the state of having much wealth (p. 808)

airlift a system of transporting food and supplies by aircraft into an area otherwise impossible to reach (p. 777)

alien an immigrant living in a country in which he or she is not a citizen (p. 271)

alleged stated as a fact but without proof (p. 791)

alliance system defense agreements among nations (p. 656)

ambush a surprise attack (p. 185)

amendment an addition to a formal document such as the Constitution (pp. 211, 219)

American System policies devised by Henry Clay to stimulate the growth of industry (p. 320)

amnesty the granting of pardon to a large number of persons; protection from prosecution for an illegal act (pp. 496, 893)

anarchist person who believes that there should be no government (p. 689)

anarchy disorder and lawlessness (p. 648)

annex to add a territory to one's own territory (p. 366)

annexation bringing an area under the control of a larger country (p. 637)

anti-Semitism hostility toward or discrimination against Jews (p. 742)

apartheid racial separation and economic and political discrimination against nonwhites, a policy formerly practiced in the Republic of South Africa (p. 898)

appeasement accepting demands in order to avoid conflict (p. 744)

apprentice assistant who is assigned to learn the trade of a skilled craftsman (p. 113)

appropriate to set aside for a particular purpose, especially funds (p. 221)

arbitration settling a dispute by agreeing to accept the decision of an impartial outsider (p. 617)

archaeology the study of ancient peoples (p. 17)

armistice a temporary peace agreement to end fighting (pp. 643, 668)

arms race the competition between the United States and the Soviet Union to build more and more weapons in an effort to surpass the other's military strength (p. 801)

arsenal a storage place for weapons and ammunition (p. 452)

article a part of a document, such as the Constitution, that deals with a single subject (p. 206)

artifact an item left behind by early people that represents their culture (p. 17)

assembly line a production system with machines and workers arranged so that each person performs an assigned task again and again as the item passes before him or her (p. 559)

assimilate to absorb a group into the culture of a larger population (p. 578)

astrolabe an instrument used by sailors to observe positions of stars (p. 39)

autocracy government in which one person has unlimited power (p. 663)

automation a system or process that uses mechanical or electronic devices that replace human workers (p. 814)

—————————— **B** ——————————

baby boom a marked increase in the birthrate, especially in the United States immediately following World War II (p. 808)

backcountry a region of hills and forests west of the Tidewater (p. 108)

balance of power the distribution of power among nations so that no single nation can dominate or interfere with another (p. 882)

bankruptcy the condition of being unable to pay one's debts; one's property is managed or sold to pay those to whom one owes money (p. 916)

barrio a Spanish-speaking neighborhood in a city, especially in the southwest U.S. (p. 627)

bicameral consisting of two houses, or chambers, especially in a legislature (p. 190)

black codes laws passed in the South just after the Civil War aimed at controlling freedmen and enabling plantation owners to exploit African American workers (p. 499)

blacklist list of persons who are disapproved of and are punished, such as by being refused jobs (p. 790)

blitzkrieg name given to the sudden, violent offensive attacks the Germans used during World War II; "lightning war" (p. 745)

blockade cut off an area by means of troops or warships to stop supplies or people from coming in or going out; to close off a country's ports (pp. 177, 463, 850)

blockade runner ship that sails into and out of a blockaded area (p. 467)

bond a note issued by the government, which promises to pay off a loan with interest (p. 259)

boomtown a community experiencing a sudden growth in business or population (p. 377)

border ruffians Missourians who traveled in armed groups to vote in Kansas's election during the mid-1850s (p. 444)

border states the states between the North and the South that were divided over whether to stay in the Union or join the Confederacy (p. 461)

bounty money given as a reward, as to encourage enlistment in the army (p. 479)

boycott to refuse to buy items from a particular country (p. 135); to refuse to use in order to show disapproval or force acceptance of one's terms (p. 824)

brand a symbol burned into an animal's hide to show ownership (p. 531)

budget deficit the amount by which spending exceeds revenue, especially in reference to the government (p. 919)

bureaucracy system in which nonelected officials carry out laws and policies (p. 337)

burgesses elected representatives to an assembly (p. 74)

cabinet a group of advisers to the president (p. 258)

Californios Mexicans who lived in California (p. 374)

canal an artificial waterway (p. 315)

capital money for investment (pp. 306, 399)

capitalism an economic system based on private property and free enterprise (p. 689)

caravel small, fast ship with a broad bow (p. 40)

carbon dating a scientific method used to determine the age of an artifact (p. 20)

carpetbaggers name given to Northern whites who moved South after the war and supported the Republicans (p. 505)

cash crop farm crop raised to be sold for money (pp. 106, 515)

casualty a military person killed, wounded, or captured (p. 469)

caucus a meeting held by a political party to choose their party's candidate for president or decide policy (pp. 269, 337)

cede to give up by treaty (p. 375)

censure to express formal disapproval of some action (p. 792)

census official count of a population (p. 313)

charter a document that gives the holder the right to organize settlements in an area (p. 72)

charter colony colony established by a group of settlers who had been given a formal document allowing them to settle (p. 111)

checks and balances the system in which each branch of government has a check on the other two branches so that no one branch becomes too powerful (pp. 207, 218)

circumnavigate to sail around the world (p. 49)

civil disobedience refusal to obey laws that are considered unjust as a nonviolent way to press for changes (p. 825)

civil service the body of nonelected government workers (p. 605)

civil war conflict between opposing groups of citizens of the same country (p. 445)

civilization a highly developed culture, usually with organized religions and laws (p. 21)

classical relating to ancient Greece and Rome (p. 38)

clipper ship a fast sailing ship with slender lines, tall masts, and large square sails (p. 386)

closed shop a workplace in which the employer by agreement hires only union members (p. 782)

coeducation the teaching of male and female students together (p. 426)

cold war a struggle over political differences between nations carried on by methods short of war (p. 777)

collective bargaining discussion between an employer and union representatives of workers over wages, hours, and working conditions (p. 567)

Columbian Exchange exchange of goods, ideas, and people between Europe and the Americas (p. 55)

commission a group of persons directed to perform some duty (p. 511)

committee of correspondence an organization that used meetings, letters, and pamphlets to spread political ideas through the colonies (p. 139)

compromise agreement between two or more sides in which each side gives up some of what it wants (p. 201)

concurrent powers powers shared by the states and the federal government (p. 218)

Conestoga wagon sturdy vehicle topped with white canvas and used by pioneers to move west (p. 281)

conquistador Spanish explorer in the Americas in the 1500s (p. 50)

conservation the protection and preservation of natural resources (p. 618)

consolidation the practice of combining separate companies into one (p. 551)

constituents people that members of Congress represent (p. 221)

constitution a formal plan of government (pp. 90, 189)

containment the policy or process of preventing the expansion of a hostile power (p. 775)

convoy a group that travels with something, such as a ship, to protect it (p. 665)

cooperative store where farmers bought products from each other; an enterprise owned and operated by those who use its services (p. 545)

corporation a group that is authorized by law to carry on an activity but having the rights and duties of a single person (p. 560)

corruption dishonest or illegal actions (p. 505)

Glossary

cotton gin a machine that removed seeds from cotton fiber (pp. 306, 397)

counterculture a social movement whose values go against those of established society (p. 859)

coup a sudden overthrow of a government by a small group (pp. 854, 912)

coureur de bois French trapper living among Native Americans (p. 62)

court-martial to try by a military court (p. 323)

credibility gap lack of belief; a term used to describe the lack of trust in the Johnson administration's statements about the Vietnam War (p. 863)

credit a form of loan; ability to buy goods based on future payment (p. 402)

culture a way of life of a group of people who share similar beliefs and customs (p. 20)

customs duties taxes on foreign imported goods (p. 279)

debtor person or country that owes money (p. 92)

decree an order or decision given by one in authority (p. 363)

default to fail to meet an obligation, especially a financial one (p. 717)

deferment an excuse, issued by the draft board, that lets a person be excused from military service for various reasons (p. 860)

deficit the shortage that occurs when spending is greater than income (p. 888)

demilitarize to remove armed forces from an area (p. 322)

demilitarized zone a region where no military forces or weapons are permitted (p. 788)

deport to send out of a country aliens who are considered dangerous (pp. 271, 690)

depreciate to fall in value (p. 194)

depression a period of low economic activity and widespread unemployment (pp. 196, 349)

deregulation the act of cutting the restrictions and regulations that government places on business (p. 906)

desert to leave without permission (p. 172)

deserter soldier who runs away from battle or war (p. 167)

détente a policy which attempts to relax or ease tensions between nations (p. 882)

dictator a leader who rules with total authority, often in a cruel or brutal manner (p. 741)

disarmament removal of weapons (pp. 322, 748)

discrimination unfair treatment of a group; unequal treatment because of a person's race, religion, ethnic background, or place of birth (pp. 391, 622)

dissent disagreement with or opposition to an opinion (pp. 78, 672)

diversity variety or difference (p. 107)

dividend a stockholder's share of a company's profits, usually as a cash payment (p. 561)

dollar diplomacy a policy of joining the business interests of a country with its diplomatic interests abroad (p. 649)

domestic tranquility maintaining peace within the nation (p. 215)

domino theory the belief that if one nation in Asia fell to the Communists, neighboring countries would follow (pp. 804, 853)

dove a person who opposes war or warlike policies, such as one who opposed the Vietnam War (p. 860)

draft the selection of persons for required military service (p. 478)

drought a long period of time with little rainfall (p. 28)

dry farming a way of farming dry land in which seeds are planted deep in ground where there is some moisture (p. 535)

due process of law idea that the government must follow procedures established by law and guaranteed by the Constitution (p. 226)

Dust Bowl the name given to the area of the southern Great Plains severely damaged by droughts and dust storms during the 1930s (p. 729)

effigy rag figure representing an unpopular individual (p. 135)

Electoral College a special group of voters selected by their state legislatures to vote for the president and vice president (p. 206)

emancipate to free from slavery (p. 473)

embargo an order prohibiting trade with another country (pp. 291, 884)

emigrant a person who leaves a country or region to live elsewhere (p. 357)

emigrate to leave one's homeland to live elsewhere (p. 576)

empresario a person who arranged for the settlement of land in Texas during the 1800s (p. 363)

encomienda system of rewarding conquistadors with tracts of land and the right to tax and demand labor from Native Americans who lived on the land (p. 54)

Enlightenment movement during the 1700s that spread the idea that knowledge, reason, and science could improve society (p. 205)

entente an understanding between nations (p. 656)

entrenched occupying a strong defensive position (p. 482)

enumerated powers powers belonging only to the federal government (p. 217)

escalate to increase or expand (p. 855)

espionage spying (p. 673)

ethnic group a minority that speaks a different language or follows different customs than the majority of people in a country (p. 576)

evolution the scientific theory that humans and other living things have evolved over time (p. 710)

executive branch the branch of government, headed by the president, that carries out the nation's laws and policies (pp. 206, 218)

executive order a rule issued by a chief executive that has the force of law (p. 848)

exile a person forced to leave his or her country (p. 848)

expansionism a policy that calls for expanding a nation's boundaries (p. 632)

expatriate a person who gives up his or her home country and chooses to live in another country (p. 706)

export a good sold abroad (p. 111)

factory system system bringing manufacturing steps together in one place to increase efficiency (p. 307)

famine an extreme shortage of food (p. 392)

fascism a political system, headed by a dictator, that calls for extreme nationalism and racism and no tolerance of opposition (p. 742)

favorite son candidate that receives the backing of his home state rather than of the national party (p. 333)

federal debt the amount of money owed by the government (p. 906)

federalism the sharing of power between federal and state governments (pp. 205, 217)

Federalists supporters of the Constitution (p. 209)

federation a type of government that links different groups together (p. 32)

feminist a person who advocates or is active in promoting women's rights (pp. 425, 838)

fixed costs regular expenses such as housing or maintaining equipment that remain about the same year after year (p. 402)

flapper a young woman of the 1920s who defied conventions in her behavior and dress (p. 703)

flexible response a plan that used special military units to fight guerrilla wars (p. 847)

forty-niners people who went to California during the gold rush of 1849 (p. 376)

Fourteen Points the peace plan to end World War I and restructure the countries of Europe, proposed by Woodrow Wilson (p. 675)

free silver the unlimited production of silver coins (p. 546)

freedman a person freed from slavery (p. 497)

frigate warship (p. 297)

front a region where warfare is taking place (p. 666)

fugitive runaway or trying to run away (p. 439)

fundamentalist a person who believes in the literal meaning of religious texts and strict obedience to religious laws (p. 900)

genocide the deliberate destruction of a racial, political, or cultural group (p. 758)

ghetto a part of a city in which a minority group lives because of social or economic pressure (p. 814)

ghost town former mining town that became deserted (p. 526)

Gilded Age the name associated with America in the late 1800s, referring to the extravagant wealth and the terrible poverty that lay underneath (p. 586)

glasnost a Soviet policy allowing more open discussion of political and social issues, as well as more widespread news and information (p. 908)

global warming a steady increase in average world temperatures (p. 928)

grandfather clause a clause that allowed individuals who did not pass the literacy test to vote if their fathers or grandfathers had voted before Reconstruction began; an exception to a law based on preexisting circumstances (p. 515)

grassroots society at the local and popular level away from political or cultural centers (p. 918)

greenback a piece of U.S. paper money first issued by the North during the Civil War (p. 480)

gross domestic product the value of all the goods and services produced in a nation during a one-year period (p. 925)

gross national product the total value of all goods and services produced by a nation's residents during a year, regardless of where production takes place (p. 698)

guerrilla referring to surprise attacks or raids rather than organized warfare (p. 346)

guerrilla warfare a hit-and-run technique used in fighting a war; fighting by small bands of warriors using tactics such as sudden ambushes (pp. 179, 847)

habeas corpus a legal order for an inquiry to determine whether a person has been lawfully imprisoned (p. 478)

hawk a person who advocates war or warlike policies, such as a supporter of the Vietnam War (p. 860)

hieroglyphics an ancient form of writing using symbols and pictures to represent words, sounds, and concepts (p. 23)

Hispanic a person from or descended from people who came from the countries of Latin America or Spain (p. 839)

Glossary

Holocaust the name given to the mass slaughter of Jews and other groups by the Nazis during World War II (p. 759)

homestead to acquire a piece of U.S. public land by living on and cultivating it (p. 534)

horizontal integration the combining of competing firms into one corporation (p. 562)

hot line a direct telephone line for emergency use (p. 851)

human rights rights such as freedom from unlawful imprisonment, torture, and execution regarded as belonging to all persons (p. 898)

Hundred Days a special session of Congress that dealt with problems of the Depression (p. 723)

Ice Age a period of extremely cold temperatures when part of the planet's surface was covered with massive ice sheets (p. 17)

impeach to formally charge a public official with misconduct in office (pp. 221, 502, 926)

impeachment charging a public official with misconduct in office; if proven guilty before a designated court, the official is removed from office (p. 890)

imperialism the actions used by one nation to exercise political or economic control over smaller or weaker nations (p. 632)

implied powers powers not specifically mentioned in the Constitution (pp. 220, 268)

import a good bought from foreign markets (p. 111)

impressment forcing people into service, as in the navy (pp. 264, 290)

inauguration the ceremony in which the president takes the oath of office (p. 257)

incumbent someone who currently holds an office or position (p. 926)

indentured servant laborer who agreed to work without pay for a certain period of time in exchange for passage to America (p. 88)

Industrial Revolution the change from an agrarian society to one based on industry which began in Great Britain and spread to the United States around 1800 (p. 306)

inflation a continuous rise in the price of goods and services (pp. 174, 480, 780)

initiative the right of citizens to place a measure or issue before the voters or the legislature for approval (p. 607)

injunction a court order to stop an action, such as a strike (p. 569)

installment buying a system of paying for goods in which customers promise to pay small, regular amounts over a period of time (p. 699)

integrate to end separation of different races and bring into equal membership in society (pp. 507, 822)

interchangeable parts uniform pieces that can be made in large quantities to replace other identical pieces (p. 309)

internal improvements federal projects, such as canals and roads, to develop the nation's transportation system (p. 319)

Internet a worldwide linking of computer networks (p. 927)

internment camps the detention centers where Japanese Americans were moved to and confined during World War II (p. 754)

interstate across state lines; connecting or existing between two or more states (p. 831)

iron curtain the political and military barrier that isolated Soviet-controlled countries of Eastern Europe after World War II (p. 775)

ironclad armored naval vessel (p. 468)

Iroquois Confederacy a powerful group of Native Americans in the eastern part of the United States made up of five nations: the Mohawk, Seneca, Cayuga, Onondaga, and Oneida (p. 117)

island hopping a strategy used during World War II that called for attacking and capturing certain key islands and using these islands as bases to leapfrog to others (p. 763)

isolationism a national policy of avoiding involvement in world affairs (pp. 631, 695)

isthmus a narrow strip of land connecting two larger land areas (p. 646)

joint occupation the possession and settling of an area shared by two or more countries (p. 356)

joint-stock company a company in which investors buy stock in the company in return for a share of its future profits (p. 72)

judicial branch the branch of government, including the federal court system, that interprets the nation's laws (pp. 206, 218)

judicial review the right of the Supreme Court to determine if a law violates the Constitution (pp. 220, 280)

kamikaze during World War II, a Japanese suicide pilot whose mission was to crash into his target (p. 763)

laissez-faire policy that government should interfere as little as possible in the nation's economy (pp. 278, 350, 618)

land-grant college originally, an agricultural college established as a result of the 1862 Morrill Act that gave states large amounts of federal land that could be sold to raise money for education (p. 591)

landslide an overwhelming victory (p. 335)

League of Nations an association of nations to preserve peace and resolve international disputes proposed in Wilson's Fourteen Points (p. 675)

lease to hand over property in return for rent (p. 694)

legislative branch the branch of government that makes the nation's laws (pp. 206, 218)

lend-lease the act passed during World War II allowing the United States to sell, lend, or lease arms or other war supplies to any nation considered "vital to the defense of the United States" (p. 748)

line of demarcation an imaginary line running down the middle of the Atlantic Ocean from the North Pole to the South Pole dividing the Americas between Spain and Portugal (p. 47)

line-item veto the power that allows the president to cancel individual spending items in a budget or bill (p. 920)

literacy the ability to read and write (p. 114)

literacy test a method used to prevent African Americans from voting by requiring prospective voters to read and write at a specified level (p. 515)

lock in a canal, an enclosure with gates at each end used in raising or lowering boats as they pass from level to level (p. 316)

lode a mass or strip of ore sandwiched between layers of rock (p. 525)

log cabin campaign name given to William Henry Harrison's campaign for the presidency in 1840, from the Whigs' use of a log cabin as their symbol (p. 350)

Loyalists American colonists who remained loyal to Britain and opposed the war for independence (pp. 146, 164)

lynching putting to death a person by the illegal action of a mob (p. 516)

M

maize an early form of corn grown by Native Americans (p. 20)

majority more than half (p. 334)

Manifest Destiny the idea popular in the United States during the 1800s that the country must expand its boundaries to the Pacific (p. 359)

manumission the freeing of some enslaved persons (p. 198)

martial law the law applied by military forces in occupied territory or in an emergency (p. 869)

martyr a person who sacrifices his or her life for a principle or cause (p. 452)

mass media types of communication that reach large numbers of people, such as newspapers, radio, and television (p. 703)

mass production the production of large quantities of goods using machinery and often an assembly line (p. 559)

materialism attaching too much importance to physical possessions and comforts (p. 815)

Mayflower Compact a formal document, written in 1620, that provided law and order to the Plymouth colony (p. 79)

Medicaid a social program that gives the states money to help those who cannot afford to pay for their hospital bills (p. 829)

Medicare a social program that helps pay for medical care for the elderly (p. 829)

mercantilism the theory that a state's or nation's power depended on its wealth (pp. 59, 110)

mercenary paid soldier who serves in the army of a foreign country (p. 164)

merger the combining of two or more businesses into one (p. 564)

MIAs soldiers classified as missing in action (p. 871)

migrant worker a person who moves from place to place to find work harvesting fruits and vegetables (p. 730)

migration a movement of a large number of people into a new homeland (p. 18)

militarism a buildup of military strength within a country (p. 656)

militia a group of civilians trained to fight in emergencies (pp. 118, 143)

minutemen companies of civilian soldiers who boasted that they were ready to fight on a minute's notice (p. 143)

mission religious settlement (pp. 54, 96)

mobilization gathering resources and preparing for war (pp. 670, 750)

moderate opposed to major social change or extreme political ideas (p. 798)

monopoly total control of a type of industry by one person or one company (p. 562)

Morse code a system for transmitting messages that uses a series of dots and dashes to represent the letters of the alphabet, numbers, and punctuation (p. 388)

mosque a Muslim house of worship (p. 41)

mountain man a frontiersman living in the wilderness, as in the Rocky Mountains (p. 356)

muckraker a journalist who uncovers abuses and corruption in a society (p. 606)

mudslinging attempt to ruin an opponent's reputation with insults (p. 335)

Glossary

N

national debt the amount of money a national government owes to other governments or its people (p. 259)

National Grange the first farmers' organization in the United States (p. 545)

nationalism loyalty to a nation and promotion of its interests above all others (pp. 294, 655)

nativism the belief that those born in a country are superior to immigrants (p. 709)

nativist a person who favors those born in his country and is opposed to immigrants (p. 393)

neutral taking no side in a conflict (p. 163)

neutral rights the right to sail the seas and not take sides in a war (p. 290)

neutrality a position of not taking sides in a conflict (p. 264)

New Deal the name given to the new laws aimed at relieving the Depression, which were passed by Congress during the Hundred Days and the months that followed (p. 723)

nomadic moving from place to place with no permanent home (p. 538)

nomads people who move from place to place, usually in search of food or grazing land (p. 18)

nominating convention system in which delegates from the states selected the party's presidential candidate (p. 337)

nonimportation an agreement not to import or use certain goods (p. 135)

normal school a two-year school for training high school graduates as teachers (p. 413)

Northwest Passage water route to Asia through North America sought by European explorers (p. 59)

nullify to cancel or make ineffective (pp. 272, 338)

O

offensive position of attacking or the attack itself (p. 464)

on margin to buy stock by paying only a fraction of the stock price and borrowing the rest (p. 715)

Open Door policy a policy that allowed each foreign nation in China to trade freely in the other nations' spheres of influence (p. 638)

open range land not fenced or divided into lots (p. 531)

ordinance a law or regulation (p. 192)

ore a mineral mined for the valuable substance it contains, such as silver (p. 525)

override to overturn or defeat, as a bill proposed in Congress (p. 500)

overseer person who supervises a large operation or its workers (pp. 108, 403)

ozone the layer of gas composed of a form of oxygen that protects the earth and its people from cancer-causing sun rays (p. 928)

P

pacifist person opposed to the use of war or violence to settle disputes (pp. 87, 673)

partisan favoring one side of an issue (p. 267)

patent a document that gives an inventor the sole legal right to an invention for a period of time (p. 307)

Patriots American colonists who were determined to fight the British until American independence was won (pp. 146, 163)

patronage another name for the spoils system, in which government jobs or favors are given out to political allies and friends (p. 604)

patroon landowner in the Dutch colonies who ruled like a king over large areas of land (p. 85)

peaceful coexistence agreement between opposing countries that they will compete with one another but will avoid war (p. 805)

pension a sum paid regularly to a person, usually after retirement (p. 734)

per capita income average income of each person in the nation (p. 808)

perestroika a policy of government and economic reform in the Soviet Union in the mid-1980s (p. 909)

perjury lying when one has sworn an oath to tell the truth (p. 790)

persecute to treat someone harshly because of that person's beliefs or practices (p. 78)

petition a formal request (pp. 149, 192)

philanthropy charitable acts or gifts of money to benefit the community (p. 563)

pilgrimage a journey to a holy place (p. 41)

Pilgrims Separatists who journeyed to the colonies during the 1600s for a religious purpose (p. 79)

plantation a large estate run by an owner or manager and farmed by laborers who lived there (p. 55)

plurality largest single share (p. 334)

political machine an organization linked to a political party that often controlled local government (p. 603)

poll tax a tax of a fixed amount per person that had to be paid before the person could vote (p. 515)

pool a group sharing in some activity, for example, among railroad barons who made secret agreements and set rates among themselves (p. 554)

popular sovereignty political theory that government is subject to the will of the people (p. 216); before the Civil War, the idea that people living in a territory had the right to decide by voting if slavery would be allowed there (p. 443)

Populist Party U.S. political party formed in 1892 representing mainly farmers, favoring free coinage of silver and government control of railroads and other monopolies (p. 546)

poverty line a level of personal or family income below which one is classified as poor according to government standards (p. 828)

preamble the introduction to a formal document, especially the Constitution (pp. 152, 215)

precedent a tradition (p. 257)

prejudice an unfair opinion not based on facts (p. 391)

presidio Spanish fort in the Americas built to protect mission settlements (p. 54)

primary an election in which voters choose their party's candidate (p. 607)

privateer armed private ship (pp. 177, 297)

productivity how much work each worker does (pp. 698, 807)

prohibition the forbidding by law of the making or selling of alcoholic beverages (p. 613)

Prohibition the nationwide ban on the manufacture, sale, and transportation of liquor in the United States that went into effect when the Eighteenth Amendment was ratified in 1920 (p. 708)

propaganda ideas or information designed and spread to influence opinion (pp. 139, 661)

proportional to be the same as or corresponding to (p. 200)

proprietary colony colony run by individuals or groups to whom land was granted (pp. 85, 112)

protectorate a country that is technically independent, but is actually under the control of another country (p. 643)

public works projects such as highways, parks, and libraries built with public funds for public use (p. 718)

pueblo home or community of homes built by Native Americans (pp. 28, 54)

Puritans Protestants who, during the 1600s, wanted to reform the Anglican Church (p. 78)

---

quota system an arrangement placing a limit on the number of immigrants from each country (p. 709)

R

radical extreme (p. 496); referring to one who favors making extreme changes to the government or society, such as the New Left (p. 859)

ragtime a type of music with a strong rhythm and a lively melody with accented notes, which was popular in early 1900s (p. 594)

ranchero Mexican ranch owner (p. 370)

rancho huge properties for raising livestock set up by Mexican settlers in California (p. 370)

ratify to give official approval to (pp. 184, 209, 474)

ration to give out scarce items on a limited basis (p. 751)

realism an approach to literature, art, and theater that shows things as they really are (p. 592)

rebate discount or return of part of a payment (p. 553)

Rebel Confederate soldier, so called because of opposition to the established government (p. 465)

recall the right that enables voters to remove unsatisfactory elected officials from office (p. 607)

recession a downward turn in business activity (p. 698)

reconciliation settling by agreement or coming together again (p. 509)

Reconstruction the reorganization and rebuilding of the former Confederate states after the Civil War (p. 495)

recruit to enlist soldiers in the army (p. 165)

referendum the practice of letting voters accept or reject measures proposed by the legislature (p. 607)

regionalism in art or literature, the practice of focusing on a particular region of the country (p. 592)

relief aid for the needy; welfare (p. 717)

relocate to force a person or group of people to move (p. 342)

Renaissance a period of intellectual and artistic creativity, c. 1300–1600 (p. 38)

rendezvous a meeting (p. 356)

reparations payment by the losing country in a war to the winner for the damages caused by the war (p. 676)

repeal to cancel an act or law (p. 135)

republic a government in which citizens rule through elected representatives (p. 190)

reservation an area of public lands set aside for Native Americans (p. 540)

reserved powers powers retained by the states (p. 217)

resolution a formal expression of opinion (p. 135)

revenue incoming money (p. 134)

revenue sharing money raised from federal taxes and given to the states for use at the state and local levels (p. 887)

revival a series of meetings conducted by a preacher to arouse religious emotions (p. 411)

S

sabotage secret action by enemy agents or sympathizers to damage a nation's war effort (p. 673)

scalawags name given by former Confederates to Southern whites who supported Republican Reconstruction of the South (p. 505)

search-and-destroy mission a strategy used in Vietnam in which American forces sought Vietcong and North Vietnamese units to destroy them (p. 856)

Glossary

secede to leave or withdraw (pp. 285, 338, 439)

secession withdrawal from the Union (p. 454)

Second New Deal a new set of programs and reforms launched by Franklin D. Roosevelt in 1935 (p. 734)

sectionalism loyalty to a region (pp. 319, 437)

sedition activities aimed at weakening established government (p. 271)

segregation the separation or isolation of a race, class, or group (pp. 516, 821)

Separatists Protestants who, during the 1600s, wanted to leave the Anglican Church in order to found their own churches (p. 78)

settlement house institution located in a poor neighborhood that provided numerous community services such as medical care, child care, libraries, and classes in English (p. 588)

sharecropping system of farming in which a farmer works land for an owner who provides equipment and seeds and receives a share of the crop (p. 507)

shareholder a person who invests in a corporation by buying stock and is a partial owner (p. 560)

shuttle diplomacy negotiations between nations carried on by a person who travels back and forth between them (p. 885)

silent majority the phrase used by Nixon to describe the majority of Americans, those who did not protest or demonstrate (p. 865)

sit-in the act of occupying seats or sitting down on the floor of an establishment as a form of organized protest (p. 830)

slave code the laws passed in the Southern states that controlled and restricted enslaved people (p. 405)

slum poor, crowded, and run-down urban neighborhoods (p. 585)

smuggling trading illegally with other nations (p. 111)

Social Security Act a law requiring workers and employers to pay a tax; the money provides a monthly pension for retired people (p. 734)

socialist person who believes industries should be publicly owned and run by the government rather than by private individuals (p. 672)

sodbuster a name given to the Plains farmer (p. 535)

speculator person who risks money in order to make a large profit (pp. 124, 260)

sphere of influence section of a country where one foreign nation enjoys special rights and powers (p. 638)

spiritual an African American religious folk song (p. 405)

spoils system practice of handing out government jobs to supporters; replacing government employees with the winning candidate's supporters (p. 337)

square deal Theodore Roosevelt's promise of fair and equal treatment for all (p. 618)

stagflation a combination of rising prices and a sluggish economy with relatively high unemployment (p. 887)

stalemate a situation during a conflict when action stops because both sides are equally powerful and neither will give in (p. 787)

standard gauge the uniform width of 4 feet, 8.5 inches for railroad tracks, adopted during the 1880s (p. 552)

standard of living a measure of people's overall wealth and quality of life; a minimum of necessities and luxuries that a group is accustomed to (p. 808)

states' rights rights and powers independent of the federal government that are reserved for the states by the Constitution; the belief that states' rights supersede federal rights and law (pp. 272, 338, 455)

steerage cramped quarters on a ship's lower decks for passengers paying the lowest fares (p. 577)

stock shares of ownership a company sells in its business which often carry voting power (p. 560)

stock exchange a place where shares in corporations are bought and sold through an organized system (p. 715)

strait a narrow passageway connecting two larger bodies of water (p. 49)

strike a stopping of work by workers to force an employer to meet demands (p. 391)

strikebreaker person hired to replace a striking worker in order to break up a strike (p. 568)

subsidy grant of money from the government to a person or a company for an action intended to benefit the public (pp. 527, 724)

subsistence farming farming in which only enough food to feed one's family is produced (p. 104)

suburbs residential areas that sprang up close to or surrounding cities as a result of improvements in transportation (p. 586)

subversion an attempt to overthrow a government by persons working secretly from within (p. 789)

suffrage the right to vote (pp. 336, 426)

suffragist a man or woman who fought for a woman's right to vote (p. 610)

summit a meeting of heads of government (p. 805)

surplus excess; amount left over after necessary expenses are paid (p. 798)

sweatshop a shop or factory where workers work long hours at low wages under unhealthy conditions (pp. 566, 578)

tariff a tax on imports or exports (pp. 261, 338)

technology the application of scientific discoveries to practical use (pp. 39, 306)

Tejano a Mexican who claims Texas as his home (p. 362)

telegraph a device or system that uses electric signals to transmit messages by a code over wires (p. 388)

temperance the use of little or no alcoholic drink (p. 412)

tenant farmer farmer who works land owned by another and pays rent either in cash or crops (pp. 95, 401)

tenement a building in which several families rent rooms or apartments, often with little sanitation or safety (p. 585)

terrace a raised piece of land with the top leveled off to promote farming (p. 25)

theocracy a form of government in which the society is ruled by religious leaders (p. 22)

Tidewater a region of flat, low-lying plains along the seacoast (p. 107)

toleration the acceptance of different beliefs (p. 81)

total war war on all aspects of the enemy's life (p. 487)

totalitarian a political system in which the government suppresses all opposition and controls most aspects of people's lives (p. 742)

trade deficit the situation when the value of a country's foreign imports exceeds the value of its exports (p. 898)

trade union organization of workers with the same trade or skill (pp. 391, 567)

Transcendentalist any of a group of New England writers who stressed the relationship between human beings and nature, spiritual things over material things, and the importance of the individual conscience (p. 414)

transcontinental extending across a continent (p. 527)

triangular trade a trade route that exchanged goods between the West Indies, the American colonies, and West Africa (p. 105)

tribute money paid for protection (pp. 51, 289)

trust a combination of firms or corporations formed by a legal agreement, especially to reduce competition (pp. 562, 605)

trustbuster someone who breaks up a trust into smaller companies (p. 617)

turnpike a road that one must pay to use; the money is used to pay for the road (p. 314)

unconstitutional not agreeing or consistent with the Constitution (p. 260)

underemployment the condition when people work at jobs for which they are overqualified or that do not utilize their skills (p. 894)

Underground Railroad a system that helped enslaved African Americans follow a network of escape routes out of the South to freedom in the North (p. 420)

unemployment insurance payments by the government for a limited period of time to people who have lost their jobs (p. 734)

utopia community based on a vision of a perfect society sought by reformers (p. 411)

vaquero Hispanic ranch hand (p. 532)

vaudeville stage entertainment made up of various acts, such as dancing, singing, comedy, and magic shows (p. 595)

vertical integration the combining of companies that supply equipment and services needed for a particular industry (p. 563)

veto to reject a bill and prevent it from becoming a law (p. 349)

viceroy person who rules a country or province as the representative of the monarch (p. 54)

Vietcong the guerrilla soldiers of the Communist faction in Vietnam, also known as the National Liberation Front (p. 853)

Vietnamization Nixon's policy that called for South Vietnam to take a more active role in fighting the war and for Americans to become less involved (p. 868)

vigilantes people who take the law into their own hands (pp. 377, 526)

War Hawks Republicans during Madison's presidency who pressed for war with Britain (p. 294)

warrant an official order (p. 226)

work relief programs that gave needy people government jobs (p. 724)

writ of assistance legal document that enabled officers to search homes and warehouses for goods that might be smuggled (p. 134)

Yankee Union soldier (p. 465)

yellow journalism writing which exaggerates sensational, dramatic, and gruesome events to attract readers, named for stories that were popular during the late 1800s (p. 592); a type of sensational, biased, and often false reporting (p. 641)

yeoman Southern owner of a small farm who did not have slaves (p. 401)

Index

Italicized page numbers refer to illustrations. The following abbreviations are used in the index:
m = map, *c* = chart, *p* = photograph or picture, *g* = graph, *crt* = cartoon, *ptg* = painting, *q* = quote

Index

D

O

P

Index

Ptolemy, 45

PT 109, 827

public health: in cities, 586–87

public housing: Eisenhower administration funding, 799; Johnson administration funding, 829

Public Works Administration (PWA), *c722,* 725, 731

Pueblo, the, 54

pueblos, *p28,* 28, 54

Puerto Rico, 630; immigration, 840; Spain, possession of, 324, 643; U.S. territory, 643, 644

Pulaski, Casimir, 173

Pulitzer, Joseph, 592, 641

Pullman, George M., 553, *c557,* 569

Pullman Strike, *m568,* 569

Pure Food and Drug Act, 606, 618

Puritans, 78, 80, 81–82, 84, 109, 113–14

Pyle, Ernie, *q755*

pyramids, 21, *p22,* 22, *p29, p33*

Quadruple Alliance, 324

Quakers, 87, 109, 114, 163; antislavery movement, 416–17, 425; antislavery society of, 197

Quayle, Dan, 910

Quebec, Canada, 62, 94, 149–50; Battle of, 123

Quechua, 25

quipus, 25

quota system, 709

Rabin, Yitzhak, 920

racism, 422, 513, 515, 821, 830; Ku Klux Klan, 506, 709; in World War I armed forces, 664, 672

radicalism: during Great Depression, fear of, 689–91; demands for reform, 733–34; increase in, 731

Radical Republicans, 496, 498; conflicts with Andrew Johnson, 500, 501, 502–03; Reconstruction plan, 496

radio, 703–04, *g704;* during Great Depression, 732; fireside chats, 723

railroads, 386–88, *m387,* 400, 551–54, *m553;* after the Civil War, 514; competition

between, 553–54; consolidation of, 551–52; corporations, 561; economic effects of, 529, 552; effect of, on buffalo, 539; effect of, on cattle industry, 531–32; expansion of, 527–29, 551–52; farmers' problems with, 544, 545, 546; government aid to, 527; impact of, on western settlement, 529, 534; improving, 552–53; rate setting, 544, 545, 553–54, 605; schedules of, 529; strike of 1877, 568, *p569;* transcontinental lines, 527–29, 551

Raleigh, Sir Walter, 71–72

Randolph, A. Philip, *p691,* 691, 752–53, 825

Randolph, Edmund, 199, 200, 202, 211; as attorney general, *ptg258,* 258

Rankin, Jeannette, *p614,* 614–15, *p615, p664,* 664

rationing, 671, 751

Reagan, Ronald, 839, A7; anticommunism, 907; appeal, 900, 906; assassination attempt, 905; defense policy, 907; domestic policy, 905–07; election, 900, *p905,* 905; 1976 election, 895; foreign policy, 907–08, *p909,* 909; Iran hostage release, 900; presidential style, 905; reelection, *q908,* 908; relations with Congress, 906, 907, 908; Supreme Court appointments, *p906,* 906

realism: in art, 593–94; in literature, 592

Rebels, 465. *See also* Confederacy

recall of elected officials, 607

recession: after World War I, 698; Bush administration, 915–16; defined, 698; Nixon administration, 887; Reagan administration, 907; Roosevelt Recession, 736

Reconstruction, 494–513; African Americans, 504–06; aftermath of, 513–16; conflict between president and Congress, 496, 500, 501, 502–03; Congressional plan, 500–01; end of, 508–11; impact of, 516; Andrew Johnson's plan, 498; Lincoln's plan, 495–96; military districts, *m501,* 502; politics during, 501, 504,

508–10; Radical, 501–02; Radical Republican plan, 496; resistance to, 505–06; state governments affected by, 495–96, 498, 502

Reconstruction Finance Corporation (RFC), 718

recycling, 932

Red Badge of Courage, The, 434–35, 593

Red Cloud, chief, *q538*

Red Scare, 690, 709, 789–92

referendum, 607

reforms, 410–28; alcohol, 412; business, 620; education, 412–13; governmental, 604, 607; labor, 546, 547; political, 546, 547; progressivism, 602–27; slavery, 416–22; social, 411–15, 603–13; women's rights and, 424–28

region, 21; U.S. physical regions, *m3*

Rehnquist, William, 886, *p927*

religion(s): of enslaved persons, 405; freedom of, 78–81, 85, 86, 219; effect of Great Awakening on, 113; of immigrants, 575–76, 579–80; of early Native Americans, 22–25; in the Netherlands, 78; reform of, 80, 411–12; toleration of, 81, 89–90. *See also* individual religions

religious intolerance, 78, 80–81, 88, 576, 758–59, *q759*

Remington, Frederic, 593, 643

Renaissance, the, 38

Reno, Janet, 926

Republican Leader, The, q441

Republican Party: beginnings of, 448–49; during Reconstruction, 504, 508–10; slavery, opposition to, 448, 451, 454–55

reservations, *m343,* 540–41, 542, 543

reserved powers, 217–18

resolution, 135

responsibilities, citizen's, 227–28

Restoration, the, 84

Revels, Hiram, *p505,* 505

revenue sharing, 887

Revere, Paul, 139; midnight ride, 143, 144, 145, *ptg181*

revivals, 411–12, *p412*

Revolutionary War, *m166;* African Americans in, 164, *ptg167,* 167, *ptg183;* American advantages, 164–65, 185; British advantages, 163–64; campaigns in,

165–66, 167–68; colonies taking sides, 146, 151, 163–64; financing, American, 174; first battles in, 144–46; Native Americans and, 176; role of European allies, 171–72; in the South, 178–80, *m178;* Valley Forge, 172–73; in the West, 176–77, *m177;* women fighting in, 165. *See also* American Revolution

Rhode Island, *mRA6, cRA4;* charter colony, 111; English settlement, 81–82; opposition to Constitution, 209, 211; ratification of Constitution, 211

Richardson, Elliot, 890

Richmond, Virginia: in the Civil War, 470, *p487,* 487; Confederate capital, 461, 464, 487

Richthofen, Baron von, 659

Rickenbacker, Eddie, 659

rights of citizens, 226–27; basic, 152, 156; bearing arms, 242; equal treatment, 226–27, 242–43; freedom of assembly, 219, 242; freedom of religion, 78–79, 81, 85, 88, 89–90, 219, 242; freedom of speech, 219, 242; limits on, 227; search and seizure, 226, 242; voting rights, 112, 190, 227, 228, 246, 247, 249, 336–37. *See also* civil rights

Riis, Jacob, *p578, q587,* 587, *q603,* 603

Rio Grande: Texas/Mexican border dispute, 372–73, 375

Rivero, Horacio, 753

river travel, 314–15, 386

"Road Not Taken, The," 924

roads, 386; to the West, 313–14, *m314*

Roanoke Island, North Carolina, *m72,* 72

Roaring Twenties, 702–06

Robeson, Paul, 706

Robinson, Jackie, *p821, q821,* 821

Rochambeau, Jean Baptiste de, *ptg182,* 182–83

Rock, Emily, *q832*

Rockefeller, John D., *p560,* 560, 561–62, 563, 564

Rockefeller, Nelson, 892

rock 'n' roll, 811–12

Rockwell, Norman, 769, 848

Rocky Mountains, *p2,* 4; Lewis and Clark expedition, 284; and mountain men, 356; and Oregon Trail, 357

Index

abolitionist/abolicionista una persona que favorece firmemente suprimir la esclavitud (p. 416)

abstain/abstenerse no tomar parte de una actividad, como de votar (p. 440)

adobe/adobe un ladrillo de lodo, seco al sol, usado para construir las casas de los Nativos Americanos (p. 31)

affirmative action/acción afirmativa un esfuerzo activo para mejorar las oportunidades de educación y empleo para grupos de minorías y de la mujer (p. 887)

affluence/afluencia la condición de tener mucha riqueza (p. 808)

airlift/puente aéreo un sistema de transportar comida y abastos por vehículos aéreos hasta una área que no se puede alcanzar de otras maneras (p. 777)

alien/extranjero una persona inmigrante que vive en un país en el cual no es ciudadano (p. 271)

alleged/alegado dicho como un hecho pero sin pruebas (p. 791)

alliance system/sistema de alianza acuerdos de defensa entre naciones (p. 656)

ambush/emboscada un ataque por sorpresa (p. 185)

amendment/enmienda una adición a un documento formal tal como la Constitución (pp. 211, 219)

American System/Sistema Americano políticas ideadas por Henry Clay para estimular el crecimiento de la industria (p. 320)

amnesty/amnistía el otorgar perdón a un número grande de personas; la protección del proceso a causa de una acción ilegal (pp. 496, 893)

anarchist/anarquista una persona que cree que no debe de haber ningún gobierno (p. 689)

anarchy/anarquía desorden y sin ley (p. 648)

annex/anexar añadir un territorio a su propio territorio (p. 366)

annexation/anexión traer una área bajo el control de un país más grande (p. 637)

anti-Semitism/antisemitismo hostilidad hacia o discriminación en contra de los judíos (p. 742)

apartheid/*apartheid* la separación racial y discriminación económica y política en contra de la gente no blanca, una política anteriormente practicada en la República de África del Sur (p. 898)

appeasement/apaciguamiento aceptar demandas para evitar conflictos (p. 744)

apprentice/aprendiz asistente asignado para aprender el oficio de un artesano experto (p. 113)

appropriate/destinar apartar para un propósito en particular, dicho especialmente de fondos (p. 221)

arbitration/arbitraje arreglo de una disputa por medio de un acuerdo para aceptar la decisión de una persona imparcial (p. 617)

archaeology/arqueología el estudio de pueblos antiguos (p. 17)

armistice/armisticio un acuerdo temporal de paz para suprimir combates (pp. 643, 668)

arms race/carrera de armas la competición entre los Estados Unidos y la Unión Soviética para construir más y más armas, cada uno con el propósito de sobrepasar el poder militar del otro (p. 801)

arsenal/arsenal un lugar para el almacenaje de armas y municiones (p. 452)

article/artículo una parte de un documento tal como la Constitución que trata de un solo tema (p. 206)

artifact/artefacto un artículo dejado por pueblos antiguos que representa su cultura (p. 17)

assembly line/línea de montaje un sistema de producción arreglado con máquinas y trabajadores para que cada persona haga vez tras vez su trabajo designado mientras el artículo pasa por en frente de él (p. 559)

assimilate/asimilar introducir a un grupo dentro de la cultura de una población más grande (p. 578)

astrolabe/astrolabio un instrumento usado por los marineros para observar las posiciones de las estrellas (p. 39)

autocracy/autocracia gobierno en el cual una persona lleva el poder sin límite (p. 663)

automation/automatización un sistema o proceso que usa aparatos mecánicos o electrónicos para reemplazar a los trabajadores humanos (p. 814)

baby boom/auge de nacimientos un aumento marcado de la proporción de nacimientos, como el de los Estados Unidos inmediatamente después de terminar la Segunda Guerra Mundial (p. 808)

backcountry/monte una región de colinas y bosques al oeste de la orilla del mar (p. 108)

balance of power/balance de poder la distribución de poder entre naciones para que ninguna nación en particular pueda dominar o interferir con otra (p. 882)

bankruptcy/bancarrota la condición de no poder pagar sus deudas; la propiedad de uno es manejada o vendida para pagar a las personas a las cuales uno debe dinero (p. 916)

barrio/barrio una vecindad hispanoparlante de una ciudad, especialmente en el sudoeste de los EE.UU. (p. 627)

bicameral/*bicameral* que consiste de dos cámaras, especialmente dicho en una legislatura (p. 190)

black codes/códigos negros leyes establecidas en el Sur al terminar la Guerra Civil para controlar a los libertos y permitir a los dueños de plantaciones la explotación de los trabajadores afroamericanos (p. 499)

blacklist/lista negra una lista de personas que son desaprobadas y castigadas, tal como rehusar a darles trabajo (p. 790)

blitzkrieg/*blitzkrieg* nombre dado a los ataques ofensivos súbitos y violentos usados por los alemanes durante la Segunda Guerra Mundial; "guerra relámpago" (p. 745)

blockade/bloqueo el cerrar una área por medio de tropas o de buques de guerra para prohibir el entrar y el salir de abastos y de personas; cerrar los puertos de un país (pp. 177, 463, 850)

English/Spanish Glossary

blockade runner/forzador de bloqueo un buque que navega adentro de y afuera de una área bloqueada (p. 467)

bond/bono una obligación hecha por el gobierno la cual promete pagar un préstamo con interés (p. 259)

boomtown/pueblo en bonanza una comunidad experimentando un auge repentino de comercio o población (p. 377)

border ruffians/rufianes fronterizos hombres de Missouri que viajaban en grupos armados a votar en la elección de Kansas a mediados de los años 1850 (p. 444)

border states/estados fronterizos los estados entre el Norte y el Sur que fueron divididos sobre el problema de quedarse en la Unión o de unirse a la Confederación (p. 461)

bounty/gratificación dinero dado como recompensa, como para animar el alistamiento en el ejército (p. 479)

boycott/boicotear rehusar comprar artículos de un país en particular (p. 135); rehusar usar (p. 824)

brand/marca a fuego un símbolo quemado en la piel de un animal para mostrar título de propiedad (p. 531)

budget deficit/déficit del presupuesto la cantidad por la cual los gastos exceden las rentas, especialmente referente al gobierno (p. 919)

bureaucracy/burocracia sistema en el cual oficiales no elegidos administran las leyes y políticas (p. 337)

burgesses/burgueses representantes elegidos para una asamblea (p. 74)

cabinet/gabinete un grupo de consejeros del presidente (p. 258)

Californios/californios mexicanos que vivían en California (p. 374)

canal/canal vía de agua artificial (p. 315)

capital/capital dinero para inversión (pp. 306, 399)

capitalism/capitalismo un sistema económico basado en la propiedad particular y la empresa libre (p. 689)

caravel/carabela un buque pequeño y veloz con una proa ancha (p. 40)

carbon dating/datar con carbón un método científico usado para determinar la edad de un artefacto (p. 20)

carpetbaggers/carpetbaggers nombre dado a los blancos norteños que se trasladaban al Sur después de la guerra y apoyaban a los republicanos (p. 505)

cash crop/cultivo comercial cosecha cultivada para vender por dinero (pp. 106, 515)

casualty/baja un miliciano muerto, herido, o capturado (p. 469)

caucus/junta electoral una reunión llevada a cabo por un partido político para escoger el candidato a la presidencia de su partido o para decidir políticas (pp. 269, 337)

cede/ceder abandonar por tratado (p. 375)

censure/censurar expresar desaprobación formal de alguna acción (p. 792)

census/censo registro oficial de una población (p. 313)

charter/carta de privilegio un documento que otorga los derechos de organizar establecimientos en una área (p. 72)

charter colony/colonia a carta colonia establecida por un grupo de colonizadores a quienes se les había dado un documento formal permitiéndoles colonizar (p. 111)

checks and balances/inspecciones y balances el sistema en el cual cada rama de gobierno refrena las otras dos ramas para que ninguna rama vuelva a ser demasiado poderosa (pp. 207, 218)

circumnavigate/circunnavegar navegar alrededor del mundo (p. 49)

civil disobedience/desobediencia civil el rehusar obedecer las leyes que uno considera injustas como una manera pacífica para inisistir en cambios (p. 825)

civil service/servicio civil el cuerpo de trabajadores gubernamentales no elegidos (p. 605)

civil war/guerra civil conflicto entre grupos opuestos de ciudadanos del mismo país (p. 445)

civilization/civilización una cultura sumamente desarrollada, generalmente con religiones y leyes organizadas (p. 21)

classical/clásico relacionado a Grecia y Roma antigua (p. 38)

clipper ship/buque clíper un buque veloz con líneas delgadas, mástiles altos, y grandes velas cuadradas (p. 386)

closed shop/taller cerrado un lugar de trabajo en el cual, por acuerdo, el empresario contrata sólo a los miembros del sindicato (p. 782)

coeducation/coeducación la enseñanza conjunta de estudiantes hombres y mujeres (p. 426)

cold war/guerra fría una lucha sobre diferencias políticas entre naciones llevada a cabo por métodos fuera de guerra (p. 777)

collective bargaining/negociaciones colectivas discusión entre el empresario y los representantes sindicales de los trabajadores sobre salario, horas, y condiciones del taller (p. 567)

Columbian Exchange/Cambio Colombiano el cambio de productos, ideas, y personas entre Europa y las Américas (p. 55)

commission/comisión un grupo de personas dirigidas a hacer algún deber (p. 511)

committee of correspondence/comité de correspondencia una organización que usaba reuniones, cartas, y panfletos para propagar ideas políticas para las colonias (p. 139)

compromise/compromiso un acuerdo entre dos o más partidos en el cual cada partido abandona algo de lo que quiere (p. 201)

concurrent powers/poderes concurrentes poderes compartidos por los estados y el gobierno federal (p. 218)

Conestoga wagon/conestoga vehículo firme cubierto de lona blanca usado por los pioneros para moverse hacia el oeste (p. 281)

conquistador/conquistador explorador español en las Américas en los años 1500 (p. 50)

conservation/conservación la protección y preservación de recursos naturales (p. 618)

consolidation/consolidación la práctica de juntar compañías particulares en una (p. 551)

constituents/constituyentes personas representadas por miembros del Congreso (p. 221)

constitution/constitución un plan formal de gobierno (pp. 90, 189)

containment/contención la política o proceso de prohibir la expansión de un poder hostil (p. 775)

convoy/*convoy* un grupo que viaja con algo, tal como un buque, para protegerlo (p. 665)

cooperative/cooperativa una tienda donde los granjeros compraban productos uno al otro; una empresa poseída y operada por los que usan sus servicios (p. 545)

corporation/sociedad anónima un grupo autorizado por ley a montar una actividad pero con los derechos y deberes de una persona particular (p. 560)

corruption/corrupción acciones deshonestas o ilegales (p. 505)

cotton gin/despepitadora de algodón una máquina que sacaba las semillas de las fibras de algodón (pp. 306, 397)

counterculture/contracultura un movimiento social cuyos valores están en contra de los de la sociedad establecida (p. 859)

coup/*coup* derrocamiento súbito de un gobierno por un grupo pequeño (pp. 854, 912)

coureur de bois/*coureur de bois* cazador de pieles francés viviendo entre los Nativos Americanos (p. 62)

court-martial/consejo de guerra someter a juicio por un tribunal militar (p. 323)

credibility gap/resquicio de credibilidad falta de creencia; un término usado para describir la falta de confianza en los anuncios de la administración de Johnson referente a la Guerra en Viet Nam (p. 863)

credit/crédito una forma de préstamo; la capacidad de comprar productos basada en pagos futuros (p. 402)

culture/cultura la manera de vivir de un grupo de personas que tienen en común sus creencias y costumbres (p. 20)

customs duties/derechos de aduana impuestos sobre productos importados del extranjero (p. 279)

D

---

debtor/deudor persona o país que debe dinero (p. 92)

decree/decreto una orden o decisión dada por alguién de autoridad (p. 363)

default/incumplimiento de pago fallar en hacer una obligación, especialmente una financiera (p. 717)

deferment/aplazamiento un perdón, aprobado por la junta de reclutamiento, que permite que sea perdonado una persona del servicio militar por varias razones (p. 860)

deficit/déficit escasez que ocurre cuando los gastos son más que los ingresos (p. 888)

demilitarize/desmilitarizar quitar fuerzas armadas de una área (p. 322)

demilitarized zone/zona desmilitarizada una región donde no se permite ninguna fuerza militar ni armas (p. 788)

deport/deportar mandar afuera de un país a los extranjeros que se consideran peligrosos (pp. 271, 690)

depreciate/depreciar caer en valor (p. 194)

depression/depresión un período de poca actividad económica y de desempleo extenso (pp. 196, 349)

deregulation/deregulación el acto de quitar las limitaciones y reglamentos que el gobierno había puesto en el comercio (p. 906)

desert/desertar salir sin permiso (p. 172)

deserter/desertor soldado que huye de la batalla o la guerra (p. 167)

détente/*détente* una política que intenta relajar o aliviar tensiones entre naciones (p. 882)

dictator/dictador un líder que manda con plena autoridad, a menudo de una manera cruel o brutal (p. 741)

disarmament/desarme el quitar armas (pp. 322, 748)

discrimination/discriminación trato injusto de un grupo; trato parcial a causa de la raza, la religión, los antecedentes étnicos, o lugar de nacimiento de alguién (pp. 391, 622)

dissent/disensión desacuerdo con u oposición a una opinión (pp. 78, 672)

diversity/diversidad variedad o diferencia (p. 107)

dividend/dividendo cheque que se paga a los accionistas, por lo general trimestralmente, representa una porción de las ganancias de la corporación (p. 561)

dollar diplomacy/diplomacia del dólar una política de unir los intereses comerciales de un país con sus intereses diplomáticos al extranjero (p. 649)

domestic tranquility/tranquilidad doméstica mantener la paz dentro de la nación (p. 215)

domino theory/teoría dominó la creencia de que si una nación de Asia hubiera caído a los comunistas los países vecinos la habrían seguido (pp. 804, 853)

dove/paloma una persona que se opone a la guerra y las políticas de guerra, tal como una persona que se oponía a la Guerra en Viet Nam (p. 860)

draft/reclutamiento la selección de personas a servicio militar requirido (p. 478)

drought/sequía un largo período con poca lluvia (p. 28)

dry farming/agricultura seca una manera de cultivar tierra seca en la cual las semillas se plantan al fondo de la tierra donde hay un poco de humedad (p. 535)

due process of law/proceso justo de ley idea de que el gobierno debe de seguir los procesos establecidos por ley y garantizados por la Constitución (p. 226)

Dust Bowl/Cuenca de Polvo el nombre dado al área del sur de las Grandes Llanuras extensivamente dañada por las sequías y las tempestades del polvo durante los años 1930 (p. 729)

E

---

effigy/efigie una figura rellenada de trapos que representa una persona impopular (p. 135)

English/Spanish Glossary

Electoral College/Colegio Electoral un grupo especial de votantes escogidos por sus legislaturas estatales para elegir al presidente y al vicepresidente (p. 206)

emancipate/emancipar liberar de la esclavitud (p. 473)

embargo/embargo una orden que prohibe el comercio con otro país (pp. 291, 884)

emigrant/emigrante una persona que sale de un país o una región para vivir en otras partes (p. 357)

emigrate/emigrar dejar su patria para vivir en otras partes (p. 576)

empresario/empresario una persona que arregló la colonización de tierra en Texas durante los años 1800 (p. 363)

encomienda/encomienda sistema de recompensar a los conquistadores con extensiones de tierra y el derecho de recaudar impuestos y exigir mano de obra a los Nativos Americanos que vivían en la tierra (p. 54)

Enlightenment/Siglo de las Luces movimiento durante los años 1700 que propagaba la idea de que el conocimiento, la razón, y la ciencia podrían mejorar la sociedad (p. 205)

entente/convenio un acuerdo entre naciones (p. 656)

entrenched/atrincherado que ocupa una posición fuerte defensiva (p. 482)

enumerated powers/poderes enumerados poderes que pertenecen solamente al gobierno federal (p. 217)

escalate/intensificar aumentar o extender (p. 855)

espionage/espionaje espiar (p. 673)

ethnic group/grupo étnico una minoría que habla un idioma diferente o que sigue costumbres diferentes que la mayoría de la gente de un país (p. 576)

evolution/evolución la teoría científica de que los seres humanos y otros seres vivos se han desarrollado tras largos períodos de tiempo (p. 710)

executive branch/rama ejecutiva la rama de gobierno, dirigida por el presidente, que administra las leyes y la política de una nación (pp. 206, 218)

executive order/orden ejecutiva una regla emitida por un jefe ejecutivo que lleva la fuerza de ley (p. 848)

exile/exilio una persona forzada a abandonar su patria (p. 848)

expansionism/expansionismo una política que demanda el extender las fronteras de una nación (p. 632)

expatriate/expatriado una persona que abandona su patria y decide vivir en otro país (p. 706)

export/exportación un producto vendido en el extranjero (p. 111)

---

factory system/sistema de fábrica sistema que junta en un solo lugar las categorías de fabricación para aumentar la eficiencia (p. 307)

famine/hambre una escasez extrema de comida (p. 392)

fascism/fascismo un sistema político, dirigido por un dictador, que demanda nacionalismo y racismo extremo, y ninguna tolerancia de oposición (p. 742)

favorite son/hijo favorito candidato que recibe el apoyo de su estado natal en lugar del partido nacional (p. 333)

federal debt/deuda federal la cantidad de dinero debido por el gobierno (p. 906)

federalism/federalismo el compartir el poder entre el gobierno federal y los gobiernos estatales (pp. 205, 217)

Federalists/federalistas apoyadores de la Constitución (p. 209)

federation/federación una forma de gobierno que une grupos diferentes (p. 32)

feminist/feminista una persona que aboga por o está activa en promulgar los derechos de la mujer (pp. 425, 838)

fixed costs/costos fijos gastos regulares tal como de vivienda o mantenimiento de equipo que se quedan casi iguales año tras año (p. 402)

flapper/*flapper* una jovencita de los años 1920 que retaba las costumbres de comportamiento e indumentaria (p. 703)

flexible response/respuesta flexible un plan que usaba unidades militares especiales para montar guerras al estilo guerrilla (p. 847)

forty-niners/*forty-niners* personas que fueron a California durante la fiebre del oro en 1849 (p. 376)

Fourteen Points/Catorce Puntos el plan de paz para suprimir la Primera Guerra Mundial y reestructurar los países de Europa, propuesto por Woodrow Wilson (p. 675)

free silver/plata libre la producción sin límite de monedas de plata (p. 546)

freedman/liberto una persona liberada de la esclavitud (p. 497)

frigate/fragata buque de guerra (p. 297)

front/frente una región donde la guerra activa se lleva a cabo (p. 666)

fugitive/fugitivo evadido que trata de huir (p. 439)

fundamentalist/fundamentalista una persona que cree en el sentido literal de escrituras religiosas y la obediencia estricta a leyes religiosas (p. 900)

---

genocide/genocidio el eradicar un grupo racial, político, o cultural (p. 758)

ghetto/*ghetto* una parte de una ciudad en la cual vive un grupo de minoría a causa de presión económica o social (p. 814)

ghost town/pueblo de espectros pueblo anterior de mineros que se dejó (p. 526)

Gilded Age/la Época Dorada el nombre asociado con América al final de los años 1800, referente a la gran riqueza de los tiempos y la terrible pobreza que estaba debajo (p. 586)

glasnost/*glasnost* una política soviética que permitía discusión más abierta de cuestiones políticas y sociales, y la promulgación más amplia de noticias e información (p. 908)

global warming/calentamiento mundial un aumento contínuo del promedio de temperaturas mundiales (p. 928)

grandfather clause/cláusula de abuelo una cláusula que permitía votar a las personas que no aprobaron el examen de alfabetismo si sus padres o sus abuelos habían votado antes de que empezó la Reconstrucción; una excepción a una ley basada en circunstancias preexistentes (p. 515)

grassroots/la gente común la sociedad al nivel local y popular afuera de los centros políticos y culturales (p. 918)

greenback/billete de dorso verde un billete de la moneda de EE.UU. expedido primeramente por el Norte durante la Guerra Civil (p. 480)

gross domestic product/producto interno bruto valor de todos los productos dentro de las fronteras nacionales de un país en un año (p. 925)

gross national product/producto nacional bruto valor total de todos los productos producidos en un año con la mano de obra y la propiedad suplidas por los residentes de un país, sin importar donde toma lugar la producción (p. 698)

guerrilla/guerrilla referente a ataques sorpresas o incursiones en lugar de la guerra organizada (p. 346)

guerrilla warfare/contienda a guerrilleros una técnica de tirar y darse a la huída usada en combates de guerra (pp. 179, 847)

H

habeas corpus/hábeas corpus una orden legal para una encuesta para determinar si una persona ha sido encarcelada legalmente (p. 478)

hawk/halcón una persona que aboga por la guerra y las políticas de guerra, tal como un apoyador de la Guerra en Viet Nam (p. 860)

hieroglyphics/jeroglíficos una forma antigua de escribir usando símbolos y dibujos para representar palabras, sonidos, y conceptos (p. 23)

Hispanic/hispánico una persona de o descendiente de la gente que vinieron de los países de Latinoamérica o de España (p. 839)

Holocaust/Holocausto el nombre dado a la matanza extensa de judíos y otros grupos por los nazis durante la Segunda Guerra Mundial (p. 759)

homestead/_homestead_ adquirir una pieza de tierra pública de los EE.UU. por medio de vivir en ella y cultivarla (p. 534)

horizontal integration/integración horizontal la asociación de firmas competitivas en una sociedad anónima (p. 562)

hot line/línea de emergencia una línea telefónica directa para uso en caso de emergencia (p. 851)

human rights/derechos humanos derechos, tal como la libertad de encarcelamiento ilegal, tortura, y ejecución, considerados como pertenecientes a todas las personas (p. 898)

Hundred Days/Cien Días una sesión especial del Congreso llamada por Franklin D. Roosevelt para tratar los problemas de la Depresión (p. 723)

Ice Age/Época Glacial un período de temperaturas extremadamente frías cuando parte de la superficie del planeta estaba cubierta de extensiones masivas de hielo (p. 17)

impeach/residenciar acusación formal a un oficial público de mala conducta en la oficina (pp. 221, 502, 926)

impeachment/residenciamiento el acusar a un oficial público de mala conducta en la oficina; si se le prueba culpable ante una corte designada, se le despide de la oficina (p. 890)

imperialism/imperialismo las acciones usadas por una nación para ejercer control político o económico sobre naciones más pequeñas y débiles (p. 632)

implied powers/poderes implícitos poderes no mencionados específicamente en la Constitución (pp. 220, 268)

import/importación un producto comprado de mercados extranjeros (p. 111)

impressment/requisición captura de marineros para forzarlos a servir en una marina extranjera (pp. 264, 290)

inauguration/inauguración la ceremonia en la cual el presidente presta el juramento de la oficina (p. 257)

incumbent/titular alguién que actualmente tiene un oficio o posición (p. 926)

indentured servant/sirviente contratado trabajador que consiente trabajar sin pago durante un cierto período de tiempo a cambio del pasaje a América (p. 88)

Industrial Revolution/Revolución Industrial el cambio de una sociedad agraria en una basada en la industria que empezó en la Gran Bretaña y se promulgó a los Estados Unidos alrededor del año 1800 (p. 306)

inflation/inflación aumento contínuo del precio de productos y servicios (pp. 174, 480, 780)

initiative/iniciativa el derecho de los ciudadanos de poner una medida o tema ante los votantes o la legislatura para aprobación (p. 607)

injunction/amonestación una orden judicial para terminar una acción, tal como una huelga (p. 569)

installment buying/compra a plazos un sistema de comprar productos en el cual los clientes prometen hacer pagos pequeños y regulares a través de un período de tiempo (p. 699)

integrate/integrar suprimir la segregación de las razas diferentes e introducir a membrecía igual y común en la sociedad (pp. 507, 822)

interchangeable parts/partes intercambiables piezas uniformes que pueden ser hechas en grandes cantidades para reemplazar otras piezas idénticas (p. 309)

internal improvements/mejoramientos internos proyectos federales, tal como canales y carreteras, para desarrollar el sistema de transportación de una nación (p. 319)

Internet/*Internet* enlaze a través de todo el mundo de redes de computadoras (p. 927)

internment camps/campos de internamiento los centros de detención adonde los americanos japoneses fueron trasladados y allí encerrados durante la Segunda Guerra Mundial (p. 754)

interstate/interestatal a través de fronteras estatales; que conecta o existe entre dos o más estados (p. 831)

iron curtain/cortina de hierro la barrera política y militar para los países de Europa Oriental controlados por los soviéticos que los aislaba después de la Segunda Guerra Mundial (p. 775)

ironclad/acorazado buque armado (p. 468)

Iroquois Confederacy/Confederación Iroquesa un grupo poderoso de Nativos Americanos de la región oriental de los Estados Unidos compuesto de cinco naciones: los pueblos mohawk, séneca, cayuga, onondaga y oneida (p. 117)

island hopping/saltar islas una estrategia usada durante la Segunda Guerra Mundial que demandó el atacar y capturar ciertas islas importantes para usarlas como bases para saltar por encima de otras (p. 763)

isolationism/aislacionismo una política nacional de evitar el involucramiento en asuntos mundiales (pp. 631, 695)

isthmus/istmo una faja estrecha de tierra que conecta dos áreas de tierra más grandes (p. 646)

joint occupation/ocupación en común la posesión y colonización de una área como esfuerzo compartido por dos o más países (p. 356)

joint-stock company/compañía por acciones una compañía en la cual los inversionistas compran acciones de la compañía a cambio de una porción de las ganancias en el futuro (p. 72)

judicial branch/rama judicial la rama de gobierno, incluyendo el sistema de tribunales federales, que interpreta las leyes de una nación (pp. 206, 218)

judicial review/repaso judicial el derecho del Tribunal Supremo para determinar si una ley viola la Constitución (pp. 220, 280)

kamikaze/kamikase durante la Segunda Guerra Mundial, un piloto suicida japonés cuya misión era chocar con el blanco (p. 763)

laissez-faire/*laissez-faire* la creencia de que el gobierno no debe de involucrarse en los asuntos comerciales y económicos del país (pp. 278, 350, 618)

land-grant college/colegio de tierras donadas originalmente, un colegio agrícola establecido como resultado del Decreto Morrill de 1862 que dio a los estados, grandes cantidades de tierras federales que podrían ser vendidas para recaudar dinero para la educación (p. 591)

landslide/victoria arrolladora una victoria abrumadora (p. 335)

League of Nations/Liga de Naciones una asociación de naciones para mantener la paz y resolver disputas internacionales propuesta en los Catorce Puntos de Wilson (p. 675)

lease/arrendar entregar propiedad en cambio de renta (p. 694)

legislative branch/rama legislativa la rama de gobierno que redacta las leyes de una nación (pp. 206, 218)

lend-lease/prestar-arrendar el decreto aprobado durante la Segunda Guerra Mundial que permitía a los Estados Unidos que vendiera, prestara, o arrendara armas u otros abastos de guerra a cualquier nación considerada "vital para la defensa de los Estados Unidos" (p. 748)

line of demarcation/línea de demarcación una línea imaginaria a lo largo del medio del Océano Atlántico desde el Polo Norte hasta el Polo Sur para dividir las Américas entre España y Portugal (p. 47)

line-item veto/veto de partida el poder que permite al presidente que cancele partidas particulares de gastos de un presupuesto o proyecto de ley (p. 920)

literacy/alfabetismo la capacidad de leer y escribir (p. 114)

literacy test/examen de alfabetismo un método usado para prohibir a los afroamericanos a votar por requerir a presuntos votantes que pudieran leer y escribir a niveles especificados (p. 515)

lock/esclusa en un canal un recinto con puertas en cada extremo y usado para levantar y bajar los buques mientras pasan de un nivel al otro (p. 316)

lode/filón una faja o venero de mena intercalada entre estratos de piedra (p. 525)

log cabin campaign/campaña de cabaña rústica el nombre dado a la campaña para la presidencia de William Henry Harrison en 1840, debido al uso de una cabaña rústica de troncos como su símbolo por los whigs (p. 350)

Loyalists/lealistas colonizadores americanos que quedaron leales a la Bretaña y se opusieron a la guerra para la independencia (pp. 146, 164)

lynching/linchamiento matar a una persona a través de la acción ilegal de una muchedumbre airada (p. 516)

maize/maíz una forma antigua de elote cultivado por los Nativos Americanos (p. 20)

majority/mayoría más de la mitad (p. 334)

Manifest Destiny/Destino Manifiesto la idea popular en los Estados Unidos durante los años 1800 de que el país debería de extender sus fronteras hasta el Pacífico (p. 359)

manumission/manumisión el liberar a unas personas esclavizadas (p. 198)

martial law/ley marcial ley administrada por las autoridades civiles en una situación de emergencia (p. 869)

martyr/mártir una persona que sacrifica su vida por un principio o una causa (p. 452)

mass media/difusoras de información formas de comunicación que alcanzan a grandes números de personas, tal como periódicos, radio, y televisión (p. 703)

mass production/fabricación en serie la producción de grandes cantidades de productos usando máquinas y muchas veces una línea de montaje (p. 559)

materialism/materialismo atribuir demasiada importancia a las posesiones y comodidades físicas (p. 815)

Mayflower Compact/Convenio del Mayflower un documento formal escrito en 1620 que proporcionó leyes para el mantimiento del orden público en la colonia de Plymouth (p. 79)

Medicaid/*Medicaid* un programa social que da dinero a los estados para ayudar a las personas que no pueden pagar la factura del hospital (p. 829)

Medicare/*Medicare* un programa social que ayuda en pagar el esmero médico para los ancianos (p. 829)

mercantilism/mercantilismo idea de que el poder de una nación dependía de ampliar su comercio y aumentar sus reservas de oro (pp. 59, 110)

mercenary/mercenario soldado remunerado para servir en el ejército de un país extranjero (p. 164)

merger/fusión de empresas la asociación de dos o más negocios en uno (p. 564)

MIAs/*MIAs* soldados clasificados como extraviados en la guerra, inglés *missing in action* (p. 871)

migrant worker/obrero migrante una persona que se mueve de un lugar a otro para buscar trabajo en la cosecha de frutas y vegetales (p. 730)

migration/migración el movimiento de un gran número de personas hacia una nueva patria (p. 18)

militarism/militarismo un desarrollo de poder militar dentro de un país (p. 656)

militia/milicia un grupo de civiles entrenados para luchar durante emergencias (pp. 118, 143)

minutemen/*minutemen* compañías de soldados civiles que se jactaban de que podrían estar listos para tomar armas en sólo un minuto (p. 143)

mission/misión una comunidad religiosa (pp. 54, 96)

mobilization/mobilización juntar recursos y preparar para la guerra (pp. 670, 750)

moderate/moderado opuesto a gran cambio social o ideas políticas extremas (p. 798)

monopoly/monopolio control total de una industria por una persona o una compañía (p. 562)

Morse code/código Morse un sistema para transmitir mensajes que usa una serie de puntos y rayas para representar las letras del abecedario, los números, y la puntuación (p. 388)

mosque/mezquita una casa de alabanza musulmana (p. 41)

mountain man/hombre montañés colonizador que vivía en el monte, como en las Montañas Rocosas (p. 356)

muckraker/expositor de corrupción periodista que descubre abusos y corrupción en una sociedad (p. 606)

mudslinging/detractar intentar arruinar la reputación de un adversario con insultos (p. 335)

national debt/deuda nacional la cantidad de dinero que un gobierno debe a otros gobiernos o a su pueblo (p. 259)

National Grange/Granja Nacional la primera organización de granjeros de los Estados Unidos (p. 545)

nationalism/nacionalismo lealtad a una nación y promoción de sus intereses sobre todos los demás (pp. 294, 655)

nativism/nativismo la creencia de que aquellos que nacieron en un país son mejores que los inmigrantes (p. 709)

nativist/nativista una persona que favorece a los nacidos en su patria y se opone a los inmigrantes (p. 393)

neutral/neutral que no toma partido a ninguna persona ni a ningún país en un conflicto (p. 163)

neutral rights/derechos neutrales el derecho para navegar en el mar sin tomar partido en una guerra (p. 290)

neutrality/neutralidad una posición de no tomar partido en un conflicto (p. 264)

New Deal/Nuevo Trato el nombre dado a las leyes nuevas con la meta de aliviar la Depresión que fueron estatuidas por el Congreso durante los Cien Días y los meses siguientes (p. 723)

nomadic/nómada que se mueve de un lugar a otro sin hogar permanente (p. 538)

nomads/nómadas personas que se mueven de lugar a lugar, generalmente en busca de comida o de tierras para pastar (p. 18)

nominating convention/convención nominadora sistema en el cual los diputados estatales escogieron al candidato para la presidencia de su partido (p. 337)

nonimportation/no importación un acuerdo de no importar ni usar ciertos productos (p. 135)

normal school/escuela normal una escuela con programa de dos años para entrenar a los graduados de preparatoria para ser maestros (p. 413)

Northwest Passage/Paso Noroeste ruta acuática para Asia por América del Norte buscada por exploradores europeos (p. 59)

nullify/anular cancelar o hacer sin efecto (pp. 272, 338)

offensive/ofensiva la posición de atacar o el mismo ataque (p. 464)

on margin/al margen comprar acciones por pagar sólo una fracción del precio del valor y el resto del préstamo recibido a un corredor (p. 715)

Open Door policy/política de Puerta Abierta una política que permitía a cada nación extranjera en China que comerciara libremente en las esferas de influencia de las otras naciones (p. 638)

English/Spanish Glossary

open range/terreno abierto tierra sin cercas ni dividida en solares (p. 531)

ordinance/ordenanza una ley o regulación (p. 192)

ore/mena un mineral minado por la sustancia valorable que contiene, tal como plata (p. 525)

override/vencer rechazar o derrotar, como un proyecto de ley propuesto en el Congreso (p. 500)

overseer/capataz persona que supervisa una operación grande o a sus trabajadores (pp. 108, 403)

ozone/ozono el estrato de gas compuesto de una forma de oxígeno que protege la tierra y a su gente de los rayos del sol que causan el cáncer (p. 928)

pacifist/pacifista persona opuesta al uso de guerra o violencia para arreglar disputas (pp. 87, 673)

partisan/partidario a favor de una parte de un asunto (p. 267)

patent/patente un documento que da al inventor el derecho exclusivo legal de una invención durante un período de tiempo (p. 307)

Patriots/patriotas colonizadores americanos que estaban determinados para luchar en contra de los británicos hasta que se ganara la independencia americana (pp. 146, 163)

patronage/patronazgo otro nombre del sistema de recompensa política en el cual puestos y favores gubernamentales se dan a aliados políticos y a amigos (p. 604)

patroon/patroon terrateniente de las colonias holandesas que gobernaba áreas grandes de tierra como un rey (p. 85)

peaceful coexistence/coexistencia pacífica acuerdo entre países opuestos de que competirán uno con el otro pero evitarán la guerra (p. 805)

pension/pensión una cantidad pagada a una persona, generalmente después de la jubilación (p. 734)

per capita income/ingresos por persona el promedio de ingresos de cada persona de la nación (p. 808)

perestroika/perestroika una política de gobierno y economía empezada por Gorbachev en la Unión Soviética a mediados de los años 1980 (p. 909)

perjury/perjurio el mentir después de haber jurado decir la verdad (p. 790)

persecute/perseguir tratar cruelmente a alguién a causa de sus creencias o prácticas (p. 78)

petition/petición una solicitud formal (pp. 149, 192)

philanthropy/filantropía acciones caritativas o donaciones de dinero para beneficiar a la comunidad (p. 563)

pilgrimage/peregrinación un viaje a un sitio sagrado (p. 41)

Pilgrims/peregrinos separatistas que viajaron a las colonias durante los años 1600 por un propósito religioso (p. 79)

plantation/plantación una finca grande manejada por el dueño o un gerente y cultivada por trabajadores que vivían allí (p. 55)

plurality/pluralidad el mayor número de individuos (p. 334)

political machine/máquina política una organización aliada con un partido político que muchas veces controlaba el gobierno local (p. 603)

poll tax/impuesto de capitación un impuesto de una cantidad fija por cada persona que tenía que ser pagada antes de que pudiera votar la persona (p. 515)

pool/consorcio un grupo compartiendo de una actividad, por ejemplo, entre barones ferrocarrileros que hacían acuerdos secretos y fijaban tipos entre ellos mismos (p. 554)

popular sovereignty/soberanía popular la teoría política de que el gobierno está sujeto a la voluntad del pueblo (p. 216); antes de la Guerra Civil, la idea de que la gente que vivía en un territorio tenía el derecho de decidir por votar si allí sería permitida la esclavitud (p. 443)

Populist Party/Partido Populista partido político de los EE.UU. formado en 1892 que representaba principalmente a los granjeros, que favorecía la acuñación libre de plata y el control gubernamental de ferrocarriles y otros monopolios (p. 546)

poverty line/línea de pobreza el nivel de ingresos personales o familiares clasificado de pobre según la norma del gobierno (p. 828)

preamble/preámbulo la introducción de un documento formal, especialmente la Constitución (pp. 152, 215)

precedent/precedente una tradición (p. 257)

prejudice/prejuicio una opinión injusta no basada en los hechos (p. 391)

presidio/presidio un fuerte español en las Américas construido para proteger las colonias misioneras (p. 54)

primary/elección preliminar una elección en la cual los votantes escogen al candidato de su partido (p. 607)

privateer/buque corsario buque armado privado (pp. 177, 297)

productivity/productividad la cantidad de trabajo que hace cada trabajador (pp. 698, 807)

prohibition/prohibición leyes que prohiben el hacer o vender de bebidas alcohólicas (p. 613)

Prohibition/Prohibición entredicho contra la fabricación, transportación, y venta de bebidas alcohólicas por todo los Estados Unidos (p. 708)

propaganda/propaganda ideas o información diseñadas para influenciar la opinión (pp. 139, 661)

proportional/proporcional que son iguales o que corresponden (p. 200)

proprietary colony/colonia propietaria colonia dirigida por personas o grupos a quienes se les había otorgado la tierra (pp. 85, 112)

protectorate/protectorado un país que es técnicamente independiente, pero que en realidad está bajo el control de otro país (p. 643)

public works/proyectos públicos proyectos tal como carreteras, parques, y bibliotecas construidos con fondos públicos para el uso del público (p. 718) pueblo/pueblo una casa o una comunidad de casas construidas por Nativos Americanos (pp. 28, 54)

Puritans/puritanos protestantes que, durante los años 1600, querían reformar la Iglesia anglicana (p. 78)

quota system/sistema de cuotas un arreglo que pone un límite en el número de inmigrantes de cada país (p. 709)

radical/radical extremo (p. 496); referente a alguién que favorece hacer cambios extremos al gobierno o a la sociedad, como la Nueva Izquierda (p. 859)

ragtime/*ragtime* una clase de música con un ritmo fuerte y una melodía animada con notas acentuadas que era popular al principio del siglo XX (p. 594)

ranchero/ranchero dueño de rancho mexicano (p. 370)

rancho/rancho propiedades grandísimas para producir ganado establecidas por colonizadores mexicanos en California (p. 370)

ratify/ratificar dar aprobación oficial para (pp. 184, 209, 474)

ration/racionar distribuir los artículos escasos sobre una base limitada (p. 751)

realism/realismo una perspectiva de literatura, arte, y teatro que representa las cosas tal como son (p. 592)

rebate/rebaja descuento o devolución de una porción de un pago (p. 553)

Rebel/rebelde soldado confederado, así nombrado a causa de su oposición al gobierno establecido (p. 465)

recall/elección de revocación el derecho que permite a los votantes que despidan de la oficina a los oficiales elegidos que son inadecuados (p. 607)

recession/recesión un deslizamiento en actividades comerciales (p. 698)

reconciliation/reconciliación arreglar por acuerdo o por reunirse de nuevo (p. 509)

Reconstruction/Reconstrucción la reorganización y la reconstrucción de los anteriores estados confederados después de la Guerra Civil (p. 495)

recruit/reclutar enlistar a soldados para el ejército (p. 165)

referendum/referéndum la práctica de permitir a los votantes que acepten o rechazen medidas propuestas por la legislatura (p. 607)

regionalism/regionalismo en arte o literatura, la práctica de enfocar en una región en particular del país (p. 592)

relief/ayuda social ayuda para los pobres; asistencia pública (p. 717)

relocate/reubicar forzar a una persona o a un grupo de personas a trasladarse (p. 342)

Renaissance/Renacimiento un período de creatividad intelectual y artística, alrededor de los años 1300–1600 (p. 38)

rendezvous/*rendezvous* una reunión (p. 356)

reparations/reparaciones pago por el país que pierde una guerra al país que gana por los daños causados por la guerra (p. 676)

repeal/revocar cancelar un decreto o ley (p. 135)

republic/república un gobierno en el cual ciudadanos gobiernan por medio de representantes elegidos (p. 190)

reservation/reservación una área de tierra pública apartada para los Nativos Americanos (p. 540)

reserved powers/poderes reservados poderes retenidos por los estados (p. 217)

resolution/resolución una expresión formal de opinión (p. 135)

revenue/ingresos entrada de dinero (p. 134)

revenue sharing/ingreso compartido dinero recaudado de impuestos federales y dado a los estados para uso a los niveles estatales y locales (p. 887)

revival/renacimiento religioso una serie de reuniones dirigidas por un predicador para animar emociones religiosas (p. 411)

sabotage/sabotaje acción secreta por agentes del enemigo o los que compadecen para dañar el esfuerzo de guerra de una nación (p. 673)

scalawags/*scalawags* nombre dado por los confederados anteriores a los blancos sureños que apoyaban la Reconstrucción republicana del Sur (p. 505)

search-and-destroy mission/misión de buscar y destruir una estrategia usada en Viet Nam en la cual las fuerzas americanas buscarían las unidades nortevietnameses y vietconenses para destruirlas (p. 856)

secede/separarse abandonar o retirar (pp. 285, 338, 439)

secession/secesión retiro de la Unión (p. 454)

Second New Deal/Segundo Nuevo Trato un nuevo juego de programas y reformas lanzados por Franklin D. Roosevelt en 1935 (p. 734)

sectionalism/regionalismo lealtad a una región (pp. 319, 437)

sedition/sedición actividades con el propósito de debilitar un gobierno establecido (p. 271)

segregation/segregación la separación o aislamiento de una raza, una clase, o un grupo (pp. 516, 821)

Separatists/separatistas protestantes que, durante los años 1600, querían dejar la Iglesia anglicana para fundar sus propias iglesias (p. 78)

settlement house/casa de beneficencia institución colocada en una vecindad pobre que proveía numerosos servicios a la comunidad tal como cuidado médico, cuidado de niños, bibliotecas, y clases de inglés (p. 588)

sharecropping/aparcería sistema de agricultura en el cual un granjero labra la tierra para un dueño que provee equipo y semillas y recibe una porción de la cosecha (p. 507)

shareholder/accionista una persona que invierte en una sociedad anónima por comprar acciones y que es un dueño parcial (p. 560)

shuttle diplomacy/diplomacia de lanzadera negociaciones entre naciones llevada a cabo por una persona que viaja entre ellas yendo y viniendo (p. 885)

silent majority/mayoría callada la frase usada por Nixon para describir la mayoría de los americanos, los que no protestaban ni demostraban (p. 865)

sit-in/plantón el acto de ocupar asientos o de sentarse en el suelo de un establecimiento como una forma de protesta organizada (p. 830)

slave code/código de esclavos las leyes aprobadas en los estados sureños que controlaban y restringían a la gente esclavizada (p. 405)

slum/barrio bajo vecindad pobre, superpoblada, y de de vecindades ruinosas (p. 585)

smuggling/contrabandear cambiar ilegalmente con otras naciones (p. 111)

Social Security Act/Decreto de Seguro Social una ley que exige a los empleados y a los empresarios que paguen un impuesto; el dinero provee una pensión mensual para personas jubiladas (p. 734)

socialist/socialista una persona que cree que las industrias deben de ser poseídas por el público y manejadas por el gobierno en lugar de personas particulares (p. 672)

sodbuster/rompedor de césped nombre dado al granjero de las Llanuras (p. 535)

speculator/especulador persona que arriesga dinero para hacer una ganancia grande (pp. 124, 260)

sphere of influence/esfera de influencia sección de un país donde una nación extranjera tiene derechos y poderes especiales (p. 638)

spiritual/espiritual una canción popular religiosa afroamericana (p. 405)

spoils system/sistema de despojos la práctica de dar puestos gubernamentales a los partidarios; reemplazar a los empleados del gobierno con los partidarios del candidato victorioso (p. 337)

square deal/trato justo la promesa de Theodore Roosevelt para el trato justo e igual para todos (p. 618)

stagflation/stagflación una combinación del alza de precios y una economía estancada con una tasa alta de desempleo (p. 887)

stalemate/estancamiento una situación durante un conflicto cuando la acción se para debido a que ambos partidos son igualmente poderosos y ningún de los dos lo abandonará (p. 787)

standard gauge/medida normal la anchura uniforme de 4 pies, 8.5 pulgadas de las vías ferroviarias, adoptada durante los años 1880 (p. 552)

standard of living/norma de vivir una medida de calidad comprensiva de vida y riqueza de la gente; el mínimo de las necesidades y lujos a los cuales un grupo está acostumbrado (p. 808)

states' rights/derechos estatales derechos y poderes independientes del gobierno federal que son reservados a los estados por la Constitución (pp. 272, 338, 455)

steerage/entrepuente los cuarteles apretados de las cubiertas bajas de un barco para los pasajeros que pagan los pasajes más bajos (p. 577)

stock/acciones valores de propiedad de comercio que vende una compañía que llevan muchas veces el poder de votar (p. 560)

stock exchange/mercado de acciones un lugar donde acciones de sociedades anónimas se venden y se compran a través de un sistema organizado (p. 715)

strait/estrecho un paso angosto que conecta dos extensiones más grandes de agua (p. 49)

strike/huelga un paro de trabajo por los trabajadores para forzar al empresario a satisfacer demandas (p. 391)

strikebreaker/esquirol una persona contratada para reemplazar a un huelguista para suprimir una huelga (p. 568)

subsidy/subsidio donación de dinero del gobierno a una persona o una compañía para una acción con el propósito de beneficiar al público (pp. 527, 724)

subsistence farming/agricultura para subsistencia labranza que produce solamente la comida que se necesita para dar de comer a la familia del trabajador (p. 104)

suburbs/suburbios áreas residenciales que brotaron cerca de o alrededor de ciudades como resultado de mejoramientos de transportación (p. 586)

subversion/subversión un esfuerzo para derrocar un gobierno montado por personas trabajando secretamente desde adentro (p. 789)

suffrage/sufragio el derecho al voto (pp. 336, 426)

suffragist/sufragista un hombre o mujer que luchaba para el derecho al voto de la mujer (p. 610)

summit/conferencia cumbre una reunión de altos jefes de gobierno (p. 805)

surplus/superávit exceso; la cantidad que sobra después de pagar los gastos necesarios (p. 798)

sweatshop/fábrica-opresora un taller o fábrica donde se explota a los trabajadores, trabajándolos muchas horas por poco pago y en condiciones malsanas (pp. 566, 578)

tariff/tarifa impuesto sobre productos importados o exportados (pp. 261, 338)

technology/tecnología el uso de conocimientos científicos para propósitos prácticos (pp. 39, 306)

Tejano/tejano un mexicano que reclama Texas como su patria (p. 362)

telegraph/telégrafo un aparato o sistema que usa señales eléctricas para transmitir mensajes a códigos a través de alambres (p. 388)

temperance/templanza el uso de poca o de ninguna bebida alcohólica (p. 412)

tenant farmer/granjero arrendatario un granjero que labra la tierra de otro dueño y paga renta ya sea con la cosecha o al contado (pp. 95, 401)

tenement/casa de vecindad un edificio en el cual varias familias alquilan cuartos o apartamentos, a menudo con pocas medidas sanitarias o seguridad (p. 585)

terrace/terraza una parcela de tierra elevada y allanada para fomentar la agricultura (p. 25)

theocracy/teocracia una forma de gobierno en la cual la sociedad está gobernada por líderes religiosos (p. 22)

Tidewater/Orilla del Mar una región de llanuras planas y bajas alrededor de la costa del mar (p. 107)

toleration/tolerancia el aceptar creencias diferentes (p. 81)

total war/guerra total la guerra en todo aspecto de la vida del enemigo (p. 487)

totalitarian/totalitario un sistema político en el cual el gobierno suprime toda oposición y controla muchos aspectos de la vida de la gente (p. 742)

trade deficit/déficit de cambio la situación cuando el valor de las importaciones de un país excede el valor de las exportaciones (p. 898)

trade union/gremio una organización de artesanos con el mismo oficio o destreza (pp. 391, 567)

Transcendentalist/transcendentalista uno de un grupo de escritores de Nueva Inglaterra que acentuaban la relación entre los seres humanos y la naturaleza, asuntos espirituales sobre asuntos materiales, y la importancia de la conciencia particular (p. 414)

transcontinental/transcontinental que se extiende a través del continente (p. 527)

triangular trade/trato triangular una ruta de comercio para cambiar productos entre las Antillas, las colonias americanas, y África del Oeste (p. 105)

tribute/tributo dinero pagado para protección (pp. 51, 289)

trust/cártel una combinación de firmas o sociedades anónimas formada por un acuerdo legal, especialmente para reducir la competición (pp. 562, 605)

trustbuster/rompedor de cárteles alguién que divide un cártel en compañías más pequeñas (p. 617)

turnpike/autopista una carretera que uno debe de pagar para usar; el dinero se usa para pagar el costo de la carretera (p. 314)

unconstitutional/anticonstitucional no de acuerdo ni consistente con la Constitución (p. 260)

underemployment/empleo insuficiente la condición cuando la gente trabaja en puestos para los cuales están sobrecalificados o que no utilizan sus destrezas (p. 894)

Underground Railroad/Ferrocarril Subterráneo un sistema que ayudó a los afroamericanos esclavizados a seguir una red de rutas de escape afuera del Sur hacia la libertad del Norte (p. 420)

unemployment insurance/seguro de desempleo pagos por el gobierno durante un cierto período limitado de tiempo a las personas que han perdido sus trabajos (p. 734)

utopia/utopía una comunidad basada en una visión de la sociedad perfecta buscada por los reformistas (p. 411)

vaquero/vaquero trabajador ranchero hispánico (p. 532)

vaudeville/teatro de variedades entretenimiento compuesto de varios actos, tal como baile, canción, comedia, y espectáculos de mágica (p. 595)

vertical integration/integración vertical la asociación de compañías que abastecen con equipo y servicios necesarios para una industria particular (p. 563)

veto/vetar rechazar un proyecto de ley y prevenir que vuelva a ser una ley (p. 349)

viceroy/virrey persona que gobierna un país o una provincia como el representante del monarca (p. 54)

Vietcong/*Vietcong* los soldados guerrillistas de la facción comunista en Viet Nam, también conocidos por el Frente Nacional para Liberación (p. 853)

Vietnamization/vietnamización la política de Nixon que demandó que Viet Nam del Sur tomara un papel más activo en luchar la guerra y que los americanos se involucaran menos (p. 868)

vigilantes/vigilantes gente que toman la ley en sus propias manos (pp. 377, 526)

War Hawks/halcones de guerra republicanos durante la presidencia de Madison que insistían en la guerra con la Bretaña (p. 294)

warrant/citación una orden oficial (p. 226)

work relief/ayuda de trabajo programas que dieron trabajos gubernamentales a los pobres (p. 724)

writ of assistance/escrito de asistencia documento legal que permitía a los oficiales que exploraran las casas y bodegas en busca de productos que tal vez pudieran ser de contrabandeado (p. 134)

Yankee/yanqui soldado de la Unión (p. 465)

yellow journalism/periodismo amarillista escritura que exageraba acontecimientos sensacionales, dramáticos, y repulsivos para atraer a los lectores, citando historias que fueron populares durante los fines de los años 1800 (p. 592); una clase de reportaje sensacional, prejuzgado, y a menudo falso (p. 641)

yeoman/terrateniente menor dueño sureño de una granja pequeña que no tenía esclavos (p. 401)

Credits and Acknowledgments

Acknowledgments

741 Excerpt from *Mein Kampf* by Adolf Hitler, translated by Ralph Manheim. Copyright © 1943, renewed 1971 by Houghton Mifflin Co. Reprinted by permission of Houghton Mifflin Co. All rights reserved.
753 From *Collected Poems* by Langston Hughes. Copyright © 1944 by the Estate of Langston Hughes. Reprinted by permission of Alfred A. Knopf Inc.
832, A20 Reprinted by arrangement with the Heirs to the Estate of Martin Luther King, Jr., c/o Writers House, Inc. as agent for the proprietor. Copyright © 1963 by Martin Luther King, Jr., copyright renewed 1991 by Coretta Scott King.
859 From *Blowin' in the Wind* by Bob Dylan. Copyright © 1962 by Warner Bros. Music, copyright renewed 1990 by Special Rider Music. All rights reserved. International copyright secured. Reprinted by permission.
979 From *Major Poems* by Jose Martí, Philip S. Foner, editor, Randall, Elinor, et al, translators. Copyright © 1982 by Holmes & Meier Publishers, Inc.
983 "Dream Boogie Variation" from *Collected Poems* by Langston Hughes. Copyright © 1994 by the Estate of Langston Hughes. Reprinted by permission of Alfred A. Knopf Inc.
986 Reprinted with the permission of Simon & Schuster from *The Longest Day* by Cornelius Ryan. Copyright © 1959 by Cornelius Ryan; copyright renewed 1987 by Victoria Ryan Bida and Geoffrey J.M. Ryan.
991 From *Private Lives* by Benita Eisler. Copyright © 1986 by Benita Eisler. Reprinted by permission of author.
992 Excerpt from *Dear Mrs. Parks: A Dialogue with Today's Youth.* Text copyright © 1996 by Rosa L. Parks. Reprinted by arrangement with Lee & Low Books, 95 Madison Avenue, New York, NY 10016.
995 From *When Heaven and Earth Changed Places,* by Le Ly Hayslip with Jay Wurts. Copyright © 1989 by Le Ly Hayslip and Charles Jay Wurts. Reprinted by permission from Doubleday.

Photo Credits

Cover Jim Barber Studio; **iii** Collection of David J. & Janice L. Frent; **iv** Chicago Historical Society; **v** Copyright, Virginia Historical Society, 1996, All rights reserved; **vi** The Historical Society of Pennsylvania; **vii** Kari Haavisto; **ix** Library of Congress; **x** Musee de L'Homme. Photo M. Delaplanche; **xi**(l)Indiana Historical Society, (r)Smithsonian Institution; **xvi**(t)Stanford University Museum of Art, (c)Collection of David J. & Janice L. Frent, (b)Collection of the Museum of American Folk Art, gift of Cyril Irwin Nelson in loving memory of his parents, Cyril Arthur & Elise Macy Nelson. 1984.27.1. Photo courtesy New York Quilt Project; **xvii**(t)Jerry Jacks/courtesy Arizona State Museum, University of Arizona, (bl)Mercantile Money Museum, (br)Collection of Michael Barson; **Reference Atlas** Larry Kunkel/FPG; **0** ©James Randklev/AllStock; **2**(t)Robert W. Madden/National Geographic Society, (b)Rich Buzzelli/Tom Stack & Assoc.; **4** (t)David M. Dennis, (b)Walter Meyers Edwards/National Geographic Society; **6** Eliot Cohn; **9** Scala/Art Resource; **12**(l)H. Armstrong Roberts, (r)University Museum of National Antiquities, Oslo Norway; **12-13** Orbis Typus Universalis; **13** Musee de L'Homme, Palais de Chateau, Paris; **14** Louise Erdrich; **15** Private Collection; **16** Doug Stern & Enrico Ferorelli/National Geographic Image Collection; **17** file photo; **21** Boltin Picture Library; **22**(l, c)Richard Alexander Cooke III, (r)David Hiser/Tony Stone Images; **23**(l)Michel Zabe'/Museo Templo Major, (r)Museum of Ethnology; **25**(l)Ed Simpson/Tony Stone Images, (r)Heye Foundation, National Museum of The American Indian/Smithsonian Institution; **27** Jerry Jacks/courtesy Arizona State Museum, Arizona University; **28** (l,c)David Muench, (r)Richard Alexander Cooke III; **29** Cahokia Mounds State Historic Site/painting by L.K. Townsend; **30** Addison Doty/Morning Star Gallery; **33** Richard Alexander Cooke III; **36** US Architect of the Capitol; **37** Brown Brothers; **38** Bodleian Library, Oxford; **39**(l)National Maritime Museum, (r)NASA; **41**(l)Giraudon/Art Resource, NY, (r)National Museum of African Art/Jeffrey Ploskonka; **43** Peabody Museum of Salem; **46**(l)Giraudon/Art Resource, NY, (r)Archivio Fotografico del Museo Preistorico Etnografico L. Pigorini, Roma; **49** Maritime Museum, Seville/Artephot/Oronoz; **50** courtesy The Oakland Museum; **51**(tl, bl, r) Michel Zabe', (c)e.t.archive; **54** Museo de Historia, Chapultepec/Bob Schalkwijk; **56**(t)Brian Lanker, (b)Bill Ballenberg; **56-57** Kevin Chadwick; **57** Lowell Georgia; **58** SuperStock; **59** Catherine Tekakwitha by father Claude Chauchetiere/Jacques Turcot, Mission Saint-Francois-Xavier, Caughnawaga, Quebec; **61** courtesy The Oakland Museum; **66**(t)Dedham Historical Society, (c)Colonial Williamsburg, (b)Peabody Museum/Harvard University/Hillel Burger; **66-67** Private Collection; **67** Plimoth Plantation; **68** Royal Albert Memorial Museum, Exeter, England; **69** National Maritime Museum, London; **70** Childs Gallery, Boston; **71** Jamestown-Yorktown Foundation; **72** Princeton University Libraries; **73** National Portrait Gallery, Smithsonian Institution/Art Resource, NY; **74** Colonial National Historic Park; **75**(l)New York Historical Society, (r)Bill Pugliano/Black Star; **76**(t)Ashmolean Museum, (b)Farrell Grehan; **76-77** Kevin Chadwick; **77** National Portrait Gallery, Smithsonian Institution/Art Resource, NY; **78** Plimoth Plantation; **80** courtesy Pilgrim Society, Plymouth, Massachusetts; **82** courtesy Haffenreffer Museum of Anthropology, Brown University; **84** courtesy Winterthur Museum; **85** New York Historical Society; **86** courtesy Museum of American Arts of the Pennsyvania Academy of the Fine Arts, Philadelphia. Gift of Mrs. Sarah Harrison (The Joseph Harrison, Jr. Collection); **88** British Museum; **90** The Association for the Preservation of Virginia Antiquities, Bacon's Castle. Library of Virigina; **92**(t)Ashmolean Museum, (tr, l)courtesy Rice Museum from VOICES OF TRIUMPH: PERSEVERANCE/Craig Moran (C)1993 Time-Life Books Inc., (c)Gibbes Museum of Art, (br)Charleston Museum; **93** Colonial Williamsburg; **94** National Archives of Canada; **95** Paul Harris Art Selections, Scotland/courtesy Joslyn Art Museum; **96** Historical Picture Collection/Stock Montage; **100** Library of Congress; **101** Doug Martin; **102** Old John Street United Methodist Church; **103** Colonial Williamsburg; **104** courtesy Museum of Fine Arts, Boston; **105**(l)courtesy Peabody & Essex Museum, Salem, MA, (r)file photo; **107**(l)Botany Library, Harvard University, (r)Peabody Essex Museum/Mark Sexton; **108** Colonial Williamsburg; **109** courtesy American Antiquarian Society; **110** Yale University Art Gallery; **111**(l, tr, tl)courtesy Historic Deerfield Inc./Amanda Merullo, (c)Addison Gallery; **113** Yale University Art Gallery; **115** Blue Ridge Institute & Museums/Ferrum College; **116** courtesy American Antiquarian Society; **118** (l)Washington & Lee University, (tr, br)Chicago Historical Society; **119** Library of Congress; **120** Musee de L'Homme/M. Delaplanche; **121** State Historical Society of Wisconsin Museum Collection; **124** Culver Pictures; **128**(t)David A. Schorsch, (b)Reza Estakhrian/Tony Stone Images; **128-129** The Metropolitan Museum of Art, Gift of John S. Kennedy, 1897. (97.34); **129** courtesy Peabody & Essex Museum, Salem, MA; **130** Bettmann Archive; **131** Library of Congress; **132** Lafayette College Art Collection, Easton, PA; **133** Crown copyright. Historic Royal Palaces. Photograph David Chalmess; **135** Massachusetts Historical Society; **136** Patrick Henry Before the Virginia House of Burgesses (1851) by Peter F. Rothermel. Red Hill, The Patrick Henry National Memorial, Brookneal, Virginia; **137** Library of Congress; **138** file photo; **140**(l)DAR Museum on loan from Boston Tea Party Chapter, (r)courtesy American Antiquarian Society; **141** The Royal Collection ©Her Majesty Queen Elizabeth II; **142**(l)Lexington Historical Society, Lexington, MA, (r)Fort Ticonderoga Museum; **145** Concord Museum, Concord, MA; **146** Chicago Historical Society; **148** Smithsonian Institution; **150** (c)Virginia Historical Society, All Rights Reserved, 1996; **151** Massachusetts Historical Society; **152** Painting by Don Troiani, photo courtesy Historical Art Prints, Ltd.; **154**(c)John Lewis Stage, (b)Thomas Gilcrease Institute of American Art, Tulsa OK; **154-155** Kevin Chadwick; **156** Raza Estakhrian/Tony Stone Images; **157**(l)George Washington At Constitutional Convention by Junius Brutus Sterns, Virginia Museum of Fine Arts, Gift of Colonel & Mrs. Edgar W. Garbisch, (c)Architect of the Capitol, Washington DC, (r)National Gallery of Art, Washington DC; **162** Library of Congress; **163** West Point Museum; **164** Library of Congress; **165**(l)UPI/Corbis-Bettmann, (r)Corbis-Bettmann; **167** Collection of A.A. McBrurney; **168** New York Historical Society; **171** Chicago Historical Society; **172** The Valley Forge Historical Society; **174** Eric P. Newman Numismatic Education Society; **176** Collection of Mark Nichipor; **179**(tl, tr, bl)Minute Man National Historical Park, Concord, MA, (c) Collection of the State of South Carolina, (br)Massachusetts Historical Society; **180** William T. Ranney, MARION CROSSING THE PEDEE, 1850, o/c, 1983.125; Amon Carter Museum, Fort Worth, Texas; **181** Private Collection; **182** Chicago Historical Society; **183** Lafayette College Art Collection, Easton, PA. Gift of Mrs. John Hubbard; **184** Trumball Collection, Yale University Art Gallery; **188** Fraunces Tavern Museum, NY; **189** The Metropolitan Museum of Art, Gift of J.H. Greenville Gilbert, 1939 (39.87ab); **190** Picture Research Consultants; **192** Chicago Historical Society; **194**(l)Independence National Historic Park, (r)Chicago Historical Society; **196** Independence National Historical Park; **197** Bettmann Archive; **198**(l)Delaware Art Museum, Wilmington. Gift of Absalom Jones School, Wilmington, (r)Moorland Spingarn Research Center, Howard University; **199**(l)Historical Society of Pennsylvania, (r)Library of Congress; **200** Columbiana Collection, Columbia University; **201** Yale University Art Gallery; **202, 204** Independence National Historic Park; **205** National Portrait Gallery; **206** Fred Maroon/Smithsonian Institution; **207**(l)Colonial Williamsburg, (tr)Peabody Essex Museum/Mark Sexton, (c)Ellen Kelleran Gardner Fund, courtesy Museum of Fine Arts, Boston, (br)Colonial Williamsburg; **208** Supreme Court Historical Society; **209** Scotchtown, VA/Katherine Wetzel; **210** Bequest of Winslow Warren, courtesy Museum of Fine Arts, Boston; **211** New York Historical Society; **214** Michael Evans/Time Magazine; **215** Independence National Historic Park; **216** Picture Research Consultants; **220** Massachusetts Historical Society; **221** SuperStock; **224**(l)White House/Gamma Liaison, (r)AP Photo/David Karp; **226** Bob Daemmrich/Tony Stone Images; **228** Sylvain Grandadam/Tony Stone Images; **230** Mark Burnett; **244** Boltin Picture Library; **249** Cobalt Productions; **251** Paul Conklin; **252**(t)Smithsonian Institution, (b)Museum of American Textile History; **252-253** courtesy Winterthur Museum; **253** Smithsonian Institution; **254** Darlene Pfister/Minneapolis Star Tribune; **255** Robert M. Friedman/Frozen Images; **256** Huntington Brooklyn Museum; **257** Frank & Marie-Therese Wood Print Collection, Alexandria, VA; **258** Library of Congress; **259** Yale University Art Gallery; **262** Atwater Kent Museum; **263** Chicago Historical Society; **266** Independence National Historic Park/Joseph Painter; **267** courtesy American Antiquarian Society; **269** courtesy American Antiquarian Society; **270** Collection of David J. & Janice L. Frent; **271** Stock Montage; **276** courtesy Peabody & Essex Museum, Salem, MA; **277** Boltin Picture Library; **279** The Huntington - San Marino, CA/SuperStock; **280** Duke University Archives; **281** West Virginia State Museum; **282** courtesy American Antiquarian Society; **284** Chicago Historical Society; **285** New York Historical Society; **286** (tl)Royal Ontario Museum, Toronto/National Geographic Society, (tr, br)National Museum of American Art, Washington, DC/Art Resource, NY, (bl)Montana Historical Society; **286-287** Kevin C. Chadwick/National Geographic Society; **287** Peabody Museum/Harvard University; **288**(t)Missouri Historical Society, (b)Missouri Historical Society; **289** Peabody Essex Museum/Mark Sexton; **291** Library of Congress; **292**(l)courtesy Peabody & Essex Museum, Salem, MA/Jeffrey Dykes, (tr, br)Colonial Williamsburg, (c)Prints Collection/Miriam & Ira D. Wallach Divison of Art, Prints & Photography, New York Public Library/Astor, Lenox & Tilden Foundation; **295**(l)Library of Congress, (r)(Tecumseh)Field Museum of Natural History; **296** Princeton University Library; **297** New York State Historical Association, Cooperstown; **299** Anne S. K. Brown Military Collection, Brown University; **301**

Missouri Historical Society; **304** Jacob Edwards Library, Southbridge, MA/Clive Russ; **305** Bob Mullenix; **306**(l)Smithsonian Institution, (r)Yale University Art Gallery, Gift of George Hoadley, B.A. 1801; **307**(l)Slater Mill Historic Site, (r)Museum of American Textile History; **309** National Gallery of Art, Washington. Gift of Edgar William & Bernice Chrysler Garbisch; **310**(l) courtesy Samuel Herrup Antiques, (r)Library Company of Philadelphia; **313** Smithsonian Institution; **315**(tr)Valentine Museum, (l)Smithsonian Institution, (c)The Metropolitan Museum of Art, Rogers Fund, 1942. (42.95.11), (br)Old Sturbridge Village/Thomas Neill; **316** New York Historical Society; **317**(t)Boot Hill Museum/Henry Groskinsky, (b)Peter Menzel; **318** James Monroe Museum & Memorial Library; **321** New York Historical Society; **322** Historic New Orleans Collection, 1855.57; **328**(l)Craig McDougal, (r)Anthony Richardson; **328-329** St. Louis Art Museum, Eliza McMillan Fund; **329** courtesy Charleston Museum; **330** Corbis-Bettmann; **331** Library of Congress; **332** Boatmen's National Bank of St. Louis; **333, 334** Collection of David J. & Janice L. Frent; **335** New York Historical Society; **336** Collection of David J. & Janice L. Frent; **337** Library of Congress; **338** Library Company of Philadelphia; **340** Archives & Manuscripts Division of the Oklahoma Historical Society; **340-341** Kevin C. Chadwick/National Geographic Society; **341**(l)White House Historical Association, (r)Archives & Manuscripts Division of the Oklahoma Historical Society; **342** National Museum of American Indian/Smithsonian Institution; **342** SuperStock; **345**(t)National Museum of American Art, Smithsonian Institution. Gift of Mrs.Joseph Harrison, JR/Art Resource, NY, (tr, bl, br)Fulton County Historical Society/Mike Kenny, (bc)Tippecanoe County History Society, Lafayette, Indiana. Gift of Mrs. Cable A. Ball; **346** Thomas Gilcrease Institute of American Art, Tulsa OK; **348** Bettmann Archive; **349** Historical Society of Pennsylvania; **350** New York Historical Society; **351**(l)National Portrait Gallery, Smithsonian Institution/Art Resource, NY, (r)Smithsonian Institution; **354** Collection of Mrs. J. Maxwell Moran; **355** Nikki Pahl; **356**(l)Colorado Historical Society, (r)Colorado Historical Society; **357** Joslyn Art Museum, Omaha; **358, 359**(l) Henry Groskinsky; **359**(r)Mongerson-Wunderlich Gallery, Chicago; **360** Collection of David J. & Janice L. Frent; **362, 363** Archives Division, Texas State Library; **364** Friends of the Governor's Mansion, Austin; **366** courtesy Bexar County & The Witte Museum, San Antonio, Texas; **367** Archives Division, Texas State Library; **368** Panhandle Plains Historical Museum; **369**(tr, bl)courtesy The Oakland Museum, (c)Thomas Gilcrease Institute of American Art, Tulsa OK, (br)Panhandle-Plains Historical Museum; **371** courtesy Matthew R. Isenburg; **372** Collection of David J. & Janice L. Frent; **373** collection of Michael F. Bremer; **375** California State Library; **376** courtesy The Oakland Museum; **377**(l)Levi Strauss & Company, (r)Doug Martin; **378** International Society Daughters of the Utah Pioneers; **379** courtesy Denver Public Library Western History Department; **382** California State Library; **383** Doug Martin; **384** Louisiana State University Museum of Art, Baton Rouge. Gift: Friends of the Museum & Mrs. Ben C. Hamilton in memory of her mother, Mrs. Tela Hamilton Meier; **385** Smithsonian Institution/Charles Phillips; **386** Peabody Essex Museum, Salem, MA/Mark Sexton; **388** The Chessie System, B7O Railroad Museum Archives (Photo by Robert Sherbow/UNIPHOTO); **390** Jack Naylor; **391** Museum of Fine Arts, Boston, M. & M. Karolik Collection; **393**(l)Museum of the City of New York, (r)Bostonian Society/Mark Sexton; **396** Grant Heilman Photography; **399** Bettmann Archive; **401** John Deere Museum; **402** The J. Paul Getty Museum; **403** New York Historical Society; **404**(l)Louisiana State Museum, New Orleans, (tr)Blue Ridge Institute & Museum, Ferrum College, (c)T. W. Wood Art Gallery/Montpelier, VT, (br)Valentine Museum; **406** Chester County Historical Society, West Chester, PA; **407**(l)National Portrait Gallery, Smithsonian Institution, Washington DC, (r)Picture Research Consultants; **410** SuperStock; **412** New York Historical Society; **413** From Fletcher's History of Oberlin College, courtesy Oberlin College; **414** courtesy Essex Institute, Salem, MA; **415** From the Collection of Edith Hariton/ Antique Textile Resource, Bethesda; **416** Massachusetts Historical Society, Boston; **417** Peabody Essex Museum/Mark Sexton; **418** American Antiquarian Society; **420** Cincinnati Art Museum; **421** Library of Congress; **424** Daughters of the American Revolution Museum. Gift of Mrs. Erwin L. Broecker; **425** Collection of William Gladstone; **426**(l)Chicago Historical Society, (r)Meserve Collection; **427** Mount Holyoke College Art Museum, South Hadley, Massachusetts; **428** Maria Mitchell Association; **429** Bettmann Archive; **432**(t)High Impact/Larry Sherer, (b)Photo Network; **432-433** The Picture Bank; **433** Mark Burnett; **434** Bettmann Archive; **435** Medford Historical Society; **436** courtesy Robert M. Hicklin, Jr.; **437** Frank & Marie-Therese Wood Print Collection, Alexandria, VA; **438** Collection of David J. & Janice L. Frent; **439** National Portrait Gallery; **442** Library of Congress; **443** Schlesinger Library, Radcliffe College; **445** The State House, Topeka, Kansas/photo courtesy Photo One; **446**(l)Jim Gensheimer; (r, b)Schomburg Center for Research in Black Culture, New York Public Library; **446-447** Kevin C. Chadwick/National Geographic Society; **448** North Wind Picture Archive; **449**(l)Collection of David J. & Janice L. Frent, (r)Museum of American Political Life/Sally Anderson Bruce; **450** Missouri State Historical Society; **451** courtesy Illinois State Historical Library; **453** Chicago Historical Society; **454** Collection of David J. & Janice L. Frent; **455**(t)Picture Research Consultants, (b)Matt Meadows; **457** National Portrait Gallery, Smithsonian Institution. Gift of Joel A. H. Webb & Mrs. Varina Webb Stewart/Art Resource, NY; **460** Painting by Don Troiani/courtesy Historical Art Print, Ltd.; **461** Stamatlos Brothers Collection, Cambridge/Larry Sherer; **462** Seventh Regiment Fund, New York City; **464** Library of Congress; **465** Picture Research Consultants; **466** Museum of the Confederacy; **467**(l)US Naval Academy Museum, Beverly R. Robinson Collection, (r)courtesy Stonewall Jackson Foundation, Lexington, VA; **468** Larry Sherer; **469** Library of Congress; **470** Museum of the Confederacy; **472** McLellan Lincoln Collection, The John Hay Library, Brown University/John Miller; **473** US Capitol Historical Society; **474** Moorland-Spingarn Research Center, Howard University, Washington DC; **476** Collection of Larry Williford; **477** Library of Congress; **478** Museum of the Confederacy; **481** Doug Martin; **482** Manassas National Battlefield Park/Larry Sherer; **485**(l)US Army Center of Military History/Exhibits Branch, (r)Brown Brothers; **487** Library of Congress; **488** West Point Museum Collections, US Military Academy/Henry Groskinsky; **490** Cincinnati Historical Society; **492** 1985 Time Life Books Inc./Smithsonian Institution/Peter Harholdt; **493** Aaron Haupt; **494** Cincinnati Art Museum/John J. Emery Fund; **495** National Museum of American History/Smithsonian Institution; **496** Gettysburg National Military Park; **497**(l)1986 Time-Life Books Inc. from the series "Civil War"/Edward Owen, (r)Illinois State Historical Library; **499** Chicago Historical Society; **500** Tennessee Botanical Gardens & Museum of Art, Nashville; **502** file photo; **503** Collection of David J. & Janice L. Frent; **504** courtesy Peter Hill Inc.; **505** Library of Congress; **506**(l)Blue Ridge Institute & Museum/Ferrum College, (tr)The State Museum of Pennsylvania, Pennsylvania Historical & Museum Commission, (c)Corcoran Gallery of Art, (br)Ananostia Museum; **507** National Museum of American History, Smithsonian Institution/Rudolf Eickmeyer; **508** North Wind Picture Archive; **509** Stock Montage; **511** Collection of David J. & Janice L. Frent; **512** Museum of American Political Life; **513** Smithsonian Institution; **515** Erich Lessing/Art Resource; **517** courtesy Babcock Galleries, NY; **518** North Wind Picture Archive; **520**(t)Morning Star Gallery, Addison Doty photo, (b)Bob Mullenix; **520-521** Collection of Mr. & Mrs. Paul Mellon, (c)1996 Board of Trustees, National Gallery of Art; **521** National Park Service Collection; **522** National Portrait Gallery, Smithsonian Institution/Art Resource, NY; **523** National Museum of American Art, Washington, DC/Art Resource, NY; **524** The Stark Museum of Art; **525** courtesy The Oakland Museum; **527** Colorado Historical Society; **529** The Andrew J. Russell Collection, The Oakland Museum; **531** Beinecke Rare Book & Manuscript Library, Yale University; **532**(l)courtesy Arizona Historical Society, (r)Thomas Gilcrease Institute of American Art, Tulsa OK; **533** Kansas Collection/University of Kansas Libraries; **534** Library of Congress; **535** Montana Historical Society, Helena; **536** Archives & Manuscript Division of the Oklahoma Historical Society; **538** The Museum of the American Indian, Hye Foundation, NY; **539**(tl, r, bl)Morning Star Gallery, Addison Doty Photo, (c)National Museum of American Art, Washington DC/Art Resource, NY; **541**(l)courtesy Smithsonian Institution, (r)Denver Public Library, Western History Collection; **544** New York Historical Society; **545** courtesy American Antiquarian Society; **546**(l)Collection of David J. & Janice L. Frent, (r)Kansas State Historical Society; **550** Westmorland Museum of Art, Greensburg, PA; **551** Picture Research Consultants; **552** Picture Research Consultants; **556** W.H. Clark/H. Armstrong Roberts; **557**(t)courtesy George Eastman House, (b) Smithsonian Institution; **558**(t)Library of Congress, (bl)Picture Research Consultants, (br)Lewis Latimer Collection, Queens Borough Public Library/ Long Island Division, NY, (br)Lewis Latimer Collection, Queens Borough Public Library/Long Island Division, NY; **559** courtesy Ford Motor Company; **560** courtesy Rockefeller Archive Center; **561** Library of Congress; **562**(l)The Oakland Museum, (tr, c)courtesy Biltmore Estate, Asheville, NC, (br)Museum of the City of New York, Gift of Mary & Charles Ogden; **563** National Portrait Gallery/Smithsonian Institution/Art Resource, NY; **565**(l)courtesy AT&T, (c)Michael Freeman, (r)Picture Research Consultants; **566, 567** Library of Congress; **569** Carnegie Library; **574** Museum of the City of New York; **575, 576** Karen Yamauchi for Chermayeff & Geismar Inc./Metaform; **577** Corbis-Bettmann; **578** Jacob A. Riis Collection, Museum of the City of New York; **579** Lewis W. Hine, courtesy New York Public Library; **582**(t)Culver Pictures, (c)courtesy California History Room, California State Library, Sacramento, (b)Montana Historical Society; **582-583** Kevin Chadwick; **583** Library of Congress; **584** Smithsonian Institution; **585**(l)Sears, Roebuck & Company, (r)Social Ethics Collection/Carpenter Center/Harvard University; **587**(tr) Museum of the City of New York, (r)Museum of the City of New York, Gift of Mrs. Andrew J. Miller, (c)courtesy New York Historical Society, (br)Museum of the City of NewYork, Gift of Phelps Warren; **588**(t)Kennedy Galleries Inc., (b)University of Illinois at Chicago. The University Library, Jane Addams Memorial Collection; **590** Collection of Sue & Lars Hotham/Rob Huntley/ Lightstream; **591** Library of Congress; **592** Picture Research Consultants; **593**(t) Collection of Mr. Arthur G. Altschul, (b)John Evans; **594** The Cleveland Museum of Art, Purchase from the J.H. Wade Fund; **595**(l)Smithsonian Institution, (r)Library of Congress; **598**(t)National Archives, (b)Collection of David J. & Janice L. Frent; **598-599** US Military Academy, West Point/Henry Groskinsky; **599** Collection of David J. & Janice L. Frent; **600** Archive Photos; **601** National Archives; **602** The Brooklyn Museum/Dick S. Ramsay Fund; **603** Doug Martin; **604**(l)Library of Congress, (r)Picture Research Consultants; **605** Culver Pictures; **606**(l)By permission of the Houghton Library, Harvard University, (r)Pelletier Library/Alleghany College; **609** Museum of the City of New York; **610** Museum of the City of New York, The Byron Collection; **612** Schlesinger Library, Radcliffe College; **613** Picture Research Consultants; **616, 617** Collection of David J. & Janice L. Frent; **618**(l)Yosemite Museum/Leroy Radanovich, (r)Museum of American Political History; **619**(l)Library of Congress, (r)file photo; **621** Theodore Roosevelt Collection/Harvard College Library/by permission of the Houghton Library/Harvard University; **622** Library of Congress; **623**(l, tr, br)Peabody Essex Museum/Jeffery Dykes, (c)Private Collection; **624**(l)Corbis-Bettmann, (r)Private Collection; **625** Culver Pictures; **626**(l)Oscar B. Willis/The Schomburg Center for Research in Black Culture, New York Public Library, (r)The Schomburg Center for Research in Black Culture, New York Public Library; **627** Wyoming Department of Cultural Resources; **630** The Franklin D. Roosevelt Library; **631** Picture Research Consultants; **632** courtesy US Naval Academy Museum; **633** Historic Seward House/James M. Via; **635** National Postal Museum; **636**(l)Bishop Museum, (r)Bishop Museum; **638** Library of Congress; **640** Brown Brothers; **641** Library of Congress; **643**(l)Remington Art Memorial, Ogdensburg, NY, (r)US Military Museum, West Point; **645** Aaron Haupt; **646** Picture Research Consultants; **647**(l)Private Collection/courtesy R.H. Love Galleries, Chicago, (r)Corbis-Bettmann; **648** Library of Congress; **649** El Paso Public Library; **654** Library of Congress; **655** Corbis-Bettmann; **657** Collection of Colonel Stuart S. Corning/Rob Huntley/Lightstream; **658**(l)UPI/Bettmann Newsphotos, (r)US Air Force; **660** Picture Research Consultants; **661**(l)Larry O. Nighswander/ National Geographic Society Image Collection, (r)Corbis-Bettmann; **664** UPI/Bettmann; **665, 667**(l, tr, br), **669** Collection of Colonel Stuart S. Corning/ Rob Huntley/Lightstream; **667**(c)Imperial War Museum; **668** The National Gallery of Art, Washington DC/Gift of Ethelyn McKinney in memory of her brother, Glenn Ford McKinney; **670** Picture Research Consultants; **671** National